ISAIAH BERLIN

FLOURISHING

LETTERS 1928–1946

Edited by Henry Hardy

Assistant to Henry Hardy · Serena Moore
Archival research · Michael Hughes
Additional research · Jennifer Holmes, Kate Payne
Consultant Russianist · Helen Rappaport

The compleat explanation of an author not systematick and consequential, but desultory and vagrant, abounding in casual allusions and light hints, is not to be expected from any single scholiast.

Samuel Johnson [*see page xlviii below*]

FLOURISHING

LETTERS 1928–1946

———

ISAIAH BERLIN

Edited by Henry Hardy

Chatto & Windus

London

Published by Chatto & Windus 2004

2 4 6 8 10 9 7 5 3 1

In the USA this book is published under the title *Letters 1928–1946*

First published in Great Britain in 2004 by
Chatto & Windus
Random House, 20 Vauxhall Bridge Road,
London SW1V 2SA

Random House Australia (Pty) Limited
20 Alfred Street, Milsons Point, Sydney,
New South Wales 2061, Australia

Random House New Zealand Limited
18 Poland Road, Glenfield,
Auckland 10, New Zealand

Random House South Africa (Pty) Limited
Endulini, 5A Jubilee Road, Parktown 2193, South Africa

The Random House Group Limited Reg. No 954009
www.randomhouse.co.uk

A CIP catalogue record for this book
is available from the British Library

ISBN 0–7011–7420–X

Designed in the Department of Typography & Graphic Communication,
The University of Reading, by Phil Reid and Paul Luna

Typeset by Deltatype Ltd, Birkenhead, Merseyside
Printed and bound in Great Britain by
Biddles Ltd, Kings Lynn

For Jenifer Hart

παντα αγαν   Isaiah Berlin, aged 16[1]

Nimiety – that's your weakness!   John Sparrow[2]

Surtout, Messieurs, point de zèle.
                         Charles-Maurice de Talleyrand[3]

---

1 'Panta agan' ('Everything to excess') – a parody of the Greek proverb 'μηδὲν ἄγαν' ('mēden agan', 'Nothing to excess') – written by IB in this unaccented form in the front of his 1925 St Paul's School diary. (For 'IB' and all other abbreviations see pp. xlv–xlviii below.)
2 Commenting on a draft typescript of IB's 'Richard Pares', an obituary published in the *Balliol College Record* 1958, and reprinted in PI. 'Nimiety' means (alleged) 'excess', i.e., in this context, over-enthusiasm in his judgements – for instance, describing Pares as 'the best and most admirable man I have ever known' (PI2 124).
3 'Above all, gentlemen, no zeal whatsoever.' For bibliographical details relevant to this maxim, a version of which IB often identified as his personal motto, see L 92, note 2.

CONTENTS

A CALL FOR LETTERS

THIS IS an earnest entreaty, addressed to any reader who possesses, or knows of, any correspondence with Isaiah Berlin that I may not have already seen, to tell me of it.

I have been collecting Isaiah Berlin's letters, with this edition in mind, since late 1990, when I left my post at Oxford University Press to begin full-time work on editing his unpublished writings. Although I have pursued a great many leads, sometimes with an obsessive persistence that must have irritated those exposed to it, there are bound to be letters that I have not tracked down, of whose existence, indeed, I am unaware. Berlin's correspondents were so numerous that I must be ignorant of a large proportion of them; those who have died may have passed their papers to members of their families or to institutions without leaving clues that I have been able to find; letters may have ended up in unpredictable hands, or may still lurk unseen wherever they were first put aside.

My hope is that the publication of this volume will stir memories, so that future volumes can be more representative, and so that further letters which fall into the time-span of this volume can be added to its future impressions, or prefixed to the next volume. Hence this request for letters and information. Berlin did not keep copies of his handwritten letters, and his secretaries did not always keep copies of those in typescript; even when they did, there were often additions to and corrections of the top copy that were not recorded on the duplicate. So I am dependent on the generosity of owners for the chance to select from the widest possible range of letters, and to use their final texts (when these survive).

I undertake to treat whatever I am shown with due discretion; and I should naturally respect any wish on the part of correspondents that particular letters or passages should not be quoted or published at all, or not within a particular time-limit. I should be glad to receive (and cover the cost of) photocopies of letters if their owners prefer not to lend originals. Any originals sent on loan can be copied and returned quickly.

A second motive for this request is to accumulate as complete a collection of Berlin's correspondence as possible, now, before it is too late; and to deposit additional items (with suitable embargoes if necessary) alongside the archive of his papers now housed at – and owned by – the Bodleian Library in Oxford. Already, with the passage of time and the death of some of his correspondents, many of his letters have been lost or destroyed.

I take this opportunity of saying that I should also be grateful for other archival material – for example, photographs, and (tape recordings or transcripts of) interviews or lectures not listed in the catalogues of such items in *The Isaiah Berlin Virtual Library*,[1] and anecdotal information about Berlin that may supplement what is already known to me.

My postal address is Wolfson College, OXFORD, OX2 6UD, UK; my email address *henry.hardy@wolfson.ox.ac.uk*.

H.H.

---

[1] The official website of the Isaiah Berlin Literary Trust – *http://berlin.wolf.ox.ac.uk/* – hereafter 'IBVL'.

ILLUSTRATIONS

CREDITS

Unless stated otherwise, all images are from The Isaiah Berlin Papers, Bodleian Library, University of Oxford, © The Isaiah Berlin Literary Trust 2004. Where items in the following list contain an oblique stroke, the photographer precedes the stroke, and the owner of the photograph or object follows it.

Letter to Chesterton: British Library, BL Add. MS. 73232A, scanned by the British Library

Invitation to Bella Schalit's party lent by Judy Sebba

Maps

Hampstead: detail from *Hampstead 1915* [Old Ordnance Survey Maps, London Sheet 27] (Consett, [2002]: Alan Godfrey Maps)

Oxford: from E. A. Greening Lamborn, *Oxford: A Short Illustrated Historical Guide* (Oxford, 1928), reproduced by permission of Oxford University Press; scan by Oxford University Libraries Imaging Service, © Bodleian Library, University of Oxford, from their G. A. Oxon 8° 1056(3)

Manhattan: from *Manhattan, New York* (New York, 1946: Hammond and Co., Inc.), copyright Hammond World Atlas Corp. # 12605; scan by the Library of Congress from their G3804 .N4 : 2M3 1946 .H 31

Midtown Manhattan: reproduced by permission of the British Library from *Nester's New York City Maps* ([London, 1952]: Nester House Publications); scanned from their Maps 34.a.1.(4.)

Central Washington: detail from *Esso Pictorial Guide to Washington, DC, and Vicinity: 1942* ([New York, 1942]: Standard Oil Company of New Jersey), copyright General Drafting Co., Inc., 21 West Street, New York, NY; scan by the Library of Congress from their G3850 1942 .G4

Central Moscow: scan of detail from 'Mil.-Geo.-Plan von Moskau II (Stadtkern)', in *Militärgeographische Angaben über das Europäische Rußland*, Map H: *Moskau* (Berlin, 1941: Generalstab des Heeres, Abteilung fur Kriegskarten und Vermessungswesen [IV. Mil.-Geo.]) by Oxford University Libraries Imaging Service, © Bodleian Library, University of Oxford, from their C40 e. 1/H*

Central Leningrad: detail from *Plan Leningrada 1939 g.* ('Plan of Leningrad 1939') ([Leningrad, 1939], Lenizdat); scan by the Anna Akhmatova Museum, St Petersburg, from their copy of the map

Photographs

  4 J. Russell & Sons, Wimbledon, 1927/8

  5 Postcard by Walker Photographer, 15 Pemberton Gardens, London N19

  6 Postcard by Valentine & Sons Ltd, Dundee and London

  7 Postcard

  9 Thomas Photos, neg. 64703/All Souls College

 10 George Leslie's Studio, Oxford

 11 Photo lent by Dr Clarita von Trott

13–15 Photos by members of the party/Noel Worswick

 16 Photo by John Ward-Perkins

 17 Nigel Francis/Sir Stuart Hampshire

 19 Postcard

 21 Photo by E. C. Hodgkin

 22 Nigel Francis/Edward Mortimer

 23 Photo lent by Nancy Nichols

 24 Raphael, 1 Wilton Place, Knightsbridge, London SW1/Lucy Gaster

 25 Ramsey & Muspratt, Oxford, 7 July 1943/Diana Hopkinson

 26 Photo lent by Penelope Newsome

 27 Photo lent by Sir Adam Ridley

 28 Cressida Ridley/Sir Adam Ridley

 29 Photo by Mary Fisher

 30 Thomas Photos?/New College Library, from A. H. Smith, *New College, Oxford, and its Buildings* (Oxford, 1952: Oxford University Press)

 31 Thomas Airviews, 1948/Rockefeller Centre Archive Center, image No 1163

 32 Postcard by Haberman's Real Photographs, GPO Box 198, NY

 33 Photo lent by Sir Stuart Hampshire

 34 Photo owned by and scanned for Amanda Opinsky

 35 Copy photo supplied by the *Daily Telegraph*

 36 From 'The British Embassy – I Washington', *Country Life*, 14 January 1939, 38–42, at p. 39; new print supplied by *Country Life* from original negative

PREFACE

Drinks before dinner

I am always disappointed when a book lacks a preface: it is like
arriving at someone's house for dinner, and being conducted
straight into the dining-room. A preface is personal, the body of
the book impersonal: the preface tells you the author's feelings
about his book, or some of them. A reader who wishes to remain
aloof can skip the preface without loss; but one who wants to be
personally introduced has, I feel, the right to be.

Michael Dummett[1]

I FIRST BROACHED the publication of his letters with Isaiah Berlin after
lunching with him in All Souls in the late 1980s. Over coffee, we were
discussing my possible departure from Oxford University Press to work on
his papers, and when the question of his letters came up I said that
publication would have to be selective. I had in mind the large quantity of
material, the likely views of publishers about what the market would stand,
and the fact that some letters were less interesting than, or repetitive of,
others, and so did not merit inclusion, at any rate in an edition intended for a
general readership. His response, which came without any noticeable pause
for reflection, surprised me, since it was so unlike his reliably self-deprecating
reaction to suggestions about publishing his academic writing. He brushed
aside my instinct for selectivity and said that, if the job was to be done, it
should be done thoroughly. The edition should be 'full-bottomed', free of
half measures.

Broadly speaking, I have since been guided by that clearly stated
preference, though it would have been unwise to follow it too literal-
mindedly. All the reasons for selectivity just cited do indeed apply, even if
they can be followed with a lighter or a heavier hand. A heavier hand would
have fashioned the one-volume selection that some publishers argued for,
but that outcome would have been unfaithful not only to Berlin's wishes,
but also to the quality of the material. Even the present degree of selection
has required strong doses of self-denial.

---

1 Preface to *Frege: Philosophy of Language* (London, 1973), opening paragraph. Though Dummett
writes as an author rather than an editor, the same applies, *mutatis mutandis*, to the present
enterprise.

The present, provisional, plan is that there should eventually be three volumes. The foundation of Wolfson College in 1966, or perhaps Berlin's retirement as President in 1975, is likely to provide the break between the second and third volumes. But all options remain open until the time comes. Indeed, this first volume was originally to have ended when Berlin left England for the USA for the first time in July 1940, but the preference of all publishers for fewer volumes than I at first envisaged, together with the more rounded impression of Berlin that emerges if his wartime output is included with his pre-war letters, led me to extend its coverage.

CORRESPONDENCE AND CORRESPONDENTS

> [Berlin] was internationally significant not only for his own achievements as philosopher, intellectual, teacher, writer and public figure, but also because he moved in so many different circles, corresponded with so many of the leading figures of his day, participated in so many momentous political and cultural events, was a beloved friend and mentor to so many others.[1]

Berlin, it hardly needs saying, was one of the most notable intellectual figures of the twentieth century. A leading liberal thinker of his time, indeed one of the most renowned English thinkers of the post-war era, he continues to be the focus of widespread interest and discussion, and the subject of conferences, books and other publications in many languages – not only because of his important ideas and the distinctive essays in which he recorded them, but because of the manner of man that he was. This is not the place to retell the story of his life – a biographical sketch giving the main details appears below,[2] and Michael Ignatieff's perceptive authorised biography[3] has already done the job splendidly – but something should be said about the correspondence.

Berlin was a prolific as well as an incomparable letter-writer throughout his life, and a very large number of his letters survive, which makes possible the publication of a selection fully representative of his multiple epistolary topics and personae. The first extant letter known to me was written in March 1928, by an eighteen-year-old St Paul's schoolboy, to G. K. Chesterton, asking him to contribute to a new school magazine, and the last at the end of October 1997 to Anatoly Naiman, Anna Akhmatova's friend and

---

1 Unnamed evaluator of the application by the Bodleian Library, Oxford, for funding to catalogue the Berlin Papers.
2 'A Personal Impression of Isaiah Berlin' (pp. xxxvii–xliv below), a slightly revised version of my obituary of Berlin, published in the *Independent* newspaper in London on 7 November 1997.
3 Michael Ignatieff, *Isaiah Berlin: A Life* (London and New York, 1998).

(latterly) secretary, less than a week before Berlin's death.[1] Spread through the almost three score years and ten between, there are thousands of other letters, covering all aspects and stages of Berlin's long, active and productive life: his time in Oxford as undergraduate, researcher, teacher, lecturer, professor and founding President of Wolfson College; his many visits to North America, Europe, Palestine/Israel and beyond; his work during the Second World War in New York, Washington and Moscow; his activities as administrator, author, critic and broadcaster. Running through the correspondence are several recurrent themes: these include his relationship with his parents, especially his mother, until their deaths, and from the 1950s with his wife Aline; his enormous and diverse network of friends and acquaintances; his love of gossip and anecdote; and his increasingly numerous interchanges with students and critics of his work. The correspondence spreads far beyond Oxford and academe into many other worlds, especially those of the arts and politics, in many countries.

The list of his correspondents includes a roll-call of men and women prominent not only in academia, but in politics, journalism, society, literature, music and art: Joseph Alsop, Noel Annan, A. J. Ayer, Lauren Bacall, Cecil Beaton, Max Beloff, Violet Bonham Carter, Elizabeth Bowen, Maurice Bowra, Alfred Brendel, E. H. Carr, Noam Chomsky, Winston Churchill, Sibyl Colefax, Emerald Cunard, Abba Eban, T. S. Eliot, Margot Fonteyn, Felix and Marion Frankfurter, Stuart Hampshire, Jacqueline Kennedy, Teddy Kollek, Harold Macmillan, Yehudi Menuhin, Nicolas Nabokov, L. B. Namier, Karl Popper, Anthony Powell, Bertrand Russell, Arthur Schlesinger, Jr, John Sparrow, Stephen Spender, Igor Stravinsky, A. J. P. Taylor, The Prince of Wales, Ava Waverley, Chaim Weizmann, Bernard Williams, Edmund Wilson and many more. But often it is the most unremarkable correspondents who receive the most remarkable letters: Berlin was scrupulous and generous in answering letters, no matter what their source; and of course he relished, above all, writing to his closest friends.

The vein of social comedy that runs through the letters and (hundreds of) postcards truthfully displays Berlin's ebulliently positive temperament: he was good company, a virtuoso in conversation, an essentially happy person, a lover of life in many of its various manifestations. Nor is he a stranger to self-mockery: 'I have always been prone to coloured descriptions of unimportant phenomena.'[2] What he writes is rarely drily academic: there

1 The letter is dated 31 October 1997; Berlin died on 5 November. Poignantly, he signed this last letter in Russian, with the diminutive version of his given name that his family and friends used in his early life: 'Шая' ('Shaya').

2 To Marion Frankfurter, 3 June 1936. More quotations appear in the IBVL under 'Quotations from Berlin'.

is, if anything, more about people – his supreme interest – than about ideas and events, especially in this first volume. Above all, he gossips: 'life is not worth living unless one can be indiscreet to intimate friends',[1] he once wrote; 'destroy this letter', he often directed, but, fortunately for us, the injunction was usually ignored.

During this initial period Berlin moved from St Paul's School, then in the London borough of Hammersmith, to Corpus Christi College, Oxford, where he took firsts in Greats in 1931 and in PPE in 1932.[2] He took up a post as Lecturer in Philosophy at New College in October 1932, and soon afterwards won a Fellowship by Examination (or 'Prize Fellowship') at All Souls – he was the first Jew to be elected to the College. In 1938, after completing the biography of Marx that primarily occupied him at All Souls, he became a Fellow of New College. In early July 1940 he left for America with Guy Burgess, intending to proceed to Moscow, but stayed in the US, apart from visits home and his famous trip in 1945–6 to the Soviet Union, until early April 1946, at which point this volume closes.

The pre-war letters are handwritten, but in America he learns to use a secretary. The secretaries had to learn to work for him, too, as these extracts from letters written in 1952 by one of them, Lelia Brodersen,[3] to a friend testify:

> He has an Oxford accent, a lisp, an inability to say r,[4] & the most inconceivably rapid "delivery" that I have ever heard outside of a patter song [. . .] On Tuesday, typewriter in hand & despair in heart, I arrived at the Deanery, where he is staying. [. . .]. I took his letters directly on the typewriter, which forced him to make pauses, since the noise of the machine forced itself upon him; he is happy to have things struck over, x'ed out, etc., & will sign literally anything; his letters are charming & occasionally pathetic; & he is movingly shy, polite, helpless, & apologetic. And – on Thursday, when I went again, & he was shortly called to the telephone, I started to read a reprint which

1 To Morton White, 7 May 1970.
2 'Greats' is the colloquial name for Lit. Hum. (Literae Humaniores, now called simply Classics), or more specifically, at this time, for the study of ancient history and philosophy, which occupied the last seven terms of the degree course. The full first part of the course, Honour Mods (i.e. Moderations), covering Greek and Latin language and literature, lasted for five terms; but because of his comparative weakness as a classical linguist, Berlin opted instead for Pass Mods, which he took at the end of his first term, sitting the final examination after three years (as against four for the full course). PPE is Philosophy, Politics and Economics, normally a three-year course, but completed by Berlin in a single year.
3 Lelia Brodersen, later chief psychologist at Bryn Mawr's child guidance clinic, worked briefly as Berlin's secretary when he was lecturing at the College. She was doing graduate work there at the time, was therefore short of money, and was picking up earnings wherever she could. These letters to Sheema Z. Buehne are postmarked 2 and 17 March 1952. For the full texts see 'Letters on Berlin' in the IBVL.
4 The latter two deficiencies were later overcome.

he had lying on his desk "Lev Tolstoy's Historical Scepticism."[1] I was at once caught up into it; & when he came back I asked him if he could spare it for a few days. "Oh, take it, take it," he said, fumbling madly among his papers. "I have them to send to people – take it – keep it." So I did, & when I had finished it I settled once & for all into the impression that here was a near-great, if not a really great man. [. . .]

I have grown curiously fond of him. I won't be sorry to conclude the secretarial part of it, but I will be sorry to see him go. There is a peculiar sweetness & charm there which grows upon one half-imperceptibly. It has really been quite an experience altogether.

THE BUILDER AND THE BUTLER

> I can't get used to your servant's manner [. . .] he behaves as if he's on equal terms, he makes *conversation* . . .[2]

> It is utterly impossible to persuade an Editor that he is nobody.
> William Hazlitt[3]

Hazlitt had a point. Nevertheless, there is sometimes a constructive role for this irritating parasite, so long as he remembers his station. What this station is varies considerably. Indeed, the notion of an editor is so capacious that one sometimes wonders how useful it is. What does the Editor of *The Times* who thunders on world issues have in common with the editor who establishes the text of Aeschylus, or the publisher's editor who tinkers with commas? Fortunately, context usually determines roughly which part of the wide editorial terrain is in question, though further particulars of the specific brief in operation are usually helpful.

Two rather different metaphors tend to come to my mind when I reflect on the peculiar editorial role that has fallen to me personally; between them they seem to me to capture many of the most important features of what I do, at any rate as I see it. The first metaphor is that of the stonemason slowly assembling a great building, perhaps a cathedral, from blocks of stone that are provided for him, some cut to size, some needing adjustment to fit into place. The other is that of the butler silently lurking behind the green baize door, his vision narrowed by its confinement within the household he serves, but also sharpened by its concentration on his restricted domain.

The mason is not (at any rate today) the architect of the cathedral; yet

---

1 *Oxford Slavonic Papers* 2 (1951), 17–54; reprinted with additions as *The Hedgehog and the Fox: An Essay on Tolstoy's View of History* (London and New York, 1953), and included in RT and PSM.

2 Words given to Alexander Herzen's mother, Luiza Haag, on p. 28 of Tom Stoppard's *Shipwreck* (London, 2002), part 2 of his trilogy of plays *The Coast of Utopia*.

3 From 'On Editors' (1830): vol. 17, p. 361, in *The Complete Works of William Hazlitt*, ed. P. P. Howe (London and Toronto, 1930–4).

the architect's vision is realised through the sympathetic work of the builder's hands on the materials he is given. The blocks may be prepared in advance, but they have to be exactly placed, and sometimes adjusted when unforeseen problems occur; the mortar for the joints between them must be well mixed in the right proportions, and the blocks must be carefully pointed, with no gaps. When the mason is done, the finished structure stands, if he has done his work well, as a monument not only to the artistic conception that made it a possibility, but to the workmanship which gave that conception physical form. Another builder could have done the job as well or better; but the building that stands for all to see was made by this one.

The butler operates from below stairs, which gives him a privileged but distorted view. He sees or hears of most of what goes on in his master's house, except for the most private episodes, but he is so myopically focused on the details of his microcosm that he finds it difficult or impossible to relate it, at any rate in a balanced or informed way, to the wider world. He knows every nuance of procedure at the social functions at which he officiates, but is tempted to believe that this is what all such functions are like, since he does not witness those in any other establishment. He is an unrivalled source of information about the minutiae of his employer's doings, but sees them out of context and out of proportion, and can therefore be naïve and un-perceptive about their implications, resonances and overtones. Once again, too, he is replaceable in a way in which his employer is not; but it is at his hands that the household's infrastructure is kept in some kind of working order.

The editor, then – this editor, at any rate – is essentially a lieutenant, a number two to the author whose work is under his care. When on duty, he does not wish to put himself forward too stridently; for this is not the purpose of the exercise. That purpose is to construct an edifice that realises the implicit vision of its designer, even if some of his plans were left in a fragmentary and ambiguous state at his death. It is to manage a social occasion that best displays the host's personality, not to distract the guests by obtrusively self-advertising antics. The glasses must seem to fill themselves. Who welcomes a waiter who interrupts his customers' conversation, still worse seeks to contribute to it, except in the most tangential and un-argumentative fashion? Who asks a builder for a lecture on architecture, or invites a butler to run a course on domestic management?

This is the rationale – sheer incompetence apart – for the absence of a strong directing critical hand in this edition. Some might seek, for example, by way of introduction, a scintillating vignette of Oxford life in the 1930s, or a résumé of the sociology of wartime America. Even if such aids were desirable, I am not the one to provide them, not being a social historian, or indeed a historian of any kind.[1] Besides, Berlin himself has well described the background of his wartime work in two pieces that I reproduce here as appendices, and the letters themselves clearly bespeak the worlds from which they emerge, as they do the personality of their author. In any event, I should not wish to interpose a particular set of spectacles between the text and its readers, as if I could tell them how to read Berlin's words. My aim, as explained in a little more detail below, has been to free readers (in Berlin's own terms, and in his spirit) negatively, not positively, to make what they pluralistically will of what he writes, by providing them with the minimum of factual information that they need in order to understand what is being said, and then to react to it as they see fit.[2] What is offered here is raw material, not a pre-processed critical package.

THE ELECTRONIC REVOLUTION

> There are, in my view, two factors that, above all others, have shaped human history in the twentieth century. One is the development of the natural sciences and technology, certainly the greatest success story of our time.
>
> Isaiah Berlin[3]

Thus begins Berlin's testamentary lecture on 'The Pursuit of the Ideal', delivered in 1988. One of the technological developments that has evolved and expanded out of all recognition even since then is the voracious invention of the Internet and email. This has already had a radical effect on the way in which we communicate with one another, on our selection of correspondents, and on the manner in which many kinds of research are most efficiently undertaken. Personal letter-writing is now in serious decline (not only under the influence of computers, of course, but also because of the increasing pressures of modern life), and hours spent in research libraries have been replaced by seconds spent with a computer search-engine.

Berlin's letter-writing, and the preparation of his letters for publication,

---

1 The latter disclaimer was sometimes proffered with markedly less plausibility by Berlin himself.

2 Inevitably, I have not followed this self-denying ordinance at every turn. Hence, for example, the epigraphs on p. vi. These too can be read in more than one way, but it may help to say that I had in mind principally (*a*) Berlin's idiosyncratic and attractive combination of exuberance of style and conception with a horror of imposing visions of life on those who do not share them; (*b*) the process of development whereby the sometimes self-conscious and purple prose of the adolescent and young undergraduate matures into the more measured and stately (but no less engaging) periods of our man in Washington.

3 PSM 1. The other factor, he wrote, 'consists in the great ideological storms that have altered the lives of virtually all mankind'.

fall on either side of this anthropological watershed in a providentially timely way. Berlin was one of the last, best exponents of the epistolary art before it was exposed to the mutating influence of this e-change; and the editing of the correspondence is one of the first generation of projects to benefit radically from the transforming potential of electronic research and communication. I am fortunate on both counts: the qualities of my material depend not only on its author's exceptional gifts but also on its having come into being before the e-revolution; and its preparation for publication would certainly have been far slower and even more deficient than it actually has been if that revolution had not gathered momentum while the work was in progress.[1]

A CRITICS' CRIB

> I pinned up before my desk a notice with the words: ACCURACY / RELEVANCE / CONCISION / INTEREST; and these were my objectives.   Anne Olivier Bell[2]

> One difficulty with his correspondence is that the flickering allusiveness would be lost on the general reader unless ponderously annotated.   John Hilton[3]

The preparation of an edition of the letters of a prolific and wide-ranging correspondent, especially one whose letters have not already been sought out and gathered together, is not to be recommended to those of a perfectionist or impatient disposition. The task is long and slow, and bristles with permanently open-ended quests and questions likely to induce despair or even nervous collapse in those whose temperament inclines them to pursue the cut-and-dried and to put every detail in its place. How far should the search for letters be pressed? How much information, and about which people, places and events mentioned in the letters, should be provided? To what extent, if at all, should this factual support be laced with comment or gossip? What should be done about passages that might wound those referred to in unflattering terms, or their surviving relatives and friends?

These are only the principal conundrums among the many that have to be faced and settled. My own decisions have been pragmatic as much as principled, and will not satisfy all (or any?) of my critics. For their benefit, and by way of introduction to the remarks that follow about editorial procedure,

---

1 For some related thoughts expressed nearer the beginning of this revolution see my 'Viewpoint' column in *The Times Literary Supplement*, 26 December 1980, 1464.
2 Anne Olivier Bell, *Editing Virginia Woolf's Diary* (London, 1990), p. 22.
3 Letter to the editor, 1 November 1991.

here is a paragraph from an imaginary hostile review that they are welcome
to plagiarise:

> The editorial support that the readers of these letters are given is defective in
> various significant ways. The information supplied in footnotes is for the most
> part relentlessly dry and factual, making the notes cumulatively thin and
> etiolated; the same is true of the occasional contextual or introductory passages
> that appear sporadically here and there, according to no clearly discernible
> principle. The prosopographical detail is monochrome and dead, the narrative
> links bland and flat, written in the style of an official report rather than with the
> hand of a biographer. In place of a Boswell we encounter a disjointed prose
> McGonagall, as if newspaper were used as a table-cloth on which to serve the
> dishes of a master-chef. What glimpses of a human response we are permitted
> are somehow pervaded by a cloying aura of uncritical sycophancy towards this
> often overestimated and overpraised writer. Even within its own terms the
> apparatus is inconsistent: dates are given for most individuals, but not for all;
> the amount of data provided about people of the same degree of importance in
> the correspondence varies considerably; odd currants of speculation and
> anecdote are randomly and unaccountably lodged in the factual dough. There
> are numerous errors, too, which undermine one's confidence in the general
> reliability of the editorial matter provided. [Here insert two or three sample
> mistakes, preferably embarrassingly laughable ones.][1] Well, half a loaf is
> better than none, but what an opportunity missed to do the job properly!
> Whenever a compiler is let loose on imaginative material, some degree of
> bathos is inevitable; but there are degrees even of bathos.

It should be clear by now that the understated interpretative presence whose
drawbacks are here (I hope) somewhat overstated is quite deliberate, 'to be
accepted or refuted by the critical reader', to use Berlin's own words.[2] It
remains only to give chapter and verse for the main editorial rules of thumb
and explanatory conventions that I have adopted.

Selection
The selection in this first volume is fuller than it can be hereafter, for three
reasons. First, fewer letters survive from this early period; second, the quality
of those that do survive is, not unexpectedly, more uniformly striking than in
later years, when (although excellent letters continue in profusion and gain
in maturity) survival is more indiscriminate; third, the sheer number of later
letters will require a more ruthless selection if the size of the volumes is not

---

1 In an enterprise of this kind errors are inevitable. For every topic there is someone who knows
more than I do, often at first hand, and could write a better note. Sources vary in reliability.
Slips of transcription occur. I shall record in the IBVL any mistakes that are notified to me, and
I encourage readers who find errors to put me right.
2 At the end of the author's preface to *The Magus of the North*: TCE 252.

to get out of hand. So not very many letters have been omitted or cut this time. When they have been, the reasons have to do either with my judgement of the intrinsic interest of the items or passages in question, or very occasionally with the need to protect the sensitivities of the living, but not, of course, with any reservations about the likely effect of the omitted material on the overall impression of Berlin given by the volume. Berlin is allowed to present himself just as he was, feet of clay and all.

One major exception to the inclusive policy of this volume should be mentioned. There is a plentiful supply of ostensible 'business' letters from Berlin's time at the British Embassy in Washington,[1] and these, apart from one or two representative samples, I have not included, in the belief that they would more naturally be published, if at all, as a separate volume, aimed at specialists in Anglo-American relations of that period. They would then complement H. G. Nicholas's edition[2] of the official dispatches drafted by Berlin for the British Ambassador, Lord Halifax. Though they are often diverting as well as perceptive – Berlin only rarely excluded the personal dimension from his professional correspondence – the general reader would probably find them too often opaque and esoteric, studded as they are with references to minor figures and events of the time that mean little to most of us today without the aid of a disproportionately vast apparatus of annotation. As Berlin himself wrote of his 'bootleg' correspondence with H. G. Nicholas during this period, his professional letters 'presuppose a somewhat more intimate knowledge of the American political scene than the majority of [. . .] readers could be expected to possess'.[3]

Arrangement

The letters are arranged in a single chronological sequence, so far as I have been able to establish one.[4] I have often been asked if I planned to group them by topic, or at least divide them into personal and academic. But not much reflection is needed before rejecting this approach, largely because of the uncompartmentalised nature of Berlin's epistolary personality. In addition, continuities and cross-references that are visible in a chronological

---

1 Many of IB's personal letters at this time were also dictated to his office secretaries, and survive only as the carbons they kept. In these cases there are often errors and confusions in the carbons that would have been put right in the top copies. I have corrected these where it is obvious what is wrong, but not otherwise; such letters are flagged '[*carbon*]' after the date as a warning that they may not correspond exactly to what was sent, especially given IB's practice of making (often prolific) handwritten additions to dictated letters.

2 H. G. Nicholas (ed.), *Washington Despatches 1941–1945: Weekly Political Reports from the British Embassy* (London and Chicago, 1981).

3 See p. 660 below.

4 The letters are often undated, and various clues as to their date have to be resorted to, when available. Sometimes only an approximate guess is possible. Any information enabling me to date them more precisely will be welcome.

sequence begin to disappear if other arrangements are adopted, and an extra
layer of signposting would then be required to compensate for this. If any
reader has a distaste for a particular subject-matter or correspondent, it
should not be difficult to identify and skip the relevant items and move on to
more appealing fare.

Editorial matter

From time to time I have inserted passages of what Berlin referred to as
'connective tissue', to provide context for the letters that immediately
follow. I have not followed a hard and fast rule as to when to supply
information in this way, and when to do so in footnotes, but my instinct has
been to opt for notes, other things being equal, so that readers who prefer to
encounter the primary texts without the distraction of commentary can
more easily do so. However, there are times when it is more economical,
and I trust more helpful, to resort to a headnote, or to introduce a series of
letters with a paragraph or two about their common hinterland. Sometimes I
have provided these paragraphs myself, sometimes I have taken them from,
or inserted into them material from, other sources – for example, the family
memoir that Mendel Berlin wrote in 1946 and subsequent years, the
autobiographical document dictated by Marie Berlin in 1971–2, or the wonderfully rich recorded interviews with Berlin conducted by Michael Ignatieff.
I have also felt free to refer readers to Ignatieff's biography[1] when
additional contextual information is available there in a form that it seemed
pointless to debase by paraphrase. Indeed, any reader who wishes to get the
most out of the letters should most certainly have read this biography, or at
least its relevant chapters, before embarking on the present volume.

The best connective tissue, where it is available, is naturally that
provided by Berlin himself. There exists a good deal of this in one form or
another – enough, perhaps, to constitute one day a patchwork autobiography of sorts – but it is somewhat scattered, and far from homogeneous in
style. The largest concentration is to be found in the pages of his *Personal
Impressions*, together with some other pieces of the same genre not included
there, and excerpts from that collection will no doubt find a place in the later
volumes of this edition. The reminiscences published by Berlin that are most
useful for this first volume are his introduction to H. G. Nicholas's selection
of the dispatches Berlin drafted in Washington (referred to above), and his
1972 Jacob Herzog Memorial Lecture, 'Zionist Politics in Wartime Washington'. Because these pieces are so intimately connected with the later letters
included here, and because they will not be readily available to all those who

---

1 By page, thus: MI 279. Interviews are referred to by archival reference number, thus: MI
Tape 7.

would like to read them in connection with the letters they illuminate, I have printed them both as appendices.

Annotation

As for the notes themselves, I quoted from Anne Olivier Bell at the head of this section more in hope than in expectation, more in admiration than in emulation – especially as regards 'interest'.[1] I have in general aimed to give only the minimum information necessary to identify, date and barely characterise the individual or other note-worthy item in question, at times adding something known to me that is relevant to the particular context. I have not sought to stand for long between readers and their encyclopaedias (in the case of those persons and topics that may be expected to appear in their pages): space and time would in any case have ruled this out; nor is it to my taste to rehearse or compress information – the selection of which would often be invidious – available in any modest reference library. If enough is said to enable readers to look up this kind of information quickly for themselves, I am content.[2]

My default format for notes on people is this: name (preferably in full), dates where discoverable without ludicrously disproportionate research,[3] occupation at the time of the letter, and before if relevant. Developments that took place after this volume closes, being unknown to Berlin and his correspondents in the period it covers, have on the whole been excluded, except where they seemed important for purposes of identification. I have not refrained from adding extra anecdotal material here and there, when it is to hand, even though this may make the notes somewhat heterogeneous – as Berlin would have liked. The same guidelines apply to the entries in the biographical glossary (on which see further below), which are not usually pen-portraits but simply collections of basic data, gathered together for ease of reference, on a selection of central and/or ubiquitous figures.

Letterheads

The format of the names, addresses and dates in the letter-headings has been

---

1 Her edition of Virginia Woolf's diaries, and the edition of Virginia Woolf's letters prepared by Nigel Nicolson and Joanne Trautmann, have indeed been my models on many levels.

2 A handful of well-known people are left unannotated.

3 Is it worth delaying publication substantially by conducting extensive genealogical enquiries to discover the dates of those who do not appear in publicly available sources, and pass briefly across the stage in a role to which precise dates are irrelevant? This is not, I hope, a counsel of idleness, rather one of avoiding complete slavery to obsession. Where necessary (and on occasion otherwise) I have set in train, sometimes with satisfying results, baroque invest-igations that would appal a professional time-manager.

standardised, and the most common addresses[1] abbreviated according to the following list:

Corpus Christi	Corpus Christi College, Oxford
New College	New College, Oxford
All Souls	All Souls College, Oxford
Hollycroft Avenue	49 Hollycroft Avenue, London NW3 (Berlin's family home from 1928)
British Information Services	The British Press Service, British Information Services, 30 Rockefeller Plaza, New York City
British Embassy, Washington, DC	British Embassy, 3100 Massachusetts Avenue, Washington, DC

The location of, and reference for, the original is given at the end of the text of letters held in archives. Otherwise it may be assumed that letters, or photocopies or carbons, either are in the Berlin Papers in the Bodleian Library in Oxford, or have been provided by their original recipients or their heirs.

Ancillary matter

People and other subjects that receive a gloss are in general footnoted on first occurrence only. The index will quickly locate this introductory note if it is needed in connection with a later reference to the subject in question. As already mentioned, figures of special importance to Berlin, and some who simply crop up with particular frequency, are also dealt with, usually at somewhat greater length, in a biographical glossary at the end of the text: an asterisk in front of a surname in a footnote or in the index signals the existence of an entry in this glossary.

The family trees that conclude the preliminary pages were compiled with astonishing investigative flair by the genealogist Jennifer Holmes; these make it easier to place Berlin's relatives, and the chronology that follows the appendices, compiled by Serena Moore and Jennifer Holmes, will usually pinpoint his whereabouts and occupation when he wrote a particular letter.

Editorial procedure

The originals of the items in the sections entitled 'London', 'Oxford' and 'New York' are in manuscript unless otherwise stated. Those in the later sections are typed unless said to be in manuscript. Manuscript items are in

---

1 It should not necessarily be assumed that a letter was written where its letterhead suggests: IB frequently used printed stationary purloined from elsewhere.

general transcribed exactly,[1] typescript letters lightly edited to eliminate the distracting and in any case irrelevant contributions of typists with differing styles, mannerisms and deficiencies. Paragraphing[2] in the texts of manuscript letters errs on the side of generosity: Berlin often wrote on narrow sheets that made it natural for him to indicate breaks by means of a wider interlinear space, or the turn of a page or a line, instead of an indent, and such indicators would disappear if the layout of the original were followed too literal-mindedly. Berlin's punctuation too – which is in any case moderately random, idiosyncratic and (sometimes) confusing[3] – tends to disappear at the ends of lines of manuscript; on the whole, however, I have not attempted to supply the desiderated points, whose presence is usually clearly enough implied by the context. But where it seemed positively unhelpful to stay my hand, I have silently introduced extra punctuation, and occasionally deleted or altered punctuation that struck me as especially misleading.

Abbreviations and other conventions

Berlin is referred to throughout the editorial matter as IB, and recipients of letters are referred to by their initials in notes to letters received by them. Undergraduates are not described as such in the notes, to avoid frequent repetition of the long word 'undergraduate': but undergraduate status may be inferred from the format 'Balliol classics 1929–33'. Also for reasons of space, the often cumbersome (and, to many, opaque) full titles of dons are not usually given: I have taken the view that readers will primarily wish to know a don's subject and College, and whether (s)he is a Fellow (and, if so, Tutor); other refinements, such as whether (s)he also holds a University Lectureship or other post, are omitted, though Professorships are given their official title. My format is 'Fellow and philosophy Tutor', the subject being attached to the Tutorship since Fellowships are not technically restricted to a particular subject; this post would be officially entitled 'Fellow and Tutor in Philosophy', a format I have eschewed as ambiguous and a fraction longer.

Angle brackets, ⟨ ⟩, enclose manuscript insertions, marginalia or postscripts in typescript letters, unless they are simply short corrections or afterthoughts that it would be excessively pedantic to distinguish in this way. The omission of part of a text, for whatever reason, is flagged by an ellipsis in brackets, thus: [. . .]. Unbracketed ellipses are authorial.

These and other abbreviations are listed on pages xlv–xlviii below,

1 Underlining is indicated by italic type.
2 A device Berlin always used too sparingly.
3 For instance, he often pairs a single inverted comma with double inverted commas.

together with a guide to short forms of names that are regularly used by
Berlin and not glossed on each occurrence.

Where no note is provided, it may be assumed either that it has not
proved possible to identify the person or other subject in question, or that it
did not seem worth the labour of doing so in the context. I should welcome
rescue from my ignorance and failure in such cases.

ACKNOWLEDGEMENTS

> I know that it is customary in works of this kind to end with some
> formula whereby the person whose name appears on the title
> page reveals that the book was in reality written by half a dozen
> other people, his own role being confined to distortion,
> plagiarism and the insertion of a few false references.
>
> R. D. Dawe[1]

> I am much indebted to conversations I have had with others over
> the years [. . .] I will not indulge in the conventional fatuity of
> remarking that they are not responsible for the errors this book
> may contain. Obviously, only I can be *held* responsible for these:
> but, if I could recognise the errors, I should have removed them,
> and, since I cannot, I am not in a position to know whether any of
> them can be traced back to the opinions of those who have
> influenced me.   Michael Dummett[2]

> This matter appears so trivial that I am afraid we cannot assist this
> time.   Secretary of the Churchill Society[3]

More than most of the other fourteen volumes of Isaiah Berlin's work that I
have so far edited or co-edited, this one has been a truly co-operative
venture, for all that I have been the main conduit for the wide-ranging
expertise incorporated herein. Not only have the resources of the Internet,
especially the miraculous Google search-engine, together with the electronic
resources of Oxford University's integrated library system – in particular
OLIS (its electronic catalogue) and online versions of *Who's Who* and *The
Dictionary of National Biography* – transformed my task, as intimated earlier;
but I have also depended heavily on the special knowledge of a number of
scholars, and of friends of Berlin, who have given out from their stores of
accumulated knowledge and wisdom with great generosity. A full history

---

1 R. D. Dawe, *The Collation and Investigation of Manuscripts of Aeschylus* (Cambridge, 1964),
   Preface, p. viii.
2 op. cit. (xv/1), p. xii, quoted here with the same proviso there invoked.
3 Email of 6 March 2003 to Kate Payne, responding to a request to identify a passage from one of
   Churchill's speeches.

of this beneficence would be a long essay in itself. But a few words must be said about my principal personal debts of gratitude, invidious as it is to single out particular individuals.

I begin with the recipients of the letters and their heirs and assigns, without whom there would have been little to edit. On almost all hands I have found them helpful and forthcoming, not only with letters but with background information, and in other ways. Their crucial contribution has only been thrown into sharper relief by the handful of cases in which I have been met by silence or refusal. Not that I begrudge those who prefer not to make their letters available: but I am glad that they are in a tiny minority.

Next, Berlin's Literary Trustees.[1] Lady Berlin has been consistently kind, generous and patient, even on the rare occasions when our judgements have not initially coincided. She has also helpfully commented on a draft text of my selection of letters. Peter Halban has always been unreservedly available for help, support and advice. Lady Berlin's generosity has also enabled me to retain the services of my brilliant Assistant Serena Moore, who, disguised as Sally Denholm-Young, was Berlin's secretary at Wolfson in 1972. In addition to contributing directly to several aspects of the work on the letters, Serena has run my office with saintly tenacity and tact since she joined me in late 1998, and her conception of her role is imaginatively large. This has left me gloriously free to concentrate on my main editorial work. I am daily aware of my dependence on her loyal support.

The other name that belongs in this company is that of Pat Utechin, Berlin's private secretary for as long as I knew him. For all those years she was the vital link with Berlin and his authorial activities, as recorded in my acknowledgements in earlier volumes. She also became one of my closest personal friends. I could not begin to summarise what she has done for me, in all sorts of ways. It is certain that my larger project has been fundamentally rooted in her expertise and enthusiasm. This is a permanent state of affairs, even though, with Berlin's death and the transfer of his papers to the Bodleian Library, her day-to-day involvement has inevitably diminished. But her input has continued, and she has nobly read the typescript and made numerous helpful comments and suggestions.

Four long-standing friends of Berlin's in particular have been irreplaceable sources of personal knowledge, especially about this early period, for which help of this kind is increasingly hard to find, and therefore of exceptional value. Mary Bennett, née Fisher, knew Berlin well from the early 1930s, as did Jenifer Hart, née Williams; Stuart Hampshire became a friend in

---

1 IB appointed Lady Berlin, Peter Halban and myself as his Literary Trustees in 1996. In 2002 Lady Berlin appointed a fourth Trustee in the person of Alan Ryan, who has readily put his wide knowledge at my disposal.

1935; Jean Floud came to know Berlin later, but is also knowledgeable about the years in question. They have all explained allusions and answered myriad questions with a will. Jenifer Hart has gone further and spent very many hours looking up the material for footnotes, and writing it down for me. Because of my gratitude to her for this heroic assistance I was specially glad when Aline Berlin suggested that this volume should be – most appropriately – dedicated to her.

Another unrivalled source of first-hand contemporary knowledge has been Arthur Schlesinger, Jr, whom Berlin met in Washington in the winter of 1943–4. Despite his many other commitments he has read the wartime letters and enabled me to annotate many of the names that appear in them, always saving me time and often telling me what I should not otherwise have discovered. Similarly generous expert readings have been provided by Susan Brewer (author of *To Win the Peace: British Propaganda in the United States during World War II*) and Nicholas Cull (author of *Selling War: The British Propaganda Campaign against American 'Neutrality' in World War II*), both of whom have supplied explanations of many allusions that would otherwise have been hard and time-consuming to unravel.

In late 2000 the Berlinian expert Joshua Cherniss, then an undergraduate at Yale in his final year, introduced himself by email, having visited the Literary Trust's website. He has become a good friend, an indefatigable correspondent and a helper of great understanding and effectiveness, and has now happily come to Oxford to do graduate work, which means that I can take advantage of him even more mercilessly than before, if this were possible.

Michael Hughes, Archivist of the Berlin Papers at the Bodleian Library, most ably assisted by Matthew Neeley, has cheerfully entered into the spirit of the enterprise, and has patiently responded to requests for information and for copies of documents now in his care. As he catalogues he discovers items (some very important) which I had overlooked or forgotten and alerts me to their significance, much to the benefit of this book.

Michael Ignatieff, Berlin's biographer, has donated to the Literary Trust in my care, for eventual onward transmission to the Bodleian Library, his recordings and transcripts of his interviews with Berlin, and all his working papers. I am very grateful to him for his exemplary open attitude to my use of the material he worked so long and hard to accumulate.

Betty Colquhoun has now been typing Berlin's (and others') difficult manuscript, and his secretaries' typescripts, for me for some thirteen years, and has become an unrivalled interpreter of Berlin's squiggles and hiero-glyphics. The great majority of the keystrokes that have generated this book

are hers, and I pay tribute to her skill, endurance and unfailing willingness
and courtesy.

For the last thirteen years my work has been supported by generous
benefactors who do not seek public recognition. This remains the case, and I
am as grateful to and dependent on them as ever; the same applies to my
debt to the late Lord Bullock, who arranged my funding at the outset and
kept an eye on it thereafter. Most recently the Ford Foundation, at the
instigation of Kenneth B. Wilson, has enabled me to seek help with some of
the time-consuming ancillary tasks that were hanging over me, and also to
improve my electronic resources: I thank Ken and the Foundation most
warmly for this timely act of rescue, whose principal fruits are described in
the next paragraph.

The life both of the project and its editor has been saved over recent
months by two tireless, meticulous, imaginative and self-effacing scholarly
researchers, Jennifer Holmes and Kate Payne. Kate has completed the
explorations in the Public Record Office at Kew that I had hardly begun,
and has there discovered several documents of the greatest interest that were
previously unknown to me. She has also most productively and patiently
double-checked my annotation, kept me relentlessly up to the mark in my
endlessly postponed attempts to plug the gaps therein, drafted many of the
missing notes, and performed numerous other thankless tasks from which
the book has greatly benefited. What is more, she and Jennifer have tracked
down numerous individuals who had eluded all previous sleuthing by myself
and others; the tale of some of their explorations has to be heard to be
believed. Jennifer, furthermore, in addition to acting as genealogist to the
project, and supplying missing annotation, has stepped into some of the
other breaches left gaping too long while my attention has been diverted
elsewhere: in particular she has drafted much of the editorial connective
tissue, as well as checking the dating and sequencing of the letters, which had
previously been seriously awry. Indeed, in the last stages of the preparation
of the volume the help I received from experts of various kinds, and from
these two supremely competent researchers in particular, became the
principal input into the editorial apparatus, especially for the war years.

For Russian matters I have turned again in the main to Helen Rappaport,
who has already helped with other volumes of Berlin's work, and have relied
as usual (as have Jennifer Holmes and Kate Payne) on her wide-ranging
expertise and exemplary efficiency. For Hebrew/Jewish questions I have
called principally on Daniel Frank, and on the eponymous wisdom of
Norman Solomon, and for Yiddish I have applied to Gennady Estraikh.

Much as I should like to continue specifying who has contributed what,
and how, the time has now come to resort to a list. Many of those whose

names appear on it have helped in ways no less crucial for being more localised. I apologise to anyone I have forgotten to mention, and hope that they will not forbear to complain, so that I can make amends. My thanks, then – together, surely, with those of the readers of this edition – to Pauline Adams, David Alan, Brigid Allen, Susan Mary Alsop, Christopher Andrew, Susan Ashcroft-Jones, Norma Aubertin-Potter, Lynda Bailey, Simon Bailey, Clare Baker, Gunnar Beck, Kate Belanova, Richard Bell, Ruth Ben Ari, Margaret Bent, Beryl Blair, Elizabeth Boardman, John Bodley, Mary Bone, Peter Boswell, Baruch Brandl, Michael Brock, Lelia Brodersen, Geoffrey Brown, Sally Brown, Ian Brunskill, Philip Burnham-Richards, Ron Bush, Becky Cape, Ursula Carlyle, Terrell Carver, John Casson, Don Chapman, Elizabeth Chilver, Mary Clapinson, Jerry Cohen, Janet Collyer, Judith Curthoys, Julie Curtis, Caroline Dalton,[1] Silvia Daniel, Robin Darwall-Smith, Kate Day, Timothy Day, Jacqueline Dean and her colleagues, Ernesto Del Valle Lehne, John Donaldson, James Douglas, Rosemary Dunhill, Mastan Ebtehaj, Valerie Eliot,[2] Kenward Elmslie, Robert Evans, Jean Fasman, Jules Feldman,[3] Jan Fellerer, Sev Fluss, Roy Foster, Nigel Francis, Lucy Gaster, John Geddes, Sir William Goodhart, Cyril and Martin Goodman, Alan Gordon, Stephen Gower, Micha Gross, Steffen Gross, John Gurney, Samuel Guttenplan, Adrian Hale, Anne Hardy, Ellen Hardy, Robin Harland, Ian Harris, Brian Harrison, Stephen Harrison, Selina Hastings, Roger Hausheer, Peter Heales, Joanna Hines, Emily Hirons, Leofranc Holford-Strevens, Park Honan, David and Diana Hopkinson, Jill Hughes, Roger Hutchins, Alastair James, Peter Jay, John Jenkins, Jeremy Johns, Myra Jones, Alexander Kabishev and family, Jim Kates, Dov-Ber Kerler, Charles L. Koch, Lionel Kochan, Barbara Kraft, Clive Lacey, Nicola Lacey, Philippe Lambert, John Landers, Matt Landrus, Stephen Latham, Midge Levy, Andrew Lownie, Henry Luce III,[4] Paul Luna, Chris McDowell, Peter McInally, Richard McKane, Archie Mackenzie, John Maddicott, Bryan Magee, Henry O. Malone, Christine Mason, Douglas Matthews, Mary Merry, Claire Miller, David Miller, Ann Mitchell, Gail Monahan, Janet Morris, Edward Mortimer, Anatoly Naiman, Peter Nelson, Aubrey Newman, Jon Newman, Penelope Newsome, Sheila Noble, Judy Nokes, Onora O'Neill, Verena Onken-von Trott, Amanda Opinsky, Peter Oppenheimer, Polly Pemberton, Chris Penney, John Penney, Ofra Perlmutter, Elliot Philipp, Roland Philipps, Gérard Philippson, Ellena Pike, Lesley Pitman, Jane Potter, Oliver Ready,

---

1 I must break my rule and add here that Caroline, the Archivist at New College, has been exposed to a remorseless succession of enquiries, which she has answered with unflinching patience, good humour and skill.
2 By courtesy of whom I publish letters to T. S. Eliot from the Faber archive.
3 An Israeli cattle-farmer who thankfully enjoys answering queries in the IBVL.
4 For permission to publish the cable of 13 August 1945 from his father to IB.

David Rechter, James Reed, Julian Reid, Phil Reid, Mario Ricciardi, Michael Riordan, Christine Ritchie, Robert Ritter, Timothy Robbins, Gareth Roberts, Ben Rogers, Ken Rose, Miriam Rothschild, Jodi Roussel, Alan Ryan, Micky Sacher, Janet Sample, Ruby Sangster, Ronald Schuchard, Sophia Schutts, Yvonne Scott, Judy Sebba, Sam Sebba, Merav Segal, Avi Shlaim, Robert Silvers, Ben Simpson, Rowena Skelton-Wallace, Gill Skidmore, Ann Pasternak Slater, R. E. F. Smith, Joanna Snelling, Natasha and Stephen Spender, Michael Stansfield, Roberta Staples, Will Sulkin, John Sutherland, Marjory Szurko, Alan Tadiello, Shabtai Teveth, Conrad Tiarks, Deirdre Toomey, Brenda Tripp, Clarita von Trott, Jeff Walden, Julian Walton, Bernard Wasserstein, Stephan Wenderhorst, Nigel West, Christopher Wickham, Mary-Kay Wilmers, Michael Wolfers, Mike Woodin, Christine Woodland, Mary Yoe. Some of these persons have died during the years of the book's gestation, but my gratitude survives them.

ENVOI

> Art, and the summer lightning of individual happiness: these are
> the only real goods we have.
>
> Alexander Herzen[1]

It is rather an anti-climax if the preface in which one welcomes one's readers fizzles out in a list of names, however needful and sincere the record of obligation may be. So I conclude with a self-regarding moment.

To know such a consummate human being[2] as Isaiah Berlin for twenty-five years, to become his friend, and to edit and publish his scattered work with his co-operation, is a pleasure that I could never have aimed at or expected. I have been by temperament one who over-plans and likes to proceed too rationally. For that reason, the fact that I have spent much of my life on an unpredictable task on which I stumbled by a series of accidents such that, if any one of them had fallen out otherwise, I should have been deprived of what has become my vocation, is a particularly delicious irony. Were Berlin a saint, I should propose that he be the patron saint of untidiness; certainly my own association with him fits a patronage of that

---

1 A. I. Gertsen, *Sobranie sochinenii v tridsati tomakh* (Moscow, 1954–66), vol. 16, p. 135, as 'translated' by Berlin in 'Herzen and his Memoirs', PSM p. 524.

2 I take this opportunity to put on record an encounter that struck me at the time, and may be thought to corroborate this judgement. I bumped into the satirist John Wells (1936–98), whom I had not previously met, as he was leaving Brooks's Club in London after the celebration of IB's 40th wedding anniversary on 7 February 1996. He already knew he had the lymphoma from which he was to die less than two years later. We each explained our connection with IB, he finishing, as he donned his scarf and turned to the staircase, with the words 'the best human being I have known'. Nimiety (cf. vi/2)? I doubt it.

character, in many ways. However that may be, luck has smiled on me, and I cannot improve on Lelia Brodersen's retrospective verdict on her dealings with him: It has really been quite an experience altogether.

HENRY HARDY

Tisvilde Lunde, Nordsjælland, Denmark, August 2002
Wolfson College, Oxford, February 2004

A PERSONAL IMPRESSION OF
ISAIAH BERLIN

ISAIAH BERLIN was one of the most remarkable men of his time, and one of the leading liberal thinkers of the twentieth century. Philosopher, political theorist, historian of ideas; Russian, Jew, Englishman; essayist, critic, teacher; he was a man of formidable intellectual power with a rare gift for understanding a wide range of human motives, hopes and fears, and a prodigiously energetic capacity for enjoyment – of life, of people in all their variety, of their ideas and idiosyncrasies, of literature, of music, of art.

His defence and refinement of what he saw as the most essential conception of freedom achieved classic status, and the presence and character of this conception in the modern mind is due in no small measure to him. He also identified and developed, with considerable originality, the pluralist view of ultimate human ideals that supports his liberal stance, and deserves to become just as deeply embedded in our outlook. In contrast to the great majority of ideologies and creeds that humanity has created, he argued that not all values can be jointly realised in one life, or in a single society or period of history, and that many ideals cannot even be compared on a common scale; so that there can be no single objective ranking of ends, no uniquely right set of principles by which to live.

From this it follows not only that people should be free (within the crucial but rather broad limits set by the demands of sheer humanity), both individually and collectively, to adopt their own guiding priorities and visions of life; but also, perhaps more radically, that a perfect, frictionless society, as well as being impossible in practice, is in principle incoherent as an ideal. Insights of this kind may seem unstartling to some today, but this, Berlin maintained, is a more recent, less widespread and less secure development than might be supposed; it is also a beneficent one, and may be laid partly at his door.

Like other great men he was a catalyst of excellence. Those who have had the good fortune to know him can testify to the strikingly positive, enlarging, warming experience of being in his company and listening to his irrepressible flow of captivating talk. He was legendary as a talker both for his imitable rapid, syllable-swallowing diction and for his inimitable range – he was astonishingly widely read in a number of languages, he knew (and deeply influenced) a great many prominent men and women in England and elsewhere, and he peppered his conversation and writings with a bewildering cascade of names. (This was not name-dropping: the names were a short-hand for their bearers' ideas.)

Though he spent his whole professional life, apart from his war service, as an Oxford academic, he did not suffer from parochialism, and moved with equal ease in the many worlds he inhabited, often simultaneously, surviving day after day, without flagging, a punishing schedule of commitments and diversions. He lectured to learned and distinguished audiences in many countries, talked to undergraduate societies (not only in Oxford), colleges of education and sixth forms, and gave generously of his time to the growing number of those who made demands on it: former students with problems, scholars studying his work, strangers who sought his advice or help in connection with projects of their own. He was often heard on the radio, especially the Third Programme, and gave numerous interviews, particularly to foreign journalists. He positively relished what others would have found intolerable pressures and, though he was perfectly serious when the occasion demanded, brought a sometimes impish sense of fun to everything that he undertook.

He was not, and would not have wished to be, any kind of saint, but he was a good man, with feet of top-quality clay, and had in abundance what in others he called 'moral charm'. This attribute was particularly striking in his manner of conversation, which could unsettle those new to it. He did not stick to the point, but would sit back, look up, and follow his interest where it led, happily digressing, digressing from digressions, and unceremoniously returning to the topic of his own previous remarks, or changing the subject, apparently oblivious of what his interlocutor may have been saying, even at some length, in the interim.

This last idiosyncrasy might have seemed impolite in other hands, but in him it was clearly unselfconscious, and demonstrated his absorption in the issue before his mind, which he would pursue almost playfully, often in odd directions. Although talking to him made one's mind race, it could be infuriating if one wanted to sort out some problem and come to a clear conclusion, and he was not always an attentive listener – sometimes because he had a shrewd idea of what one was going to say before one had said it.

He had little taste for (or skill in) purely verbal word-play, but his wit, in the wider sense, was matchless. He could be bewilderingly quick in the uptake, and equally quick with an illuminating response. He was refreshingly direct and, for a man of his generation, unusually open: he made the obsessive circumspection of some parts of the Oxford establishment seem mean and life-denying by comparison. Gossip and anecdote abounded, but not malevolently: indeed, he was virtually incapable of innuendo, and did not seek to score points. Even when he propounded an unfavourable view of someone, it could seem more like a move in a game than a damning judgement. He loved ranking people, and sorting them into types: most famously, hedgehogs and foxes – those in the grip of a single, all-embracing vision as against those who are more receptive to variousness. Indeed, his taste for light-hearted categorisation was an informal manifestation of his ability to extract and display the essence of a person or a difficult writer.

As a lecturer he had complete command of his material, and was spellbinding to listen to (fortunately several of his lectures were recorded, and can now be heard at the National Sound Archive in London).[1] He was consciously but not self-consciously Jewish, and a lifelong Zionist: his role in the creation of the State of Israel was not insignificant. He was a Director of Covent Garden and a devoted opera-goer; he was a Trustee of the National Gallery. He did not lack recognition – a knighthood, the OM, many honorary doctorates, the Mellon Lectureship, the Presidency of the British Academy, the Jerusalem, Erasmus, Agnelli and Lippincott Prizes – but always protested that he was being given more than his due, that his achievements had been systematically overestimated. He was larger than life, entirely *sui generis*, a phenomenon, irreplaceable.

Isaiah Mendelevich Berlin was born in 1909 to Russian-speaking Jewish parents in Riga, the future capital of Latvia, but then under Russian rule. His father, Mendel, owned a timber business (chiefly providing sleepers for the Russian railways); his mother, Marie, was a lively, cultured woman, enthusiastically interested in the arts. She bequeathed her enthusiasm in full measure to her only surviving child, whose love of music in particular, especially but by no means only opera, was a thread of deep and growing importance to him which ran through his life from boyhood onwards.

In 1915 the German army was closing on Riga, and the Berlins moved to Russia proper. They lived first in Andreapol, then, from 1917, in Petrograd, where in that year Isaiah witnessed both the Social Democratic and the Bolshevik Revolution. On one occasion he saw a terrified, white-faced man being dragged and kicked through the streets by a mob; this was a formative experience which left him with an ineradicable loathing of any form of violence.

In 1920 the Berlins returned to Riga, under a treaty with the Communists, and Mendel decided to move to England, where he had friends and business connections. Arriving in early 1921, they lived first in Surbiton, then in London – in Kensington and, a few years later, Hampstead. After prep school Isaiah went to St Paul's and, without ever losing touch with his Russian or Jewish identities, continued a thoroughgoing process of

---

1 His 1965 Mellon Lectures on romanticism can also be heard at the National Gallery of Art in Washington, DC.

Anglicisation that enabled him to become a prominent figure in the English culture of his day.

In 1928 he went up as a scholar to Corpus Christi College, Oxford. He took Firsts in Greats and PPE in 1931 and 1932. Thereafter he was interviewed (unsuccessfully) for the *Manchester Guardian* and made preparations to read for the bar; but Richard Crossman, then a don at New College, gave him his first post, as a lecturer in philosophy. Almost immediately he was also elected to a fellowship at All Souls which ran concurrently with his lectureship until 1938, when he became a Fellow of New College. It was during this first spell at All Souls that he wrote his brilliant biographical study of Marx for the Home University Library (*Karl Marx: His Life and Environment*, 1939): ironically he was by no means the series editors' first choice for the job.

During the early years of the Second World War Berlin continued to teach. Then, in 1941, he was posted to New York by the Ministry of Information. In 1942 he was transferred to the British Embassy in Washington, DC, where he served until 1946 (apart from a few months in Moscow) as head of a team charged with reporting the changing political mood of the United States. The dispatches sent to Whitehall from Washington, not in his name but mostly drafted by him, attracted the attention of Winston Churchill, and have long had a reputation for their brilliance; a selection (*Washington Despatches 1941–1945*, edited by H. G. Nicholas) was published in 1981.

Berlin has written most engagingly about aspects of these years: in particular, his descriptions of his meetings in Russia with Boris Pasternak, Anna Akhmatova and other writers are extremely moving. His encounter with Akhmatova had an especially profound effect on him; and the many passages about him in her poems bear witness to its fundamental significance for her too. 'He will not be a beloved husband to me / But what we accomplish, he and I, / Will disturb the Twentieth Century': she was convinced that there was a direct link between Stalin's reaction to their meeting in 1945 and the beginning of the Cold War in 1946.

By the end of the War Berlin had decided that he wanted to give up philosophy for the history of ideas, 'a field in which one could hope to know more at the end of one's life than when one had begun'.[1] In 1950, with this in view, he returned to All Souls, where in 1957 he was elected to the Chichele chair of Social and Political Theory in succession to G. D. H. Cole. His inaugural lecture, *Two Concepts of Liberty*, is one of his best-known works, and certainly the most influential. In it, with great passion and subtlety, he stands up for 'negative' liberty – freedom from obstruction by others,

[1] CC viii.

freedom to follow one's own choices – and shows how easily 'positive' liberty, the (desirable) freedom of self-mastery, is perverted into the 'freedom' to achieve 'self-realisation' according to criteria laid down and often forcibly imposed by self-appointed arbiters of the true ends of human life. His account has remained an indispensable reference-point for thought about freedom ever since, and permeates all subsequent informed discussion of the subject; nevertheless, perhaps partly because of the unassertive and deliberately unsystematic nature of his ideas, and his rejection of panaceas of any kind, he did not (to his relief) in any narrow sense acquire disciples or found a school of thought.

The year before his election to the chair, abandoning his apparently settled bachelor existence, he had married Aline Halban (née de Gunzbourg). In his late forties he had found the partner who would be the linchpin of his life from that time onwards; and, in his three stepsons (he had no children of his own), a mutually devoted family. He always recommended marriage to others.

In 1966 Berlin became the first President of the newly founded Oxford graduate college, Wolfson, relinquishing his professorship the following year. Wolfson College, where he remained until his 'retirement' in 1975, would not have come into existence in its present form and under its present name (it began as Iffley College) without his efficacy as fund-raiser and charismatic inspirer of new institutional forms, traditions and loyalties. The generosity of the Wolfson and Ford Foundations in funding the building and endowment of the College was in direct response to his personal involvement.

Wolfson apart, Berlin's chief legacy to the future is what he wrote: a large, enormously varied *oeuvre* of unmistakable style and penetration. In his own, reasonable, estimation his most important work is represented by his exploration of four fields of enquiry: liberalism; pluralism; nineteenth-century Russian thought; and the origins and development of the romantic movement. Under all these headings he shed much new light, and the way he did so still retains the power to excite which it had when his contributions were first made public.

For most of his life his reputation as a writer lagged behind his actual output, much of which was in the form of occasional essays ('I am like a taxi: I have to be hailed'), often published obscurely. Comparatively little had appeared in book form – principally *Karl Marx*, *The Hedgehog and the Fox* (a long essay on Tolstoy's view of history), and the collection *Four Essays on Liberty*, which included his inaugural lecture. But then in 1976 came *Vico and Herder*, and shortly thereafter four volumes of collected essays (1978–80).

These books gave the lie to a remark made by his friend Maurice Bowra when Berlin was appointed to the Order of Merit in 1971: 'Though like Our Lord and Socrates he does not publish much, he thinks and says a great deal and has had an enormous influence on our times.'[1] Other volumes followed in the 1990s, including two devoted to work he had left unpublished when it was first written, and The Proper Study of Mankind, a retrospective anthology of his work published early in the year of his death.

By contrast with Bowra's case, a good deal of Berlin's way of speaking is captured, happily, in his published work, which is imbued with his personality and sets forth his cardinal intellectual preoccupations with the greatest clarity and fecundity, if often through the medium of his enquiries into the ideas of others. One of the most attractive characteristics of his writing is that he is never merely the detached scholar, never forgetful that the point of the enquiry, in the end, is to increase understanding and moral insight. Since, as another friend, Noel Annan, has put it 'He will always use two words where one will not do',[2] his message – a notion he would have hated – is impossible to summarise without losing all of its characteristic mode of expression. But its central content can be baldly stated.

Berlin once described the main burden of his work as 'distrust of all claims to the possession of incorrigible knowledge about issues of fact or principle in any sphere of human behaviour'.[3] His most fundamental conviction, which he applauded when he discerned it in the writings of others, and adopted in an enriched form as his own, was that there can never be any single, universal, final, complete, demonstrable answer to the most ultimate moral question of all: How should men live? This he presents as a denial of one of the oldest and most dominant assumptions of Western thought, expressed in its most uncompromising form in the eighteenth century under the banner of the French Enlightenment.

Contrary to the Enlightenment vision of an eventual orderly and untroubled synthesis of all objectives and aspirations, Berlin insisted that there exists an indefinite number of competing and often irreconcilable ultimate values and ideals between which each of us often has to make a choice – a choice which, precisely because it cannot be given a conclusive rational justification, must not be forced on others, however committed we may be to it ourselves. 'Life may be seen through many windows, none of

---

1 Letter to Noel Annan, quoted in Annan's 'A Man I Loved', in Hugh Lloyd-Jones (ed.), *Maurice Bowra: A Celebration* (London, 1974), 53.
2 PI2 xxiii.
3 RT viii.

them necessarily clear or opaque, less or more distorting than any of the others.'[1]

Each individual, each culture, each nation, each historical period has differing goals and standards, and these cannot be combined, practically or theoretically, into a single coherent overarching system in which all ends are fully realised without loss, compromise or clashes. The same tension exists within each individual consciousness. More equality may mean less excellence, or less liberty; justice may obstruct mercy; honesty may exclude kindness; self-knowledge may impair creativity or happiness, efficiency inhibit spontaneity. But these are not temporary local difficulties: they are general, indelible and sometimes tragic features of the moral landscape; tragedy, indeed, far from being the result of avoidable error, is an endemic feature of the human condition. Instead of a splendid synthesis there must be a permanent, at times painful, piecemeal process of untidy trade-offs and careful balancings of contradictory claims.

Intimately connected with this pluralist thesis – sometimes mistaken for relativism, which he rejected, and which is in fact quite distinct – is a belief in freedom from interference, especially by those who think they know better, that they can choose for us in a more enlightened way than we can choose for ourselves. Berlin's pluralism justifies his deep-seated rejection of coercion and manipulation by authoritarians and totalitarians of all kinds: Communists, Fascists, bureaucrats, missionaries, terrorists, revolutionaries and all other despots, levellers, systematisers or purveyors of 'organised happiness'. Like one of his heroes, the Russian thinker Alexander Herzen, many of whose characteristics he manifested himself, Berlin had a horror of the sacrifices that have been exacted in the name of Utopian ideals due to be realised at some unspecifiable point in the distant future: real people should not have to suffer and die today for the sake of a chimera of eventual universal bliss.

Berlin always discussed these ideas in terms of specific individuals, not in the abstract, remembering that it is the impact of ideas on people's lives that give them their point. Here he was served by his unusual capacity for imaginative identification with people whose visions of life varied greatly and were often distant from his own. This enabled him to write rich and convincing accounts of a wide range of figures, historical and contemporary: Belinsky, Hamann, Herder, Herzen, Machiavelli, Maistre, Tolstoy, Turgenev, Vico; Churchill, Namier, Roosevelt, Weizmann; and many others. His descriptions of those with whom he is in the closest sympathy often have a marked autobiographical resonance: he said of others, with dazzling virtuosity, what he would not have been willing to say of himself, what he

1 PI 4.

probably did not believe of himself, though his words sometimes fit his own case precisely. Had he been sufficiently interested in his life and opinions for their own sakes, he would have been his own ideal biographer; but he would also have been a different man.

Isaiah Berlin was often described, especially in his old age, by means of superlatives: the world's greatest talker, the century's most inspired reader, one of the finest minds of our time – even, indeed, a genius. It may be too early to be sure about such strong claims. But there is no doubt that he showed in more than one direction the unexpectedly large possibilities open to us at the top end of the range of human potential, and the power of the wisely directed intellect to illuminate, without undue solemnity or needless obscurity, the ultimate moral questions that face mankind.

H.H.

ABBREVIATIONS

All Oxford colleges except New College are referred to in the notes without the word 'College'. Information in the form 'Balliol classics 1929–33' indicates that the person concerned was an undergraduate reading that subject at that Oxford college during that period. Page references are not introduced with 'p.' or 'pp.' when the context makes it obvious that that is what they are. Cross references of the form '(256/6)' mean 'see page 256, note 6'. An asterisk before a surname indicates that there is an entry on the person in question in the biographical glossary.

⟨ ⟩	enclose manuscript addition to typed item
{ }	enclose matter mistakenly present in manuscript
[?]	uncertain transcription (follows doubtful word without intervening space)
[ ]	gap in carbon typescript where typist could not interpret IB's dictation
[. . .]	matter omitted by editor
AC	IB, *Against the Current: Essays in the History of Ideas*
b.	born (the absence of a date of death does not necessarily mean that the person concerned is still living)
BIS	British Information Services (whose main office was in New York until 1942, then in Washington)
BL	British Library
BPS	British Press Service
CC	IB, *Concepts and Categories: Philosophical Essays*
CCC	Corpus Christi College, Oxford
Ch. Ch.	Christ Church (Oxford College)
Corpus	Corpus Christi College, Oxford
Corpuscles	Brian Harrison (ed.), *Corpuscles: A History of Corpus Christi College, Oxford, in the Twentieth Century, Written by its Members* (Oxford, 1994)
d.	died (the absence of a date of birth does not necessarily mean that the person concerned was never born)
Dept	Department
DNB	*The Dictionary of National Biography*
FDR	(US President) Franklin Delano Roosevelt
FO	Foreign Office (London)
FORD	Foreign Office Research Department (London)
FRPS	Foreign Research and Press Service (based in Balliol)
Greats	Literae Humaniores, the second part of the classics course at Oxford, comprising (in the relevant period) philosophy and ancient history: see p. xviii above, note 2

IB	Isaiah Berlin
the IBVL	*The Isaiah Berlin Virtual Library*, website at http://berlin.wolf.ox.ac.uk/
ILO	International Labour Organization
Kt	Knight
KM	IB, *Karl Marx*
L	IB, *Liberty*
LMH	Lady Margaret Hall (Oxford women's college)
LSE	London School of Economics [and Political Science]
MEW	Ministry of Economic Warfare
MI	Michael Ignatieff, *Isaiah Berlin: A Life* (page references are given by number alone, thus: MI 97)
MI Tape	recording of interview by Michael Ignatieff (interviews conducted 1988–97)
MOI/M. of I.	Ministry of Information (London)
MP	Member of Parliament
n.d.	no date
n.p.	no place
NY	New York
OSS	Office of Strategic Services (USA)
OUA	Oxford University Archives
OWI	Office of War Information (USA)
PI; PI2	IB, *Personal Impressions* (both editions); 2nd edition thereof
PPE	Philosophy, Politics and Economics (Oxford University undergraduate course)
PRO	Public Record Office (Kew, London)
PSM	IB, *The Proper Study of Mankind: An Anthology of Essays*
PWE	Political Warfare Executive (a branch of British Intelligence)
q.v.	*quod/quem/quam vide*: 'which [or 'whom' – male or female] see', i.e. see the entry for the item/person in question
RT	IB, *Russian Thinkers*
SCR	Senior Common Room
SD	State Department
SHAEF	Supreme Headquarters Allied Expeditionary Force
SIS	Secret Intelligence Service (also known as MI6)
SM	IB, *The Soviet Mind: Russian Culture under Communism*
SSEES	School of Slavonic and Eastern European Studies (London)
TCE	IB, *Three Critics of the Enlightenment: Vico, Hamann, Herder*
Univ.	University College, Oxford
UNRRA	United Nations Relief and Rehabilitation Administration
WD	H. G. Nicholas (ed.), *Washington Despatches 1941–1945: Weekly Political Reports from the British Embassy*
WIZO	Women's International Zionist Organization

Listed below are the people most frequently referred to in the letters in this volume. The incomplete versions of their names in the left-hand column are not annotated except on first occurrence; rather, these names can be assumed to refer to the individuals in the right-hand column unless otherwise stated.

Adam	Adam von Trott
Aubrey	Aubrey Morgan
Austin	J. L. Austin
Ayer	A. J. Ayer
Ben	Ben Nicolson
BJ	Baby Junior, i.e. Maire ('Moira') Lynd
Butler	Sir Harold Butler
Chaim, Charles	Chaim Weizmann
Chip	Charles Bohlen
Christopher	Christopher Cox
Con	Constance Morgan
David	Lord David Cecil
Diana	Diana Hubback (later Hopkinson)
Dick	Richard Crossman
Douglas	Douglas Jay (also 'Dougle')
Felix, F.F.	Felix Frankfurter
Foster	John Foster
Francis	Francis Graham-Harrison
Fred	Fred Rau
Freddie	A. J. Ayer (occasionally 'Freddy'; Ayer himself wrote 'Freddie')
the Gazelle	Stuart Hampshire
G[oronwy]	Goronwy Rees
Guy	Guy Chilver
Hants	Stuart Hampshire
Herbert	H. L. A. Hart
Hodgkin	Thomas Hodgkin
Ida	Ida Samunov, IB's maternal aunt
Inez	Inez Spender, née Pearn, later Madge
Jenifer	Jenifer Williams, later Hart
Jeremy	Jeremy Hutchinson
Joseph	H. W. B. Joseph
the Justice	Felix Frankfurter
Mary	Mary Fisher (later Bennett)
Maud	John (Redcliffe-)Maud
Maurice	Maurice Bowra
Miss (Fis[c]her)(-)	
Williams	Jenifer Williams
Moore	Moore Crosthwaite
Mrs Cameron	Elizabeth Bowen

Mrs Chilver	Sally Chilver, née Graves
Pares	Richard Pares
Peggy	Margaret Jay, née Garnett
Rach	Solomon Rachmilevich
Ridley	Jasper Ridley (the younger)
Robin	Robin Cruikshank
Rosamond	Rosamond Lehmann
Rowse	A. L. Rowse
Roy	Roy Harrod
Salter	Sir Arthur Salter
Shiela	Shiela Grant Duff (later Newsome, then Sokolov Grant)
Sigle	Sigle ('Sheila') Lynd
(Mr) Smith	A. H. Smith
Stephen	Stephen Spender
Stuart	Stuart Hampshire
Tony	Antony Andrewes
Victor	Victor Rothschild
Wallace	David Wallace
Woodward	E. L. Woodward
X, Xtopher	Christopher Cox
Yitzhak, Yitz(c)hok	Yitzhak Samunov, IB's maternal uncle

Most but not all of these individuals, together with other frequently mentioned people, are subjects of the brief biographical summaries in the biographical glossary that precedes the index. The people in that list are only briefly glossed on first occurrence in the text, and on that occasion an asterisk at the beginning of the surname indicates that an entry is to be found in the glossary, thus: 'Stephen Harold *Spender'.

—

The quotation on the first page of this volume is from Samuel Johnson's preface to *The Plays of William Shakespeare, in Eight volumes, with the Corrections and Illustrations of Various Commentators; to which are added Notes by Sam. Johnson* (London, 1765), p. lix: p. 103 in *Johnson on Shakespeare*, ed. Arthur Sherbio, first vol. (New Haven and London, 1968) [*The Yale Edition of the works of Samuel Johnson*, vol. 7].

The quotation on the last page (after the index) is from Hegel's foreword to *Grundlinien der Philosophie des Rechts*: p. 37 in Georg Wilhelm Friedrich Hegel, *Sämtliche Werke*, ed. Hermann Glockner (Stuttgart, 1927–51), vol. 7. The translation is mine.

FAMILY TREES

These notes explain the conventions adopted in the three family trees that follow:

Persons in italics appear with more detail elsewhere.

Only selected members of these extensive families are shown. Preference has been given to the relations IB mentions.

East European Jews did not adopt fixed surnames until well into the nineteenth century; so the earliest generations of the Schneerson family are shown without surnames. Even thereafter variation persisted, as in the Fradkin family, some of whose members used the name 'Ladier'.

The question of given names is even more complicated. Any given name may, at different times and in different places, appear in a multiplicity of different forms: Hebrew, Yiddish, Russian and English, with a range of diminutives in each language. The many versions of 'Isaac' shown in these trees demonstrate this variation. The names given in the trees are mainly Yiddish for the earlier generations, including that of IB's grandparents. Later names are those used by IB.

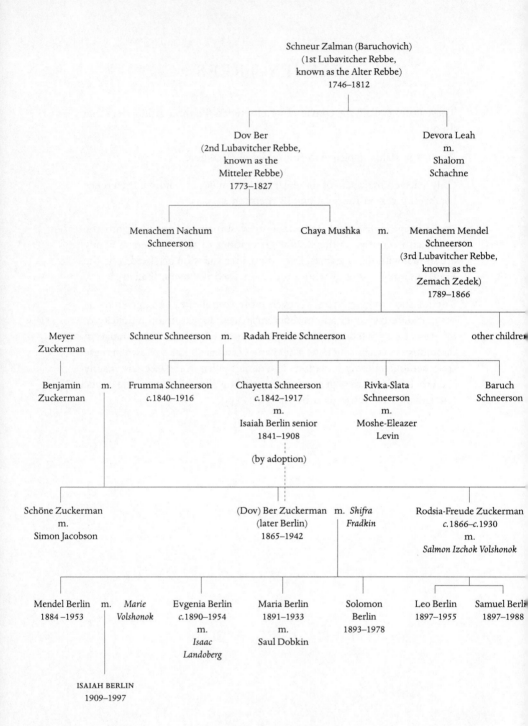

THE BERLIN FAMILY

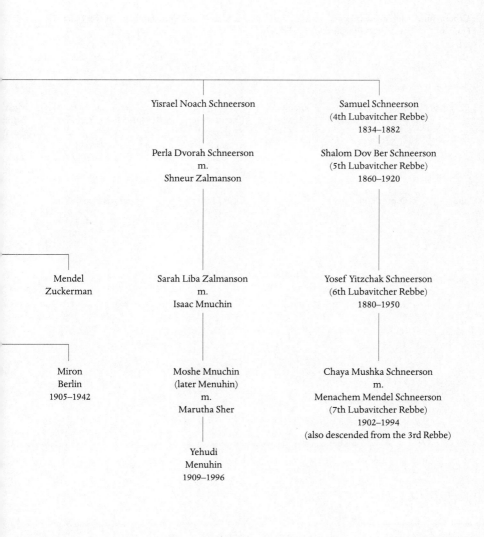

Yisrael Noach Schneerson

Samuel Schneerson
(4th Lubavitcher Rebbe)
1834–1882

Perla Dvorah Schneerson
m.
Shneur Zalmanson

Shalom Dov Ber Schneerson
(5th Lubavitcher Rebbe)
1860–1920

Mendel
Zuckerman

Sarah Liba Zalmanson
m.
Isaac Mnuchin

Yosef Yitzchak Schneerson
(6th Lubavitcher Rebbe)
1880–1950

Miron
Berlin
1905–1942

Moshe Mnuchin
(later Menuhin)
m.
Marutha Sher

Chaya Mushka Schneerson
m.
Menachem Mendel Schneerson
(7th Lubavitcher Rebbe)
1902–1994
(also descended from the 3rd Rebbe)

Yehudi
Menuhin
1909–1996

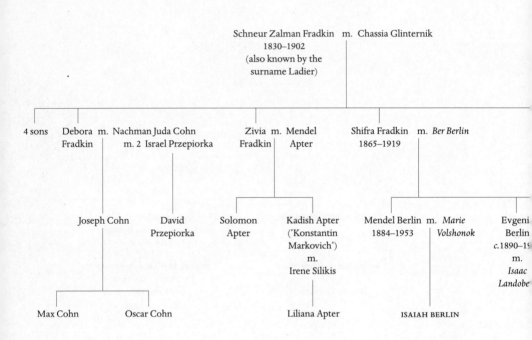

Schneur Zalman Fradkin m. Chassia Glinternik
1830–1902
(also known by the
surname Ladier)

| 4 sons | Debora m. Nachman Juda Cohn | | Zivia m. Mendel | Shifra Fradkin m. *Ber Berlin* |
| Fradkin | m. 2 Israel Przepiorka | Fradkin | Apter | 1865–1919 |

Joseph Cohn   David Przepiorka   Solomon Apter   Kadish Apter ('Konstantin Markovich') m. Irene Silikis   Mendel Berlin m. *Marie Volshonok*   Evgeni Berlin *c.*1890–19 m. *Isaac Landober*
1884–1953

Max Cohn   Oscar Cohn   Liliana Apter   ISAIAH BERLIN

THE FRADKIN FAMILY

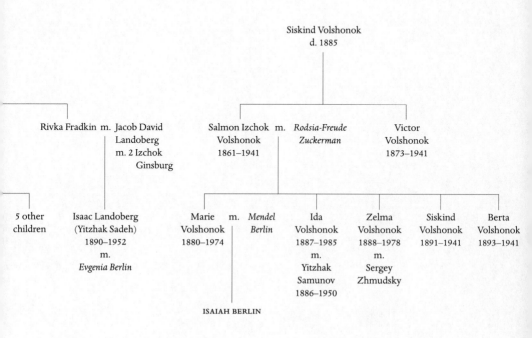

Siskind Volshonok
d. 1885

Rivka Fradkin m. Jacob David
Landoberg
m. 2 Izchok
Ginsburg

Salmon Izchok m. *Rodsia-Freude*
Volshonok   *Zuckerman*
1861–1941

Victor
Volshonok
1873–1941

5 other
children

Isaac Landoberg
(Yitzhak Sadeh)
1890–1952
m.
Evgenia Berlin

Marie m. *Mendel*
Volshonok   *Berlin*
1880–1974

Ida
Volshonok
1887–1985
m.
Yitzhak
Samunov
1886–1950

Zelma
Volshonok
1888–1978
m.
Sergey
Zhmudsky

Siskind
Volshonok
1891–1941

Berta
Volshonok
1893–1941

ISAIAH BERLIN

THE VOLSHONOK FAMILY

THE LETTERS

Called
rere

Promise
given
17/5/28

33, Upper Addison
Gardens 105
W. Kensington W. 14

31/3/28

Dear Mr Chesterton

My friends and I make bold to address this letter to you because
we regard ourselves as, in a sense, continuing a tradition
which you and your friends had started at St. Paul's School.
The boast and peculiarity of St. Paul's has for a long time been
that it did not produce a uniform type of men for export to
the universities, — that Paulines are totally unlike men from
any other school, and totally unlike each other; this fact in
itself is not remarkable in a day-school; what is remarkable
is that this peculiarity finds no articulate expression
anywhere: the Speaking societies, viz. the Union and the Junior
Debating Society, both of which have now all the forces of tradition
behind them, are normally anaemic and languishing bodies.
'The Pauline' magazine is still an arid and gloomy publication,
which reflects no side of school life whatever. 'The Debater,'
which in theory represents the rebels, has been declining into
a tame collection of writings of the prize-essay type, and has all but

The first page of the earliest surviving letter, to G. K. Chesterton, 31 March 1928

LONDON

The only great and tremendous satisfaction I had in my life was that my son is growing up and studying among people who consider him clever and good-hearted.

Marie Berlin, autobiographical notes[1]

---

1 Marie *Berlin (1880–1974; an asterisk signals an entry in the biographical glossary), mother of Isaiah *Berlin (hereafter 'IB').

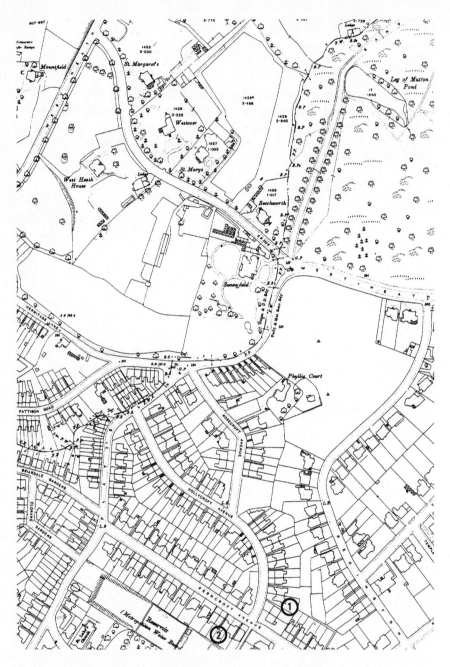

*Part of Hampstead: the Berlin family moved into 49 Hollycroft Avenue (1) in October 1928;
the Philipp family (see p. 253 below, note 6) lived at 6 Ferncroft Avenue (2)*

IB first took his Higher Certificate examinations at St Paul's School,
Hammersmith, London, in July 1927.[1] He passed, though without
winning any distinctions. In December 1927, having been rejected twice
by Balliol College, Oxford, in the spring (once for a scholarship, once for
a place), he won a Scholarship[2] to Corpus Christi College to read
'modern subjects', i.e. Classical Mods[3] followed by history. But after a
conversation soon afterwards between IB and G. B. Grundy,[4] the
Corpus don who claimed to have secured him his award, the history
element was replaced by Greats.

TO G. K. CHESTERTON[5]

31 March 1928

33 Upper Addison Gardens, West Kensington, London W14

Dear Mr Chesterton

My friends and I make bold to address this letter to you because we regard ourselves as, in a sense, continuing a tradition which you and your friends had started at St. Paul's School. The boast and peculiarity of St. Paul's has for a long time been that it did not produce a uniform type of men for export to the universities, – that Paulines are totally unlike men from any other school, and totally unlike each other; this fact in itself is not remarkable in a day-school; what is remarkable is that this peculiarity finds no articulate expression anywhere; the Speaking societies, i.e. the Union and the Junior

1 He offered Classical Studies (Latin, Greek, Ancient History, Literature), with English Literature as a Subsidiary Subject: *Oxford and Cambridge Schools Examination Board: Examinations for Certificates, July 1927, List of Successful Candidates* [Cambridge, 1927; bound as part of OUA OC 10/43], p. 21.

2 According to IB, 'I probably got in on the essay paper, writing on "bias in history". We were a fairly sophisticated London school, we used to read highbrow journals, e.g. T. S. Eliot's *Criterion*: that had recently published an anti-Western article by an Indian whose name I don't recollect called "Bias in History" – the very title of the set essay – and I reproduced what I remembered of it, and was elected.' From his contribution to Brian Harrison (ed.), *Corpuscles: A History of Corpus Christi College, Oxford, in the Twentieth Century, Written by its Members* (Oxford, 1994), 44–50, at p. 44. The article he remembers is Vasudeo B. Metta, 'Bias in History', *Criterion* 6 No 5 (November 1927), 418–25. The school gave him Logan Pearsall Smith's *Little Essays Drawn from the Writings of George Santayana* (London, 1920) as a scholarship prize.

3 For Mods and Greats see xviii/2.

4 George Beardoe Grundy, Fellow and ancient history Tutor, Corpus Christi College (CCC), 1903–31, Senior Tutor 1928–31.

5 Gilbert Keith Chesterton (1874–1936), journalist, novelist, critic, poet; illustrator and co-author of *The First Clerihews* (Oxford, 1982), a facsimile of the notebook in which Edmund Clerihew Bentley (485/8) and his contemporaries at St Paul's recorded the first examples of this genre, including two by GKC (on Cervantes and Carlyle) that were later published by Bentley as his own. At St Paul's, aged sixteen, GKC founded the Junior Debating Club and a magazine entitled *The Debater*. GKC attended St Paul's from 1887 to 1892, IB from 1922 to 1928.

Debating Society, both of which have now all the force of tradition behind them, are normally anaemic and languishing bodies. 'The Pauline' magazine is still an arid and gloomy publication, which reflects no side of school life whatever. 'The Debater', which in theory represents the rebels, has been declining into a tame collection of writings of the prize-essay type, and has all but lost touch with the livelier elements in the School.[1] There is no doubt that the School is as full of original talent as ever; but this talent is extraordinarily shy and refuses to show its face in public, and must therefore be coaxed into doing so patiently and delicately. We have therefore considered it advisable to found a new School magazine whose sole and whole purpose would be to print anything submitted by Paulines, if it is well-enough written, and more or less sincere, however irresponsible, or immature, or fantastic it may be. We shall attempt to concentrate on contents and vigour rather than faultlessness of style, and have selected for this purpose an editorial committee from among the most unconventional elements in the School: the Union, and the Lower School are both represented upon it. We naturally intend Paulines rather than Old Paulines to be the chief contributors; but it is all-important that 'The Radiator' should be inaugurated with great éclat, and be at once read as widely as possible, and as the impetus, which anything written by you in it would produce on the sales, is infinitely great, we appeal to you, sir, to help us in our task. The first number of 'The Radiator' will probably be issued on the 1st of June (permission for a 'new satirical Journal' has been granted by the High Master),[2] and we shall be grateful to you, sir, for anything you choose to send us; – a poem or an essay or a story or an open letter will be equally welcomed by us. Once more allow me to implore you, sir, in the name of Exuberance and Outspokenness which will surely be the distinctive characteristics of our magazine, to give us your support.

    I remain

        yours sincerely

           I M Berlin[3]

           (Joint-Editor).

British Library, BL Add. MS. 73232A

The letter is annotated by Chesterton: 'Called here / Promise given 17/5/28'. The first issue of the Radiator *was published on 5 June, too soon to*

1 IB himself contributed to the *Pauline* and the *Debater* in 1928: one of his contributions (631/1) appears in this volume; the others may be read in the IBVL under 'Uncollected publications'. No doubt he also wrote some of the other material in the first issue of the *Radiator* (vol. 1, No 1, Summer 1928, sixpence), as well as the article on pp. 7–8 below, but no item is signed by him.
2 John Bell (1890–1958), High Master 1927–38.
3 M = Mendelevich, a patronymic IB later dropped.

include the promised contribution, but this unsigned description of the encounter (surely by IB) does appear therein:[1]

OUR INTERVIEW WITH GKC

We came replete and in good humour to our goal – Topmeadow, Beaconsfield,[2] nor had we been long upon our journey. The house glowed in the warm sunlight, and proved a perfect picture of contentment. Timidly and with halting steps we advanced along a flagged path to the great oak door; with deference we pressed the electric bell, and politely stated our request. We were told that the great man was busy, but that he would see us. We almost fell over each other in our eagerness to be the first to grip him by the hand. We found ourselves (we know not quite how) in the presence. We were motioned with a wave of the hand and sat nervously upright upon the edge of a sofa drenched in large orange cushions, tracing imaginary patterns with our walking sticks upon the ample carpet. The whole room seemed a luxurious surfeit of cushions, large orange cushions. We felt as in a trance. GKC waved a hand – *the* hand, we reflected, that had written . . . – we were recalled from our reverie by a Voice, 'Americans . . .'. We listened, and heard how some incredible American had thought of some medieval Chesterton building that house, of Chestertons from generation to generation adding to it, and lastly of GKC sitting in this ancestral pile writing of men who were Thursday and of the innocent Father Brown.[3] From the depths of the chair he uttered his quiet studious laugh . . . 'built it ourselves twelve years ago . . .'.[4] Yes, the oak certainly *looked* old; but we pictured the low-ceilinged Tudor houses and shuddered.

This was the epitome of comfort itself. We got decidedly sorry for America, in so far as one can feel pity for a nation that sings not the praises of beer.

'When I revisit the shadows of the moon' (happy phrase!) murmured the voice in the chair 'what always strikes me is Digby La Motte.[5] Still as young as ever he was when I was a small boy. I would like to take him about in my pocket, and produce him and say "See how young I am! Here am I, a disreputable old journalist: there's my old schoolmaster!"' There came a period of chuckles . . .

We shook hands.

The last thing we were conscious of was a booming voice, 'The cross roads . . . Windsor . . . through the town . . . good luck . . .'

1 On pp. 24–5.
2 Where Chesterton and his wife Frances (d. 1938) continued to live for the rest of their lives.
3 Chesterton's *The Man Who Was Thursday* appeared in 1928, his *The Innocence of Father Brown* in 1911.
4 The house was indeed built by the Chestertons, to their specification.
5 Digby La Motte (1861–1946), a young master at St Paul's in Chesterton's time.

We felt that we had been in the presence of the great, and the great had not disappointed us.

Chesterton redeemed his promise with a poem, 'Debellare Superbos',[1] which appeared in the second issue of the magazine,[2] re-titled St Paul's School Radiator *because the Albion Motor Co. in Glasgow, whose trade journal was called* The Radiator, *had lodged an objection.*

From May to October 1928, while moving house from Kensington to Hampstead, the Berlin family lived at the Royal Palace Hotel, Kensington. During this intermission IB's parents, together with Marie's sister Ida,[3] visited their relations in Riga, to help IB's aunt Berta[4] care for her ailing mother.[5] IB appears to have divided his time between the hotel and the Samunovs' home in Sinclair Road (near St Paul's School), where Yitzhak,[6] Ida's husband and Mendel Berlin's[7] business partner, would have kept him company. Mendel evidently returned before Marie: see the letter from Rotterdam below.[8]

TO MARIE AND MENDEL BERLIN

Sunday [3 June 1928]

57 Sinclair Road

Dear Mother & Father.

Both Itzchock[9] & his sister regard me as having definitely advanced in the science of looking after myself. For instance I commit no grave mistakes in connection with my diet, I get my clothes pressed, I go to bed & rise in time, and generally behave better than the Schlemihl[10] which I am usually made out to be. To day for instance I sent off 7 letters to M-r I. Goldston informing him that though father would simply leap for joy if he could

---

1 'To subdue the proud in war', from Vergil, *Aeneid* 6. 853. The poem is not included in *The Collected Poems of G. K. Chesterton*, 3rd ed. (London, 1933), the first edition of which (London, 1927) IB reviewed anonymously in the February 1928 issue of the *Pauline* – vol. 46 (1928), 13–15 – nor listed in John Sullivan, *G. K. Chesterton: A Bibliography* (London, 1958).

2 Winter 1928 number, p. 39.

3 Ida Samunov (1887–1985).

4 Berta Volshonok (1893–1941), Marie's unmarried sister.

5 Rodsia-Freude ('Rosa') Volshonok (*c.*1866–*c.*1930).

6 Yitzhak Samunov (1886–1950). His surname sometimes became Germanised as 'Zamenhof', as in the case of the Russian-speaking Polish Jew who invented Esperanto, Ludwik Lejzer Zamenhof (1859–1917), to whom it intrigued IB to think himself connected.

7 Mendel *Berlin (1884–1953), IB's father.

8 p. 12.

9 Yiddish transliteration of Hebrew version of 'Isaac' (usually 'Yitzhak' among Hebrew-speakers); also 'Yitzchok'.

10 Yiddish for 'unfortunate but amiable bungler'.

contribute some £1000 to the N[ew] West End Synagogue,[1] yet, because he is away, the joy is still to come; to Women Zionists[2] I write that it is hopeless for them to start anything so long as you, their head, brain, heart, muscles, intelligence, energy, (oh mother!) are away. To Councillor Arthur Howitt[3] I write of my sympathy in that he is going to be deprived of both your companies when he opens a Talmud Torah;[4] in fact, perhaps he can postpone it? it won't be the same without you. As for the Bnei Brith[5] they have decided to liquidate the whole business if you are not going to help them. What are ten thousand Snowmans[6] to one you? And so on. Your social duties seem to extend from Lady Aberdeen[7] to Harrods who indignantly demand payment for certain scent & eau de cologne which father seems to have purchased. Moreover P. S. Allen,[8] the President of Corpus,[9] has written to ask for my Higher Certificate; I had to answer that I had no access to it. Perhaps father can write Yitzchok where it is lying, because one does not want to keep University waiting. The valet de chambre is frankly surprised at the quantity of fathers suits, shoes, etc. He says nothing but looks on me (am I not also partly owner of them?) with vast respect.

The Hall-Porter regards himself as 'in loco parentis' i.e. my adopted father, and rings up to Yitzchok whenever there are letters. My relations with him, if not actually intimate, are of special 'деликатность'.[10] I lead a very comfortable double existence. Mostly I sleep here, with Yitzchok, but sometimes I pass the night at the hotel. Last night I went to [the] theatre with Ettinghausen,[11] and so as not to disturb anyone, I slept at the Hotel. All meals, of course, in school-time and during the weekend I take at Sinclair

---

1 A fashionable Ashkenazi synagogue in St Petersburgh Place, London W2, on whose behalf, it seems, Mr Goldston was running an appeal.

2 Marie, always an active Zionist, was for many years the Chairwoman of the Brondesbury and District Women's Zionist Society, a branch of the Federation of Women Zionists of Great Britain and Ireland.

3 A councillor in the SW London district of Richmond, of which he had been Mayor in 1924–5.

4 Religious secondary school for Jewish children, attended on Sundays.

5 B'nei B'rith ('Sons of the Covenant') is the most prominent world-wide philanthropic Jewish association.

6 A prominent Hampstead Jewish family; cf. 529/4.

7 Lady (Ishbel Maria) Aberdeen (1857–1939), née Marjoribanks, wife of John Campbell Gordon, 7th Earl of Aberdeen and 1st Marquess of Aberdeen and Temair, youngest daughter of 1st Baron Tweedmouth.

8 Percy Stafford Allen (1869–1933), President of CCC 1924–33.

9 Whither IB would be bound in October 1928.

10 'Delikatnost'' ('tact').

11 Walter George Ettinghausen (1910–2001), born in Munich, one of three children of a successful book-dealer; IB's contemporary at St Paul's 1923–8 and Oxford (Queen's modern languages 1928–32); after the war he changed his surname to Eytan, and was later (1948–59) first Director-General of Israel's Foreign Ministry.

Road. M-rs Swan¹ who is terribly excited about L'affaire Halevi² looks after me devotedly. At last (now I may write definitely) (do not wire congratulations till a day after – *please*.) it has come off officially. So to-day the Braut & Brautigam³ went off to Jasha Heifetz⁴ as a kind of quasi-honeymoon. Both are very pleased, and Yitzchock's worst fears are allayed because Halevi has come in a different suit and a new shape of collar. I have already announced my definite intention to avail myself often of their hospitality, and they seem less downcast than one might suppose. A pleasant, if slightly elderly pair. Will they have children? but there, I am getting indelicate. Rivkah is slowly learning English but persists in commanding me not [to] speak Turkish, which is a language which she seems to detest above others. Russian is Turkish, English is Turkish, French is Turkish, Hebrew is almost Turkish, but Yiddish is *not* Turkish. Why? A deep problem. When you come back bring Bertha with you. (My digestion is perfect, Eno's Fruit Salts is a heavenly drink, and I am looking better.)

　　Yours with love etc. etc. etc.

　　Shaya

P.S. To see Halevi & Rivkah blush before each other is a romantic and remarkable sight which those who have not seen it cannot imagine. IMB.

TO IDA SAMUNOV⁵

　　[June 1928]

　　　　　　　　　　　　　　　　　[57 Sinclair Road, London W14?]

Dear Idussia.

　　I am now engaged in the exciting pursuit of literary fame i.e. I have become the editor of a new School paper which is quite difficult to publish.⁶ It is written definitely for the lower classes and plays up to the gallery; which is very amusing and pleasant. One cannot soar in high intellectual sublimities all the time: and even a little commonness is a relief. I am sending you a copy. As usual I write about myself, because to tell the

---

1 Perhaps the housekeeper.
2 A reference to the engagement between Yitzhak's sister Rivka and Eliezer Halevy, the future parents of Ephraim Halevy, Head of Mossad (the Israeli secret service) 1998–2002.
3 'Braut' and 'Braütigam' are German for 'bride' and 'bridegroom'.
4 Jascha Heifetz (1901–87), American violinist originally from Russia, gave a recital in the Albert Hall, London, on the afternoon of Sunday 3 June 1928, with his main accompanist at that time, Isidor Achron; the programme included Grieg's Sonata in C Minor and Lalo's *Symphonie Espagnole*.
5 A PS added to a letter, of which only the last (second) page survives, from Yitzhak to Ida.
6 The *Radiator*: see pp. 5–6 above.

truth I cannot find a more interesting topic. My admiration for Gandhi[1] grows every day. A very great man. My prize[2] is for Shakespeare & Carlyle.

Yours with love
    Shaya.

P.S. I am more than delighted by the Halevi-affaire. To watch it grow under one's eyes was a delight and an experience. Nor did it lack in positive beauty. There is something to be said for the Jewish method of marriage after all.[3] In every sense a Mazal Tov.[4] Mrs Swan feels it as a personal achievement, and her pride is great. The whole house is therefore in an uplifted mood of joyful expectancy. As it ought to be. Anyhow I, who am vowed to eternal celibacy, am very glad. Which, from me is enough. Needless to say, so are the couple concerned. Which is more than enough.

Yours
    Shaya

In July 1928 IB re-took Higher Certificate, gaining a distinction in Latin and Greek, and again passing in English Literature.[5] In the same month the Governors of St Paul's awarded him a leaving exhibition in classics.[6] In his final report on IB the High Master commented: 'He has the prospect of a brilliant career at Oxford; I entirely endorse the opinion of his Form Masters, and the work he has already done in English is that

1 Mohandas Karamchand Gandhi (1869–1948) was at this time working in particular for the non-violent elimination of conflict within Indian society; his response to inter-communal violence was to fast.
2 The Butterworth Prize (awarded at the 'Apposition' ceremony on 25 July) for performance in an examination set after the Easter holidays (4 April to 1 May) on Shakespeare's play *Henry IV*, parts 1 and 2, and *Heroes and Hero-Worship* – in full, *On Heroes, Hero-Worship and the Heroic in History* (London, 1841) – by Thomas Carlyle (1795–1881), historian, translator and essayist, for whom strong, heroic individuals, in their different spheres of influence, provide crucial leadership for their fellow-men. Joshua Whitehead Butterworth (1817–95), Master of the Stationers' Company and head of the well-known firm of law publishers based in Fleet Street, was at St Paul's 1828–32, and founded his prize for English Literature in 1889. IB also won the Lord Chancellor's Prize and Truro Medal (endowed by Thomas Wilde, 1st Baron Truro, sometime Lord Chancellor, once a pupil at St Paul's) for an essay on freedom that had to be handed in on the first day of the summer term (2 May): this is reprinted on pp. 631–7 below.
3 This suggests that match-making played a role.
4 'Mazal tov' means 'Congratulations!', but also, if taken more literally, 'a piece of good fortune'.
5 *Oxford and Cambridge Schools Examination Board: Examinations for Certificates, July 1928, List of Successful Candidates* [Cambridge, 1928; bound as part of OUA OC 10/44], p. 22.
6 St Paul's School, Governors' 'Minute Book', vol. 16, 1925–30 (privately printed), 25 July 1928 (Mercers' Company Archives). IB's '2nd exhibition' was worth £60 per annum (p. 13) for four years: he was awarded 1,001 marks out of a possible 1,350 in the classics examination, and came 2nd out of the 9 candidates from St Paul's (p. 11).

of an absolutely first class "Greats" man; it is remarkably mature for his age.'[1]

TO MARIE BERLIN

[1928?]

Grand Hotel Weimar, Rotterdam

Dear Mother

To-day I saw the Museum at Amsterdam and was deeply impressed. I want to go to London to-morrow (Father goes from Ostende on Friday) so we would only arrive at London, I at 9 a.m. he 12 hrs later at 9 P.M. But I may go with him. We shall see. Anyhow on Friday we are both in London. About Bertha: what has happenned?[2] Is it that grandmother's condition simply prevents her from coming, or that she does not want to go at all? if it is the former then I cannot say more than that you know best when you can go. If the latter then for God's sake impress on her not that it is her last chance, or any such cruel statement, but that you think that she & Gabay[?] are suited, and that she is to regard it purely as a holiday trip, to take her away from her present dark surroundings, and not as [a] marriage-journey, that if she finds the slightest fault in him, nothing will be said, and everything will peacefully be ended: that she is *not* a burden on the family who *must* marry: that has embittered her in the past, for she thinks that she has sacrificed her career for her parents' welfare, and that we are all very grateful to her for it. I know that your position is not sweet. Nevertheless personalities like yours, chosen souls, bear greater responsibilities, heavier burdens, than we others. It is therefore your imperative duty, and not a too pleasant one, to sweeten others' lives even while there is nothing but bitterness in your own heart. This is not at present the case: you are not bitter, and you never will be: since you are too strong to be poisoned by adverse circumstances, but that you must pacify people like Bertha, resist the melancholy of Ida and your father,

1 This does not perhaps entirely bear out IB's frequent insistence that he was in no way exceptional as a schoolboy. Nor does this comment of his English teacher, Leslie Henry Staverton Mathews (1875–1946), in the same report: 'There is a certain danger that he may not get down to close work at a subject; otherwise his writing is as attractive, and as effective, as anything I have had from a pupil.' In Autumn 1927 Mathews had written: 'He is sometimes inclined to write about ultimates, instead of addressing himself to the question in hand.' Also, IB had won the Lower Fifth first prize in 1923, the Lower Eighth first prize in 1925 and the Middle Eighth first prize – Leonard Whibley (ed.), *A Companion to Greek Studies* (Cambridge, 1916) – in 1926, when he also shared the Composition Prize. In 1928 he won the Eighth Form second prize. Several, at least, of the books he received as prizes remained in his possession until the end of his life, but since most of the bookplates were not filled in, it is usually impossible to match books to prizes.
2 IB often spelled this word thus in his early life, and made other similar mistakes.

and generally what you call keeping your human semblance, i.e. natural energy born of hope and not of despair, that is obvious. I know that you will say that one cannot hear theorising like mine in the midst of such actual trouble. Well, perhaps not. But I know that you instinctively feel all that I have, and all that I could have said: and I know that you recognise your burdens. Father wants you{r} very badly: (in future I call him the Lover, you Die Ferne Geliebte,)[1] but you know what to do.

All that I have said must have been obvious too always. Remember: Life is Good; and always will be Good however ugly it looks: for Beauty and Goodness are not the same thing. But enough of vain philosophy,

Yours Love & Kisses.

Shaya

---

1 'An die ferne Geliebte' ('To the Distant Beloved') is a song-cycle by Beethoven.

OXFORD

I have a natural tendency to gossip, to describing things, to noticing things, to interest in human beings and their characters, to interplay between human beings, which is completely independent of my intellectual pursuits.

IB talking to Michael Ignatieff [1]

1 MI Tape 21.

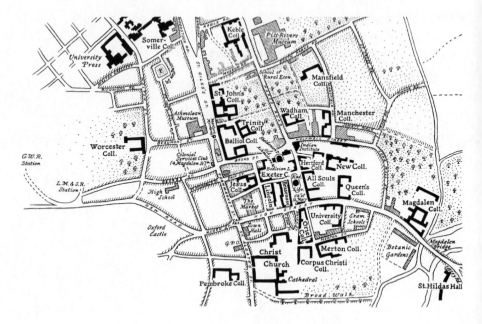

Oxford University in 1928

*IB came up to Oxford for Michaelmas Term 1928, which began on 14
October. He matriculated (that is, was formally admitted to the
University) on 16 October. He arrived at the end of Oxford's so-called
Golden Age, which, as he later described it, was characterised by the
tribal loyalties of two rival groups of students:*

There were two lots of people, there were aesthetes and there were
hearties. The hearties wore huge woollen scarves and had enormous
muscles and rowed and went about in groups and drank beer. Aesthetes
went about by themselves and wore more elaborately expensive clothes
and had very elaborate pansy manners. So when the hearties met
aesthetes, they tended to want to beat them up. [. . .] The aesthetes used
to detach chains from lavatories which they wound round their arm,
which then was a weapon: if you unwound the knob and swung it
round, it could hold off the hearties. [. . .] It was a very different
university, I can tell you, than any you've ever known. And by the time
I came up it was already ebbing; and that went on until the middle of
the financial crisis of '31, which killed it stone dead. [. . .] You had to have
£400 a year in order to be an aesthete because you knew you'd be sent
down. You knew that if you couldn't get a degree here [. . .], you had to
have some kind of income. But after '31 the parents could no longer pay
for the clothes, no longer give you the private income.

   Then [. . .] the Communists came up. And they gave much more
trouble to the dons than the aesthetes. The aesthetes were just sent down
– for doing no work and getting drunk and misbehaving [. . .] – whereas
the Communists asked lots of questions in their essays: that was much
more troublesome. [. . .] The literary societies died overnight, and were
succeeded by political societies. My last year as an undergraduate was
politicised.[1]

*Fortunately, Corpus was a small and inward-looking college, relatively
unaffected by these antagonisms. As IB later remembered:*

Corpus in my time was a very tolerant society [. . .] the general
atmosphere was of cosiness and friendship. The undergraduates were all a
bit like dons and schoolmasters already. On the whole they tended to
wear dark blue suits. There was not much temperament; the general
atmosphere was of cosiness and friendship; it was an equal society –
nobody stood out or dominated; I was perfectly happy at Corpus.[2]

*Nevertheless it was a quite different life from the one he had known with
his parents.*

1 MI Tape 12.
2 *Corpuscles*, p. 49.

TO MARIE BERLIN

Sunday [autumn 1928]

Corpus Christi

Dear Mother.

Thank you very much indeed for your very very sympathetic letter. You guessed my thoughts so accurately that I was almost surprised to see them set down on paper. Thank you very much indeed. My life in College is really very pleasant; Ettinghausen also seems happy enough, Halpern[1] a little less so. No one disturbs me in my work, which is a mercy. I shall definitely expect either you or father on Sunday next when a hot lunch will be provided: please write whether you or father are coming, as I cannot possibly see you both together:[2] but I should really like to see you and father next Sunday and on the Sunday after. So please write and I will meet you at the station. Now as for money-matters here is a short report: I have left of the money which father gave me in cash £6. In the bank: the only cheques I have given out are £1-5-0[3] for books and 17 and 6^D for an Old Pauline Tie, mortar-board, and white tie. The Battels[4] (i.e. weekly account) is £2./7./1. which is not very much in comparison with other people's. This need not be paid until next term. This also does not include subscriptions to College and University Societies, scholastic fees etc.[5]

TO MENDEL BERLIN

Tuesday [autumn 1928?, *postcard*]

Corpus Christi

Dear Father,

My battels are as follows:

Kitchen account	15-1-6
Buttery (i.e. cider, biscuits, cheese, butter)	0-16-7
University & College dues, Rates etc	1-18-8
General Service	7-0-0
Messenger	0-2-6

1 Wolf Abiram ('Abe') Halpern (1909–43), German-born, IB's contemporary at St Paul's (1923–8) and Oxford (Exeter classical mods and PPE 1928–32), naturalised 1932, worked for Derby & Co., London metal-brokers; married Barbara Strachey, killed in action (flying) 1943.

2 Perhaps because Marie talked so much that IB and Mendel would not have been able to communicate.

3 IB's renditions of pounds, shillings and pence vary somewhat, but are clear enough. The ties and motar-board cost 17s. 6d.

4 College domestic bill.

5 The rest of the letter is missing.

Gate bill	0-7-1
Letters	0-0-5
Laundry	1-15-2
Room rent	5-6-8
Fuel	2-11-0
Tuition	9-0-0
Junior Common Room	0-5-0
Hire of Furniture	1-6-8
Electric light	1-0-0
College Clubs (Sports—	5-0-0
Insurance	0-2-0
Plate fund	0-1-0
Examination fees	8-0-0
Pelican Record[1] (Magazine)	0-5-0
Altogether	59-19-3
Scholarship	10-0-0
	49-19-3

I must pay this fairly soon, i.e. in two or three days time. And moreover I have had to spend a lot on books, about £10 in fact: together forming £59·19·3 as my expenditure if you send me £30 all that is left of £30 + 30 = ninepence. So please send me £40 or £50 if you can.

On 5 December 1928 IB started his Holy Scripture examination,[2] and on 10 December his Pass Moderations,[3] which entailed examinations in Latin, Greek, Greek Literature, and Logic.[4] He was successful in both.

1 See 22/4.
2 Every undergraduate had to take this test, but Jews were allowed to substitute non-Biblical texts: in 1928 Plato's *Apology* and *Meno*.
3 See xviii/2. This examination could be taken in any of the three terms.
4 Cicero, *Philippics* I and II, Vergil, *Aeneid*, books 2, 4 and 6, prose composition and unprepared translation; Homer, *The Odyssey*, books 7–11, and unprepared translation; the history of Greek tragedy in the fifth century BC, with special reference to Aristotle, *Poetics*, Aeschylus, *Eumenides*, Sophocles, *Antigone*, and Euripides, *Bacchae*; and the elements of deductive and inductive logic – more fully, 'The Elements of Deductive and Inductive Logic as comprised in [Thomas] Fowler's *Elements of Deductive Logic* and in the first five chapters of Fowler's *Elements of Inductive Logic* (omitting the sections on Classification, Nomenclature and Terminology, and the notes appended at the end of each chapter)'; the subject could be studied in these works of Fowler or in W. S. Jevons's *Elementary Lessons in Logic: Deductive and Inductive* or in S. H. Mellone's *An Introductory Text-book of Logic*, or 'in any other works which cover the same ground'. The source for IB's selection of options is Oxford University's handwritten 'Undergraduate Register' (volume for A–C, 1928–9), OUA UR 2/1/165. The options among which he chose are listed in *The Examination Statutes [. . .] Revised to 7 July, 1928* (Oxford, 1928), pp. 43–5 (Pass Moderations) and 39 (Holy Scripture); and the dates of the examinations appear on p. 7 of the same volume.

Those who had come up in 1927 would take Honour Moderations the
following term (Hilary Term). IB thus began Greats a term before these
mainstream candidates.

TO MARIE BERLIN

18 May 1929 [*picture postcard of Rudolph Valentino*]

Corpus Christi

Dear Madam:

I propose for the next week or so, to make you acquainted with our
leading and talented film-stars in some of whom you may no longer [be]
interested. This beautiful and delicate series of photographs is issued by those
wonderfully artistic people, Messrs Woolworth, whom I recommend to you,
as a shop of rare taste and charm. A more serious letter will soon follow.

For the first two years of IB's undergraduate career, most of his activities
were College-based. His sociability was already in evidence. He recalled
that 'I think I belonged to every society there was at Corpus. I made
friends with almost everyone. I think I had what critics might call an
undiscriminating taste in people.'[1] *As the President of Corpus later*
phrased it, 'his rooms were a place of resort',[2] *often full of other students*
looking for company and conversation. And although Corpus
undergraduates tended not to stir much from their College, they did
receive visits from outside. When, for example, Louis MacNeice[3] *was*
planning to bring some tourists to Oxford:

he told the only person he knew in Corpus, which was John Hilton[4]
[. . .] that he was going to bring them, and they really rather liked
ceremonies, and if he could bring them at some time when there was
some ceremony going, that would impress them. Some of them were
quite rich – might even give some money to Oxford or London. And
Hilton and I [and one or two others] wore gowns and mortar-boards,

1 *Corpuscles*, p. 50.
2 ibid., p. 49.
3 (Frederick) Louis MacNeice (1907–63), poet and dramatist; Merton classics 1926–30; Lecturer
in Classics, Birmingham, 1930–6; Lecturer in Greek, Bedford College, London, 1936–40;
feature writer and producer, BBC 1940–9.
4 John Robert Hilton (1908–94), CCC classics 1926–9; then architect and archaeologist
(Director of Antiquities, Cyprus, 1934–6); later diplomat and deputy Head of MI6; married
Margaret ('Peggy') Frances Stephens 1933.

and we stood round the Pelican,[1] and we threw a silver jug at each other
and bowed every time we received one, and then threw it to the next
man, and we did it 44 times round the Pelican; then we bowed, and we
shook hands very formally, and left as a procession. It was an invented
ceremony for the benefit of the tourists, who goggled very satisfactorily.[2]

*IB had the best of memories of his undergraduate years: 'My total
happiness and cosiness [. . .] in Corpus certainly gave me security which
I might not otherwise have possessed.'[3]*

TO MENDEL BERLIN

20 October 1929 [*card*][4]

[Corpus Christi]

How are you? I am well. That is the sum and substance of all I have to say.
Eh?

your very dutiful son
I. Berlin
Sch. of C.C.C.
Oxon.

*IB's involvement with the life of the University as a whole started when
he became joint editor of the* Oxford Outlook, *'a somewhat highbrow
university journal'.[5] Although IB initially accepted the editorship on
condition that he did not have to meet the (probably aesthete)
contributors, his new role inevitably brought him into contact with a wide
range of brilliant and cultivated minds, both at Oxford and beyond. As he
later admitted, his involvement with the* Oxford Outlook *'sort of got me
on'.[6]*

1 A stone pelican, symbol of Corpus, stood (as a successor now stands) on a column in the
  front quadrangle.
2 Interview with Brian Harrison for *Corpuscles*, 19 October 1992.
3 ibid.
4 On the other side of the card, above the address, IB has written 'postcard' in English, French,
  Italian, German, Russian and Hebrew – the six languages with which he was most familiar.
5 Interview for *Corpuscles*. IB edited six issues of this undergraduate periodical, from vol. 10 No
  52 (May 1930) until vol. 12 No 57 (February 1932), jointly with Arthur Calder-Marshall for No
  52, and with Richard Goodman (165/4) for Nos 55 (June 1931) to 57. He wrote twelve pieces
  for it himself.
6 MI Tape 5.

TO T. S. ELIOT[1]

27 May 1930

Corpus Christi

Dear Mr Eliot,

A copy of the 'Oxford Outlook' has been sent to you because it was thought that you might feel some interest in the kind of thing that is now being written, and possibly believed, in Oxford; the most notable characteristic of this journal is its almost entirely critical content – three years ago it was full of poetry and short stories only. I hope that you will not think me importunate in sending you this.

I am
 yours sincerely
  I. Berlin

The Faber archive

TO JOHN HILTON

[November 1930]

Corpus Christi

Hardie[2] & I have just been dancing a small jig in the quad about your Locke.[3] a great puff in the Pelican R[4] is being prepared. Hardie does not want 'Success of Past Editor' in block letters, but consents to have it in small type. Anyhow it is a most astonishing performance. This is to be taken as a pure compliment. There is no element of real surprise in it.

 yrs etc.
  I Berlin

---

1 Thomas Stearns Eliot (1888–1965), poet, publisher, critic, playwright, editor of the *Criterion* since 1922.

2 William Francis ('Frank') Ross *Hardie (1902–90), Fellow and Tutor in philosophy, CCC, 1926–50, later (1950–69) President.

3 JRH had just won the John Locke Scholarship in Mental Philosophy, awarded annually by examination, and open to postgraduate philosophy students as well as undergraduates. IB was to win the prize jointly with Sidney Budden of Merton in 1931.

4 The *Pelican Record*, the magazine of CCC. IB was one of the editors from vol. 19 No 4 (December 1929) to vol. 20 No 4 (June 1932).

TO JOHN HILTON

December 1930

Corpus Christi

Dear John Hilton John Locke was good to him

My Apologies for lateness in reply: the story and the poem both pleased me greatly: the story largely because I once tried to write something of the sort more unsuccessfully, much more. The poem has genuine solidity which I do not know if you would confess to.

Anyhow both will see the light,[1] hoffentlich,[2] that is.

Meanwhile Hardie & I have decided to give you a definite boost in the P. Record,[3] so as to hurt Dr Grundy's[4] feelings a little but not very much. they (Hardie & Henderson)[5] expelled a small quotation which I wished to have printed on a blank page by itself, viz 'Mind you, the class Mr Dickie[6] will obtain depends entirely on the opinion the examiners will take of his papers!" Hardie was very adamant, but I still think it would have been very nice.[7]

What will you do with the £100 or the glory? oughtn't you to endow a small Modern Greats prize in Corpus with the condition that the winner be forced to recite in full Hall the story of the toils & troubles of the prehistoric founder of the prize, and how the dark forces of the College were overcome, and the light triumphed at last? and if not, why not?

1 Both appear in the *Oxford Outlook* 11 No 54 (March 1931): 'Flip-Flap', 4–7; 'Poem', 16–17.
2 'Hopefully', in the sense 'it is to be hoped'.
3 The (untitled) notice that appeared runs as follows: 'We offer our congratulations and admiration to a former member of our staff, Mr J. R. Hilton, on his winning the John Locke Scholarship in Mental Philosophy. Mr Hilton achieved a First in 1929. Some of our readers will recall that he was the first (not the last) member of this College to read the school of "Modern Greats". He is also (we ascertain) the first "modernist" in the University to win a prize which has hitherto been won only by men who have read "Ancient Greats". The performance is the more remarkable in that, during the last year, Mr Hilton has been fully engaged in preparing, at the University of London, for the profession of architect. Almost all past winners of the Scholarship have become professional teachers of philosophy. We again congratulate Mr Hilton on his unique distinction.' *Pelican Record* 20 No 1 (December 1930), 2. IB was later to become the 2nd PPE undergraduate at Corpus.
4 Grundy strongly disapproved of PPE ('Modern Greats').
5 Charles Gordon Henderson (1900–33), history Lecturer, CCC, 1928, Fellow and Tutor 1929–33; married (Mary) Isobel Munro (Fellow and ancient history Tutor, Somerville).
6 Alexander Hugh Hamon Massy Dickie (1907–87), CCC classics 1926–30, became a solicitor at the London firm of Freshfields, which later acted for IB.
7 JRH comments: 'I can only be sad that none of Isaiah's – and Frank Hardie's – wilder fantasies passed (perhaps never reached) the editorial blue pencil; maybe it would have been thought unkind to tease Dr Grundy (a great croquet player) in his last days as senior tutor. He and Phelps, the Dean, were my major antagonists in the battle to change to PPE. The College knew, when it gave me a maths scholarship, that I intended this change; then took away my emoluments – later restored – but left me my gown. Much talk of Girls' Greats, Soft Options etc. etc.' JRH to the editor, 21 November 1991.

I hear that A. H. H. M. Dickie has just promised to come up next term to read a paper on Henniker Heaton:[1] H. P. Kingdon[2] will defend the sacred memory of an expresident, and W. F. R. Hardie will say a few words. I do not believe that there are any limits to the monstrosities H.D. will produce, and that it will be genuinely libellous and very funny. His father (H.H.'s) is related to have told someone that his son had a Byronic profile.

I find I've no more to say, express general benevolence, and remind you to give signs of life sometime.

I.B.

TO BELLA SCHALIT[3]

[13 December 1930]

49 Hollycroft Avenue

Written on the *Thirteenth* day of the month, which read backwards stands for *the Day itself*, leaving a gap of *one bare lifetime* between the two, if numerically computed in the Holy Tongue. This is intended to be slightly obscure.

ABANDON HOPE ALL YE WHO ENTER HERE
(of boredom)

miss bella schalit

has the pleasure of inviting

you
to

spend new years eve with her in

hell

(for the occasion transplanted to 28, arkwright road, n.w.3)

garments suitable for the nether regions de rigeur though cerberus might admit you in evening dress if you ask him nicely.

9 p.m.—brooms and chariots at dawn.
R.S.V.P.

Invitation to Bella Schalit's 21st birthday party

1 Peter Joseph Henniker Heaton (1907–76), journalist; CCC classics 1926–30; President, Pelican Essay Club, 1929.
2 Henry Paul Kingdon (1907–89), theologian; CCC classics 1926–31; priest 1934.
3 Daughter of Lipman Schalit of Riga, a business associate and friend of IB's father who also emigrated to England. Her dates, 1909–97, are the same as IB's.

mr isaiah berlin begs to acknowledge miss bella schalit's penetrating suggestion as to where he is peculiarly fit to go, and is forced to admit the appropriateness of the direction.[1]

He regrets that he was unable to reply during the preceding week which was passed in a somewhat subdued manner in reflecting on his destiny and in making a final settlement of all his affairs on earth during the few days that are left him.

He clearly realises that it is quite useless to attempt to disguise his identity: he feels that a life of crime and excesses (and who can deny that his was such?) has made him a marked man with Hell's legal officers, and that simple, modest clothing may make an agreeable impression and soften the hearts in question more than clumsy efforts at unrecognizability could do. He has, alas, no doubt that Cerberus* will not withhold his right to enter an environment where he belongs so eminently well, however unassuming his attire.

Of the two alternatives, could he have a chariot, please; should insufficient of him be left to make real use of this last, he begs that what little is left over be religiously registered to the above address, with some explanation attached; he has masked his real character so well at his home, that they, simple souls, may not understand . . .

*or perhaps honeyed dog-biscuits will do it; there is at least one case recorded in which it definitely worked.[2]

IB took a First[3] in Greats in the summer of 1931. As he had one year of his four-year scholarship at Corpus yet to run, he planned to read another subject at first-degree level before pursuing an academic or legal career. He considered history, but eventually opted for PPE (Philosophy, Politics and Economics). In the intervening long vacation he made the second of his many musical pilgrimages to Salzburg.[4]

1 A reply to an invitation to Bella Schalit's twenty-first birthday party (she was born on 30 December 1909). The invitation reads: 'ABANDON HOPE (of boredom) ALL YE WHO ENTER HERE / miss bella schalit has the pleasure of inviting you to spend new year's eve with her in hell (for the occasion transplanted to 28, arkwright road, n.w.3) / garments suitable for the nether regions de rigeur though cerberus might admit you in evening dress if you ask him nicely. / 9 p.m. – brooms and chariots at dawn. / R.S.V.P.'

2 In classical mythology Cerberus was the (at least) three-headed dog who guarded the entrance to Hades. Few passed him. But when, according to Virgil's *Aeneid*, the Sybil of Cumae escorted Aeneas there, she threw Cerberus a cake made with honey and poppy-seeds, which sent him to sleep and allowed them to enter the underworld.

3 i.e. was awarded a first-class degree (Oxford degrees were then divided into four classes).

4 For IB's visits to Salzburg see MI 54–5.

TO CHARLES HENDERSON

14 August 1931

Pension Mussoni, Bürglsteinstrasse 6, Salzburg etc.

My dear Чарльзъ,[1]

Your letter expresses genuine happiness. Plainly the power of Stimmung[2] upon you is so great that nothing, not even the unspeakable weather of which you must have felt something, can mar your bliss. I shall not attempt to do that, but only, if possible, to make [you] envious of our local, Salzburg conditions, which are still attractive enough. The cons are evident enough: the foulness of the unceasing downpours, and the droves of tourists who are washed by these into the cafés, and make of them vast shambles of human steam and general disagreeableness. But the pros: never in anyone's life have the last two movements of Mozart's Jupiter symphony been conducted & played, as they have here been done by Herr Heger[3] & Vienna Philharmonic: never has such a Clarinettist trilled roulades to the galleries of the Karabienersaal[4] as the incomparable Professor Viktor Polatschek:[5] and, greatest of all, never has anything so lovely, so moving and symmetrical and in all ways perfect been revealed to the eye & ear as the Aufführung[6] of Cosi fan Tutte in the Stadttheater. The impression of this is altogether incommunicable. But for the fact that the interval of that performance was spoilt for me by a certain young man from New College, who, having killed a man in the usual manner, i.e. in a motor-car after a Commem. Ball, was apparently allowed to go to Salzburg, and having come, introduced himself to me in the brazennest manner possible, by simply telling me that we belonged to the same university, seized the opportunity, and introduced me to a series of sisters, each duller, uglier and generally more unutterable than the last, who waylay me singly & in batches in every street, café and Vergnügungsort[7] in Salzburg. However Cosi fan Tutte was so good that I would be willing to go again though a hundred murderers with a thousand hideous sisters each might accost me in the foyer.

Otherwise I enjoy my very epicurean self, (*very* epicurean indeed) a good deal. I sleep till quite 9.30, all except for one morning when

1 'Charles'.
2 'Mood'.
3 Robert Heger (1886–1978) was a guest conductor in Salzburg in the 1930s.
4 'Karabinersaal' [*sic*]: literally 'Carbine Hall'.
5 Viktor Polatschek (1889–1948) taught at the Vienna Conservatoire and played at the Vienna Opera and in the Vienna Philharmonic Orchestra before moving to America to become principal clarinettist of the Boston Symphony Orchestra.
6 'Performance'.
7 'Place of entertainment'.

Watson[1] of our college had himself announced impromptu. He lives with a Munich baroness, and has had several serious conversations with the mysterious Kluckhohn[2] who went to Munich to escape from Vienna, ostensibly because of the heat, but as you & I know, to fly from *them* really, and ranted for a long time at the somewhat bewildered Watson about the insufficiently physiological character of Oxford philosophy. Watson seemed melancholy about his career – he is going to be a solicitor in Edinburgh: when I asked him whether he wanted to become that, he replied that he never ventured to put the question to himself at all: his father was one, it was assumed that he would be, and that was that. All this in the most doleful tone. I immediately reflected that a good many people must be continually pitched headlong into similar cul-de-sacs, and myself stopped thinking about it.

We stay here until the 25th, and then I go back, to London or Meran.[3]

On the day of the plebiscite[4] I obtained my first glimpse of a real Nazi – a great corpulent creature in the official brown uniform, with a red & black Swastika on his sleeve, & wearing a small black demi-astrakhan hat with silver symbols embroidered thereon: he was very drunk, rolled into my café, & was led out by 3 waiters. Sandy Rendel[5] sent me a most charming note – I have not got his address, so if you write to him, please send him my thanks for it. if you feel that a historic Umgebung[6] is working a serious change in your character do write & inform me please: it has been known to do all that & more.

yrs

Шая[7]

TO MARIE BERLIN

2 September 1931

49 Hollycroft Avenue

Dear mother

Father left for Holland last night (to-day is Wednesday) and will go to

1 John Parker Watson (1909–89), solicitor; CCC classics 1927–31.
2 Clyde Kay Mayben Kluckhohn (1905–60), anthropologist; American Rhodes Scholar, CCC, 1928–32, first director of Russian Research Center, Harvard, 1948–54; despised by IB. He suffered from paranoid delusions that he was being pursued by unspecified enemies.
3 The Italian town of Merano in the South Tyrol.
4 The Nazis had held a referendum in the hope of overthrowing the Social Democratic government of Prussia, but failed to win a majority.
5 Alexander Meadows Rendel (1910–91), CCC classics 1929–33, then diplomat and solicitor by turns; agent for the Greek resistance in Crete in the war.
6 'Setting'.
7 'Shaya'.

Berlin on Thursday night, & back to London on Sunday. His mood when leaving was so-so, better than when I arrived. The man who is really bearing up very well is Bick,[1] who is in a hopeless position. Generally the Schalit's position seems to be dreadful, and ours much much better. I sent your letter, which encouraged father, to him. I hope he will receive it. I read it through myself, and found it very good, except for the reference to Bick – that is a little irritating, esp. as the partnership is bound one of these days to come to a forcible end.

And now more interesting news: and news *of the first importance:*

The President has written to me to say that his friend the editor of the Manchester Guardian[2] wants a recruit for their personnel, "a good greats man, with knowledge of foreign subjects'. What about me? it is a most tempting offer, & kind of him to send [it] to me. I wrote back & said that I was very grateful, certainly did not decline it, but was thinking of an academic career.

So I would write to Hardie, my philosophy tutor, and find out whether he thinks I can get a fellowship somewhere. If he thinks I can't, then I would like to consider the Manchester Guardian: it seems a very good thing: as the President says. To be taken on the staff of one of the best European newspapers at the age of 22, & to be paid a regular salary by it, seems to me a very fine idea. I am very sorry that neither father nor you are here to advise me. So I had to act by myself. As I said, all I did [was] to postpone the thing for about a week, till I hear from Hardie. "Foreign subjects" means, I think, that I shall be required to read French or German papers and to write little resumés on the situation. Most attractive, but it means that I have to give up my 4th year at Oxford. Please reflect about it all & give me yr opinion when you come back. Of course I can go on reading for the Bar[3] even while working for the Guardian. I am a little excited by it all.

Love (I am very, very well. Johanna cooks excellently, & the house is in the best of order).

Shaya.

1 Myer Oscar Bick (1865–1940), a business partner of Mendel's; they were involved in a co-operative venture on the Russian timber market with the Schalit family which had run into serious trouble.
2 Charles Prestwich Scott (1846–1932, CCC classics 1865–9), at this point strictly Governing Director of the *Manchester Guardian* (Editor 1872–1929).
3 IB briefly considered a legal career at this stage.

TO CHARLES HENDERSON[1]

[shortly before 20 September 1931]

49 Hollycroft Avenue

Милейший Чарльз[2]

I am writing this at an hour long after midnight, for I cannot go to sleep when I think of the stirring part which, I have persuaded myself, you & Sandy Rendel, must have played in the recent political history of Austria. Count Lamberg,[3] says the local press here, is in prison. You I know from your own admissions are (a) staying with his close relative (b) on terms of intimate acquaintance with other schloss owners who are, no doubt, all mixed up in it. How could you help being pushed into the vortex? a romantically appealingly helpless beautiful country, slowly dying under a prosaic regime. I do not blame you in the least. You could not avoid it. Any gentleman would have acted so. I know, I know. *You* were not enthusiastic at all at first. You sought safety and remembered Louis XVIII and how prudent it is to be prudent. But Sandy R, his eyes flashing etc. hurried you into it. Prince Starhemberg[4] & Frau Gräfin Lamberg, well comprehending the difference between your outlooks, began on him, and you could not lag behind: you remembered all your Stendhal and how very like this was, and Sandy R. remembered Zenda and Hentzau[5] & so on, & acting from your different motives, you plunged. And what if you are now being conveyed in plain vans to the Federal Prison: what if you are going to be tried for breaking every verboten[6] possible? Yet I say it was worth it. Especially the assumption of the good Austrian name which you did assume, placarding the country with your autocratic calls to revolt.

[for if you are not the spiders behind the web, why should 'he' alone have remained officially uncaught? but it is you of course. I admit it was very skilfully engineered].[7]

Your letters from prison should prove fascinating reading in the common

1 c/o Countess ['Gräfin'] Lamberg in Austria.
2 'Mileishii ["Dearest"] Charles'.
3 Count (Karl) Ottomar Konstantin Anton Raimund Michael Lamberg (1898–1942), who lived at the castle of Pichlarn by Steinach in Styria, was associated with the putsch by Walter Pfrimer, leader of the local Heimwehr, the right-radical paramilitary organisation powerful throughout inter-war Austria. On 12/13 September 1931 Pfrimer made an abortive attempt to assume power in Styria and beyond. Lamberg died in Auschwitz.
4 Prince Ernst Rüdiger Starhemberg (1899–1956), one of the best-known politicians of inter-war Austria, was overall leader of the Fascist Heimwehr ('Home Guard') and deputy premier under Schuschnigg 1934–6. The most charismatic figure of the radical right, he grew disenchanted with Hitler and fled the country when the latter took it over.
5 Anthony Hope's novels *The Prisoner of Zenda* and *Rupert of Hentzau*.
6 'Prohibition'.
7 IB's square brackets.

rooms where you are notorious. And I am sure the Old Rugbeian Club will do something. But I am ready to print all you send in the Oxford Outlook: for once it will sell like h. cakes. etc. etc. etc. in this style etc. etc. etc.

You note the weakness of mind which has evidently seized on me. It is all due to the abnormal excitement to which I have been lately subjected by the President's sudden & violent interest in my career & furious activity resulting therefrom. I have been indulging in an orgy of correspondence with him & others, sensation followed on sensation (this last untrue but bene trovato),[1] and I am at the moment in a welter of loyalties, feelings, reflections etc. and rather anxious to consult you if you are at any definite address for any length of time. Please do not go to any trouble to find out the situation, as, though I naturally am somewhat agitated about it, I do realise that it is not really very important, and you certainly need not communicate till you return to England, & not then for a time, if you are at all busy. It is all to do with openings in journalism clashing with P.P.E., All Souls etc., nothing more.

I do not know if you have been reading the Times lately wherever you may be, but if you have, I am sure even your Conservative soul was shocked by some of its leading articles: 2 or 3 of them were so undignified, unctuous & reactionary in the worst, continental sense of the word, that not only was the New Statesman wildly enraged till it talked of the justifiability of communism when such things were printed,[2] but even the staid Week-End Review,[3] & still staider Manchester Guardian[4] were rude to it. They might, as far as what they contained was concerned, have been written by Lord Brentford[5] or Mr Churchill,[6] and it was excessively splenetic even for them. Politics have become so interesting that even I have begun to follow them with some avidity; the peace of our suburbia will be disturbed by Mr Gandhi who is coming to live as our not very distant neighbour,[7] and he draws crowds larger than any man of note for the last 25 yrs, including D. Fairbanks & Charlie C.[8]

1 'A good invention'.
2 'Critic', in 'A London Diary', New Statesman and Nation, 12 September 1931, 302–3, at p. 303, mentions the City articles in The Times in these terms as well as 'the main article on Tuesday's debate', probably the first leader, 'The Opposing Case', 8 September 1931, 13.
3 Possibly a reference to a mild remark in the anonymous 'Comments of the Week', Week-End Review, 12 September 1931, 293.
4 Reference untraced.
5 William Joynson-Hicks (1865–1932), Home Secretary 1924–9, 1st Viscount Brentford 1929, an ultra-Conservative anti-Communist.
6 Rt Hon. Winston Leonard Spencer Churchill (1874–1965), soldier, journalist, author and politician (of variable allegiance); Chancellor of the Exchequer 1924–9, First Lord of the Admiralty 1939–40, Prime Minister 1940–5, Leader of the Opposition 1945–51. Churchill held strongly anti-Bolshevik views before the rise of Hitler made Nazism appear the greater threat.
7 An exaggeration: Gandhi spent 3 months in late 1931 living in the Kingsley Hall Settlement, a commune in Bromley-by-Bow, while negotiating the future of India.
8 Douglas Elton Thomas Ulman Fairbanks (1883–1939), American actor famous for his

Jerry's[1] career seems to be completely settled. I am happier about it than I can say, in spite of a slightly bitter letter about Africa from Cruikshank[2] which I unexpectedly received.

I have at last obtained a book called

ВВЕДЕНИЕ В ФИЛОСОФИЮ
ДИАЛЕКТИЧЕСКОГО
МАТЕРИАЛИЗМА[3]

by the official philosopher, President of the Academy, Deborin,[4] which is very large, dull, unintelligent, & which I am devouring with vast interest, & the worse the arguments the better I feel. It is utterly unlike anything ever written on philosophy or economics in England: I am sure of that. And seems to have been written on another & coarser planet. But the doctrines seem to have caused a greater influence almost than Rousseau,[5] and it is all, despite the dulness of the author, exciting & interesting and not written for foreigners. I am sure Rowse[6] would be captured by it, though he would set about rewriting it at once. I hope you met Prof Clark[7] in Austria: he must be wonderfully charming against an Austrian landscape.

yrs

Шая

swashbuckling roles in silent films such as *The Mask of Zorro* (1920) and *The Three Musketeers* (1921); father of actor Douglas Fairbanks, Jr.; Charles ('Charlie') Spencer Chaplin (1889–1977), British-born film actor, producer and director; star of *The Kid* (1921) and *The Gold Rush* (1925).

1 John Frederick ('Jerry') Cornes, CCC history 1928–31, entered the Colonial Service in 1931.

2 John Augustus Cockburn Cruikshank, CCC history 1927–30, joined the Colonial Service in Nigeria in 1930.

3 'VVEDENIE V FILOSOFIYU DIALEKTICHESKOGO MATERIALIZMA' ('Introduction to the philosophy of dialectical materialism'), published in Moscow in 1922.

4 Abram Moiseevich Deborin (1881–1963), Soviet Marxist, philosopher, political theorist.

5 Jean Jacques Rousseau (1712–78), Swiss-French philosopher, novelist and composer who spent much of his life in France. He argued that the current structures of human society corrupted the inherent goodness of human nature and suggested revolutionary changes in political and social organisation, and in educational systems, to counter this; his work made a major and distinct contribution to the development of political theory (as well as encouraging the sensibility to the natural world characteristic of the Romantic era).

6 Alfred Leslie Rowse (1903–97), historian, Fellow of All Souls 1925–74; a socialist early, a conservative late; vigorous opponent of appeasement; an egotist to the point of imbalance, loathed by IB.

7 Albert Curtis Clark (1859–1937), Corpus Christi Professor of Latin, 1913–34. In *Corpuscles* (p. 48) IB writes that Clark was 'a friend. He was old, eccentric and alarming. I used to take him to the cinema. Everyone – Hardie, Ronald Syme [338/1] particularly – mimicked his voice, which was unusually high. Typical quotations were: "I was staying in a hotel in Italy with a very pretty woman. She came down once and said she'd been bitten by a flea. I said 'Oh fortunate creature!' "; or, "Fresh tomatoes can be a poem; stewed tomatoes are the lowest form of boarding house filth." Clark was a distinguished scholar, bored at being in Corpus. He used to come to lunch with me in All Souls; "I hate salt", he piped, "but I dote on pepper."'

For the benefit of the Austrian Police should they inadvertently open this:
Alles was darin steht ist ja nur ein dummer dummer Witz – Verzeihet![1]
I.B.

TO CHARLES HENDERSON

20 September 1931

49 Hollycroft Avenue

Dear Charles

This will, I believe, grow into a very full and big-bellied letter: I shall, that
is to say, try and compress myself as far as possible: but I doubt if anything
will come of my intentions.

I

First a warning and an apology; and a request. Some days ago, between the
hours of two and three in the morning I sat down to write you a letter.[2]
I must have been very tired, or the very odd modern music to which I had
been listening all the evening must have driven me temporarily crazy: at any
rate I wrote an entirely insane and fantastic letter: I remember it very dimly
now, but I believe it was a hotch-potch of the most ludicrous and stupid
nonsense. I sent it to Gräfin Lamberg: who may send it on to you: I fervently
hope that you left no address behind: for I have no desire at all that you
should read it: I do believe it was a genuinely frightful attempt at humour,
and teemed with awkward, dull, elephantine wit which is better dead.
However I must face issues: if you do get hold of it, you would be doing an
inestimable service if you destroyed it unread. If this is too much to ask – the
letter was addressed to you and is legally your inalienable property – I can
only beg to you to forget it. I shall do any penance you choose to impose. So
much for that.

II

Even in that incoherent outpour I did, I believe, try to say something about
certain minor events which the President originated and which robbed me of
peace of mind. I shall now try to give a chronological account with
psychological asides thrown in.

---

1 'Everything herein is of course only a stupid stupid joke – sorry!'
2 The previous letter.

Chap. 1

Some ten days ago, or more, I received a letter from PSA[1] which informed me that C. P. Scott Editor of the Manchester Guardian, had written to him, declaring that a man was wanted as a recruit to their staff, who was to be a 'good Greats man, interested in foreign politics', since he was required to deal with "foreign subjects', and who had to possess an 'easy knack of writing.' This PSA followed up by saying that 'so good an opening into public life' was well worth giving a Fourth Year up for: and would I please write quickly & say whether I wanted it.

I was quite alone in London at the time, with no friends or relatives to ask advice from – and being a vacillating & very unself-confident person I always require moral support of some kind – and after a night spent in brooding on the problem, wrote a letter (1) to PSA, in which I told him that though I had entertained no such thoughts before, yet my First had inflated my conceit & made me think, however vaguely, of an academic career: to which I was drawn, more than by anything else, by my present eager interest in philosophy. Did he think a Fellowship was at all feasible? if not, I should prefer journalism to the Bar, prefer it infinitely, since my attempts in that direction had always been half-hearted. All this I couched as stiltedly as possible and sent off with a trembling hand.

(2) I wrote a much opener & better letter to Hardie in Edinburgh, asking the same question more frankly, also for his personal opinion of my philosophical capacities.

Chap II

(1) The President replied that Fellowships were very precarious but that + P.P.E. + John Locke + other magnificent achievements a man *might just* stand a chance. Whereas the M.G. was a magnificent opening etc. etc. etc. clearly urging me in favour of that.

(2) Hardie sent long letters, and altogether behaved with fervour & warmth & general enthusiastic desire to help which I had hardly expected from a man of his cool temper, and for which I am very grateful indeed. He also thought that considering the average age of Oxford philosophers chances of fellowships were small even if not nothing. Nevertheless he encouraged me to go on with P.P.E. as equally useful whatever I was going to do, mentioned All Souls and the 'Times',[2] but of course did not want to

1 P. S. Allen.
2 Geoffrey Dawson, né Robinson (1874–1944), historian, then Editor of The Times, was at All

do anything to prevent me from following my natural inclinations, and said very wisely that everything depended on the precise nature of the M.G. job.

Meanwhile I, torn between two worlds, could not decide between the peaceful philosophical life, provided that was practicable, between P.P.E. & an attempt at All Souls, and finally between the possibility of going on the M.G. at once and then, perhaps, being sent to foreign parts, Moscow even . . . Anyhow I wrote to the President requesting him to arrange for an interview with Scott, and telling him that I should, at the interview ask Scott whether he would allow me to go back to Oxford for a time, for P.P.E., in which event I could try for All Souls without breaking connexion with the M.G., which I do admire as a newspaper, and always have done.

The Pres. wrote that he had written to Scott, suggested at Hardie's instance an exam. at Merton for a research fellowship for 3 years, (which I rejected as leading nowhere at all), and there the matter ended for the time being. The situation on the whole may be represented as PSA pulling hard in M.G. direction, though outwardly committing himself in neither direction, Hardie strongly championing P.P.E., and myself wobbling miserably in indecision.

All this happened about a week ago. End of reel one.

III

I continued for a week in suspense in Hampstead, occasionally feeding the swans in the Hamp. Heath pond. Nothing happened. a Russian atmosphere of total eventlessness began growing denser and denser. The Pres. explicitly stated that the next step was with Scott. This step the latter has so far refused to take: goodness knows what description of me was sent by PSA to Scott: Hardie too, I believe, was made to write about me.

After a week's vain waiting I wrote to PSA last Thursday night, informing him of the state of stagnation, and suggesting that as I was plainly not wanted, I was, was I not, to assume that I was returning to do P.P.E. And anyhow it was impolite of Scott not to let me know that I was not wanted. All this I expressed with angelic mildness. PSA must have received my letter sometime on Friday, but on Saturday (yesterday) I had no reply; it may be that he is out of Oxford, and has been for the past week, and that Scott may have written to him instead of to me, and that the letter is waiting, unread, in C.C.C. alongside of mine. Or I may get a reply on Monday. Or did Scott

Souls 1898–1906, 1911–44, and Hardie might have suggested that he was on the look-out for suitable young Fellows to recruit to his staff. (Dawson's change of surname, in 1917, was required under the terms of a property inheritance.)

expect me to write to him direct, enclosing a short self-extolling autobiography? I have not the faintest notion of what is done in such cases. Meanwhile minor difficulties with regard to rooms which I contracted to take for this coming year, and which I could get rid of, if I acted sufficiently rapidly, but not if I allow a week to pass, act as a small but effective irritant.

I am, as you see, in a complete welter of conflicting emotions, circumstances, hopes etc. etc. aggravated by a most unpleasant ignorance of what is happening.

I should be really obliged, grateful, beholden etc. etc. etc. if, weighing the evidence carefully (I think I've told you all I know, but if more light is wanted I could probably supply it. But I do not think it is.), you would write what you think I ought to do, or what you yourself would have done had you been standing in my – at present very uncomfortable – shoes;

You asked for a full letter, and you cannot deny that this one is overflowing with, at any rate, words. And though we both agreed, not very long ago, that excessive self-centredness and demands to have things done for one and absence of feeling for others is very culpable, yet in this case I am perhaps not altogether wrong in filling this letter with me and my affairs: I plead extenuating circumstances without number.

———

I entirely agree about the increasing corruption of Germans as you advance North: I am not very fond of Bavarians, and a comparison of Würzburg & Salzburg is an insult. It really is. Würzburg is heavy and dark & dull, though dignified after a fashion, whereas Salzburg is young & beautiful. I am more passionately fond of it now than ever before. But in Cologne people are abominable, & so are streets, and Belgium is always, everywhere, to everyone endlessly unspeakable. But a charming people lives between Würzburg & Cologne, notably round Frankfurt, in Baden & Würtemburg. Delightful men and fine, if ugly, women. However.

I am very happy indeed about Jerry, who is mortified about his marks,[1] but is slowly recovering to true proportions of things after receiving a kind of moral cauterization of pride and ill-founded opinion of himself from me, who did it with zest and in my namesake's style. I am waiting for yr letter with bated breath. Write.

yrs

Шая

1 Jerry Cornes took a Second.

TO CHARLES HENDERSON

24 September 1931

49 Hollycroft Avenue

Dear Charles,

A rapid scribble to let you know the temporary solution of the
Manchester Question: Scott wrote & said that circumstances had somewhat
changed, & that the opening was no longer immediate, though they would
still like to see me. I was much relieved. This means that I definitely come up
for a year. And if they want to see me they can have that curious pleasure,
though I doubt if aught will come of it. I strongly suspect on the basis of your
evidence & otherwise that the rat, having failed to creep off the ship, is the
cause of the non-emptiness of his hole which I should have been expected
to fill: is the rat a certain Ayerst[1] of whom people have talked to me? and
is the College Oriel? and is my hypothesis not plausible? none of these
questions need be answered if they are at all illicit.[2]

Did you see that Jerry had got in at the tail of the ICS[3] list, now that he
no longer wants it? and Crofton?[4] & Dixon?[5]

I am particularly happy about the middle one: it was a dream of a
lifetime, so far as I know.

When I inquire into the state of my mind I find that I can report that I am
more than glad that I am to have another year of Oxford – even though it be
in the far from epicurean suburb of Wellington Square.[6]

yours

Шая

In October, as part of his PPE course, IB started studying politics (though
he was largely self-taught, since he received no formal tuition in the
subject). It was an interesting moment to do so. The financial crisis of
1931 had put an end to the aesthetes as an Oxford phenomenon, and
Japan's invasion of Manchuria, which started in September 1931, gave an
impetus to the increasing politicisation of the undergraduates, which
continued, at a faster or slower rate, for the rest of the decade.

1 David George Ogilvy Ayerst (1904–92), Christ Church history 1923–6, journalist on the
   Manchester Guardian 1929–31, 1932–4, later author of *Guardian: Biography of a Newspaper*
   (London, 1971) and editor of *The Guardian Omnibus, 1821–1971: An Anthology of 150 Years of*
   Guardian Writing (London, 1973).
2 Nor can they be answered, or even fully understood, by the present editor.
3 Indian Civil Service.
4 Denis Hayes Crofton, CCC classics 1927–32.
5 Algernon Drew Dixon, CCC classics 1926–30.
6 Where many Oxford undergraduates lodged, then and later.

By now many of IB's friends had left Oxford and were starting their careers. For his own part, IB began to write reports for publishers on proposals they were considering. The earliest specimens to survive (possibly also the first he wrote) were commissioned by Geoffrey Faber,[1] founder of Faber & Faber, who was at All Souls, and therefore soon afterwards IB's colleague. Though the reports are sometimes cast in the form of a letter, they are printed, because of their length and distinctive character, as an appendix rather than in their chronological position in the main text. The first reports were written in January 1932.

The next letter exemplifies IB's critical powers in a private capacity.

TO GORONWY REES[2]

4 July 1932 [*postcard*]

Pensioni Mussoni, Bürglsternstr. 6, Salzburg

I swallow my pride and write first. I feel strongly however that I must at this stage put it on record that I believe all your reviewers to be wrong both in their positive & their negative epithets.[3] I finished it in the second week after term, and, believe me, it is (1) immature (2) sometimes awkward and pretentious in form (3) in parts dull (4) tasteless in the Hamish E. part or what I assume to be that.[4] But it is (1) not average in any sense (2) not over-introspective (3) humid, genuinely romantic, really pregnant, not set, not ossifying, early, potential sort of writing, (3) [*sic*] the dialogue is interesting and warm and sympathisch,[5] (4) the banalities are not the banalities of professional padding, but insufficiently felt, or insufficiently worked upon patches of material, in itself interesting, genuine, and capable of igniting properly if treated with greater experience than you possess. I want to stress the fact that you do depend on actual experiences, that the value of what you produce largely consists in its actuality, by which I do not mean that you are, or ought to try to be, naturalistic, but that even when you symbolise, your business is to symbolise – and use as symbols – everything wie es eigentlich

1 Geoffrey Cust Faber (1889–1961), lawyer and publisher; Fellow of All Souls 1919–61 (Estates Bursar 1923–51).

2 (Morgan) Goronwy *Rees (1909–79), historian and journalist; New College history, then after his first year PPE, 1928–31; Fellow of All Souls 1931–46.

3 Rees had just published his first novel *The Summer Flood* (London, 1932), whose spine styles him 'Garonwy Rees'.

4 A very intense section of the book on a homosexual affair between the hero, Owen Morgan, and an Oxford friend, Sasha, who are based, IB assumes, on GR and James ('Hamish') Alexander Wedderburn St Clair-Erskine (1909–73), New College 1928–c.1931 (left with no degree), Nancy Mitford's first love, who did not marry. See especially chapter 4, 'The Strawberry Mare'.

5 'Congenial', 'likeable'.

ist[1] and not as [it] ought, might, or, per fairy tale impossibile, could – be. All my criticism is vitiated by inability to dissociate the writer, when I know him, from the work. This disqualifies my judgments both in your case and Stephen Spender's.[2] When I read I see the face & hear the voice of the man. Hence the lack of objectivity in what I say. The reason for my saying anything is that you once asked me what I thought, & I couldn't then say, because I hadn't read your novel. I daresay your critics and Humphry[3] may be right, & I totally wrong. But if I don't mean anything to them, neither do they mean much to me. I write for entirely personal reasons. I am not, in this case, fit to judge the truth. I liked your novel and shall read it again.

I.B.

IB achieved a first-class degree in PPE in summer 1932. R. H.
Crossman[4] offered him a lectureship teaching philosophy at New
College, which he was to take up that October, after his annual trip to
Salzburg.

TO JOHN HILTON

Postmark 11 August 1932

Villa Mussoni, Salzburg

[. . .]

Here everything is very normal and English: *Sigle* Lynd[5] has arrived escorted by Felix Markham,[6] and begs her love to be sent to you: on this more intimate side I may tell you that I like her quite well, anyhow as a considerable relief (a) from Hardie who left yesterday and was in the end höchstens[7] boring and (b) from the singularly idealistic and high-minded

---

1 'As it really is'.
2 Stephen Harold *Spender (1909–95), poet and critic, friend of IB for life from 1929 or 1930; Univ. PPE 1927–30.
3 (Arthur) Humphry *House (1908–55), Hertford classics 1925–29, history 1929–30, teacher, Repton School, 1930–1, Chaplain-Fellow and English Lecturer, Wadham, 1931–2 (resigned after a crisis of faith); Special Assistant Lecturer in Classics, University College, Exeter, 1933–5.
4 Richard ('Dick') Howard Stafford *Crossman (1907–74), New College classics 1926–30, Fellow and Tutor in philosophy, 1930–7.
5 Sigle ('Sheila') *Lynd (1910–76), Somerville chemistry and biology 1929–30, left after four terms (too busy dancing); member of the CP; worked for the publisher Victor Gollancz until 1939, the year in which she had married Peter Wheeler.
6 Felix Maurice Hippisley Markham (1908–92), Fellow and history Tutor, Hertford, 1931–73.
7 'At best'.

generation of young women attached to All Souls & New College, who incessantly talk about the good life (that is New College and Joseph[1] in the end) and look for aims. Anyhow she is quite nice.

Tell Mr Kahana[2] (who in distant memory is fast growing into a red & green dragon with insistent ways) that his book is safe in my keeping, and that as soon as I return I shall give [it] to you for him, or whatever arrangement suits him best. I am very stricken by terror of him. But I expect it is my well-known Englishness which is frightened by dynamic continentalism. Anyhow pay no attention to my words in any serious crisis. I haven't read Apocalypse[3] but I observed H. House reading it and look into the pages over his shoulder: it then seemed to me definitely of a quality and mostly good. I leave here on the 16th and go straight back. I have been buying impressive looking German philosophy books to leave open on my table as a desperate last resort for impressing my very, very Wykehamist[4] pupils. I have been giving v. concentrated thought to all kinds of things relating to you and will try to be interesting on the subject when I return: as soon as I do I shall write or phone etc.

Love

I.B.

IB's new life as a don started in October. His first impressions of his colleagues at New College were not favourable: he later described them as 'the most boring, priggish, pompous collection of people I've ever come across'.[5] And although he enjoyed the teaching, he was depressed by the lack of intellectual stimulation that New College then offered: 'It's the first time a young man like me discovers he can't say what he likes. People are too conventional. They talk about bypasses, about cars, what they read in newspapers. It was impossible to say anything genuine.'[6]

1 Horace William Brindley Joseph (1867–1943), philosopher, Fellow of New College 1891–32, Supernumerary Fellow 1932–43; 'Jobags' to some of his friends.
2 JRH writes: 'Uriel Kahana [1903–65], a fellow student of mine at the Bartlett School of Architecture (University College London). After qualifying (1933) we started an embryonic partnership that ended when I went next year to Cyprus. Born in Russia, he had worked in Berlin before coming to London; after I left he went into Erich Mendelsohn's offices, where he was unhappy; then set up on his own in Israel. Died 1 September 1965 after finishing "98% of the drawings" for the Shalom-Aleichem House (dedicated to the memory of his wife's "illustrious grandfather", a noted writer). Powerful in voice, and everything else.' JRH to the editor, 7 November 1991.
3 By D. H. Lawrence (Florence, 1931; London, [1932]).
4 i.e. from the leading English public (i.e. private) school, Winchester College.
5 MI Tape 5.
6 MI Tape 10.

TO SHIELA GRANT DUFF[1]

Thursday [13 October 1932]

New College

Dear Shiela

(Though if Goronwy had his way I should be forced to call you Miss Grant Duff. On the other hand A. v Trott[2] thinks that I know you well enough. I trust him implicitly and this settled my doubts.)

I was genuinely disappointed when I heard that you were not going to come to the very dinner dinner which is to be held in the Barn[3] to-night. I have, after all, been seeing the other members of that dinner party with some regularity, and I looked forward to making very small small talk with you during, at any rate, the first portion of the dinner. This is very sad. Moreover you have robbed me of any opportunity of proving to you by irrefragable logic + appeal to moral sense why you should come and inspect Stephen Spender. I do not intend to pursue you with a tract on the subject here and now: I can only make a direct, sincere, simple appeal to your sense of values, & of how great a one you would be realising in coming to lunch on Saturday. But if you really cannot come there is, I suppose, nothing to be done. And I hope to see you in the near future. We might even go for a walk perhaps.

yours sinc.

I.B.

IB's unhappiness at New College made the prospect of a Fellowship at All Souls all the more inviting. His father later recorded his memories of that year's events:

In the spring of [1932] I visited you in Oxford and you were agitated by the problem of whether to apply for a job at (if I remember well) Exeter College. You were not keen on joining Exeter, but did not think that any of the Colleges which you fancied would take you. Still you decided to

---

1 Shiela (*sic*) *Grant Duff (b. 1913), Lady Margaret Hall (LMH) PPE 1931–4, then Foreign Correspondent in Germany and Czechoslovakia; Foreign Research and Press Service (FRPS) 1939–41, BBC Foreign Service 1941–44.

2 In IB's words, Adam von *Trott was 'a German Rhodes scholar who took part in the 1944 plot [to assassinate Adolf Hitler] and was brutally killed by Hitler. We became friends in his Oxford years, and I liked and admired him greatly'; he also refers to 'aspects of his outlook and behaviour that at times seemed inscrutable to some of his most devoted friends'. Contribution to 'Books of the Year: A Personal Choice', *Observer*, 22 December 1968, 17, recommending Christopher Sykes's biography of von Trott, *Troubled Loyalty* (London, 1968).

3 A New College building in New College Lane, then the home of Richard Crossman and his German wife, Erika.

wait and the opportunity of a lectureship at New College occurred, which you took.

Soon afterwards the examination at All Souls took place. I don't know how you felt but possibly you were more encouraged by some of your friends, particularly Hardy.[1] I was sure in my mind that a College known for their great selectivity, full of bishops and statesmen, will not plump for a foreign born Jew. There I believe was scarcely a Jew ever on record having been a Fellow of All Souls. And I believe the first reaction of Lord Chelmsford,[2] the Warden, after your examination, was 'I hope *he* will not join our College.'[3] I remember having written to you, in order to soften the blow of the expected rejection, that your election[4] could only be a miracle, and that miracles nowadays don't happen. The reply next day was a telegram from you: 'A miracle has happened.' I think the moment when Reece[5] was sent to see you and inform you of your success must have been one of the proudest in your life. I remember old Lenanton of Foy Morgan & Co.[6] telephoning me to congratulate, in the belief that I was not fully conscious of the honour and importance of election to an All Souls Fellowship, trying to explain to me what it meant and how impressed he was, knowing your antecedents. The Jewish Chronicle devoted an article[7] to this important event in the Jewish Community and the Chief Rabbi wrote to congratulate you (addressing you, if I remember correctly, as 'Irving' Berlin).[8] This election established your position in Oxford.[9]

1 sc. W. F. R. Hardie.
2 Frederic John Napier Thesiger (1868–1933), 1st Viscount Chelmsford, Warden of All Souls 1932–3.
3 IB's usual version was 'At least we don't have to take *that* one!'
4 Which took place on 3 November.
5 sc. Goronwy Rees.
6 William Ray Lenanton (1863–1944), father of Gerald (506/2); Foy Morgan & Co. were London timber-brokers.
7 'A Jewish Fellow at Oxford', 11 November 1932, 8. The piece pointed out that the only previous Jewish Fellow at the University was 'Professor Samuel Alexander fifty years ago. Professor Sylvester's case is scarcely in point, for he was elected to a Fellowship in virtue of his Professorship.' Cambridge, by contrast, 'can already show a list of five Jewish Fellows'. The philosopher Samuel Alexander (1859–1938) was Fellow of Lincoln 1882–93; the mathematician James Joseph Sylvester (1814–97) was Savilian Professor of Geometry and Fellow of New College from 1883 to his death (though effectively retired for his final years); each was notable for his personality as well as for his intellect.
8 He does: the letter, dated 25 November 1932, from Joseph Herman Hertz (1872–1946), Chief Rabbi since 1913, is addressed to 'Irving Berlin, Esq., New College'.
9 Mendel Berlin, family memoir. This manuscript, dated 11 March 1946, is addressed to IB, for reasons made clear by its opening words: 'I started several times to write down my autobiography and some facets of my life for the benefit of my son, but during the War I could not concentrate sufficiently; now, when the extinction of nearly all the members of my wife's and my family by the Nazis has been confirmed, I feel the necessity for these records is real; the living link between the past and the future, the link who still remembers the past, is practically only myself.'

IB moved from New College to All Souls[1] almost at once, but his
excitement led to too little sleep, too much talking, and then nervous
exhaustion. He returned home to recuperate.

TO STEPHEN SPENDER

5 December [1932]

49 Hollycroft Avenue

Dear Stephen

Thank you for your letter: I am much better, very bored, but in a self
satisfied and complacent frame of mind which I am prone to and which
anyone who really has experienced it is bound to detest in retrospect. I have
suddenly begun to read Turgenev in Russian and am now reading him wildly
in a sort of intoxication. I have read Rudin, On the Eve, Torrents of Spring
(again) Smoke, First Love, & about 15 short stories and plays. I shall soon
read his poems. Rudin has a frightful, inhibiting effect on one: one becomes
instantly ashamed (why should I say 'one'? I mean I) of all The loose
enthusiastic speeches I sometimes make about books or persons: the more
I know I have impressed the audience I mean to impress, the more
uncomfortable I felt after reading successive chapters of Rudin.[2] I believe
Turgenev did not mean that at all: I believe he often does much better than
he intends: that he starts out by trying to sketch some general well known
type of Russian and cannot help noting various personal characteristics
which are irrelevant to the type, but produce living individuals: whereas
Tolstoy is trying quite consciously, almost aloud, not to lose himself in
generalities, but is continually & successfully pumping temperament &
blood into his characters knowing what he is doing:[3] Turgenev's ambition
is to produce universal types but he is too much an artist & too little of an
intellectual to be able to prevent himself from creating individuals so
individual that their universal significance is a very secondary fact about
them. This, I suppose, is self-evident to anyone who reads them. I have only
just discovered it. I am rather sorry you left Malaga: I was on the point of
trying to persuade my parents to go there & might have succeeded when

1 Despite the move, he was still to teach philosophy for New College.
2 The eponymous central character of Turgenev's first novel, *Rudin* (1856), is said to have been
  modelled on his friend Bakunin, the archetypical disaffected intellectual of the 1840s. Rudin is
  fired by the romantic idealism and philosophical debate he encountered at university, holds
  forth at length about life and liberty, but achieves little. He is also exposed as lacking not just
  political but also emotional will: he is loved by the beautiful young Natal'ya, but cannot
  bring himself to a declaration. Restless and rootless in Russia, he throws himself into events
  in Paris in 1848, only to die a futile and forgotten death on the barricades.
3 An early adumbration of the thesis of IB's *The Hedgehog and the Fox* (xix/1).

your second letter arrived. As a result I have succeeded at any rate in scotching S. France, which wd have been frightful quite obviously & succeeded in getting them to buy a ticket to Naples: I shall let them stay at Amalfi for a little and then will drag them to Sicily: to Taormina I expect. I wish you would take a barge & pick your way to Majorca and Sardinia & Sicily. But this is obviously a chimera, I suppose.

I am glad you like your neat Hellmut:[1] I am in some fear of Oxford next term: I am growing very conscious not of the barrenness of academicism in general but of the futility of the particular wrangles indulged in by my colleagues, young especially. Consequently I shall read a lot of Hegel,[2] Marx,[3] Engels[4] & the Russians in order to climb out into a different even if not wider universe. Also I shall become suspect by Joseph etc. A good thing.

I pray you to be in Spain at Easter.[5]

I believe that next term I shall have to teach philosophy to B.J. (Lynd:[6] the poetical one) and to Shiela Gr. Duff: this frightens me: philosophy with me tends to become personal occasionally when in the despair of a disagreement I appeal to my pupils' inner consciousness: embarrassing tho' it may be, it may be good for me: in spite of my obvious and excessive interest in people I do tend to live in a framework of quite good, but nevertheless obviously thin abstractions. Such jolts as I've had so far, such as finding that my pupils lied about their feelings, or had a different set from mine, excited me a great deal and made me think & actually – the excitement there was enormous – come to independent & personal conclusions about what I had before taken public opinion in Oxford philosophy for granted. If these women aren't frightened (God knows what there is frightening about

1 Hellmut Schroeder, a young German with whom Spender was then having a relationship in Spain.

2 Georg Wilhelm Friedrich Hegel (1770–1831), German historicist philosopher and major influence on Marx: see chapter on him in FIB.

3 Karl Heinrich Marx (1818–83), German socialist and founder (with Friedrich Engels) of Communism; lived in London from 1849; see KM. His major work, *Das Kapital* (1867–94) expounded his economic, social and political views and was largely responsible for the widespread influence of Marx's thinking.

4 Friedrich Engels (1820–95), German socialist and businessman; collaborator with Marx on the Communist manifesto, *Manifest der Kommunistichen Partei* (London, 1848); editor, after Marx's death, of the second and third volumes of *Das Kapital*.

5 Before this sentence the following is crossed out: 'in a sense I suppose I could induce my parents to go, I can hardly demand that you shall be where I want you at any particular time. Nevertheless I do.' After it this: 'I repeat I do want to go to Malaga v. much indeed. I'll talk about it to my parents: but the chances of going are small: we shall see.'

6 Maire ('BJ', i.e. 'Baby Junior') *Lynd (1912–90), classics Home Student, Oxford, 1930–4, then a distinguished publisher's reader for William Heinemann; married Jack Gaster 1938; member of the CP.

me but even Sheila Lynd – think – was frightened for a few hours) or nervous or insincere, it may be very good.[1]

TO SHEILA GRANT DUFF

Thursday 8th [December 1932]

All Souls

Dear Shiela

Your letter was melancholy and sympathetic. Having soaked myself in the most enervating and good Turgénev for some weeks I was in a flaccid state in which the least encouragement would make me wistful. This is so rare a state that it escapes from being included under the category of normal introspection (which, we agree, is an unnecessary & on the whole bad occupation) & is the object of real objective curiosity. However, all this is in no way your fault. It is not a good time in which to go to Vienna. It is cold there and probably very like Oxford. Collingwood[2] is very exciting and risky. He is a very sly lively continental sort of philosopher: if he takes an interest in you you will, I think, find him interesting & even sensational. I know really very little about [him] save that I always found him entertaining, enormously ingenious, and frequently deceitful and unsound. He is the only philosophy tutor in Oxford who is also a man of genuine culture. This is all very good and I wish he taught me too. I am glad the Fulton[3] comedy is over. Even so cautious a man as my own good Hardie declares that he is a farcical philosopher.

If Goronwy takes his job[4] seriously he ought to be better at it than at anything else whatever at the present moment. I wish, for his sake, that there were a war somewhere. He would report it most brilliantly. Or any sort of turmoil: my general charge that he tends to live from hand to mouth still stands, but that sort of capacity for concentration on everything as it happens is obviously very useful for anyone who describes actual states of affairs. I am uneasily aware of beginning a lecture on someone's character, which, we are agreed, must stop. Have you ever seen *Speculum Mentis*, your future tutor's masterpiece? I read it at school and have forgotten it entirely. It is, I believe, shallow and exhilarating. But I may be hopelessly unfair. As for discussing

1 Letter incomplete?
2 Robin George Collingwood (1889–1943), Fellow of Pembroke and University Lecturer in Philosophy and Roman History 1912–35; his *Speculum Mentis, or the Map of Knowledge* was published in 1924.
3 John Scott Fulton (1902–86), Fellow and Tutor (philosophy 1928–35, politics 1935–47), Balliol, 1928–47; previously SGD's (presumably unsatisfactory) tutor.
4 Journalism.

philosophy with you I shall not be able to prevent myself from doing it whatever you do. So that is secure. If you write to Goronwy will you tell him that Stephen Spender has left Malaga and is in Barcelona which he dislikes? I may forget to, & he is interested, I believe. His address is c/o Cooks, Barcelona. I wish you were coming to Sicily. It would be so much more delightful to talk about anything, Locke even, than in Oxford. But of course you won't come, & some Bowen[1] will. I hope you enjoyed the party on Wednesday. The plot to inveigle me into it, which failed miserably, as anyone who knows me at all, would know. But I travelled to Oxford this morning opposite 2 young men entirely unknown to me, who were there, & discussed everyone to my admittedly unlimited delight. Finally I could resist no more & appearing from behind the Times asked a pertinent & personal question. They were very astonished and excited and embarrassed and just had time to ask me whether I did not think that Sigle Lynd looked like the Duke of Wellington, when we arrived. Instead of consisting, as I intended, of (1) a lot of information about Childhood, Adolescence etc.[2] which I possess & (2) an encomium to Adam v[on] T[rott] this letter has degenerated into this tittle tattle. I am so sorry.

Shaya.

Tolstoy. It is extremely important to note the descriptions of (1) how he always found his face very ugly & (2) the speculation on what would be said after his suicide. Both are very considerable chunks of my early life.

TO SHIELA GRANT DUFF

Monday 12th [December 1932]

49 Hollycroft Avenue

Dear Shiela,

I hope the enclosed[3] is not too much out of date. I wrote it days ago & put [it] into my pocket. Nothing happened after this. This morning I rediscovered it. Secretly, I suppose, I am rather pleased to be absent minded. I cannot remember anything of what is inside except that I was feeling warm and grateful in a general way when I wrote it. I don't even

---

1 A reference to (Ivor) Ian Bowen (1908–84), economist, Fellow of All Souls 1930–7, Lecturer, Brasenose, 1931–40, Chief Statistical Officer, Ministry of Works, 1940–5, Lecturer, Hertford, 1946–7; married Erica Baillie 1934 (divorced 1950); author with John Creasey, under the joint pseudonym 'Charles Hogarth', of *Murder on Largo Island* (London, 1944).
2 Tolstoy's fictionalised but autobiographical *Detstvo, otrochestvo i yunost'* (separately 1852–7, collected 1886), usually translated as *Childhood, Boyhood and Youth*.
3 Letter of 8 December 1932.

know whether it is worth sending it. I leave for Sicily the day after to-morrow in poor company. It is obviously good for me to be bored and not to talk for a long period. I have suddenly found Descartes,[1] whom I used to hate, very exciting & great. [I] used to think of him as a collection of irritating bits, each to be explored in turn, most out of a sense of duty. Now he appears as an obvious monolith. This is very good. I have genuinely moved from somewhere to somewhere which happens very rarely. I cannot even remember the last time it happened.

    yours
      Shaiah

TO JOHN HILTON

    26th [December 1932]

                         Hotel Santa Caterina, Amalfi

My dear John,

    Your fears were groundless. There is no hope of my going to Sicily. My parents are of Moore's[2] views completely: they will not stir hence save to return: which we'll do in three or four days. Going slowly via Naples, Rome, Florence. The walks are far too steep for me to be blamed if I do not take them. My parents hobnob with everyone and I am gloomily cenobitic. I am regarded as the degenerate son of worthy parents and am addressed carefully and very timidly. This pleases me a lot and I take no exercise & look better every day and read bad books with mild enjoyment and don't dress for the Xmas dinner. The latter, Xmas tree, Amalfi children receiving rich gifts from benevolent English milady etc. all occurred with most admirable precision: the whole thing was unfortunately ruined by the loud excesses of a tipsy American who behaved so badly that no dance was held: all our ladies declaring that they were frightened of his possible advances: he ended by bullying my unhappy father into splitting a bottle of champagne (he called it bubbly I am almost certain) with him at a little table all by themselves. He then insulted the proprietor & said he was four times richer than the proprietor, in a provocative manner. To day I was the only person to greet him: (I am not in any way a sensationalist. But I do seem to be doing everything to make myself unpopular) he informed me that I was a man of

1 René Descartes (1596–1650), French scientist, mathematician and philosopher, often referred to as the 'father' of modern philosophy; his attempt to reconcile philosophy with science (while not discarding religion), through the deconstruction and reconstruction of all human beliefs, marked a major change of enduring influence in philosophy.

2 (Ponsonby) Moore *Crosthwaite (1907–89), CCC classics 1926–30; Laming Fellow, Queen's College, Oxford, 1931–2; Diplomatic Service from 1932.

the world & knew how these things were. His wife asked me to agree with her that life was a little merrygoround, the same old wheel, huh? I said my life wasn't & left her abruptly. Even she is now offended. By now you will have gathered that the place is an Anglo-American pension with one unhappy Italian couple who strayed into the place by error, & are nightly driven out from the English speaking drawing room where the Sterling Group nightly gather (there is a Dane & Norwegian or two. They dare speak no language but English.)

For me it is quite a cheerful existence: I live wonderfully lazily, more so than at Oxford. Forgive me if I write no more: I am very sleepy at this hour & propose to slumber over the watery, sensible, & beautifully soporific pages of M. Emile Meyerson on Identity & Reality.[1]

Good night.

I shall be back on about the 7th? will you telephone?

I.B.

TO SHIELA GRANT DUFF (IN BERLIN)

Tuesday [postmark April[?] 1933]

49 Hollycroft Avenue

Dear Shiela

Thank you for your beautiful soothing letter: I was very wrought up about something at the time and it produced a very swift serenifying effect. My memories of Holland are very curious: I passed part of last summer there, waiting for my P.P.E. viva, partly in the sea, partly at concerts, & received excellent letters from Maurice[2] who was in Verona, I think. Holland I loved: it was absolutely pre-war in character: the music normally played was just the sort of amiable, rather cheap, rather nice ninth rate stuff I imagine 1912 was full of: everyone was dull, happy and agreeable: everything was old fashioned, comfortable, provincial, hospitable, stolid and touchingly childish: there really were windmills, clogs, and malarial planters from Malay States. I enjoyed myself very much, loved the Dutch because they were so bourgeois and gentle and tidy, & then had awful feelings of horror because I suddenly discovered that they were what I had long feared I was myself: I had suddenly found myself in a pre-war mildly liberal universe where everything violent was muffled and there was no movement at all. Having discovered this (true all but for the new buildings which you drew

---

1 Émile Meyerson, *Identité et réalité*, 4th ed. (Paris, 1932).

2 (Cecil) Maurice *Bowra (1898–1971), classicist; New College 1918–22; Fellow and Tutor, Wadham, 1922–38, Warden 1938–70.

with considerable expression: the best was an absolutely mad polygon which is a lunatic asylum near the Hague where I was. The Hague is unbelievably calm and sweet and Victorian. I don't believe any town in England was so staid ever as The Hague. Lovely it was) I immediately, or rather the I which requires, so you say, being put back, which on this occasion observed the other self to be thus Dutch, became very self conscious and unhappy, & I left almost immediately. But I loved it before this revelation. I was taught about music by a very excitable Polish conductor: I was driven about the country by an enormous bald Dutchman who was very nice: and I enjoyed anything that happened. Especially the old ladies: there were two, Germans, and they rang for tea ('Bellen' I may add means 'to ring' in Dutch and 'to bark' in German). The waiter appeared & said 'Haben Sie gebellt?'[1] which caused a panic: It was very, very funny indeed. The food was wonderful, I was for once completely contented with the company of my parents. The chief musical guest was the so-called Sir Wood[2] who was described in the local press as 'mächtig'.[3] I talked to him and he was nice but stupid in the extreme. No, no, no. I have stopped worrying about you & G. Why should I talk about it to e.g. Sigle? Stephen I may have spoken to about it, because he is the most sympathetic person about personal relations that I know. Douglas[4] I am not on intimate enough terms with. Anyhow it is too much the sort of ground I have taught myself to regard as semi-sacred, certainly to fear to tread, for it to be a subject of ordinary conversation. I have begun to think about politics. It is very disagreeable: I do not understand anything, except that I must try & compromise myself in some way & commit myself to something in order to see the thing from the inside: if only, that is, to revolt against my first position. I propose therefore to make a fool of myself at first and be scoffed at: no braver act did man ever embark on: it really is a right act one chooses without in the least wanting to do it. I haven't yet heard from G. but since you say I will, no doubt you're right.

As for the concert I shall probably take Humphrey Spender,[5] who is very nice indeed.

---

1 'You rang/barked?'

2 The conductor Sir Henry Wood (1869–1944).

3 'Masterful'.

4 Douglas Patrick Thomas *Jay (1907–96), economist; Fellow of All Souls 1930–7; married Margaret (Peggy) Garnett 1933; journalist 1929–40.

5 Stephen Spender's brother, (John) Humphrey Spender (b. 1910), architect, photographer and artist, at this time working as a photographer for the *Daily Mail* under the name 'Lensman'; principal photographer 1937–8 for the Mass-Observation programme of social research, for which he took over 800 photographs as part of a detailed investigation into and recording of working-class life in Bolton and Blackpool; photojournalist for *Picture Post* 1938–42, then joined British Intelligence to work on photo-interpretation.

G. if he goes with you cuts a semi-important college meeting. But you must make him. I shall, after all. Hume on causality is frightfully crucial: Everything he says, or nearly everything is true: & at this point the whole discussion gets taken up by Kant & becomes important, exciting, & vital to the nth degree.[1] I want to know more about the Toy merchant: Nüremberg does he come from? if he is the one I know (fat, fair, rosy, gruff, like a sheep in sheep's clothing, a great fleece of white hear [sic] parted in the centre on his head,) his children are all very ugly.

I very much look [forward] to seeing you again: it will be a magnificent summer (Douglas is lengthy about that) and I too will be more gentle than unfortunate in manner.

Love
    Shaya.

If you've time in Berlin and (1) Blech[2] is conducting Carmen or Mozart it is important to go. (2) was going to be about Klemperer.[3] But it isn't now.

TO JOHN HILTON

Wednesday [June 1933?]

All Souls

Dear John
    Not a breath passes here where all is very still. I am about to write a tractate on God's chasing his own predictions for you but am so idiotically busy that I haven't been able to find a cool hour yet. I am mildly oppressed by the heat which you wd love. Why don't you come? please: we shall leave Oxford at once & go somewhere. Especially if you have a car. But even if not. The only piece of really stimulating gossip there is is the unmentionable fact (do be careful) that the President being weak & adying demands blood.[4] The Fellows gallantly offered theirs. Chas Henderson offered but

---

1 Hume pointed out that we cannot derive the idea of causation from observation on its own: all we can do is observe phenomena which, because they constantly occur one after the other, we assume to be causally linked. This shows that we have a mental predisposition to ascribe causation to constantly conjoined phenomena. This in turn led Kant to his theory that our minds are hard-wired (as we now say) with 'a priori' categories (such as those of time and space) that force us to interpret our experiences in particular ways so that they shall be intelligible.

2 Leo Blech (1871–1958), Jewish conductor and composer; music director of the Berlin State Opera 1913–23 and 1926–37.

3 Otto Klemperer (1885–1973), conductor.

4 P. S. Allen died on 16 June 1933.

was forbidden to give by his future father in law who explained how, if so, there might be no children at all, there being just enough as it was, so he thought. Hardie was found to have none to offer. Pidduck & Phelps,[1] though something was running furious in their veins, were discovered in its not being blood, but some sharper, inferior liquid: a lot of it there was (what is this extremely bogus style I am developing?) but not blood. So Blakeway[2] paid two pints. They are now blood brothers, & he will be invited to all intimate functions. A very pleasing thought. But do come. And can I write a compelling letter to Dunedin?[3] or Bowra? who longs to do something quite genuinely.

My love
    Shaya

In late June 1933 (and again in 1934, 1935 and 1938) IB went on holiday to Ireland with three Oxford friends: Mary Fisher,[4] daughter of H. A. L. Fisher,[5] then Warden of New College; Maire Lynd, known as 'BJ', who lived with the Fishers while she was at Oxford, and was at the time one of Berlin's pupils; and Christopher Cox,[6] tutor in ancient history at New College. They ended up staying on a small island in a small lake, Lough Annilaun, near Maam Cross in County Galway; the island belonged to the Countess (Ruth) Metaxa, who was the mother-in-law of a friend of Christopher Cox, and lived in nearby Oughterard. On their way north on this first trip they paid an impromptu visit to the novelist

1 Fellows of CCC: Frederick Bernard Pidduck (1885–1952), mathematician, Fellow 1921–50; William Phelps (1882–1963), classicist, Fellow 1906–50, Tutor 1924–50. In *Corpuscles* (p. 48) IB wrote: 'Pidduck wrote Oxford obituaries for *The Times*, and explained that when he changed his view of someone, he modified the text, usually pejoratively [. . .] Phelps was an intelligent man, clever and formidable, a personality of the first order. He liked gentlemanly games-players and disliked intellectuals and aesthetes. He was a snob of a straightforward old-fashioned British kind.'

2 Blakeway, Alan Albert Antisdel (1898–1936), archaeologist of ancient Greece; Fellow and Tutor, CCC, 1931–6; Director, British School at Athens, 1936; married Alison Hope (later Mrs Antony [Tony] Andrewes) 1935; died 1 October 1936 at Winchester (where he was a master 1924–31), of blood-poisoning; 'Ferocious but loveable' (Mary Bennett to the editor, 11 September 1996).

3 If this is the judge Sir Andrew Graham Murray, Viscount Dunedin (1849–1942), his connection with IB and the purpose of writing him a 'compelling letter' (on JH's behalf?) are unknown to me. It is more likely to be a slip for 'Dunbabin', and therefore a reference to the classical archaeologist Thomas James Dunbabin (211/1), who would have been in a position to help JRH fulfil his archaeological ambitions.

4 Mary Letitia Somerville *Fisher (b. 1913), Somerville classics 1931–5.

5 Herbert Albert Laurens *Fisher (1865–1940), historian, statesman, Warden 1925–40.

6 Christopher William Machell *Cox (1899–1982), ancient historian, Fellow of New College 1926–70.

Elizabeth Bowen[1] (Mrs Alan Cameron) at Bowen's Court, her family home near Kildorrery in County Cork (she also had a house in Headington, near Oxford); this was at the suggestion of Berlin's friend Humphry House, tutor in English at Wadham, who was having an affair with Bowen and was staying at Bowen's Court at the time. IB and Bowen became friends: many letters passed between them, and in 1938 Berlin stayed at Bowen's Court to finish his biography of Marx.

Writing to her mother from Bowen's Court on 27 June, Mary Fisher, as yet unaware of the spelling of Humphry House's first name, and correcting a false impression of his status at Bowen's Court, describes the visit vividly:

This is the only house in the neighbourhood that wasn't burnt down[2] & is an immense & hideous 18th century grey stone box standing in a wide park full of trees in clumps & sheep & herons [. . .] The house incidentally belongs not so much to Humphrey House (who is a large slightly bent & rather forbidding young man) as to Elizabeth Bowen, otherwise Mrs Cameron, who is a charming creature & immensely hospitable, tho' worse made up than you can imagine, all shiney wet white & badly put on rouge [. . .] It was an alarming arrival as we came up the drive in the car, all very disreputable, with maps & mackintoshes & Christopher's hats oozing out of every chink, to find the two ladies [EB and a friend, Miss Brown] in beautiful striped silk frocks sitting on the stone steps from the front door elegantly topping & tailing gooseberries [. . .] I've never laughed so much so continuously as during these adventurous two days – BJ & I in fits of giggles all the time in the car while Isaiah sings in a high falsetto in the back.

Two days later, after a depressing day in Kilkee, on the coast of County Clare, she writes from Killaloe, north-east of Limerick, at the south end of Lough Derg on the banks of the Shannon: 'Isaiah was a brilliant idea [of BJ's]: he never fails to be amusing even in moments of the deepest gloom.' On the Friday, in Galway, after a 'slight crisis' – the accident described in the next letter – she adds:

Isaiah is a godsend: he is most efficient & continues to be amusing at the same time [. . .] he is really a great dear – much nicer and not nearly so tiresome as I expected. Goodness knows what B.J. & I should have done without him at the slight crisis [. . .] it is a relief to have a Man to Turn To.

1 Elizabeth *Bowen (1899–1973), novelist.
2 In the Troubles over a decade earlier, many of the great Anglo-Irish houses were seen by the Irish as symbols of oppression, and destroyed.

TO ELIZABETH BOWEN

30 June 1933

Great Southern Hotel, Galway

Dear Mrs Cameron

I should like to tell you how grateful I am for that night and day in your house and your company. It is a very remote and beautiful experience now, because of the reversal of fortune which has suddenly occurred. After very agreeable empty days with & after Humphry,[1] the larger parts of which I spent in mild self-dramatising day dreams, as usual, while the rest of the party talked solidly about birds for hours & hours, we drove into a little old woman on a donkey cart, and went to pieces. It was an entirely empty spot, but about 70 persons immediately gathered. The old woman was more dazed than hurt, but proceeded to exaggerate her wounds very disreputably.

If you have a taste for that sort of thing I am quite willing to give you an account of the serio-comic scenes that followed. The Gardai[2] were gay and honourable men and we made great friends with them, the scene in the police-barracks when we made our depositions, ("while Miss Lynd consoled her ladyship Mr Berlin felt a bomp and saw an ass with bits of shaft to him . . ." etc.) was a pure René Clair Le Million[3] scene which I hope I shall never forget. All this is rather spoilt by the fact that one of Cox's fingers is badly damaged, & he is in hospital now, while the rest of us gloomily circulate from the garage to the barracks, from the barracks to the hospital, from the hospital to the railway hotel. The entire town appears to be informed, since we are continually stopped by unknown men and asked sympathetic questions. We have managed to keep it out of the papers, for the news value of the two young women is rather large: also they are mortally frightened lest their parents hear of it: consequently it has to be preserved as a very dark secret: some ingenious theory will have to be built to account for the shortening of Cox's finger. I shall say that we had a scrap and I bit it off. I shall say it in a voice which will make it impossible to know whether it is true, or only a poorish joke in dubious taste. For it must never be revealed. B.J. has emerged out of this in full splendour, looks after everything, has created without any aid, a genuinely romantic (slightly

1 Humphry House, who was at that time, according to IB 'unhappy, jobless, a prey to religious doubts, and only too ready for emotional involvement', had found Maire Lynd 'irresistibly attractive' at first sight, followed her around Bowen's Court 'like a huge, lovelorn dog' and claimed within hours to have fallen 'in love, deeply, irrevocably' with her (to IB's disapproval). The next day House had insisted on accompanying the group for some distance on their journey. Letter from IB to Maire Gaster, January 1982.
2 The Irish police.
3 René Clair (1898–1981) wrote and directed this classic early sound film in 1931.

wartime) atmosphere, in which I merely feel awkward and inefficient, but which I do admire.

I am so sorry. I hadn't meant to go off on this tangent: my original intention was to say how grateful we all were for your hospitality: & how much I hope to see you again & entertain you, if you'll allow me, in Oxford. Oh yes: the Countess Metaxa is a large, nice, motherly kind woman: her son is abominably hearty and a crashing bore.

Yours v. sincerely

I. Berlin

Saturday [postmark 1 July 1933]

Great Southern Hotel, Galway

Dear Sigle

This is a very funny nice party, & I only hope I shall remember enough of the mass of odd events which have occurred to tell you when I'm back: That the Italian tour will be a great success I am now convinced: if this hasn't been a failure the other, a fortiori, is bound to be a roaring success. B.J. is growing liquider and fonder every day, Mary more and more positive and nordic.

Christopher is restlessly happy, & I preserve long silences and have mildly self-dramatising day dreams. Mrs Cameron with whom we stayed a night was charming, and v. much my cup of tea I thought. She is, I hold, a great acquisition in Oxford. We have lived on practically nothing but great samovarfuls of tea and eggs & bacon all the time: the population is infinitely charming, very romantic & unconscious of time, but occasionally for practical purposes, slightly tiresome because vague. Not that that is anything I feel disposed to quarrel with. If ever I marry I shall certainly choose an Irishwoman. I shall almost certainly come to your party, on the 6th, or is it the 7th, I treat this whole tour not so much as a positive experience as an amiable gap between events, a very agreeable empty intereventual vacuum in which nothing is done by me nor demanded from me. My embottled loquacity will no doubt burst upon our Italian scene in a terrific shower. Mr Cox's party. Very funny indeed

yrs

Shaya

The next day Mary Fisher writes home from Lough Annilaun:

Oh such bliss! We are encamped in two little wooden huts in the middle of an island in the middle of a lake in the middle of mountains [our] hut was *incredibly* dirty when we got in, but it is nevertheless heaven. Isaiah is surprisingly handy in the home – he whipped off his coat & cleaned the sink before I had turned round yesterday & quite willingly dug a pit for eggshells & tins when it was suggested to him [. . .] BJ & I spent the morning swimming naked thro' black water while they discreetly slept on the verandah. All is bliss.

They stayed on the island for two more nights, returning home on the Dublin–Holyhead ferry on Wednesday 5 July. Then, before continuing his travels with Oxford contemporaries, IB spent some time on holiday with his father.

TO MARIE BERLIN

[July 1933]

Hôtel Atlantic, Le Touquet

Dear Mother:

I have sent father away to the Casino and have stayed behind to read and write letters: I am very well: and leaving for Paris & Italy to-morrow: the non-arrival of your telegram till this morning produced a little crisis here, but it was soon got over. We enjoyed our holiday very much: as for Switzerland: it is v. expensive for Father, & what he really worries about is what he should do during bank holiday with even Bick away. He is in the humiliating position of being at once friendless and dependent on company. I am the latter but at least not the former. I hope your passage through Germany[1] was without incident. Here there is not a Jewish soul: Frida Markovna, old, broken, shabby, was seen by us through a café window one evening, shambling quickly with somebody – she was not seen again. Father looks splendid, is rested, & I look well too. I may spend the 10 days before I go to Prague with Crosthwaite somewhere – in Italy or Switzerland. He sends his greetings to my parents. A v. continental character in some ways. When he is 40 he will be a pompous snob, but he is still all right at present.

I'll write you next from Portofino. Father is not back yet so I'll send this without his knowledge even. To work on a holiday with him is impossible – he does not read for more than ¾ hours at a time *and* he hates to be left alone. But he is a very nice man: I occasionally get a sort of objective vision of him, not as a son, but absolutely, and he is an excellent person – even his egoism is

---

1 Since Hitler had become Chancellor of Germany in January, anti-Jewish propaganda and legislation, as well as Nazi-provoked public persecution of Jews, had already come to characterise Germany under the Nazi regime.

of an human & amiable character. It is a pleasure to see a man who has been so little battered by life: you will say that it is the tent built by you that has saved him from friction – maybe: but some people look for sharp corners, потереться о них[1] – he – having no natural bristles, if you protect him from roughnesses, develops none of his own. For which I say thank you. I wish you much joy of Mr Bick. His sentimentality will be boundless.

love.

Shaya.

IB's holiday companions in Portofino were Roy Harrod,[2] his mother Frances,[3] Thomas Hodgkin[4] and the Lynd sisters. But the party found their hotel there inconvenient and Portofino overcrowded, and on 2 August they moved to San Vigilio on Lake Garda. Derek Kahn[5] and Edward (Teddy) Hodgkin[6] had planned to join them in Portofino soon afterwards. Thomas wrote to Teddy about the change of plan but could not contact Derek, who therefore went to Portofino, cabling on 4 August to ask to be met in Bolzano, but not giving an exact rendezvous. IB, Thomas and Teddy searched for Derek in Bolzano without success. IB then travelled via Innsbruck to Marienbad before continuing to Salzburg, where he had invited the Hodgkins to join him from 20 August.

TO CHRISTOPHER COX

14 [August][7] 1933

As from Hauptpostlagernd, Salzburg

Dear X.

How are you? why do you never write? Are you satisfied about Greats? how is your finger? is B.J. perceptibly sadder after Italy?[8] or on the other hand perceptibly less so? what are the details about Greats? is the great house

---

1 'Poteret'sya o nikh', 'to rub up against them'.
2 (Henry) Roy Forbes *Harrod (1900–78), economist, Student (i.e. Fellow) and Tutor, Christ Church, 1924–67.
3 Frances Marie Desirée Harrod (1866–1956), widowed novelist, sister of the actor Sir Johnston Forbes-Robertson.
4 Thomas Lionel *Hodgkin (1910–82), Balliol classics 1928–32, Senior Demy (i.e. graduate scholar), Magdalen, 1933, was returning to England via Europe after living in Palestine as a trainee archaeologist from 26 December 1932 to 24 July 1933.
5 Derek Edward Walter Blaikie (1912–44), né Kahn, Balliol classics 1930–4, changed his surname in 1933; killed in action in Burma 14 February 1944.
6 Thomas Hodgkin's younger brother Edward Christian Hodgkin (b. 1913), known as Teddy by his family, Balliol history 1932–5, later (1969–72) Deputy Editor of *The Times*.
7 Misdated July.
8 For reasons unknown, but presumably amatory.

of Ford in mourning?[1] are you aware of the fact that I am slowly turning into the E. Waugh Prime Minister who always complained that no one ever told him anything?[2] evidently there is much that you could write about. Please fill in at least the above questionnaire. and for God's sake keep the above address a secret. It would be fatal if the Lynds, e.g., knew. I am rapidly turning a Slav philosopher: all the local notables are professors & very clever men: The picture on the stamp combines, don't you think, the austere nobility of the Vice-Chancellor with the urbane charm of Prof. Clark.[3]

Shaya.

Surely the Lit Hum results are just right?

New College Archive

TO ROY HARROD

15 August 1933

G. Hotel Klinger, Marienbad

Thank you v. much for your most welcome letter. My poverty was becoming acute.[4] How well you know the suspense that induces. However, I had less reason for it than you. Bolzano was quite agreeable: no trace of Derek Kahn could be discovered. The number of other Kahns was astonishing: but no Derek. I fear he must be suffering from a feeling of neglect which will deepen his melancholy to a still darker shade. From Bolzano we continued to Innsbruck, where on a high and lonely eminence I left the brothers Hodgkin, T. resigned but brave.[5] Marienbad is aglow with every type of Central European opinion, is full of exiles, revolutionaries, agitators, counter-agitators, is very jolly, in fact. At Innsbruck by pure accident I came across Miss Strachey[6] and her young man who were travelling to my wild surprise – to Marienbad. We continued together:

1 Edward William Spencer Ford (b. 1910), New College classics 1929–33, Law Student (Harmsworth Scholar), Middle Temple, 1934–5, later (1975) Secretary and Registrar of the Order of Merit, of distinguished lineage, had missed a First in Greats at New College.

2 Mr Outrage, 'last week's Prime Minister' (but soon reinstated) in Evelyn Waugh's *Vile Bodies* (1930).

3 The Czechoslovak stamp bears a portrait of Tomáš Masaryk, then (first) President of Czechoslovakia. The Vice-Chancellor was Francis John Lys (1863–1947), Provost of Worcester; 'Prof. Clark' is A. C. Clark.

4 It sounds from the letter to which this is a reply as if RH's mother somehow intervened to enable IB to replenish his supply of cash while he was abroad.

5 BJ had been engaged to Tommy Hodgkin, but had broken the engagement off before Tommy went to Palestine.

6 Barbara Strachey (1912–99), daughter of Oliver (brother of Lytton) and Ray Strachey, LMH history 1930–3, Ministry of Information (MOI) 1940–1, BBC 1940–74 (Foreign News Assistant 1942), married Olav Hultin on 17 January 1934 (they were divorced in 1937), and thereafter Wolf Halpern (18/1), the 'young man' here referred to.

a grotesque comedy was then enacted here before the young man's father,[1] to whom I was forced to introduce Miss S. as Belinda Grier.[2] I pant to tell you the whole story but there is no room. There is a Rockefeller student called Michel Angelo Heilperin[3] here who passionately desires to meet you. Will you tell your mother how much we all enjoyed ourselves & how grateful we feel?

Shaya.

I hope you note the striking facial resemblance of the stamp to Prof. Clark and/or the Vice Chancellor.

British Library, BL Add. MS. 71191

TO CHRISTOPHER COX

Friday 26th. [sc. 25 August 1933]

bei Oberstleutnant Richard Edler von Kosatzky
59 Plainstrasse, Salzburg
But it is easier to write to the Hauptpost.

Dear X:

Forgive me my apparently rude neglectful silence, but the arrangements for forwarding letters in my home are wretched: I received your 3 letters simultaneously:[4] the cumulative effect of them read in chronological order was terrific: I was flattered, moved, delighted, being alone, unembarrassed, and finally distressed at apparent difficulties. At least they may not be apparent. They are: (the professional imitation of me is always: one. two. three.)

1) Money. If I am too poor to come that will be quite fatal. I can't say yet how much I shall be left with. I wd rather not borrow immediately on arrival.

2) I have been away so long that (a) it is immoral, a waste of labour-time, soul destroying, nostalgia-developing occupation. I could at best come for 2 days or so. Which seems slightly absurd.

My desire to go to Ruthenia[5] is become very feeble: but G. & S.[6]

1 Georg Gad Halpern (93/3).
2 A name perhaps suggested by that of Lynda Grier, Principal of LMH (250/1).
3 Mich(a)el Angelo Heilperin (b. 1909), economist; Professor of International Monetary Relations, Graduate Institute for International Studies, Geneva, 1935–8.
4 CWMC had invited IB to 'Sligger' Urquhart's Chalet des Mélèzes in the French Alps (above St Gervais-les-Bains on the slopes of Mont Blanc): he had taken over the running of one of the New College reading parties there because of Urquhart's failing health.
5 Subcarpathian Ruthenia is now divided between Slovakia and Ukraine.
6 Goronwy Rees and Shiela Grant Duff. SGD gives a good account of the trip (made at IB's

have arrived (this I regard as solely due to my insistence that they arrive by different routes at different times. S v. melancholy before G.'s arrival. Now such scenes of open affection occur as wd melt any heart save mine. I try to curb them at my own great peril.) and I feel committed. It is a ludicrous situation: we all find Salzburg the fulfilment of all our dreams (I have for the past 4 years) & wd like to stay, but if we don't now go to Ruthenia we may never go, & may miss something. Also Shiela pines for the country. I have unsuccessfully tried to frighten them with stories of the hideous diseases which riddle every Ruthenian, of political dangers, etc. So we are going. We leave this paradise on Monday morning, go by water to Bratislava which we reach on Tuesday morning, & Kosiče & Užhorod on Wednesday. The names are undoubtedly exciting. I don't want to stay more than 3 days. If I leave on Sunday the 4th I may get to Zurich late on the 5th. If I were to come to the Chalet, I should probably arrive at some odd hour on the 6th & stay till the 8th or so or the 9th. Is that worth anyone's while? Admittedly:

(1) I should love to see you. To begin & end the summer in your company gives a pleasing roundedness to it.

(2) If I don't break it somewhere, my journey becomes pure torture towards the end. 40 hours in 3 class carriages uninterruptedly destroys one's human semblance. The motives of money, conscience, & also, I suppose, my parents' growing impatience still weigh heavily. However if you on receipt of this were to send a letter by airmail to Poste Restante, Kosiče [Koschau]^1 Czechoslovakia, informing me of how one reaches you from Zurich or Bâle, & whether 2 days or so is not ridiculous in view of the difficulties & length of access, if you do that, I hope I shall wire to you happily. (your wire, by the way, only got here yesterday afternoon) I have a great deal to tell you, but I shall release it in small quanta, & cause no havoc in daily work. The Hodgkins were both in Italy & here, & Tommy, whom I hardly knew, is a very sweet touching character. His relations with B.J. were very moving, very sweet, very honourable & slightly silly throughout: Roy Harrod took up the attitude that young people must enjoy themselves, an attitude which revolted Sigle who found it sentimental & more than B J deserves. Mrs H[arrod] deserves 60 to 70 pp. to herself. She alternately cried & asked us all if she showed too much back. In retrospect she is a rich and lovely figure, at the time she was more revolting than comic.

Do write therefore.

I'll wire anyhow somewhere round the 4th Sept.

suggestion: 'He wished to investigate the "basic Slav" which he understood was spoken in that eastern tip of Czechoslovakia') to Subcarpathian Ruthenia – ceded by Hungary to Czechoslovakia in 1920 – in her book *The Parting of Ways: A Personal Account of the Thirties* (London and Boston, 1982), 50–3.

1 IB's gloss and brackets.

Greats was quite right, I agree. The Philosophy standard must have come down if Stopford[1] got a phil. 1ˢᵗ.

S. & G. are up a mountain to-day and I am alone save for the Edler von Kosatzky who talks about the relative merits of the Serbs & Croats. & about his late master, the Archduke Joseph.[2] (?). This town is absolute heaven in every way. The shadows of a political night are closing about it: This is probably my last occasion here: you cannot believe how diluted and weakly romantical I become here: I had obviously better end.

 Yrs
  Sh.

It is v. v. kind of you to offer about books. But I have Kant's works. What more can I want.

New College Archive

After leaving Salzburg, IB, with Goronwy Rees and Shiela Grant Duff, paid a short visit to Subcarpathian Ruthenia. On the way back he stayed in Vienna (3 September) and Zurich (4 September) and then joined Christopher Cox and friends at the Urquhart chalet in the French Alps for a few days.[3]

TO MENDEL BERLIN

Sunday. [3 September 1933, *postcard*]

Zilina (5 hrs from Vienna)

I am slowly returning. As Subc[arpathian] Ruth[enia] was somewhat deficient in natural scenery, I propose to spend 2–3 days in a chalet at St. Gervais in Savoie whither I've been invited by 7 or 8 letters & telegrams by various new College people who have it for the summer. I hope to be in London on Saturday or Sunday.

 love
  Shaya.

---

1 Edward Kennedy Stopford (1911–83), New College classics 1930–3, entered War Office 1936.
2 Presumably Archduke Joseph Karl (1833–1905), a member of the Hungarian line of the Austrian royal family.
3 In the Chalet Book where visitors record their attendance IB has entered his dates as 5–10 September (CWMC's dates were 2–22 September, and IB appears in a number of his photographs from that occasion). Also there during IB's visit (apparently the only time he was at the Chalet) were Richard Chilver (60/1), Herbert *Hart, Frederick Walter How, Thomas George Odling, Mark Dalcour Tennant, Richard Wilberforce (65/5), Oliver Frederick John Bradley Woods and Shaun Wylie. The last six, apart from Wilberforce, were New College men.

TO CHRISTOPHER COX

12th [postmark September 1933]

49 Hollycroft Avenue

Dear X

I am in one of your own tearing hurries. Enclosed: £7. Third cl[ass] sleep[ing] c[a]r. admirable, fellow passengers shake hands on entering & on leaving; mine was a charming cavalry officer, v. interesting about Italian Menace. Scurrilous references about High Personages: I am most grateful to you for Chalet: I enjoyed myself v. much indeed, I recovered after a long fit of depression and disease, altogether I am most thankful. They are all golden in various ways, each inhabitant of the Chalet. Tell Richard[1] that his missive is safely despatched. Douglas in v. high spirits, his leader on Brown Book[2] got 'Economist' confiscated in Germany – everyone v. pleased, even Layton[3] not rude. G & Shiela are here, I believe, & they & the Jays going away for week-end until they quarrel. At present everyone v. happy, including, it is said, B.J. Wonderful it all sounds. As for me I shall see no one & work very hard indeed. I wish I cd have stayed longer. Here there is only rain & weddings.[4] God how stupid this is. Sorry.

Shaya

New College Archive

TO ISOBEL HENDERSON[5]

28 September 1933

49 Hollycroft Avenue

Dear Mrs Henderson,

I am wholly incapable of saying what I want to say, for I cannot bring myself to realise the full meaning of the few lines in the 'Times' which I read yesterday, by accident almost; I beg you to forgive me for this. I am ashamed and embarrassed that it required this to make me aware of how deeply I was attached to Charles, and how much he [had] done for me and with me.

1 Richard Clementson Chilver (1912–85), New College classics 1931–4; entered Civil Service 1934; married Sally Graves 1937.
2 'The Hitler Terror' (unsigned), *Economist*, 2 September 1933, 440–1. The 'Brown Book' is *The Brown Book of the Hitler Terror and the Burning of the Reichstag*, 'prepared by the World Committee for the Victims of German Fascism' under the presidency of Albert Einstein (London, 1933). Interestingly (in view of later uncertainty about IB's knowledge of Hitler's extermination of the Jews), chapter 8, 'The Persecution of the Jews', contains a section on p. 283 headed 'Liquidation of the Jewish Question'; reference is made here to 'the war of extermination which is being waged against 600,000 Jews'. Did IB read this?
3 Walter Thomas Layton (1884–1966), Editor, *Economist*, 1922–38.
4 Including that of Charles Henderson to Isobel Munro.
5 Charles Henderson died of pleurisy in Rome on his honeymoon on 24 September.

When I arrived in Corpus, on the same day and year as he himself, we were both equally lost and unhappy for a time. I wish now I had told him explicitly how grateful I was for seeking me out: he was the only genuinely humane and civilized man in that Common Room. his great good taste, shyness, gentleness and affectionateness made him feel isolated in the icy atmosphere in which he found himself; nevertheless he refused to freeze, and his room was the only place I, and I suppose his other, later, friends, knew in Oxford, in which we could look for sympathy and a warmth of emotion which hardly exist elsewhere in the University: also he was very sensible and grown up (in a sense I never felt a difference in age, I suppose because I am myself elderly in many respects; in practical matters I was very young and stupid and he very helpful) and told me what to do whenever I grew silly and disheartened: he arranged my entire career at Corpus in face of violent opposition: and sent me to All Souls and supported me in every way; I am sorry if I seem to obtrude myself and my affairs in this: but I do feel greater gratitude to him than to any man in Oxford, or anywhere, during those four years: and this is the only way of stating it. You know better than I that his sensitiveness and Europeanism which made him hate and feel foreign to what he thought of as the bourgeois pedantry, the narrowness of interests at Oxford, made him mildly melancholy during all those four years, until he met you in fact. He became more and more restless and pathetic, at the same time preserved, as a human being, genuine size and nobility. I neither can nor want to write an obituary of him, however intimate, and all this which I could, and perhaps some day may be allowed to tell you, is emerging cold and awkward in writing. On the few occasions on which I saw him since his engagement, he was very happy and very much in love, and altogether larger and richer. This is the most painful event that has ever happened in my personal history: I only hope that my self consciousness and inability to find adequate words will not prevent you from understanding the sympathy which I am trying to convey. I have expressed myself very badly. I am sorry.

    yours ever
       Isaiah Berlin

IB regarded his deliverance from the conversational sterility of New College as 'total liberation'.[1] All Souls provided a completely different environment: 'Everybody there was young and bright and talkative, and all the old men had to be on their toes, because they were outnumbered.'[2]

1 MI Tape 5.
2 MI Tape 10.

*The old men in question were the generation then in positions of influence
in the academic world or in public life; most were deeply conservative in
outlook. Those not based in Oxford paid weekend visits to All Souls, and
although amicable relations were preserved with the younger,
predominantly left-wing, academics, there were nevertheless two distinct
groupings within the Fellowship. What united them was a passion for
discussion, especially of politics: international policy, the governance of
Britain and the future of Europe were all dissected by acute minds at the
centre of events. Just listening to these conversations was an exceptional
political education.[1] The one recorded in the next letter was evidently not
up to this standard.*

TO ADAM VON TROTT

26 October [1933]

[All Souls]

Dear Adam

I should have written long ago. As I write the usual All Souls scene is
going on. By the fire Rowse & Rees are discussing the prospects of politics in
Germany. I am unable to listen, Rowse is again saying the same things. This
conversation rotates in ever-recurrent cycles, 3 or 4 are over the fifth is
beginning, the same thing is being said for the fifth time. The candidates
(*why* didn't you come? so bad is everyone that they are thinking of electing
nobody) are poor. Humphry House wrote poor papers, & a tremendous
struggle will take place over his body which I dread. I slowly revive under
the influence of Cassirer who is here & enjoying success with all schools
of young philosophers. Foster[2] & Ryle[3] & Price[4] & Ayer[5] all lie meekly side
by side to listen to him. I boldly speak of this having decided that you won't
think it petty. Rather shrilly I insist that it *isn't* petty. Cassirer is lucid,
interesting and learned. I am slowly orientating towards something or other
now at last.

1 See IB's interview with Françoise Sorbier, 'Sir Isaiah Berlin, esprit hardi', in *Oxford, 1919–1939*
   (Paris, 1991), 66.
2 John Galway *Foster (1904–82), lawyer and historian; Fellow of All Souls 1924–82, legal
   adviser, British Embassy, Washington, 1939–43, then legal adviser, SHAEF; Conservative
   Member of Parliament (MP) for Northwich, Cheshire, 1945–74.
3 Gilbert Ryle (1900–76), Student and philosophy Tutor, Christ Church, 1925–45; Waynflete
   Professor of Metaphysical Philosophy and Fellow of Magdalen 1945–68.
4 Henry Habberley *Price (1899–1984), Fellow and philosophy Lecturer, Trinity, 1924–35;
   Wykeham Professor of Logic and Fellow of New College, 1935–59; President of the Society
   for Psychical Research 1939–40.
5 Alfred ('Freddie') Jules *Ayer (1910–89), Christ Church classics 1928–32; married (Grace
   Isabel) Renée Lees (1909–80) 1932; philosophy Lecturer, Christ Church, 1932–5, Research
   Student, 1935–44; Fellow and philosophy Lecturer, Wadham, 1944–6.

My summer was quite mad, from Ireland to Italy, from Italy to Austria, from Austria to Ruthenia, (mad country. squalid, bad, interesting ambitious population. No majority at all. 5 principal languages, 7 subsidiary ones, 4 frontiers, picturesque and mad Jews, petty Ukranian squabblers), from Ruthenia to Switzerland, to France, home. Surely Central Europe, so crowded, so ambitious, so jealous, so undecadent in its very Balkanism is bound to produce something soon. They can't go on stewing in their own juice forever. I can't go on writing. Rowse talks & talks & talks & talks in a close repetitive pattern. It dulls the mind & torpifies the imagination and irks the spirit and is probably right in all his views and must be supported & helped. "The point is, my dear Goronwy, the point is *not* to listen to what people *say* they think, but what they *do*. Marx said that people are determined to do certain things in the political sphere which is after all the national spirit on the level of national consciousness by what happened to them not by what they think they intend to do . . ." etc etc etc. I can't go on – Do write to me. I require every sort of support from spiritually vigorous people.

yours

    Shaya

Charles'[1] death absolutely crushed me for a time. I was fonder of him than I thought I was. I cannot realise that I shall never see him again.

TO DIANA HUBBACK[2]

Monday [30 October 1933]

All Souls

Dear Diana

I wish I had seen you under more favourable conditions: there were too many people about & I don't much care for Miss Sperry. The last is probably my fault as she has, it is universally asserted, gaiety, wit, and beautiful velvety eyes. The fact remains that her presence & that of the sweet but irrelevant Hudson[3] made the occasion overpublic. You are, I suppose, not likely to be in Oxford again soon, nor I in London: so if I am to see you at all, (and,

---

1 Charles Henderson.
2 Diana Mary Hubback (b. 1912), great, great, great niece of Jane Austen through the latter's fifth brother, Francis; St Paul's Girls School, LMH 1931–2; close friend of Adam von Trott; trained and worked as a copywriter and was employed in refugee work for Basque, German and Czech children 1936–40; married David Hopkinson 1939.
3 Geoffrey Francis Hudson (1903–74), historian, Fellow of All Souls 1926–54.

apart from the general advantages of such a course, such unsatisfactory meetings as our last must never be allowed to remain the last experience to be remembered,) it will have to be in December which is a long way off. My universe is instead of expanding, contracting rapidly, & such inhabitants of it as are still undead and unestranged, grow daily more valuable through scarcity.

Was your remark re Martin Cooper[1] really fruitful and may I write to him about it, if so what? do tell me.[2] He is most anxious to make some money: must he return to London to write these captions: anyhow he'll be returning at Xmas. I can't refrain from telling you how puzzled I was 10 minutes ago when, in the middle of this letter, Prof. Ernst Cassirer,[3] called to ask if his Seminar was to take place at Christmas. Before that I hope I said politely: he looked at me as tho' I was quite mad. Christmas turned out to be Christchurch[4] which you guessed already. Forgive me, it is a poorish story but it occurred just now & people here are unappreciative. Please write about Martin: & anything else you please: I am sorry you couldn't come to lunch with Professor [A. C.] Clark: it was an unforgettable occasion.

　　　Yours
　　　Shaya B.

TO THOMAS HODGKIN

　　　[early November 1933][5]

　　　　　　　　　　　　　　　　　　　　　　　　　All Souls

Dear T.H.

　　　Let me tell you all I can without breaking my oath of secrecy. You weren't elected[6] because the examiners recommended only Austin.[7] Consequently all those who either had no chance of reading the papers or

---

1 Martin du Pré Cooper (1910–86), music critic and musician; St Edmund Hall modern languages 1928–31, music critic of *London Mercury* 1934–9, *Daily Herald* 1945–50.

2 Cooper seems to have requested some form of recommendation from DH.

3 The historian of ideas Ernst Cassirer (1873–1945) was a refugee from Germany who came to Oxford with his wife Toni in September 1933 as a Chichele Lecturer (on 'Die Philosophie des Rechts' – 'The philosophy of law'), at the invitation of All Souls, and supported financially by All Souls and CCC, and stayed until 1935; his *Die Philosophie der Aufklärung* ('The philosophy of the Enlightenment') had appeared in 1932.

4 A solecism uncharacteristic of IB, but one he repeats elsewhere: the Oxford College is Christ Church; there are Christchurches in New Zealand and Dorset.

5 TH's reply is dated 8 November 1933.

6 To an All Souls Fellowship.

7 John Langshaw *Austin (1911–60), Fellow of All Souls 1933–5, Fellow and philosophy Tutor, Magdalen, 1935–52.

trusted the examiners voted for Austin alone. A large party mustered round you including the most distinguished names you could wish for. There was a long & closely run contest in which you lost by literally the narrowest possible margin. Everyone old & young made speeches about you, whether they wanted to have you or not, saying how nice you were, how well you got on with everyone you met, how anything you said was bound to be original & interesting, & how fond of you everyone who knew you was. This went on for a very long time. The Warden[1] was in tears after the result was known. Grant Robertson[2] made some sharp remarks. Woodward[3] & Pares[4] cursed under their breaths. Various people who might have voted for you were absent for various causes. Altogether your memory is indelible in everyone's heart. I personally see no reason why you shouldn't come in again, though you may indignantly repudiate the suggestion. But I instance Archbishop Lang & Wilberforce.[5] I told your mother all I dared to say: I didn't tell her what I think true i.e. that I think this College treated you somewhat shabbily when it asked you to come in again. No one pretended that your papers had deteriorated: but the examiners' standard appears to have shifted: I can't otherwise explain it. At any rate let me tell you that inductively speaking it is true that no one who tries twice ever gets in (e.g. Felix, House, Preston, Figgures, Barger etc.)[6] whereas those who try thrice do (q.v. above). I see no reason why you should be melancholy (I hope you aren't? what is glory.) & give up. Especially if like Reilly[7] you can bribe them by producing modern history.

I own indeed (though since you don't ask you may think it excessively officious on my part. Don't. or else I apologise. Whichever you prefer) that in some of your papers, notably the essay you didn't do yourself justice.

I don't know whether it is but a cold comfort, but at any rate you ought

1 (William) George Stewart *Adams (1874–1966), Warden of All Souls 1933–45.

2 Sir Charles Grant Robertson (1869–1948), historian, Fellow of All Souls 1893–1948, Vice-Chancellor, Birmingham, since 1927.

3 Ernest Llewellyn Woodward (1890–1971), historian, Fellow of All Souls 1919–44, Lecturer, New College 1922–39; Montague Burton Professor of International Relations 1944–7.

4 Richard Pares (1902–58), historian; Fellow of All Souls 1921–45, 1954–8; Lecturer, New College, 1929–40; Professor of History, Edinburgh, 1945–54; joint editor, *English Historical Review*, 1939–58; the subject of a memoir by IB in PI.

5 Cosmo Gordon Lang (1864–1945), Fellow 1889–93 and 1897–1928, Archbishop of Canterbury 1928–42, stood only in 1886 and 1889, not three times as IB implies below, and was therefore successful at his second attempt, which makes him an exception to IB's rule that those who try twice don't get in. Richard Orme Wilberforce (1907–2003), stood unsuccessfully in 1930 and 1931, but successfully in 1932.

6 Felix Markham (stood in 1929 and 1930); Arthur Humphry House (1930, 1933); Cecil Herbert Sansome Preston (1932, 1933); Frank Edward Figgures (1931, 1932); Evert Hugh Barger (1932 only: IB appears to have included him in error in this list of those who failed twice).

7 (D'Arcy) Patrick Reilly (1909–99), historian, diplomat, Fellow of All Souls 1932–9, 1969–99.

to know how long & obstinate a fight was waged over you by the losers. If ever you want a job in Oxford (good God how like a K. Bell[1] or somebody I write. Forgive me it is horrible) you have at least 10–15 or so golden opinions among the locally influential to draw on, not to speak of our sort of fry. If you come back during term please visit me. God bless you many times. This is a poor sort of letter.

 I.B.

TO THOMAS HODGKIN

 [November 1933][2]

All Souls

Dear Thomas

 I wish I could, but I can't. Your Miss Moore may be of the greatest genius, but, alas, I, having spent the past four days in bed pursued by a nameless & undiagnosable disease which has just begun to leave me, cannot travel at all. This is a great nuisance & pity. And you imply you won't come to Oxford which is even more so. Your letter was a much finer document than mine – I only hope I didn't give the impression of having made heroic but unavailing efforts on behalf of you – I ought to have probably, but I own I didn't. I behaved more ignobly than your other admirers, God be with me. Having got this off my chest I reiterate even more insistently my sorrow at the consequences of my ailments (The Warden calls every other day & never really finds more to say than 'you must go on eating oranges, they're terribly good for you my dear man.') and my hope of seeing you not too unsoon (I am sorry, but what is opposite of soon?) I return unread I am surprised to say a packet of correspondence which during my illness my scout uprooted among my books. I cannot think how it came there. It's all the Frau Oberstleutnant's[3] packing I expect: she retained the letters for her own use but either found them difficult, or boring, or finished with them & sent them home in the only un-self-inculpatory way.

 yrs
  Isaiah B.

---

1 Kenneth Norman Bell (1884–1951), Balliol history 1903–7, Fellow of All Souls 1907–14, Fellow and history Tutor, Balliol, 1914–41, ordained 1946.
2 A reply to TH's letters of 8 and 13 November. The classical pianist Vera Moore was to give a concert in London on 16 November. TH invited IB to dine and attend the concert.
3 IB's Gasthof hostess in August in Salzburg, the wife of Richard Edler von Kosatzky.

*At this point IB took on a task that came to dominate his next five years,
and led to new, lifelong, intellectual interests:*

The Warden of New College, Fisher, in 1933, asked me to write a book
on Karl Marx for the Home University Library.[1] It was first offered to
Laski,[2] who refused. It was then offered to Frank Pakenham, Lord
Longford,[3] who refused. It was then offered to Cole,[4] who refused.
It was then offered to four or five other people, I expect.[5] In the end,
in despair,[6] they offered it to me, and I thought, well – I'd read a little
bit of Marx because I had to in PPE, where *Kapital* was a set text: I could
never get through it, but I read a certain amount of it – obviously Marx
is [going to be] a great deal more important, not less. If I don't write
about it I'll never read it, and I'll never know what they're talking about
– just as I haven't read Freud,[7] and I shall never know, because it's too
lengthy, too boring. [. . .] So I said yes, all right. Then I began reading
the forerunners, and I began reading the French Encyclopaedists,[8]
beginning in the 1750s. That gave me a great taste: I thought they were
wonderful. And Plekhanov[9] wrote about them in a very appetising
way. [. . .] So I read Helvétius[10] and Holbach[11] and Diderot and
Rousseau and everybody [. . .] Then I read various Germans [. . .]

1 The Home University Library of Modern Knowledge was at the time published by Thornton
Butterworth, and Fisher was one of its Editors.
2 In February 1932. Harold Joseph Laski (1893–1950), Professor of Political Science at the
London School of Economics from 1926.
3 Francis ('Frank') Aungier Pakenham (1905–2001), Baron Pakenham 1945, later (1961) 7th Earl
of Longford; New College PPE 1924–7; Lecturer in Politics, Christ Church, 1932, Student
1934–46; later Labour politician, author and campaigner for penal reform.
4 (George) Douglas Howard Cole (1889–1959), socialist, political theorist, economist, historian
of the Labour movement, journalist and, with his wife Margaret (155/7), writer of detective
stories. The surviving letters in Fisher's papers do not bear out the offer to Cole, but do
record one to Sidney Webb, Lord Passfield.
5 There is no evidence that this was so.
6 Fisher writes to one of his co-editors on 6 November 1933: 'Berlin is one of the most brilliant
of our younger men, and I am sure that he would do us a very good book.'
7 Sigmund Freud (1856–1939), Austrian neurologist turned psychologist responsible for the
revolutionary and widely influential theory and technique of psychoanalysis. IB visited him
at his home in London when Freud was in the terminal stage of cancer of the jaw: see MI
91–2.
8 A group of philosophers and writers, notably the editors Denis Diderot (1713–84) and Jean le
Rond d'Alembert (1717–83), who produced the highly influential *Encyclopédie*, a comprehensive account of the sciences and arts (first edition 1751), the Bible of the Enlightenment, and a
work whose rational, secular and sceptical approach prepared the intellectual ground for the
French Revolution.
9 Georgy Valentinovich Plekhanov (1856–1918), founder of Russian Marxism: see IB's article on
him in POI. 'Plekhanov is a mordant and extremely clear and rather sharp writer, of all the
Marxists far the most readable,' IB adds here on the tape.
10 Claude Adrien Helvétius (1715–71), French utilitarian philosopher and Encyclopaedist; the
subject of a chapter in FIB.
11 Paul Henri Thiry, baron d'Holbach (1723–89), German-born but brought up in France;
strongly anti-religious Encyclopaedist.

Rodbertus, von Stein, [. . .] Lasalle[1] – and that gave me a general taste. And finally of course in London I went to the London Library and by pure accident stumbled on Herzen,[2] [. . .] I knew there was a bearded sage – nineteenth-century, heavy stuff – and then I saw his name, so out of pure curiosity I took out one volume, and never looked back. He became a central figure in my life. [. . .] Then I began lecturing on these French Encyclopaedists. Well, nobody took the slightest interest in that in Oxford, but I got an audience. God knows where they came from. [. . .] And that's how I got into that world, simply in order to write a book on Marx.[3]

At the end of the month Virginia Woolf[4] dined in New College, and IB was a guest. The account he gives of this meeting in the next two letters is complemented by extra (sometimes conflicting) details in the memoir of Woolf he wrote in 1989.[5] The seating plan for the dinner survives among the papers of the Warden's wife, Lettice Fisher:[6]

The Warden

Mrs Woolf	Mr Berlin
John Sparrow[7]	BJ.
Mary	Mr Crossman
A Ker[8]	Mr Lewis[9]

LF

1 Karl Johann Rodbertus (1805–75), economic theorist and moderate socialist; Lorenz von Stein (1815–90), sociologist and economist; Ferdinand Lassalle (1825–64), prominent socialist discussed in KM.

2 Aleksandr Ivanovich Herzen (1812–70), Russian revolutionary thinker, journalist and writer; lived in London from 1852, publishing the influential newspaper *Kolokol* ('The bell', 1857–67), which campaigned vigorously for political reform in Russia. His major works were his political essays, collected as *S togo berega* ('From the other shore', 1847–50), and his memoirs, *My Past and Thoughts* (1867), regarded by IB as one of the great works of world literature; IB's introduction to Constance Garnett's translation (1968) is reprinted in AC and PSM.

3 MI Tape 6.

4 (Adeline) Virginia Woolf (1882–1941), née Stephen, novelist, short-story writer, essayist and literary critic; drowned herself on 31 March 1941 after many years of intermittent mental problems.

5 'Memories of Virginia Woolf', in PI2.

6 Lettice *Fisher (1875–1956), economist and historian, married H. A. L. Fisher 1899.

7 John Hanbury Angus *Sparrow (1906–92), barrister, historian, Fellow of All Souls 1929–52, author of *Half-lines and Repetitions in Virgil* (Oxford, 1931), later (1952–77) Warden of All Souls.

8 Alan Ker (1904–67), New College classics 1923–7, Fellow of Brasenose 1931–46.

9 Clive Staples Lewis (1898–1963), Fellow and English Tutor, Magdalen, 1925–54, author of *The Pilgrim's Regress: An Allegorical Apology for Christianity, Reason and Romanticism* (London, 1933).

Woolf herself wrote to her nephew Quentin Bell[1] on 3 December: 'There was the great Isaiah Berlin, a Portuguese Jew by the look of him, Oxford's leading light; a communist, I think, a fire eater'; but to Elizabeth Bowen on 6 January 1934: 'I never realised which of [150 undergraduates] Mr Berlin was, but had to piece him together from descriptions afterwards.'[2]

TO MARY FISHER

[30 November 1933]

All Souls

Dear Mary

X[3] was v. funny on the way home. 'There was the Warden talking about Rosebery[4] and talking *well*, and Virginia gently questioning him, when a bellow from the lower end of the table – you know who I mean – Crossman or Crosspatch or whatever the name is – 'Uppingham is a HEARTY school, I *like* Uppingham' & so on.* I do think she is the most beautiful person I've ever seen. I can also imagine what she looks like when she goes mad, as I believe, she occasionally does. I can't say how much altogether I enjoyed myself. I'll be grateful if it is half as pleasant to-morrow night at the Clarks'.[5]

yrs

Shaya

1 a.m.

*surely untrue? I mean about X & his voice, not Uppingham.[6]

1 Quentin Claudian Stephen Bell (1910–96), son of Woolf's sister Vanessa and Clive Bell; artist, potter, author, critic; later (1972) Woolf's biographer. His wife, Anne Olivier Bell (cf. p. xxii above), edited Woolf's diaries, which do not mention this occasion.

2 *The Sickle Side of the Moon, The Letters of Virginia Woolf Volume V: 1932–1935*, ed. Nigel Nicolson (London, 1979), pp. 255, 360.

3 Mary Bennett believes this to be John Sparrow. (IB usually uses 'X' to refer to Christopher Cox, who, however, was not present at this dinner, though he was – as the next letter records – among those to whom Woolf was introduced afterwards.)

4 Archibald Philip Primrose, 5th Earl of Rosebery (1847–1929), Prime Minister 1894–5.

5 Probably George Norman Clark (1890–1979), Chichele Professor of Economic History and Fellow of All Souls 1931–43, Regius Professor of Modern History, Cambridge, 1943–7, Provost of Oriel, 1947–57, and his wife Barbara.

6 In the next letter, to Elizabeth Bowen, IB has Mrs Fisher hold forth on Uppingham: so presumably he means that Sparrow misattributed the Uppingham remarks to Crossman (confusingly if more naturally also referred to as 'X').

30 November 1933, 1 a.m.

All Souls

Dear Elizabeth

A most trivial peg to hang a letter on, but you will I hope forgive me. It is this: After huge preliminary preparations and a great deal of consulting and rearranging Mrs Woolf was finally induced to come & stay a night with The Warden of New College – her first cousin. She was asked for a week-end but funked that and came for one night. John Sparrow was specially got down from Town via me as intermediary and at 7.45 tonight we commenced. Mrs Fisher whom I saw on the previous night & whom I asked whether it was true, as alleged, that Mrs W. was very shy, especially of new faces, said 'yes. she must pull herself together, that's all. I met her last when [she] was 17 and most priggish & horrible I thought her. I hope she's improved since then. Anyway there won't be many new faces. Only 20 or 30 or so".

During dinner I sat opposite her in petrified and satisfied silence admiring her beauty which is very, very great. The Warden talked gently & rather well about Rosebery, & she egged him on very gracefully with a minimum of effort. Now & then John Sp. murmured half and quarter sentences which mingled with the current without either augmenting or diverting it. We then trooped out led by a screaming Mrs F. who was shouting that she liked Uppingham it was so sincere and hearty, where chosen undergraduates and undergraduettes one or two titled, one or two possessing the even greater advantage of really humble birth + self-taught knowledge of literature ('700 books on Shakespeare alone, & some of them quite good ones, you must talk to him Virginia' The Warden said 'he's very poor') were awaiting us. There Virginia settled comfortably among the worshipping pop-eyed New College boys and girls (among whom Cox) and talked about Meredith.[1] But we weren't allowed to listen (she was talking & behaving very nobly) but were constantly re-formed by Mrs F., who ill at ease and idle handed jumbled everyone into a sort of game of musical chairs in which nobody talked to anybody for more than 2 minutes, except me, who tired of this & hopeless of conversation however broken with Mrs Woolf, retired sulkily into a corner with a man called Lewis and talked about God, Shakespeare, and the comedy of life. (Literally. He is a pious man & believes that God is a dramatist in a most literal way. It was rather exciting, really.) Mary F., B.J., others would stray into our neighbourhood, & be frozen away by the apparent repulsiveness of the subject & the unction in

---

1 The novelist and poet George Meredith (1828–1909), acknowledged by Woolf as an early influence on her work.

our voices. (I develop my interlocutor's voice to a ludicrous degree). Mrs F. like Anna Pavlovna Scherer in War & Peace continually refashioned her uneasy little groups into more & more ill fitting combinations. Only Virginia's corner was sacred, & there I had no apparent access. So matters dragged themselves till 10.30. Mrs F. now began to fidget & I grew angry at my spoilt evening, not wholly spoilt, for I enjoyed her appearance & gestures enormously (this sounds gross, but the feeling was really exquisite, really exquisite); 11 p.m.: finally we got up & water, I think, was handed round. Mrs W was talking to Sparrow: '. . . Mrs Bowen' (sic) she said, B.J. and I automatically turned towards her. 'We know her too' we both wanted to say grasping at an opening. It was here that my shameful act must be recorded, God give me strength. I stepped forward: 'She is in America' B.J. said 'I received a postcard from her' I said blushing as furiously as even you could have wished me to. 'What does she say?' said Mrs Woolf, I mumbled something unintelligible and quickly swallowing said 'which poet do you think will get the King's new medal?' etc. I cannot tell you how that lie which I shall think white to-morrow, but certainly don't to-night, revolved in my head, like some ludicrous autobiographical Russian's. I really had the feeling of a man who had committed an unscrupulous desperate act & had, moreover, been rewarded for it by a few Elysian moments. I am trying to make this as Tchekhovian as possible (I do think it is a theme worthy of no better author. But also of no worse a one) to melt your heart into not merely forgiving me (which I don't deserve, but you will, I hope, do, seeing how I grovel) but into not even being excessively amused, nor being as amused as I should be, for instance, if it had happened to someone else, being heartless in such matters, but on the contrary rather touched. After this the story ends abruptly. After some 3 minutes on Olympus I told myself that I must perform an act of will, obey the Warden's warning yawns, & leave before everything petered out. So I bowed stiffly and went. I've never felt more like an inferior character in a Russian story who goes through a gamut of trivial emotions which he dramatises ad infinitum, including a minor crime which looms enormous & pursues him and grows into quite an alastor.[1] She really is a most beautiful and godlike person whom it is a pity that anyone should know intimately. I hope I shall meet her again.

Humphry[2] I've neither seen nor written to nor heard from not sent a gram or anything because I've been ill in bed for a fortnight with a disease which the doctor failed to diagnose: my neighbour Lionel Curtis[3] thinks

1 Greek for 'avenger'.
2 Humphry House was now living in Exeter.
3 Lionel George Curtis (1872–1955), public servant and historian, Fellow of All Souls 1921–55, who was writing his Civitas Dei, published in three volumes 1934–7, in which he argued for world democratic unity; 'a fanatic of the British Empire, who founded Chatham House, and

it's the bacillus abortivus, which when it attacks cattle is a harmless cause of sterility (Please forgive me. I write on & on as I talk, & how tiresome that must often be. But I cannot think of stopping therefore) but in Lady Winterton[1] produced my symptoms. I hope he is well (Humphry, not the bacillus), as well as I who have recovered and am going to write a book on Marx in 2 years time:[2] Roy now approves the scheme provided I go to tutorials with him on economics & incorporate his views. Nothing will make me prouder I am sure than to owe views to him 'for which however I alone am responsible' etc. the last brings me back to Mrs W. to whom I said that you'd be back within 3 weeks for which I am of course alone responsible – I hope this account of an in some ways v. drab evening to which I had looked forward too much might amuse you, but perhaps I have made it too long: & the central point – *my* centre – the Lie is after all only caused by your breaking your promise to write which you haven't yet done – or perhaps the post is very slow – only thus, by turning my sense of guilt into a grievance designed to cause it in you can I get rid of it.

I am reading the philosopher Malebranche[3] who says that a better world than ours might exist but it would be far more complicated, & God being good, & desiring to give us a world not wholly unintelligible produced this compromise between simplicity & goodness, which are he thinks (odd interesting view!) incompatible. Hence our miserable makeshift universe. Indeed if our universe is the best of all possible worlds what must the others be like? (I am not sure the last pensée fits me at all well). Did not Kant say 'out of the crooked timber of humanity no straight thing was ever made?'[4] this [is] irrelevant but impressive don't you agree. I hope sincerely that [when] you return you will let me know, to the above address. I don't know where I shall be. in Town probably. By way of filling in space I reproduce a French play of the 18th century composed of the letters of the French

---

who was an *éminence grise* of a tremendous kind behind the scenes. He had no money and no great ambition for power, but he manipulated people: if you wanted your letter to be signed by both Archbishops on the next day, he and he alone could do it' (MI Tape 8).
1 (Cecilia) Monica Winterton (1902–74), wife of Edward Turnour, 6th Earl Winterton.
2 He finished it five years later.
3 Nicolas Malebranche (1638–1715), French philosopher who attempted to reconcile science and Christian theology.
4 This (so far as I know) is IB's earliest surviving use of this quotation (which he first heard at a lecture given by Collingwood), now well known through his frequent later deployment of it. I drew on it for the title of one of my collections of his essays, *The Crooked Timber of Humanity* (1990): see the penultimate paragraph of my preface to that volume for the Collingwood connection. The quotation is taken from Kant's 'Idea for a Universal History with a Cosmopolitan Purpose' (1784): see *Kant's gesammelte Schriften* (Berlin, 1900–), vol. 8, p. 23, line 22. (And cf. Ecclesiastes 7. 13: 'Consider the work of God: for who can make that straight, which he hath made crooked?')

alphabet, it helps you to remember them, & is somewhere in Pushkin.[1]
yours
Shaya B.

Tragédie.
Acte Unique
Scène unique

Caractères: Le Prince Eno, aimant de la princesse; La Princesse Kaël; L'abbé
Pécu, son rival; Ixe, Igrec, Zède, pages.

Prince Eno: 'Abbé! cédez!"
L'abbé 'Eh? ffff . . . (s'etouffant de rage)
Prince E. "J'ai hâche!"
Princesse "Ikaël aime Éno"
Prince E (se tournant vers l'abbé qui tremble affreusement) "Pécu est resté?
(avec dégoût) uh! Ixe, Igrec, Zède, prenez M. l'abbé et jetez-le dehors de la
fenêtre!"

Finis.

2 a.m.

TO DIANA HUBBACK

[November 1933]

49 Hollycroft Avenue

Dear Diana
The story I am about to relate causes me the deepest shame and
embarrassment: pray God you think of it more lightly than I do: for what
I have to confess is that I am nothing better than a THIEF. Having brought
this off my chest I can now begin afresh with more composure [I have been
reading Miss Austen lately. Hence this caricature). You will remember, my
dear Diana, you will remember the birthday party last Saturday which you

---

1 Aleksandr Sergeevich Pushkin (1799–1837), Russia's national poet. His most widely-known
work is the verse novel *Evgenii Onegin* ('Eugene Onegin', 1823–31), in which the critical event
is a death from a duel, Pushkin's own fate (578/3). The 'somewhere' is A. S. Pushkin, *Polnoe
sobranie sochinenii v shesti tomakh*, ed. M. A. Tsyavlovsky (Moscow/Leningrad, 1936), vol. 5,
p. 454. Berlin also published a somewhat different version of this 'tragedy', under the title
'Eno et Ikaël', in an Editorial in *Oxford Outlook* II (1931), 2, where the correct 'amant' appears
in place of 'aimant', but not 'hache' for the incorrect 'hâche'. Pushkin's errors differ.

so amiably provided for our delight.[1] In the course of it I suddenly found myself face to face with a man whom I had met once only, and that over five years ago, & who greeted me with the kindliest effusiveness. While nervously fidgeting under his enquiries, I lifted a small matchbox, handsomely encased in a silver frame, from off one of the tables. Absently I played with this bibelot, occasionally offering matches to myself and others. Some forty minutes passed, or more. I was talking to Stephen Spender. In the course of it I felt for matches in my pocket and extracted the silver object already referred to. With an exclamation of feigned disgust I revealed to Stephen my curious kleptomania. He, with a great guffaw, child of nature that he is, not infrequently referred to by German clairvoyantes as 'Sonnenkind',[2] seized the bagatelle from me and giggling madly put it into his inside breastpocket. I assumed (how rashly!) that he would presently tire of it and restore, but was wrong. I spent the rest of the evening with him: in the course of it, guiltily I own, he produced the fatal object and returned it to me. I mildly remonstrated, & decided to return it on the next day with a suitable letter of apology. Later that evening we all went to the Café Royal, our company grew and grew, the box was used, for it contained a fantastic quantity of matches for its size (2½ " x 1½ " would you say?). We then went home. I totally forgot the whole matter. But on Monday morning I woke up with a strong sense of guilt about something. I remembered the box. feverishly I searched for it. All my pockets. It was gone. I telephoned Stephen yesterday, & the Café Royal: they knew nothing of it. Last night, it appeared in a nightmare in the most grisly manner. I am reduced to nervous collapse: I yammer at my family and am rude to the maid. I dart idiotically forward at the glitter of anything silvery. I am very like a character in Poe.[3] Now what am I to do? I do hope that its absence hasn't been missed (it is *so* small), & that unworthy suspicions have not been allowed to fall. I ought to have told you sooner. I am very sorry. I think it best to purchase another, as like it as may be, & send it + a letter of apology to your grandmother: I am prepared to grovel to almost any extent I feel so guilty.

Meanwhile will you have lunch with me on Friday at (say) Commercio at 1.30, & help me to choose the replica? if, that is, I am still fit to be associated with by the self respecting. Please.

Yours in deepest anguish

Shaya B.

---

1 DH was born on 26 November 1912. Perhaps this twenty-first birthday party took place on Saturday 25 November 1933.

2 'Sun-child'.

3 The works of Edgar Allan Poe (1809–49), American poet and short-story writer, often described actions of frenzied intensity undertaken by guilty and neurotic characters.

B.J. who says that she always advises something underhand recommends me to beg you to say nothing to your grandmother if her suspicions are not aroused already: & to substitute the object I present in the hope that its suppositiousness may be overlooked.

Diana Hopkinson (as she became) quoted from this letter in her autobiography, The Incense-Tree *(London, 1968), on p. 121. But she made some minor alterations at the request of IB, who was embarrassed by the tone of what he had written.*

TO SHIELA GRANT DUFF

1 a.m. [1933?]

All Souls

Dear S.

I think I have been wrong and tiresome. I am liable to sudden fits of depression and feelings of friendlessness which is no excuse but at best an explanation. I daresay that my post-malarial collapse and the sight of an elaborate useless lunch which neither you nor I found possible to enjoy accentuated what is in any case not a very reputable state of mind. The whole thing is merely a stupid piece of my own history which I tried to blame you for, wrongly and inexcusably as I now think: I am extremely sorry. You behaved very well. I am completely devoted to you.

 Yours
  Sh.

I

I should be very embarrassed if you showed this to Goronwy. He would only accuse me, on the strength of the last sentiment of being in love with you or something silly. I sometimes wish I were: if I am not, the cause is not in you. ('Same if you were'[1] you can say).

II

You haven't discovered *Trade & Industry* by a man called Marshall[2] I suppose?

1 A repeated catchphrase in IB's correspondence with SGD, who thinks it came from a nanny she had from the age of seven, and was always amused by what she saw as its total contradiction.
2 Alfred Marshall, *Industry and Trade* (London, 1919; 3rd ed. 1920).

III

Monday.[1]

TO SHIELA GRANT DUFF

[1933?]

49 Hollycroft Avenue

Dear S.

When I sat down to write letters to my relations I had no intention of writing to you: the impulse, however, grew irresistible. This is an instance of a gruff compliment: the fact that you will somehow necessarily misinterpret it into something wounding, does not alter its nature. Whenever you feel this desire to misread you must say to yourself, as you do to G., 'No, no, no!'

I must now get on to the subject which I touch on so sparsely, namely myself.

I pass many hours in reading books & taking notes, as I used to when I was an undergraduate, which was a time during which I was very happy. Thus even now such hours are quiet and lovely. The men who grip me at the moment are K. Marx, Hyndman (related to Tony)[2] & your own Sir J. Lubbock.[3] The last mustn't surprise you. It is very odd & interesting that all the men who wrote about the natural sciences then wrote so well. Huxley[4] is beautiful. Darwin (did you know that he demanded a happy ending to every story, & said that if the central figure was a pretty woman why then so much the better?) Wallace,[5] Tyndall[6] all were excellent. The subject – popular science – is an abomination of the lowest order. But they did write well: Sir J. Lubbock who was a man much less interesting than his friends, but much more amiable: therefore I like him better. He refutes Blok's[7] stuff about the neurotic & panicky state of the whole XIX century,

1 Had IB forgotten to finish this letter?

2 Henry Mayers Hyndman (1842–1921), socialist leader and author, main founder of the (later Social) Democratic Federation in 1881. Thomas Arthur Rowett ('Tony') Hyndman (1911–80), was Stephen Spender's boyfriend in the 1930s, and fought in the Spanish Civil War.

3 SGD's maternal grandfather, Sir John Lubbock, 1st Baron Avebury (1834–1913), scientist and Liberal MP.

4 Thomas Henry Huxley (1825–95), biologist, champion of Darwin and agnosticism, educator.

5 Alfred Russel Wallace (1823–1913), naturalist, co-proposer with Darwin of the theory of evolution by natural selection.

6 John Tyndall (1820–93), scientist and populariser of science, close friend of Lubbock. Tyndall's works were widely translated.

7 Aleksandr Aleksandrovich Blok (1880–1921), revered Russian symbolist poet of the revolutionary era, best known for his narrative poem The Twelve (1918), a vivid depiction of the turmoil of the October Revolution. Blok's dreams for a new moral and political world order inspired by the Revolution soon faded away after 1917, and he sank into a deep

tho' it is obviously true of Russia & Germany. I never knew what a patriot K. Marx was: he refused to sign a peace-manifesto in the F.-Prussian war unless it was stated that Germany fought a defensive war. Sir J. Lubbock's optimism is now wildly irritating: but he was [a] very acute man all the same: think, think of the brilliance of his remarks on Bergson[1] whom he must have read in deep old age: Bergson produced his stuff about the perverting nature of reason and the necessity of trusting Intuition. Your grandfather upon this remarked that it reminded him of the story of the man who was groping for the path in a dark forest at night by the aid of a weak lantern: 'put out your light' said the Erlking[2] 'you will find the path far better by trusting instinct.' To have said it then was a very notable act, everyone else was on his knees, worshipping.

I admit whenever I think of him I think of Canon Barnett[3] also. Why am I writing all this down for you? you'll think uncommonly silly.

You must philosophise. Supposing you say that a chair has changed, what do you mean? Surely that some properties are gone, some have replaced them, & some are there still which also were before. Now: what has changed? not the qualities: they can only come & go: their coming & going leads you to say that the chair has changed: the red of 1929 is gone, the red of 1933 is there, but what is gone is not changed, it is gone. What is there now is not changed, it is there. But neither can it be the owner of qualities that have changed (if any. Berkeley denies, you remember). For if the chair is still in any sense the same now as in 1929, 'it' must be unchanged, though it may have lost some, & acquired other, attributes. If 'it' doesn't persist, nothing will, & if *nothing* persists 'change' loses meaning. Things can only be said to change in relation to something else which relatively to them doesn't. So nothing changes. But change is real surely? Bradley[4] boldly denied that it was: very boldly since it can convince no one. I hope this means something to you. Now where I wonder could Miss Russell[5] have heard of the fact that you & I alone send Ian [Bowen] sympathetic letters? I cannot think. Very embarrassing moment it was. I yammered & said nothing. Douglas's Christopher[6] which I inadvertently kicked has recovered: had it not, Douglas

---

melancholia, writing little and dying in poverty. IB translated his 'The Collapse of Humanism', *Oxford Outlook* II (1931), 89–112.

1 Henri Bergson (1859–1941), French philosopher.

2 In German mythology the Erlking was an evil goblin who haunted forests and lured the unwary to their destruction.

3 Samuel Augustus Barnett (1844–1913), divine, social reformer, first Warden of Toynbee Hall.

4 Francis Herbert Bradley (1846–1924), leading British Idealist philosopher.

5 Betty Parr Russell (1912–2000), LMH modern languages 1931–4, married Col. William H. Whitbread 1941.

6 Probably Douglas Jay's cat (he hated dogs, but liked cats). Peg (usually Peggy) is Jay's wife Margaret.

would not, he told Peg privately, ever speak to me again. How lucky. But I am slightly embarrassed by the thought of how thin is the thread upon which hangs his willingness to speak to me.

Stephen is genuinely interesting on symbols & poetry. He thinks of poets as divided into those who think in prose & translate & intensify this prose by writing poetry, & those who use poetry as a means of conveying emotion as one might use prose or a drug, i.e. a parallel independent means, never reducible to the other except by accident. I shall teach this to my more tender minded pupils. You know James'[1] distinction of philosophers & men generally into tough- and tender-minded? Spinoza & Kant & [T. H.] Green are tender minded, Hume and Mill and James tough, he thought. Which are you? I think a sort of seashore, part sand, part shingle, part pretty shells, which, you'll own, is a fair judgment on my part, since for myself I light only on the pebbles, & those not the smoothest either. I am happy beyond measure.

Shaya.

TO ELIZABETH BOWEN

2 January [1934]

49 Hollycroft Avenue

Dear Elizabeth

Thank you very much indeed for your letter:[2] it arrived at a time when I was mildly depressed by two or three letters from old friends who patently accused me in the kindliest possible manner of totally lacking in sensibility or capacity to understand either them or their past present and possible relations with other old friends. This, which regularly happens, automatically produces in me first fury then petulance, then pathos, then an artificial and pompous resolve to accept my own inhumanity as an unignorable but somehow also rather grand fact, & apply myself exclusively to my own proper abstractions, with special attention to Descartes' arguments to prove that animals are automata, with a view of extending his hypothesis to my correspondents who have been so vulgar as to accuse me of what I can coldly point to as a virtue which they can never know. Unfortunately for me I invariably call my own bluff almost before I strike up

---

1 William James (1842–1910), philosopher, in his *Pragmatism: A New Way for Some Old Ways of Thinking* (1907), divided (to put it roughly) tender-minded rationalists from tough-minded empiricists.

2 In her letter of 18 December 1933 EB, replying to IB's of 30 November, writes: 'It made me – your letter, I mean – very much less blankly homesick [for New York, whence she had recently returned] than I had expected to feel.'

an attitude. I find that I have been aware all the time that I am at least as interested in persons & their relations as in the presuppositions of mathematics. This is at once humiliating and delightful: your letter arrived & tipped the balance, and it is definitely delightful, and I no longer mind what people say. Not but that invulnerability seems attractive at times – and crude and very small and vulgar at others.

No no your remarks on America so far from being boring were, as either of the Misses Lynd might say, but this time genuinely, fascinating. I now, for the first time, really want to go there very much: though I shall always be too frightened ever really to go unless dragged or towed. Such Americans as one meets in Oxford are farcical characters mostly, the two whom I remember best are one who madly looked for a mistress in the women's colleges saying (to A. H. Smith!)[1] that he'd always had a coed before, but in this blasted place he was being forced to pick up a fallen woman. (The last words a nice concession to Smith's peculiar expression). The second was a fascinating maniac called Kluckhohn who enticed two Blues to U.S.A. where one of them nearly committed suicide, & the other left for the colonies immediately after. He (the Amer.) was a handsome and interesting man & corresponded regularly with Freud & Adler.[2] The third was a loony called Dr Kraus in Balliol who wrote a silly book called Sick Society,[3] who ran about Oxford in cold weather & whenever he saw any two men in conversation would squash them against each other: & stuff green apples into their pockets. The fourth is my pupil, who turns out the same 4 essays, in [the] same order, every term with unflagging freshness and a vast toothy smile. He thanks me at the end of every tutorial & tells me what a privilege it is to be taught by me. I am wandering. But I should very much like to go to U.S.A., except that I am rather afraid of finding there people too similar to myself: I shall never forget the horror with which I discovered the enormous temperamental affinities between myself and the inhabitants of Holland.

You are very kind about Mrs Woolf whom I continue to adulate. I am very *very* frightened of meeting her.[4] When nervous & embarrassed she is rather brusque, I noted, like a frightened terrier which barks nervously. Since I shall probably be extremely embarrassed myself if & when I meet her, that may communicate itself to her. Which wd be tragic. I feel so frightened of miscarriage that I would almost rather not meet her at all. No no, that is silly & childish. I cannot resist interpolating that B.J., who has dined with her,

1 Alic Halford *Smith (1883–1958), Fellow and philosophy Tutor, New College, 1914–44, Acting Warden 1940–4, Warden 1944–58.
2 Alfred Adler (1870–1937), Austrian psychologist whose early association with Freud gave way to increasing divergence between their interpretations of human behaviour.
3 Arthur James Israel Kraus (b. 1896), Balliol 1928–30, wrote *Sick Society* (Chicago, 1929).
4 At a private dinner which EB had offered to host.

thinks of nothing else, in spite of being ragged about philosophy by Leonard W.[1] who reduced her – very unkindly – to saying that phil. though unintelligible, was heavenly. Sylvia L[ynd][2] is seriously frightened of B.J.'s immense passion, and doesn't know what to do. As a mother she is even stupider than Mrs Fisher.

Dear Elizabeth, I should very much like to see you as soon as possible: I shall be in London till about the 11th, then I return to Oxford. Will you be in Town? I live in 49, Hollycroft Av., N.W.3, & my number is Ham 0912. I leave the rest to you. As for Humphry: I had one short, tired, tolerant note saying how tired he was, & vague about marriage-dates.[3] This was followed by a long, apologetic, typical, humouring letter, declaring he was happy & overflowing with affection for Madeleine (?). Most typical piece of Humphrian Prose: 'At last I can settle down to my work here living in peace, comma, fruitfully.' Basso profundo, rhythm, are all there. I must send my dumb waiter[4] to-morrow.

I have not read much this winter. Apart from professional philosophers (oh you cannot imagine how exciting $\sqrt{-1}$, or even more a thing shaped $\aleph$[5] called transfinite number invented in U.S.A. by a man called Jacob Cantor[6] can be) I have torn myself from my Russians (after ordering a book of 65 photographs of Turgenev) & read nothing but Jane Austen and Henry James. Miss Austen's preoccupation with marriage, everything, (is this a truism?) analysis of emotions, description of situations, is subordinated to this single end: it is terrifying and only too psychoanalysable. It is odd that Maurice B. cannot read her ("yes, yes, Austen, can't abide her, don't talk of her, not a real subject at all . . .). As for 'The Ambassadors' which Stephen bullied me into, it is a most melancholy, self-pitying, tragic, terrifying book: everyone is bound to think of Proust,[7] I suppose; but Proust's experience is much broader and deeper, his analyses don't simply unwind and unwind, & when all the strands are separated & flattened on a table, create intermediate cobwebs in order to hover in and about them too: they *cut*. It may be the result of not reading enough of him, but I am left with the impression that James with all his genius for slow, courteous, ruthless evisceration of every situation, was unable to find sufficient real

1 Leonard Woolf (1880–1969), Virginia's husband; publisher, author and editor.
2 Sylvia Lynd (1888–1952), née Dryhurst, poet and novelist, wife of Irish journalist Robert Lynd (1879–1949), and mother of Sigle and Maire.
3 House married Madeline (*sic*) Edith Church (1903–78) (to EB's chagrin) in December 1933.
4 Presumably a wedding present to the Houses.
5 IB's rendition suggests that he was not aware that this symbol is the Hebrew character 'aleph', $\aleph$.
6 Actually Georg Ferdinand Ludwig Philipp Cantor (1845–1918), inventor of set theory.
7 (Valentin-Louis-Georges-Eugène-)Marcel Proust (1871–1922), French novelist, author of *À la recherche du temps perdu* ('In search of lost time').

material in his direct experience to satisfy his craftsmanship, and frequently invented annexes which – this is my complaint, remain artificial, dead addenda: whereas with Proust, even with Tolstoy, the more one is told, the more is revealed, the more is left untold, the more precise and minute the distinctions, the richer and more interpenetrating and fluid the experience one is [reading?] about seems to become. With James everything is too granulated the analysis is always a little too leisurely, like a post mortem: not only will your material not run away or change if you wait, but you may hope to analyse & distinguish so thoroughly that nothing will be left over, a psychological triumph: once real experience is done with, imagination self consciously adds a lot more invented by analogy: only one at once feels the crack, the partition between what is 'real' & what is the craftsman's triumph, the sham continuation of the 'real' which 'would deceive any but the most practised eye'. So self-conscious is the superstructure however that it cannot deceive anyone about itself, the perfecter it is, the more it fulfils its end, the more similar to the original, the deader it is, & the more melancholy.

I really must *not* go on and on. Please forgive me. I shall next see how much I can get into a postcard.

yrs

Shaya

TO MARIE BERLIN

Undated [mid-January 1934?]

New College

My dear mother:

in answer to your questions in order:

1) I am taking my medicine

2) I feel much better. The stomach is less troublesome. I am taking care about diet.

3.) I have *not* taken the new handkerchieves with me so far as I know. I'll look again, but I think not.

4) I have had 2 baths!

5. Nails etc. fairly, not very, clean. Doing my best.

6. Please continue to remind me of my appearance. But I do not promise always to do what told.

7. Please send the Studs etc. if possible on Tuesday. But no matter if you send them only on Wednesday.

8. I am not sure that Friday night is a possible Friedmann[1] night,

1 Possibly Georges Friedmann (1902–77), French philosopher and sociologist.

because I may have to dine with Mrs Cameron if she has V. Woolf there. So best have Friedmann on, I suggest, the Friday *after*. Let us fix this as definite, & invite him at once.

9. Suit has arrived. I have not put it on yet. Oxford is an absolute dream in snow, à la Russian late 19th century paintings.[1]

TO MARIE BERLIN

Tuesday evening. 10 o'clock.

All Souls

Dear Mama

I hasten to inform you that 15 min.s after you went (too early!) желудок[2] arrived uninvited, without the Marienbad Salts. I may take them anyhow: but this is a sign that I am well even in this respect. I cannot tell you how sorry I am that you left, how nice your being here was, how melancholy I now feel without you, how I look forward to seeing you on Friday. This is almost like a love letter, though it begins a little prosaically. It is not almost & not like, but *is* a love letter.

Shaya.

TO SHIELA GRANT DUFF

[Shortly before 14 March 1934]

All Souls

Dear Shiela,

Not a word, not a line, before you left – at least I assume you have left Oxford – why, even Mr Ensor,[3] with whom my acquaintance is of the most superficial kind, sent me a kind message before he went away – you really must not display so little natural affection – however perhaps you [are] very busy – but again you cannot have been busier than I was – .

Could you do me a kindness? and tell me Goronwy's telephone number: I go down on Wednesday & propose to see Wozzeck as done by the

1 The letter is incomplete and/or unsigned.
2 'Zheludok' – literally 'stomach', but here apparently used as a euphemism for relief from digestive problems.
3 Robert Charles Kirkwood Ensor (1877–1958), journalist and historian, deputised as Gladstone Professor of Political Theory and Institutions (a post attached to All Souls) in Michaelmas Term 1933 and Hilary Term 1934, after Adams's resignation from the chair on his appointment as Warden of All Souls; he was succeeded as Professor in Trinity Term 1934 by Sir Arthur Salter.

B.B.C.,[1] & wondered if he wd like to come – he has, I was told by Mrs C[ameron], met her, & also a man called Cyril Connolly[2] whom I've never seen, but who is alleged to be the most malicious man in the world. Will you tell Goronwy to be very careful indeed of what he says e.g. of Pares or Maurice. Rows really are hideous things. Hoping this finds you as it leaves me, better contented than at most times,

    yrs
       Shaya.

1. The Times really is *disgusting*: no other newspaper of its standing could refuse to print a letter by a man of Cripps's position,[3] & yet print Rowse because he is Fellow of A.S. Its Austrian news,[4] written by that demented & revolting creature, Arthur Barker, son to Ernest,[5] is more unctuous & reactionary than the Morning Post, which preserved a certain dignity & didn't openly exult.

2. I hadn't read On the Eve[6] for 8 years. I read its beginning in bed last night. The stuff about giving & taking – meant to show callow & wordy[?] idealism represents painfully closely my own reflections on the subject. Really embarrassing – it is really very very rarely that one feels seen through by a novelist – no, no more to say. IB.

By this time it was well known that the Nazi regime in Germany had started persecuting the Jews. So when Adam von Trott wrote to the Manchester Guardian in February 1934 to refute an article alleging anti-Jewish discrimination in the German courts, IB had been outraged, and had made his views known to many of their mutual friends, who in general had remained sympathetic to von Trott.

1 *Wozzeck*, the opera by Alban Berg (1885–1935), was performed on 14 March 1934 in the Queen's Hall by the BBC Symphony Orchestra under Adrian Boult.
2 Cyril Connolly (1903–74), journalist and author.
3 Sir (Richard) Stafford Cripps (1889–1952), Labour MP for East Bristol 1931–50, British Ambassador to the USSR 1940–2, later (1947–50) Chancellor of the Exchequer. 'Policy and the Party', a letter from Rowse discussing Cripps's proposals for constitutional reform, appeared in *The Times* on 26 January 1934, 8, and there is indeed no letter from Cripps thenabouts.
4 Chancellor Engelbert Dollfuss (1892–1934), in an attempt to save Austria from Nazism and Communism, had established one-party rule in Austria during 1933; socialist opposition to this move led to a brief though violent civil war in February 1934 which included the bombardment of a housing project in Vienna by government forces. The government and the Heimwehr (29/4) suppressed the uprising and disarmed the Schützbund ('Protection Force', the social democratic militia). Socialist leaders fled or were arrested. Dollfuss was murdered by Nazis a few months later.
5 Ernest Barker (1874–1960), Professor of Political Science, Cambridge, 1928–39.
6 Turgenev's 1860 novel.

TO SHIELA GRANT DUFF

[March 1934][1]

49 Hollycroft Avenue

Dear S.

This is stimulated by the fact that accidentally I lit upon your note re
Adam, & it suddenly appeared to me that although your defence was not
plausible, my attack must be withdrawn. From time to time I imagine that
I really can take an impartial survey over the situation, & that my criticisms
are objectively grounded. That this is not so one minute's honest introspection proves. I am hopelessly a parti pris in the question of Nazis &
Jews: & this probably colours everything I think about Nazis in general. I do
not feel nearly such violent feelings about the Italians, who being more
cynical, are really worse. All I am entitled to say about Adam is that he is no
hero – that the facts are other than such as he states I am more or less
convinced of by the universal agreement of all newspaper correspondents –
that he naturally seeks & finds those relatively honourable people whom he
mentions is natural – that he is a patriotic person before everything was
patent always. I cannot say that I think him a person of particularly big
stature. I like him as a person and admire a certain grandioseness which,
although collapsible, nevertheless has genuine sweep while it lasts. His
charm is very great indeed, his intellectual honesty mediocre. But I look on
what any German does with a jaundiced eye: I cannot help it, but I must beg
you to discount it: my indignation is a fact about myself: to have exhibited it
to you & to Xtopher as tho' it was founded on a dispassionate consideration
of the facts, was unconsciously dishonest, and, I suppose, transparently
personal. So well do I know this feeling & its results that I am almost certain
that Adam felt it when he wrote his letter: tho' I daresay his limitations in
this matter are wider than mine, which are really rather narrow. But to foist
them on other people is less excusable in my case than in his. What really
distresses me is that he should by his action have shifted himself into the
region which I see in terms of sheer black & white, from the rest of the
universe where I really can discriminate, in which I was determined that he
should, because I liked him very much indeed (& still do, I suppose,)
permanently remain. I write all this mainly because I am alone at home with

1 So dated by SGD, who would have supported Adam von Trott when his letter to the
Manchester Guardian defending Germany against charges of anti-Semitism was published on
21 February 1934. See Christopher Sykes, *Troubled Loyalty: A Biography of Adam von Trott zu
Solz* (London, 1968), 104–11. The impression given by IB of his view of von Trott, after this
episode and subsequently, is conveyed by Paul Gore-Booth in a letter from Washington to
the Foreign Office (FO) dated 25 September 1944: 'Isaiah Berlin knew Adam von Trott zu
Solz very well and thought well of him until 1934 when his German patriotism clearly
proved stronger than his adherence to the Social Democratic Party.' FO 371/39066.

nothing to do, (no books.). Also because my tirade was more passionate than mere annoyance with the errors of a friend: finding how grossly I deceive myself, I hasten to confess it at once. If & when you write to Diana do tell her that I cannot be expected to be reasonable on this matter. We walk to-morrow!

    Yours
      Sh.

TO MARIE BERLIN

    Wednesday. [21? March 1934]

                                      All Souls

Dear Ma
    I am back in All Souls after a week's wanderings. It was very very agreeable to hear the 2 Mozart operas – they are heavenly – & then to go to Devon to stay with Humphry House. There I found the Houses rather melancholy and had to act as a sort of ice-breaker: you know how difficult that is even when your husband or your son are melancholy & require restoration: but if one *is* going to enjoy oneself one must try & cheer one's hosts up. Somewhat exhausted I returned to Oxford & dined to meet Virginia Woolf, who was charming to me: very beautiful very cold very nice. Now I sit down to work for a month. Father became v. worried about your silence: he always telephones or wires, every year as you know, especially when I am not there to distract him: you must not mind that: but what you have always told me about "even small postcards etc." applies to him now, since he is alone.[1] I am glad I am here, it is peaceful & I can & do work. Brighton would *not* have done. Write me about the doctor, briefly but write. I also met T. S. Eliot the poet, who also was v. kind.

    love
      Shaya.

TO SHIELA GRANT DUFF

    [May 1934?]

                                        All Souls

Dear Shiela
    Your letter (I read it in the middle of a tutorial) suddenly made me very

---

1 Presumably there was a regular annual arrangement whereby Mendel remained in London to attend to business while Marie stayed in a hotel in Brighton for a spring break.

happy and washed away the last traces of resentment. Yes yes I shall take both you and G[oronwy] to the Opera (he would surely want to come) and everything I said or suggested before is foolish and makes me a little ashamed. As for Sunday, to show you how moved and affectionate I am, I declare myself willing to get up at some frightful hour – 9 or something – and go with you to Abingdon then – or indeed anywhere – even a Jay reservation.[1] But if this is to happen you will in any case have to put your lunch off: I can't, really can't begin anything with the end set so near. However it's all in your hands. After your letter my tutorial which began sleepily gained in vigour and boldness and my dull little pupils became very nearly excited.

As for Opera, Otello, I certainly shall not go now unless you come. I enlarge on your sentiment, not to go with you is much worse than not going at all. There. I have, as usual, succeeded in reducing myself to embarrassment. I have now bought the most beautiful records I have ever listened to in my life. Will you tell me what hour in the morning to meet you & where. The bus?

    Yours

      Shaya

TO ELIZABETH BOWEN

    Tuesday [shortly after 6 July 1934]

                   Breslin's Hotel, Bunbeg, Co. Donegal

Dear Elizabeth

I cannot write a diary by candlelight, but I do find that reading books by it for an hour or more is fascinating. Normally I read very fast. Here I am forced (1) to go to bed early since Cox & Mary do so, which leaves me alone with B.J., who unless either made love to, talked to idealistically, or gently flattered, grows melancholy & develops into something in Celtic Twilight[2] at its thinnest and artiest. To avoid this I too retire early. Inability to break old habits keeps me up: I therefore read Mr Yeats' Autobiography[3] which I enjoy very much indeed: his vanity and his unself-consciousness are, after a term in Oxford, unusually delicious. Cox complains that he has no sense of humour and then, with sudden fury, that as a man he despises him.

---

1 In the letter to to which IB is replying, dated only 'Tuesday', SGD writes that 'it would be lovely to have breakfast with you at Abingdon [on Sunday], but you do not like getting up early'.

2 W. B. Yeats, *The Celtic Twilight: Men and Women, Dhouls and Faeries* (London, 1893, and subsequent enlarged editions).

3 *Autobiographies* (London, 1926). William Butler Yeats (1865–1939), Irish poet and playwright; awarded the Nobel Prize for Literature 1923.

He remembers him in Oxford in 1922[1] & how vain and boastful and foolish and cowardly he was, & how eagerly he drank in the rivers of flattery directed at him. I indulge in my usual game of supporting the other side into something outrageous & then suddenly withdrawing support & turning. In this case he was provoked into complaining that Yeats looks dreadful and ought to lead an opener air life & talks nothing but shop. At this last I no longer pretended to myself that this was entertaining and we very nearly did quarrel. However the terror in Mary's & B.J.'s eyes restrained me. Now all the old and usual jokes are in force again & we get along swimmingly. They go up mountains & I talk to ravishingly beautiful but rather dull youths, who freely speak of politics and their private lives. Soon we shall reach our island and the dear Contessa, and I shall accustom myself to fruitful solitudes. Humphry – the word fruitful always recalls him to me – we saw with Madeline in Belfast; she livelier, securer, more of a person, almost a mother already:[2] he, reduced, I thought rather gloomy, altogether deflated, un-naturally flexible, fangless, and gentle, it rather frightened me. He was plainly expecting to be taken joyriding by us, but my companions thought it inconceivable that he be asked without her, so nothing was suggested, to his obvious chagrin. However he is married and why should he be allowed to forget it? this sounds unkind but he mustn't be tempted deliberately to desert her. That he is not happy I now have no doubt of.

The country is deliciously wet and straggly. I find I like Irish villages, winding in crooked lines of scattered houses, now & then broken by almost 18th century houses, more than anything. And the faces are beautiful. There is an odd shrinking from the sea, which is hard to get to. Few roads lead to it oddly unmaritime the Irish are, there are few even of fishing villages: their enterprise was, I suppose, killed in the 16th century. Still it seems odd in an island to find such a conspiracy to ignore the sea. I find that [I] like beyond bounds to play with the sand & the tide. I build great sand castles & wait for them & me to be flooded. I notice B.J. looking at me with great surprise and scorn as if she had detected, against her will, a most contemptible Achilles' heel, while Cox looks with a games master's approval, touchingly; both attitudes please me more than I can say. But I like being childish for its own sake & not for the sake of new sensations, or people's surprise. Though no one, you included, will believe me for an instant. This I accept as inevitable. I was given, last night, a new book of stories by you called The Cat Jumps & Other Stories,[3] by B.J., who had it from her sister I suppose. I read you

---

1 Yeats was a frequent visitor to Oxford and in 1919 had leased a house in Broad Street.
2 By now Madeline would have been expecting her first child.
3 Published 6 July 1934 by Gollancz, where Sigle Lynd worked. The quasi-supernatural title

instead of Mr Yeats & shall continue to for a week. After which I'll write
again. Last night I read 'The Cat Jumps' which frightened B.J. so much that
she asked Mary to accompany her to her bedroom. I like it very much: it
seems to me to succeed in all its effects: it is very amusing & good in the
beginning, it produces acute discomfort of the proper vague kind, it terrifies
quite genuinely not by what it says but by what it omits about relations
between people in general And finally ends on a mixed note of horror & fun
in which each goes on increasing the effect of the other indefinitely the more
one thinks, so that if I were at home and not afraid of the consequences
I should want & in fact would, giggle semi-hysterically & deny it to my
family afterwards. Even now I haven't fully recovered – I am easily fright-
enable it is true – & fall into pleasantly gloomy reveries which evokes bright
banter from Cox, this time the sympathetic man on a tobacco tin
advertisement, hat over eyes, pipe, shirt blowing out in front & back, and a
foully contented air. I must not be so malicious. I like him very much. And it
is a considerable concession on the part of public school principles that he
should go away with me. But he is not as neutral a character as I should have
liked – I respect him quite a lot – after all he has discovered for himself the
truth about Goronwy. My companions are calling – I must go – I'll write
again from the island, I am devoted devoted to Ireland

    yrs
      Shaya

TO JOHN AND PEGGY HILTON

    Tuesday [postmark 10 July 1934, *postcard*]

                                                  Eire

I wish you were here. The villages are lovely to look at, everything is
fantastic, the inhabitants are wonderfully handsome and boring by nature.
Soon we reach the Island (In Lough Annilaun) & the dear Countess.

    Is your Frl. Ingrid Warburg[1] really researching into a 17th century trans-
lation of Lucretius? I saw Louis Macneice[2] in Oxford the other day. A very,
very good person I thought. My love. I shall phone in the last week of this
month.

    story is set in a house where a grisly murder has been committed. Hysteria mounts and at
    the end of the story all the characters are locked in their bedrooms in a state of panic.
  1 Ingrid *Warburg(-Spinelli) (1910–2000), whose parents came from Hamburg, studied English
    unofficially for a time at Somerville in 1932. She married Veniero Spinelli in the US in 1941.
    JRH was her second cousin through her mother and third cousin through her father.
  2 MacNeice later bequeathed IB 'a saucer of milk' in 'Auden and MacNeice: Last Will and
    Testament', in his *Letters from Iceland* (1937), written with W. H. Auden. Thereafter IB's
    opinion was less positive.

TO ADAM VON TROTT

[late July 1934]

Droitwich

Dear Adam,

Forgive me for my very long silence. I was extremely moved by your letter, both by its contents and by the fact that you wrote it. I never intended to raise an issue between you and me – the M[anchester] G[uardian] incident led to a very small explosion on my part, I admit, both because I thought it in itself harmful, not in keeping with your character and beliefs, and more particularly because of the idiotic defences of you put up in a spirit of uncritical loyalty by all your other friends. This last must please you – had the rôles been reversed it would have pleased me enormously – but I, who felt that for once I was arguing with an almost disinterested passion, and had got away from personalities, felt irritation that all my arguments were taken as evidence of personal treachery and not estimated *an sich*.[1] You yourself are so much better aware of the pros and cons of such actions than your allies – if I were you I really should declare *non tali auxilio nec defensoribus istis*.[2] I should very much like to see you: in later August I shall probably go to Venice via Salzburg – there is no chance of seeing you I suppose? I should very, very much like to – on every sort of ground, because I am attached to you, because I want to learn your views on a variety of subjects, because one ought to meet at regular intervals and give an account of the past and the future, because the thought of seeing you would excite me for some time to come. If there is the remotest possibility will you let me know? From Venice I propose to take a boat, in company with John Foster of my College, for Egypt, & thence to Jerusalem – there I shall call on Tommy, your cousin[3] Tommy, who appears to have become Secretary to the Governor of Jerusalem, and writes anti-imperialistic letters – as for Oxford, I should give almost anything to have you back there this coming term. The place is going to be a Mausoleum next year, the constants all there, the variables all gone: This last summer marks a break, an end of a period of one's personal life. All the young women will have gone down – Shiela, to whom I have been behaving tiresomely, after a very decent Second in P.P.E., B.J. (no, you call her Moira) after an excellent 3^D in Greats, a gap in Cox's life far more than in mine perhaps. Goronwy will not be in Oxford, either to fascinate or to irritate – he has been ill-behaved for longer than was thought

1 'In their own terms'.

2 Vergil, *Aeneid* 2. 521. The beginning of the next line, 'tempus eget', is understood: 'The occasion does not need help of that kind or defenders such as those.'

3 This seems likely to be a reference to the closely interlocking circles of friends to which von Trott and Hodgkin both belonged; no family connection between them is known to me.

possible – on the other hand I actually have accumulated a certain amount of material for books, and a long, dark, I hope warmly lined but unbroken tunnel will begin for me in October. I shall be in every night – I shall talk civilly to Holdsworth,[1] I shall be regularly embraced by the dear Warden who after every remark of mine will say, as to everyone else – I am so glad to know what is in your mind – I shall see nothing or nearly nothing of Harrod, & less than I need to even of Mr Bowra. I look on all this with great contentment: the period 1932–34 was expensive as far as time and emotional energy were concerned, and leaves a certain stock of agreeable memories, but the taste of triviality exaggerates into importance, and a definitely moralistic outlook and the need for a severe diet – like the autumn after a gay and wasted summer punctuated by a shaming succession of small and banal crises. Is it impossible to see you? do let me know in All Souls. I should value a meeting very much indeed.

Your Fraülein Ingrid W. is, I think, intelligent and well brought up, and ought to visit the Middle East to supply her with a stock of visual images of the sort of things she is prepared to praise without knowing about them. Which is indeed my own purpose in going there.

All our friends are well. As for my disapproval of your behaviour, I never was violent on this point. I do think that without in any way deceiving anybody, you are allowing a situation to develop which is bound to lead to a great deal of suffering – you know this yourself – but I am honestly obtuse about human relations, and am nearly always wrong – nor allowed to forget it – so that I suspend judgment. I really have no criticisms to offer of your personal affairs, and I do not think I ever shall. Forgive me, I must end. This horrible hotel where I came to see my mother[2] – I came for a fortnight, I leave in 5 minutes after 30 hrs – the food is prunes & prawns in aspic and rice pudding, the whole dining room talks loudly over my head – I am seated in the centre, a meeting place of two independently circulating draughts – they speak of weathers, past, present, future, improbable, and feared but unfulfilled, and the rate of mortality among Bedlington & Sealyham puppies. Whereas I belong to a Mediterranean culture. I have not really adequately conveyed what I wished to convey: how unpleasant it was to prevent oneself from writing, with what relief your letter was received, (I am sentimental and was very greatly moved), how much I want to see you, how unshaken and unchanged everything to the last tittle is at Oxford, how you ought to come and spend a week during a vacation, just at the beginning of one, in All Souls – I must go, but write write.

Shaya

1 Sir William Searle Holdsworth (1871–1944), Vinerian Professor in English Law and Fellow of All Souls 1922–44; noted for his 12-volume *A History of English Law* (London, 1903–38).
2 Presumably Marie was enjoying the benefits of the spa at Droitwich.

*IB reiterated these sentiments to Shiela Grant Duff in Paris later. She
wrote to Adam von Trott from Basle on 4 September: 'Met Shiah and
Stuart Hampshire[1] in Paris. Shiah talked a lot about you – how much
he admired you, and thought you noble and good in everything you did!
I said we none of us trusted him or his admiration, and he protested, but
he knew that you did not trust him, and seems to want you to.'[2]*

TO MARY FISHER

Saturday [August 1934]

Hotel Metropole, Brighton

Dear Mary

This hotel is very gay to-night and my parents, I believe, are roistering
wildly. This means that I, in a grave and elderly way, am expected to, & do
retire. I am surprised to have to inform you that I like this town. It is vulgar
gay & unaffectedly happy. Which is more than I can say for this hotel which
is vulgar but also pretentious, weary and definitely garish. This last is not
a word which I've ever been able to use before, but it precisely fits: I strongly
suspect that Subcarpathian Ruthenia, Jerusalem in its modern parts & my
present surroundings belong to the same stratum of existence.

My journey is becoming more & more difficult: my parents have to be
deceived re my détour to Salzburg, to which I am now committed to going:
the rest of my party are there already I imagine. The scheme for alibi is now
so complikex, as Prof. Cassirer would say, as to involve persons called Bill
Aitken[3] & John Pentland,[4] whom I believe to be nephews & sons of
Lords Beaverbrook[5] & Pentland – or perhaps Pentland is a Lord himself –
friends of Cyril Strauss[6] you will be delighted to hear – all, all acting in
some vague way as my agents for the purpose of posting deceiving letters to
my parents. Perhaps you ought to meet them as persons of consequence?
Beaverbrook's relations are a little raffish perhaps, but Lord Pentland? but

1 Stuart Newton *Hampshire (b. 1914), Balliol classics 1933–6, Fellow of All Souls 1936–40,
philosophy Lecturer, Queen's, 1936–9, military intelligence 1940–5.
2 Quoted in notes taken by Christabel Bielenberg from a letter whose present whereabouts (if
it survives) I have not been able to trace.
3 Perhaps William Traven Aitken (1905–64), newspaperman and politician.
4 Henry John Sinclair (1907–84), 2nd Baron Pentland of Lyth, Caithness: his father, the 1st
Baron, was John Sinclair (1860–1925).
5 William Maxwell Aitken (1879–1964), 1st Baron Beaverbrook 1917, newspaper proprietor;
Minister for Aircraft Production 1940–41, Minister of State 1941, Minister of Supply 1941–2,
Lord Privy Seal September 1943 to July 1945.
6 Is this Cyril Anthony Strauss (1913–44), author of *A Soldier Looks Back* (London, 1951), Strauss's
journals, edited by Derek Patmore?

you have met him. He was brought to tea & B.J. achieved one of her rare failures by attempting to interest him in the works of G. M. Hopkins.[1] Though I may have got the name wrong . . .

This is really meant to thank you for the Perkins[2] photographs. Our relations are, so far as I know excellent if not very close: I put it down firmly to shyness. Here is an item: Stephen Spender (he too, by the way, will be in Salzburg. Will your friend my pupil[3] like to meet him? or his friend the ex-Guardsman? he is charming but if you can conceive a party consisting of him, Mr Tony Hyndman (the ex-G.), the other Tony,[4] & Miss Walker, also Sigle & Lady J. and the five inevitable acquaintances – Wykehamists all – you conceive better than I who frankly boggle) writes that he met a youth whom he disliked called Lafitte who remarked among other things that Oxford was, of course, not the same since Moira Lynd went communist. I've reported this to B.J. but doubt whether it will please. Distant strains of a thing called a Rumba I believe (I do like this elderly pose. I hope it won't be begrudged me) are slowly entering this room which contains no one save me and a fascinating Russian couple – he is a Cossack I believe – a rich & prosperous & glossy Cossack – odd concept I own – who is at the moment engaged in telling his little mongoloid wife that she is grown too fat & *must* diet. She replies, inconsequently, that she "has spent 3 hours this afternoon in looking for him & in despair addressed me by mistake for him (odder & odder) while he walks to outlying inns & has double whiskies & soda" (pronounced sweetly & in full). I find it hard to look stern & uncomprehending. The Rumba (Ramba? Romba? Rumba? is that right Miss Fisher? yes, yes I was sure you would know) reminds me of Mrs Ayer[5] & oddly enough of your Miss Shannon & her song for which I am still genuinely grateful.[6] It could [not]

---

1 The poet Gerard Manley Hopkins (1844–89).

2 John Bryan Ward-Perkins (1910–90), New College classics 1931–4, Senior Demy, Magdalen, 1934–6, contemporary and friend of BJ and MF, classical archaeologist, later Director of the British School at Rome (1946–74). The photographs were of the group of friends who attended the New College commem ball on Tuesday 19 June 1934: Richard Chilver, Guy Chilver (III/4), Ward-Perkins, Herbert Hart, MF, BJ, Lady Julia (Agnes Cynthia) Pakenham (1913–56; daughter of 5th Earl of Longford, Somerville PPE 1931–4), Rachel ('Tips') *Walker, Priscilla Chilver (sister of Guy and Richard) and IB. One of these snaps is reproduced in this volume as Plate 16.

3 Rachel ('Tips') *Walker (1913–92), Somerville PPE 1931–4; pupil and close friend of IB; later became mentally ill.

4 Antony Andrewes (1910–90), ancient historian; New College classics 1929–33, Fellow of Pembroke 1933–46, married Alison Blakeway, née Hope, 1938, Intelligence Corps 1941–5, later (1953–77) Wykeham Professor of Ancient History and Fellow of New College.

5 Renée, wife of A. J. Ayer since 1932.

6 The song was *Frankie and Johnny*. Mary Bennett reports that Sheila Dunbar Shannon (1913–2002), who married Patric Dickinson in 1945, remembers singing it in New College Lane (though what the 'background' was neither of them has the slightest idea).

have been done at a better moment or against a more affecting background. Do thank her once more for me sometime – How I do run on.

    yrs

       Shaya

I did tell you of Price's letter to me with its end of "it must have been very amusing for you to teach Miss Lynd [suppressed from B.J.] – I should say an $\alpha\delta$!" [reported]?[1]

IB was the first of his immediate family to go to Palestine. Since his mother was a committed Zionist and an active member of the Federation of Women Zionists, his family would have moved, in London, in the same circles as leading Zionists who were now in Palestine. (Keren Hayesod, the financial wing of the World Zionist Organisation, was founded in London in 1920 and remained there until 1926, when it moved to Jerusalem. Among its first Directors were Berthold Feiwel,[2] Georg Halpern,[3] Shmarya Levin[4] and Hillel Zlatopolsky.)[5] IB's visit coincided with a lull in the inter-communal violence. He appears to have undertaken a round of courtesy calls, dutifully recorded in his letters home, on Zionist notables. But his later reminiscences emphasise the other perspective in these letters: his enthusiasm for absorbing all the different experiences that this new land, in its strangeness and familiarity, had to offer, and for meeting as many as possible of its inhabitants – Jewish, Arab and British, Zionist and anti-Semitic; officials, politicians, academics, businessmen and ordinary people.

1 The brackets in this PS are IB's. As for the Greek letters, Oxford examinations are often marked with the first few letters of the Greek alphabet – alpha, beta, gamma, delta, epsilon: α, β, γ, δ, ε (equivalent to English A, B, G, D, E: Greek puts G third rather than C as in the English alphabet) – in various combinations and permutations (see, e.g., letter of 29 July 1936 to Giles Robertson), and this system was (and is) applied more generally in conversational judgements. So here '$\alpha\delta$' characterises work displaying a mixture of first- (predominantly: the order counts) and fourth-class ingredients.

2 Berthold Feiwel (1875–1937), poet and Zionist leader.

3 Georg Gad Halpern (1878–1962), German-born economist and leading Zionist, director of the Jewish Colonial Trust 1921–33 and founder member of Keren Hayesod; emigrated from London to Palestine 1933 and set up the Migdal Insurance Co. in Jerusalem.

4 Shmarya Levin (1867–1935), Zionist politician and writer.

5 Hillel Zlatopolsky (1868–1932), Zionist leader, industrialist and philanthropist; born in Russia, which he left in 1919; murdered in Paris.

TO CHRISTOPHER COX

5 September 1934 [*postcard*]

Egypt

I've never known such heat, every movement is a torture. Robbers abound: the boat[1] was v. curious, full of loud & rather handsome Zionist women, The Egyptian Acting High Commissioner[2] & his party, v. pukka officers, (with whom via Foster I consorted! very odd experience.) & Friends of the King.[3] Foster's Arabic is a great success.

IB.

New College Archive

TO MARIE AND MENDEL BERLIN

Thursday [6 September 1934]

Pension Romm, King George Avenue, Jerusalem

My dear parents

I enjoyed the journey from Cairo very much indeed. The first sight of Palestine was most beautiful – it is not too hot here – the normal hours which I intend to keep are 8–12 a.m. Rest, 4 – till evening. or even 7–11. perhaps. One wakes easily in this weather & sleeps equally easily. Am staying with Yitzchok & Ida,[4] while Foster is staying at the K. David.[5] There has been trouble there – all the Jewish employées were suddenly dismissed – labour trouble – so it is unpopular for Jews to stay there at the moment. This Pension is very nice, the room is open & cool – & I shall eat where I like. Cairo was rather hot I must say, but I survived it very well. The first thing which greeted me here was Ettinghausen + Marmorstein[6] – the latter has a job on a Palestine paper – illegal* as he has no right to stay – & is extremely happy. Ettinghausen is not perhaps so happy, & angry that his mother should have sent him a shirt – it makes her ridiculous he thinks. Нюта

1 The *SS Ausonia*, which docked in Alexandria on the afternoon of 4 September 1934.

2 Maurice Drummond Peterson (1889–1952), acting High Commissioner for Egypt while the High Commissioner was on leave; Ambassador to Iraq 1938–9, to Spain 1939–40, Controller of Overseas Publicity, MOI, 1940–1, Under-Secretary of State, FO, 1942, Ambassador in Ankara 1944–6, in Moscow 1946–9.

3 Fuad I (1868–1936), Sultan 1917–22 as Ahmad Fuad, King 1922–36.

4 Earlier in 1934 the Samunovs, both of whom were ardent Zionists, had emigrated from London to Palestine, where they lived in a pension before establishing a home of their own.

5 The King David Hotel, built in 1931, the most famous hotel in the Middle East, and one of the most impressive buildings in Jerusalem; later (July 1946) one wing was blown up by the Jewish resistance movement Irgun, while the building was in use as a British military and administrative base.

6 Emil Marmorstein (1909–83), a contemporary of IB at St Paul's, worked in the European Dept of the BBC.

Шнеерсонь[1] asked Ida when I was getting married! apparently Mrs Goldberg has invented a rumour that I am engaged & will marry soon! This is rather disagreeable, but I shall take no trouble to kill it. Only it is ridiculous to hear rumours created out of literally Gunischt[2] + envy. She is a v. bad woman. To night Foster & I dine with a lot of young officials & Yitzchok wants me to 'pump' them. This I will not do. Ida is a little full of 'atrocity propaganda' about British injustice, articles in the Times etc. but this is not new. The town is lovely – I haven't seen much yet – Marmorstein knows the whole ancient city intimately – all the Bokhara Jews bow to him – & it is a Jewish country. More Hebrew is heard than anything & the Arabs all speak it. The English lower officials are a poor tired washed out lot, the upper, patient, disillusioned, uninterested policemen. I shall call on the Feiwels,[3] on the Acting High Commissioner,[4] possibly on Ussishkin.[5] We'll see. The bananas are wonderful – such a fresh taste I've never tasted: you see that I am v. happy. Everyone is charming, the Jewish officials are the rudest people on earth. A mixture of Chutzpa & inferiority complex. Otherwise the Jews seem nice. But wait. I'll write more fully later. I am really v. well.

love

Shaya.

*it is *most* important that you should not tell *anybody* it – everything gets round here in 24 hrs & people get exposed.

1 'Nyuta Schneerson'', perhaps the wife of A. M. Schneerson, Financial Secretary of the Hebrew University. She may have been a distant relation of IB's.

2 IB's version of the Yiddish word 'gurnisht', roughly 'nothing at all' or 'rubbish' (cf. German 'gar nichts').

3 Berthold Feiwel's wife Sterna (née Schneersohn) was a distant cousin of IB.

4 John Hathorn Hall (1894–1979), technically 'Officer Administering the Government' while the High Commissioner was on leave.

5 Avraham Menachem Mendel Ussishkin (1863–1941), Chairman of the Jewish National Fund 1923–41, president of the 20th Zionist Congress (1937), permanent president of the World Zionist Organization's Zionist Action Committee, member of the Executive of the Jewish Agency (96/10).

TO MENDEL AND MARIE BERLIN

בד׳[1]

Rosh Hashana. יום א[2]
Monday [10 September 1934]

as from Pension Romm,
King George V Avenue, Jerusalem

My dear parents

I am enjoying myself enormously here. Everyone is being very kind indeed. I have met in my 3 days:

1. English officials, of not v. high rank but v. friendly. Yitzchok regards them as all antisemites. Needless to say so does Ida. Hodgkin[3] is being very obliging

2. The local Bloomsbury i.e. Prof. Roth[4] with whom I've had tea and dinner asked a party to meet Foster & me consisting of:

Achad Haam's son who is registrar of the University,[5] Shmarya Levin, Dr Scholem the Kabbalist,[6] Avinoam Yellin[7] who is son to David Y.[8] & a govt. official, Mr Viteles[9] who is American Big Business, Jewish Agency[10] & head of Cooperatives in Palestine as well as Ruthenia, Rumania, Poland etc. & others. In cafe's I've met Labour leaders & Fay Orgel[11] whom I promised

1 These Hebrew characters are unclear, and are possibly an abbreviation for a conventional expression for 'With God's help' that would normally stand at the head of a letter.

2 'Yom aleph', 'first day of': Rosh Hashanah is the Jewish New Year, at the beginning of the month of Tishri, which usually falls in September.

3 IB's friend Thomas Hodgkin was working for the British High Commissioner to Palestine.

4 Leon Roth (1896–1963), first professor of philosophy at the Hebrew University of Jerusalem, brother of the historian Cecil Roth.

5 Ahad Ha'am (Asher Hirsch Ginsberg, 1856–1927), leading Hebrew essayist and proponent of cultural Zionism; his son was Mordecai Zalman (Shlomo) Ginsberg.

6 Gershom Gerhard Scholem (1897–1982), professor of Jewish mysticism and cabbala at the Hebrew University. IB remembers him as 'young, lively, slightly mad – dashed about, obviously wanted attention to be paid to him [. . .] He was rather gifted and romantic and interesting as a man' (MI Tape 11).

7 Teacher of Arabic (1900–37), and a leading promoter of the teaching of Arabic in the Jewish School System; later an Inspector of Schools for the Mandate Government. Killed by Arab terrorists in October 1937.

8 David Yellin (1864–1941), Hebraist, Zionist, educator, previously Deputy Mayor of Jerusalem, founder of the first public library in the city. He is remembered primarily for his leading role in the 'Language War' between German and Hebrew, in which connection his name is second only to that of Eliezer Ben Yehuda, the 'Reviver of the Hebrew Tongue'.

9 Harry Viteles (1894–1971) wrote extensively about co-operatives and kibbutzim.

10 The Jewish Agency for Palestine (now the Jewish Agency of Israel), an international institution working on behalf of the World Zionist Organization, with a brief to support Jews anywhere in the world who wish to participate directly or indirectly in the settlement and development of Israel.

11 Fay Orgel, whose parents lived in London, worked for the Levant Fair Publicity Bureau, and married Gabriel Moscovitz in Tel Aviv in 1937. Her father Calman Orgel (d. 1946) was an active Zionist.

to ring up when I go to Tel-Aviv. I haven't been yet. Two days ago I witnessed Police Sports at Nablus! Gerizim & Ebal are very impressive.[1] The place is Arab; this morning I went, not wholly to Yitzchok's satisfaction, to the Mosque of Omar[2] with the H.E. The High Commissioner's Arab Secretary who likes Baneth of the University.[3] Baneth showed me over the library of the University which is splendidly equipped. Really good. Philosophy books more numerous than at Oxford. Roth is quite nice, pure Bnei Brith Brondesbury,[4] his wife even more so, he is a little משוגע [5] but treats me well.

Shmarya Levin told a good joke: he spoke to an Englishman who said he was in full sympathy with Zionism save for 3 points:

1) Why have the Hebrew language? cumbersome, difficult Uneuropean etc. (Wedgwood[6] thinks the same)

2. If colonization is desirable why choose Palestine? barren, dull, hot, full of Arabs?

3. If England was determined to embark on the experiment, why, of all nations choose *the Jews*? otherwise he approved.

Last night we called on Meir Berlin.[7] Clever cunning man with an unpleasant son in law, who teaches the Yerushalmi[8] at the University.

I had lunch with a Syrian anti-semite called Antonius,[9] a charming,

1 Twin mountains immediately south of Nablus (biblical Shechem) – see Deuteronomy 11: 29. Fifty-five years later IB still remembered this occasion: 'We were invited to go to the police sports in Nablus. We went, we sat there, police sports occurred – boring beyond belief! A kind of gymkhana with people on motor bicycles, and cars whizzing past. I sat next to a man wearing short trousers who was obviously a British official [District Commissioner], and I said to him, "We are looking at two hills: I think they must be the biblical Ebal and Gerizim [. . .] Which is Ebal, which Gerizim?" He said, "I don't know. Just hills to me. No good asking me that kind of question." He later became Lord Caradon [Hugh Mackintosh Foot (1907–90), Baron Caradon 1964].' MI Tape 11.

2 Seventh-century Muslim shrine, known today as the Dome of the Rock, an outstanding landmark in Jerusalem and one of Islam's holiest places. Muslims believe that Muhammad ascended to heaven from the rock over which the dome is built. IB's description, commonly used at the time, is a misnomer: the shrine is a place of pilgrimage rather than a mosque, and though sometimes associated in the past with the Caliph Omar, the first Muslim conqueror of Jerusalem, it was in fact built by the Caliph Abd el-Malik half a century after Omar's death.

3 The High Commissioner was Lt. Gen. Sir Arthur Grenfell Wauchope (1874–1947); David Hartwig Baneth (1893–1973) was lecturer in Arabic at the Hebrew University.

4 'Brondesbury' is an ironical reference to the Anglo-Jewish assimilationist, suburban, bourgeois intelligentsia of the period, centred in the London districts of Brondesbury, Kilburn, Maida Vale etc.

5 'Meshuga' ('crazy').

6 Josiah Clement Wedgwood (1872–1943), MP for Newcastle-under-Lyme 1906–42 (as a member of the Labour Party from 1919), one of the 'gentile Zionists', visited Palestine in 1934.

7 Meir Berlin (Bar-Ilan) (1880–1949), leading exponent of religious Zionism and head of the Mizrahi (the religious-Zionist movement in Europe and then in Israel).

8 The Jerusalem or Palestinian Talmud.

9 George Antonius (1891–1941), author of *The Arab Awakening* (London, 1958).

polished, highly educated clever, unscrupulous man. Very formidable enemy. I want to see everyone. If I could lunch with the Mufti[1] I would. To-day I will call on Doukhan,[2] whom I met in the street & who inquired after you both, on Feiwel, who rang up, & on the Libovitch family, I should like to meet the celebrated Shaya L. at last.[3] On Thursday I may go on a tour of S. Palestine & Transjordan, if so no letters for 4 days at least. The postal & telephone services are terrible. The colonies I have not yet seen. All in good time. Jerusalem, כותל המערבי[4] etc. is wonderful. Very beautiful. So is the rest of the land. Most picturesque. Mosque of Omar, & El Aqsa which stand on Moriah[5] are magnificent. Interesting are the Stables of Solomon underneath the Temple. Wauchope is away so I shall probably not use my dinner jacket after all. I am in a state of such enthusiasm, so well, so happy, so unhot! (the heat is very bearable, no more than London, & only lasts for 3 hrs)

    yrs

      Shaya

During his visit IB travelled to Transjordan with Thomas Hodgkin, who, he remembered, 'was violently anti-Jewish from a purely left-wing point of view – natives. [. . .] I think he would have denied [being anti-Semitic] ferociously [. . .] We went on the backs of donkeys, and when we came back to Jerusalem, it was Friday afternoon and we were stoned by the pious Jews. Just like Christ – "Hosanna!"'[6]

1 Hajj Amin al-Husseini (c.1897–1974), Mufti of Jerusalem and Arab Nationalist.

2 Probably Moses Doukhan, barrister from St Petersburg, Assistant Director of the Dept of Lands in Palestine till 1936.

3 Yeshayahu Leibowitz (1903–94), scientist, philosopher and Zionist (later professor of organic chemistry, biochemistry and neurophysiology, the Hebrew University), was the subject of a tribute by IB (published in Hebrew translation as 'The Conscience of Israel' in *Ha'aretz*, 4 March 1983, 8) in which mention is also made of Leibowitz's sister Nechama, a biblical scholar with a great popular following. The family was altogether remarkable: devout, polymath and outspoken.

4 'Kotel ha-ma'aravi', 'the Western Wall': all that remains of the Jewish Temple built by Herod the Great and destroyed by the Romans. Traditionally known as 'the Wailing Wall', it is a focus of pilgrimage for Jews from all over the world.

5 In Genesis 22 God calls on Abraham to sacrifice his son Isaac on an unnamed mountain in 'the land of Moriah'. The place in question has traditionally been identified, under the name 'Mount Moriah', with the site of the First and Second Jewish Temples in Jerusalem. All that remains today is the great platform known to Jews as the Temple Mount, and to Muslims as the Noble Sanctuary. The Temple Mount is now occupied by the Dome of the Rock and the al-Aqsa Mosque, the most important in Jerusalem, regarded by Muslims as the third holiest after those in Mecca and Medina. A flight of steps nearby leads down to the so-called Solomon's Stables, a large vaulted area (used as stables by the Crusaders) whose pillars support the south-east corner of the Temple Mount.

6 MI Tape 11. IB alludes here to Jesus' entry into Jerusalem on a donkey shortly before his trial,

TO CHRISTOPHER COX

[1934, *postcard*]

Palestine

Since Foster's departure I am sunk in missionary circles. This is really a very interesting country – the Municipal elections were very exciting, the Vote-Exchange[1] fluctuates wonderfully, I was nearly given a vote. The Archaeological circles are impatiently expecting you. I have passed a night on that very interesting inscription of Hadrian's at Djerash,[2] the D, very big – smarts still. Everyone refers to Iliff[3] as that Museum Wallah.

love

IB.

New College Archive

TO MENDEL AND MARIE BERLIN

Monday [24 September 1934]

[King David Hotel, Jerusalem]

My dear parents

My tour of Palestine is now over & I shall rest here for a week & leave by the Pilsna (Jewish Capt. – Mr Steindler) as will also Ettinghausen, on the 3[D], arriving London on the 9th. I shall be with you for two days – then I'll go up to Oxford & try & return for the week-end before going back. I feel very well. I shall now give you a fairly full account of my journey from London.

to an enthusiastic reception by people shouting 'Hosanna' (details vary in the accounts in the Christian Gospels).

1 A reference to the exchange of blocks of Jewish votes for blocks of Arab votes. The municipal elections were held on a basis of ward voting, the wards being drawn mainly along ethnic lines and the predominant group within each ward generally presenting a single agreed candidate, so that elections were not required in such wards. In Jerusalem in 1934, however, these groups failed to reach unanimity, and in some wards two candidates opposed each other. The contest was sometimes so bitter that candidates of the majority group sought support within the local minority community. As a result Jewish votes were 'exchanged' for Arab votes in different wards.

2 Roman Gerasa (one of the cities of the Decapolis) in present-day Jordan. A triumphal arch marks the Emperor Hadrian's visit in AD 130. The inscription fell from the arch soon after it was built, probably as the result of an earthquake, and was rediscovered only in June 1934, buried under debris. It seems that IB must have used it as a bed while it was lying on the ground awaiting re-erection. IB later explained that he didn't get a bed for the night in Amman (some 20 miles to the south) 'because I stood looking at the ruins of Djerash for too long, and I slept on a stone inscription which said the Emperor Hadrian visited, and every letter absolutely carved itself into my back during the night' (MI tape 11). Since the inscription is in Greek, 'D' may mean 'Δ'; but the story has the ring of embellishment, particularly since the letters are not deeply incised or especially large.

3 John Henry Iliffe (1902–60), first curator (known as 'Keeper' under the Mandate) of the Palestine Archaeological Museum in Jerusalem 1931–48.

My luggage proved a much greater difficulty than I let you suppose at the time. It was stopped at the Italian–Swiss frontier & after endless negotiations from Verona I had to go back to the frontier for it + my keys which [Tony] Andrewes brought. I arrived there in the evening with Andrewes who urged me to return with him to Salzburg for 1 night in order to hear a certain Toscanini concert,[1] instead of returning to Verona of which we had had enough. Perhaps you noticed a certain gap in my letters of 36 hrs – it was due to a secret visit to Salzburg for 2 nights & 1 day – I would have written abt. it but I was afraid father might worry. The concert was the greatest experience of my whole life. Toscanini is an enormous genius. Sh. Lynd had already gone & so had all my friends save the Hardies[2] & Lady J[ulia] Pakenham who made me an ovation when I arrived. I had a terrible sense of guilt about hiding it from you, so I stayed as little as I could – 1 day – in the course of which I met 2 persons, one of whom I was happy to meet, the other not – one was – Foster! who was however proceeding by car, & whom I only really met in Venice. The other was Mrs Shneerson![3] who said she was incognito – would I please not reveal her presence to her children: so I said I was incognito too – you knew I was in Central Europe but not exactly where – as I did not wish to worry you as Austria was thought unsafe wd she keep my presence as a secret if she wanted me to keep hers: it was said as a joke of course: but if you see her do not mention it, as she may think I betrayed her – I don't know why she was hiding – & she will want revenge. One must attempt not to cross the path of ill-willed persons. I hope you do not really mind my brief escapade – it gave me a strong sense of guilt at the time – but Salzburg was very safe, Andrewes very pressing – I only spent 1 day there – it was lovely & *full* of Jews. I don't know why – Toscanini I suppose – & on the next day my luggage & I left for Venice. Venice was simply wonderful. Do write & say you forgive me Salzburg, or I shall be tortured. Venice is heavenly, absolutely unreal like a toy. The journey on the sea was uneventful. Palestine is *extremely* interesting: I do not mind not living in the

---

1 Arturo Toscanini (1867–1957), Italian conductor; Guest Conductor at Salzburg Festival 1934–7; one of IB's heroes, both morally, because of his opposition to Nazism, and musically. Toscanini conducted in Salzburg on 23, 24 and 30 August 1934. The first concert seems the most likely candidate to have been 'the greatest experience of [IB's] whole life', since it comprised music by Mozart, Brahms and Beethoven. The second concert consisted exclusively of music by Wagner, which IB did not usually like, and the last was a mixed bag, as well as having occurred very close to IB's arrival in Egypt in early September.

2 Probably W. F. R. Hardie and his brother Colin Graham Hardie (1906–98), Fellow and classics Tutor, Magdalen, 1936–73.

3 Mrs L. Shneerson was on the committee of the Brondesbury and District Women's Zionist Society, a pillar of the community well known to IB's mother.

K. David, it is empty, expensive, & I have meals here often anyhow. I have now met: Mills[1] the Chief Immigration Officer, who is a clever, disillusioned, cynical person, who does not believe in, nor takes much interest in the whole experiment & has deep contempt for the whole Zionist Organization – & they are men of v. 2^D rate intelligence. With Hodgkin my relations are very close, he takes me about: I have met an important Syrian anti-Zionist called Antonius, if I could meet the grand Mufti I would. Ettinghausen is wandering happily about Palestine, I think the Rothschild Pica[2] may give him a small job. Tel Aviv is dreadful – like the Klondyke – imagine a whole lot of Jewish gold-diggers suddenly swooping on to the place – some live in houses, some in huts, shacks, tin palaces – noisy, dirty, streets too narrow because of dearth of room – Jews have no taste. Same applies to Hadar Hacarmel.[3] And yet the atmosphere, though hectic is beautiful: Jews. Everywhere Jews. On the holidays you feel rest: a lot of Hebrew singing not too loud & vulgar in the Jewish suburbs of Jerusalem, people going about in Talésim[4] openly etc.

I called with the Samunovs on Ussishkin & D[o]ukhans – the latter very welcoming, she is a nice woman. Also on Feiwels. Berthold did *not* descend – pleaded illness – was seen in the street next day – *very* rude, not to me but to Samunovs whom he obviously does not want to see. They experience a lot of little rebuffs I think,[5] Ida as usual is unhappy. I'll tell you all about them when I return. Yitzchok is pleased to be in Palestine but joblessness is weighing on him. To distract him I went for a tour of the North – Metulla[6] etc. with him – most interesting – fine types really, the Kvutzoth[7] are very *unaggressive* and hospitable & no proletarian pride in the offensive sense. It is a *fascinating* country: every sort of climate & every sort of person. Yom

1 Eric Mills (1892–1961), appointed Commissioner for Migration and Statistics in Palestine (the official previously styled 'Director of Immigration') April 1934.

2 The Palestine Jewish Colonisation Association, established by Baron Edmond de *Rothschild (1845–1934) in 1923 to promote Jewish agricultural settlement in Palestine. (The 'I' in 'PICA' is a result of the near-interchangeability of 'I' and 'J' – which have a shared origin – and the fact that 'PICA' works better than 'PJCA' as an acronym.)

3 The central area of the Mediterranean port of Haifa, one of its earliest Jewish neighbourhoods and its shopping and commercial centre.

4 Jewish prayer-shawls (today usually transliterated 'tallithim').

5 Yitzhak Samunov, being distantly related to Rabbi Meir Berlin, had access to the leading Zionists in Palestine; but he appears to have been regarded as a tedious hanger-on and not to have received the help with his career that he had expected when he emigrated.

6 Small town (the country's northernmost) on the Lebanese border, founded by Russian immigrants as a farming settlement in 1896 on land purchased by Edmond de Rothschild.

7 Plural of *kvutza* – a communal settlement in Palestine, typically smaller than a kibbutz. The establishment of the *kvutzot* began in 1909.

Kippur in Haifa. The *top* of the Carmel,[1] not Hadar, but the *top* is beautiful. If to build a house then either in Rehavia,[2] which looks like Le Touquet before it was built – white houses with big empty stretches – or on top of Carmel. A *little* money – only a little – £200 say, might be invested in Beersheba,[3] very unsafe. I'll report when I return. Yitzchok cannot come now, ready to come for Peisach.[4] I hope he passed his exam. Erev[5] Yom Kippur Foster & I happenned to be near Beirut: there discovered a whole group of husbands who ran away from their wives *and* Jewish public opinion (you remember the Halpern case?) for Y. Kippur – party of 4 consisting of Van Vriesland,[6] Smoira (lawyer),[7] Pflaum (philologian)[8] & a doctor, to whom we talked. They were surprised to be discovered by us, but were very polite. So too were (polite I mean) [the] L[e]ibovitches, with whom I saw Mulya Schalit[9] – very well & contented – & Myer Berlin,[10] who was specially courteous towards me. Jewish opinion is v. bitter against the English. Not so much abt. policy in general as abt. small rudenesses, brutalities, insults. The English *are* C3.

To-morrow I visit Shukri Bey Taji el Farugi, millionaire father of my Arab pupil[11] who sells land to the Jews & writes against it. So you see I see everyone. I shall be *full* of stuff when I return. I get no sensations when I see biblical places: they are so different now – perhaps father will. You *must* come. I am very well & very happy, not eating 'fancy dishes'! I look forward to another conversation with Mills, to a Stay of 3 days in Tel Aviv, I'll call on

---

1 Haifa is built on three levels: the older, port area, the main town (Hadar), and above them the more exclusive residential areas of the Carmel Hills.

2 Fashionable residential area of Jerusalem, built in the 1920s and 1930s, home to intellectuals, Zionists and politicians and to many German Jews fleeing the Nazi regime.

3 Town on the edge of the Negev desert about 50 miles south-west of Jerusalem, often mentioned in the Bible as marking the southernmost limit of Israelite territory.

4 Passover.

5 '[On the] evening [of].'

6 Zadok A. Van Vriesland (1886–1939), General Manager of Palestine Potash Ltd 1923–38, then General Manager of the Marine Trust, which administered the port of Tel Aviv; Consul General for Holland since 1929. He shot himself.

7 Moshe Smoira (1888–1961), Chairman of the Jewish Bar Association, later President of the Supreme Court and Chief Justice of Israel.

8 Heinz Pflaum (1900–1962), born in Berlin, emigrated to Palestine in 1925, later (by 1949) changed name to Hiram Peri; from October 1934 Lecturer (Professor from 1948) in Romance Languages and Medieval Literature at the Hebrew University.

9 Samuel ('Mulya') Schalit, son of Mark (Morduch) Schalit of London (originally from Riga), and cousin of Lionel and Bella Schalit. Mulya had emigrated to Palestine and remained there for life.

10 The Meir Berlin referred to on 10 September 1934.

11 Abdul Majid Taji Farouki (1912–86), previously of the American University in Beirut, New College PPE 1932–5. His father, Ahmed Shukri Taji, was a landowner from Wadi Hunain, Palestine.

Lusia Schalit[1] & Persitz,[2] & then home. I can't write daily diaries. One is too tired in the evenings & goes to bed too early –

love

Shaya

TO MAIRE LYND

Postmark 26 October 1934

All Souls

Dear B.J.

I sympathise most actively, i.e. I sink into depression myself whenever I think of the pointless and sapping scenes which must occur – I shd. have thought your mother wd have been practical enough to come to terms with the situation: your father[3] appears to have behaved with old fashioned nobility of the kind I desire to possess very strongly. As matters are, therefore, your visit to Mrs P.[4] is entirely good, a relief etc.

Goronwy may be expected here, I think, and the college will be full & swarming which I loathe. on the other hand I shd like to see you about this & in general. What to do. The only thing I can offer is a walk on Sunday morning before lunch at about 12.15 or so, in New College garden. I'll cause the porter to remind me ½ hr before. Otherwise anything may happen. My memory & mind are going to bits. If I am in a room choc a bloc with chaps & not really properly got up from bed I need the most urgent reminders that any action is expected & not just indefinite continuance of the status quo. I am aware that I risk offending you, but this is a psychological fact: in normal conditions I act & behave responsibly, loyally & rationally. Given more than 6 persons I become fogged, dazed, pleased in an intoxicated sort of way & totally forgetful of everything. Having written all this however, there is now really no danger of my forgetting. None whatever. Therefore if you are in New College by 12.15 or, better 12.30 (definitive), I'll be there without fail or lateness. If you don't reply, I'll assume it.

love

Shaya.

---

1 Lionel ('Lusia') Leopold Schalit (1906–85), son of Lipman Schalit of London (originally from Riga). Lionel moved to Palestine in 1934 but returned to London in 1937 because his father was ill.

2 Akiva Persitz (1912–83), Univ. law 1930–3, later a lawyer in Tel Aviv, where his mother Shoshana, daughter of Hillel Zlatopolsky (93/5), was a prominent Zionist politician.

3 Robert Lynd (80/2).

4 Mrs Pilkington, with whose son (Edward Cecil) Arnold Pilkington ('Pilks') (1907–94), New College PPE 1926–9, BJ had a mild emotional entanglement – the background to these opening remarks. The Pilkingtons belonged to the family that manufactured glass in St Helen's, and lived on Boar's Hill, outside Oxford to the west.

TO MARION AND FELIX FRANKFURTER[1]

7 December 1934

All Souls

Dear Marion & F.F.

It has taken me all these weeks to recover from my summer – which now seems infinitely remote, as distant as you say Oxford does to you. It was a very peculiar journey – I was very frightened when I began it and relieved when it was over and passed not a single bored moment during its course. The only method I know of recording it is the chronological: it may make this too long but it will give me so much pleasure to remember everything that I cannot resist, I do so like living in the past. After a brief visit to Salzburg and Toscanini, made difficult by my parents' fear of stray bullets which made me arrange to have all my letters posted from Verona, I went to Venice, which I thought absolutely wonderful. I cannot think of it as a city at all, only as a clump of fragments of dry soil set in water: the people – the women especially, are beautiful & degenerate, the tempo of everything is so slow – I almost felt myself back in Oxford in that respect. I met Foster there – he was gay, good-tempered, tolerant, prepared to be serious if required, practical, helpful, ironical, even kind, all the time. An irreproachable co-traveller. And *not* a bore whatever Maurice may say. But he loves cads & we met them all the way & he adored them & I hated them more the handsomer and better mannered they were – all my traditional & puritan upbringing swam up – finally we took a boat and arrived in Alexandria. One doesn't know what noise is if one hasn't been there. At once a vast swarm of niggers – generic term – in coloured nightshirts rushed on deck, one of them seized my bag & bolted. Worried, passportless, hot, I followed slowly. Suddenly he threw my bag at my feet and said 'I am not porter, I am a business man' he was an agent for a porter who again was only allowed to go a certain distance before another took over etc. finally I found myself in a taxi with three porters on a journey about as distant as All Souls to Wadham.[2] We haggled, they screamed, everything as in comic descriptions. Cairo was hot but wonderful. The museum is breathtaking. But all Egypt is horrible, slimy, weary, corrupt, anything can happen, you can rely on nothing and nobody, everything is oily & sticky and decaying & beastly. Everything is like a perpetual hang-over after exhausting experiences. Oo it was absolutely vile. Crossing the canal on a raft was rather exciting, Arabs

---

1 Felix *Frankfurter (1882–1965), Byrne Professor of Administrative Law, Harvard, 1914–39, George Eastman Visiting Professor, Oxford, 1933–4. For the visit to Oxford by Frankfurter and his wife Marion A. *Frankfurter (1890–1975), née Denman, see MI 82, PI2 112 ff.

2 About 400 yards.

like persons in the Arabian nights, Greek women, policemen, nondescripts at
1 a.m. The customs of Kantara East[1] are ludicrous. Now that the customs
officials have been promised 90% of what contraband they find for
themselves & their families, they look on your bag as a lucky dip, search and
search & if they find nothing begin again – time is nothing, the train can wait
– then one was searched for arms & when I was being looked at Foster said
'Oh I'd advise you to search him carefully. Well known smuggler. 4 or 5
pistols at least.' The Egyptians have no sense of humour. They took him
seriously. You don't know what it is to be stroked by an Egyptian official up
and down your flanks. Very tiresome it was. I admit that that night I
definitely could not sleep. Foster giggled a lot, but I was genuinely excited by
the first sight of the country. The first oasis somewhere between Gaza and
El-Arish looked almost stagey – it was not so romantic – but all this is very
trivial so far. I found some relations as soon as I arrived and thenceforward
lived two separate lives, one with Foster, the British officials Hodgkin, (who
is the most honest pseudo-romantic I know, childish, honourable, capable
about routine things and silly about the general situation – idealistic in the
most infantile and irritating sense – but very good and kind and generous,
the Arabs like him for his conscientious stammering Arabic, the Jews like
him because he is transparently sincere, both sides regard him as deceivable
easily, and capable of the hugest mistakes – everyone loves him, no one
respects him, some people want to use him, others want to protect him –
from all of which it followed that he ought not to be there at all but is much
better than his probable successors wd be – but enough of him.) to go on
with List I, some Arabs who enjoy official patronage (of them later) & the
officially favoured Jews. I met all the latter at a party of intellectuals and
general prominents given us by the Professor of Philosophy, Mr Roth, at
which the Viteleses, the Yellins, various captains of business & Old Zionists
were present: they were fairly stiff & not very interesting. As a result of them
& Foster's British looks we were given to the official guide Mr J. Gordon
who took us about. It was all impossibly bureaucratic – he was very kind, &
we did see everything from his car – but all that belongs to Life N° 1. Life N°
2 was lived through my relations in private houses in Jerusalem and colonies.
The two Palestines are absolutely different. The official situation is as of a
huge secondary school staffed by public school men – of an inferior brand,
not as good as Wykehamists even – who feel acutely class conscious and
develop the sort of snobisme which only the lower middle classes have. The
High Commissioner (who was away on leave) is obviously regarded as an
old Headmaster, decorative, full of sincere & noble sentiments, slightly

1 On the East of the Suez Canal, 30 km north of Ismailia on the main road from Ismailia to
  Port Said, at the beginning of the railway line to Palestine.

behind the times, a very representative figure, good with parents and Governors (the Colonial Officer & distinguished visitors) but unable, owing to excessive high-mindedness to see the daily issues clearly: therefore he has to be mildly and systematically managed all the time. The Col. Office are the Board of Governors – rich, stupid, far distant, continually sending inspectors who have to be led round & sent back as quickly as possible, tho' the Governors occasionally make things easier by previously prompting the local ushers about what to answer. The boys are the Arabs: gay, affectionate, high spirited & tough, occasionally liable to break out & have a rag & break the skulls of a few Jews or an Englishman perhaps, if so, they are given lines or detention, in the hope that they will emerge with a heightened conception of British justice. This, I may add, is not a hypocritical but a sincere belief of the local government. The problem is the Jewish House: abler & richer than the other boys, allowed too much pocket money by their parents, rude, conceited, ugly, ostentatious, suspected of swapping stamps unfairly with the other boys, always saying they know better, liable to work too hard & not to play games with the rest. Such is the general atmosphere as I found it. The Government seemed to have no policy at all: just to engage in ad hoc justice, as though there were no mandate, but two excitable populations each highly unreasonable & dishonest, and intent on cheating the government. Of course the Jews don't make it any easier: they will not believe in simplicity of motive as possible at all: if an English official cuts an appointment & goes & plays tennis this is ascribed not to ordinary rudeness but to a complicated collusion with the Colonial office, & countermeasures are taken at once: these do, of course, endlessly complicate everything. The law is regarded by the majority of the Jews from Poland & Russia – so still by some of my relations – as something created only to be circumvented. I met a man who was indignant because the local passport authorities were difficult about his passport, in which he was said to be 53 years old, his wife 54 & his daughter 59. His plea that in Russia everyone raised their ages to avoid conscription was regarded as odd in the case of a woman – he explained that as men raised their ages women did so out of solidarity – & was indignant, very indignant when this was regarded as an unsatisfactory reply. But in spite of that sort of thing the official attitude is cold, rude, & monstrous: the average official is either a disgruntled, melancholy, bitter, clever failure like Mills, whom I did meet and spoke to or else an earnest, stupid, godseeking missionary young man who understands nothing & expects courteous and unruffled manners, & wants to go to the Gold Coast where you are either black or white and your status & its duties are easy & clear. I met a lot of the latter & went on picnics with them to the Dead Sea, beautiful and terrifying, marred by the Scotch-Jewish Café Kallia where portly Arabs lead newly landed German

Jewish filles de joie, slowly & with suppressed excitement, into the filthy
water, to Jerash in Transjordan – a really beautiful Hellenistic city, full of
curious Circassians with long fair beards – I used to think all Circassians were
women once – not far from Ammân – where lives the Emir Abdullah,[1] in
a palace full of stuffy Victorian bibelots and a huge Singer Sowing [sic]
Machine advertisement fixed to the back of the Palace. On these picnics I
really got to know them, & they are honourable and quite gay but
impossible in Palestine: too simple, silly, & impatient, they say they
understand Zionism is mystical, but they understand nothing, & are divided
into those who think the Jews more amusing & interesting than they are
vulgar, & those who think the opposite. As for the Jews they are most odd &
fascinating, & I felt equally uneasy with them & away from them, like
relations one hasn't seen for 30 years or something, to whom one knows one
is, even feels, related, but whom one doesn't really know, & is afraid of, &
has to treat on an oddly familiar footing, tho' knowing nothing about them,
& even afraid of them. Jerusalem is a most beautiful town, you'll agree, &
the Mosque of Omar is unspeakably beautiful, & the old Town is like the
Arabian Nights, little asses & bells, and potters pottering, & dimly lit caves
with blinded camels slowly gyrating grinding sesame, & everything to please
the wildest medievalist, the Arabs sometimes very beautiful, & pummeling
each other like schoolboys, the Jews graver, & in the new German pension
country happy in a restrained quite unexpectedly dignified way. Tel-Aviv
incredible, like my conception of the Klondyke, full of gold-rush, built on
sands in every sense, with more telephone calls per person per day than even
New York, only 100,000 strong, with the tempo of a town of 600,000, hot,
sticky, the sea so full you cannot see it, the German refugees swarming about
with little portfolios under their arms doing business everywhere – in cafés,
in buses, in bathing huts, in the sea, everywhere save their offices, the
policeman checking traffic with a stick which he lashes with like a conductor's bâton, using Hebrew when cool but loud and passionate Yiddish
when excited, the car-drivers all shouting advice, cursing, laughing like
Greeks or Syrians, already levantinized, suddenly checked by a long caravan
of camels, very beautiful & like a tourist advertisement, led by a little Polish
Jew in a black bowler hat making suitable Arab noises to the camels, learnt
overnight, followed by a group of official intellectuals, poets, editors & the
like, a peripatetic academy arguing about the possibility of coining a new
word, etc. etc. etc. unbelievable it is, like the performance of Pergolesi's
Serva Padrona[2] in Hebrew in the University theatre overlooking the Hills

1 Abdullah ibn Husayn (1882–1951), Emir of Jordan 1921–46, later King of Transjordan (1946–50)
  and King of the Hashemite Kingdom of Jordan (1950–1); assassinated in Jerusalem.
2 La serva padrona ('The servant as mistress'), a short and relatively lightweight opera in the

of Moab & the Dead Sea – Pergolesi certainly never thought of Hebrew as a fate of his libretto – this followed by a visit to some crusader church & a conversation in halting French with an infinitely polite monk, you see I am getting lost, there are too many impressions, & we haven't even got to the colonies yet, or the waterfalls in the North, or the Sea of Galilee & the incredible city of Safed and its mystics. I must stop & go to tea with Mrs Cameron & find out if Fraenkel[1] is Professor of Latin – the Election is to-day – I shall recommence as soon as I return.

8 December

Someone has just brought the news of Fränkel's election to the Professorship of Latin. This is really splendid. All the forces of darkness are, momentarily at least, defeated, I have just sent a wire to Maurice in Berlin: he is very pleased & amused about the Bousios[2] correspondence – so are Roy, Sylvester Gates,[3] Ayer etc. to whom it has been shown – 'The loving-living Greeks' is very fine. Maurice is willing to write anything for anyone, if well paid, or so he says. It is nice to be able to afford that sort of joke. Meanwhile the Ayers' situation is gloomier & gloomier[4] – Renée can certainly not go on living in Oxford – she will live in London whatever happens. It is really important to have Freddie elected – to be ejected now would ruin him in all sorts of ways – the only way out is an American lectureship: perhaps there is something going? it would be a service to him to civilization and to us all (in that order) if he could be got something in America somewhere – they would come like a shot I think – & he really is very good indeed as even his

---

tradition of the Italian *commedia dell'arte* (designed to be performed between the acts of more substantial works), with music by Giovanni Battista Pergolesi (1710–36) and libretto by Gennaro Antonio Federico (d. c.1745); first performed 1733.

1 Eduard David Mortier Fraenkel (1888–1970), Jewish émigré from Germany, Corpus Christi Professor of Latin, Oxford, 1935–53.

2 The Greek student Basil Nicholas Hellenagoras Bousios wrote a somewhat comical letter to Felix Frankfurter, 'Twentieth-Century-Educational-Leader', from New York on 5 November 1934, asking him to contribute to a book about the influence of ancient Greek culture on the modern world. Frankfurter replied on 8 December recommending Bowra as a more suitable person to approach, and sent the exchange to IB, asking him to make sure that it came to Bowra's attention, and suggesting 'the desirability of reading this correspondence in the presence of a very intimate circle, composed, say, of Roy, Sylvester Gates, and Ayer'.

3 Sylvester Govett Gates (1901–72), British barrister and (later) banker; Commonwealth Fund Fellow (Private International Law), Harvard, 1925–7 (where he had been a pupil of Felix Frankfurter); Controller of Home Publicity, MOI, 1941–4; attached to Office of Minister of Reconstruction 1944.

4 The Studentship Ayer had hoped for at Christ Church had been awarded to Frank Pakenham instead, and his Lectureship there had been extended only until June 1935. With no apparent prospect of a better post in philosophy – and despite being deeply engaged in writing *Language, Truth and Logic* – Ayer was contemplating a change of career.

worst enemies now realise – even those who denied it 4 or 5 months ago. You will be seeing Fraenkel soon – he really is an excellent man – I asked him what he thought of Maurice once & he rapidly answered 'He is a very learned and tender man.' people in Oxford shiver slightly, as you know, when real adjectives are suddenly used instead of vague blanket-terms like charming or sweet or nice. Fraenkel will tell you how disturbed everyone is getting re the Ayers & he will have direct Christchurch intelligence too, such as I have not. Roy insists on sending some of his work to Whitehead:[1] it is v. important that this should be favourably commented on – perhaps you could explain the situation – it is a severer test than any of us has had to undergo. I don't know why Freddie is punished thus: anyhow I hope you will be able to do something for him, whether by recommending him for some philosophy post – he is *far* more stimulating than the average incumbent, apart from his value as a philosopher – and/or by preventing Whitehead from dismissing him as a jejune dry little sophist with bad intellectual manners. This really is important. And – I might be writing a begging letter for myself so lacrymose am I growing – you are the only friends in America he possesses.

To return to Palestine: The people in the colonies are handsomer, franker, more interesting, more stable & more reliable in crises than the gay little townees. I enjoyed talking to the ex-social democrats from Russia a very great deal. They are the old 1848 idealist type of person who somehow do work the land by day & read poetry by night without making it seem impossibly arty and affected. I liked them better than I've ever liked any body of men tho' I couldn't live among them, they are too noble, simple, & oppressively good. But visiting them is delightful.

The passage from the severe red hills of Judaea to the relatively voluptuous rolling lands of Samaria is interesting in itself, one sees how the various strains of Jew arose – all the taxi-men spoke of nothing but their prowess as smugglers of illegal immigrants & the land they could sell you cheap – they look & behave like Sicilian bandits. Syria is wonderful: Damascus squalid but Baalbec & Beyrout & the great road South, with the magnificent green slopes of the Lebanon on the left & the Sea on the right – it really is so beautiful that even I who have no eyes was absolutely amazed & stopped talking and even Foster who hates Nature was impressed: Sidon is the most lovely of fishing villages, with red & yellow sails bobbing in the dark blue water & fishermen in bright white swathings emptying their silver

---

1 Alfred North Whitehead (1861–1947), English mathematician, Professor of Philosophy, Harvard, 1924–37.

catch – I am becoming, for me, lyrical, & therefore embarrassed, & must stop. I do think that the Palestine Jews are the happiest & securest people I have ever met. I don't feel absolute kinship, alas, but if I lived there for a bit I am sure I should. I must go & catch a train. In a few days time I shall produce a second & probably even longer instalment of this – more serious, more impersonal, about the Govt. & the university & the levantinization of the people: but now I must stop.

Thank you for the Spender review:[1] even the New Yorker has cracked a joke about him, more than which no man may aspire to. I do hope you will keep your word and come here in June – please do – I shall stay here after term for any indefinite length of time & wait for you if you come – I solemnly promise that – nor will I make absurd excuses for absence, but really will be here – & so too, I am sure all your friends. There is little news of them: Maurice is grimly settling down to persuading himself into middle age, Roy is corresponding with Dr Marie Stopes[2] about birth control, Rees has thrown up research & is on the Times – it really is a racket that – Crossman is trying to sell his soul again & finding no buyers even among those who think he had one.

I do apologise for the length, the scattered nature, the emptiness of this letter – I wish I could write a better – I'll try again shortly – Fraenkel has just called himself, he cannot go to America, he says the old guys won't let him, they have shown such enormous courage in electing him at all that he cannot afford at this stage to cause friction.

Do come in June. I am sorry about this letter. I can't even face reading it again it conveys so little.

    Love
       Shaya

TO MARY FISHER

    [1934, *opening 6 pages of letter missing*]

                                     All Souls College

[. . .] As for Miss Kisch,[3] I hope her essays will prove to you the mine of curious information they've been for me: she really is qualified to do a book on the Curiosities of Philosophy. But I daresay her history essays are brilliant.

---

1 A review of or by Spender? Untraced, as is the joke cracked by the *New Yorker*.
2 Marie Charlotte Carmichael Stopes (1880–1958), scientist and sexual reformer.
3 Eve(lyn) Myra Kisch (1912–45), Somerville classics 1931–4, switched to music in 1933 after Mods.

She used to play Blakeway & me off against one another most unskilfully. In the end we compared notes & both cornered her, which was most necessary & unedifying.

I am instructed by B.J. who is away somewhere to look in the Times every morning re the possible demise of Mr Cox.[1] I'm very remiss & miss everything. Will you be kind & tell her if this happens? I have no feelings about people I've never seen: unless they're very very grand indeed. I've just received a nice silly note from him[2] which indicates macabre gaiety. I hope he's well. Here there is no news except a fragment of a teaparty the guests at which were: Mr Eliot, Mr Bowra, Mr Spender & Mrs Woolf. Hostess: Lady Ottoline Morell.[3] But I haven't collated enough to describe this as it ought to be described. As soon as enough material accumulates, I'll make it up, & send you a vignette. Otherwise I live virtuously & without excitements (the end of term was really very exhausting), until I go to Florence on the 7th, where I meet Guy.[4] To whom I shall be very nice, since he's been most hardly treated & has complained the least.

Unlike the old lady with rimless glasses in the corner of the restaurant-car in which Dick & I travelled up to Town on Wednesday, who upon Dick's rather loud quotation in German from some Nazi friend followed by a banging of the table to emphasise the sincerity of the sentiment, said querulously & to nobody at all 'I wish foreigners wd behave in English trains' & then blushed scarlet & plunged into the menu with enormous embarrass-ment. I told Dick about this, I think, but he wasn't listening, & didn't hear.

I never knew Mrs Lynd was violently superstitious: but it is the case that B.J.'s opal earrings had to be thrown into the White Stone Pond[5] or something when[6] her cheek, to the chagrin of her daughters, suddenly got better.

    yrs

      Shaya

I haven't re-read. But you are very discreet.

---

1 Christopher Cox's father was dying.

2 sc. Christopher Cox.

3 Lady Ottoline Violet Anne Morrell (1873–1938), well described by David Cecil (153/6) in the DNB as 'the centre and patroness of a bohemian and intellectual circle which was to include some of the most distinguished artists and writers of the age', notably her sometime lover Bertrand Russell.

4 Guy Edward Farquhar *Chilver (1910–82), Merton classics 1932–4; Fellow and Praelector, Queen's, 1934–63.

5 A reservoir in Hampstead, London NW3.

6 sc. 'whereupon'.

TO MARY FISHER

[After 16 December 1934][1]

All Souls

Dear Mary

Plainly you enjoyed Paris: I do genuinely envy you – I have begun to adore the city – I am passionately anxious to hear about the appearance & personal habits of M. Lalande:[2] please thank my ex-pupil[3] for her demure, amiable, elegant and felicitously phrased billet. Alas, I have just offended Mr Ryle. I met him at a wedding (!) at which he sat with his head in his hands, to all appearances devout & moved. Actually he is bored & sleeps (genuinely). I regard him as a man who always unconsciously makes gestures & assumes expressions which convey more & intrigue one greatlier than the content deserves. Anyhow on being asked why I wouldn't accompany him to the subsequent reception I said that I wasn't dressed nearly well enough: only then did I observe that Mr Ryle was wearing a gay check suit. Mr Ryle reddened, said 'you're all right" angrily & left me. I'll have to ask him to a meal, *please* come.

The Fraenkel news is wonderful. He burst into my room to thank me for my letter to him & was dreadfully moved. Did you see the foul correspondence in the D. Telegraph about him? Started by a rat called Arthur J. M. Cohen who speaking as a British Jew & Old Oxford Man objected to choices at Oxford being dictated by sentimental reasons: a Miss May, Aryan indeed, but somehow connected with Palestine, rightly replied that it takes a British Jew to lean so far backwards in the effort to appear upright.* I endorse the sentiment.[4] If you get a Baring[5] book at any time don't acknowledge it.

---

1 In the Christmas vacation MF visited Rachel Walker and French friends in Paris.
2 André Lalande (1867–1963), philosopher of science, Professor at the Sorbonne since 1904.
3 Rachel Walker.
4 The announcment was published in the *Daily Telegraph* on 13 December, p. 16, under the heading 'German Elected to Chair at Oxford: Refugee from Nazis', and begins: 'Oxford University has acted on the suggestion, made when brilliant scholars were turned out of German universities under the Nazi regime, that posts should be found for them in English Universities.' Fraenkel had been Professor at Freiburg until his resignation in 1933; he now succeeded A. C. Clark as Corpus Professor of Latin. Arthur Cohen's letter appeared on 14 December, p. 14, that from D. H. C. May (male, with no stated Palestinian connection) on 15 December, p. 10. The latter begins: 'It takes an English Jew to lean as far backwards, in his efforts to appear perfectly upright, as Mr A. J. M. Cohen . . .'. On 17 December, p. 9, there are three further letters, all supporting May.
5 Maurice Baring (1875–1945), British diplomat, journalist and writer of novels, criticism, essays, poems and an autobiography; a brilliant linguist, and a devoted Russophile before the Revolution. IB adored his books.

Social News:

(1) Guy & Miss Oppé[1] were definitely seen by me in apparently warmly friendly conversation – I was meantime being harangued by a gesticulating Swiss Diplomat who is also a French mystic about the difference between S. John of the Cross (referred to as S. Juan della Cruz) & J. Boehme,[2] he gesticulating, a lot of Wykehamists & Edward Ford giggling, I helpless & embarrassed.

2. Peggy Jay believes a horrible thing is being said about her 'every where', she is trying to find out what it is & to track it down. She met Boase[3] & asked him what the horrible thing was, he, however, paid her nine compliments at once. She really is delightfully flatterable: I do it as a joke, crudely, & it is unexpectedly repaying.

3. Miss Chilver & Mr Davidson,[4] my dear, are said to be *engaged to be married*! but it is a *great* secret, & *no one* must hear. If true this is v. neutralising & pro tanto unobjectionable. I must catch the post. Enjoy Xmas. Much touched by your mother's pencil.

yrs
     Shaya

*Mr Bowra is exultant in Berlin & says it is so good, that some vast blow is about to descend.

TO JENIFER WILLIAMS[5]

[Late January 1935?][6]

All Souls

Dear Miss F.-W.

I feel no less than you that the elaborate and delicate principles on which this correspondence has so far been modelled should, if possible, not be allowed to collapse. On the other hand I also agree that there are times when even to attempt that would involve one in the risk of mere dull preciosity, to no end. I therefore bluntly renew & confirm my request to you to come to

1 Armide Lyonesse Tollemache Oppé (b. 1910), Somerville classics 1928–32, friend of Rachel Walker's sister Mary.

2 St John of the Cross (273/2) and Jakob Böhme (1575–1624), mystics.

3 Thomas ('Tom') Sherrer Ross Boase (1898–1974), Fellow and history Tutor, Hertford, 1922–37 (taught and examined Jenifer Williams); Director of Courtauld Institute of Art, London, 1937–47. According to IB, he 'had a glass eye which occasionally generated tears' (interview with Brian Harrison, 25 April 1988).

4 Priscilla Chilver did indeed, in 1935, marry Brian Davidson (1909–95), New College classics 1928–32, who became a lawyer.

5 Jenifer Margaret *Williams (b. 1914), Somerville history 1932–5; Civil Service 1936–47; married Herbert (H. L. A.) Hart 1941; close and lifelong friend of IB.

6 JW's reply is dated 31 January.

lunch next Saturday as ever is, though I can no longer guarantee the presence of Mr A. Smith (I have only just learnt of the existence of Alec Brown);[1] or to revert to the courtesy which you deplore in the young,[2] I declare that I anticipate yr coming with feelings of eager expectancy. As for the ratio of entertaining letters, what can I, what do you expect me, to say? beyond expressing appreciation of your own contribution in that medium, nothing. Indeed I am far from being certain that I know what you intended to convey: all that remains is a faint residue of not wholly agreeable nachgefühl,[3] mild sense of persecution, a beboasedness, Boasegefühl, Ver-boasenheit.[4] And yet I know that of all people you are aware of the phenomenon and its disastrous effect. Consequently I cannot acquit you of acting deliberately, at least not altogether. To that extent I profess ignorance of your motives, and vainly ask myself what constituted me into a fitting object for such an act.[5] But it is a very transient feeling and leaves no traces, as a rule, and by to-morrow I shall have recovered completely. But anything that lingers is annoying. Surely you agree.

 Yrs sincerely
  Isaiah Berlin

TO JENIFER WILLIAMS

 [Early February 1935?]

                All Souls

Dear Miss F.-W.!

 In my anxiety not to be embarrassing I find I am made to relapse half a stage backwards in which I am far from comfortable. Your suggestion that skirmishing is involved I should like to rebut: in the sense that if you are right, and such tactics are necessarily involved, then I prefer not to play at all, since it detracts from peace of mind and does not even kill time enjoyably. As for temporarily suspending my habits i.e. in the direction of simultaneous reticence and naturalness, I only promised to do so because I gathered that such a course would meet your criticisms: I was prepared to think them just and act accordingly. But if either you were misreported or alternatively such restraints may set up unpredictable inhibitions, I am only too delighted to

1 Presumably Alec John Charles Brown (1900–62), revolutionary socialist novelist, poet, and translator.
2 According to Jenifer Hart, this is a reference to a letter from Vienna.
3 'Empathy'.
4 References to Tom Boase, JW's tutor and examiner.
5 Jenifer Hart has forgotten what this was. Here and elsewhere (she suggests) it is perhaps relevant to point out that, especially at this stage in his life, IB had a slightly melodramatic tendency, at least in letters, so that trivial episodes are portrayed as significant.

relapse into the familiar mannered garrulity, which because of my low voice
is at present so successful with the Warden of New College, where more
bracing personalities have failed. I must point out that A.[1] is Alick & not
Alec: which is bizarre & even slight romantic (there is a gipsy hero in the
poet Pushkin called Aléko)[2] but enormously non-political. I am glad that
you see his beauty of character. And I hope that you will share my
indignation if & when you observe with what ghastly familiarity that man of
exquisite sensibility is treated by the present regent of New College.[3] That
you do pay attention to modes of address is made plain by the move on your
part which precipitates my retreat (q.v.). I am really very glad indeed that
you are coming.

Yours sincerely

Isaiah Berlin.

*By now IB's life had settled into a pattern, but as he recalled, 'Teaching
philosophy was so remote from Marx or anything to do with it that I did
lead two lives.'[4] His explorations into Karl Marx were demanding:*

I read an enormous amount, because I'm always very nervous about
being ignorant. So I sat there reading volume after volume of the
Marx–Engels *Ausgabe*,[5] in German, badly – my German is not good –
with dictionaries, but if I could read anything in translation, I did it, the
same way as I used cribs at school. The edition was stopped in '33 – by
Hitler. Then it began to appear in Russian. I was able to acquire volumes
of it from the Soviet bookshop. So I read everything he wrote,
absolutely, and took notes.

In contrast there was the routine of life as an Oxford don:

I lived in College. On weekdays I taught, five hours a day, morning and
afternoon. I talked to Austin, who was elected the year after me. I went
for walks with him or Maurice Bowra or some other friend. I dined at
All Souls night after night. There were about seven or eight people to
dinner on weekdays and about twenty-five at weekends. I had a very
regular life. I was an Oxford don absolutely, much more than I have ever
been since, and fitted into the Oxford texture, absolutely – felt perfectly
cosy and comfortable in Oxford academic life – and was very very
academic, I really was a super-don in those days. I was friendly with the
other philosophers; I used to meet them, and was cosy with them, and

1 In 'A. Smith' (see previous letter): for Alic [*sic*] Smith see 79/1.
2 In Pushkin's *The Gypsies* (1824).
3 R. H. S. Crossman, Sub-Warden, acted as Warden during Fisher's absence on sick leave.
4 MI Tape 8, from which the other extracts in this headnote are also taken.
5 'Edition'.

we talked about the same sort of subjects. I used to dine with Ryle, or Ryle dined with me, and I would ask philosophers to dinner, or we had tea together, or I met them in Blackwells[1] and talked to them. But I was among brothers. I lived a purely donnish life, I didn't know the great world. I didn't go to London much. I wasn't asked out to dinner in London much. I didn't go to country houses. This happened later in my life.

TO ELIZABETH BOWEN

Wednesday [13 March 1935] 2.30 p.m.

All Souls

Dear Elizabeth

Your telephone is as unresponsive as you allege mine to be, certainly it was so 3 minutes ago. I have for many days been wanting to see [you] on every ground: may I come sometime on Sunday? will you be here? Friday – I should have loved to come but for my Saturday lecture which drives me dotty on all Fridays, however this Saturday is the last.[2] Last time a man came up who, after my lecture on sympathy, said quietly & with dignity, 'what about pity?' very moving he was about it too, & has since pestered me with notes about his own experience. If there is one thing I am dangerous as it is as a psychoanalyst, since I am unperceptive, & tread gaily & brutally on people's more delicate shades of meaning. So I shall put some end to that correspondence. But it is very disturbing. May I come up early on Sunday afternoon? if you ring up on any morning between 11 & 1, I am *always* in.[3] And almost always between 5.30 & 7. I must give you an account of Maurice's intoxicated pranks on Saturday night. I am reading thro' the proofs of a critical book by Stephen S. on Henry James, Eliot etc.[4] it is good in parts, but sticky, very moralistic & extremely depressing & guilt inducing. The party – its pleasures – ended with your departure: Sparrow & Rees both became intolerably rude to each other, Rees more & more drunk, truculent and vulgar, Sparrow more & more pedantic, difficult & irritating. I suppose this had better not reach their ears.

    love

      Shaya

1 The main bookshop in Oxford, founded in 1879 by Benjamin Henry Blackwell.
2 IB lectured on 'Hume's Ethical Views' on Saturdays at 10 am in All Souls in Hilary Term 1935. The last lecture would have been delivered on 16 March, the last Saturday of Full Term.
3 Discussing philosophy with J. L. Austin, as he did most mornings.
4 Stephen Spender's *The Destructive Element: A Study of Modern Writers and Beliefs* was published by Jonathan Cape in London in April 1935.

TO JOHN HILTON

Thursday, most probably the 14th March [14 March 1935]

All Souls

Dear John

How can you be so silent. This wealth of new & violent impressions must make you want to speak.[1] Therefore your silence is due to some repression to do with me, which I take hardly. It is natural enough for me to remain silent, since all that ever happens here is an intrigue or two, or a fuss about whether we should have a great illuminated G.R. suspended on All Souls in honour of H. M. The K.[2] if so with or without red lights, or could we have an electric sign like Piccadilly Circus of the King taking off his bowler hat every five minutes while a mechanical mallard, our emblem, said quack each time it happenned, or would floodlighting be enough, and how much was the King worth to us, £200, or only £2.10.0 or nothing? Whilst you & Peggy live in the midst of Beauty. Has the rebellion[3] repercussed on you at all? wd it be true to say of the Cypriots what Ronald Storrs said here of the Jerusalem Jews, that they were unscrupulous, tiresome but never boring? have you squared or suppressed Mr Gunness? and so on.

We are in throes of elections of philosophical professors, J.A. & Joachim are going, Collingwood & Price are nuclei, the slave market is heaving like a jelly and the logical positivists, Braithwaite, Ayer & such are spreading havoc wherever possible.[4] My intrigue to get Miss Stebbing[5] into New College may yet work. A Mr Wisdom[6] has published an opus[7] in which he proves that if one is a determinist one must believe in prenatal existence since it is

1 JRH was Director of Antiquities in Cyprus 1934–6. He arrived in Cyprus with his wife in the autumn of 1934, charged with the task (on probation) of establishing and directing a department of antiquities. Sir Ronald Storrs (1881–1955), Governor and Commander-in-Chief, Cyprus, 1926–32, had appointed his ADC, Rupert Gunnis (*sic*), 'Inspector of Antiquities' when he left the island. Gunnis gave Hilton a lot of trouble. Storrs had also served in Palestine (as Governor of Jerusalem 1917–26) and Rhodesia.

2 The silver jubilee of King George V (6 May 1935) was approaching.

3 The attempted coup (defeated on 12 March) by the former President of Greece, Eleutherios Venizelos.

4 'J.A.' is John Alexander Smith (1863–1939), Waynflete Professor of Moral and Metaphysical Philosophy 1910–35; Harold Henry Joachim (1868–1938) was Wykeham Professor of Logic 1919–35; Robin George Collingwood (1889–1943) succeeded Smith, and Price succeeded Joachim; Richard Bevan Braithwaite (1900–90) was Sidgwick Lecturer in Moral Science at Cambridge 1934–53, whereafter he became Knightbridge Professor of Casuistry, Moral Theology and Moral Philosophy.

5 (Lizzie) Susan Stebbing (1885–1943) had been Professor of Philosophy, London, since 1933.

6 (Arthur) John Terence Dibben Wisdom (1904–93), Lecturer in Moral Sciences, Trinity College, Cambridge, later (1952) Professor of Philosophy, Cambridge.

7 John Wisdom, *Problems of Mind and Matter* (Cambridge, 1934).

unreasonable to stop with the merely adventitious occasion called birth. This is explained by the fact his father was a Calvinist but evinced blame. Broad in the meantime has in the course of an interesting new book ostensibly about McTaggart,[1] been making more improper jokes e.g. 'this possibility was first suggested by Mr Russell[2] but like so many of his progeny has been abandoned on the steps of his Infant Welfare Centre for illegitimate conception, while he has gone off to try & make an honest woman of Behaviourism'.[3] This I quote from memory, i.e. having looked it up, but inattentively. Louis Macneice has published a charming poem in New Verse,[4] terrific fuss is going on about Stephen's Vienna:[5] (last recorded remark "Now that I find I like women I don't mind what people say about my poetry so much.' and 'Poor Tony [Hyndman], he is so homosexual.') This is being a very petty chronique scandaleuse, I ought to attempt to rise. Who is Miss Aline Lion[6] whom I am to meet to-morrow? I had a letter about her saying she wishes to talk about Diamat* & was called 'tu' by Mussolini[7] & wasn't made a don at L.M.H. because she made mischief alla Romana.[8] Have you ever heard of her?

Come to Salzburg in summer. Toscanini will conduct Otello, symphonies, & [Bruno] Walter the rest. It will, as Sigle wd say, be heavenly. Do you know her David [Wallace]?[9] he is a firm, reputable, solid, boring man who will not talk of anything save in so far as it affects The Party. Possibly Lenin was like that, except that in the margin of Soviet aesthetician's works

1 John McTaggart Ellis McTaggart (1866–1925), philosopher. His major contribution to the field was the two-volume work The Nature of Existence (Cambridge, 1921–7), about which Broad wrote the two-volume Examination of McTaggart's Philosophy (Cambridge, 1933–8). Charlie Dunbar Broad (1887–1971) was Braithwaite's predecessor (1933–53) as Knightbridge Professor at Cambridge (117/4).

2 Bertrand Arthur William Russell (1872–1970), 3rd Earl Russell, the philosopher.

3 op. cit. (note 1 above), vol. 1, pp. 61–2: 'no one, so far as I know, before Russell, had made the important suggestion that the judging-relation might be more than dyadic; whilst he, I suppose, abandoned it, like so many of his philosophic offspring, on the steps of some Foundling Hospital for illegitimate conceptions, when he decided to make an honest woman of Behaviourism'.

4 Presumably 'Birmingham', New Verse No 7 (February 1934), 3–4.

5 A poem published as a book by Faber & Faber in 1934.

6 Aline Augusta Lion (1891–1964), philosopher, educated privately and at Rome University, was a scholar of LMH 1926–30, where she took a B.Litt. and a D.Phil. The letter IB has had is from the ancient historian Isobel Henderson at Somerville, who writes inter alia that Aline Lion is a pupil of Giovanni Gentile, has published a book on the philosophy of Fascism – The Pedigree of Fascism: A Popular Essay on the Western Philosophy of Politics (London, [1927]) – and now teaches at Roedean.

7 Benito Amilcare Andrea Mussolini (1883–1945), Italian prime minister 1922–43.

8 'In the Roman fashion.' His metaphor is drawn from cookery.

9 David John *Wallace (1914–44), Balliol classics 1933–6; married Prudence Major 1939, killed in action in Greece.

on Art & the Proletcult,[1] he often wrote 'Ha-Ha!' My love to Peggy & please write. Then I can write more gravely.[2]

*Dialectic materialism.

TO FELIX FRANKFURTER

20 March 1935

All Souls

Dear F.F.

Very many thanks for your document:[3] I agree with, I think, every word: the only thing I cannot understand is how you, who must have moved in relatively exalted company throughout, said very much the same as I who, on the whole, lived among the rabble. Only you put it all very much better than anyone else has. I do not propose to enumerate points of agreement. But the one or two points on which I differ I might as well state: perhaps they aren't real points of difference, but of emphasis. You'll forgive me if I am donnish and pedantic & say one, two three. Obviously fear of pedantry if one is serious is the worst sort of fear. 1. The British are not malevolent, but they are not benevolent either. H.E. may be sympathetic & the three or four Hodgkins & odd men about the place, architects & such, may try & be thrilled. The rest are instinctively repelled, & if they do pursue any sort of constructive policy it is malgré soi, against, I mean, their personal inclinations. Every thing that is done is done either patronisingly or grudgingly or amusedly or all three. Storrs came to breakfast here with, I think, Malcolm,[4] & said to Foster (I wasn't here) that the Jews were unscrupulous tiresome but never boring. On a lower level this is Millsism.[5] In India the conscientious & the self-deluded civil servants both

---

1 The Proletkul't ('Proletarskie kulturno-prosvetitel'skie organizatsii', 'Proletarian cultural and educational organisations') was founded in February 1917, and in October was placed under the direction of Lunacharsky, People's Commissar for Culture and Education. It set out to create a whole new proletarian culture and system of education for Soviet workers that would replace the existing class-based culture. It survived until 1932, although Lenin frequently criticised its divergences from the official line. Despite his punctuation, it is not clear whether IB has one aesthetician or more in mind, but the leading Proletkul't theoretician was Aleksandr Aleksandrovich Bogdanov (1873–1928), who wrote, among other things, O proletarskoi kul'ture, 1904–1924 ['On proletarian culture . . .'] (Leningrad, 1924).

2 If complete, the letter is unsigned.

3 Frankfurter's confidential report (dated 8 June 1934) on a visit to Palestine, 3–14 April 1934. The carbon copy he sent to IB survives.

4 Dougal Orme Malcolm (1877–1955), historian, Fellow of All Souls 1899–1915, 1924–47, Director of the British South Africa Company.

5 For Mills see 101/1.

conceive themselves as Kulturträger[1] of some sort; in Palestine the Jews are obviously that, so the moral façade simply cannot be built up. To be mere traffic-policemen is not v. glorious. The only possible moral approach (which all these missionaries and Wykehamists have – save that they really come from my school St. Paul's & are correspondingly inferior) is to regard themselves as the protectors of the Arabs against the recognizedly irresistible forward movement of the Jews. That as much as anything causes Revisionism. Coupland[2] believes that England is in an immoral mess out there, & if Coupland governed me I should turn violent too. Obviously if a mandate means the ruling of a territory solely to make the then inhabitants self-governing there is no justification for settling Jews. Historic right, the good of the world at large securable by Zionism which does not do harm to Arabs, etc. which is the real moral justification from the British point of view of the mandate, is a non-Wilsonian approach,[3] though perfectly good in itself. Only if one embraces that transplantation of whole populations becomes justifiable. I personally believe that it is. Only the average English civil servant is only capable of two points of view: either cynical exploitation or liberal self-determination of landed peoples. Jewish Palestine does not fit into either formula. From either point of view the Jews are a nuisance. All the high minded Oxford dons – the whole Balliol Sittlichkeit[4] – would behave exactly as those people do. Unless someone can be sent who takes a wider view & sees that the genuine grievance of the Arabs – who say they prefer to be self-governed badly rather than verjudet[5] however mildly – must be overridden by stronger considerations instead of conceded by some officials, painfully ignored by others, despised by still others etc., the present guilt-complex which is fairly acute in English Palestinian circles will last: it is as much this as traditional policy that leads to absence of decision, general fear of action, & ad hoc steps. As for the Jews they feel much too ill-used, too happy, & too possessorial to adopt an au-dessus de la mêlée[6] position & explain their rights, while not simply exposing the Arabs as a gang of paid agitators. Of course the present Antoniuses & Muftis[7] are corrupt to the last degree. But in fifteen years time the Arab nationalists will be sincere, incorruptible, utterly brutal fascists. It is then that the real fun will begin. Unless something is done now, however, by way of self-explanation, the

1 'Vehicles of culture'.
2 Reginald Coupland (1884–1952), Beit Professor of the History of the British Empire and Fellow of All Souls 1920–48.
3 A reference to Woodrow Wilson's doctrine of national self-determination.
4 'Ethics'.
5 'Jewified'.
6 'Above the fray'.
7 For George Antonius and the Mufti, see IB's letter of 10 September 1934 to his parents, pp. 96–8 above.

opportunity will be missed. And it is difficult for anyone, even Weizmann[1] to do this without being howled down as a traitor. The labour problem is directly relevant – you are quite right:

2. Arab labour should not be employed but not for the reasons – monstrous reasons – that are given. The duty of the government is to enact some sort of social legislation to undermine effendi-ism & not to refuse to employ Jews because Arabs are cheaper, or else to employ Jews generously, as a gesture. The Histadrut[2] is quite a decent body of men as our Warden[3] wd say, but bureaucratic & slightly ossified. For a socialist vested interest singularly uncorrupt.

3. The Revisionists[4] are a vile party. But their political attitude is more political than that of the Centre. That is they are not opportunists. It is necessary no doubt to be flexible, sensible & gradualist. But it is possible to go on saying this too long, until everyone gets slightly cynical, rather bored & used to a sort of mild & crooked manus manum lavat[5] with a none too scrupulous government. One can only retain (a) honesty (b) enthusiasm if one not merely has, but from time to time reasserts certain rigid principles. The Palestinian labourites don't. They boast about their opportunism, they luxuriate in being seen to be practical & not dreamers. This is unattractive & demoralizes. I wish you'ld tell them not to: why should Jabotinsky monopolise the stock of conscious integrity which Jewish politicians all in some measure possess? perhaps the habit of evading laws is largely incorrigible: but couldn't some superior persons sometimes make clear statements of belief which are not formulae, not collects which look repulsively boring & mechanical & like yesterday's news, when printed?

4. Why aren't there *any* superior persons in Palestine? only amiably imaginative publicists like Shmarya Levin & efficient demagogues like Ben Gurion?[6] If there is anything the English respect it is genuine size. But I suppose this is inevitable.

1 Chaim *Weizmann (1874–1952), chemist and statesman; President, World Zionist Organisation and Jewish Agency for Palestine, 1921–31, 1935–46.
2 The largest Jewish trade union organisation in Palestine.
3 Adams.
4 The Revisionist Zionist party (the ancestor of Likud), founded in 1925 by Ze'ev (Vladimir) Jabotinsky (332/4), wanted a Jewish State on both sides of the Jordan, occupying the whole of Mandate Palestine. The party's tactics were militant, and it refused to compromise with the national aspirations of the Palestinian Arabs. These hardline policies brought the Revisionists into conflict with the gradualist Labour Zionists, led by Chaim Weizmann and David Ben-Gurion. The party spawned two dissident military organisations, ETZEL (or Irgun), led by Menachem Begin, and LEHI, better known as the Stern Gang after its founder, Avraham Stern.
5 'One hand washes the other.'
6 The future first Prime Minister of Israel, David Ben-Gurion (1886–1973), led Mapai, the Zionist labour party, when it was formed in 1930, and in 1935 became chairman of the Zionist Executive and head of the Jewish Agency for Palestine.

God knows why I go on – maundering like this. You are a busy man &
otherwise occupied & should not be torn from a nation's business because
our term has come to an end and I feel at a loose end & can't collect myself
to face my research into the splendid but repulsive Marx and the flâneurish
but enchanting Hume.[1] There is a lot of local gossip, but I shall spare you.
And go on about [it] instead to Mrs F[rankfurter] who has more time and is
therefore more open to exploitation.

Is there no chance of your return this summer? we should all willingly
stay up into the vacation if you could –

Yrs

    Shaya B.

*In April IB, with Guy Chilver, visited Rachel 'Tips' Walker,[2] his former
pupil, who was studying philosophy in Paris. Tips had previously
expressed intense feelings for IB, but at this time had just received a
proposal of marriage from French philosopher Jean Cavaillès.[3] IB, Guy
Chilver, Tips and her close friend Mary Fisher, then also staying in Paris,
went to the opera (Beethoven's* Fidelio) *before Mary and Tips left for a
holiday in the South of France.*

TO MARIE BERLIN

7 May 1935

                                      All Souls

Dear mother

Again I have hardly time to write. This is very bad. I really shall sit down
to-morrow & write you a proper letter. Realising that father would "зейерь
скучаень"[4] in the Mme Croll expression during the Jubilee week-end,[5]
I spent Sat. night in London. He seemed well, he looks v. well, & even
cheerful. Here in Oxford huge crowds filled the streets, but all were very
quiet, subdued, obviously waiting for somebody to do something. The
undergraduates are *so* different from those abroad, gentler, politer, stupider,
more childish, less interesting, kinder, nicer, more liveable with, less
barbarian. I simply cannot understand how they can be made into either

1 cf. 253/3.
2 See pp. 719–20 below.
3 Jean Cavaillès (1903–1944), French philosopher; later a hero of the French Resistance, shot by
  the Gestapo.
4 'Zeier' skuchaen'', apparently a hybrid of a Russian transliteration of the German word *sehr*,
  'very', and 'skuchen'', the Russian for 'bored'; i.e. IB's father would have been 'very bored'.
  Mme Croll was presumably IB's German governess when he was a child.
5 The silver jubilee of King George V fell on 6 May 1935.

Fascist or Communist material. Everyone, grown ups & boys are so charmingly childish. I am now going to a concert with H. A. L. Fisher, which I shall therefore enjoy.

love

Shaya

TO STEPHEN SPENDER

[19 May 1935]

All Souls

Dear Stephen:

It is very rude of me not to have replied to you for so long: but I do answer your letters with a certain sense of responsibility. I don't want simply to write as I talk i.e. in loose bits. Diana says that you are in Yugoslavia or somewhere, I don't know when this will get to you: anyhow I enclose the Salzburg tickets, the ones I ordered: if you want others, as I think you said you did, write & I'll buy some more: the only difference will be that they may be rather worse: which is not serious. Your remarks on George[1] I think are absolutely true. I think he was a divine poet sometimes the Teppich des Lebens[2] is magnificent, so are odd things in the other books: as for the passages you quote, I think he was a persecuted megalomaniac, nor can any of the pleas of his closest followers save him from the fact that he was a man of repulsive views or actual modes of living, that he ruined many of his friends, exploited them, used them, etc. as sometimes Wagner did, did not simply burn them up as George Sand or Dostoyevsky did, or tortured them as Lawrence sometimes must have done (is this nonsense?) but definitely used them coldly & that not in virtue of his nature but in virtue of what he believed himself to be, or at any rate in virtue of the part he was determined to act.

The intolerance, the systematic ignoration of say Rilke[3] by the George circle, the cheap personal grandeur does lead occasionally to shaming pompous platitudes, or even Nazi-ism: obviously the Georgians are engaged in defending him against the charge of having caused all this: but Gundolf[4] quarrelled with him on precisely the grounds of political & personal views which he thought horrible, & the difference between him &

1 The German poet Stefan George (1868–1933).
2 George published his book of poems Der Teppich des Lebens ('The tapestry of life') in 1900.
3 Rainer Maria Rilke (1875–1926), German lyric poet.
4 Friedrich Gundolf (1880–1931), German poet and critic.

Yeats both engaged, as you say, on propping up collapsing possibly collapsed systems is that Yeats does in terms of his own genuine un-invented imagination which really does seem naturally to be steeped in mythology tradition etc. & is unhappy without archaism, whereas George, like Wagner, does not feel the emotions directly at all, but only wants to feel them on the grounds of certain intellectual or emotional convictions, so that just as Wagner has to ask himself 'what is erotic passion? what is jealousy?" & then invents painfully an elaborate construct which is miraculously made, full of genius, but horrible & unreal in that it is a sort of paraphrase, an attempt to describe what has never been experienced, an everlasting approximation to what he is not acquainted with, (while Verdi more crudely gets down what he actually knows), so George produces catchwords to trap emotion, which is not spontaneous at all, works at second hand which it seems to be the fate of all German artists, even Goethe, even Schiller who really was direct & genuine, sometimes to be doing. I daresay it is part of romanticism to be able to be illuded by bogus things, only they are sometimes so obviously artificial or so obviously degraded that it seems strange to more prosaic but more self-critical persons that such creative gifts & sensitive feeling can be combined with this total blindness which mistakes a tortured thirst for certain states of mind with the states of mind. Is this all nonsense? I can't see otherwise how to understand the Germans. I think heroic qualities always go with terrible stupidity & what seems frightful nonsense: which the enormous and careful seriousness of the French has always avoided, at [the] expense of a specially German sublimity.

To change over: I haven't read reviews of your book save one by McCarthy:[1] I can see what he means: he thinks: I've had lunch with Henry James so often, he liked good food & the rich so much, it *must* be nonsense to call him a communist: must be silly. I cannot remember how far you call him that: all you say (I may be wrong) is that his analysis of individuals in society is such that anyone reading it must know that the society is suffocating & is so poverty stricken that it must alter with an explosion. I think this is true. And I think it is true that he saw this & was a melancholy writer. I think it is not true that he was a revolutionary, in that he really liked the rich & would sink with them: when he saw people too rich or too vulgar or too cruel his New Englandism made him castigate: but he would have hated any form of revolution. He had a sense of tragedy but no desire for the solution. He was a clear sighted, tortured, unillusioned reactionary. This is

---

1 Desmond MacCarthy (1877–1952), critic and author. The review of *The Destructive Element* referred to here is 'Communism and Henry James: Mr Stephen Spender's Theory', *Sunday Times*, 5 May 1935, 8.

all McCarthy can claim. He complains that you don't mention Shaw[1] & Wells:[2] why should you? Every generation has official satirists & preachers: who lash out against the more obvious anomalies. James or Lawrence don't rant in this sense, aren't tendencious in the sense in which Shaw or communist authors or even Victor Hugo or Dickens were: but present individuals or societies in decay which are far more terrible indictments than tracts: just because no adjectives are used or obvious laughs or groans invited: nobody even felt impelled to suicide or violent upheaval as a result of Shaw–Wells: their disciples are smug characters like Joad[3] or Rowse or Sir A. Salter.[4] Just as Marx's economic history is a thousand times more effective as propaganda than all the books by later socialists, Lenin even, so James's analyses hurt more than the loudest thunderbolts flung at the public. So at least I think: McCarthy seems a fool, tho' I can see his well meaningness. I think he is right about the looseness of your book: I don't see that as a vice: though in ten years time I daresay you could produce a more organic whole. Did I not correct 'Spinozan' into 'Leibnitian'? what, if not for this, am I good for? I thought I had. Mortifying.

T. E. Lawrence died this morning.[5] He must have been an attractive person, since all his friends say so: a mysterious end, he must have been the only person as famous & as valuable, so to speak, who rode a motor-cycle: class-conscious sentiment. I am sorry I did not meet him in this college, he used to come in at 2 a.m. or so, my sort of time: he was said to be simple & charming so that we might have got on. You said in your book that Kafka doubted his vision. I want to go further & say that he was ironical about it, made jokes about it, as people can to whom a landscape is so familiar that it is the natural object of reference, jokes & all. That is what makes it so clear, so terrifying, so natural-unnatural, so plainly genius & sui generis & not oddly talented. I can't go on writing I am fearfully tired, I work hard & teach too much, it is like striking matches on soap.

1 George Bernard Shaw (1856–1950), Irish playwright, author and socialist, whose works often embodied a moral or political message; awarded the Nobel Prize for Literature 1925.
2 Herbert George Wells (1866–1946), English novelist and social thinker: cf. 145/4.
3 Cyril Edwin Mitchinson Joad (1891–1953), head of the Dept of Philosophy at Birkbeck College, London, popular broadcaster and writer on philosophy, famous for beginning his answers on the radio programme *The Brains Trust* with the formula 'It all depends what you mean by . . .'.
4 Sir (James) Arthur *Salter (1881–1975), Gladstone Professor of Political Theory and Institutions and Fellow of All Souls, 1934–44, MP (Independent) for Oxford University 1937–50.
5 Thomas Edward Lawrence (1888–1935), 'Lawrence of Arabia', British soldier and writer of strongly Arab sympathies (legally adopted the surname Shaw 1927); Fellow of All Souls 1919–26, according to IB as part of 'an attempt to make All Souls a centre for liberal imperialism', although 'he never came to the College in my time' (MI Tape 8). Lawrence's death resulted from a motorcycle accident some days earlier.

Von Trott has been here, Shiela Grant Duff, Diana, Bernard,[1] everyone, all this weekend I am almost dead. Mr Norris[2] is delightful. Archie[3] says he did not like its being said that his chin is like a concertina. Otherwise he approved. I'll write again re arrangements.

love to Tony[4]

Shaya

TO STEPHEN SPENDER

Wednesday [26 June 1935]

All Souls

Dear Stephen

I am writing this in great haste. You see from this hour on I begin moving about from place to place for about a week before I finally return here to do 5 weeks uninterrupted work in July, a period I look forward to I cannot tell you how much. I wish I cd find your poem which I left on the table of my colleague [Ian] Bowen because I was listening to a Toscanini concert there: since when it disappeared: I read it through once quickly & don't remember it well: I can't even remember what I thought when I read it: I should be most grateful if you had another copy. The one in the Mercury I liked v. much, misprints and all.[5]

Faber brought Eliot to the Encaenia[6] lunch to-day and I was intro-

1 Charles Bernard Spencer (1909–63), CCC classics 1928–32, poet and schoolmaster. IB had shared lodgings with him (and two others) in St John Street during his PPE year, and described him in 1992 as 'a gifted poet whose verse can still be found in more than one anthology [. . .] an uncompromising aesthete, a friend and disciple of Louis MacNeice': in 'Mixing It' (letter), *Oxford Magazine*, Noughth Week, Hilary Term 1992, 8.

2 A reference to *Mr Norris Changes Trains*, published in 1935, a novel by Christopher (William Bradley-)Isherwood (1904–86), English novelist and playwright who emigrated to the US with his close friend W. H. Auden in 1939, and like him became an American citizen in 1946. This was the first of a linked pair of novels about 1930s Berlin; the second, *Goodbye to Berlin*, was published in 1939.

3 Archibald Hunter Campbell (1902–89), Fellow of All Souls 1928–30, 1936–89, Stowell Civil Law Fellow, Univ., 1930–5, Barber Professor of Jurisprudence, Birmingham, 1935–45, Regius Professor of Public Law, Edinburgh, 1945–72; friend of IB, Stuart Hampshire, Auden, Isherwood and Auden's other Berlin friends; homosexual, Bohemian; introduced SS to Auden in 1930.

4 Hyndman.

5 'Three Poems' by SS – 'An Elementary School Classroom', 'At Night' and 'The Exiles' – appeared in the *London Mercury* 32 No 187 (May 1935), 8–11.

6 Encaenia is the summer ceremony held annually in Oxford at which the University awards honorary degrees to distinguished men and women and commemorates its benefactors. 'Encaenia' is Greek for 'festival of renewal/dedication', and corresponds to 'Commencement', from Latin, the name used in many North American universities for the chief ceremony of the academic year. In 1935 Encaenia was held on 26 June.

duced to him: I thought he was very nice, I talked to him with too much freedom I think, too fast and too gesticulously if you see what I mean: he appeared to want to talk about serious subjects but under the circumstances, with Bishops, admirals, lords & my own guests intervening it was practically impossible.

And now I am still in a haze of wine, conversation, idiots like Sir Thomas Bazley[1] cross & re-cross the quad and Maurice keeps ringing up to say he is feeling low, or to give the latest news. Whenever he does the latter I bless him, since it definitely offers one a firm gay support, a positive note, in the same sense as the poet Blok said he felt exhilarated whenever he thought of the name Pushkin, a gay name he said.

The Auden–Isherwood play[2] is not so very good. The poetry by Auden which intervenes is very beautiful indeed sometimes, but the dialogue is not good enough: its purpose is to be great fun: fun it is but not great fun: sometimes better sometimes worse than Noel Coward[3] or Gilbert.[4] Never generically superior. Comparable to & not so good as, say, Bert Brecht.[5] I am rather angry that this should be so: since, being very simple & intelligible, it will, I suppose, be widely read, & all the Sparrovians[6] will acquire a new stick to beat new poets with, this time alleging cheapness, which is a more effective insult than obscurity. I shall enjoy meeting you in Salzburg very much indeed: it will be full of people as usual I suppose: I shall definitely stay at the Gasthof Höllbraü. The chief virtue of the Dog B.T.S. is its readableness. But it is not good enough: it is not even an ambitious failure. Failure after all (I am uneasily conscious of being about to eject an aphorism.) means not aiming too high, but trying to persuade oneself that (or assuming through stupidity that) one has succeeded when in fact one knows one hasn't begun. A sort of systematization of sour grapes as a policy. To defend this

1 Sir Thomas (Stafford) Bazley (1907–97), Harrow, Magdalen (pass degree) 1927–30.

2 *The Dog Beneath the Skin: or, Where is Francis?* (London, 1935). Wystan Hugh Auden (1907–73), English poet, critic, essayist and playwright; Christ Church natural sciences, then English, 1925–8; moved to US 1939 and became an American citizen in 1946.

3 Noël Pierce Coward (1899–1973), English actor, playwright, novelist and composer of light music.

4 William Schwenck Gilbert (1836–1911), English playwright and librettist of the Savoy operas, for which Sir Arthur (Seymour) Sullivan (1842–1900) wrote the music.

5 Bertolt (né Eugen Berthold Friedrich) Brecht (1898–1956), German poet and playwright whose innovative theatrical approach, especially in his later works, was designed to stimulate (Marxist) thought rather than emotion in the audience. Here IB is presumably referring to Brecht's early work *The Threepenny Opera* (1928), and possibly to *The Rise and Fall of the City of Mahagonny* (1930).

6 A reference to John Sparrow's controversial book *Sense and Poetry: Essays on the Place of Meaning in Contemporary Verse* (London, 1934).

book as part of the united front wd be deception I think. Thank God I haven't to review it.

love to Tony.

Shaya

Cd you add 60 sch. to your debt? I shan't remember.

TO MARY FISHER

[Probably early July 1935]

All Souls

Dear Mary

There is a class of slightly depressed not quite Fellows of colleges outside examiners who when in common rooms seek to please and vigorously set themselves to sparkle. Of such the company at Pembroke was composed, they were all very agreeable & flattering and I spent an unexpectedly gay evening. If Pares be trusted yours was no less so, he showed, for the first time in his life to my knowledge, inquisitiveness & wanted to know who you all were. I broached Saturday to Tony who owned to expecting you, but thought that to transfer yourselves here would be discourteous. It is always funny & ludicrous when the maximum happiness of [a] collection of people or at least of a majority of them cannot be compassed owing to the imaginary (at least I think so) reactions of members of it, which convention prevents one from examining openly, or revealing when one knows. At the same time conventions are themselves so delightful & necessary that to question them in order to produce and have pleasure is wrong: & makes them more valuable the more uselessly & for their own sakes they are obeyed. The simple conclusion is that I hope you will pay me a brief visit if a long, or a long visit if a brief viva takes place. This is certainly the most tortuous and convoluted set of remarks I have ever addressed to you: I really don't know what possessed me to weave this pseudo-Henry James stuff on so simple a text. I apologise.

yrs

Shaya

I did meet Tips & Mlle Parodi[1] for 6 or so seconds: it was so brief as hardly to be even embarrassing.

---

1 Jacqueline Parodi, Rachel Walker's main friend in Paris at this time, younger daughter of Dominique Parodi, who was Inspecteur Général de l'Education Nationale, and an old friend of the historian Elie Halévy. Rachel Walker had been introduced into Halévy's circle by the Fishers, also long-standing friends of Halévy's.

TO MARIE BERLIN

[?July 1935]

All Souls

Dear Ma

I am working hard & well. Here absolute stillness, I occasionally see Pares (whom you once asked if he was my pupil) and Hardie whom you like. Mr Bowra being gone life is tranquil. Marx is a *very* Jewish character. His bad early poems, his satire of society, his sentimentality snobbery & learning, all *so* like Jacob Schapiro,[1] as I wrote you before. Even the antisemitism of both. Miss Averbach has written again.[2] This time I think I will again ignore her letter, or answer formally. It is not my fault if she wants to speak of her inmost feelings to someone. I am *not* a suitable confidant for young women, & would hate to get into a false position. But you may rely on it, I shall act, if anything, too frigidly. You must have a Nachkur:[3] if at the beginning of August I may come & stay with you. You must eat more, that is clear, otherwise weakness + depression. I am *very* well. Father seems well too, though very bored.

love
Shaya

TO MARIE BERLIN

[Late July 1935]

All Souls

Dear Mama:

Thank you very much for your two letters, Beethoven Denkmal,[4] picture of yourself (which I find ravissant) the article on R. Strauss etc.

I am still working well. You speak of Masaryk's book on Marx:[5] the only other person I know who talked about it was the late Shmarya Levin in Jerusalem who said it was very good. I must read it, but German books,

---

1 Jacob Salwyn Schapiro (1879–1973), a Professor of History at the City University of New York, wrote a number of books on intellectual history.
2 The eighteen-year-old Hilda Averbach had most recently written on 5 May and 27 June 1935, from Haifa in Israel. She describes her father as 'an old friend of your mother's from Riga, years ago', and adds 'We met you in London about three and a half years ago.' Hilda asks for advice about studying in London, but then decides on a course at the Hebrew University in Jerusalem, for financial reasons.
3 'Convalescence' (after the health cure in Karlsbad now in progress).
4 'Memorial.' Possibly a small plaster bust: IB collected many such and some he painted blue.
5 T. G. Masaryk, *Otázka sociální: zklady marxismu, filosofické a sociologické* ['The social question: philosophical and social foundations of Marxism'] (Prague, 1898).

especially long ones, this one is 400 or so pages frighten me. Perhaps you would be kind enough to get it for me & bring it? or, better, have it sent. Anything on Marx even by Masaryk who is anti-Marx, may not be safe to take through Germany. But could you order it to be sent to me, in some Karlsbad bookshop? I should be grateful, & you would pay less in crowns than I in shillings. Yes Oxford is empty, warm and delightful. Everything is subdued and pianissimo, even conversation has taken on a sort of matt hue. Meanwhile I am perplexed with a dilemma: there has been an air accident recently[1] & a man called Mr Newhouse aged 55 was killed. Hans New-house stockbroker. Is he or is he not the father of Willie Martin's wife?[2] if he is I must write and condole, if not how dreadful if I do. I do not know how to find out, but I'll try. All my pupils are having their viva voce exam-inations now, & run in excitedly to tell me what has happened to them. There is no news. A public scandal has broken out about there not being enough food at one of the Naval receptions:[3] a photograph of the French Ambassador offering the Portuguese ambassador a few cold peas, very funny. No doubt important officials will now be dismissed. Where, after all, do you intend to have a Nachkur? you really ought to have one, I do not care if it is the local doctor's method of enriching the Czech exchequer, yet it can do you only good. Please don't hurry home, father is lonely, but bears up, I visit him at week-ends. I must now go – & have a haircut. My appearance is very respectable these days.

    yrs
        love,
            Shaya

I did *not* know that Strauss's schwiegertochter[4] is a Jewess! they are all idiots.

IB's work on Marx was interrupted by an attack of quinsy, for which he was treated in a nursing home; on his recovery he travelled to Salzburg to join a group of friends. He returned home via Paris.

---

1 On 16 July, reported in *The Times* of 17 July, 14.
2 Margery Martin née Newhouse was indeed the daughter of this accident victim. According to IB she later married a Mr Brown of the British Museum.
3 Perhaps held in connection with the Anglo-German naval accord, signed on 8 June, whereby the Germans were permitted to build up their naval resources.
4 Daughter-in-law. Richard Strauss was associated with the Nazis.

TO LETTICE FISHER

27 August 1935

Achenseehof, Tyrol

Dear Mrs Fisher

I ought to have thanked you long ago for the letter you sent to the Acland[1] – I cannot tell you how nice it is to receive sympathetic notes if one has quinsies; that and the visit of Prof. Lightfoot[2] were my chief comforts in what was otherwise really extremely disagreeable. I do not know how I came to acquire a quinsy. Tonsilitis with which I began sounds somehow quite respectable, but quinsy, I always thought, is what butlers' mothers & very small children principally tend to get, and really my life has been blamelessly regular – I expect I talked too much. It is the only explanation which seems to me at all plausible and in character.

I hurried off to Salzburg as soon as I was able – it is the only town in which I know that I shall be entirely happy all the time – and found Mary and B.J. there looking extremely well and beautiful and happy. Richard Pares, who stayed in the same hotel, can always be counted on to be very good and courteous company, Toscanini was really magnificent, we all enjoyed ourselves a very great deal. We have now moved off to this lake until Saturday: both B.J. and Mary look as well and appear to be as contented as they were in Ireland, which is saying a vast deal. It really is a most heavenly place with very dramatic mountains and very blue water and wheeling buzzards to keep B.J. happy, we all hope that Christopher may visit us on his way back from Vienna, but I expect his every hour is counted, he probably has appointments with pupils at every important town en route where he gives them rapid tutorials, we shall be regarded as a mere pleasure & brushed aside.

yours
Isaiah Berlin

TO ELIZABETH BOWEN

Thursday [shortly before 27 September 1935][3]

49 Hollycroft Avenue

Dear Elizabeth

My family has retired to bed early this evening and I am reduced to

---

1 The Acland Home, a private nursing home (later a hospital) in the Banbury Road, Oxford.
2 Revd Robert Henry Lightfoot (1883–1953), Fellow of New College 1921–49, Ireland Professor of Exegesis of Holy Scripture 1934–49, also for some of this period Tutor and Chaplain.
3 The date of EB's reply.

twiddling with my wireless and wondering irritably about my book, the
shadows of which grow bigger & bigger. Having rationally persuaded myself
that this was futile I sat down, like Maurice, to count up my gains & losses
this summer. Everything was slightly out of joint, as a result of my Acland
days I daresay. Salzburg was really very comic. I arrived to be met by six
persons most of whom had by that time settled comfortably into mutually
antagonistic cliques. I have never seen young women persecute one another
before, nor been put into the embarrassing position of having openly to
protect the victim. She was a technically pretty, rather repulsive young
woman, who had had a success in America, but here was dreadfully snubbed
by many highbrows, therefore tinkled & exclaimed incessantly, read aloud,
shrieked with pleasure, plainly believed that womanliness was enough. She
was chaperoned by a hideous but intelligent young duenna, with a face like
something in an elongating mirror, 28 or so years old, of difficult French-
Jewish origin (like your Mr Ebhart[1] but of that later), persecuted to
a degree, who used to visit me late at night to inquire if I knew what the
meaning of the word love was, or how one could bring oneself to surrender
one's everything to a practically unknown man, & what she would do if she
were ravished (actual word used) in a forest. This last is so hypothetical a fact
that at one point I was obliged to leave the room & compose my features:
the place was full of English musical men and persons with villas near
Venice; Stephen burst into my delicately poised party, surrounded by boys &
girls. Every year he tends to have ghastly American admirers trailing after
him: but this year he definitely arrived surrounded by a semi-permanent
collection of worshippers. Tony was eliminated I don't know how or why,
& Stephen wandered loosely attended by 2 young women, an elderly spinster, and two ludicrous little boys, one Giles Romilly[2] who broke out of
bounds, you remember, the other a Cambridge poet: I now know what is
required to attract Stephen, in women at least; a long 'poetical' face, slow
speech, & snaky black locks. He kept interrupting all his remarks with 'where
are the girls?" or "where are the boys"? & talked interestingly but a little too
heavily about Hölderlin[3] before a large wandering audience, of whom

1 Max Ebhart, hero of EB's *The House in Paris* (133/3): see p. 135 below.
2 An allusion to *Out of Bounds*, a periodical opposed to the ethos of public schools, started in
   1934 by Esmond Romilly (1918–41), younger brother of Giles Samuel Bertram Romilly
   (1916–67), after he had absconded from his own school, Wellington, at the age of fifteen.
   Giles was a contributor, and in November 1935 they published a joint book, also entitled *Out
   of Bounds*, containing their brief autobiographies, in the course of which they describe their
   education and their conversion to radicalism. Giles was also at Wellington, then a classical
   scholar at Lincoln from 1934 to 1936, when he left suddenly for Spain, without sitting any
   examinations: see further *Lincoln College Record*, 1966–7, pp. 28–9. During the war he was
   held in Colditz Castle for two years as an important prisoner-of-war (he was a nephew of
   Churchill), and subsequently testified at Nüremberg.
3 (Johann Christian) Friedrich Hölderlin (1770–1843), German poet.

only B.J. was prepared to sit & uncritically worship. Miss Graves[1] arrived for an afternoon & did not go down at all with Stephen. She is definitely not poetical I fear. He thought her too mondaine. She is very intelligent about Maurice, thinks she is not his style, & intends to drop out: her mother has just died in Germany, ought one to write, but how can one. The music which was wonderful crystallised for me, as for all the Americans etc. into vulgar Toscanini worship. I bought 20 postcards of him & look at them occasionally with great naiveté & feeling. From Salzburg I escaped gratefully to the Achensee in the Tyrol. Save that I was pursued by the black duenna who forced me to make intelligent conversation all the time, which was tiresome. I went to Paris, saw Mary Fisher off to Dieppe where she was met by her friend Henriette Noufflard:[2] imagine my excitement when on opening your book[3] shortly after, Miss Fisher & Henrietta occurred at once. I enjoyed this latter enormously & I own painfully, since my experiences in the last fortnight were in some respects too similar to certain things which you describe with fearful acuteness, so that real events & descriptions in your book became fused into a very heightened but very painful state of consciousness. I have at least, temporarily, put an end to my relations with Miss Walker. I think I have behaved self-indulgently and badly, she was plainly terrified of me and under the most passionate illusion that her life must be dedicated to my happiness. Our meeting in the Zoo opposite the Python was exciting and tormenting in the extreme. Your remark about the seriousness & literalness of inter-racial conversation is absolutely true. I was conscious of talking with vast effort throughout, entirely unaware of any.effect my words had (a very unfamiliar sensation,) & also of talking the most dreadful & unintelligible elaborate nonsense throughout. We went on aiming at each other, missing mostly, with desperate gravity. Dear me. I can't possibly marry her. She thinks I can. We should be miserable at once. The last scene in which I forced myself to be sensible & pedestrian & analyse the situation calmly & declare that I must stop, was awful beyond words. I always found I had to begin afresh, & talked almost of the weather, to begin with. Then a silence. Then I would get up & make as if to go. We both felt that something had to be said. We gulped & floundered & I felt unscrupulous & a cad. The climax was reached when she inquired how far my recent declarations resembled my final end with Sigle Lynd.[4] It was

1 Elizabeth Leila Millicent ('Sally') Graves (b. 1914), Somerville history 1932–5, married Richard Chilver 1937; later Principal of Bedford College, London (1964–71), and LMH (1971–9).
2 Dr Henriette Noufflard was a niece of Elie Halévy.
3 *The House in Paris* (Gollancz, 1935). The characters include Henrietta Mountjoy, an English child travelling through Paris, and Naomi Fisher, the half-English half-French fiancée of the hero, Max Ebhart.
4 IB had become briefly attached to Sigle Lynd in a repressed way in summer 1931: see MI 57.

past all bearing. But I was always in love with her when with her, & in a state of electric excitement for days after, but not for weeks. The affair with Sigle was relatively plain & vulgar. We understood each other perfectly, & her complaints of ill treatment lifted some of the burden of guilt from me. (my coldness in recording all this is really shocking). In the case of Miss Walker, the whole was really much more real & splendid & much the most shaking experience I shall ever have. The fact that I, the umbrella & general uncle should have been metamorphosed into a protagonist, frequently struck me as unreal. Dear me, what silly difficulties arose. I once sent her 3 books, Tolstoy's Childhood & Youth, Les Enfants Terribles, & The Awkward Age.[1] I am grossly insensitive (that really is true: to have a thin skin & be insensitive, a quality I share with K. Marx), & never thought of the effect of juxtaposing these. It was taken to be a brutal insinuation of her infantilism etc. & I was v. nearly sent De Senectute[2] which wd have been funny & good. Do you know I never thought of the Awkward Age as meaning what it does mean, but {a} rather a brilliant description of a historical period. And the fate of the 2 girls in it – plainly my prognostication of her future – appears to have driven her to a pitch of dementia. Her mother was shocked to discover the book in the house. It is repulsive, of course, I do think, I hadn't read it when I sent it.

Anyone who regards my conduct as symbolic or meaningful makes big mistakes, oof I honestly cannot live on such mountains. I have always sympathised with my fellow-corpulents, Pierre Besuhoff, Sancho, even William in Night & Day, & hated the Prince Andrés and Del Dongos.[3] Miss Walker having gone to stay with a Sir A. Lawrence[4] in Venice, I am, like a low organism which grows limbs, recovering frightfully fast. I am not sure that the visit to Paris was not an error, but I am, of course, glad to have committed it. The oddity is that never never did we climb down from off our exalted plane into any pedestrian valleys, though even she must spend most of her life in such, disapprovingly. (the last sentence is in Humphry rhythm). I do not deny that it is with some pride & pleasure that I am able to look down on sub-lives & sub-romances such as go trailing on through London &

1 The latter books are by Jean Cocteau and Henry James.
2 'On Old Age', by Cicero.
3 Pierre Bezukhov and Prince Andrey Bolkonsky are characters in Tolstoy's *War and Peace*, Sancho Panza is Don Quixote's squire in Cervantes' novel, William Rodney appears in Virginia Woolf's novel *Night and Day*, and Fabrice del Dongo is the hero of Stendhal's *Charterhouse of Parma*.
4 Sir Alexander (Waldermar) Lawrence (1874–1939), a graduate of New College and a Justice of the Peace in the county of Somerset. One of his three residences was in Asolo, in the Veneto, north of Padua.

Dublin between B.J. & Mr Guinness[1] on & on. Yes, Maurice, who curtly opened relations by writing: we ought to enter into correspondence, after observing that the Portuguese were naive & very, very disillusioned, & that they built & demolished walls in your bedroom while you were in bed, reported that Roy had nearly got married this summer to someone typically described only as being somewhere between the Upper Middle & Upper Class: Miss Headlam Morley we ask ourselves? dear Maurice he is a very good wise man, & Mr Eliot doesn't think he will be Professor of Greek after all. This would be a bad thing. For our own sakes he must become something grand soon. Is Leopold like Freddie in appearance?[2] I am sure, as a child, he may well have behaved so. I suddenly thought of Freddie as my child by Miss Walker & did laugh aloud, & was asked by my mother what I was laughing at, & had to produce a reply, & said that I had met an American who had said "I was told Popes lived at Avignon. But I reckon that can't be so, for if they had, it would have been heard of." Dear me how silly I am becoming. Have you ever read the work of Karin Michaelis?[3] she is a living & famous Danish author I believe. A Danish Jewess even perhaps, very rare & interesting. And Braithwaite.[4] All these lovely known names, Miss Fisher, Henrietta, etc. save that Mme Fisher (who really is wonderful of you I think. The conversations are really bloodfreezing & fascinating. My future course with Miss W. is directly & deeply influenced by this book. Which you can certainly not have intended. Nor will I believe that you can possibly know how much there is contained in that book) is not at all like Mrs H. A. L. Fisher. Who wrote a collection of very kind, very nauseating letters.

Max is a macabre character whom I'm grateful not to resemble, altogether the effect on me is of a play where one identifies oneself with situations & characters, about which one has nightmares & dreams, in terms of which one talks for a long character [*sic*], having torn the characters from their contexts & made them operate like marionettes of one's own. Freddie-Leopold has stuck in my head. But I do think altogether that it is an

---

1 Bryan Guinness, who, between the end of his first marriage (to Diana Mitford) and his second, was one of BJ's admirers.

2 Leopold Grant Moody is the hyper-analytic, hyper-curious illegitimate child of Max Ebhart and the heroine, Karen Michaelis, in *The House in Paris*: IB seems to see A. J. ('Freddie') Ayer as a possible model.

3 Karin Michaelis (1872–1950), Danish novelist, author of *Den farlige alder* ('The dangerous age'), 1910. Presumably EB had read KM's book and borrowed her name for her heroine. The hero, Max, is a brilliant French-Jewish financier who commits suicide; much is made of the racial divide between Max and the very English Karen, with whom he is in love – hence IB's comments, and indeed his powerful reaction to the novel, which he evidently read in terms of his relationship with Rachel Walker.

4 In the novel, butler to the Michaelis family at their house in Chester Terrace, Regent's Park, London: for the real-life Braithwaite see letter to John Hilton of 14 March 1935.

absorbing & fascinating book, which, as soon as I am sufficiently composed, I shall read again. And if you will let me, talk to you about.

I wish I could come to Ireland. But my father is in Moscow,[1] & I can't leave my mother, who is vaguely unwell, though very gay. I hear you have Mr Plomer[2] who I am persuaded is nice, intelligent & gay. I really must settle down in Oxford to the tranquil life which it is the general impression that I lead. No young women. It really is disturbing if one is so anxious to please as I. A delightful vista of empty boring days & walks with Maurice. When shall I see you? it really depends on you now, you know. I shall go to Oxford roughly on the 1st Oct. When do you come to Town? this has been much the most serious summer in my life. I am plainly an extravert & hate real experiences. But against that is the fact that, as in this letter, I seem unable to discuss anything but myself. It is awful, I apologize.

Shaya

I ask you: have *you* ever been in an atmosphere in which everything you say & do is symbolic, portentously important, frightfully serious, decisive?

TO JOHN HILTON

[received 13 October 1935]

49 Hollycroft Avenue

Dearest John:

This is far from proper.[3] You must, I suppose, have been appointed in a fit of conscience on the part of the Bucklers[4] etc. & corresponding un-popularity of Gunness etc. a year, having elapsed, & sense of guilt ap-peased, the original crooks came up again. When I see Mr Buckler I shall cross-examine him disagreeably. No, I have made no new friends: as you think I have trouble enough as it is to keep them at peace with [each] other: which I do by urging everyone all the time to put all the cards on the table:

---

1 In connection with his timber business.

2 The writer William Plomer (1903–73), a close friend of EB, had been staying at Bowen's Court.

3 By this time JRH had been told that his probation was terminated, though he was allowed to say he was resigning. In the undated letter to which IB is here replying, JRH doesn't know who his replacement will be, but reports that 'The Daily Mirror gossip column has already referred to a "Nigel Gunnis, director general of antiquities in Cyprus".'

4 William Hepburn Buckler (1867–1952), American lawyer teaching archaeology at Balliol 1925–52, and his wife Georgina. JRH writes: 'Through a set of curious chances I was known to Buckler [. . .] and professors Beazley, Wace and Norman Baynes. Architecture was in slump. Though regarding myself as a pioneer of "modern architecture", I was offered simultaneously a philosophy lectureship at Birmingham and – after vetting by George Hill of the BM and Charles Peers of the Office of Works, Ancient Monuments branch – the Cyprus job (with a warning from Hill about Gunnis).' JRH to the editor, 7 November 1991.

a disreputable occupation, I own, but occasionally enjoyable. My summer was peculiar: I am trying desperately to write a book on Marx: & find myself (a) unable to write at all for at least an hour after settling to, (b) when I begin I suddenly let loose a flood of words about Rousseau's influence on the romantic style, & then remember that the relevance needs proving. It really is torture: anyhow I spent a month thus, & then fell ill of the quinzy as I daresay I wrote: & then went to Salzburg where my companions were jealous and I went about in a haze, partly induced by disordered tonsils, partly by the emotional tensity of the whole fortnight: which was not ended in England where I was suddenly turned from the observer & Figaro of situations into an active agent: which was so sudden & surprising that, with horror, I observed the unbelievable callowness & naiveté with which I, without any doubt whatever, continued to act. This period is also left behind however. Erica Mrs Crossman was in Salzburg, her introduction of one to her man was so curious: she used in previous years to call him her uncle: but this year she merely said 'this is my . . . er . . . my . . . er?' & then a lot of leering etc. all rather agreeable. Toscanini, however, is the greatest man in the world. I met Warden Fisher in Bond Street yesterday, & he inquired as to whom I thought the greatest man etc. I said unhesitatingly 'Toscanini', is it possible that he was offended? I should, I suppose, have referred to someone lately dead.

What do you really intend to do if & when you return (will you let me know?): let me acquaint you with the state of the philosophical slave market: Price has been promoted to Joachim's professorship, & there is consequently a vacancy at Trinity: Balliol is decomposing in some way: Fulton has gone to U.S.A. for a year, and Morris[1] is muttering about wanting to go & slum somewhere (which reminds me of a report in the Irish Press of Mrs Elizabeth Pakenham's speech,[2] to a lot of farmers, on the insufficiently active part played by women "there are only 2 female philosophy dons in Oxford' she observed 'the only place I know much about'. Very odd.), there is, I believe a lectureship under Professor Heath[3] in Swansea, I believe; and also there is a Professorship at Cairo at £E950 p.a., minus seventy or so pounds for 'stamp duties'. that is all I personally know, Hardie may know a little more: your substitute at Birmingham is a disaster.

The literary world is shaken by the creation of the Group theatre[4] to

1 Charles Richard Morris (1898–1990), philosopher, Fellow and classics Tutor, Balliol, 1922–41.
2 Elizabeth Pakenham (1906–2002), née Harman, married to Frank since 1931, lectured for the Workers' Educational Association 1929–35.
3 Archie Edward Heath (1887–1961), Professor of Philosophy, University College of Swansea, 1925–52.
4 Innovative theatre company which commissioned and performed works by leading writers

produce Mr Eliot, Auden & such: The first night of Sweeney Agonistes + The Dance of Death, was remarkable chiefly for its audience: they were all pure Oxford 1927–28, supported by a certain quantity of Promenaders: it looked like the regular Punch picture of aesthetes: have you read the Dance of Death, or The Dog Beneath the Skin?[1] the latter contains intercalary poems which I think are very good: and a great deal of patter not as good as Gilbert, sub-Coward sometimes: both works are undoubtedly written to help struggling humanity in some way: it is very difficult to say which way: action seems to be preached: & so people sunbathe, live artily etc. etc. because one must act: so also Mr Auden writes because one must be doing: I can extract nothing more: in The Dog there are 2 inefficient parodies of Nazis, & heavy blows aimed at the Public School Man: the Jewish financier & other cardboard figures enter: the dialogue is just not slick enough: there the most moving speech by far is put in the mouth of the enemy: so too in the D. of Death: it is as though Auden, fundamentally a patriotic poet, writes most eloquently when vaguely fascist, & conscientiously has to transfer this to the enemy because people he respects are all left-wing. The general atmosphere of the Auden–Eliot revival stirred me to pompous ideological reflection: it really was very much as I imagine Berlin in 1926–7 was, the same eager & hobohemian audience, the same rather thin acting. Dr Goebbels[2] wd have found it all very unhealthy This, cyclically pursued, threatens Fascism in England in 1942 or thereabout, unless it collapses elsewhere first: a curious race of objective tendencies, a ballet of historical universals & the like which I daresay someone could write quite well. Or is it more orthodox Marxism to maintain that the sated imperialist powers, having smashed up their hungrier younger rivals, & induced left wing revolutions in them, then go Fascist themselves as the last technique for keeping hard won gains & preserving the status quo? I don't understand world movements, & everyone seems to be blandly discussing the imminent collapse of European civilization, though I cannot see what can possibly be meant: this is becoming like a Topsy letter.[3]

Do go & visit Jerusalem before you return, if you can, it is very

including Auden, Eliot, Isherwood, MacNeice and Spender. This double bill – Auden's *The Dance of Death* (London, 1933) and Eliot's *Sweeney Agonistes* (London, 1932) – ran at London's Westminster Theatre 1–12 October.

1 *The Dog Beneath the Skin* was written for the Group Theatre, who performed the play in 1936, also at the Westminster.

2 (Paul) Joseph Goebbels (1897–1945), Nazi Minister for Public Enlightenment and Propaganda 1933–45, who was trying to cleanse the arts in Germany of everything alien to the Nazi ideal.

3 A. P. Herbert's *The Trials of Topsy* (London, 1928) collects his fictional letters from Topsy to Trix, first published in *Punch*. Their style is somewhat breathless and uncomprehending, and there are many malapropisms. An example from the first page (p. 7) of the first letter, 'A Brush with the Highbrows': 'last night I went to a perfectly *fallacious* party with the Antons, my dear all Russians and High Art and beards and everything'.

handsome: the Dead Sea is definitely stunning, & in Tel-Aviv, unless you also have atavistic longings like Sir A. Mond's daughter,[1] there is nothing enjoyable save the ice-cream: they say that Mitzpaz is a good orangeade. Do not wear a cork hat since you will be taken for a newly arrived clothes-proud immigrant from Bukuresti,[2] or else an adviser to a small Sheik, they have to wear them because of the mistakeable appearance of the rest of their clothes. I must plainly stop [. . .]

My love to Peggy, will you let me know when you return: I have two really funny stories about Irish persons.

yours

Shaya

TO MARY FISHER

[Mid-October 1935]

All Souls

Dear Mary

Can you mean Puvis de Chavannes?[3] an appalling painter, grey-blue in colour. But the degree of depression reached by me in reading that book has never, can never (yet) have been equalled. I am reviewing a book which makes embarrassing jokes all the time which set one's teeth on edge:[4] I hardly like to commit them to paper, as Sparrow wd say: words like: Mendelssohnnies, Schumannikins, Stravinskyttens. The author is a respectable British composer, about as Dutch as G. N. Clark, called Van Dieren. Where I cannot conceive the state of mind I cannot even criticise: I am not sure that, to some extent, is not the case with regard to the House in Paris.[5] However not this was the original end of this letter: but will you, for God's sake etc., come to lunch on Sunday + Miss Sée?[6] I've written to her; or would this displease your mother excessively in view of the 1st group of undergraduates etc.[7] If so I offer Monday instead (I was written to by

1 A reference to one of the three daughters of Sir Alfred Moritz Mond (1868–1930), 1st Baronet 1910, 1st Baron Melchett 1928. Mustapha Mond in Aldous Huxley's *Brave New World* was named after him.

2 Bucharest.

3 Pierre Puvis de Chavannes (1824–98), French mural painter.

4 Bernard van Dieren, *Down Among the Dead Men*. The review, entitled 'Musiciens d'autrefois', appeared in the *Spectator*, 1 November 1935, p. 732 (see also IB's letter in the 29 November issue, p. 906).

5 Elizabeth Bowen's novel.

6 Anne Sée, sister of Peter (140/1), was encountered by MF, BJ and IB in Salzburg earlier in 1935, and joined them on a trip to the Achensee.

7 The Fishers usually had an undergraduate lunch party on Sundays in term. The first such party this academic year would have been on 13 or 20 October.

her & invited to invite her, & I must have support). I do not know who else
to ask, Richard Pares, Christopher; Maurice says he hates Peter Sée[1] &
definitely would dislike meeting Anne. So that is that. If we have it on
Monday, I am afraid Guy may not come. Which would be too unusual.
I shan't take steps about the others, if any, until you answer. Could you ring
up before lunch? I should be touchingly grateful. I found myself to-night in
the foyer of the Queen's Hall crushed against & gazing into the eyes of Mr
Rink.[2] As a result of entertaining candidates I have amassed a whole lot of
new points against Wykehamists.

    yrs
        Shaya

*Music was a lifelong passion for IB and he often wrote about it. His
earliest published pieces were the 'Music Chronicle' section of the* Oxford
Outlook, *which he wrote from 1930 to 1932, initially under the
pseudonym 'Albert Alfred Apricott'.[3] From 1934 he wrote occasional
reviews of books on music for the* Spectator. *But the need for a wireless,
mentioned in several of the following letters, is more likely to relate to his
reviews of concerts and gramophone records which appeared at intervals
in the* Oxford Magazine *from 1936 until he left Oxford in 1940.*

TO MARIE BERLIN

    [Early November 1935]

                                                            All Souls

Dear Mother
    Thank you for your letter: in voting, as we have no liberal candidate,
I shall vote for J. L. Stocks,[4] a professor of philosophy in Manchester, who
loves the Jews & is standing as a socialist: actually he is a mildly pink liberal.
I am very well having lost my cold completely: I met Dr Hobson[5] at a
concert & was tenderly inquired after. Ettinghausen is slowly recovering. It
is very good about being a musical critic! if you really can manage it. As for
father's question about how do I know about Busoni[6] I admit I got all that

---

1 Peter Henri Sée (1910–63), New College classics 1929–33, Harmsworth Law Scholar 1933–4,
    called to the Bar 1935.
2 George Arnold Rink (1902–83), barrister, an unwelcome admirer of Rachel Walker.
3 Conceivably inspired by Alan Albert Antisdel Blakeway (50/2)?
4 John Leofric Stocks (1882–1937), Fellow and Tutor, St John's, 1906–24, Professor of
    Philosophy, Manchester, 1924–37, Vice-Chancellor, Liverpool, 1937; unsuccessful Labour
    candidate for Oxford University 1935.
5 Dr Frederick Greig Hobson (1891–1961), doctor to IB and many other dons; drank, and had a
    poor reputation.
6 Ferruccio Dante Michelangelo Benvenuto Busoni (1866–1924), Italian pianist and composer.

from the v. reliable Rachmilevich.[1] I wd rather not come to London if possible: but if you feel worried abt. my health, let father come & *dine* with me on a weekday. he can take the 4.45 train up (or 5.15) & return by the 9.37 p.m., say on Saturday even. That will convince you.

Au revoir

Shaya.

I am glad action is being taken about chairs, I never thought my sharp letter wd have effect, but you see!

Re wireless: it will *not* disturb work, only keep me more in my rooms which is desirable. I wrote a v. nice letter abt. Beloff[2] to Corpus, & he is grateful. I.B.

I return here on circa 15th *Dec.* but don't come home till Jan, why spend horrible Xmas in England.

TO STEPHEN SPENDER

Wednesday [13 November 1935]

All Souls

Dear Stephen

I am far from being altogether happy having sprained a toe, so that I hobble miserably about and read too much and meditate on the psychology of cripples & how interesting it might be to be one for a short terminable period. I shall, however, be entirely well by the time you arrive, that is certain. The only difficulty is about Sunday night: having promised dinner to my guest in Hall, I cannot now very well not give it him there: Maurice will be in Cambridge; what I shd really like wd be for you to lunch with me on Sunday (I cd invite anyone you wanted or nobody) + Tony, & dine or sup with the Carritts.[3] Is that feasible? if not, I prefer to give you dinner myself + my guest who will probably be too enchanted to meet you to mind about Hall. Cd you let me know? this is a very bogus fuss that I am making: but if you could go to the Carritts for supper & return circa 10.30 or so (taxis are very cheap in Oxford now), that wd be ideal. But do let me know at once.

1 Solomon Rachmilevich (usually known as 'Rach') (*c*.1892–1953), a Russian Jewish intellectual born in Riga and living in exile in London, was a close and influential friend of IB, whom he met through the Schalits. In his preface to his book on Marx IB thanks him for his help; he also said: 'He was the first person who gave me a taste for ideas in general, interesting ideas *tel quel*' (MI Tape 6). See also MI 42–4.

2 Max Beloff (1913–99), CCC history 1932–5, later (1981) Baron Beloff of Wolvercote; he took a First in 1935.

3 Edgar Frederick Carritt (1876–1964), Fellow and Praelector in Philosophy, Univ., was for a while Stephen Spender's tutor.

I look forward to you & Tony exceedingly. [Cyril] Connolly's review of a don's novel in the last New Statesman[1] is the funniest & cleverest thing I've ever read. Perhaps it comes of knowing the man: but C.'s malice is definitely a social asset. It is sad, like Maurice to hate Connolly so much that one refuses to enjoy his malice. I tried to persuade him that if one hates two men it is agreeable to see the snakes coiled round each other but he seems dubious. The same number has an awful passage abt. Oxford by Dadie Rylands.[2] When I pointed this out to Maurice he said: "Shut up. I write like that myself'.

 love.
  Shaya

TO MARIE BERLIN

 Tuesday. [mid/late November 1935]

               All Souls

Dear Ma

 Thank you for your letter & pamphlet.[3] I read the pamphlet in its original form when it appeared in the Times, it is *very* outspoken, but still does not tell all. Last night I spoke to the Jewish Society[4] – it was a *very* crowded meeting. I think I pleased quite well: except for one remark of mine about the dirty condition of the streets of Tel-Aviv & its chaotic buildings, which gave offence to somebody, so I withdrew about half of it. Otherwise I think they liked me. I must ask Sebba[5] to tea. Levine[6] I completely forgot about: I knew he was coming & vaguely intended to go, but forgot. I am rather sorry, but there it is. Perhaps if you see him you could tell him

---

1 Cyril Connolly, 'New Novels', New Statesman, 9 November 1935, 699–700, starts with a review of J. C. Masterman, Fate Cannot Harm Me (London, 1935).

2 George ('Dadie') Rylands (216/1), in 'An Ambitious Anthology' – a review of The New Book of English Verse (London, 1935) – writes of (Arthur) Q(uiller-Couch)'s The Oxford Book of English Verse, 1250–1900 (Oxford, 1900): 'Q's counsellor was the adorable dreamer, whose heart has been so romantic, who has given herself so prodigally but never to the Philistines; the beautiful city, so unravaged by the fierce intellectual life of the century, so serene; the Oxford of Newman, Arnold, Jowett, Pater.'

3 Unidentified.

4 An undergraduate society.

5 Sam Sebba (b. 1915), St John's law 1934–7, came from Riga like IB and knew him before they met at Oxford, where Sebba took his turn as President of the Jewish Society. He also attended St Paul's School.

6 The Revd Ephraim Levine (1885–1966), Minister of the New West End Synagogue (9/1), author and noted orator.

that I had hurt my foot & could not walk that day (it is true: I bruised my toe, & though it has completely passed now, it was painful for about 2 days, I even had a masseur to do it, who did it very well. It was not a real injury, only I hit it against a stone; I can no longer remember now what it even felt like; I was otherwise quite well, but could not walk for about 2 days.). *Wireless*: do do something PLEASE: I can do *nothing*: reviewing musical books in non-musical magazines is not a sufficient cause. You can say anything, but I am sure it will not help. But do do it soon, I want to have it still this term. Please. As for father, would he consider coming next Sunday? I am out to lunch, so perhaps it is a not v. good idea: why shouldn't he take the 4.45 train from London on, say, Monday, or later even, say the 5 something, arriving about 7 & dine with me here, & then go back at 9.30 or so? it is much the most convenient for me, I am sure. But do do something re wireless.

    love.

       Shaya.

I enclose Russian stamps, off some books my colleague sent me.

    I cannot tell you *how well I am at the moment*. Hair cut, nails clean etc.

TO MARIE AND MENDEL BERLIN

    [Late November 1935]

                                      All Souls

My dear Pa & Ma.

    I am really perfectly well. (1) Re the visit: If all you wd like is to see me, I might contrive to come & dine with you next Monday; if on the other hand father wishes definitely to come here, then I suggest Sunday the 1st Dec.

    To-morrow 2 Jews, Mr Isaac Saul & Mr Abraham Harman[1] are coming to tea with me. Solidarity.

    Wireless: I *cannot* say to the local people: I am a musical person, I write reviews etc. I'll try if you like, but if I fail, have I your authority to order a set for the full price? please authorize. Ettinghausen is better. I have no more to tell you really, at the moment, at all.

    love,

       yrs

          Shaya

---

1 Avraham Harman (1914–92), British-born, later Israeli diplomat (Ambassador to US 1960–7), subsequently President of the Hebrew University, Jerusalem. Isaac Saul is unidentified.

I am sorry if I sounded brusque on the telephone to-day, but I was covered with shaving soap!

TO MARIE BERLIN

[Late November 1935]

All Souls

Dear Ma,

I am now *perfectly* well. *All* traces of cold have left me. With regard to McMichael,[1] I cannot possibly write myself to anybody. You see I am *not* a musical critic & to say that I am (reviewing books on music is not = musical criticism) would be legally prosecutable as obtaining money under false pretences, what *you* do I am not responsible for, if necessary I can always say I knew nothing about it, so your dealings with Mr Jenks do not concern me. So please tell him to send me a set, the earlier the better. If he wants to know why I cannot write say I am away or ill or anything you like. I simply must not get involved in inaccurate statements.

love

yrs

Shaya

TO JENIFER WILLIAMS

[November 1935?]

All Souls

I enclose a document which may give you a little mild pleasure.[2] The whole letter is of a courtliness which pleases me more than I can say. How nice it is when old men are ceremonious. But you disagree, I expect. How unlike this Douglas's letter will be in 1970. The pencilled superscription[3] belongs to Mr Bowra & is one of his best known ways of clarifying the read & the unread, + the implication that the read should be removed, so that he may not have to rummage on one's table if one is out only to fish out tedious familiar stuff.

I.B.

1 A make of wireless.
2 A letter from George James Turner (1867–1946), lawyer (Ford's Lecturer, Oxford, 1937), a Visiting Fellow of All Souls, inviting IB to dinner. A PS reads: 'You no doubt noticed the name of Jenifer F.W in 1st class in the History Schools last summer.'
3 'Noted'.

TO STUART HAMPSHIRE

[1935?]

All Souls

[. . .]¹ a chalet turn, & we agreed that William III knew his stuff & would have got congratulated by the P.P.E. examiners though not a friend of any of them, & Henry VIII & Elizabeth would also, & George II wd have got a bad second, & Victoria would be viva'd for a first & not get it, and James I would get a second as a clever fool, & Charles II a second for being a Villiers, & Stephen a fourth, etc. I enjoyed it very much, I remember.

I don't believe Macaulay² was a reactionary at all. He may have been an intolerable character & got everything wrong, but his scale of values was constructed by reference to an ideal which was of the right kind i.e. (a) not reactionary in the Cobbett–Belloc–Fascist³ sense (b) not dreary & vulgar in the Wells–Huxley⁴ sense or else merely verbal, collections of attributes etc. which make all utopias unreadable (c) above all not consisting in rules i.e. moralistic and irrational & ugly. You may say that he is smug and self-deceived almost literally deafened & taken in by his own rhetoric. Possibly. His actual ideal may be disreputable, crude, unimaginative, worthless. Anybody, you will say, who resisted Benthamism then was doing so for consciously or unconsciously disreputable motives i.e. desire to escape from the truth, fear of being expelled from a profitable fiction etc. This, I think, is quite true. Nevertheless there are some forms of cowardice infinitely more sympathetic than others. Plato also escaped, particularly in the Laws which is a cold blooded ignoration of moral issues, but his asylum is really repulsive.

The virtues of Macaulay reside in the fact that the words, images etc. which he stopped doubts with are idealistic in the proper sense, that is to say, not mere words to him, not, as you allege, revolutionary phrases turned into weapons of reaction (which is Fascism) but retaining the greater part of their original meaning, and capable of being used for radical ends without modification: only they are used as if they described an actual state of affairs, hence self-satisfaction etc. when in fact they don't and it may be criminal

---

1 Beginning of letter missing.
2 Thomas Babington Macaulay (1800–c.1860), 1st Baron Macaulay, English poet, historian, Whig politician and advocate of political reform.
3 William Cobbett (1763–1835), journalist, campaigned for political and social reforms designed to re-establish an agrarian society; (Joseph) Hilaire Pierre Belloc (1870–1953), prolific writer, partly French but brought up in England, warned against the dangers of increasing State control, including welfare benefits, in his book *The Servile State* (1925).
4 A number of Wells's novels portray Utopian societies, especially *The Shape of Things to Come* (London, 1933), in which scientists rule the world after a disastrous war. Aldous Leonard Huxley (1894–1963), English novelist and essayist, whose most famous work, *Brave New World* (1932), is a satire that warns what a society ruled by technology might be like.

blindness to suggest that they do. But they are not contaminated, as by Fascism, not directly & indissolubly connected with black causes, but kept in a state of insulated integrity, capable of being reinterpreted & reapplied at any moment, & therefore not corrupted & made unbearable to contemplate. Baldwin[1] is not an ideologist at all, he merely uses slogans in order to prevent injustice from emerging too nakedly. This is ordinary political cheating, an attempt to give reputable patina to what is not even a deliberate blatant reactionary policy, but only politics in the sense in which politicians are not thought of as ever pursuing distinct ends. Whereas Macaulay's scale of values is a perfectly intelligible and on the whole genuinely libertarian, & not inhumane schema, which neither discredits reason nor repels because it is realist (as e.g. much in Mill repels. Mill is much honester, more upright, more truthful, but bleaches everything and is only not depressing if one supplies the desiderata, i.e. positive admiration for certain types of life, character, colour, gesture etc. oneself).

Strachey,[2] I think, was not interested either in social characteristics or in ideas. He specialises in individuals, their emotional dispositions & precise reactions to crucial situations. Words which had a minimum of sharp personal associations, & could therefore be shouted as easily as spoken, therefore offended him as such, since they presupposed nothing private or idiosyncratic. Macaulay however monstrous his own activity was, divorced himself as a writer sufficiently to convey that one kind of life, in general, was good, another abominable, & that, however valuable the individuals produced by it, & however repulsive the individuals produced by the former, i.e. Millism[?] which is a frontal attack on Stracheyism; it is crude, histrionic, costs him nothing to say, but not hostile & contemptuous.

IB.

I must go & dress, else I should write something new.

TO JOHN HILTON

[1935/6, *card*]

All Souls

Dear John

I have no notion of where you are, if I did I should write, possibly come,

---

1 Stanley Baldwin (1867–1947), 1st Earl Baldwin 1937, Conservative politician, Prime Minister 1923–4, 1924–9, 1935–7.
2 (Giles) Lytton Strachey (1880–1932), English critic and biographer.

& altogether be stimulated into friendly & sympathetic activity. Which reminds me of the fact that Mrs Beazley[1] has re-conceived a gigantic passion for you brought on by the general intensification of her feelings due to the nefarious activities of the professional seducer Katzmann[2] whose crimes were given me in the course of a séance lasting some 3–4 hours of uninterruped Medea-talk. The combination of tigress, bore, & femme fatale is really very odd: the effect is violent claustrophobia & a desire for solitude, with me as rare as rare – love to Peggy.

IB

TO GILES ROBERTSON[3]

20 January [1936]

All Souls

Dear Robertson

I am overwhelmed with delight and gratitude. I could no more think of returning it to you, (unless you yourself demanded it urgently and for serious reasons of your own) than a dim figure of the Renaissance could return an episode of his life painted by, let us say, Gozzoli;[4] but ravished as I am I could no more think of sending it back to you than of accepting its frame or its canvas at your expense – you must let me pay for these if I am not to lose my picture altogether.[5] And I am most determined to keep it and take daily pleasure in it, for – in this I may make up in personal enthusiasm and feeling what I lack in critical power – I think it more attractive than anything I've seen in the galleries for many a year: everyone who has seen it in these last few hours have been equally affected: my delight grows greater &

1 Marie, wife since 1919 of John Davidson Beazley (1885–1970), Professor of Classical Archaeology and Art at Oxford.

2 The Russian-American Jew Charles Katzman (1909–79), who came to Brasenose in late 1934 (with a BA from Rollins College) to study for a B.Litt. in Russian literature, had lodged with the Beazleys, through whom he met Louis MacNeice's wife Mary, Mrs Beazley's daughter by a previous marriage. Mary left her husband for Katzman in November 1935. Early the next year Katzman and Mary left for the US, despite Mrs Beazley's attempt to stop Mary being granted a visa. For the details see Jon Stallworthy, *Louis MacNeice* (London and Boston, 1995), esp. 171, 176. See also pp. 155–6 below.

3 Giles Henry Robertson (1913–87), New College classics 1933–6, philosophy pupil of IB; later taught fine art at Edinburgh (from 1946, becoming Watson Gordon Professor of Fine Art 1972–81).

4 Benozzo di Lese di Sandro Gozzoli (1420–97), painter in the Florentine School, mainly known for his frescoes.

5 Giles Robertson had given IB a painting (Plate 17) depicting an episode from IB's childhood: IB had related how as a two-year-old in Riga he leant dangerously out of a window while anxious adults stood below in case he fell (which he didn't). After IB's death Aline Berlin gave the painting to Stuart Hampshire.

greater. As for Blunt & Burgess[1] they are probably so made as to see the truth more brightly drunk than sober, if their tipsiness equalled what either was or ought to have been the warmth of their approval, they must have been past aid. Which I for one wd much have enjoyed had I been there. Meanwhile I must thank you personally. So will you come to dinner at my High Table next Sunday (Jan. the 26ᵗʰ?) at 7.30, dressed? If Prof. Fraenkel is really instrumental about this he deserves his chair, & much more, & I must thank him too. Yes, your masterpiece really is delicious, the colours are so vigorous & full, the whole scene is so gay & so humane, the late Roger Fry[2] would have loved it so much, it is altogether too valuable for me to accept it like that. What would you like in – however inadequate – return? what is my most valued single possession? my records of the Beethoven Society.[3] You can have them all, or nearly all. But even if you won't have them, come to dinner on Sunday week. a suitable inscription, relating the story, will have to be engraved & attached, as in Daumiers or Goyas.[4] I hope you can come.

   your touched & once more grateful beneficiary
      Shaya Berlin

It would be silly for you after this to continue to address me as Mr. anything. If you feel embarrassed about handle-less names pray don't use any vocative at all. But you certainly can no longer call me Mr.

TO DIANA HUBBACK

   [Shortly before 7 February 1936][5]

                                                All Souls

Dear Diana,
   I wanted to write immediately after your party & thank you, since I enjoyed myself a great deal, having been allowed to talk freely. I thought

1 Anthony Frederick Blunt (1907–83), art historian, Fellow of Trinity College, Cambridge, and Guy Francis de Moncy Burgess (1911–63), Trinity (Cambridge) history 1930–3, both later exposed as Communist spies for the USSR.
2 Roger Eliot Fry (1866–1934), artist and art critic.
3 The Society series were comprehensive collections of recordings of the great composers' works. The Beethoven Society series of all the piano sonatas, played by Artur Schnabel, were issued by His Master's Voice between 1932 and 1939: vols 1–9 of the eventual total of 15 vols are listed in the 1936 catalogue. The scheme also included Beethoven's violin sonatas, played by Fritz Kreisler (violin) and Frank Rupp (piano): vols 1 and 2 are in the 1936 list.
4 Honoré Daumier (1808–79), French artist, lithographer and caricaturist, imprisoned for a caricature of King Louis-Philippe; Francisco de Goya y Lucientes (1746–1828), Spanish painter. In the event no inscription was attached.
5 The date of DH's reply.

very highly (this is pure testimonial writing reminiscence) of all the young men I hadn't seen before: particularly one called Davison[1] (?) who had a nice sympathetic sort of face made of costly though unvarnished wood. And your Mr Gluckman[2] who obviously is a specialist, which is very nice & rare. Are you coming up to Oxford this term, and if so when? if you warn me I shall see to it that no irrelevant episodes occur. I hope that your sister does not detest me too much for consistently lying all the way home about my mode of life: I explained very carefully how full and varied the life of a tender of sick Oxford birds was, and even displayed esoteric informedness which made, I hope, some impression. But having been told that I was a mere name to her and invited to describe myself, I could hardly do otherwise.

Is it right to have written & condoled with your grandmother?[3] I much respected the general type represented by your grandfather – a tiny class with hardly any members – one of the very, very *very* few English Jews of any station by whom one was in no way embarrassed. Which is really exceptional.

Shaya

I have just looked at my letter to your grandmother: it is slightly pompous – more than slightly – but quite sincere. I hope she won't regard it as a forward act.

TO JENIFER WILLIAMS

Wednesday [25 February 1936]

All Souls

Dear Jenifer

I am slightly bemused this evening as a result of an agreeable but strenuous evening of Miss G. Stein,[4] who talked in lucid moving and simple English and propounded an excellent and original thesis. So that in a sense it was disappointing, and in a sense not: I longed to get up and say 'could you not be a little obscure, please, just a shade perhaps? and lower

---

1 Possibly Howard William Davidson (1911–95), Oriel classics 1931–4, who later joined the Colonial Service.
2 (Herman) Max Gluckman (1911–75), South African Rhodes Scholar, social anthropologist.
3 On the death of DH's grandfather, Sir Meyer Spielman (1856–1936).
4 Gertrude Stein (1874–1936), the American writer. In his diary entry for 25 February Jasper Ridley writes: 'went with NOB [N. O. Brown] to Jowett [Society], to hear American Miss Stein (gentle face figure, delicate, but voice like a bull) on causal reciprocity. she used whitehead prehensions etc, which was unintelligible and funny. Farrell answered her with the gravity and ridiculousness of a man of 60 philosophising.'

your voice, since we hear too well and understand everything before you say it;' but she was formidable with hecklers, told them what was wrong with their lives, asked them what Schools they were at, embarrassed them, trampled on them, & winked a great deal at Alice B. Toklas[1] & Lord Berners.[2] I saw no reason for immolating myself in this manner and sat in rather agreeable silence while one after the other my pupils asked questions & were slaughtered with enormous gusto & genius by Miss Stein. Mr Boase (the shareability of my sentiments about whom with you I prize beyond measure) was not only benevolently present but followed me into All Souls afterwards (calling on the Comte de Biéville[3] on the way). There is no question but he bears us both great good will. Which makes him an even greater source of discomfort than ever. I am sorry. I did not mean to write this wandering introduction. I wanted to tell you only how enormously your letter set me up, as they say, and that it improves steadily upon rereading. Thank you v. much. I also recollect the earlier afternoon with unalloyed pleasure: as for the latter half, the gigantic mountain up which I was led by Professor Price was not relieved by our intensive fieldwork on sense data done while I was staring at the horizon, setting sun (forced so frequently on me by Douglas's exclamations of rapture & orders to look and describe one's feelings – you can't mind his introduction here for a purely frivolous part –) etc. while I desperately wondered whether the suggestion that we might sit down for a while on some picturesque boulder would be regarded as morally despicable and evidence of not taking one's subject seriously. All Wykehamists, I indignantly suggest to you, approach everything with a strong moral attitude & judge one entirely by one's behaviour and are themselves everywhere in chains and go about forcing people to be free who are free already and merely have imaginary chains thrust upon them which are then dramatically removed. If this is extravagant it is only a coloured exaggeration in the right direction, and being in & among Wykehamists permanently I feel strongly. I suddenly expressed myself passionately about this to Professor Price: who looked startled, and brought our walk to an end. It is about 3 a.m. and having been enfeebled by agreeable but exhausting visits

1 Alice Babette Toklas (1877–1967) was Stein's companion, secretary, general organiser and cook.

2 Gerald Hugh Tyrwhitt-Wilson (1883–1950), 14th Baron Berners, composer, author, eccentric; author of *Far from the Madding War* (London, 1941), in which the character Mr Jericho is based on IB: see Mark Amory, *Lord Berners: The Last Eccentric* (London, 1998), 182–4.

3 Anne de Biéville, a withdrawn, narcissistic, homosexual French aristocrat (a member of the homintern) from an old Protestant family, came to Oxford in 1933 (with no formal position). He occupied a flat above Blackwell's in Broad Street and dined at Balliol, where he sat next to David Wallace. He started a French society with Wallace, Ben Nicolson and Stuart Hampshire: invitations were accepted by Gertrude Stein, Poulenc and (on the same evening as Gertrude Stein's talk to the society, the day after the one to the Jowett Society described here) Salvador Dali (153/2), who brought his wife Gala.

from the good looking Branch[1] (who also commented adversely on Mr B[oase] on that afternoon) for four days in succession from midnight till 5 a.m., I am voiceless and limp. There is a sense of infinite leisure and a general melting quality which occurs at about 2.30 a.m. which has already begun now & which I must put a severe end to. It would be nice if you would come to tea sometime: on Friday next for example. Pray do not come into Oxford for the specific purpose. But if you do, I shall provide the tea for which we are so famed.

    Yrs

       Shaya B.

Ah yes. My colleague Rees has expressed an overwhelming desire to meet you, fired by Douglas's unceasing talk. I do not see why I should, unless at your request, or at least by your consent, bring you together with the (suite et fin)[2] most celebrated lover of my generation. If you wish it, certainly. But if not, I see no reason for returning to my old and ill played part of chaperon, not to speak of my dreadful danger in incurring the certain fury of Douglas (who whatever one may say does act, burns one's room, pours things over one etc.) who with Peggy looks on Rees as a satanic character. If he really were that, I should afford you the pleasure of such a rare phenomenon. As he is not, I shall not act unless at a sign from you. I have decided that both (a) self-dramatization & (b) dramatizing others to them-selves are the most shocking crimes there are. Incidentally did you know that in French there is a charming French word 'life-struggler'?[3] it is a good clear concept, & I am not sure you don't rather like that.

    I.B.

TO STEPHEN SPENDER

    26 February [1936][4]

                             All Souls

Dear Stephen:

    I am very very very sorry indeed not to have answered your letter for so long, but I have never had a more congested overworked term in my life. I do not know why it should have been so, partly work on my book, partly

1 Guy Branch (1913–40), Balliol English 1932–5; friend of IB at Oxford; member of OUDS; married Lady Prudence Pelham March 1939; joined British Council; killed in the Battle of Britain.
2 'Continued and concluded'; written at the beginning of a supplementary card.
3 Namely?
4 Dated from SS's to IB, 10 January [1936], to which this replies.

a seminar[1] I have been conducting where fairly clever people have forced me to get things up, partly the necessity of having to write a paper to read in Cambridge,[2] partly late hours, have killed all capacity for thinking, writing, any thing save talking, really. I hope you have lived a more leisurely & less broken-into-quanta sort of life: I hate discontinuities of all kinds, which is only another way of saying that I am a slow starter & hate to be uprooted which Maurice said about me once: consequently I passionately defend all small societies, fixed disciplines etc. which merely rationalizes my love of the womb I expect (a womb with a view, a womb of one's own etc.)

Señor Miguel de Unamuno[3] lectured here, & looks splendid, a short-bearded idéologue combined out of Anatole France,[4] Fleuriau[5] & Mazzini:[6] he said that we were too oppressed by our history to be able to act, too debilitated by the burden of the knowledge of the past to do anything but hesitate, perhaps Rousseau was right & we needed a new barbarism etc. in order to get rid of our burdens: I think this only applies to cultivated high minded Spaniards of to-day or Russians of 1917 who live somewhere in 1848: nobody else seems to be overburdened with a sense of the endlessness of pros & cons for anything because of vistas of historical memory, except the Jews possibly. Long memories are obviously a hideous defect, it tends to poison everything with the taste of possible corruption: Americans seem to have it in an odd unhistorical way, like a synthetic memory, compounded to resemble the real one they so much need: which being artificial dessicates them in a bogus sort of way even more, if you see what I mean.

Which reminds me of the fact that Gertrude Stein lectured here. She was definite too clear & quite good. She said that Americans had to go to Paris because they need a mythology, England won't do because its history happenned, definitely happenned, & might get mixed up with American history & bully & impinge & enslave as it did Henry James: while French history did not happen, (not in the American time series it didn't), & Paris took nothing from you, left you all you had, at least before the war, & supplied a mythology. 'In the 19ᵗʰ century all Parisian painters were French'

---

1 IB and J. L. Austin held a class on C. I. Lewis's *Mind and the World Order* (NY, 1929) at All Souls on Mondays at 5.30 pm in Hilary Term 1936. It was, IB believed, the first philosophy class held in Oxford on a contemporary work.

2 IB gave a paper to the Moral Sciences Club in Cambridge, probably on 'Pleasure', on 28 February.

3 Miguel de Unamuno y Jugo (1864–1936), Spanish author and philosopher. He and the three people out of whom IB says he is composed all wore beards.

4 Anatole France, pseudonym of Jacques Anatole Thibault (1844–1924), French novelist and critic in the classical tradition, who won the 1921 Nobel Prize for Literature.

5 Aimé Joseph de Fleuriau (1870–1938), French ambassador to London 1924–33.

6 Giuseppe Mazzini (1805–72), Italian nationalist leader, a central figure in the movement for the reunification of Italy.

she said, 'but in the 20th they are Spanish, & that's something.' Also 'must things have something to do with everything', Also 'when we do we don't do what we do & also do it' 'How do you mean?' said someone 'do & don't do in the same sense?" "Well! don't we?' she said 'don't we do & don't do what we do? I mean *don't* we?" She was splendid with hecklers 'you sit down my boy, you don't *want* to know what I mean, you just want me to use your language: Well! I won't. I don't create for a public only for myself etc." She obviously is rather clever & genuine in a sort of way. She said that all American writing was sui generis in style, you could pick it out if you didn't know who the author was. Even Henry James. 'Hemingway?'[1] said somebody 'why Ernest Hemingway came to me as a kid of twenty' she said '& I taught him how to write: just like one of your professors here: I told him what to do & how to do it: of course he's *different* that's because I taught him.' very unrealistic about our professors, I must own. The cortège of Lord Berners + 6 peeresses + Alice B. Toklas + Stein was splendid, very Roy-like. Altogether, under the lead of Comte de Biéville, leader of the French Huguenot nobility, we are enjoying a thorough aesthetic renaissance. Salvator Dali[2] is here this evening, apparently going to do his stuff which includes half-shaving the head of a woman & then frying an omelette on her head + a lot of average obscenity. Ben Nicolson[3] is terrified he may do it again. He & Hutchinson[4] are like the chess king & chess queen in Oxford highbrow circles: Ben slow, only one move a time, vulnerable, solid, honourable, round, three dimensional but all-important: if he were to go, it would all disrupt. Jeremy bitter, active, effective, whizzing all over the board sticking things into people, but definitely N° 2.

I enjoy the sociology as much as ever. Communism is at a temporary dead-end, all interest in politics has subsided, surréalism is being discussed again. Obviously this is v. temporary. The only active movement now, given that in every society there is a residue of persons who just do what they do ill or well but wd have done it in any age, like Davids Garnett[5] & Cecil,[6] or Mrs Cameron, or Maurice, or I for that matter, given that, there is the element which again whether ill or well is making whatever difference is being made, like Bloomsbury in 1907 (when protesting against protests

1 Ernest Miller Hemingway (1899–1961), American novelist, journalist, short-story writer and essayist.
2 Salvador Dali (1904–89), Spanish surrealist painter.
3 (Lionel) Ben(edict) *Nicolson (1914–78), son of Harold Nicolson and Vita Sackville-West, Balliol history 1933–6, later art historian.
4 Jeremy Nicolas St John *Hutchinson (b. 1915), Magdalen PPE 1933–6, had lodgings in Beaumont Street with Stuart Hampshire and Ben Nicolson.
5 The author David Garnett (1892–1981).
6 Lord (Edward Christian) David (Gascoyne) *Cecil (1902–86), Fellow of Wadham 1924–30, Fellow of New College 1939–69 (Goldsmiths' Professor of English Literature from 1948).

against free-love was a real attitude, burning question etc.), now there are certainly the so called Communists, who are mostly really liberals like you, i.e. do not expect an actual bloody revolution, & wouldn't know quite what [to] do if it happened, but feel that Socialism is ineffective, imposes no burdens, is bureaucratic & discredited, & is a highbrow revolt in a way, of high-minded individualistic ideologists . . . [a] pure intelligentsia movement, only thinly modified by genuine workers: communists seem to understand one's language, socialists usually patter much more & are vulgarer. This is not intended as at all a description of surfaces: it may be fatal to communism that it is so genuinely idea-ridden: in the Kulturwelt[1] anyhow it is they & they alone who seem to make the pace. I suppose because once more this is a case of starved intellectuals provided with a reputable mythology. I suppose all great poetry which goes on & on from poem to poem relevantly is quasi-mythological: only hand to mouth lyrical poets, however full of genius, like Catullus or Heine[2] don't need it & can talk directly without interposing a framework & a specially built up non-everyday world. Beethoven in a certain sense obviously has a mythology whereas Schubert has not: Berlioz certainly has, or Wagner, or Mussorgsky, but no French composer, after Berlioz. But I suppose the French have a language which is already so traditional & disciplined that they have no need of it at all.

You speak of reading Greek:[3] if I were you I should read Plato & Herodotus with cribs: the Phaedrus, the Symposium, the Phaedo, possibly the Ion, & the earlier books of Herodotus: as for tragedy, the Agamemnon, the Oedipus Coloneus, the Bacchae is what you are bound to like, whatever may be with the rest. Yeats' translation of the Oedipus in Colonus is very beautiful I think. Euripides's Alcestis is an easy play, & attractive in a way.

I shd have thought the Oxford Book[4] was too difficult – it is so for me on the whole – Maurice has just published his big book on Greek Lyric Poetry,[5] I haven't read it yet, it is well timed: pray God he gets his professorship we shall all be undone if he doesn't:[6] Prof. Rose (your

1 'World of culture'.
2 Both Gaius Valerius Catullus (*c*.84–*c*.54 BC), Roman lyric poet, and (Christian Johann) Heinrich (né Harry) Heine (1797–1856), German poet whose works included love lyrics, were inspired by their personal amatory circumstances.
3 With the ultimate aim, SS explains, of reading Greek tragedy.
4 *The Oxford Book of Greek Verse* (Oxford, 1930).
5 C. M. Bowra, *Greek Lyric Poetry: From Alcman to Simonides* (Oxford, 1936).
6 Bowra was a candidate for the Regius Professorship of Greek, which in the event went to Eric Robinson Dodds (1893–1979), Professor of Greek at Birmingham since 1924. The other main candidate was John Dewar Denniston (1887–1949), Fellow and classics Tutor, Hertford, 1913–49. Denniston was the best candidate so far as exact knowledge of Greek was concerned, but Gilbert Murray (169/4), the current Professor, and thus a Student of Christ Church, thought him insufficiently original, and preferred Dodds, a far better scholar than Bowra.

enemy over Pound-Propertius)[1] is his chief rival, eine lächerliche Figur.[2] Write again please. I am very very tired & must go to bed simply. Sparrow has published a funny malicious article about N. Mitchison's last book[3] with quotations like 'a delicious slack hanging piece of she-flesh' or 'what should a socialist woman do?' + bits of Joseph tartly interspersed. Elizabeth Pakenham says she really asks herself that frequently – she is growing duller & dimmer daily. Crossman is delivering foul anti-democratic lectures on 'The philosophy of war-guilt' & is aureated with scandals of a squalid sort. Write.

Shaya.

Will you send me bits of your play, the thought of which definitely excites me & (b) tell me more about Portugal etc. I see that about Byron & grottoes very clearly.[4]

Separate Entry.

News: Humphry has sailed for India. Freddie Ayer has a daughter (a son wd have been *inconceivable* as Moore wd say) called Valerie.[5] Mrs Crosthwaite has written enquiring in abstract what is the view of our generation about the mari complaisant?[6] The Cole-Mitchisons wd say I suppose that it is his duty to help the lover up with his career.[7] Louis Macneice is stricken by

1 Herbert Jennings Rose (1883–1961), Professor of Greek at St Andrew's 1927–53. Ezra Pound's translations of Propertius may be regarded either as a tribute by poet to poet or as a collection of howlers. For example, he translates 'sitiens', which means 'thirsting', as 'sitting': *Homage to Propertius* (London, 1934), 2. 6 (p. 12).

2 'A ridiculous figure'.

3 John Sparrow, 'What does a Socialist woman do?', review of Naomi Mitchison, *We Have Been Warned: A Novel* (London, 1935), *Spectator*, 7 February 1936, 209–10. The first of the quotations that struck IB was a description of a character in the novel, the Russian girl Oksana: 'a slack delicious weight of she-flesh' (p. 330).

4 The play was published as *Trial of a Judge: A Tragedy in Five Acts* (London, [1938]), but an earlier version sent to IB by SS on 11 March 1936 is entitled 'Death of a Justice'. SS had taken a house in Portugal with friends. He describes the hills behind the house as 'romantically rocky' and adds: 'Byron thought Sintra was the most beautiful place he had ever been to: and one can quite see why, because it is very like the eighteenth century. In these hills one realises what grottos really are: there are scores of them here, damp now, with pretty but slightly clammy newts hibernating on their ledges.'

5 Born on 21 February 1936; died 1981.

6 The letter from Moore Crosthwaite's mother about what she calls 'complacent husbands' is dated 2 February 1936.

7 A reference to two married couples: (George) Douglas Howard Cole (1889–1959) and Margaret Isabel Cole (1893–1980), and their close friends (Gilbert) Richard Mitchison (1890–1970) and Naomi Mary Margaret Mitchison (1897–1998), née Haldane. There was a special attachment, perhaps sexual, between Margaret Cole and Dick Mitchison, accepted by the gentle and undersexed Douglas and the progressive Naomi; and Douglas helped Dick in his career. See Betty D. Vernon, *Margaret Cole 1893–1980: A Political Biography* (London, 1986), 67–71, and Jenni Calder, *The Nine Lives of Naomi Mitchison* (London, 1997), 103.

his wife's elopement with an American Jew called Katzmann,[1] but Mrs
Beazley is said to have stopped her visa to U.S.A. & his to England: terrific
amount of bumbling all round. Rowse is quoting Rimbaud ad nauseam
(Abyssinian association I suppose)[2] & has attacked me physically this
evening, for laughing too much at him. I scratched & he complained that I
ought to cut my nails more often. You agree a very unreal S.C.R. situation.
Archie Campbell wd have liked it.

P.S. About stating & describing:[3] is statement always in direct terms &
non-mythological in character, whereas description being a definite attempt
to supply a coherent love of symbols is, as it were, even in the short run the
presentation of an ad hoc myth? the words 'myth' etc. suggest too much,
nothing so pompous is wanted: but anyhow a personal world, or bits of one,
with the suggestion that what is revealed is unfinished, there is indefinitely
more there etc. I am sorry this is so obscure: but I do take it that you are not
merely beguiled by the bald-seeming nature of Greek, which is only so in
translation: the bible could also be *made* to seem so, yet I take it describes
a great deal?

> *SS replied on 2 March. In his letter he says he is writing a book about
> liberalism and communism. IB annotates the letter with this note to an
> unidentified friend:*

The book if published is bound to start a newspaper controversy, quotations
etc. & probably he ought to be told not to write it just now: in which case
violent protests from me, might just stop him: please tell me what you think
[. . .]

> *A passage in Jasper Ridley's*[4] *diary starting on Wednesday 4 March
> conjures up the atmosphere in IB's rooms at this period:*

went to Berlin's room to hear Berlioz Messe de Morts and Symphonie
Funèbre et Triomphale on wireless. Follow Dies Irae in 1530 missal IB
produced (worm eaten, splendidly, and celestial type). [. . .]

---

1 147/2.
2 The French poet (Jean-Nicolas-)Arthur Rimbaud (1854–91) was a skins and coffee trader for a
   year in Harrar, Abyssinia, in 1880–1; Mussolini was attacking Abyssinia at the time of this
   letter.
3 In his discussion of Greek SS suggested that 'Greek poetry always states, and our poetry
   always describes.'
4 Jasper Maurice Alexander *Ridley (1913–43), Balliol classics 1932–6; married Cressida Bonham
   Carter 1939; killed in the war.

Giles Robertson came in in the middle and stood lower stomach out, fixed, open mouthed thick lipped grin, turning everything to Cambridge gossip and inexpressibly toad-like and repulsive. IB says youd like him if he were a picture. But he isn't.

IB magnificent report on reading his paper on pleasure in Cambridge – esp. Hardy's[1] enquiries after Valerian Wellesley.[2] Broad having a picture of Gallie[3] on his table (thinks him succulent), imitation of Moore,[4] madness of Wisdom. No one else spoke, but it was agreeable. Austin came in in the middle so did Russell – looked more shy embarrassed unhappy than conceivable – as if everyone in the room were being insolent to him. Then went out. He wore a check overcoat and a belt in such a way as IRA revolutionaries wd wear one if they lost their raincoats.

Thursday March 5

Lunch with Berlin – went to his room and found Villiers[5] finishing tutorial. dramatic confrontation. IB shaved played an Engelbach[6] record eccentrically – conversion of diatonic to atonic, result magnificent human wails and what Wagner wd have written if he had dared, because his diatonic progression clearly meant to suggest what this achieved. In buttery Pember[7] who is 74 and whitehaired and reposeful and handsome, and Pares. Austin appeared afterwards in IB's room, and as predicted opened 'what about quantities of pleasure?' which lasted half an hour.

TO STEPHEN SPENDER

[mid-March 1936]

All Souls

Dear Stephen
Your play arrived safely. I haven't read it yet: I shall write a longish letter

---

1 Godfrey Harold Hardy (1877–1947), Savilian Professor of Geometry and Fellow of New College 1919–31 (Hon. Fellow 1936–47), Sadleirian Professor of Pure Mathematics, Cambridge, 1931–42.
2 Arthur Valerian Wellesley (b. 1915), later (1972) 8th Duke of Wellington, New College 1934–8, where he took a pass degree in history and French.
3 Perhaps (Walter) Bryce Gallie (1915–98), Balliol classics 1931–5, Assistant Lecturer in Philosophy, University College of Swansea, 1935–8.
4 George Edward Moore (1873–1958), Professor of Philosophy, Cambridge, 1925–39.
5 Charles Hyde Villiers (1912–92), New College PPE 1933–6, later (1976) Chairman of the British Steel Corporation.
6 Perhaps an error for the composer Johann Christoff Engelmann, né Kaffka (1754–1815), whose music might so sound if the record was placed off-centre ('eccentrically') on the turntable.
7 Francis William Pember (1862–1954), lawyer, Warden of All Souls 1914–32, Hon. Fellow 1932–54.

to c/o Cook, Barcelona as soon as I have unless you indicate some other address. Here D[esmond] McCarthy has been writing rubbish about Read's book on Shelley;[1] emboldened by Sparrow's little book[2] all the old men now bravely say 'rubbish', 'unintelligible' etc. to ordinary not v. exciting but clear propositions, under the impression that the impostors' bluff has been called, & no dangerous reprisals followed: like Hitler's occupation of the Rhineland.[3] The political situation seems frightful: Dawson in the Times is doing great anti-Russian turns while Locker Lampson[4] is issuing little anti-Hitler pamphlets saying 'England Awake!' 'German Spies buy English secrets!' etc., & between them a genuine pre-war panic is slowly being created. I cannot see that one can do other than either a) say we won't go to war whatever happens or (b) be thoroughly disagreeable to the Germans. These are policies, the rest seems intrigue.

Write about your very next whereabouts: I am likely to go to Nice with my parents,[5] I expect a hostile mood in France which affects even metics[6] like me. We have elected someone even more terrifyingly un-English than I am, namely a Montenegrin called J. Petroff Plamenatz,[7]

---

1 Herbert Read, *In Defence of Shelley and other essays* (London, [1936]). DM's review, 'Shelley and the Psycho-analysts: Mr Herbert Read's Criticism', is in the *Sunday Times*, 1 March 1936, 8.

2 *Sense and Poetry* (127/6).

3 On 7 March German troops had re-entered the demilitarised Rhineland. This was in direct contravention of the 1925 Treaty of Locarno, which had established as permanent both the frontiers between Germany, France and Belgium laid down in the Treaty of Versailles and Germany's undertaking that its forces would not enter the Rhineland. Germany now claimed that a recent military alliance between France and the USSR violated the Locarno Treaty and that the German action was justified in self-defence. At the League of Nations Council meeting soon afterwards, Britain and Belgium were among the countries who accepted that, whatever the legalities of the matter, the re-occupation of the Rhineland was not a sufficient reason for war.

4 Commander Oliver Stillingfleet Locker-Lampson (1880–1954), barrister and journalist; his exploits as Commander of the Russian Armoured Car Division of the Royal Navy in the First World War included involvement in a plan for the Tsar's escape; Conservative MP for the Handsworth Division of Birmingham 1922–45; a friend of Churchill who, like him, moved from strong anti-Bolshevism to even stronger anti-Nazism; prime mover in Einstein's escape from Nazi Germany. His campaigns against persecution of the Jews resulted, later in 1936, in the imprisonment of an author who had accused Jews in Britain of ritual murder.

5 For Passover.

6 A favourite self-description by IB and some of his immigrant friends. 'Metic' is a word of ancient Greek origin meaning an alien living in a Greek city with some privileges of citizenship.

7 John Petrov Plamenatz (1912–75), Fellow of All Souls 1936–51, later (1967) succeeded IB as Chichele Professor of Social and Political Philosophy. An address on Plamenatz by IB appears in PI, and IB contributed an entry on Plamenatz to the DNB. It is clear from these accounts that Plamenatz turned out not to fulfil IB's lurid expectations.

I expect he will do a lot of terrorism at college meetings. Comes of an old Cetinje family & looks a brigand.

love.

Shaya

TO MARY FISHER (IN SPAIN)

Postmark 23 March 1936

All Souls

Dear Mary

B.J. says that she has already informed you of the fate of Richard Pares.[1] As my friend Mr Turner[2] wd certainly have observed, Pares has fallen. Yet I am not really disposed to exclaim in the words of my pastiche de Wagner record 'Oh malheúr, / oh désastre, / oh catastrophe inévitablé'. Of course I do not know Miss Powicke: it seems a thoroughly dynastic alliance, if, as I fear, she is called Sheila, & is niece to Erica Lindsay, this intrusion of pseudo-names into a universe where certain titles have irrefragable associations, is highly inconvenient and disturbing. Not but what Miss P. obviously answers to the celebrated table of desiderata which I once extracted from Richard. She is round-faced, docile, reasonably stay at home, looks on North Oxford as both inevitable and agreeable, and in other respects is like the ideal negress – Oxford negress – we decided he wanted. Mrs Maud[3] when told, said 'I must tell Maud[4] at once.' but before that 'oh ruddy cripes' I apologise for even setting this down, but I had to tell someone in whom it wd produce a sympathetic frisson. The three men who sent Pares telegrams in special gilt envelopes now obtainable, were Curtis, Coupland and Cox. The C class is not as distinguished or nice a class really as the Smith class (I have enumerated them to you? the very unlowering group consisting of Adam Smith, the Sydney Smiths, the Rejected Addresses Smiths, F. E. Smith, J. A. Smith, Sir George Adam Smith, & A. H. Smith, all

---

1 Marriage to Janet Lindsay Powicke, daughter of (Frederick) Maurice Powicke (1879–1963), Regius Professor of Modern History and Fellow of Oriel 1928–47, and his wife Susan (née Lindsay), and niece of Alexander Dunlop Lindsay (1879–1952), philosopher, Christian socialist, Master of Balliol 1924–49, Vice-Chancellor 1935–8, and his wife Erica (née Storr). IB gets Janet Powicke's first name wrong.

2 Probably G. J. Turner (144/2).

3 (Margaret) Jean Hay (Redcliffe-)Maud (1904–93), née Hamilton, wife of John (Redcliffe-)Maud (see next note).

4 John Primatt Redcliffe Redcliffe-Maud (1906–82), Baron Redcliffe-Maud (of the City and County of Bristol) 1967; Fellow and politics and economics Tutor, Univ., 1932–9, Dean 1933–9; Master of Birkbeck College, London, 1939–43; Deputy Secretary, later Second Secretary, Ministry of Food, 1941–4; Second Secretary, Office of the Minister of Reconstruction, 1944–5; Secretary, Office of Lord President of the Council, 1945; Permanent Secretary, Ministry of Education, 1945–52.

enormously positive and robust figures with a strain of gaiety and sturdy but not offensive though occasionally slightly vulgar sense).[1] I cannot think, as they say, that marriage will make any difference, I think he married with that end in view. I think every thing will remain exactly the same: though if they shd take it into their heads to go to, say, Salzburg next summer, every thing, will not, I admit, be at all the same. I know nothing about her save that I suddenly met him three times running in her society, made some slightly unsuitable comments, was told that Mrs Powicke was really extraordinarily nice, giggled even more unsuitably, was greeted with charming Jane Austen embarrassments & blushes, realized I was treading real ground, abstained from further comment, & was rewarded by an early confession for my sympathy & tact. Still if you think it horrible I hold that I see what you mean. The alternative wd have been for him to turn tart & acid to an even greater extent, which would indeed have been artistically better, but so uncomfortable that at a certain point I at any rate would, if asked, opt for a conventionally happy ending, however crudely managed and aesthetically offensive. What must not, I think, be supposed is that he could have married anyone in herself either remarkable or exquisite. Remember that in spite of everything Pares is a Wykehamist of the Price–Guy period,[2] and therefore seeks security and respectability, and being Pares, non-impingement. Also a wife who is a wife. Nothing very costly can be acquired with these specifications, only something durable, practical, and in decent taste. But I must stop from this libel on a person unknown to me (as if that ever prevented me in the past...).[3] My days have chiefly been spent in working honestly at Marx, and elaborating propositions against Logical Positivism (such as that all inductive proposition, acc. to Carnap,[4] must be either tautologies or self-contradictions, which pleases me frightfully):[5]

1 Not previously identified Smiths (if it matters?): the political economist Adam Smith (1723–90); the writer Sydney Smith (1771–1845), Canon of St Paul's Cathedral, and (of several other SSs) possibly Sydney Goodsir Smith (1915–74), poet, playwright and critic; Frederick Edwin Smith (1872–1930), 1st Earl of Birkenhead, Lord Chancellor 1919–22; Sir George Adam Smith (1856–1942), biblical scholar, until 1935 Principal and Vice-Chancellor of Aberdeen University.

2 Presumably the period spanning or including the Winchester dates of H. H. Price (1899–1984) and Guy Chilver (1910–82). Richard Pares (1902–58) would have overlapped with Price there.

3 IB would later have written of Mrs Pares more warmly. Indeed, his obituary of Pares, in which he refers to 'the loving-kindness of his wife', makes clear that he came to recognise the success of this marriage, and shared the general admiration felt for Mrs Pares's courage and intelligence in looking after her progressively disabled husband.

4 Rudolf Carnap (1891–1970), German logical positivist philosopher, leading member of the Vienna Circle.

5 He was working on the paper (a reply to Margaret MacDonald) published as 'Induction and Hypothesis' in Proceedings of the Aristotelian Society supplementary vol. 16 (1937), 63–102.

I have read E. M. Forster's miscellany[1] which is very interesting and painfully sensitive and makes one genuinely terrified of meeting the author who is obviously skinless, very observant, capable of making one feel embarrassed about almost anything one says or does, but always with an irrefutable reason provided, very much what people think Sumner[2] (oh so falsely) to be. Also Stephen has sent me a play in verse. He is threatening to become a sort of V. Hugo, concerned with the lacrimae rerum[3] exclusively, having taken the dictum that the poetry is in the pity too literally. The perpetual ad misericordiam[4] appeal, the larmes[5] which are carefully set in every three lines of verse, are being overplayed. I intend to write a severe and deflating letter. It is not in character but Stephen always automatically provokes donnishness in me, & I become governessy almost at once. And now, dear me, Blakeway's last party. One cannot deny, can one, that all his parties have a certain really grand terribilitá about them, which not all Alison's[6] bathos can wholly destroy. The terrified, charged atmosphere, in which *everything* is unreal, & every one is playing for something, effect, or mischief, or safety or simply home, is a tribute to something absolutely unique and not of our century. I was glad to be able to refuse to go to the actual dinner, owing to a Gaudy, and arrived at about 11 p.m. The mise en scène was far from dull. Conceive Blakeway's room in Corpus. In the centre a sofa. On the sofa, 3 figures. In the centre Miss Graves, mildly tipsy but possessed. On her left R. Chilver, with a possessive but exhausted look: on her right Maurice, dark purple, very aggressive, and full of wine, shouting things at Richard. Their behaviour to each other was that of pugilists after about 27 rounds, a colossal number of points, both very very exhausted, hitting out groggily, missing as often as not, but going on & on & on. I learnt later that Richard took much punishment during dinner, & terrific blows which wd have knocked out a man less tightly grim. I can't describe to you the 130° tension of the duel which fused even Blakeway's ferocity into dim insignificance. Tony sat there, happy & oblivious of anything untoward, & Blakeway kept repeating to him, by way of keeping

---

1 (Edward) Morgan Forster (1879–1970), novelist. The miscellany is *Abinger Harvest* (London, 1936), a collection of literary criticism, essays, poems and fiction named after the village in Surrey where Forster had inherited a house.
2 (Benedict) Humphrey Sumner (1893–1951), Fellow and history Tutor, Balliol, 1925–44, Professor of History, Edinburgh, 1944–5, Warden of All Souls 1945–51.
3 Almost untranslatable phrase from Vergil *Aeneid* 1. 642: literally 'tears of things'.
4 'To pity'.
5 'Tears'.
6 Alison Blakeway, née Hope (1913–83), Somerville English 1932–5, then literary critic for the *Sunday Times*. She married Alan Blakeway in 1935; he died in 1936, and she married Tony Andrewes (92/4) in 1938.

the rest of the room alive (the Mortimers,[1] Miss Cook,[2] Miss Fischer-
W.,[3] Guy) 'Do you realise that Crossman's brother[4] is coming to
Corpus – My God etc.' this had by this time an incantatory ring, if you get
me, of one of the remarks which he must have produced at least 20 times
that evening & wanted to have made to him, being as we know, fond of
endlessly identical stimuli followed by a grateful release of pent up emotion.
Guy & Jenifer stood in the window, a very tranquil frightened couple, but a
quiet pool of culture & of rest in the surrounding typhoon. Maurice had
apparently begun the evening by arriving a little too gay, & shaking Mrs
Mortimer violently by the shoulders: which Miss Oppé for instance would
have liked, or even B.J. but hardly Mrs M. He was then sat between Miss
Cook & Alison, which meant violent uphill work in two directions. By the
time I arrived he was avenging himself vertiginoso con furia.[5] Whenever
he moved I fled in the opposite direction, seeking shelter & trivial
conversation. Even Blakeway seemed a little embarrassed by the spirits
he had unwittingly called up. It really is monstrous that Maurice shd be reduced to this by Miss Graves who after all etc. not but what (what
a good idiom that is) she has a renaissance touch about her inasmuch as, so
one is informed, two of her rejected suitors, Mr Bell[6] & Mr Mcmillan (of
B.J.'s firm),[7] burning with jealousy & indignation, joined forces, arrived in
Oxford during this same week-end, in order to keep watch over the
movements over this female Juan (there is a place in literature somewhere
where the Dons Quixote & Juan meet? I can't remember what happens but it
obviously calls for the highest genius). Finally I, acting as an aunt as usual,
broke the party up, packed Guy & Miss F.-W. into a taxi together, & took
Maurice, singing very very loudly, & anxious to call on All Souls, where had
he in his then condition met Dawson, all wd have been up with the Regius
chair, to Wadham. And returned to find Sparrow & Rees arguing about the
difference between being sensitive & sensitized or something. But these
episodes (+ Miss Sée's party where the spectacle of Richard + Miss Graves +

1 Robert Mortimer (1902–76), Student of Christ Church 1930–44, Canon and Regius Professor
   of Moral and Pastoral Theology 1944–9, later (1949–73) Bishop of Exeter, and his wife Mary
   ('Mollie'), née Walker, Rachel Walker's elder sister.
2 Probably Helen Cooke, much admired in Oxford in the 1930s, daughter of the Revd George
   Albert Cooke, Canon of Christ Church and Regius Professor of Hebrew 1914–36.
3 Jenifer Williams.
4 Thomas Edward Stafford Crossman (1917–40), CCC classics 1936–9.
5 'With vertiginous rage'.
6 Oliver Sydney Bell (1913–80), Balliol PPE 1932–5; later (1949–57) Editor, Educational Matters,
   New York Times; son of Kenneth Bell (66/1).
7 On coming down from Oxford in 1934 BJ joined the publishers William Heinemann as a
   reader at £3 a week. Her colleague there, John McMillan, later went to the US and became a
   reviewer for the New York Times Book Review.

Miss Scott-James[1] all in difficult silence & no telepathy either rewarded one for a waste of appalling bores) are becoming rarer, & I find to my surprise (a humiliating thing to confess) that I spend about 3 times the time I used to in professional chat. It has I believe been arranged that Miss Anrep[2] be enslaved by Mr Stephens[3] of Magdalen. Please write me a letter (about Spain[4] for which I truly long) how your father is – do you think the fact that All Souls has elected a Montenegrin called John Petroff Plamenatz to a thesis fellowship wd excite him? 'What nationality is he?' said Oman.[5] He was given the answer. 'A Montenegrin!!!!!!' he said & almost swooned. It was v. funny. Headlam[6] said he shd be searched for bombs before entering college meetings but that he approved of Southern Slavs since he had himself suggested that a statue of him, done by Mestrovic,[7] should be executed in white marble & erected outside Gloucester cathedral (the chapter had suggested a portrait). Plamenatz is repulsively ugly & looks like a currant & dates merchant. And is a philosopher. Will you *please* remember to remind me to reproduce for you: (a) Oman on psychology when anthropology was discussed (b) Oman on women pursuing abnormal studies in the library (c) Coupland on Codrington college Barbadoes[8] ("there they are, I can see them now, fifteen blacks, five coffee & five whites"). One Mauricism: I told him that I had never met anyone who dates so much as Eddie Sackville West.[9] 'Dates, dates' he said 'dates, why he is a box of dates'. $\beta+$[10] wd you say? will you think about Salzburg?

  Shaya

  1 Before he married Sally Graves, Richard Chilver had been in love with the writer Anne Scott-James (b. 1913), who was at this point working for *Vogue*, having gone down from Somerville at the end of her third year because, although she took a First in Classical Mods, she did not take to Greats.
  2 Anastasia Anrep (b. 1912), daughter of Boris and Helen (Roger Fry's mistress), was a contemporary of Jenifer Williams and Sally Graves at Somerville: history 1932–4, English 1935–6, failed her degree.
  3 Courtenay Edward Stephens (1905–76; known for some reason by the nickname 'Tom Brown'), ancient historian, Fellow of Magdalen 1933–72. He liked to get his pupils to perform practical tasks for him, and they willingly acquiesced in this arrangement: so the reference to slavery is good-natured.
  4 The three Fishers were staying with Lettice Fisher's sister and brother-in-law, Sir George and Lady (Jessie, sometimes 'Helen') Young, after a breakdown in H. A. L. Fisher's health. The Youngs had a house at Torremolinos, then a small village.
  5 Sir Charles (William Chadwick) Oman (1860–1946), historian, Fellow of All Souls 1883–1946.
  6 Rt Revd Arthur Cayley Headlam (1862–1947), historian, Bishop of Gloucester, Fellow of All Souls 1885–97, 1924–47.
  7 Ivan Mestrovic (1883–1962), Croatian sculptor of gigantic statues.
  8 Christopher Codrington (1668–1710), soldier, Fellow of All Souls 1690–7; his munificence (in his will) financed the Codrington Library in All Souls as well as Codrington College, Barbados.
  9 Edward ('Eddie') Charles Sackville-West (1901–65), music critic and author; later (1962) 5th Baron Sackville.
  10 For Greek letters see 93/1.

TO JENIFER WILLIAMS

[March? 1936]

All Souls

Dear Jenifer,

There is nothing I should like to do more than to expound to you the errors which, I hold, vitiate Alfred J. Ayer's book.[1] Particularly as I shall thus clearly apprehend them myself for the first time. Some of this I shall write down during to-morrow's college meeting: the rest on Sunday evening. I look forward to this with genuine pleasure. Meanwhile let me recommend to you an enchanting work by Professor Price published in a journal called Philosophy during, I think, 1935, called 'Theology and Logical Positivism',[2] which also bristles with errors, but is delightful in every way; perhaps not bristles, but has a great whopping one in the centre. I contemplate my visit to-morrow with very mixed feelings. I hope that by the time I arrive whatever was bound to happen will either have already happened or was determined not to happen.[3]

Possibly I shall not manage my opuscule[4] quite so soon, in that event (the sentence is composed solely to end in this way) it may offer curious reading during your Tour of Wales. I suggest as a night-thought that there are *three* distinctions between human beings

A) Tolstoy's distinction of those who understand from those who don't.

B) Those who are sympathetic about human affairs, those who are not, and the lunatics & eccentrics.

C) Those who are finite and rounded and those who are unbounded and in no sense aggregates of characteristics.

This is not very happily expressed, but classification along these lines is fascinating & instructive and not gossip, but uses it in a serious and creative manner.

I venture to end the asymmetry and remain

Yours

Shaya.

1 *Language, Truth and Logic* (London, 1936).
2 H. H. Price, 'Logical Positivism and Theology', *Philosophy* 10 (1935), 313–31.
3 Jenifer Hart can't remember what this was.
4 Jenifer Hart doesn't know what this was. She has a letter from Jasper Ridley dated March 1936 asking to see a letter from IB that refers to his opuscule: if this is the letter in question, it must have been written before or during March 1936.

25 April 1936

All Souls

Dear Stephen

I am sorry not to have written you for so long: I was in France and worked very hard, and then came back & there was chaos and disorder about my pupils etc. which took time. I have read your MS.[1] twice: and, of course, as you know, I like everything you write an & für sich,[2] the subject, as you said, we have talked about, and I have to discount both that & my natural liking if I am to say anything useful. The chief danger so far as I can see is that however good your poetry and however effective your order of scenes – the cumulative effect of even as much as you have written up to date I thought very moving and beautiful – there is too much morality, conscious morality, in the words themselves. Too much larmes; the danger to any poet, I shd have thought (forgive me for speaking like a don), who writes about a social issue about which he feels really passionately, is that unless he screams like Toller[3] – who is fundamentally silly, & in all respects utterly unlike you & really a sort of Goodman[4] in parts – is that of becoming a Hugo. Hugo you remember sent an uncut diamond after seeing Sarah Bernhardt perform, + the inscription 'une larme de Victor Hugo'. It was I think a perfectly sincere gesture, & what is wrong is not merely that it is silly or rhetorical, but that he did become a sort of specialist about being moved, tears etc. and consequently acted in his real capacity, & not an assumed part. I grant that you are not like that, that you don't make a corner in emotions excited by political injustice or tragedy. But there is too little relief in the sense in which Eliot's choruses, which are, when good, pure poetry which neither describes, nor states, but is what it means, is relief to his didactic or polemical stuff. In your play every line, every word (this is exaggerated) wrings the vitals. There is too much concentrated emotiveness, if you see what I mean.

I know nothing about poetry, and nothing about plays, and my criticism

---

1 *Trial of a Judge* (155/4). Spender, referring to the Fascists' destruction of the political independence of the judiciary, described the theme as German justice. The judge (following the law) has sentenced to death both a gang of Nazi thugs, for the murder of Petra, a half Jew, half Christian Pole, and three Communists, for the lesser crimes of self-defence and disseminating propaganda. He decides as a matter of conscience that the Communists should be reprieved by the President, but there is a Nazi putsch, after which the Home Secretary reverses this decision, so that only Petra's murderers are reprieved. The judge resigns in protest and is shot.

2 'In and for itself'.

3 The émigré German author Ernst Toller (1893–1939).

4 Probably Richard Hackett Goodman, New College PPE 1929–32, co-editor of the *Oxford Outlook* with IB (21/5).

& my advice, I should have thought (if I were an impartial critic) are of no use. All I want to say is that I, no one else, desiderate a certain spaciousness & abstractness, a non-parti-pris element, which seems to me to be swamped by the enormous ad hocness of your lines. I think there are some absolutely lovely lines, and I should like to read the rest very much, & shall think it very good, in fact, because I believe I possess your moral taste. This is all I can say at present: I should do a lot to meet you somewhere in order to discuss the play further – I have made out a list of minor corrections, which I'll send you when you want it. At present I am not sure to what address to write to you.

I have read Forster's book,[1] & I admire it very much, but I am continually repelled by a broken, resentment-full, self-torturing, crippled, patriotic, shrill, element which somehow seems to penetrate everything he writes & twists it & leaves a bitter taste, not objectively, morally, bitter, like the romantics' indignation or genuine pain, but little malicious, self-conscious, self-pitying stabs which make both his malice, & his sentimentality more intolerable than the sentimentality of, say, Havelock Ellis[2] (whose essay on Restif de la Bretonne[3] is v. interesting) or the malice of, say, Eliot. Forster is getting his own back, & has [a] frightful contorted indirect way of doing it. But his book is really very good: the individual things are absolutely unique & full of an intellectual sincerity which I like & admire v. much. Meanwhile that silly Desmond McCarthy (to borrow a Rowsian expression) encouraged obviously by Sparrow's book,[4] which now I regard as a disaster & not merely bad, accuses Hubert Read, (abt his book on Shelley)[5] of being silly, obscure, unintelligible, perverse etc. & quotes things like "the contour of an idea' as being typically unintelligible ('only mountain ranges have contours not ideas'), when they are obviously plain. He greeted Sparrow's book, I remember, as something too good to be true, a young man saying all these things which had accumulated for years in the hearts of the old, so now the bluff of the modernists has been called, one can at last boldly show them up. This makes me feel genuinely indignant, so that were I to meet McCarthy, I should, I think, not speak to him, though I don't doubt that as a man I should like him better than Read.

Freddie Ayer says Lindemann[6] says he saw you in Barcelona. I think

---

1 *Abinger Harvest* (161/1).
2 (Henry) Havelock Ellis (1859–1939), doctor, writer, student of sexual behaviour, which he believed should be openly discussed.
3 Nicolas-Edme Restif (1734–1806), French novelist and shoe-fetishist, described the seamy side of eighteenth-century French life.
4 *Sense and Poetry* (127/6).
5 See 158/1.
6 Frederick Alexander Lindemann (1886–1957), physicist and politician, scientific adviser to the government, Professor of Experimental Philosophy, Oxford, and Fellow of Wadham 1919–56, Dr Lee's Reader in Experimental Philosophy and Student of Christ Church 1921–57;

him a horrible man, Roy admires him enormously, Maurice hedges. What did you think of him. News (via Grigson)[1] that you have joined the C.P. seems to me to alter nothing. You are quite right about it in England. On the continent, where in any case there was a tradition of government persecution, revolutionary parties automatically were conspiratorial, met abroad, talked about nothing save tactics & revolution, had no time for life or art, & were like Lenin so to speak. In England where this is not so, the C.P., is as you say, neo-liberal. It is a radical-intellectual revolt against the bureaucracy & stale corruptness of the Labour-Party, i.e. those who were socialists in 1920 are now communists, they don't really hope for a revolution, & are more highbrow than Socialists, & more intelligent & less vulgar. Sigle Lynd says that only applies to the insignificant handful of intellectuals, while real party is different. Possibly. Only the former really alter the tone of the process.

Mr Van Dieren, the composer, whose book I once reviewed, & so that I was attacked by him in a letter, answered it etc.[2] died yesterday, & now I feel like Lockhart who snuffed out Keats with a review,[3] (or Cardan,[4] who according to Forster, was nearly killed by Scaliger)[5] i.e. very grand & malevolent: but really had I known how ill he was, I should have moderated my tone. Maurice relates that in Day-Lewis's new novel there is a don who is vulgarly like himself,[6] & that he is much embarrassed. Will have to be looked into.

My colleague O'Neill[7] writes excellent letters from Germany: he says that in Heidelberg the professor of English, lecturing in post-war English

personal assistant to Winston Churchill from 1939, created Lord Cherwell 1941.

1 The poet and critic Geoffrey Edward Harvey Grigson (1905–85).

2 For the details see 139/4.

3 John Gibson Lockhart (1794–1854), famous as Walter Scott's biographer, is thought to be the pseudonymous author, 'Z', of a hostile review of Keats's *Endymion* (1818) published under the heading 'Cockney School of Poetry No IV' in *Blackwood's Edinburgh Magazine* 3 No 17 (August 1818), 519–24. This review and another of great virulence (by John Wilson Croker, published anonymously in the *Quarterly Review* 19 No 37 (April 1818), 204–8) preyed on Keats's mind, though they can hardly be said to have caused Keats's death (1821).

4 Gerolamo Cardano (1501–76), in English Jerome Cardan, Italian physician and mathematician.

5 Julius Caesar Scaliger (1484–1558), classical scholar and literary critic. See *Abinger Harvest* (161/1), 194–5. In fact, according to Forster, Cardan was not literally 'nearly killed', though he was certainly got down by Scaliger's published attack on his work: rather his death was reported as a joke.

6 Philip Starling, 'fellow of All Saints and the foremost authority in England on Homeric civilisation and literature' (p. 47), in *Thou Shell of Death* (London, 1936), published under the pseudonym Nicholas Blake, which Day Lewis used for his crime-writing. Day Lewis's widow doubts that Starling is closely based on Bowra, to whom her husband was devoted.

7 Hon. Con Douglas Walter O'Neill (1912–88), lawyer, Fellow of All Souls 1935–46, Diplomatic Service 1936–9.

literature, has selected, to lecture on, J. B. Priestley,[1] Mary Webb,[2] & Sir Philip Gibbs.[3] Also that he went to a law Court where a man was condemned to 4 months for throwing a stone at a bird – against Goering's new Reichsjagdgesetzbuch[4] – because that is bestial cruelty and the National Socialist régime is opposed to cruelty in every shape & form. He quotes very funnily from Faust: when in Auerbach's Keller the company is tipsy

Alle (Singen)	Uns geht es ganz kanibalisch gut
	Als wie fünfhundert Säuen
Mephisto.	Das Volk ist frei . . .[5]

which is v. funny I think. He declares (how enthusiastic about his letters I am being. However I respect him a lot.) that Germany is like an enormous female spider, which has lain inertly in central Europe for many years, while the rest of Europe tried vainly to impregnate her. At last they succeeded. A tiny egg has been laid. the spider shifted ominously & with a huge loving look turned to her mate to devour him.[6] Please write your address, about Spain, Greece, anything, & I shall write you a better letter.

Love to Tony.

Shaya

1 John Boynton Priestley (1894–1984), prolific English journalist, novelist, playwright and essayist; published over 120 books on a wide range of subjects. *The Good Companions* (1929) and *Angel Pavement* (1930) were highly successful popular novels; his play *An Inspector Calls* (1946) is often revived.

2 Mary Gladys Webb (1881–1927), English novelist associated especially with the landscape of her native Shropshire. Her novel *Precious Bane* (London, 1924) was enormously successful, and was parodied by Stella Gibbons in *Cold Comfort Farm* (London, 1932).

3 Sir Philip Gibbs (1877–1962), Roman Catholic English writer and journalist, war correspondent in both world wars, author of several books on political and autobiographical subjects; reputed the first journalist ever to have secured an interview with the Pope (Benedict XV, in 1919).

4 'Reich hunting code'.

5 In David Luke's translation (Oxford, 1987): 'ALL [*singing*]: Oh now we're having a cannibal feast, / Happy as five hundred swine! / MEPHISTOPHELES This mob's on the free [. . .].' Characteristically, IB slightly misquotes (Goethe wrote 'Uns ist ganz kanibalisch wohl / Als wie fünfhundert Säuen!'). O'Neill gets it right, and gives the reference (*Faust*, part 1, lines 2293–5). Auerbachs Keller is a beer-cellar in Leipzig.

6 O'Neill continues: 'But no doubt the meal will be decently ordered, as a sacrament, and the victim will suffer for his own good and the greater glory of the new religion.' The remarks by O'Neill that IB quotes are in a letter from Heidelberg dated 25 March and one from Freiburg dated 20 April.

Burning Cactus[1] arrived to-day, I have not had time to look at it even. Did you like Connolly's review in I think the Daily Telegraph?

TO MARION FRANKFURTER

3 June 1936

All Souls

Dear Marion,

A letter exists, in fact, which I began writing to you about 4 months ago, when there seemed no prospect of your return, which I have not indeed destroyed, but which has grown to the dimension of a quasi-diary & which cannot possibly be sent, because it is too detailed, too inconsequent and too dull. So that having written this, the other will be destroyed this evening.[2] At first I was very sorry that you weren't both coming, but then I fell ill with a quinsy and recovered slowly and secludedly, and wouldn't have been able to stay in Oxford or anywhere where I might have seen you. After which my life repeated itself with pedantic accuracy. I went to Salzburg as I always do, to the Riviera in spring with my parents, and so on. I pretend that this repetitiveness is precisely what I require, it provides a framework, makes deviations possible etc. the truth being that I stay put, dislike anything unknown, dislike being uprooted and so on, which is really very shaming. The effect is that little in my life or anyone's here has changed. You will find Oxford exactly the same aquarium as you left it. The Goodharts[3] it is true live in [a] large white house. It is very white indeed. No difference has been made to anyone. Social life in any case does not (happily) exist, ever since Maurice stopped entertaining on a large scale, and everything is, if anything, more sedate, less lively & malicious, than when you were here last. Maurice himself (it is impossible not to start with him) is on tenterhooks about his professorship. I doubt if he will get it. Murray,[4] being himself a popularizer, has a naturall passion for austerity rigorism etc., & suspects

---

1 Stephen Spender, The Burning Cactus (1936), a book of short stories: the title story first appeared (dedicated to IB) in the New Oxford Outlook 1 No 1 (May 1933), 24–42. This previous incarnation is not mentioned in the book; nor is the dedication repeated there, perhaps because the book as a whole is dedicated to W. H. Auden and Tony Hyndman.

2 He did not destroy it, but enclosed it with a letter to MF dated 26 July 1951.

3 Arthur Lehman Goodhart (1891–1978), Professor of Jurisprudence and Fellow of Univ. 1931–51, later (1951–63) Master, and his wife Cecily.

4 (George) Gilbert Aimé Murray (1866–1957), born in Australia but educated in England, Greek scholar, author, translator and internationalist; Professor of Greek, Glasgow, 1889–99; Regius Professor of Greek, Oxford, 1908–36; pacifist in inclination, active supporter of the League of Nations, campaigner for women's rights. The character of Adolphus Cusins in Shaw's play Major Barbara (1905) is based on him.

Maurice of slipshodness & so on. Lady Mary hates him.[1] His faculty is
a jealous body of men, full of resentment and secret hatred of their subject.
I wish this tension were to end however, since it is very wearing. He is still
the most fascinating man I know, and infinitely responsive to every inflexion
& accent. But somehow a little too resigned to academic failure. But I may
be wrong. The Ayers have a child and are quite happy. There cannot be
complete tranquillity anywhere where Freddie is, future crises are already
looming, but on the whole even they seem settled. Their prosperity, their
life in London etc. has tranquillized them a great deal, but still they are the
most exotic persons, with an infinite quantity of style, whom one has ever
met, & refreshing & exhilarating to the last degree. Freddie's unwavering
loyalty to his friends is a childlike, pathetic, very endearing quality which
always moves me a great deal. The mixture of sophistication & simplicity is
very odd & attractive. He grows no older, & seems permanently fixed, still
anxious to be the enfant terrible of the philosophers. In this he succeeds, save
that now his colleagues like & respect him a good deal more than they used
to. Elizabeth Cameron's success with her last novel[2] has repercussed here
nearly as much as in U.S.A. I think. She lives in London since her husband
has a job there, and has relapsed into not exactly Bloomsbury, but anyhow
a very non-Oxford atmosphere. She continues to be a delightful person,
understands everything one says, and loves low life, toughs, blood, and
anything violent. I don't see her at all often, & always enjoy it when I do. She
makes one feel cleverer, more sympathetic, more nicely poised than one is,
one cannot talk about nothing, one is kept up to the mark, & she never does
not respond at all, but always reacts in some way to all one does or says,
which is nice. I read her books with only moderate pleasure: they are like
very good conversation, but perfectly motionless, with no direction, and like
artificially constructed universes made deliberately to shut out anything at all
sizeable outside. All the individual pages & chapters are very good but the
whole is a loose collection, held by nothing, connected capriciously, &
always violently self-conscious. I am not expressing this at all well. My point
is that there is no grand single line, everything is in bits, & often absolutely
dead, & always very unheimlich,[3] almost macabre. They are more unlike
her ordinary conversation than one could well believe. The house in
Regent's Park in which she lives, & entertains David Cecil & Mrs Woolf, is

1 Murray was married to Lady Mary (Henrietta) (1865–1956), née Howard, daughter of the 9th
   Earl of Carlisle. A lady of firm convictions, left-wing in politics, teetotal and vegetarian, she
   had rejected in favour of a brother her inheritance from her feminist mother of the family
   home of Castle Howard in Yorkshire.
2 *The House in Paris* (133/3).
3 'Eerie'.

1 Marie Berlin as a young woman

2 Marie and Mendel Berlin on a seaside holiday

3 Yitzhak and Ida Samunov, IB's uncle and aunt

4 As a pupil at St Paul's School

5 49 Hollycroft Avenue, Hampstead

6 Front quadrangle, Corpus Christi College

7 In his Corpus room, *c.*1932

8 In St Giles', Oxford, outside the Taylorian Institution

9 The Great Quadrangle, All Souls, where IB had rooms

10 Mary Fisher with her father, Herbert Fisher

11 Adam von Trott in the Cloisters, New College, with the Bell Tower in the background

12 Jenifer Williams

13 At the Chalet des Mélèzes in the French Alps, September 1933:
(*standing*) Oliver Woods, IB, George Odling, Shaun Wylie, Christopher Cox, Richard Chilver, Frederick How; (*sitting*) Herbert Hart, Richard Wilberforce, Mark Tennant

14 Man in cloak at the Chalet   15 Christopher Cox at the Chalet

16 In New College garden in a break from the Commem Ball on 22 June 1934:
(*back*) Richard Chilver, Guy Chilver, John Ward-Perkins; (*front*) Herbert Hart, Mary Fisher,
Maire Lynd, Julia Pakenham, Rachel Walker, Priscilla Chilver, IB

17 Painting by Giles Robertson,
January 1935, of a scene from
IB's childhood in Riga

18 Stephen Spender in an ancient
theatre of uncertain
Mediterranean location

19 About to tour a salt mine, Salzburg, August 1935, in celebration of the end of Mary Fisher's finals: 5th–8th from left are Maire Lynd, Mary Fisher, IB, Richard Pares

20 Gap of Dunloe, Killarney, 3 September 1936: Con O'Neill, IB, Stuart Hampshire

delightfully pretty, like an object in art. Alan Cameron[1] is daily becoming kinder and more intolerable.

Then there is Rees, who is more featherweight than ever, who having quarreled with his girl,[2] is now deliciously free & happy. He really is a purely gaminious figure. Very untrustworthy, very gay. Actually last summer was not quite so simple as I said. Things did happen to Maurice & even to me which I cannot put in a letter, & hardly even into conversation. If you ask me questions I expect I shall answer, but I cannot set anything down in cold blood. I dislike my equilibrium destroyed so much that even the memory of it is disturbing. But we must go for a walk on this subject if you are interested.

The Warden of New College, for whose great style & really well & artistically self-built up personality I have genuine admiration, has been ill, & is now back, very pale & transparent, & still full of epigrams which all come off. He recently described a pupil to me as 'a man of wavering and opalescent intelligence who may be interesting at the age of forty'. Really he is much younger than anybody here, & more distinguished. You are bound to see him sometime. I assure you it will be a pleasure. The chief real difference here is that the crisis is over. The Fellows elected in my College this year are pre-war types, or at any rate post-political. The break is evident everywhere. Society is becoming interested in Mozart. Less & less politics is being produced by undergraduates. The really terrific political tension of 18 months ago, is over. The prospect is in no sense bright: People have somehow become more neat, tidy, hard-working, ordered, sensible, kind, polite, & reputable. Also more callous, boring, & priggish. There is a sort of expensive aluminium feeling about one's best pupils, they are so very nice, courteous, decent, clever, industrious and charming. There is not a single human note anywhere. I exaggerate: but there really is far more insensitiveness, & a sort of respectable anxious-to-be-of-use-to-the-world admirably poised but entirely frigid niceness about, which absolutely terrifies me. I prefer cads provided they now & then perform an unnecessary gesture. However you will see for yourself. I wish you could meet Stephen Spender, who will I suppose still be in Greece, who is v. symbolic of a now slightly démodé romanticism, which alone means anything at all to me. At present all young men are tremendously interested in the arts, in facts about them, in

1 Alan Charles Cameron (1893–1952), educationalist, husband of Elizabeth Bowen since 1923. He had recently started working for the BBC in London, so the Camerons had moved from Waldencote, their house in Old Headington, in north-east Oxford, to the Regent's Park area of London.

2 Presumably Shiela Grant Duff. If Rees had a mistress less than 3 weeks later (174/7), perhaps the end of his delicious freedom was near.

dates, attributions, details etc. they are all reputable scholarly & lucid, but their actual feelings on seeing something are negligible. Can you conceive of a universe full of enlightened, tolerant, amiable, handsome, absolutely repulsive people? but I have always been prone to coloured descriptions of unimportant phenomena. It will be very nice indeed seeing you again. My love to F.F. & I shall tell Maurice etc. Roy e.g. is in terrific form, writing a book in which he believes he has struck oil at last, mad, & gay, & eccentric, & snobbish & sweet. Au revoir, I am really delighted that you are coming. Shaya.

TO STEPHEN SPENDER

20 June [1936]

All Souls

Dear Stephen

Thank you very much for your letter & postcard.[1] I enjoy everything you send so much that if I really thought that by writing more frequently I should extract more from you, I should do so. Assure me that this is so, & I will. For otherwise there is too little incentive, since I haven't much to say at present. There is another change of mood in Oxford, & I as you know attach some importance to this: since as Curtius[2] once correctly said, the barometers of culture in England were in Oxford & Cambridge & not in London. Not but what a congress of libertarian intellectuals is going on there at present: all the great Frenchmen, Gide, Malraux etc. the English names begin with a sudden descent: Bates.[3] Forster & Huxley, being apparently nervous about being compromised with communism, sent Heard,[4] whom they can trust to be non political & pacifist, to represent them. Eyeless in Gaza[5] by Aldous H. I have just bought & not yet read. It looks rather awful, but like all he writes has a certain sympathetic quality which overrides one's repulsion in the end: but he creates a lot of unnecessary obstacles: his images are squalid & nauseating, and he seems unable to keep them out: the whole thing is done in a sinister understated sort of way: we are used to war

1 Letter of 6 May 1936, postcard of 10 June 1936.
2 The humanist Ernst Robert Curtius (1884–1956). But where did he say it? Perhaps in conversation.
3 Herbert Ernest Bates (1905–74), English novelist and short-story writer, many of whose works celebrate the English countryside and rural life.
4 Henry Fitzgerald ('Gerald') Heard (1889–1971), of Irish descent but born and educated in England; BBC science correspondent 1930–4; moved to US 1937; writer and lecturer on religion, mysticism, anthropology and human development; as H. F. Heard, author of mystery stories.
5 London, 1936.

horrors, consequently he produces a scene in which the mangled remains of a terrier plop down from an aeroplane on two lovers naked on a roof, & spatter them with blood. Quiet horror is a speciality of the French in the last century, but whereas Baudelaire & Huysmans[1] do so for purely artistic reasons & standing aloof from it present it without comment, Huxley, a puritan moralist makes a sort of propaganda of it, & merely lowers & sordidifies the scene. One is touched or nauseated or pierced in some way, but not moved or at all profoundly affected or made capable of seeing something or understanding anything save abstract general propositions. He is clever & humane and morally sympathetic, but there is a bottled up ressentiment[2] which makes one always uneasy when one reads him, just as one is with really distinguished & sincere people if something is all the time simmering away inside them & from time to time disfigures whatever they do. All this before reading the book. More afterwards.

Maurice Bowra is in a difficult state. Gilbert Murray has told Baldwin[3] to appoint someone else to the Greek Chair, & Maurice is tossing to & fro, & I have been ordered to [be] bloody bold & resolute & attack the Warden of New College.[4] I shall have to leave Oxford when he fails to be appointed. The strain will be intolerable. I don't think I shall come to Salzburg this year: Moore will be there I think: the atmosphere of the place has begun to oppress even me; the huge cowed smart audiences and the complete absence of privacy. Toscanini one ought, I admit, to do anything rather than not hear, what I shd really like to do is to go & hear him in Jerusalem in September: the scene wd really be remarkable: he wd conduct on a red hill with thousands of very variegated Jews absolutely worshipping round him & the possibility of Arab bombs. I can imagine how such a scene wd be described by say Stefan Zweig:[5] it wd undoubtedly be the most repulsive piece of writing ever read: the last chords of the 3^d movement of the 7th Symphony, then a bomb etc. But I should very much like to be present. When are you returning to England? whenever that be, if I am there & it is not term, I should like to go & stay in the country with you for 3–4 days at least & make up accounts so to speak. I am convinced that another generation has come to an end (in Oxford to go back), & that now unlike

1 Joris Karl (né Charles-Marie-Georges) Huysmans (1848–1907), French-Dutch civil servant, novelist and art critic. The naturalism of his early novels was replaced firstly by exotic decadence and an interest in Satanism, then by a concentration on the spiritual journey which led to his late conversion to Roman Catholicism.

2 'Resentment'.

3 The Regius Chair of Greek was in the gift of the Prime Minister, then Stanley Baldwin.

4 Maybe Bowra (who had, incidentally, been an undergraduate at New College) felt that Fisher had Baldwin's ear, and that Berlin could persuade Fisher to support him in that quarter.

5 Austrian-born biographer, novelist and essayist (1881–1942); a close friend of Toscanini.

previous years, we are going to get some intelligent and sensitive Marxists. Marxism is at present a movement with more nonsense attached to it than Fascism: there is no Fascist arithmetic: only if sufficiently honest & intelligent people begin writing (as unlike Blaikie[1] as possible) will the nonsense be got rid of: at present too many silly anti-Marxist attacks are necessarily successful, when there is no need to drag about this incubus of rubbish. There are some undergraduates here, not, I regret to say much encouraged by Maurice or Roy, who are both nice & intelligent, & without the enormous sectarian pride of the scientists in Cambridge. Roy is I think frankly anti-socialist now: & is altogether breaking out sexually & otherwise. But this I can only convey in conversation. It is far from unamusing. Connolly has published a book, costing 50 francs, called the Rock Pool.[2] Faber refused to publish it on the ground that it was about a little group of decadents in Paris & nobody could be interested in them. A fuss is going on about the surréalist exhibition in London.[3] Everyone, even the Evening Standard is anxious not to repeat the mistake about the post-impressionist one.[4] It is said to be charming & restful. It was opened by André Breton,[5] a dapper little figure, who got up on a hard sprung sofa, rocked a little, & then in an absolutely enormous voice roared: 'Changez la Vie!'[6] Goronwy is responsible for this story. He has finally abandoned Shiela & has an awful mistress, a Mrs Pamela Warburg,[7] for whom I can find nothing to say. She is pretentious, vicious, boring, & not even beautiful. Casson?[8] you rather waste good adjectives on him I think.[9] He is all you say, but less. An absolutely unimportant, unlearned persecuted little buffoon who calls himself a communist, & raises laughs at New College. He acts as vulgar light relief &

1 55/5.
2 Paris, 1936: Obelisk Press. The book's failure to find an English publisher was really due to the fear that it would be regarded as obscene.
3 The first 'International Surrealist Exhibition', held at London's Burlington Galleries in June and July. There were 25,000 visitors, and the opening caused a massive traffic jam.
4 Possibly a reference to the 1910 and 1912 post-Impressionist exhibitions organised by Roger Fry, which brought recent developments in French painting to a British audience for the first time, and caused a furore. The *Standard* tended to be down on 'modern art'.
5 André Breton (1896–1966), one of the leading founders of surrealism.
6 'Change Life!', a rallying-cry derived from a sentence in *Une saison en enfer* ('A season in hell', 1873), by the rebellious homosexual teenage French poet Arthur Rimbaud (156/2), 'Il a peut-être des secrets pour *changer la vie*?': 'Délires I: Vierge folle – L'Époux infernal'; p. 189 in Arthur Rimbaud, *Poésies, Une saison en enfer, Illuminations*, ed. Louis Forestier ([Paris], 1999). The phrase became a central tenet of surrealism.
7 Pamela de Bayou, wife of Fredric John *Warburg (1898–1981), Chairman of the London publishing house of Martin Secker & Warburg (their first book was published on 4 April 1936).
8 Stanley Casson (1889–1944), classical archaeologist, Fellow of New College 1920–44, killed in action.
9 SS describes him in his postcard as a 'vain, self-conscious, spiteful, ashamed, talkative, nervous man'.

nobody thinks of him seriously. Ashamed is quite right, his spitefulness is pure defence: hence his squalor. Lindemann is a bad man on a much bigger scale: a genuinely horrible figure, who symbolizes everything that one hates most passionately, from general cryptoness & snobbery to a love of inflicting pain on the weak & hatred of himself. Roy claims to be devoted [to] him & praises his intelligence & his sensitiveness. I dramatize him as a hostis generis humani[1] & really hate him more than anybody. He is the only person, I think, whom I have ardently wished to murder. How unusual such a sentiment is in me you can well conceive.

What am I to do with your play?[2] I have read it again & read & reread your letter, & I understand all you say, I don't regard you as in [the] least defeatist, as e.g. Huxley is or even Forster, and I even understand why he should have been pseudo-scrupulous & frightened of admitting any possible self-identification. What I complain of is not the sadness of your characters, but the fact that you sometimes accompany them with overheard personal lamentation. You once said yourself that the poet must not shove himself into his work. In your play you stand too near your characters, you pity too much and are contorted with horror & pain too often: Eliot, e.g. rushes to the opposite extreme & practises a sort of exhibitionistic restraint and wry jokes: pseudo-grimness is also ridiculous. But I am sure that when Blake said Damn Braces Bless Relaxes,[3] over & above the obvious meaning he also intended to say that Damnation stiffens, Blessing relaxes, & that one must therefore convey a sort of hard, elastic, relentless quality into the characters themselves. Otherwise the audience is touched & not moved, looks at you & sympathises instead of at your work & sees, and your work becomes symbolic of you & your generation, & nothing but (cf your remarks about Wertherishness).[4] The horror & sense of destruction in Malraux or even Kafka (not to speak of Henry James, which you discovered for me) is achieved by terrific externalization & suppression of description as opposed to statement: my charge is that you sometimes forget to be rigorous enough & begin to palpitate slightly. But as I told you before I was enormously moved, as I am by almost all you write.

Will you write me about your immediate movements? I shall be in

---

1 'Enemy of the human race'.

2 155/4.

3 'Damn braces: Bless relaxes.' William Blake, The Marriage of Heaven and Hell, 'The Proverbs of Hell', plate 9.

4 Near the beginning of his letter: 'I suppose I am now going through a romantic, Wertherish period in my work, as in my life, from which I see and feel no relief, except in so far as I can work it off in my writing . . .'. Goethe's Die Leiden des jungen Werthers (1774), 'The sorrows of the young Werther' (the basis of Massenet's opera Werther), glamorised the romantic notion of a glorious suicide.

England till about 20th Aug, when I shall probably go to Ireland. The Palestine situation[1] is depressing me a lot, I am sure it is largely the government's fault for having no policy at all & soothing both sides down all the time. One subsists on such occasional good jokes as Maurice makes: the last one was about Boase: You know the Boase series: Boase, Boasey, the Boaseye (which waters or falls out or something) the Boase-Lyon, Böslein Böslein Böslein Rot Böslein auf der Heide.[2] And now to crown all the Boase oeil as opposed to the Beaux Yeux.

    Love to Tony
      yrs
        Shaya.

I am not by nature a lover of violent sensations but if you send me anything you've written the tremor preliminary to reading is there, & I really do begin (& usually end) fairly breathlessly. Do keep me supplied. I am your most ardent admirer: be careful to feed the flame of my devotion, it will come in useful in my autobiography & biography of you: both interesting & valuable documents.

Moore with vast pride has shown me a bill from his tailors:[3]

coat – £45
trousers – £12
sword, sash & scabbard etc. – £8.8.0

There are 40 carats of gold on the coat alone, & buttons on the tails: he is leading a charmed life: hours of work are from 11 a.m.–1 p.m, & 3 p.m–5 p.m. But I suppose my own job doesn't allow me to mock or be indignant. I wish we could meet on some island between Sicily & Spain, Majorca or

---

1 After months of tension between Arabs and Jews the Arab parties had in April called a general strike to protest against increasing Jewish immigration to Palestine, and violent clashes had broken out between the opposing sides. In May the British government announced the setting up of a commission of enquiry (246/3).

2 'Bosey' was the nickname of Oscar Wilde's friend Lord Alfred Douglas; Bowes-Lyon is the family name of the late Queen Mother; in the parody of Goethe's 'Röslein, Röslein, Röslein rot, / Röslein auf der Heiden' ('Little red rose from the heath'), from his 'Heidenröslein' (1771) – *Goethes Werke* (Weimar, 1887–1919), vol. 1, p. 16 – 'Böslein' is a coinage intended to mean 'evil little thing'; 'beaux yeux' is French for 'beautiful eyes', and 'oeil' is the singular of 'yeux'.

3 FO regulations specified in minute detail the uniforms to be worn by staff serving abroad: IB may be referring to Crosthwaite's Levee Dress, comprising coat, trousers, hat, sword (with sword-knot and belt) and boots. Although his rank (Third Secretary) entailed less embellishment than on the uniform of more senior officials, his coat would have had gold embroidery on collar, cuffs, back and pocket-flaps, and gilt buttons (displaying the Royal Arms and Imperial Crown) front and back.

somewhere. I leave here on Monday the 12th. If you write to London they will forward. All hope of Malaga is not lost, but nearly all. I shall report your words to Bernard [Spencer?]: he is working solidly but happily on some film: it is a small & poor company in which everyone does everything: it is all squalid & pathetic & he likes it v. much. I've not seen O.P.[1]

love.

Shaya

TO ELIZABETH BOWEN

[June 1936]

All Souls

Dear Elizabeth

I haven't seen you for an infinitely long period of time, your telephone is alleged to be out of order, Goronwy's reminders of you whet one's feelings so that steps have to be taken to deflect them, consequently what is to be done? I may be in Town on Friday morning: wd you be visible then? or early on Thursday afternoon? I don't know when I shall finally return to London, on Monday week conceivably. And I am making vague plans towards a visit to Ireland in late August–September with a quasi ex-pupil (male).[2] Will you be there? here I am scorched by the reflected rage and dismay on the part of Maurice to whom the news has just been broken that Murray recommended a man called Dodds for the professorship. Nothing has been announced yet, a desperate last minute action is being fought: I have been told to be bloody bold & resolute & have assailed Fisher: Roy has attacked the Dean of Christchurch: K. Clark[3] is treacherous & does nothing. David Cecil was thought of as likely to have access to Ormsby-Gore[4] who is loved by Baldwin (it is said), but is thought to be too slow to act at all, & too listless & not enough of a friend. But if you do chance to see him . . . I am sure we shall lose, but like the Viennese rising, it is a sacred duty to be defeated under aesthetically non-shaming circumstances. What has Mr

---

1 *Oxford Poetry*, an annual publication of poems by Oxford graduates and undergraduates founded in 1910 by Basil Blackwell. Spender had been the editor in 1929 and 1930 but there had been a gap in publication from 1932 to 1936.

2 Stuart Hampshire.

3 Kenneth Mackenzie Clark (1903–83), Keeper, Dept of Fine Art, Ashmolean Museum, Oxford, 1931–3, Director, National Gallery, 1934–45, MOI 1939–41, later (1969) Baron Clark.

4 William George Arthur Ormsby-Gore (1885–1964), Conservative politician, Secretary of State for the Colonies 1936–8, MP for Stafford 1918–38, 4th Baron Harlech 1938, married Lady Beatrice Cecil, sister to David Cecil, 1913.

Rowse been writing to Billy? addressing envelopes to your lodger excites me
a great deal.[1]

    love
      Shaya

The Frankfurters are announced here for to-morrow: do you look on that as
relevant?

TO MARION FRANKFURTER

   [24 June 1936]

                                  All Souls

Dear Marion

   I discovered your arrival & address by means of a telephone call to
Freddie Ayer, which I performed in order to convey my gloom about three
waves of disaster each greater than the other, of which I leave you to judge
the relative magnitude:

   1) The assassination of a really valuable philosopher named Schlick[2] in
Vienna, a man of great beauty, probably killed by a jealous Austrian rival.

   2) Maurice's non-elevation to the professorship of Greek. Genuine
dismay greeted the announcement that a man called Dodds got it. Mostly for
wrong reasons, such as that he was a conscientious objector during the war,
or a Sinn Feiner or the like. The real objection is that he is interested in late
& mystical Greek writers, is a queer idéologue as a character, and does not
care for style & form. Which are qualities in a man which secretly (from
Maurice at least) attract me for instance, but are obviously unsuitable in
a Professor of Greek: the only chance of that language resides in its formal
properties & not in what they said. Anyhow we were all divided into
Bowristas & Dennistonites[3] & this is a gratuitous insult. I rushed off to see
M. at once & spent an evening with him, which as you can well believe, was
not altogether easy. I passionately pointed out that in Oxford & Cambridge
only personalities counted & not posts, that striking & original figures always
overshadowed dim professors, etc. which it was absurd to have to say. He
seemed to need it however since it was received eagerly. To-day he has

---

1 William de l'Aigle Buchan (b. 1916, 2nd son of the author John Buchan), 3rd Baron
  Tweedsmuir 1996, who went up to New College in 1934 but failed pass moderations twice
  and left in summer 1935, was for a period the Camerons' lodger at Clarence Terrace,
  London, where they moved in about August 1935.
2 Moritz Schlick (1882–1936), professor of the philosophy of inductive sciences in Vienna,
  founder and leading member of the Vienna Circle, died on 22 June, having been shot by a
  disturbed student.
3 Supporters of J. D. Denniston (154/6).

almost completely recovered, was definitely jaunty, & went off to dine with the other disappointed candidate, carrying two bottles of red wine. He bitterly complained that [A. D.] Lindsay & Murray who seem to have a hand in this, definitely not only did not count war-services in one's favour – which was, he agreed, correct of them – but positively against one, which was hard.

The 3ᵈ disaster is a trial of Basil Murray, not a very nice man it must be said, & an undergraduate called Floud (held to-day), accused of breaking up a Mosley meeting.[1] The Fascist witnesses were terrifying neurotic figures, Goebbelses & Goerings, and the police seemed to be in their pocket, & cannot have spoken the truth, & were obviously encouraged by our Lady Mayoress,[2] a handsome steely diehard woman; the whole trial sent cold shivers down one's spine, for one has never been actually face to face with such miscarriage of justice: all your host[3] says in his books about parti pris justice in England seemed to come true in a most vivid & terrifying manner.

So that I feel to-day limp & exhausted as after an enormously dreary journey full of small irritations & with occasional patches of frightening scenery. Freddie's news of your arrival is the only gay factor in this situation, & the Warden's C.H.[4] which [was] very funny & nice & innocuous & no one can grudge it him & we all drank his health in water quite happily. When are you arriving? I hope v. soon. I don't know if you got my long letter.

Love
        Shaya

I must add some facts.

1.) The enormous sudden gaiety of the scene in Court when Roy appeared, in cap & gown which he carries everywhere, accompanied by the Earl and Countess of Birkenhead,[5] who, what with the Pakenhams,[6] Lady Mary Murray, Maurice & my better born pupils sudden[ly] made the court

1 This Fascist meeting took place in the Carfax Assembly Rooms, Oxford, on 25 May. Basil Andrew Murray (1902–37), journalist, second son of Gilbert Murray, and the Communist Bernard Francis Castle Floud (1915–67), Wadham history 1934–7, later (1964) Labour MP for Acton, were both accused of 'acting in a disorderly manner' and 'inciting persons to act in a disorderly manner'. The trial took place on 23–4 June; Murray was fined £2 for each offence and ordered to pay £3 3s. costs; Floud's case was dismissed.

2 Councillor Mrs Mary Georgiana Townsend was Mayoress of Oxford in 1935, 1936 (when she took over after the death of the incumbent) and 1958.

3 Presumably Harold Laski, who was a longstanding friend of Felix Frankfurter and held Marxist views at this time.

4 The recent appointment of W. G. S. Adams, Warden of All Souls, as a Companion of Honour.

5 Frederick Winston Furneaux Smith (1907–75), 2nd Earl of Birkenhead, and his wife Sheila, née Berry (1913–92), biographers.

6 Frank (67/3) and Elizabeth (137/2).

a sort of Encaenia scene. The combination of these with the Fascist thugs, the Bench of greengrocers, communist young men & women, busmen (on strike) and a sprinkling of generally queer types was a really rich Shakespearian scene. Jolly & slightly terrifying (a word which occurs too often in this note). The other thing is that Salter is longing for F.F. & so is Pares, & I have a young man I should v. much like him to meet. Pares is engaged to be married & speaks lyrically of you.

TO A. J. AYER

Friday [summer 1936, *postcard*]¹

All Souls

[. . .] I continue to give Mrs Frankfurter α++.² Have you read the Essays presented to Whitehead?³

yrs –
    Shaya.

TO ELIZABETH BOWEN

[Summer 1936]

All Souls

Dear Elizabeth
    I have inspected the files of the Oxford Outlook with mingled excitement and embarrassment, mostly embarrassment. Everything I myself wrote is both clumsy, priggish, & occasionally vulgar. Not a single sentence is natural, everything is said in a strangled, artificial, almost arty crafty manner, the jokes are terrible, the meditations ponderous, senile, & insincere. On the other hand everyone else is excellent. There is a beautiful review of the Waves by Stephen, & an equally good article on Eliot & the pylon boys by Goronwy, a simple & moving obituary notice by Arthur Calder Marshall,⁴ an excellent, illuminating, electric article by Freddie

---

1 Addressed (to 11 Foubert's Place, Regent Street, W) but not stamped: not sent?
2 i.e. A double plus: for Greek letters see 93/1.
3 F. S. C. Northrop and others, *Philosophical Essays for Alfred North Whitehead, February Fifteenth Nineteen Hundred and Thirty-Six* (London, [March] 1936).
4 Arthur Calder-Marshall (1908–92), author, contemporary of IB at St Paul's, Hertford classics 1927–30.

etc.[1] I append the issue containing Stephen's story.[2] I still find it tender, charming, & extremely moving. The characters are: the bully – Crossman, the little flautist a certain Swingler[3] who used to write inoffensive verses, the Mrs Ramsay – Mrs Carritt, wife of the emaciated don at Univ. the girl is probably imaginary & faintly connected with Gabriel Carritt[4] with whom Stephen was in love, & who systematically left him, every third term or so, for Crossman; he was a silly, nice, girlish little boy, brave, sentimental, & not very pretty, & a friend of Auden which cost him his reputation in Christchurch. Now, I believe, a communist. Perhaps it is the familiar mise-en-scène which touches one, but I really think still that this is a better story than any Stephen published subsequently, being like his earlier poems, more simple, more lyrical, & therefore inevitably to be abandoned, but better in its own right than the more difficult, conscientious, responsible later works.

The discovery of what a prig I was almost brought relief. I now know why I have to invent metaphors about gold, silver, paper etc., why I accuse Maurice of unscrupulousness, Goronwy of piracy etc.: it is obvious defence of what Marxists wd say were the values of a crumbling world which wd be scoffed at by the bourgeoisie itself in an earlier & healthier stage of development, i.e. defence of all that Connolly is so genuinely ferocious about in the didactic passages in his book.[5] What by the way, am I to do with it? I mean do you want it sent anywhere, or may I keep it till your return to London? or am I to smuggle it to Bowen's Court? I dare not give it to O'Neill to read for it will depress his noble & melancholy state of mind still further: nor to Hampshire, since he is (I am relieved to discover) with his uprightness, respect for Humphry etc. my kind of prig which is why I like him I think. I am sure that is what I originally fell for in Humphry: the splendid reactionary violence, a sort of Fascist sternness which contrasted with the surréaliste undergraduates of my first year in Oxford. I devour the works of M. Malraux[6] with a special passion for his weakest & most histrionic

1 Obituary by Arthur Calder-Marshall of the poet Clere Trevor James Herbert Parsons (1908–1931), *Oxford Outlook* 11 No 55 (June 1931), 138–40; A. J. Ayer, 'The Case for Behaviourism', *New Oxford Outlook* 1 No 2 (November 1933), 229–42; Goronwy Rees, 'Mr Eliot and some others', ibid., 243–7. The 'pylon boys' as a name for the Auden school, called 'MacSpaunday' by Roy Campbell in 'Talking Bronco' – p. 79 in *Talking Bronco* (London, 1946) – derives from Spender's poem 'The Pylons' in *Poems* (London, 1933).

2 'The Haymaking (For Gabriel Carritt)', *Oxford Outlook* 10 No 53 (November 1930), 579–97. By 'Mrs Ramsay' IB means Mrs Graham.

3 Randall Carline Swingler (1909–67), New College classics 1928–32, a protégé of Crossman whose poetry appears in the *Oxford Outlook*.

4 Gabriel C. Carritt, son of the E. F. Carritts; 'Tristan' in Spender's autobiography, *World Within World* (London, 1951), which is dedicated to IB (on whom see pp. 70–2 therein). IB's tentative identification of the girl with Carritt is perhaps implausible, since Carritt is almost certainly the basis of one of the three brothers in the story.

5 *The Rock Pool* (Paris, [1936]).

6 André Malraux (1901–76), French novelist; opponent of French imperialism in south-east

element, i.e. the fatalité, necessity of throwing oneself beneath Chiang Kai Shek's[1] car etc. which seems very solid & golden & dependable.

I saw Maurice a few days ago, & he was extremely troubled about your charges with regard to Goronwy.[2] He now thinks that G. has won you over to his side, that his hitherto tranquil relations with you are troubled, & complains that the old rule – wherever Goronwy there sooner or later trouble – holds more than ever. I am glad he is off to Harvard[3] since otherwise his genuinely cruel prosecution of G. would certainly be delivered with more violence than ever, as having used unfair means against him by bringing you, whom he cannot assail, to the front. I refuse to play, & said so to him.

I dined with Goronwy the other night, & he was so nice and friendly & sincere & charming that I shall never say a word against him again. I remembered how enormously helpful he had been when I was ill in Oxford last year, & am at present brimming over with affection and even the general jealousy of him which I used to feel is abated. I really am determined to reform & set up a tranquil friendship with him & be very loyal behind his back. It may be an illusory hope: I know that as soon as I find myself standing with a bundle of crisp, bright, really gay, really picturesque paper notes in my hands, with exhilarating inscriptions in an invented language, pressed on me by Goronwy ('Where is that elf, Rees?' can you guess the utterer? answer: Humphry), I shall once again feel an outraged, outplayed member of the bourgeoisie, & have pensées d'escalier,[4] swear pompous revenge etc. On the other hand my resolve may last. At present I cannot imagine what it is to feel indignation with him. Like feeling indignant about the levity of the French, or the salacity of Flaubert (which Tourgénev is alleged to have felt.). But soon Stephen will be returning from Austria, earnestness will reassert itself, creative depression will return, every second woman will resemble Miss Walker (I have wonderful terrors daily, even now), & I shall become

Asia, fighter for the Republican cause in the Spanish Civil War and the French Resistance in the Second World War; later (1960–9) French Minister of Culture.

1 Chiang Kai-shek was head of the Nationalist government in China 1928–49. This is a reference to Malraux's 1933 novel *La Condition humaine* (first published in English in 1934 as *Storm in Shanghai*), in which the young revolutionary Tchen, a passionate believer in expressing ideals through action, attempts to assassinate Chiang by throwing himself on to his car holding a bomb.

2 I have found no record of what these were. But EB had recently become an intimate friend of Goronwy Rees, who must have conveyed to Maurice Bowra her disapproval of his behaviour towards Rees. It is clear from what follows that Rees engendered mixed feelings in more than one direction.

3 Bowra was at Harvard from early September 1936 until early February 1937.

4 'Staircase thoughts', i.e. a riposte that comes to one too late to be used, on one's way downstairs after a verbal encounter.

insufferable once more. I look forward enormously to Bowen's Court: do you think it will be possible to have even one conversation tete a tete?

love

Shaya.

TO MARIE BERLIN

Wednesday [22 July 1936]

All Souls

Dear Mama

I am glad to hear that you have arrived safely: about me there is little to say: I am happy & working in Oxford which is too deserted to distract me & not deserted enough to drive me mad with loneliness. Mrs Ettinghausen & Walter came to tea to-day, she is *enormously* enthusiastic about Tel Aviv & will not listen to *any* criticisms of Palestine. Do you know a name Blumberg in Riga? A man called William(!) Blumberg has written a slightly antisemitic, but in my opinion able article about Palestine in the *Spectator* where he blames the Jews for not initially taking the Arabs into their economy, & treating them not as enemies but as if they were non-existent, and only of interest when they made trouble.[1] This seems exaggerated but true. Mrs E. brought back quite a funny story from Tel Aviv: the German Jews, as soon as they arrive, of course begin by buying a Fahrplan[2] of the omnibuses: Fahrplan is the first thing they think of. They come at 10 a.m. to the place, no bus. They ask whether there will be a bus soon, the Jew in charge says no, no bus, no hope of bus. The German Jew begins 'aber im Fahrplan . . .'[3] the other interrupts & says 'Weil en Jid will machen gutes geschäft und verkaüft aich a Fahrplan, missen *wir* fahren wie *er* willt!'[4] also in the buses, it is said, instead of the usual notices 'It is forbidden to speak with the driver', in the Jewish buses it says 'müssen sie ausgerechnet mit dem chauffeur sprechen?'[5] or 'Lehnen sie sich schon aus, werden schon sehen was wird passieren'[6] etc. Каламбуры.[7]

love

Shaya

1 William Blumberg, 'The Arab and Zionist Policy', *Spectator*, 17 July 1936, 96.
2 'Timetable'.
3 'But in the timetable . . .'.
4 A mixture of German and Yiddish. Freely translated: 'Just because some Jew has made a quick buck flogging you a timetable, that doesn't mean *we* have to run the buses to suit *him*!'
5 'Must you speak with the driver, of all people?'
6 'Just you lean out, and you'll soon see what'll happen/go past.'
7 'Kalambury' ('puns').

TO GILES ROBERTSON

Postmark 29 July 1936

All Souls

Dear Giles,

Now that I have discovered your marks I sympathise even more profoundly than I shd otherwise, your closeness to a Second is a vanishing quantity. Your marks were:

Logic	$\beta=$[1]
Morals & Politics	β
Phil. Books	$\gamma\beta$
Ancient Hist.	β
Greek "	$\beta?+$
Roman "	β
Phil. Trans.	$\beta\delta$
Gk Hist. Trans.	$\beta?+$
Roman " "	$\beta++$
Unseens	$\gamma.$
Latin Pr.	γ
Greek Prose	$\gamma.$

—

Aristotle & he alone torpedoed you: Ryle & Hardie both spontaneously asserted that you plainly were an intelligent person & a bad examinee and Hardie particularly expressed distress at the necessity of their choice, and said that had you given them the slightest opportunity of raising you in the viva, or had there been a plus somewhere on which to make a stand, they would eagerly have embraced such an opportunity. I honestly believe that to some extent you are a victim of the De Burgh[2] régime, & that the Capuan state that induced was never remedied. Anyhow, as you are not going to be either a schoolmaster or a civil servant, I cannot see that this matters. Mrs Beazley[3] has been persecuting me fairly persistently by suggesting that I was tired of her & her affairs: she makes life if not impossible at any rate ludicrously uncomfortable in a farcical sort of way: she is, however, au fond a reputable

1 For a full note on the first five letters of the Greek alphabet ($\alpha=$ A, $\beta=$ B, $\gamma=$ G, $\delta=$ D, $\varepsilon=$ E), see 93/1. Here '$\beta=$', for example, is 'B double minus', i.e. two steps down from plain B, and '$\gamma\beta$' is 'GB', i.e. third class with some second-class elements.

2 Perhaps a reference to W[illiam] G[eorge] de Burgh (1866–1943), author of *The Legacy of the Ancient World* (London/New York, 1924). If this book was not very challenging, GR might have been lulled into a false 'Capuan' (i.e. decadent) sense of security about his examination prospects.

3 See p. 147 above.

being & fond of you. She suspects you were jealous of Mr Katzmann on her account: please let her continue to do so since she plainly is made happy by the thought & should on the whole be allowed to gratify her in the end very innocent desires. I find I approve of her more than I should like to.

[Jasper] Ridley's marks are fantastic: he did a tremendously impressive viva on logic, was vastly well thought of by philosophers & produced δs and $\gamma\varepsilon$ in history of which he knew literally none.[1] I regard both him & you as having cheated yourselves of your due by sheer inadvertence and insufficient stolidity:[2] M. J. Smith[3] obtained the best first of his year, and is plainly not a being whose mind you would willingly exchange for anybody's whom you respect, let alone your own. Which entails all sorts of propositions which I shall not embarrass you by educing. David Wallace's first was exceedingly borderline, & was obtained as a result of a history viva: if there were such a thing as a II, I,[4] that is what I think he would have got. Hampshire was plainly the best philosopher of his year.[5] There is nothing of any interest about Jeremy.[6] Odgers[7] was viva'd for 90 minutes, & was finally demoted by the historians, for, so far as I can judge, insufficient general brightness. Anyhow he did not get an a on his coins, & special subjects are obviously a snare & a delusion. Darby[8] produced an extremely jejune line of βs & β?+s, which are obviously the result of a sort of grim self-discipline as a result of general disenchantment. Lepper[9] was a pure historian who must have made titanic efforts. John Griffith[10] did a little too well in ethics, βa or something, for any real satisfaction to be extracted

1 Ridley's own account in his diary for 7 August: 'letter from CRM[orris] giving details – Logic βa, M[oral] & P[olitical] $a\beta$, Plato and A[ristotle] $a\beta$, Anc Hist $\beta\gamma$, Gk H. $\gamma\delta$, R[oman] H. $\gamma\delta$. viva. H $\delta\gamma$, phil a. $\gamma\delta$s incredible. δ as Jo [Grimond, Balliol contemporary] says must imply almost moral disapproval. but polishes 2nd considerably – esp as postcard from Ryle "philosophy of real good 1st class quality, esp viva" – at any rate my viva illusion has not been shattered, and IB says "if only you had risen to a solid γ". but hell, if I had, what an agreable [sic] 1st it wd have been. all good points if it was a 2nd wd have been 10 times as sharp if it had been a 1st.' Sir Adam Ridley, Jasper Ridley's son, relates that in his father's viva 'the ancient historians searched desperately for a question – one at least – which he could answer correctly. When he was unable even to remember the date of the battle of Marathon, they had to give up . . .'.
2 Ridley took a 2nd in Greats, Robertson a 3rd in PPE.
3 Maurice Judson Smith (b. 1913), New College classics 1932–6.
4 i.e. a divided second class in the final examination results, first adopted in Oxford in 1986.
5 He took a 1st in Greats.
6 Jeremy Hutchinson took a 2nd in PPE.
7 Paul Randell Odgers (b. 1915), New College classics 1933–6, took a 2nd in Greats.
8 Samuel Leonard Darby (1914–2002), New College classics 1932–6, took a 2nd in Greats.
9 Francis (Frank) Alfred Lepper (b. 1913), New College classics 1932–6, Fellow of CCC 1939–80, Tutor in Ancient History 1949–80, took a 1st.
10 John Godfrey Griffith (1913–91), New College classics 1932–6, took a 2nd; Fellow and classics Tutor, Jesus, 1938–80.

for his fate, but still it will do. The slaughter in P.P.E. is dreadful. McLaren[1] was unlucky, but more so Swingler,[2] demoted for his French, & poor miserable Robinson[3] accused of not reading Kant (if Smith had a conscience . . .) or Meinertzhagen[4] found out by his speciousness: but the general unimportance of classes – which like scholarships & their absence are enormously trivial in themselves, & have at best or worst, only financial importance – is being borne in on me only now. One goes on teaching on the consciously false assumption that one's job is the production of specialists: this is luckily false, & wd be pernicious if true, & so far as I can see only its falseness justifies both your existence and mine during the past three, four years. I cannot refrain from repeating that you carry away the last shreds of a continuous & definite tradition, K. Clark, Kahn, even Brett[5] & Goodhart Rendel,[6] a perfectly positive, describable culture, as definite & examinable as, say, Bloomsbury. You chronologically & personally, you will be pleased to learn, belong to the genuinely gay, interesting, occasionally brilliant, completely unforced climax of all this, for which I shall always feel mild nostalgia, but like all my feelings, it will be feebly felt, & dramatized in introspection. And I shall miss you more than any of your contemporaries, which may or may not surprise you, but is quite clear to me; I have not had time in which to analyse the reasons. Please stay when you come for your degree, & let me know the date.

    yrs
       Shaya B

Unless stopped I'll write to Maurice B. & tell him to tell K. Clark to put you in the Nat. Gal. & Ben in the Tate. Why won't Anthony B[lunt] go to Rome?

In 1936 All Souls College, which had recently established a chair in social anthropology (first held by A. R. Radcliffe-Brown), was contemplating appointing a psychologist as well. Among Berlin's papers there is a draft letter to the Warden of the College (W. G. S. Adams), and draft material, much of it in virtually final form, for a memorandum on the subject. The final version (if there was one) has not yet surfaced. The letter and

---

1 Martin McLaren (1914–79), New College PPE 1933–6, took a 2nd; soldier and politician.
2 Stephen Thomas Swingler (1915–69), New College PPE 1933–6, younger brother of Randall Swingler (181/3), later (1945) a Labour MP, took a 3rd.
3 Frederick James Robinson (1906–88), New College PPE 1934–6, took a 3rd.
4 Daniel Meinertzhagen (1915–91), New College PPE 1933–6, took a 3rd.
5 Reginald Baliol Brett (1852–1930), 2nd Viscount Esher; Liberal politician, historian, deputy governor, then governor, of Windsor Castle 1901–30.
6 Harry Stuart Goodhart-Rendel (1887–1959), architect, Slade Professor of Fine Art, Oxford, 1933–6.

memorandum have been published together elsewhere,[1] *but the letter is included here too, in its proper place.*

The memorandum seems to have been circulated in late September. In a letter dated 2 October Geoffrey Faber writes: 'I read your memorandum on psychology last night [. . .] it is the ablest statement of a tangled matter that I remember to have seen: & if the College doesn't recognize it for what it is, there's no balm in Gilead.' The proposed appointment was not made.

TO W. G. S. ADAMS
Warden of All Souls

5 August 1936 [*draft*]

All Souls College

Dear Mr Warden,

As I understand that the letter circulated to the College last year proposing to establish a Professorship of Psychology, signed by Woodward and Faber, is under consideration by the relevant Committee, and as I am in complete agreement with its general purpose (although I should myself suggest that in the present absence of wide facilities for psychology here in Oxford, a Fellowship would do better as a beginning than a full fledged Professorship unsupported by Readers or an organized undergraduate school), I should like to submit a memorandum on the present state of psychological studies in England and elsewhere, which, as you yourself suggested, may be of assistance to the committee and possibly the College in arriving at a decision on this issue.

As I am myself not even an amateur psychologist, and my entire knowledge of the subject is gathered from scattered and unsystematic reading and conversation with experts, I do not suppose that the document which I have prepared is anything like as exact and exhaustive as it ought to be: I believe, however, that there are not positive misstatements in it. I have done my best to verify my classification by reference to the published writings of psychologists, and by relevant questions to the Professor of Psychology in Cambridge and the Reader in Nottingham,[2] both of whom discussed the present scope and division of the subject with me – without, however, being told the motive for my questions, which I was obviously at present not free to reveal.

1 Isaiah Berlin, 'The State of Psychology in 1936', *History and Philosophy of Psychology* 3 No 1 (2001), 76–83.
2 Frederic Charles Bartlett (1886–1969), (first) Professor of Experimental Psychology, Cambridge, 1931–52; Walter John Herbert ('Jack') Sprott (1897–1971), Reader in Philosophy, Nottingham, 1928–48.

I append certain conclusions which seem to me to follow from the evidence I have collected. If this is the kind of document which is wanted, I should be grateful if you would circulate this letter and the memorandum to the relevant Committee, or to the College, whichever you think proper.

Yours sincerely,

    I. Berlin

The outbreak of the Spanish Civil War in July intensified political divisions in Oxford, as it did in the country as a whole. Like most of his circle, IB was totally opposed to Franco[1] and made his own modest contribution to helping the Republican government: 'I packed parcels for Spain quite enthusiastically.'[2] But his experiences as a child in Petrograd during the Russian Revolution guaranteed that he was never tempted by Communism, to which many of his friends had succumbed.

TO SHIELA GRANT DUFF

[10 August 1936]

                                    All Souls

Dear Shiela,

Goronwy said that you wanted Mrs Olden's[3] address: he is away somewhere at the moment, so I can only send this to Chelsea. It is: c/o Dr Schuz, 5, Mölkergasse(strasse) Wien VIII.

I hope you are as well as possible: the Spanish issue[4] is the best Farbekenner[5] in the world: one only needs to ask people what they think, no further questions about their politics are ever necessary; it is somehow more terrifying than anything which has happened yet. The necessity of knowing what one is prepared to do if what is more personally urgent than it was before: the Spanish issue is the only absolutely clear cut, the Huxley[6] position, barring Fascists etc., the only plainly bogus one; on all other issues (e.g. Palestine) no clear proposition can be uttered which is not in some

---

1 General Francisco Franco y Bahamonde (1892–1975), leader of the Nationalist forces during the Civil War of 1936–9 and subsequently Spanish head of State until his death.

2 MI Tape 7.

3 Rudolf Olden's wife. He was a strong anti-Nazi and they were taken in by the Gilbert Murrays, on Boar's Hill. They were drowned in the ship, sunk by the Germans, in which Britain sent many German refugees to Canada.

4 Less than four weeks earlier, civil war had broken out in Spain when a group of generals mutinied against the left-wing republican government. Most public intellectuals in England rapidly committed themselves to the republican cause.

5 'Colour distinguisher', i.e. litmus test.

6 Aldous Huxley contributed to *Authors Take Sides on the Spanish War* (London, [1937]), arguing for pacifism.

degree unjust to someone. What is so nice about Malraux (whose novels I devour with enormous admiration, one by one, v. fast) is that he always pays in gold, never with paper or cheques: his sentences are all completely verified, guaranteed, oversubscribed. What, I wonder, are Humphry's present views? I remember his quasi-fascist period: there were vague rumours of interceptibility of letters etc, sounded fantastic and ridiculous to me, but I am ill informed.

I saw Miss [Ingrid] Warburg once or twice in London. She is a very honest and sympathetic character, and ought to be put in charge of some genuine enterprise.

Undergraduates are serious and honourable once more, interested in knowledge and impressively undilettanteish about politics, and while as B.J. would say not fascinating, also not prigs and not in the least dreary. Everything resembles 1830, therefore, popular uprisings & bloody suppressions and the decline of aestheticsm and the appearance of an idealistic generation doomed to perish or turn into reactionaries.

I really do hope you are well.

yrs

Shaya

TO JOHN HILTON (IN DORSET)

Postmark 18 August 1936 [*postcard*]

49 Hollycroft Avenue

I feel acute guilt & displeasure about not having visited you after undoubtedly giving trouble. But in fact I mustn't. I am trying to write a book on K. Marx very very fast, I dislike the job very much and want to rid myself of it in as little time as possible. I don't know how to turn myself into a socially indignant figure, which is the only possible mood in which to do justice to my vulgar & disagreeable hero, I admit the Spanish events have helped a great deal, they simplify everything e.g. questions about politics, one need never ask anyone again about that once his views on the present situation are made clear, it is an ideal Farbekenner. To return: my aim is not to leave this house for as much as a night since that ruins my artificially propped & unnaturally tense continuity, but (a) will you and/or Peggy be in Town before the 26th when I go to Ireland for 14 days, & if so where when, I shall fly to see you I swear. (b) can you have me on about 12th, 13th Sept? given the slightest encouragement I'll come. Please write.

IB.

Please forgive me. But a week-end in the country means dislocation for 4 days at least, & my present self-discipline is rare & wonderful.

TO ELIZABETH BOWEN

[Before 26 August 1936]

49 Hollycroft Avenue

Dear Elizabeth,

Thank you very much for your letter. It is agreeable to reflect about a society of prigs announcing their stubborn adherence to the Gold Standard, whether it assists prosperity or not; Stephen who arrived yesterday (and said he greatly wanted to meet you) plainly belongs. So does his faithful Tony (for whom a job was found by another member of the organization – that most defence-needing & defence-conscious figure, Mr E. M. Forster). Like Goronwy I now feel among friends & happier. Let me rapidly dispel any exaggerated impression my letter may have given about Maurice.[1] It was almost certainly a pure product of the mild persecution epidemic which seems to have been travelling in the air & affected even me slightly. No: he is not in the least annoyed, only frightened, & that not very. Frightened, that is to say, of the unknown rather than the known, he will not believe that Goronwy puts up a disinterested defence of him behind his back, as e.g. to the disapproving Coopers,[2] and suspects G.'s presence anywhere as likely to lead to complications in unexpected quarters at unexpected times. It is, I think, no more than general nervousness about a known non-loyalist: attack in his case is certainly a method of defence, hence these occasional spells of kindness, meals at the Savoy etc., when hope revives that something may still be achieved by kindness; the thing has now become circular: first M. attacks, then G. complains, then M. takes this to be a counter-move of the most perilous type, & counter-propagandizes, & organizes an annihilating attack, which in its turn leads to trouble etc. I despair of achieving any abatement, which I object to purely on the ground that the war is an unnecessary nuisance, now certainly fought for no real stakes or principles, any longer, whatever the original causes. Consequently I intend to go on inventing good blood, acting as a general Switzerland, and hope that presently ammunition will be exhausted, and a truce follow which insensibly unless broken by outside agencies, emotional armaments agents, persons who (Maurice's old conception of Connolly. I do not know how far up to

1 A reference to the passage about Bowra in the preceding letter to EB (p. 182 above).
2 The MP and author (Alfred) Duff Cooper (1890–1954), British Ambassador to France 1944–8, and his wife Lady Diana Cooper (1892–1986), later (1952) Viscount and Viscountess Norwich.

date now) supply both sides with weapons, work up scares, & grow rich on the proceeds, may glide into what newspapers call a durable peace. Anyhow you are regarded as an immensely valued & friendly power which has suddenly issued a diplomatic démarche. The slightest warmth of feeling of a sympathetic kind – the sort of letter you said you might write, will certainly produce an enormously grateful effect. But I do apologise, if I have inflated this at all; there is no situation really, & benevolence is still at a high premium all round.

I leave England on the evening of the 26th [August] & go to Belfast & meet O'Neill there & proceed to Sligo & thence to the Blaskets. I am not afraid of rain. I was born in a semi-Scandinavian town[1] & look on pastel colours as natural & friendly, & on the Italian-Palestinian landscape as absolute paradise but too splendid & like a dream. The only surroundings I really dislike is the adventurous, Peter Fleming type,[2] very high mountains, very low valleys, angry torrents, pure & snowy peaks etc. The sublime in nature directly connects with Nazi heroes, T. E. Lawrence, Mr Day Lewis's lines[3] on Auden as a kestrel, bully boy etc. & moral bullying. This in its turn leads to reactionary romanticism, the Germans, chivalry & the beauty of danger, & Mr Huxley's exhortation to us to prepare ourselves for a contest of more than Olympic importance.[4] I cannot conceive why I suddenly have begun to go on like this, unless it is that it is nice to take sides, & seems relevant now.

Please keep the O. Outlook if you want to, I have another copy: if I remember rightly it contains a shaming work by A. A. Apricott (who is myself),[5] which led to a year's acrimonious correspondence & the friendship of Martin Cooper. I am sure reminiscence is not a vice, & Mr Huxley in making Proust sit in a bath reingurgitating the bath water in cupfuls is being intolerably awful & squalid & vulgar.[6]

I am not absolutely sure of the precise date of our arrival in Bowen's Court: it depends on O'Neill's arrangements, Hampshire is an easy character & will remain or go as requested; I shall know on the 28 or 29th I think &

---

1 Riga, now capital of Latvia, near the Baltic coast.

2 (Robert) Peter Fleming (1907–71), soldier and travel writer.

3 In *The Magnetic Mountain* (London, 1933), part 3, section 16 (p. 29).

4 Aldous Huxley, *What are you going to do about it? The case for constructive peace* (London, 1936), 34: 'Constructive Pacifists are athletes in training for an event of much more than Olympic importance.'

5 The work in question is 'Music Chronicle', *Oxford Outlook* 10 (1930), 616–27. Between 1930 and 1932 IB wrote five reviews of music in Oxford under this title for the *Oxford Outlook*, first (on this occasion) as Albert Alfred Apricott, then twice as A.A.A., then twice over his own initials.

6 In *Eyeless in Gaza* (172/5), 8.

write absolutely at once. Rosamund[1] I like very much, & I am sure Mr Senhouse[2] (Bloomsbury novel more even than Bloomsbury name) will be nice.

What can I tell you of my companions which I haven't already said? The resumé of their presses may be helpful. O'Neill is regarded as difficult by Rowse, fascinating by Goronwy, prickly by Maurice, a snob by Mr Bowen & charming by Boase. I like him very much, am oppressed by his shynesses & silences, & admire him enormously as a distinguished character. Hampshire is more undergraduaty, approved by Maurice who declares that he has a keen sense of enjoyment & is a good loyal boy, thought silly by Goronwy, unfascinating by B.J., is much admired by Freddie Ayer; I feel both respect & affection, the former because of Cambridgy qualities, intelligence, integrity, purity of character, awkwardness, donnishness etc., the latter for the same reasons again, &, I suppose, because I seem to be able to talk about my subject to him more successfully than to most people, also he likes music & bullies me politically. He is & looks a gentle, antelopelike, herbivorous character. I have just read The House in Paris again: it connects with something or other, since it moves & harrows me literally more than anything I've ever read, & is an extremely major event. I really do think it most enormously good. I have long known myself to be doomed to late development, & have just ordered your complete oeuvres & those of M. Malraux.

    love

      Shaya

the picnic you propose fills me with a real sense of gaiety & anticipation. *Please* let us have it not once but twice. As for Humphry, I shan't write till I see you, since I might seem unnatural, that having heard nothing, I should send a passionate appeal for his return.[3] As you say, to what?

At the end of their Irish holiday, IB, Stuart Hampshire and Con O'Neill joined a house-party at Bowen's Court, hosted by Elizabeth Bowen and her husband Alan Cameron. While there, IB became aware that his fellow-guest Goronwy Rees – with whom Elizabeth Bowen was in love – was starting an affair with her friend Rosamond Lehmann, who thereafter

1 Rosamond Nina *Lehmann (1901–90), novelist; married Hon. Wogan Philipps 1928 (marriage dissolved 1944).

2 Roger Henry Pocklington Senhouse (1899–1970), previously personal assistant to Lytton Strachey, co-founder in 1936, with Fredric Warburg, of Martin Secker & Warburg.

3 From Calcutta. EB had evidently enlisted IB's support in encouraging him to come back within reach.

referred to this episode as 'the Weekend where a Great Deal
Happened'.¹ Saying nothing to his hostess, and advising others to do
likewise, IB left to stay with Stephen Spender in the Lake District.
Elizabeth Bowen discovered the truth only some weeks later.

TO ELIZABETH BOWEN

Monday [14 September 1936]²

Skelgill Farm, Newlands,
Keswick, Cumberland

Dear Elizabeth,

Being in a more equable & normal frame of mind, I can now describe
our recent experiences here. Life is very pastoral. The country is beautiful
but uneven & the long walks which plainly are intended to be taken on it,
with no seats obtaining, terrify me. I cannot think, or speak, or therefore be
happy while moving uphill. Not so Stephen. He confesses to a natural piety
towards the land & is in that respect more religious than I, I suppose.
Meanwhile our greatest excitement is Mr Walpole.³ We went to tea there
a few days ago: you know Mr Walpole? he says he admires your books
immensely – a fat, rosy, happy largeish dimpled man came bouncing out to
meet us, and then served tea coyly, like a shy provincial spinster, anxiously
inquiring about milk and sugar. He bounded at once on to William Plomer
& Mrs Woolf. He was proud & pleased about his knowledge of them, &
spoke of them with a curious mixture of patronage & admiration. Mrs Woolf
– who plainly persecutes him & plays him & turns him over & over – he said
was a very humourous woman. His letter from her was humorous: he gave
one to understand that he lived with her on easy, gay, unconcerned terms,
each a head of a non-competitive profession: he enjoys everything equally &
easily: he loves good literature, good pictures, good food, with enormous
naive enthusiasm. He is like a Glaxo baby, to do with cream, honey, jam and
so. He is absolutely uncritical: he thinks 'The Waves' splendid & his own
books also splendid: above all one should enjoy oneself, & not be gloomy
like Quennell.⁴ For this latter – he was an absolutely isolated case – he had
no love. Some review must have done it. Even Mr Plomer had once sinned
in that respect; so Walpole wrote & severely warned him about the
consequences of such acts. Since when peace prevails. He discussed Henry

1 Not 'when', oddly: Rosamund Lehmann, *Rosamund Lehmann's Album* (London, 1985), 98.
These events became the genesis of Elizabeth Bowen's novel *The Death of the Heart* (London,
1938): see 288/5.
2 IB was staying in Keswick from 8 to 15 September.
3 Hugh Seymour Walpole (1884–1941), popular novelist, Kt 1937.
4 Peter Quennell (1905–93), poet, critic and biographer.

James, who, one was given to understand, had been in love with him, with great enthusiasm, affection, and, it must be added, understanding. And was slightly embarrassed about his own association with Mr Priestley. He discussed Bloomsbury gingerly – a fine body of men & women for whom he made special terms – & his own world rather disdainfully: most of them made over £1000 a year, which on the whole he thought slightly contemptible. Mr Cronin[1] came in for some harsh words. The culte of him at Keswick is really gigantic. Every window has pictures of him with & without (a) his dog (b) Priestley. He is followed about by a huge detective who enormously resembles him, is obviously devotedly attached, & differs only by a certain sullen & suspicious expression, & pronounced taciturnity. Hugh himself prattles away: he is really charming & affecting about James, is himself singularly unenvious and sweet in character. His passion for keeping in touch with the young – & relief when informed that I at any rate intended no creative experiments – was v. touching. He happily goes on Hellenic cruises, to Hollywood, to the Coronation,[2] though no longer to Germany, because of the Nazis, a country he used to visit, as he said, 'for the music'. He likes & enjoys everything everything everything, all the time. He adores honey. His relish during the conducted tour of his study, which is really full of touchingly pretty things, was enormous: he was a little embarrassed when a huge new photograph of himself was ceremoniously brought in in the middle of this by his man, but conquered his reservations, & enjoyed that too. In the presence of so expansive a nature how can one not be happy oneself? Stephen & I played up terrifically to everything: one conscientious protest against the Book Society by Stephen was the only blow struck for integrity: & my praise for William Plomer as a reviewer was not well received for the reason stated above: otherwise we swam in endless, richly provided, butter. He praised Rosamond (which I think is a real passion) & Isherwood in the same terms, & did a terrific, & by now genuinely generous turn about Somerset Maugham,[3] who had given him pain in the past. He told us what we didn't know before, that James had an insatiable appetite for information about all sexual experiences whatever: everyone supplied him with stories but he never had enough. He praised Harold Nicolson's[4] character, his wife's writings, Aldous Huxley's gentle manners, Martin

---

1 Archibald Joseph Cronin (1896–1981), Scottish novelist whose work combined realism, romance and social criticism, often reflecting his own experiences as a doctor; gave up medical practice after the success of his first novel, *Hatter's Castle* (London, 1931); many of his stories were adapted for film or television.

2 Presumably Walpole planned to attend the Coronation of Edward VIII scheduled for May 1937.

3 (William) Somerset Maugham (1879–1965), playwright, novelist, short-story writer.

4 Hon. Harold George Nicolson (1886–1968), diplomat and author, father of Ben Nicolson and husband of Vita Sackville-West; MP (National Labour), West Leicester, 1935–45.

Secker's poverty. We left him warmed & charmed. He came to tea this afternoon & the delicious kindliness continued. Everyone forgotten last time was remembered & praised, & this with real sincerity, he really likes the valuable & the original, like so much turkish delight. The suggestion that he should write, like Forster, a homosexual novel, which wd really be truthful & a masterpiece excited him inordinately. He was worried, flattered, delighted. He kept returning to the subject, looking slyly both at me & at Stephen, wondering about the relations between us. He placed his arm several times heavily on my shoulders, explaining later that Henry James used to do it to his favourites. He wears huge scarabs on both hands, Stephen wanted, as a delicate compliment, to buy some cheap ones & wear them for him. His relations with the Sitwells and Mrs Hutchinson[1] were touched on. Not a name was mentioned but soft streams of praise would begin-{ning} to flow from his lips, he became in turns gay, avuncular, serious about Mrs Woolf's insanities, jolly about the Buchans,[2] understanding towards us, sympathetic about Isherwood & his boy, everything everything. I am absolutely fascinated by so much receptiveness, so much insensitiveness. He has an enormous sense of inferiority untinged by self pity, untouched by unhappiness. His capacity for mixed feeding, for enjoyment in general is enormous. He is very unlike Flaubert indeed. In fact he is a sort of glorified Bouvard:[3] I can see why Maugham, why any sharp toothed person, could not resist the temptation of getting his teeth into flesh so pink & innocent, so obviously made for cannibals: Mr Connolly might well be unleashed at him; his nicest traits are his genuine affectionateness, & real purity of character. I hope I shall meet him again: a figure so distant from persecutors & persecutees is rare in our world. His pleasure when anyone is run down is also full of innocent delight. How he has managed to survive embitterment, in spite of periodic dips into Bloomsbury where he must be spitted & roasted with regularity, is truly astonishing. I am sure he would give you infinite pleasure. A valuable acquaintance.

Last night Stephen & I played a new game, answering questions in the manner of Mr Eliot. Once you get into it you cannot easily get out again. You answer very slowly, carefully & deliberately, avoiding no obvious platitudes, but embellishing them by clothing them with carefully placed words. Above all the tempo must be kept very slow & even, & nothing

---

1 Mary Barnes Hutchinson (1889–1977), writer and associate of the Bloomsbury group, mother of Jeremy Hutchinson and Barbara Rothschild (215/3); mistress of Clive Bell.

2 The author John Buchan (1875–1940), 1st Baron Tweedsmuir 1935, Governor-General of Canada 1935–40, and his wife Susan; they lived at Elsfield Manor, Oxford.

3 One of the anti-heroes of Flaubert's unfinished novel *Bouvard and Pécuchet*, about two copying clerks who leave their jobs in order to write a book about the entire realm of human knowledge. They fail.

ordinary left unspoken.: E.g. I: 'one can only get to know people adequately
by meeting them. It is very difficult to form a satisfactory impression
vicariously.' Stephen 'Yes, Berlin. That is quite true. But how else can one
get to know the dead?' etc. After three hours of this we discovered that we
were conscious of a deeper insight into Eliot's character, & into that of the
beauties of New England Prose. All this quite genuinely. The great test is
saying 'Yes' in a properly melancholy manner, with a sincere & pensive
inflexion. But curious though the conjunction may seem, both Mr Eliot and
Mr Walpole are both beautiful characters, both have loyal & affectionate
natures, & neither abounds in ideas. In fact I am laying the old, Oxford-
induced, emphasis on qualities of the heart. While one is with Stephen it is
difficult to resist such direction: I antidote myself with imagining how
Maurice would say 'yes, yes, a very kind, very very *kind* man' (I think Mr G.
Hopkins was so last described), nevertheless it is agreeable to reflect that this
reliable characteristic still inhabits one's universe: the chief difference
between them is that while Walpole owns a beautiful Renoir, Mr Eliot
almost certainly doesn't: like his the works of both are modern classics.

If Goronwy is still with you give him & Alan my love: my Irish journey is
very symphonic in structure: first a very uncertain, rapid allegro full of very
odd episodes, not very skilfully interwoven. Then an extremely beautiful and
absolutely blissful andante in Bowen's Court with distinguishable themes &
variations built with balance & symmetry, possessing a definitely enchanted
quality: then a silly & agreeable little menuet & trio with Mr Walpole +
broad touches of religious feeling supplied by Stephen. I go home on Wed.
My family are always good for a leisurely allegro & obvious finale.

    Love,
        Shaya.

Is this too arty? Stephen sends his love. He really has a charming character.
Why shouldn't Mr Eliot write a special short story? I must stop. Do write me
a letter as soon as may be.

TO JOSEPH HERTZ[1]

19 September 1936

All Souls

Dear Dr Hertz,

I should like to express my great distress, and profound sympathy with you in your sorrow. I only learnt of your son's untimely end four days ago when I was in Ireland[2] and could not therefore write sooner as otherwise I should have done: I knew him, not intimately, but quite well, since he was a junior contemporary of mine at St. Paul's, and we met occasionally in Oxford: I was very fond of him and had great and growing respect for his character, his abilities, his general style of life, his dignity as a Jew and a man. His contemporaries, & his tutors, some of whom are now my colleagues, spoke of him always with admiration and affection; as for me I was very glad that he should be in Oxford in particular, since the number of Jews who create a fund of positive goodwill, by neither shrinking from, nor seeking excessive contact with their gentile fellows, is really rather small: Daniel's independence of character, his integrity as a scientist and human being, his seriousness and his charm won him a circle of admirers at New College of which he was probably unaware: indeed his unawareness of such things largely constituted that purity of character for which so many among his contemporaries consciously or unconsciously respected him. I am sure that the shock and distress of such as I have met is shared by a much larger number than any I am acquainted with: if the knowledge of genuine and universal sympathy can do anything towards the alleviation of your feelings, I should like to assure [you] that it is felt, and will continue to be felt, by all who knew your son. My parents would like me to convey to you their deep sympathy – and I my own.

yrs sincerely

Isaiah Berlin

Hertz Archives, Southampton University

---

1 An extract from this letter appeared in *Daniel Henry Hertz: In Memoriam* (London, 1936: privately printed), 7. Daniel Hertz, son of the Chief Rabbi, Dr Joseph Hertz, and a successful doctor and medical researcher, was born in Johannesburg in 1909, and committed suicide on 29 August 1936. Rumours surround his death. Did he misdiagnose his glandular fever as Hodgkin's disease? Was he addicted to the opium he started taking after a tennis injury? He was an undergraduate at New College 1928–31, and took a 1st in animal physiology.
2 He was in fact in Cumberland.

TO ELIZABETH BOWEN

[Shortly after 23 September 1936][1]

All Souls

Dear Elizabeth,

Please forgive me for having kept this book until to-day: I enclose Maurice's letter as an atonement. Mr Rowse[2] is a little unwell and therefore tender and polite and anxious to coo and be cooed to: knowing how infinitely on my nerves he usually gets it is not difficult not to melt before his anxious attentions: I really think that as dagoes go Jews are more reliable & firmly made than Celts. The only frivolous moment was when he said: 'I must have one of the two new Fellows. I always have, especially now Richard (Pares) is getting married. Do you want Hampshire?' You are a thousand times right and one is living among impossible sex maniacs & one's estimate of everything & even use of words is insensibly distorted by it. I hope you don't think I behaved weakly or too passively about Mrs Phillips: it was the easiest way of putting an end to the nonsense, the alternative wd have meant endless accusing letters from Goronwy, + an impossible explanatory scene with Stephen who wd be complained to: as it is it is all over & done with & I am once more an acquaintance with liability to acquire protective covering as soon as any danger of dramatization arises. This was my motive (I claim success) but I am tortured by the thought that it may have appeared as disloyalty, even appearances should not be allowed to intervene – will you please, on Monday say what you actually thought?

Shaya.

TO JENIFER WILLIAMS

[c.30 September 1936]

on M.V. Ulster Queen writing paper,
'As from All Souls'[3]

Dear Jenifer

This is v. belated in all respects, I apologize. During the week-end I was in bed and very happy, owing to a certain recurrent migraine which strikes me at fixed seasons, and produces a vivid state of consciousness and exhilarated feelings, but kept me, on this occasion, from thinking of either K.

---

1 The date of the letter from EB to which IB is replying.
2 A. L. Rowse.
3 Probably actually from there: certainly not on the vessel from which he removed this writing paper earlier.

Marx or the Civil Services. About the former.[1] You must admit that it is very satisfactory. I am dining with Douglas this evening, & I doubt if any other subject will be discussed: I believe that it is reported that he is mad with joy.[2] In his tranquiller fashion Mr Turner[3] will no doubt be warmed by the thought, I wish I could meet him now: as for me, I think I can describe my sensations briefly and accurately: I was told that you occurred 3^d on the list [4] by, of all people, Mr [Max] Beloff, who had come to – I really cannot use any other term – solicit about All Souls. The news gave one the sort of instant physical satisfaction produced by a deep smile inside one's chest.[5] That is exactly how it was, and I am delighted to report it. Beyond that all available emotive noises (as Messrs Ayer or Ridley wd express it) must have been used up already in your enormous incoming correspondence: pray choose amongst these whichever are the most sympathetic and least embarrassing and accept them from me. Oh dear. I really am enormously pleased but in our convention, one is, for some reason, not allowed to express such things directly. I apologize for breaking through even so far as this. How much easier for Salter or Douglas who proceed by shortest distances between two points (in the case of the former at least, and once or twice the latter, not very attractive points perhaps. Still, it is enviable freedom & economy of means). What Dept. will you go to? at first I mean? before your inevitable translation? I think to be in the Home Office under Mr Henderson[6] must be absolute heaven. Do not reject it too hastily; think of the power of protecting conspirators you acquire. Which brings us to our next subject.

Marx.: I have now read Messrs N. & M-H.,[7] & by internal evidence I judge that the latter wrote the first, the former the second part of the book. The former, if so, is much the better. The first chapter is quite pleasant, &

1 sc. latter.
2 Douglas Jay was a close friend and admirer of JW.
3 G. J. Turner (144/2).
4 The list, in order of merit, of results of the Civil Service entry examination.
5 This phrase occurs in a letter from Elizabeth Bowen to IB dated 23 September 1936: presumably one of them had used it when speaking or writing to the other at some earlier point.
6 John F. Henderson (b. c.1902), Assistant Secretary in the Home Office, head of the Children's Branch. See Jenifer Hart, *Ask Me No More: An Autobiography* (London, 1998), 83–5.
7 Boris Nicolaievsky and Otto Maenchen-Helfen, *Karl Marx: Man and Fighter* (London, 1936). JW was reviewing this book for *The Economist* at the request of her friend Douglas Jay, who was on the staff of the magazine, and she asked IB for his assistance, being out of her depth. Her short unsigned notice, largely drawn from this letter, appears in the issue dated 12 December 1936, 56. The book was reissued in a revised edition (with references added) in French in 1970, and in English in 1973: the page references in subsequent notes give the page(s) in the 1936 edition before an oblique stroke, in the 1973 edition after it, thus: p. 382/407.

has no business not to be, but not much better than Mr Carr.[1] Mr Carr wrote a frivolous patronizing book, & thinks of K.M. as a grotesque old monster, very able & curious & interesting, & now & then tells you he was a man of genius, but offers no evidence. Still he does try & answer questions: about M's ideological evolution, about his relations with Hess, Lassalle, Bakunin[2] etc. He is always superficial, intolerably jocose, & usually wrong, but he is aware, dimly, that he has solved nothing. These two are aware of nothing of the kind: they go happily on & on without any attempt to ask or answer such questions as the difference between 'True Socialism' & Marx, or why he in Berlin preferred the Hegelian lecturer Gans[3] to the conservative Savigny [4] (which is really interesting & throws light) or how liberals turn into revolutionaries, or why it was right for Engels to join Willich's[5] democratic army but wrong for Herwegh[6] to lead a fine body of men from Paris for the same purpose. I mention this only because the authors definitely spend words on this & say nothing. However you want to know about the alleged new material: I only know what Mehring[7] & Mr Carr & my new Russian Biochronik[8] know: I can therefore not vouch for anything, but this much is, I believe, new: or rather I never knew that:

1) he fought a duel in Bonn.[9]

2) the Rheinische Zeitung[10] was stopped as a result of representations by the Russian Govt.[11] This is a genuine scoop I think. Marx's fanatical anti-slavism is luckily under-explored.

3. The professor's story about the meeting of the Workers Educational Ass. in London is charming, & I think quite new.[12]

1 E[dward] H[allett] Carr, *Karl Marx: A Study in Fanaticism* (London, [1934]). For Carr see p. 694.
2 Moses Hess (1812–75), German journalist and socialist treated in AC; Ferdinand Lassalle (1825–64), prominent German socialist discussed in KM; Mikhail Aleksandrovich Bakunin (1814–76), Russian anarchist compared to Alexander Herzen in RT.
3 Eduard Gans (1798–1839), disciple of Hegel and German jurist.
4 Friedrich Karl von Savigny (1779–1861), German jurist.
5 August Willich (1810–78), revolutionary, formerly a Prussian officer; see p. 201/213.
6 Georg Herwegh (1817–75), German poet and revolutionary.
7 Franz Mehring, *Karl Marx: The Story of his Life*, 5th ed., trans. Edward Fitzgerald (London, 1936; 1st ed. published in German 1918, 5th ed. 1933).
8 Presumably Karl Marx, *Chronik seines Lebens in Einzeldaten* (Moscow, 1934), 'Russian' only in the sense that it was published by the Moscow-based Marx–Engels–Lenin-Institut.
9 p. 20/21–2.
10 A liberal democratic newspaper founded at the beginning of 1842. Marx was the editor by October, and the paper was suppressed in March 1843.
11 p. 59/64.
12 Possibly pp. 204–5/217, where a newspaper report is quoted that describes members of the German Communist Workers' Educational Union 'stamping raw pelts at a German fur factory in East London'; the skins are made supple and durable by the workers' sweat, so that 'our rich ladies, with their boas and muffs, though they do not suspect it, are literally clothed in the sweat of the Democrats'.

4. I didn't know that Danish spies watched Engels in Bremen & Barmen.[1]

5. Good funny description of M.'s life in London by a Prussian spy.[2] But the visit of Louis Blanc[3] is even funnier, & of this not a word here. If one fills one's pages with anecdotes of this sort – obviously a good thing to do on the whole – they ought to be the funniest, don't you agree? So, they leave out Annenkov's stuff about him, save for one extract, & that, admittedly, the best.[4]

6. There are bits about the obscure Belgian De Paepe, new to me.[5] They seem vaguely important for the history of the International.

7. The chapter on Bakunin[6] is better than anything on Marx. Guillaume[7] & the aged Wrangel[8] were obviously worth reprinting. We are still in regions of light memoirs. The whole Nechaiev story,[9] nice in itself, [is] not fearfully relevant. I think this must be Nicolaievsky who knows about Russian revolutionaries and likes telling stories of their lives. I approve.

8. Scoop 2. Engels' plan to help the Commune in Paris.[10] Seems quite new.

9. They make a fuss about discoveries in 1927 of the Lassalle–Bismarck

1 pp. 90/96–7.

2 pp. 241–2/255–7.

3 Jean-Joseph Charles-Louis Blanc (1811–82), French socialist, organised a Communist banquet at the Highbury Barn Tavern, now in the London Borough of Islington, on 24 February 1851 to commemorate the revolution of February 1848. Marx was excluded, since he belonged to the wrong faction, but he sent two spies. In a letter written to Engels that night, after one of the spies reported back, he tells a story which may be the one IB is referring to. The banqueters 'began to grow restive. They set up a shout of "Spy, spy" [. . .] whereupon Schramm and Pieper were man-handled out of the hall, their hats torn off; in the courtyard outside the hall they were kicked, stamped on, cuffed, nearly rent in pieces, handfuls of hair torn out, etc.' Letter dated 24 February 1851: Karl Marx, Frederick Engels, *Collected Works* (London, 1975–   ), vol. 38, p. 298 (the words in capitals were written by Marx in English).

4 p. 118/125. Pavel Vasil'evich Annenkov (1812–87) watched Marx debating in 1846. The quoted passage occurs in his 'A Remarkable Decade', chapter 31, first published in *Vestnik evropy* 1880 No 2 (March–April): see p. 497. See also P. V. Annenkov, *Vospominaniya i kriticheskie ocherki* (St Petersburg, 1877–81), vol. 3, *Zamechatel'noe desyatiletie (1838–1848)*, 156.

5 Passing mentions only, on pp. 274/292, 300/319. César de Paepe (1842–90), Belgian anarcho-syndicalist and follower of Bakunin.

6 Chapter 18.

7 James Guillaume, *Karl Marx, pangermaniste et l'Association internationale des travailleurs de 1864 à 1870* (Paris, 1915), quoted from (IB's 'reprinting') on pp. 290–2/308–11.

8 Baron Nikolay Egorovich Wrangel (1847–1920), 'father of the well-known [White] General [Petr Nikolaevich] Wrangel [1878–1928], who fought against the Bolsheviks in South Russia in 1919 and 1920', 286 [not 336 as the index has it]/303. Baron" N. Vrangel', *Vospominaniya (ot" krepostnogo prava do bol'shevikov")* ('Memoirs: from serfdom to the Bolsheviks') was published in Berlin in 1924 (and subsequently in an abridged French translation, itself translated into English), and a passage about Bakunin's speaking style (pp. 61–2) is quoted on p. 285/303.

9 pp. 345–53/368–76.

10 IB somewhat misdescribes a passage on pp. 318–19/339–40.

letters,[1] but then peter out, & don't say a word about their actual contents. This is absolutely maddening.

    10. Funny occasional descriptions of K.:[2]

'a nice unaffected fellow' (Freiligrath)[3]
'like a gentleman farmer' (anonymous Dutchman)
'bad host' (the Prussian Spy.)

The conclusion: I really cannot see, what material difference is made by their researches. They fly from all theory like poison; I am not sure I shan't follow their example in that respect, it seems impossible to discuss Hegel, or his revolting disciples, without becoming obscure & bombastic oneself. I keep writing précis of their views, & they look like enthusiastic partisan nonsense, I tear them up, & the next version is jejuner but still silly in some in-eliminable way.

    The chapter on Germany 1848–49[4] is appallingly chaotic, so is the whole 1849–1862 period: as soon as Bakunin & the Russians enter, the style improves. The omission of an account of K.'s relations with (a) Hess (b) Heine (c) Lassalle, is intolerable. There are bits of chronique semi-scandaleuse about all of them, but even Mr Carr, with his patronizing showmanship, is more detailed & better. I can't discover anything epochmaking save the two scoops, & they aren't. Now & then, cf p. 373, funny quotations about, e.g. Turkey occur. But they definitely boast of shedding light on the history of the International: I don't know if their account of its meeting in the Hague[5] & assassination by K. & Engels seems convincing to you; it seems to me to pour floods of darkness on that madly unintelligible situation.

    Yet it is not exactly a bad book, I suppose. Except that it does not prove its case, that M. was a great man. It refutes the totally ignorant like Dick C[rossman], who publicly maintain that M. was not a man of action. But that cd have been done out of Mehring with no difficulty. I think it does communicate a sense of general activity. But apart from the bits towards the end, from Bakunin onwards, which look like translations from the Russian, & do possess an agreeable sort of liveliness, it is a dead book. The test of such lives is what they do about 1848, which it is criminal to leave drab & boring

1 p. 258/275.
2 pp. 100/106 ('that nice, interesting, unassuming, resolute fellow'), 359/382 ('the impression that Marx made on him [a Belgian journalist in the Hague] was that of "a gentleman farmer"'), 241/256.
3 (Hermann) Ferdinand Freiligrath (1810–76), German political poet, friend of Marx.
4 Chapter 14.
5 In September 1872: pp. 358–67/381–91.

as they do. Not but what I shall probably be guilty of that myself. If so, so much the worse for me. I shall be the first, if not to acknowledge, at any rate to mind such criticism. I am sorry this is so scattered, & that I am so ignorant. Please do not think, however, that N.O. Brown[1] wd have done better. Perhaps he would, but I cannot bear the thought. I go to Headington, to a bedroom in the village, where I shall live incognito with a member of the Board of Education till Monday. If ever you return, pray let me know: I long to hear about Miss K.[2] & I cannot bring myself to ring you up, I cannot speak to strangers.

    Yrs

      Shaya.

Upon referring to yr letter I find I havent answered yr question: the 2 bits of new information seems to me quite interesting but absolutely inessential, the documents seem perfectly first hand & trustworthy.

TO ROSAMOND LEHMANN

    [Early October 1936]

All Souls

Dear Rosamond,

    This is very late notice but I didn't have your address. The faithful Stuart, now being examined in my college, informed me, I don't know how he knows, but he gave it away as a sort of private datum of his own. Both he & other charming – I think unusually sympathetic & attractive undergraduates long to meet you. I am sorry I still haven't managed to express that I am inviting you to lunch for next Sunday, here. The undergraduates in question – they have just gone down in point of fact – are David Wallace & Jasper Ridley, connected with each other & with you I believe, via a Mrs Ridley is this right? whom you are said to know. Please come if you possibly can, I very much want to talk about Ireland etc.

    I went away from an enchanted atmosphere: Goronwy's description of all of us sitting in timeless Toulouse-Lautrec postures has re-established

1 Norman Oliver Brown (1913–2002), communist – but see Jenifer Hart, op. cit. (199/6), 103 – Balliol classics 1932–6 (taught by IB); after leaving Oxford he studied for a PhD at Wisconsin and remained a US academic apart from service with the US Office of Strategic Services (OSS) as a research analyst during the war.

2 Eve Kisch went on holiday to Yugoslavia with JW, Herbert Hart and Arnold Pilkington. She was not a close friend of JW, who recruited her to the party only to appease her parents, since they thought it desirable that it should contain another woman. She was academically very able, but not always sensitive in her personal relations, and proved a rather trying holiday companion: hence, perhaps, IB's interest.

everything vividly, also the man in the black tie, Roger S[enhouse]'s check Swedish tie, Alan's popping blue eyes and Elizabeth [Bowen] curiously on edge, communicating an electric & thrilling quality to everything, the American minister,[1] the infinite sense of leisure & the sense that something terrific wd very soon occur operating together, & finally the entrance of Goronwy, with nothing but his genius to declare like the youthful Rousseau among a company of official mid-eighteenth century philosophes – the whole thing was as good as art & I shall never forget it or want it otherwise.

Please come if you can.

yrs

Shaya.

Lehmann Papers, Modern Archive Centre,
King's College, Cambridge

TO STEPHEN SPENDER

[8/9 October 1936]

All Souls

Dear Stephen

I have come to the conclusion that I must certainly apologize.[2] I am not, as Moore, who has just left, wd say, *hopelessly* in the wrong, but the balance of right is certainly on your side. What happened was: I wrote, you recollect, that I wd meet you etc. if I heard no answer. Suddenly I became panic stricken about whether you were at any reachable address, since if not, you would not reply, for a cause other than stipulated in my letter. The thought gave me no rest. I began to telephone both to Abercorn & to Riverside[3] at regular intervals, & worked myself into a feverish expectancy. The builders in Riverside were friendly but uninformative. On Tuesday I sent you a desperate telegram to Abercorn-Randolph, to which there was no reply. I assumed that they wd send it on to wherever you then were. I wrote to Moore who communicated with Tony who said you wd not be back till Thursday. At this point I assumed that you had forgotten about our date, & since I was terrified of the prospect of a lonely evening with, I feared, really

---

1 Probably Alvin Mansfield Owsley (1888–1967), US Minister to the Irish Free State 1935–7, a sturdy Texan Democrat.
2 SS had written on 8 October remonstrating (mildly) at IB's failure to appear on Wednesday 7 October at a meeting-place he himself had suggested.
3 Riverside 3990 was Spender's telephone number at 11 Queen's Mansions, Brook Green, London W6; Abercorn 1763 was the number of his previous address, 25 Randolph Crescent, London W9.

awful music, I asked to be invited to dine by [Martin] Cooper – particularly as
Sparrow & Maurice had painted a hideously funny picture of his married life
with Ralph Ricketts[1] – a huge, gentle, ludicrous man, like a muffin as
Elizabeth Bowen said. It was a repaying meal, & I am prepared to be fairly
malicious to you about it by way of general reward. One of my tickets
remained mine, the other I sold under squalid circumstances to Sir J.
Squire[2] who is detestable (friend to Ricketts). You missed little: the music
was tortured and psychologically or pathologically rare, but musically a sort
of pious, devout, honest pastiche: as Vincent d'Indy[3] to the Latin tradition,
so van-D[ieren] seemed to be to some sort of hybrid English-Seventeenth
Century one. One couldn't exactly say that it was imitative, nor that [it] was
more like Delius than anybody tho' there were bits, at the same time it was
not independent or totally original or even good: if you can imagine a truly
highbrow artyness, not vulgar, very self-conscious, affected by genuine
feeling for the past, learning, suffering etc. on the whole it had a cultural but
not much musical significance. Mr Turner was not present. There was a
gang of Burras,[4] Shaw Taylors[5] etc. which always puts me off a little. On
the other hand I have now stopped being uneasy about having persecuted a genius unawares.[6]

I am v. sorry about our misappointment: to sit & wait for someone who
doesn't arrive is absolutely awful always, there is nothing I know better. You
ought to be rewarded by learning that (a) the Cooper dinner was terrifyingly
instructive about the possibility of human transformation. You will say you
saw the process earlier, & nothing else either (b) the music was painful (c) I
left a dress coat & a bowl[7] in a taxi hurrying back to Oxford (d) Moore has
lectured me a great deal, (e) I am in further difficulty: you may not know it
but Rosamond & you are coming to lunch here on Sunday. I have asked to
meet you Hampshire & Jasper Ridley (a charming eccentric), David Wallace
& probably the nice, but you say ugly, Graham Harrison.[8] This makes 6
men v. one woman. But at least they are all very nice. Now Cooper has
written, could I ask R. Lehmann whom, he says, I know, to lunch on Sunday,

1 Ralph Robert Ricketts (1902–98), Magdalen 1921–5 (pass school, no degree), writer; sub-
editor, *London Mercury*, 1934–9; subsequently a market-gardener and farmer.
2 Sir John Collings Squire (1884–1958), minor Georgian poet; editor, *London Mercury*, 1919–34,
co-author with John Lloyd Balderston of the play *Berkeley Square* (1926).
3 (Paul-Marie-Theodore-)Vincent D'Indy (1851–1931), French composer.
4 Presumably a reference to the painter Edward John Burra (1905–76), who worked as a
designer for ballet and opera.
5 Desmond Christopher Shawe-Taylor (*sic*) (1907–95), music critic; at this time writing for *The
Times* and the *Spectator*, mainly on literature, though sometimes on music.
6 Probably a reference to IB's review of van Dieren's *Down Among the Dead Men* (139/4).
7 i.e. a bowler hat?
8 Francis Laurence Theodore Graham-Harrison (1914–2001), Magdalen classics 1933–7; civil
servant from 1938, indexer of KM.

because Ralph & he want to meet her & will be here then. Ordinarily I should just not have done anything. What am I to do? this is a pure & awful coincidence. 8 men v. one woman seems fantastic. Anyhow You dislike Martin C. & Ricketts, though soft & harmless, doesn't add as Maurice wd say. I shd mind him less than Martin C. It is difficult to lie to them since they are sure to discover, & it is a squalid thing to do. Myself as hostess is only funnier than myself as member of a house party. I wish Hugh [Walpole] were here to help me. I am sure he & Henry James must have evolved a definite rule for meeting situations of this kind. No, but really what am I to do? tell me quickly (as B.J. wd say). If the worst comes to the worst, i.e. no solution is provided, I shall ask everyone, it will be enormously populous & you won't mind Cooper who will, hoffentlich[1] be lost amongst them. It will be like a Roy party. Perhaps I might divide the mob into lunch & tea sections. I shall see. Meanwhile tell me if you can absolutely not tolerate Martin C., which, if true, wd at any rate ease matters by being decisive. I'll ask Giles Romilly to a meal, & discover about the Austrian club.[2] Write spedito. "This is a *dreadful* mess, my dear Isaiah, how *could* you let it happen".

Shaya

TO JOHN HILTON

[Mid-October 1936, *card*]

All Souls

Do you know Dodds? he seems quite nice & reputable but very gray on gray, & self-consciously provincial & lustreless. Like Mr Eliot he believes in bleaching subjects. He looks, tho' no one agrees with me, like Beaverbrook. Blakeway? he died with a faintly hostile remark about C.C.C. on his lips. Mr Bowra writing from Cambridge Mass thinks it is God's third smack at the neo-Hellenists, first Payne's death,[3] then his own failure with the professorship, now Blakeway: which shows that God observes the rule of Three. The immediate cause of B.'s death was inflammation of kidney + phlebitis. The ultimate cause was whatever made him limp. Hardie being celibate escapes the curse on junior married Fellows of C.C.C. doubtless imposed by Phelps.

yrs

Shaya

1 'It is to be hoped'.
2 IB had been invited to stay with Spender and other friends in Mieders, a small Austrian village in the Tyrol south of Innsbruck, but in the event he did not join them there.
3 Humfry Gilbert Garth Payne (1902–36), Director of the British School of Archaeology, Athens, since 1929. He was Blakeway's predecessor in this post, and also died prematurely – of blood-poisoning, on 9 May 1936.

TO STUART HAMPSHIRE[1]

Postmark 21 October 1936

All Souls

Dear Stuart,

I enjoyed your letter very much indeed. I was sorry you didn't include the Warden who is, after all, a very rich grotesque figure, nor the silent neurotic figure of Mr Henderson[2] with whom I left you in obvious distress in order to discover Woodward's view of you. He thought you were very nice. That is all he said. Doubtless, since he is an examiner the rest will be evinced by action, a subject on which at present I really cannot enlarge, save to say that you have done yourself no injustice & no injustice is likely to be done to you. But one never knows, really not, save that your expertise in the philosophy paper did make this difference, that Salter & Woodward after informing me that the trouble about my darn questions was that the examiners couldn't understand the answers, turned the papers over to me for a report: also to Woozley:[3] I presented a verbal report full of sharp exclusive descriptions of every one which I enjoyed very much. Don't, will you, leave England. I am glad you met Salter. He is bezaubert[4] by Rowse whom he believes to be the most fascinating man he has ever met on equal terms, and the flirtation is at once entertaining & disgusting. Disgusting only because Salter is now Rowse's sole contact with what he vaguely thinks of as power & as this is not the case, i.e. Salter is somehow strangely out of affairs, they form a binary closed system, a sort of isolated ellipse, or possibly something rather like the thing in Jules Verne's voyage to the Moon:[5] travellers in a projectile fired at the moon, shoot straight at it until they meet a small asteroid which is pursuing a vague & enormously remote path, to this they become attracted & their shell becomes its satellite. They still imagine however that their path to the moon & a new world continues with more than ordinary rapidity. In the end, I think, they drop into the Pacific ocean, and are fished out playing dominoes. But perhaps Salter, unlike the meteoroid, won't explode, but will land himself back into the lunar system:

1 At 8 Clareville Grove, London SW7. SH had just attempted the fellowship examination at All Souls.
2 Henry Ludwig Henderson (1880–1963), classicist, Fellow and Tutor, New College, 1905–45. The obituary note on him in the *New College Record* for 1963–4 (pp. 2–3) is recommended. One sample: 'As a classical scholar he belonged to a long-vanished era when a pupil's errors of syntax or prosody were regarded as indications of moral obliquity.'
3 Anthony Douglas Woozley (b. 1912), philosopher, Fellow of All Souls 1935–7.
4 'Enchanted'.
5 Jules Verne, *De la terre à la lune: trajet direct en 97 heures 20 minutes* (Paris, 1865). IB read the Russian translation (in his set of Verne's works, *Polnoe sobranie sochinenii Zhiulia Verna*, St Petersburg, 1906–7) as a child, and preferred it to the English version (1873); he appears to have near-perfect recall of the plot.

at present he is saying that he won't be bought off with an under-secretaryship. As for your philosophical views, I am glad you are worried about metalanguage, about which you on the whole refuse to commit yourself: you (rightly) say that it is not tautological in the sense in which an artificial language is, but you tend to suggest that if so it is not significant [at] all, or if significant, evocative, i.e. issuing commands: a horse is an animal, as you observe, is not an order 'use horse etc.' but an illustration of how this is obeyed: Mr Lewis's[1] concepts at work etc. But what one wants to know is how one manufactures concepts: what one presupposes in the process of arranging the data in any convenient semi-arbitrary pattern: it is only the transcendental question asked about language, if you like, instead of laws of physics: necessity being verbal ('I have a Humean right to say this', as Ridley somewhere observes) how is it possible? language cannot = chess, or we cd only speak but not say. nobody else writes about anything a quarter as interesting as that. You kill coloured-extended a little too easily, since in that case the mysterious (to me) property of colour by operating in two dimensions, extensive & intensive, seems very unlike an etymological convention: & what about heat? extended things can certainly feel con-tinuously hot, but sharp stabs of heat do not seem capable of being called extended;

All [H. H.] Price's pupils or influences (e.g. Peck)[2] gaily discuss things as bluish, purplish, etc. without seeming aware of oddity of outlook: it is an obvious airman's view of colours,[3] but it seems curious to find it popularized & made mechanical.

The metaphor about Charles Morris[4] is repulsively true. I was, as I shd like to put on record conspicuously wrong to advise P.P.E. as a course: possibly it is pure reproductivism, i.e. because I was bullied into doing it myself, therefore it is a discipline I should like to see others suffer: because I have to be forced to be free therefore I cannot conceive of freedom without force (early Marx would have perpetrated something about '. . . therefore I am freed to urge force' or something equally awful). Anyhow Sumner etc.

1 Clarence Irving Lewis (1883–1964), American philosopher, author of *Mind and the World-Order* (152/1).
2 Antony (Tony) Dilwyn Peck (1914–87), philosopher, Trinity PPE 1933–6 (pupil of H. H. Price), Fellow 1938–46, then a civil servant.
3 Price's main hobby was aviation: he was a founder member of the Oxford University and City Gliding Club.
4 Morris was described to the editor by SNH, his pupil at Balliol, in these terms: 'Bad philosopher, later successful post-war Vice-Chancellor (Leeds [1948–63]), public man'; later still (1967) he became Baron Morris of Grasmere. In his undated letter SNH had written: 'Charles Morris' attitude to me and logical positivism is still that of the frequenter of Promenade Concerts on Beethoven nights to a performance of Hindemith – or rather that is how he would represent it to himself.'

are obviously right. Anyhow this may become an academic question. I must sometime report to you a conversation between Sparrow & Plamenatz which could not have been more grotesque.

Rosamond Lehmann: I don't quite know the answer.[1] Wait. I don't quite understand either, your remark about hating to let situations trail away into insignificance because of your lack of self-consciousness (you mean awareness of yourself & your environment? you can't be said to lack the other kind): e.g. if even you were offered a bridge, would you cross it? or do you simply want the luxury of refusing to do so, instead of simply being conscious of the stream, & of your reflection in its waters to those on the other bank, but ignorant of the possibilities of crossing & presenting yourself in person to be concretely treated by these mysterious figures. Explain if you please. Anyhow I, who on no account want bridges offered, being in such respects, as [Goronwy] Rees has bitterly observed on more than one occasion, a fanatic & a monster, am in danger myself of paying a brief visit to that, I do think, very unglamorous shore. In other words, another meeting seems inevitable, I shall see to it (here the monster touch appears) that it is on my own ground. After this I shall report more accurately what you are conceived of as: I agree you have every right to know, ignorance persecutes. I shall ask direct questions, & give you the direct answer. I am sure they will be that. Nothing becomes a genuine conversation so little as subtlety. I have had a visit from Jeremy & a postcard from Ben: the former definitely made himself agreeable, stayed, chatted, and indeed seems to have decided to accomodate himself to circumstances and think everybody charming (except Boase. I suddenly thought that Boase stands in the relation in which Belgians stand to Paris, to something really good). Ben was unbelievably sentimental, said 'shall I never see again meadows meadows wet with rain?' or the like: is this Housman or his mother?

yrs

Shaya.

TO MARY FISHER (IN PARIS)

Postmark 23 October 1936

All Souls

Dear Mary,

It is undoubtedly something to be complacent: a virtue I mean. So far

---

[1] In the same letter SNH writes: 'I would be grateful if you would tell me what is my persona for Rosamund Lehman [sic]: I feel she moves in an arena of masked figures and it suddenly occurred to me yesterday that I might be miscast. I dislike situations trailing away into insignificance from my lack of self-consciousness – which seemed to me to be happening.'

only Mrs Blakeway and I have shown this virtue, and Guy too I suppose, &
I mark them (us?) accordingly. The double & crossing stream of events of
which I am a sort of dead centre are (1) Blakeway's death. (2) repercussions
after Ireland. With Christopher jittering about and pacing up & down the
front quad of New College in a neurasthenic and unnecessary manner. The
second – Irish affairs – are really only squalid: Miss Lehmann is chiefly
responsible, a lot of Bloomsbury nonsense has occurred by which everybody
suspected everybody of saying they weren't going to have affairs with
everybody else, & ludicrous persecutions developed: I can't begin to take
them seriously even: the atmosphere is essentially grotesque, there is no real
suffering only a lot of behaviour as if; and everyone has applied to me for
data, since I am (rightly) regarded as a disinterested spectator of events: what
appears to be less clear [is] that there is a limit to even my curiosity, i.e. at the
point where squalor begins: the upshot is letters from Miss Lehmann full of
embarrassing sentences, which one cannot leave unanswered: she may be
a very beautiful and tremendously important woman, but I find her dull and
sentimental, and kindness is certainly not enough: but, as you might have
guessed, I play up, and write everyone soothing letters, & feel a Christopher,
and long to make jokes about this to someone: only the only possible
audience seem all to be protagonists.

As for Blakeway: I heard of it from Hardie which is obviously suitable:
and it is a disaster of an order one has never experienced before, & finally
marks the end of jeunesse.[1] Dundas[2] wrote a good obituary in the Oxford
Magazine,[3] of which, if you like I'll send you a copy: Wade-Gery[4] wrote a v.
good characteristic one in the *Times*,[5] which you probably saw, about B's
being a man all flame and passion, ribald, direct, vehement or something of
this kind: Mr Leeson,[6] gathering a group of Wykehamists round him
stuttered through 'A great light is gone' twice: & then complained of the
obituary on the ground that 'it omitted to describe the underlying gentleness
of the man'.

I am sorry my letter is getting so irascible: but you sympathise: to go on:

1 'Youth'.
2 Robert Hamilton Dundas (1884–1960), classicist, Student and Tutor of Christ Church 1910–57.
3 An unofficial University magazine, then as now published weekly in full term. 'Alan Albert
  Antisdel Blakeway', by 'R.H.D.', appeared in the issue dated 22 October 1936, 50.
4 Henry Theodore Wade-Gery (1888–1972), ancient historian, Fellow of Wadham 1914–39, then
  Wykeham Professor of Ancient History and Fellow of New College.
5 'Mr Alan Blakeway: Director of the British School at Athens' (unsigned), *The Times*, 12
  October 1936, 19, in which Wade-Gery calls Blakeway a 'violent man, all fire and spirit, and
  born with a body to match' and adds that 'he will be remembered as a man of reckless
  vitality' and that 'He was a quite uncompromising fighter, ribald, personal, direct [. . .]'.
6 Spencer Leeson (1892–1956), Headmaster of Winchester 1935–46.

Guy behaved exceedingly well, & didn't pretend he was unable to laugh for
a fortnight: Alison [Blakeway] behaved in an astonishingly adequate manner:
neither crushed nor unnaturally tough: this is partly, I suppose, due to the
fact that she really doesn't see things at all: imagines she is going to have an
important literary career in London etc. however it was excellent however
caused. I feel sure that R. Chilver–Miss Graves behaved oddly or wrongly
somewhere about something, but I have no evidence. Tony was very very
difficult indeed. He had every reason to. If anyone is left utterly stranded it is
he. He dined with me about three days after, and not once was Alan's name
mentioned. I resented that a little. I don't think Tony was dramatizing the
situation, after all dramatization is only exaggeration of something there
(hardly a platitude even) & there are situations which being maximal are
unexaggeratable, but must appear bogus because of their general out-of-
focusness. Anyhow Tony moped, & left rooms with muffled sounds,
laughed mirthlessly, said 'stop stop' in the middle of harmless sentences, and
indeed hardly lived at all.

If Maurice were here I believe by sheer toughness he'd keep everyone
disciplined better: Roy & Ryle, not essentially among the late B.'s friends,
appeared at the memorial service: I don't quite know why but they were like
state officials present at the funeral of a convicted revolutionary, who
nevertheless was too great not to be regarded, in spite of mutinousness, as
a great national figure. Dunbabin[1] also behaved excellently, grew much
handsomer suddenly, like a beautiful native of somewhere, very typical, &
polynesian, & left for Perachora[2] in a businesslike way: The late B. died
very gaily, so it is reported, after making some fairly obscure but hostile
remarks about Corpus. You don't mind all this funerary detail? I can't help
regarding even such events as are so nearly connected with one, as semi-real,
objects in art etc.

How by the way does one define a highbrow? I can only think of
highbrow accounts of it: (the case arises in connexion with Herr Köpler,[3]
once described by [Frank] Pakenham as Dick's black servant, the German
who co-occupied the Barn, who wants to know why he isn't, because all the
suggested formulae fit him & he obviously (to all but himself) is the v.
opposite of one) is a highbrow a person acquainted (i.e. not knowing by
description) with the indefinable qualities in works of art & artists, who also

1 Thomas James Dunbabin (1911–55), Assistant Director, British School of Archaeology,
Athens, 1936–45, Fellow of All Souls 1937–55, a hero of the Cretan resistance.
2 Greek archaeological site (north of Corinth) where the British School were excavating at the
time.
3 Heinz/Henry Köppler (1912–79) had recently completed his D.Phil. at Magdalen, where he
became a Senior Demy in 1937. He was later employed by the British to re-educate
Germans.

finds these same in nature, & when he finds them is thrilled? anyhow a person who abstracts relations between X and Y in life, X and Y being relatively unimportant, & then begins to do geometrical things i.e. to produce them, to ask as X is to Y, what is to Z? Mr Forster observes somewhere 'Everything is like something; what is this [I can't remember what] like?'[1] that is surely a typical aesthete's question (also incidentally being concerned with lists, series, assigning parts etc, makes you & me into first rate aesthetes, which I, at any rate, find agreeable enough . . . (three dots however is always middlebrow. Mr Meiggs[2] uses them a lot! exclamation marks are upper & lower class: or is all this nonsense? I think so); pursuing this line of thought we get: aesthetes distort because they abstract relations or nuances or whatnot, & operate them in surprising media: or not as the case may be: e.g. Tolstoy: he produced W & P. which happens, because that is how he chose to embody the relations he was uniquely acquainted with, in circumstances of real life: that happened to be his medium: but only happened: thus middlebrows enjoy him too because it happens, per accidens, to be reasonably photographic: imitation of that aspect of it is bound to lead to The Good Companions:[3] in essential it is much more like Proust (your father wd not agree). Lowbrows or base persons are themselves acquainted with sensation passion etc, & want nothing else: highbrows are acquainted with what these emotions, passions etc. feel like precisely: middlebrows are not acquainted at all, they are like children who paint the other side of the head into profiles, because they know it's there, although, not being either simple, or Manet, they don't know they don't see it: they therefore alone claim (v. falsely) to want works where people move 'as in real life' i.e. mechanically. Woodward e.g. who is a typical middle-brow who makes his position explicit, objects to films because they don't inform, merely repeat life, which is dull enough, whereas of course he would go, if more news were given. The distraction of everyday life & really interesting facts, news etc. exists neither for real lowbrows nor real highbrows: your father e.g. who likes picturesque & dramatic relationships to exist between persons or situations in history, & wd almost encourage them to happen more often, and approves of Napoleon[4] because he possessed a lot of style (I observe that all this is really an inflated paean to this last quality), plainly is identified

1 'Everything must be like something, so what is this like?' E. M. Forster, 'Our Diversions', 3, 'The Doll Souse' (1924): p. 49 in *Abinger Harvest* (161/1). 'This' is Queen Mary's dolls' house. Cf. Gertrude Stein's remark quoted earlier (p. 153 above), 'Must things have something to do with everything?'
2 Russell Meiggs (1902–89), ancient historian, Fellow of Keble 1930–9.
3 Picaresque novel by J. B. Priestley (London, 1929).
4 See H. A. L. Fisher, *Napoleon* (London, 1912).

with ultra-highbrows. Not so Mr [H. G.] Wells who has a vested interest in the mediocre.

Out of this emerge further: bogus highbrows: i.e. persons who know there is a state of acquaintance & indefinabilia to be acquainted with, but have never been in contact with these themselves, behave as if, & are difficult to detect because, ex hypothesi, if the objects are indefinable, one does not, without telepathy, know whether they are aware of them or not: one has to deduce from behaviour, which if skilfully done (the old world Oxford aesthetes) passes scrutiny. Also bogus middlebrows (a) Sumner & Cox who in their differing degrees are aware of the truth but suppress, & talk an unnatural language of the imaginary man in the street (b) Mrs Bowen, a natural lowbrow, who talks pompously a language which is at once boring in itself & above her head. Dear me: I always seem to be talking about the same thing in the end: I do apologise for writing half obituary gossip, half aesthetic theory. I meant to write a letter. The term is very slow, the trough is thoroughly there, we are soon going to elect, Mr Hampshire (I hope) (not without some reason) & possibly Routh[1] or Beaumont:[2] the Arab & the Jew are both out of it: & so soon as anything occurs I shall write.

love
    Shaya

TO ELIZABETH BOWEN

[Autumn 1936?]

All Souls

Dear Elizabeth:

I left Regent's Park and arrived in a mood of almost unnatural exhilaration, the clan of hacks whom I found waiting for me, must have been surprised by the uncharacteristic gaiety & briskness with which they were treated:[3] I was asked who was responsible for the revival of philosophy in the XVI century: they said afterwards that I said it was the Renaissance boys who did that, Italian fellows – had they never heard of them? later I developed a long cold, which indeed is still there: consequently I'd rather not come up for my concert to-morrow (Monday), I tried to ring up to say so this morning, but you were said to be out till late in the evening. The week has been wonderfully uneventful: partly due to the dense mist in which one lives

---

1 Dennis Alan Routh (1912–91), New College PPE 1931–5, Laming Travelling Fellow at Queen's 1935–6, Fellow of All Souls 1936–61, Central Office of Information 1940–8.
2 Robert Leslie Beaumont (1914–38), Christ Church classics 1932–5, Fellow and ancient history Tutor, Corpus, 1937–8. The Arab is probably Albert Hourani (292/6), and the Jew perhaps Max Beloff (141/2), then a Senior Demy at Magdalen.
3 Presumably IB was giving a talk.

if one moves about with a great overpowering cold on one, looking helpless and giving a specious impression of kindness and benevolence. When one is in that condition, one naturally makes for nice, stupid, obstinate, comfortable, slightly self-pitying, but in the whole solidly rooted figures like Geoffrey Faber: with whom I have now had 3 enormous pointless heart to hearts about (1) modern poetry & philosophy: of incredible fatuity: (2) treatment of sexual criminals. He spoke with the terrific passion of all the members of the great International. (3) Mr Hayward,[1] of whom he is scared. He gave a for him really very vivid description of Mr Hayward, for 40 seconds, clinging like a monkey to his chauffeur's neck: he is extremely excited by the thought, that he, Faber, a solid, unimaginative beefy figure (dramatization 1) should wander about so familiarly amongst these remarkable and significant figures: like a Vollard[2] among the impressionists: he is to a ludicrous extent a young man's elderly man, because he likes asking 'what is philosophy?' what is art? etc, & we all love explaining. But the extent to which his innocent self-dramatization goes serves as a sort of awful warning of how fatally easy it is, & how rapidly it destroys all sense of truth & reality: it is a temptation which, unless one in fact occupies a very simple & very peculiar position of one's own, like say Stephen, never completely leaves one: the watchfulness required is a strain, but the retrospection of dangers & humiliations successfully avoided is agreeable, and when one meets anyone who (like yourself. I apologize for apparently putting you into a class. But then we agree that personalities *must* be avoided at all costs & always. So it is a stylistic dodge) who either in fact avoids it, or much better, consciously discounts and neutralizes it, one gets the delicious sensation felt, I regret to say by a disagreeable figure in Turgenev's Rudin,[3] & expressed by 'long live intelligent people'. I feel, perhaps falsely, that I am armed absolutely and for ever against all kinds of common bluff, and against some of the expensive important ones too. I may be too cowardly or indolent to call it; but by not playing up at all, not even appearing to, yawning almost, one seems to be able to induce a natural evaporation of it which is as effective, & possibly leaves fewer scars. Or is this simply another dramatization of oneself as invulnerable? like the devil's most fatal device of inducing disbelief in his own existence? I do not know. You are quite right. I do live in a society of suppressed or incompletely suppressed maniacs who compensate themselves sometimes in proper ways, by learning etc. sometimes squalidly by paddling, or talking or having important & elaborate feelings which are absolutely

---

1 John Davy Hayward (1905–65), man of letters, anthologist, bibliophile, who suffered from muscular dystrophy. Geoffrey Faber was part of his minor salon in London.
2 Ambroise Vollard (1836–1939), art dealer.
3 The first of Turgenev's novels, published in 1856.

worthless. For myself I cannot honestly complain at all. When e.g. Goronwy exclaims about our colleagues that they are all brutes & beasts, I see what he means, or even that he may be right, but it means practically nothing to me in real i.e. bullion terms. I only get involved when I find myself by accident or design involved in a complex created without me, & then I behave like a frightened tourist and run into troops etc. (like Mr Pickwick who by accident became mixed up with the review of troops at Chatham. The magistrate said 'the punishment for this is death.' but the Clerk of the Court corrected him, & was obviously right?)

    love

       Shaya

I must write to Mrs Phillips & put her off. I don't really hope that this will be the last instalment.

TO ELIZABETH BOWEN

[November/December 1936?]

All Souls

Dear Elizabeth

    Mr Rees whom I saw for about 4 minutes on Saturday, said you had gone to bed with general weariness: and Mr Hampshire that you were going to Japan:[1] I questioned none of their authorities but would be greatly relieved if you would produce a démenti at any rate to the former rumour which is v. worrying: as for Japan, you will probably enjoy it very much: and acquire an extra subject of conversation with Reneé Ayer which is more than anyone else can discover even with my capacity for patient research. I only saw Messrs Rees & Verschoyle[2] fleetingly because I went to Cambridge, almost as soon as they arrived: there I stayed with the Rothschilds;[3] my sole fellow guest was Aldous Huxley; he had a cold, sniffed whenever he spoke, which made everything he said sound querulous: I didn't think him even very clever: but very well informed and lucid. He sat there literally with an encyclopaedia (the new Columbia one in one volume) held at about 3″ from his eyes, and from time to time read out bits about diseases and the novelist Eugène Sue.[4] We went to a party in Trinity almost as soon as we

1 With her husband Alan Cameron, who later cancelled the visit, to EB's relief.
2 Derek Hugo Verschoyle (1911–73), literary editor, *Spectator*, 1932–40.
3 (Nathaniel Mayer) Victor (1910–90), 3rd Baron *Rothschild 1937, and his first wife Barbara Judith Rothschild (1911–89), née Hutchinson.
4 Pseudonym of Marie-Joseph Sue (1804–57), who wrote sensationalist novels about urban degradation.

arrived – given by Anthony Blunt – and it really seems as if the life which died in Oxford roundabout 1931 continues in Cambridge: before the delighted eyes of Messrs Rylands,[1] [Raymond] Mortimer,[2] Bishop (who is charming)[3] etc. a group of young men with pink faces and in fur coats made their second or third début: elderly American women wandered about the room with the arms of bored but gallant young men about them: Mr Huxley started talking to somebody about Poussin[4] learnedly at once: somebody who didn't know me tapped me smartly on the shoulder and said loudly: 'don't listen to him, old boy, don't listen to him: this is la vie (leer) and we don't get too much of it either in these days.' the sense of the past, but in no sense nostalgia, occurred with great intensity. I suppose this is what Mr Mortimer means by praising the social aspects of Cambridge. My weekend was enjoyable on the whole: the house is enormously comfortable, my host, so rude to his intimate friends is polite to me, but Mr Huxley is too unspontaneous. Things are said, nothing happens for some time, then after the process of absorption, assimilation, classification, cross-reference, is over, you get the response, carefully & slowly stated, with the last embers of life carefully snuffed out, absolutely bleak and sterilized. He was not at all shy, about Balliol[5] he spoke with great passion and hatred, but again as if slowly compounding a nostrum out of a number of labelled retorts round him, done with no mysterious or sinister air, nor even very rapidly and deftly, but slowly, deliberately and lifelessly. His conversation, while often informative & never bogus, was never positively interesting: and the only phenomenon which ever produced a spark out of him was hatred: a Cambridge scientist's dislike of his wife, Balzac's dislike of peasants etc. He seems somehow the apotheosis of the intelligent, serious, self-taught, envious ugly grammar-schoolboy, levelling everything, not by systematic debunking, but by describing everything in the same unemphatic, colourless

1 George Humphrey Wolferstan ('Dadie') Rylands (1902–99), Fellow of King's College, Cambridge.

2 (Charles) Raymond (Bell) Mortimer (1895–1980), critic, literary editor of the *New Statesman* 1935–47.

3 Herbert Francis 'Adrian' Bishop (c.1900–42), King's College, Cambridge, classics 1919–23; homosexual; worked in education and journalism in various countries for several years then became a monk after a religious experience following an illness; volunteered for war service and became Intelligence officer in Egypt and Persia; attached to the British Embassy in Baghdad at the time of his death; a friend of Bowra, who writes about him in his *Memories* (London, 1966).

4 Nicolas Poussin (1594–1665), French painter who spent much of his working life in Italy; his doctrine that a work of art should stimulate the intellect as well as please the eye became fundamental to the classical tradition of art in France over the next two centuries.

5 In 1918 Aldous Huxley sounded out Balliol, where he had been an often unhappy undergraduate (English 1913–17), to see if there was any prospect of a job, but was told they had taken on a good man during the war and wished to keep him. With this account of Huxley compare PI 191.

disgusted way: which naturally overcompensates itself by patches of absolutely soft and awful sentimentality, principally directed at music, which he
rarely leaves untarnished. And yet his intellectual snobbery is, I suppose a
very admirable quality, and he is probably a kind, generous, sensitive,
admirable person. But enormously unsympathetic, I think.

Mr Alistair Buchan[1] I found terrifying. But I'd rather leave him for some
other occasion. Odd association of ideas. Mr Rothschild sent me home by
aeroplane which was fantastic & delightful. The whole week-end was so like
the rich that I enormously wish I were a writer. The dinner party on Sunday,
half Mayfair half Cambridge–Bloomsbury, half upper class exclamatory
style ('do you mean to say you have heard *nothing* you dreary bore?')
half Cambridge science (Mr Huxley brought everything to the story of some
tumour on somebody's lung, immediately exaggerated by Victor R. into
something grisly to shock the guests. Everything there happens par
épatage.)[2] + quasi-philosophy when I wd be called on, & again & again did
the piece I was expected to do, was a genuine subject for sophisticated
fiction. They are not exactly a nice couple, the Rothschilds, but they are
extremely picturesque, have a great deal of style, do not conceal their
passions, and are nice to stay with. I like them far more than principle wd
allow. Which cannot be said for Miss Pearn.[3] Proceeding on the well
known assumption, how often justified that it is useless to advise against,
I shall attempt to come to terms with Inez. My first step was to try & save
Stephen some embarrassment & persuade her to change it to Agnes. She
consented. You will say it is much too nice a name, but let us think of
Stephen. That she is an adventuress I have no doubt at all. I only hope that
her ambition will end here, & won't go on to, shall we say, Mr Eliot. In
which case, so tough and heartless is she, it may even be a success for
a number of years at least. She must have behaved in the hideously vulgar
way you described partly through terror of you: which proves nothing, since
behaviour under terror is an absolutely certain sign, like smiling. She is at
least as unspontaneous as Mr Huxley, which, I now think, is the most
dreadful of all qualities. I shall be as courteous to her as I can. Indeed I shall

1 Hon. Alastair Francis Buchan (1918–76), third son of John Buchan; Christ Church history
  1936–9; 'fundamentally a Scot, with formidable powers of work and a granite-hard integrity
  which impressed people even more than did his intellectual ability and the literary fluency
  he inherited from his father' (Michael Howard, DNB). He took a 2nd class degree.
2 'By shock tactics'.
3 Stephen Spender's first wife, Marie Agnes ('Inez') Pearn (1913–76), Somerville modern
  languages 1933–6. She and SS married on 15 December 1936 and were divorced in 1941; in
  1942 Inez married Charles Madge, who had previously been married to Kathleen Raine.

behave as I did to Tony, & all Stephen's other mutable adjectival beings. May I stay the night after Mr Hayward? & call for you at 7? or even ten to? Frankfurter wires that Maurice has been offered something enormous at Harvard. He wd be mad to accept it: but it may only be for bargaining power.

    love

      Shaya

TO JOHN HILTON

    [Early December 1936, *card*]

                                         All Souls

Dear John

    Point by point answer by answer.

    Anarchism. Is there any post-Bakunin literature which is not in Italian or Spanish? even the Reflexions sur la violence[1] are more syndicalist than anarchist: & Kropotkin's[2] gentle little volumes are pure Ruskin & Tolstoy. Plekhanov has a good vicious attack in a pamphlet called Anarchism & Syndicalism, I doubt if translated, very gay and readable: otherwise a lot of Spaniards.

    Time: lawful, yes. But you should get it like me from Chicago & read endless details about Mrs Simpson, the Arbp. of C-n-t-r-b-r-y, Mr Simpson, H.M., etc. etc. never was such pleasure experienced. 'The King in Love'. 'Monarch builds love nest for cutie' etc. I don't think I want my books because I cannot remember what you have: Marx is appearing next year I suppose.

Amongst the younger dons and undergraduates there was considerable agreement on matters of foreign policy. But the great domestic issue, the abdication of King Edward VIII, was a different matter, as IB recalled:

The great rows occurred over the abdication. One Fellow of Exeter threw a glass of wine at another Fellow of Exeter for being against King Edward VIII. There were passionate feelings. Roy Harrod canvassed the London–Oxford train, compartment by compartment, to find out if they

---

  1 By Georges Sorel.
  2 Petr Alekseevich Kropotkin (1842–1921), Russian geographer, anarchist and revolutionary, whose books include *Mutual Aid* (1892, in English 1902).

were in favour or not in favour after the Bishop of Somewhere had revealed the facts about Mrs Simpson,[1] and found on the whole that the great majority were in favour of the King. I was in favour of the abdication. I thought there was something very wrong with him. Her pro-Nazi sympathies were already known.[2]

TO MARY FISHER

[*c.*17 December 1936]

All Souls

Dear Mary

I meant and meant to write: for every kind of reason, and as an end in itself. The end of term is always intolerable, and scholarships which succeed it, but for the Crossman–Henderson[3] (my co-examiners') interchanges, very boring and lowering. Scenes occur thus: we meet: there is an argument about the nature & purpose of vivas between C. and H. C: my purpose is to elect the *best men we can*. H: (swelling like a turkey cock & gobbling) 'you will no doubt be surprised to learn that curiously enough that too is my intention' etc. & then I pacify.

Before all I wish to express my enormous gratitude for Toscanini:[4] it is absolutely enchanting, it stands on my mantelpiece; I hope that it will seem to have been presented by the subject: there is a puzzling point about the collar, whether or not there is a stud anywhere at all, & about a certain tab. Meanwhile events have to some degree happenned: they are in order: all disastrous.

1) The abdication of Edward VIII.[5] You may be surprised to note this as a private event. Nevertheless I am sure it is. I listened to his valedictory speech & it was a neurotic & intensely moving event. The private significance of it is that it marks the end of the Twenties finally and absolutely, & represents the victory of the old men and the entrance of the Forties. Which is profoundly melancholy. In his vulgar and awful way he did stand for the Weimar Republic, libertarianism, being allowed to be spontaneous, say what one wished, etc. The victory of the Church affects one's private life

1 Wallis Warfield Simpson (1896–1986), American wife of Ernest Aldrich Simpson, her second husband, became Duchess of Windsor in June 1937 when she married the former King Edward VIII (1894–1972). The Bishop of Bradford, Dr Alfred Walter Frank Blunt (1879–1957), criticised the King in a speech on 1 December that precipitated the first coverage in UK newspapers of his relationship with Mrs Simpson.
2 MI Tape 8.
3 Richard Crossman and H. L. Henderson.
4 A postcard.
5 On 11 December 1936.

and puts a social premium on Mr Boase and a taste for respectability as opposed to even worth (Pares–Cox. Which is slightly depressing but I am sorry to say not acutely unsympathetic). This is intensified by

2) the offer of a Greek professorship to Maurice in Harvard. I suddenly received a telegram from Frankfurter which said 'distinguished offer to Maurice here. Oxford will have to be handsome to keep him. Frankfurter.' I really didn't know what I was expected to do: I inferred a professorship, I don't know whether rightly. I rang up: Mynors,[1] Wade Gery, Dundas, & suggested a round robin in which 40 persons implored him not to leave them. Fraenkel supported this. I don't think more will be done than remarkable letters from Dundas, Wade-G. & Mynors; the latter came flying to my room in a state of great concern. I had a charming letter from Mrs Frankf. in which Maurice is alleged to be swimming happily on a tide of his own making: his last mot: 'The trouble about Americans is that they don't know when they're being bored.' He threw himself vigorously into the Presidential election, sat up by the wireless all night, from time to time saying 'What of Arkansas?' 'We've heard nothing from Indiana.' It must have been heavenly. I don't know what he has been offerred: but I think he would be mad to accept. He will certainly become bored very rapidly, & the Americans would note only the most violently exaggerated characteristics. (3 or 4 days later).

I hear from B.J. that you are back. This intensifies my feeling of guilt, (in part expiation of which I enclose a relevant cutting + facsimile of Mrs Frankf.) but does not inhibit from continuing with the narrative. In order that you may once more realize that, as M[aurice] wd say, God observes the rule of three in the short as well as the long run, the third blow in November is the engagement of Stephen Spender to Miss Inez Pearn. You will have heard of it, perhaps. I do not know whether I need enlarge? it is all in a sense my fault, since they met in my room, on an occasion when, having invited Miss Lehmann + entourage, and realizing there wd be no other women, and having received a visit of condolence (for Blakeway) from Miss Beecham[2] + Miss Pearn representing the widow, I, very hesitantly (so Miss Pearn truthfully later alleged to Stephen), at the iron gate, invited them both. It was in any case a ludicrous lunch party followed by trivial, irritating, low level emotional complications for the guests, and some clerical work for me. On the next occasion when Stephen was in Oxford, he said he was going to tea

1 Roger Aubrey Baskerville Mynors (1903–89), classicist, Fellow of Balliol 1926–44.
2 (Helen) Audrey Beecham (1915–89), Somerville PPE 1934–7, later engaged for a time to Maurice Bowra.

at 4.30, at Somerville. With whom? I said, with Inez, said he. Then, I cannot conceive how or why, I suddenly said 'are you going to marry her?' & he, blushing, I must own, 'Yes, as a matter of fact I think so, I mean I think I am going to, marry her I mean'. They were married two days ago, & although officially I don't disapprove, I couldn't bring myself to attend the ceremony. I suppose that all poets' wives are dreadful, that she is quite pretty & quite nice, but she is (1) arty crafty (b) frightfully dull. Well informed about Spain, but unspontaneous, lifeless, artificial etc. (c) an open adventuress: will she regard Stephen as high enough (they both declare they are in love. When is one to believe what?) or will she forsake him for Mr Eliot? Elizabeth Cameron wrote me a very violent letter about her, saying she was common, ate food with repellent greed & rapidity, stared raptly at the ceiling & whenever addressed came to with a reluctant start, as if called away from a valuable esoteric meditation, etc. & in fact provoked all her most snobbish feelings. In a sense she'll do as his wife: because it wd be appalling if he married someone vulgar & soft: vulgar & tough, common and on the make:

a further lapse of days interrupted this narrative: in the course of which I met Peggy on a bus who said (after a warm welcome: I believe that is at least half the reason why one likes meeting her so much: the chaleur[1] is so enormous and – I believe – genuine, the excitement of meeting anyone at all is always gigantic –) that Dougle had just been appointed to a post with £1000 p.a. attached, a secretary of his own etc. etc. Peggy in wealth will be most agreeable: telling one in a whisper of the enormous prices paid for everything, and going to Indo-China or the Orinoco River in the company of H. Hart[2] (certainly one of our most prosperous friends: Sparrow will also make money, but it will only mean still shabbier clothes). Mrs Cameron, by the way, wishes to annul her previous judgment, she now finds Mrs Spender full of charm etc. Mr Connolly of the New Statesman says, on the other hand, that had we wished we could all have mugged up pre-Cervantes Spanish literature, and as for going to Brussels to read, that must be bogus for it has the worst public library in the world. The press is on the whole bad rather than good, my attitude being that of the Nazi Press towards Edward VIII, artificial, unreal neutrality, & a refusal to be involved in anything at all. I see that Miss Laski,[3] unable to hold herself any longer, now that Miss Graves, Miss Pearn, Miss Hope[4] etc., has announced her engagement in

---

1 'Warmth'.

2 Herbert Lionel Adolphus Hart (1907–92), New College classics Oxford 1926–9, Chancery Bar 1932–40, future husband of Jenifer Williams.

3 Marghanita Laski (1915–88), novelist, critic, journalist and broadcaster; married publisher John Eldred Howard in 1937.

4 Somerville contemporaries of MF's, all of whom had now married.

the *Times*. Her horrible father's official position[1] will provoke an outcry in the non-Aryan press. This I shall enjoy, considering the wonderful triviality of the values involved.

I have now (the association of thought is faintly uncomplimentary) met Mr H. L. Henderson every night: our tastes are absolutely coincident: in restaurants, in the theatre (we saw Parnell.[2] H.L. was much moved by repulsive acting. I must, however, reproduce accurately for you the scene in the restaurant, when he suddenly embraced me from behind & uttered a prepared sentence). A set of terrible fatalities also occurred because I spent a week-end at Cambridge, & Mr Rees (as he is now frequently known to even his nearest friends) rifled my room, discovered a letter about himself full of violence, and a fuss began.[3]

But let us rather consider the advantages of the week-end: I went to stay with the Rothschilds: the luxury is a little too unashamed: the continual atmosphere of footmen oppressive, but the comforts enormous. My only fellow guest was Mr Aldous Huxley. He was, I regret to state, dull. He suffered from a cold, stared at every thing through 3 inches of glass, sniffed, swallowed vitamins, began remarks with 'it is wonderfully cu-rious to reflect that' or 'how remarkable it is' when it didn't begin to be, in this respect resembling Woodward; he resembled him otherwise too: in being plainly a lacerated figure, anxious to turn himself inside out for inspection, hoping for confidences, promising to respect them, never getting them, wanting to discover the precise mechanism of human behaviour even in the case of his friends, & so asking scientific questions & killing all possibility of spontaneity in a room. He is a v. kind, sensitive, gentle, humane man. Three quarters dead and, I regret to have to repeat, boring. Not very, but still sufficiently. While there I complained of the difficulty of going home via Bletchley. My host said why don't you go by air? which I took to mean why not by underground or the like. When I rose in the morning, Victor R. had gone to his laboratory, Mrs R. was in bed, my co-breakfaster, a Mrs Venetia Montagu[4] (wife to a dead Secretary for India, Edwin M., handsome, smart, awful woman, celebrated society wit I am told, but quite genuinely clever and entertaining, only very awful. With two dogs, and 3 aeroplanes, piloted

1 Neville Jonas Laski (1890–1969), QC 1930, President, London Committee of Deputies of British Jews, 1933–40, Recorder of Burnley 1935–56.

2 A play by Elsie T. Schauffler about the Irish nationalist politician Charles Stewart Parnell (1846–91), leader of the Home Rule party in the British Parliament.

3 Elizabeth Bowen's letter to IB of 23 September 1936, in which she describes the events of the infamous house-party in detail, and refers to Rees's 'ruthless incontinence'.

4 (Beatrice) Venetia Stanley (1887–1948) had married in 1915, to the great grief of the Prime Minister H. H. Asquith, who was deeply in love with her. Her husband, Edwin Samuel Montagu (1879–1924), son of 1st Baron Swaythling and Liberal politician, played a major role in obtaining constitutional reform for India during his time as its Secretary of State 1917–22.

by a ravishing young man[1] with whom she visits Persia, Tibet etc.) was
not helpful. At this point the butler approached & said the car was ready
whenever I wished it. My difficulties seemed solved. (this story cd be
expanded a la Smith–Cox: is it known which of them adopted the method of
infinite elasticity first? pre-established harmony?). I entered the car. I was
driven to an aerodrome. I was very very frightened indeed. I was offered
a choice of 2 machines, one covered, the other not. I chose the former. I sat
in the wrong seat. Great difficulties were experienced in moving me. My
pilot looked like all pilots, very handsome, clipped moustache, distinguished
voice, very smart. We flew over a large number of country homes in
Bedfordshire in some of which my pilot had either stayed or flown people to,
anyhow he asked me if I had ever been inside 'em, they made one
wonderfully comfortable there considering what a crusty old stick the old
man was etc. We arrived at Stanton St. John after appearing to strike trees
houses etc. where a Citax[2] was already waiting. I shook hands with my
pilot, the taxi man approached & said, 'where do you wish to be driven to
my Lord?' a very unreal scene, however you look at it. I left Cambridge
at 12.10 p.m. and entered All Souls at 12.55 p.m. As a mode of travel
I recommend it: the country from the air is very pretty, & the sensation of
immobility above a very slowly changing complex of formal patterns (made
by avenues of trees, drives etc.) extraordinary. Some dislocation was caused
to my Eustachian tube, since I began to hear a faint murmuring which rose
to a continuous susurrus which became louder & louder & mediated very
disagreeably between me & the external world: field work on sense data
(reported to Price) was not a sufficient reward: in the end Dr Macbeth[3]
blew up my ear drum & restored me. That was v. odd too. Will you greet
your parents for me & say how v. much I enjoyed the dinner party in
November: it couldn't be fuller of style and was exhilarating and shapely at
every moment. And will you please write? I may go to Paris in Jan.

    yrs
      Shaya

2 added vignettes.

    it is wonderful how far your mother's & my views coincide about the
sudden proximity of the Sée family

    Miss [Betty] Russell, now vulgarly regarded as a nuisance by Guy, has
been giving me a deal of trouble.

1 One Rupert Bellville (1905–62), the heir to Papillon Hall in Leicestershire, who fought for
Franco in the Spanish Civil War.
2 City taxi.
3 Presumably Ronald Graeme Macbeth (1903–92), FRCS, an Oxford aural surgeon.

TO SHIELA GRANT DUFF

[1936?, 2 postcards]

[All Souls?]

Bad about Isaiah.[1]

Dear Shiela:

(These points are ranged in an order of importance.)

1. Will you let me know sometime the exact reference to Hume on abstracts & numbers, as I propose to scrutinise him on that for my own sake as well as for yours.

2. Will you ingeminate into Goronwy (in Warden Pember's[2] sonorous words) that Stephen feels vaguely cheated of a weekend and perhaps something might be done when he comes to Appleton[3] in the beginning of term?

3. Should the question of Goronwy's debt of a letter to me ever arise, then, should he have failed (but why should he) to lose or destroy the letter from me which created the debt, I think it better that you shouldn't read it. By better I only mean that it would embarrass me very much to know that you have; I do not retract any portion of it: repeat that it is a letter I should have been pleased to have got myself: and beg you not to read it (you, after all, are not, like us, inquisitive) (though whether you do or not is ultimately very unimportant even to me) but instead to believe me that the return I got for it was unjust and inadequate. I admit that it is only very recently that I discovered what a luxury it is to feel injured. I insist, by the way, that I feel & am injured not in the observer or external, but the observed or inner or real self. I can't think why you want to redintegrate me.

Finally (4) will you give Goronwy this cheque.

I am sorry that you pass so without stopping. I was looking forward to choosing some really important concert, & spending half days on explaining why it was going to be so uniquely wonderful for you. Douglas's laugh on a telephone is absolutely fantastic: it was evoked by Erica or Tittle by Tattle.[4] Enjoy yourself.

love.

Shaya.

---

1 Perhaps a reference to the pictures on the obverses of the two postcards, which show painted wooden masks from Ceylon, worn by 'devil-dancers' to cure patients suffering from blindness or disease.

2 Francis Pember (157/7); presumably IB wanted Goronwy Rees to invite Stephen Spender to All Souls.

3 A village west of Oxford.

4 Erika [sic] Crossman, first wife of Richard Crossman (but not mentioned by him in his Who's Who entry), was generally considered rather a joke. Eric, or, Little by Little (1858) by F. W. Farrar was a popular children's book in which Eric went to the bad 'little by little'.

[Mid-January 1937?]

All Souls

Dear Elizabeth,

When will you come to a meal? this term, without Maurice, has suddenly opened out with a great room of work to be done & lectures to be delivered, which I personally find rather nice. One does in fact, it must be owned, do more work in the evenings during Maurice's absence. However I think, in spite of Mr Boase, (I have never met a man more anxious for Maurice to stay in U.S.A. One of the chief reasons for wanting him back is the pleasure of those who will [be] pleased.[1] Boase, very. Goronwy, openly. Half his colleagues. Freddie (oddly enough, & not confessedly. However it is the case. M's existence vaguely persecutes him). Mr Longden.[2] Sparrow (v. secretly). And that, you see, is really intolerable. Roy has written him a letter which must be wonderful. You remember the last one, on the Regius professorship, when he spoke of 'your growing reputation as a scholar & a wit'? on those lines. All about the unimportance of who was & who wasn't professor, on the beauties of life in Wadham (with citations from David Cecil) on the fact that what is important is not Maurice's books or reviews of them, but what he says about Yeats, what he writes about Valéry.[3] However it is a sincere & loyal document. I met old J. A. Spender[4] last night. From Stephen's accounts one would have deduced a repulsive monster, stupid, bullying and blindly reactionary. He is very silly, but charming, gentle, with funny stories about the Kaiser, and essentially sweet and very courtly. I am sure that no member of my generation will, at his age, be so unembittered, unressentimental, gay, affable, scrupulous and affectingly truthful. His views are awful and his thing about Stephen v. funny. 'Stephen is a good boy, a *good* boy. But it's these friends of his, who encourage the perversion of his true, limpid, style. It's Mr Auden. Always, everywhere, this Auden. It's he, I am sure, who makes him write about decaying teeth and so on. I am sure Stephen doesn't really think of them at all. But then, whenever I open my mouth he says 'you *would* say that' (at this point a Mrs Harrod look came into his face, – 'the woman whom Pater loved & in whose company Swinburne & Meredith delighted,'[5] or whatever it

1 i.e. 'One of the chief reasons for wanting him back is [to frustrate] the pleasure of those who will be pleased [if he stays].'
2 Robert ('Bobby') Paton Longden (1903–40), Student of Christ Church 1929–40, Master of Wellington College 1937–40 (killed in a German bombing raid on the school).
3 (Ambroise-)Paul(-Toussaint-Jules) Valéry (1871–1945), French poet and essayist.
4 (John) Alfred Spender (1862–1942), journalist and author, editor of the *Westminster Gazette* 1896–1922, uncle to Stephen Spender.
5 Untraced.

was, except that I suppose he was quite eminent in 1908). It all sounded pathetic & a little squalid. He is a v. humbled old liberal.

Are you going to write about pet fallacies for Miss Macaulay[1] & Mr Connolly? I am more than honoured to find myself in such company: but genuinely don't know what to answer. Why hasn't Mr Eliot been included? he'd be fearfully pleased. Or John Hayward: it was more than right to omit the pylon boys.[2]

Will you come to Oxford soon? next week? please, if you can, on any day. I hope you are well. I rang you up this morning, & they said you were out, with no date of return. I conclude that your operation left no lowering effects. Please come as soon as you find convenient

   yrs
      Shaya

Yes: wd you, since you are said to know him, find it frightfully inconvenient to ask Mr Bliss[3] whether he would talk to undergraduates & dons here about anything he likes about music some time? nobody here seems to know him & I am in charge of a sort of musical Florentine society.[4]

TO ELIZABETH BOWEN

   [Late January 1937][5]

                                     All Souls

Dear Elizabeth

Please come to lunch on Tuesday. I shall ask nobody else then, but perhaps, in order to save you from a sense of guilt or a desire to leave too early to avoid it, I might ask Mr Boase & Mr Hampshire to tea. Wd that be suitable? If not, pray let me know, else I'll ask them: I owe something to the former but you may reasonably protest against being made the means of paying it. My sentences are affected by a kind of Sparrow-All Souls smartness which I must avoid. Talking of unsmartness brings us to Arthur C-M. I shall buy his book[6] and Humphrey's,[7] & write complimentary letters to both, I

---

1 (Emilie) Rose Macaulay (1881–1958), prolific novelist, poet, journalist, historian and travel-writer. This literary project seems not to have borne fruit.

2 181/1.

3 Arthur Edward Drummond Bliss (1891–1975), composer, later (1953) Master of the Queen's Music.

4 A discussion group called the Florentine Club: see MI 90.

5 EB's reply speaks of 1 February as 'Monday next'.

6 Arthur Calder-Marshall, *Pie in the Sky* (London, January 1937).

7 Humphry House's edition of *The Note-Books and Papers of Gerard Manley Hopkins* (London, January 1937).

expect. I agree about the necessity for glamour (I can't help hating the word, it enables bohemians & philistines to bully one – or Flaubert who killed romanticism – equally – & philistines & bohemians are, as I am delighted to find K. Marx thought, equally vulgarizations of middle classness.) but strenuously object, and indeed have physical discomforts, not only when it is injected crudely & artificially (i.e. your category of nonsense) but when it is done by way of relieving the author's feelings, & assumes the form of a sincere but intolerably vulgar self-expression, a genuine, non-self-dramatized exhibition of ineradicable cheapness. E.g., Arthur's previous books. But I shall read this one & Dead Centre.[1] We can talk about Rose Macaulay's book on Tuesday – I think it will probably be unequal & in parts very bogus & the result what you say, hence personal & professional qualms, vanity etc. I don't know what to do. I'll go to the library now & read Sir T. Browne,[2] & then I know I shall refuse.

'I don't wish to be called Hants'[3] the Gazelle firmly said to our Professor Macgregor,[4] who was being tipsily playful. He strongly denies that others should have strong emotions, that the universe should move in dramatic leaps, that people should continually fall out of one mode & into another without débris on the way. Himself he recoils from Goronwy's coarser formulations, & has a{n} child-neurotic terror of paper games. I am regularly rallied for hating change & seeking to preserve and carefully restoring old outlines of important events in one's life, & find the attacks full of generous spirit and enjoyable. The sense of elderliness they give me, donnish, avuncular, governessy, Eliotlike benevolence is also highly enjoyable. Very very nice in fact. There may be such a thing as an excessive absence of self pity, a swing in the opposite direction. I am sure I suffer from it. I am not sure that you don't too.

love

Shaya

I shall tell you too of Miss Graves's wedding,[5] Mr Verschoyle, Miss de Baillou.[6]

1 Arthur Calder-Marshall, *Dead Centre* (London, 1935).
2 Sir Thomas Browne (1605–82), doctor, author of *Religio Medici* (1643) and (alluded to here) *Pseudodoxia Epidemica: or, Enquiries into Very Many Received Tenents, and Commonly Presumed Truths* (London, 1646).
3 'Hants' is the standard postal abbreviation for the English county of Hampshire. The qualities of Stuart Hampshire's that led to his other nickname were his slight build and grace of movement.
4 David Hutchinson Macgregor (1877–1953), Drummond Professor of Political Economy, Fellow of All Souls 1922–45.
5 To Richard Chilver.
6 Probably Goronwy Rees's sometime mistress Pamela de Bayou (174/7).

TO H. A. L. FISHER
Warden of New College

1 February 1937

All Souls

Dear Mr Warden

I should like to offer you my warmest congratulations on your O.M.;[1] in spite of the superb connotation of that Order it remains true that you bring to it even more distinction than you could possibly derive from it: your title to it has been self evident for so long, my colleagues in this college & I have so often commented on its obvious appropriateness, that now that you have it, one obtains the sense of equilibrium restored, of a gap filled between value and existence (if you will forgive my professional jargon) rather than that of a new and remarkable event in the universe. I very much doubt whether all the masses of outward respect however sincere can begin to convey to you the absolutely unique position which you occupy in the eyes both of dons and of undergraduates, particularly of those who are able to meet you and talk with you. Oxford is a very tight, self-contained system with a private and sometimes unreal and perverse system of symbols and values, usually out of relation with the outer world: I can think of nobody, in this century, no individual that is, towards whom so many inhabitants of this town have felt & feel such unqualified and direct admiration. I could have said this of myself alone, but I am sure there is great virtue in numbers in personal issues: but you as a historian may disagree.

yours sincerely
Isaiah Berlin

Bodleian, MS. Fisher 74, fol. 82

After complications following flu, IB spent a month in a nursing home.

---

1 The Order of Merit, in the personal gift of the Sovereign, and limited to 24 members. Founded by Edward VII in 1902, it is 'given to such persons . . . as may have rendered exceptionally meritorious service in Our Crown Services or towards the advancement of the Arts, Learning, Literature, and Science or such other exceptional service as We are fit to recognise'. IB was himself appointed OM by the Queen in 1971.

TO ELIZABETH BOWEN

Wed. [3 March 1937]

All Souls

Dear Elizabeth

4 weeks of absolute inertia were not at all disagreeable. After the first horrors were over, I discovered that the whitewashed walls & Irish nurses & infinite sense of leisure were almost agreeable: I felt enormously tranquil and absolutely invulnerable & at some absolute point of rest. I knew I was in an abnormal condition when I realized that I wanted to see no one, that reflection on various disagreeable incidents of the past caused no pain, & that I was, as nearly as I could be, in a Mrs Woolf state, in which everything occurred with the greatest lucidity and dramatic value but under a thin crust, not of glass, but of ice, which absorbed all first hand qualities, & only allowed a schematized, nevertheless very full & vivid version of everything to appear. This is really a very unusual state for me, who live from hand to mouth & in the present far more than I like. It was heaven while it lasted. I read books very slowly with a conscious air of priggish tranquillity, made agreeable non-significant conversation with my 2–3 daily visitors. Your flowers I was very grateful for: they completed a mise-en-scène & made everything full of style & finish. It really was very nice. Reading slowly, & understanding every word with enormous clarity, & being receptive & invulnerable, because on an observatorial level, is the most agreeable state there is. I am sorry to have lost it. I now lead a rigidly controlled valetudinarian existence, get up earlier, go to bed earlier. Next month I want to go to Italy or anywhere where there is a hot sun. I have temporarily developed tropical Freddyish characteristics, & pine in cold, a very incongruous state, if you think of it, for me.

Maurice is very gay, & plainly determined not to return. Felix F. wrote me a letter saying, Maurice was to be given patient admiring audiences for his stories, America wasn't to be minimized in his presence, & he was to be received as a hero. Adding that in the last analysis etc. etc. perhaps their milieu wasn't altogether suitable. Obviously he will stay, & I am v. glad. I tried to persuade him to ask Roger Senhouse to stay. He won't. Agrees he is a v. nice man, but says that he can't stand guests, they hang about. Mr Boase is displeased about Maurice's desire to stay. Maurice responds that Mr Boase *likes everybody*, only some more than others. I am frightfully upset about Stephen's public renunciation of his book[1] & joining of the Com. Party.

1 In his book *Forward from Liberalism* (London, 1937), Spender had argued that the show-trials and execution (in August 1936) of Zinov'ev and other Trotskyists indicated a need for liberalism in the USSR in the form of a democratic constitution allowing criticism of the Soviet government. Soon afterwards Harry Pollitt, the head of the CP in Britain, persuaded him that those executed had been plotting against the State. Spender joined the CP on 16 February and

partly out of pique, because of my wasted eloquence (you remember, at lunch).[1] I think it is all due to Tony & sentimental and therefore is bound to lead to embarrassing silliness. I had a most passionate card from him in Port Bou.[2] As usual, I shall deflate; I thought his essay on Keats & Shelley in Mr Dobrée's omnibus[3] v. good. & John Hayward was extremely moving about the physical debilites of Swift.[4] And Sparrow autobiographical & comic about Lord Mansfield.[5] But Mr Eliot on Byron[6] – treated as a Scottish anti-religious poet with a strongly disapproved of face – tendency to corpulence etc. very splendid & unexpected. Have you read it? it is very intelligent & shows what an enormously good temper he is in.

Mr Walpole is addressing an anti-cruelty league in Oxford this evening. I don't know why I think this so comic.[7]

Hampshire, gazelle tho' he be, is, I have come to the conclusion a vampire. I always feel slightly bled after talking to him. And that complexion is due to enormous draughts of blood from somewhere. I am sorry I cannot come to-morrow: but journeys are said to be fatal to me.

    love

      Shaya

IB then accompanied his parents on their spring holiday in Italy.

TO MARY FISHER (IN ROME)

Friday [9 April 1937, *postcard*]

Hotel Danieli, Venice

I was given a really enormous amount of pleasure by your letter.[8] I can hardly express the degree of my passion for Rome: the unity seems to be created by the irresistible centripetal influence of the hills: it is the only town

on 19 February the *Daily Worker* published his retraction of the liberal views expressed in his book (Stephen Spender, 'I join the . . . Communist Party' [what does the ellipsis signify?], *Daily Worker*, 19 February 1937, 4).

1 Presumably the occasion on which IB begged Spender 'on bended knee' not to join the Communist Party (MI Tape 9).

2 On the north-east Spanish coast, not far from the French border.

3 Stephen Spender, 'Keats and Shelley (1795–1821: 1792–1822)', in Bonamy Dobrée (ed.), *From Anne to Victoria: Essays by Various Hands* (London etc., 1937), 574–87.

4 John Hayward, 'Jonathan Swift (1667–1745)', ibid., 29–40.

5 John Sparrow, 'Lord Mansfield (1705–1793)', ibid., 252–64.

6 T. S. Eliot, 'Byron (1788–1824)', ibid., 601–19.

7 Hugh Walpole, as Vice-President of the National Society for the Abolition of Cruel Sports, addressed the Oxford University Association Against Cruel Sports at the Carfax Assembly Rooms on 3 March.

8 MF's letter of 29 March describes her favourable impressions of Rome, where she had gone with the support of a travelling bursary from Somerville, ostensibly to study Roman history.

in which I had literary exclamatory feelings of a low but intense order. Not but what this is also a far from negligible city. I have only just read the Aspern papers,[1] and I am moved by everything here. I wish I had a book of the right period in which somebody says 'It is a pleasing and potent fact, madam, which has not been frequently remarked, that some others are capable of giving charm or terror to places which else' etc. 'Yes indeed' she said, and then once more 'yes indeed'. Have you read The Years?[2] I waft in a sort of cloud. I find it hard to compose a paper on Induction for Proc. Arist. Soc.[3]

Shaya

TO SHIELA GRANT DUFF (IN PRAGUE)

3 May 1937

All Souls

Dear Shiela,

Thank you very much indeed for your letter. I would have replied at once if there had been any conceivable chance of my being able to go to Praha [Prague]. There wasn't: I dutifully followed my parents to Merano, one of the great centres of central European bourgeois pilgrimage: I am absolutely fascinated by towns of the Marienbad-Merano type: anyhow, as you know, I like anything pre-war, Holland, Ireland, etc. then I went to Vicenza which is absolutely heavenly. You know that I have practically no eyes & spend time in not seeing things. Whereas Padua or Verona are magnificent, full of beautiful, impressive, enormously old, very literary very fascinating buildings and streets, one cannot live there for that reason. Whereas Vicenza is pure renaissance, full of green leaves & surrounded [by] small hills with trees, & gay Palladio buildings with endless non-oppressive, not claustrophobic arcades, and a renaissance theatre with painted perspectives, which is I can't tell you how wonderful. I should come from China to hear Monteverdi sung there. I am sorry if all this sounds connoisseurial, but it describes genuine feeling. Then I went to Venice. But Vicenza would be magnificent to live in: nor should I object to dying there, especially as death is not a real thought at all, not being, if you see what I mean, an event in

1 Henry James's novella *The Aspern Papers* (1888) is set in Venice.
2 Virginia Woolf's novel *The Years* was published in 1937.
3 The paper (160/5) was delivered on the morning of Saturday 10 July at Bristol University.

one's life.[1] Venice is wonderfully wicked, & would certainly have been destroyed by God if there were one (I do apologize: this whole letter has now begun to become epistolary to a grotesque degree).

It is wildly beautiful and is so cut off that acute claustrophobia assails one, & one wants to escape a great deal. On the other hand I am beginning to have genuine feelings about pictures – I can't remember if you have them or not. One used not to discuss them much, I am prepared to begin. Have you read the Aspern Papers? to read it in Venice is a literary experience of the first order. Also – On the Eve.[2] But what is so delightful & silly is to go in a gondola through a fairly squalid canal, & realize this is like a v. second rate novel, & then suddenly hear Chopin played from the window of a not very beautiful palazzo & realize that one is part of a sentimental and ridiculous film set. It is, in fact, an enchanting sensation. The Scala in Milan was a scene of indescribable Stendhalian magnificence. Firstly it has six tiers of boxes, secondly they are full of cads in magnificent uniforms and women more boldly and beautifully dressed than I've ever seen. Thirdly the stalls are full & if [one] looks down from the gallery the white shirtfronts glitter like water, & the dim illumination in the boxes produces an early XIX effect of the most superb operatic kind. Also Donizetti was sung: also I had finished a paper for the Aristotelian Society and was contented. I wish you were there: as a scene it was so magnificent that you would have enjoyed both it and conversation about it. The opera was called Elisir d'Amore[3] & was exquisite. I wish, I really wish I could be talking to you & use intonations & gestures instead of adjectives. My affection for you which reawoke on the occasion on which we had tea somewhere in Berkeley Square after a period of some frigidity and was intensified by your letter, is now an enormous swelling tide:[4] I was v. sorry not to have seen you when you were in London for 2 days or whatever it was: then someone made bad blood, I don't know who, between Adam and me, & I was preoccupied with that, & spent some tormented weeks, then I found your letter again (but Douglas says the address is not valid) & the river rose again: & it is inundating its banks at the moment.

I went to a party given by Jane Rendel,[5] at which everyone one knew

---

1 cf. Ludwig Wittgenstein, *Tractatus Logico-Philosophicus* (London, 1922), proposition 6.4311: 'Death is not an event in life.'

2 Turgenev's novel (1860).

3 'Elixir of love'.

4 IB's relationship with SGD seems to have generated a series of episodes of frigidity and reconciliation. In her reply to this letter she writes (on 11 May, from Prague): 'I'm afraid your affection for me has always been in the nature of a tide & the giant ebb which it took in this country has never quite been balanced by a giant flow. Perhaps this flow will be terrific.' The 'giant ebb' might be a reference to their trip to Subcarpathian Ruthenia in early September 1933, about which SGD writes in an undated letter: 'I will always behave beautifully towards you & try & take to heart the things you said in Zilina.'

5 Jane Rendel (1912–91), LMH PPE 1931–5, formerly Head Girl of St Paul's School for Girls.

duly appeared: even your mother & brother attended, and Peggy etc. I don't know why but the whole thing seemed absolutely artificial, & like a friendly caricature of the past: not at all persecuting, very sympathetic, but faintly silly. Certain figures on the other hand, e.g. Stephen, Goronwy and, I suppose, Maurice, continue solid and not attached to dates. Christopher, being gone, has ceased to be altogether for the time being. He is said to be bored. Can you believe this? I maintain that he will have a dreadful conflict which [sc. when?] he nostalgically returns in summer. A great deal of fuss is being made in connection with the Crossman affair. Was or was he not cited as co-respondent in Mrs Baker's[1] divorce case? some say no, but Pilkington[2] swears he saw it in print: & Sir Arthur Salter isn't certain he didn't. Is the Warden[3] driving him out from politics, or he is really resigning? nobody knows. It is, at present, our major scandal. But the same hectic interest is not being taken as before. I haven't read Goronwy's novel[4] yet. It was lukewarmly greeted. I shall read it & am sure to be moved since I hear people's voices when I know them at all. Your life is a profound mystery: what do you do? whom do you know? how much on top of the universe (is that a vulgar phrase?) are you? when will one see you? I should gladly come to Prague in late July or late August if that was suitable? but don't reflect on it if not. At the same time I should like to see you. Will you kindly write me another letter? the last was too short. And as you know continuity is my end in itself. Please write.

Your meeting with Douglas in winter in the snow was a pure piece of Jay romanticism as he related it. I think perhaps I ought to marry.

love

Shaya

By this time IB's daily philosophical discussions with J. L. Austin had evolved into a larger forum. Austin and IB had invited Freddie Ayer, Stuart Hampshire, Donald MacKinnon,[5] Donald Macnabb[6] and

---

1 Inez ('Inezita' / 'Zita') Hilda Baker (1900–52), wife since 1923 of Dr John Randal Baker (1900–84), New College zoology 1918–21, member of Senior Common Room since 1932, in 1937 University Demonstrator and Lecturer in Zoology and Comparative Anatomy. Crossman married Zita Baker on 18 December 1937.

2 Arnold Pilkington (at New College with Crossman), or possibly his father.

3 H. A. L. Fisher was at this time urging Crossman to go into politics. Crossman did resign his Fellowship, saving the Governing Body the awkwardness of having to decide how to respond to the divorce case.

4 *A Bridge to Divide Them* (London, 1937).

5 Donald MacKenzie MacKinnon (1913–94), Fellow and philosophy Tutor, Keble, 1937–47, Director of special courses in philosophy for RN and RAF cadets at Oxford 1942–5, philosophy Lecturer, Balliol, 1945–7.

6 Donald George Cecil Macnabb (1905–91), philosopher, Fellow of Pembroke 1935–69.

Anthony Woozley to join them. The gatherings took place in IB's room on
Thursday evenings during 1937–9, and the group's 'ordinary language'
approach became a characteristic feature of 'Oxford philosophy'.
Perception, a priori truths, personal identity and the verification and
logical character of counter-factual statements were the main topics
discussed. The opposing views of Austin and Ayer – sworn enemies at any
rate as far as philosophy was concerned – made for a dynamic exchange
of ideas. '[T]hey were in a state of almost continuous collision – Ayer like
an irresistible missile, Austin like an immovable obstacle' – which
according to IB produced 'the most interesting, free and lively discussions
of philosophy that I have ever known'.[1]

TO ALFRED ZIMMERN[2]

[*c.*10 June 1937]

All Souls

Dear Zimmern,

In connexion with the P.P.E. meeting which has been summoned for
Sunday morning,[3] & your invitation to write what one thinks, I should like
to outline some suggestions which it might be useful to discuss.

It is my view – I do not know how far shared by my colleagues in the
Sub-faculty of Philosophy – that P.P.E. as it exists at present is a greatly
overweighted School, which achieves a unity which is often highly artificial,
at the expense of the two ends to which it ought to be devoted i.e. the
promotion of knowledge and of the capacity for clear thought. It is a widely
recognized fact that practically no one can be expected to devote him or
herself to three subjects and hope to be proficient in them all, however
emphasis between them is distributed. Consequently it is customary for
undergraduates who do P.P.E. to neglect one of the three subjects, a practice
which no P.P.E tutor is either able or willing to control, since he knows
better than anyone that his pupils are being asked to do the impossible. This
state of affairs makes the whole School rest on a cynical foundation, since its
success in individual cases entails the systematic sabotage of one or other of
the three subjects. If these premises [are] correct, the conclusion follows
that this situation can only be remedied by the curtailment of subjects. The
most natural solution would seem to consist in allowing pupils to do only

1 Pl2 144.
2 Sir Alfred (Eckhard) Zimmern (1879–1957), New College classics 1898–1902, Fellow and
  Lecturer in Ancient History 1904–9, (the first) Montague Burton Professor of International
  Relations 1930–44, Supernumerary Fellow, New College, from 1931.
3 13 June 1937.

two subjects out of three, any two being permitted. To this it may be objected, not altogether invalidly I think, that undergraduates when they come up cannot tell which two subjects they are most capable of doing; & only discover by doing all three. To meet this I suggest the following scheme:

1. That an intermediate honours examination be introduced in the middle of the P.P.E. course, after either three or preferably (in order that the First long Vacation might not be lost) after four terms, in the three existing subjects: this would contain 3 classes, i.e. a First, Second & Pass in order to stimulate ambition & industry. The details could be worked out without very much difficulty, I think.

2. That the second part consist of two subjects only, any two being combinable;[1] Politics seems to me, on a priori grounds, more easily combinable with either Philosophy or Economics, than Economics with Philosophy. But I may well be mistaken in this.

3. Languages, which ought, I think to be an integral part of the School, since no one should be allowed to go down without some knowledge of at least two languages other than English, could be included in the first part of the School, in the form of set books in German & French. This would allow the elimination of the present unseens, for which very little can be said.

4. Freed from a third subject, each of the remaining two could be pursued far more intensively, and a higher standard attained. This seems desirable. It seems commonly thought that the e.g. philosophy standard in P.P.E. is lower than it is in Greats. The removal [of] the present asymmetry between the two would perhaps remedy this.

5. Although they would be able to obtain an honours degree after 3 years, such graduates as wish to specialize ought, I think to be allowed to do so by doing a course resembling the B.C.L.[2] course in law, in one subject only. Three years is not really sufficient for anyone wishing to obtain specialized knowledge of a subject: a fourth year with a special degree attached, would draw the type of man who at present, rather hesitantly, writes a thesis for a B.Litt.: an organized semi-research School would be far better: in, e.g. philosophy it would draw members from among those who had done Greats, as well as P.P.E. This last plan although it fits into the other scheme, in the sense of forming an apex of the pyramid of gradually increasing specialization, can be considered independently of it, since it could be grafted on the present unreformed School, just as successfully.

1 The bipartite Final Honour School in PPE was introduced with effect from 1 October 1970, for first examination in 1971. See the lengthy explanatory note to the relevant decree of Hebdomadal Council (responsible for the academic policy of the University) in the *Oxford University Gazette*, 16 October 1969, 91.
2 Bachelor of Civil Law.

These are my suggestions, without arguments. I do not know whether next Sunday in New College is the time & place to discuss them, but if you think they are, perhaps you would tell me whether you think them worth considering, & whether there is any support of the kind of arrangement suggested in the views of others who will have written to you. This scrappy document is certainly not worth communicating to any one else: but perhaps I might be allowed to say a word about it at the meeting.

    yours sincerely
    I. Berlin.

Bodleian, MS. Zimmern 116, fols 67–8

In the last paragraph of the next letter IB refers to Toscanini's concert with the BBC Symphony Orchestra in Oxford's New Theatre on 8 June 1937, given for the Oxford University Appeal Fund, which he reviewed anonymously in the Oxford Magazine.[1] *When I invited him towards the end of his life to confirm that he was the author of the review, he replied: 'I cannot deny that the piece on Toscanini must have been written by me – all the sentiments are so identical to what I still feel about him (and others do not) . . .'. In the review he writes:*

This magnificent gesture on the part of the greatest of living conductors is likely to be remembered as the most notable artistic event in the history of the University in this part of the century; perhaps the greatest musical honour conferred upon it since the visit of Josef Haydn a century and a half ago, commemorated by the title of a celebrated symphony. It was a personal experience of the first magnitude for everyone present: those who had never heard him before may well have found that for them it shifted the boundaries of artistic possibility, and in this respect fundamentally altered the nature of their musical experience.[2]

TO STEPHEN SPENDER

[Summer 1937]

All Souls

Dear Stephen,

I ought to have written to you many weeks ago, to apologize about Toscanini: I couldn't come at the last moment out of purely personal considerations: a man called Dr Marschak[3] was reading a paper on my

---

1 10 June 1937, 719–20. The unsigned article in the *Oxford Mail* on the following day ('Oxford Diary' on p. 3) was scarcely less lyrical.

2 p. 719.

3 Jacob Marschak (1898–1977), Chichele Lecturer in Economics at All Souls, 1933–5, Reader in

subject, I thought few wd go, he is very nice, learned, a refugee etc. & so
I had to go if you see what I mean. I sent Sigle Lynd largely because I had
awful guilt about not having seen her for so long, or communicated. At this
point you will justly remark that sending her to meet you doesn't remedy
that. That is why I apologize. On the second occasion I went with Guy
Branch, one of my loyalties acc. to Inez & you, & Derek [Kahn?] blew up to
us & said in a harsh & breezy voice 'hallo boys!'. I do not know why, but
I was physically affected by this (which doesn't happen often) & fled from
him into some crowded space. I hope he wasn't offended, I couldn't have
acted differently anyhow. Will Miss B[eecham] accept Maurice's hand? I am
in the curious state of knowing I shall regret whichever happens, or even if
nothing happens at all. I met Mrs Carritt[1] for the first time last week: at a
party of the Mauds which both of us disliked a great deal. She was absolutely
sweet I thought. She reported your visit & seems enormously devoted to
you: she talked about Wystan & Heinz:[2] I have never had so free a conversation with any elderly person in a conventional drawing room &
enjoyed it very much indeed. Please tell her so if you see her. She told me to
ring up & visit them any Sunday, but this I am incapable of doing. But I want
to show appreciation in some way.

I have received a presentation copy of Crossman's book;[3] it is quite well
written & very shocking, & quite sincere; it is not, in spite of the terrific
reviews, selling well. I wonder why not. Rowse has at last sailed into the field
with his book:[4] he spends his time in telling me how he squares reviewers.
One will never be able to hear that (like extract from early letters by some
Victorian Saint of rationalism) with equanimity. I think I hate opportunist
boasting more than oiliness & complacency: don't you?

Toscanini here was wonderful. However the first movement of the 1st
Brahms symphony, being like soup, can't be unstranded as it is by him: like
spaghetti: it can't afford it I mean & sounds poor & ill compounded.

Why does V. Woolf use so many clichés?

Shaya

Statistics and Director of the Institute of Statistics, Oxford, 1935–9, Professor of Economics,
New School for Social Research, New York, 1939–42, Director, Cowles Foundation for
Research in Economics, Yale, 1943–8.

1 Winifred Margaret Frampton Carritt, née Etty, wife of E. F. Carritt.
2 The German Heinz Neddermeyer was a boyfriend of SS's friend Christopher Isherwood from
1932. He evaded conscription until May 1937, when he was expelled from Luxembourg. He
returned to Germany, where he was imprisoned for homosexual practices.
3 *Plato Today* (London, May 1937).
4 *Sir Richard Grenville of the* Revenge: *An Elizabethan Hero* (London, June 1937).

TO ELIZABETH BOWEN

[July 1937?]

All Souls

Dear Elizabeth

I feel fearfully guilty about not having written – I cannot even come to lunch on Sunday, having slumming to perform – you'll meet my guest (Guy Branch) & Mr Bishop (now a religious maniac) & I shall come in early afterwards (my slumming = Lord Erleigh[1] & Prof. Namier,[2] Zionists) & ask you to take a walk in Magdalen, and come to tea: Salzburg arrangements have taken an oddish turn: I mean the house: one is now offered an "old fashioned house full of old world charm which I am sure will appeal to you" in an unspecified place in the old town. I wonder what will become of us. I shall take it unless you protest, please do if you feel it advisable: I hate responsibility. John Hayward turned up with Roger Senhouse here yesterday, he was very very malicious indeed about Roy – most agreeable it was – after he tried out Rub Roy etc. Roger said Harrod Antipas, & we all dispersed & went to bed satisfied. The gazelle enjoyed it all prodigiously.

    love

      Shaya

TO STUART HAMPSHIRE

Thursday [July 1937?]

Hotel Metropole, Brighton

Dear Stuart.

Revulsion. I think now that I am behaving atrociously. To cause you to modulate and adjust yourself at such a moment is pure inconsiderateness.[3] Consequently it would be best if you stayed in London & I in Brighton until, at any rate next week. This has many advantages. In particular that your experience, considered retrospectively will arrange itself, the essential & the trivial will fall into place, you will not have the tortures (which I often endure) of stressing the unimportant at the time with vast emotional emphasis, & later being ashamed of magnifying, inflating, wasting even. Of

---

1 Gerald Rufus Isaacs (1889–1960), 2nd Marquess of Reading, Earl Reading, Viscount Erleigh, Viscount Reading, Baron Reading, Bencher, Middle Temple.

2 Lewis (Bernstein) Namier (1888–1960), Political Secretary of the Jewish Agency for Palestine, 1929–31, Professor of Modern History, Manchester, 1931–53. See IB's essay on him in PI.

3 The letter is about SNH's relationship with A. J. Ayer's wife Renée (whom SNH married in 1961), and IB's negative attitude to it.

course I shall ask to be told: and you are quite right: either all or nothing. But you'd best tell me nothing until you can trust yourself not to fall into embarrassment or remorse in the middle. I can, I know, decide to speak: I assume an artificially even voice, speak with that pseudo-hardness which I find sympathetic in Mrs Chilver[1] – knowing as I do that it consists of the same material – a determination to objectify so as to avoid projecting oneself, one's demands & fears, into the recital, which would make every conversation a personal overture, an advance or withdrawal, anyhow an emotional campaign, a personal skirmish, which I certainly, & she at any rate with me, are desperately anxious to avoid. I don't know whether you don't require longer to adjust yourself to the rectilinear style in which I live. As for Freddie in his case insensitiveness to surroundings is not a vice but a great virtue: Such as he is he can only survive as somebody made of one piece (monolith is a little silly perhaps) with a burnished shining surface to which nothing sticks: it would be both intolerable & undignified if he suddenly began to react: he cannot modulate at all: this insensitiveness alone made the marriage possible by which Renée gave precisely as much as she wanted, & no more was suspected to exist or asked for. I respect & like him or at any rate am non-neutral: I read Herzen when I am not writing about Marx, & I cannot say how much I sympathise, how admirable I find his vigorous moral standards about both life & politics. What you call facing facts is often (tho' not in your, Proust's or H. James's cases) a mask for emotional neutrality, a love of chiaroscuro for its own sake, an indeterminate Harrod like wobbling for the sake of the blurred, the sweet, the gently nerve-wracking. Hoffmansthal, Strauss[2] are the experts: & I abominate. Elizabeth [Bowen] likes blood to flow melodramatically, which is quite different, & distinguishes the American school. Your irritation with Freddie's gaiety is to me intelligible, but I cannot see how you can fail to see that that is precisely the reason why I admire, like, him, but cannot be intimate: he is a set of remarkable properties to me: if you add sensitiveness to others, you don't heighten, you tarnish them, make them wet, blotting paper like: jealousy, dramatization, squalid scenes is what happens then. He ultimately is a two & not three dimensional being – nobody knows this better than Renée, & also how this left her intact & allowed her to live as she wished more or less. One must hope that he will go on being blind: or at least this obscuration will go on: only to take positive advantage seems to me immoral. Stop. I begin to moralize. On the subject of ethical neutrality I shall read you a sermon when we meet: abstract, literary, & not allusive. Meanwhile keep me posted with

---

1 Sally Graves had married Richard Chilver in spring 1937.
2 Hugo von Hofmannsthal (1874–1929), German dramatist, collaborated with Richard Strauss (1864–1949) in a number of operas.

at least your states of mind: whether you are exhilarated, lacerated, or in a twilight: & I shall try & guess the facts which possibly I shall never verify. I cannot now conceive why we were so stupid as to suppose for one instant that Renée would plunge everything into disaster & lose control entirely by telling Freddie unnecessarily. In any case I think, from your account that her conception of distance covered in Paris, because of the meanings & values she attaches to words, is smaller than yours, who look on implication as ¾ facts already.

My love.
Shaya

TO ELIZABETH BOWEN

Thursday [July 1937?][1]

[Hotel Metropole, Brighton; as from] All Souls

Dear Elizabeth

I am in occupation of a fairly large room facing the Brighton Parade. I like it very much indeed. The intense liveliness outside creates a vicarious scene of activity and removes necessity for doing anything violent, like long walks, from oneself. Consequently I am writing K. Marx quite successfully. I am entirely alone, which is also unusual. My mother is abroad, my father in London: after 1 day's acute melancholy, sense of abandonment etc. I adjusted insensibly and am definitely contented. Every time this happens to me when alone, I am surprised afresh: yet it is only [in] such conditions, or in the company of one person, whom I don't see except at meals that I can work at any length at all. This is really the determining motive which has decided me not to come to Ireland. I cannot say how much I want to: there is an *enormous* mass of accumulated material which I should be grateful to offer you for examination: my passion for Bowen's Court (+ the reverence which Goronwy finds so artificializing & static-making) is, as you know, enormous. I like Alan, who possesses certain characteristics in common with Fortinbras. You are the only person (not excluding Maurice or Stephen) towards whom, apart from other, simpler & warmer feelings, I feel absolute trust and respect and admiration: my natural dogmatism and conceit (as opposed to vanity which is actually not great) collapses completely & I feel entirely happy when it does. Remarks about absolute trust usually lead up to something, are bullying in a peculiarly awful way, a prelude to burdening with something

1 Perhaps written at the same time as the previous letter, certainly from the Hotel Metropole, Brighton, probably in the summer vacation. A summer date is also suggested by the reference to not visiting EB in Ireland.

particularly disagreeable to bear. In this case they prelude nothing. And indeed I already feel a revulsion from the sentimentality of the words, which please abstract: the meaning is not obscure, and I cannot see why it should not be stated. But to go back: I had best not come to Ireland I think: not indeed because of elocution[1] (that tragicomedy is about to commence: if I cannot turn it to something rewardingly funny I shall stop it) but because I cannot do any work if attractive alternatives exist. This has been proven over & over again: you said something about the Cecils & Mr [E. M.] Forster: of course I should love to meet them. But I do so little work on the whole, that guilt might outweigh pleasure: &, after all, I must account to myself for the priggishness & disciplinarianism I show in so many other respects, towards my younger contemporaries ('What some people don't seem to realize, is that people have *appetites*' Mrs Chilver) by doing severe things to myself now & then: i.e. when some profit is to be extracted, not a dramatic self-mortification, certainly.

Those are my reasons: if I thought I could go on with K.M. steadily in Ireland I should come without hesitation, & not wait to be invited twice. Oh dear: why did I let Mr Fisher persuade me? here it is grey rain + occasional arty sunsets Henry James weather of a certain type. I am slowly taking against the great writer. Bullied by Stephen & Stuart, I began to read him in earnest. His obvious merits I concede. He is a serious writer: he undoubtedly tells the truth about the nature of vanity and humiliation, & the necessity for protective masks & the fantastic power of words, & the non-existence of various fictions like 'the world' or pure action. But I revolt against the neutrality of the attitude. Neutrality pretends to be attitude-lessness, a facing of facts unmarred by emotional or moral prejudice: a not taking of sides, anti-Russian, anti-Balzac, ultimately anti-Stendhal & Flaubert (who both in their attitude to the romantics & to the various forms of stifling dreariness took v. positive, almost crudely partisan attitudes: Stendhal's hatred of the reaction and passion for haute bourgeoisie, Flaubert's loathing for the middle classes and bourgeois democracy and adoration of intellectual toughness and style are far more undisguised than the views of Hugo & Zola, the 'partisans': from which I wish to infer that the post-naturalists, James, Proust, Mrs Woolf even up to a point (though she does not strictly pretend to deal with situations: there is no more search for verisme[2] than in poetry) abstract quite deliberately, and not from a capacity for minuter vision or greater tolerance or dispassionateness, but from direct timidity, not anaemia exactly, but certainly insecurity, and terror of being committed, of saying something

---

1 Was IB having lessons to enable him not to be misunderstood by his typist? See communications of 31 July 1937 and 15 April 1938 to Mary Fisher, pp. 244 and 270 below.
2 'Realism'.

irrevocable: Proust is braver than James: and indeed one has to be in French which does not allow emotional timorousness to be translated into such indeterminate vagueness as English. I find James unsympathetic not because of the miserable fear of all his characters of losing something which apparently they *can* be robbed of – nothing in his universe is indestructable – I prefer the rhetorical exclamations of the 19th century about love or honour & immortal properties, inner freedom etc. James's characters are all possessed, all jittering because their private world may be taken away from them (the ultimate tragedy is when it is), the premiss of which is that all human relations are predatory, the question is how much territory you yield, + the accompanying fear of staking too much at once, of sending all your forces to defend one position leaving yourself unprotected somewhere else. In the earlier authors you couldn't *wholly* lose ever because of the substance of which you were composed: in James etc. you can only survive if the *secret* arsenal is untouched, the other life to which you escape, the system is one of constant duplicity. And for this reason nobody can ever advance more than ¾ way in any direction, the risk is too great. This is of course not deliberate policy, but an emotional disposition, an epidemic almost. Kafka, where also one is helpless, presents a much deeper (hateful word) thesis: that since defeat in some sense is inevitable: it must be written off: it cannot be avoided by secret funds: indeed their very possession, the need for them is a symptom of defeat before you begin: the curse is on you: so you may as well continue as if it could be avoided, take steps, cope, knowing that it is hopeless, but that it is silly & undignified to admit this. This point is truer, because it does not assume that human forces can annihilate other human beings completely (which is shallow pessimism: & precisely what the romantics rejected, & Flaubert also: & indeed everyone one admires, the Russians, the Japanese even: only not the Germans: Goethe's stuff on that is artificial rhetoric, the 19th century writers are embarrassing precisely because their pessimism is false in this way, a frightful persecution mania both in George & in Wassermann:[1] Nietzsche overstates the case against: still it is symptomatic of the morass in which his contemporaries wallowed) but, to continue with Kafka, only supernatural forces: which alters the problem & destroys the very possibility of cheap self-pity (as e.g. found in even Chekhov – who to this extent dates, & is fin-de-siècliste).

The over-sensitiveness with which James (and alas, Mr Forster) deal, leads logically to the theory that we – the intellectuals, the sensitives, the observers, the persons who discuss – are cripples: able to peer from all sorts of unusual angles, able to move ourselves simultaneously %10 way in *every*

---

1 Jakob Wassermann (1873–1934), German novelist sometimes compared to Dostoevsky.

direction: but thereby we deprive ourselves of the right of life, which James vaguely accords to the rare normal figures, who occur at the edge of his world – Forster quite openly offers Nazi portraits of gross athletes, & allows no bridge between us & them: I can see why Stephen, or Stuart, or Mr Forster or Mr [Raymond] Mortimer might adopt such a theory of themselves: but (tho' possibly this is self-defence – but what remark is not, if pressed with sufficient malice & skill?) I wish to maintain that the doctrine is simply false, that relations are possible, & daily occur, in broad daylight, neurotic perhaps, but direct, not a perpetual generation and corruption, but a direct activity between persons. Tolstoy over-simplified perhaps: but fundamentally he, & even the Victorian conventionals are right: people give themselves wholly & lose nothing irrecoverable: & unless one does, & has confidence, & is deceived, & generally plunges, plumps, commits, a close subterranean atmosphere will continue to enclose & enervate all attempts at stabilizing oneself at this or that level, nothing will ever be anything rather [than] something else, one will endlessly slip and lose grip. No doubt generating pearls like Proust, but at the expense of an ultimate falsehood about the possible relations between men & women. Everything he says is true, piecemeal, so to speak, but false in the aggregate because he distrusts – for personal reasons I believe, or the climate of the age, but not as a result of patient observation – the possibility of the constellations which Dostoyevsky or Tolstoy or even Trollope, miserable shortsighted proficient entertaining hack, allege to exist, & even offer portraits of. I cannot conceive why I am being so vehement. Deflation is required. But as Mr Mortimer feels bullied by the young, so I by the continual evidences to the effect that the best combinations are patchwork, & may be taken to bits, & other people snip off what they like, & make their own quilts & are in their turn harried & robbed, or else get bored, & that all arrangements are temporary & everybody pulling at & against everyone else, warming themselves off fires lit by others, lit to spite someone probably, & never at the same temperature, with the end always in sight. How obscure is all this? & how simple & naively not-competitive but co-operative am I being? & how far is the whole thing a wish fulfilment, because I hate vibrating in nine directions at once, & seek stability & comfort? I cannot go on: please write to London. I long to see you.

 love

  Shaya.

There may be a lot of theoretical nonsense here: I can never trust myself to re-read letters, for fear of revulsions, imagine Flaubert's indignant contempt of so elementary a cowardice. if encouraged, I'll go on about the short story.

Later.[1]

As a matter of private gossip: I hazily gather that there is an estrangement between Freddie Ayer & Stephen, since the former made unsuitable proposals to Mrs Spender.[2] So squalid that I refuse to probe further. But Stephen's silence towards me may be connected. I believe Goronwy is the authority, but *above all* he mustn't know that I have wind of it. Else awful things are threatened. Freddie is an absolute Italian, but I am surprised that Inez is thought suitable even for a temporary flutter. This unfamiliar language! I haven't yet written to Maurice.[3] I shall. But I don't really know what to say.

TO MARY FISHER

31 July 1937

Ashton Wold, Peterborough[4]

Dear Mary

It is 7.45, & one must dine soon. Not a moment of time has there been: or such as there has was spent in interviewing the elocutionist provided by Mr K. Barnes,[5] & in thanking yr parents. Suitably enough this for the Rothschild estates. These are not the aeroplane ones,[6] but their mother, quite a dignified old lady, originally from Hungary. The house is full of vicious members of the aristocracy: e.g. Lady Prudence Pelham,[7] friend of

1 This appears on a separate card, and has been assigned to this letter because it came next in the packet of letters returned to IB on Elizabeth Bowen's death. If it belongs here, a date earlier than July seems likely, given that the estrangement between Ayer and Spender took place in January 1937: see Ben Rogers, *A. J. Ayer: A Life* (London, 1999), 138. So perhaps the fragment belongs to an earlier letter, though the ink appears to match.

2 According to Spender's widow, Natasha, the estrangement arose from more than 'unsuitable proposals' (Rees was an unreliable informant). Ayer and Spender were to have co-authored a book, but Spender withdrew when he discovered that Ayer had been having an affair with Inez before she and Spender married, and that it had continued during their courtship. It may or may not have lasted into the marriage. Philip Toynbee, with whom she was also involved at the same time, recorded these events in his diaries.

3 Presumably (if the July date is right) to congratulate him on his (short-lived) engagement to Audrey Beecham.

4 Home of Rozsika Rothschild (1870–1940), née von Wertheimstein, widow of Hon. (Nathaniel) Charles Rothschild (1877–1923), mother of Victor and Miriam Rothschild; the latter still occupies the house.

5 Perhaps Kenneth Ralph Barnes (1878–57), Kt 1938, principal of the Royal Academy of Dramatic Art 1909–55.

6 Victor and Barbara (215/3).

7 Younger daughter (1910–52) of Jocelyn Brudenell Pelham, sixth Earl of Chichester, Prudence Pelham was a sculptor and a lettering pupil and friend of Eric Gill, and also a friend of the painter and poet David Jones; Victor Rothschild was in love with her before he married. In 1939 she married Guy Branch, killed in the Second World War; she later lived with the painter

the Hodgkins. And about 4 other such. A son of Lord Mt. Carmel[1] called Godfrey Samuel.[2] Foster. Ld Phillimore.[3] A Mrs Pitt-Rivers.[4] etc. The house is not nearly so moneyed & vulgar as Waddesdon.[5] J[ames] de Rothschild, is a man with remarkable hands, but no taste in anything, except a certain general style. I agree about the non-visuelness [sic] of the Jews. Even their taste in pictures when right, is generally a function of its commercial advantages. It arises, I daresay, partly from Bible on graven images, partly from the squalor of their medieval surroundings. Foster I continue to like, but only, I think probably, because I knew him 5 years ago, when he wasn't nearly so vulgar. Now, I grant, his raffishness has grown too unbuttoned & too great. I avoid the question of Mrs Frankel,[6] to whom I did not indeed suggest you, but whom, for my own pleasure, I admit, I goaded about the Barn.[7] On Mrs Chilver you are right: she is enormously taste-lacking, self confident, large. I am glad she is coming to Salzburg, because one obviously needs someone for Elizabeth Cameron, who warms her up, to put it crudely. Neither Hampshire nor I can do that: & Mrs C. is a substitute for Rees. I don't know what it'll be like, at all. I shall report from there. The great advantage of Mrs Ch. is that she pulls her own weight to any degree: & anyone who is as easy as that, & at the same time not impossible, I am prepared to welcome, considering that autokineticity[8] is frightfully rare. I hear Christopher is in England: since he gives no sign of life to anyone,

Robert Buhler, changing her surname to his by deed poll, but not marrying him (she needed her widow's pension). She referred to psychologists as 'spychologists', and taught a friend how to drive in reverse, on the theory that this would make driving forwards easy by contrast. She died of multiple sclerosis, blind at the end. She called IB 'the Burler bear', and wrote a limerick about him with E. C. Hodgkin: 'Com'è molto gentile ce Burler / Who dislikes to be woken too earler / He probes all his friends / But to make them amends / He'll make debutante talk to a girler.' (The opening reference is to the aria 'Com'è gentil notte a mezzo april!' in Donizetti's opera Don Pasquale; the debutante reference is to a conversation IB was observed to have with one of the Paget twins, daughters of the 6th Marquess of Anglesey.)

1 Sir Herbert (Louis) Samuel (1870–1963), Liberal politician, (first) High Commissioner for Palestine 1920–5, created 1st Viscount Samuel of Mount Carmel and of Toxteth, Liverpool, and appointed Liberal leader in the House of Lords 1937.

2 Godfrey Herbert Samuel (1904–82), third son of Herbert Samuel; architect, designer (as part of the architectural firm Tecton) of the modernist gorilla house (now listed Grade I) at London Zoo 1933.

3 Godfrey Walter Phillimore, 2nd Baron Phillimore (1879–1947).

4 Presumably Dr Rosalind Venetia Pitt-Rivers (1907–1990), chemist, wife of Captain George Henry Lane Fox Pitt-Rivers.

5 Waddesdon Manor, the Buckinghamshire home of James Armand Edmond de *Rothschild (1878–1957), 2nd cousin once removed of Roszika's husband; MP for Isle of Ely 1929–45, Joint Parliamentary Secretary, Minister of Supply, 1945.

6 Ruth Fraenkel, wife of Eduard.

7 Perhaps it was as a lodger that IB didn't suggest MF to Mrs Fraenkel, and perhaps the Barn (for which see letter of 13 October 1932 to Shiela Grant Duff) is a symbol of sexual irregularity among dons and their wives, given that Crossman, who lived there until about this time, was having an affair with the wife of a College colleague.

8 Literally 'self-movingness', i.e. self-propulsion.

it seems, save BJ I don't know of it. He wd have wished to go to Ireland, it seems, which is nice: I am sorry, really v. v. sorry I can't. Oh dear. I must go down & dine. A car has just disgorged some more very fairhaired women & an enormous Rothschild tough with a moustache. Why Jews love enormous bullying men I don't know. But they do. I shall not enjoy dinner. I hate talking in smart society & equally hate being silent & am frustrated whichever I do. But in retrospect the whole thing is enormously funny, always. I shall write from S'burg.

    love
      Shaya

Miriam R.[1] I like for her altjüdisch[2] appearance, & curious wit.

TO FELIX FRANKFURTER

23 August 1937

                                    Salzburg

Dear Felix,

Your letter has only just arrived here, forwarded through countless hands. If I attempt to answer your questions in full, & comments, general expression of emotion etc. I don't know how large it will become. All the issues are burning, one might say. I am genuinely delighted to have an opportunity of touching on them. The first move, remembering Toscanini who entirely dominates this neighbourhood, is to establish order & discipline. Even in letters, I am sure, one must be careful not to lose grip. I shall begin, with the pedantry of my profession, by dividing the matter into A: Public. B: Private.

A. The Jews. The Pal. Report[3] is largely written by our friend C.[4] (as he would like to be mysteriously referred to). Have you ever heard him speak of B. K. D. etc. to people, sotto voce in All Souls? it is very fine & impressive. That is: he wrote the promised historical section (which, don't you agree, is creditable? though embodying a skillfully draped central lie, I mean about the acutely conflicting promises: e.g. to the Jews of an autonomous state: so as to make them as incompatible as possible: hence

---

1 Hon. (from 1938) Miriam Louisa *Rothschild (b. 1908), entomologist, married George Lane 1943 (divorced 1957).

2 Literally 'old-Jewish', i.e. she looks like a Biblical Jew, as she still does; she agrees with, and likes, this description.

3 The 'Peel Report' (July 1937), the Report of the Royal Commission of Inquiry to Palestine, headed by Lord (Robert) Peel (1867–1937), appointed in August 1936 by the British government to investigate tensions between Palestinian Arabs and Jews.

4 Coupland.

according to the Jews more than they dared to hope for, in the beginning section, in order to take it all away in the end. In London they lapped it up like anything. 77 Great Russell Street[1] was a happy place on the day of publication, & sold copies of the Report at a discount, literally. I bought a copy from them, at a cheaper rate: they could not contain their transports. A not very dignified or acute body of men.), he also wrote the recommendation at the end, hurriedly. He is very proud of the sentence in the peroration about the Thrice Hallowed land.[2] He told me that he was not an anti-Zionist, but realized how unpopular he would become. His manner of pronouncing the words 'National Home' is far from agreeable however: a gentle old fashioned anti-Semitism, like that of Lord Rennell,[3] whose letter you may have seen in the Times: quoting Nazis about Jewish subversiveness, quietly reminding the audience of Jewish unpopularity in 40 A.D., and suggesting that all the Jews might become naturalized Palestinians 'which wd surely give them more than a few yards of barren territory'.[4] Can you not see the Germans, with shrieks of joy, embarking thousands of Jews to 'repatriate' them? However to return:

No one seems to know exactly who wrote what: none of the Commissioners exc. Coupland seems enthusiastic about it: they were seriously embarrassed when Philby wrote an article in Time & Tide as a counterblast to a pale thing by Bentwich, saying that not half a loaf but $^{19}\!/_{20}$ ths had been given to the Arabs, which was only right.[5] Coupland's line hasn't changed since he talked to me about it in 1935: Palestine is a great nuisance, a serious flaw in the moral facade of the Brit. Emp. as defended &

1 Great Russell Street was the headquarters of Zionism in Britain during the 1930s and 1940s. The London Executive of the Jewish Agency was at 77 Great Russell Street, the Zionist Federation of Great Britain and Ireland at 75 Great Russell Street. The Jewish Agency was identical, de facto, with the World Zionist Organisation.

2 The sentence in question, which concludes the main text of the report, is 'Numberless men and women all over the world would feel a sense of deep relief if somehow an end could be put to strife and bloodshed in a thrice hallowed land' (p. 297).

3 James Rennell Rodd, 1st Baron Rennell (1858–1941), diplomat and scholar. His letter was published under the heading 'The National Home: Importance of State Organization: Jewish Citizenship and Passports' in The Times, 26 July 1937, 13.

4 Rennell actually wrote that, if the 'conception of the National Home' favoured by Peel 'were acceptable to the Jews, to whom it should offer greater advantages than a few additional square miles of territory, their timely adherence to the Report might discount the preoccupations of the Arabs, who, ambitious of complete autonomy themselves, should sympathize with the desire of the Jews to establish a legal status for people of their own race.'

5 Norman de Mattos Bentwich and H. St John Philby, 'The Palestine Report', Time and Tide 18 No 29 (17 July 1937), 969–73. Norman Bentwich (1883–1971), who had been Attorney-General in the Palestine Government 1920–31, was Professor of International Relations at the Hebrew University of Jerusalem 1932–51. A moderate in Zionist politics, he worked for a bi-national State. Harry St John Bridger Philby (1885–1960), orientalist and explorer, expert on Arab affairs, had become a Muslim, and was at this time based in Jedda. His words (p. 972) are: 'Stated arithmetically, the Arabs win their case as to $^{23}\!/_{24}$ ths of their claim. [. . .] Twenty-three-twenty-fourths of a loaf (not half, as the Commission states) is better than no bread.'

romanticized by [Lionel] Curtis etc. it goes on proving a ludicrous source of embarrassment, & is not worth continuing with: the thing to do is to get rid of it by offering it as an attractive gift after pushing up the price, to a bemused company of clever fools: to facilitate which the report was written. Coupland is certainly the person, who contrary to expectation is more directly responsible for everything than anyone else: to me he praised Shertock[1] a great deal, said he was much the best witness, paid an encomium to Weizmann who invented the joke about the over promised land, declared the country was in his view hideously ugly: & said that Namier for once behaved with statesmanlike tact and, tho' in the same hotel, did not speak till spoken to. I have at last met Namier. A frightful man, I thought, who ought certainly [to] be put on to something. It will be far worse if he is frustrated. In the meanwhile the London executive threatened to resign if he was added to it: he v. nearly was, having successfully wooed the labourites – I always follow the aristocracy he said. I assume that Coupland was personally responsible for everything because (a) everyone else assumes it (b) Maud kept on mysteriously hinting, while it was being written, that Coupland was in some way being very great (c) because he as good as says so. Partition is certainly his idea. I wish you could tell me what is going to happen. It looks now as if everyone is going to leave open doors to everyone else, & the situation will moulder on in an awful sort of way, until Palestine is finally annexed by someone. But I may be wrong. Weizmann certainly seems to have promised acceptance of Partition to O[rmsby]-Gore, over the heads of the Congress. I daresay he knows them by now. Can you conceive the consequences? one enormous cylindrical town from Haifa to Tel-Aviv of Talith[2]-sellers, with the fashion for Bar Mitzvah boys to be 'confirmed' in the Holy Land, & a nation of Jewish hotel keepers & souvenir-vendors to receive them? that is what a nation of 1.500.000 will certainly become. I expect I am quite wrong & it will really be as soundly Blut & Boden,[3] as, say, Luxemburg. Coupland is regarded as the historical expert on the problem. Your 3 hours with him, diluted into his own inimitable pan-synthesising sauce with which he covers everything he touches is probably what is meant. Anyhow you obviously performed a most needed service to the J. People: since his superior knowledge made him pleased, authoritative over his colleagues, & in a way not as anti-Zionist as he might otherwise have been. Meanwhile Curtis has been entertaining Saudi Arabians, in All Souls. Very handsome group they all made; 'a lot of Harabs about the

---

1 Moshe Shertok (Sharrett) (1894–1965), head of the Jewish Agency's political department 1933–48.
2 Prayer-shawls: cf. 101/4.
3 'Blood and soil', the phrase used in Nazi ideology to mark an alleged exclusive connection between the German race (or *Volk*) and its land.

college to-day sir' said my scout when calling me 'Harabs, sir, a lot of Harabs. Mr Curtis, he's said to be very good with them, with Harabs sir. Harabs all over the place to-day.'

I suppose Coupland will get his knighthood, but he is v. dissatisfied with the debate in Parliament. He thinks he's got Ormsby Gore: so does Weizmann: so does Baffy:[1] I expect they all have. Chamberlain[2] is said to have explained to King Carol[3] who came to inquire, that the Cabinet is not enthusiastic about the recommendations, & doesn't care what happens in the Mandatory Commission:[4] so nobody knows anything at all, & Gore is angry because the Congress came to no decision, & Herbert Samuel's[5] life has been threatened by Revisionists. Lord Mt. Carmel & Toxteth one ought to call him. Smart Jewish circles refer to him as Lord Tooting:[6] he, again, has displeased everyone except the Nashashibists.[7] This is all I know which isn't absolutely public. If you know of anyone who wants to make Coupland's life & thought his doctorate thesis, I should be glad to give him an accurate, if slightly malicious description, of his mixture of pride, desire to be indiscreet, Wykehamist reserve and passion for painting word pictures of his own progress, with which he addressed me in All Souls on his return. He thinks of Partition, as a strong, heroic, non-academic act, a move bloody bold & resolute with which to save the Empire. At bottom he is both sincere & naive I think: but the surface is unattractive. So much for that. Another tit-bit which might give you pleasure, is the hectic haste with which the deputation to Göttingen[8] was frustrated. First Council voted to send me: votes 13 to 7 (the proceedings are of course very secret): then Salter very decently &

1 Blanche Elizabeth Campbell Dugdale (1880–1948), née Balfour, enthusiastic non-Jewish Zionist, niece and biographer of the politician Arthur James Balfour, 1st Earl of Balfour; head of Intelligence Dept, League of Nations Union, 1920–8; member of UK Delegation to League of Nations Assembly 1932. The nickname 'Baffy' comes from her attempts to pronounce 'Balfour' when she was a child.

2 (Arthur) Neville Chamberlain (1869–1940), originally Liberal, later Conservative politician; Prime Minister 1937–40.

3 King Carol II of Romania (1893–1953).

4 sc. the Royal Commission of Inquiry to Palestine (246/3).

5 Herbert Louis Samuel (1870–1963), 1st Viscount Samuel, politician, High Commissioner, Palestine, 1920–5, Liberal Leader, House of Lords, 1944–55.

6 An unfashionable area of London: presumably an allusion to Samuel's choice of the unfashionable Liverpool district of Toxteth (his birthplace) as part of his title.

7 Supporters of the Nashashibis, the main party in opposition to the Husseinis. Palestinian politics under the mandate were dominated by the rivalry between (especially these) prominent Palestinian families. The Husseinis, led by Hajj Amin al-Husseini, the Grand Mufti of Jerusalem, rejected partition, while the Nashashibis were inclined to accept it, at least in private.

8 The minutes of the meeting of the Hebdomadal Council held on 1 March 1937 state that it was agreed by 10 votes to 9 to send a representative and an address to the Bicentenary Celebration of the University of Göttingen; the 26 April minutes state that it was decided by 14 votes to 7 to reverse Council's decision to send a representative but to adhere to the decision to send an address.

unexpectedly wrote to Lindsay protesting: another meeting was summoned. Actually I acted. I asked Maurice to talk to his friends, Roy to Miss Grier,[1] your talkative Derby-companion Austin to bully Parker[2] etc., a lot of dramatic telephoning by everyone on the actual morning (genuinely exciting) & it was turned down, 13 v. 12. Next issue was Russell, (Bertrand)[3] to whom Chicago seems to have offered a professorship. Again plots, intrigues, cabals, to get him to lecture in Oxford for one term: my conversation with the Warden I cannot reproduce, it was absolutely wonderful: he plainly hates Russell & all connected with him, but finally said 'I suppose, at bottom, he is a very lovable kind of man?' really I didn't know what to say. I might have said, I suppose, 'Many women appear to have found him so, sir' but didn't, only just though. The Principal of Jesus[4] said if R. came to Oxford, he wd convert the morals of the place into those of a stockyard: Farkie[5] supported this: somebody had the dubious taste to refer to Amanulla's morals, who has a Hon Ll.D. here.[6] Majority for Russell: 13 v. 12. Oh dear. They are very exciting, these campaigns, but the risk of loss, & the consequent damages too great. So far, no losses. Incidentally: what will the Palestine Jewish diplomatic representative be called? The Jewish Minister? what will the Rev. Mattuck[7] & Mr Hore Belisha[8] say?

Private Affairs

Maurice: Sheer Disaster. It was, in my view, a mad choice, she[9] would have bored him in no time, a young, earnest, impulsive, feministic anarchist: anyhow after a whirlwind flirtation, apparent acceptance, a solemn vetting by friends etc. she appeared to have declined at the eleventh hour. Being obviously & rightly, I suppose, frightened by the prospect. If only she had done it earlier. Now M. feels humiliated & angry & spends time in answering

1 (Mary) Lynda Dorothea Grier (1880–1967), economist and administrator, Principal of LMH 1921–45, member of Council 1926–45.

2 Henry Michael Denne Parker (1894–1971), Roman historian, Fellow of Magdalen, member of Council 1928–41. Austin, also a Fellow of Magdalen, was in a position to approach Parker. It seems he had been to the Derby with Frankfurter.

3 Bertrand Arthur William Russell, 3rd Earl Russell (1872–1970), philosopher, mathematician, pacifist and advocate of free love.

4 Alfred Ernest William Hazel (1869–1944), lawyer, Principal of Jesus 1925–44.

5 Brevet Lt. Col. Arthur Spenser Loat Farquharson (1871–1942), philosopher, Fellow and Tutor of Univ. 1899–1942.

6 A DCL by Diploma (not strictly an honorary degree) was conferred on King Amanullah of Afghanistan in Oxford on 23 March 1928.

7 Rabbi Dr Israel Isidore Mattuck (1883–1954), Minister of the Liberal Jewish Synagogue, St John's Wood, 1912–48. Born in Lithuania but trained in the US, he was one of the pioneers in the UK of the Liberal Jewish movement, which did not regard Judaism as entailing Zionism.

8 (Isaac) Leslie Hore-Belisha (1893–1957), Jew, Liberal politician, Secretary of State for War and President of the Army Council 1937–40.

9 Audrey Beecham (220/2).

letters of congratulation from all over Europe. He wrote to me here, saying that Audrey – for so as you know she is called, had 'a bad attack of doubts'. I assume all is over, else he wouldn't have written. I can't say how distressed I feel. Blow after blow, of a flattening kind. Pray God he is elected Warden of Wadham. I don't know what to write to him, at all. He really passionately wants to have a wife, he cannot bear his sexless existence any longer, (as he would put it), & he can obviously not do as Pares has done, who married a worthless, homely little nitwit (daughter to Powicke, niece to Lindsay) who is below criticism [. . .]. Anyhow there it is; I can't deny that I think that there is something he lacks in the precipitancy of his advances, his view that towns & villages can be not only captured but held after a single rush, his ignoration of the less perceptible reactions on the part of the people at whom his enormous impact is directed. Also his life is lived in full limelight: & the jibes of the Night & Day[1] contributors (in private) disturb more than they ought: only oh why didn't you find him an intelligent & decorative wife in America? between 25 & 35, and with dignity? Night & Day is not really very good. Elizabeth Bowen & Evelyn Waugh alone are good. Betjeman writes embarrassing rubbish, & Peter Fleming is even worse. Not a patch, not a tenth part of a patch on the New Yorker which it imitates.

Prof. W. Notestein[2] has been staying in All Souls. What about him? I have never met a man so anxious to please, to adapt himself to the strange but distinguished English. Sparrow likes him very much. So do Rowse & Pares. I could not help finding him agreeable but (a) squalid (b) reactionary in a nicely slimy sort of way. He is a nice man really I expect. The part he plays is that of a pleasant old academic racketeer. Please say something about him. Roy pursues pleasure. Weekly he is seen in College garden with one or more tipsy, fat, red lipped young women, hardly able to walk for drink. Descriptions of him, with his head on someone's lap, in a low London dive, talking gently & seriously about the trade cycle, are fascinating. He is very, very unchanged. Mr Keynes[3] is unwell, in a nursing home: if people visit him he opens by saying he hasn't a minute to spare. The bed overflows with periodicals. Round him are rooms in which corpulent peers are trying to lose

---

1 A short-lived weekly magazine, partly modelled on the New Yorker, edited by Graham Greene and published by Chatto & Windus from July to December 1937. An anthology was published in book form under the same title, by the same publisher, in 1985, edited by Christopher Hawtree. According to Virginia Woolf, writing to her sister Vanessa Bell on 28 December 1937, Lydia Keynes (500/1), wife of J. M. Keynes (note 3 below), preferred Night & Day to the New Statesman.

2 Wallace Notestein (1878–1969), historian of 17th-century Britain, Sterling Professor of History at Yale 1928–47.

3 John Maynard Keynes (1883–1946), economist (created Baron Keynes of Tilton 1942), had fallen ill with heart trouble in May.

weight. The bulletins of their competitive activity are reported to Mr Keynes daily. He refers to them as the elephants. There is going to be a new Ayer crisis roundabout 1939: you must forgive me for pestering, but *could* something be done about him in U.S.A.? he is really celebrated by now, & no longer as much an enfant terrible as he used to be: if he published a heavyish book, wd that help? if you could help, it would add to the sum total of good in the universe enormously: I shd be most grateful if you wd let me know: Oxford Colleges are grotesquely frightened of him: Couldn't he be asked to lecture for a term in America, somewhere fairly reputable, even if not Harvard itself? Also this: his life with Renée is approaching a crisis too: I can't tell you what enormous admiration I now feel for Marions[1] analysis or rather prognosis of this, when last we met: America would settle this too, & as the crisis is essentially weatherable, & depends on environmental rather than permanent emotional conditions. More than this at present I cannot trust myself to say. Would you were both here, & inspected the situation, which is by no means desperate or even tragic at present: only downhill-facing. At All Souls we have elected a young man from Balliol called Stuart Hampshire to whom I am attached, & another called Routh, a protegé of Pares & Salter, to whom I am v. much less attached, a useful Wykehamist hack. Crossman, I am surprized to inform you, may be leaving us. I fear this may be a greater loss to the world than gain to us, consequently utilitarian reasons, require us to keep him here, harmless. If he goes, that creates a minor crisis for me. I think I can manage it quite easily.

I really must stop you know. Logorrhoea is an unattractive property, & shd be kept in check.

One more point: a young pupil of mine called Pat Nowell Smith,[2] a philosopher of radical views, & in himself a bright, slightly childish little man, clever, well behaved, assiduous, tidy, conscientious, slightly affected, & v. much the son of his father, a professionally broad minded ex-don ex-headmaster – head secretary of [the] League of Nations Union, is sailing to Cambridge as a Commonwealth Fellow; he is to be supervised by C. I. Lewis. I think he would seem pleasant enough to you: there is no great need to take trouble about him, but if he comes & sees you I recommend him fairly warmly. He is not exactly interesting, but bright, ingenious, & I think, very technically clever. He got a First in Greats this year, was my No 1 pupil & asked to be recommended to you. He was educated at Winchester, & being a good boy, was doted on by all his schoolmasters & dons, including me. He has a kind of charm.

---

1 Marion Frankfurter.
2 Patrick Horace Nowell-Smith (b. 1914), New College classics 1933–7, Commonwealth Fellow, Harvard, 1937–9, army service 1939–45, Fellow and Lecturer in philosophy, Trinity, 1946–57.

When shall I see you & Marion again? When are you returning to Europe? I can't believe I shall ever cross any ocean: tho' Maurice's accounts of Harvard pupils, who obviously paid proper homage, was glowing to a degree. He was v. hard on Dr Nicholas M. Butler:[1] & resentfully respectful about Conant.[2] I shall write more of this to Marion, very soon.

Love

Shaya B.

Marx appears next year, Hume in 1940.[3]

I cannot bear to read through all this: I hope it is not too endlessly discursive & thinly buttered.

TO MARIE BERLIN

Thursday [early September 1937]

Anglo-Palestine Club, London W1

Dear Ma.

We have just dined here simply but very well: the food is fresh, cheap, and pleasantly served: the atmosphere is one of a vegetarian rather than a Kosher restaurant. I arrived from Paris on Tuesday: you ought to go through Paris & see the exhibition:[4] the things inside are not v. interesting, but the general atmosphere marvellously gay. At home there is no chaos: the charwoman is quiet, polite & efficient: I lunch at home & dine in town with Father: so far all our meals have been Jewish and not 'exotic'. As Saturday, Sunday, Monday Tuesday are non-office days, & your husband likes развлечения,[5] I think we'll go to Brighton for a long week-end, returning in the middle of the week. Mrs Phillip[6] says that 53 Hollycroft Av. is a v. decent Jewish boarding house: perhaps when you return we could eat there

---

1 Nicholas Murray Butler (1862–1947), President of Columbia University 1902–45.

2 James Bryant Conant (1893–1978), organic chemist and educationalist, President of Harvard 1933–53.

3 It seems clear from Frankfurter's letter (23 July) that IB was at this time planning to write a book on Hume (cf. p. 122 above), which never materialised. On 13 February 1940 Yitzhak Samunov writes to IB's parents: 'Is he now working on Hume? I hope it will be as pleasant reading as Marx.'

4 The Paris World's Fair (Exposition Internationale des Arts et des Techniques dans la Vie Moderne), May–November 1937.

5 'Razvlecheniya' ('entertainments').

6 Clarisse Philipp (sic) (1888–1971), a near neighbour and friend of the Berlins. She and her husband Oscar (316/6) lived in Ferncroft Avenue, adjoining Hollycroft Avenue: the Berlins' house could be seen from the Philipps', No 6; see p. 4.

till you find a maid. Anyhow I intend trying it. After dinner we return home & don't go out: much quieter & nicer.

I hope Riga[1] is nice: my regards of course to everyone: wonderfully long lived they are, e.g. Beines Berlin,[2] Mr Shaye Berlin etc.[3] here my friend Rothschild[4] – But one can't congratulate!

yrs
Shaya

TO BEN NICOLSON

[Late September? 1937]

as from All Souls

Dear Ben,

I was very glad to get your letter.[5] To begin with your sensations in and about Venice I find sympathetic, so sympathetic that I [am] almost glad you have them, although I found them acutely embarrassing and painful myself. It is the most isolated and unreal town in the world: Henry James phrase about the drawing room of Europe is not merely untrue and silly but an insult if one feels as I felt, & as I imagine to some extent you do. The sense of claustrophobia, of being cut off in a small, alarming, vicious, anti-humane, personality-sapping corrosive world, not the end of something, an agreeably decaying cul de sac, where one is left to oneself, & nothing eats one or impinges on one, but in a shut in sinister cannibalistic place, which the enormous crowds and the unwanted acquaintances make seem even more sinister, as the familiar does, as in a nightmare.

Oh dear, I am exaggerating as usual. What I wish to say is that it is the only town in the world in which I, who don't respond easily to environment, felt that I was going mildly insane. I was alone for two days, then Giles [Robertson] arrived, & his patter about the outside world, his gossip, his familiar malice, his appreciation, the return of Oxford & Cambridge restored my equilibrium. I was v. grateful to him for it at the time: but I sent some mad letters & telegrams before he arrived.

1 Marie was visiting her family there.
2 Presumably Beinus, nephew (b. c.1867) of Isaiah Berlin senior, IB's great-great-uncle and adoptive great-grandfather, after whose death (in IB's infancy) Beinus was briefly in partnership with Mendel. Mendel describes Beinus in his memoir as 'a most incalculable, unreliable, dishonest man and liar'.
3 Probably a distant cousin who briefly housed Mendel, Marie and IB on their return to Riga in 1920; possibly the brother-in-law of Beinus.
4 Victor Rothschild had just succeeded his uncle (Lionel) Walter Rothschild, 2nd Baron Rothschild (who had died on 27 August at the hardly advanced age of 69), as Lord Rothschild.
5 Dated 18 September 1937. His reply to the present letter is dated 2 October.

I didn't in the least wish to begin in this tone: but Venice is a symbol to me now, & my growing antipathy to Henry James is part of it: they are not dissimilar: his characters also possess the appalling characteristic of not having things happen to them, but looking, digging, scratching sometimes, for experience: they prepare themselves like emotional vampires, to absorb & accumulate: the perpetual haunting fear is that it may fall short, there may not be enough blood, the stream will one day run dry: and – this the worst thing of all, – they don't *live* through their sought for experience at all, they avoid. They stack up the avoided crises behind them in closer & closer layers, & this vast mass of carefully wrapped up emotional and intellectual events, tied up with bits of string quickly, for fear of explosions, vulgar humiliations, climaxes which end, instead of leading on to, other situations, this badly assorted dead matter, or rather unalive perhaps, is what the reader is given. I dislike it & admire it: I admire it because like Dostoyevsky he examines the unfamiliar and establishes one truth which everyone *must* admit is true: that the most terrific tragedies, the most dramatic, thrilling, moving, genuine catastrophes occur in milieus where nobody does anything, where people merely talk and understand, where everyone trembles in an inhibited way at the approach of everyone else and the writing on an envelope or the sight of [a] lifted curtain fringe creates a turmoil far more violent than so called action could produce. I admit at once that I abhor twilight: that I don't believe that all primary colours, & all solid-seeming primary emotional relations, all the three dimensional architecture of a Tolstoy novel are, on closer inspection, seen to break up into infinite gradations of hardly isolable, opalescent (cf H.A.L.F. you remember: the account of Mr Darby?)[1] shades, which blend & vanish and alone are real, so that in terms of them alone can anything be properly described. Proust, by being so much sharper & bolder in his account, bribes one into accepting that because others (including oneself) have been unable (or have shrunk from) to probe to and describe the emotions, motives, appearances which he alone has done, bribes us into accepting the false proposition that this alone is real, & for that reason & no other has proved too frightening or too obscure to ordinary men or ordinary novelists. I deny from the outset that nobody lives in sunlight, that all relations are rapacious, that one must eat or be eaten, that everything is in disequilibrium & tension always, that sensitiveness & kindness are therefore the only real virtues, + (cleverness where & how to be), as of course they would necessarily be in wartime, at the front, not far from the First Aid Red Cross stations, where no peace is expected, and such armistices as are declared only exist to relieve tension, to allow new armaments to be made. In a vulgarer way this is also the assumption of Aldous Huxley, of everybody

1 See letter of 29 July 1936 to Giles Robertson, p. 185 above.

who preaches the necessity of kindness & easy toleration: being unmoved by the continual impingement of individual on individual, of persons using others as means, of emotional exploitation, cannibalism, which I think I dislike more than anything else in the world.

At this point I was called away, and although I do not propose to re-read what I have written, I am surprised at the violence of my sentiment & at the motive which prompted me to convert a private letter into a tract. Let us return to private affairs. Salzburg was on the whole very enjoyable: Rain, cramped rooms, etc. cast a blight over the Francis week, which added to his natural lack of confidence & tendency to eat himself, probably made him miserable. The Ridleys, I mean J. & Cressida B-C.[1] arrived and stated that in their view he was fearfully unhappy, implying that we were monsters not to notice it, or take steps etc. I don't think that what they saw was there. That Francis gnaws away at himself and contorts himself into painful postures is true: but there is no cosmic change: I mean no great overwhelming sense of futility has suddenly come on him: it is a hand to mouth, day by day, discontinuous state of nervousness & misery, which anything might cure for a time, and nothing in particular is responsible for promoting. I suspect Ridley of looking for lesions, not indeed like Rosamond Lehmann, for a definite love of them for their own sakes, but as a function of his own dissatisfaction.

Now as for the cloak:[2] the ugly rumour is partially justified: there is an entity, best called a cloak, owned by me now for 5 years, bought under the influence of the Hodgkin brothers, an ugly, dark blue, shapeless sheet, which is extremely useful in Austrian tropical rain, warm, and never worn except in bad weather in Austria. With it goes a hideous flat German hat – whereas the cloak is an Austrian bourgeois town-garment, worn by the lower & lower middle classes, the hat, is, I have to confess, Tyrolean. It has no brush, feather, ribbon, it is also shapeless, & again is worn only in rain when it is warm & waterproof. The cloak nobody thought arty (it isn't) & I was allowed to wear in peace: Stuart & Mrs C[ameron] praised it officially. The hat was severely criticized by Stuart for its sheer ugliness: but it was seen that I wish to demonstrate nothing by wearing it, it was not a symbol, gesture, state of mind: so that too passed. Until Ridley, making a fearful thing out of the hat, where was it, how monstrous if Stuart's, but permissible if mine, asked for it. I gave it to him with relief & pleasure. He looked handsome and central European in it. His companion, Miss B-C. protested against this

---

1 (Helen Laura) Cressida Bonham Carter (1917–98), daughter of Sir Maurice and Lady Violet Bonham Carter, married Jasper Ridley in 1939.
2 In his 18 September letter Nicolson had reported the 'wicked rumour . . . that you were seen in Salzburg in Tyrolese hat and cloak, had it seized by Ridley and subsequently pounded on the ground by Mrs Ridley'. The cloak appears in Plate 14 – in France.

sudden rapacity, but was not permitted to say anything. My meetings with them are full of the acutest embarrassment: why I can't quite say, it is Ridley's fault mainly: he feels self-conscious, talks faster than usual, & having seized a subject, won't relinquish it, & is piqued & insulted if one even faintly shows signs of wanting to modulate away from it. Miss B-C. is acutely nervous & afraid of some terrible accident, wound to vanity, or misunderstanding, interprets away, & doesn't look at me (what Stuart is accused of with regard to her, I believe). I, embarrassed and excited, play faster & faster tennis – it is more like badminton really, the shuttlecocks come all awry & one hits crookedly at awkward feathers & it flies off at unexpected angles, & if it falls, it does so inelegantly, the thing is a pure misfortune, it doesn't bounce but stays on its side & has to be obviously picked up again clumsily – with Ridley & then we leave out of breath, having achieved nothing, only exhibition of our styles. I have never met her without him – all my talent for accommodatingness is wasted – consequently we are now in a groove where only embarrassments can occur. I don't think it important since I never see her – it is a mild nuisance. As for Stuart, why is it so important that he should display active liking for her? he quite likes [her], I believe, but again, meeting her, as he does, solely with Ridley, the mis en scène is Ridley's, the objects placed in his eccentric way, normal relations are impossible; if you want to bring them together without friction or obvious effort, you must ask them both to something without R. – but why this siege which both you & Wallace are so vigorously conducting, of a fortress which doesn't mind whether it is taken or not? please explain: I am interested.[1]

The Cloak was left on a seat, taken to the police station, Stuart's attempts to retrieve it failed because he is not accustomed to Austrian officials, I asked Pares (whose wife is more dreadful in Salzburg than even in Oxford. Something unspeakable. Academic negress is much too kind) to get it, since I had to leave myself, & to give it to Ridley if he didn't want it (as obviously he couldn't). But what did you say Mrs R. did with it? grounded it? hounded? bounded it? your word can't be read:[2] how does one bound a cloak? hounded I understand, & it is a vigorous & beautiful picture, but is that what you said? please explain this too. Ridley & Miss B-C. were plainly very unanxious to see us: or perhaps it was she who was embarrassed by me in particular: on this point too light would be welcome.[3] Please research &

1 BN's careful reply of 2 October cannot be briefly summarised, but it begins: 'It is of course partly one's natural inclination to want two very nice people who are frightened of one another for absurdly superficial reasons to know one another.' He was also concerned to prevent an All Souls/London 'rift'.

2 In the same letter BN writes: 'I wish I had written "hounded" it is a fine phrase. But in fact I used the perfectly good English word "Pounded", like coffee or granite.'

3 BN explains that Cressida disapproves of IB behaving as an Oxford personage even in

tell me: I dislike ambiguous situations, I can't probe myself without thereby altering the situation: I look to you for precise knowledge. In any case I have no notion of what anyone feels. In Salzburg tact had to be & was employed: else there wd have been friction: which is a nuisance. I analyse everything in terms of comfort only, I take it her emotions are so seriously involved that this attitude is frivolous & vulgar: again I may be mistaken – again you must elucidate: I trust your acumen in this, v. much.

Biéville: I shdn't have minded meeting him, he is nothing to me, perhaps mild amusement might have been had. Stuart was not exactly adamant, but disapproved, & it fell through: For this I kept my pupils away too. In fact our plan not to get caught up was amazingly successful. In Salzburg it is absolutely essential. Which brings me to the subject of gangs in general. I approve of gangs, Stuart disapproves. He points out rightly that living one's life in public is hateful, that three cornered situations lead to muddles, because even in cases of absolutely non-erotic relationships, given individuals A, B, C, B can always tell C that he doesn't understand A at all & it will always be true, & vice versa, & trouble ensues. All of which is quite true. On the other hand I quote my noble 19th century Russians & maintain that only in nuclei does anything worth while develop, unless one is an exceptional Dostoyevskian hermit, that one gains enormously from having oneself observed & responded to, that one never knows what one thinks & feels until one says it, that one can only say it in a context & milieu where there is no restraint & absolute confidence and a wall of disinterested friendship protects one from all the things which inhibit one in public, or even where one is alone & therefore open to a hostile (real or imaginary, doesn't matter which) world, & that this civilized inhabited area, where one is free, & spontaneous, & happy can only be created, in the majority of cases, by the establishment of machinery for spontaneous discussion, & unself conscious, ungrammatical communication, where standards are not lived up to, and one knows that one's words are valued simply as being one's own, & not for their relevance, content, effects, intentions. Hence my pro-Russian anti-Florentine turns. Your daily letters to the B-C. family seem to me – who hold such doctrines – entirely excellent. Particularly unforced narratives, where pearls & jewels are not looked for, & the effect is cumulative & results from reliance & affection, not admiration & criticism. Am I really singular in holding that one must be able to express oneself simply & copiously to someone at regular intervals, if one is to express oneself at all, & not find oneself in a private world, full of ghosts and terrors? Proust said that friends were a waste of time & the real world was a private universe into which the

Salzburg: 'She has a concept of "All-Souls-foregathering-in-Salzburg-during-august" [sic] which is repellent.'

artist withdraws with relief. This again holds only of the bruised, the humiliated, the cripples, even when their passion is for the truth alone, & they are men of genius. The paranoia of mystics, poets, & Proustian writers may increase their neurosis to the point of genius, but as a quality of life I can not protest against it more vehemently than I do. And the windows can be kept open only when outside them there are other persons, who are fond of one, & of whom one is fond, neither side expecting anything in return. I shall never cease believing this: hence my escape literature is the Russian 19th century: like Don Quixote & his knights-errant, when he used to say Amadis of Gaul wd not have said this, what would Bel-somebody of Greece have done etc. so I think in terms of Herzen's or Belinsky's[1] reaction to something: you use an imaginary portrait of Stuart for this purpose (you seem to me to dramatize & romanticize him immensely – but this only illustrates the correctness of A, B, C, above, B's view of C must always seem oddly fantastic to A): unless one lives among people whose reactions one respects, (& therefore one's own reactions to them are less suspect than in more dubious cases) how can one orientate oneself? & not to do so is the worst of all disasters. As for Giles I do see what you mean quite clearly. Jeremy wd say he was squalid: there is indeed a querulous, envious ex-ploiting quality about him, which I don't mind, since I appreciate the vir-tue of the vice i.e. that he is one of the few people who can sympathize genuinely with all one's lowest, & most trivial griefs without making one feel ashamed of them, without by implication morally embarrassing one. A most valuable property in a universe of rigorous testers by standards. When one is low, he is sympathetic. Irritating, fussy, loquacious, but sympathetic. His malice is wonderfully de-inhibiting. He has taste, he is genuinely sensitive, he is not a prig, & he likes one. His opportunism is honourable, & his tortures about being disliked or slighted, endearing. As for your relations, you probably cannot genuinely like anyone unless you (a) admire & (b) respect them. You don't admire Giles at all, & you respect only certain selected qualities, not the pattern: & therefore not spontaneously but because you infer, that the qualities being there, & respectworthy, you must respect. On the other hand you cannot possibly dislike or disapprove of him ever seriously, since he will never commit an act of serious treachery to anything you hold sacred & think of him as devoted to, too. Hence your relations will always remain in this firmly precarious condition, securely rivited to the edge of a precipice, you in perpetual fear & distress about the perils, & consequently liable to minor quarrels, he irritating & wooing by turns, malicious in minor matters, undeviatingly loyal in major. I am sure in this particular case you have nothing to be worried about: no major situation

---

1 For these thinkers see RT.

for good or for evil could possibly develop: the scale on which Giles is conceived is too narrow: the materials of which he is composed are quite expensive, but there are gaps, eked out by inferior stuff: of this he is aware, hence occasional shrill yelps + long thin scrannel moans at your massive qualities. He is more attached to you than you to him: which is never wholly unsatisfactory to the person who receives – or at least is offered – more than he gives.

Your description of Mrs H.[1] I enjoyed very much: I have never properly speaking met her, & am more terrified than ever of doing so. I must stop & go to All Souls & help with the philosophy paper: the examination is as usual a family affair, with Wallace, Davis,[2] Francis, etc. etc. all in. I expect I shall give one of my usual populous lunch parties after which someone will marry someone else unsuitably. I expect you to say something unexpectedly savage to me in a letter shortly (almost a Blunt touch this), but whether or not you do, write. And sometime next term I shall beg you to visit me & explain about the B-C. situation. It is obviously easy to remove all difficulty: making molehills out of bogus mountains is the greatest pleasure.

Shaya.

TO SHIELA GRANT DUFF

[Shortly after Monday 18 October 1937]

All Souls

Dear Shiela,

Our relations continue good.[3] With regard to lunch: I am prepared & more than prepared to ask you & *Agnes*[4] next Wednesday, provided you allow me, favour for favour, to work off Boase & the Pareses[5] at the same time: I don't insist on Boase, but the Pareses I beg for: Macartney[6] doesn't seem to be here: if he comes he & his noxious wife shall be asked too. Will

1 Mary Hutchinson.
2 Henry Whitcliffe ('Bill') Davies (*sic*) (1914–42), Communist, Balliol classics 1933–7, Fellow of All Souls 1938–42, killed in action in the navy in the Battle of Java Sea, 27 February 1942.
3 SGD had asked in a letter of 18 October: 'Are our relations still v. cordial?'
4 Agnes Headlam-Morley (1902–86), SGD's politics and economics tutor; author of *The New Democratic Constitutions of Europe: A Comparative Study of Post-War European Constitutions with special reference to Germany, Czechoslovakia, Poland, Finland, the Kingdom of the Serbs, Croats & Slovenes and the Baltic States* (Oxford, 1928), Fellow and history and politics Tutor, St Hugh's, 1932–70.
5 Richard Pares and his wife Janet.
6 Carlile Aylmer Macartney (1895–1978), expert and writer on Hungary; married the Bulgarian Nedella Mamarchev; Intelligence Dept, League of Nations Union (under Maxwell Garnett), 1928–36; Research Fellow of All Souls 1936–65.

you accept on these terms? I feel this is a case for hard headed higgling of the market: pray state your minimum demands. As it will be no fun if you go with the rest, I demand that you stay – outstay Miss H-M, & perhaps even till tea. Kindly tell me if you are prepared to acquiesce in all this. If you are I shall look forward immensely.[1]

love

Shaya

TO STEPHEN SPENDER

5 January 1938

Hotel Bristol, Beaulieu-s/-Mer[2]

as from All Souls

Dear Stephen,

The Riviera is dreary & hateful beyond belief. I had no choice but to go to this place, since I wished to finish Marx & at the same time not be totally isolated since in absolute solitude I tend to go mad. As a result I am living in luxury against which I have violent petit bourgeois feelings: look at Sir J. Simon[3] & your uncle sitting under the trees of the jardin exotique: but am in fact writing very fast & ferociously. The weather is very good, which for one I dislike, since it gives open pleasure to so many detestable people: really you ought to come here in order to get a taste of the kind of society which produced the anarchists & dynamiters of 1880–1890: do you know about them, Ravachol,[4] Vaillant[5] etc.? extremely awful men, but very interest-ing. I read Herzen whom I like more & more: I like the rhetoric, dulness & all. His description of the English is very good indeed: he maintains that the Germans look on the English as a superior brand of the same article as they are themselves, & say yes for ja long before it is necessary.

If I buy you a copy of 'My life & thoughts' will you read it? I still haven't lost all hope of the critical quarterly:[6] but have suffered a bouleversement

---

1 At this point IB has written 'Goronwy', but crossed it out, and annotated the deletion thus: 'new method of persecution. I apologize. But I had never thought of it before. It is meant to be an illustration *only* not a real case.'

2 Beaulieu-sur-Mer is 7 km east of Nice on the south coast of France.

3 Sir John Allsebrook Simon (1873–1954), barrister and Liberal politician, Chancellor of the Exchequer 1937–40, 1st Viscount Simon of Stackpole Elidor 1940.

4 François Claudius Koeningstein ('Ravachol') (1859–92), Dutch-French anarchist, exploded bombs at Clichy and Fourmies in March 1892.

5 Auguste Vaillant (1861–94), French anarchist, exploded a bomb in the French Chamber of Deputies on 9 December 1893.

6 A letter of 22 October 1937 from Stephen Spender refers to discussions of this planned publication with Leonard and Virginia Woolf at the Hogarth Press, and suggests other possible publishers. It seems that IB had provided a scheme for a sample issue.

of ideas concerning it & how it ought [to] be run. Will you be in London in
Jan–Feb? or will you stay a night in Oxford? do write, since I should like to
meet. A very odd & frightening pamphlet has been written by Humphry
House called 'I spy with my little eye'[1] sent to [William] Plomer via Elizabeth [Bowen]: it is wildly paranoiac, asserts its own kinship with Milton
which is remote, & attacks Eliot for ignorance of Greek: or no, that is not the
pamphlet, which is anti England in India, but the letter with it. I tremble to
think, what, with his natural rankness of mind & tendency to overgrow with
long dark dank creepers, must have happened to him in the congenial society
of a lot of inferior Mulk Anands.[2] I honestly fear a right–left mystical–physical violence, inverted Yeats Brown.[3] But this may be pure phantasy on my
part. I feel in a highly malicious mood owing to the unspeakable, as Moore
wd say, creatures who teem all round. Write
    Shaya

TO ELIZABETH BOWEN

    [January 1938?]

                                       Hotel Bristol, Beaulieu-s/-Mer
Dear Elizabeth
    I meant & meant to write, but lowness of life is such that one can do
nothing save routine labours. I write ferociously on Marx every day, & have
accomplished the 290th page of a book of 256 p.p. which is like hurrying it
towards the date by which it was promised i.e. autumn 1937 etc.
    The hotel in which my family lives is awful. I can choose no simpler or
more conveying words. It is English in the worst sense & also contains one
or two Germans who, as the great Herzen observed early in the 19th century
(the remark absolutely obsesses me) regard themselves as inferior products
of the same machine as the English, coarse fruit of the same tree, & behave
accordingly, & become bad English. These are: 1 English yachtsman + a
detestable formally good looking fishlike wife 1 knowing American to do
with films: for 2 days Charles Laughton[4] (enormous excitement) & 1 ex-
Mayor of Kensington who daily suggests that I play golf with him. Apart

---

1 Untraced.
2 Mulk Raj Anand (b. 1905), Indian novelist.
3 Francis Charles Claypon Yeats-Brown (1886–1944), author, had served in and written about
   India; he moved from physical violence (as a Bengal Lancer) to an interest in Yoga and Hindu
   philosophy. House seemed to be going in the opposite direction.
4 Charles Laughton (1899–1962), film actor, British by birth, famous for roles such as Henry VIII
   (in *The Private Life of Henry VIII*, 1933) and Captain Bligh (in *Mutiny on the Bounty*, 1935).

from going up to La Turbie[1] & trying to have the bleak feelings which Mr Eliot said he had, & liked having, up there, I know no pleasures. But Marx is really getting on, 1½ chapters only require writing, & in a melancholy sort of way I am satisfied. But really. It is difficult not to go communist, anarchist, anything in this repulsive zoo. No feelings, no behaviour, not even manners: I infinitely prefer the petite bourgeoisie, where at least something happens. I do, for me, incredible things. I go to the Opera in Nice, which is appalling, in order to talk to my lower class neighbours, who at least provide couleur.[2] My parents are very patient with me. Social indignation has never shaken me before: & doubtless when I return to All Souls, Rowse, Routh, Rees, etc. will reduce me back to accomodating moderation. In the meanwhile I fulminate: & write about Marx like an irritated wage slave racked with social inferiorities. Everyone here (in the press) speaks of Malraux's new book on Spain,[3] & M. Céline's[4] unexpected antisemitism. I have bought Montherlant[5] but cannot read anything save daily Parisian papers which have an agreeable bitter tang like coffee or the Gare du Nord. I return this week.

love,

Shaya

This is a fearfully silly letter, I believe: if so I beg your forgiveness. Solitude enrages me over my llamalike condition.

TO MARY FISHER

Forwarding postmark [Wednesday] 12 January 1938 [*postcard*]

Beaulieu, France

Everything is incontinently & indecently rich & luxurious. Not a word of the French language is anywhere to be heard. Only Italian & English. The name of Mr Berkeley[6] is unknown to the local informatifs: the Mayor of

---

1 A pretty village high above Beaulieu, famous for its Roman remains and its fine panoramic views. T. S. Eliot stayed at the Savoy Hotel there for most of November and December 1925, to recover from an operation and to begin his 1926 Clark Lectures on metaphysical poetry.

2 i.e. local colour.

3 *L'Espoir* (Paris, 1937), translated as *Days of Hope* (London, 1938).

4 Louis-Ferdinard Céline, pseudonym of Louis-Ferdinand Destouches (1894–1961), French doctor and writer. The first of his three notoriously anti-Semitic pamphlets, *Bagatelles pour un massacre*, appeared in Paris in 1937.

5 Henri de Montherlant (1896–1972), French novelist, also wrote the travel book *Flèche du sud* (Paris, 1937). It is impossible to be sure which work IB is referring to.

6 George Fitz-Hardinge Berkeley (1870–1955), Keble history 1889–93, a friend of MF's parents, believed to be in Beaulieu or nearby by MF at this point, perhaps working on his 3-volume

Kensington is more familiar & disagreeable every day, & the Maître d'Hôtel's son studies philosophy in Cannes: he thinks it may be better taught in Aix les Bains. I have already recommended Chamonix as better than either. The Maitre d'Hotel declares he regrets he didn't send him to Eton. I return on Thursday to a Ch. Ch. gaudy.

Shaya

TO MARIE AND MENDEL BERLIN

Tuesday. [after 13 January 1938]

All Souls

Dear Ma & Pa,

I am sorry we speak so briefly – the phone last night, but my room was full of pupils: I get up at 9.30, & go to bed at 11. I work at Marx in the Library from 11 till 1 on some mornings (e.g. Sunday from 12 till 1 & 3 till 5) or from 4.15 till 7. So it is getting on. Hampshire has sinusitis in London (All Souls' effect again, draughts etc.) so I have no one to talk to & work much harder.

In Christchurch I sat next to a crypto-Jew called Clive, in Erlanger's bank,[1] who praised Blum[2] as only a Jew can, esp. one who wishes to pretend he isn't, & on the other side I had a bluff B.B.C. Official who said he wd send me all tickets for everything whenever I wanted them. Mr Sacher jun.[3] arrived to be taught to day: he looks like his mother & has a thin, vulgar, Manchester voice. I am sure we shall get on excellently. At least I hope so. Mr Bowra is v. well & so is Mary Fisher, both send their love. Jay & Salter both predict a real slump in 1940–41, when the armaments boom is over, this one being a passing little one, since manufactures (e.g. cotton) is already picking up again. But the coming slump will be *terrific*, & wd have been here now except for the artificial deflection of it by the armaments expenditure. Which all sounds reasonable: hence the mixed atmosphere of boom on top & slump suppressed, like a suppressed headache, underneath this dose of aspirin, which as soon as the effects of the drug wear away will re-emerge: unless of course a war intervenes, as in the slump which began in June 1914. Harold Nicolson dined here & sat next to me & was very affable, & said how wonderful it was to be a fellow of All Souls & how he wished he

---

Italy in the Making (Cambridge, 1932–40, repr. 1968), written jointly with his second wife Joan.

1 The d'Erlanger family's banking house in Frankfurt, Paris and London.

2 Léon Blum (1872–1950), first Jewish (and first socialist) prime minister of France.

3 Gabriel David Sacher (1920–2001), New College PPE 1937–40. His elder brother, Michael Moses Sacher (1917–86; also PPE), preceded him at New College by two years.

was, but he stood & failed.[1] He generally feels himself a failure. An amusing, clever, but not *very* nice man: a little dirty minded, like Mr W. Wolf, but less bitter. Mr Carr, who wrote Bakunin, has written me a *very* flattering letter[2] which I shall forward to you when I answer it. I suddenly feel like a powerful reviewer before whom poor authors are obliged to crawl. Soon I shall be a poor author myself. Mrs Fisher has offered to read the proofs of my book. I am well & happy.

 love

  Shaya

TO MARIE AND MENDEL BERLIN

 [After 14 January 1938]

All Souls

Dear Pa & Ma

 Thank you for your letter: I am v. well still: & work quite hard, another chapter is finished, 1¼ more to do: I enclose Carr's letter. Don't destroy it. I am a little tired of writing having just written him five pages about Bakunin:[3] after all he is a professor & may come in useful one day, so forgive me if I don't write now: nothing to say anyhow: Beloff coming to tea in 15 minutes about a Rumanian Jew with a mad proposal about colonizing the Negev. Do telephone Sunday 11.30 or so.

 love

  Shaya.

TO CRESSIDA BONHAM CARTER

 30 January [1938]

All Souls

Dear Miss Bonham Carter

 Could you please come and have lunch with me here, in All Souls, during this next month? it seems to be asking a good deal to invite anyone to perform the not necessarily agreeable journey to Oxford in February when there are rains and storms (the sensation of being almost levitated out of bed through the cardboard walls of one's bedroom by terrific gusts is very odd.

---

1 I can find no evidence that this last statement is true.
2 Dated 6 January [1938], sent in response to IB's review of E. H. Carr's *Michael Bakunin* in the *Spectator*, 31 December 1937, 1186.
3 This letter appears not to have survived.

The image may be rather grotesque & like the pictures in German Max &
Moritz books:[1] but the sensation is incommunicable) but I can only
promise that if you were to come on, e.g. Wednesday the 9th, there would be
a performance by Kreisler[2] at 3 o'clock: his desire to recover long abandoned integrity is so enormous that it may be a phenomenon worth
observing in itself: and he was, by all accounts, once upon a time a man of
enormous genius. The programme is not too attractive: and yet and yet. All
that is fioritura.[3] Really I shd be extremely glad if you wd come to lunch,
then or on the Wednesday after, or indeed on any Wednesday, or indeed on
some other day this next month.

    Yrs sincerely
      Isaiah Berlin

TO CRESSIDA BONHAM CARTER

[February 1938]

All Souls

Dear Miss Bonham Carter,

I am most genuinely grateful. I hadn't realized that Mahler–Asquith[4]
happenned next Wednesday, & although this doesn't involve reorganization,
it involves a new pattern for the day: which I am more than content with: if
you are to be at Mahler too this won't seem a surfeit? I don't think it will,
since Kreisler is playing a shocking programme: beginning with the Franck
Sonata and rapidly descending into Pugnani-Kreisler, Nardini Kreisler,
Viotti–Kreisler etc.[5] So what I said about his remorse etc. seems quite false
and you may still reasonably refuse to go. The other virtuoso performing
here on Wednesday is Bertrand Russell, whose lecture[6] is at 5: to go to
Mahler one must take the 5.50 train at the latest: but if you have never heard
him, possibly you may like to: he really is trying to save his soul, and is doing

1 The children's book *Max und Moritz* by Wilhelm Busch (1832–1908), published in 1865 (and in
  an English translation in 1874), a cautionary tale in verse about two boys who play cruel and
  dangerous tricks on their neighbours but come to a gruesome end, was well known at the
  time.
2 Fritz Kreisler (1875–1962), violinist and composer.
3 'Embellishment'.
4 The film director Anthony Asquith (1902–68), CBC's uncle, was a fanatical lover of Mahler and
  a serious amateur musician. He had organised a Mahler concert in London.
5 Fritz Kreisler wrote various pieces in the style of earlier composers, pretending they were
  authentic. He admitted his hoax in 1935.
6 Bertrand Russell lectured on Wednesdays and Fridays at 5pm in the Examination Schools on
  'Language and Fact', starting on Wednesday 26 January.

excellently at the moment: his audiences are splendid, the Warden of N[ew] College[1] says he is very *magistral* pronouncing it as in French: the whole thing is very feierlich[2] & fine. As for trains: admittedly the 11.20 from Paddington only arrives at 1.25, but the 11.15 arrives at 12.40 or so, & is a much nicer train in every way: but I shall be glad of your arrival at either time: & may well meet the earlier train unless you counter-instruct.

    yours

      Isaiah Berlin

TO CRESSIDA BONHAM CARTER

    [February 1938?]

All Souls

Dear Cressida,

    I write in great haste only to entreat you if books arrive not to think it at all necessary to acknowledge, really *not*. Shaw I am not sure about: Bassetto[3] I was afraid you might already have acquired in the meantime: Tolstoy[4] I can recommend with all my heart: episodes in one's own life are groupable round episodes in the book to an almost indefinite degree: it acts as a focus, a criterion, a string, everything is like something there etc.

    I enjoyed last Wednesday to a really immoderate degree. From the beginning to the final end when I travelled back in mildly vile body society, Mr & Mrs Roy F. Harrod, slightly tipsy and immensely affable. Wallace wished to know why we carried an air of conspiracy against him when we entered: I assured him that he was mistaken in a non-confidence conveying voice. I cannot say how pleased I was & am by your open adherence to the sunlit parts of the universe & ones which contain solid three dimensional objects and not swift successions of antennae-requiring light-and-shade variations to be reacted to at once for their own sake as an end in itself not to be retained: nothing, I wish to maintain, which cannot be conserved and produced again and again, fitted into new situations & then both rescued and looked at again & reaffirmed so to speak, possessed any value or interest. Pictures without frames are mere decorative wall paper, and fragments only fragments and not indications to some transcendental region. But at this

---

1 H. A. L. Fisher.

2 'Solemn', 'ceremonial'.

3 *London Music in 1888–89 as Heard by Corno di Bassetto (Later Known as Bernard Shaw) with Some Further Autobiographical Particulars* (London, 1937), an anthology of GBS's pseudonymous music criticism.

4 *Childhood, Adolescence and Youth* (1852–7).

point (my hate increases, my pupils wait & chafe all this is v. immoral according to my own standards) I hurry to say that Kafka is to be excluded from the general condemnation: he is naif and not sentimental: his figures are life size & solid, not either exaggeratedly big or thin & transparent & excessively mobile. his values are really a fanatical version of the democratic middle class ones so nakedly presented and vehemently asserted as to seem mad & mystical. Mystical however only because isolated & presented in an undated unspatialized sort of way, by themselves, not because of some inability to express what is seen beyond the world as or in the case of genuine mystics: it is almost the solidest universe I know, only very bare and with no conceivable use for even inferior & gross antennae of any kind. So it is really an exaggeration in one's own direction, & one applauds excess of this kind: Alas I must go at once. I very much hope we meet again

    yrs
      Shaya B.

TO MENDEL BERLIN

   [Early 1938][1]

All Souls

Dear Pa

   I am really delighted about Toscanini with the example of concert No 1 (for which I am provided) I only really care about 1 seat for myself for as many of the rest as possible. The residue is immensely easy to get rid of: & better get them, else the Box Office will remember it against one on the next occasion. I am v. well: the shorthand here costs 3/- an hour which is a lot. Perhaps I might begin to type myself? will you buy & send me a typewriter? I mean this seriously: I am prepared to type out my own stuff evening by evening. I think I shall learn quickly & indeed enjoy it v. much. I come on Friday next.

---

1 In May and June 1938 Toscanini conducted the BBC Symphony Orchestra in a series of concerts, playing music by a wide range of composers, in the Queen's Hall, London.

TO STEPHEN SPENDER

[Soon after 18 March 1938]

All Souls

Dear Stephen

I wished to see you for a few minutes longer on Friday night after your play,[1] but it was altogether too social an evening: the Connollys in themselves wd have made it so, not to speak of Moore (who was charming) & Lady Bonham Carter[2] who is an unbelievably repaying caricature of mondanity if you see what I mean, I mean a kind of New Yorker hostess translated into English terms, with all the serious qualities removed & the comic ones enormously stylized. But I wished to make remarks about the play, which I was enormously moved by, not more, but as much as by reading it: I have now read it twice and the cumulative effect is very great. So far as the production is concerned, the Judge is a little too much a character actor, which one can be, but one then cannot also speak poetry as poetry: somehow one must convey the sense of futility, brokenness, probity, pedantry, etc. by means other than having a futile, pedantic etc. voice & diction: otherwise one fails to become a properly universal symbol altogether: but he was dignified and sincere & didn't overact: the Nazis were v. good, particularly the leader: whose ferocity, since he is, I suppose, a communist, is reassuring: but even they are too boyish & not bestial enough: I assume you don't want them to be public school casualties, gâtés[3] figures generally, but brutish: if so you must have coarser types. The play itself seems to me fearfully good & effective: save for the Judge's wife, who starts invoking all that is corrupt & horrible within her too early & too naively: wd it not be better to let that occur gradually rather than let her explode at once with apostrophes to all that is old & bad & rotten? the whole thing is so musical & stands to an ordinary prose play so much like an oratorio to an opera, that I almost wd like the actors to have better singing voices, & speak your poetry with less conscious underemphasis: I am now converted to the word 'clocked'[4] which genuinely stuck before. I don't like the stage much & never go to see plays, & prefer to read, since when I do I hear someone's voice in any case, in this case yours, which is more suitable, apart from any other reason, than your actors'. I shall now read it for a third time & so acquire a certain amount by heart: the whole Fidelio–Destructive element

1 *Trial of a Judge* (155/4, 165/1) staged on 18 March by the Group Theatre.
2 Charlotte (1893–1989), wife of Cressida's uncle Sir Edgar Bonham-Carter (1870–1956).
3 'Spoiled'.
4 In act 3 (p. 66) a character speaks of 'the sun clocked in primitive time'.

theme is more sympathetic than I can say. I am reading Isherwood:[1] it is slightly disappointing, not sharp enough & who is Chalmers? & too silly in parts & too conventionally described for him: also the Mangeot bits are a little too Dickensy for me, it is all spoilt by knowing what a bogus musician he is & how badly he plays. I have also read Chateaubriand[2] who is, I think, absolutely magnificent: corrupt, but also pure with a Bellini sort of cantilena, with tremendous capacity for detaching, intensifying & adorning primary emotions, so that in spite of neo-medievalism, of fine writing etc. the prose is genuinely noble & expressive & has Miltonic properties of creating a world of colossal strength & beauty from the earliest beginning of any sentence. Have you ever read him? I shd like to see [you] & to see Inez, please; may I come to tea this or next week or even the week after? I hope you got good notices, I read none. I heard from someone Goronwy I think who was v. indignant that Lionel Hale[3] was rude: he always, you'll admit, was a repulsive & sordid figure, a Riverside aesthete, & one of the few genuine militant philistines, a Christian fascist when the hour comes.

Shaya

TO MARY FISHER

Postmark 15 April 1938 [*postcard*]

[49 Hollycroft Avenue]

I wish I could come: but my days are filled with a new source of discomfort: I have begun dictating Marx, my typist produced results which not only are a nuisance but shame me: e.g. when I say 'later' she writes 'letter': for 'Jew' 'due': & this is far the worst, for 'wise' 'ways': my elocutrix[4] has evidently produced no effect: the misprints are results not of an obscure but of a genteel voice. The book is 2½ times too long: I may take a bold course, &

---

1 *Lions and Shadows: An Education in the Twenties* (London, 1938). 'Chalmers' is Edward Upward (b. 1903), schoolmaster and author. Isherwood had been part-time secretary for a year to the Belgian violinist André Mangeot's string quartet in Chelsea, and remained a friend to his subsequently estranged wife Olive Mangeot ('Madame Cheuret' in *Lions and Shadows*), with whom he had an affair.

2 François Auguste René, Vicomte de Chateaubriand (1768–1848), French statesman (of varying allegiances), writer and influential precursor of the romantic movement in literature. IB may be referring to Chateaubriand's posthumously published autobiography *Mémoires d'Outre-Tombe* ('Memories from Beyond the Tomb'; Paris, 1849–50), to his accounts of travels in North America and Europe, or to his novels *Atala* (1801) and *René* (1802); his writings extolling Christianity seem less likely recipients of IB's enthusiasm.

3 Lionel Ramsay Hale (1909–77), journalist and playwright; theatre critic for the *News Chronicle* 1937–40.

4 See letters of July 1937 to Elizabeth Bowen from Brighton and 31 July 1937 to Mary Fisher, pp. 241 and 244 above.

propose to call on your father with it in the near future: I suddenly saw Dougle as Don G[iovanni] & Peggy as Leporello singing the Catalogue aria[1] the other day.

2 points: 1. Will you be in Oxford next week?

2. Would you like to come to Glyndebourne to Don Pasquale[2] for which I have 2 10/- tickets? on July 8.

TO JENIFER WILLIAMS

[1938?][3]

All Souls

Dear Jenifer

I own I was surprized when your Miss Pilley[4] without a murmur scribbled away in response to sentences a page or two pages long. From time to time I said, 'you might put in some colons commas etc.' & she nodded as if she had known me all her life (& mine). I ought, too to have thanked you before, she gave me lot of irrelevant pleasure by her obiter dicta: "is it all going to be like this, sir?" or "I think Miss Williams intends to read your book, sir, but you aren't making it easy for her': also I knew what she wanted exactly: she wanted K. Marx to be the son of a v. rich man who gave up all & died in poverty not far from Miss P.'s home. The second I more or less gave her, but I could not lie about the first: she asked wistfully once or twice whether Marx hadn't given up his family fortune to the struggle, & I did my best by pushing Engels forward: from time to time she wd exclaim 'you don't seem to like Mr Marx' & after I complete[d] a fulsome vignette of Frau Marx 'she seems to have all the virtues' 'she was rather boring' I said 'ah,' said Miss P. with pleasure 'it never does to be *that*'. She was plaintive about your office, sceptical about your love for it, & sympathique towards Mr [J. F.] Henderson, whose tears seemed to her well justified (as indeed all forms of protest). Cd you beg her to accelerate her typing? I feel hot & cold when I think of isolated sentences presented to your judgment: & shut out the thought. Douglas was here this week-end, quiet, subdued, polite, respectful, modest: I dare say because philosophy was discussed which fills

1 The aria in which Don Giovanni's conquests are listed for Elvira's benefit, sung by his servant Leporello in Mozart's eponymous opera.
2 Donizetti's opera.
3 See previous letter.
4 Probably a shorthand typist in the Home Office whom JW had produced to work for IB.

him with sentimental reverence. Will you be in O. at all this summer? Will you say?

Shaya.

I have forgotten the number of Hamp Sq. Wd you & Herbert[1] come to Don G. in July?

TO CRESSIDA BONHAM CARTER

[1938?]

All Souls

Dear Cressida:

The Busch Quartet,[2] Beethoven, Tolstoy, Kafka all belong to the same moral universe with clearly defined frontiers and an absolutely rigid scale of values which one can accept or reject, or, above all, defend or attack openly knowing what one will gain or lose. I suppose by Kafka I do mean the Castle: & not the Gt. Wall of China[3] etc. About which I want to say that: whereas Henry James & Debussy is accurate and as right as can be, Kafka is not a semitone[?] distortion of the normal universe which makes it therefore terrifying: in a sense the quality is that of a nightmare but it is so lucid and so not unexpected that the continual frustration which meets every move in every direction is not a growing terror or despair but on the contrary tends to throw into relief, of an almost Racine nobility, the characters & qualities round which the plot revolves, which are unexaggerated & undistorted, not sinister, not neurotic in the least, and above all communicable, whereas mystics are unable & unwilling to translate, & atonalists are all exploiting something, inventing new modes of reception, astonishing one by the reshuffling of old, slightly retouched cards, evoking neglected sensations etc. Kafka's figures are precisely lifesize, the values which are recognized by them are intelligible & familiar, the horror arises only if one deliberately ignores his semi-religious solution & justification: his purpose being so to explain that if you consider it with his eyes, there is no horror.

The irony also is not an ab extra[4] sardonic mockery but on the contrary the normal jokes which anyone makes & can afford to make about his familiar environment, in this case the mystic about his vision, save that the

1 JW and Herbert Hart lived together in Hampstead Square from 1937 to 1939.
2 In IB's (and others') view the finest string quartet of the inter-war period, founded by Adolf Busch (1891–1952). Its members were staunchly anti-Nazi and exiled themselves from Germany in the early 1930s.
3 A short story by Franz Kafka (1883–1924), written in 1918 or 1919 and left unpublished at his death.
4 'From outside'.

mystic is concerned with the outlines of a public *not* a private universe (although all the translators & reviewers chatter about the privacy of his world, grossly mistaking his innigkeit[1] for privacy, which is true of Debussy or Proust or even Mr Forster, but certainly not of Kafka who is a moralist & ipso facto about external affairs, affari esteri, the common world) in this case, & the vision is not a blinding revelation, v. white etc. as with St J. of the Cross[2] e.g., but a scrupulously & methodically constructed edifice made up of observed, untampered with, data of human behaviour & relations to the inanimate world of causal objects. The purpose is not either merely to describe or to analyse or to explain but to discover & proclaim means to freedom – once more the bourgeois virtues, the passionate working of the not to be transgressed against rights of the individual, the subject of Beethoven, Tolstoy the Busch quartet etc. etc. (all the frightful patter about self-realizing individuals & freedom in obedience to law appears unsullied & true in the playing of the Busch family, I wish I didn't have to repeat them so often it is a wonderfully silly name) the musical analogies, I admit, are partly in Bartok partly in Berg, but most of all in the posthumous quartets, in the A minor in particular, because the distortions, when they do occur, are not new uses for trite phrases, but an attempt to put stress even more sharply & unambiguously on permanent subjects, which now force themselves on attention, & even frighten, because of the extreme nakedness and colossal seriousness with which they are presented. Do you remember the remarkable account in Tolstoy, C. A. & Y.,[3] of the student who was supported by the professor who unfailingly ploughed him in the viva? or something like that: he is intended as a gigantic human symbol, & is a pure Kafka figure extremely unoverdrawn, not touching and in a sense rather repulsive & inwardly perhaps rather vulgar, but guilt-making & moving to the last degree. Whereas Schlick's murderer[4] & Dostoyevskian Christian peasants etc. are excluded as being carriers of some exaggerated, non-human, mad, non-secular mission, very terrifying and holy, but not human, & not to do with the regular, recurrent, obvious problems, therefore not of interest to the democrats in question.

It is, I am deeply sorry to say, 3 a.m. and I can literally not go on writing: else who knows how long & how serious this might not have become? and how repetitive & boring too. Not difficult to read but flatter & flatter. I must stop: I shall doubtless see you this evening: I extracted an enormous quantity of naive pleasure last Monday: Also I enjoyed my brief words with Wallace

1 'Depth'.
2 St John of the Cross, né Juan de Yepes y Alvarez (1542–91), Spanish Christian mystic and reformer of the Carmelite Order of monks.
3 *Childhood, Adolescence and Youth* (45/2).
4 See 178/2.

to an unexpected degree: I discover I like him very much, except that it is probably necessary to punish him ostentatiously for deliberate misbehaviour from time to time & for insufficient appreciation of the sacrosanct figure of Francis.

I agree entirely about one's own motives for flying from unexplained darkness, overpraising the light, repeating things about right & wrong because one doesn't do with impunity X, Y & Z whereas A & B do & nothing happens & every one (oneself included) likes it very much; but I cannot see that anything can be done about this at all: one announces that one only deals by the light of the sun: having said this openly & clearly one's sour grapes about the moon are perfectly honourable & one makes a thing of that in itself: one even sometimes goes to the length of saying slightly persecutingly that what cannot bear the rays of the sun cannot bear inspection at all, & had better not be. The somnambulist party respond with some acerbity. One answers back; being what one is, what else is one to do, & surely this is better than pseudo fairness according to which everything is of equal value & one must not make fuss about anything at all, only move unobtrusively & be kind?

    yrs
       Shaya

I ought to have said at once, I enjoyed your letter v. much indeed: the very fact that you are prepared to discuss is enormously nice.

The summer of 1938 was dominated politically by the events leading up to the Munich agreement, and for IB personally by his publishers' demand that he shorten his book on Marx. Also, since the completion of the book was imminent, and New College had offered him a Fellowship, he had resigned his seven-year All Souls Fellowship by Examination a year early, with effect from the end of the academic year 1937–8, and was preparing to move into New College.

TO HUMPHRY HOUSE

    Postmark 2 August 1938

                          49 Hollycroft Avenue

Dear Humphry,

I apologize profoundly for not writing until now, but I was prostrated by a discovery, not essentially very unexpected – about my book, which threw all my plans into disorder. The discovery is that, having been commissioned to write 50.000 words for the Home University L. I have, in fact, composed 85.000. They have no option but to make me cut. How does one eliminate 25.000 words?[1] at any rate how is a person like me to do it? having planned to be free & revise at leisure, with the agreeable sense of the transposability of bits & the insertability of others, I am now doomed to absolute torture. At least if they won't accept my bold plan which is to write 2 books in place of one. If they reject this – & how can they not – I can't possibly leave London, simply because of the need of environment in which I am allowed to be openly irritable at meals – you may not imagine the possibility – but it occurs to a sordid extent. If they do accept the division into 2 books, I shall finish the first within 3 days, & am free to come & stay & should love to, & would finish it while staying with you. I agree that meetings in London proper are detestable and constricted, but why should you not come & sit on the Heath here one afternoon or evening, it is delusively remote and extremely agreeable, cool, neither under nor overpopulated and with one or two inoffensive beer gardens about which are funny but not repulsive. That cd happen any day: I still hope to be able to come: but if not, will you not appear instead? say on Thursday afternoon?

Shaya.

TO ELISABETH JOACHIM[2]

5 August 1938

All Souls College

Dear Mrs Joachim

I cannot say how painfully the obituary notice in the *Times*[3] which came quite unexpectedly affected me. I shd like to say how greatly I, & my philosophical generation, respected and even revered your late husband – long before I met him I realized that he possessed the most distinguished and beautiful philosophical mind in Oxford – and indeed represented a combination of moral purity and strength and exquisite European culture which by merely existing creates standards and humanizes its surroundings. After I met him at New College I conceived and preserved an affection and admiration for his personal qualities – indeed let me sincerely assure you that all my philosophical contemporaries, whatever their views, agreements and

---

1 'I was no good at mathematics.' IB interviewed by Beata Polanowska-Sygulska, April 1988.
2 Elisabeth Joachim, widow of Harold Henry Joachim (1868–1938), Wykeham Professor of Logic and Fellow of New College 1919–35, who died on 30 July.
3 2 August 1938, 12.

disagreements, profoundly appreciated Professor Joachim, the remarkable harmoniousness of his life, his beliefs, his tastes, the fact that he alone among all the men who taught them and were set up over them, did possess a genuine, single, Weltanschauung, a[n] integrated outlook which expressed itself in all he did and said, and which allowed us all to realize the dignity of the subject and of a life spent in genuine cultivation of it: – a possibility which mere competence or even excellence at a subject treated as a technical accomplishment, does not convey. I am afraid I have not managed to say all that I wished to express – that your husband possessed an intellectual, moral, personal nobility and dignity – and charm and disinterestedness – that whereas others commented and niggled he not only philosophized but made his audiences and colleagues realize this fact – & that I never hope to meet his like again. Once more I beg you to accept my warmest and most genuine sympathy.

 yrs v. sincerely
  Isaiah Berlin

please do not trouble to acknowledge this

New College Archive

TO JOHN HILTON

 [August? 1938]

49 Hollycroft Avenue

Dearest John:

 I sat patiently within earshot & waited all day. So you see what comes of flirting or making light promises. Your 2^d & 3^d cousine[1] I saw, she is very nice & highly energetic. She expressed a warm desire to see you. As for me: I cannot say what vinegar your words about K. Marx are to my wounds: indeed I am leaving to-day (Monday) for Folkestone (Hotel Metropole. Very gay.) to cut 30.000 words out of my MS. in 4 days.[2] God knows how this is done. Then I go to Ireland till about 12th Sept. Then probably to Oxford. *When* will you be in Burford? write to Folkestone or All Souls: something may quite well be arrangeable provided you abandon your view of me as in general not there & about nothing. My love to Peggy whom I haven't seen

---

1 Ingrid Warburg: see 88/1.
2 Both IB's original manuscript and the first, longer, typescript, survive almost complete (despite IB's professed belief that he threw them away). Perhaps the full version, or at any rate the most significant excised passages, may one day be published.

for a decade, literally,[1] & whose stylized image I faithfully carry with me, anxious for content.

yrs
    Isaiah

TO MENDEL BERLIN

Friday [26 August 1938, *postcard*]

Loughan[n]ilaun, Eire

Book practically finished in sense of being cut: to 58-000 words. Now: quotations, insertions, copying. Very well indeed. Leaving here Sunday, maybe with Day in Dublin interpolated.

Shaya.

TO CRESSIDA BONHAM CARTER

[28 August 1938]

Shelbourne Hotel, Dublin

Dear Cressida
    You must believe me. I am sitting in the Writing and Reading Room of the Shelbourne Hotel Dublin. On my left are two fishermen from the West talking about fish. But on my write [*sic*] (believe me) is Mr Yeats chanting verse in a corner to a young woman & what appears to be her brother.[2] It is perfectly audible & the verse may be hers, & is to me quite unknown. It is absurd and sublime that being forced to spend a night here alone, one immediately comes upon Mr Yeats, in full tide. My last week was spent under exceedingly primitive and genuinely agreeable conditions on an island in a lake. It gives me opportunities of producing Austrian[?] dishes which I am quite good at making. A man has just come in who began at once (to his Irish host) 'As you know I am a Republican Senator: and I hate Roosevelt[3]

---

1 An exaggeration: he cannot have met her earlier than 1930, according to JRH.
2 Ethel Edith Mannin (1900–84), popular novelist, and her fiancé (whom she married later that year) Reginald Reynolds (1905–58), Quaker, pacifist, writer, traveller, friend of Gandhi. They looked alike: hence IB's guess that they were siblings. Yeats, who had had an affair with Mannin a few years before and remained close to her, gave them dinner at the hotel on 28 August.
3 Franklin Delano Roosevelt (FDR) (1882–1945), lawyer, Democrat, US President 1933–45 (the only President to be re-elected three times) during the Depression – in response to which he instigated his 'New Deal' legislation – and the Second World War. Brought the US into the war after the attack on Pearl Harbor (December 1941), died with victory in sight, a fortnight before the inaugural UN conference (April 1945) for which he had campaigned. He contracted polio in the 1920s and never regained the use of his legs. His portrait is on the dime (ten-cent coin).

politically; but I like a man with ideas. . .' etc. intrinsically not particularly
interesting: but there is something absolutely overwhelming about a city in
which everybody is fully coloured, in which everyone is always saying
everything explicitly, over-explicitly & to the extent of lying very often in
order to convince themselves & others of their own possession of properties,
if you see what I mean, the Country is incurably beautiful & like art: the
grass is a violent green: the avenues of trees rivers & people's faces are
expressive to the last degree, the people in the Smoking room of this hotel,
with & without mad eyes or whiskers cd all occur in Turgenev short stories.
I am in fact both happy and nostalgic, because, of course, the fact that there
should be a pocket of the 19ᵗʰ century preserved is merely exceptional, & not
in itself so very exhilarating. Life on an island however – I don't know how
nesophile[1] you are – by candlelight etc. at an immensely easy level, with
unprofessional fishing & a really enormous sense of leisure is my conception
of 19ᵗʰ century Russian small gentry, which is what I really mean by saying
I like Russians so much, not the genuine aristocracy which is mostly horrible
& really corrupt & dull. Which brings us to Herzen. I am very glad indeed
that you like it. Do you find it at all dull? You see, if one, for example, really
prefers French or Latin literature generally to the Russo-Germans, how can
one not find it dull? at least in long patches? I admire French inquisitiveness
& sharpness & a certain unsentimental appetite for first hand experience etc.
very much, as e.g. in Diderot, Balzac, Maupassant, but really I feel fearfully
unsympathetic to it on the whole: I can't bear so much cut out, such linearity
& anxiety to come to the point, to say it once, & then to move on. Whereas
the Russians (& up to a point the Germans in general) except Dostoyevsky,
describe long, solid emotions & characters, on & on, which inevitably involves moralizing & irrelevance, but on the other absorbs one, so that,
unlike one's attitude when reading e.g. Henry James or Flaubert, one is not,
all the time, aware of how good it is, or how well expressed, page by page &
description by description: but proceeds at some submarine level, at which
what[?] [one] reads[?] is absorbed & expanded, & it does not occur to one to
note the quality of the water: or even to note that one is in fact in water, or
how deep. I am sorry: this is like a Sunday newspaper. Meanwhile the two
American politicians are racketing on & on in dull monotonic voices, screen-
ing Mr Yeats & his party, who are romantically bending forward round
a dimly lit tobacco-table. I wish I had the courage to introduce myself to
Mr Yeats, explain that I did sit next to him at lunch once, etc. but in fact no
such thing can be done. To-morrow I go to stay with Elizabeth Cameron, &
then back to Oxford. Where furnishing etc. begins. Mrs Ayer has, I think

---

1 A neologism from Greek: 'island-loving'.

suddenly lost interest, & her carpenter won't answer my letters. If one lived in Ireland all colour problems wd settle themselves so easily. Will you not come to Ireland one day? really, I assure you, one doesn't look about like a curious dilettante or conoisseur: one genuinely experiences emotions. I have had a series of affectionate telephone conversations with Con,[1] but didn't go to stay, since I am frightened of his family. His voice on trunk calls is even more endearing than in life, he continues to say 'Mmm?'. his vividness of language is, I am sure, greatly accounted for by the appearance of every thing here. I wish the Americans wd stop their chatter: Mr Yeats looks wonderfully majestic at the moment. I had a letter from David [Wallace] too, & one from Ben, who, being plainly offended with Jeremy reports curtly that he (David) cannot have him (Ben) to stay because Jeremy gave him jaundice in Karlsbad; K. is a *hideous* town and I am sorry for D. who is extremely funny about the person[2] he calls his one time mother. Ben has no taste in persons whatever. He has just met a fearful bore to whom he expresses warm admiration. However, on introspection, I find I like him, without exact reason, a good deal. Much more than Jeremy. Herzen wd not have liked either, I think. Oh dear, Herzen. There is no writer, & indeed no man I shd like to be like, & to write like, more. I agree with every judgment, & whenever I read in the ten volumes, almost anywhere, I become fascinated & moved at once. The entire, rather ponderous, moralistic attitude, the wit, malice, imagination, umanitá,[3] uninhibitedness about going on for as long as the moral emotion persists, gaiety, civilizedness, etc. etc. I admire more than I can say. His short stories are weak Turgénev like things, but again such as make one admire the author, dull but noble failures, the ends are so sympathetic. The test really is whether or not one is bored. I must stop if I am not to imitate his least good qualities. I did write you a letter some 3 weeks ago, about 4 days after our visit to the theatre, rather trivial & slightly incoherent, I think to ask you about where you had seen the horses or the material for curtains, also + a lot of stuff about the Gaité Parisienne[4] which I had just then seen: it began as a postcard, climbed over on the back, no envelope large enough could be found, it entered two envelopes, I think I actually got to the point of putting a stamp on it, but then didn't send it off because it seemed too silly. On the whole I am sure that is a mistake: one ought to write whatever one feels inclined & risk one's correspondent's feelings: it is extremely agreeable to receive letters written for their own

---

1 Con O'Neill's family (his father was Sir Hugh O'Neill, later Lord Rathcavan) lived in Bally-mena, Co. Antrim.
2 Namely?
3 'Humanity' (normally 'umanità').
4 *La Gaîté parisienne* is a ballet put together in 1938 from Offenbach's music.

sakes, almost the nicest thing there is, & I was most grateful for yours. Reading anything by candlelight is infinitely delightful, one reads more slowly & much more enjoyably. I believe that when you say that your letter is awful etc. you really believe this, since I am so excessively well acquainted with that feeling: experiencing it myself as I do at the moment, genuinely. but as I am prolix & you are not, it is likely to be truer in my case. Mr Yeats has gone, the Americans are intolerable. To morrow I return to candlelight (malicious words suddenly came up – about the fact that anyone cd get anything out of David W. with sufficient wine & Nell Gwynn candles) I *must* finish K. Marx, of which now only 7000 words remain to be cut: it is an absolutely hateful process, every evening I count up little drops of blood & measure the cup: all the purple passages are gone, & now the turn of the facts has come, towards which I now feel vindictive & eliminate them gaily. One last word about Herzen – that if anyone were alive now who talked as he must have done – vide the memoirs of others about him – one wd never listen to anyone else. I am really sorry about this idiotic straggling document.
 Shaya.

I think even this[1] attractive, is it so, or does Dublin merely glow for me after finishing 'Hail and Farewell'?[2]

I haven't read a word of this. Even for me an absolute jungle. As for Ben, David, Samson, & Delilah *surely* you know the feeling of saying things which one knows one mustn't, for no reason at all, with a sense of agreeable fatality; not even being terribly fascinated?

TO MENDEL BERLIN

 Sunday [28 August 1938, *postcard*]

            Shelbourne Hotel, Dublin

Here I am, in civilization again. To-morrow I go to Bowen's Court, Kildorrery, C° Cork. Marx shall be sent off on the 31st. As I am allowed 65 000 words[3] (publish[er's] letter) a great load has dropped off, hooray!
 Shaya

---

1 By now the letter has overflowed on to a card that displays a green shamrock bearing the hotel's name.
2 The Irish writer George Moore's three-volume autobiography (1911–14).
3 As published the book runs to some 75,000 words.

TO CRESSIDA BONHAM CARTER

2 September 1938 [*postcard*]

Bowen's Court, Kildorrery, Co. Cork

[. . .]¹ Dublin excessively mad? *If so* I *apologize.* [. . .] thrown into a state by the truly odd surroundings, Mr Yeats the [. . .] Senators etc. & in any case was in the heightened state one is in after a very long rickety journey, a meal at the end of a fast, and being suddenly abandoned by all one's companions. My mise en scène has altered once more: I am now gravely engaged on transcribing my MS in an immensely tall, bare, handsome room, with four candles burning and a general[?] Rembrandt, dramatized foreground. Bats beat against the windows and herons squawk, and one writes slowly with colossal pleasure over each letter. The only thing I still stand by is feeling about Herzen, the combination of public & private properties, humanism & grand seigneurishness, understanding one's jokes and old fashioned sublimity. But again I must stop.

IB

[. . .] about the curtains, wd you [. . .] – here, or to All Souls: but [. . .] Ireland is much nicer, I am now convinced [. . .] Vicenza with any number of Tiepolos: do you know Hythe?²

TO MENDEL BERLIN

Postmark 8 September 1938 [*postcard*]

[Cork, Eire]

Thank you for your letter. I shall come home *next week.* K. Marx will be finished this week-end. The mere transcription of unreadable pages takes so long. I am in Cork this evening. Very agreeable town.

Love.

Shaya

1 The stamp has been cut out of the card: hence the gaps, here and in the postscript. IB evidently begins with a query about his 28 August letter from the Shelbourne Hotel (pp. 277–80 above).
2 Near Folkestone in Kent. Elizabeth Bowen had lived there as a child.

TO MENDEL BERLIN

Postmark [Saturday] 10 September 1938 [*postcard*]

Bowen's Court

I now have plans clear: Marx will be posted on Monday: I shall leave on Wednesday & arrive in Oxford on Thursday to watch my man mix paint for my room: & may come home the same evening & go back to move furniture. Plait-il?[1] wd you send letters on Monday, if they look private, still here?

Love
    Shaya

IB returned to England at a time of political crisis. The Prime Minister, Neville Chamberlain, had begun a series of meetings with Hitler in an attempt to avert the threat of a war over Germany's demand that it should annexe the Sudetenland. The first of these, at Berchtesgarden on 15 September,[2] raised hopes that war might be avoided, but disagreements, and hence preparations for war, continued until the Munich Conference of 29–30 September, when Britain and France accepted that Czechoslovakia should cede the Sudetenland to Germany.

TO ELIZABETH BOWEN

Saturday [after 15 September 1938]

All Souls

Dear Elizabeth,
    I have never – this is really true – had so much to thank for before in my life, I don't in the least know how to convey it, the overcompensation against my emotional mother + life in England & in Oxford has so far atrophied all my natural capacity for expressing direct personal feeling, that I must necessarily hope that they will get expressed by some cumulative effect of everything else one says, the alternative is frightful Henry James circumnavigation with allusions to a state too sacred to be unlocked or described etc. & all this fearful embarrassment because I don't know how to say that I enjoyed myself enormously, that in the middle of it I was conscious of inability to repay, that I theoretically condemned {that} the whole complex of payment-repayment, but that for all that I was pursued by a sense

1 'Is that all right?'
2 Where the Foreign Secretary Lord Halifax is reputed to have mistaken Hitler for a doorman.

of insufficient sensibility to offer in return, that I hope that my well known ponderous inadaptability didn't get on your nerves too much, that the possibility of finishing K. Marx in peace is due to you solely, that my affection, admiration, & a circumambient complex of unstateable feeling has risen to a point which I shd be angry if I could articulate – I can't continue with this, I hope I hope I convey, that I have induced ideas. Let me rather give an account of the succeeding hours.

Upon leaving you all at Fermoy[1] (as astringent a scene as even I cd desire) I found myself in the company, as you know, of Mrs Walton,[2] who spoke to me with the special air adapted to one who was at once a literary funny & a friend of the picaresque Foster.[3] That is, she spoke slowly, & apologized for every reference to local life, lamented her husband's ruthless devotion to his Irish home[4] and the pleasures of her youth & of London: she complained too of her husband's light head, & predicted that he would behave badly after a sherry party, when he wd dine in Bowen's Court to meet Mr Lennox Robinson.[5] She supposed she wd hear of it later: these things had happened more than once, & she was tired of inventing ad hoc explanations of it to allay shocked neighbours. This increasing intimacy, which I supported by a series of pontoon like Maurice 'yes' sounds, was interrupted by the arrival of a friend of hers, called Reggie certainly, & possibly also Stern or Stearn or Stirn. He greeted me with great affability, told gallant stories of insults to foreign station masters, & was finally left alone with me, after Mrs W.'s departure. Thereupon we settled down to a solid hour of discussion of the horse trade – I inquired, with I thought not really excessive crassness, about yearlings, hunters etc. being definitely pleased to see no look of frustration in my companion's eyes: I learnt a great deal about the habits of Cork horsebreeders, verified the story of the President's descent,[6] & altogether enjoyed the full pleasures of a highbrow behaving unfamiliarly without excessive loss of dignity. We became very

1 Town in County Cork.
2 Diana Florence Walton (1904–83), a neighbour of Elizabeth Bowen. One of her sons remembers her talking of the train journey from Fermoy with IB, and reports that he 'resolutely disdained any interest in looking through the window'. In the 1920s she had lived at Islip, near Oxford, where – as a beautiful young woman living close by – she was much in demand at undergraduate dances. Maybe these are among 'the pleasures of her youth' that she lamented, and also one of the reasons why she regretted 'her husband's ruthless devotion to his Irish home', for whose management she was responsible.
3 John Foster is alleged to have had an affair with a relative of Diana Walton, Diana Hill (1911–98), an allegation whose plausibility is perhaps increased by IB's remark, however hyperbolic it may be, that Foster 'went to bed with more ladies than anybody in the twentieth century' (MI Tape 20).
4 Clifford, in a magnificent setting in the north of Co. Cork, overlooking the river Blackwater.
5 (Esmé Stuart) Lennox Robinson (1886–1958), Irish playwright and theatre director.
6 Douglas Hyde (1860–1949), of Elizabethan settler descent, became first President of Ireland in 1938.

attached on the boat & in the English train – he is a revolting little man – it
was very full & we shared a sleeping car. In some wayside station at 6. am.
men in pyjamas ran out & bought newspapers, with Chamberlain's journey
in them: 'the war is postponed' said my horsedealer & then something like
'whizzbang' & went to sleep again. I never, as Turgenev, wd say, saw him
again. He was a very minor cad of about 1870, & continued the cord with the
past, which didn't snap till one reached London. Oxford was in a state of
absolute enchantment. The sun shone, the town was empty & extremely
beautiful, the Warden of New College was walking very slowly in a panama
hat, & Mr Rowse was mild & almost deferential. I spent a few hours there, &
the sleepless night & the general state of unrest kept me afloat – I am sure
you know the condition, in a state of abnormally acute sensibility, irrational
ecstasy & suspended animation, all until one reached London, & collapsed
into the pedestrian mood of my parents. On the next morning & through the
whole of the next day I went through a period of misery and nostalgia which
persists still & which nothing can cure. All the faces of ordinary passers-by –
even one's friends, Freddie whom I called on, & who said how much he
wished he'd been in Ireland – in Bowenscourt I mean – & Stuart whom I met
by accident waiting for Renée, & who looked at me really like a frightened
gazelle lest she come & find us together & demand some explanation, until
I left him feeling at least 25 years his senior, & very grave, bearded, operatic,
melancholy & wise, all lacked lustre – I don't know how else to put it, after
the terrific temperament & glitter of everything in County Cork, persons,
physical objects, the weather. I saw Stephen almost out of desire to achieve
contact with a definite person, & he was that, certainly, but plaintive, saying
Inez had written a wonderful novel sadly, & then on & on again about Spain.
The sense of being driven out of paradise was so acute – I suppose Turgenev
felt it when forced to leave the West & return to his literary coterie in Russia
– that I am resolved not to let it happen so easily, to create possibility of
returning to Ireland, at specified intervals however rare, but definite, which
wd give stability to one's hopes. You will perhaps rightly suspect a Salzburg
once more. Possibly. Except that Salzburg scenes used to return definitely
theatricalized, definitely as artificial & sentimentalized as they were meant to
be by Reinhardt[1] or somebody, whereas my memory of isolated place &
times in Bowen's Court: notably the broad stairs, & the moment before
turning the handle of the dining room in the morning, & the beginning of
enchanted life (I apologize if this is badly put), the moment of carrying a
candlestick from one room into the other, the stern reality of aunt Annie's[2]

1 Max Reinhardt (429/1).
2 Anne Marcella Cole Bowen, one of EB's paternal aunts.

room, & the splendid sensation of the sanctity & hardships of a dedicated life, the infinite pleasure of one's bed afterwards, & Curiosities of Literature[1] & To the North[2] by candlelight (the latter I've been stupid about, & left in Oxford on Thursday & cannot finish till Tuesday when I return & then I will send back promptly) the (I thought) much too short walk with you & David C. – again like M. de Charlus,[3] why couldn't it go on & on? releasing one during its second portion & allowing one to say all sorts of things? Even the official theatre – Mr O'Mahoney[4] in knickerbockers drinking claret decoratively on the steps, & treating the company to his fund of laid up erudition & charm & the evening walk among the sneezing troops, & the complete unbelievability of it even at the time to me (I should *never* dare to confess this to you at the moment, I am certain) & above all the terrific allusiveness of everything to everything else, the sense of everything as chargé du passé et gros de l'avenir, I can't go on; here there is a lull, the newspapers read like a cheap serial, Chamberlain from having been a sad, mean, bedraggled figure is a national hero, Runciman[5] sold the Czechs piecemeal & bit by bit while he prepared I think to sell them wholesale – Miss Grant Duff's book at 6[d] in Pelican on Czechoslovakia[6] comes out in a half million edition to-morrow – theatres are half-empty, the ballet more so still, I shall return to Oxford with relief, it is very self-possessed & frigid: I can hardly believe that I have been as happy as I have: I shall return his detective story to Alan I think it is very good. My love to Noreen[7] who has no flaws. And to Humphry when he comes I can't bear to finish this letter. I must go.

This is inconceivably inadequate – these & not when writing K.M. is what I really long to be able to write, a sentiment which is absolutely truthfully stated – & wd rightly have been despised by Flaubert or Tolstoy equally. This is like inability to go to bed. The pleasure of nostalgia is too acute. I've now suddenly recollected the Victorian evening in Cork, & the appearance of everyone in the box, & the directness and keenness of all one's

---

1 *Curiosities of Literature: Consisting of Anecdotes, Characters, Sketches, and Observations, Literary, Critical, and Historical* (London, 1791), published anonymously by Isaac d'Israeli, father of Benjamin Disraeli.

2 EB's novel, published by Gollancz in 1932.

3 Baron (Palamède) de Charlus, a character in Marcel Proust's *À la recherche du temps perdu* (Paris, 1913–27). Probably a reference to the male brothel scene early in the last volume, *Le Temps retrouvé*, where Charlus is beaten and then stays to chat.

4 Eoin 'Pope' O'Mahony (1904–70), barrister by profession, a great raconteur and broadcaster who frequently discussed clan history on the radio, a familiar bearded figure travelling the roads of Ireland, and a well-known visitor at Bowen's Court.

5 Walter Runciman, 1st Viscount Runciman of Doxford (1870–1949), head of the mission to Czechoslovakia July–September 1938. See Shiela Grant Duff, *The Parting of Ways* (57/6: see p. 58), 173 ff.

6 S. Grant Duff, *Europe and the Czechs* (Harmondsworth, 1938).

7 Noreen Colley, a much younger cousin of EB, daughter of her Aunt Edie Colley.

sensations, as if filtered & intensified by the period frame in which they occurred. I must end on a cautionary note. As I was driving out of Oxford in a taxi, the Broad being blocked, past Wadham, I saw Maurice contentedly in its doorway, surveying & approving. I stopped the taxi, & was at once rushed over the house, the red carpets, late Victorian desks (hideous I thought I must confess, & oddly vulgar for M. is this the David C. virus working insensibly? I *must* acquire an antidote *at once*) cellars, attics, bathrooms, bedrooms, sculleries & kitchens, he was well, benevolent, extremely nice, & colossally happy, & not wholly unlike Markie[1] – a character I am prepared to defend always & against anyone.

My love
Shaya

[W[arden] Fisher quite polite about K.M.].[2]

TO ELIZABETH BOWEN

Tuesday [27 September 1938]

All Souls

Dear Elizabeth,

I am now here, in the process of moving, & it is really the most unexpectedly melancholy procedure. It is drizzling slightly, as always when one is moving, & all my colleagues are seated round me, in muted gloom, even the boisterous irresponsible very old shamed by the elderly & priggish. Maurice is roaring away indeed, but more quietly than usual, Wade Gery has decided that liberalism is at an end, & one must act resolutely, & declares that he weeds his garden with greater ferocity than usual, pulling & cutting bitterly. I escaped from the horrors of my half evacuated room to the town hall, where I was detailed to assemble gas masks, which I enjoyed very much. It was a scene of indescribable confusion. The organ played, a vast number of don's wives sat hunched over tables tying & cutting, while N. Oxford ladies & even scouts wives, with a pleasing sense of equality before this common danger, mixed freely & loudly among them; my partner was a formidable harridan of about fifty who said she had been through six wars and two revolutions, & then, after a pause, 'and matrimonial trouble' she added. I more than ever believe in the necessity of preserving standards of civilized life against the frightful warmth & intimacy of wartime cosiness which here at any rate has begun to develop already. I suppose I had better

1 A character in *To the North* based on Maurice Bowra: see 288/4.
2 IB's outer brackets.

think of evacuating my parents, to Headington perhaps. Rumours are wonderfully rife, agitated groups in streets & all.

The government is alleged to be coming here (which is v. unwelcome), the university is not to begin, refugees are being prepared for or rather not being prepared for, dons have been told to sit & wait & not move anywhere, everyone is busy filling forms all the time; but making gasmasks gives one an agreeable sensation of truly productive labour, like being a doctor, I have all sorts of Zola sentiments while pulling on & smoothing thick rubber bands, while in another corner my friend Mr Chilver is teaching a baller[1] from N. Oxford this and that. I perceive that it will be more necessary than ever to dig mines & furnish one's means of intellectual security – I don't think the emotions will be touched much this time. I couldn't not send you the books I did – I beg you not to acknowledge them as such[2] – since they form part of my ramparts, & were what I was brought up on to a large extent (not Diderot I add), & now fuse with Ireland & Bowen's Court, & the particular pieces of furniture & appearance of places, at particular times, & memories of particular hours of the day, & genuinely form a solid nineteenth century whole which I shall never abandon. I am sure my sentiments about B' Court & everything which belongs to that is much more solid & unsentimental & affects all one does much more, than simply the recollection of particular forms of pleasure in particular places (e.g. Salzburg) being in my case much more closely interwoven with what I look for anyhow. I shd be fascinated to hear what you think of Herzen himself – whether you think him dull e.g. – I feel a passion for him, & a dislike for his poetical wife which is more sustained than one's feeling about real people, or Tolstoy characters. His particular gentlemanliness & irony & unsqualid disillusionment & undramatized rhetoric I find alluring beyond words.

Maurice has invented some new jokes such as (when asked abstruse questions of a certain kind) 'In such cases I always ask who is Pernod Père',[3] & a few more which will doubtless assist us during the troubled days. In my train Lord Tweedsmuir & Billy[4] travelled in sombre silence at diagonally opposite ends of a carriage. Sparrow (this is an awful petite chronique) finds it difficult to decide between peace & honour. I told M. about the Denniston–Maynard K[eynes] conversation,[5] it was excellently received, D.

---

1 Defined in the *OED* as 'a workman who charges puddled bars into a balling or reheating furnace'.
2 On 30 September she thanked him for 'Tolstoi's *Childhood and Youth* [. . .] [Sergey Aksakov's] *A Russian Gentleman* [. . .] The Herzen memoirs, the Diderots, the others [. . .]'.
3 Jules François Pernod (1827–1916), founder of Pernod Père et Fils, maker of the liqueur.
4 John Buchan and his son William.
5 Not recorded by Robert Skidelsky in his three-volume biography of Keynes.

earned marks, & May. K. lost none. Oh dear. More & more triviality, I am
sure, will alone rescue us. The attempt to live up to the situation, face the
facts, etc. is bound to lead to dreary insincerity. When will you return?
perhaps it wd be best not to? I shall return To the North to-morrow. [. . .]¹

Interpolated:² cd you please tell Humphry, if there, that I shall be in Oxford
probably uninterruptedly now: & that he had better come & stay a night if
the Oxford & Bucks Light something or other³ don't take all my rooms.

I like To the North enormously: Markie is wonderfully unhorrifying &
even sympathetic, Emmeline is, to me personally, almost repugnant, but
Lady Waters is more horrible, more like something frisson causing out of a
childhood terror, more loathsome, unbearable even to think of, than any
character real or imaginary. About Cecilia I shd like to write separately, if I
may.⁴

In October 1938 IB became a Fellow of New College.

TO ELIZABETH BOWEN

[*c.*3 October 1938]

New College

Dear Elizabeth
    Thank you for your letter & for your book.⁵ I am reading the latter
now in the best early Bloomsbury tradition, on packing cases, in chaos, in a
curious liver coloured room where nothing will ever fall into any kind of
pattern. A sudden gust of indignation against Mrs Ayer & fripperies swept
over me this morning, which took the form of tearing out all the plywood
frou-frous made by her underling, revealing the original ugly marble & brass

---

1 The rest of the letter is missing.
2 What IB introduces as 'Interpolated' is written on the back of a sheet, and therefore cannot be
   assigned a definite position.
3 The Oxfordshire and Buckinghamshire Light Infantry, usually known as the Ox & Bucks.
4 Markie, the gross, over-assertive bullying male protagonist of *To the North* is superficially based
   on the personal style and appearance of Maurice Bowra, as EB admitted. Emmeline is the
   masochistic heroine, Cecilia her sister-in-law. Lady Waters is an overwhelming and interfering
   minor character.
5 *The Death of the Heart* (published by Gollancz on 3 October 1938), in which the beautiful,
   intense, unhappy, potentially very neurotic sixteen-year-old orphan Portia Quayne may owe
   something to IB's account of Rachel Walker, though IB would not necessarily have been
   forcibly stuck by this. The loathsome Eddie (no surname), to whom Portia attaches herself, is
   openly and closely based on Goronwy Rees (who threatened to sue), including his tendency to
   burst into tears.

which I now look contentedly upon, as representing the 19th century & solid worth. I definitely prefer hideous thick stone to the prettiest thin painted concealments with which everything was enshrouded. Your novel robs me of sleep at nights, it is colossally absorbing, although I doubt if I shall ever experience sensations comparable to those induced by the House in Paris which I read in a night in a condition approaching my equivalent of hysteria & exalténess. I couldn't *stop* the Warden from asking you to lunch so I suppose we shall meet there: It wouldn't, I suppose, be conceivably possible for you to take a train earlier than 11.15? By teatime my guest wd have arrived – but perhaps there cd be a walk in my new, dank, but rather fine garden – full of heavy reliable character, & growing plants like Bishop of Llandaff.[1] The Ayers are arriving en famille (i.e. + Stuart) to-morrow, I am not sure I am not glad to have secured dignified isolation from that situation. My last night at All Souls was very sentimental. Mr Rowse said he wasn't a great friend of Mr de Beer,[2] & was astonished to hear he had enquired so tenderly after him. The Proustian malice we use vis a vis each other at least serves to remind me of the necessity of keeping up standards against the ocean of mediocrity and amiable crassness in which I now move so self-consciously. I have bought Flaubert's letters, & wish Maurice were a nicer character & not nice only. It is 1.15 a.m. & I must return to Death of the Heart. I shall talk ceaselessly of it when we meet.

love
   Shaya

Many of the older generation of non-academic Fellows whom IB knew at All Souls had supported a policy of appeasement throughout the 1930s, particularly Geoffrey Dawson, Lionel Curtis and their circle. As IB put it, 'They didn't say "Hurray for Hitler";[3] they said that resisting him was unlikely to succeed. 'They didn't talk about appeasement openly with us, but they brought sympathisers with them and talked in the privacy of their own rooms. There they would practically have committee meetings.' The younger generation of dons, almost all fiercely opposed to Hitler, Mussolini and Franco, were more militant. The Munich Agreement consequently evoked mixed reactions, but IB's response was unequivocal:

From 1933 onwards, I was fully aware of Nazi horrors, more than most. I knew it was unique, terrible and didn't for a single moment think we

---

1 A variety of dahlia.
2 Probably Gavin Rylands be Beer (1899–1972), Prize Fellow, Merton, 1923–38, Jenkinson Lecturer in Embryology 1926–38.
3 MI Tape 8, from which the two following extracts are also taken.

could have peace with them. My father didn't. When Munich happened, my father said exactly what Blum said in Paris: shame and relief. Thank God no war. I felt indignant. Upset. Deeply depressed by Munich. A betrayal. Straightforwardly. People divided in quite interesting ways in Oxford. [. . .] In All Souls there was a lot of open disagreement.

TO MENDEL BERLIN

[October/November 1938]

As from New College

Dear Pa,

Thank you for your letter. I am settling in slowly, continually causing minor alterations to be made to this or that in my room. The painting of the walls downstairs is still incomplete. Upstairs is virtually finished. Mother can come on Wed. if she wd like; at 3 p.m. wd be the best time, I wd meet her at the platform, but *only* if she wd wait on the platform itself till I arrive. I'll go into my financial position in the bank to-day, & send you your cheque made out to Brown Shipley:[1] is that correct? Otherwise no news. I am really quite happy in my new milieu: everyone is anxious to be nice, even Joseph; in All Souls all the old conservatives are very nervous, & do not really defend Chamberlain. Dawson has not yet dared to appear. They all want to fight for the colonies. But they won't. I feel absolutely certain that one day a Russian–Slav bloc will form in Europe & sweep away the German penetration. The mood is depressed. Everyone is conscious of defeat. Buy next week's Spectator my colleague Hudson is writing an interesting article on Palestine for it.[2]

Vale.

Shaya

In later years IB was dismissive of his talents as a tutor and feared his students had not benefited from his teaching: 'I used to take to pieces what they said. I didn't really feed them with positive doctrine. I probably left too many of them in a broken state. That's possible. The clever ones were all right. The second- and third-rate ones may not have profited.'[3] But the memories of one of IB's pupils at this time, James Douglas,[4] are

---

1 Merchant bank in London.
2 Two unsigned articles on Palestine appeared in the *Spectator* at about this time: 'The Problem of Palestine', 21 October 1938, 641–2, and 'Deadlock in Palestine', 11 November 1938, 797–8.
3 MI Tape 5.
4 James Alexandre Thomas Douglas (b. 1919), New College PPE 1938–41.

entirely favourable, even though a tutorial with IB could be an unsettling experience:

He was much the most brilliant and stimulating teacher I ever met. My tutorials with him would be in his rooms in the New Buildings. There he kept an odd collection of things which he had bought off the street traders who in those days sold things from the pavement in Regent Street, and also a magnificent gramophone with a hand-made papier mâché trumpet, the then current equivalent of today's high fidelity equipment. As I would read my essay to him, he would wander round the room toying with his collection: a toy cow would fall off an inclined plane – 'I am so sorry! Please continue'; a blast of Verdi would emerge from the gramophone's trumpet as he accidentally dropped the needle on the disc – 'I am so sorry! Please continue.' Until I got used to it, I would be firmly convinced that he had not heard a word. This was a fatal illusion. 'At one point you say . . .' – and a careful exhaustive cross-examination of the whole argument would develop. At the end of the tutorial, I would be exhausted but also stimulated and interested.[1]

TO JOHN HILTON

[Late 1938?][2]

New College

Dear John

It is some time since you've written or shown any signs of being: apart from reflexions on my lack of chivalry no rumours about you have even begun to reach me. The enclosure will remind you of an arrangement entered into long ago. But it is v. important that you should write. Very. I am at the moment busily teaching incomplete inversion[3] to a class of Etonian rowing men. Whenever the incongruity of the situation overcomes me I have to go into my bedroom for a few moments to drink water and recover. It is extremely odd.

    yrs

      I.B.

---

1 From an email from James Douglas to the editor, 28 May 2003.
2 Placed here by pure guesswork.
3 A phenomenon in formal logic.

TO MARIE AND MENDEL BERLIN

[Early March 1939]

New College

Dear Pa & Ma,

1. I am writing my lecture in note-form

2. *Please* send me Tosc. Tickets.[1] I *promise* that I shall only barter away a maximum of 1–2 tickets for such as I haven't got. Which will leave (a) 1 ticket for each concert (b) extra tickets for about 3 of them which I shall send back to you at once. Do you want anything for the Beethoven *Missa Solemnis*? Or only orchestral concerts? & will you order 2 tickets for Menuhin[2] in Alb. Hall (at about 8/6) or 3 if mother can come? (I have 3 Missa Solemnis tickets. If you don't require any, I shall get rid of 2).

I have absolutel no news, as Mr Kaplan wd say.[3] Had dinner with the Ettinghausens + Bentschen[4] etc. wonderful corner of traditionalism in this town. If only they weren't both so terribly ugly. I shrink from all thought of the child's[5] appearance.

I am arranging the future of a local Arab,[6] whose friend I have become. I feel sure that this sort of bienveillance, quite apart from my liking for him will bear some sort of agreeable fruit one day. Our relations are touching – he is a Syrian, a *presbyterian*! (missionaries). A. von Trott has been here. Honest he cannot be called. But with much charm.

love

Shaya

1 Toscanini conducted the BBC Symphony Orchestra in an all-Beethoven series of concerts at the Queen's Hall, London, in May 1939; the *Missa Solemnis* was performed at the final concert, on 28 May.

2 The violinist Yehudi Menuhin (1916–96), a distant cousin of IB, gave a concert in the Royal Albert Hall on 16 April 1939 which raised substantial funds towards the relief of Jewish women and children emigrating to Palestine as refugees from Germany and Austria.

3 A reference to a collection of humorous *New Yorker* pieces by Leonard Q. Ross (pseudonym of Leo Calvin Rosten), immensely popular at the time, about an English night-class for immigrants to America, and collected as *The Education of Hyman Kaplan* (London, 1937). In a letter he composes as an exercise in one of the classes, Kaplan, the Jewish hero, writes to his 'brodder': 'You should absolutel coming to NY and belonging in mine school!' ('Mr K*a*p*l*a*n the Magnificent', 45).

4 'Blessing': here the Hebrew grace after meals (prescribed in Deuteronomy 8: 10), important in observant Jewish homes.

5 David Richard Ettinghausen, first child of Walter Ettinghausen and his wife Vera (née Schiff), was born in December 1938.

6 Albert Habib Hourani (1915–93), Magdalen PPE 1933–6, lecturer at the American University of Beirut 1937–9, Foreign Office, Cairo, 1939–45, Arab Office, Jerusalem and London, 1945–6.

TO CRESSIDA BONHAM CARTER

[Mid-March 1939]

New College

Dear Cressida,

I enjoyed the evening very much, and was indeed unable to go to bed for at least as long as you I am sure. On the next day a cultivated Presbyterian Arab[1] called on me and promised he would shortly re-visit me and then play Sacchini's[2] beautiful piano Sonatas if I provided a piano: and in the meanwhile Sacchini's even more beautiful works for the flute. He would then, if I pressed him, play systematically through all single instrument works of Fesch, Porpora and the Elder Stamitz: Pergolesi he thought over-rated. In return I am to (a) discover the musical and artistic origins of the Bach unaccompanied violin sonatas which are so utterly unlike Corelli & the Italians generally: (b) help him with his career in general. This I promised to do. An absurd episode, which I can hardly describe occurred the next night, when [Guy] Branch suddenly arrived and asked for a bed. The Warden of Wadham[3] said would we call at 10 that evening as he wd then be back from a Domus Dinner[4] in his college. At 9.45 p.m. D. Cecil & Mr Coldstream[5] came in & we thought we would go together. On the way David C., attempting to describe the Warden's house to Branch, said (you must supply dynamics etc.) 'it's rather like, rather like, actually rather like a Trust-House,[6] I mean the drawing room is *exactly* like one'. I elaborated on this considerably. We entered the house. Darkness everywhere. We ascended to the drawing room. Still darkness. Somebody switched on the light. David lunged forward & said to Branch 'You see *exactly* what I mean now, don't you?' Branch giggled and agreed it was wonderfully like a Trusthouse (to me a new term). I pointed to a particularly awful object & said 'look look at this'. At this point a dull tapping at an unnoticed door in the corner occurred. Nobody officially took notice but conversation died. Branch started a new sentence but the ghostly sound occurred again. He marched forward & no

---

1 Albert Hourani.
2 Antonio Maria Gasparo Gioacchino Sacchini (1730–86), Italian composer. The other composers mentioned in this letter are the Dutch violinist Willem de Fesch (1687–1761), the Italian singing teacher Nicola Antonio Porpora (1686–1768), the Bohemian violinist and teacher Johann Wenzel Anton Stamitz (1717–57), the Italian composer Giovanni Battista Pergolesi (1710–36) and the Italian violinist Arcangelo Corelli (1653–1713).
3 Maurice Bowra.
4 A dinner for Fellows of the College, held on this occasion in the first week of March.
5 William Menzies Coldstream (1908–87), painter.
6 A hotel owned by Trust Houses, a company founded in 1903 to restore the traditional standards of the old coaching inns. (Trust Houses merged with Forte Holdings in 1970 to form Trusthouse Forte.)

sooner did he touch the door than it sprang open & revealed the Warden in dinner jacket & a frightful rage. The next hour was a nightmare. David who behaved as if nothing [had happened] started lightly on topics & was crushed again & again. Mr Coldstream looked dazed & uncomfortable, Branch fidgeted, I suffered. Everything anybody said was snubbed out of existence, at 11 p.m. David got up & said he must be going: The Warden made no effort to retain him, but said to me & Branch 'You needn't go'. For a moment I was prey to terrible hesitations, whether se solidariser[1] with D. or not. Then I decided that I was more afraid of the W. of W. than of anybody, & stayed. He then became easy, affable & gay, except that at times his face darkened, like remembering sorrow. On the next morning my colleague Cecil was in a very shattered state: 'after ten years of building up & up, it's all in pieces again; really it is *too* awful: but then he mustn't go snooping about in cupboards & eavesdropping: I suppose Rachel[2] will have to give him an enormous *gift*, but it can't be anything for the house now, *can* it?' Their relations are back to nadir, the [Warden of] Wadham looks angry and ressentimental[3] when he looks at him, I am obscurely speculating on the cause of his rage. Because he overheard? because the joke of hiding behind doors, which wd have done with Branch & me was awkward with his own late colleague & Duchesse de Guermantes,[4] & quite intolerable before Mr Coldstream, a stranger to whom he is the [Warden of] Wadham & full of dignity? because of the unfortunate phrase Trusthouse? because 'exactly what I mean' suggested unknowable depths of malice? is this really rather a trivial local story demanding a strict context? or do I convey the almost Dostoyevskian atmosphere of homicidal anger in which we stayed for an hour chatting about I believe, croquet? Everything is terrifically magnified by the narrowness of environment, but possibly is literally made greater & not merely to seem so. I told you (while on this sort of thing) that upon some professor's asking Mrs Ayer what she wd do in case of war, Freddie suddenly intervening said quite unconsciously 'Oh Renée has a refuge in Hampshire' which is literally true in the most literal sense as well, & made my informant gasp audibly & embarrassingly & pretend to have swallowed something. I return your gloves & £1 which you really ought to have reminded me of – I borrowed it at [David] Wallace's Wedding – *Toscanini*: I have 1, possibly 2 tickets for the 3ᵈ May (1ˢᵗ Concert?) have you anything for symphs 5 & 6 or 7

1 'To show solidarity'.
2 David Cecil's wife.
3 'Resentful'.
4 One of the main characters in Proust, between whom and the Baron de Charlus there was strong mutual admiration: presumably IB is alluding to a tendency on David Cecil's part to flatter Maurice Bowra.

& 8? or 9? if so wd you wire? (if not, not.) & will you or Jasper buy tickets for Casals?[1] Valery delivered an agreeable but dull lecture here.[2] He said words were like thin planks over precipices, & if you crossed rapidly nothing happenned, but if you stopped on any of them & stared into the gulf you wd get vertigo & that was what philosophers were doing.

    yrs
      Shaya

TO DOUGLAS JAY

    [1939?]

                                    All Souls

My dear Douglas,
    With regard to Hotels: 1) Cap Martin Hotel.[3] Mr Yeats died there but Herbert knows far more about it than I; it may be shut at the moment: but if not it is ideal in the middle of a wooded hilly eminence over the sea. Not. v. expensive. 2) Hotel, I think, Metropole,[4] Beaulieu sur Mer, between Monte Carlo & Nice. Food is superb, & not awfully expensive: quiet, English, re-tired generals & maids of honour. I have forgotten its exact name, there are only two first class hotels in Beaulieu one is French & called Reserve, the other English & this one. You discover via the Gordon Hotels[5] in London to whom it belongs. Beaulieu is small & Cheltenham-dreary. You can walk (a) along the sea: along the sea you can walk to any distance to Monte Carlo or Nice. On the other hand you can (b) walk up to the Turbie terrace, a terrace of houses & streets till you get to the top, from which views etc. but all enormously cultivated & touriste with Hotels dotted about. I wrote my book there. There is no sign of traffic near the hotel. That's all I know. There are lots of smart hotels in Monte Carlo, but you won't want to know about them. I recommend Beaulieu to live in, but as a small luxury town it is in itself rather depressing, buses take you very efficiently elsewhere. Mentone is death. All the hotels are equally good or bad & everyone is over 60. Nice is

1 Pablo Casals (1876–1973), Spanish cellist, conductor, composer and fierce opponent of Franco's regime, gave a concert with the London Symphony Orchestra on 28 March 1939 at the Royal Albert Hall to raise funds for Spanish children; the programme consisted of music by Mozart, Haydn, Bizet, Elgar and Dvorak.

2 Valéry gave the Sir Basil Zaharoff Lecture at Oxford's Taylor Institution on 1 March on 'Poésie et pensée abstraite en France' ('Poetry and abstract thought in France').

3 Hotel Idéal-Séjour, Cap Martin, where W. B. Yeats (87/1) had settled for health reasons in December 1938, dying there on 28 January 1939.

4 A confusion with Brighton. The Hotel he had stayed at in Beaulieu was the Bristol (see p. 261 above).

5 The owners of the Dorchester Hotel in London, which had opened in 1931.

Brighton, as such noisy vulgar & v. nice. When are you & Peggy likely to be in Oxford: Goronwy has been suspiciously absent.[1]

Shaya

IB's book, Karl Marx: His Life and Environment, *was published soon after the outbreak of the Second World War, forcing some of IB's former colleagues at All Souls to revise their opinions of him:*

I was terribly disapproved of by the academic senior Fellows, because they thought I was a time-wasting chatterbox who would never write anything and wasted the time of people who might. I felt waves of disapproval, not from the politicians, who were quite nice to me, but from the people of fifty – Sumner, who later became Warden, a man called Woodward, famous English historian [. . .] G. N. Clark, who became Regius Professor of History at Cambridge [. . .] they thought I didn't show any signs of settling down to work and getting things out. It's quite true, I didn't in my first three or four years. When I produced a book on Karl Marx, they were totally astonished that I could have generated anything at all.[2]

TO A. D. LINDSAY
Master of Balliol

31 October 1939

New College

Dear Master,

Thank you for your very illuminating letter,[3] which I wish I could have read before writing my book (I am ashamed to say I hadn't even heard of the Geistige Gestalt d. M. Arbeiters).[4]

I agree with a very great deal. I agree (1) that Marx was not at all determined to understand above everything else. Knowledge was a means to an end, disinterested pursuit of the truth was, in any case, a bourgeois

1 In April 1939 Goronwy Rees joined the Royal Artillery Territorial Army in London, to the amazement and disapproval of many of his Oxford friends, who had little sympathy for the Conservative government of Neville Chamberlain which this action appeared to support.

2 MI Tape 5.

3 Dated 15 October. IB had sent Lindsay a copy of his book on Marx, and in his reply Lindsay wrote: 'I think you a little overdo the empirical side and underdo the prophetic side of Marx [. . .] None can miss the passion in [. . .] Marx and it isn't – I rejoice to say – the pure scientific passion. I feel you to be hedging a little about this [. . .]'.

4 Gertrud Hermes, *Die geistige Gestalt des Marxistischen Arbeiters und die Arbeiterbildungsfrage* ['The intellectual cast of the Marxist worker and the question of workers' education'] (Tübingen, 1926).

illusion, and the desire to do down other theorists and ideologies was enormous & not compatible with a passion for the truth an sich.[1]

(2) that Marx wanted neither simple & intelligible social units like Bentham[2] (who was his bête noire) nor efficiency for its own sake, whatever the ends it was meant to secure. I don't think that he really cared about motives very much: the cosmic process (the vision of which, I entirely agree, was central in his thought, only he thought he had proved its existence scientifically) would realize some, and frustrate other purposes. The process was imposed on us and not divertible: so, therefore, were our ends. He hated bunglers, but misunderstanding of what ends the cosmic process made achievable was just as fatal & contemptible as inefficiency with means. Ends were good or bad, behaviour moral or immoral entirely according to whether they were or were not being forwarded by the cosmic process. I agree with all this – & if I seemed to disagree it can only be because I had not expressed it clearly and forcibly enough in my book. Where I still disagree is, I think, about the quality of his emotion. The vision of the classless society, the march of history etc. seems to me metaphysical and not religious: metaphysical and not moral. The world seemed to him orderly & governed by an immutable, non-repetitive process, but society was chaotic and full of stupidity and knaves imposing on fools: he did not merely disapprove of this, he hated and loathed it passionately, it seemed to him degrading to the dignity of the human being as he ought to be, & one day would be, and this is a moral sentiment in a sense, but one founded on pride in human possessions & not on a love of justice. This seems to me to come out very strongly if one compares Marx with men genuinely burning with moral passion, like Proudhon[3] or Mazzini or even Carlyle: they were very different, & Mazzini and Carlyle are sometimes histrionic and induce states in themselves as Marx never did: but they attacked society from the viewpoint of an ardently felt ideal to which they were committed beyond redemption, whatever were or were not the facts of history and the views of their opponents: whereas Marx seems to me to have suffered bitterly himself from the stupidity, disorder and smugness of the world, and to have generalized his condition to cover the human race, or at any rate the working class, which became a kind of projection of himself seen as a potentially free and powerful being held down and humiliated by miserable little Lilliputians. And this, if it is moral passion, seems to me of a different

---

1 'In itself'.

2 Jeremy Bentham (1748–1832), British philosopher and social reformer, who argued that social policy should conform to a principle of utility and hence promote 'the greatest happiness of the greatest number'.

3 Pierre-Joseph Proudhon (1809–65), French socialist-anarchist famous for declaring 'Property is theft' in the first paragraph of his *Qu'est-ce que la propriété?* (Paris, 1840).

order to that commonly so called, and something which permeates but is not what is most valuable in M's work, although, like all eloquence it can and has kindle [*sic*] very different & nobler & profounder feelings in those who read him with eyes different from his. I apologize once more for going on so. But I couldn't leave all this unsaid. I hope you don't mind.

> yrs sincerely
> I. Berlin

Keele University, Lindsay Papers, L193

Lindsay replied on 6 November, sticking somewhat to his guns.

TO MARY FISHER

Thursday, [18] April 1940

New College

Dear Mary

There is nothing I can possibly say. My scout told me early this morning,[1] after which neither of us spoke at all for the rest of the morning. Conversation in the Common Room is artificial to a degree, nobody refers to it at all, Sir Hugh A[llen],[2] is ferocious and morose which represses the others, except Legg,[3] who whispers in corners about arrangements. David is not here, to whom alone I could have spoken. Your father was the only grand'homme I have ever known face to face, so to speak, and I cannot speak of him without saying that, which the colleagues would think affected and socially de haut en bas. I may have to speak to Smith[4] in order to have spoken to somebody. I wish I were ordered to write an éloge[5] in some obscure publication, then I could set down and so create a concrete image for myself which I could permanently carry. Oh dear, this sounds endlessly pompous and selfish but what I wish to convey is that I feel the need for something upon which to concentrate all the emotions of devotion, large scale admiration, gratitude, etc. which have accumulated for years and now swum up into acute consciousness, which sudden distress & frustration produces. I am sorry, I am producing words. I hope you are not undone, & weren't even for a moment: in a sense you must have considered the

---

1 That H. A. L. Fisher had died: he had walked into the path of a lorry in London, and died of his injuries some days later in hospital.

2 Sir Hugh Percy Allen (1869–1946), Organist, New College, 1901–18, Fellow 1908–46, Heather Professor of Music 1918–46.

3 Leopold George Wickham Legg (1877–1962), historian, Fellow of New College 1908–48.

4 A. H. Smith was Acting Warden of New College after Fisher's death.

5 'Tribute'.

possibility – but I imagine when events happen they produce an impact which is genuine whereas the previous thoughts were not. I apologize I am being both clumsy and obscure – the effect of Oxford is that one loses all power of direct statement or even direct feeling and has to circumnavigate in the hope that the outline of what one is unfortunately not simple enough to say directly, is conveyed, & with it the undescribed content. I will, if you will let me, tell you what I should have done had I been called upon to describe your father to others, and what I think I personally owe him, when I see you. If you would rather not, I won't. If I am in London next week I shall telephone. If not, will you be in Oxford? I can't, do what I will, make my words less like sticks, and convey something. I don't understand, I have always been told, what profound suffering is, I have always thrown screens between the possibility of it and myself, and I can only wish that you may not be feeling it, or will have ceased to do so as soon as possible, since I think it bad, and capable of teaching nothing. And that may be a shallow view, but it is the only one I have direct experience as evidence for. I have the most passionate belief in the value of disciplines & frameworks (as indeed had your father, I believe) and the necessity to enroutiner[1] oneself to an extent which makes dégringolades[2] virtually impossible, and that monotony is better than even the smallest disintegration. Hence ferocious snobs, who preserve the values for whatever reasons, are preferable to ferocious anti-snobs, who pull everything down for the pleasure of seeing one or two tin characters humiliated. Also I believe, though rather less than I used to, in the possibility of pleasure, dignity, style, civilized life, ends in themselves pursued with passion, personal relations not falsified by continual analysis, indeed all our common assumptions. I do not know why I should have chosen this moment for preaching this secular sermon, except that I never don't moralize. Also I believe you to hold to all this if anything more uncompromisingly than I, who have on occasions betrayed here and there.

I cant say how symbolic of all this your father was, what a mythological regard I had for him, & how much his head was taller than anyone else's whatever company he was in. Again I can't continue, whereas had I been brought up in the 19th century I could. And if I were actually to see you I certainly could. Meanwhile, until I do, in a few days time or whenever, I shall, I suppose, continue with my routine, and if Mr Smith & Mr Boult[3] are removed by the Govt. (the last of which I may be able to compass by my

---

1 'Establish a routine for'.
2 'Breakdowns'.
3 David Robert Boult (1910–44), New College law 1935–7, Fellow and law Tutor 1938–44, Dean from 1940.

own efforts) I shall be left to rule the college with Prof. Lightfoot. There is nothing to tell you. I dined with [. . .]. It is very touching and gentle and complete, but too resigned, like deuxièmes noces.[1] There is a complete lack of any motion principle at all, the monotony is not superimposed on any desires, hopes, ambitions, but is the core of their life. They neither expect nor fear much. Their characters are so good, and manners so beautiful, that one is prepared to accept that as idyllic: but it is not. Both have stabilized at some compromise level [. . .]. The Ridleys who are much more dissatisfied & frustrated, have a direction, & are much more admirable. I preach once more. I therefore stop. Wd you say (or ring up from here) if you are coming to Oxford: I think I am almost bound to be in London very soon. I shall write to your mother separately. This is an appalling letter, even for me. I apologize.

   love
      Shaya.

Friday

Mr Smith wants Lloyd George to deliver the éloge,[2] it has been decided to consult your mother & yourself: officially. Mr Legg is a little frightened that he may be 'political'. The more so the better, Dr McCallum[3] & I think. Would he come? are you yourself coming to the service here, i.e. on Thursday or Friday or Saturday next, whenever it is to happen? it will I suppose be at 2.15 or so, would you lunch with me, or have tea later, would your mother come to lunch? do suggest something, I long to see you. Prof. Lightfoot is in his element what with two memorial Services in one week. Somebody suggested [H. W. B.] Joseph as the élogien, his éloges are very good formal ones, but in my view he cannot have admired rightly or understood anything to do with your father except as the public in general did: which is not good enough. However he may have to do as a pis aller. Sir Hugh [Allen] thinks it would be graceful to ask P. Matheson,[4] but he is said to be in feeble voice. The Warden of Wadham longs to be asked, I cannot explain that he is thought to be of too light calibre, apart from everything

---

1 'Second marriage'.
2 There were two services, but Lloyd George did not speak at either. The address at the memorial service in St Margaret's Westminster on 23 April was given by Cyril Garbett, then Bishop of Winchester. There was no address at the funeral in the College chapel on 27 April.
3 Ronald Buchanan McCallum (1898–1973), historian, Fellow of Pembroke 1925–55, later (1955–67) Master, authority on the Liberal Party.
4 Percy Ewing Matheson (1859–1946), classicist, Emeritus Fellow, New College, President of the New College Society 1939–40.

else. I suppose intrigues will soon start now. I am not looking forward to them in the least. I wd rather have anybody – Seton Watson,[1] Ormsby Gore,[2] anybody than Moberly,[3] whose smile is said to be as big as a cathedral. Do let me know about arrival. If I don't hear, I shall telephone on about Monday or Tuesday.

    love

      Shaya

TO LETTICE FISHER

    Thursday [18 April 1940]

                                  New College

Dear Mrs Fisher

    Everyone here is genuinely and deeply distressed, the scouts pad softly and don't raise their voices. As for me, you know my feelings. I admired the Warden, his life, his works, all that he stood for more than anyone I had ever personally known. I was absolutely devoted to him, would have done anything at any time, and owed him a debt of which you know the size and magnitude, both for his personal kindness, at a time when I was greatly in need of it, and indirectly, as setting standards of life and behaviour which dwarfed those of most of his contemporaries in Oxford. Indeed I cannot conceive that anything will ever again fill in my life the place that the Warden's lodgings held during all these years: Could you and Mary not come and live there still? while no one else lives there? I do not suppose that even you can fully know how much it meant not only to your friends but to everyone, dons, undergraduates, every one, how much bigger in scope and stature it was, how much more distinguished and interesting and unique, what quality its hospitality possessed; the closing of that period means much more to me – it only shows how unpolitical and domestic I am [I] expect – than even the changes of the war. I suppose there is nothing I can do? I do hope that people are not being too importunate or cluttering up your hours with trivial things at this moment: if there is anything I cd possibly do now or at any time anywhere in any way, I really should be distressed if I wasn't told to do it. They are speaking here of asking the Warden of Winchester[4] to

1 Robert William Seton-Watson (1879–1951), New College history 1898–1902, Masaryk Professor of Central European History, London, 1922–45.

2 Ormsby-Gore (177/4), by this time Lord Harlech, New College history 1904–7, had been an Honorary Fellow of the College since 1936.

3 Sir Walter Moberly (1881–1974), New College classics 1900–3, Chairman of University Grants Committee 1935–49.

4 Rt Hon. Harold Trevor Baker (1877–1960).

write to the Oxford Magazine:[1] and of asking you whether you wd like Lloyd George to speak in chapel next week: most of them are anxious to have him I think: but they wd accept anyone you suggest: they have no minds of their own.

I hope a memoir is published soon; I suppose George Trevelyan[2] could do it, or perhaps it ought to be composite with a galaxy of great names: I do think – I don't wish to sound pompous but I think it passionately – that a volume ought to appear soon, as relevant particularly to the present, to commemorate and reveal to public view the virtues and the ideals which nobody seems eloquent or sincere enough to proclaim so as to catch the imagination, which we all believe in, which we are told we are fighting for, of which the Warden was a most noble incarnation. I apologize for being so lame, but I always did write badly.

> yrs ever
>   Shaya Berlin

By this time most of IB's friends and colleagues had been called up or were working as government officials. IB's weak left arm, damaged at birth, and his foreign origins barred him from contributing in either way to the war effort, and he became increasingly frustrated by his marginalisation.

TO LORD HALIFAX[3]

21 June 1940

As from All Souls

Dear Lord Halifax

I must apologize for intruding at such a moment – I hope you will forgive my importunity. I write to you on the advice of the Warden, and Lionel Curtis before whom I laid my proposal; they both thought it worth bringing to your notice. It is briefly this: I am 31 years of age, physically unfit for military service on account of a bad arm and other defects, and so at once

---

1 The *Oxford Magazine* published 'The Warden of New College', an appreciation of Fisher by P. E. M[atheson], in their issue dated 2 May 1940, 286–8.

2 George Macaulay Trevelyan (1976–1962), Regius Professor of Modern History, Cambridge 1927–40; Master of Trinity College, Cambridge, 1940–51; a family friend of the Fishers.

3 Edward Frederick Lindley Wood (1881–1959), 1st Earl of Halifax, 3rd Viscount Halifax, 1st Baron Irwin, Secretary of State for Foreign Affairs 1938–40, British Ambassador, Washington, 1941–6. This letter appears not to have been sent in this form, but it may be a draft of a letter that *was* sent.

reserved and, save for L.D.V.,[1] unemployed. I was born in Riga and educated to speak both English and Russian, and indeed I am virtually bilingual:
no Russian on merely hearing me speak would assume that I was any sort of
foreigner. I get on with such Russians as I have met in England easily and
well. And I possess, as a result of reading both U.S.S.R and émigré Russian
newspapers and books fairly continuously during the last 15 years, a fairly
detailed knowledge of Russian affairs: I am far from being a political or
economic expert on Russia, or indeed any country, since my interests used to
be largely historical and literary. But as a result of such general reading, and
conversation with people, I may, I think, without presuming too much,
claim to possess a fairly wide and sympathetic knowledge of the background
for the last half century. Perhaps this does not amount to real expertise: I am
most anxious not to make an exaggerated claim. What I could say with
confidence is that Russia, the contemporary condition of its institutions and
its peoples, is the subject which absorbs me most next to my proper
academic studies. I therefore thought that I could perhaps be of service to the
country, to however small [a] degree, if I could go to Moscow in some semi-
official or official capacity, and, while doing any work which our representatives there might wish me to do, e.g. in connection with the press or
the like – I should willingly do any hackwork they may want done – I also
tried to establish contacts not so much in Moscow where this is notoriously
difficult, although I would try, but in the provinces, where my accent,
appearance and interests would not make me as conspicuous as a foreigner.
There are a good many useful things which it seems to me that I could do,
which are not easy for official persons, by way of establishing friendly
relations with literary and artistic circles, particularly outside Moscow, who
often give better indications of [the] general state of feeling than political
circles which, one gathers, are exceedingly inaccessible. I should very greatly
prefer to develop this to you, however briefly, in person if you could possibly
grant me a short interview. I quite realize that this may at the present
moment be impracticable. But if you could see me for a few moments I think
I could lay my suggestion before you more briefly and more clearly than I
have done in this letter. I have a recollection of once having had a conversation with yourself on this very subject, at dinner in All Souls six or
seven years ago, when I was a very junior Fellow, very flown with my new
status, and probably talked a great deal of nonsense which you were too
courteous to arrest. That, and the fact that I genuinely believe that this is the
way in which I could be most useful to the country in the present crisis,
made me bold to write as I have. I could, of course, come up to London at

1 Local Defence Volunteers (later Home Guard).

the shortest notice at any time. Once again I must apologize for taking up your time. Mrs H. A. L. Fisher, to whom I spoke of the matter, said she too proposed to write, as the late Warden of New College had intended to do so on his own initiative shortly before he died. This is only to explain the cause for her letter, in case it should have arrived.

yours sincerely
I. Berlin.

TO MARION FRANKFURTER

23 June 1940

New College

Dear Marion,

I meant to write on almost every day, or every other day, since the beginning of the war. It became increasingly difficult, since the private relationships and personal facts which used to absorb my life were pushed back and almost obliterated from the day the war was declared. And in their place at first too little happened, and then too much. So that I became sunk, so far as I could, in the routine tasks of my academic life. Oxford changed relatively little: the undergraduates worked far harder and more seriously than before: in the examination papers which I am now correcting there is not a trace of war neurosis: Maurice, if in a lower-keyed register, is making the same jokes as before, the emphasis falls on the same words. He is in charge, I believe, of some 160 postal workers. So our mails are safe at any rate. David Cecil still runs in and out, with a voice like a crate of hens carried across a field. Our general morale is good, only our refugees cast a certain gloom, and I wish indeed that they were gently segregated somewhere in safety instead of being allowed to act like mild vampires and lower our vitality. The events in France have removed the centre of some peoples' lives – Elizabeth Cameron's for example – who obviously orientated herself by an imaginary Paris. Before the Blitzkrieg,[1] Oxford was singularly unaffected. And even now it has not lost its, I think, admirable cold discipline in the Common Rooms and streets. Blackwells is very full. Do you think this too ancien régime and pseudo-Roman? I have such a terror of things falling into soft decay that even bogus stoicism seems better to me than none at all. One or two eccentrics have joined us. Lord Berners who is, as you probably know, a noted eccentric millionaire, who paints & writes and composes

---

1 Literally 'lightning war', a military tactic relying on surprise, tanks and precise air–ground co-ordination to break through defences and advance rapidly into enemy territory. The Germans had successfully used this approach when invading the Netherlands, Belgium and France.

good musical satire. He has come because he found life in his enormous house[1] with painted cockatoos and budgerigars too depressing in solitude in war, and after a short and not too happy stay with Maurice who terrified him, settled in a room with a piano, calls on us all, & has to have his morale kept up. He is the most obviously gifted man (at this point, literally, I stopped on account of our first air raid alarm) I've met, but a pure luxury, pathetic and ill adapted to the present times. He, David C., a few Asquiths and Churchills form a sort of upper class enclave in Oxford who meet at parties in a slightly Decameron sort of way. Maurice disapproves, and I rather like them and enjoy the extreme independence and first handness of their conversation. Freddie is a successful and picturesque soldier, in the Welsh Guards: he obviously enjoys it very much indeed: he talks of his regiment with a real esprit de corps feeling: with contempt for dull weaklings and admiration for brilliant originals: he looks like a Chasseur Alpin,[2] and will, if given the chance, make a wonderful success of soldiering. At least so I think. He so obviously enjoys unpredicted conformity after a long & slightly dreary tradition of being the revolté, the enfant terrible etc. Hampshire is waiting to be called up: the triangle continues in an awful sort of way, there is plenty of new scandal about Mrs A. but it can no longer be borne to be thought about. Dr [Guy] Chilver (you remember him?) is in the Ministry of Food, Maurice after having been forbidden by his College to be a machine gunner in an aeroplane, continues here. As for me, I am not physically fit for the army, was stopped for the minor Govt. jobs[3] I was offered in the beginning of the war by my late Warden – I am glad he is dead, he would have disliked all this past endurance – & so am largely at a loose end, examining in philosophy with the Master of Balliol[4] with whom I've made moderate friends. Apart from the now mutually conceded fact that we remain unsmiling during the other's jokes, we get on well enough. Warden Adams is like a farmer whose ricks have been fired, deafer, and even more affectionate. Indeed, since I have left All Souls, I have grown quite genuinely fond of him. Whom else have I been seeing? Mrs Woolf and Dr Weizmann. She is a woman of such genius and beauty as I can hardly describe. I experience terror and admiration when I meet her and tremble before and after. Dr W. is a public face rather, and talks gloomily of ending his life in a concentration camp, preferably he says, in Palestine. When this mood passes, he talks with passion about the Jews

---

1 Faringdon House, Berkshire.
2 'Alpine hunter', French mountain light infantry, specially trained for combat in mountainous regions such as the Alps and the Pyrenees.
3 A 'rather lowly post' in the Education Ministry was mentioned to IB by a friend there: Fisher advised him not to accept it, but in the event it could not in any case be offered to him because of his Latvian birth (MI Tape 7).
4 A. D. Lindsay.

and his schemes for Palestine. He seems to admire a banana King called Zemurray[1] in the U.S.A. a good deal. (Zemurray? Zecameron? ZeMacdonald? one could go on) he fails to fascinate me. I can't understand why it is I fail to fall under the spell of well known charmers, Weizmann, Desmond McCarthy, Harold Nicolson, but I do. And I find both their voices and their silver tongued sentences slightly nauseating. I join on the whole in the general chorus of condemnation of Auden, Isherwood, Macneice, who have removed to the U.S.A.: they were, as some one said, recruiting sergeants of the left, they gladly accepted the part of prophets, social critics, directors of consciences. They preached passionately and effectively against the others who locked themselves into ivory towers. That self preservation should have taken this form is sordid and discredits their moral pathos. Mr Spender, my old friend, who is here, emerges as a tragic liberal figure, less inspired and far more dignified. I see no excuse for anyone leaving unless directly in the interests of their political institutions, directly by orders of their government, or else because they are exposed racially or politically, and the end has come.

We are not on the edge of disintegration: the government did not send Auden to China, or to the U.S.A.: what was personal discontent was now seen only too obviously to mask itself in the form of a social creed and generalize itself to acquire more dignity and eloquence. And to exploit public issues in a private cause is to me a very bad and dangerous activity for artists, and has led to D'Annunzio[2] and Dr Goebbels. Personal survival is no doubt a legitimate end: one fights while one can & then one either dies or escapes. I am not a soldier, & can't be one, and am in certain respects highly exposed, if only because I am a Jew & have written on Marx: I shd do my best not to be caught: if I could induce some institution in the U.S.A. to invite me, I would. But cold blooded flight is monstrous. And indifference to a conflict on which the outcome of which all art & thought depend, repulsive and stupid.

I perceive that I am being violent and unusually public minded. That is perhaps a genuine change. The private world has cracked in numerous places. I should terribly like to be able to help in the great historical process in some way. We shall win if we can be made into a vast aerodrome by yourselves and the Canadians, & if I could help in that process, or in Russia because I know the people & the language, or somewhere somehow, I should be made happy. And I really share Maurice's feeling about the

---

1 In 1911 Samuel Zemurray (1877–1961), 'Sam the banana man', led a group of American adventurers and investors out of New Orleans to seize Honduras, where he took power, established the Cuyamel Fruit Company, combined forces with the United Fruit Company of Boston (of which he became President in 1938), and turned Honduras into a 'banana republic'.
2 Gabriele d'Annunzio (1863–1938), Italian poet and Fascist.

desirability of *mourir en combattant*.[1] The only horror is Pétainisme.[2] To save what they want to save seems very detestable: our Franco chickens are coming home to roost. If that ever happened in England I should want to emigrate or die. There are no signs of it at present. And if the war is a long one the national revival (which is acutely needed after 20 years swift decay) will at the end be terrific, in spite of the waste & weakened social structure. Meanwhile I cannot say how much I should like to see you and Felix, and the circumstances of peace & civilized life. I should not feel this so acutely perhaps if I was in the army, & so relatively carefree & employed. As it is, I am full of yearning. Since I cannot see you I will send greetings by a somewhat inferior ex-manager of my father's called Aronson[3] who is emigrating to the U.S.A. from Finland via this country. He will probably telephone to you when he arrives but there is no necessity to see him or do anything about him. He is a tough, and quite capable of looking after himself. I'll write again as soon as I can. All my love to Felix who, I am sure is active in our cause. You were here just a year ago, I suppose. Yet it seems out of all relation to ordinary time sequence: I hope you are very happy and well.

Shaya.

1 'Dying in combat'.
2 A reference to Marshal Henri-Philippe Pétain (1856–1951), Commander-in-Chief of the French Army in the First World War, War Minister 1934, head of the collaborationist Vichy Government 1940–4. He was found guilty of treason, but his death sentence was commuted to life imprisonment.
3 Samuel ('Mulya') Aronson, formerly manager of Mendel's pit-prop business in Finland.

NEW YORK

A particularly brilliant star in the galaxy around the Director-General[1] [of British Information Services in New York] was Mr Isaiah Berlin, who, having arrived in Washington in the summer of 1940 ostensibly en route to Moscow as Press Attaché, was prevailed upon by Lord Lothian[2] to remain in an advisory capacity to the Press Counsellor. Under Sir Gerald, Mr Berlin was charged with relations with labour and Jewish press and personalities.[3] In reality, however, his profound wisdom made him a much sought-after adviser in wider fields. He was subsequently transferred by Mr Butler[4] to the Office of the Minister in charge of Information Affairs in Washington, where he became responsible for all survey matters there and, in particular, [for] composing the weekly political summaries which the Ambassador sent to London.

John Wheeler-Bennett, writing in 1946[5]

1 Sir Gerald Campbell (1879–1964), Director-General of British Information Services (BIS), New York (NY) 1941–2. In an interview held on 29 September 1987 with Nicholas Cull for his book *Selling War: The British Propaganda Campaign against American 'Neutrality' in World War II* (NY and Oxford, 1995), IB remarked that, while Campbell 'was likeable, his talents were strictly limited to the delivery of good but empty after-dinner speeches'.

2 Philip Henry Kerr, 11th Marquess of Lothian (1882–1940), British Ambassador in Washington from August 1939 until his untimely death in December 1940, notably strengthened Anglo-American relations. Wheeler-Bennett here exaggerates his role in persuading IB to stay; indeed the accuracy of his account is in general somewhat approximate, and should not be relied on, but it is included to show how IB was regarded in the immediate aftermath of his war service.

3 In his interview with Cull IB added Negroes and Catholics to Jews and organised labour, and spoke of 'propaganda to minority groups'. The official chart of the British Press Service (BPS) lists IB as one of the 'specialists', 'Labour and Jewish interests' as his remit, and his monthly salary as £300 (FO 371/30667, A/701/399/45, OEPCC 1126, Appendix B, Plan III).

4 Harold Beresford Butler (1883–1951), Minister and Head of BIS at the British Embassy, Washington, 1942–6.

5 From 'History of British Information in the USA', unpublished typescript (British Information Services, NY, 1946), fos 27–8. John Wheeler (*sic*) *Wheeler-Bennett (1902–75), attached to British Library of Information, NY, 1939–40; Assistant Director, BPS, NY, 1940–1; Special Assistant to Director-General of BIS in the US 1941–42; Head of NY Office of British Political Warfare Mission in the US 1942–44; Intelligence Dept, FO, 1944; Assistant Director-General 1945; Assistant to British Political Adviser to SHAEF 1944–5.

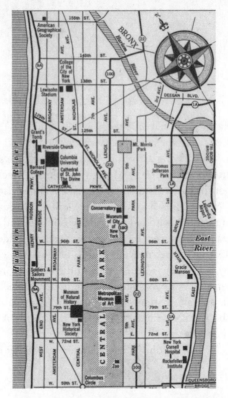

Manhattan, showing the Rockefeller Center

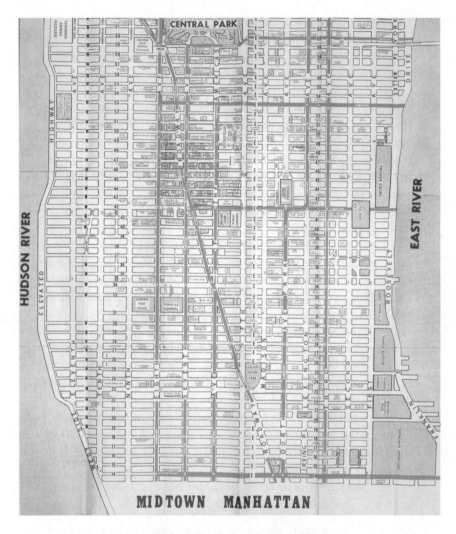

CENTRAL PARK

HUDSON RIVER

EAST RIVER

MIDTOWN MANHATTAN

*Midtown Manhattan, showing the Rockefeller Center
and 55th Street, on which IB stayed at various hotels*

IB's pre-war Oxford existence essentially ended when he made his first
trip to the US, recorded in the letters that follow. Though it was some
time before he became settled in New York, this is the natural place to
begin a new chapter in his life.

In late June he received an unexpected and surprising visit from an
old friend, Guy Burgess. He regarded Burgess as agreeable and entertaining, though clearly amoral and unstable, later recalling: 'Not only did

I not know he was an agent, but I had no suspicion of him being a member of the Party, though most people did.'[1] *Their previous meetings had usually consisted of long talks about books and people, never about politics; IB would remain sober while Burgess became increasingly drunk.*

This occasion was different. Claiming to be working for the Intelligence Services, Burgess said that his great friend Harold Nicolson (then a junior Minister at the Ministry of Information) wanted IB to become British Press Attaché in Moscow 'because you know Russian, and they think it might be rather useful'. Attracted by the idea, despite its implausibility and the obvious irregularity of Burgess's intervention, IB went to see first Harold Nicolson, and then Gladwyn Jebb[2] *in the Foreign Office, both of whom had been persuaded that IB would be useful in the proposed role.*

It was agreed that IB would go to Moscow, and that Burgess would travel with him. Burgess had of course instigated the trip himself, hoping to use IB as cover for his own visit to the USSR. The purpose of this visit was probably to enable Burgess to make contact with the NKVD[3] *(the Soviet secret police), since their London resident had been withdrawn earlier in the year, and normal contact was impossible.*

So it was that on 1 July Lord Halifax signed a Courier's Passport requesting 'free passage for Mr Isaiah Berlin, proceeding to Moscow, via USA and Japan, and returning to London, charged with Despatches'. He did the same for Burgess.

Bemused by the speed of developments and increasingly worried about why he was being sent, IB travelled with Burgess by train to Liverpool where they were to board the SS Antonia. He later described his last-minute panic: 'I then thought I must tell somebody what I'm doing, because I may never come back – somebody ought to know.' He thought of Lionel Curtis at All Souls.

So I wrote him a letter: 'Dear Lionel, I don't really understand why I am going or what I am expected to do, but I thought I had better tell you what is happening. We're going to Washington in order that I might get

1 MI Tape 7, from which the other unfootnoted quotations from IB in this and subsequent headnotes for 1940 are also taken.

2 (Hubert Miles) Gladwyn Jebb (1900–96), later (1960) 1st Baron Gladwyn, Private Secretary to Permanent Under-Secretary of State, FO, 1937–40, seconded to the Ministry of Economic Warfare (MEW) 1940–2, Executive Secretary of the Preparatory Commission of the UN 1945, Acting Secretary-General of the UN 1946.

3 Narodnyi komissariat vnutrennykh del ('People's commissariat for internal affairs'), the name of the secret police 1934–43; previously (1923–34) its name was OGPU, Otdelenie gosudarstvennoi politicheskoi upravy . . ., 'United State political administration [for struggle against counter-espionage and counter-revolution]', subsequently (1943–6) NKGB, Narodnyi komissariat gosudarstvennoi bezopasnosti, 'People's commissariat for State security'.

a Visa from Oumansky,¹ and I thought perhaps if anyone ought to know, you ought to – you can tell members of the Government, should it be necessary, about what is happening. You are the most politically important person I know.' Roughly.

The letter was intercepted by the Censor and Curtis was interrogated. 'He was frightfully displeased,' Berlin remembered: 'thought I'd in some awful way compromised him, [by] intriguing somehow. I remember when I saw him later he complained, but [. . .] when I became important in Washington he suddenly totally changed his view and said how clever of me to have written to him. He was a time-server if ever there was one.'

As usual IB made no mention of his worries in the letters he wrote to his parents.

TO MARIE AND MENDEL BERLIN

Tuesday [9 July 1940]

Cunard White Star

Dear Father & Mother,

I could not be more comfortable, confident or happy. We are very full, of course, the food so far as one meal can tell, is excellent. I shall communicate as soon as is possible, which may not be for a week or more as you know. The embarkation was a triumph of our official positions. I observe among my companions (1) Miss Bergner² & husband (2) Cohen Next Door!³ (at least I *think* it is he. Like me he is writing furiously before ship moves.) My travelling companion is completely under my thumb (not a very oppressive one you will complain) I have conveyed to him the suspicions of the House of R.⁴ which will keep him in order. The telephone number of his office is Whitehall 8066 (write down!) for renseignements.⁵ They are, I must say, marvellous at arranging exits for their officials, the whole proceeds with streamlined smoothness. I think you would find them helpful in a crisis: they would be told to be by us if one arose. I need hardly

1 Constantine Aleksandrovich Oumansky (1902–45), Soviet Ambassador to the US 1938–41, Soviet Ambassador to Mexico from May 1943 until his death in a plane crash in January 1945.
2 Elisabeth Bergner (1900–86), actress, married to Dr Paul Czinner.
3 Joseph Cohen, joint managing director, British and Colonial Furniture Co., joint assistant managing director, Cavendish Furniture Co., had previously lived at 26 Heath Drive, Hampstead, where he was a neighbour of Mendel Berlin's former business partner, Myer Bick, at No 27. The sobriquet, which evidently survived his move from this address, doubtless served to differentiate Cohen from numerous other acquaintances of the same name, as in the Welsh practice of referring to 'Jones the milk' etc.
4 Miriam Rothschild had advised IB against friendship with Burgess; but the reference may also/instead be to her brother Victor, who was then in the Secret Intelligence Service (SIS).
5 'Information'.

assure you again how careful of my health, behaviour etc. I shall be: as I said when I left I am oppressed by the thought of my own felicity as opposed to yours more than by anything. I am *very* well & happy. All my love to both of you: we shall soon see each other again: whatever happens.

    love,

      Shaya

TO MARIE AND MENDEL BERLIN

    Wednesday [10 July 1940]

                               Cunard White Star

Dear Pa & Ma.

    We haven't moved yet. Dead secret. Everyone has settled comfortably to their prison. There are besides Cohen-Next-Door (whom I have still not quite verified. Очень подвижной)[1] 25 Oxford dons' wives, 3 Canadians whom I have just examined in Oxford; my cabin-sharer is a Prof. Schüller,[2] I suspect the ex-Austrian ambassador to Rome,[3] a very marrano[4] Jew, once cream of Viennese Society, and father or uncle of a girl whom [Wolf] Halpern once thought he wished to marry. If he is the man I mean[5] he knows the Warden of All Souls, and is a mild pro-Habsburg. We shall see. At the moment neither of us talks much. But all the stewards confidently say that it takes at least 14 days to Montreal zig-zagging as we shall. The last 3 days up the St. Lawrence are said to be both safe & beautiful. Miss Bergner is freckled, trousered and ugly. Herr Czinner, her husband, likes her very much. Both are red haired. He looks like a hog, like Stresemann.[6] Our women in the 1st class (the Oxford wives are 3^{d} – I shall soon go on a dame patronesse visit to the slums) are very smart now. The men are not so smart. The food and water are good. Mr Burgess promises to drink $\frac{1}{2}$ bottle of wine a day and no spirits. The food is astonishingly plentiful. The bread is a dream. We have a certain number of Frenchmen who listened with obvious mixed

---

  1 'Ochen' podvizhnoi' ('very lively').

  2 Dr Richard Schüller (1870–1972) was Permanent Under-Secretary of State, Austrian Board of Trade, before the First World War; after the war he became Chief Economic Adviser to the Austrian Government, and in 1934 Austrian Minister at the League of Nations. He left Vienna in late 1938, and was Professor of Economics, New School for Social Research, NY, 1940–52. See IB's further observations on him in his letter of 16 July, p. 317 below.

  3 Schüller was not in fact Ambassador to Rome, though he did know Mussolini.

  4 A Spanish word meaning a Jew (or originally also a Muslim) ostensibly converted to Christianity in response to actual or threatened persecution; whence also a Jew seeking to conceal his Jewishness.

  5 He was.

  6 Gustav Stresemann, Chancellor (1923) and Foreign Minister (1923, 1924–9) of Germany's Weimar Republic.

feelings to the story about the Richelieu.[1] My mackintosh is either at (a) Parker Duofold Shop, Bush House, Strand where I bought pen. or (b) in photographer – Jerome, also Strand, near Tivoli I think. I am very gay indeed.

Love.

I would recommend transfer of say £1000 to Bermuda[2] without further delay, & see how it goes, mentioning J. G. Foster. Or smaller sum. Why not?

TO MARIE AND MENDEL BERLIN

Tuesday 16 July 1940

Cunard White Star

My dear parents

Life in this ship is monotonous but perfectly agreeable. To-morrow we reach Newfoundland, on Thursday Quebec, on Friday Montreal. We may disembark in Quebec to avoid the immense chaos of disembarkation of the millions of children. Or we may go on. In any case we are likely to be in Washington by the week-end. The journey was very uneventful. We are very full; the ship only moved on Wednesday, & then slowly and un-certainly. We zig-zag elaborately under Admiralty orders. Some depth charges may or may not have been dropped in the course of our journey, nobody is quite sure. My plans are to let my companion[3] proceed further if he feels he is in a hurry. And stay myself until the path is clear. Anyhow to do whatever they think best at the Embassy. Now for the company. There are of my acquaintances:

(1) 3 Oxford dons' wives whom I know well. Altogether there are 25 + 75 Oxford children. The noise they make is terrific. The ship is endlessly full of restless children behind, on, in, above, below every piece of furniture and rigging. Peace only comes after 7 p.m. and then it breaks out again some-where far away below, in the 3^{d} class. We 1st class passengers are peacefully insulated from the lower life below decks. But for the mothers – & the motherless children – it must be hell. The dons' wives come up & spend the evening with me occasionally. One of them is the sister of [Stafford] Cripps' secretary, now 3^{d} secretary in Moscow.[4] We discuss the world & our friends. It is very peaceful.

---

1 French battleship, forced to evacuate to Dakar, Senegal, on 18 June 1940, in a not fully commissioned state.
2 To support Marie's family in Riga: see letter of 2 August, p. 325 below.
3 Guy Burgess.
4 John Wriothesley Russell (1914–84), diplomat; Moscow 1939–42, Washington 1942–5, Warsaw

(2) The Jews. These are imprimis:[1] Cohen Next Door, Mrs Cohen Next Door & Levitt.[2] The firm is travelling en bloc. With them I have no official relations. We look at each other piercingly but without recognition. I suspect them of going to their Canadian branch. Levitt is entirely silent and very gloomy. Is his wife dead? Cohen is also not gay. They play cards in the evenings with each other. But quietly. Without the old brio. No hint of Hinton Court. In strong contrast to them are Mr & Mrs Lincoln.[3] Mrs addressed me *at once*: said she knew Mrs Berlin who is a very smart capable woman. Has met her in the Golders Green Hippodrome. Their son, Ashe Lincoln, M.A., barrister, member of Kashrut[4] committee, knew me, so they said, at Oxford. A very cosy and lively couple. You would be glad of their company. Firstly they discovered within 3–4 hours everything about everyone on board. Where Cohen is going. Which is Elizabeth Bergner's husband & which her friend. What the Canadian general said to the captain & what the captain refused to say to him. How much money everyone was carrying (I skilfully evaded examination. They are a little puzzled & annoyed I think, but have not lost all hope). Their corner in the evening is pure Brondesbury[5] boarding house. He used to be a reverend, & knows the intimate histories of all our friends. Exactly where Mr O. Philipps's[6] house is in Goring by Brighton. When & why he left it. What Mr Elsley Zeitlyn[7] did during the last war. Why he was in New York & why later in China. Where the Geneens[8] are. I have dutifully [read] their son's book on Jewish ideals tastefully published as a present for pious homes & praised it.[9] They + another 100 passengers eat Kosher food which they say is excellent. They have been to the States every year for years. Their three sons are in the

1945–8. His sister Camilla Georgiana (1912–83), was married to the author and journalist Christopher Hugh Sykes (1907–86), who was not in fact a don.

1 'In the first place'.

2 Joseph E. Levitt, chairman and joint managing director, British and Colonial Furniture Co., assistant managing director, Cavendish Furniture Co.

3 Reuben and Fanny Lincoln, parents of F(redman) Ashe Lincoln (1907–98), Exeter law 1925–8, BCL 1928–9, minesweeping in the Royal Naval Volunteer Reserve during the war, an eminent QC after it.

4 Kashrut is the body of Jewish law that lays down what foods Jews can eat and how these are to be prepared and eaten. Food that meets these standards is 'kosher' (from the same root).

5 See 97/4.

6 Oscar Philipp (1887–1965), metal-broker, lived in Ferncroft Avenue, which adjoins Hollycroft Avenue (see p. 4 above): the Berlins' house could be seen from OP's, and he became a good friend of Marie Berlin. At the beginning of the war the family left London for West Worthing, near Brighton in Sussex.

7 Elsley Zeitlin (1878–1959), an anti-Zionist who had lived in China, was a barrister in London. He lived in Hampstead, and was active in the London Lodge of B'nei B'rith.

8 The Geneen family from Golders Hill Park in north-west London owned an antique shop in the Grosvenor House Hotel, Park Lane.

9 F. Ashe Lincoln, *Is Orthodoxy Worth While?* (London, 1934).

Navy, & a fourth in America. They are Zionists. I enjoy occasional gossip with them very much. They made an attempt to introduce me to a young lady (married.) from Riga, which I have successfully avoided. They point out that she has a perfectly good husband from Dublin on board, & that I have nothing to fear. But memories of Miss Finkelstein[1] haunt me & I refuse. In the mornings I apply to the Lincolns (I think he is by origin an East End Jew born here. Not at all stupid. Nor is she. She used to sit next to you in the Golders Green Synagogue) for the news of the ship's social history. They are definitely desirable, if vulgar, citizens. The most interesting is my cabin-mate, Dr Schüller. Father of a girl once engaged to Halpern (a fact my knowledge of which I conceal). He has been for 40 years in the Austrian Foreign Ministry, & signed the peace of Brest Litovsk & St-Germain.[2] He is very interesting on Trotsky, whom he knew in Vienna in 1907, & again at Brest-L., on Aerenthal,[3] Franz Joseph,[4] Dollfuss[5] etc. He used to come & stay with Adams at All Souls, and knows Lothian, Mussolini, Ribbentrop[6] etc. Hardly a Jew, except, as Frau Cassirer[7] said to Mr [H. W. B.] Joseph, for Hitler & for me. He has a daughter in U.S.A., is 72, & will doubtless stay there. A typical Austro-Jewish imperial tactful bien pensant official.

There are also officers' wives with nurses & children whom they treat not too well, a few consular officials, the Bergner ménage, some soldiers, returning Canadians (the nicest people) a collection of Frenchmen, Chinese, etc. Our diplomatic status secures exceptional respect from the stewards. We are now definitely out of danger, being likely to be in sight of land this evening{s}. The weather is wonderful. But you will doubtless get my telegram before this. I propose to go Montreal (or Quebec) – N. York – Washington, report at the Embassy, & wire my next step.

Also about our friends in Bermuda.[8] I am in very high spirits and

1 When Tatjana Finkelstein (1914–74), from Riga, went to St Hugh's in 1935 (where she read for a B.Litt. in international law) after three years at University College London (where she took an LL.B.), Mendel's partner Myer Bick asked IB to 'introduce her to a nice circle and, whenever you have time, look after her': letter of 9 October 1935. Her father was later a victim of the Nazis in Riga.

2 Under the Treaty of Brest-Litovsk (3 March 1918) Austria and the other Central Powers imposed harsh peace terms on Russia. But that of St Germain (10 September 1919) led to the dismemberment of the Austro-Hungarian Empire.

3 Aloys Leopold Johann Baptist, Count Lexa von Aehrenthal (1854–1912), Austro-Hungarian diplomat and Foreign Minister (1906–12).

4 Franz Joseph (1830–1916), Emperor of Austria (1848–1916) and King of Hungary (1867–1916).

5 Engelbert Dollfuss (1892–1934), Chancellor of Austria 1932–4.

6 Joachim von Ribbentrop (1893–1946), German Foreign Minister 1933–45.

7 Possibly Toni Cassirer, wife (and cousin) of Ernst, or perhaps Else Cassirer, wife of Ernst's cousin, the Oxford publisher Bruno Cassirer, and sister of Bruno's cousin Paul Cassirer.

8 The puzzling references in this and later letters to friends and relatives in the West Indies seem to be a simple code to deflect the censor's attention from any possible irregularity in the transfer of funds from Mendel's investments in Bermuda to Marie's family, who remained in Riga.

confident about England, ourselves, and everything else. I hope to find Aronson's address in Commodore, New York. If I stay in Washington I'll wire address. Pro tem, c/o John Foster, B. Embassy, Washington, D.C.

　　Love

　　　Shaya.

IB and Burgess disembarked at Quebec and made their way to New York, remaining there for the weekend. Burgess sought out Michael Straight,[1] later revealed as another member of the Cambridge spy ring.[2] IB visited Felix Frankfurter in Heath, Massachusetts, and was introduced to Reinhold Niebuhr,[3] who offered to contact Sir Stafford Cripps on his behalf. When IB and Burgess eventually reached Washington, an encrypted telegram was sent to Gladwyn Jebb at the Foreign Office, under the name of Lord Lothian as British Ambassador, but consisting in substance of the following message from IB:

TO GLADWYN JEBB

24 July 1940 [en clair *typed transcript of encrypted telegram*]

[British Embassy, Washington, DC]

Russians here unexpectedly helpful. Frankfurter and other prominent persons very friendly and prepared to intercede in the manner contemplated. Russian visa granted but do not in any event propose to proceed until and unless His Majesty's Ambassador formally requests appointment of Press Attaché and Moscow and London agree. Hope this meets with your approval.

FO 371/24847, N6063/40/38[4]

Meanwhile Miriam Rothschild, who happened to be in Washington at the time, was horrified to hear of IB's plan to go on to Moscow with Guy

1 Michael Whitney Straight (1916–2004), American economist, author, lecturer and committed supporter of liberal causes; economist for the State Department (SD) 1937–8, 1940–1; editor of *New Republic*, a liberal journal founded by his parents, 1941–3, 1946–56. (His admission in 1963 of his link to the Cambridge spy ring, formed while he was reading for an MA there in 1937, led to the unmasking of Anthony Blunt.)

2 Guy Burgess, Donald Maclean and Harold Kim Philby met as undergraduates in Cambridge in the early 1930s and were recruited as spies by the NKVD, as was Anthony Blunt. Burgess and Maclean subsequently worked for the FO, Philby and (during the war) Blunt for British Intelligence. For years they supplied the USSR with highly sensitive information, until the defection of Burgess and Maclean in 1951 and Philby in 1963. Blunt was publicly unmasked in 1979, having secretly confessed to the British authorities in 1964.

3 Revd Professor Reinhold Niebuhr (1892–1971), Graduate Professor Emeritus of Ethics and Theology, Union Theological Seminary, NY City, since 1928.

4 From which the quotations in the 1940 headnotes that follow are also taken.

Burgess, of whom she had long held a low opinion. At her prompting, her
close friend John Foster, who shared her suspicions of Burgess, urged the
Head of Chancery, Derick Hoyer Millar,[1] *to have Burgess's plans*
blocked. Hoyer Millar agreed to recommend accordingly. IB appears to
have known nothing of these machinations, and to have been taken aback
when on 27 July Fitzroy Maclean[2] *replied to Lothian: 'It is not desired*
that either Berlin or Burgess should proceed to Moscow. Burgess should
return to United Kingdom immediately. Berlin, who is not in the employ
of His Majesty's Government, must do what he thinks best.'

TO MARY FISHER

30 July 1940

as from 2414 Tracy Place, Washington, DC

Dear Mary

I was delighted to receive your letter which arrived this morning. My
voyage was uneventful. We had on board – but I wrote you about all that I
think. The United States is both predictable and not. At first it seems familiar
enough – particularly if one comes via Canada & so gradually into it. Soon
the illusion is dispelled. The chief advantage is that everyone and everything
is very easy. Nothing lacks to human comfort. Everything has been foreseen.
Food is excellent. Trains are comfortable. One can fly anywhere. Temperature is between 94 & 99, but there are air cooled establishments in which
even that is foiled. The population is extravert, friendly and divided into Mrs
Page[3] (or Mrs Plaskett[4] or any American don's wife) Brogan[5] and Prof.
Chamberlain.[6] Mrs Frankfurter here seems much simpler and much more
directly the outcome of surroundings. Not needing to work hard to com-
prehend our complex system she relaxes and obeys reflexes. One can only
admire the extraordinary acuteness of her perceptions in Oxford when

1 Frederick Robert Hoyer Millar (1900–89), Head of Chancery and Counsellor, British Embassy,
  Washington; a relative of John Foster; later (1961) 1st Baron Inchyra.
2 Fitzroy Hew Royle Maclean (1911–96), diplomat, soldier, MP, writer, historian; widely thought
  to have inspired Ian Fleming's James Bond; at this point in the Northern Dept, FO, London;
  parachuted into Yugoslavia 1943 as Churchill's personal envoy to Tito; later (1957) 1st Baronet
  Maclean of Dunconnel.
3 Katharine Elizabeth Page, American wife of the classicist Denys Page (Student and Tutor,
  Christ Church, 1932–50).
4 Edith Alice Plaskett, Canadian wife of H. H. Plaskett, Savilian Professor of Astronomy and
  Fellow of New College 1932–60.
5 Denis William Brogan (1900–74), historian, Fellow and Tutor, Corpus, 1934–9, Professor of
  Political Science, Cambridge, 1939–68.
6 Probably Lawrence Henry Chamberlain (1906–89), assistant professor of Political Science,
  Idaho, 1932–40.

one realizes the lack of effort with which she – & everyone else – lives here. Everything, in comparison with us, is geared down. It goes faster owing to the flatness of the country, the streamlined mechanism, the lack of the unexpected. But in fact neither intellectual nor nervous energy is in demand. I quite see why they find the English unnecessarily complicated about nothing, why they are surprised and wounded by the elaborate, & as seems to them, deliberately difficult attitude adopted to their simple behaviour. New York is in parts like rive droite Paris,[1] in parts like a modern German town, there is no resemblance to London whatever. It is a southern town in spite of skyscrapers, indoor life etc. Only the streets & piazzas are indoors as often as not. New England (Boston I haven't seen) may be like Holland. Other towns are like Sweden etc. There may be individual introversion, mystery etc. There is no social mystery, no special social mazes which in principle cannot be represented by a definite plan, as e.g. Oxford, Cambridge, Bloomsbury, even Edinburgh I expect. This is very grave. There is a total lack of salt, pepper, mustard etc. No spark, at least none I've met yet. *Everything* is stated. If you omit, you are politely but relentlessly pressed for it. Since it can not really be supplied in so many words, systematic misunderstanding, charges of hypocrisy, snobbery, obscurity etc. are bound to arise. I suspect Henry James wrote as he wrote because of a vain effort to render it all explicit, knowing one couldn't, but tantalized all the same. The chief charge against America is its extreme flatness. Mr Connelly[2] is by no means exceptional. Washington is very handsome, very formal, white pillared 1803 palladian buildings surrounded by green trees, very wide streets (avenues they would say) with a clear unequivocal purpose. The population is artificial & very welcoming & courtly. Diplomats, journalists & politicians compose the dominant stratum. I cling to the English desperately. I passionately long to [come] home. England is *infinitely* preferable to the best discoverable here. No doubt this is exactly what the end of the 18th century thought about the 19th. The 19th dealt with much larger issues & despised the 18th for niggling & being blind to $\frac{9}{10}$ of what was going on. We too agree in theory with the 19th as against the 18th century. The 18th century complained chiefly about the absence of feeling for very small differences in the 19th. The broad sweep is here & not in England, it is bolder, more in tune with what the facts demand (I dare say) etc. but tasteless. If one's eye is used to minor shades, the local view is very monotonous. Not to the natives who have macroscopic vision & see in larger units. Politically they are jittering & really frightened, but I can't believe that they can act rapidly. The government is as good as at war, psychologically at least. Every British success is played up.

1 The part of Paris on the right bank (*rive droite*) of the Seine, i.e. the north of the city.
2 Willard Connely (*sic*) (1888–1967), New College English 1925–7.

Our propaganda here is far from good, the policy of no propaganda may have been good a year ago, it is no longer so.[1] The French, Belgians, Germans, Italians do better. We ought to send (1) Gen. Swinton[2] (2) Mr [Harold] Laski (3) Mr Tawney[3] (4) perhaps Mr Spender, perhaps Mr Garvin.[4] The first 3 are Frankfurter's choices, so do tell someone. They wd all do *far* better than the M. of I. people. Audiences for them exist, millions of students worship Laski, Tawney wrote a letter to the, I think, N.Y. Times which had a colossal effect, Swinton would enchant the anti-Roosevellites. Lothian is very popular, easy, affable, fluid, scattered, quick, able, improvisateur. Lothian & Foster are a success. The rest of the Embassy are sticks.

My own affairs are going a little slowly, the Foreign Office is sluggish & not over-eager, but I am mustering ammunition, & will strike before the end of the week. Then, I hope, for Omsk & Tomsk. I met the U.S.A. Ambassador to Moscow yesterday, Mr Laurence A. Steinhardt.[5] A tough, clever, well informed Jewish lawyer. He denounced Seeds[6] passionately (a) for laziness & stupidity (b) for being socially cold towards himself. He is genuinely Anglophile, & ought to be cultivated. If you meet anyone in the Foreign Office, do tell them that it is essential that Cripps should be gushingly nice to him there. If I ever arrive I shall genuinely try & build a bridge myself. He really was, as they wd say here, hopping mad about the treatment of himself, & went on for ½ hour before we got on to my affairs. This holds good in general – Anglophile sentiment, which exists in the middle classes, is not nearly intensively enough cultivated. Even the Pakenhams, operating jointly, could call it forth. I feel irked by staying idly here, & intriguing as slowly as I am doing. But I am assured that this is the only possible tempo. I suspected that my mother would, having been very brave during my departure, then slightly collapse.[7] The whole problem of emotional investment, the rights, duties, and proper technique for investors & investees

---

1 This assessment anticipates the major policy change that began in August 1940. Britain had adopted a low-key approach in the early months of the war because of US mistrust of propaganda, and had relied on US opinion-formers to alter the previously isolationist mood of their country. The fall of France, and the realisation that Britain could not survive without US support, coincided with a growing willingness in the US to contemplate aid for the Allies. Soon after this letter was written, Britain adopted a more active propaganda policy. See also 337/2.

2 Major-General Sir Ernest (Dunlop) Swinton, Chichele Professor of Military History and Fellow of All Souls 1925–39.

3 Richard Henry Tawney (1880–1962), Professor of Economic History, London, 1931–49.

4 James Louis Garvin (1868–1947), Editor of the *Observer* 1908–42.

5 Laurence Adolph Steinhardt (1892–1950), US Ambassador to the USSR 1939–41, to Turkey 1942–5, to Czechoslovakia 1945–8, then (1948–50) to Canada (killed in a plane crash).

6 Sir William Seeds (1882–1973), British Ambassador to the USSR 1939–40.

7 Marie Berlin had written in her diary: 'S[haya] is gone on July the 11. The Lord help me. O, God!'

is very difficult and to me opaque. I *knew* the Jerome pictures would look appalling. I am not photogène, & the sooner, I say tartly, my mother learns that, the better.

My love to your mother, & to Mr Smith, of whom alas Lord Lothian, who wants to know about Wardenship at New Coll. has never heard. Local opinion is hardening against Harlech.[1] The blockade specialist here wants Hichens,[2] & thinks John Maud wd like it. Jean [Maud] is expected shortly with babies. Mrs Falk[3] & Evelyn P-B.[4] both look well. I'll write shortly.

    love

      Shaya

Guy B[urgess] has left for England to-day. The F.O. takes not much interest in me, & I must obviously create my own job. I can't say how bad at this I probably am.

TO MARIE AND MENDEL BERLIN

    31 July 1940

                    2414 Tracy Place, Washington, DC

Dear Pa & Ma,

Here I am, in the lap of luxury. I am living here by the kind hospitality of John Foster, to whom this beautiful house[5] was lent by its owner. I meet journalists and New Dealers, and gently plot for my own further journey. Guy B. has been recalled and will by now have telephoned to you: the Clipper–Lisbon,[6] and Lisbon–England services are now regular if expensive. If I have to return that way I'll try to pay in £, so you may get wire requiring you to pay someone something in London. Fred Rau[7] who has

---

1 Lord Harlech was an Honorary Fellow of New College.
2 William Lionel Hichens (1874–1940), New College classics 1893–97, member of Lord Milner's 'kindergarten' in South Africa, prominent businessman.
3 Wife of (Werner) David Falk (1906–91), German-born moral philosopher, New College PPE 1936–8, philosophy Tutor 1942–50 (moved to Australia 1950, to US 1959).
4 Dorothy Evelyn Mostyn Phelps-Brown, wife of Henry Phelps-Brown, economist, New College.
5 Oddly, when I went to look at this house in 1998, it seemed much less impressive than others in the street, and hardly beautiful.
6 The transatlantic sea-planes of this period were known as clippers, after the sailing ships.
7 Frederick Solomon Rau (1906–56), junior partner in Derby & Co., London metal-brokers. He was not called up because of the importance of his work for the war, and went to the US to ply his trade. He was also active in the London lodge of B'nei B'rith, and known to IB because his mother (see p. 331 below) was a friend of Marie Berlin.

kindly offered me part of his hotel apartment when I am in N. York (on the whole more comfortable & less committal than staying with Mulya)[1] is surrounded by relations as always. His office is Philipp Bros,[2] 70, Pine Street N. York, & his hotel the Shoreham in 55th Street. Aronsons live in a small, dear, noisy flat off Broadway, he complains of lack of connections, could I put him in touch with Warburgs[3] etc. naturally I neither can nor would do any such thing which he by now comprehends. He listens to Radio all day & all night and panics about England, very unnecessarily and without basis of fact. I saw Mr Laurence Steinhardt yesterday, the U.S.A. Ambassador to U.S.S.R., a very interesting, tough, realistic lawyer who strongly encouraged me, and invited me to meals should I ever be in his vicinity. He belongs to the vigorous pushing Jewish type which achieves a lot, and was illuminating both about Russia and about our own very gentlemanly people there. He hopes much from Cripps. Molotov[4] is due to make a statement to-day, so we shall see. Mother would like America v. much: open, vigorous, $2 \times 2 = 4$ sort of people, who want yes or no for an answer. No nuances. Food is superb everywhere. There is a lot of pro-British sentiment, some not yet adequately tapped, Lothian and Foster are both great successes. The Frankfurters could not be nicer to me, he does what he can, introduces, encourages etc. Their view is that I either go on or go back, but all agree that much negotiation still remains to be done. To-day I lunch with Ben Cohen[5] one of the President's closest New Deal advisers, the man who drafts the whole legislation. A very open, straight, honest, good, solid, excellent Jew, 200% American. Goodhart[6] has not responded yet, he may be on vacation: I sent him his brother's note of recommendation. A visa to my ultimate goal has been given me without trouble, so there is no hitch there. I'll wire at

1 Samuel Aronson.

2 A leading metal-broking company, founded by Oscar Philipp on behalf of himself and his brother in England in 1909, in NY in 1914.

3 The prominent American banking family, to whom Ingrid Warburg and her parents were closely related. See pp. 720–1 below.

4 Vyacheslav Mikhailovich Molotov, né Skriyabin (1890–1986), Soviet politician and staunch supporter of Stalin; Chairman of the Council of People's Commissars of the USSR 1930–41, Deputy Chairman 1941–2 (after Stalin himself took over as head of government), First Deputy Chairman 1942–6; People's Commissar for Foreign Affairs 1939–46; negotiated Molotov–Ribbentrop pact with Nazi Germany in 1939. The 'Molotov cocktail', a crude incendiary weapon, was named after him.

5 Benjamin Victor Cohen (1894–1983), lawyer and (from 1933) presidential adviser, key figure in FDR and Truman administrations, draftsman of much New Deal legislation; Assistant General Counsel, National Power Policy Commission, 1934–41, Special Assistant (on public utility holding company litigation) to US Attorney General 1941–2, Assistant to Director, Office of Economic Stabilization, 1942–3, General Counsel, Office of War Mobilization, 1943–5, Counsellor, State Dept, 1945–7.

6 Howard Lehman Goodhart (1885–1951), US stockbroker, brother of Arthur Lehman Goodhart (1891–1978), Professor of Jurisprudence at Oxford 1931–51.

regular intervals. My health is *excellent*, I sleep, eat, talk better than in England or anywhere. Nothing to say.

love

Shaya.

Lord Lothian sent another telegram on 1 August:

Mr Berlin's statement, reported in my telegram[1] [. . .] that Russian visa has been granted him is not exactly accurate. The real position is as follows: when, before the receipt of your telegram [. . .] we asked Soviet Embassy whether they would ask for diplomatic visa for Burgess to enable him to proceed to Moscow with bag, they replied that they had received instructions to grant diplomatic visas not only to Burgess but also to Berlin on receipt of passports from us. We have however so far not sent Berlin's passport to the Soviet Embassy to be visa'd. Burgess returned to the United Kingdom to-day. Berlin himself is anxious to proceed to Moscow in a week or so, he hopes through contacts with the Soviet Embassy here to obtain positive confirmation that he would not be non-persona grata in Moscow. He considers, apparently with reason, that this is already indicated by the fact that instructions have been sent to give him a diplomatic visa. Before proceeding to Moscow he would in any case communicate with Cripps. I should be glad to learn if I may forward his passport to Soviet Embassy to enable him to obtain a diplomatic visa. It seems questionable whether they would give him an ordinary visa without our intervention.

TO MARIE AND MENDEL BERLIN

2 August 1940

2414 Tracy Place, Washington, DC

Dear Pa & Ma.

I have got both your letters of the 22·7 & the 25·7 which arrived simultaneously. I am still here and glad to hear you are so well. As for me I am patiently plying my Embassy for continuation of voyage. It will take some time I think. Burgess was suddenly recalled – he will have phoned by now – but the F.O. telegram explicitly stated in answer to enquiry from our Embassy that I was not a HMG. servant & could use my own best judgment as to what to do. Which I am in fact doing.

Every local attempt possible is being made to induce the Americans to part with some of their destroyers, but the Presidential election – the inability to take decisive steps because they may be used as material by the other

1 The telegram relaying IB's message to Jebb, reproduced above, p. 318.

side, spoils everything. No doubt Hitler knows this too. But Lothian & Foster are both very active and popular, & something may yet be done. Thank you for the Oxford Greats report. I am greatly relieved about Ev. Standard: not only wd anything in that have been *most* unwelcome publicity but as I am still not officially appointed, any statement wd irritate the F.O. terribly & prejudice my appointment a good deal. So do keep them away.[1] I wonder who told them. The heat has declined, the weather is very agreeable. Fred Rau has established himself in the Hotel Shoreham, 55th Street, New York, where he has kindly offered me indefinite hospitality, so in N. York I'll occupy a bed in his suite, which is again nicer than isolation: as for Bermuda the points are (1) it is perfectly legal to send money there to our relations, but it is not withdrawable at will, (2) Butterfields[2] are probably over-invested in relatively to their assets, Jamaica is advised where they can easily get it. Best do nothing at the moment, the relations probably have enough to live on at present in W. Indies. Have not seen Goodhart yet. I am *v. well* & will go on wiring weekly,

> Love
>
> > Shaya.

On 3 August Fitzroy Maclean at the Foreign Office comments: 'Mr Berlin is intolerable', and drafts a reply to Lord Lothian: 'You should do nothing to assist Mr Berlin in obtaining Soviet visa. As he has already been informed, it is not desired to employ him at Moscow.'

IB's new contacts in America had their own ideas as to where he might best serve his country. John Wheeler-Bennett had met IB on his first evening in Washington and had been deeply impressed. He later recalled that IB 'had been in America scarcely forty-eight hours but his comments on the situation would seem to betoken a lifetime of acquaintance with that country'.[3] As IB would clearly be a valuable addition to the British contingent in America, Wheeler-Bennett, Aubrey Morgan[4] and others started to exert pressure within the Embassy to find him a post. IB himself remained determined to go on to Moscow or back to Oxford.

1 Presumably they were seeking an interview on IB's proposed role in the USSR.
2 One of the main banks in Bermuda, established in 1858.
3 Sir John Wheeler-Bennett, *Special Relationships: America in Peace and War* (London, 1975), 87.
4 Aubrey Niel *Morgan (1904–85), Survey Section, British Library of Information, 1939–40; BPS 1940–2 (Special Assistant to the Director-General of BIS 1941–2); Deputy Director-General of BIS and head of BIS NY 1942–5.

TO MARION FRANKFURTER

Monday [5 August 1940]

2414 Tracy Place, Washington

Dear Marion,

My affairs are moving, but ever so slowly. I suddenly feel acutely depressed. The stock of bouyancy [*sic*] with which I arrived from England
has now become exhausted and both the public and the private situation
seem overcast. John Foster keeps assuring us all that the destroyer situation
is really acute: that these 50 American boats may well make the whole
difference between survival and defeat: that if the German invasion succeeds
and the American people is then told that but for these few ships it might
have been averted they will, justifiably enough, say that they didn't realize it
was as critical as that, and that because no adequate steps are being taken to
inform them in spite of General Pershing[1] or William Allen White.[2] The
Embassy does its best but it is unimaginative and giftless as a propaganda
agency, etc. I suppose radio commentators ought to be told directly, but no
one seems to know how this is done.

As for my private affairs, my Foreign Office has now turned slightly sour
and said that they never said that any assistance from me was wanted in
Moscow – which is the very opposite of what I set out with, after conversations in London. I see the Russian Ambassador to-morrow morning:
even if the Russians put up no obstacles, there is still Cripps to be won
& even then London may cut up rough. They don't seem to care what one
is doing & urge similar indifference upon the Embassy. My personal relations with this latter body are very affable, but I am slowly turning anti-
British and mildly embittered about my treatment. The French are in a
disgusting state of personal sauve qui peut-ism, repeating proudly whenever
one talks to them: 'we are defeated nation' as if that was a perfectly recognized honourable status conferring certain definite rights and protecting
the holder from attack. And they perpetually harp on Oran[3] and the loss of
1400 Frenchmen. The Belgians are just as bad. Everyone is having a sort of
dreary good time, while the citizens of the U.S.A. rightly marvel and are
indignant. If my intrigue proceeds at its present snail's pace I think the best

1 John Joseph Pershing (1860–1948), Commander-in-Chief, American Expeditionary Force, First
   World War. In a national radio broadcast on 4 August General Pershing had recommended
   that at least 50 superannuated destroyers be handed over to Britain.
2 William Allen White (1868–1944), influential Kansas editor, in 1940 founding chairman of the
   Committee to Defend America by Aiding the Allies, whose aim was to encourage 'all aid short
   of war' for the Allies. White was also allegedly responsible for suggesting to FDR that
   Frankfurter be appointed to the Supreme Court.
3 On the Algerian coast; scene of British naval action against French ships in early July 1940, to
   prevent them being taken over by Germany.

thing would perhaps be to take a boat & proceed back while it is still possible: I shall return to equal inactivity in England, but at least in a familiar context and with no guilt about deserting my family and countrymen in order to do nothing. My family will protest, my countrymen will be indifferent, but at least this peculiarly painful suspense in the bogus atmosphere of Washington diplomatic life will be ended. There is talk, if the Russia scheme fails, of attaching me to the local Embassy, but unless there is something vital to do, I cannot see how, whatever may threaten at home, I can possibly accept without profound dishonour. I do apologize for maundering so, I shall recover by to-morrow, and face the same objective situation in a less enfeebled mood. I haven't met Mr Macleish[1] yet, as he has had to go away suddenly for 10 days: I have been on [an] appallingly ill-conceived diplomatic picnic in the course of which I delivered a passionate defence of the French Rothschilds whom I disapprove of: I have met Mr Krock[2] who is a monster, a leaner over backwards, a hollow, ashamed, dishonest, uncomfortable, pourri[3] figure, an appeaser of the first water, a general traitor and symptom of the spineless attitude of the crypto-Jews of this remarkable land. As for the U.S.A. I haven't seen it. Such odd corners of it as I have come across strike me as full of individuals endowed with far greater vitality, honesty and simplicity than anyone in Europe: everything is clear, explicit, floodlit even. They seem to me to be on better moral terms with their environment and problems than we are: i.e. they don't shrink from discovering where the centre of moral gravity lies, what is fundamental, what requires to be done in a particular situation. Sometimes they may not do it, but then it is explicit lying or betrayal, not the decayed atmosphere of half truth half self deception, which blurs the issue and makes all courses of action seem equally crude and not wholly justified by the facts, in which Europe, even the Nazis, live. I am myself a little disturbed by this terrific clarity & emphasis: where nothing is taken for granted, everything is stated in so many unambiguous terms, no secret seasoning is tasteable, everything is what it is and proclaims itself sometimes at great length, to be so. But it is superior to the nuances and evasions of England or France. Aesthetically inferior but morally superior. It destroys art but conduces to life, liberty and the pursuit of happiness. So must the 19th century have seemed to the last survivals of the 18th – effete old men who finessed away about what to the 19th century seemed despicable trifles in comparison with what needed doing, avoidance of daylight

1 Archibald MacLeish (1892–1982), poet, Librarian of Congress 1939–44, Director, Office of Facts and Figures, 1941–2, Assistant Director, Office of War Information (OWI), 1942–3, Assistant Secretary of State for Public and Cultural Relations 1944–5.
2 Arthur Krock (1886–1974), Washington correspondent, New York Times, 1932–53.
3 'Rotten'.

& relegation of the great issues for the sake of private games, but was nevertheless everything to them (the 18th century survivals). We really are ghosts compared to you. I see what stopped Maurice from remaining here, in spite of the bitternesses of Oxford. And I see what would suit Freddie who is not very pervious to atmosphere, and likes one to say 2 + 2 = 4, yes or no. Everything here – not only estates, distances, fortunes, but faces, thought behaviour is large, clear, articulate, deliberate but on occasion slightly taste-less & flat, by comparison with the unnecessary and meaningless (by now) tortuosities of Europe. Perhaps England was like that vis a vis France or Austria in 1840. I admire it, envy it, even feel sympathy with it, but am overpowered by the over-simplification. There is no defence for our obsolete refinements. They may offer escape to dissatisfied Americans, & may [be] good for the Kleinkunst[1] we produce, but are intrinsically bad, ruin lives & countries to no end, have long outlived even their decorative function, like the etiquette of Spain. But I am used to them, and still unfamiliar with this wholemeal diet. My love to Felix and to your sister if she is still with you (and even if not) & I hope to see you soon.

    Yours

      Shaya

Supplement on Baroness.[2]

I saw a photograph[3] of her the other day, & it is alas definitely not our old Wangenheim[4] – more's the pity. Wheeler Bennett defended Trott passion-ately to me as a good European or something, how *can* we win the war? the Westrick[5] job has been very well done. I am still full of memories of Mr Krock, how *did* you manage to breed such a caricature of a Munichois English gent.? so cowardly, so corrupt, so malignant? is this too strong?

---

1 'Cabaret'.
2 Baroness Ingrid von Wallenheim, secretary to Gerhard Westrick (see note 5 below).
3 Enclosed with letter.
4 Luise, Baroness Götz von Wangenheim (1899–1985).
5 Gerhard Alois Westrick, one-legged German Commercial Counsellor, corporate lawyer, high-ranking Nazi and commercial spy, in the US from March 1940 to ensure that American production met Germany's war needs rather than those of Britain. In June, Westrick's associates in the top echelons of the US business community gave a party for him at the Waldorf-Astoria Hotel to celebrate the fall of France to the Nazis. British Intelligence alerted the *New York Herald Tribune*, who duly informed the nation. When the FBI decided that he had obtained a driving licence illegally, having concealed his disability, Westrick was recalled to Germany.

TO SIR STAFFORD CRIPPS[1]

7 August 1940 [en clair *typed transcript of encrypted telegram*]

2414 Tracy Place, Washington, DC

UNDERSTAND NIEBUHR[2] KINDLY COMMUNICATED ABOUT ME HAVE ARRIVED
WASHINGTON ON STRENGTH UNDERSTANDING WITH LONDON THAT IF
CONSIDERED SUITABLE BY YOURSELF AND IF SOVIET GOVERNMENT AGREE-
ABLE LONDON WILLING APPOINT ME ATTACH[É] STOP COURIERS VISA
MOSCOW NOW WAITING FOR ME SOVIET EMBASSY HERE STOP HAVE
REQUESTED SOVIET AMBASSADOR INFORMALLY TO INQUIRE WHETHER IN
EVENT OF APPLICATION APPROPRIATE VISA LIKELY TO BE GRANTED IF REPLY
FAVOURABLE MAY I COMMUNICATE AGAIN.

FO 371/24847, N6063/40/38

*Fitzroy Maclean annotates: 'Mr. Berlin is trying to double cross us. We
had better telegraph to Sir S Cripps.'*

TO MARIE AND MENDEL BERLIN

8 August [1940]

2414 Tracy Place, Washington, DC

Dear Ma & Pa,

My situation is now this: the Russians seem quite disposed to give me
facilities, but Sir S. Cripps is convinced he does not need me: I shall go on
faintly hammering at him, but I think it may now safely be assumed that the
Embassy scheme will probably come to absolutely nothing. With this my
raison d'être in Washington disappears: the Embassy here would probably be
quite glad to use me as a cipher clerk, but that is not a sufficient reason for
remaining. On the other hand Mr Childs[3] – you may remember Hugh
Seton Watson's[4] despatches from Belgrade – is here for the Ministry of
Information and he does need staff in the British Library of Information in

---

1 Cripps had arrived in Moscow in June.
2 The decipherment of his telegram to Cripps (also dated 7 August) appears on the same sheet,
  and reads: 'CONFIDENT I BERLIN OF ALL SOULS NOW HERE WOULD BE OF REAL HELP TO YOU
  AND URGE YOUR USE OF HIM MAN OF GREAT DISCRETION AND EXCEPTIONAL SUITABLE
  ATTAINMENTS FELIX KNOWS HIM INTIMATELY AND HOLDS HIM IN HIGHEST ESTEEM'.
3 Stephen Lawford Childs (1896–1943) had previously worked in southern Russia (economic
  rebuilding of anti-Bolshevik areas 1918–20), Geneva (refugee work with League of Nations
  1921–6 and from 1929) and South America (1926–9); later apparently with the ILO in Geneva;
  diplomatic service Belgrade 1939–40 and briefly in Paris 1940; Embassy Press Office, BIS
  Washington 1940–2. He was killed in an air crash between Iraq and Iran in January 1943.
4 (George) Hugh Nicholas Seton-Watson (1916–84), son of Robert (301/1), served in British
  Legations in Belgrade and Bucharest 1940–1; Fellow and Praelector in Politics, University
  College London, 1946–51.

New York. He wants me to go and see him to-morrow (Friday), I may be useful as a contact with Jews etc.: If I am really needed there I may stay, as in England, being neither fit for even L.D.V. nor in any government dept, I should be doing nothing at all. So I may promise to stay on if they need me, for a few weeks at any rate. To-morrow also I make my first contact with Howard Goodhart and dine with Ingrid [Warburg]. I hope Burgess gave you my greetings: he ought to be home by now: there is a battle here about giving us the needed destroyers – they are all tied up in their own legal difficulties, Munich attitudes etc. but our cause is undoubtedly making headway. I hope it will be in time. I am, of course, very well, and longing to get back home: I don't really adore America at all, the English here are oases in a desert. As soon as I get to N.Y. I shall (1) check your bristles – that will be in order I am sure (2) ask Fred about help to our relations in W. Indies – he'll know more about official British regulations than they seem to know in the Embassy. Have met v. nice treasury man called Stopford[1] who was with Runciman in Prague.[2]

Love

Shaya

TO CRESSIDA RIDLEY

11 August 1940 [*postcard*]

2414 Tracy Place, Washington, DC

I address it queerly[3] because I am not sure of the address again. I am still vainly struggling eastwards: I cannot tell you what mountains I've already moved, it is all but perfected and yet I believe there will be a loose link somewhere & I shall return ignominiously v. soon. Mrs Heathcote Amory[4] (called Gaynor perhaps?) sends her love. I shall tell you & Jasper about Washington life: it is very odd. The Americans are very pro-Allied, but befuddled & frightened. I cannot bear – I mean I can & hate – being here, intriguing, being frustrated, alone, doubtfully placed.

yrs

Shaya

---

1 Robert Jemmett Stopford (1895–1978), banker, member of Runciman Commission to Czechoslovakia, 1938, Financial Counsellor, British Embassy, Washington, 1940–3, War Office 1943–5.

2 Runciman's mission to Czechoslovakia (285/5), designed to put pressure on the Czech Government, led to Munich.

3 i.e. c/o her father, Sir Maurice Bonham Carter.

4 Hon. (Margaret Irène) Gaenor Heathcoat Amory (1919–2002), daughter of 8th Baron Howard de Walden, wife since 1938 of Richard Frank Heathcoat Amory, who worked in the Washington Embassy 1939–42.

TO MARIE AND MENDEL BERLIN

Monday 12 August [1940]

The Shoreham, New York City

Dear Ma & Pa,

It is about 12.30 at night, I am in quiet and comfortable room, wondering sadly how you all are. I am far too well considering the state of the world. My negotiations have reached this point: the Russians seem to have no special objection. The obstacle is Sir S. Cripps himself who says (1) there is no accomodation(!) (2) no chance of work. This is a little infuriating considering the effort involved. I may go on battering at him, meanwhile there may be work here: Childs (the villain of the Seton Watson letters) who is a v. nice man, wants me to stay here & do some work in the British Library of Information. And there may be some work to do co-ordinating the Jews to help the Cause. They are all very eager – I am busily interviewing Zionists, anti-Zionists, Labour etc – to help & complain that not enough is being made of their enthusiasm. So something may be doable. I went for a week-end to stay with the Wilmerses[1] in Stamford near N. Y. City. He is an old friend of Rau. She is an Eitingon,[2] of the Moscow & Lodz furriers, speaks Russian & is quite nice. In the afternoon Ingrid Warburg came over. She helps me a lot with the Jews.

Mrs Rau junior[3] is here now & reports that Mrs Rau senior[4] in Montreal is full of small but bitter complaints about this and that. They don't seem to get on excessively well. Arthur Rau[5] seems to have [gone] for a holiday to N. Wales: why don't you? or the Lakes? find out where Dr Falk of New College has gone – he says it is a nice hotel in the lakes which he knows & recommends. I am here till Thursday when I go to Washington with a small report for the Embassy. Foster has gone to California for a holiday, so I shall stay with an old Embassy Englishman called Elmslie[6] who has invited me, probably for a few days. So between 15th & 19th my address is uncertain, but 2414 Tracy Place or the Embassy c/o Elmslie wd find me. I really cannot

---

1 Charles Kossman Wilmers (1909–80), from London, managing director of a Belgian company, had met his Polish-born wife Cesia Eitingon (1907–99) on the transatlantic liner *Aquitania* when she was returning from a trip to the USSR with her uncle Motty Eitingon (336/6).
2 The Eitingon family firm had a near-monopoly of the export trade in Russian furs, with a branch in the US as well as in several European countries. One of Sigmund Freud's closest colleagues was an Eitingon, as was the NKVD general who organised the murder of Trotsky a few days after this letter was written.
3 Fred Rau's wife, Johanna ('Hanna'/'Natiya') Rau (c.1911–57).
4 Fred Rau's mother, Käthe Rau.
5 Fred Rau's elder brother, Arthur Aron Rau (b. 1898).
6 William Gray Elmslie (b. 1896), Honorary Attaché, British Embassy, Washington, since 1939.

bring myself to stay with Aronson again, tho' he presses & Fanny is really v. kind. Their rooms are hot, noisy and too small, the child etc. Fred Rau is being v. nice to me & gives sound advice on all points. I visit (1) Brown Harriman,[1] to-morrow (b) Howard Goodhart with whom I dine. Also the Presidents of the Zionist & anti-Zionist factions[2] respectively. I'll lunch with Akzine.[3] It is sad that Jabotinsky[4] is dead. He was a very colourful, sympathetic, if wild figure, from a nicer age. Haven't seen Felix for sometime. Nice about Mrs Woolf.[5] Do whatever you think fit about my £2000 or so – invest them where you please – mention John as reference if you want to. I have not yet visited the World's Fair!

    love

        Shaya

I cannot say how much I *long* to go home. How much nicer England is. The pro-British campaign is in full swing here. I can't believe that they believe that they will manage to keep out of war. But our propaganda *must* be strengthened.

Meanwhile events in Europe reinforced the arguments for retaining IB as a British official in America. In his words:

Then I began to be offered British jobs in Washington. I could see what it was. By this time we'd reached mid-August, Battle of Britain; they thought, 'Hey, the Germans might win, they might invade Britain' – in which case, if I was there, I'd be caught and tortured and killed, and I must be saved. Not a word was said about this, but it was clear to me that was the secret agenda. I was touched, but nobody said it, and I began to be offered posts.[6]

---

1 The oldest and largest partnership bank in the US.

2 Rabbi Solomon Goldman (1893–1953), President of the Zionist Organization of America 1938–40, and probably the lawyer Solomon Marcuse Stroock (1874–1945), then President of the American Jewish Committee.

3 Benjamin Akzin (b. 1904), native of Riga, constitutional lawyer and political scientist, early supporter of the Revisionist party, head of the political division of the New Zionist Organization 1936–41, political adviser then secretary to the Zionist Emergency Committee in the US 1945–7.

4 Ze'ev (Vladimir) Jabotinsky (1880–1940), Russian-Jewish Zionist leader, founder of the Revisionist Zionist Movement, died in the US on 3 August while visiting Betar, the youth organisation of the Revisionist Zionist Party.

5 This may be the occasion, recounted by IB, on which Virginia Woolf sent IB an invitation that he was unable to accept because he was abroad.

6 MI Tape 7.

TO MARIE AND MENDEL BERLIN

16 August [1940]

2414 Tracy Place, Washington, but
As from Shoreham Hotel, 55th Street, New York

My dear parents

The papers this morning are full of the attacks on Croydon[1] etc. more credence is given to English than to German versions.

My position is largely unchanged. New organizations, sponsored by the British Embassy, are being constructed, and they wish, Frankfurters approving, to fit me in while waiting for the Russians to decide, which I suspect they will never do at all. It is, of course, best to say nothing at all about this to anyone: whatever I do is confidential & neither Burgess, nor the Evening Standard, nor anyone ought to be told: people talk & that necessarily leads to distortion & bureaucratic trouble. So if asked, say you know nothing: that I am a bad correspondent (which after all is true) etc. Mr Willkie[2] makes his "acceptance" speech to-morrow, & after that Roosevelt may become bolder in his foreign policy. He is too reticent at present. I live in the Shoreham in N.Y. because (1) I must have an address (2) Rau lives there, & when he goes away I occupy his room which costs me less. Life is very dear, of course, but people are kind, & I stay with them de temps en temps.[3] I rang up Holdstein[4] yesterday: Sophie is away on holiday, he was very affable, enthusiastic, anxious to help me in any way, to have me to stay at the seaside etc. Obviously a very nice man; Aronson also, of course, presses me to stay with him, in New York, but his bedroom is small, hot, noisy, & he snores louder than anyone I've ever heard. However I'll humour all these people in some way. Theodore Gaster[5] is here, attached to the American-Jewish Committee, which is the rich Jews' anti-Zionist organization, which, if I stay, I will persuade to co-operate with us. (Perlzweig[6] is supposed to be coming

1 Croydon airfield had been one of the targets for heavy Luftwaffe bombing on 15 August; however, Luftwaffe losses were so severe that the German pilots named it 'Black Thursday'. Soon afterwards the Germans mistakenly transferred the main focus of their attack from military targets to London, thereby allowing the RAF the opportunity to recover from their own losses. This misjudgement eventually determined the outcome of the Battle of Britain.

2 Wendell Lewis Willkie (1892–1944), Republican presidential nominee 1940, candidate for re-nomination 1944; against the New Deal, but liberal, in favour of civil rights, and internationalist.

3 'From time to time'.

4 Walter Holdstein (1895–1968) founded General Sportcraft Co. Ltd (now Sportcraft Ltd) in NY. His wife Sophie died in 2002 aged 100.

5 Theodore Herzl Gaster (1906–92), expert on Judaism, comparative religion, and folklore.

6 Maurice L. Perlzweig (1895–1985), one of the leaders of the Liberal Jewish movement in the UK before the war, serving in several London synagogues; founding member of World Jewish Congress 1936 (first chairman of British section), nominated head of World Jewish Congress Dept of International Affairs, NY, 1942.

late in August, I am sure to see him) I had lunch with Dr Akzin, who sends his regards: I think he fancies himself as Jabotinsky's successor: he is a pompous, artificially tactful little man, but by no means a fool. There is no news here about Riga,[1] I don't suppose you have much in London. I ought to try & find the Raskin's,[2] I don't know their address. Perhaps via Mrs Wilmers-Eitingon & the fur trade. Messrs Brown H. & Co were very polite & have promised to supply a full list of bristle cases:[3] they said they gathered it was insured. If you wd like to wire me what you think the list to be I could check it, if you think it necessary, & confirm. But possibly this is not required. I circulate between N.Y. & Washington. I am sure you are in good spirits. I am enormously well.

love,
    Isaiah Berlin.

It is best to write to Shoreham, W. 55th Street N. York.: of course Tracy Place, or British Embassy will forward.

> On 18 August the Foreign Office sent a telegram to Stafford Cripps (repeated to Washington): 'I understand that Mr Berlin has suggested in a telegram to you from Washington that in principle we agree to his being attached to your staff. This is not the case. Indeed we have repeatedly informed Mr Berlin that it is not desired to employ him at Moscow.'
>
>   The episode led to a flurry of enquiries in London in January 1941, in response to a remark by Fitzroy Maclean that 'If we had been consulted, we should certainly have had something to say about [Mr Berlin] being sent to Moscow.'[4] It emerges that the passport was issued at the request of a Colonel J. N. Tomlinson[5] of the Passport Control Department.[6] Maclean comments: 'It seems odd that Colonel Tomlinson should have

1 The latest surviving communication sent from Riga to IB's parents is from Marie's father, and dated 8 August 1940, some two months after Riga came under Soviet control. He says they are well, and concludes: 'Keep well my dear children, from me your father who wishes you all the Good and hopes to see you.' An earlier postcard, dated 9 January 1940, has been stamped with the eagle and swastika by the Nazi postal censor in Königsberg, Germany, on its way to London – an uncanny harbinger of the Nazi occupation of Riga in mid-1941: the Nazis murdered virtually the entire Jewish population of the city within months.

2 sc. the Raskins, Russian émigrés in the fur trade, friends of the Berlins, who lived in London, in Avenue Mansions in the Finchley Road, but were often in NY on business. They had a son who emigrated from Russia direct to the US, and a daughter, Rosa, who went to NY during the war, and emigrated to the US after her parents' death. The reference here is probably to the parents.

3 Presumably the containers in which the bristles were shipped.

4 See IB's comment in his letter of 15 September to his parents, p. 347 below.

5 Apparently on secondment from the Royal Engineers.

6 Code name for the SIS.

taken it upon himself to send Mr Berlin to Moscow at a time when we
were doing what we could to prevent him from going there. I really think
that Northern Department[1] *might have been consulted. It would be*
interesting to know what D's organisation[2] *intended that Mr Berlin and*
Mr Burgess should do in Moscow.' The reply to this (from J. M. Addis)[3]
is that 'Colonel Tomlinson did no more than give a telephone message on
behalf of a superior[4] *(now happily liquidated, I understand). He remembers*
no more of the incident.' At this point the matter is allowed to drop.

TO MARIE AND MENDEL BERLIN

20 August [1940]

The Shoreham, New York

Dear Pa & Ma

There is really nothing to report. My position is as undetermined as
before, tho' the next few days may work a change & stabilize me. As for
[Brown] Harrimans, there is nothing beyond what I've already stated. We
naturally cling to our radios & listen from hour to hour: "ils arrivent
lentement mais enfin ils arrivent"[5] is true of the Americans: Cambon[6] said
it about the English in the last war. Frankfurters could not be kinder or nicer
– this applies to everyone – I am now au fait with Embassy affairs, the
blockade people are now working extremely well, all the non-diplomats –
Lothian, Foster, the financial, economic, trade people are 1000% more
efficient than the diplomats who are comic characters. What they need here
is an economic dictator à la Reading[7] in the last war – Wilfred Green[8] wd

---

1 The department of the FO then responsible for Scandinavia, the Baltic States, the USSR and
   Afghanistan.
2 A reference to (Edward) Hugh (John Neale) Dalton (1887–1962), who in July 1940 set up the
   SOE (Special Operations Executive), incorporating (coincidentally, but appropriately enough)
   Section D of the SIS ('D' for 'destruction'), then under Colonel Laurence Grand (whom IB had
   visited before his departure).
3 John Mansfield Addis (1914–83), Christ Church classics 1933–6, diplomat 1938–74; later
   Ambassador to, successively, Laos, the Philippines and China.
4 Unidentified.
5 'They are slow to come but they come in the end'.
6 Jules Martin Cambon (1845–1935), French diplomat, Ambassador to Germany 1907–14;
   chairman of the Council of Ambassadors charged with enforcement of the Treaty of Versailles
   1920–2.
7 Rufus Daniel Isaacs (1860–1935), 1st Marquess of Reading, Lord Chief Justice 1913–21, employed
   during the First World War in special duties to further the war effort; President of Anglo-
   French Loan Mission to US 1915, Special Envoy to US 1917, High Commissioner and Ambassador to US 1918.
8 Sir Wilfrid Arthur Greene (1883–1952), lawyer, Fellow of All Souls 1907–14, 1932–52, 1st Baron
   Greene 1941, Master of the Rolls 1937–49.

do it very well. If it wasn't only for the pace, which is so slow. Bullitt's[1] speech was simply terrific spoken in a kind of white passion, designed to remove the doubtful taste left by his utterances when he returned from France. There is naturally an isolationist outcry of 'warmonger, near-traitor! etc,' but the effect is bound to outweigh Lindbergh.[2] The extraordinary thing about the latter is that he is supposed to be really fonder of France than of the Reich, yet too proud to say so in case it looks like a concession to his opponents. He is said to lack all influence now: his wife[3] is worried but loyal – generally opinion is, wherever I have moved, terrifically pro-British. The chief anti-British element are, by our friends, said to be the Irish – Cudahy[4] etc.

Perlzweig is supposed – so Nahum Goldmann[5] of the World Jewish Congress told me – to be coming here with some official statement from the F.O. perhaps you cd tell him how, by that time, you & mother are, & whether you contemplate staying in London, it will probably be quicker than by letter, telegrams conveying so little. I told you I think about Holdstein's affability to me & his promise to do anything to help – invitations to his house etc. Yesterday I met the furrier Moté Ettingon,[6] precise equivalent of a Hampstead Russian Jew à l'Americaine. I must research & look for the Raskins. Do write to New York. I am *exceedingly* well. The news from England are so far really wonderful.[7]

Yr affec. son
    Isaiah Berlin.

---

1 William Christian Bullitt (1891–1967), first US Ambassador to the USSR 1933–6 (later fiercely anti-Soviet), Ambassador to France 1936–41, Ambassador at Large 1941–2, Special Assistant to the Secretary of the Navy 1942–4, Major in the Free French Army 1944–5; co-author with Sigmund Freud of *Thomas Woodrow Wilson, Twenty-Eighth President of the United States: A Psychological Study* (London, 1937).

2 Charles Augustus Lindbergh (1902–74), pilot, inventor, author, became an international hero in 1927 after making the first non-stop flight across the Atlantic; widely criticised for accepting a decoration from Germany in 1938 and for his strongly isolationist views in the early years of the war, when his campaign for American neutrality (later as a speaker for the America First Committee) led also to accusations of anti-Semitism.

3 Anne Spencer Morrow (Lindbergh) (1906–2001), writer, aviator, daughter of Dwight Morrow, sister-in-law of Aubrey Morgan, married Lindbergh 1929; in 1932 their son was kidnapped and murdered.

4 John Clarence Cudahy (1887–1943), US Minister to Ireland 1937–40.

5 The Zionist Nahum Goldmann represented the Jewish Agency in NY at this time. IB later wrote a memoir of him: 'Nahum Goldmann (1895–1982): A Personal Impression', in William Frankel (ed.), *Survey of Jewish Affairs 1983* (Rutherford/Madison/Teaneck and London/Toronto, 1985), 238–43.

6 Motty (*sic*) Eitingon (*sic*) (1885–1956), born in Russia; wholesale fur dealer on the grand scale.

7 In the intensifying Battle of Britain there had been massive German bombing raids the previous week over the south of England, and the Luftwaffe had sustained much heavier losses than the RAF. In the House of Commons on the evening of the day this letter was

21 August 1940

The Shoreham, New York

Dear Mary,

I continue to be miserable. Instead of serving my country in a dashing & individual (as they wd say here) fashion, I am stuck ingloriously here waiting for what daily grows more certain disappointment. And moreover I am pressed to do odd jobs here for the Brit. Library of Information, which I can't exactly decline, but which seem to me not worth sitting here for. A new galvanizer, called Mr Childs, accompanied by a Lord Strathallan,[1] Lord Perth's son, are trying to inject life into what is at present a pretty dull concern.[2] Everywhere there are obstacles to everything. I have begun for want of anything better to try & get up some sort of contact between the Embassy and the Jews, who can, should, & aren't being exploited by us at all. The Americans are by now enormously frightened, & if they believed in us sufficiently would certainly hurl themselves to our help with no thought of either yesterday or to-morrow: or rather with vague thought about the day after to-morrow. Remaining here in any capacity is a nightmare to me. No one I've met – the nicest even, have the slightest element of the suppressed reserve of European life which functions as a background unfelt until one is withdrawn from it into this great big glaring sunlit extravert over-articulated scene. I cling with pathos to even the most squalid representatives of our civilization, drawing the line at Mrs Ayer alone. Even Mrs Frankfurter to whom I continue devoted loses half her mystery here. My admiration for Roosevelt has greatly grown when one realizes the crassness he is faced with: to like Americans *very* much – as opposed to admiring, respecting, enjoying, believing in, them, is, I am now sure, a mark of absence of soul: of a passion for the aerated, hygienic and wholesome, an open air attitude which you cannot, I suddenly say testily, expect *me* to sympathize with.

I had a letter from my parents, full of high morale, praising you prodigiously. Do tell them about getting this letter, they *will* be bucked.

---

written Churchill delivered his famous tribute to the British pilots, 'Never in the field of human conflict was so much owed by so many to so few.' *Winston S. Churchill: His Complete Speeches 1897–1963*, ed. Robert Rhodes James (New York, 1974), vol. 6, p. 6266.

1 John David Drummond, Viscount Strathallan (1907–2002), Lieutenant, Intelligence Corps, 1940, War Cabinet Offices 1942–3, Ministry of Production 1944–5; 17th Earl of Perth 1951.

2 A reference to the major intensification of British propaganda in summer 1940 (321/1).

I can now classify all our friends[1] in American political terms: Lightfoot, Dr Creed, Dr Watson, Joseph, Dundas, Masterman are staunch Republicans, Smith, Xtopher, Phelps Brown are left Republicans who voted for Roosevelt in 1932 & now support Willkie, You, I, Master of Balliol, Maurice, Billa, Guy, Wade Gery are Rooseveltites & New Dealers, Dr McCallum, Yorke, Tony, Dodds, Syme, W. J. Turner are isolationists, Jenifer & B.J. are both hauled up for unAmerican activities. I don't know how much longer I am to be kept here, alone in hotel bedroom, waiting for my case to go through. I read Dickens in bulk & feel like a comic litigant ground by the law courts into farcical squalor of some sort. I long to return & dare not for fear that suddenly I may be motioned on by some magical power, & reach Russia after all: meanwhile I hack here more usefully than in England, but drearily enough. Do write, no one does & this increases one's insulation & low morale. The newspapers are terrifically pro-us: success is what they admire: if the R.A.F. go on like this they will plump soon.

love to your mother –
Shaya

TO SHIELA GRANT DUFF

22 August 1940

The Shoreham, New York

I imagine the censor requires me to say: from I. Berlin Esqre, en route eastwards held up by the slow pace of official progress. Oh dear.

Dearest Shiela,

I am ambiguously situated & thoroughly miserable. The Russians are on the point of yielding to my skilled wooing. The Ambassador, who is far from nice, has been won by my discretion. The U.S. State Dept. cd not be more helpful. The Embassy takes no interest: there are individually nice & able people in it, but collectively it is sunk in a bureaucratic swamp to an extent

---

1 Those in this list who have not previously been identified are: Richard Stephen Creed (1898–1964), physiologist, Fellow and Tutor of New College 1925–60; Sydney Watson (1903–91), Organist of New College 1933–8, Master of Music, Winchester College, 1938–45; John Cecil Masterman (1891–1977), historian, Student of Christ Church 1919–46; (Ernest) Henry Phelps-Brown (1906–94), economist, Fellow of New College 1930–47; Wilhelmine 'Billa' Harrod (b. 1911), wife of Roy Harrod; Eric Cecil Yorke (1901–97), classicist, Fellow and Tutor of New College 1927–69; Ronald Syme (1903–89), ancient historian, Fellow of Trinity 1929–49; Walter James Redfern Turner (1889–1946), poet, music and literary critic, colleague of MF on the Joint Broadcasting Committee (under Hilda Matheson), which supplied overseas broadcasting stations with pro-Allied material.

which wd surprise even Balogh.[1] Lothian is very good indeed. So are
Messrs Foster, Rumbold[2] (who used to know Adam) & the entire financial-
economic group. Mr Stopford, late of the Runciman mission is here, & very
sweet & good. all the extra persons drafted in since the war are interesting,
able, energetic, and successful. The purchasing commission works well, it
seems. The only blots are the diplomats. We cannot be attracting the best
minds in the British Isles to the Foreign Office. My misfortunes arise from
the to put it mildly, negative attitude of the F.O. & Sir Staff[ord Cripps],
hence my bitter outlook. I am still struggling. New York is full of persons
who look like (a) Balogh (b) me (c) you (d) the Gauleiter.[3] Nobody much
looks like Hill[4] or Beeley[5] or Douglas. Peggy is a very common type, but in a
weaker, diluted, German form. Herbert occurs more in the Middle West.
Washington where I have spent a miserable fortnight in diplomatic circles
(the French are frightful: the Brit. Emb. is at least personally honest, brave
and reputable. Their fault – this applies to about 5 – is stupidity and internal
strife. The French are personally contemptible.) abounds in Clark-like[6] men,
seasoned with occasional Laffans and Lathams.[7] Christopher is the rarest
type & practically extinct. You & I go down well here, being taken for
granted in our respective ways. I quite seriously think that you wd do far
better here, among the Czechs, than in England: they are rich, & powerful as
you know, but lack proper contact with the English, in spite of Jan Masaryk.[8]
You might ask Wheeler Bennett about that if he is still in England, who is
here in the Brit. Library of Information. A very affable & nice man who
admires everyone, & is a strong Adamite.[9] Ingrid W[arburg] is working on
refugees solidly in her grave fashion & longs to see you. So do I. I hope

1 Thomas Balogh (1905–85), economist, National Institute of Economic Research 1938–42,
   Institute of Statistics, Oxford, 1940–55, later (1968) Baron Balogh of Hampstead.
2 Sir (Horace) Anthony (Claude) *Rumbold (1911–83), diplomat, Washington 1937–42.
3 It is unclear to whom this insulting nickname refers (a Gauleiter was the head of a territorial
   division of the Nazi party).
4 (John Edward) Christopher Hill (1912–2003), Fellow and history Tutor, Balliol 1938–65, later
   (1965–78) Master.
5 Harold Beeley (1909–2001), Queen's history 1931–5, Foreign Research and Press Service (FRPS)
   1939–43, FO Research Dept (FORD) 1943–45. The FRPS was the wartime branch of the Royal
   Institute of International Affairs, set up in 1939 at Balliol under Arnold Toynbee (491/1),
   moving to London in 1943 and merging with the FO's Political Intelligence Dept to form
   FORD.
6 Probably a reference to A. C. Clark. G. N. Clark and Kenneth M. Clark are other possibilities.
7 References to Robert George Dalrymple Laffan (1887–1972), historian, FRPS 1939–43, FORD
   1943–6, and the Australian Richard Thomas Edwin Latham (1909–43), Magdalen law Rhodes
   Scholar 1931–3, Fellow of All Souls 1934–43, FO 1935–41, RAF 1942, shot down 1943.
8 Jan Garrigue Masaryk (1886–1948), son of Thomas Masaryk; Foreign Minister in the émigré
   Czech government in London during the war.
9 Supporter of Adam von Trott.

to move east as soon as possible, but still, altho' most unlikely, if you did come we might meet: unlikely because if Russia falls through I shall return unless violent demand is made for me here: so violent that it is clearly more useless for me to be in Oxford doing nothing, than here doing something: but it wd have to be very genuine to offset the misery of not being with yourself, Hourani, Katkov,[1] my family, in England; as it is I live, do little, & mope in a room by myself in a N.Y. hotel, because I cdn't bear Washington where everyone was very nice & hospitable to me, or to stay with the Frankfurters, until I know my future. I can't express the degree of misery: personal physical security is a burden & a blight, as it wd be to you, if you get me, under the circumstances: one wd infinitely rather do nothing but at least be exposed to some sort of danger. This country seems to me enormously pro-British, in spite of a definite Irish hostility, & the far from stupid activities of the Germans & their agents. You wd like the journalists very much. I omitted to add that the next frequentest type after Balogh is that of Keyes.[2] Balogh & he fill all cafeteries [sic], cinemas, squares, subways and strands of the sea. Miss Fischer-W[illiams] occurs more Boston way, & tends to be Anglophobe & Anglophile at once. The Oxford upper class loook [sic] is nowhere seen. half Woolworth, half Balliol is what it is. You really wd (a) get on fearfully well (b) therefore do a great deal of pro-allied good if you came, say to talk to women's clubs on Czechs & English. It cd easily be arranged once you were here.

 Love
  Shaya

[on back of envelope] Do write: it will get to me somewhere.

> *Eventually IB was offered something specific, if short-term, to do. As he remembered it:*
>
> Finally they said, 'Well, will you just do one job for us?' 'What?' 'Would you look through all the dispatches for the Associated Press to see whether they are anti-British, as we think they are, and defeatist and generally very much not in our interests?' I said, 'Where do I do this?' 'You do this in New York, in the British Library of Information, under a man called Angus Fletcher.'[3] 'And how long will that take?' I said. 'It

---

1 George (Georgy Mikhailovich) Katkov (1903–85), BBC Monitoring Service 1940–6, later (1959–71) University Lecturer in Soviet Institutions, Oxford, and Fellow of St Antony's.
2 Herbert Morgan Roger Keyes (b. 1913), Oriel graduate student (English B.Litt.) 1934–7, Fellow of Balliol 1937/8–46.
3 Angus Somerville Fletcher (1883–1960), Deputy Director of the British Library of Information in NY 1922–8, Director 1928–41, Kt 1941.

might take two or three weeks', because there were hundreds of them, not only from England but from France, Germany, wherever the AP was. [. . .] I did do the job, and I did report that they were unfriendly, which was what they wanted to know.

TO MARION FRANKFURTER

Friday [23 August 1940]

The Shoreham, 33 West 55,
New York City

Dear Marion,

I have now more or less recovered, although the climate disagrees with me even more than does that of Oxford. I was also much cheered by our telephone conversation, I am not sure why, probably as an oasis in this awful desert. I telephoned to Renée,[1] who seemed, for the first & possibly last time in our lives, overjoyed to hear my voice. She declared she hadn't got my letter, was miserable, & pressed me to come & see her. Which I intend to do to-morrow, I think. I also interviewed the British Library of Information, where I was told I would find a granite faced old bully who would say no to everything. His name was to be Fletcher. The last only is true. His name is certainly Fletcher. But what I found was a tired, bored, silly selfconscious old creature, anxious to discuss bogus philosophical questions, the ends of education in general, the problem as to why Stalin[2] is not a Christian, the possibility of Gandhi converting Stalin to non-aggression etc. *that* sort of stuff I know of old, it is the way elderly officials like to sublimate themselves in the presence of persons they suspect of being intellectuals. I got on shamefully well with him, but cannot conceive how such a man can have been appointed to pursue a dynamic policy of cultural infiltration. With him was a Prof. Allardyce Nicoll,[3] of Yale, of whom I had vaguely heard in London, who seems also to belong to the Brit. Library & pressed me to visit him in New Haven. They both hinted that great issues were at stake, that reorganization i.e. chaos was occurring in the Brit. Library, & that I was to report for potential duty on Monday. I don't know what this means, but I shall certainly go, and see if it is serious, and then come to New Milford[4] on

1 Renée Ayer had brought her children to the US because of the threat of invasion at home. Freddie was training to be an officer at the Royal Military College, Sandhurst.
2 Joseph Vissarionovich Stalin, né Djugashvili (1879–1953), General Secretary of the Central Committee of the Communist Party (and eventually virtual dictator of the USSR) 1922–53.
3 (John Ramsay) Allardyce Nicoll (1894–1976), attached to British Embassy, Washington, 1942–45, Professor of English Language and Literature, Birmingham, 1945–61 (his special expertise was in the history of drama).
4 The Frankfurters' home in Connecticut.

Monday afternoon, after tea, or alternatively on Tuesday, if that is all right. I'll wire in any case. If the organization seems hopeless, & I am merely likely to be bureaucratically enmeshed, then, in spite of Childs, the new boanerges and cleanser of the Augean stable, I shall not stay. If there seems to be a chance of doing really useful work, and especially, of bridging the at present foolishly wide gap between the local Jews and the British, then I shall see; perhaps I might stay for 14 days or so, provisionally. That will, I hope be clear on Monday. I would rather come & see you after, not before, the issues clear. I therefore propose to go to New Haven to see Renée to-morrow (Saturday) and come back to New York on Sunday. She seems to have found someone in New York to look after her children. My mind is absolutely confused about what to do: I haven't altogether abandoned hope of converting the foolish Cripps: that too I would like to consult Felix about on Monday or Tuesday. My general misery reached a climax when, in bed with this absurd chill, I was ashamed of enduring purely personal moral crises when everyone I knew was probably going through a far more genuinely worse time. Mr Auden's sudden unexpected visit, and his queer views did not improve matters much: he came, driven by the guilt induced by isolation I suppose, & Macleish's suddenly withdrawn alliance: since he never really knew or liked me much. Our conversation was stiff and artificial and led nowhere. Then, a day later, I went out and to a cinema and felt better, and had an interesting evening with the art expert Mr Shapiro,[1] and felt equally ashamed of enjoying anything at the present time. I wish I knew what I ought to do. Renée is quite right if she disapproves of me for cowardice and disliking to face painful issues: I only feel happy when I feel the solidarity of the majority of people I respect with & behind me. And at present I am cut off from this alliance. Hence my essentially petty vacillations. Once launched in any direction, backed by the beliefs of people I believe in more than in myself I shall re-emerge from the tunnel.

    Love

    Shaya

TO MARIE AND MENDEL BERLIN

    26 August [1940]

Shoreham Hotel, 35 W 55 St,
New York City

My dear parents.

    Your cable this morning with its cheerful and optimistic tone relieved me

---

1 Meyer *Schapiro (sic) (1904–96), art historian at Columbia University.

greatly, as papers here naturally colour things as luridly as they can. I know I ought not to believe them, nevertheless the cumulative effect is difficult to avoid. I am hurrying the Russians to decide one way or the other: even then there is Cripps to persuade etc. etc. Meanwhile Childs's organization is still not properly organized so that too waits fire for the present, in short all is in a state of flux. I consulted about Butterfields etc. to-day and enclose a form + some specimen signatures in case they are wanted. I quite understand too about Shipleys, and unless instructed, will do nothing. I met a young Belgian banker to-day called Phillipson[1] who married a Mocatta.[2] He has had exciting experiences in the Belgian & British-Belgian armies, before he got away. He is interesting on the financial position of various colonies: the Dutch e.g. are incomparably better off than the French, whose Martinique bank depended on the banque de France. Only those people were saved who invested in, say, mortgages or building societies: in the perpetual dispute between cash v. investment, hoarding v. investment, Keynes v. the rest this is most instructive. In similar circumstances were I so placed I should probably act similarly. There is plenty of advice on such subjects here, not all of it sound.[3] Our British name stands high here, financially, politically, morally, socially. America seems to be preparing to do her bit at last. I am still evading the need to stay with Aronson, but in order not to offend him, I will do so very soon. Everyone is terribly nice to me & I am exceedingly well.

    love

      Shaya.

Tell Mary F[isher] & everyone that I am pressing on eastwards as energetically as they will let me. That the blockages are *most* disheartening.

TO MARION FRANKFURTER

    2 a.m. [26 August 1940]

                      The Shoreham, 33 West 55,
                                 New York City

Dear Marion,

    I am sorry this sheet of paper is so dirty, it is the only one possible to obtain at this hour of the night. My affairs are in a worse mess than ever: Childs, the man who wishes me to stay, has reduced himself and the British

---

1 Paul Louis Philippson (1910–78).

2 Ann Marian Mocatta (b. 1919), from the banking family: Moses Mocatta founded Mocatta & Goldsmid, the oldest members of the London gold market, in 1671.

3 Crossed out here: 'But you were too cautious I think'.

Library of Information which he was sent to reform, into a state of chaos and resentment. Their telegrams to London are misinterpreted, their local arrangements break down daily, they beg me to wait at least until Friday to allow things to settle down until they and/or I make up my/their mind. So I suppose I had better stay in New York at least till Friday morning: could I come to New Milford then? if things settle themselves before that, or even relatively, so that I know where I stand, or even what precise job I am being asked to perform, I should like to come before, on Wed. or Thursday. The confusion is indescribable. And is due to the inferior personnel, tired idle, defeated old men. Nothing else.

Renée came to New York yesterday and spent some hours with me. She was very frank and discussed every thing. When she said Maurice to you, she meant Freddie. She – wishes to return:

(a) Because she cannot bear Yale, neither its kindness nor its prejudices. She thinks she is there on show, and cannot bear being asked so many questions about England. Also she has met some Nazi scientists there. And she has bloodcurdling stories of anti-Jewish remarks and cannot bear to tell them that she is married to even half a Jew. Also there is the money problem. Allowing for all her tendency to colour things luridly, she is plainly miserable. I agree too about the elaborate exquisite old world elegance, a combination of pathos, malice and fine workmanship which is consciously directed against the extremely matter of fact background against which she moves. And yet New York is much more her town than London, I should say. But I may be mistaken.

(b) the real reason for returning is, however, Hampshire's letters from the army. He is miserable, near nervous breakdown and asks her to come back. 'Sex' as she observed simply 'helps'. Freddie, she is sure, is happy more or less wherever he may be: he may need nursing but not spiritual comfort, having, she suspects, no such needs. She regards him, quite obviously, as a toy character, lost in a serious world, who had once taken her in, by whom she is deceived no longer. Hampshire is a gentle stream plashing at the foot of her garden, by whose side it is possible to live forever. To it she wishes to return. The next Cunard boat sails to-morrow (Tuesday) then nothing – from N. York, till Sept 10 or so. She thinks it is safer to go from here than from Canada. Perhaps this is so. She thinks I ought to stay on account of being able to extricate them all if anything happens. I couldn't & it would be no reason if I could and she, on the whole knows it. She would like to travel back with me. I am flattered and depressed. I shall send a wire if I may, on Wednesday or so: my love to Felix.

Shaya

Renée thinks her children will be very happy with Mrs – I cannot remember her name – of Rye.[1] She is terrified that Valerie may suddenly say she has two daddies. I had a most eloquent and passionate account of the beauty of Julian,[2] & of the unbridled affection in which Valerie holds him. She is content, I think, to let them grow up as Americans in America if necessary. She hopes you never thought she meant to plant them on you. I assured her that that thought never crossed your mind.

I thought Dr Cohn's[3] Willkie letter was very good. There's not a Roosevelt button to be seen here.

I have written three memoranda for Mr Childs & dictated them: by the effect they produced one would think no one in local English circles could read or write. It is all most depressing. They are all Republican & admire Roger Mynors & have never heard of Maurice.

TO MARIE AND MENDEL BERLIN

3 September [1940]

Shoreham Hotel, 35 W. 85[4] Street,
New York

Dear Parents

I am spending a few days with the Aronsons for courtesy's sake. Letters etc. had best still go to Shoreham or Washington, 2414 Tracy Place; Here, in 250 W. 85th Street it is a little noisy, Broadway traffic is too near. I had dinner again with Howard Goodhart, he is not quite my type, a little too snobbish – Eugene Rothschild[5] who was once host to the Duke of Windsor[6] was there, exhausted, ½ ruined (but he arrived with a bag of jewels, so the U.S. press said, worth \$1000.000 which he declared) writing a book on Titian. My position is this: Childs wants, I think, to employ me as an intermediary between our Embassy and the local Jews. This I would, I think do v. well. If he appoints, which will be clear during next few days, I should like to hop back to England, see some people, Lord Lloyd,[7] Weizmann, etc. arrange

1 The Godleys of Rye in Westchester County, on the outskirts of NY, had taken the Ayers in.
2 Born in January 1939; his father is Stuart Hampshire.
3 Alfred Einstein Cohn (1879–1957), physician and scientist with broad cultural interests, frequent correspondent with Frankfurter.
4 He means 55: 85 is the number of Aronson's house.
5 Eugène Daniel de *Rothschild (1884–1976), a distant cousin of Edmond, James and Victor Rothschild, from Vienna.
6 'Ex-King Edward, now Duke of Windsor, is to stay for an indefinite period as the guest of Baron Eugene de Rothschild at the latter's castle at Enzesfeld, 25 miles south of Vienna.' *Manchester Guardian*, 14 December 1936, 9.
7 George Ambrose Lloyd, 1st Baron Lloyd of Dolobran (1879–1941), Secretary of State for the Colonies 1940–1.

with Oxford, & skip back again, preferably by Clipper. As I haven't much money I shall try to get you to pay my fare from England, at least the Lisbon–London & return bit: from London to N.Y. it is certainly possible. I am not sure about N.Y–London. I don't think there is much chance of getting on the Clare[1] which goes to Ireland & carries more important persons than me. I shall not do this until I've cleared up matters with Childs, who is very benevolently disposed. I am working interestingly now in the British Library and have sent a report on it to Harold Nicolson, who may be wondering as to what I am doing. You might telephone to Miriam Rothschild (please do this) chez Jimmy Rothschild in Telephone Directory since she seems worried about what I am doing & tell her that as soon as my immediate job is over, which it will be by the time you get this, I am returning home at once. Here there is general optimism about the R.A.F. powers of resistance, a terrific swing towards us of feeling etc. The news this morning was (1) about the destroyers coming to England which is splendid[2] (2) about formation of a Jewish army, which the Revisionists have long agitated for, but which here appeared as a statement not from the British Govt but from a Mr Abrahams[3] of London. Has he any authority? is this an attempt to force everyone's hand? it seems a little premature, insufficiently well prepared for in America. Could you phone Mary Fisher (Joint Broadcasting Committee, in phone book), & Christopher Cox (Colonial Office) to tell the first I intend returning v. soon, & the second ditto + to enquire of him if Smith is in Oxford in September since I shall have to see him. I shall complete cast-iron arrangements here to step back into work when I return. Frankfurters thoroughly approve my scheme & think I wd be very valuable. Hope you got my wire about aunt Berta who ought, if it is possible, to be sent to Jamaica[4] where she cd be supported. Aronsons both send love – they are a little gloomy about absence of business & the toughness of local business people & dishonesty of local shops: they much prefer England, it seems.

    love

       Isaiah Berlin.

Rau is gone to Montreal for a fortnight. He was v. nice to me & helpful. If

---

1 One of the clippers.

2 On 2 September the US agreed to provide Britain with 50 elderly destroyers in exchange for 99-year leases on bases in the West Indies, Bermuda and Canada.

3 Abraham Abrahams (1987–1955), head of the Political Dept of the revisionist New Zionist Organization in London during the war, editor of the *Jewish Standard* 1940–8.

4 It is not clear whether IB is using Jamaica as a code-name for somewhere else. In the event Berta and other relatives remained in Riga and were killed by the Nazis in 1941 (see 334/1).

treated friendlily and not with condescension, he is very nice to live with even if a little gross.

IB's analysis of the Associated Press dispatches was, according to Wheeler-Bennett, 'a masterly, penetrating and droll survey'.[1] Its high quality gave added impetus to the continuing discussions about a possible long-term role for IB in the US.

TO MARIE AND MENDEL BERLIN

15 September [1940]

Shoreham Hotel, 35 W 55th Street,
New York City
sometimes varied by 250 W 85 Street (Aronson)

My dear parents,

It is so nice and relieving to get your letters and wires, particularly the one from Llandudno. I am glad you finally decided to go, the noise must have been excruciating. Are you both permanently settled in 3 Victoria Road,[2] or does Pa still go to London occasionally? or is it all done by telephone? I had a letter from Harrimans saying that I was sole master, but that if I did anything they would be pleased to credit Brown Shipley with whatever it is. As I propose to do *absolutely nothing*, as per instructions, the case does not arise. Sobol[3] is said to be here, having arrived from Madrid, but I shall not contact him if I can help it, since I have nothing to say to him, and would not act whatever anyone, save yourself, said. So much for that. The newspapers here play the London bombardment up to a terrific extent. But to-day the 170 Nazi aeroplanes got down made a deep impression.[4] There are voices definitely suggesting that America go to war, which is new. Our propaganda still needs gingering up, which is now being begun. The F.O. now takes the line that they never dreamt of sending me to Moscow, anyhow. Which means that someone must have done me down there. Well, if they choose to be deliberately unaware of what I could do, I cannot help it. My situation is this: Childs, my present patron, is the re-organizer sent out by Duff Cooper to wake the Embassy etc. up. I got Felix to ask us both to breakfast in New York, which raised my stock in Child's eyes & has produced the following effect: he definitely wants me to work for him: it will take him 14–20 days from the 10th i.e. till Oct 1. or so & put his new Press Service on an

---

1 loc. cit. (325/3).
2 In Landudno, where IB's parents had retreated for a long holiday.
3 Boris Sobolewitz of Montreal did business with Mendel's company, Britain and Overseas Trading Co., which owed him over £5,000 for Russian bristles, paid in November.
4 These aircraft were among some 1,000 sent on raids to England that day: only 27 British losses were reported.

organized footing, there is a lot of wiring & counter-wiring to London going on. He is willing to pay me a certain sum – say £200 or so to give me facilities for getting from home as much more as, in this terribly expensive land, I need, he suggests up to 5000 dollars a year. That would suit me. The College might pay another £200–£300 and the rest I could get out of my bank in the ordinary way. Please see there is enough there for the purpose. I explained I wanted to go home on a brief visit before settling down to work. He is willing, provided, I set things up here first. Felix blesses the arrangement. Childs says that he must obtain my inclusion by wire to the M of Information, since I am not on any official staff. This he will do when he sends his budgetary requests on Sep 25th or so. I hope they will not make difficulties, but they are capable of anything, & have muddled things before. So I remain here pro. tem. in hopes. I have had letters from Hourani, Beeley, Mary Fisher (who was v. nice about our Hollycroft air-shelter etc.) and David Cecil & Marmorstein who transmitted messages from yourselves designed to keep me happy & so definitely of a propagandist nature. Rau having gone to Montreal (he returns to-morrow) & I hating solitude moved myself to the Aronsons for a bit – I pay them a trifle which is much better. The advantage of Rau was that I paid for sharing a suite with him, which cost much less. On the 17th I go for 3 days to Virginia on a short visit to a journalist friend called Joseph Alsop,[1] a cousin of the President, who I think will be elected. Willkie is very unreliable, F.D.R. is wonderful. The Jews here are a tough nut but I hope to crack them for the benefit of H.M.G. Please go on writing,

  love
   Shaya

I need hardly add that I am physically extremely well, the food & cool weather & regular hours in the Brit. Library suit me. Either address →[2] will find me. I have met a nice banker from Brussels, called Philippson, married to Mocatta. I get on very well with the Brit. Library (50 Rockefeller Plaza, N.Y.) staff.

P.S. Aronson is depressed by lack of credit here when so much good business, both with England & with S. America can be had. He is a little hurt by lack of response to his cables. They send their love.

what about either Butterfield or the R[oyal] B[ank] of C[anada]? New York is a coarse city, very prose.

1 Joseph Wright *Alsop (1910–89), syndicated newspaper columnist.
2 In the original this postscript appears at the head of the letter, so that the arrow points to the two addresses.

I am (1) looking for the Raskins (2) not bored at all, but nostalgic (3) shipping Mrs Ayer back to England to-morrow.

TO MARIE AND MENDEL BERLIN

23 September [1940]

The Fairfax Hotel,
2100 Massachusetts Ave., Washington, DC

My dear parents,

Just because you have left London, it is surely no reason for ceasing to write: possibly your letters take a long while to get here, but then you can always cable – I do it less (a) because I am under normal conditions whereas you are not (b) because it costs me more than you, so to speak. My permanent address is Shoreham Hotel N. York, 35 W 55 street because the Brit. Library is in New York. I came here to-day to see my patron Childs: I now have a fairly probable job, the arrangements are that the Govt is to pay a part & I a part (i.e. New College + private means) up to about £1200. That is satisfactory, & the job is after my heart. My condition is that I should be allowed to return to England for a week or 10 days and then go straight back. The whole thing awaits confirmation by the Ministry of Information which has to agree. If they agree, I'll clipper back towards the end of this month & then try & Clare back again. To-day Foster had no room for me in his house, hence a night at a Hotel. Letters should come *either* to Shoreham in N. York or c/o Foster, Embassy, preferably the former, since I there live in a double set with F. Rau, whose mother lately in New York, sends greetings. So does Mrs Frankfurter. A diary it is impossible to keep, one's experience is too monotonous. To-morrow I shall return to the Shoreham and try to establish contact with Raskins & Holdstein. Both for my own pleasure & not your préstige. I stayed for 14 days with Aronsons on account of its being cheaper (I paid 1 dollar a day) they pretended not to want money, but wanted it all the same. Mulya is offended by the pointed silence from London, whereas Oiserman[1] writes to him. I don't enclose letter from grandfather, since its substance is that they are well, how are you, etc, otherwise dull. If I return by Clipper, I shall instruct my bank to pay the fare to U.S. Lines, 7, Haymarket. And I morally feel I must return for a week or so.

love

Shaya

1 Anna Oiserman, a distant Schneerson cousin of Mendel and Marie, was married to Zemach Oiserman, possibly a business connection as well. They lived in London at this point and knew the Berlins and the Samunovs well.

TO MARIE AND MENDEL BERLIN

Sunday 5 October 1940

The Shoreham, 33 West 55th Street,
New York

My dearest parents,

Happy New Year[1] & many thanks for your letters & cables. They give me inexpressible pleasure. My job here is practically fixed. I am to work both under Childs & under Fletcher of the British Library of Information, indirectly both under F.O. & M of I. I had a nice letter from Harold N. explaining why Moscow was impracticable,[2] & telling me to trust Childs in everything. Which I am doing. In spite of my unimpaired moral position I propose to return now because:

1. It will be more difficult in January, with weather colder, ice forming on Clipper wings, & transport generally harder.

2. Smith's cable grudgingly (letters *cannot* explain things to them. Still I'll get the F.O. to tell them something.) consents to wait till January. But my job here is for the duration, & New College will be justly aggrieved if I then cannot come because I shall be right in the middle of things. So I'd better settle all now. And there will be more to do after the Presidential election.

I propose therefore:

1) to get Childs to (a) inquire of the F.O. and M of I, or get the Ambassador to enquire, whether they are prepared to re-export me at once.

2) to get our Treasury people here to tell the B[ank] of E[ngland] to let you or the Oxford Bank pay my air fare to U.S. Lines: I think of going via Portugal both times by air to & from Lisbon, I mean by air New York–Lisbon–London, by air London Lisbon, then either by Clipper or by U.S. boat. That at present is obviously safer than it may be by January: this will be a long war, & the U.S. may soon come into it with us, & be liable to attack. But this can't happen till Nov. 5 at the earliest, when the President is elected. That I am sure you will find rational. I shall cable date of departure, of course. I shall not set out without terribly impressive documents, explaining my full importance.

Perlzweig is here, I don't like him terribly, but had a perfectly amiable interview under Nahum Goldmann's auspices, I shall always seek to co-operate with & not antagonize potential co-meddlers in Jewish affairs. Chaim [Weizmann] is apparently not coming just yet, partly because

1 See 96/2.

2 In a letter dated 9 September Nicolson had claimed that Cripps' objections to an extra member of staff and Gladwyn Jebb's move from the FO to the MEW were the reasons for the change in the FO's attitude.

noblesse oblige, maybe because both his sons are fighting & Vera[1] won't leave. Sobolevich[2] has not accosted me, so I let sleeping dogs lie. I now definitely live here, not with Aronson, whom I can't bear in large doses. I stayed partly for economy (but paid them, tho' not much, about a dollar a day all included, laundry, food) partly not to offend. Living here with Rau is also economical & much nicer – he is a simple fellow, with an inferiority complex vis a vis me, which now has passed away: he was much upset by Ika's[3] end. You ask how I spend my time. In the morning I breakfast on coffee, smetana,[4] rolls, toast etc. & go at about 9.30 to the British Library in Rockefeller Centre, about 5 blocks away i.e. 7 minutes walk. There I work till lunch, & then eat either with some 'business' friend, a Jewish journalist or useful American, or with a colleague. The Director[5] likes me & takes me out occasionally. The food is continental, & in my opinion delicious. Too good for war time. I return & work till 6.30 or so. Then I dine with someone – if no one else then Rau in a Kosher establishment, Segal[6] or Poliakoff,[7] or else with others: I have not seen Howard Goodhart for some time, he is a little too dully snobbish for me, but I'll see him before I leave: I dined with the Holdsteins, gave them Bick's greetings, & was told he had died. Embarrassed silence. Wally likes Mr Berlin very much, & offers if need be, to lend money: he is a very nice man. Sophy is more restrained but friendly. Wally can safely be entrusted with anything, much more generous than the rich. I also called on the Raskins. The Riga Raskins[8] were there too. A most agreeable evening. A postcard from Victor [Volshonok] to Aronson to say he is very well & safe etc. & so is whole family, second time Riga communicated. Both Mrs Raskins very sweet to me. In the evenings occasionally one goes to cinemas. When I go to Washington about once a fortnight or more rarely, I stay either with Foster, or with an Oxford don called Opie[9] in the Embassy, (he has an American wife & was here when war broke out) or other friends. A portuguese pupil of mine is here, & is to furnish me with introductions in Lisbon in case I get stuck for a day or two & need assistance or distraction. [Jacob] Marschak is also most agreeable. I am

1 Vera Weizmann (1881–1966), Chaim Weizmann's wife, paediatrician, co-founder in 1920 with Rebecca Sieff (416/2) and others of the Women's International Zionist Organization (WIZO).

2 See 347/3.

3 A dog?

4 Russian for sour cream.

5 Alan Alves Dudley (1907–71), Assistant Director, British Library of Information, NY, 1930–40; Director, British Press Service (BPS) and BIS, NY, 1940–2; FO 1942–9.

6 Probably Louis Segal (1894–1964), US Zionist labour leader, served on executives of World Zionist Organization and Jewish Agency.

7 Arthur Poliakoff (b. 1909), prosperous furrier, contemporary of IB at St Paul's.

8 Probably the brother of IB's parents' friend, and his wife; see also 334/2.

9 Redvers Opie (1900–84), Fellow and economics Tutor, Magdalen, 1931–45, Counsellor and economic adviser to the British Embassy in Washington 1939–46, became a US citizen 1948.

not alone at all. Rau may go to S. Africa, then I shall look for a man to share a
flat with: some old & reliable friend.

love

Isaiah Berlin

I gather the office is chez Rach, i.e. old London Northern?[1] I am overwhelmed by the niceness of both the English here, & all {our} the Jews I deal
with. The rich alone are not so nice.

In mid-October IB set off for home, travelling via Portugal.

TO MARIE AND MENDEL BERLIN

Friday 18 October 1940

Estoril Palacio Hotel

My dear parents,

Here I am, having arrived by Clipper, waiting for transport to England. I
hope you are not unduly worried by my escapade – but I really *had* to return,
I could not put my heart into my work without having openly made *full and
explicit* arrangements with the College etc. I do not suppose I shall stay in
England long, I carry letters to the F.O. & the M.O.I. which demand my
immediate return. Portugal is very agreeable. Full of refugees of every
nation, waiting, some hopelessly for transport to U.S.A.[2] The quotas have
been opened; e.g. the Latvian which was previously full, hence many
Parisian Latvians are impatiently sitting here, daily visiting the travel
agencies. I am terribly comfortable in a luxury hotel: the food is good, the
people exciting to look at, Lisbon full of remarkable faces & buildings. The
Embassy here, which has had a cable about me from Washington is very
polite, but not sure when transport is next available. Possibly next Thursday.
The Holdsteins were *very* wise & useful, they can be relied on altogether. I
tried to give them Bick's regards when they informed me that [he] had died

---

1 IB's father had recently set up a timber company in partnership with Lionel Schalit, based in
   the Moorgate offices of the Schalit family's previous (collapsed) business, the London and
   Northern Trading Company; Solomon Rachmilevich worked for his cousin Lionel in both
   ventures.
2 Portugal, a neutral country relatively friendly towards the Allies, provided in the port of
   Lisbon continental Europe's only point of departure for the Americas. Would-be refugees to
   the US faced lengthy and often fruitless bureaucratic procedures in their efforts to secure
   immigration visas and passage on a ship. Despite increasing pressure for liberalisation because
   of the situation in Europe, US immigration laws, based on quotas related to national origin,
   remained complex and restrictive (cf. 362/1).

shortly before: A man named Rosenthal here from Paris, a friend of Reb. Barber claims acquaintance with you. He is en route to U.S.A. Estoril is a watering sea resort hour from Lisbon, quieter & nicer than the city. To visit officials I perform a short train journey: the most frequently heard language is, I think, Polish. I shall go straight to Oxford or Llandudno on arrival, depends where we arrive. I am very well & even happy. I know the Daily Telegraph correspondent & others & am not bored. I shall write here a report on U.S. conditions in case the Ministry wants one before letting me go.

> All my love
> Isaiah Berlin

I hope to be off 24th Oct. but may not get off then. Lord Lothian with wh I crossed from N. York[1] cannot take me with him. But unlike the private passengers I can claim a Govt. priority from the Air Attaché.

Cd you immediately wire Smith (& Aronson) at Oxford & 250 W 85 Street respectively, that I am here till 25th through no fault of mine, weatherbound.

TO MARIE AND MENDEL BERLIN

> Saturday 19 October 1940

> Estoril Palacio Hotel

Dear Pa & Ma

[. . .] It would be *terribly* kind of you, if, on receipt of this, you would wire Palacio – Estoril, Portugal, that you are well. Wires here cost a lot & my stack of dollars is not great. I really am extremely well, read Portuguese papers which talk of the forthcoming invasion by England, and talk occasionally to the astonishing collection of refugees from all lands who live in this luxury hotel & bewilder the simple Portuguese. I hope very soon to be with you. I would have kept my return secret from you, knowing how opposed you were, but this delay forces me to give news of myself. The Frankfurters & everyone else approved the journey. I feel my behaviour must be modelled on Caesar's wife: & that I cannot keep out of what is happening to you all, however important my work in U.S: anyhow I shall have made full arrangements for return. My love & cable or even write.

> Your bored but flourishing,
> Isaiah B.

1 IB had been on the same outward flight as Lothian, who was on his way to London for consultations.

*When IB was eventually able to obtain transport to England, his sea-
plane landed at Bristol at a dramatic moment. IB, guilt-ridden at having
so far escaped the war's dangers, felt only relief: 'There was an air raid
going on when we arrived; I was delighted, I thought this was what I
had come for, I felt better [. . .] Then I took a train from Bristol to
Oxford, went back to New College where I was living, and started life
again [. . .] Nobody asked any questions. I began teaching.' But this
return to his old way of life was short-lived:*

Then, in late November, I received a letter from the Ministry of
Information saying, 'Dear Mr Berlin, You appear to us to be overstaying
your leave. Would you kindly explain what you are doing?' I wrote back
to the American Department and said as far as I knew I wasn't employed
by the Ministry of Information, or indeed anybody else; therefore I didn't
think I could have leave. What did this mean? They said, 'Oh well, yes, I
see, I think there's been some confusion, perhaps you would come and
visit us?' So I went to London, quite happily, to the Ministry of
Information, saw a man whose name I can't remember, some drunken
journalist, who said to me, 'Look, you've been appointed to the British
Information Services in New York.' 'When?' 'Oh, three weeks ago.' 'But
you failed to tell me!' 'I'm afraid we did.' Now, why was I appointed?
Because during my AP days I met two people who took to me: one was
a man called Aubrey Morgan [. . .] and the other was called Wheeler-
Bennett. And they were working in the British Library of Information,
which had been turned [. . .] into a propaganda bureau of sorts. And they
took to me – they liked me quite, thought I might be useful, and
recommended to the Ministry of Information that I be appointed –
wanted to have me back. Very sweet, but nothing was said to me![1]

TO CHAIM WEIZMANN

[December 1940]

The Dorchester Hotel,
Park Lane, London

I have tried to communicate, but in vain. In the Hotel they couldn't trace
you and the 2.0. number[2] is said to be out of order. I am due to leave on

---

1 There is a contradiction between this account and IB's statements in several of the previous
   letters that he was definitely to return to a job in the US. Perhaps to his parents he presented
   arrangements still under discussion as settled in order to calm their fears about his returning to
   wartime Britain at all. The letter of 3 January 1941 to Maire Gaster (pp. 355 ff. below) offers a
   possible explanation of what really happened.
2 The Weizmanns made Suite 210 at the Dorchester their permanent London home during the
   war. IB's '2.0.' may be an error for '210'.

Friday the 3^d [January] – I shall spend the night before in Bournemouth (the Royal Bath Hotel) and Tuesday & Wednesday in Oxford. I shall try to telephone you from there at regular intervals. I may be held up by the Portuguese Consulate which delays and delays over the transit visa – if so I shall make a gigantic effort to see you once again before I go. I cannot say how greatly excited I was by your last Lloyd interview[1] and how arrestingly absorbing the whole of last Monday evening seemed to me to be – I was sorry only not to see Mrs Weizmann to whom I offer my devotion. Could you write or wire to me in Oxford where & when you are to be expected in Lisbon and whom I could ask, while there, about your probable where-abouts? I should be very grateful. Both for that and for many other things.

Yrs

Shaya Berlin

TO MAIRE GASTER[2]

3 January 1941

Royal Bath Hotel, Bournemouth

Dearest B.J.

You have every right to your remonstrance, and I feel guilt, gloom, and general misery. Has anyone told you of my sad adventures? How I thought I was going to Moscow by orders of at least two Govt. departments as press attaché (a thought which excited me immoderately as you can imagine – a plot in which even Mrs Fisher assisted) – there is no town in which it would be more interesting to be at this moment, or you would say at any moment. Beside which the misery of doing nothing in Oxford in mid-July was becoming too much and I passionately wanted to be identified in some way with this war (do you still sympathize? perhaps no longer). So off I went as a

1 Lord Lloyd had met Weizmann on 13 September to convey the British Government's agreement to the establishment, in due course, of specifically Jewish units within the British Army, for which the Jewish Agency had long pressed, but which had been blocked by the previous Prime Minister, Neville Chamberlain. Churchill, appointed Prime Minister in May 1940, was more sympathetic to the Zionist cause, and the resulting breakthrough in September left Weizmann 'elated and solemn': Blanche E. C. Dugdale, *Baffy: The Diaries of Blanche Dugdale, 1936–1947*, ed. N. A. Rose (London, 1973), 175. But the agreement was the subject of continuing argument and uncertainty, and Lloyd and Weizmann met on a number of other occasions in late 1940 and early 1941 to discuss its detailed implementation. Weizmann's mood fluctuated in step with the outcomes of the meetings; Baffy Dugdale does not record the specific meeting referred to here, but it was evidently encouraging. In the event, continued opposition by elements in the Army and officials in Palestine led to a series of delays and the Jewish Brigade Group was not established until 1944 (and disbanded in 1946).

2 Maire Lynd married Jack Gaster (b. 1907), lawyer and Communist activist, in 1938.

courier with a bag & on getting to Washington after a literally frightful voyage was neither recalled nor sent on but stopped, told to wait, & given no instructions. That America is hateful I hardly have to tell you. The inhabitants have no souls, only hearts at the most. Everybody is enormously relentlessly boring in a sense which extends the concept of the activity. They are all guilty, uneasy, frightened, brazen, stupid, muddled and generally intolerable. After about a fortnight I hysterically announced to the Frankfurters that I was going home. I was then offered various English jobs by officials. These I conscientiously refused until a Jewish one turned up which seemed both more real & important & less possible to refuse. I said I might accept if a thousand conditions were fulfilled among them that I should be allowed to return & consult everyone & look for something in England. By this time I felt a deserter, a fool, & miserably undecided about what to do. I therefore returned & was immediately set upon by the Foreign Office & Information Ministry – the latter is gay, raffish, ineffective & full of old friends, essentially nice to visit but not impressive. I like being their official very much, it wasn't in the least like being a civil servant, and since efficient grimness is nowhere to be found, it was at least fairly humane. I was swiftly made No something, made to sign the official secrets act, and told to return to America at once. I vacillated and played for time which was fatal. The more demands I made the swifter they were granted. I desperately angled for jobs in England which all collapsed. So I am off again as 'specialist attached to the British Press Service,' 30 Rockefeller Plaza, New York. I really cannot describe the blackness of my misery. Firstly I don't want to leave at all, having spent the happiest months of my life in England now. Secondly there is no doubt that there is a job to perform & my new God Dr Weizmann is wooing me ardently into doing it. Thirdly every time news of England of a particularly harrowing sort appears in American papers I become neurotically anxious to return, & have the reputation in America – you won't believe it – for melancholy & neurosis. There is no doubt that the only way in which I can at all affect the course of events, however minutely, is either at Moscow or at New York. I would infinitely prefer the former. They won't let me get there: the Russians don't mind it seems, only Whitehall does. Russians & Jews are the only public subjects I have any relevance to. I have two other jobs in New York, not connected with Jews, but these anyone could do. I am also to create all sorts of contacts with the 8 or so million American Jews, 5 million real ones, 3 of the Zimmern type.[1] I am acutely unhappy. Everyone says it is my duty to go. Except Maurice who

---

1 A reference to Alfred Zimmern (234/2). Although Jewish by birth, he adopted a cosmopolitan outlook with no specific focus on Jewish interests.

is displeased. I shall in fact go, & be tortured throughout. The only thing to do is to accept some principle & conform. I wish to help to win the war. This [is] the only way allowed to me. But please pray for me in general. My feelings I am sure you will guess at. Thank you very much for the picture of your child which I am sure you rightly think heavenly. At last even I think the old days gone, & bitterly do I regret it. What would you do in my place? I am touchingly grateful for any word of general sympathy. Darling B.J. I wish I could see you immediately, I am nearer general (the word oddly recrops up) dissolution than ever before in my life.

God bless you.

Shaya.

Do write to me whenever you can. You cannot imagine what enormous effect letters have in exile. If anything really happens here I shall rush back, duty or no duty. I wish one wasn't so irrevocably attached to small universes & familiar objects. To be lost at the age of 31 is most humiliating. I had letters from Goronwy who (I cling to gossip as to so many straws) is married to a Miss Morris[1] who likes jazz, from Humphry in the army. Christopher has urged me to go throughout. Love to Jack.

I.B.

Mendel writes in his family memoir:

On the 1st January 1941 you went to Bournemouth to join a plane from there for Lisbon and from thence [by ship] to New York. We accompanied you and for 8–9 days we stayed together as the weather was too bad for the plane to take off. You were not too happy there [. . .] and of course the perilous journey worried us. Your decision to go turned out very wise and proper. Imagine your staying on through the war years in Oxford, or perhaps having to take some minor and very uncongenial government office. It would have not only repressed you but possibly sapped your great vitality and you would have shrunk inwardly, turned you perhaps into a hack. Instead, thanks of course to your gifts and personality, you grasped the opportunity and developed enormously in America. You must have done very good work for the Government, or you would not have been so praised and appreciated, but you have done good work for yourself. You have enlarged and expanded your personality, came into contact with a greater and larger world than academic Oxford [. . .] and gained a great deal of self-confidence. You have obtained a knowledge of politics and diplomacy and cannot so easily be led up the garden, as many academicians were and are.

1 Margaret ('Margie') Ewing Morris (1920–76) married Goronwy Rees in December 1940.

TO MARIE AND MENDEL BERLIN

10 [January]¹ 1941, 2.30 p.m.

Estoril Palacio Hotel,
Costa do Sol, Portugal²

Dear Pa & Ma,

The sky is blue with a few white clouds. The sea calm. I have a cabin (unlike 25 other passengers) shared with a very nice, solid American financial journalist and head of a firm in England who supplies trade statistics to private firms and our Govt. departments. His name is Scriven and he was with us in the hotel. He knows half America and is very interesting. The Palacio Hotel greeted me like a long lost friend and gave me a wonderful double bedroom in which I slept comfortably for 14 hours after an exceedingly rough flight. Nearly everyone was sick: there was a debate – imagine it – between the passengers as to whether it was best to be sick there & then, or try to conquer one's nausea. One of the most disgusting but somehow, in the circumstances, intelligible conversations I have ever taken part in. I just managed to escape without disgrace. The extraordinary thing was that as soon as we landed & breathed a little fresh air we all felt wonderfully well, and Scriven ([Ian] Bowen knows him by the way. Common interest in statistics I suppose) & I dined very well & then slept comfortably and the next day (yesterday) was pure happiness, Lisbon gay and delightful; Panamerican Airways behaved in their usual negligent fashion, talked about flights in March, & gave me a transfer to Export Line. Even so I had to pay 40 dollars extra which is adding injury to insult.

The boats are said to be very comfortable, but to take 8–9 days to reach New York. I dined with one of our Embassy officials called Innes, but fortunately had no need to ask the Embassy to do anything. Everything went most smoothly. I have purchased a pair of terribly warm soft flannel pyjamas. To day is cold & fine & clear & windless. We sail at 5 or 6. The odd crowd of refugees in the Palacio is not much changed, the same tired but hopeful faces, daily besieging the British or American consul[a]t[e]s. Kadiss³ still here, but lives in a large handsome flat, with 2 maids in the main thoroughfare of Lisbon; he has almost got an American visa: his wife⁴ intends to engage in home production of chocolates in the U.S. of which she

1 Misdated 10 December 1941.
2 Written on board the passenger steamer *Excambion*, on hotel writing-paper. It was on this journey that he first saw, and noticed, his future wife Aline Strauss, who was travelling from France. But on this occasion he did not meet her; nor did he mention her to his parents in his report on the voyage in the next letter.
3 Kadish Mendelovich Apter (after emigration Konstantin Markovich Apters), Mendel's cousin.
4 Irene Apter, née Silikis.

supplied me with a sample. Everyone knows them. They are far from poor, & would be better advised to stay here. But K. is burning to do business & sees himself as an American captain of industry, conquering the Americas by charm of manner, iron logic, and genius as a business man. This is a delightful land and I am sorry to leave it. Our victories over the Italians have produced a profound impression here: the Italians are hated even more than the Germans, and our victories are emphasized in all the papers with terrific headlines. I hope the American press is equally friendly:

I am *extremely* well, looking forward with genuine eagerness to my work, my life, even my voyage. I am about to buy some delicious dried fruit for my journey, which will offset the inevitable overfeeding and lack of exercise. If any bills arrive in New College, please settle them: I cannot do so from America and I don't wish Blackwells etc. to think I've slipped them for the duration. Write often and fully to the Shoreham or to my office, & encourage others to do so.

I hope you'll have a nice tea party with the Adamses and that Oxford will continue as immune as heretofore. I am in excellent health & spirits & send you all my love. God bless you

    yrs

        Isaiah Berlin.

Chaim said he was going – the 15th – he might appreciate it if you wished him bon voyage. But it is not necessary.

    IB

TO MARIE AND MENDEL BERLIN

    Tuesday 28 January [1941]

                          British Information Services

My dear parents

You won't believe me but ever since I arrived I have been in a perpetual hurry, busy, agitated, happy, active, on the move. Very different from the long, dull, unhappy days in August–September. The air journey to Lisbon was pretty rough, a violent tailwind, everyone except me & my American friend Scriven, very sick. Two agreeable days in Portugal about which I wrote you from Lisbon. Then 9 days on the Excambion, first day a definite gale, your son sick for the first time in his life for 2 hours or so, after that happy for the rest of his voyage. A mixed, very mixed company, a Duchess, a lot of rich expatriate repatriated Americans, the *Times* correspondent from Lisbon, a plump Jewess from Geneva called Frieda Vogel who insisted, to the general amusement that she was a Turk, a member of an old Turkish family etc. The voyage as such was not eventful, I ate a lot, slept a lot, and according to people here, look much better than when I left the U.S. in October. I was welcomed rapturously by all my colleagues both here and in Washington. I am very happy here now. My own colleagues are exceptionally nice & helpful, my old British Library friends even gave a dinner for me, the F.F.s in Washington were very sweet & hospitable, I talk to Mrs Childs[1] in Russian, the Embassy has suddenly begun to attach weight to me & to invite me to stay nights with various members of itself. I attended a luncheon in Washington of the United Palestine Appeal & met Stephen Wise,[2] Lipsky,[3] Mrs de Sola Pool (President of Hadassa.).[4] Wise is very lovable. Absurd, unbalanced, erratic, noisy, unreliable he is also generous, large, clever, understands who is who and what is what, has imagination, courage, & a golden heart. Lipsky is nothing. Mrs de S. Pool is gentle, quiet, sweet, a Mrs Solomon[5] with more savoir faire, intelligence and charm. I got on well with her.

Sometime soon I must call on Brandeis,[6] who is regarded as a saint & gentleman, a kind of Jewish Lord Balfour, but even finer, & who has been urging other people to get in touch with me. F.F. again I suppose. My next quarry are the millionaires. Swiftly I must traverse the whole jungle of American Jewish social life. Chaim is expected, but has not yet arrived. he & Brandeis are said to be on not good terms, but I am an old hand at preserving friends who are jealous of each other. There is plenty of work, I am well, busy and contented. I moved because the Shoreham was a little too dear for what it gave – a service flat is really what I ought to have – meanwhile I pay less & am happier in the Devon, 2 steps from my work, 70 West 55th Street; snow lies white upon the ground, hard and brilliant as in Baltic countries,

1 The former Larissa Choumakoff (b. c.1903), apparently Russian by birth, who had married Stephen Lawford Childs in 1922 in Sofia.

2 Stephen Samuel Wise (1874–1949), Reform rabbi, social reformer and Zionist leader. President of the American Jewish Congress 1925–49.

3 Louis Lipsky (1876–1963), Polish-born US Zionist leader, journalist and author; President, Zionist Organization of America, 1922–30.

4 Tamar de Sola Pool (1890–1981) was from 1939 to 1943 President of Hadassah, the Women's Zionist Organization of America, a very powerful fund-raising body founded in 1912.

5 Flora Solomon (1895–1984), daughter of Russian millionaire Grigory Benenson; married to Harold Solomon, a British Army officer; lived in London and briefly in Jerusalem (1920–4), where her husband was permanently crippled in a riding accident; Zionist and friend of Chaim and Vera Weizmann. After the Benenson fortune was lost in 1931, she joined Marks and Spencer and devised their welfare scheme for employees.

6 Louis Dembitz Brandeis (1856–1941), influential as a justice of the US Supreme Court (1916–39) and as a Zionist.

& the view from my 44th floor window over New York is breathtaking.[1] Political opinion – pro-British sentiment – has advanced very rapidly since I was here before. Bernard Joseph,[2] the legal adviser of the Jewish Agency in Palestine, is here, & saying that Gen. Dolbiac[3] is very pleased with the Jewish airmen operating in Greece. That is really most encouraging. The Aronsons are not too well – first he, then she, now the child are ill with the local flu, which has now passed, leaving only the little Adir Aronson with a fever. Fanny is very pathetic. They have, without any bitterness, given up all hope of any initiative on father's part in any respect whatever – I have convinced them that what he really cares for is his A.R.P.[4] duty, as for business, that can wait till after the war. This thesis has been accepted. If mother were to write a line to Fanny it would be well received, she is hungry for a little cosiness. They seem genuinely fond of me, with no obvious desire to exploit. Dr B. Joseph told a good joke. During an air alarm in Tel Aviv, a Jew was observed not taking cover. An air raid warden urged him to do so. 'Why should *I* go inside?' said the Jew 'I am not from Tel Aviv. I am from Jerusalem.' Palestine he said would, if attacked, go the way of Finland, not of Vichy. And I am sure that's so.

Halifax was very well received.[5] And the news from Willkie[6] seems good. Altogether a better & better mood. I shall write again soon.
 love.
  Shaya.

IB's initial role in New York (soon extended) was to encourage support for Britain from one of the major groups within American society: the Jews. The earliest of his official US letters to survive are written to the Governor of New York State.

1 The 44th floor is just over half way up the section of the then RCA building (30 Rockefeller Plaza) between the first and second steps in its eastern façade. Some views from the BIS offices appear in Frank Thistlethwaite, *Our War, 1938–1945* (Cambridge, 1997); see also Plates 31–2.
2 Bernard (later Dov) Joseph (1899–1980), Canadian-born lawyer, politician and author, legal adviser to Jewish Agency's political department 1936–45.
3 John Henry D'Albiac (1894–1963), Air Officer Commanding British Air Forces, Greece, 1940–1.
4 Air-Raid Precautions.
5 Lord Halifax had arrived on 25 January to take up the position of British Ambassador after Lord Lothian's death (from uraemic poisoning, for which, as a Christian Scientist, he had refused treatment) on 12 December.
6 After FDR's re-election in November 1940 Willkie, the defeated candidate, devoted himself to unifying the US behind a policy of increasing military aid to Britain. He also gave unqualified support to FDR's Lend-Lease proposal (367/2) – in support of which he was currently on a visit to Britain – and crusaded against isolationism.

TO HERBERT H. LEHMAN[1]

5 February 1941

British Information Services

Dear Governor Lehman

I beg to enclose a letter addressed to you on my behalf by my friend Arthur Goodhart which he gave me when I was leaving Oxford over a month ago. I am naturally not a little perplexed and bewildered in this teeming new world in which I so unexpectedly find myself, and should very deeply appreciate it if you would be so good as to allow me to consult you with regard to several problems with which at present I am faced. I quite understand that you have many far more important matters to occupy your attention than the giving of advice to a young man greatly in need of it – I should be most grateful if you could let me know when it would be most convenient for you to let me inflict myself upon you – naturally all times suit me beginning from next week. I do apologize for adding to your burdens.

    Yours sincerely
    Isaiah Berlin

TO HERBERT H. LEHMAN

27 February 1941 [*typescript*]

British Information Services

Dear Governor Lehman,

Thank you for your letter of February 24th, and also for your kindness in enclosing letters of introduction to the various eminent persons who may be able to help me in my work. I should like to take this opportunity of explaining what, perhaps, I did not make clear during our meeting – that the principal aim, both of my organisation in general and of my own section of it in particular, is the acquisition of information for transmission to England. We are naturally anxious to remove any misconceptions which prevail about our intrinsically excellent case and to present it honestly and well. But

---

1 Hon. Herbert Henry Lehman (1878–1963), pronounced 'Leeman', banker, liberal Democrat Governor of NY State 1932–42, first Director-General (1943–6) of the United Nations Relief and Rehabilitation Administration (UNRRA), set up in November 1943 to provide aid to liberated areas. After the announcement of the Nüremberg Laws in 1935, Lehman urged that the US double the number of German Jews admitted annually. FDR responded sympathetically, but the immigration laws remained unchanged.

equally we are anxious not to make any direct pro-Allied propaganda or pressure which in any case is undesirable, and in the case of the Jews can never have been required.

Permit me to say how grateful I am for your kindness in giving me so much of your time and for your advice upon the questions which we discussed – advice which has already proved most valuable to me. I should like to say once more how deeply I appreciated your kindness.

Yours sincerely,
Isaiah Berlin

TO MARIE AND MENDEL BERLIN

Feb. something, perhaps 27ᵗʰ [1941]

Devon Hotel, 70 West 55th Street,
New York

My dear parents

I am, of course, very well indeed. I see a great many people. This is a strange country. People are, in spite of all the odd modernity of life – everything laid on – light, heat, music, art, love – laid on like water. Yet the people are simple, naive, slow, uncivilized, like peasants in town, tough, sentimental, suspicious, generous at the same time. But you want to know about my life. I live in [a] large, warm, airy room. I rise at 9.30, dress, & breakfast en route to my office, after a cup of coffee in my room. I work till lunch, & then eat usually with someone I have professional reasons for seeing. Jewish life is permeated with jealousies, etc. & one has to walk carefully. I saw Gov. Lehman the other day, a very nice, comfortable man, like a little brown bear, swinging his little legs from his chair, honest, brave, slow and a personality. also Mrs de Sola Pool, the head of Hadassah, very nice indeed, who asked me to dinner. A lot of odd Londoners are here: Istorik,[1] who accosted me in a hotel, & seems quite nice, shrewd, & funny about his employers. I went to a public dinner which revealed Gildesgame[2] whom Istorik declares he defeated in a court of law. Very affable, not very

---

1 According to IB in his memoir of Alexander and Salome Halpern (366/3), Istorik was 'a general manager of the Zionist Bank, at that time called the "Jewish Colonial Trust". At the end of the 1930s I had become acquainted with Istorik in connection with the Zionist movement in London. He was in New York on some kind of financial business.'

2 Pierre Gildesgame (1903–81), Chairman of the Maccabi World Union (the international Jewish sports organisation), and closely involved with the quadrennial World Maccabiah Games, a competition for Jewish athletes similar to the Olympics in style and standard.

nice. Libermann[1] who is nice, sends his love, and wants to help the Allies with his friends. Lunched with him. A friend I think. Rabbi Shneerson[2] wants to get in touch via his son in law, Rashag. Sends greetings. The Apters have arrived. In no hurry to see them. You need have no fear about my being financially or otherwise exploited by them. Aronson unable to find work, melancholy, listening to radio 25 hours a day. Holdsteins, very friendly. I visited Brandeis the other day. Most impressive: puritanical, fierce, 84 years of age, respected religiously by all, denounced rich Jews and speaks & looks like a Misnagdic[3] saint. Edward Warburg,[4] charming, decadent, wistful, oppressed by his sense of duty to Jews, rich man's son enfant perdu. But to return to my day. I work till 7, dine, usually in company (again Jewish social persons) sometimes work after dinner. Beautiful, quiet room, marvellous view from 44th floor. Wish I were in England.

Shaya

TO MENDEL BERLIN

Postmark 5 March 1941 [*end of incomplete letter*]

British Information Services

I had a letter from Smith saying the College wouldn't pay me any extra money giving good reasons, & asking me to regard your low rent[5] as equi-

---

1 Probably Alexander Liberman (1912–99), sculptor, painter, photographer, film-maker, writer and later (1962–94) editorial director of all Condé Nast publications, including *Vogue*. He and his mother emigrated from Russia to London in 1921; after some years in Paris, he came to NY in 1941. Alternatively his father Simon Liberman (see 504/1), a friend of IB's parents who, like Mendel Berlin, worked in the timber business.

2 Yosef Yitzchak Schneerson (1880–1950), a distant cousin of the Berlin family (see p. li above), the sixth Lubavitcher Rebbe, that is the leader of the Chabad sect of Hasidic Judaism. His eldest daughter Chana married Rav Shemaryahu Gurary, known by the acronym 'Rashag'. The Lubavitcher Rebbes take their name from the small town of Lubavitch (between Vitebsk and Smolensk), where the Chabad sect was based for over a century. The sect combines a distinctive attitude to human knowledge of the divine and scholarly respect for the sacred texts with the emotional fervour in prayer and religious observance introduced by the original Hasidim.

3 Hebrew term meaning 'opposed' to Hasidism, i.e. stressing the need for detailed study of the Talmud and rejecting Hasidism's emotional aspects; later used more generally to imply scholarly, rational, analytic-minded, sceptical and anti-mystical.

4 Edward Mortimer Morris *Warburg (1908–92), collector and patron of the arts, American cousin of Ingrid Warburg, son of Felix Warburg, and thus nephew of Ingrid's father Fritz.

5 Mendel occupied IB's rooms in the house at the east end of New College's 'New Buildings' from late 1940 until early 1945, travelling to London as required by his business commitments and duties as an air-raid warden. Marie was obliged to live in a boarding-house run by a Mrs Hall in Holywell Street (part of whose south side is formed by the New Buildings), but used the New College kitchens to cook their meals: Mendel, who suffered from inflammation of the gall-bladder for several years during the war, had to follow a strict diet.

valent. Very well. I am, they say, to have no false shame in accepting a
further £300 p.a. from you in lieu of Fellowship allowance if you'll give it me.
I have applied for permission to import same, & Childs has written to
London recommending the course. I hope it will go through the Treasury or
Foreign Office or whoever it is before 1945. A man called Edelbaum, a
religious Jewish lecturer from London, who says he has met you is here,
trying to extend his exit permit.[1] The Jews are certainly no less crass &
ignorant of Europe, strange as it may seem, than their fellow citizens, & the
most familiar truths have to be hammered into them again & again in baby
language. This I do to the best of my ability. I am v. popular with Hadassah,
more so than with the male counterparts, with whom my relations are good
but not enthusiastic. As soon as war is over I shall return to private life with
relief & gratitude. Meanwhile this is interesting if exhausting. American
food, particularly the cuisine induced by Fred, agrees with me better than
anything ever has.

    All my love
      Isaiah Berlin.

TO MARIE AND MENDEL BERLIN

   15 March [1941]

The Shoreham,
Connecticut Avenue at Calvert Street,
Washington, DC

My dear parents,

    Here I am once again in Washington. The town is very crowded since a
new picture gallery – Mellon's[2] bequest, (mostly from the Hermitage) is
being opened. This is an event of high social importance, hence no room in
hotels. You ask about my life. I cannot recollect all your questions, but in
brief, I am absolutely full from morning till night. People telephone continually, curious visitors call, business accumulates. I rise at 9·30. I consume
one cup of tea, dress, & walk to my office. On the way I enter a drug store &
consume: 1 cup of coffee, a Frankfurter or a sandwich, another cup of
coffee etc. sometimes a tomato juice. I begin work at 10·30 & work till

---

1 Required during the war in order to leave Britain.
2 Andrew William Mellon (1855–37), American lawyer, banker, philanthropist and art-collector;
  Secretary of the Treasury 1920–32, US Ambassador in London 1932–3. In 1930–1 he bought 21
  masterpieces from the Hermitage Museum in Leningrad; the ensuing criticism of his lavish
  spending, and a tax investigation, led to his resignation from the Treasury. In 1937, shortly
  before his death, he donated the paintings as the nucleus of what became the National Gallery
  of Art in Washington.

one. I then lunch, usually with someone, in my own building, till 2·30. I then return to work. My secretary[1] at last understands every word I say. Great triumph. At tea time cups of tea are brought in as a tribute to our English status. Americans take no tea. I work till 7·30. I then dine, again usually in company, & if I can get away politely, return to the office. There are usually 3 or 4 people there, the typists & clarks are gone, & one chats amiably at midnight. By 12·30 I am in bed. I have acquired, from Woolworth's a complete set of crockery, cutlery, etc. so that I can make my own meals if necessary. Anyhow here everything can be brought canned & scrupulously clean & medically perfect. So far I have had no occasion to develop autarky. Rau is back, & I may invite him to share an apartment – i.e. a small flat – with me. It is both cheaper & nicer than a hotel & has all its advantages. I haven't seen him yet as he has gone to see his mother in Canada, but I am told he looks very sunburnt & imperial after a tour of Rhodesia. I have been exceptionally well throughout; I am sorry to hear father had flu (aha, how do I know?) & is now well. Mulya, poor man, is much deflated. I hope he will get some work soon. At present he seems to be living on his capital. I am here to confer at the British Embassy: John Foster (tell Miss Carruthers)[2] is being more & more invaluable to them. I am intriguing hard to get him away from the Embassy & attached to the British Press Service, where I think he would do even more good. But the Embassy evidently regard him as too valuable. I met a nice old gentleman, Alexander Halpern,[3] (I think he was something in the liberal government in Russia in 1917) head of ORT[4] in London, here; he has arrived to collect money for them, dollars for H.M.G., sterling for the refugees in England I suppose. Anyhow he is a courtly person of a past age, a friend of all exiled liberals & Maurice Baring & the Benckendorffs[5] & Ridleys, a little snobbish, a little superficial, but still well

1 At this time, a Mrs Alice B. Irwin.

2 John Foster's former governess, who brought him up after his parents separated, continued to share his home and enjoyed his life-long devotion.

3 Alexander Yakovlevich Halpern (c.1879–1956), lawyer from St Petersburg, assistant to the Secretary to the Provisional Government 1917–18, then emigrated to London. In NY during the war he moved in left-wing Russian émigré circles. His genuine work there for ORT (see next note) provided cover for his activities with British Intelligence, namely, at the time of this letter, responsibility for controlling various foreign-language broadcasts made by a supposedly independent short-wave radio station in Boston. His wife Salome (1888–1982) had belonged to the literary and artistic worlds of pre-revolutionary St Petersburg and between-the-wars Paris. See IB's 'Alexander and Salome Halpern', in Mikhail Parkhomovsky (ed.), *Jews in the Culture of Russia Abroad: Collected Articles, Publications, Memoirs and Essays*, vol. 1, *1919–1939* (Jerusalem, 1992) – as yet published only in Russian translation in this Russian collection.

4 Selective acronym of the organisation's original Russian name 'Obshchestvo remeslennogo i zemledel'cheskogo truda', 'The society for trade and agricultural labour [amongst Jews in Russia]'; later 'Society for the dissemination of labour'.

5 Jasper Ridley's mother Nathalie (1887–1968) was the daughter of Count Alexander Konstantinovich Benckendorff (1849–1917), Russian Ambassador in London from 1903 until his death. The Benckendorff family had a long tradition of loyal service to the Tsars. Nathalie's

preserved, civilized, refined and an oasis in New York. He is returning to
England shortly & is looking forward to it. The amount of goodwill Britain
has here is colossal. It is a subject which any fool – which even you – could
have triumph with, however badly you speak. Any mention of England, of
Churchill, of London brings volleys of cheers, release of pent up sentiment.
Considering how much money & effort the Germans are thought to be
spending here,[1] the result seems very negligible. The test came over the
Lease-Lend bill.[2] The administration, the Embassy, we, all the good and the
wise, really felt a little nervous. The opposition was so very loud, the radio &
papers seemed full of them, then Wheeler[3] (who is a really bad man) made
a speech in the Senate about "the Rothschilds, the Sassoons,[4] the Warburgs'
which brought *that* in too (as Proust somewhere calls it), & then this
enormous Roosevelt triumph, the heavy majority, the national relief, the
congratulations, the pleasure, all most agreeable. To return to private life.
Chaim is expected here next week which will make all our lives more dramatic, I am sure. My appearance is very soigneusement kept: as a representative of the H.M.G. I regard myself as an official entity & take steps to
conform to a norm which otherwise I cannot pretend to admire: my hair
is cut regularly, my suits pressed, my shoes shined by enthusiastic negroes at
street corners, my evenings spent to some extent among very picturesque
Jewish journalists, with wild hair, & manners of second rate actors of the
Yiddish theatre, wearing green smoking jackets, or red kimonos or both, but
full of genuine gusto, & a juicy, racy, primitive wit which has largely died out
in Europe. I lunched with [Jacob] Marshak who is not happy about having
left England: but he *is* doing definite work among the students in the
universities of a very necessary pro-British kind. Here there is a definite
student class, as in Russia before the 1st war & in Germany, & they tend to be
isolationist. They are silly & sophisticated at the same time, & I am glad I
don't have to teach them. They are sceptical about opinions & naïve about
facts which they swallow uncritically, which is the wrong way round. After
Oxford, Harvard is a desert. What I enjoy is the brimming vitality, the

husband was Jasper Ridley senior (1887–1951; Kt 1946); her daughter Catherine married Genia
Lampert.
1 cf. 328/5.
2 Lend-Lease was a means whereby the US helped its allies with war equipment and supplies
that they could not afford to pay for in cash. FDR proposed the lend-lease system in December
1940, and his Lend-Lease Act was passed in March 1941. The Act allowed repayment 'in kind or
property, or any other direct or indirect benefit which the President deems satisfactory'.
3 Burton Kendall Wheeler (1882–1975), Democratic Senator from Montana 1923–47; Chairman of
the Interstate Commerce Committee 1935–40, 1943–6; originally a supporter of FDR and the
New Deal, became a leading isolationist, violently opposed to any American involvement in
the war and an outspoken critic of Lend-Lease.
4 A wealthy and influential Jewish family of merchants in India, China and Britain; many of
them were also philanthropists and scholars of Hebrew culture.

unexhausted passion for life, the enormous appetite & childish affectionate-ness, of some young Americans, particularly when they have southern European blood; they are simple, idealistic, hot blooded, generous and full of fire. Out of such material a world may yet be buildable, if only they let themselves be affected a little by the more fastidious taste of our hemisphere, & not shout shout shout so much, & always the same, & always as if one were intellectually & even physically deaf.

I met Bronislaw Huberman[1] the other day – did I tell you that? very nice & distinguished man, the only difficulty is to know whether he is looking at you or your neighbour. Full of noble sentiments. I met him first at dinner with Sieff[2] who seems to be here to sell his goods, & doesn't seem too happy about his own state, he has with him his daughter in law, a girl from Brooklyn, vulgarity itself, platinum hair & purple finger nails & a sharp eye for money. Then I met the violinist again at lunch with Arthur Lourie,[3] a very nice, very modest Zionist official, whose father comes from Liban & mother from Goldingen, another Raskin marriage, he an old fashioned Courland[4] Jew, who has made some money in S. Africa, she a delicate gentle civilized woman, full of blue-eyed old fashioned sentiment, married to a nice bear. They have lived in S. Africa for 30 or 40 years, he still remembers a little Russian, she never knew it I suspect, but she knows some Hebrew & they are Zionists. Huberman I talked a little Russian to – he has learnt it he says, it is a foreign language to him, figurez vous[5] he is still a patriotic Pole – he said that in Riga he had had his best & most successful artistic experiences, more than in Petersburg or in Leipzig. I find I have too little time for music or concerts – our old friend Istorik full of gossip of the most amusing & malicious kind about all our old acquaintances, is dragging me to Horo-witz.[6] So you see, I am in a 'neutral' peaceful country, & cannot bear to think of the dulness & dreariness of your life in England. I know it is neither very terrifying nor very difficult. But dull. The belief in England here grows with the stories of every returning American traveller. I told Benjamin Cohen, who is on Winant's[7] staff, & a great friend of FF to ring you up if he

1 Polish violinist (1882–1947), toured internationally from the age of 11, protested publicly against Nazi treatment of Jewish musicians, subsequently set up the Palestine Symphony Orchestra with Toscanini as its first conductor, spent the war in the US.

2 Israel Moses Sieff (1899–1972), businessman working for Marks and Spencer (retail chain founded by his father-in-law), philanthropist and Zionist.

3 Arthur Lourie (1903–78), South African lawyer, political secretary of the Jewish Agency in London 1933–48 (for part of this time under Chaim Weizmann), a Zionist activist in the US during the war.

4 A district of Latvia (also 'Kurland').

5 'Just imagine'.

6 Vladimir Horowitz (1903–89), Ukrainian-born virtuoso pianist (married to Toscanini's daughter Wanda), had resumed his US concert career in 1940 after a gap of some years.

7 John Gilbert Winant (1889–1947), teacher, liberal Republican politician, Assistant Director,

is ever in Oxford & give you my love. He is a nice, serious, slow, able, unmarried elephant. What more do you want to know? I find one of my letters to you was never finished, & was produced by my secretary out of a heap of papers (I am still not terribly tidy) so one of the letters I said I had written, never went.

love

Isaiah B.

TO MENDEL BERLIN

9 April 1941 [*postcard*]

British Information Services

Mr Churchill['s] sombre speech[1] will increase American efforts I believe. They have crossed a moral Rubicon and will not go back. I am physically very well, in the thick of work. I work till 1 a.m. often but do not rise too early. I appreciate your letters more than I can say. Go on writing. Chaim & Felix both much nicer to me than to each other. Fascinating life but difficult to be so far from you.

Shaya

cd you tell Blackwells to send me half dozen copies of my own book?

TO MARIE AND MENDEL BERLIN

28 [April 1941]

British Information Services

My dear parents,

The scarcity of letters from me is due solely to the fact that being obliged to write a great deal in the course of my duties, I am both too tired & too distracted to be able to sit down to a proper letter. Physically I am extremely well. Not a cold not a headache. So far as I know my relations with everyone, superiors, inferiors, friends, etc. are excellent. Chaim & Felix both brighten my life, I function as an occasional buffer when they don't want to

International Labour Organization (ILO), in Switzerland 1935–40, US Ambassador in London 1941–6. Committed suicide.

1 In his radio broadcast of 9 February, addressed largely to the US, Churchill had stressed Britain's urgent need for 'an immense and continuous supply of war materials and technical apparatus of all kinds' – supplies which were to be forthcoming as a result of the Lend-Lease Bill, at the time still under debate in Congress. Churchill concluded his speech with a direct appeal to FDR: 'Give us the tools, and we will finish the job.' op.cit. (336/7), vol. 6, p. 6350.

communicate directly. Both are great & good men but each is on a pedestal & conscious of his public position etc. and not disposed to make concessions to the other. I saw a nice man the other day, Louis Ginsberg,[1] professor at the Jewish Seminary,[2] born in Kovno, talmudist & author of an excellent book on Jewish legends. Very modest, scholarly, learned and sweet. A happy old man contented with his work & himself, with a terrible wife[3] whose qualities he hardly notices. Also Salmann Shocken,[4] administrator of the University of Jerusalem, & publisher, a really cultivated man who likes poetry & with whom I get on. In Washington I meet celebrities who are interesting for an hour or two & leave images on one's mind which colour memories of historical events. When one reads newspapers one then hears certain voices & sees certain faces. America is a fascinating semi-barbarous land. The president governs it, excellently; step by step he brings them nearer realization of what to do. It is patrols to-day, it will be convoys to-morrow. He judges popular temper, he never loses a trick, the Gallup poll shows 23% or something like in favour of complete participation in war if Britain cannot do without it – inconceivable 3 months ago. So long as he is in power we have nothing to fear. I had lunch with Mrs Lauterpacht,[5] the evacuated wife of the Cambridge professor of law;[6] very nice, very pales-tinian, wanted to be remembered to you. I think I am leaving the Devon for the Shoreham again – opposite, in the same street, not only because Fred Rau is there, but because it is friendlier in general. I shall let you know immediately if I do so. John Foster is very well & popular. His aunt[7] in Oxford seems agitated about his desire to move to New York from Washington – he is much annoyed by the fuss she has been making cables

1 Louis Ginzberg (1873–1953), leading Jewish scholar born in the Lithuanian city of Kovno (present-day Kaunas); immigrant to US 1899; editor of the rabbinic department of *The Jewish Encyclopedia* (NY/London, 1901–6) 1900–3; for the rest of his life a teacher of Talmud at the Jewish Theological Seminary of America (see next note); leading figure in Conservative Judaism, which combined national and religious values. His major work, *The Legends of the Jews*, appeared in six volumes between 1909 and 1938.

2 The Jewish Theological Seminary of America, founded in NY in 1886 to preserve the knowledge and practice of historical Judaism.

3 Adele Ginzberg née Katzenstein (1886–1980), who became engaged to Louis Ginzberg in 1908 while he was on a visit to Berlin. The shock of this engagement led Ginzberg's close friend Henrietta Szold (1860–1945), the translator of much of his work and the first female student at the Jewish Theological Seminary, to reassess her life, a process which eventually led her to found Hadassah in 1912.

4 Salman (*sic*) Schocken (1877–1959), Polish-born businessman, publisher, art and book collector and active Zionist; established publishing houses in Berlin, Tel Aviv and NY; moved from Berlin to Jerusalem in 1934 and to the US in 1940; chairman of the Executive Council of the Hebrew University in Jerusalem 1934–45.

5 Rachel Lauterpacht, née Steinberg.

6 Hersch Lauterpacht (1897–1960), Whewell Professor of International Law, Cambridge, 1938–55.

7 Miss Carruthers (366/2) was an honorary aunt rather than a true relation.

she has sent him etc. She is very devoted & very indiscreet it seems. I wish you wd write to Ben Cohen of the American Embassy & tell him you would like to see him when & if next he comes to Oxford, or in London even. He is a silent, serious, heavy, nice, good, kind excellent man. He won't have much to say but you would enjoy meeting him for a short while, & you can say I asked you to. he is a great friend of Felix. I haven't yet written to Hourani or Beeley but will this week. So far only David Cecil & Mary Fisher write. My affection for them rises daily. Mr Bowra may be sulky because of my complaints of his letter here in September. I have written him a nice letter. Stephen Spender is married[1] again I hear. I keep cousin Constantine [Konstantin Apters] at arms length, but no further. He is harmless if one doesn't trust him too far. Samuel [Aronson] I haven't seen for a month – I really am busy, but very well & happy.

I hear Arthur Goodhart is coming on a visit. I'll try & see him. The more such people the better.

I haven't seen Sir A. Salter yet, but he is a definite success.

TO MARIE AND MENDEL BERLIN

17 May 1941

The British Press Service,
33 West 55th Street, New York

My dear parents
    What on earth am I to describe to you now? My mode of life you know. My hours are 11 a.m.–1, 2.30–7, 10–12 in the evening. Your last letter was very interesting and delightful – particularly the gossip. Miss Litvine (Spender's new wife) is at the very least ½ a Jewess, and, as Mr Bowra said in a letter to me, worn out. Why, as Mr B. also said, has he this passion for marriage? the best remark about the war, quoted by Mr B. is by the wife of [a] Cambridge don, a relation of Mary Fisher, Fredegonde Shove[2] who said "the war has shown up all foreigners as such".
    The Weizmanns are very nice to me, occasionally I dine with them alone – an honour much sought after by local persons – and then take her to

---

1 To Natasha Litvin (b. 1921), pianist, lecturer, gardener and author.
2 Fredegond Shove (1899–1949), poet, Mary Fisher's first cousin, daughter of Frederic William Maitland and Florence Maitland (elder sister of H. A. L. Fisher), niece of Ralph Vaughan Williams, who set some of her poems to music. Her husband Gerald Frank Shove (1887–1947) was a Fellow of King's College and Reader in Economics, Cambridge.

the cinema. He is worn out by his journeys across U.S.A & Canada, but still full of life. Very funny when he talks on the telephone to somebody unknown, smiles sweetly, says "How *are* you Mr Heineman, yes, of course, we must meet soon, it will be *very* nice to see you, we must arrange . . .' then turns to me while the other talks and whispers loudly *"money"* then turns back "it would be delightful to see you how is your daughter' etc. I ask 'is he rich?" W. answers "vehrry. A terrible fellow. But *very* rich". Two nights ago I visited Yale university & chatted to some intelligent but isolationist students. At a certain point their intelligence suddenly becomes exhausted and they repeat communist slogans. To-morrow I go to Princeton where lives my old friend Elias Lowe, professor of palaeography.[1] He has promised to take me to see Einstein.[2]

How nice of Ben Cohen to call on you so often. Alsop who introduced me to him (or was it Felix?) is a "columnist" in the Herald Tribune, a cousin of the President, a fanatical Anglophile, intelligent, young, snobbish, a little pompous, and my permanent host in Washington. To-day I lunched with [Arthur] Goodhart & Wilfred Greene. The latter is very angry by the off hand way in which the British Embassy treated him: John Foster alone had met Americans, he declared, the rest knew nobody & muddled his tour. The Master of the Rolls was an important person and if our Embassies do not realize that, they should be spoken to, etc. etc. so to soothe him down I brought two of my nicest colleagues to lunch with him and buttered him up and made All Souls small talk. I hope he will be mollified by the time he returns. He was a great success with a large number of Congressmen, the greatest in fact, since Lothian died. He goes about blasting British officials in a way found exhilarating by Americans, & I suppose indirectly does us good. This week I go on a pilgrimage to Keynes & Salter. So the days pass. I work 12 hours a day, look well, sleep well, & don't think about anything.

    love

      Shaya

IB's letters home give a selective account of his life in New York, passing over the sense of isolation he later remembered:

I was very unhappy in New York. I used to stand on the 44th floor of the Rockefeller Building, and look down into the street with a certain

1 Elias Avery Lowe (1879–1969), US palaeographer, Lecturer and Reader in Palaeography, Oxford, 1913–48, Professor in Palaeography, Institute for Advanced Study, Princeton, from 1936.

2 Albert Einstein (1879–1955), discoverer of relativity, Zionist, permanent member of the Institute for Advanced Study, Princeton, from 1933, had won the Nobel Prize for Physics in 1921.

desire to commit suicide. All these little ants running around, one more, one less, it couldn't make any difference. I felt somehow I was just a cypher, a number, no individual personality at all. In Washington I felt quite different.

Also, mindful of his parents' sensitivities about his well-being, he habitually concealed any health problems. Marie and Mendel discovered only some months later that IB had spent time in hospital and that the next letter was written during his convalescence.

TO MARIE AND MENDEL BERLIN

Sunday 31 July [1941]¹

South Londonderry, Vermont

My dear parents,

I am really very full of remorse about not having written for so long. But I cannot say how unconducive to writing one's surroundings are. One reads, dictates, talks all day and at the end of it one is exhausted mentally and quite incapable of writing anything but a few words of greeting. But you are quite right. Firstly because it cannot really be as desperate as that. Secondly because even inanities are better than nothing, postcards better than silence. I shall reform. And I shall find out from John Foster the secret of his rapid postal technique. You say you wish to have details of my life, personal relations etc. My routine I think you know. I rise at 10 a.m. and go to bed at 12–1 a.m. I am in the office at 10.30 and read letters, make an enormous number of telephone calls, etc. until 1 p.m. I then lunch, either alone in which case it takes about half an hour, or with "clients" or colleagues in which case I am back at 2.30, 2.45. More interviews, files to be read, endless conferences. My region of work has considerably expanded. I am not surprised that Raymond Gram Swing² should look on me as a Middle Eastern expert (Hourani probably won't like that at all) since my only long conversation with him was concerned with the Iraq rebellion,³ then at its

1 Though 31 July was a Thursday in 1941.
2 Raymond Gram Swing (1887–1968), journalist and radio commentator, *Philadelphia Public Ledger* and *New York Evening Post*, London, 1924–34; influential (anti-Nazi) commentator for the BBC 1935–45, the Mutual Broadcasting System 1936–45, and ABC 1942–8; married to feminist Betty Gram, whose name he had adopted.
3 When Iraq gained independence from Britain in 1930, Britain retained rights of transit for troops between India, Egypt and Palestine, while Iraq was obliged to offer aid and access to Britain in wartime, and to protect the pipeline from the northern Iraq oilfields to Haifa on the Mediterranean. Arab nationalism in the Army and resentment at the continuing presence of two RAF bases in Iraq, combined with the violently anti-British and anti-Semitic zeal of the former Grand Mufti of Jerusalem, now in Baghdad, prompted the pro-Axis Prime Minister,

height, when he took a pessimistic view of British prospects, and I – the only
person in our office with the remotest knowledge of Middle Eastern
conditions – reassured him. Since we did so well in Iraq his opinion of me
rose. I have met him only once or twice: he is one of the nicest of men,
sincere, serious, high minded, realistic, and immensely anxious personally
to help all good causes. In that respect American journalists & radio
commentators of the better sort – (at their worst they are unbelievably bad,
inaccurate, sensational, cheap, alarmist, vulgar) have passionate moral
convictions which they do not conceal. Swing, Mowrer,[1] Dorothy
Thompson[2] (she was at Charles's Seder,[3] and is a woman of tremendous
physical energy and animal spirits – she addresses one like a public meeting
and preaches her doctrines with fury – the rest of the company is silent &
gapes – Charles being a little used to that himself found in her an insuperable
obstacle. In the end they divided the available time & talked in a kind of
dialogue while the rest of us sat spellbound or frustrated, according to
temperament.) and the others are passionate anti-fascist fighters and look on
themselves as dedicated people, not as detached commentators but as priests
& prophets and guides of the American people. The President takes the same
view – he consults with them & calls upon them as moral and political allies
and sometimes causes them to say what he cannot say himself. Their
influence is far greater than that of any comparable figure in England.
Possibly Garvin in his prime, or J. A. Spender had the same influence. But I
doubt it. I often work in the evenings, after dinner, between 9 and midnight,
since it is quiet, the telephone is silent, and one can read & write in peace.
My colleagues often do the same. At midnight we gather & discuss events &
local gossip. At 12·30 we disperse.

My work now covers Labour & other special groups[4] as well as Jews
etc. I have been provided with an assistant[5] whom I hardly know, & I have
been united to a very nice, pleasant, sensitive, intelligent man called Donald

Rashid Ali el Gailani, to depose the four-year-old King and his uncle, the Regent, in April 1941.
At Churchill's insistence British troops and air-power were diverted from other commitments
to protect the British bases; they then crushed the revolt and reinstated the previous regime
before Axis support could reach Iraq.

1 Edgar Ansel Mowrer (1892–1977), Pulitzer Prize-winning foreign correspondent, *Chicago Daily
   News*; fiercely anti-Nazi (and later equally anti-Communist), he had been expelled from
   Germany, Italy and the USSR for his reports; Goebbels allegedly said that he would give a
   division of troops to capture Mowrer. Once the US had entered the war, he became deputy
   director of the US Office of Facts and Figures under Archibald MacLeish.
2 Dorothy Thompson (1894–1961), author, outspoken anti-Nazi journalist and radio broadcaster,
   married to Sinclair Lewis.
3 Chaim Weizmann was sometimes known as Charles. Seder is the Jewish celebration of
   Passover, centrally important in the Jewish year.
4 Specifically, Mormons, Roman Catholics and (in the terminology of that era) Negroes.
5 J. Alan Judson, later a researcher on IB's staff in Washington.

Hall[1] as joint head of a department of the Press Service. He writes bad novels, and as so often with bad novelists, is a gentle and sympathetic human being. In short I like working with him.

You inquire about my relations to my superiors: so far as I am aware they are excellent. All sorts of changes have occurred, as you may have read in the papers, Sir G. Campbell is now our master (in his absence John Foster comes from Washington to deputize) but the changes and alliances and bureaucratic battles and alterations of status of various persons hardly touches me. It is possible that in the course of one of our regular internal upheavals (which take place on an average only once a year – which is a tribute to the general harmony) I shall be elevated to a place directly connected with Sir G. Campbell's office as opposed to the Press Service which is now one of the bodies co-ordinated by him – but this would alter neither the nature of my work (which is v. interesting) nor my abode (which will continue in New York) nor my salary (which is still £900 + £300 of my own) so I am not really much concerned whether this occurs or not. I am sorry Alsop left for India as a drafted U.S. official[2] – I lose a friend and gain nothing in return. In New York, although I professionally meet quite important and interesting people, I have found no one exceptionally attractive. The Jewish world is divisible into (a) the dignified dead, of German descent, dull, benevolent, pompous, far from brave, unwilling to act, rich and not very generous, either deadly dull like Samuel [Aronson], or eccentric like Elkan Adler.[3] Even Bentwich was disappointed in their lack of public spirit. Governor Lehman is far & away the best among them, brave, sincere, energetic and straightforward. The rest are gargoyles & mummies.

(2) The lively intriguers. Some are nice & some are not. The Zionists are full of life, have clear aims, but are torn with internal fights and are unskilful in attracting young men to their ranks. The 5 million Jews of the U.S. – a fundamentally lower middle class population, like the Czechs, – are sentimentally pro-Zionist (at least 90% of them are I should say), but lack leadership and so, unless some public event or turn of policy with regard to Palestine moves them to enthusiasm or indignation, they remain quiescent and hope for the best. It is difficult to bring home to them the implications of the war & their duty in this respect as they are, above all things, terrified of being thought warmongers and to be acting in their own, rather than general American interests. If they were integrated & led, they could be an immense power.

1 Donald John Hall (b. 1903), travel-writer and novelist, Special Assistant to the Director-General, BIS NY, 1941, private secretary to the Minister of State in the FO 1945.
2 Joseph Alsop had enlisted in the US Navy.
3 Elkan Nathan Adler (1861–1946), English lawyer, bibliophile and author, son of former Chief Rabbi Herman Adler.

(3) the Jewish Trade Unions. The leaders – Hillman,[1] Dubinsky[2] etc. are nice people and quite brave, but are not sure what they want. They have invested everything in Roosevelt and if he is ever defeated, or if the Democratic Party is out, their influence will suffer a corresponding eclipse.

All these groups are very pro-British and speak of what they regard as unjust treatment in Palestine more in sorrow than in anger. They are prepared to forget this issue if they are not forcibly reminded of it from outside. Weizmann says their attitude to Britain is one of unrequited love.

Working with these people is very interesting. Weizmann's relation to his followers is exactly like that of Parnell[3] – they resent his pride, his contempt for them, his autocratic behaviour, his personal isolationism, his general de haut en bas attitude, his unique position among the governing elements both here & in England, yet they know they cannot do without him, they admire him, worship him, and swallow all the minor insults which they receive from him. He delivered a series of brilliant speeches all over the U.S. – the tenor being: (a) Allied victory is the sole hope of the Jews everywhere. All other issues should be shelved (b) The future of the Jews in Europe will be dark even after a British victory. The status quo is irrecoverable. Other arrangements must be made. Palestine the only solid hope. (c) Attacks on the British about Palestine, appeasement etc. are idiotic and, at the present moment, suicidal. Britain is at present the conscience of the world. The Jews can put complete trust in Mr Churchill & Mr Roosevelt

His (b) irritated the German refugees – Max Warburg[4] with whom I lunched, a typical Hohenzollern Jew[5] who cannot forget his intimacy with the Kaiser – who all want to settle in Europe comfortably again and regard Weizmann's pessimism as defeatist & treacherous. The majority of the refugees both Jewish & non-Jewish are so blind politically, and have so little understanding of what has been, is, and may be happenning to them, that the opposite of their views is always likely to be true. I have never met such hopeless ostriches in my life. Weizmann amused the Commonwealth Club in San Francisco by saying "All the 135 million American citizens came to this country on the 'Mayflower' – all except the Jews. The Jews hurried after

1 Sidney Hillman (1887–1946), President of the Amalgamated Clothing Workers of America 1914–46, strong supporter of FDR and New Deal, member of the National Defense Advisory Commission and Associate Director-General of the Office of Production Management 1940–2.
2 David Dubinsky (1892–1982), President of the International Ladies' Garment Workers' Union 1932–66.
3 See 222/2. Parnell was called 'the uncrowned king of Ireland' because of his great influence over his followers; his career had been ruined by a divorce scandal in 1890.
4 Max *Warburg (1867–1946), banker, Jewish leader in Germany until his emigration to the US in 1938; brother of Aby, Paul, Felix and Fritz, uncle of Ingrid and Edward.
5 i.e. a Jew who retains the sense of a secure place in society enjoyed by the wealthy German Jewish community under the Hohenzollern Emperors (1871–1919).

them on the 'Normandie' and the 'Queen Mary' faster, bigger, better but never quite caught up, despite the most desperate efforts."

To return to my private affairs. I go to Washington about once in three weeks on business – and invariably, after visiting the Embassy, see my All Souls colleagues – Bob Brand[1] head of the Food Mission, Salter, Anthony (now Sir A.) Rumbold who is much the most intelligent of my contemporaries in the Embassy, John Foster, occasionally Keynes, Childs, a Labour leader or two, Ben Cohen who, I think, will not return, the Felixes, and various young officials, & one or two older ones, in American government offices, who have an energy, idealism, and faith in their own powers to alter the world which is very scarce in Europe. I used to stay with Joe Alsop – now I divide my attentions between my ex-colleague, Captain John Sparrow who is here as a member of our military mission, the Rumbolds,[2] and occasionally, out of sentiment, I stay in Alsop's house now rented by a very hospitable member of the Embassy named Elmslie who presses one to stay with him. One of my chief pleasures is to talk to visiting Englishmen all of whom tell the same story – of the incredibly high English morale, as high as when I left in January – the greater efficiency & collaboration in Govt. departments – and the false impression of the degree of American belligerency. Wint[3] said that the impression in England was that all the women knitted bundles for Britain day & night while the men were panting to go to war. This, in spite of the vast volume of pro-British sentiment, is still far from true. Both the President & our people here have a vast task before them yet. But you would prefer me to discuss my private life more fully. I hardly have any. But I will try next time.

love
    Isaiah.

1 Robert Henry Brand (1878–1963), merchant banker, historian, Fellow of All Souls 1901–32, 1937–63, head of the British Food Mission in Washington 1941–4, Representative of HM Treasury in Washington, 1944–46, 1st Lord Brand of Eydon 1946.
2 Anthony Rumbold's wife was Felicity Ann, née Bailey (1917–84).
3 (Frank) Guy Atherton Wint (1910–69), administrator, historian and (later) journalist; Oriel PPE 1928–31, then additional study at Berlin University; research secretary, League of Nations 1932–6; Leverhulme Research Fellowship 1937–40; External Affairs department, Government of India, 1940–6; author (with George Schuster) of *India and Democracy* (London, 1941).

TO LILLIAN SCHAPIRO[1]

[early August 1941]

Statler Hotel[2]
but as from Shoreham Hotel, 33 W 55 Street

Dear Mrs Schapiro

I apologize deeply for not writing for so long. But as soon as I returned into the steambath in New York I became enveloped in routine – back to my old evil habits of staying up till the early morning. I am now deep in the most tortuous labour politics – to me strange and rather depressing – involving journeys like this one to visit 'important' people, and my work in your house seems a remote and no longer attainable pleasure. I really did enjoy myself enormously. I am sure, whatever you may say, that I was a nuisance to some degree, especially as I was in the low state of an immediate convalescent, & for this I beg you to forgive me. I am also very grateful indeed. I don't know how best to express my gratitude in a sachlich[3] form. I am vainly searching New York for a copy of Alexander Herzen's memoirs a book which altered my life and became a point of reference both intellectually & morally, but only bits of it in bad translations seem available here. I am still searching and will send it as soon as it turns up. My vividest memories are the taste & smell of corn in the open and the sight of Ernest[4] on a stone in the middle of the stream. My love to him and to Miriam. I burn to resume the issues Meyer & I discussed in the early morning. I am off to Washington for 3 weeks & will try & reach you in September. I much envy the very decorative jacket M. wears when it is cool. Once more I am v. grateful.

yrs
Isaiah B.

Guilt pursues me. Ought I to have left something for your nice maid? I liked her very much. Will you indemnify me later?

Although IB's remit nominally covered the interests of minorities such as Negroes, Catholics and Mormons, his chief preoccupations during his time in New York were Jews and organised labour. The Jewish world was of course familiar to him, and he had already encountered a number of its leading figures in England; there was an occasional conflict of loyalties

1 Dr Lillian Milgram Schapiro (b. c.1903), paediatrician, wife of Meyer Schapiro.
2 In Cornell University, Ithaca, NY (part of their School of Hotel Administration).
3 'Material'.
4 Ernest and Miriam were the Schapiros' children.

between his Zionist sympathies and his official responsibilities, but on the
whole he contrived to be faithful to both. Organised labour offered a
different challenge: it was an unfamiliar milieu whose political nuances he
had to master – in particular the antagonism between trade unions
sympathetic to Britain and those whose long-standing prejudices against
imperialism in any form ensured their continuing isolationism.

TO MARY FISHER

25 October 1941

The Shoreham, New York

Dear Mary,

You are quite quite right to be silent since I am, but believe me it is
infinitely harder to write here than in the most bombed moment in England.
It is impossible to throw even those temporary half hour roots which are
presupposed in writing a letter. Everything is artificial, made of some plastic,
durable, but ignoble matter, disposing to perpetual restlessness. I have
acquired about 2 mildly [sic] friendships with young American New Dealers,
but against the background of European stability, stability which is not
related to precariousness of life, [they] are absolutely unreal. When I go to
Washington & mingle with the English I am pathetically relieved, but
immediately accuse myself of self indulgence & plunge back into the noisy
universe in which, I say pompously, my work lies. Xtopher wd probably, for
all his English qualities, get on far better. I admire them very much &
genuinely. The amount of unspent vitality, belief in their own powers to set
the world right, general capacity for coping is terrific. They (the Americans)
are very inefficient, confused, vague, genuinely uncivilized, insensitive (but
neurotic) and unprofound. But on the other hand what they express they
express very directly, there is a good deal of first hand grappling, but all shot
through with infantilism – the cruelty, grossness & freshness are all frightfully childish qualities, so is the roaring round in masses & the rankling
resentment at the superiority of the effete grown up English. I now deal with
Labour & see fine British Trade Union leaders, wonderful Yorkshire toughs
with glittering eyes & enormous temperament with whom I mysteriously
get on well. To-day a quantity of British civil servants from the Ministry of
Labour appeared on the scene for the I.L.O. Conference now held here and I
must confess that the Americans shine by comparison. Fishlike, bored, &
dreary, they are several grades below the well washed shiny perpetually
welcoming faces of the U.S. government, with square spectacles, flat hair,
and general air of aggressively hygienic people. The nicest delegates are the

Greeks and Czechs (you remember your father once thought Mr Bowra offered to write a book on Czech literature, misreading the word, & congratulated him on his versatility but said that the subject was surely somewhat narrow?). If you see Lightfoot do give him not only my love (which will be received with justified scepticism) but that of Mrs Niebuhr, once his pupil as Miss Keppel Compton,[1] who carries Oxford with her wherever she moves, & would be irritating there, but here is civilization itself. Mrs Robert Hall I cannot bear.[2] I last saw her at a sale for unmarried mothers.[3] She works in Washington & is coy, arch, vulgar, has disagreeable views, is devoted to the family of Ramsay McDonald, and is acutely embarrassing. Where is Syme?[4] Turkey? your cousin is said to be here as Mrs Commander Coleridge,[5] attached like Sparrow to the Joint Staff Mission in Washington. She looks amiable, but I am far too nervous to approach her inasmuch as she is English and I cannot do my American turn at which I am, in a shameful way, quite good now, provided I am not disturbed by the intrusion of some genuine i.e. English factor. The Commander is very popular & thought a good fellow by everyone including Frankfurter. Mrs F. wears trailing dresses of white satin & moves in a very disembodied fashion, collecting all available fragments relating to the death of Mrs Woolf. I long to come back more than I can say – as in my notorious letter to Smith, even Wickham Legg etc. even Binnie,[6] even Sir Hugh [Allen] so you see how intense the feeling. You couldn't contrive to come here via the Foreign Office I suppose? or to help with the B.B.C. which is not too efficient? or in any capacity? I would do anything to compass that. Everything for me would fall into place & acquire proper proportion if I could confide everything daily, and you would find enormous possibilities of work – if only among women whom Prof. Cullis[7] copes with & a Somervillian called Miss M. Walters[8] – the ignorance & snobbery are terrific

1 Ursula Keppel-Compton Niebuhr (1907–97), wife of Reinhold Niebuhr.
2 Laura Margaret Hall, née Linfoot, wife 1932–68 of: Robert Lowe Hall (1901–88), Lecturer in Economics, Trinity College, Cambridge, 1926–47, Ministry of Supply 1939–46, British Raw Materials Mission, Washington, 1942–4, Baron Roberthall 1969.
3 These were run by Lettice Fisher at New College every year and were a standing joke. (Mrs Fisher had in 1918 founded the National Council for the Unmarried Mother and her Child, now the National Council for One Parent Families.)
4 Ronald Syme was Press Attaché at the British Embassy, Ankara, 1941–2.
5 Rosamund Coleridge, MF's first cousin, daughter of Admiral Sir W. W. Fisher (427/4) and wife of Richard Duke Coleridge (1905–84), later 4th Baron Coleridge of Ottery St Mary, who had joined the Joint Staff Mission, Washington, in May.
6 Alfred Maurice Binnie (1901–86), Lecturer in Engineering, New College, 1933–44.
7 Winifred Clara Cullis (1875–1956), physiologist, Head of Women's Section, BIS NY, 1941–3.
8 Marjorie Walters (1915–89), graduate student Somerville 1938–40 (D.Phil. on Francis Bacon 1941), BIS NY 1941–2, MOI (American Division) London 1942–5, Principal, Ministry of

& you could satisfy both needs so well. I feel like the Sybil & really do apologize for this letter. I wish I had some thing to say.

Shaya

This *proves* that letters cannot be adequately written from America.

TO MARIE AND MENDEL BERLIN

26 October 1941

The Shoreham Hotel, New York

My dear parents,

Do not reproach me. It is really terribly difficult to write. And I did send a stream of about 3 postcards. My work owing to expansion into labour & allied things has become fascinating. Everyone is extremely nice to me. I now spend 2½ weeks in New York – Fred Rau whom I see only in the morning & evening is just what I require not to go to bed alone without a human contact – & 5 days or so in Washington. The hotels are overcrowded there so I exploit the hospitality of members of the Embassy – Sir A. Rumbold, a 2d secretary, Etherington Smith[1] a 3d Secretary, John Foster (who is still earning golden opinions here altho' Lord Halifax is said to disapprove of him & his reputation in England is said to be in tatters) & the Childses who like me more than I them. About my life there is really nothing to say. My idiotic secretary Mrs Irwin is devoted to me but developed a crise de nerfs[2] when she thought I winked behind her shoulder at a remark of hers & tried to resign but failed & is now a slave. Even my irregular habits don't upset her any more. I have found some young American intellectuals, ex-pupils of Felix, one called Graham,[3] one called Pritchard[4] & one called Rauh[5] who are all in the U.S. government, very nice, enlightened, charming, share my views, & whom I see now that my old friend, the hostess-like Mr Alsop has gone to China. Ben Cohen is in depths of hypochondria which is a state normal in him, is resigning from the government

Education 1945–9, married Sir Patrick Linstead 1942.

1 (Raymond) Gordon Antony Etherington-Smith (b. 1914), diplomat serving in Washington 1940–2.

2 'Fit of hysterics'.

3 Philip Leslie Graham (1915–63), lawyer, journalist and publisher, worked on the Lend-Lease programme 1941–2; US Army Air Corps 1942–4 and 1944–5; Intelligence Service 1944; from 1946 publisher of the *Washington Post* in succession to his father-in-law, Eugene Meyer; committed suicide after several years of manic depression.

4 Edward ('Ed') *Prichard (sic; 'Prich') (1915–84), large lawyer who achieved notoriety in 1948 for stuffing a ballot-box in Bourbon County, Kentucky, an offence for which he was jailed.

5 Joseph Louis Rauh (1911–92), lawyer; worked for the US government 1939–42; US Army 1942–5; later a prominent civil rights activist.

& wants someone to pull him out of the swamp. no one is prepared, everyone is either too busy or too unhappy themselves, & Marion Frankfurter thoroughly disapproves of his self-indulgence in melancholy and generally cannot bear him. Felix is still full of life & action, someone has written a hostile article about him entitled 'Felix Frankfurter – Conservative'[1] do ask Mr Bowra if he wants to be sent it, if so I will, if he promises that he will not tell the Frankfurters that I did so. A very clever and malicious work, by an ex-pupil, ausgerechnet[2] also a Jew. The Jews continue in a state of combined cowardice & indignation which is the most immoral combination. The deaths of Ussishkin & Brandeis are very sad – both were proud unbending rocklike men, Ussishkin an eastern potentate, Brandeis a Boston puritan, dry, not interested in ideas, absolutely pure, absorbed in facts, universally admired & respected. Felix's éloge was a little too Viennese, he was nervous & unnatural. My relations with the Frankfurters are extremely warm. Marion wears dresses of white silk & sails about like [a] neurotic & distinguished Vestal.[3] Mrs Pool of Hadassah invites me to dinner in the Succah[4] & complains that Major Attlee[5] answers her invitations impolitely. Soon I am to provide 12 Jewish editors to lunch with Sir Gerald Campbell, my chief, who is a v. nice man, a trifle too Aaronic[6] in temper. As Halifax is no Moses either, our life is tranquil. Miriam Rothschild sent me a v. nice cable for the New Year, don't tell Miss Carruthers who hates her. The Halifaxes are very remote & viceregal, equally distant from English & Americans, she quite popular locally in the Washington ambit, he

1 'Felix Frankfurter, Conservative', by Fred Rodell, né Roedelheim (1907–80), Professor of Law at Yale from 1939, appeared in *Harpers Magazine*, October 1941, 449–59. There were long-standing differences of opinion between the Yale and Harvard Law Schools, and Frankfurter of Harvard (whose liberal views had been less in evidence, since his appointment to the Supreme Court in 1939, than his commitment to judicial restraint) was frequently criticised on legal, political and personal grounds by Justices Douglas and Black of Yale, Rodell's colleagues. Rodell was renowned as a relentless and scathing critic of lawyers, the legal system and legal language; a typical example of his incisively iconoclastic approach is 'There are two things wrong with almost all legal writing. One is its style. The other is its content. That, I think, about covers the ground': 'Goodbye to Law Reviews', *Virginia Law Review* 23 (1936–7), No 1 (November 1936), 38–45, at 38. He particularly condemned footnotes as productive of 'sloppy thinking, clumsy writing, and bad eyes' (ibid., 41).

2 'Emphatically'.

3 In Ancient Rome the Vestal Virgins were the guardians of the sacred fire in the temple of Vesta, goddess of the hearth; the proper performance of their duties was considered vital to the safety of the Roman State.

4 A temporary hut essential to the celebration of the Jewish festival of Succot, which commemorates the wanderings of the Jewish people in the wilderness after their exodus from Egypt. For the seven or more days of Succot observant Jews eat meals in the Succah.

5 Clement Richard Attlee (1883–1967), later (1955) 1st Earl Attlee, Labour politician, Major in the British Army during the First World War; Leader of the Opposition 1935–40, Lord Privy Seal 1940–2, Deputy Prime Minister 1942–5, Prime Minister 1945–51.

6 In the Old Testament Aaron is the mouthpiece of his brother Moses, the active leader of the Jewish people.

neither known nor liked. I see him occasionally & he is always charming, but the problem of building a bridge between him & the public seems insoluble. My clientèle now officially includes British Trade Union leaders, a really fine body of men, far superior in quality to the local product. Here bridge building seems more possible. Everyone asks about Harold Laski, whom they think of as a very important & dangerous man, I find it difficult to convince them that he is a harmless megalomaniac. To-morrow I dine with Prof. Ginzberg, the outstanding Jewish scholar of this land, a charming, learned, gay Litvak[1] with a terrible loud, bright, shiny Snowmanesque wife from Furth.[2] On Wednesday I dine with the Editor of the St Louis Post Dispatch,[3] on Thursday with Webster[4] whom you took to be a tramp in Oxford once & with Tawney our new labour luminary, on Friday with two U.S. radio commentators. So you see my life is variegated enough. Istorik wrote me a nice letter, & I am glad you like Bentwich. I don't write to David, Mary, Maurice B., because to write letters an atmosphere of tranquillity when one is neither too tired or too preoccupied with the next move is necessary, & U.S. civilization, at least in New York, does not provide for that. I am really active well, slept, fed, haircut, shaven, & about to be photographed. Fred who thinks his brother is slandering him, sends greetings.

    Love

      Shaya

TO MARIE AND MENDEL BERLIN

18 November 1941

                    Book-Cadillac Hotel, Detroit

My dear parents

    The govt. C.I.O.[5] Labour convention is occurring here & I am an interested member of the audience. The U.S. Labour world is in a primitive but exciting condition and I am very excited at being in a position to record

---

1 Term often used to denote a Lithuanian Jew; sometimes connotes learning and rationality, since Lithuania had been the Misnagid centre (see 364/3).

2 Fürth in Bavaria.

3 Presumably Oliver Kirby Bovard (1872–1945), managing editor of the *St Louis Post-Dispatch*.

4 Charles Kingsley Webster (1886–1961), Professor of International History, London School of Economics and Political Science (LSE), 1932–53, FRPS 1939–41, Director, BIS NY, 1941–2; FORD 1943–6.

5 The Congress of Industrial Organizations (so named since 1938), originally part of the American Federation of Labor, but independent and in competition with the AFL from 1936; its initial goal was the unionisation of workers in the steel, car-making, electrical, rubber, glass, textile and similar mass-production industries.

its doings. Carter Goodrich[1] of the I.L.O. has told me that he saw you chez Adams, & Roger Makins[2] of the Foreign Office (& All Souls) has been here & would tell you how well I am if you ask him. I also saw Attlee who was nice but painfully shy and bleak, & the rest of the I.L.O. delegation among whom there were some very hefty specimens of British manhood. To-morrow I move to Chicago where I've been – one must see the U.S. sometime, not merely N.Y. & Washington – & thence back to Washington. The C.I.O. this morning passed a rousing pro-Roosevelt-foreign-policy resolution & all the German-born delegates from Milwaukee & Wisconsin & Minnesota bought 'thumbs up' badges of British War Relief offered to them by a very homely Jew who later took me to a Kosher restaurant. A lunatic world. I am now hurrying off, to see the British Consul[3] who claims to be eager to make my acquaintance. I am *terribly* well. You said K. Clark was living in sin! You meant K[enneth] Bell! Libel!

> Yours
> Shaya

TO MARIE AND MENDEL BERLIN

Saturday 29 November [1941]

> The Shoreham, 33 West 55,
> New York City

My dear parents

What am [I] to say to you that is new or interesting? You have imposed a rigid policy of sanctions. No more letters. David Cecil now writes oftener than you without, as Spinoza defined the true amor intellectualis Dei,[4] expecting to be loved in return. I have been travelling. First I went to Detroit – a hideous city of more than a million inhabitants, without the ugly cosiness of English industrial towns. A C.I.O. convention was occurring at the time, John L. Lewis[5] conspicuously absented himself and pro-British sentiments

---

1 Carter Goodrich (1897–1971), Professor of Economics, Columbia, 1931–63; Special Assistant to US Ambassador, London, 1941; US Government Member of Governing Body, ILO, 1936–46, Chairman 1939–45.

2 Roger Mellor Makins (1904–96), later (1964) 1st Baron Sherfield of Sherfield-on-Lodden, Southampton; Fellow of All Souls 1925–39, Counsellor, FO, 1942, British Embassy, Washington, 1945 (as Minister from May 1945), Ambassador 1953–6.

3 Cyril Hubert Cane (1891–1959), British diplomat; Consul at Detroit 1939–43, Consul-General 1943–5.

4 'Intellectual love of God'.

5 John Llewellyn Lewis (1880–1969), labour leader, President of the United Mine Workers of America 1920–60, first President, Congress (originally Committee) of Industrial Organizations, 1936–40. Previously a Republican, he had supported FDR during his first two terms, but opposed his bid for a third term (partly because he considered FDR's foreign policy too interventionist), and carried out a threat to resign as CIO President should FDR be re-elected.

were rampant. The ludicrous spectacle of Communists trying to force the
rest of the delegates into a pro-British attitude which they would have taken
up in any case occurred – What Rousseau calls forcing men to be free.[1]
Thence I went to Chicago which is a strange town. The waterfront – Lake
Michigan – is magnificent, broad embankment, imaginatively built skyscrapers, a sense of width & wind and hanseatic opulence – behind this miles
on miles of hideous noisy slums – a hell beside which Kilburn High Street[2]
on Saturday night is a peaceful Arcadia – with trams, overhead railways,
buses, cars, pouring masses of standardized human beings, a vast confusion
of electric signs going on & off, blinding one – & yet the people are simpler,
more generous, homelier than in the East coast – like old pre-war Moscow
in, say, 1890 versus Petersburg at the same time, ignorant, hospitable, 1000
miles away from the Atlantic, from Europe, from the war, a population
much more *peasant* – Czech, Polish, Irish peasants, with all the freshness,
picturesque speech & brutality of peasants – then after one night Washington stately, elegant, frigid – I must go to bed.
    love
      Shaya

Sorry about this *torn paper* it is 1 a.m. & none other available now. My
secretary Mrs Irwin says if you come here you *must* stay with her in Brooklyn
(Brooklyn = Stamford Hill in London.[3] "Follow me a going" as Jews say.)

*For much of his time in the US, IB sent regular telegrams (often weekly)
to his parents, to reassure them that he was well, which they were
constitutionally disinclined to believe. His hopeless efforts to convince them
are a mixture of humour and desperation. Again and again he describes
his condition in a one-word message as 'flourishing', which explains the
telegram that appears below (the censors had problems with it, thinking it
might refer to code words, and delayed its passage).*

TO MARIE AND MENDEL BERLIN

2 December 1941 [*telegram*]

New York

PLEASE SUGGEST SYNONYMS FOR FLOURISHING = BERLIN

1 In *Du contrat social* (1762), book 1, chapter 7.
2 In north-west London.
3 Both districts had large Jewish populations.

IB's admiration for President Roosevelt did not blind him to FDR's reluctance to commit American troops to the European war, and he later recalled:

Roosevelt thought he would win the war without fighting it. [. . .] He thought that by supplying the British, but not actually declar[ing] war, so no American boys would actually get killed, [. . .] at the end he'd be in the neutral position of being able to dictate the kind of world he wanted.[1]

When the Japanese attack on Pearl Harbor, on 7 December, did bring the US into the war, one of the major aims of the British Press Service was accomplished.

TO MARIE AND MENDEL BERLIN

12 December 1941 [*typescript*]

British Information Services

My dear parents,

Here is a letter written in the full glory of official accoutrement. This is the guise in which I present myself to most of the persons who hear from me officially and I thought it would give you a certain mild pleasure to be approached in this way for once. I really do apologise for the extreme scarcity of letters from me lately but I have almost completely got out of the habit of writing with my own hand, preferring the greater joys of dictation. I have become quite a good spontaneous composer of official documents – my pomp and stiffness in official communications cannot be exaggerated, I do not see why I should ever return to the cosier ways of private life. Naturally the events of the last two days[2] have shaken us up considerably – we feel like a sailing boat being towed by a fast motor launch – events are succeeding each other so rapidly, and yet they have made less impact upon the lives of ordinary New Yorkers so far as I can observe than the corresponding events in England in 1939. This is said to be an exact replica of New York in 1917 when America entered the last war. Russian and Libyan successes[3] are very pleasing and America is in a determined and unanimous

1 MI Tape 20.
2 On 8 December, the day after Pearl Harbor, the US had declared war against Japan. On the same day the Japanese began their invasion of Malaya; on 10 December they sank two British ships and began their invasion of the Philippines. On 11 December Germany and Italy declared war against the US.
3 On 18 November a British offensive (Operation Crusader) had started in Libya. A massive

mood. The President's genius in conducting internal policy can hardly be exaggerated – he is not only a very clever man and a very liberal man and a man generous both intellectually and emotionally but he is not afraid of the future and proposes to ride it when it comes which gives him an immeasurable advantage over all the timid and cautious and isolationist individuals who find him too sweeping for their taste. Churchill's popularity here continues to be immense – a Norwegian speaker at a meeting, I think recently, drew rounds of applause when he observed that whatever else Norway may or may not have done it did, by being invaded,[1] succeed in putting Mr Churchill into office, which was the most fortunate event, and the most important, of the entire war.

Now, as for my private condition. I received all your six letters from mid-October till late November simultaneously, so you see air mail can be as precarious as sea mail. I am very distressed indeed that Bowen should have upset you in this idiotic way about my alleged illness. He is a hypochondriac and squalid dabbler in the world of diseases and hospitals and this is his natural topic of conversation, like a sordid bedridden old boarding house keeper. Tell him so for me. The facts are these: I did have an attack of sinusitis as Rau told you in his cable towards the end of June, it arose as it usually does with me, out of an ordinary cold. I acted with a wisdom with which you cannot ever credit me and departed for a hospital immediately where I lay in perfect comfort in a private room with no pain for five days, being much visited and delighted to have opportunity of reading books. They are much more efficient than in England at my sort of complaint. Every conceivable technique was brought into play, while one doctor suffused my forehead with electric rays another tickled my nostrils with elaborate and delicate weapons while a third performed a sort of general massage and a fourth administered gargles. Under this blitz I recovered in record time and moved off to Vermont from where I wrote you at the time. I then spent hot but painless days in Washington and have since then not had a twinge of this or any other ailment. But I do find it useful now and then to behave as a malade imaginaire to avoid the too persistent attentions of certain persons from whom I take refuge in proclaiming myself indisposed for a day or so, usually on Sundays when I do in fact tend to sleep exceedingly late. Among these persons is the highly charmless Mrs Bowen who pursues me from time to time and from whom any excuse is better than none. My opinion in this respect is shared by the lately arrived Lt Alfred J.

Soviet counter-offensive on 5–6 December had halted and repulsed the German advance on Moscow.

1 The Allied failure to stop the invasion of Norway by Germany, and the subsequent resignation of Neville Chamberlain in May 1940, led to Churchill's appointment as Prime Minister.

Ayer, whose wife, I understand, is still in England, while Hampshire, according to the Warden of Wadham, is in Sierra Leone[1] – what she can be doing without her two men I cannot conceive. She is not made for solitary life. This last remark I am sorry to say acutely resembles the sort of remark which I am made to say in Lord Berners's novel 'Far from the Madding War' which has just arrived here and in which I am distressed to observe I form at least a part of a character referred to as Mr Jericho.[2] Do read it. David Cecil will tell you who the other characters are. The book is after all dedicated to him.

I am glad you met Lord Greene. He is a genuinely distinguished person with very sharp views on us all. The Bishop of Gloucester[3] is a wicked old man with shocking views on every subject, but I am sorry to say I have personally always got on excellently with him and enjoyed his extremely cutting comments on his colleagues both in the church and the laity immeasurably. Your view of Mrs Rees is borne out by Ayer, who also thinks that she, as Dr Bowra would say, does not add. I promise I will not send him the article on Felix Frankfurter since I agree with you that he would not make the best or most harmless social use of it.

I am not particularly lonely but occasionally say so out of politeness. Lest this should seem too cynical I do suffer most acutely from nostalgia and every ten days long to be back with you. But I am *not* lonely and there is quite enough work and general activity in this now to me absolutely fascinating country to occupy much more time than I have. I promise not to fly during the winter. I hope that greetings from me will be conveyed (a) by R. B. McCallum who is a don at Pembroke College who passed this way en route for China which he never reached but went home instead. Telephone him at Pembroke and ask after me: I had no time to tell him to get in touch with you. (b) Another possible person is Jack Jones,[4] a Welsh miner and novelist who lectured here under my auspices as labour specialist and was a greater success than any British visitor has ever been since the days of Lord Balfour. He promised to telephone to you, a very nice man; ask him to tea with David Cecil, who will like him. I take it that what you attended was

1 After military training, Hampshire, a member of the Artillery, had been posted to Sierra Leone to organise the transfer of local recruits to Burma, where substantial numbers of West and East African soldiers formed part of the British forces attempting (unsuccessfully) to prevent a Japanese invasion and (successfully) to defend the land route to India. He returned to Britain in early 1942 and joined MI6 at the instigation of Hugh Trevor-Roper (1914–2003; Lord Dacre of Glanton 1979).

2 To say the least: Mr Jericho in Berners's novel (London, 1941) is clearly based on IB.

3 Arthur Headlam.

4 Jack Jones (1884–1970), Welsh labour leader, had toured the US for the BPS. Jones was a founder member of the British Communist Party, but became a Liberal supporter after a spell as a member of Oswald Mosley's New Party. His novel *Bidden to the Feast* appeared in 1938.

the All Souls Day reception at the Warden's, the highest peak of social attainment possible to the inhabitants of North Oxford. I shall send you my photograph as soon as I have had a haircut. That will bring it home to you how little has changed in my life. Love to David and Mary.

yrs

    Isaiah Berlin.

⟨(c) I have just heard that Capt. John Sparrow is going home. Sometime he is bound to visit All Souls. I have seen him too v. lately.⟩

    Isaiah

TO MARIE AND MENDEL BERLIN

    2 January 1942 [*typescript*]

British Information Services

My dear parents,

I hope you approve of the formality of this address which will doubtless give the entire letter a strong Victorian flavour. My natural indolence emerges in the fact that I prefer to dictate to even the very small amount of physical exercise involved in moving a pen across a sheet of paper. From which you will have gathered that my fundamental habits remain unaltered.

Your letters continue to give me the greatest possible pleasure and excitement, particularly the gossip and news which you report. I was much amused by the scene, which I have no difficulty in imagining, of Mrs Berlin bellowing into the Bishop of Gloucester's ear or the conversation with Lord Greene. I have received letters from Mary Fisher (for which please thank her) and from Richard Pares. I have met a man who claims to have known you both a quarter of a century ago and to have lost touch in about 1908. His name is Druck and he claims to have offered gallant attentions to Mrs Berlin in Warsaw or it may have been Riga, at the beginning of the century. He seemed to me a very nice man, gentle, scholarly, sentimental and devoted to the memories of his youth. He was tremendously excited by seeing my name in print in one of the New York Jewish papers – the Morning Journal[1] – on whose staff he more or less is. I cross-examined him on his knowledge of our family and he emerged with flying colours and remembered a great many trivial and important facts, e.g. the beauty of Mrs Berlin, upon which he was very eloquent to one of my assistants who had been a colleague of

---

1 The *Jewish Morning Journal*, founded in 1901, a Yiddish newspaper with Zionist sympathies which promoted traditional Judaic values. IB's work with Jewish interests had brought him into contact with the influential Yiddish press, for whose benefit he had arranged for MOI material to be translated into Yiddish.

Druck's in some previous existence. What is your recollection of him? He seems exceedingly happy to have met me but is also genuinely shy and will not occur again unless I search him out, which I may yet do. What further gossip would you like?

Mrs Bowen, the nurse who, you will recollect, married Ian Bowen and is the source of the story of my ill health which worried you so long and so unnecessarily, lives very gaily in New Haven and is clearly not anxious to be restored to her former drab existence with Mr Bowen. They are a decayed couple and on the whole hostile to life which is a very damning thing to say of anyone but in this case true, I am sure.

Mr Ayer also seems gay: his wife, who is in England, refuses to join him here and demands her children whom she originally brought here; this from his point of view is both humiliating and difficult as it is not easy to find volunteers among those returning to England who are prepared to take responsibility for looking after children aged four and two on a sea voyage. However, as Marion [Frankfurter] acidly points out, Mrs Ayer will undoubtedly succeed in bullying someone into this course of action; she is very unanxious to see Freddie, who is on the contrary most anxious to see her. Placed as I am between the two, I play my usual precarious delicate and tactful part of friend of all the world. Nothing, as I observed above, has changed my fundamental habits.

The declaration of war by the U.S. has changed everything of course. Our functions can clearly not continue to be the same although sheer inertia of a large organisation carries us on in a semi-automatic fashion. Some think that we ought to cease to exist altogether; others that we ought to change our technique, etc. What is certain is that some sort of liaison must be preserved between the British and American organs of public opinion since after our honeymoon, which is still in progress, the more sordid aspects of marriage are bound to emerge and a certain amount of friction and misunderstanding must, however much good will and understanding of one another exists on both sides, occur which only persons on the spot can cure. Whether this view will recommend itself to our superiors, and if so in what form who can tell.

In the meanwhile the effect of the Prime Minister's arrival[1] was magical. The U.S. was going through a period of relative depression due to the effect of the first shock of war – we had something similar in October

---

1 Churchill had arrived in the US on 22 December 1941 for 'Arcadia', the first conference of the war, at which he was accompanied by his Chiefs of Staff. He addressed Congress on 26 December, visited Canada 29–31 December, delivering the 'Some chicken! Some neck!' speech to the Canadian Parliament on 30 December, and flew out on 14 January 1942. For this remark see op. cit. (336/7), vol. 6, p. 6544.

1939 – and the Far Eastern disasters. The coming of Churchill, emerging in his regular sea uniform, smoking his official cigar, looking like a representation of himself on the stage, was a tonic whose effect can hardly be described. He is incapable of being downed either in speech or in action; the life and gaiety which his mere presence communicates to his surroundings spreads far and wide. The speech to Congress, which you may have heard, was magnificent in content and public effect; so was the speech in Canada. The President and he obviously enjoy each other's company enormously. They admire each other publicly and privately, both have the same taste for vitality, fire, any large form of expression, both have a very acute sense of historical context; they do what they do and say what they say against a very dramatically and excitingly conceived historical background, both are conscious and rightly so that they are persons of very large historical dimensions and will be acted on innumerable stages for a long time to come. In an age when the individuals concerned seem on the whole incapable of conceiving the magnitude of the events in which they live, or if capable tend merely to gape at them, it is fortunate that there should be at least two men on our side who possess a tremendous appetite for the future and are prepared to let the wave come in the full confidence that they will ride it triumphantly. I believe that it is this omnivorous appetite – the sense that anything life may bring can be absorbed, assimilated and turned to use – that inspires the peoples and the democrats in the world, not any specific professed views but the strength and boldness of the behaviour of Roosevelt and Churchill, which can only spring from a genuine sense of being at home, of being adequately oriented vis-à-vis the forces rampant at the moment. Stalin, oddly enough, does not give me that feeling. The whole thing is much duller and blinder although perhaps no less powerful for that.

Having indulged in a sufficient number of profound reflections, I may now turn to lighter things and beg you to pay the income tax demanded from you, and, I suppose, the New College battels if they seem reasonable and do not include rent, etc., which is supposed to be covered by my unpaid Fellowship. I am well, healthy, wealthy, busy, happy, versatile, perpetually mobile: on excellent terms with everyone owing to my continuing absence of ambition, which not even the passionate local competition has to my regret done anything to stimulate. If one is born emotionally vegetarian the sight of blood makes one more not less so. Enough of these pensées approfondies.[1]

love

Isaiah Berlin.

1 'Deep thoughts'.

TO MARIE AND MENDEL BERLIN

14 February 1942 [*typescript*]

British Information Services

My dear Pa and Ma,

Thank you for your last two letters to which a third was added yesterday. Before expanding into more interesting topics, let us kill some routine subjects:

1. I am entirely and continuously well and there is really nothing which can possibly be said on that score ever again.

2. Money.

(a) Would you get in touch with the London Library, or perhaps not, as I seem to remember my arrangement quite clearly and it meant discontinuance of payment while I was abroad. I will therefore enclose a note to my bank mentioning the items in question.

(b) College Battels. I suppose you must go on paying whatever they ask, but I do think they might pay my insurance premiums if nothing else. But as I do not relish a controversy about this, and neither, I fancy, do you, my case had best go by default. So much for being a gentleman. I will have a power of attorney made out in your name and sent to you as soon as possible. In general please deal with all bills as seems to you best in your wisdom. Could you ask Blackwells to send me Rohan Butler's book on the origins of national socialism,[1] Lord Berners's works and anything else you regard as suitable reading for me, including half a dozen more copies of my own book. You suggest having it republished here. This, I feel, is not an appropriate season for it for every reason. So let us be patient and produce a glorious revised, 'aggrandised' as the Jewish Prayer Book[2] often says, edition later.[3]

Please thank Mrs [Lettice] Fisher for her letter, which was most welcome. You need not tell her that I have so far been unable to read one single word of it.[4] One day when there is little work and I have no books to read or newspapers, I will sit down to it. Meanwhile I will attempt to reply in a manner which creates the illusion of being an answer to it. I have also had a charming letter from David Cecil for which please thank him. He wonders

---

1 Rohan d'O. Butler, *The Roots of National Socialism 1783–1933* (London, 1941). Rohan d'Olier Butler (1917–96), son of Harold Butler; Balliol history 1935–8, Fellow of All Souls 1938–84.

2 *The Authorised Daily Prayer Book of the United Hebrew Congregations of the British Empire*, with a new translation by S[imeon] Singer (London, 1890) became the standard prayer book for Anglo-Jewry. Popularly known as 'Singer's Prayer Book', it had reappeared in many new editions, some of which were merely reprints; but usually a new edition would claim to have been enlarged or 'aggrandised'.

3 The second edition (of an eventual four) was published by Oxford University Press in Oxford in 1948, in NY in 1949, but with few changes.

4 Her writing is indeed execrable.

whether the new situation makes my presence here as essential as it might have been thought to be before, at any rate by others. I wonder too, and am affected by periodic waves of nostalgia which I find it progressively more difficult to resist. Of course we are all told that whatever we do is more needed than ever, that Anglo-American harmony on all subjects is crucial and that only complete access to information can make this certain. This is quite true, but it does little to console one for so long an absence.

Now as to Mr Berlin's business future. I entirely agree that retirement at the age of 58 is unthinkable. You say that there is a proposition in the air concerning the export of Canadian timber, an operation to be undertaken by unnamed Rothschilds, unnamed Warburgs (concerning these you know as much as I: the conjunction is surely the first in the history of Big Business), Messrs Benson, private bankers (a member of that firm, an agreeable man and very social but not a genius is our Military Attaché in Washington: I know him very slightly but John Foster of course knows him well: his name is Rex),[1] and Sir Malcolm Stewart,[2] concerning whom I know nothing. Seems sound enough, I must say. And I warmly approve of anything which breaks inertia, starts something fresh, and ties you up with Canada, which, like the rest of the Western Hemisphere, including Australia and New Zealand, is likely to have a terrific future if 1% of the consensus of local prophets is even remotely correct. On the other hand sea voyages are not to be indulged in light-heartedly at the present moment. In your place I would wait a month or two, and then, with the rest of your mission, definitely come. I imagine that Mrs Berlin would be anxious to accompany you. As to my desire for a consummation of such a scheme, whereby I could see you in Montreal or you me in New York, I need not speak. On the other hand the thought of parting once more is almost unbearable. My future is a trifle obscure; I may go to Washington or I may come home. In any case I would like to get leave to visit England if only for a relatively short while. Poor Lauterpacht is eating his heart out (and his wife's as well) while waiting for a superior form of transport, which he does not seem destined to get. Meanwhile, being under 44 he is required to register himself in the American draft, which worries him. I am continuously consulted and have no advice to give except a general recommendation to fast, pray and hope for the best. I am apparently not required to register, as I am a British official who is 'UK based', and appear on a special list produced by the Embassy. Charles seems to have deferred his arrival on account of news that his son, who is in the

1 Rex Lindsay Benson (1889–1968), Military Attaché, Washington, 1941–4; British Intelligence agent and well-known social figure.
2 Sir (Percy) Malcolm Stewart (1872–1951), industrialist, chairman of London Brick Co.

RAF, is missing.[1] I know that he is exceptionally fond of him, so that his condition must be acutely painful. I am sorry that Mr Druck should have borrowed 50 roubles from you in 1908. I have not seen him again, but he has shown no similar inclinations so far as I am concerned. Indeed he seems far too shy and retired ever to have had the boldness and adroitness to obtain this sum so easily from you. Perhaps a cunning and unprincipled nature cowers within that unassuming frame, but I think it very unlikely. Fred seems to have arrived in South Africa and is no doubt tippling freely with our Colonial Service. I miss him, but not nearly as much as I had supposed I would.[2]

My life flows very uneventfully. So, I imagine, in spite of everything, does yours. Ultimately I do not really see how one could go on living in New York, unless one enclosed oneself in one of the little enclaves of social, racial, or intellectual persons who live lives in New York absolutely insulated from each other: there are to be found in this city Greek, Armenian, Italian, German, Hungarian, Polish, Jewish cultures absolutely untouched by the environment – the food, the wallpaper in the restaurants, the newspapers, the interests, lifted bodily out of Europe and unassimilated to a degree only possible where the surrounding civilization is not itself powerful or intolerant enough to compress the immigrants into conformity.

I went to a Jewish court[3] the other day, presided over by Rabbi Goldstein[4] and Judge Null,[5] both of whom I vaguely know. A most remarkable case. A Jewish beggar, long beard and sidecurls, straight out of Russia in 1880, came in on a wooden leg. He had a very serious complaint: when the surgeon in the Jewish hospital amputated his leg he solemnly promised to bury it in consecrated ground, not too far away from the man himself. The leg had however, through some oversight been disposed of in some other way. When the Messiah comes, and the dead are resurrected, all the various limbs will be reassembled, but limbs which have been destroyed are lost forever. 'I am willing to walk with a wooden leg for fifty years' said the man 'for a hundred years – for two hundred years – but for eternity?' The court was clearly puzzled. 'What do you expect the Court to do {you} for you?' he was asked 'That's what I want to know' said the beggar 'what can the court do for me?' the thing really was most pathetic. A man condemned

---

1 Chaim Weizmann's second son, Michael Oser Weizmann (1916–42), an RAF pilot, had gone missing in action over the Bay of Biscay on 11 February. Weizmann was deeply affected by his son's death, and his wife Vera never recovered from it.
2 Here typescript yields to manuscript.
3 Such a court (a Beth Din) would often be convened to hear religious arguments.
4 Israel Goldstein (1896–1986), rabbi, leading Zionist and author, President of the Zionist Organization of America 1943–61.
5 Samuel Null (1893–1949), Justice in the Supreme Court of NY 1944–8.

to wander about on one leg for eternity, unenviable even in Paradise, as the man pointed out. Nobody laughed, nobody smiled, the mood of the most intense seriousness prevailed throughout. The court adjourned. No one knew what would happen. The beggar (I suppose he must have been a man of about 80 or 90) remained silent & gloomy. Finally the Court decided that if a token object – a part of his body, a hair, or a nail, were buried with appropriate rites, it being solemnly announced that this should function as a substitute for the leg, then the Almighty, who has done queerer things before, would, in all probability, recognize the just claim supported by the New York Court, and produce a leg at the required moment. The man was content and the case was closed. The ceremony of burying the hair & nails must have been exceedingly odd.

The next case concerned a woman to whom her brother in law would not grant a release from marriage vows – a Ketubah[1] case in fact – and she maintained that unless the brother relented, her late husband's soul would lie face downwards through all eternity – that all Jews believe this – and that something really must be done. All this in New York in 1942, all treated with the most exquisite gravity by all concerned. In this way I keep myself amused. I have been reading Roth's[2] great invocations[3] to the Jews of England to retain their faith & integrity, and I must say I am not deeply impressed. If adhering to Judaism entails a permanent link with Cecil Roth, the motives for desertion are extremely strong. I have not been to Washington very lately, & so have not seen the Felixes.[4] He, fundamentally, is a gay, lively, frivolous Viennese of about 1900, ready to do a good turn here or there, editor of a liberal Viennese paper, or an intimate of liberal Hapsburg statesmen, but in no sense an earnest progressive new world American, with a touch of puritanism, such as Brandeis was, not a great man, but a very nice one.

The Ayer's matrimonial life must have become complicated again by Hampshire's return to England: she now demands (a) the children (b) a divorce, a blow both to vanity & hopes of a comfortable future to Alfred Jules Ayer. Heaven only knows what S. Aronson is doing. And I must look up the Raskins. No one has gone to England lately except my old benefactor

---

1 Hebrew marriage contract stating the bridegroom's obligations to his bride: in Rabbinic law a pre-requisite for marriage, usually written in Aramaic; provides economic protection for a divorced or widowed woman.

2 Cecil Roth (1899–1970), Reader in Post-Biblical Jewish Studies, Oxford, 1939–64, President, Jewish Historical Society of England, 1936–45, 1955–6.

3 Perhaps a reference to Roth's *A History of the Jews in England* (Oxford, 1941) and/or to his contributions to the *Jewish Chronicle*.

4 Felix and Marion Frankfurter.

S. L. Childs of the Embassy who has made himself immensely disliked all round – even I find myself incapable of defending him any longer. I really have no more to say. My life does not bear description. I sleep, eat, work etc. I have had a photograph taken but it is too shocking to send. You know how vain I am.

   love

      Isaiah Berlin.

TO CHAIM WEIZMANN[1]

   25 February 1942 [*telegram*]

New York

HAVE BEEN WAITING FOR DEFINITE NEWS BEFORE EXPRESSING ALL MY LOVE AND DISTRESS STOP PASSIONATELY CONVINCED THAT THERE IS NO REASON FOR LOSING HOPE STOP NATURALLY VERY GLAD TO LEARN YOU BOTH EXPECTED HERE SOON STOP IS THERE ANYTHING I COULD CONCEIVABLY DO STOP I CANNOT CONVEY HOW ANXIOUS I AM TO DO ANYTHING POSSIBLE AT THIS MOMENT = ISAIAH BERLIN.

---

1 At the Dorchester Hotel.

WASHINGTON

My British buddy,
We're as diff'rent as can be;
He thinks he's winning the war,
And I think it's me.
But we're in there pitching,
And on one thing we agree:
When the job is done
And the war is won,
We'll be clasping hands across the sea.

Irving Berlin[1]

I wish to help to win the war.

Isaiah Berlin to Maire Gaster[2]

1 From 'My British Buddy', written for the British version of *This is the Army* (1943). Irving Berlin, né Israel Baline (1888–1989), Russian-born song-writer, emigrated to America in 1893; he wrote more than 900 songs, including *God Bless America* and *White Christmas*, and nineteen musicals, one of which, *This is the Army* (1942), was written specifically as a morale-booster for America and performed on stage and screen by a racially integrated (at Irving Berlin's insistence) company of soldiers, the only such company in the US Army during the war: its substantial profits were donated to the Army Emergency Relief Fund.

2 Letter of 3 January 1941: see p. 357 above.

Central Washington, showing the British Embassy (top left) and Tracy Place (1)

Once the US had entered the war, IB's task of explaining Britain to the Americans diminished in importance. The pressing need now was to explain America to the British. On the strength of IB's reports about the special-interest groups within his remit, IB was appointed to run an enlarged Political Survey Section attached to the Washington Embassy. The unit's principal task was to draft the Weekly Political Summary, Whitehall's main official briefing on the American political scene. This document had previously been a routine summary of press reports, and IB set about injecting the inside information he acquired from his wide range of personal contacts.

TO MENDEL BERLIN

18 June 1942 [*postcard*]

2500 Massachusetts Avenue,
Washington, DC

My life (which in spite of Miss McGeachy's[1] words) has not during the last year been broken by a single day in bed, is now divided into two: 4 days in N.Y., 3 in the Embassy in Washington. I travel only in trains (airlines are too busy) see large number of persons in both towns & thrive. I preserve the peace between Charles & Felix which is amusing.

love
    Shaya

On 6 July 1942 Derick Hoyer Millar wrote from Washington to Nevile Butler[2] in London enclosing 'a paper produced by one or two members of the staff here setting out various points which Americans are apt to hold against the British'.[3] He urged him not to think that the authors believed that the views described were justified. It was revealed in a letter

---

1 (Mary Agnes) Craig McGeachy (1901–91), MEW, First Secretary, British Embassy, Washington, 1942–4, director of Welfare, UNRRA 1944–6, married the banker Erwin Schuller (1909–67, nephew of Richard Schüller) in 1944, and then used the surnames Schuller and Schuller-McGeachy. She was the first woman to be given British diplomatic rank, and as such was the subject of an article by Carolyn Bell entitled 'Petticoat Diplomat' in the *Washington Post*, 13 October 1942. In a letter to Herbert Nicholas (9–11 November 1943) about one of her exploits IB describes her as a 'minx', adding 'What a woman!' She got on well with IB's parents and had presumably said or written something to them about his state of health.

2 Nevile Montagu Butler (1893–1973), Counsellor, British Embassy, Washington, 1940, Minister 1940–1; Head, North American (later American) Dept, FO, 1941–4; Assistant Under-Secretary of State, FO, 1944–7.

3 FO 371/30656, A6681/60/45, from which the other quotations in this headnote are also taken.

intercepted later that month that the author was in fact Isaiah Berlin, described in the letter as 'A v. clever Jew who works in the British Propaganda dept here. [The paper] has the schadenfreude of the Jew finding that another race [sic] is disliked also – but it is very shrewd and about 60% of it is accurate.'

In September the paper was reproduced in a slightly reorganised form in a 'Postal & Telegraph Censorship Report' on the US compiled at the Embassy. The editorial note begins:

Mail from the United States of America examined during the last two months indicates that in spite of the admiration for Britain and friendliness towards her people evidently felt by many Americans, and in spite of a frequently expressed desire that the United Nations should join together as closely as possible in a supreme effort to bring about the defeat of the Axis, there still exists in America a considerable amount of animosity towards the British. This does not appear to be attributable to any one particular cause. The criticisms aimed at Britain are diverse, and sometimes contradictory, and are for the most part caused by racial, inherited and political prejudices and widespread ignorance.

IB's list is then mentioned, though not attributed – 'One writer has compiled a list, which is intended to be helpful . . .' – and its reproduction in the report is justified by the 60 per cent accuracy attributed to it in the intercepted letter. A transcript of the original paper follows.

THINGS WHICH AMERICANS HOLD AGAINST THE BRITISH

The items in this list are chosen from among popularly entertained notions, few of which are justified. The order is not meant to be any indication of relative importance.

1. The British are imperialistic. They do not believe in the equality of men. British colonial policy has been oppressive, stupid, inefficient and insulting to the natives, with the result that Malays and Burmese have been conspicuously disloyal in contrast to the loyalty of the Filipinos. British hypocrisy in India, etc.

2. Rigid class system in Britain. The British aristocracy hold rank and position through birth and not through merit or election. The British are ruled by feudal landlords who are either hard-faced men, grinding the faces of the poor, or decayed parasites living on the toil of others.

3. The British are going red. From a society where feudal reactionaries oppress would-be socialist workers, England is turning into a regime where

native Reds will oppress feudal reactionaries. Either alternative is equally unattractive and equally remote from the American way of life.

4. The British bunglers in high places: over-cautious, contemptuous of all new ideas and defensively minded, tired old men bored with their own task.

5. The British are sitting safely on their island with 3,500,000 men under arms.

6. The British always seem to be being defeated and having to retreat. They are prepared to die bravely but not to take trouble. They sipped tea at Singapore while the Japs were at the gate; British officers are either Bourbons or lackadaisical.

7. Lend-Lease is stripping America to supply the British who have not even paid their war debts. The British use US imports to compete with the US in Latin America, and are generally feathering their nests rather than winning the war. They are thinking more intensely about their own post-war position vis-à-vis America than of how to win the war.

8. The British are much too adroit for simple, honest Americans. They believe in 'balance of power', in 'divide and rule'. They virtually encourage wars, provided these preserve their own position as arbiters of other people's destinies. The Treaty of Versailles, to which Hitler and all other evils are due, is a typical example of cunning British diplomacy, which wants to keep the world divided.

9. US foreign-language groups tend to think of the British as belonging to the class of the wicked landlord nations whose victims fled to the US in search of liberty. The Irish naturally originated this view, but the Poles or Slovaks think of the British as analogous to their own Central European tyrants. Britain alone of the original group of 'master' nations survives comparatively unimpaired, since the Austrians and the Russians are no longer possible targets.

10. Anti-British sentiment is a part of the central patriotic American tradition. Whereas e.g. anti-Semitism or anti-Catholicism is equally definitely disreputable, prejudiced etc., Anglophobia is compatible with any given set of other sentiments. The interventionists, for example, have been known to express relief at the fact that since Pearl Harbour they could once more give vent to anti-British sentiments without thereby playing their enemies' game. Anglophobia is a proof of vigorous Americanism.

11. Superior airs of British persons in America and their unspoken attitude that theirs is the right way of doing things, by the mere fact that they do it that way. Their 'when in Rome, do as the English do' attitude.

12. British lack of forthrightness in speech. Englishmen in America substitute caution and reserve for tact, do not allow themselves to agree or

disagree vehemently with the American speaker's point of view, but are expected to remark that it is 'very interesting'. They are professional seers of both (or more) sides of every question, which irritates all parties, and consequently appear to have no strongly held, honest convictions of their own on any subject. They are therefore either frivolous or concealing something.

13. Fear of treading on American corns and embarrassment at American gusto and over-emphasis produce a nervous reserve on the part of the British, which in its turn embarrasses Americans and makes them distrustful. Hence greater popularity of hearty British extroverts over more delicate natures.

14. Irritation caused by over-civilised English accent as opposed to Scots, Welsh or any other home-bred accent. Any burr is preferred to the smooth, well-bred English voice, which conveys artificiality, insincerity etc. This is more important than might at first appear. A strong Yorkshire or Lancashire accent is a greater asset to e.g. a British lecturer than anything else, without qualification. This includes a good strong cockney accent.

15. *Washington*

The mere concentration of British in Washington causes a certain amount of adverse feeling due to the tendency of British people to take refuge in each other's company. The Embassy in particular as opposed to the technical missions has a quite fantastically low reputation. It is regarded as snobbish, arrogant, patronising, dim, asleep and a home of reactionary and generally disreputable views. It is thought of as containing large numbers of effete diplomats who make no attempt to keep in touch with what is happening outside their own restricted circle. This belief is shared and to some extent encouraged by many members of the missions themselves. Believing that the Embassy staff is very numerous, and not having the remotest idea what it does, they think themselves entitled to be constantly looked after by the Embassy, and if their contacts with the Embassy turn out to be few and far between they blame it on the laziness and snobbery of the staff.

16. Absence of an adequate impression of British industrial and military effort, which is at least partly due to the poor and shallow quality of news dispatches from American correspondents in England, notably in the *New York Times*.

17. Ricochet of the lack of understanding of the US in England (owing to the null-and-voidness of US diplomats in London). Winant, who is very popular, is unfavourable to the prospect of US propaganda in England.

18. Unpopular character of US Anglophiles, who are regarded as a group

of idle rich, concentrated on the East coast; their love of the English is regarded as a species of snobbery and un-Americanism.

19. A certain embarrassment vis-à-vis the English on account of the relatively small degree of suffering which the US has so far borne as a result of the war. This is a function of the 'phoney war' atmosphere which is still prevalent here and corresponds to the embarrassment felt by the English and French in the face of Poles and Norwegians before May 1940.

20. Stonewall attitude on the part of British officials in dealing with aggrieved groups, e.g. Chinese, Jews etc. Few high British officials display or simulate a sufficient degree of interest or understanding of the problems submitted to them, and display mild weariness, which causes more irritation than actual failure to comply with requests, so that even when grievances are remedied, resentment continues.

21. Certain British books and films (notably the film *Ships with Wings*)[1] display a falsity of feeling and an acute class-consciousness that does great damage.

22. The Chinese and Indians, although present in relatively small quantities, attract a great deal of romantic interest, and have put across a very dark picture of the British in Asia.

23. All the Roosevelt-haters hate the English because they are held to be popular with the President.

                                                FO 371/30656, A6681/60/45

In early August IB returned to the UK for leave and briefings with the Foreign Office and the Ministry of Information.

TO CRESSIDA RIDLEY

7 September 1942 [*manuscript postcard*]

                                                New College

Dear Cressida

I enjoyed my evening & morning at M'beggars[2] far more than any settled and non-nomadic person can conceive; I am self consciously aware of the need to return to my Thebais[3] with a mass of protective prophylactic

1 This somewhat escapist war film, directed by Sergei Nolbandov, was premièred in November 1941.
2 Mockbeggars Hall, Ipswich, home of Jasper and Nathalie Ridley, parents of Cressida's husband Jasper.
3 Presumably a comparison of Washington with the ancient Greek city of Thebes, the scene of

images visual but mainly auditory i.e. of conversation in particular places with persons. Please assure Mrs Ridley of my gratitude and of the fact that I think of the whole thing as so much armour too. I repeat my seriously considered invitation to you: will you telephone to M.O.I.?

I.B.

I met Fulford[1] on the evening I left you. Like a v. nice clergyman. When he speaks of H.M. Queen his voice changes genuinely.

IB's return to the US in late September involved a week's wait in Ireland for an onward flight. While there he developed pneumonia, but nevertheless caught his plane. Reports of his illness soon reached his parents.

Your several visits to England during that time were sources of great pleasure to us, but also of great anxiety owing to the hazards of wartime travel. Particularly was this the case in 1942, I believe, when, after having received your usual cheerful cable announcing safe arrival in New York, I was rung up by Rach, advising me to buy an Evening Standard where there were some news of you. His tone was so funereal that I hastened to obtain a copy and there were the news that you were taken ill and had to be transferred from the airfield to a hospital (which turned out to be not quite true). Mother, who already went to Paddington Station to catch a train to Oxford, and whom I was to join at the station, was hastily recalled by me back to our London house and we frantically started telephoning to your Ministry – at that time the Ministry of Information – to obtain news and information. About 10 p.m. that night we had from them the news that a Mr Thomas[2] visited you in hospital and that you were as well as you could be. This sacramental English phrase can mean anything you like. We only knew that you were alive, but that is all. An idea struck us, to telegraph to Dr Weizman[n], who was then in New York, to enquire about you, and we shall never forget his kindness in sending us such a reassuring cable that we really started believing that you were not in great danger. You yourself were very good in cabling and writing us reassuring letters making light of the

bloody internecine conflicts described by Statius in his epic the *Thebaid* and dramatised by Sophocles in his play *Antigone*.

1 Roger Thomas Baldwin Fulford (1902–83), Liberal politician, journalist, author of books on the British Royal Family; part-time Lecturer in English, King's College, London, 1937–48, Civil Assistant, War Office, 1940–2, Assistant Private Secretary to the Secretary of State for Air 1942–5.

2 See 411/2.

whole affair. Still for 10–14 days we passed through great anxiety and worry. You contracted pneumonia owing to an open window in the Shannon Hotel, where you had to wait a night for the next New York plane. Our great consolation at several times when we worried about you was only that you were not in London under the bombs, particularly knowing that when you were in London during air raids you never took cover and exposed yourself fearlessly (and perhaps foolishly) to all possible dangers. We sometimes read articles and remarks about you in the papers, filling us always with justifiable, and in parents so understandable, pride.[1]

TO MENDEL BERLIN

1 October 1942 [*telegram*]

Gotham Hotel, New York

FLOURISHING ISAIAH BERLIN GOTHAM HOTEL NY

On 2 October the following report appeared in an early edition of London's Evening Standard *newspaper:*

Altitude Sickness

I hear that Dr Isaiah Berlin is seriously ill in New York. He was taken to hospital after crossing the Atlantic by air from London; it is believed that a sinusitis condition may have been brought about by flying at some altitude.

Dr Berlin, of Russian origin, is one of Oxford's most brilliant philosophers. Not long ago he was the preceptor there of Miss Clarissa Churchill,[2] who was taking a course in philosophy. He is one of three Fellows of All Souls now in America; the others are Lord Halifax and Mr John Foster, the barrister who is First Secretary at our Washington Embassy.

Talks at MOI

Dr Berlin is one of the principal advisers to Mr Harold Butler, the British Minister in Washington. He had been in London for consultations at the Ministry of Information. As head of the Report Section of the British Information Services in the United States, Dr Berlin is responsible for a regular American political analysis prepared for cabling to London.

1 Mendel Berlin, family memoir.
2 (Anne) Clarissa Churchill (b. 1920), daughter of Winston Churchill's brother John Strange Spencer-Churchill (1880–1947), later (1952) married Anthony Eden (431/1). She did not take a formal course in philosophy, and was not taught by IB, but was tutored informally by A. J. Ayer for a few months in 1939–40, and came to know IB through that connection.

*In later editions this was somewhat altered. It began: 'I hear that Dr
Isaiah Berlin, the Oxford philosopher, has arrived in New York by air
from London. I gather that he did not enjoy the journey and after landing
went to hospital.' As if to make up for this moderation of the initial
report, IB is now described as 'short and tubby' and 'one of the characters
of Oxford'. Again, 'He has the large head of the intellectual and wears
thick glasses.' And the following new section is added:*

Misunderstood

Although he is a brilliant conversationalist, Dr Berlin is a man not easy to
understand.

Miss Dixie Tighe,[1] the American reporter, who arrived here last
night, was telling me to-day of a meeting she had with him in
Washington. Dr Berlin spoke fluently for some minutes. When he paused
Dixie Tighe leaned forward.

'Pardonnez-moi,' she said, 'Je ne parle pas français.'[2]

TO MARIE AND MENDEL BERLIN

Friday 2 October 1942 [*manuscript postcard*]

New York Hospital,
525 East 68th Street, New York

I must admit that perhaps it was not very wise or true to cable to you, as I did
yesterday, that I was 'flourishing', which was an exaggeration. The week of
waiting in Ireland produced a cold in the head – by the time I arrived in New
York, the old, well known, familiar, no longer frightening symptoms of sinus
trouble were on. Acting in accordance with your own oft given advice I
decided that a hospital – which here is equivalent to nursing homes i.e.
provides private rooms & nurses & is certainly no cheaper – would generally
be a good thing. Wheeler Bennett, I decided, being both wealthy & ailing[3] wd
be *bound* to have a good doctor. So on the next day I found myself here,
under his Dr Hauser in great comfort, no pain, with a temp. of about 38 (this
morning 37.7 as stated in my cable. This afternoon 37.4.) in a room kindly
filled with flowers by my friends. Everyone is most considerate. My old
Jewish "clients" suddenly began pouring in & had to be stopped. The Felixes
sent their friend Alfred Cohn to make a report (Mr Bowra can tell you who
he is) & he told them not to worry. Charles is in the mountains & after I
leave here I think I'll join him for a rest cure. What nonsense did the Evening

---

1 Dixie Tighe (1905–46) was at that time foreign correspondent for the *New York Post*.
2 *Evening Standard*, 2 October 1942, 2, 'Londoner's Diary' (unsigned). On 5 October his father
   sent him two cuttings, and wrote: 'The earlier edition said that you were "seriously" ill, which
   you imagine was upsetting, the 2nd edition toned it somewhat down.'
3 He suffered from unstable blood pressure, exhaustation and other ailments.

Standard print? do send me the cutting. I am, au fond, flourishing.

Isaiah Berlin

F. Rau is here & greets you. So does Wheeler Bennett.

To allay what I imagine must be your feelings I'll try to telephone but I'm sure it can't be done. I'll write again to-morrow

TO MARIE AND MENDEL BERLIN

Monday 5 October 1942 [*manuscript postcard*]

New York Hospital

The whole story is really very simple. I suppose I became unwell on my first Monday from home (I left on Sunday, you remember) in Ireland while waiting for transport. My sinuses gave trouble, but I slept well and my appetite was astonishingly vigorous, my digestion digested well, I was not in pain. However repeated journeys to the airport in a windy bus, each time ending in frustration did not improve the sinuses. By the time I arrived here a week ago my condition was classical. I knew all the symptoms and acted almost mechanically – doctor, low temperature – one night in the hotel – higher temperature, brief consultation with doctor (who is very nice & *very* good) and with Fred Rau (who is shortly going to England pour l'honneur[1] I think) off to a large & airy room in this hospital with a special nurse, quantities of flowers from Wh-Bennett, Charles, Sidney Bernstein[2] (our film director. A very smart smooth, polite, nice man who owned theatres in London, who behaved exceptionally kindly to me, took me to hospital, sent me flowers & books, looked after your requests etc.) Bernstein returns home shortly & will I hope get in touch with you. Meanwhile endless enquiries from F.F., my colleagues, Butler etc. until the doctor stopped all communication. He thinks I need a complete rest, & Vera W. has written me a v. nice letter begging me to come to them in the hills where absolute quiet etc. exists. I shall go next week. On Thursday when I cabled you that I was flourishing I *was* flourishing: my temperature was normal and I was lying pleasantly in bed, reading a life of Liszt. The Evening Standard must be v. hard up for news if has to use me as copy. Anyhow its correspondent, A. Cooke,[3] was scolded severely by his colleagues for worrying you. Having

---

[1] 'As a matter of honour', i.e. presumably to show it wasn't cowardice that took him to the US.

[2] Sidney Lewis Bernstein (1899–1993), anti-Nazi activist, film businessman with contacts in Hollywood and with the US media; Films Adviser, MOI, 1940–5; Liaison, British Embassy, Washington, 1942; Chief, Film Section, Allied Forces Headquarters, North Africa, 1942–3; Chief, Film Section, SHAEF, 1943–5.

[3] Not Alistair Cooke, who recollects that Allison Cooke of the *Evening Standard* often traded on the confusion.

nothing to do except to be rubbed with alcohol (very new & agreeable), I feel far better than ever in my life. Everyone is most kind. Life is v. interesting. Do write me c/o B.I.S. 30 Rock. Center, about what you did in London & how you communicated with M.O.I. (who sent me v. sympathetic cables of condolence –) triumph! glory! I am a dip. 1st Secretary!

    love

      Shaya

TO MARIE AND MENDEL BERLIN

    7 October 1942 [*manuscript postcard*]

New York Hospital

There is, I note, a subtle difference between the worried and sceptical cables of Mendel Berlin ("please cable *truth*". "Is treatment surgical?" etc.) and the much more peaceful style of Marie. Actually no special treatment is being given to my sinus – the technique is fundamentally Acland–Hobson[1] in type. When I leave this place (the expense is appalling, but I shall not leave till driven out, as it is *so* comfortable. Also I'll try to get sterling out of the Ministry as my last claim upon them before the new arrangement comes in. So cd you replenish my bank a/c if needed) the question is: should I go to Charles in his New York Hills *or* shd I boldly persuade Wheeler-Bennett to come to Arizona (warm, high, dry, remote) or both? anyhow this time I propose to do exactly what my excellent doctor orders. You will probably have seen Lady Fraser[2] by now. The next bulletin will come via Sid. Bernstein. Tell Miriam [Rothschild] to write to me here.

    love

      Shaya

TO MARIE AND MENDEL BERLIN

    16 October [1942, *manuscript postcard*]

New York Hospital,
525 E 68 Street, N.Y.C.

Your letter gratefully received. First let me answer it: no operation can permanently cure sinus trouble – its poipose is only to reduce acute inflammation which I did not have. My treatment is infra-red rays, not v. per-

---

1 A reference to the Acland (nursing) Home (131/1) and IB's doctor (140/5).
2 Unidentified.

manent perhaps but certainly pleasant in the short run. Now let me be more explicit. I knew I was ill in Ireland, because I got occasional temperatures, tho' my appetite remained excellent. Had I revealed my condition I shd have had to go to bed in, say, Limerick. I don't know if you know average Irish convent-owned hospitals. Cox (when we had our famous motor accident) can tell you. Consequently I preferred to go on. I am sure I was right. There are *no* nursing homes in U.S.A., only private wards in hospitals, e.g. mine. My room is large, sunny, whitewashed, full of flowers (sent by Charles, [Wheeler-]Bennett, Rothschilds, lots of others you don't know. Also books from all my ex-secretaries etc.) I am to-day well in the sense that: my temperature is 36–36.6, X rays reveal no trace of infection left, digestion & appetite are normal. The only thing which my doctor stresses is that after every 2 phone calls my pulse rises 10 beats. i.e. I am a little weak. He advises but doesn't insist that I stay 3–4 days cut off from all visitors & phones before leaving. I accept. Charles is impatiently calling for me. Thanks for the clippings: I can well understand what you must have felt. Mrs Lauterpacht goes home soon & will visit me before.

    love,

      Shaya

I toy with the idea of importing mother here – I need no nurse, but it is attractive as such – but the winter is a bad time for crossing. I'll try to work something for summer – to sit in Lisbon for 8 weeks is not attractive.

    love

      Shaya

TO MARIE AND MENDEL BERLIN

17 October 1942 [*manuscript*]

New York Hospital

My dear parents:

All my ex-secretaries offer to come and be dictated to: but I feel that you will feel it to be more real if I write. As you rightly point out in your letter I am letting the facts of my "illness" out bit by bit: the principal cause, as Mrs Berlin with what the Warden of Wadham calls her 'appalling penetration' so justly guessed, was not sinus as such: though for want of a name the Evening Standard called it that. It was general exhaustion. Nor do I think that however long I stayed in England that wd have been cured: Oxford is too full of interest, people, books, telephones, and to go away would have been too meaningless & dull. Ireland was, of course, a very odd experience: as I told you in my last card (I hope you got them all) my general health seemed good enough except for causeless fevers – and I was not going to be trapped into experiencing an Irish hospital if I could avoid it. I decided that the flight by Clipper to New York was no more dangerous than a similar flight + train journeys + endless complications + waiting if I asked to return to England (because of a slight temperature. The whole thing was too silly). So I flew on. On arrival in N. York I knew perfectly well that I would have to go to hospital. The Shoreham hotel had no room (for me – an old customer – I made a fearful scene) but produced Fred Rau. That was very comforting. I now knew that if the worst came to the worst I could always fall back on his help. I then argued that as Wheeler-B. was (a) an invalid (b) far from poor, his doctor would be good. So it was. Dr Hauser, came to see me at the Gotham Hotel (55th & 5th Avenue) opposite the Shoreham. The Gotham is smarter than Shoreham, dearer, but since I am now a diplomat, reduces rates for me. My temperature was somewhere round 38.4 so next morning I removed to hospital. There are no nursing homes in U.S. & their place is taken by private wards in hospitals which are exactly the same, i.e. rooms, nurses etc. & at least as expensive. I was seen off into hospital by Sidney Bernstein, our film director, who is going back to England shortly, & who will, I hope, call on you. He is an amusing shrewd, elegant, slightly boulevardier character, but most considerate & v. kind to me. I have, by the way, been thinking that I must send a present to the stenographer at M.o.I. who looked after me so well: in the meantime, while thinking of what to send, I asked Bernstein's secretary to send you some trifling cosmetics etc. & a box of cigars to our friend Chester:[1] you will both doubtless have to pay duty on this somewhere sometime. So. To go on: I was fed on Sulfadiazene tablets – the great new drug they all believe in.[2] It did reduce the fever, so that by the time I cabled 'flourishing' I was. A little jesuitical perhaps but what was I to say? 'confined to hospital with mysterious fever?' however Evening Standard spoilt it all by chattering. Everyone poured attentions: not only Charles & Vera [Weizmann] who are waiting for me in the Grossinger Hotel,[3]

1 Possibly (Daniel) Norman Chester (1907–86), Lecturer in Public Administration, Manchester, 1936–45, Economic Section, War Cabinet Secretariat, 1940–45, Fellow of Nuffield 1945–54, then Warden (1954–78).

2 The antibacterial sulphonamide ('sulpha') drugs were developed by Gerhard Domagk at the I.G. Farbenindustrie laboratory in Wuppertal, Germany. They were effective against a range of streptococcal infections, and became commercially available in 1935. Before penicillin (not available to civilians until the later 1940s) they were regarded as the first wonder-drug. For this work Domagk was awarded the 1939 Nobel Prize for Medicine.

3 Grossinger's Hotel, founded in 1919 by Austrian immigrant, Jennie Grossinger, was famous for high-quality food, entertainment and sports facilities, as well as its rural location.

Ferndale, N.Y., (a thickly Jewish neighbourhood. When Secretary Morgenthau[1] heard that this was C.'s address he was deeply shocked) but millions of others – my colleagues [Wheeler-]Bennett and Thomas,[2] & the
Morgans[3] when they came back, 4 typists contributed 4 dollars for books
for me (about 25 books have arrived), my friend Guy Rothschild,[4] The
Countess Ilyinska[5] (Flora Solomon's couturière sister married to a Polish
officer with Sikorski)[6] cooks special soups, Felix sent a book & Marion a
very long letter with promise of more – a lot for her. Mrs Lauterpacht, about
to return to her dull husband in Cambridge, brought flowers, so did Sir A.
Rumbold – both are returning, both will ring you. My friend Alsop the
journalist, returned from Jap. internment[7] came in, so did countless others.
While this was very gay, & my fever had dropped to normal already since a
fortnight, the visitors & telephone were not too good for an exhausted
person, & about a week ago my pulse began to go to 90 or so, too high. So
by a colossal act of self-abnegation I cut off all human contacts. No visitors,
no phone calls for say 5 days. Everything improved immediately. I get up, my
pulse is taken before & after, my temperature is no longer measured. I eat
normally, i.e. chops & steaks & chickens, & drink about 2 gallons of fruit
juices a day. It is a kind of Baden Baden rest cure. I need no night nurse – I
know what mother means so well – but I sleep perfectly normally & I have a
private day nurse from 8 a.m. to 8 p.m. of course the corridor is alive with
nurses whom the slightest pressure on my bell brings, also an athletic orderly
who is a specialist in enemas (clysters) & always tries to induce me to have
one, as if it was an illicit pleasure. He says he enjoys administering them, the
patient feels nothing, & everything is much brighter afterwards. I rely on
prunes, figs etc. which work better.

Let me describe a typical day: the room is cream coloured, with a distant

1 Henry Morgenthau, Jr (1891–1967), Secretary of the Treasury 1934–45, conservative in his
   economic views; often clashed with FDR, though they remained friends.
2 Ben(jamin) Crewdson Thomas (1902–75), barrister; Press Censorship 1939–41; Finance and
   Establishment, BIS NY, 1941–6; 6 feet 7 inches tall.
3 Aubrey Morgan and his second wife Con(stance), who worked in the Survey Section of the
   BPS, BIS NY.
4 Guy de *Rothschild (b. 1909), French banker, weary of being (in his words) a 'Jew under
   Pétain', had arrived in NY with his wife Alix in October 1941, had enlisted with the Free
   French, and was waiting to be ordered to their Headquarters in London (419/3). See his *The
   Whims of Fortune* (London, 1985), 272.
5 Countess Ilinska (*sic*) is Fira Benenson (1898–1977), fashion designer for the prestigious NY
   fashion store Bonwit Teller; married to Count Janusz Ilinsky.
6 Wladyslaw Sikorski (1881–1943), Polish politician and general, left Poland in 1939 to build up an
   army abroad, became commander-in-chief of all Polish military forces abroad and premier of
   the Polish government in exile, based in London; he was killed in a plane crash at Gibraltar.
7 Joe Alsop had transferred from the Navy to the American Volunteer Group (Flying Tigers)
   and had been captured by the Japanese in Hong Kong, but released as part of an exchange of
   prisoners in August 1942.

view, from the 12th floor, over N. York. it has two pink armchairs, & many flower strewn tables & knick knacks. I wake circa 8.30 a.m. in spite of the blinds & silence, & pull at my bell. Enter Miss Wallace the nurse (she is type paÿsan, efficient, attentive, unromantic, allegedly best nurse here. Illiterate, kind, & works like a clock) who (a) washes my face & hands & teeth (b) makes me swallow 2 vitamin tablets which are supposed to be good & taste like cocoa. (c) gives me a glass of hot orange juice (d) gives me the N.Y. Times (e) finally brings breakfast. I eat semalina [*sic*], an egg or two, coffee, a baked apple or figs, rolls. After this strenuous discipline I rest 20–25 minutes while the nurse reads a lowbrow newspaper. I am then ceremoniously handed my electric razor. I shave. I then rise, half dress, & repose in an armchair, where I read, & when visitors are allowed, hold the morning levée. at about noon the doctor examines me & tells me that I am getting on well. Once a week blood tests are taken, occasional sinus X rays. My blood composition & pressure are apparently perfect. At 12.15 I take a bath. I used to be washed in alcohol which was even nicer. At 1 p.m. I lunch: I eat a bouillon, an escalope, hundreds of green vegetables, buttermilk, more stewed fruit. At 2 p.m. I sleep. I wake at 4 p.m. perspiring and fresh. I am rubbed with eau de cologne, & rise again & drink coffee. more vitamin tablets. I telephone Washington & collect the gossip. at 6 p.m. I dine. I eat more soup, a fish, or chicken, a salad, fruit. jugs of orange & pineapple juice circulate. at 6.30 I either read, or someone comes to play 1 game of chess with me. At 7.30 my face, hands, teeth are cleaned again. At 7.45 I am in bed surrounded by books, a radio, orange juice, a spray for sinus, an electric lamp for sinus if it should trouble me (it hardly does), the radio aerial + bell rope + telephone wire, are stretched across the room & form a barrier to all comers. At this moment (it is about 9 p.m.) I am listening to Mozart's Bassoon concerto, about to read myself asleep with a funny book by Bemelmans[1] about the life of waiters. What cd be more idyllic? John Foster came to see me, nice of him. Rumbold also came all the way from Washington. John advised barring visitors, or else not answering them, just nodding wisely, to save energy. Very funny as always. I may be here a week more, or less. Depends on how strong I feel. I shall not return to Embassy for at least 1 month. no more to say now. I shall write again soon –

    love

       Isaiah Berlin

---

1 Ludwig Bemelmans (1898–1962), Austrian-born US author. The book is probably *Hotel Splendide* (London, 1942).

TO MARIE AND MENDEL BERLIN

Friday 23 October [1942, *manuscript*]

Private Patients Pavilion,
525 East 68 Street, New York City

My dear Pa & Ma,

Your (Father's) letter of the 15th Oct. to hand, as they say, via the Bag[1] forwarded by Nicholas.[2] I shall send this by the same route i.e. by Bag via Nicholas, & see what happens. I have a general idea that airmail letters & cards sent direct get through quicker. But in your letter of the 15th you say nothing about my numerous cards, sent by ordinary airmail since late in Sept. Please tell me in your next letter whether this (won't reach Washington before Saturday – to-morrow – 24th Oct.) arrives before or after a postcard marked Saturday 24th I shall airmail at the exact moment the official British messenger leaves with this for Washington i.e. 11 a.m. to-morrow morning. There messengers are known as 'Safe Hands' & lead a dog's life. Now: you rightly reproach me with lying. *Of course* if I could have kept knowledge of my sinus trouble from you I would have done so. Just as Father's digestive troubles were kept from me. I would in the end have told you something because the whole thing is lasting so long. I thought sinus infection = 3 days temperature + 3 days diet and basta.[3] The trouble is that apart from the mild bronchitis (which lasted about a week) the real cause was *not* sinus (which was not very acute, & just like on previous occasions) but a general physical exhaustion. So that when the official disease was over – 4, 5 days no more – I was diagnosed as weak generally, & unfit to work, & needing rest & quiet. Now of course if we had a house in U.S. – not in a hotel – but a house I suppose I could go there straightaway. Or I could go to the seaside with a nurse. But it seemed to me – & to the good doctor, & he *is* good – that nothing cd be more peaceful than a room here, if the nurses were told to bar visitors. At first I *wanted* visitors: it warms one psychologically to realize how many people are prepared to do so much for one 3000 miles from home – the Guy Rothschilds offered me a room &

1 By international agreement items sent in a diplomatic bag between an embassy and its government are not subject to inspection or interference by the host country; although intended for official documents, the bag from America was also used to supply Churchill with Cuban cigars throughout the war.

2 Herbert George *Nicholas (1911–98), New College classics 1931–5, Commonwealth Fund Fellow in Modern History, Yale, 1935–7, Lecturer in Politics, Exeter, 1938, Fellow 1946–51. At this time he was in the American Division of the MOI in London, where he was IB's main contact and a channel of (mis)information from IB to his parents: he observed that concealing IB's real state of health had required an 'orgy of perjury' (letter to IB, 14 May 1943).

3 Italian (and Spanish) for 'enough'.

absolute quiet, so did Alsop, Charles of course, Wheeler B[ennett] is still brooding about going to Arizona with me, etc. but the visitors were plainly not good for me.

As I told you truthfully before, my temperature digestion etc. are absolutely normal. The only thing which was not normal was that after some exertion – a bath, or a walk in the sun – my pulse rose from 72 to 86, or 90. People do go about their business with pulses of 85 & gradually it calms down, but as Butler told me not to hurry (if he had only said that when I was in Oxford!), & my day nurse is a severe disciplinarian, a régime has been adopted whereby *no* visitors are admitted & *no* phone calls made except if it's brief & urgent. The result is that my pulse is now about 80, it may take a bit longer & it will fall to 72. I was told that I could leave whenever I wished but that this was not advisable: but that people have done it & been no worse off. That is the full truth about my continuing here. I have no night nurse because I sleep soundly at night & need none. I have a day nurse from 8 a.m. till 4 p.m. – the minimum hours, because I need someone to keep away the friends, give me vitamin tablets, rinse my sinus, keep people out – nurses etc – when I sleep in the afternoons, etc. After 4 p.m. the general nurses do all this. I suppose they could do it anyhow: but the doctor prefers reports from one person, so I keep her. The only way of really convincing you is by eye-witness accounts I suppose. Do you remember Guy Chilver – tall, curly brown hair, also a don, who I think once came to 49, & certainly to Oxford? he is returning to England shortly & has seen me öfters.[1] I'll ask him to ring you, ask him to tea in London before he returns to the Food Ministry in Colwyn Bay. I think my doctor good because he doesn't hurry anything, wants me not to return to work for some time, feels so strongly that he is going to write to Butler to say so, & is generally behaving like a friend. I have had a letter from Nicholas to say he'd seen you. He is a trifle – no after all I am sending this through him – only he belongs to the оскорбленные[2] and is a little мелочный[3] but I think у меня есть место для него тут[4] so he временно очень преданн.[5] The radio is playing Boris Godunov. I have just (it is 6.30 pm) finished consuming: cream of chicken; a Wiener Schnitzel with asparagus tips, carrots julienne, and cole slaw which is a kind of mild sauerkraut; this was followed by buttermilk, a cup of chocolate (coffee *might* keep me awake. I am eating heartily but with *infinite* care) stewed prunes (not to tempt fate.) and a mass of green salad. Sometimes I even go to the

1 'Now and then'.
2 'Oskorblennie' ('insulted'). The same word is used in the title of Dostoevsky's novel *The Insulted and Injured* (*Oskorblennie i unizhennie*).
3 'Melochnii' ('petty', 'small-minded').
4 'U menya est' mesto dlya nego tut' ('I have a place for him here').
5 'Vremenno ochen' predann' ('for the moment is very devoted').

gentile extreme of devouring masses of spinach purée – groz, if I remember the word rightly. I *think* that next week, doctor or no doctor, I shall leave, I feel too well to stay. Very nice of Sir H. Allen to wish me well, but I was never seriously enough ill to have to 'pull through'. I wish the E. Standard would lose interest in me. I don't like being called tubby & the story about Dixie Tighe is false. But if they do say, please send me cuttings: But you'll never believe me again.

    love

       Shaya

I hope you realize that such energy in lulling your fears as I've displayed cannot proceed from a *very* sick man: or do you not believe in Pilpul?[1] talking of that, love to Rach.

(Yesterday's postcard had some fantastic date on it, 26 or something.)

> *When he left hospital at the end of October, IB joined Chaim Weizmann, also recuperating from illness, and his wife Vera at Grossinger's Hotel in the Catskill Mountains, New York State, for a brief convalescence before returning to New York.*

TO MARIE AND MENDEL BERLIN

9 November 1942 [*manuscript*]

                            The Gotham, New York

My dear Pa & Ma,

    From the distinguished notepaper you will have gathered that I have gone up in the world since my days in the Shoreham. Actually this is about 400 yards from the Shoreham (whose joys Fred Rau, who must surely have arrived in England by now – nobody here believed that he would *ever* return – he is expecting one or two unkind remarks I think) and opposite the St. Regis where Charles lives, socially between the two. Both the St. Regis and the Gotham make a reduction for diplomats (!) so after careful reflection I decided that this was about as much as it was decent to afford. The holiday with Charles was a great success. They lived in a v. pretty chalet in the hills. The hotel (owned by Galician immigrants) refused to charge them anything, but in return Charles was forced to give a brief interview to the local religious dignitaries. On the other hand when two Hadassah ladies made

1 The use of subtle or casuistical distinctions in the study and exposition of the Talmud.

their way into the garden & started to accost Charles, Vera said in her haughtiest voice "can't you read?" (the hedge & gate outside said 'Private') & shooed them away like cats. Her hatred of the bourgeoisie is a little extreme, to servants she is nicer. She thinks Romana Goodman[1] a fool for living so regular a life & having such philistine tastes (imagine: Romana lives in a boarding house in the country & says 'such nice people. Retired Indian civil servants' imagine it!") hates Rebecca Sieff,[2] & detests Mrs Eder,[3] who, she says, always makes her feel that she has said or done something wrong. Her sister who has arrived here is very Russian & exactly as she herself would have been if she hadn't married Charles, elegant, social, & unmemorable. Charles is in excellent health, terribly happy about the African campaign, & obviously well over the shock about his son. She has collapsed. Her heart is probably affected – anyhow while I was there she spent most of the day in bed, looked terrible, wept at meals, didn't smoke, didn't play cards, & was very tender & attentive to me. Occasionally friends arrived & went away again. Now you want to know exactly how & why I was ill, & why I wanted to go to Arizona etc. I think I was quite well, if tired, when I left, & caught my cold in Ireland where the B.O.A.C.[4] is not a very attentive host to its distinguished passengers (people sleep two or three in unheated rooms when better arrangements are infinitely easy) I knew that I wasn't well because my temperature began to rise in the middle of the day with regularity after the third day of waiting. I thought I had ordinary flu, but on arrival in N. York found that a general kind of exhaustion had seized on me – I was X-rayed, fed on sulfa drugs (these really are marvellous – they kill infection rapidly & absolutely. They exhaust one but any streptococci, pneumococci or other viruses which might produce pneumonia or pleurisy or anything else are killed immediately. Consequently my crisis was over between Monday 28th Sept. and Thursday 31st Sept.[5] My temperature was normal by Thursday so that my cheerful cables contained that much truth. The doctor thought that I would be able to leave hospital about a week after i.e. about the 7th Oct. but when that date arrived my legs felt like jelly – my pulse was about 95 – my temperature was subnormal. Consequently it was decided to keep me and

1 Romana Goodman, née Manczyk, wife of the leading British Zionist Paul Goodman (1975–1948); one of the founders and leading members of WIZO.

2 Rebecca Sieff (1890–1966), daughter of Michael Marks, who started the Marks and Spencer retail chain, and wife of Israel Sieff, who described his wife and Vera Weizmann as 'basically life-long friends who fought each other all the time': Israel Sieff, *Memoirs* (London, [1970]), 123. Their dissension partly concerned the running of WIZO, which they had co-founded in 1920.

3 Edith Eder, née Low (1872–1944), married first to Leslie Haden-Guest, then to psychoanalyst and leading British Zionist (Montague) David Eder (1865–1936); one of the founding members of WIZO.

4 British Overseas Airways Corporation, Britain's state airline from 1939; later part of British Airways.

5 i.e. 1 October.

feed me properly. So for another 3 weeks I stayed there, having my sinus washed etc. eating vast meals & drinking gallons of fruit juices. It was noticed that my pulse rose after telephone conversations, so for those 3 weeks I was kept in monastic solitude by my own wish: I had no great desire to see anyone, & enjoyed my sanatorium life enormously. Now both Charles & I are back here. I have seen my doctor who thinks there is no need for Arizona (which is the classical high & dry & sunny cure for all sinus etc. cases. Far from the sea & from anything, mountainous, empty, always sunny, windless it must be very good) but that I must not return to Washington for a[t] least 1 week–10 days, & live quietly here. Charles wanted me to come to his hotel (for supervision) but Mrs C. is so weak & demands so much attention that it depresses & exhausts me. Rumbold who is in N. York today is leaving v. soon & will dine with me to-night & ring you up in London when he gets back. I feel perfectly well – but to please the doctor I shall remain in bed till midday & go to bed at 10 p.m. and take two little walks daily of half an hour each & drink & sleep at lot. To-morrow my friend Joe Alsop dines here he too is going to England as a U.S. official. I shall return myself soon if things get too dull here.

    Love
      Shaya

The most difficult thing I had to do this week was to write Lord Halifax about the death of his son[1] whom I knew. The effect on Vera was also not easy to bear.

TO MARIE AND MENDEL BERLIN

   14 November 1942 [*manuscript*]

                     The Gotham, New York

My dear Pa & Ma

   I still inhabit my luxurious suite in this hotel, sleep late in the mornings, in bed by 10 p.m. in the evenings & am told by everyone that I look far better than when I left America in August. I am still tempted to go to Arizona for a fortnight (maybe for Xmas) as a kind of substitute for Amalfi and the Mediterranean. Actually my health is v. good, the electrical treatment has produced the result that my sinus gives no trouble at all for the moment. But I am now in a position to explain the entire medical situation as evidenced by the Xrays etc.–:

1 (Francis Hugh) Peter Courtenay Wood (1916–42), second of Halifax's three sons, Major, Queen's Own Yorkshire Dragoons, had been killed in action in Egypt on 26 October.

(1) the source of the trouble is the narrowness of apertures between the sinuses (i.e. cavities above the eyes) and the antrums (i.e. upper cheeks) through the nose. The draining process is not v. perfect. This leads to blockages (i.e. catarrhs) & accumulation of stuff. (b) My throat is a breeding ground for streptococcal bacteria. All throats have some, but mine has too many.

Now: to kill the streptococci I am to be vaccinated with an anti-streptococcal culture which is guaranteed to eliminate them permanently, or at least for 7 years, as opposed to sulfa drugs which only remove infection & inflammation, from which I no longer suffer. Instead of having one strong injection I am to have 3 very mild ones at intervals of 1 week each. The doctor in New York is a man called Palmer (attached to the N.Y. Hospital) who seems to me very sensible & good, & he has a friend in Washington, another doctor, who will, if necessary, work under his instructions if I don't want to travel to N.Y. to have each injection. I was, as usual, asked if I wanted to have an operation on the side of the nostril, to have the channel between it & the antrums widened, and refused. There is no urgency about this, I am not ill, & I can well wait a year or so & see if I still have attacks before taking action. And anyhow I don't believe in the operation in question – I haven't yet met anyone who has really profited by it. My general doctor – a man named Edwin T. Hauser, says my general condition is very good & nobody would even have known that I had had any time in hospital. Tonight I dined with the Morgans who have pressed me to come & stay in Wheeler Bennett's quarters (he lives with them in N.Y. & is at present in the South. Charles calls the "South" "Soith" & finds that a v. funny joke. Mr Bick used to pronounce it that way without finding it funny) until the latter returns i.e. about 25 or 26th, & this I shall do. It is as comfortable as here, cheaper, & Mrs Morgan will certainly see to it that I lead a quiet life. As you don't know her, there is no need to acknowledge anything. Your telegram to Mrs Charles [Vera Weizmann] thanking her for my stay with them was delayed by the U.S. censor who wanted to know who "Isaiah" was. Upon being told that he was a 1st Sec. of the Brit. Embassy, they apologized. Mrs Charles is now in an almost hysterical condition about her missing Michael – to-day is his birthday & she is surrounded by doctors & nurses & weeps without ceasing – while Charles looks blooming & is in a good mood. Just received your cable saying that Fred Sidney[1] gave good accounts of me. If you see Fred tell him I am saddled with his less interesting books which I cart about with me in a tin box wherever I move. Tony Rumbold will have given you greetings, & my friend Joe Alsop, the Roosevelt-cousin-journalist whom

1 i.e. Fred Rau and Sidney Bernstein: either a slip of the pen or a reflection of a cost-saving omission of 'and' in the cable.

Ben Cohen mentioned to you is going to England soon: tell me all about All Souls Day tea party. Ld Halifax has written charmingly to me in reply to my note condoling on the loss of his son Peter. I am looking after myself with wonderful assiduity & success. I drink Sanka[1] coffee & sleep well at nights.
    love
        Shaya

I have just seen Victor R.[2] who came here for a fortnight on H.M.G.'s business. I didn't ask him to ring you because I was sure he wouldn't have, not being well brought up. He was most friendly.

Although most of IB's 'business' letters are omitted from this selection, for reasons explained in the Preface, the next two items (unsent at any rate in the form in which they survive) exemplify the atmosphere of intra-office intrigue that prevailed at the Embassy, as well as demonstrating the volume of annotation needed to render IB's professional correspondence intelligible to non-specialists.

The first item may also stand for IB's extensive 'bootleg' corres-pondence with his Oxford colleague Herbert Nicholas at the MOI in London. The official dispatches drafted by IB and sent in Lord Halifax's name were a diplomatic distillation from sources of many kinds, and of varying degrees of confidentiality and reliability; much of what had to be omitted found its way into the often spicy, but somewhat impenetrable, Berlin–Nicholas exchanges.

These particular letters were written in the wake of Operation Torch, the Anglo-American invasion of Algeria and Morocco (8–11 November).

TO HERBERT NICHOLAS

26 November 1942 [*manuscript, not sent*]

158 East 70th Street, New York

Dear Herbert,

    I am still semi-hors de combat, and cannot therefore institute proper research about the attitude of the local authorities to De Gaulle[3] etc, but

---

1 A make of decaffeinated coffee (from the French 'sans caffeine').

2 This was the second occasion on which Aline Strauss met IB, who was with Victor Rothschild in his NY apartment when she called on him. She was so preoccupied with learning the Rothschild news that she ignored IB almost totally.

3 General Charles de Gaulle (1890–1970), leader of the Free French Movement in exile in London 1940–3, viewed by the US as an unmanageable troublemaker; President of the

this much is certainly true: the local Gaullists are furious & depressed by turns. The policy towards them of the State Department which is in the hands of A. A. Berle[1] who does not love them (or any Free Movements other than the Austrian) seems to me not exactly to set up Giraud[2] or Darlan,[3] but to break the whole French set up into constituent elements, reduce the subject to confusion, and then mould the fragments into some structure acceptable to the U.S. Let me explain: the F. French at present rule Equatorial Africa, Madagascar, Pacific islands, & in theory Syria. They are, I believe, to be allowed to continue to do this. Darlan – or anybody else who turns up, Giraud, Herriot,[4] anybody – will manage N. & W. Africa with U.S. in charge. Admiral Robert[5] will be left in control of Martinique, & possibly Guiana, & will deal directly with Washington. Pétain & the Germans will occupy France. There will be no source of central authority, no single object of anti-Nazi allegiance. Whether De G. does or does not reach an understanding with Giraud is of little import, since the State Dept. believes that friction, intrigues, and open disloyalties will continue so long as Messrs Noguès,[6] Esteva,[7] Boisson[8] etc. are about, i.e. men so deeply committed

Committee of National Liberation 1943–4, President of the French Provisional Government 1944–6; later Prime Minister (1958–9) and first President of the Fifth Republic (1959–69).

1 Adolf Augustus Berle, Jr. (1895–1971), lawyer, economist and diplomat, member of FDR's 'Brain Trust', Assistant Secretary of State 1938–44, Ambassador to Brazil 1945–6, later adviser to President Kennedy. Noted for his strong dislikes, paramount among which were the British, whose whole propaganda effort he had tried to shut down in early 1942.

2 General Henri-Honoré Giraud (1879–1949), Commander of France's Seventh Army; after France's surrender, prisoner-of-war in Germany until April 1942; selected by Eisenhower before Operation Torch as a future French military leader in the vain hope that he could persuade Vichy French troops in North Africa to remain neutral during the invasion. He became the civil and military chief of French North and West Africa after Admiral Darlan's death and later briefly shared the Presidency of the French Committee of National Liberation with de Gaulle, before being outmanoeuvred by him.

3 Admiral Jean Louis Xavier François Darlan (1881–1942), French Chief of Naval Staff 1936–40, then senior member of Vichy Government; in 1942 Commander-in-Chief of French Forces and High Commissioner in North Africa. He surrendered to the Anglo-American invasion of French North-West Africa on 11 November and, though known to be strongly anti-British, was considered by Eisenhower the only person capable of ensuring that French Africa remained neutral or friendly to the Allies, and was therefore appointed as the civil and military chief of French North Africa. He was assassinated on 24 December by Fernand Bonnier de la Chapelle, a young resistance fighter.

4 Édouard Herriot (1872–1957), former Prime Minister of France, initially a supporter of Pétain but later arrested by the Vichy authorities and handed over to the Germans.

5 Admiral Georges Robert (1875–1965), High Commissioner of Martinique, Saint-Pierre and Miquelon, Guadaloupe and French Guiana 1939–43.

6 General Auguste Paul Charles Albert Noguès (1871–1971), Commander in Chief French North Africa, Resident General of Morocco 1936–42.

7 Admiral Jean-Pierre Esteva (1880–1951), Resident General of Tunisia 1940–3.

8 Pierre François Boisson (1893–1948), Governor General of French West Africa 1938–9, 1940–3, supporter of Vichy Government.

against De Gaulle that no real understanding, however loose, is possible. The reason with which Mr Hull[1] & Mr Welles[2] justify this apparently cynical opportunism on their part to themselves, is that neither De Gaulle nor any other French leader represents the future France (which is true) and that it would be fatal to jell anything now which would mortgage the future. The only way to keep things at once unjelled and yet pro-allied (& in particular pro-U.S.: Martinique & Rabat continue to broadcast anti-British stuff unimpeded by our allies) is to set them against each other. You ask whether Giraud is being propped up against De Gaulle: yes, but not too much. Having heralded him for a day or two, the S.D. have now more or less dropped him. The President is, of course, behind all this, far more than the S.D., which rarely has views of its own on Europe. He is merely practising his normal method in internal politics – keep two parties going & occasionally egg them on into competition, & preserve power by arbitration. (e.g. Welles v. Wallace,[3] Nelson[4] v. Somervell,[5] McNutt[6] v. Hershey[7] & Perkins,[8] Elmer Davis[9] v. Donovan,[10] Jesse Jones[11] v. Morgenthau etc.). The Austrian legion (created by the combined influences of Hull, whose wife is an Austrian, Berle, & it is said, Frankfurter) is under very anti-democratic archdukes, its chief organizer, Windischgraetz[12] is talking about the future of Benes[13] etc. in a very bloodcurdling way. The purpose is apparently to create a Danubian federation round Austria. F.D.R., when

1 Cordell Hull (1871–1955), lawyer, Democratic Congressman and Senator, US Secretary of State 1933–44. Committed to an internationalist stance in foreign affairs; spent the later war years working towards the establishment of a new international organisation for the post-war era, and (having been nominated by FDR) was awarded the Nobel Peace Prize in 1945 for his contribution to the setting up of the United Nations.

2 Sumner Welles (1892–1961), diplomat, Assistant Secretary of State 1933–7, Under-Secretary of State (under Cordell Hull) 1937–43.

3 Henry Agard Wallace (1888–1965), former Secretary of Agriculture, Vice-President 1940–4.

4 Donald Marr Nelson (1888–1959), Chairman of the War Production Board (set up in January 1942 to control the domestic economy) 1942–4.

5 General Brehon Burke Somervell (1892–1955), Assistant Chief of Staff (Supply), War Dept, 1941, Commanding General, Services of Supply and Army Service Forces, 1942.

6 Paul Vories McNutt (1891–1955), Director of the Office of Defense Health and Welfare Services 1941–3; Chairman of the War Manpower Commission 1942–5.

7 Major-General Lewis Blaine Hershey (1893–1977), Director of the Bureau of Selective Service 1941–6.

8 Frances Perkins (1882–1965), Secretary of Labor 1933–45.

9 Elmer Holmes Davis (1890–1958), journalist, news analyst at CBS 1939–42, Director of OWI 1942–5.

10 General William ('Wild Bill') Joseph Donovan (1883–1959), lawyer, Director of OSS 1942–5.

11 Jesse Holman Jones (1874–1956), Secretary of Commerce 1940–5.

12 The aristocratic Windisch-Graetz family were linked by marriage to the royal family of the former Austro-Hungarian Empire.

13 Edvard Beneš (1884–1948), President of Czechoslovakia 1935–8, 1945–8; at this point in exile in London.

asked what wd happen if the Czechs resisted & the Atlantic Charter[1] which is unequivocal about self determination is invoked, is said to have answered that in that event the U.S. army of occupation wd stay 5 or 10 years until the Czechs saw reason & agreed to a settlement. Now, if you apply this to the French case, you will, will you not, agree that the same tactic – fragmentation of French groups with a view to leaving the settlement in the hands of the victors, preferably U.S. – is being used. To set Austrians against Czechs (which is being deliberately done – Benes is out of favour heavily with F.D.R.) is the game in Mittel-Europa. As for the dear old F.O. no opposition is anticipated, particularly if they can be assured that they can continue to keep De Gaulle & Syria while N. & W. Africa go to the temporary U.S. sphere of influence: and occasional snubs (Mr Mack's[2] delay in Gibraltar, e.g., about which you doubtless know) will help to impress the need for cooperation. I admit that I am writing with a 'Nation'[3] like bitterness, but I cannot help being offended by the nakedness with which Mr Berle admits to this policy of not letting the French solidify round anyone or anything – & the extraordinary feebleness which we display. The best London source for all this, if he is willing to talk, is my old host & friend Sir A. Rumbold (whom Cruickshank[4] knows) who is lately added to the French Department of the F.O. – this knowledge of U.S–French policy is very genuine. The strongest single influence in the business is still Mr Murphy[5] in Algiers; I have met him and his view is that only by systematically playing Weygand[6] (or whoever) against De Gaulle on the one hand, & Laval[7] on

1 Signed by FDR and Churchill in July 1941; laid down principles justifying the war against Fascism and intended as the basis for the post-war world-order; a key element was the right of all peoples to self-determination.

2 (William) Henry Bradshaw Mack (1894–1974), Irish-born British diplomat; civil liaison officer with General Dwight D. Eisenhower (allied commander-in-chief North Africa) 1942–3.

3 The NY current affairs weekly.

4 Robert ('Robin') James Cruikshank (1898–1956), journalist, American correspondent, News Chronicle, 1928–36, Assistant Editor 1936 (Editor 1948–54), Director of American Division, MOI, 1941–5, Deputy Director-General of BIS in US 1941–2, 'a delightful man to work for: all the people in the office adored him' (IB interviewed by Nicholas Cull: see 309/1).

5 Robert Daniel Murphy (1894–1978), free-ranging US intelligence officer, fixer, diplomat and trouble-shooter, FDR's political representative in North Africa 1941–43, set up an intelligence network in preparation for Eisenhower's landings there.

6 General Maxime Weygand (1867–1965), named Allied Commander-in-Chief of the French Army in May 1940; after the French surrender, made Delegate-General of French North Africa and commander of French forces in Africa; he was openly anti-Axis, and relieved of his command in November 1941 at the insistence of the Germans. In 1942 he was arrested and imprisoned in Germany. On his return to France in 1945 he was arrested and tried for treason, but acquitted.

7 Pierre Laval (1883–1945), Prime Minister of France 1931–2, 1935–6 (when his government fell because of his proposed concessions to Italy over Abyssinia), Prime Minister in the Vichy Government 1940, 1942–4, strong advocate of collaboration with Nazi Germany, complicit in

the other, can adequately post war malleability be achieved, & wartime loyalty of various French groups be kept up. When I return to Washington next week I shall endeavour to collect details. Thankyou v. much for forwarding the enclosed.

Yrs
   Isaiah B.

TO LADY DAPHNE STRAIGHT[1]

26 November 1942 [*manuscript, unfinished, not sent*]

158 East 70th Street, New York

Dear Daphne,

Your reply[2] plunges me into genuine melancholy. Our need is not trumped up but genuine. Con is flooded with work & Aubrey not unnaturally objects – Judson who has being getting out of hand, is a difficult collaborator. Your letter was enormously admired: *please* send another swiftly, to explain Cripps, Cranborne[3] etc. Is Cripps afraid of becoming a Hore Belisha[4] if he resigns? does he think that M.A.P.[5] will enable him to visit U.S. & get together with Wallace which he so passionately desires? & is Cranborne to go to India? & why O. Stanley?[6] Your letter to H. Armstrong[7] was fulsomely praised by him, I gather. So that your future as a political commentator is genuinely bright. Ronnie's[8] letter to [Harold]

the persecution and deportation of Jews; executed for treason 1945.

1 Lady Daphne (Margarita) *Straight (1913–2003), wife of the American-born member of the RAF Whitney Willard Straight, had worked with IB in the BPS in NY and was now a secretary in the American Division of the MOI in London. IB was very fond of her (as she was of him) and admired her abilities. Unfortunately most of IB's personal letters to DS have not survived (this one, not having been sent, at any rate in this form, is a happy exception).

2 To IB's request for DS to join his team in Washington. There are many letters, over a long period, to Herbert Nicholas in London about her possible transfer. One of them has as its repeated refrain 'What about Daphne?', surely the perfect title for a volume of IB's professional wartime correspondence.

3 Robert Arthur James Gascoyne-Cecil, Viscount Cranborne (1893–1972), Unionist MP, South Dorset, 1929–41, Paymaster-General 1940, Secretary of State for Dominion Affairs 1940–2, 1943–5, Secretary of State for the Colonies 1942, Lord Privy Seal 1942–3, Leader of the House of Lords 1942–5, later (1947) 5th Marquess of Salisbury.

4 Hore-Belisha had resigned in January 1940 over military policy in France.

5 The Ministry of Aircraft Production.

6 Rt Hon. Oliver Frederick George Stanley (1896–1950), son of 17th Earl of Derby, held many Government posts including Secretary of State for War 1940, Secretary of State for the Colonies 1942–5.

7 Hamilton ('Ham') Fish Armstrong (1893–1973), former Director of the Council on Foreign Relations, editor of its journal *Foreign Affairs* 1928–72.

8 Ronald Tree (1897–1976), Conservative MP, Harborough division of Leicestershire, 1933–45, Parliamentary Private Secretary to Sir John Reith (Minister of Information), Alfred Duff Cooper and Brendan Bracken 1940–3.

Butler, if sent, is shewn to no one. But Washington is in such a frightful mess that this is not surprising. John [Foster] is miserable in P.W.E., [David] Wills[1] has antagonized Mr Grubb[2] ('the man is just a squirt. I shall see to it that London is told') so back we are to Childs & the old nightmares. Winocour,[3] having bought chips at the wrong time, now finds himself bankrupt – Wills has offered him a job as outside contact – a glorified tout, who sits all day at the bar of the Press Club, & says 'I say, have you heard . . .' the Survey alone seems unaffected: I cling to an isolationist policy & a general sham silly attitude. Grant Mackenzie[4] who refuses to do any work has been entrusted with guidances: I have a plan which will cure all ills, provide general & total employment, & redirect attention to the war; I feel a pocket Rosenman[5] & doomed to failure. Butler is like prince Lvov[6] (first premier of the Russ revolution – liberal, vague, respected, elderly, impotent & slightly meaningless) & I don't wonder Robin declined to be his Kerensky.[7] The N.Y. office runs exceptionally well: Aubrey is popular once more, & happy because of the prospect of a scrap with Wills, a man of slightly less than his own weight, but worth a fight. Ben [Thomas] is unaltered. Mrs Edmondson[8] is melancholy. Mr E.[9] gets on with his job. Sunday evenings are not what they were. Now for public facts.

Before we get to these however, I must add that the first page[10] of this lay unattended in some obscure pocket of my coat while events occurred, I went to Washington, and as M[onsieur][11] Lenin once said, 'it became better to act than to write'. Not that I have done much of either, but the thought of the need of each inhibited the other. The first Morgan–Wills round was fought amid terrific public feeling – Aubrey won that one amid almost universal acclamation. Winocour (what hands will this fall into? for G.'[s] sake take a care!) goes about muttering that W. is a wrong 'un, the loathing of him comes from such unexpected places as Miss McG. & our toy general

---

1 Member of the British Embassy staff in Washington.
2 Kenneth Grubb, MOI London.
3 Jack Winocour (1913–1978), US journalist in the BPS at BIS NY, working in Washington at the time of this letter.
4 Member of the British Embassy staff in Washington.
5 Samuel Irving Rosenman (1896–73), lawyer; justice, NY Supreme Court, 1932–43, confidential adviser and speechwriter to Presidents Roosevelt and Truman 1943–6. FDR named him 'Sammy the Rose'.
6 Georgy Evgenievich Lvov (1861–1925), head of the provisional government after the Russian Revolution of February 1917.
7 Aleksandr Fedorovich Kerensky (1881–1970), successor to Lvov, July–October 1917.
8 The wife of D'Arcy Edmondson (see next note).
9 (George) D'Arcy Edmondson (1904–1976), head of BIS's Information Service, NY; from 1946 head of whole of BIS.
10 Which ends with the previous sentence.
11 Presumably a somewhat arch use of French as the language of diplomacy.

Sir R. Campbell[1] is clamouring for Robin, Rodgers (whom I hope you have never even heard of)[2] is supporting subversive elements, Aubrey is contemplating a small expeditionary force to rescue Jolly Jack for a while & keep a second front open, my frontiers are still inviolate, altho' Capt. Crawford's suicide has plunged Paul[3] into continuous hysteria. Oh dear. This will kill your appetite for return if anything could but let me hasten to assure you that the Survey Dept is a haven of calm blue water while the tempest rages about 3 miles away. I am too exhausted to continue. The next page must wait awhile. Oh dear. I am in as violent a state of partisan indignation if you must know (tho' why you must I cannot think) as during the Act period.[4] We appear to have engaged a doubtful character named David Cohn,[5] a friend of J. Foster & Angus MacDonnell,[6] who, I am sure, will give immense trouble. The question of salaries has ripped open a great many wounds, and Bathurst[7] wanders about, crouching & hissing that his legal advice will prove useful yet, that the atmosphere is too terrible even for him, that the latest Butler plan is a Munich, that W. will be at Prague by March, that he longs to go to Canada where he knows of a job. Rennie[8] declares that instead of the cow in a china shop – Sir G[erald Campbell] – we now have an ox & may yet get a bull – Mrs Rea[9] alone looks radiantly happy as she leads that new life to which you originally yourself called my distracted attention. The pen drops from my limp hand.

When IB returned to Washington, he settled into a pattern of life and work which was to continue for the next two and a half years. The

1 Sir Ronald Ian Campbell (1890–1983), diplomat, British Minister at Belgrade 1939–41, Minister to the US 1941–5, Assistant Under-Secretary of State, FO, 1945–6, Ambassador to Egypt 1946–50.

2 I certainly haven't.

3 Paul Scott Rankine (1908–83), at this time working for IB in Washington (previously head of the BIS survey section, NY); left to join Reuters in early 1944.

4 The time leading up to the passage of the Foreign Agents Registration Act in April 1942. Isolationist Under-Secretary-of-State Adolf Berle (420/1) had put forward proposals for legislation which would constrain and expose British propaganda activity in the US. These proposals were eventually vetoed by FDR and the Act that was passed took full account of British interests.

5 Might this have been American author David Lewis Cohn (1896–1960)?

6 Angus McDonnell (1881–1966), son of 7th Earl of Antrim, Attaché to British Embassy, Washington, 1941–5.

7 Maurice Edward Bathurst (b. 1913), international lawyer, legal adviser to BIS 1941–3 and to the British Embassy, Washington, 1943–6, legal member, UK Delegation to UN, 1946–8.

8 John ('Jack') Ogilvy Rennie (1914–81), BPS, NY, 1941, BIS 1942–6, FO 1946–9, later (1968) head of MI6.

9 (Margaret) Hermione Rea (b. 1911) worked at BIS and began a new life with René MacColl (1905–71), Director of the Press and Radio Division, BIS, NY, 1941–5, whom she married in 1946.

following letters emphasise the routine aspects of his existence, but in contrast his friends testified to IB's ability to enliven the dullest of contexts by his very presence. This is Guy de Rothschild's memory of encountering IB in America:

[T]he man who probably made the deepest impression on me was Isaiah Berlin [. . .] the most immediately striking thing about him was his unconventional appearance: his peculiar air of seeming to float in his clothing, a strange face that seemed almost a caricature of his two dominating characteristics: subtle intellect and Russian-Jewish ancestry. [. . .] Isaiah was then serving as one of the most important members on the staff of the British Embassy in Washington. He knew all the secrets of American politics, and proved to be of inestimable aid to Anglo-American relations. Brilliant, original, witty and bold, truly erudite, he was unanimously admired as much for what he was as for what he did, and he was universally recognized as an exceptional, fascinating human being.[1]

TO MARIE AND MENDEL BERLIN

Sunday 21 February 1943 [*manuscript*]

British Embassy, Washington

From Isaiah Berlin[2] (in English, implausible tho' this sounds)

My dear parents

I cannot think why I should find it so difficult to write you letters – except that I am genuinely so busy that *writing*, as opposed to other things, is difficult, and my new secretary who is a very good & efficient Canadian girl does not press me to write to you as frequently as did my American widow[3] in New York, and the Embassy being awe inspiring, prevents me from wasting government time on private affairs (I hope censors will copy this out for the benefit of my dear Ministry). My life: I still live in the Shoreham Hotel, Washington, which unlike the Shoreham Hotel in N. York is large, opulent, and very comfortable, but costs 6 dollars a day, which is a trifle dear. Every morning I walk across a park to the Embassy which is in a wooded neighbourhood, and work until 7.30 p.m. or so. There really is nothing to

1 Guy de Rothschild, op. cit. (411/4), 115–16.
2 Many of the wartime letters are so superscribed, for the censor's benefit (this also explains IB's frequent inclusion of his surname in his signature at this time). I have reproduced the superscription, untypically, in this case because of the parenthesis that follows.
3 Alice Irwin.

report of private life except that I miss the Rumbolds (ring A. Rumbold in French Dept. of F.O., he saw me in hospital & out of it in November) & propose to set up in a house or large flat with someone else. My present choice is a certain Edward Prichard, an immensely fat American expupil of Felix, who works in the White House, a very witty, malicious, & idealistic person, about 28 years old, (I'll try & send 'Time' Magazine in which he & Ben Cohen his boss are photographed)[1] comes from Kentucky and suits me temperamentally. He is social, &, I am afraid, as untidy as I am, so possibly when Guy Chilver arrives for the Food Mission (he must be leaving shortly. If you want to send your love – your last greeting, via Nicholas, was most warmly appreciated by me, very nice of you to send it – tell him to via Food Ministry where I think he must now be, if not still in Colwyn Bay) may be allured by me into sharing the house or flat, as he is very tidy & precise & orderly. Houses are terribly difficult to get, and expensive, the last offered cost 350 dollars which is too much even if I pay half. By the way I cashed a cheque for £250 to defray my illness via Ministry, so do see to it that the bank pays it. As for College battels, how can I tell from here what is required justly & what is not – pay it please as it is probably due. I am physically extremely well – the injections lasted for a short time, seemed to me to have little effect except that my sinus has in fact not troubled me for a long time now, whether because of them, or because of the very sensible & regular life I lead (easier here than in distracting New York) I cannot tell. Jack Stephenson[2] wrote me, I am glad, all old friendships are wonderfully touching at this distance, I shall reply. Please thank David & Mary for their letters. I met Mary['s] first cousin, Rosamund or Rosalind Coleridge,[3] daughter of Admiral William Fisher,[4] not in the least like Mary & not fond of her, hard, gay, smart, & considered, but not in fact, beautiful. As for work, it is absorbingly interesting, I find it difficult to keep an even balance between demands of Ministry & Foreign Office[5] as both want things done, & both suspect I give too much time to the other. But my immediate chiefs seem satisfied. I lunched with the Halifaxes at last – he most gracious, a being not of this century, remote, mildly curious about this strange environment, she looking gentle and sweet and subdued but in fact full of toughness. The death of one son & the crippling[6] of another had no outward effect on

---

1 *Time*, 11 January 1943, 19: a splendid picture of Prichard.

2 John Vere Stephenson (1909–73), contemporary of IB at St Paul's School 1922–8, Jesus (Cambridge) classics 1928–32, civil servant, MOI.

3 Rosamund (380/5).

4 Admiral Sir William Wordsworth Fisher (1875–1937), a younger brother of H. A. L. Fisher.

5 IB's Weekly Political Summaries were produced for the FO, but he was technically an employee of MOI until 1945, and reported to them on other aspects of his work.

6 Halifax's youngest son, Richard Frederick Wood (1920–2002), had lost both his legs in the North African campaign, where his brother had been killed (417/1).

them, stoicism of persons brought up in & devoted to public life & duty, all of which increased his popularity very definitely with Americans. I get on quite well with Sir R. Campbell, the diplomatic Minister, who is a half Jew, his mother was a Lehman[n], aunt of Rosamond L. a charming, shy, musical old world diplomat de métier.[1] Mr [Harold] Butler is also nice to me, & my old affectionate collaboration with Morgan & Wheeler B. continues. So you see that I am perfectly contented. I took a long time to recover, I only really got going in mid-January, but now it all marches well. I had a letter from aunt Ida, it said nothing, but was nice to get, Rabbi Meir B[erlin] who is here, saw them recently & said that Isaac[2] is now in the Public Custodian's office in Jerusalem, & is happy, but wants more money & better "contacts". Well, well. Nicholas[3] wishes me to point out that his staying a night with me & my writing of this letter are no accident. Do write, however little I do to encourage you, remember the lonely lot of exiles. I envy Moore Crosthwaite who is off to Moscow.

love

Isaiah Berlin

Miss McGeachy sends her love to you & Adamses).

TO MARIE AND MENDEL BERLIN

21 April 1943 [manuscript]

British Embassy, Washington, D.C.

My dear parents

This is just a brief scribble to celebrate (a) the Passover[4] (b) my new fountain pen. You cannot believe how much difference the object makes. Everything the advertisement says is true. Writing becomes tempting. I write. Well: there were some serious social complications about the Sedarim[5] this year. I was invited to the first Seder by: (a) Weizmann (b) his factotum, a certain Weisgal[6] who gives noisy bohemian Seders for Dorothy

1 'Career diplomat'.
2 Yitzhak Samunov.
3 Herbert Nicholas spent January–May on an extended visit to MOI New York.
4 19–20 April.
5 The two domestic celebrations of Passover, consisting of large formal dinners to which as many guests as possible are invited. ('Sedarim' is the plural of 'Seder'.)
6 Meyer Wolf Weisgal (1894–1977), Polish-born Zionist, emigrated to US 1905; editor of books and newspapers, producer of plays; national secretary of Zionist Organization of America 1921–38; Secretary General of US section of Jewish Agency for Palestine 1940–6; Organising Secretary of American Jewish Conference 1943; Chaim Weizmann's personal political representative in the US.

Thompson + Max Reinhardt[1] + heaven knows who. (c) Meyer Berlin & his daughter Judith.[2] He is here from Palestine & is going to England. He will tell you all about Yitzchok etc. Incidentally Mr Mindel,[3] the agent of Rabbi Schneursohn[4] has written asking for the address of 'your father Mendel'. I have not replied. If I do I shall ask him to send his letters to me for forwarding. Otherwise all kinds of nonsense may flow across the ocean: the Rabbi may or may not be in his right mind. Our family has always been gifted with a certain luxuriant imagination. (d) Mrs D. de Sola Pool, of Hadassah. (e) Holdstein. For the second Seder by the same, minus Weizmann & Holdstein. Meyer Berlin – Mrs Pool – Vera W. are reciprocally not on speaking terms. To go to one is to insult the other two automatically. After a wild desire to stay in Wash. & plague all their houses, I decided to make a secret pilgrimage to Weizmanns, after insuring my incognito. It was very quiet & gentle & small. Only the hosts – a rich Jewish merchant named Kramazsky from Hamburg originally (Fred can tell you of him) & the Weizmanns. I told him but not her about Abie Halpern's[5] death – you, I notice, tell me nothing. But somebody's sister wrote to her brother here & so it leaked out. I was immensely shaken & for about 3 hrs had to stop work. He died better than he lived, & he lived very well really. Poor Godya.[6] Two children is too much,[7] he deserved some suffering but surely not this. I must write to Barbara – I imagine her new religion is really a help now: she was, I believe, in her mad way, very fond of him. So was I. he lived so much of his life near me that memories are very interwoven. I never really liked him very much, but I was attached to him, as one is to cousins whom one takes for granted. I suppose I ought to write to Jerusalem too. Dr W. is very tough & swallows it all in 5 seconds. But she is very frail now: the only way of making her gay is by mentioning Mrs Sieff, & then she fulminates.

Talking of my contemporaries, Freddie Ayer (with his children) should be home by now, & so shd my friends Raimund von Hoffmannsthal[8] &

1 Max Reinhardt, né Maximilian Goldmann (1873–1943), Austrian stage producer and director, dominated German (and European) theatre in the early 20th century and indirectly influenced German and world cinema; founded the annual Salzburg Festival 1920, with Hugo von Hofmannsthal and Richard Strauss; emigrated to the US 1937.
2 Judith Berlin Lieberman (1904–1978), educator, Hebrew Principal then Dean of Hebrew Studies at Shulamith School for Girls, New York; married to talmudic scholar Saul Lieberman.
3 Dr Nissan Mindel (1912–99), rabbi, author, translator and editor, researcher of Jewish and Yiddish stories, closely associated with successive Lubavitcher Rebbes.
4 Yosef Yitzchak Schneerson (364/2).
5 Wolf Halpern, Barbara Strachey's husband, had been killed on 10 March while serving in the RAF Volunteer Reserve.
6 Wolf Halpern's father, Georg Halpern (93/3).
7 Presumably the Halperns had lost another child.
8 Raimund von Hofmannsthal (sic) (1906–74), son of Austrian poet and dramatist Hugo von Hofmannsthal, London correspondent for Time in 1943.

Guy de Rothschild.[1] The last may not remember to phone you, but Ayer should. Send him a message to Christchurch if he forgets. Also Nicholas will be returning & can testify to my continued good health. My Second Seder was fantastic: given by Mr M. Weisgal, it included: André Meyer[2] of Lazards in Paris: the Baronne Guy de Rothschild:[3] Max Reinhardt + his wife Helene Thimig[4] (I remember her sitting on the right of the Archbishop of Salzburg[5] in 1935 – a really fantastic change) a New Deal banker called Alexander Sachs[6] (born in Lithuania. But to me he talks for hours about the fact that his *real* name is Saichas, he comes *really* from Portugal,[7] his family is *really* aristocratic etc. etc. you remember how Gaster[8] was *really* de Castro?) + a collection of Zionists, Hollywoodites, stam Jews,[9] & Mr First Secretary Berlin. The effect was v. oriental & curious, Reinhardt is very decayed, the host, who is son of a Polish Chazan[10] was very melodramatic, the whole thing most bizarre. Now I must grovel to Rabbi Meyer Berlin (no point in offending him) & explain it all away to him & Mrs Tamar de Sola Pool, great Zionist powers, with whom diplomatic relations must be

---

1 Who had sailed to join the Free French in London in March, surviving the sinking of his ship by a torpedo in mid-Atlantic.

2 André Benoit Mathieu Meyer (1898–1979), French banker, until 1940 partner in Lazard Frères in Paris but now in their New York branch, which he went on to build into one of the leading investment banks of America; he was personally credited with the single-handed revitalisation of post-war American business.

3 Alix Hermine Jeannette Rothschild, née Schey de Koromla (1911–82); cf. p. 715 below.

4 Helene Thimig (1889–1974), Austrian actress, Reinhardt's second wife.

5 Sigismund Waitz (1864–1941), noted for his concern about social problems and his outspoken opposition to Nazism.

6 Alexander Sachs (1893–1973), long-winded economist, banker and self-appointed presidential adviser; collaborated with physicist Leo Szilard in writing the letter, signed by Albert Einstein, calling for research into and development of atomic energy, and personally delivered it to FDR in October 1939.

7 Sephardi Jews, ancestrally from Spain and Portugal, were often regarded as socially more refined than the Ashkenazi Jews, whose families had emigrated from Eastern Europe in the late nineteenth century and afterwards. This was especially true in England, but also in the US, where the very early settlement of Sephardi Jews would give them a claim to 'aristocracy' in American-Jewish society, by contrast with descendants of the Eastern European Jews whose mass immigration to both the US and Western Europe created the bulk of the Jewish communities there by the mid-twentieth century. The Portuguese spelling of Sachs's purported name is 'Seixas': cf. the American tennis player of the early post-war period, Victor Seixas, who even as Wimbledon singles champion in 1953 had trouble being admitted to Forest Hills Lawn Tennis Club in New York, on account of his Jewishness. He was the occasion of the following limerick: 'The Wimbledon champion Seixas / Has a service that's quite efficeixas. / With incredible pace / He delivers his ace, / While the rest of us murmur "Good greixas!" '

8 Moses Gaster (1856–1939), rabbi, scholar and leading Zionist; born in Romania, settled in England as a young man, became the head of the English Sephardi community; father-in-law of Maire Lynd.

9 Ordinary Jewish laymen: 'stam' is Yiddish for 'simply'.

10 Cantor in a synagogue.

preserved. Meanwhile my work is still fascinating, my colleagues affable, Butler has gone to England, I think he quite approves (he is totally ineffective I may say, & has no idea of what any one of us does, & hideously unpopular, but on all that silence. He is v. nice to me), Mr Eden's[1] entourage were a gay throng with which I mixed up to a point – Strang[2] is v. intelligent & cross examined me like a really capable inquisitor – I am altogether well, & propose to continue in this comfortable & indeed luxurious hotel for the present. Au revoir. I am really well.

yrs
    Isaiah

I haven't seen any old friends lately – Holdstein once, he is doing quite a good business – but no Raskins or Aronsons or Libermans – what is Rach's explanation of the execution of Alter and Ehrlich?[3] does he weep [at?] Miliukov's[4] death (in Aix les Bains) he wd be thoroughly in his element in local left v. right controversies which are *pure* 19th century. But don't say so to him.

TO MARIE AND MENDEL BERLIN

4 May 1943

British Embassy, Washington

My dear parents,

Thank you for your last telegram.

Cruikshank's letter saying that some meddling busy-body had been turning your blood cold with accounts of me in a condition resembling the last acts of *Traviata* or *La Bohème* was very amusing. I can assure you there is no truth in this.

I have so far been unable to get to New York to see our pseudo cousin,

---

1 (Robert) Anthony Eden, 1st Earl of Avon (1897–1977), Conservative MP (1923–57), Secretary of State for Foreign Affairs 1935–8, 1940–45.

2 Sir William Strang (1893–1978), Acting Assistant Under-Secretary of State 1939, UK Representative, European Advisory Commission (with personal rank of Ambassador) 1943, Political Adviser to Montgomery (Commander-in-Chief, Germany) 1945–7.

3 Victor Alter (1890–1941), engineer, and Henryk Erlich [*sic*] (1882–1941), journalist and lawyer, Polish leaders of the Bund, the anti-Zionist Jewish Socialist Party. They escaped from Poland at the time of the German invasion in September 1939 but were arrested by the Soviets and executed in December 1941. News of their execution did not become public until 1943.

4 Pavel Nikolaevich Milyukov (1859–1943), Russian liberal, briefly Minister of Foreign Affairs in the Provisional Government in 1917, then leader of the liberal Constitutional Democratic Party (acronymically 'Kadets'), founded in 1905; left Russia for Western Europe November 1918.

Meyer B[erlin][1] who is going to England and whom I should therefore see before he goes.

Could you possibly buy Mr Bowra's ⟨⟨to whom give my love⟩⟩ book[2] for me and send it to me via Foreign Office bag, simply marked I. Berlin, British Embassy, per favour of bag? Indeed I see no reason why you should not do what Miss Carruthers does and send all your letters that way. At worst they will be read by someone in the FO, which is no worse than a casual censor. I should also be grateful if you would open a subscription for me with the *New Statesman* and the *Times* which could equally be sent to me either by bag or straight – the publishers could tell you if you telephone.

[Herbert] Nicholas will be bringing you concrete regards from me.

Old Percy Baker's youngest daughter, under some new name has written me and asked me to go and see her, which I shall probably do.

Love,

Shaya

⟨I really am in enormously excellent health & spirits.⟩

Your last letter just received containing [Guy] Wint's revelations. So the truth is out at last. Yes, I must confess that what I had was pneumonia of the virus kind. It was not dangerous at any stage nor were there any relapses. There is nothing very detailed to tell you about that except that it was thought to be sinusitis at first because the symptoms of virus pneumonia can only be detected by X-ray and not by the usual listening devices. Sulfa drugs had little effect and I recovered from sheer natural resources. Of course this was the reason for my prolonged stay in the hospital. I must say that everyone who knew the facts behaved most discreetly on the subject and I would not have wished it otherwise even though it involved a certain deception of you. John Foster's view is that Miss Carruthers should not have revealed the truth to you even now but we assume that the Berlins' third degree efforts would finally elicit the truth from everyone. The Ministry knew the facts of course and behaved like gentlemen. It was all very pleasant as it was accompanied by no physical discomfort of any kind and a month in bed with no pain and a great deal of attention and comfort was really very agreeable. If one must be ill that is the ideal method. I observed that Mr Churchill suffered from the same complaint. The holiday which I took after the illness did me a great deal of good and I have had no recurrence of any kind (Wint's relapses are pure imagination and probably due to the fact that I declined to see him once or twice, as he is a terrible bore, on grounds of

1 Meir Berlin was a distant cousin of IB's uncle Yitzhak Samunov, but no relation to IB himself.
2 *The Heritage of Symbolism* (London, 1943), a study of post-Symbolist poetry.

colds, etc.). However, I will keep you carefully posted about my condition. I sleep a great deal, spend half Sunday in bed, and am in blooming health.

I wish I knew who 'Stephenson' is who said these nice things about me. I recollect no such person or name.[1]

There is really nothing to add except that I shall certainly try to take a holiday in August in some cool, hilly place since the heat here in August is very great, although it does not affect me particularly – I was quite comfortable here both in 1940, 1941, and July 1942.

A colleague of mine, Graham Hutton,[2] may telephone you in Oxford where he has a brother-in-law called Evan Durbin.[3] He and Nicholas are on the worst of terms and threaten to throw each other overboard from the ship on which they will probably both arrive. Both promised to communicate.

Love,
Shaya

TO W. G. S. ADAMS
Warden of All Souls

23 June 1943 [*carbon*]

British Embassy, Washington

Dear Mr Warden:

I hope you will forgive me for not having written for so long but my life, although professionally interesting enough, is in all externals uneventful. I have become an Embassy desk rat of the most humdrum variety, almost undistinguishable from the files and professional civil servants among whom I have my being. As for the general situation it is fair to say that there is a wave of anti-isolationism blowing at the moment which makes even the rabidest opponent of collaboration trim their sails somewhat, and makes one think that while the sun is shining as it is doing at the moment British and American statesmen ought to get busy making hay. The atmosphere is better than at any time since Pearl Harbor. [. . .]

Yours sincerely,
Isaiah Berlin

1 Possibly William Stephenson, head of British Security Co-ordination (436/4).
2 (David) Graham Hutton (1904–88), economist, barrister, author; Assistant Editor, *The Economist*, 1933–8, FO and MOI 1939–45; at this time running the Chicago branch of MOI.
3 Evan Frank Mottram Durbin (1906–48), economist and author; New College zoology 1924–7, PPE 1927–9, Ricardo scholar in economics, University College London, 1929; Lecturer, then Senior Lecturer, in economics, LSE, 1930–47 (also economics Lecturer, New College, Trinity term 1939); economic section War Cabinet Secretariat 1940; personal assistant to Deputy Prime Minister (Clement Attlee) 1942; later (1945) Labour MP for Edmonton; drowned in a swimming accident.

TO SIR DAVID SCOTT[1]
Foreign Office

8 July 1943 [carbon]

British Embassy, Washington

I must ask your pardon with great deference and respect for having left your letter unanswered for so long. It arrived in the midst of great alarums and excursions, when the S[ecretary] of S[tate][2] and his suite were amongst us, shortly followed by the PM with all his hosts; we felt like a small (Jane Austen) town when the regiment came, and fluttered and flew (each as much as his dignity permitted) in all directions, and even after our distinguished visitors had left, the hearts of certain of my colleagues were still pounding with every kind of emotion, public and private. As I once tried to expound to Sir R. Campbell (who is apt to treat me with indulgence about such things) our general establishment is really very like a public school: The Chancery is the School House, with a somewhat remote Head Master (or perhaps Sir R. is Head Master and Lord H. the remote Provost), William Hayter[3] is clearly the Sixth Form Master who knows a great deal of Latin and also Greek, with few illusions about the boys; while Michael Wright[4] is an Old Boy of the School, returned as keen young House Master, a new broom, tense, virtuous, and determined to raise the batting average, come what may; [J. W.] Russell the clever boy who has lived abroad too long and makes rude remarks in Italian (or it may be Coptic) and then titters at the Masters who do not understand but dimly suspect; but this is made up by Gore-Booth,[5] who has his House Colours already, and is keen as mustard and whose impatient muscular Christianity may be relied on to preserve the House from too much musing and brooding, but he is not so elegant a writer of elegiacs as the slow and gentle Barkley,[6] who used to be bullied a lot until the new House Master stopped all that. Then there is the French Master, Mr D. Hall, whom the boys rag mercilessly but who is really very nice, and tries not to mind when he finds white mice in all his pockets; and of course there are Foster and Blake Tyler,[7] whose parents are in India, much too mature to be in the School at all, raggish and with a roving eye, apt to slip off to the

1 Sir David John Montagu-Douglas-Scott (1887–1986), FO 1911–47, Assistant Under-Secretary of State for Foreign Affairs 1938–44, Deputy Under-Secretary of State for Administration 1944–7.
2 Anthony Eden.
3 William Goodenough Hayter (1906–95), diplomat 1930–58, in Washington 1941–4, later Ambassador to USSR (1953–7) and Warden of New College (1958–76).
4 Michael Robert Wright (1901–76), diplomat; Washington 1943–6.
5 Paul Henry Gore-Booth (1909–84), diplomat; Washington 1942–5; later (1968–9) Head of the Diplomatic Service.
6 Roderick Edward Barclay (sic) (1909–96), diplomat; Washington 1941–4.
7 H. B. Blake-Tyler.

races under the very eye of Mr Wright, (they have never been caught; one day they will be and then Barkley, who is senior House Prefect, will be told to beat them, and will do it very badly).

The other houses are quite different, rather less smart. There is, of course, Magowan's,[1] a safe, solid house, which has always been there and wins the same not very high number of school prizes, and is not bad at games but not good. Parents know exactly what to expect. Noel Hall's[2] is full of pallid scholarship boys, who are thought to be very clever, but rather mixed. They cram like mad but often don't quite come off. Bowes Lyon's[3] house is new and very small, and thought to be rather select and nobody quite knows what will come of it. It has not done much so far but the older Masters say that it is too early to judge. As for Butler's,[4] it is a very odd house indeed, most uneven, liable to flurries, with boys expelled now and then or else beaten in front of the entire school for unspeakable offences. Everybody is very concerned about it and its reputation. It is a concession to modern life, and new subjects are taught privately in it, which makes the older Masters shake their heads. Some think it too easy to get into and it has no social panache. Individually the boys are thought to be really rather nice and some of them quite able, but there is a curious atmosphere about the place that make things very uncosy, and there has been serious thought of transferring part of it to the School House as soon as there is room, when the Army Form has sent its contingent to Sandhurst and there is a little more room.

The problem of whether Sir G. Sansom[5] should or should not have a house has been debated for so long that nobody now expects an answer. It is raised every time any of the Governors come down, Mr Law[6] or Mr Eden, and there is a good deal of serious reflection but nothing ever comes of it – if only Butler's would keep a little quieter, similarly if the boys in Noel Hall's

1 John Hall Magowan (1893–51), Minister, Commercial Adviser to British Ambassador, Washington, 1942–8.
2 Sir Noel (Frederick) Hall (1902–83), Professor of Political Economy, University College London, 1935–8, Joint Director, MEW, 1940, Minister in charge of War Trade Development, British Embassy, Washington, 1941–3; later (1960–73) Principal of Brasenose.
3 Hon. Sir David Bowes-Lyon (1902–61), MEW 1940–1, Head of Political Warfare Mission, British Embassy, Washington, 1942–4; brother of the then Queen Elizabeth.
4 BIS, of which Harold Butler was Minister.
5 Sir George Bailey Sansom (1883–1965), retired from Diplomatic Service 1940, member of Far Eastern War Council, Singapore, 1941–2, appointed adviser to British Ambassador, Washington, 1942. He headed a committee of MOI/BIS personnel, including IB, to consider the propaganda problem in America posed by the British Empire; the committee presumably discussed whether Sansom should have his own staff.
6 Richard Kidston Law (1901–80), son of former Prime Minister Andrew Bonar Law; Conservative MP, Financial Secretary to War Office 1940–1, Parliamentary Under-Secretary of State, FO, 1941–3, Minister of State 1943–5, later (1954) 1st Baron Coleraine.

were not found using cribs and cheating in examinations, and Magowan's would assert itself a little more, and Bowes Lyon's show its quality.

The Old School House will always be criticised, principally by other schools, Llewellyn[1] College and the Phillips[2] Academy, and even Salter's Free School for the sons of Captains in the Merchant Marine,[3] and Mr Stevenson's[4] disreputable Correspondence College. But it has given its share to the life of the nation, and undoubtedly always will, even if its manners are a bit old-fashioned, and its boys wear top hats all the year round, and are taught to use quill pens until a very advanced age, and behave a little stiffly when they meet with other schools at OTC camps.

So we go on, wonderfully unaffected by the powerful influences beating vainly from without. I really must apologise for all this shocking nonsense, but it seems the shortest method of describing our environment.

[. . .]

Dear me! You will never forgive me for the monstrous length of this screed if you have had the patience to reach this far.[5] Rightly. I cannot say how sick with nostalgia I am and how I wish there were a job for me to do in England. I should return hot foot. Be it ever so humble!

You will have John Foster with you soon and shall certainly not want for gossip, which will make my Creeveying[6] quite unnecessary.

Yours ever,

---

1 Col. John Jestyn Llewellin (1893–1957), 1st Baron Llewellin of Upton 1945; Conservative MP 1929–45; President of the Board of Trade and Minister of Aircraft Production 1942; Minister Resident in Washington for Supply 1942–3; Minister of Food 1943–5.

2 Just possibly William Phillips (1878–1968), US diplomat; Ambassador to Italy 1936–41; Director, OSS, London, July–December 1942; personal representative of the President to India, December 1942; Political Officer (US) on Eisenhower's staff, London, 1943–4. Also (or instead?) a somewhat opaque reference to the prestigious Phillips Academy, Andover, near Boston, the oldest incorporated boarding-school in the US.

3 The British Shipping Mission, headed by Arthur Salter.

4 Presumably William Samuel Stephenson (1896–1989), Canadian businessman and inventor, head from 1940 of what became British Security Co-ordination (BSC), based in New York, and hence responsible for the establishment of Britain's spy network in the West during the war, for co-ordination of intelligence between Britain and the US, and for covert propaganda; known by BSC's cable address, 'Intrepid'.

5 The passage omitted before this paragraph is a lengthy commentary on recent political events, including the visits by Eden and Churchill.

6 Thomas Creevey (1768–1838), English politician famous for his diaries, which are full of illuminating and irreverent gossip.

TO LADY DAPHNE STRAIGHT
American Division, Ministry of Information

19 July 1943 [*carbon*]

British Embassy, Washington

Dear Daphne,

[. . .]

My friend Dr Weizmann, now in England, to whom I have praised you in passionate terms in an off and on sort of way, expressed a very strong desire to meet you while in England. His wife is somewhat tiresome, Russian exile type, made more pathetic by the death of their son in the RAF, a rather touching fading snob. But he is a great man, a grand nineteenth-century figure in the Italian tradition and worth meeting, at any rate once, as a kind of person whose like we shall never see again (Cavour [and] Gambetta[1] must have been a little like that). But if you do not feel inclined, do not hesitate to refuse any advance he may possibly make on my account. He looks like a very distinguished and rather tragic camel, not unlike Lenin, has a caressing voice and a passion for the English which, as in the case of Mr Hopkins,[2] becomes particularly strong in the case of the upper classes.

[. . .]

Love,

Zionism occupied only a small part of IB's official life, so his dual loyalties were not often tested. But Zionist pressures in America were on the increase, to the concern of the British Government. IB's reminiscences of 'Zionist Politics in Wartime Washington'[3] provide the background to the events described in the following letters.

---

1 Count Camillo Benso di Cavour (1810–61), Italian statesman and liberal, played a major role in the creation of a unified Kingdom of Italy. Leon Michel Gambetta (1838–82), French statesman.

2 Presumably Harry Lloyd Hopkins (1890–1946), Presidential adviser 1933–45, and from 1940 FDR's closest aide; Secretary of Commerce 1938–40, from 1941 administrator of Lend-Lease.

3 See pp. 663–93 below.

TO ANGUS MALCOLM[1]
Foreign Office

2 August 1943 [*carbon*]

British Embassy, Washington

Dear Angus,

I have a small but definite bone to pick, though possibly not with you. I am filled with dark suspicions.

The other day Alling,[2] Head of the Near Eastern Department of the SD, suddenly asked William Hayter whether he knew a man called Berlin. Was he a Rabbi (don't giggle)? Was he a Zionist? Was he an intimate of Weizmann? He said by way of explanation that 'a document' had been read by the SD containing a report of Weizmann's political activities in this country. William at first understood that this was a censorship intercept of a letter possibly written by me, but this was cleared up (a) by the fact that I had not written one, and (b) by the fact that Alling later said that it was not a censorship intercept but a document, not indeed read by him, but shown to 'his people' by 'our people', presumably in London, and dealing with Weizmann's political activities here, in detail. The Rabbinical clue led to the door of my disreputable namesake (but fortunately no relative) the Rabbi M. Berlin of Palestine and Riverside Drive,[3] an enemy of Weizmann and a clerical maximalist. Our censorship people were instructed feverishly to search and, for all I know, may be doing so still.

William then proceeded, I gather from him, to whitewash me with immense thoroughness, explaining (1) that I was not a Rabbi, (2) that I had written no political report on Weizmann. (The fact that I have written several minutes on the general subject in your day and after, duly communicated to the FO, was kept from A.) (3) that I was not 'a political Zionist' in the sense in which the SD understands it, at least not more than, let us say, Mr Welles,[4] and that no Zionist could possibly acknowledge me as a member of the faithful. (Wise is frightfully suspicious of me, and now that I have stubbornly denied all knowledge of the coming joint Anglo-American statement, so are the rest. They think William far more sympathetic to the cause (now that Weizmann is gone and his personal fascination removed I am not sure that this is not so). I have not got to the

---

1 Angus Christian Edward Malcolm (1908–71), diplomat; Madrid 1936–8, Washington 1938–42, North American Dept, FO, 1942–4, Rome 1944–7.

2 Paul Humiston Alling (1896–1949), diplomat, Assistant Chief of the Division of Near Eastern Affairs in the State Dept (SD) 1934–42, Chief, 1942–4; Deputy Director, Office of Near Eastern and African Affairs 1944–5.

3 In Manhattan.

4 Sumner Welles was sympathetic to the Zionists.

stage of telling lies to the Zionists, but even supressio veri is uncomfortable. I wish the declaration were over and done with.) (4) that I was really an Oxford Don in disguise. This last apparently proved the clinching point in favour of my respectability. The episode was thereby exhausted (not that it was really serious, only rather odd).

Picture my indignation at being charged with the appalling crime of Zionism when I was wearing myself out on the telephone persuading Sir N. Angell[1] not to attend the protest meetings and the Jewish Army rallies[2] (successfully: the Americans failed to do the same for Ickes[3] or anybody); reporting faithfully the appalling conspiracies proliferating here around the Joint Statement, news of which vaguely leaked through the White House and (probably) appeared in a perverted form in a Cairo Sulzberger[4] dispatch in *The Times* of 30 July; engaging in the most affable correspondence with various Arabs, and generally perjuring myself out of my pew in Paradise in an excess of pseudo-bureaucratic zeal. What am I to think? Did you, could you (or one of your colleagues) have communicated one of my super secret minutes on Weizmann (sent to FO) to Americans in London?

Let me tell you (fiercely) that we here (and this goes for all of us Embassy hacks) are perfectly convinced that nothing we send you remains in your files for more than three days without (a) being disseminated to every American agency in London, (b) being recabled here by them, (c) being read by Mr Berle and interpreted in a very damaging fashion. With this general background, I doubt if anything you say will convince us of the opposite but you may as well try. (I add that there is a school, probably the right one, which accepts this fact and holds that such leaks are the inevitable price of that closeness of relations which exists between you and the American Embassy in London, but not between SD and Embassy here, and that the price is well worth it. I am sure that is the right view. But, whatever the facts,

---

1 Sir Norman Angell, né Ralph Norman Angell Lane (1872–1967), newspaperman, writer and lecturer on international relations; Labour MP 1928–31; pacifist, winner of Nobel Peace Prize 1933. In mid-1943 he had written an article supporting Zionism and suggesting that the current Arab occupants of Palestine would move voluntarily to other Arab areas if sufficiently favourable terms were offered.

2 The Bergson group of right-wing Jews from Palestine, headed by 'Peter Bergson' (Hillel Kook), had pressed for the creation of a Jewish Army to fight alongside the Allies, but when rumours of the impending destruction of European Jewry reached the US in 1942, diverted their efforts to a campaign – endorsed by several influential American public figures, including Ickes – for the rescue of the Jews of Europe.

3 Harold LeClair Ickes (1874–1952), journalist, lawyer, author and politician; Secretary of the Interior 1933–46; unwavering liberal and vigorous New Dealer famous for his invective, strong supporter of action to save the Jews of Europe.

4 Cyrus Leo Sulzberger (1912–93), journalist; foreign correspondent covering the Balkans, Russia and the Middle East for the *New York Times* 1940–4.

don't let us make a thing out of this. If it is small ado about nothing, it is certainly not worth raising at any higher – e.g. Mr Butler – level.)

My own best testimonial to date is that of Mr Kettaneh,[1] a rabid Arab nationalist warned by 'the Zionists' against me as a well-known member of the British Secret Service who has sold them right and left. Since then a flood of letters from Mr Kettenah [*sic*], who, I believe, actually has been employed by our SS in the past as well as by the American equivalent.

But it really would be useful to know how much Judenlehre[2] you do show the Americans in London, as general uneasiness on this topic tends to cramp all our styles.

[. . .]

    Yours ever,
      Isaiah Berlin

TO LADY DAPHNE STRAIGHT

    4 August 1943 [*carbon*]

                    British Embassy, Washington

Dear Daphne,

    [. . .]

I am glad you have met the infinitely charming Weizmann. I am sure you cannot like his wife. One thing worries me, that is that he may well attempt to exploit you for his cause, i.e. try to get through to Mr E[den] or others through you. Do not on any account allow yourself to be so used. I should feel very ashamed and distressed if I thought that I was a party to that sort of thing. Zionism may be a worthy movement, but do not I beseech you allow yourself to be used. If he shows unscrupulousness in that direction, with which, like all great men, he is generously gifted, stall him and retreat.

    Love,

TO ANGUS MALCOLM

    9 August 1943 [*carbon*]

                    British Embassy, Washington

Dear Angus,

In an excess of bureaucratic remorse and warmed by the Head of your

---

1 Presumably Francis A. Kettaneh, a Palestinian Christian who in April had sent a memorandum to Anthony Eden about the future of his country.
2 'Jewish lore'.

Department's[1] kinder words about the political summary and its sadly reduced length, I feel that I ought to recant my somewhat mock violent words to you in my last letter about local views concerning your probable 'leaks' to Americans in London. After Drew Pearson's[2] last column on the Zionists it will be apparent that the State Department is far worse; and anyhow the whole thing was not really worth comment, certainly not serious brooding. So give it no further thought.

I attach an account of the extraordinary intrigues which, so far as I can discover, surround the abortive Anglo-American Joint Declaration on Palestine. I don't suppose I have anything like all the facts, but it shows the almost clinical pattern of Washington lobbying, reminiscent of the dear old days of Harding[3] and Coolidge.[4] In my view, the Zionists' tactic, whatever it may gain in the short run, is very dangerous {to the} à la longue.[5] They must have irritated the State Department to a degree; I should imagine the President is really displeased; and they are bound to pay for this sooner or later. Judging the situation with that remote objectivity which you used to find so queer in me, I should say that the Zionist pressure group, while it may be powerful enough to avert this or that impending action by full exercise of all its resources, is not powerful enough to sustain such tactics; it would be better advised to use methods of persuasion rather than brutal political pressure, since the latter is bound to boomerang and sow dragon's teeth (if you see what I mean), which will do them in, at any rate to some degree, in the long run. The State Department hate them worse than Communists now, and, like all established institutions, the State Department nagging patiently, and standing their ground, will probably win in the end. I do not say that the Zionists will not get much of what they want, but they would get it sooner, and more of it, and with less trouble and damage to everyone else, if they stopped their agitation (which can succeed, it seems to me, only where the vital interests of a nation are engaged, as they are conspicuously not in the case of America and Palestine), and instead operated solely by means of private conversations on the part of sensible persons with relevant Government officials in England and here. I say this to persons like Dr N. Goldmann, the only Zionist I ever see regularly, i.e. about once in six weeks, and it is obviously not at all well received and viewed simply as routine HMG tactics to keep things quiet. When the explosion

1 Nevile Butler (399/2), Head of North American Dept.
2 Andrew Russell Pearson (1897–1969), newspaper columnist notorious for his sensational investigative reporting.
3 Warren Gamaliel Harding (1865–1923), whose US Presidency 1921–3 was noted for scandals and corruption.
4 Calvin Coolidge (1872–1933), Vice-President under Harding from 1921; President from Harding's death in 1923 until 1929.
5 'In the long run'.

comes, whether as a result of a revolt in Palestine or otherwise, it will be a cold comfort to tell them that I told them so.

In the meanwhile the elections for the Zionist Organisation of America are completed. The rivals have both been assuaged. Pearly Twig[1] told William [Hayter] that whereas Goldstein wished to appease USG and confine attacks to HMG, Silver,[2] who is a Cleveland Willkieite Republican (and led the fight for Willkie there in 1940), believes in attacking both. The compromise is that Goldstein is to be President of the ZOA while Silver (Rabbi Abba Hillel) is to be Chairman of the Executive Committee of the Emergency Committee, which is a real political pressure group.

There really was value in Weizmann's presence here – it confined irresponsibility to irresponsibles and kept the big battalions with their real financial and political strength in relative check.

If the American Jewish Conference is held (and there is now some slender chance that it will not be – see my other letter sub. fin. and reference to the Welles caveat)[3] the Zionists with their 92 per cent majority and no Weizmann may really do something silly. Meanwhile we have at last secured an invitation for Freya Stark,[4] and that may serve to adjust the balance a little. Oh dear! I am sick and tired of it all after two and a half years of it.

To cheer you up I have only one small pleasantry – the fact that the Free French now talk of the two Marshals, Badaud and Giroglio,[5] and predict that Uncle Joe [Stalin] will lop their heads off in the great Purge of the Marshals, to include most of his own, which he will institute as the Liberator of Europe. You see what a sardonic mood we are in. Donald Hall and Jack Wheeler-Bennett say you all are too. I expect it's the heat.

Do write me again.

Yours,

1 This so far unidentified person may be a creation of IB's typist, corrected on the top copy.
2 Abba Hillel Silver (1893–1963), Lithuanian-born Reform rabbi, prominent Zionist, member of the American Emergency Committee for Zionist Affairs (from autumn 1943 its co-chairman, and chairman of its Executive Committee), largely responsible for a surge in its activities as a pressure-group; eloquent orator and prolific writer.
3 See p. 443 below.
4 Freya Madeline Stark (1893–1993), traveller and writer about the Arab world; during the war engaged in political and publicity work for the British government. It had been IB's idea to invite her to the US.
5 For Giraud see 420/2; Pietro Badoglio (1871–1956), Italian soldier and politician, had been appointed Prime Minister after Mussolini's dismissal in July.

TO ANGUS MALCOLM
Foreign Office

9 August 1943 [*carbon*]

British Embassy, Washington

Dear Angus,

You and, perhaps, the Eastern Department[1] may wish to know something of the background of the (apparently) final abandonment of the Joint
Anglo-American Declaration on Palestine, Zionist agitation, etc. Naturally
I do not know anything like all the facts of this dark story, but here is what
William [Hayter] and I have been able to reconstruct more or less reliably. I
tell the story at some length because it is an absolutely clinical case of how
things are done in Washington nowadays.

The history of the initial negotiations you know. Nothing leaked here so
far as we know until about four weeks ago. Dr N. Goldmann of the Jewish
Agency came to see me early in July and said that he had vaguely heard that
something 'disagreeable' (he did not know what) was being planned in
London in connection with the toings and froings of Arab statesmen in the
Middle East. I expressed total (and quite honest) ignorance. He then seems to
have gone to Welles, who has been playing with the Zionists all along and,
according to people in this Embassy, seems to have been out of step with
the rest of the Department on a number of related topics, e.g. refugee
arrangements in Sweden, etc. Welles appears to have told him, or some
other Zionist emissary, that there had been some idea of an official statement
on Palestine but that he, Welles, thought the thing premature and had
managed to stop it. According to Goldman, he promised to keep an eye on
Zionist affairs and stop or, at any rate, warn his friends among them of
anything impending. Welles then went to Bar Harbor[2] for a month's
vacation.

After this nothing happened for a bit, virtually until the date for the Joint
Statement had been fixed. About three days, at the most, before that, there
was another leak,[3] equally vague. This time so far as I could gather it was
probably the Current Affairs Division of the State Department (which would
be responsible for releasing the Declaration here), but this is very uncertain,
which conveyed to a newspaperman or editor in New York that something
on Palestine was due to appear. It seems possible that something was being
done discreetly to prepare the press, in particular in New York, where Jewish

---

1 The FO Dept responsible for 'Afghanistan, Iran, Iraq, Saudi Arabia, Syria and the Lebanon, the
  Yemen, and the foreign relations of Palestine, Transjordan and the minor Arabian States'
  (*Foreign Office List* 1943).
2 Coastal resort in Maine.
3 It was leaked by IB, as he admitted to his biographer at the end of his life: MI 117–18.

influence is strong, to give prominent and sympathetic treatment to the statement. Anyhow the Zionists learned from some newspaperman in New York that a statement by the USG was imminent (nothing was known until much later of HMG's part in it), condemning Zionist agitation here. At once there was an immense flurry: and Wise was sent to see the President, who is said to be partial to him as an old Wilsonian ally. A hasty message was also sent to Welles at Bar Harbor to say that all sorts of sinister things were going on while he was away. Welles did not react at all so far as I know, doubtless anxious not to be embroiled in State Department politics at a period when he was commonly thought, not without justice, to be on particularly sharp terms with Mr Hull and his section of the SD. The President saw Wise almost immediately. No one knows what exactly occurred. Wise told his followers that the President had reassured him completely; nothing was due to be said; he was to go home and set his followers' minds at rest; the whole thing was a baseless rumour. He also told him about his invitation to Ibn Saud,[1] or his son, to visit Washington, which was the first intimation to us that this, later confirmed by SD, was on foot. And he told him about Hoskins's mission[2] too. At first there was much Zionist joy; then, as Stephen Wise is really getting very gaga, and gave confused and very different accounts to various persons of his interview with the President, the Zionists decided to check up, and after extensive consultations with various janissaries, Sam Rosenman, who as you know is close to the President, was persuaded to make a cautious enquiry. His story was apparently very different; the President said that Wise had indeed enquired, and that he, the President, had replied that a statement was coming out, and a very good one too, but perfectly innocuous from the point of view of the Zionists. He then seems to have shown Rosenman the file relating to all this and told him to go and allay anxieties among the Jews. Rosenman kept the Eastern Department of the SD, i.e. Wallace Murray,[3] informed of his activities. Rosenman did as instructed and naturally enough his report of what was coming, instead of allaying, blew the lid off in Zionist circles, and Goldman came rushing to see me to ask if anything could be done to stop the Declaration: with which, by this time, HMG was revealed by Rosenman as being associated. Until they had heard Rosenman on the subject they were really very much in the dark as to what if anything was going on. The real fuss begins with Rosenman's

---

1 Abdul-Aziz Ibn Saud (1880–1953), King of Saudi Arabia 1932–53.
2 Colonel Harold B. Hoskins, textile executive born in Beirut who acted as one of FDR's advisers on the Middle East, had been sent on an abortive mission to establish whether Ibn Saud might be prepared to discuss with Weizmann the future of the Palestinian Arabs.
3 Wallace Smith Murray (1887–1965), diplomat, Chief of the Division of Near Eastern Affairs, SD, 1929–42; Adviser on Political Relations, SD, 1942–3; Director, Office of Near Eastern and African Affairs 1944–5; US Ambassador to Iran 1945–6.

report. Before that there were only dark suspicions, slightly intenser than routine. This must have been the day before the scheduled publication. I took the line that what he told me might well be true; but that if Rosenman's account of the President's attitude was correct, and it probably was, the President had made up his mind and that was that. I could not see what they could do. Certainly agitation would not help them and only serve to irritate the President. Goldman, quite genuinely I think, accepted this, departed in gloom, and went into a huddle with various Washington Jewish officials, e.g. Rosenman, Wagner's[1] Secretary, Ben Cohen, David Niles[2] etc., all of whom, he told me, viewed the prospect with disquiet. The disquiet arose, I think, not from inherent Zionism on the part of such Jewish officials, as much as from a general fear that the Zionists would inevitably issue a shriek, that a public controversy involving Senators, etc., would follow, which would ultimately give the Jews, whether Zionists or not, dangerous publicity as playing politics in a time of crisis. As you will see, this fear proved the dominant factor in the whole situation. Had the statement appeared on the date originally scheduled there probably would still have been a counter-demonstration by the Zionists but it probably would not have achieved much. And although Republicans might have tried to split the Jewish vote on this issue, with much attendant publicity, the immediate purpose – the allaying of Arab fears of an American conspiracy against them, and the strengthening of the hands of Jewish moderates against unbridled agitation here – might perhaps have been achieved, although at some ultimate cost. Both William Hayter and I thought that it was now or never, and that delay would automatically invite intrigue. We were, therefore, somewhat dismayed to learn that the statement had been postponed in order to get the War Department to vet it and if necessary strengthen it. The delay produced tenterhooks, on which the Zionists proceeded to sit, giving every public sign of profound agitation. Terrific lobbying followed. What had happened apparently was that the State Department, or someone in it, had suddenly got cold feet about publishing the statement as a purely political document, which would expose them to violent attack by Jews and liberals, who would accuse them of appeasing the Arabs, etc. You must know that the Darlan flurry[3] has had its effect here in the sense that the State Department are determined not to go through such a nightmare again, however righteous they may feel and however poorly they think of the strength of their

1 Robert Ferdinand Wagner (1877–1953), German-born lawyer and politician, Democratic Senator 1927–49, liberal pro-Zionist New Dealer, particularly committed to improving working conditions.
2 David K. Niles (1892–1952), Presidential Administrative Assistant 1942–51, close associate of Hopkins; liberal and humanitarian, anti-racist, pro-Zionist.
3 See pp. 419–23 above, esp. 420/3.

opponents; their caution over Italian matters is a direct result of having got their fingers burnt earlier this year, and some among them probably feared that the Zionist issue might be used as a minor spearhead for an attack upon them by Willkie, the left-wing Press (Mr Hull is almost neurotically sensitive to criticism in the obscurest journals: if *P.M.*[1] prints anything he apparently talks about 'the entire Press is against me'), etc. They therefore wrote to the War Department saying that what they wanted was a specific and clear request from the Army for a statement of this kind on strict security grounds. As the American G2[2] had been pressing for a damper on Zionist agitation, the soldiers were apparently only too willing to give the green light. I do not know what the revised draft contained, but according to rumour it was much more strongly worded than the first – discussed the possibility of an outbreak by Jewish irresponsibles in Palestine, etc., and implied that agitation here endangered the lives of American soldiers abroad. Tactically this may have been a sound self-protecting move on the part of the State Department, but with surprising innocence they seemed not to have taken into account the usual Washington factors. Two things happened almost immediately: Morgenthau, as you know, ever since about March 1941 when you and I had to cope with his sudden conversion, has been sentimentally if ignorantly pro-Zionist. The Zionists went to him as soon as he returned from his vacation. He told them that he had seen the papers which had been supplied to the White House on this issue, and was 'inexpressibly shocked' by the ferocity of the language (whether of the first or second draft is not clear); he would do his best to stop it; he added that if HMG are anxious about security in Palestine they must ask USG for more troops, and not seek to deprive US citizens of their constitutional liberties of freedom of speech; never before in the history of the United States had any such attempt been made to silence a minority of citizens, etc., etc., etc.

Meanwhile Herbert Bayard Swope,[3] who is somehow connected with War Department public relations, saw the file in a routine fashion. Swope is a Jewish assimilationist and anti-Zionist but seems to have reacted rather like Rosenman. According to his story to Felix Frankfurter (who was away from Washington throughout and telephoned to me from some distant city after the event was over), Swope argued somewhat oddly that if it was indeed true that the Jews in Palestine were straining at the leash and Arab–Jewish riots might break out at any moment, the publication of this document would be

1 Outspoken New York newspaper (1940–8), independent of party allegiance (and initially of advertising), but anti-Fascist and pro-FDR.
2 Military Intelligence (strictly 'G-2').
3 Herbert Bayard Swope (1882–1958), journalist, author, chairman of the New York Racing Commission 1934–45, public relations consultant, close friend of and adviser to Bernard Baruch.

the very thing to set them off. In that case the Jews would inevitably be blamed for the ensuing bloodshed and obstruction of the Allied military effort. The wave of unpopularity would overtake them here and not discriminate between Zionists and non-Zionists. Above all, therefore, things must be kept quiet. He saw Baruch,[1] whose factotum he has been for over a quarter of a century. Baruch agreed that anything said about Jews at the present moment would increase US anti-Semitism, which was anyhow rising fast, and is worrying people like Baruch intensely. Swope then (according to his own story to John Foster) persuaded Under-Secretary of War Patterson,[2] who probably has no views either way, that politically the War Department was 'silly to stick its neck out' quite unnecessarily by accepting responsibility for a dubious move of this kind – the Jews would be very upset, etc., and there would be a political brouhaha of the first order. If the State Department wanted to ask for trouble let them do so without bringing the War Department in.

In the meanwhile Morgenthau seems to have persuaded Stimson[3] of this also, and Baruch had a talk with his old friend, Cordell Hull. (It seems harder and harder to vouch for the absolute accuracy of all this as the story mounts to its climax.) At any rate a pincer movement by Messrs Baruch and Morgenthau (who don't, in fact, get on with each other at all well) had its effect. As you probably know, Hull told HE[4] that he had always had his qualms on the advisability of such a statement (I very much doubt this) and, as Stimson would not do his bit of it, he thought it on the whole wiser not to proceed. And that was that. Welles had been back for some days during this denouement and may or may not have had something to do with it. His vote would certainly be against the statement if the Zionists' account of their conversations with him has the least truth in it. The President, however, seems earlier to have told Rosenman that he really 'could not help it if Wise or Willkie were displeased by the statement: the war had to be won and the statement was a salutary one'. There was one funny moment in the story when Rosenman, whom I had never before met, was sent to see me by Frankfurter. He told me about his own and the Wise–Roosevelt conversation; and asked whether I could not help in keeping down Zionist clamours. I explained that I was of no possible use if only in virtue of my official position, and in any case had no effect on such people, and that Weizmann, with whom alone I could really talk, was gone. Rosenman seemed to me a very

---

1 Bernard Mannes Baruch (1870–1965), financier and Presidential adviser, adviser to the War Mobilization Board 1943–5.
2 Robert Porter Patterson (1891–1952), lawyer, judge, Under-Secretary of War 1940–5, Secretary of War 1945–7.
3 Henry Lewis Stimson (1867–1950), lawyer, Republican, Secretary of War 1940–5.
4 His Excellency the British Ambassador, Lord Halifax.

sensible and level-headed trouble-shooter, largely ignorant of the entire problem and very troubled. His principal purpose is to calm troubled Washington waters for the President. I reported my talk to William H[ayter], who told the Eastern Department of the SD, who said that they knew that Rosenman was functioning in the matter and approved.

One curious touch: On the morning of the day on which HE left, i.e. when the matter was declared finally closed by Mr Hull, Drew Pearson's column gave what purported to be a full account of the entire 'lowdown' on the matter. In spite of a few crude mistakes (BIS survey reaching you on 9 August gives a précis of it)[1] such as the dragging in of Hurley,[2] Berle (note that I refrain from the obvious), a fictional account of Wise's part in this, etc., the story is largely accurate even in detail. While most of it could certainly have been furnished to him by Swope, who is one of his most regular sources, and most of it by the Zionists, there is one point which, so far as I know, the Zionists certainly could not know – I mean Pearson's bit about the fact that the American suggestion about the Joint Statement had originally been coldly received by the FO. This, so far as I know, was known only to British and American officials. Where did Pearson get it from? Nobody here sees him, or so far as we know has talked to any but relevant American officials about any of this. It follows that he must have got it from either State or War Department or White House sources. Perhaps this is the obvious explanation. I myself am inclined to the view that the person who told him is none other than Welles himself. My reason for this is (1) they are great friends, (2) that he must have picked up the story originally from some Jew who must have brought in Welles in some fashion since the Zionists keep in permanent touch with him. Pearson's State Department stories usually represent Welles as leading the forces of the light against the 'dark' figures of Berle, Wallace Murray etc., who are represented as pro-Fascists. This regular pattern was followed except that Welles's name was conspicuously left out. You may think this all too ingenious, but I go on the principles of the 'difficilior lectio', 'lucus a non lucendo',[3] etc., and argue that Welles would have occurred in the story – the Zionists kept on trotting out his name in all their conversations – if someone had not asked Pearson not to mention him. Welles had a very good reason for wishing to be kept out of a gossip column

1 WD 235.
2 Patrick Jay Hurley (1883–1968), FDR's personal representative in various foreign countries 1942–4.
3 'Difficilior lectio potior' ('the more difficult reading is preferable') is a principle of textual criticism according to which scribal error is more likely to turn an unusual word into a familiar one rather than vice versa. The other remark, 'called *lucus* from its not being lucent', is not fully translatable since it depends on a play on the Latin words 'lucus', 'a dark grove', and 'lucere', 'to shine'; it offers a defeatist, paradoxical 'etymology' for a name that appears to suggest the opposite of its bearer's actual nature.

since the stories of his quarrels with Hull, etc., are getting too notorious publicly for his comfort. He may, therefore, piqued at not being consulted, have told Pearson that he was against the statement, so were the British originally, so was everyone except the wicked men in the SD who had prevailed on HMG, etc., or something like that, and asked to be kept out of the story himself. That is my elaborate hypothesis. Perhaps I like it because of an inherent tendency to look on Washington politics as a Sardou melodrama.[1]

The simpler view is that Herbert Swope (or, less probably, somebody in the War Department or the White House) who had access to the file which had been travelling about, read Winant's telegrams, and told the whole tale to Drew Pearson. Swope does tell Pearson everything, and Pearson's story coincided with Stimson's final refusal to help. Everything is possible, but the whole story is an almost clinical case of Washington intrigue, Washington pressure, Washington indiscretion, etc., and generally of the way things are done here. There were similar elements in the abortive lend lease white paper incident.[2] My inclination is to shake my head wisely and say that had the original statement been published, as scheduled, none of this could possibly have happened.

I rather get the impression (from Rosenman at second hand) that the President was a trifle nettled by all this Jewish barrage – after all, what it comes to is the triumph of the Zionist lobby – and that in line with his statement to Rosenman about the war having to be fought on despite Wise, etc., he will, as I gather he told HE, say something about it sooner or later, Morgenthau or no Morgenthau; only make it more conciliatory all round; which would, I firmly believe, do some good.

Meanwhile Rosenman, who is neither Zionist nor really anything in particular, and a very simple sort of man, went to New York to persuade Wise to stop Jewish Army advertisements, etc., in return for suppression of the statement. Wise pointed out, quite justly, that he had no control over the Jewish Army people, but that he would see what could be done. Negotiations to this end are vaguely proceeding.

Zionists steadily deny that they have had anything to do with Pearson's piece, saying that it could not do them any good when things were flowing so nicely in their direction anyhow. I do not know whether to believe this or not, but in any case nothing hangs on it. The Zionists say the Jewish Army

1 Victorien Sardou (1831–1908), French dramatist whose works include a play called *La Tosca*, on which Puccini's opera is based.
2 For Lend-Lease see 367/2. To meet American complaints, the British voluntarily issued a White Paper in September 1941 which laid down that no Lend-Lease supplies were to be used for exports. The only thanks they got was the setting up of an American Committee to see that the promises of the White Paper were kept.

people (their regular scapegoat and alibi), told P. Possibly it is not worth elaborate investigation, any more than his other, often well founded, stories which drive the SD purple with rage. Wise is said to have written a general letter to Mr Hull asking him to do nothing about Palestine etc. without telling him first. Not very surprisingly no answer from Hull as yet. More Zionist consternation.

I do not know what moral should be drawn from all this, except that the Zionist lobby seems strong enough to achieve at any rate short-lived triumphs, and this fact should be taken into consideration. It is a melancholy thing that on the one occasion when the Eastern Department of the SD, which, as you know, has not been too friendly to HMG in the past, had seemed to wish to do something for us, they should have failed so ignominiously. Nor will this make Hoskins's task any easier, but that looks hopeless in any case.

Meanwhile the American Jewish Conference, scheduled for the end of this month, is due, with its 92 per cent Zionist majority. Goldman says he asked Wallace Murray if it was 'all right to hold it' and that the latter said that there was no objection provided that they 'behaved with tact'. I cannot see what amount of tact is going to prevent effects on the Arabs of affirmations about a Jewish Commonwealth, on both sides of the Jordan for all I know. The Arabs, according to Sulzberger's and others' dispatches in the *NY Times*, plan the same in Cairo. So we are in for fun. Much as I sympathise with some of the Zionists' aims, I see nothing but harm in a brouhaha. Apparently Welles told Goldman that he thought the Conference would be a very bad thing, if held when planned. So the Zionists may put it off after all, as they are terribly anxious to please Welles, who is regarded as a staunch ally.

Two further things:

1. One of Cyrus Sulzberger's dispatches to the *NY Times* talked of a forthcoming Allied statement on Palestine's future (20 August, *NYT*) and quoted from a statement by Shertok. This increased Zionist simmering, and caused Wise to protest against Sulzberger's 'alarmist' articles in a letter to the *NYT*.

2. A press release issued on 12 August by Congressman Emmanuel Celler,[1] a New York Jew, crying to high heaven against Mr Roosevelt's projected Statement. Celler, of course, could by that date have got hold of his information from anyone – from Baruch, Morgenthau, to Drew Pearson etc. (or any Zionist). A copy of his release was sent by him to HE. Celler talks of Sulzberger's articles as obvious preliminary barrage to this monstrous offensive on Zion.

---

1 Emanuel (*sic*) Celler (1888–1981), lawyer, Democratic Congressman 1923–73, strong supporter of New Deal and stalwart liberal.

I must apologise for the length of this but it is the only relatively complete story of this type in our possession and may serve as an instructive model to those who wish to know how the foreign policy of the United States is sometimes moulded. You may be sure that the Catholic and every other lobby uses precisely the same methods. I do not know how much of all this is known to Zionists in London – but a cable from Locker[1] of the Jewish Agency seems to have arrived (through the ordinary censorship) some four days ago to the Zionists here saying that he had learned 'from reliable sources' in London that 'a statement' here was expected and asking that Wise be informed. I expect the entire topic will be duly discussed between the great in the near future and that this is a mere bubble in the stream, soon to be forgotten in the flood of great events.

Yours,

TO MARIE AND MENDEL BERLIN

16 August 1943

British Embassy, Washington

Dear Ma and Pa,

I have, as you will doubtless recollect, made a series of promises regarding a letter of exceptional length.[2] I have begun writing but it used to trail off and I would begin again feeling that you deserved a masterpiece. However, as no masterpiece emerged, you shall have this. I hope that length will atone for quality.

What you principally want to know, I assume, is my general mode of life, having heard too much about it from various visitors. Let me begin by saying firmly and truthfully that I never cough at all (I notice a certain undercurrent of anxiety on this score in your letters). Pneumonia is of two types, pneumococcal and virus. The first is subdivided into lobar and some other kind. As to this first kind I cannot tell at all. Perhaps it does lead to coughing for the rest of one's life. Mine, oddly enough, involved no coughing at any stage, even at its height. A certain amount of phlegm and the usual disagreeable spitting, etc., but no cough. I recovered completely somewhere in February. Mr Wint, though doubtless a charming fellow,

---

1 Berl Locker (1887–1982), leading member of the Labour Zionist Party and editor of the Party newspaper; head of the political bureau of the Jewish Agency in London from 1938.

2 In early August Herbert Nicholas had written to IB: 'Your parents remark acidly that you may still be writing but that for their part they would prefer a minor opus which they received to a magnum which was continually in process of composition.' In a letter of 25 August to Nicholas IB reports: 'I have written my parents a letter. This marks a milestone in my life.'

suffers from an abnormal fantasy in any case. I have had no 'relapses' and nothing has been wrong with me since.

You are also worried about the Washington heat. It does hover around eighty degrees, but suitably clad in airy tropical garments it is not really intolerable. ⟨To-day is 65° & wonderful weather. Really marvellous.⟩ The only thing which constitutes a danger is air-conditioning – ice-cold bed-rooms followed by tropical sun. As my bedroom was not and is not in any way air-conditioned, and at most I enjoy the use of a small fan, that pleasure with its attendant dangers is not available. But I do not in general suffer excessively from the heat, much more from cold. Jerusalem in 1934 was hotter than Washington. I tend to be hot in the daytime but I sleep like a log at night – longer when it is hot, I find (and I wear no clothes) than at other times. Consequently I am very well.

I originally intended to go in mid-August to stay on a small farm which my friend and master Aubrey Morgan owns in the remote north-western State of Washington, some 3,000 miles from here, say the distance from London to Vologda.[1] One travels by train in extreme comfort and sees a new world at the end of it, forests, mountains, with an immense industrial future tied up with Pacific trade. It is precisely what I need after the excessive social life of Washington. ⟨Weekly Magazines keep pressing me for biographical detail. I resist, feeling it is not good in the long run. Remember Evening Standard?⟩[2] I thought after a week there I would very slowly make my way down (still by train) through California to New Mexico and Arizona, high, dry, sunlit, lingering for two and three days at a time in comfortable hotels, etc., and then back to Washington. I still intend to carry out this programme, travelling out with the Morgans and back with a Secretary of this Embassy who may be returning from Los Angeles, called John Russell, who is full of gaiety and efficiency. But as neither the Morgans nor he propose to start until September owing to their own arrangements here, I see no point in going off alone (you know how I hate solitude) and propose to wait until September and start on about the 7th and return sometime in early October.

There seems not much chance of returning to England this year, although Nicholas temptingly writes asking why shouldn't I go for a month or so. I shall write to him and say that all I need is a little pressing from the Ministry of Information – I cannot each time make a fuss myself, but at a word from them I should go over with all possible speed and enthusiasm.

My present ambition is to try and get someone to send me to Moscow for a month or two to get 'a global view' of the general situation. Naturally I

1 Russian city some 300 miles north of Moscow.
2 See pp. 405–6 above.

should have to go through London if I did that, but I must try and construct some convincing reasons. I happen to know three or four members of the Embassy in Moscow, starting with Moore Crosthwaite, which would never, I fear, happen again. The Foreign Office and the Ministry of Information ought to seize this opportunity on the wing but I somehow doubt if they will and I am not really optimistic about this scheme but you can see why I am keen. Perhaps next summer would be a better time for that. We shall see. ⟨Be not afraid. I have started nothing yet in this matter.⟩

Now as for my life: I left the Shoreham Hotel despite your excellent advice because I really do not like hotels, particularly large and luxurious ones with crowds of tipsy colonels in the evenings. It was very comfortable and I was well looked after and I made a strict arrangement, not easy in Washington at present, whereby I can return there in October if I choose, which stirs everyone to great envy. The house I moved into is in George-town and belongs to Mrs Anne Fremantle.[1] Let me explain. Georgetown is the most charming possible suburb of Washington, at the tip of which is the British Embassy itself. It is full of small pink houses with white pillars here and there and with quite an immense quantity of spreading trees which drown it in shade during the hottest days. On Sunday mornings church bells toll, negro choirs sing, and negro children play in the streets, as in any Southern city. The whole thing could not be remoter from political Washington and has a strong Oxford flavour, if you know what I mean, which I much prefer to the grandeurs of life in towns. You see why I was tempted. On Sunday evenings the spreading gardens and cosy rhythm of negro life, which is a kind of pedestal on which more elegant white inhabitants have built their homes, gives it a domestic flavour of a small town or even village which is very attractive. Mrs Fremantle is a cousin of Sheila Grant-Duff[2] ⟨who, I hear, has a child!⟩,[3] a well-educated, slightly mad wife of a bad painter who is some peer's son and lives in England. I have known her since my undergraduate days. She annoys most other people by a naive gush of simple emotions. Since all I care about is a certain degree of style, this memory of highbrow life in England is very agreeable. However, I am not staying here as the story will indicate. Her house contains three bedrooms, a large living/dining room, and garden. Normally she, who came as an evacuated mother and works for the Indian Agency General (which is a kind of legation), lives here with her children. Her children have gone away

---

1 Anne(-Marie) Huth Fremantle (1910–2002), née Jackson, writer, broadcaster, editor, translator, lecturer and Georgetown hostess; successively Anglican, Muslim and from 1943 Catholic; research assistant in Indian section, British Embassy, Washington, 1942–5; married to Christopher Evelyn Fremantle, son of 3rd Baron Cottesloe.
2 Anne Fremantle's mother was the sister of Shiela Grant Duff's father.
3 Penelope Newsome, economist.

somewhere for the summer and she has relegated herself to the basement, where she lives in sordid conditions, not unlike an air-raid shelter. However, being physically very tough, she says she does not mind. The upper portions are occupied by me and until recently my friend Ed Prichard. A negress with the strange name of Kehola looked after us and still looks after me. The result: I get breakfast in bed, which at the Shoreham was impossible under wartime conditions. What that means to me you well know. Prichard is a protégé of Felix, an immensely fat man weighing something like 300 pounds, full of the most brilliant life and wit. He used to work in one of the Washington Government offices but now, in spite of his almost monstrous proportions, has been called up by the Army and is no more. He is a very intelligent, amusing and agreeable man with whom I got on exceptionally well. Having been compelled to live in this country I decided to throw in my lot with as expressive and interesting a native of it as I could find. However he is gone now and that is that. Mrs Fremantle and he got on exceptionally badly. She is a Bohemian character, and a very silly one at that (although she runs her house quite efficiently), and that he could not bear. Also, she kept on dropping in for a chat, which I, having known her for eleven years, did not mind and in fact quite liked, but Prichard, who is not given to hiding his feelings, every time she appeared at the door, with a slight idiot-like smile on her face, murmuring 'May I come in?', would sigh loudly, groan, cover his face with his hands, and display every possible sign of disgust and hostility. All very difficult. Ask Dr Bowra about her. I am sure he dislikes her equally acutely. I have never minded simple geese, which is what she is. However, so critical did the Prichard–Fremantle relations become that I was forced to consider some other arrangement and eventually found another house where we could live in privacy. It is absolutely exquisite. Similarly in George-town, it lies high on a hill, which makes it cool in summer. It is small (two bedrooms, one dressing room, interconnecting dining room and parlour, kitchen, cellar), centrally heated, overlooking the River Potomac on one side and the gardens of Georgetown on the other. Houses in Washington are almost impossible to find and small houses are out of the question. It is, therefore, particularly fortunate that it should suddenly have become vacant through the death of an unfortunate official who used to inhabit it.[1] The next problem is that of a maid. Through the kind offices of a nice Government

---

1 In a letter of 16 August IB was more explicit to Herbert Nicholas: 'I am about to move into a house where the stains of murder are still fresh upon the floor (literally).' According to Mrs Fremantle IB had solved the notoriously difficult problem of finding accommodation in Washington 'by arriving at the same time as the police after a secretary in the British Embassy had been murdered by her lover. He used to put fresh red ink where the blood had been on the floor when he gave dinner parties.' Anne Fremantle, *Three-Cornered Heart* (London, 1971), 294.

worker called, of all things, Mrs Franzblau, we have secured a very competent negress from South Carolina, the wife of a local cobbler and a Seventh-day Adventist (Mrs Frankfurter says the religious ones are the best). This means that she works on Sundays and not on Saturdays. Splendid. Sunday is when one is in and needs attention. She is an excellent cook and will be in the house all day, a reliable forty-year-old solid figure who has a remarkable ability for washing linen and frying chicken. I propose to share the house with my old friend Guy Chilver, whom you know, having decided to abandon the search for Americans, and on the grounds that old friends are best. The Frankfurters, who watch over my fortunes, have indicated their strong approval, having disapproved of the Fremantle arrangement on the ground that one cannot safely live in a house with a red-haired bluestocking. I propose to move on 1 September. A little more furniture – a rug and a bookshelf – may have to be bought. I know my immediate neighbours too; one of them is the daughter of one of the most eminent judges in this country and a great friend of the Frankfurters. So all is working out extremely well. I can always go back to the Shoreham. Really I prefer domestic life. You will begin thinking of matrimony. Let me assure you such a prospect is out of the question here to anyone with the least degree of sensibility. I leave it at that.

What more can I tell you? My days are very regular and so is my work. Life is much more like Oxford, duller and quieter than in New York. The fun of the ghetto is gone. The British colony hems me in. There is not much good music or good conversation, but everything flows very gently and peacefully and it is all very good for one's health and one's nerves.

You need not be afraid that any of Ida's relations pester me. They are all in New York and I am never there now, so that opportunities of contact do not arise.

I am glad you think all that of Charles. He is a noble and tragic figure whereas his wife is merely tragic – Mother's analysis of her is absolutely correct.

The quick pattern of social life has slowed down and there is nothing to replace it. The only interesting person I have met lately is a gifted composer called Nicolas Nabokov,[1] nephew of the late Cadet,[2] who teaches music in a nearby school. He is a person of great vitality and charm, neither White nor Red but a member of the old intelligentsia whom Rach would enjoy meeting very much. I talk to him about music, Russia, books, persons, in fact all the subjects that I like talking about best.

I intend to write letters to David and Mary almost immediately and tell

1 Nicolas Nabokov (1903–78), composer, writer, impresario; cousin (*pace* IB) of writer Vladimir Nabokov (a member of the Constitutional Democratic Party); later secretary-general of the Congress for Cultural Freedom.
2 See 431/4.

them what they know already, that it is almost impossible to write from here as nothing happens. One's life has no background. As I told you when I came back it all seemed to vanish like a dream when one touched Europe again. But I will write. Tell Mary and David (separately) that I spent a long evening with Rosamond Coleridge, née Fisher, who talked with great enjoyment about the early '30s. ⟨⟨She didn't seem to like Mary much: but disliked Mrs Fisher more. Acid girl.⟩

I have no thoughts of the slightest interest on any topic and enjoy my work very much. My relations with my colleagues are immensely harmonious and I really have nothing to complain of. Who would have thought that from teaching philosophy at Oxford with otherwise a passion only for music, I should become avidly interested in American politics and a sort of chroniqueur of the most day-to-day type? It must be because American political life is very personal in quality. Institutions play a far smaller part than individuals, and relations between individuals, the pattern of which is so strongly laid in Oxford itself, has, of course, always fascinated a gossip-loving character like me. The President really is very queer – not at all what you think he is. I have reached the conclusion that despite the gay and generous nature and all the manners and sweep of an old-established landowning squire, he is (a) absolutely cold, (b) completely ruthless, (c) has no friends, (d) becoming a megalomaniac and is pulling our Mr Churchill along rather than vice versa. This may work out quite well so far as the world in general is concerned, since his intentions are humane and decent, but the idea that one can trust him or look on him as a sort of Gladstone[1] is completely false. He does not like the rich, it is true, but neither does he like the poor or really anyone. Better so perhaps but it is not the usual picture of him. His wife[2] is the opposite in every respect, a sentimental, gushing, heavy liberal, with a great deal of native shrewdness which the very ugly often develop.

What more can I tell you? The Aronsons have left Maine and gone to North Carolina, where there appears to be some timber to cut. They have kindly written to me and asked me to stay in their village. I have not answered but may during my homeward journey from the West Coast stop a night and have a look at them. I am sure rural life will be infinitely more suitable to them than New York.

1 William Ewart Gladstone (1809–98), Liberal Prime Minister on four occasions between 1868 and 1894; opposed oppression by Turkey in the Balkans and Armenia, and by the land-owning class in Ireland; as a private citizen tried to rescue prostitutes from their life on the streets.
2 (Anna) Eleanor Roosevelt (1884–1962), niece of former President Theodore Roosevelt, thus a distant cousin of her husband FDR; newspaper columnist and campaigner for humanitarian causes; FDR's personal envoy to London October–November 1942; delegate to the first UN assembly 1946; later (1947–51) Chairman of UN Human Rights Commission.

I propose also to go to Harvard to have a look at the philosophers there. After all it would be silly to be in America and have no intercourse with one's own colleagues in one's own field.

Your old friend from Wilno, or was it Warsaw – David something, the small thin man who knew Mother thirty years ago[1] – has, I regret to say, died. Which reminds me that I must write to Barbara Halpern. It is so difficult to know what to say, but write I must.

If you see Walter E[ttinghausen][2] tell him that his friend King[3] shared a house with me for a few weeks, is very nice, and wants to be remembered to him.

As for Walter Bell[4] whom Lionel [Curtis] has met, he is a nice man, a little boring, with whom I did think of setting up a house and am on the whole glad I did not as, although he is very nice and attached to me, he would, I think, have bored me to extinction in the long run.

John Foster is to return to England for four months in September. A very good idea, I think, as it will enable him to decide where he prefers to remain. The need of him here is very great and if he shows the slightest signs of being ready to return he will be called back with the greatest possible enthusiasm by everyone in this Embassy from the Ambassador downwards. His personal services to the Ambassador have been exceptionally high and the Ambassador needed them, God knows, and would probably have been lost without him. There is no doubt that if anyone has deserved well of his country abroad it is John – the fact that he enjoyed his activity only made it more effective, him more popular, and England better liked in this city, where he penetrated into Anglophobe circles normally closed against any Englishman. He will come to see you, I expect.

John Wheeler-Bennett has returned, speaks with great affection of both of you. So does Donald Hall. They are both men of sweetest character, and both, happily for them, return to England, John for an interval, Hall possibly permanently. Alas, I may be more elegantly dressed, but no femme fatale is responsible.[5] My desire to return is very acute and I shall say so to Cruikshank in my next letter, not that it will make much effect – no Ministry likes change – and as Bracken[6] has just sent me his regards I assume that it is

1 See p. 389 above.
2 Then working in the code-breaking operation at Bletchley Park.
3 Possibly Alexander King (b. 1909), Head of UK Scientific Mission, Washington, and Scientific Attaché, British Embassy, 1943–7.
4 Walter Fancourt Bell (b. 1909), British diplomat; Acting Vice-Consul, NY, 1935–40 and 1941–2; FO, London, 1942–5.
5 Somewhat disingenuous. IB was suffering from unrequited love for the femme fatale Patricia de Bendern (see MI 111–12).
6 Brendan Bracken (1901–58), later (1952) 1st Viscount Bracken; Conservative politician and

thought well to keep me where I am.

One of my fastest friendships is with the man who gave me pneumonia, a Naval Commander called Matthews with whom I shared, fatally as it turned out, a bedroom in Ireland, a very nice man and with a permanent sense of debt to me now, anxious to please me on every occasion.

I really do not know what to say about Father and his business after the war. It seems to me that, as before, Russia and Canada will remain the great timber-exporting centres, and that his Russian connection is the one to keep alive. Could he not contrive to be sent out to Russia as an expert as soon as traffic between Britain and Russia becomes easier? Is there nobody in London among the Russian representatives with whom he can chat on that subject? But perhaps it is too early to think about all that.

Did Barber[1] tell you about his lunch with me?

Really I have no more to say at present. I am perfectly contented, well, well looked after, and have arranged my life in a surprisingly tidy and efficient manner.

Two practical things. You have not, have you, sent me Mr Bowra's book[2] or ordered the *New Statesman* (through our British Embassy)? As for writing me letters, why do you not try to send me sealed letters addressed to me as 'Isaiah Berlin Esq., First Secretary, British Embassy, Washington, DC', and on the outer envelope 'Communications Department, Foreign Office', with, in the first letter, a short note saying that you trust this is the correct Department to which to send letters addressed to me in the United States. I think they will take four or five days if you do that. You can, of course, always send them through Nicholas as often as you like. I do not think he will mind. The censor's intrusive eye really does cramp one's style and letters become mere sticks instead of talking, and from a low voice. I propose to send all my letters to you by this method anyway.

I have not seen the Raskins or anyone else of that sort for a very long time. It is exactly like not living in London and living at Oxford.

Love,

Shaya

⟨This is a terribly boring letter! perhaps mother with her really sharp eye will realize that it springs from a terribly peaceful, uneventful, productive & quiet life.⟩

businessman, Churchill's close friend and ally and his Parliamentary Private Secretary 1940–1; Minister of Information 1941–5; First Lord of the Admiralty 1945.

1 Eric Arthur Barber (1888–1965), Fellow, Tutor and Lecturer in Classics, Exeter, 1913–43, Rector 1943–56.

2 432/2.

21 Shaving in a glass held by Lady Prudence Pelham at her home
(Mill House, Falmer, Sussex), *c*.1936

22 Rachel Walker painted in
1937 by her mother's sister
Winifred Macnabb

23 Sigle Lynd

24 Maire Lynd

25 Diana Hubback

26 Shiela Grant Duff

27 Cressida Ridley, née Bonham Carter

28 Jasper Ridley

29 On the island in
Lough Annilaun, 1938:
IB, Christopher Cox, Maire Lynd

30 New Buildings and Chapel, New College, with the huts built after the war to
accommodate returning undergraduates

31 The Rockefeller Center, New York

32 Postcard of the Rockefeller Center on which IB has attempted to mark the 44th floor, but he is a whole section of the building too high; on the reverse he writes to his father (6 March 1941), 'On the other side my window is marked. The view is really breathtaking.'

33 Renée Ayer dispatch-riding in London in the war

34 Lady Daphne Straight

35 Lady Patricia de Bendern

36 The British Embassy, Washington

37 'The Sleeping Beauty': in a sleeping car between California and Washington, 1943

38 The rear of the British Embassy, Moscow, from the Moskva river

39 Fontanny Dom (No 34, Fontanka
Canal), Leningrad; from 1926 to 1952
Akhmatova lived in flat 44, on the top
floor of three in the south wing overlook-
ing the garden, where the main
Akhmatova Museum is now housed

40 Anna Akhmatova: photograph given
by AA to IB when he called to take his
leave, January 1946; on the back she has
written 'A. 2 янв. 1946' (январь, 'yanvar''
= January)

TO URSULA NIEBUHR

16 August 1943 [*carbon*]

[British Embassy, Washington]

Dear Ursula,

It is appalling of me not to have answered your letter of 3 June at all – but I can hardly describe to you the conditions in which I have been living during the last eight weeks, the heat, the discomfort, the peculiar domestic conditions, the amount of irrelevant work, the total exhaustion which boredom and the climate induces – finally the fact that I have not moved from Washington during the last three months and see no prospect of doing so until September.

I read all Reinhold [Niebuhr]'s articles with the greatest pleasure. I assume all your news of England will be much fresher now than any of mine; I have had nothing to do with Beveridge[1] and have really sunk in my files, a form of melancholy escapism whose value can be underestimated. I have talked to no labour leaders nor intellectuals, nobody but officials now for so long that I am beginning to acquire that frosted glass view of events – dim contours each very much like the other – which I realise is the typical official's normal panorama and not a cynical defeatist vision at all.

You, I suppose, are never in Washington? Nor Reinhold except for very special occasions? I attempted to telephone to you about three weeks ago but was told that you were out of New York and then finally gave up. It is just possible that I may be in that city next Saturday or Monday in which case I shall certainly at any rate telephone. Do please forgive me for this gigantic gap.

Yours sincerely,
Isaiah Berlin

---

1 William Henry Beveridge (1879–1963), 1st Baron Beveridge of Tuggal 1946, civil servant, director of the LSE 1919–37. His lifelong passion for solving the problems of poverty and unemployment led him to use a routine committee responsible for the social security system to set out a blueprint for the Welfare State (the Beveridge Report on Social Insurance and Allied Services, issued November 1942). Beveridge and his new bride (his former secretary, the widow of a cousin) spent May–August 1943 in the US on a trip organised by BIS NY to publicise the report.

TO MEYER SCHAPIRO

16 August 1943 [*carbon*]

[British Embassy, Washington]

Dear Meyer,

My absence from New York has continued on and on and I have not been there since May or possibly April for more than a few hours at a time, and since June not at all. I shall probably be there in September, however, when I shall try to get in touch with you. I should like to see you very much indeed after this monstrous interval, during which I have sunk into the most shameful bureaucratic routine, with a passion, born of indolence, for files and telephones as a barrier against what is called experience in any form to which I have always been prone and to which I am now paid to succumb.

As for Freddie, he reached England after, I gather, a shipwreck (this is not certain). He was apparently very happy in London at first and wished to lead a gay existence, according to Roy Harrod, the Oxford economist, who reported that above all Freddie wished to live in London and go to night clubs every evening. Owing to, I imagine, some intrigue he was whisked off almost immediately to the Gold Coast or somewhere else in West Africa.[1] While there is a certain poetic injustice about the riddance of all[2] Mrs A's husbands to the West Coast of Africa (Hampshire did time in Sierra Leone) I am really very sorry for Freddie since it must be hateful in every way. I imagine strings are being pulled to get him back to London.

I have not managed to secure a copy of Dr Bowra's book although, maddening thought, Felix Frankfurter has. I shall try and extract this from him and then send it to you. Can it not be ordered here through the usual channels?

I hope your son has not forgotten the excitable conductor – that is how I am sure I should like to be remembered. Please give my love to Lillian.

You never come to Washington I suppose?

    Yours sincerely,

    Isaiah Berlin

IB's closest assistant at that time, Archie Mackenzie,[3] *later recorded the impression IB made on the Washington social scene:*

1 Ayer's SOE posting to Accra in the Gold Coast (now Ghana) lasted 9 days, after which he was interned on disciplinary recall because he complained that the job was not worth doing.
2 i.e. both.
3 Archibald Robert Kerr Mackenzie (b. 1915), diplomat, working with IB in the Washington Embassy 1943–5.

He broke every rule of social etiquette – regularly forgetting appointments or addresses – and yet he remained one of the top catches of all Washington hostesses. He was a brilliant conversationalist and raconteur; witty but rarely acerbic; sceptical but not cynical; mischievous yet not malicious; exasperating yet disarming and possessed of an immense bonhomie.[1]

The following letter illustrates the hazards of inviting IB to dinner.

TO MARIA FRIAS
Brazilian Embassy

26 August 1943 [*carbon*]

British Embassy, Washington

I fear that you will never wish to speak to me again or think of me without acute distaste, but I assure you that only a peculiar kind of force majeure prevented me from dining with you last night. So humiliating is this experience I can scarcely bring myself to describe it to you. Believe me, at 7.45 p.m. on Wednesday 25 August, I set out solemnly and with the keenest expectation of much pleasure to come, hailed me a taxi and asked to be taken to 1239 35th Street, which, I discovered only too soon, not only could not have been the address which you gave me but did not, in fact, exist at all.[2] It was at this point that I made my first fatal blunder in allowing the cab in which I had arrived to go away, leaving me on the picturesque but blasted wilderness of 35th Street as it overhangs the Potomac rolling slowly below. I thought feverishly and telephoned the Brazilian Embassy. No reply. The Brazilian Ambassador's house. No reply. Information, and gave your name. No trace of your existence could be found. I then telephoned in the following order: Guitou Knoop.[3] No answer. Mr Rastko Petrovich.[4] He was in but could only remember that you lived somewhere in O Street and was unable to remember the precise address (this occurred at about 8.20 p.m. and is my only solid alibi) and referred me to Ala Kent. I telephoned her. No answer. I telephoned three or four other people who either did not know or did not reply. By this time it was 8.35 and the heat in the telephone booth was indescribable. Finally I telephoned John Russell, who thought that he might find it in a car in daylight but had no notion of the address, and referred me to a Brazilian diplomat whose name I cannot now remember, but of whom, in any case, there was no record in the telephone book or anywhere else.

1 Archie Mackenzie, *Faith in Diplomacy* (Caux/London, 2002), 32.
2 The correct address was 1239 31st Street.
3 Guitou Knoop (b. 1912), French sculptor.
4 Rastko Petrovich (d. 1949), Serbian poet.

Black despair seized on me. Never, I said to myself, did anyone fail to appear at a dinner to which he had been invited for so foolish and humiliating a reason. However, there was nothing to be done, so I spent the evening quietly weeping to John Russell to whom I went for comfort.

I really cannot say how very sorry I am for all this nonsense. I suppose I must have put your address down wrong in my diary, but I still do not realize the gravity of my error since I still do not know where you live. The only person I might have thought of and did not was my naval neighbour, Ed Mathews.[1] But I am sure that he, like everyone else, was out at the impossible hour of 8.30. Dear me, I cannot say what feelings I have endured. Please believe me, forgive me, and give me a telephone call at the Embassy – an act which I cannot bring myself to perform without the most acute torment. There now, if I have conveyed a tithe of my sorrow and my sense of guilt, you will not be too hard on me.

Yours,

TO MRS A. COHN[2]

31 August 1943 [*carbon*]

[British Embassy, Washington, DC]

Dear Mrs Cohn,

I ought to have written long ago to say how much I enjoyed myself. It is difficult to convey what 'an occupied territory' Washington is, how tight, taut, and close everything is, how everyone supervises everyone else and there is no air or light anywhere. New York is the beginning of 'unoccupied territory', and the freedom in your house, remote as it seems now, had a truly liberating effect for at least one of your visitors. The contrast between the illumination and open spaces around Washington and the cramped darkness within is really arresting. I am sure that international relations would improve immediately if they were transacted somewhere in the Dakotas. I really am most grateful for the light and sustenance offered to me.

I enclose what I so remissly forgot in the hope that it is not too inadequate. And I do hope that when Dr Cohn or yourself, or both of you, come to Washington next you will not omit to invite yourself to the little white house which I have acquired, but can only inhabit after I find a habitat for my coloured maid – an infinitely more difficult task than acquiring anything for myself but – with powerful efforts on the part of all concerned, with tentacles reaching to Connecticut and Cincinnati, an edifice should be

---

1 Presumably the Commander Mat(t)hews who gave him pneumonia (see p. 458 above).
2 Wife of Alfred E. Cohn (345/3).

ready by early September. International politics and even philosophy make infinitely smaller demands on one's resources.

I hope you are all as well and as peaceful as when I saw you. I think back on that wistfully.

Yours

PS Could you communicate to the Justice[1] that the Rt Hon Joseph Chamberlain, by his first marriage, had a daughter called Beatrice Mary, and by his second wife had daughters with no less strikingly original names, Florence Ida, Caroline Hilda, and, triumph of imagination, Ethel? I cannot recollect if this solves the problem or, on the contrary, aggravates it. Mr Elman,[2] alas, is away *sine die*.

IB

TO LADY DAPHNE STRAIGHT

4 September 1943 [*carbon*]

British Embassy, Washington

Dear Daphne,

A few hurried lines on M. Gromyko:[3] He is a very gentle, dim creature who went through some sort of courses in economics (and possibly engineering) in the USSR and was Head of the Economic Section of either the Academy of Sciences or the Red Institute of Professors,[4] but was obviously that as a politically reliable rather than economically brilliant figure. He is regarded by the State Department as an honest man with whom they had good relations when he was head of the American Section of the Narkomindel.[5] He is very silent and buttoned up and serious. When I met him about a year ago I thought he was one of the typical 'new men', earnest, dull, devoted, enormously inhibited, quite able, an excellent type of functionary with little initiative, rather timid, and not really political in any significant sense. He is not ambassadorial timber at all but, on the other

---

1 Felix Frankfurter was a great friend of the Cohns.

2 Perhaps Philip Elman (b. 1918), who had been Frankfurter's law clerk 1941–3, was at the time in the SD, and went on to be assistant to the Solicitor General 1944–61.

3 Andrey Andreevich Gromyko (1909–89), head of the US division of the People's Commissariat of Foreign Affairs 1939, on the staff of the Soviet Embassy in Washington 1939–43; Soviet Ambassador to the US and Cuba 1943–6 (his predecessor, Maksim Litvinov, had been recalled because his independence of thought was unacceptable to Stalin); later Ambassador to the UK (1952–3) and Foreign Minister (1957–85); he dealt with nine US Presidents during his career.

4 Gromyko had studied agricultural economics in Minsk; he worked in Moscow 1936–9 as senior research associate at the Institute of Economics of the Academy of Sciences, and as a lecturer in political economy at the Moscow Institute of Civil Engineering.

5 The People's Commissariat of Foreign Affairs, renamed the Ministry of Foreign Affairs in 1946.

hand, has no Ogpu[1] past like Oumansky and your new incumbent M. Gusev,[2] and is really more like a sober, decent schoolmaster, say a teacher of mathematics and geometrical drawing in a provincial Russian school, than anything else. He is married to a plump and dowdy wife,[3] lives very quietly, is respected by his foreign colleagues and allows a good deal to be done by his more showy assistants Bazykin and Fedotov, the last of whom is a very sparkling character. I cannot remember the name of the Ogpu man in the Embassy but he really holds the strings.

Yours,

Isaiah Berlin

TO PAUL GORE-BOOTH

4 September 1943 [*carbon*]

[British Embassy, Washington]

Aviation (civil); Post War
Reference – *IB:GF 522/165/43*
SECRET

Mr *Gore-Booth:*

I should say about Berle that he is a very clever man with a very tortuous mind, whose early academic success went to his head for good and all. He is a queer combination with a typical German passion (he is only half German in fact – through his father) for the most ingenious modern methods of doing things – has, e.g., considerable admiration for Schacht[4] and unorthodox economics, believes in New Deal unbalanced budgeting, etc., and is, therefore, the *bête noire* of the painfully orthodox Pasvolsky.[5] At the same time he hates capitalism, imperialism, liberalism, and the entire heritage of the nineteenth century, and has a nostalgia for pre-industrial civilisation and

---

1 312/3.

2 Fedor Tarasovich Gusev (*c*.1905–87), Soviet Ambassador in London 1943–6.

3 Lidiya Dmitrievna, née Grinevich (b. *c*.1913). Like Gromyko, she was from a peasant family near Minsk: the couple had met as students. Years later Gromyko wrote of their courtship: 'I just couldn't get her out of my mind . . . I was conquered by her beauty, her modesty and other magical qualities harder to name.' Andrei Gromyko, *Memories*, trans. Harold Shukman (London, 1989), 17.

4 Hjalmar Horace Greeley Schacht (1877–1970), German banker, President of the Reichsbank 1923–30 and intermittently until 1939, Minister of Economics 1934–7; suspected by the Nazis of complicity in plots against Hitler; tried at Nüremberg but acquitted.

5 Leo Pasvolsky (1893–1953), Russian-born economist, Special Assistant to the Secretary of State 1936–8, 1939–46 (Hull's speechwriter), Chief of the Division of Special Research, SD, 1941–2, adviser at the Dumbarton Oaks and Bretton Woods conferences.

the Middle Ages to which his wife[1] is also devoted, with the result that he has a horror of cartels and corporations. A pupil of Brandeis, he hates all forms of 'bigness' in private hands, and inclines towards a sort of R. Catholic ideal of small owners under general State control (which in his case replaces the Church). The British Empire used to be for him the symbol of all he hated – industrialism, imperialist exploitation, nineteenth-century liberalism, an obstacle to a united Christian Europe, etc., and in 1940–1 he believed that it was disintegrating and a good thing too, and wished to speed it on its way. He now believes that it will probably survive and remain quite strong and, being a complete opportunist, wishes to get on terms with it and has, therefore, been unusually civil to its representatives. He is, so far as is known, prepared to co-operate with us on quite sensible lines provided that we curb our imperialist greed and offer him support against the excessive demands by American big business which hates Berle and is hated by him in return. He is very vain, likes elaborately constructed intellectual patterns, which he weaves ingeniously, and falls easily for the flattery of foreigners for whose intellect he has respect. He likes to think of himself as half dreamer, half *éminence grise*, a Holstein[2] due one day to become a sort of modern Talleyrand,[3] fighting, however, always for the highest good but inevitably misunderstood and attacked by the ignorant, e.g., over the North African policy for which he proudly claims full and sole responsibility. He is in fact a megalomaniac, who has to be humoured.

Isaiah Berlin

TO W. J. LEANING[4]
BIS, San Francisco

22 September 1943 [*carbon*]

British Embassy, Washington

Dear Leaning,

I am about to carry out my threat to you over the telephone a Sunday or two ago and propose to descend on San Francisco in the middle of next month. My schedule is to leave New York on 26 September, arrive in Chicago on the 27th, leave Chicago on the 28th, and arrive in Portland,

---

1 Adolf Berle's wife Dr Beatrice Bishop Berle (1902–93), daughter of Cortlandt Field Bishop, was a psychiatric social worker.

2 Friedrich von Holstein (1837–1909), German diplomat, political counsellor in the German foreign office 1878–1906, especially influential after the fall of Bismarck in 1890.

3 Charles Maurice de Talleyrand-Périgord (1754–1838), French politician and diplomat famous for his ability to survive political upheavals.

4 W. John Leaning, previously serving under Graham Hutton in BIS Chicago, had been promoted to run the BIS office in San Francisco when it opened in March 1942.

Oregon, on the 30th. There I shall stay with Aubrey Morgan until 12 October and arrive in your City on the 13th (I shall let you know, if I may, the precise hour as soon as I know myself) by train. Could you be so kind as to book me a single bedroom for two nights, i.e. 13 and 14 October, at some respectable establishment not too far from anywhere.

I plan to leave San Francisco on 15 October and have no particular engagements while there save that I should like to pay you a visit and have an extensive talk at last. I am not anxious to meet a string of key individuals so do not, please, take any very special trouble, but if there is anyone whom, in your opinion, it would be profitable to talk to I should fall in easily with any arrangement you may make. But I would really be perfectly content to look at the Bay and behave like a wide-eyed tourist and not go about cross-examining people about Anglo-American relations or anything else. And I am really terrified of parties of more than four or five, so pray treat me as a casual transient. Put yourself to no trouble. If you could keep yourself free for dinner on one of my few nights I should welcome it.

I shall let you know again about the precise hour of my contemplated arrival.

Yours,

Isaiah Berlin

TO MARIE AND MENDEL BERLIN

26 September 1943 [*manuscript*]

The St Regis, New York

My dear parents

I am just about to set off to the Far West: The Morgans have a farm there to which they invited me, it sounds excellent. I am in the best possible health & the trip in American drawing rooms[1] & pullmans is v. comfortable. I arrive there, via Chicago on the 30th Sept, to stay till 12th Oct., then to San Francisco & Los Angeles (in Hollywood 1 day – I call on Harpo Marx[2] but don't tell it in Oxford, it sounds too frivolous for wartime) & then slowly via Arizona & Texas to New Orleans & so back to Washington (Nov. 2). If I don't see America now I never will, & I combine business with pleasure. You will have news of me from (a) Miss McGeachy who is devoted to Ma (b) The Donald Halls (he has become Private Sec. to Richard Law)

---

1 A drawing room, a feature of the latest generation of Pullman trains, was the largest compartment, providing sleeping accommodation for three.

2 (Adolph) Arthur ('Harpo') Marx (1888–1964), second oldest of the anarchic Marx brothers team of stage and film comedians; his trademarks in their films were that he played the harp, chased blondes, created general mayhem, and never spoke.

(c) John Foster who goes back for, we all hope, not more than 4 months. So you will hear enough. The Halls are a v. sweet couple & infinitely kind to me & really fond of me I think. But don't talk about me the *whole* time. My new house is charming. The negress *most* efficient & an excellent cook. I described it, I think. Small, white, on the slope of a hill (Hall has seen it) & Mr Chilver a *very* soothing & efficient wife. I have just acquired some gay cheap chintzes (which one resells to some other diplomat before leaving) for it & look forward immensely to life there. No letters from you for some time. Sanctions?

I shall write again from the West Coast. Nothing to say. Life flows v. evenly. I have not had even the slightest little cold since about March (touch wood). The negress washes, irons, cleans, presses & fries wonderful chicken. The street looks like something in Amalfi. My relations with colleagues continue excellent (I return from Los A. with a colleague called John Russell, whose efficiency guarantees our travel arrangements) I saw Richard Law for 2 hours, & shook hands with the P.M.[1] who said (not knowing in the least who he was talking to) – "interesting work – carry on – continue – go on." on the general principle of giving encouragement to anything which is happening – cheering on the forces of life. He was wearing his 'siren suit', looked like a sweet old man out of Dickens – & I was v. pleased even with this momentary contact with a genius (he quite clearly is that the moment you meet him). The Felixes are well. She thinner & whiter than ever, he gay as a cricket chirping along, talking sense & nonsense, but with brio & spirit & optimism. I am really looking forward to my journey enormously and shall certainly attempt some sort of Reisebriefe[2] on the way, but I doubt if time & leisure enough will occur really to let me fill myself with impressions first, + an hour or two to write them all down. As you know I loathe the very idea of diaries. Please give my love to David & Mary. Fred R. wants me to help to repatriate Katie[3] + his wife & children. I see little hope. Evacuated mothers are standing in a queue for ships 1½ years long.

love

Shaya

I am sorry to break off like this – train waiting – you know how late I am for

1 Churchill had been in Washington for the first ten days of September, after talks in Quebec with FDR and the Canadian Prime Minister, Mackenzie King. The visit, which included a successful speech at Harvard, where Churchill was awarded an honorary degree, was well-received. IB (who had this encounter with Churchill when he was asked to deliver a cable to him in person at the White House: MI 125), had written in his dispatch of 12 September: 'Mr Churchill's presence here, his talk to press and Harvard speech, together with flood of excellent war news, induced uncommon exhilaration in Washington' (WD 244).

2 'Travel letters'.

3 Fred Rau's mother (331/4).

everything – etc. לשנה טובה[1] Yom Kippur in Portland, Oregon – I wonder what the ק״ק[2] Portland will turn out to look like.

IB.

IB was away from Washington, DC, from 26 September to 2 November on a trip that combined relaxation on Aubrey Morgan's farm in the north-western State of Washington with a journey of exploration through some of the western and southern States.

TO BLANCHE KNOPF[3]

22 November 1943 [*carbon*]

British Embassy, Washington

Dear Mrs Knopf,

Thank you for your letter of 15 November.[4] I fear I do not at all know what book Mr Gollancz can have been referring to, as I am most reluctant to set pen to paper on any subject, having done so once already[5] without much satisfaction to myself or, for that matter, to others.

I shall probably be in New York next Monday, 29 November, and shall be reachable via the British Information Services (Circle 6-5100). I shall be delighted to meet you if my uselessness as a possible author is not a fatal bar.

Yours sincerely,

Isaiah Berlin

TO MARIE AND MENDEL BERLIN

7 December 1943 [*manuscript*]

The St Regis, New York

My dear Ma & Pa,

You complain of absence of letters. One of the reasons is that I now change secretaries once in 3–4 months, & so do not get on sufficiently easy

---

1 'Leshanah tova' ('Happy New Year').
2 Abbreviation of 'k[ehila] k[edosha]' ('holy congregation', i.e the Jewish community or the synagogue in Portland).
3 Blanche Wolf Knopf (1894–1966), President of her husband's publishing company, Alfred A. Knopf, Inc., and responsible for discovering, encouraging and publishing many authors previously unknown in America.
4 In which she writes, 'I am just back from England where Victor Gollancz told me about you regarding the possibility of your writing a book', and suggests a meeting in New York.
5 He is referring to *Karl Marx*.

terms to dictate private as well as public letters. And after a day spent in dictation of reports & official letters it is v. hard to sit down & write a genuine letter even to you. This is being written in a train from N.Y. to Wash (I *never* use planes now. I hate them anyway & priorities are wanted which I am too lazy to work for) as we roll past Philadelphia. My house has worked out idyllically. You know how in a sea of foreign things one likes to anchor oneself to something stable, familiar and solid. Miss Grant Duff (now Mrs something)[1] writes to say 'was it really necessary to go so far away to end up so near?' i.e. Mrs Fremantle (the religious mystic) or Chilver. The answer is 'yes'. The further the more necessary to have a point d'appui.[2] The religious mystic was really not so bad. She is a lady, tho' a mad lady, & I prefer mad English ladies to sane, coarse women of any nationality. The religious mystic was very devoted to me & looked after me assiduously. Now I live (& have done ever since my return from the West, which occurred after John Foster left) in a charming tiny white house on a hill high above a river, which is nevertheless v. dry & warm (heated by central heating fed by a gas stove) Guy Chilver is a very reliable, devoted & agreeable housemate, & we are looked after by a severe but efficient & hardworking clean negress, who is a puritanical субботнича[3] or Seventh Day Adventist, which means that she ceases work on Friday evening (like certain other people) & returns on Sunday. The problem is her wages. The original scheme was: 15 dollars a week (for which she washes, irons, presses, mends etc.) which is less than most maids here, + 5 dollars for her room + 1.65 for car fares for the tram. We have now arranged for her to live in the house, but she demands the original 21 dollars – very unreasonable. If we refuse, she will go, knowing that maids are unobtainable, & that she only got us via my Jewish contacts in Cincinnati (!). Dilemma. Blackmail. We can only reduce her wages if we get the Seventh Day Adventist Pastor's diplomatic support. Hence need for delicate negotiation. Otherwise all is well. My clothes are in order, tho' another blue suit identical with the London September 1942 one wd be quite nice – but not at all urgently wanted. Alternatively a dark brown flannel suit cut on the same lines. But it really doesn't matter. I am glad Charles is well. I heard about him from D[aphne Straight] too, same sort of thing, but it seems quite mad to me. A) I am far too occupied B) it would not be liked C) I should be the object of justified suspicion to all, & make things worse. Do you remember Heine on the derivation of the word Schlemihl? from Schelumiel ben Zurishadai who got

1 Mrs Noel Francis Newsome 1942–52.
2 'Rallying-point'.
3 'Subbotnicha', the wrong word: a *subbotnicha* in Soviet usage meant a woman who did voluntary, socially useful unpaid work on her days off.

in between Pinchas's spear & his victim (Leviticus?).[1] Well – that is what I should be. The idea is hers anyway I think, & no use at all. I have had a v. nice letter from the Warden of Wadham describing Joseph's obsequies with great verve & malice, & reporting that Mr Berlin attended, & "behaved with decorum" i.e. didn't spit etc. I cannot pretend to any sorrow at this sad event. Lightfoot must be v. excited. Wheeler Bennett will be coming soon & will call. You & we are both said to be swept by a flu epidemic, but I am quite unaffected. Not a sneeze, not a cough. What more can I tell you? Your sad admirer David – what was his name – the little Jewish writer, is dead. The Frankfurters, on the other hand, particularly he, are tremendously alive. John Foster is greatly missed, both technically & personally. I told you about my cable from Hon. Miriam Lane[2] (Lanyi) reproaching me for not taking more notice of her act? S. Goldberg is here. Very sensible & nice. My colleague Aubrey Morgan is in London c/o M.o.I. etc. in case you want to see.

love
　　Shaya

TO S. N. BEHRMAN[3]

16 December 1943 [*carbon*]

[Washington]

Dear Mr Behrman,

I began writing you a letter overflowing with gratitude on the train which took me back from New York, but the entire expedition was attended by disasters, and I duly lost the fragment of my manuscript. The whole thing was like a mixture of Gogol[4] and Proust,[5] but I will spare you the details, particularly in the second category. Had I only managed to catch the 9.55 am

---

1 Shelumiel the son of Zurishaddai in fact appears only in Numbers (e.g. 7: 36), though not explicitly in this episode (25: 6–15). The etymology proposed by the German poet Heinrich Heine (1797–1856) appears in his poem 'Jehuda ben Halevy': see *Heinrich Heines Sämtliche Werke*, ed. Oskar Walzel (Leipzig, 1911–20), vol. 3, pp. 168–70. For the background to this complex matter see S. S. Prawer, *Heine's Jewish Comedy: A Study of his Portraits of Jews and Judaism* (Oxford, 1983), 587–91, and (only for the stout-hearted) Robert M. Copeland and Nathan Süsskind, *The Language of Herz's 'Esther': A Study in Judeo-German Dialectology* (Alabama, 1976), 167–74.

2 Miriam Rothschild had married George Lane (né Lanyi) earlier in 1943.

3 Samuel Nathaniel Behrman (1893–1973), playwright and essayist, whose sophisticated comedies had been successful on Broadway; brother-in-law of violinist Jascha Heifetz.

4 Nikolay Vasil'evich Gogol (1809–52), Russian novelist and dramatist, many of whose stories tell of bizarre misfortunes suffered by minor civil servants.

5 Proust's major work, *À la recherche du temps perdu*, portrays hopeless love for unavailable and faithless women.

from Washington on last Saturday morning all might have gone well. But the motor car in which I was driven to the station lost its back axle some two yards from Union Station and subsided softly among the slightly dazed surrounding traffic. I therefore caught the 10.00 am train, which should have brought me to New York in time, had it not caught fire in its luggage van between Philadelphia and Newark, which caused it to stand still in the open (and, I dare say, beautiful) country for over an hour. My insistent enquiries as to why it was necessary to stop the train in order to extinguish the flames which surely could be done equally well as we moved were not well received by anyone. We arrived in New York at 3.20 pm, and I arrived at the theatre at 3.35, that is 55 minutes after the beginning of the performance. There was a line of considerable length in front of the box office slowly and painfully buying tickets for March and April and May, which, had I been born of different nature, I would have ignored. As it was, I stood meekly in line until my turn came, when two tickets were hurriedly pressed into the hand, indicating that my companion[1] had not arrived either. After this, a series of even more complicated misfortunes fell upon me involving immense long-distance calls, explanations, tears, etc. (This is the part a recital of which, although true, might by some be called inartistic exaggeration. I have no passion for the truth and will omit it.)

I heard the second half of *Oklahoma* with great delight, however. Indeed, even the close proximity of Senator Reynolds[2] did nothing to spoil it. The physical affinity of the actors' faces in general appearance to the persons they were meant to portray would seem to me, with possibly European experience in mind, so close as to make the illusion very powerful and give the whole thing what is called a highly convincing quality. In short, your desire to have me instructed was very successful. My actual memories of the Great West are completely superseded by this far more vivid and memorable series of sounds and sights. As soon as it was over I wished to hear, at any rate, the second act over again, and propose to do so as soon as is feasible. I do not suppose so close a relationship between the mood induced by the performance and the real memories of their own real and historic emotions about the place on the part of the audience can have been possible since Fledermaus[3] and before. I was, in fact, perhaps more profoundly moved by a vast number of imagined associations than the normal American could be –

1 Almost certainly Patricia de Bendern (507/3). This may well have been the occasion when, after seeing a performance of *Oklahoma*, IB spent a sleepless night in his hotel, tormented by the sounds of P de B and her Franco-Cuban lover Jacques Abreu in the next room.

2 Robert Rice Reynolds (1884–1963), eccentric, flamboyant Democratic Senator from North Carolina 1932–45, isolationist, enthusiastic New Dealer.

3 *Die Fledermaus* ('The bat'), operetta with music by Johann Strauss junior, libretto by Carl Haffner and Richard Genée, was set in Vienna at around the time of its first performance there in 1874.

I am sure that in the ultimate picture of America which I shall take over with me when I return to my cloistered world, growing as it will more and more artificial and stylised as the years go on, this brief and vivid fragment will linger very near the centre. For all this I am really most truly grateful to you (but you ought to allow me to pay you for the ticket).

I should give much to know what you yourself thought of it all, and assuming as I do that nothing but the most bitter need would ever bring you to Washington, I hope you will let me see you in New York at some not too distant date.

Dear me, but it really was a most painful and enjoyable day and one which for various reasons I shall in fact never forget at all. Thank you very much, indeed.

Yours sincerely,
Isaiah Berlin

TO MARIE AND MENDEL BERLIN

31 January 1944

British Embassy, Washington

My dear parents,

I must apologise for not writing for so long, but although one seems to be doing a great many useless and unnecessary things one cannot find time for much private life. I shall try to reply to all your various questions accumulated over months:

1. The post-war reconstruction of the Berlin family concerning which you have addressed an enquête.[1] My view on this is that you will not find life in the country lively enough for persons of your temperament. Life in the country in England depends entirely on (a) motor cars (b) rural tastes. As you possess neither, it is my considered view that apart from a weekend cottage or something of that sort life in the country would bore you stiff within a very short time. On the other hand, my distaste for the Hampstead house continues. So that I should suggest that a smaller house be acquired nearer the centre of London, say in St John's Wood or even Kensington or Knightsbridge (unless this lies too low for you) or Campden Hill perhaps. I do not believe in flats and have a sentimental view of privacy and houses provided that they are not too hard to keep up – 7 rooms should be enough, I suppose, but I cannot see how we can manage with fewer than four bedrooms. Also I believe in the indestructible value of real estate, particularly in post-war periods. The alternative is a house within easy reach of London

1 'Enquiry'.

(and Oxford) (in one of the little towns on the GWR[1] plus a flat in London). But a house *somewhere* I am convinced.

2. You will also presumably wish to hear about my mode of life here. Everything is running infinitely well. The house is very romantically situated far above a rushing river. It is very small and easy to run. The coloured servant is immensely energetic, clean, and being highly religious (a Seventh[-day] Adventist, which means that she does not work on Saturday but does on Sundays and does not touch the flesh of the pig) exceptionally honest and a good cook and apparently devoted to Mr Chilver and myself (we are Mr Guy and Mr Berlin respectively). We entertain small and carefully selected dinner parties (our table holds a maximum of six), and everything runs with perfect smoothness. She charges us an extravagant sum of over $20 a week, but for this washes our laundry, presses our suits and generally keeps the texture of life in repair. One cannot really ask for anything better. Before this I spent three troubled months accompanied by theft and robbery – although in the end I found that in all my losses amounted to about $7 in money and a pair of cufflinks kindly brought by [Herbert] Nicholas – Mrs Fremantle who employed these robbers is now in England, and my period of association with her and her mysticism is at an end.

3. What else is there to tell you? I see a good many official persons and had a very agreeable half hour with Sir A. Clark Kerr[2] who was visiting us from Moscow and conveyed to me Moore Crosthwaithe's regards. He asked me when I would be going to visit him in Moscow. I said 'At once, tonight.' He asked me what conditions I imposed. I replied 'None. Unconditional surrender was what I was prepared for.' I do not know how far these pleasantries have any serious basis, but I would not at all mind paying a visit provided they did not last too long, as I think that Moscow after a bit may be rather tedious. I hope you are enjoying the new Russian National Anthem[3] as much as I – it does indicate a change of tempo more vividly than anything else so far. Crosthwaithe also sent me a letter by one of the returning American diplomats in which he describes his own somewhat dull life. I do not feel somehow that he is ideally cut out for the New Russia.

4. There are various plans afoot for a visit by me to London, probably in July for a very short time I am told, as I cannot be spared, etc. I should not mind that at all as I am in blooming health and long to get back if only for

---

1 The Great Western Railway linked Oxford and London.
2 Archibald John Kerr Clark Kerr (1882–1951), 1st Baron Inverchapel 1946, diplomat, eccentric; British Ambassador to China 1938–42, Moscow 1942–6 and Washington 1946–8.
3 *The Unbreakable Union of Freeborn Republics* (lyrics by S. V. Mihalkov and G. G. El-Registran, music by A. V. Aleksandrov) had replaced the *Internationale* (lyrics by Eugène Pottier, music by Pierre Degeyter).

two or three weeks. Craig McGeachy brought news of you. She has just been offered, and, I imagine, accepted, a job as Welfare Director of UNRRA, where she will have Lehman and Salter, dull competent men entirely suitable to her temperamentally, to wheedle and cajole. I am sure she will be popping up in various parts of Europe and the East with soup kitchens and warm bedding – she has gaily offered me a job under her – I cannot conceive anything less suitable to my particular genius, I must confess. If you can conceive me in the company of, say, a Dutchman, a Croat and a Siamese, tucking up some Polish nationalist refugees in Teheran, that is the sort of image which the offer provokes. Not quite my sort of thing I feel.

6.[1] What is the news of Foster? What of Miss Carruthers? Is he still standing for Parliament?[2] His definite decision not to return has distressed everyone here as he was a great source of life and ideas. I hope that Roy Harrod gave you my love. I saw a good deal of him here. He seemed melancholy and somewhat bitter, perhaps because he feels that the war effort does not depend on him quite to the extent to which it should (last sentence not for reproduction, above all not to Dr Bowra from whom I had a nice letter). Your brushes arrived safely, and I saw the bearer who will also communicate my flourishing condition to you. I had a telegram from Charles about the transportation of one of his men, and complaining that I do not write. The reason for that is that I feel cramped by the official circumstances of open writing, and to produce completely harmless letters which one knows, because of the addressee, are bound to be copied out to various irrelevant officials makes writing too artificial to be a pleasure. I wish you would convey this to him if and when you see him.

7. It is true that I have secured, at least in principle, the visit of Lady D[aphne Straight], but as she shows no signs of coming you might jog Herbert and tell him that the Ambassador is passionately curious about her approaching arrival.

8. The Jewish issue is certainly about to boil up seriously here, and I try as much as possible to have nothing to do with it, without success, as everything ultimately comes to rest on my desk and I have to perform miracles of diplomatic contortion. In short, my life is as it always has been, peaceful, regular, full of talk, a little music, few books (thank you for the *New Statesman*) and a permanent desire to go home. Everyone is most kind and charming and polite; this country is undoubtedly the largest assemblage of fundamentally benevolent human beings ever gathered together, but the thought of staying here remains a nightmare. On the very first day after even

---

1 There is no 5.
2 In 1945 John Foster was elected Conservative MP for Northwich, Cheshire.

the European war is over, I shall probably make a frantic attempt to return to Oxford.

9. I cannot pretend to be sorry that Mr Joseph is gathered to his fathers and am almost embarrassed by his brother's request (transmitted by you) about some personal memento. I suppose I shall have to write to him direct and ask for a book or something. Please convey my regards not only to David and Mary and Mrs F[isher] and Sir Leon[1] but also to Smith if you meet him in the quad, and to Lightfoot with whom, I suppose, I shall have to live. As I grow older my tendency to appeasement increases, I find, and my capacity for moral indignation grows weaker and weaker.

Really there is nothing more to write about, everything is so composed and tranquil.[2]

I really do hope that you are both very well. From time to time someone writes to say 'your father is, of course, much better' which is the first I even hear about your ill health.[3] But I trustfully assume that you really are well. (I visited Harvard the other day. Very beautiful & tranquil. I see a lot of Felix & Mrs F. still, they are wonderfully unchanging: he still a boy, she still wistful & full of unfulfilled longings and an extraordinary dream life. To-night I dine with Robert Brand, my All Souls colleague & head of our Food Mission. To-morrow I have to go to a diplomatic (Polish!) reception.

So you see my life is in a sense full, but very empty too. I think occasionally about marriage very abstractly: I am sure that if ever I do marry I shall (a) have to fall in love (b) she will probably have every possible dis-advantage – be much too old or much too young: a Moslem or a Catholic: 4 times divorced, heavily in debt, with six children, extremely stupid, deaf in one ear. Dear me, perhaps it is really best to have many friends, write long letters, stay week-ends with other people, & remain single. I am in a very tranquil and contented mood, nothing seems very disturbing, & if I can come home in July that is all I ask for. All my love to you & I shall see you this year.

Shaya

---

1 Leon Simon (1881–1965), Kt 1944, resident of Hampstead, civil servant, Zionist leader and Hebrew expert; Director, Post Office Savings Bank, 1935–44; member of Commission of Inquiry into Jewish Education in Palestine 1945–6.
2 Here typescript yields to manuscript.
3 See 364/5.

TO ANGUS MALCOLM
North American Department, Foreign Office

1 February 1944 [*carbon*]

British Embassy, Washington

Dear Angus,

Thank you for your last letter – there are one or two things which I think I had better say at once to you and leave gossip etc. until the weekend when I shall have a little more leisure and try to acquire the right Sicilian[1] mood – I will send a budget of oddities then. Meanwhile there is this:

Our old friend Jacob Landau[2] of the Jewish Telegraphic Agency, lately returned from Mexico (where I suspect he has been trying to do a job for Nahum Goldmann, for all his professed anti-Zionist sentiments, in sounding out Oumansky about the possibility of his, Goldmann's, possible visit to Russia about Jews) came to see me today and said (1) that the resolution at present before Congress recording the sympathy etc. of the US Congress for the opening of Palestine to Jewish immigration and the establishment of a 'Democratic Jewish Commonwealth' will, as things look now, pass both Houses within about six weeks. Blum[3] can certainly not afford to block it in the Foreign Affairs Committee since his own political life in New York is very much at stake, and will indeed probably push it. Supported as it is by both McCormick[4] and Martin,[5] it will probably pass the House and ultimately the Senate as well. While admittedly it is a hollow gesture involving Americans in no kind of executive action and would under ordinary circumstances be relegated to a dusty file, the American Jews are not likely to allow that to happen and will doubtless claim it as a new political charter and quote it at every possible and impossible occasion. The State Department has apparently assured the Zionists that it would remain 'neutral', and indeed it is difficult to see what else they could really do, except to ask favoured Congressmen about who is expected to provide the bayonets

1 Presumably IB was preparing to indulge in some character assassination worthy of the Mafia.
2 Jacob Landau (1892–1952), journalist and publisher, founded the Jewish Telegraphic Agency, a bureau for the gathering and distribution of Jewish news, in the Hague in 1914 (when it was called the Jewish Correspondence Bureau), transferring its HQ to London in 1919 and New York in 1922.
3 Sol Bloom (1870–1949), Democratic Congressman for the largely Jewish South Bronx area of New York 1923–45 (and for an adjacent area 1945–9); at the time of this letter chairman of the Committee on Foreign Affairs; US delegate to the 1943 Bermuda Conference on refugees and widely criticised for following the SD line instead of pressing for more action to save European Jewry; former show-business promoter who coined the term 'belly dance'.
4 Presumably Robert Rutherford McCormick (1880–1955), strongly Republican editor and publisher of the right-wing *Chicago Tribune*.
5 Joseph William Martin, Jr (1884–1968), Republican Congressman, at the time minority leader in the House of Representatives.

doubtless required for the forcing of the large Jewish immigration into Palestine in the face of wild Arab resistance. This someone like Berle will probably do, but the only way to stop it is precipitating the debate in Congress which the State Department would rather doubt than permit especially as it is bound to result in victory for the Zionists.[1] These latter are pressing every available [advantage?] and have got all their friends lined up very thoroughly, and that is, as they say here, something I can assure you.

2. The American Jewish Committee are vaguely disturbed about the whole thing, and William and I have been trying to get them to express some sort of views, however informally, if only to us, so that someone in London may know what kind of support certain solutions could be expected to have among Jews, who, however weak institutionally, have a good deal of influence individually. They may produce something, but I doubt if it will be of great interest. Meanwhile, they seem to have written to Sir R. Waley Cohen[2] in London asking him to come and talk to them, but so far have received no reply. Perhaps he is afraid of being cast in jail by the Justice Department on some anti-trust suit or other. Anyhow, while the idea of a London Proscauer[3] is probably a good one – the Jewish conservatives and moneyed men have had nobody of their own kind to talk to – I doubt if Waley Cohen, who seems to be a hectoring and unpopular figure, is the right person. What about Lord Samuel? Or is he gaga? Or Lord Reading? Or is he too much under his wife's[4] influence? Or Jimmy Rothschild?[5] Or is he too Zionist? If you can think of a suitable nabob, and if you and our betters approve in principle (it might really have a sobering effect), tell me and I can put the idea into people's minds here and an invitation will duly be issued. Landau's view is that the Congressional resolution (which would, I suppose, have disastrous effects on the Arabs and drive poor charming Miss Stark, whom I think the world of, quite crazy in her Middle Western wilderness) will take six weeks to pass both Houses, but Weizmann will presumably only pour cold water if assured of something concrete by HMG after the war as the price of present moderation. I gather from the latest telegram that we do not intend to do or say anything until the war ends, and if this is so the suggestion is obviously impracticable. However, there it is for

---

1 This corrupted sentence was doubtless corrected in the top copy.
2 Sir Robert Waley Cohen (1877–1952), businessman (in Shell group of companies), leading Jewish layman in Britain, by this time anti-Zionist, President of the United Synagogue (a powerful association of Ashkenazi congregations in London) from 1942.
3 Joseph Meyer Proskauer (1877–1971), lawyer; justice, Supreme Court of New York, 1923–30; long-standing friend and adviser to Governor Alfred Smith of New York; while President of the American Jewish Committee (1943–9) he became a convert to Zionism; consultant to US delegation at the 1945 conference in San Francisco that established the UN.
4 The domineering Eva Violet Mond, daughter of the 1st Baron Melchett.
5 The strongly Zionist James de Rothschild (245/5).

what it is worth, which is probably less than nothing. You are, of course, quite right about the probable ability of US Jews to frustrate any change of mandate by blocking it in Congress, and if this really needs saying, it will be incorporated in some relevant report. But if we intend to stand pat, which indeed seems an excessively unimaginative policy even for HMG, this danger will not arise, and I agree too that the menace of being forced to opt for Palestine nationalities is exceedingly hollow, however useful, as a debating point with the more pusillanimous.

Yours ever,

Isaiah Berlin

On Wednesday 9 February there occurred an event which, although IB was not present, brought him as much fame as any event in his own life. The story exists in many variants,[1] often wildly inconsistent with one another, and all no doubt embellished in various ways. Here is one of the versions told by IB himself:

Mrs Churchill[2] said to Winston: 'Irving Berlin[3] is in town, he's been very generous to us' – he'd given a large sum of money to a war charity, I don't know which, with which she was connected.[4] 'If you meet him, do tell him we're very pleased with him.'

Mr Churchill said, 'I want him to come to lunch.'

She said, 'No, no, no, I didn't mean that. I mean, if you meet him in the Churchill Club,' she said, 'just pat him on the shoulder and say we're very grateful to him.'

'I want him to come to lunch,' he said, but she couldn't understand why.

He said, 'I don't want many people to be there – small party.'

Well, he came, very excited; present were the Prime Minister, Mrs Churchill, his daughter Mary,[5] the Chief Whip of the Government, Sir

1 For example: John Colville, 'A Tale of Two Berlins', chapter 30 of *Footprints in Time* (London, 1984), 168–70, and *The Fringes of Power: Downing Street Diaries 1939–55* (London, 1985), 471–2; Michael Freedland, *Irving Berlin* (London, 1974), 220–1; Laurence Bergreen, *As Thousands Cheer: The Life of Irving Berlin* (London, 1990), 430–2 (derivative from, and similar but not identical to, Freedland's account).

2 Clementine Ogilvy Churchill (1885–1977), née Hozier, later (1965) Baroness Spencer-Churchill.

3 Irving Berlin brought his successful musical *This is the Army* to Britain in November 1943. It first played in London, then toured the provinces. A performance on 6 February for General Eisenhower so impressed him that he immediately arranged for the show to be seen by all US units overseas. So a few days after the lunch with Churchill, Irving Berlin and his company embarked on a dangerous and demanding tour, lasting till late 1945, of US units in North Africa, Italy, Egypt, New Guinea and the Pacific.

4 Probably the Red Cross Aid to Russia Fund, of which Clementine Churchill was chairman.

5 Mary Churchill (b. 1922), the Churchills' youngest daughter, later (1947) married Christopher Soames (Lord Soames 1978).

James Stuart,[1] the two secretaries – Colville[2] and Martin[3] – and I
think that, perhaps, was it;[4] and each one of these people then told me
what happened, and I conflated these versions, so I have some sense of
what occurred.

Mrs Churchill didn't say much, because she thought I might be
rather embarrassed or offended, so she played it down. The others were
not at all anxious to play it down. Irving Berlin sat next to Winston
Churchill. Conversation didn't flourish. Mrs Churchill got rather worried
about this non-meeting of minds; she said, 'You know, Winston, we
ought to be very grateful to Mr Berlin, he's been very generous to us.'

Mr Churchill said 'Generous? To us? I don't understand.'

Then there was a deathly silence. She'd never heard of me: there
was no reason why she should have done. The war was on, and she
wasn't going to argue. Churchill said to him, 'Mr Berlin, what is the most
important piece of work you have done for us lately, in your opinion?'

Poor Berlin obviously couldn't quite make out what this man had
said. After some hesitation, 'I don't know, it should be *A White Christmas*,
I guess.' And Winston said 'Are you an American?' – there was this thick
American accent.

Berlin said, 'What? Why? Why? Yes.'

Then Winston again turned to Mr Berlin and he said, 'Do you think
Roosevelt will be re-elected this year?'

Irving said, 'Well, in the past I've voted for him myself, this year I
am not so sure.'

At this point Mr Churchill became rather gloomy: he couldn't
understand who he was dealing with. He still thought it was me.
Obviously my dispatches were quite coherent, but he obviously had an
idiot before him. Finally he said, 'Mr Berlin, when do you think the
European War is going to end?'

Berlin said, 'Sir, I shall never forget this moment. When I go back to
my own country I shall tell my children and my children's children that
in the spring of 1944 the Prime Minister of Great Britain asked *me* when
the European War was going to end.'

---

1 James Gray Stuart (1897–1971), later 1st Viscount Stuart of Findhorn; Joint Parliamentary
Secretary to the Treasury and Government Chief Whip 1941–5.

2 John Rupert Colville (1915–87), Churchill's Assistant Private Secretary 1940–1 and 1943–5; Pilot,
RAF Volunteer Reserve, 1941–4.

3 John Miller Martin (1904–91), Churchill's Private Secretary 1940–5 (Principal Private Secretary
from 1941); but Martin's diary entry for the day makes no mention of the event.

4 Other accounts suggest that some or all of the following may also have been present: Field-
Marshal Sir Alan Francis Brooke (1883–1963), later (1946) 1st Viscount Alanbrooke, Chief of
Imperial General Staff 1941–6, ADC General to the King 1942–6; Brooke's second wife Benita
Blanche, daughter of Sir Horace Pelly; Lady (Helen) Cynthia Colville (1884–1968), Woman of
the Bedchamber to Queen Mary 1923–53, John Colville's mother; (Vreda Esther) Mary
('Molly') Montagu-Douglas-Scott, Duchess of Buccleuch and of Queensberry (1900–93), née
Lascelles; and Juliet Olive Henley (b. 1917).

Winston was very displeased about this: he really more or less lost his temper, got up – lunch was over.

Poor Irving Berlin went off to the Savoy, where he was sharing rooms with Sir Alexander Korda,[1] and he said to Korda, 'You know, Mr Churchill is probably the greatest man in England, or in the world maybe, but I don't know what it was, I somehow felt we didn't click. I don't know what it was. Now she's a wonderful woman, I could talk to her always. With him, I don't know, something, something – I just can't make it out.'

Meanwhile John Colville had revealed that the Mr I. Berlin who had seemed such a disappointing lunch-guest was a song-writer and not, as Churchill had supposed, the Mr I. Berlin who drafted entertaining and perceptive surveys of the American political scene. To resume IB's account:

Winston immediately went to a Cabinet meeting, after lunch, told them the story with the greatest pleasure.

He asked me to lunch when he was in the Opposition, and he began by saying something like: 'You will doubtless have heard of a very grave solecism which I was so unfortunate as to have perpetrated.'[2]

This episode did not come to IB's attention immediately, but references to it as an established anecdote occur in due course.

TO JOSEPH ALSOP

11 February [1944, *carbon*][3]

[British Embassy, Washington]

My dear Joe,

Of course I owe you a letter and have for a long time, but I cannot altogether explain why it is frightfully difficult to write to anyone from Washington. One's life is filled with events which seem quite vivid and important when they occur, and fade and evaporate very quickly, leaving one cluttered up, however, with no paths through the extraordinary mountain of accumulated junk, a general sense of exhaustion and a kind of absence of a third dimension – an accumulation of unarticulate experience – from which alone one can possibly write at all expressively. So I shall confine myself to a general chronicle unless that suddenly peters out in the middle,

---

1 Sir Alexander Korda (1893–1956), Hungarian-born British film-producer who moved between London and Hollywood during the war.

2 From an interview with Sue Lawley for *Desert Island Discs*, broadcast on BBC Radio 4, 19 April 1992; some material cut from the broadcast version has been restored. See also MI 125–6.

3 An uncorrected carbon particularly full of gaps where the typist couldn't interpret IB's dictation; the top copy has not been found.

which is always liable to happen to me when I hear myself talk too much and suddenly stop out of sheer embarrassment.

I see something of our friends, the Pattens,[1] and Susan Mary told me extraordinary stories of your heroic exploits, gleaned apparently from Mr Youngman.[2] I am sure it is all true and have firmly spread the general impression, although not any specific facts since I do not know them, abroad. I find that I get on well with Sergeant, now Lieutenant, Whitney,[3] who is a truly charming old-world personality, and I find Chip Bohlen's[4] conversation about his recent journeys full of intelligence, and always find that to be [so] even when he produces unsympathetic views.

I much enjoyed meeting Sir A. Clark Kerr, who seemed to me the very best sort of ageing actor – with a dash of Wilmot Lewis[5] as he must have been ten or fifteen years ago, and the firm manner of a young man of 25, which is obviously the part he plays. What life in the Embassy in Moscow must be like with the only too diplomatic Jock Balfour,[6] who is very wholly very mad, Moore Crosthwaite and John Read[7] I cannot even begin to think. Balfour, eccentric, dotty, to be seen in his Foreign Office striped trousers, spats, a walking-stick with an ivory knob and a bowler hat, mounted on a bicycle, will convey the sort of Edward Lear figure he is, something like a Quangle-Wangle or a Dong,[8] observed usually on the back of his chair with his feet on his desk, balanced so precariously that often he does actually fall backwards (he was head of the North American Department of the Foreign Office in 1940–1,[9] of all things, which may explain much, but is infinitely more attractive than his successor Nevile Butler). The last vivid picture of

1 William Samuel Patten (1909–52), diplomat, attaché at US Embassy in London until 1945, Foreign Service Reserve Officer, Paris, 1945–52, and his wife Susan Mary, née Jay (b. 1918), later wife (1961–75) of Joseph Alsop and well known as a writer and society hostess.

2 William Sterling Youngman, Jr. (1907–94), New Deal lawyer, partner of Thomas G. Corcoran, provider of assistance to General Claire Chennault (615/5) and Chiang Kai-shek.

3 Probably John Hay Whitney (1904–82), businessman and philanthropist; later Ambassador to Britain (1957–61) and publisher of the *New York Herald Tribune*.

4 Charles ('Chip') Eustis Bohlen (1904–74), great friend of IB, US diplomat and Soviet specialist, later Ambassador to the USSR (1953–7) and to France (1962–8).

5 Sir Willmott Harsant Lewis (1877–1950), journalist, Washington correspondent of *The Times* 1920–48, grand old man of the foreign correspondents, noted social figure in Washington. Said of his profession: 'I think it well to remember that [. . .] we are writing for an elderly lady in Hastings who has two cats of which she is passionately fond. Unless our stuff can successfully compete for her interest with those cats, it is no good.' Claud Cockburn, *In Time of Trouble: An Autobiography* (London, 1956), 189.

6 John Balfour (1894–1983), diplomat; Head of American Dept, FO, 1938–41, Minister in British Embassies in Lisbon 1941–3, Moscow 1943–5 (he knew Russian) and Washington 1945–8.

7 John Leigh Reed (*sic*) (b. 1910), diplomat, Washington 1941–2; Moscow 1942–4; Ankara 1944–7.

8 In Edward Lear's nonsense poems, the Quangle Wangle had a fantastically ornamented 'Beaver Hat [. . .] a hundred and two feet wide' in which all manner of creatures made their homes, and the Dong had a luminous nose.

9 In all 1938–41.

him which anyone has is of [him] standing on his desk in the Foreign Office surrounded by six or seven colleagues, who in turn screamed out 'Napoleon!' (Balfour will shake his head silently), 'Frederick', 'Barbarossa' (no), 'Henry VIII' (no), 'Bismarck', 'Copernicus', etc. etc. 'You are all wrong,' he said, 'I am William the Silent.' Mr Crosthwaite, his First Secretary in Moscow, is an Egyptian-looking aesthete, whose life is embalmed in the more sentimental moments of Weimar Germany, *circa* 1927 or so. I knew him well at Oxford and after, and he is a charming sensitive persecuted private-face, a friend of Greenway Wescott,[1] the novelist, and might well have been at Harvard, finicky, old-maidish and irritable with very few friends, to whom he is passionately devoted, and dreams of glory, with a mother who is the only literally pot-bellied person I have ever seen. John Read, who probably met her – a rather thin, slightly-made Italianate creature, happy only in Bucharest, who used to drive me in his car under Washington bridges screaming murder and occasionally lapse into unprintable anti-Semitism until scolded by me sharply . . . How all this works in Moscow with Sir A. Kerr adding a pinch of salt here and a dash of pepper there I cannot conceive. Doubtless this is why history proceeds in peculiar ways. Kerr asked me if I wished to go to Moscow with him. I expressed enthusiasm. This has, however, I suspect, been spiked by my local authorities here, who cling to me pathetically in an election year, poor fools.

In November I went to Harvard on a visit and met your friend Ted Spencer,[2] whom I thought wistful and charming to a degree. I talked away like mad, and so the sheer volume of my words overwhelmed and drowned him completely, but I liked him very much and hope to see him when he comes to stay at Dumbarton Oaks.[3] He spoke warmly of you, and after that we discussed Othello for two hours. He knew everyone I knew in Cambridge, England, and we sailed off on that very cosily and well. I conceived the most violent admiration for Harvard, which seemed to me the only academic institute here which was large enough and proud enough to develop a strong and almost bullying personality of its own. I thought that, if I remain in America, there alone could I survive, despite all the narrowness

1 Glenway Wescott (1901–87), US novelist, short-story writer, poet and essayist, best known for his novel *The Grandmothers* (NY, 1927), published in England as *A Family Portrait* (London, 1927). Lived in Paris in the 1920s, mixing with the American expatriate community, e.g. Gertrude Stein, Ernest Hemingway and Scott Fitzgerald. The character of Robert Prentiss in Hemingway's *The Sun Also Rises* (NY, 1926) was based on Wescott.

2 Theodore Spencer (1902–49), academic and poet; associate professor of English at Harvard 1940–6.

3 A 19th-century house and garden in Georgetown donated by Mr and Mrs Robert Woods Bliss to Harvard in 1940, thereafter housing specialised research collections. Later in 1944 (21 August to 7 October) the venue for meetings between delegates from the US, UK, USSR and China to draw up proposals for the international organisation which would become the United Nations.

and prejudices. I like Boston very much. I think I like the appearance of books in windows more than anything else in the world – certainly more than any natural object.

Shortly before that I performed an enormous tour of the United States, alone, to Oregon and Washington in which everything teems like mad, racoons in the woods, fish in the rivers (I caught some to my immense astonishment, and not just fish, but sturgeon and a [ ] salmon), and next door to that Kaiser's yards[1] grinding away. I was picked up on the train by the gallery director from Portland who was under the impression that I was the accompanist of Mons. Szigeti,[2] the eminent violinist, and was much distressed that I was not – 'I had it all figured out,' he said. Obviously I might have been and, as the Hegelians would say, in a [very real?] sense, probably more. We talked through the night, and he told me all about Portland life and what the rich were like and what an enormous future the whole thing had after Japan was knocked out, and indeed it has, and there is a lot of Horace Greelyism[3] around the place. I was much affected. San Francisco was like Naples, full of natives and quite separate from its environment. Los Angeles is a hell of [such] depth and blackness as I never hope to see again. I loathed Hollywood, where everyone was either [ ] nasty or passionately anxious to be something else, and the accumulation of European decay in a series of rock pools is unsurpassed. The only agreeable thought is that since all these people are accumulated there, they cannot also be somewhere else, which is a great source of relief. There I picked up John Russell and went to the Grand Canyon and New Orleans. When you return I shall tell you a funny story about our experiences on Los Angeles station, symptomatic of both our characters if nothing else. It is too long a story to tell here and requires inflexions of voice and gestures which cannot be conveyed in writing.

On New Year's Day I went to lunch with Mrs Beale[4] and found: Mr and Mrs Michael Wright of my Embassy (have you met them? if not there is a subject there); Miss Freya Stark, a noted Arabian explorer and champion of the Arab cause (with whom I get on well on the principle of incompatibles);

---

1 The industrialist Henry J. Kaiser (1882–1967) had a large shipbuilding yard in Vancouver, Washington (across the Columbia River from Portland, Oregon), which played a major role in the wartime emergency shipbuilding programme.

2 Joseph Szigeti (1892–1973), Hungarian-born violinist, settled in the US in 1940.

3 Horace Greeley (sic) (1811–72), founder and editor of the New York Tribune; an idealist and social reformer, he consistently advocated organised settlement of western America and in 1841 advised his readers to 'turn your face to The Great West and there build up your home and fortune'.

4 Marie Chase Oge Beale (1880–1956), widow of diplomat Truxton Beale; Washington hostess, renowned for her historic home on Lafayette Square near the White House and for the annual dinner she gave for the diplomatic corps.

Mr and Mrs Adolf Berle; and Mrs N. Longworth.[1] I cannot say how well I liked meeting her – my analogy between her faith and Catherine the Great went very well with a lot of shouting, and in order to steady ourselves we then conducted a gentler conversation about whether Italian primitive painters would have found Wyoming a suitable background. After the [ ] Ambassador had left and Mrs Beale stopped calling me 'Mr Isha Berlin', Mr Berle, who was taking his leave, finally approached me, shook me by the hand and observed sombrely that he had heard a very very great deal about me. I never know what to say on such occasions and stammered out that I had heard perhaps even more about him and that that was surely less surprising, whereupon he seemed to pale, and retired talking fast to himself in a low voice, seized his wife's hand and said something in her ear and was off. The new view of him among my colleagues is that he is full of charm, good sense, benevolent towards themselves, altogether a splendid official. The new 'reorganisation' of the State Department (you will enjoy the broadcasts by the Department very very much, I fear) appears to take away control of finance from him and puts Jimmy Dunn[2] in the position of a kind of permanent Under-Secretary. Altogether there is much to tell you about this sort of thing, but it will bore you too much now, I am sure, if you have real things to do.

The Republican position is peculiar in that the Party seems to me to be behaving like a little boy who has been given a large sum of pocket-money which it must spend before a given date or forfeit. He is naturally in an agreeably excited state and roams around shop windows seeing things which are very nearly, very very nearly, what he wants but never quite. He has the tantalising feeling that if he waits too long he may find precisely what he wants but will no longer have the money to spend. They don't quite seem to

---

1 Alice Lee Roosevelt Longworth (1884–1980), daughter of former Republican President Theodore Roosevelt, widow of Nicholas Longworth; famed Washington hostess and wit, who remained a friend of IB until her death. In his words: 'She was a grande dame of the first order [. . .] she wanted to be amused, and therefore liked clever, interesting people of intellectual vitality [. . .] or those who fed her acute sense of the ridiculous in life [. . .] what she liked was heroism, boldness, power, pride, unashamed ambition, grandeur of character: she disliked dimness, servility, convention [. . .] and therefore took pleasure, in a defiant, perverse sort of way, in denouncing liberals, do-gooders etc., which is what gave her the reputation (not undeserved, of course) of being an acute reactionary. She believed in élites, and felt herself to be part of one, and disliked democracy and general American ideals, save in the form in which her father accepted them [. . .] She was a very clever, indeed, very brilliant talker – deliberately unfair, but loyal and affectionate towards those she liked, and open about her likes and dislikes. There was no touch of hypocrisy or desire to appease those for whom she did not care, in any degree' (letter to Carol Felsenthal, 16 September 1985).
2 James Clement Dunn (1890–1979), diplomat, adviser on political relations 1937–44, Assistant Secretary of State 1944–6.

want Dewey,[1] but they want Willkie less, and Bricker[2] or Taft[3] may not roll up the votes. So there is a kind of maddening frustration at the moment.

The Justice is well, very well I should say, which means that Mrs F. is particularly prone to note the seamier side of everything. Justices Black[4] and Murphy[5] suddenly assailed him openly in Court, accusing him of substituting his own private ethics for the law, etc. There were great headlines in the *Washington Post* (which has finally secured Wayne Coy[6] as successor to Mr Meyer,[7] who is not retiring), but it blew over. The Justice's capacity for gaiety when he is surrounded by enormous Indians sharpening enormous knives is magnificent. I am reminded of Mr E. C. Bentley's clerihew about 'Karl Marx / Was invariably surrounded by sharks. / He sorely missed 'em / When preoccupied with the capitalist system.'[8] I suppose it is the Justice's indestructible innocence which makes him so impregnable. I wish I had a similar capacity for ignoring dangers. The other day I found that I trod rather hard upon what turned out to be one of Arthur Krock's toes at a dinner party. Before I knew who he was I spun round [and said] that I was frightfully sorry. 'You are not frightfully sorry,' he said, 'you are perhaps a little sorry but I should doubt even that. But frightfully sorry you are certainly not', and so on and so on. After that, however, he appeased – so that even physical assault, even accidental physical assault, evidently automatically produces submission on his part.

1 Thomas Edmund Dewey (1902–71), lawyer; special prosecutor against organised crime in New York 1935–7, District Attorney 1937–40, Governor of New York 1942–54; unsuccessful candidate for Republican presidential nomination 1940; Republican presidential candidate 1944 and 1948. IB described him as 'a cold, shrewd, routine little dummy', observing that 'Not even his closest friends attribute any beliefs or purposes to him' (letter to H. G. Nicholas, 13 July 1944).

2 John William Bricker (1893–1986), lawyer; Governor of Ohio 1939–45, Republican nominee for Vice-President 1944.

3 Robert Alphonso Taft (1889–1953), son of President William Howard Taft; lawyer, Republican Senator from Ohio 1939–53.

4 Hugo LaFayette Black (1886–1971), lawyer; pro-New Deal Senator from Alabama 1927–37, Justice of the Supreme Court 1937–71; a liberal and a defender of civil liberties, despite early membership of the Ku Klux Klan, but even more strongly committed to upholding the letter of the Constitution.

5 Frank Murphy (1890–1949), lawyer, Democratic Governor of Michigan 1936–8, Attorney General 1939–40, Justice of the Supreme Court 1940–9; a consistent champion of civil rights, especially of racial and religious minorities.

6 (Albert) Wayne Coy (1903–57), Assistant Administrator of the Federal Security Agency 1939–41, Special Assistant to the President and Liaison Officer, Office for Emergency Management, 1941–3, Assistant Director, Bureau of the Budget, 1942–4; assistant to the publisher of the *Washington Post* 1944–7.

7 Eugene Meyer (1875–1959), banker; editor and publisher of the *Washington Post* 1933–46, father of Kay Graham. Meyer's successor as publisher of the *Washington Post* was his son-in-law Phil Graham.

8 Edmund Clerihew Bentley (1875–1956), author of the classic detective story *Trent's Last Case* (London, [1913]) and inventor of the clerihew (cf. 5/5). This one (in *Biography for Beginners*, 1905) runs: 'Karl Marx / Was completely wrapped up in his sharks. / The poor creatures seriously missed him / While he was attacking the capitalist system.'

Everyone else you know is exactly where you left them. Pritch is in terrific form after peculiar experiences in the Army, from which he was removed after two or three months and the pulling of innumerable strings (at least so I suppose) for 'excessive obesity'. Phil Graham[1] is thought to be coming back to Washington in some mysterious capacity. Anglo-American relations once more are giving everyone grave concern, and indeed there is a great deal of boiling going on. I have made up my mind (a) that this does not matter, as what Americans fundamentally object to about the English is (1) that they are English, (2) that they exist, and similarly the English with regard to Americans, and all objection to specific attributes is rationalisation; (b) that the problem is not political, since anti-isolationist gestures are bound to be made even under Bricker, but economic, since, on my whole wide tour of the USA, I found everyone I talked to (I talked to farmers and you must not giggle) profoundly convinced that as soon as the War is over we will all settle down to happy cut-throat competition and that the largest proportional number of throats cut will certainly be British as the Russians have no throats; they are a sort of monolith. If this happens nothing is any good, as far as I can see, but it can only be prevented by a lot of crusaders (the sort of thing that went on in 1939–41) meeting and urging, with some very simple sane programme provided by some lucid draftsmen. This does not seem too likely at present, and Keith Kane[2] and I, who occasionally talked about it, join each other into appalling glooms. Jim Forrestal's[3] line that the future is going to be a poker game between the US and USSR, and only very affluent players can be allowed – perhaps baccarat is a better example – a real big thing which it would be kinder not to let anyone except the very very rich take part in (e.g. not Britain), is probably fairly widely felt in what is called influential circles. A very heavily armed US glare and a very heavily armed USSR, buying and selling merrily and preserving world peace for many years to come, with everyone else adjusting themselves to this new unnecessary kind of twin alliance, is the sort of thing. I suppose that Chip feels that sort of thing too.

As for your old foe J. Wiley,[4] he goes about saying that he is bored by

---

1 Phil Graham had been teaching at the Air Intelligence School in Pennsylvania, but soon after this letter was written he joined a section of the Intelligence Services in Washington that interpreted information obtained through code-breaking.

2 Richmond Keith Kane (1900–74), lawyer, special assistant to the US Attorney General 1940–2 and to the Navy Secretary (at this time William Knox, from May 1944 James Forrestal – see next note) 1943–5.

3 James Vincent Forrestal (1892–1949), Under-Secretary of the US Navy, responsible for procurement and production, August 1940 to May 1944, when he became Navy Secretary; strongly anti-Communist.

4 John Cooper Wiley (1893–1967), American diplomat; Minister to Latvia and Estonia 1938–40; SD 1940–4.

World War 2; it is World War 3 that interests him, and you can imagine with whom he thinks that war will break out. Never having met me, he suddenly denounced me to various of my friends as a thoroughly dangerous figure, owing to my alleged Russophile tendencies. I was apparently invited to dinner by Irena,[1] sounded out, turned over and around, handed to Mrs Bacon,[2] taken back again, tested by various characters, finally packed up again and returned home, with J. Wiley now saying that we were fundamentally agreed on all points and that conversation with me was scarcely worthwhile from his point of view as there was nothing to argue about – [a] strange and curious figure, viewed not too seriously by his own henchmen, moving in an atmosphere of little notes written by himself about Englishmen he has talked to, or notes from tame foreigners about such conversations, sitting in his own house every afternoon at 5 like an exiled boyar sent to his country yesterday and waiting for brighter times, talking with ferocious gloom about the evil [times] upon which all good men have fallen. Yet I like him and even his wife. I can scarcely say as much for Dr Savitsch,[3] who at present is being attacked furiously in the *Times-Herald*,[4] which accuses Senator Guffey[5] of exercising undue pressure to try to get him into Gallinger Hospital.[6] Cissy,[7] who seems to have quarrelled with her doctor, now slaughters him daily in her newspaper – a noble spectacle for all good liberals.

Couldn't you contrive to get yourself to England in, say, July, when I am likely to be there? We should constitute a formidable alliance for the cementing of relations and make an unforgettable impression. Meanwhile Brendan [Bracken] is lying awake at nights thinking 'Who will be the

---

1 Wiley's wife, Irena Monique, née Baruch; according to IB, a Polish-Jewish Countess who ran a White Russian salon where IB met the Russian specialists in the SD (MI Tape 21).

2 Virginia Murray Bacon (1890–1980), widow of Republican Congressman Robert Low Bacon; with Mrs Bliss and Mrs Beale, one of three *grandes dames* who dominated Washington society.

3 Eugene Constantine de Savitsch (1903–59), doctor and surgeon; born in Russia but qualified in the US, whose citizen he had become.

4 A Washington newspaper. In an article published on 4 February (p. 2) it is suggested that Guffey (see next note) lost his chairmanship of the Democratic Senatorial Campaign Committee because his attempts from 1942 onwards 'to force appointment of Dr Eugene Savitsch, his protégé, to a District Public Health Service [operating] post were exposed by the Times-Herald'.

5 Joseph Finch Guffey (1870–1959), businessman previously indicted for misuse of government funds, Democratic Senator from Pennsylvania 1935–47, New Deal supporter who also favoured political patronage as organisationally efficient.

6 Washington's municipal hospital.

7 Eleanor ('Cissy') Medill Patterson (1884–1948), member of a leading newspaper dynasty, novelist, socialite, furious isolationist, former editor of the *Washington Herald*, from 1939 publisher of the Washington *Times-Herald*.

Sackville-West[1] of this election? Surely not Butler?' It is far more likely to be Winston himself if you ask me. Chip said that translating him was an almost impossible task. It all began in Moscow when the British translator found himself unable to understand one word of what Mr Hull was saying, and he was brought in instead – and then had to translate things like 'the depth of sublime unwisdom' into rapid Russian for Uncle Joe's benefit. Very nerve-racking, I can see.

An interesting phenomenon in this country is the fact that Anglophile and Russophile feeling move in inverse ratio to each other. Up with the Russians, down with the British, in almost exact proportions. I have now checked and rechecked this, and it seems to be a well-founded sociological generalisation.

I have had two affable letters from Tony and Felicity [Rumbold] with very opposed versions of their relations with Mrs M. N.[2] From all of which you will see that I am determined to remain persistently frivolous, a quality which goes down with the Ambassador but no one else in this establishment, despite all, and confine the serious side of my nature to academic subjects [and] private life. I now know that solemnity and public seriousness are fatal qualities in the conduct of public affairs and shall never believe anything else.

In late March IB was recalled to London for talks with the Ministry of Information and the Foreign Office. His unconventional journey back to England led him to a decision that shaped the rest of his life:

I had to travel back to England in 1944 in a bomber. In those days bombers were not pressurised, and so we were told we had to take oxygen. That meant that one was not allowed to sleep, because there was some danger of falling on the oxygen pipe and so suffocating. There was no light, and therefore one couldn't read. One was therefore reduced

. 1 Lionel Sackville Sackville-West (1827–1908), 2nd Baron Sackville, diplomat, appointed British Ambassador to the US in 1881, was tricked by the Republican Party into declaring a preference for the re-election of a Democratic President in the 1888 election and recalled to London soon afterwards; grandfather of Vita Sackville-West.

2 Barbara Mercer Nairne (d. 1965), née Chase, American wife of George John Charles Mercer Nairne (1912–99), who in August 1944 became 8th Marquess of Lansdowne (and adopted the surname Mercer Nairne Petty-Fitzmaurice). In the letter of 27 November 1943 to which IB refers, Tony Rumbold had reported that she 'works in the Ministry of Information (in close but hostile proximity to Daphne Straight) [. . .] We all dine and go to parties together and she is as charming as ever'; Felicity Rumbold's (presumably less favourable) comments have not survived. At the time of her death in a shooting accident at her Scottish home, the Marchioness of Lansdowne was described as 'a woman of great charm and an accomplished hostess. At one time she ran a ranch in America. She was an expert shot and was a former British clay pigeon shooting champion' (*The Times*, 18 February 1965, 14).

to a most terrible thing – to having to think – and I had to think for about seven or eight hours in this bomber going from Canada to England.

I came to the conclusion that what I really wanted was to know more at the end of my life than I knew at the beginning; that philosophy was a most marvellous subject which taxed the intelligence of man to its highest degree, in which human genius had shown some of its most important aspects and achievements, but it was not for me. I didn't really want the answers to these philosophical questions with that degree of urgency with which a true philosopher must want them. I didn't lie awake at night puzzling about philosophical problems, although I could quite enjoy them. On the other hand, when I read, for example, essays on moral and social subjects, say by Russian thinkers in the nineteenth century, whom I'd always dabbled with a little – the kind of things which troubled them and the kind of questions they asked did produce the kind of intellectual excitement which I think is necessary for the purpose of pursuing an abstract subject for a length of years.

I then became terribly interested in the history of these thinkers, because I thought that they were relevant, not only to the modern world, but to the human condition in general; and when I came back to England I told my startled colleagues in New College, Oxford, of which I was a Fellow, that I didn't really wish to go on doing philosophy, but wished to turn myself into a historian of thought. This was not very well received, because this was not a subject much encouraged in England, then or now. However, I was allowed to do this after promising to continue to teach philosophy at least for two or three years after the war, when the number of pupils, all coming back simultaneously from the war, would be very great, and therefore there would be a need to have qualified teachers to teach them.

And so in 1950 I stopped being a professional philosopher and devoted myself, so far as I could, to the history of Russian ideas in the nineteenth century.[1]

IB was kept busy during his time in England. As well as negotiating with New College and briefing Ministers and colleagues, he found time to address a meeting on Zionism in America, a talk which fervent Zionist Blanche 'Baffy' Dugdale described as 'supercilious, cynical, and not spoken like a Zionist'.[2]

By the time IB returned to Washington in mid-May, the story of Churchill and the two Berlins had become widely known.

1 From the English original of an interview with Frans Boenders on RT and CC, broadcast on Belgian Radio in February 1979, published in Dutch translation as 'Wijsbegeerte, geschiedenis en vrijheid' ('Philosophy, history and freedom') in *Sprekend gedacht: Interviews van Frans Boenders* ('Thinking out loud . . .') (Bussum, 1980), 171–90, at 179–80.
2 See p. 682 below.

TO MARIE AND MENDEL BERLIN

16 May 1944

British Embassy, Washington, DC

My dear parents,

I arrived after a very rapid and agreeable crossing, involving six hours in Irish sunshine in a deck-chair. I could not have wished for anything nicer or better.

I return my ration books which I forgot to surrender to the Customs Authorities. The best thing to do is to send them quietly back to the Oxford Food Office. Knowing your nature, I did not accept the local advice which indicated that the best thing to do was to do nothing, in which case nothing would happen.

Everyone is very amiable, my house is in perfect order, the cook in a[n] excellent temper, and altogether everything is very well. I go to New York for the weekend, travelling slowly by train in the company of my friend M. Nabokov with whom I shall discuss the poetry of Fet.[1] I could not have enjoyed myself more in England, and I look forward to my return in nine months' time more than I can say.

I must now write two polite letters to Woodward and Smith.

Love,

Isaiah.

⟨I shall ask Nicholas to transmit this. I am really *remarkably* well. Bad things do *not* happen twice. It was so nice to sit in the sun in the very place in which I caught pneumonia in 1942.⟩

TO W. S. G. ADAMS
Warden of All Souls

17 May 1944 [*carbon*]

British Embassy, Washington, DC

Dear Mr Warden,

I am afraid that, despite my extremely rapid journey, I failed to catch Salter, who will, I assume, be with you now and available for all decisions.

During my voyage two more names came into my mind with regard to the various chairs. One is Tom Marshall,[2] now in FORD under

---

1 Afanasy Afanasievich Fet (1820–92), Russian lyric poet and translator.
2 Thomas Humphrey Marshall (1893–1981), sociologist; Head of German Section and Deputy

Toynbee,[1] who, from all accounts, is an expert sociologist and a person of rare perception, originality and insight. I scarcely know him, but I am sure that Humphrey Sumner, Toynbee, Hodson[2] or anybody now in FORD could tell you about him. He is probably more suited to political institutions but might easily be an eminent political and social theorist if stimulated. The other person I thought of – this time for the chair of military history in case it is desired to fill that – is my friend John Wheeler-Bennett, whose brilliant works on the Treaty of Brest-Litovsk and Hindenberg[3] you will doubtless know. He is in PWE in London at the moment and is slated (although this is secret) to be one of the Masters of the new colleges in the University of Virginia at Charlottesville – having been Professor there for some time. He is a very attractive and brilliant person – perhaps you will remember that I brought him to dinner at All Souls in the summer of 1942 when he was staying with his brother-in-law Heaton[4] of Christ Church, and is an expert military historian with a very rich cultural background. I do hope he will be considered if the topic ever arises. He is remarkably well informed about American politics and if ever in Oxford well worth talking to. He is reachable via the Political Intelligence Department of the Foreign Office, on the 7th floor of Bush House (under Bruce Lockhart).[5]

Now that I have started gushing forth names, I hope you will not think me too importunate if I warmly recommend to you my friend Bob Hooker,[6] who is personal assistant to Berle in the State Department, a very nice and good man about to leave for England any day, and likely to be there by the time this arrives. He is a member of the Committee on Internal Transport in Post-War Europe, which is being assembled in London. He says

Director FRPS, Royal Institute of International Affairs (at Balliol), 1939–43, FORD 1943–4; Head of Social Science Dept, LSE, 1944–50.

1 Arnold Joseph Toynbee (1889–1975), historian; Director of Studies, Royal Institute of International Affairs, and Research Professor of International History, London, 1925–55; Director, FRPS, 1939–43, FORD 1943–6.

2 Henry Vincent Hodson (1906–99), economist; Fellow of All Souls 1928–35; Director, Empire Division, MOI, 1939–41; Reforms Commissioner, Government of India, 1941–2; Principal Assistant Secretary, then Head of Non-Munitions Division, Ministry of Production, 1942–5; Assistant Editor, *Sunday Times*, 1946–50 (Editor 1950–61).

3 Field Marshal Paul Ludwig Hans Anton von Beneckendorf und von Hindenburg (1847–1934), German soldier and politician; brought out of retirement and made supreme commander of German army during First World War; President of Germany 1925–33.

4 Trevor Braby Heaton (1886–1972), Dr Lee's Reader in Anatomy and Student of Christ Church, 1920–54; married to John Wheeler-Bennett's sister Constance Irene.

5 Sir Robert (Hamilton) Bruce Lockhart (1887–1970), diplomat, banker, editor, author; Political Intelligence Dept, FO, 1939–40; British Representative with Provisional Czechoslovak Government, London, 1940–1; Deputy Under-Secretary of State, FO, and Director-General, Political Warfare Executive (PWE), 1941–5.

6 Robert G. Hooker, American diplomat, assistant to Berle in the SD.

that he will be there for only a week or two (I should think he is contactable via the American Embassy). I am sure he would appreciate a visit to Oxford, however brief, if that is not taxing your hospitality too highly. He is a very amiable anglophile person from California, of Boston origin and upbringing, and as he is close to Berle and other persons here, it would be nice if he went away with happy memories of his brief English visit.

I expect you will have met Turner[1] by now. It is, I believe, a very dead secret indeed that he is to be Professor of History at Yale and to retire from his official duties fairly shortly. I cannot but think that you liked his generous spirit. Archie MacLeish has come back with very lyrical praise for yourself – he got on wonderfully well, it seems, with Lord Simon, of all people – and came back with a highly damaging story about the fact that Mr Irving Berlin was asked to lunch by mistake for Professor Isaiah Bowman[2] instead of the usual attribution.

I am very sorry indeed not to have seen Mrs Adams. I should be grateful if you could convey to her my regrets and apologies. I shall scan *The Times* daily for news of the Oxford elections, in which my heart, I find, is far more deeply embedded than in the ephemeral events that surround me here.

With best wishes,
    Yours ever,
      Isaiah Berlin

TO DONALD HALL
Minister of State's Office, Foreign Office

    18 May 1944 [*carbon*]

British Embassy, Washington

My dear Donald,
    I can scarcely believe that I am here after an unbelievably swift journey. On the other hand, the wonderfully unaltered condition of our colleagues convinces me that I am indeed here. It is curiously depressing to find after one had been through so much oneself in London that almost literally nothing has happened here. Everyone one meets shows mild surprise at the

---

1 Ralph Edmund Turner (1893–1964), US pioneer in cultural history; economic historian, Social Security Board 1936–41; Cultural Relations Division, SD, 1942–4; appointed Professor of History, Yale, 1944.

2 Isaiah Bowman (1878–1950), physical geographer; special adviser to the Secretary of State 1943–5; member of the US delegation to Dumbarton Oaks (482/3). For the lunch invitation see pp. 478–80 above.

fact that one has been away for, so one says, some seven weeks. Nothing, they say, marks the flow of time here. The only change I find in myself is a sudden gush of affection for Americans in general, due, I suppose, to finding them so much nicer than they had appeared at the end of an unbroken year and a half in Washington. I gave your love to Colonel Hoskins, who was more affable and informed me that he had been trying to 'get ahold of me' for two months and promptly invited me to two meals. Every American I have spoken to seems to me now 14 times nicer and wiser than my local colleagues. Perhaps this is an artificial tender feeling caused by the thought that soon I shall leave them for ever. Anyhow, the effect is violent pro-American sentiment such as I have never yet felt before in my life. [. . .]

Yours ever,
Isaiah Berlin

TO MARIE AND MENDEL BERLIN

2 June 1944

British Embassy, Washington, DC

My dear parents,

I am really exceptionally well. It is nice to find upon return how different one's stay in Ireland and one's condition here is as compared to 1942. I am in something of a hurry at the moment as the accumulation of work is still considerable, so you will forgive me if this is brief.

My friend Alexander Yakovlevich Halpern may telephone you or call personally. I do not remember if I have talked to you about him. he is a very cultivated and dignified old person, who was the first Secretary of the Provisional Government in Petrograd in 1917, then became a lawyer in London, and now works for us here. He is a great friend of mine and of John Wheeler-Bennett's and is a very charming old snob to whom you can talk Russian or English. His wife is even nicer than he, a gay old Georgian princess of no pretensions and splendid temperament.

The house continues to run in a very orderly fashion. Our maid complains that we did not give her a birthday present. She is, I fear, very grasping although reasonably attached to Chilver and myself. I still adhere to my intention of returning to England in December or January, but nobody can really tell. Everyone continues to be very nice and attentive.

Mrs Frankfurter sends her greetings. Please convey my love to David Cecil and apologies to him for my pestering him so before I left.

Love,
Isaiah

⟨I enclose an extraordinary collection of photographs, taken during the celebrated journey from California to Washington last summer. IB.

The Спящая Красавица[1] series were taken in a sleeping car. One picture is of my travelling companion, John Russell.

June 6. I am not likely to forget the coincidence of my birthday with great events.⟩[2]

TO FREYA STARK

12 June 1944 [*carbon*]

British Embassy, Washington

Is it really to be that I am not to see you before you leave for England? Alas, I cannot be in New York before you go to your Island with Esther Wright,[3] which I gather is happening on the 16th, although I shall be in New York on the 18th for a day. But if you are returning via New York or intend to be in New York for any other purpose before you actually set sail or wing, please let me know and I shall try to arrange to be in New York at some relevant date and do this most gladly if I possibly can.

London is heaven, but Oxford seventh heaven. After four days in my own room, and a conversation or two with the Cecils and our friends (Lord Berners has, you will be glad to hear, written a national anthem for and accepted by Saudi Arabia which he played to me on the piano), I lost all desire to see telegrams, dispatches, important persons, etc., and indeed, although I fear to say it, actually began to lose interest in all the subjects with which they dealt. Before this enchantment could pass, I made a date with my College to return to them in January and settle down to life of contemplation (which genuinely seems to me fuller of tangible and palpable objects than my present existence – certainly no politics are more real than those of academic life, no loves deeper, no hatreds more burning, no principles more sacred).

I shall, if I may, take you at your word about your house in Venezia. Who knows, but we may go into the Holy Land together from there one day, but not yet I hasten to add. As I told Colonel Hoskins the other day, I find I have no stomach for the ingredients of that fearful cauldron and find a position on its edge, scalded from time to time by its fearful exhalations,

1 'Spyashchaya Krasavitsa' ('Sleeping Beauty'): for an example see Plate 37.
2 D-Day was IB's 35th birthday.
3 Esther Ursula Wright, née Long, wife of Michael.

futile as well as uncomfortable. I should dearly love to tell you about my benedictory talks on that subject with various official persons in London – of how Lord Melchett[1] offered me a job as a Messiah (with sound financial guarantees) and of what America looks like from there.

I do hope that you will reply and say that you will be in New York some time after the 16th. I do envy you your early return – Europeans understand more with their little finger than – with the possible exception of Boston and Umgebung[2] – this splendid nation in all its energy and might.

Between mid-July and mid-August IB took a month's holiday from the Washington routine and climate.

TO MARIE AND MENDEL BERLIN

9 August 1944 [*manuscript*]

As from British Embassy,
Washington, DC

My dearest parents,

I am really extremely well. After the Great Heat began in the Washington Congo, I took your advice & went to the Mountains. Do not say it widely – people in England rightly think this no time for pleasure – but I heard 4 wonderful Mozart concerts under Sergey Koussevitzky[3] – a pseudo-aristocrat who looks & is a 120% Russian жидок[4] surrounded by such other Russian nobility as the composer Lourié,[5] M. Paul Gunzbourg, & his secretary Mme Hirschmann,[6] sister of Vladimir Poliakov ('Augur')[7]

---

1 Henry Mond, 2nd Baron Melchett (1898–1949), businessman; at the time Chairman of the Council of the Jewish Agency. Does 'Messiah' mean more than that the job offered would take IB back to Palestine?

2 'Environs'.

3 Serge (né Sergey Aleksandrovich) Koussevitzky (1874–1951), Russian-born US conductor; Director of the Boston Symphony Orchestra 1924–49; founding Director of the Berkshire Music Center, Tanglewood, Mass., 1940.

4 'Zhidok' ('little Jew', in a pejorative and/or ironically affectionate sense).

5 Arthur Vincent Lourié (1892–1966), né Artur Sergeevich Lur'e, Russian composer and musicologist, member of the Russian Avant-Garde movement in St Petersburg; after the Revolution, Commissar of the music division of the Ministry of Public Education; left the USSR in 1922 and lived mainly in Paris until emigrating to the US in 1941.

6 Henrietta Leopoldovna Girshman, née Leon (1885–1970), widow of Moscow manufacturer, collector and art patron Vladimir Osipovich Girshman (1867–1936) and frequent model for painter Valentin Serov (594/6).

7 Vladimir Solomonovich Polyakov (1910–77), Russian-born author and political commentator under the pseudonym 'Augur', regular contributor to *The Times*.

of London, related to the real Berlins,[1] so one of our quasi-pseudo relations. All v. Russian. I entered the entourage, talked Russian ('Г–нь Берлинь, вы как то и эрудит и в мире бываете ... и русскйи вид очень интересно ...')[2] & enjoyed myself. Then I visited Princeton (the Prof. of philosophy[3] is an Englishman) & Harvard & came to stay with the charming, gentle, jeder Zoll eine Lady,[4] Alix de Rothschild, wife of Guy, on Cape Cod, where it is cool & lovely (as it was also at the concerts) & I have a little cottage & black servant to myself. All is peace & most beautiful. On the 14th, alas, I return to Washington, but after 1 full month's holiday. So I am really O.K. The Hindemith–Schönberg joke – & Rach at the demolition squad – both very good I thought. I still intend to return in December–January, but might stay another month if hard pressed. R Law muttered something about Moscow but obscurely. I asked him to dinner with 3 young New Dealers of my acquaintance & it was all a v. great success. By the time Lord B.[5] came I had gone, better so I thought, & not mix one's loyalties. I look to having a fine time with Prof. Webster, who is one of our World Organisation negotiators & Ben Cohen who is one of the American ditto. Chilver returns on the 9th & on the 15th we resume our married establishment. I got Morgan to live there in my absence, & so got paid. As you see I am really much more practical & solid than you think, even tho' my nails are not always quite clean. Sorry this so dull but I am really so peaceful & contented, as tho' sea wind blows me about.

Shaya

Nice of Lightfoot about sweet peas. Give him my love, & to Smith & Co & Mary.

---

1 The family to which Rabbi Meir Berlin belonged and to which IB's aunt was related by marriage (432/1); IB's grandfather Dov Ber Zuckerman had taken Berlin as his surname on his adoption in childhood by his uncle Isaiah Berlin senior.

2 'G[ospodi]n" Berlin", vy kak to i erudit i v mire byvaete ... i russkii vid ochen' interesno' ('Mr Berlin, you are something of a polymath and are a man of the world ... and your Russian perspective is very interesting ...').

3 Walter Terence Stace (1886–1967), from a British military family; as a civil servant in Ceylon 1910–32 studied and wrote on philosophy in his spare time; Stuart Professor of Philosophy at Princeton 1935–55.

4 'Every inch a lady'.

5 IB had been Beaverbrook's house-guest, on Brendan Bracken's orders, for a weekend during his last visit home. At this encounter, as at an earlier dinner in 1942, IB had been repelled by Beaverbrook's coarseness; he later described him as 'one of the nastiest men ... I had ever met' (MI Tape 21).

TO HERBERT HART

[Early October 1944, *manuscript*][1]

[Washington]

My dear Herbert,

Of course you must accept. Why do I propose to half abandon the subject? really only because I cannot find convincing arguments for a priori philosophy of any save [a] mathematical kind – & that I am not v. good at or interested in [it] – & to go about knocking down metaphysical errors for 30 years or whatever is too unfruitful. But since you believe that non-empirical elements, not invented by us but discovered in the object itself – are there it is your direct intellectual duty to testify to the truth. The logistical technique is dreary but perfectly easy to learn if you don't boil against it constantly like H.W.B.J[oseph], & to equip yourself to take on your adversaries you may have to take off X number of months & just acquire it. Perhaps we cd do that together since I have been very idle about ⟨it⟩ myself. But the issue of total positivism versus the philosophy ⟨of⟩ the last 1500 years is desperate enough to deserve the dedication of even your whole talent. When you say that Ewing's[2] is the voice you find most convincing, that is only because he repeats what we have all been taught, in slightly brushed up language. The same applies to Broad. But you won't put up with that under the strenuous attack of say Ayer & Austin, who will be back in Wadham & Magd. respectively, & will have to build a new line of defense. This you will find absorbing, believe me. And nothing could be better for New College & Oxford than stout opposition of this sort. You will enjoy being a don very much. You will enjoy local administrative post-war issues more than you may think, since they will be quite real & provide a possible platform for defending intellectual etc. positions which real politics won't. That there will be a fight of standards v. adulteration I am convinced. As for your not knowing Latin & Greek, what stuff! the less Plato & Ar. are taught as ancient texts, with Joseph's puzzles about whether we should read κλεπτής τις or κλεπτὴς τίς[3] the better. There are plenty of Hardies, Mures,[4] Murphys,[5]

1 A small strip of the letter is torn off or eaten away: in this letter ⟨ ⟩ = conjectural restoration of matter in missing portion.

2 Alfred Cyril Ewing (1899–1973), Lecturer in Moral Science, Cambridge, 1931–54.

3 The accents on κλεπτης τις (*kleptēs tis*) affect the meaning: 'a certain thief' or 'Who is the thief?'

4 Geoffrey Reginald Gilchrist Mure (1893–1979), Fellow and philosophy Tutor, Merton, 1920–47; University Lecturer in Philosophy 1929–37; propaganda work with SHAEF 1939–45; later (1947–63) Warden of Merton.

5 Presumably Neville Richard Murphy (1890–1971), Fellow and philosophy Tutor, Hertford, 1919–39, Principal 1939–59.

Donald Allans,[1] Michael Fosters,[2] Maclagans[3] to look after that. And I shall be most content to be a Smith to your Joseph (don't leap in the air at that tiny sting). Smith will, I suppose, be made Warden:[4] he & I & you = 2 tutors, if I am to be allowed to recede to half time with the rest for history (God but I am frightened of my choice. It has become almost a matter of disinterested obstinacy to persevere). I see no *possible* objection. All that is necessary to absorb you & make you function is an atmosphere of sufficient intellectual activity, & with Ayer, Austin, Hants, & possible minor figures like McNab,[5] possibly ? Nowell Smith, M'Kinnon,[6] aside from Ryle & Price I think one can guarantee that. Dr F. Waismann[7] will be there to teach us all the techniques required. How can you hesitate? the only point of the Bar I shd have thought is fame & money. If you don't mind too much about the latter you must certainly abandon it since the death of the soul it produces is automatic & inevitable. As for Maurice B. ⟨that⟩ too is nonsense (as you in fact know well). He is to-day ⟨a⟩ sated power: & not a very formidable one: rather like Italy ⟨in⟩ 1900. To return to the subject: moral questions, the question ⟨of⟩ where the mirror image is, & what physicists are saying & a⟨bout⟩ what will always be the real ones, not whether the Theory of Types performs an adequate reduction of algebra to formal logic: & if I don't want to go on with this only for the rest of my life it is because I don't believe that I burn enough about it: i.e. have something important enough to say & insist on & fight for: you plainly have since the latest empiricists haven't convinced you: so that unless you speak you let the truth go by default. Why, then, hesitate? the only real objection wd be anticipations of boredom & misery in S.C.R.S. But you like Oxford & books. I am quite clear on all this. By the time I return in December or January I shall be bitterly disappointed if it – the life in Chipping Cam[p]den & all – with you & Jen commuting – won't have gone through. I didn't cable[8] because saying 'yes yes of course accept' wd have sounded hearty & silly. So much for that. Felkin[9] says you said Sparrow was missing. Surely not? Write

1 Donald James Allan (1907–78), Fellow and classics Tutor, Balliol, 1931–47; FO 1940–5; later (1957–71) Professor of Greek, Glasgow.

2 Michael Beresford Foster (1903–59), Student and philosophy Tutor, Christ Church, 1930–48.

3 William Gauld Maclagan (1903–72), Lecturer in Philosophy (from 1931 Fellow), Oriel, 1930–46; temporary civil servant HM Treasury 1940–6; Professor of Moral Philosophy, Glasgow, 1946–69.

4 This occurred on 11 October.

5 Donald Macnabb (233/6).

6 Donald MacKinnon (233/5).

7 Friedrich Waismann (1896–1959), Austrian philosopher and member of Vienna Circle; Lecturer in Moral Sciences, Cambridge, 1937–9; life member of New College from 1942, Lecturer in the Philosophy of Science and of Mathematics 1946–8.

8 HLAH had offered to pay for IB's reply.

9 (Arthur) Elliott Felkin (1892–1968), international civil servant; member of the economic

about all this at once. I am sure Xtopher supports me.

love.

Isaiah

On 7 November FDR and his Vice-Presidential running-mate Harry S. Truman[1] defeated Thomas Dewey and John Bricker, giving FDR an unprecedented fourth term in office.

TO LADY DAPHNE STRAIGHT

20 November 1944 *[carbon]*

British Embassy, Washington

My dear Daphne,

I cannot allow the elections to pass without briefly pointing out that I propose to take enormous credit not only for predicting F.D.R. but also on the controversial matter of the Republican House, concerning which you reported scepticism as early as the middle of last year. All the predictions of the real panic-mongers, particularly the really American experts – Graham H[utton] and John W[heeler]-B[ennett] – about the famous impasse between the President and Congress is now disposed of. If Capehart[2] is elected, as I suppose he will be, but Davis[3] defeated, the isolationists will be able to muster just about 32 votes in the Senate. I think things look really bright for political internationalism, as they look gloomy for economic ditto in this country.

I now move on to my election evening, which began with dinner with the Ambassador, as the paid minstrel of political reporting. I have made my peace with the latter, i.e. he has admitted that he had over-estimated Lippmann's[4] judgment on the temper of Congress, and I am now allowed

section of the Secretariat of the League of Nations under Arthur Salter; as Secretary to the Permanent Central Opium Board in Geneva (and during the War in Washington), responsible for setting up international surveillance of the illegal narcotics trade.

1 Harry S. Truman (1884–1972), farmer, haberdasher, Democratic Senator from Missouri 1935–45, Chairman of the Truman Committee to investigate the war effort, Vice-President January 1945, President from April 1945 to 1953. (The 'S.' in his name is not an abbreviation but a compromise between the names of his grandfathers, Anderson Shipp Truman and Solomon Young.)

2 Homer Earl Capehart (1897–1979), isolationist Republican Senator from Indiana 1945–63.

3 James John Davis (1873–1947), Welsh-born Pittsburgh steel-worker, Secretary of Labor 1921–30, Republican Senator from Pennsylvania 1930–45; defeated in the 1944 elections.

4 Walter Lippmann (1889–1974), political journalist and author, wrote for the *New York Herald Tribune* a nationally syndicated column, 'Today and Tomorrow', 1931–62; liberal early in his long career but later more pragmatic.

to go full steam ahead and blast our faint-hearted and pusillanimous friends
and advisers. Frankfurter, who feels my sentiments about Walter, provided
me with a beautiful photostat of a 1941 pre-Pearl Harbor column by him in
which contraction of the US is demanded, since American forces cannot ever
invade the continent of Europe. Very pleasing and agreeable and I enclose it
for your delectation or in case you have to use a secret weapon at some
crucial moment. Dinner was made eccentric by the presence of the Keyneses
– he is charming and very clever and so on; she seems to say anything that
comes to her head, and interrupted Lord H[alifax], who was trying to score
the returns for Ohio and Michigan – on whose importance I had lectured
him – when she said, 'Do you think the early poetry of Archie MacLeish is
better than his late?' 'Shhh, Lydia,'[1] said Baron K[eynes]. She was silent and
looked chastened and tried her hardest to take a serious interest in what the
radio was blaring out. It suddenly said, 'Returns from Mississippi: Roosevelt,
7,500; Dewey, 66.' 'That is very important,' said Lady Keynes, 'isn't it?
Mississippi is very important. It is for Roosevelt. Are you for Roosevelt? I am
for Roosie. Mississippi is very important. It is a big majority. I am very glad.
Are you glad? Are you for Roosevelt?' etc. etc. etc. She had to be stopped
again and then looked genuinely miserable and perplexed. Finally, sitting
next to Lord H. on the sofa, with me on her other side, she said in a normal
loud voice, 'He is wonderful, the Ambassador, so charming and so wise and
good. He had a terrible time here before, didn't he, because of Munich and
appeasement and all that? But he got over that, and they love him now, do
they not? He had a political past, didn't he? Do you remember in 1939 he
hated Chamberlain more than Maynard did, but Lord Halifax is now much
better than he was, isn't he?' I could only make mooing noises while Lord
Halifax rose on some pretext and wandered round the room playing with his
dog. Then there was a telephone call, and he went to talk to Hopkins, who
reported at about 10.45 p.m. that everything was in the bag, that the
President had told him from Hyde Park, 'Hell, it's fine', that he, Lord Halifax,
was to telephone Winston immediately to give him the news. 'I said "How's
Louise?",'[2] said Lord H. to us. 'He said, "Oh, *she's* all right, she is *quite* all
right."' 'Was he tiddley?' asked Lady H. 'A bit,' said Lord H., 'not more than
usual I should say.' 'What does the Professor say to that?' said Lady K.
innocently. I protested about being called a Professor. 'I am always being
called Professor,' said Lord K., but I answer 'I do not relish the insult without
the emolument.'

I refuse, I decline, to say anything serious to you about the election,

---

1 Lydia Keynes, née Lopokhova (1892–1981), Russian ballerina and actress.
2 Louise Hopkins, née Macy, Harry Hopkins's third wife.

which has really gone well, to the dismay of Dr Gallup[1] – Roper, if he didn't get cold feet at the last moment, would have scored a bull's eye, and still tries to maintain that he did. The President's majorities in New York, Illinois, Pennsylvania, Massachusetts, Missouri etc. are really most satisfactory. The interesting thing is that Senator Wagner ran ahead of him in New York, Mrs Douglas[2] ahead of him in Chicago (the victor over Day),[3] and so did Lucas.[4] Taft might easily be defeated (there is a fuss about alleged voting frauds in Ohio, but it may not come to much). Capehart is an absolutely frightful man, a real crook it seems, whereas Schricker[5] was splendid. Is the PAC[6] the beginning of the new labour party? Butler and Opie say yes. Curtin[7] says no. I do not know.

Yours ever,

Isaiah Berlin

TO G. B. GRUNDY

23 November 1944

British Embassy, Washington

Dear Dr Grundy,

Thank you for your letter of 21 October and your kind words. I am very glad to hear that you are working on the revised edition of your Thucydides.[8]

I hear scarcely any news of Oxford but was glad to see that A. H. Smith, whom I always liked and respected greatly, has been elected my Warden at New College.

As for me, I expect to be coming home in March, to Oxford and for good, I hope. I have had enough of government service, although I have enjoyed it all greatly and have had an incomparably more interesting war

1 Dr George Horace Gallup (1901–84) and Elmo Roper (1900–71), opinion poll pioneers, both forecast a victory for FDR, so perhaps this reference is by nickname to amateur forecasters in the Embassy.
2 Helen Gahagan Douglas (1900–1980), actress and opera singer, Democratic Congresswoman from California 1945–51.
3 Stephen Albion Day (1882–1950), lawyer, Republican Congressman from Illinois 1941–5.
4 Scott Wike Lucas (1892–1968), lawyer, Democratic Senator from Illinois 1939–51.
5 Henry Frederick Schricker (1883–1966), Democratic Governor of Indiana 1941–5, 1949–53.
6 The Polish American Congress had been founded at a rally in Buffalo, New York, in May 1944 to put pressure on the US Government to work for Poland's independence after the war.
7 British Embassy official responsible for Trade Unions.
8 The first volume of Grundy's *Thucydides and the History of his Age* appeared in 1911; a second edition of this (barely altered), together with the somewhat delayed second volume, in 1948.

than those of my contemporaries who have had to fight it, of which I duly feel ashamed. Of Corpus men, I can only think of Davison[1] here, as a Major working in the British Joint Staff Mission, and Dunnett[2] has been over from time to time from the Treasury. I live comfortably enough and, being unmarried, share a house with my friend Guy Chilver, whom you may remember as the ancient history tutor at Queen's and who is here as the much respected expert in the British Food Mission.

As for my official status, I enjoy the local rank of First Secretary in the British Embassy at Washington and am head of the Reports Office, itself a part of the Information Office headed by Harold Butler (once heading the ILO in Geneva, then of Nuffield College) of Balliol and All Souls – you must have known his father at BNC.[3] My office is shortly to be transferred to the Foreign Office, but by that time I shall probably be gone; at present it is technically a branch of the Ministry of Information. This has been very much a dons' war – with Franks[4] and Maud practically controlling the home departments in London and everyone else in tactical positions – on the whole, it does not seem to me to be too badly run by our profession, which seems to have destroyed its reputation for starry-eyed incompetence once and for all. Nobody is so fiercely bureaucratic, or so stern with soldiers and regular civil servants, as the don disguised as temporary government official armed with an indestructible superiority complex. I think with proper modesty of the fact that, had you not jockeyed CCC into electing me in 1927, I should not have been in a position now to say any of these things, and send you my warmest regards.

Yours sincerely,
Isaiah Berlin

---

1 John Armstrong Davison (1906–66), CCC classics 1925–9, Major, Cheshire Regiment, 1939–45, Military Assistant Secretary to War Cabinet, Joint British Staff Mission, Washington, 1943–5.
2 George Sangster Dunnett (1907–84), CCC classics 1925–9, British civil servant, Treasury 1931–46, Ministry of Civil Aviation 1946–7.
3 Brasenose college.
4 Oliver Shewell Franks (1905–92), Baron Franks 1962, Professor of Moral Philosophy, Glasgow, 1937–45; civil servant, Ministry of Supply, 1939–46, Permanent Secretary 1945–6.

TO ALAN DUDLEY
Foreign Office

5 December 1944 [*carbon*]

British Embassy, Washington

My dear Alan,

[. . .]

As for myself, I plan to be home late in March and to go back to New College, scarcely pausing in London where I have nothing to do. There is vague talk here about retaining me in public service, for which I am said to have developed an incurable taste, but as so far nothing concrete has been advanced, I cannot see how anything is to come of that. Michael Wright, who leads this party, regards me as suited for a job in the Foreign Office, concerning which he proposes to write to Sir D. Scott. It sounds cosy and attractive, but I am by nature a stayer-put and am not sure that there really is a job of work to be done (without which I am, to my surprise, restless and unhappy), and Oxford seems immensely concrete (although I dare say, like an old circus horse, I shall neigh like mad when the smell of public sawdust reaches me, and irritate my colleagues, much as the late Warden of New College used to when he invariably opened all his sentences with the words 'When I was in the Cabinet . . .'). If Sir D. Scott lets drop anything about that, I shall be curious to know what the reactions are. No one at all (least of all in M. of I., but in fact no one at all) knows anything about this. I am glad that Darvall[1] has finally landed – at least I hope he has – in Denver; Sir G[erald] C[ampbell] was not at all easy about this, as you may imagine. Harold Butler has, I think, wisely declined the Secretary of State's offer to him[2] – as unsuitable to his temperament and years. Brendan [Bracken] is said to be trying to make him Provost of Eton. I still enjoy my work greatly (to be conducted under the F.O. mantle, I hope, as from 1 January. Archie Mackenzie should be visiting you towards Christmas). I have two new sources in the White House and go through periods of alternate pleasure and shame at the thought that I occasionally scoop Drew Pearson. I really must return to civilised habits and solid values and leave gossip to real trivia.

Yours ever,

Isaiah Berlin

1 Frank Ongley Darvall (1906–87), Deputy Director, American Division, MOI, 1939–45; British Consul, Denver, 1945–6 (the appointment to which IB here refers); First Secretary, British Embassy, Washington, 1946–9; IB later recalled him as 'a caricature liberal' (interview with Nicholas Cull cited at 309/1), and Daphne Straight found him so unbearably tedious that she couldn't help yawning or giggling in his presence (letter to IB of 14 August 1943).

2 Untraced.

TO THE NEW YORKER STORE

7 December 1944 [*carbon*]

[British Embassy, Washington]

Dear Sirs,

I should be grateful if you could send to Mrs John G. Leaf, 4624 Van Ness Street, NW, Washington, DC, at your earliest convenience one wide brimmed Stetson hat (size 7¼; colour, light grey), which I gather would cost about $10.00. The widest available type of hat is what I have in view.

If you could let me know the precise price, I should be glad to send you a cheque for this without delay.

Yours sincerely,

Isaiah Berlin

TO MARIE AND MENDEL BERLIN

12 December 1944

British Embassy, Washington

My dear parents

I feel profoundly ashamed of my excessive silence but hasten to remedy the matter. Everything goes on perfectly peaceful here. My household affairs are in complete order, I am physically flourishing, and my present plan is to return towards the end of March.

I am very glad indeed that Smith has been elected as he is an exceptionally nice and distinguished man and a great friend of ours. I have had a nice letter and telegram from him thanking me for my congratulations and other letters from fellows of the college on college business of various sorts. There is some evident reluctance here to let me leave government service altogether, but I do not know whether anything will come of the various vague schemes for retaining me in some capacity. I do not encourage or discourage but only refuse to solicit and await offers if only to have the pleasure of refusing them. There was a vague message from the Paris Embassy wondering if I would like to go there for a while, but I do not know the French and do not particularly like them and would be no good there, I am sure. And it also sounds very cold and cheerless.

Your friend Mr Simon Liberman[1] has written a rather sweet book (in

---

1 Simon Isaevich Liberman (1881–?1960), before the Revolution a Menshevik and wealthy businessman in the Russian timber industry; worked for the Communist regime until leaving the USSR in 1926; father of Alexander Liberman (364/1), in whose obituary he was described as 'An epicure and luxury lover [. . .] renowned for his immaculate appearance': *The Times*, 27 November 1999, 24. His book was *Dela i lyudi: na sovetskoy stroike* ['Things and people: in the

Russian) on his contacts with early Soviet notables from Lenin onwards, about which he has asked me advice (with a view to an English translation). It is too detailed an account of the early timber organisation in the USSR but I dare say it would be of interest to you and I propose to send it to you one of these days – the censorship will probably have to read it from cover to cover first, but I will try to send it through some official by bag.

Guy de Rothschild has arrived here from Paris on some sort of Jewish business, and I hope to hear the latest news of Victor R., who is also in Paris from him. Miriam is said to be very low – I am not clear that she hasn't had a second still-born child, if so I do not wonder.

As for myself, I really have no news of the least interest. I have not been to New York for a long time, but last time I went, which was in October, I telephoned to Mrs Raskin and their affairs seem to be going much as before. I may go to New York for Christmas, in which case I shall look them up and generally fill myself with news of everybody to bring home to you when I return for good. I think your Bournemouth scheme[1] sounds excellent to me, I am sure the milder climate will do you a great deal of good and as for the distance from Oxford, it is, I suppose, a mere three hours which, after the vast distances I travelled here, will seem like nothing at all. The Apters have suddenly started pursuing me madly again, and Liliana, the girl, was sent to see me in Washington. She seemed to me incredibly dreary, boring, and a general embarrassment. Madam Apter (or Apters, as they call themselves here, faithful to the old country),[2] is obviously intent on throwing her into my company, the poor girl does not like me in the least, nor I her, but a great deal of hypocrisy probably goes on between mother and daughter. I have so far successfully avoided seeing the parents, despite pressing invitations to stay with them in New York – their business affairs seem to be going quite well, as everyone else's here during the boom – but you really do not need to warn me against a closer approach. I shall look after that myself quite adequately even if it means a series of deliberate snubs. The latest embarrassment is that a box of socks have suddenly been forwarded to me by Mrs A., for which I shall have to insist on paying; I do not know how much (they are of quite good quality!), she will refuse to take payment and we shall have a fearful time, all this in the way of comic relief.

The Aronsons seem to have disappeared into North Carolina, and there is not a sound from them. So much the better. I had Ida's regards from

construction of the Soviet State'] (NY, 1944), trans. as *Building Lenin's Russia* (Chicago, 1945).

1 IB's parents were planning a holiday there in January.

2 An odd remark, since the dominant version of the name in Dvinsk (now Daugavpils), Konstantin Apters's home town in south-east Latvia, was 'Apter'.

visitors from her country recently, they seem to be doing quite well and are much respected by the community.

To return to the Apters – Solomon[1] seems to have cropped up of, in all places, Afghanistan, whence he reported the deaths under doubtless appalling circumstances of the rest of the family; the American Apters are very displeased at so disturbing a piece of information being conveyed to them in so heartless a manner. All this I know from the solitary visit of Lilliana, may it never be repeated again. It is agreeable to invent reasons for Mrs A. when she telephones as to why I cannot be in New York unhappily at the precise moment at which Miss A. is down from her New England university, when it would be such a joy to see her again. Dear me, what villains relations make of us all.

I had an agreeable lunch with Lenanton,[2] who said that he would inform you of what business opportunities there might be, I gather not much is as yet in view, it will all be cartelised, I expect. Next week I expect to meet the aged Dan,[3] the Russian Social Democrat, a relic of very long ago, historically he may be quite amusing as, on the eve of approaching 90, he is said to be quite lively still.

The Frankfurters are very well and send you their love, as does Dr Chilver. I may, although this is far from certain, take a train down to Mexico before I finally return to England, just to see that remarkable land. I have finally met a real life-size Soviet diplomat who warmly pressed me to stay with him in Moscow. Stranger things have happened. I am encouraged to cultivate him by the Embassy and may, therefore, do so a little now that the new and beautiful era of our relations with that country has dawned. The question is, is he a Jew? There are some definite signs pointing in that direction and yet one cannot be sure; he was born in Moscow in 1906, evidence against; his name is Gromov,[4] evidence against; but his voice and manner, and still more his wife's, point suspiciously in the other direction. I shall sooner or later discover the truth. ⟨don't mention this to anyone. The poor man may suffer if you do.⟩

Lord Halifax has expressed suitable distress at my departure and still tells the story about me and Irving Berlin to all and sundry. Sometimes I am made to tell it myself, sometimes he is willing to do so. His legless son is very nice.

---

1 Solomon Mendelevich Apter, brother of Konstantin (358/3).
2 Gerald Lenanton (1896–1952), businessman; Chairman of Foy Morgan & Co., Director of Home Timber Production 1941–6.
3 If this is Fedor Il'ich Dan, né Fedor Ivanovich Gurvich (1871–1947), doctor and Menshevik, expelled from USSR 1922, IB or his typist exaggerates his age.
4 Anatoly Borisovich Gromov (b. 1907), real name Anatoly Veniaminovich Gorsky, from September 1944 First Secretary in the Soviet Embassy, Washington; NKGB *rezident* there (code-name Vadim), as he had been for the previous four years in London, where he had been the Cambridge spy-ring's controller. As IB suspected, he was Jewish.

I have had a letter from Mrs Falk enquiring what the future in New College of her husband is – I must know this better here than she in Oxford, etc. Do not mention this to her, please, but I will reply to this fishing expedition in a suitably ambiguous manner which, indeed, is all I am capable of. I feel morally certain that her man, though nice and quite able, will not, in fact, be given a Fellowship at New College,[1] but shall try to break this to her gently or, better still, not break it at all and plead ignorance.

John Foster[2] is said to be living in a comfortable flat in Paris; I should love to visit him there. Now that I have my French Rothschild connection, I count on comfort when I go to Paris.

Really, this letter is tapering off into nothing, and I must stop. My emotional life is wonderfully placid and disturbed by nothing, and I mean that. ⟨(my 'friend'[3] left U.S. 6 months ago.)⟩ It is exactly the same as at Oxford, say in 1939. I cannot really deplore the passing of Mr Boult[4] too much, I did not know him well and he was not particularly nice. I had a letter from Mary Fisher saying how tiresome it was that his wife should have chosen to commit suicide in the Warden's lodgings just when Mrs Fisher was moving out. It does sound very ill-planned, I must say. Dear me, how heartless one is about the unknown. I really was very distressed to hear that Jasper Ridley was killed[5] and still cannot bring myself to write a suitable letter to Cressida.[6] I have had far too comfortable a war. It is nice to think that I shall see you both so soon. ⟨I am sorry this letter is so fearfully empty. But I shall really *soon* be home.

    love

       Isaiah
       Shayah?
       Shaya?
       or as some say Shire?
       which do you prefer?⟩

---

1 He wasn't: cf. 322/3.
2 At this point a Brigadier on General Service.
3 Lady Patricia Sybil Douglas (1918–91), daughter of the 11th Marquess of Queensberry and thus great-niece of Lord Alfred Douglas (Oscar Wilde's 'Bosie'); at the time married to Count John de Bendern, on whose liberation from an Italian prisoner-of-war camp she and her daughter had returned to England from their wartime home in Cambridge, Mass.
4 David Boult, who had a weak heart, died on 1 November at the age of 34, and his distraught wife Nancy Patricia Norah Boult, aged 23, committed suicide two days later.
5 On 13 December 1943 in Italy, while serving as a Lieutenant in the King's Royal Rifle Corps.
6 See pp. 530–3 below.

TO ROBIN CRUIKSHANK

12 December 1944 [*carbon*]

British Embassy, Washington, DC

Dear Robin,

Here it is.[1] It is agreeable to order one's own coffin with exact specifications as to the type of wood and the sober ornamentation embossed on the lid. I feel like Sarah Bernhardt:[2] one more Aiglon, possibly one more Cyrano, and then the little farm near Mendon with a yellowing bundle of letters and an elderly maid who understands one's gradually less and less intelligible patter about the days when the prince himself used to look in.

My faithful Archibald[3] will give you all the talk of the town. It isn't what it used to be when we were young. I suppose they all say that.

Yours ever,

Isaiah Berlin

TO ANDY LOGAN[4]
New Yorker

14 December 1944 [*carbon*]

[British Embassy, Washington]

Dear Mr Logan,

Thank you for your letter of 11 December.[5] I fear that I am unlikely to be in New York until, at any rate, sometime next year, when I shall pay a farewell visit before returning to England for good. In any case, I shall be greatly distressed if anything was said about me in the pages of your remarkable journal, for which I have the greatest love and admiration, or indeed in any other public print, since I suffer from a (perhaps unreasoning) horror of personal publicity from which I have thus far been relatively spared, to my great relief. My words about love and admiration are, I can

---

1 Perhaps a memorandum on his Washington job, written for the benefit of RJC and any successor(s) of his own?

2 Sarah Bernhardt, née Henriette-Rosine Bernard (1844–1923), French actress and theatre manager. She continued acting into old age even after losing a leg; amongst her many famous roles were Roxane and Cyrano in Edmond Rostand's *Cyrano de Bergerac* and the Duc de Reichstadt in the same author's *L'Aiglon*; she had a home near Mendon in Southern Brittany; one of her many lovers was Henri, Prince de Ligne, by whom she had a son.

3 Archie Mackenzie.

4 Andy Logan (female), née Isabel Ann Logan (1920–2000), journalist.

5 Asking to interview IB: 'There are several groups among whom you are becoming a legend (and I'm not referring to the great Irving Berlin–Churchill saga) and we make a specialty of tracking down legends around here.'

assure you, not idle, and if there is anything I could do to please its editors, short of offering myself for copy, I should gladly do it at any time.

I understand from one of your Washington contributors that only New York personalities were of interest to you, and perhaps this would exclude me automatically; I sincerely hope that my reluctance to fall in with your very flattering suggestion is no passing modesty, but founded on a profound and unshakable conviction that an interview would be a sad waste of your valuable time and talents.

Yours sincerely,
Isaiah Berlin

TO HENRY PRICE

18 December 1944 [*carbon*]

British Embassy, Washington

Dear Henry,

I sent you a long and, I hope, not too confused cable the other day, as your letter about Hart only arrived on the 9th, owing to being sent to New York. This is doubtless due to the fact that this is the last address left in the hands of the New College authorities, but I have, in fact, worked at the Embassy in Washington since 1942, a fact I seem to have jealously concealed from the relevant authorities, and you said that a meeting might be held on this subject in the middle of December.

Now, as to the topic itself: I have known Herbert Hart for the last twelve years and do not really know quite what to say. He is a man, as you say, of very first-rate ability and philosophical capacity. The main advantages seem to me to be:

(a) That he has a generally good, tough, formidable mind and a capacity for clear exposition. I still remember him as the President of the Jowett Society, when he was an undergraduate, and he was an excellent solid Cook Wilsonian[1] then. He has not really kept up terribly much since and is very modest and self-distrustful about this himself. Indeed, I knew something of what was in the wind, since he wrote me a long letter about it himself a month or two ago, asking me to keep it confidential. What he is tortured by is the thought that he will never be better than Ewing and will never hold other views than Ewing. He realises himself that this is not a very exciting state of mind to be in, and doubtless has the feeling of a person who finds

---

1 John Cook Wilson (1849–1915), Wykeham Professor of Logic, Oxford, 1889–1915, Fellow of New College 1901–15; influential in establishing epistemological realism in the Oxford philosophy syllabus.

himself in the company of illustrious intellectuals who speak a foreign tongue, with one compatriot of somewhat inferior capacities who speaks his own language, and this is very tantalising and frustrating. Nevertheless, even given all this, he cannot be worse than Ewing, who, after all, is, in his own way, not contemptible. I feel that what New College needs is at least two philosophers, one of whom is everything that we can get so far as pure intellectual distinction and philosophical 'brow height' (as Gilbert Ryle used to call it) can make him. I do not know Urmson[1] at all well, but I should imagine that he possesses these properties, or may one day do so. At the same time, someone may turn up in a year or two equally so endowed. But the other should, so long as Lit. Hum. remains roughly what it is, be a solid teacher of Plato and Aristotle, ethics and possibly metaphysics and even politics, and generally provide the dependable background of the traditional curriculum. This would provide an even balance, and the gifts required for one purpose are scarcely ever enshrined in the same individual as those required by the other, although there have, of course, been exceptions. Now: if I am gradually to evaporate as a full-time philosopher, or indeed as the official philosopher at all, perhaps the person elected in my place in, say, two or three years' time (or earlier, if circumstances seem to point to this) might be a really distinguished epistemologico-logical highbrow, so to speak, someone who would both lecture and write in a manner worthy of the traditions of the College, which are not, I grant you, to be far advanced, even if they are not in any way lowered, by Herbert Hart. But I do think that Hart will, if he is willing to come at all, make a very admirable teacher of the staple diet, without attaining to heights or Indian rope-tricks of any kind. I do not mean to convey that he will merely be a hack of even the highest order, although I suppose that even such persons are not to be despised, but much better than this, and will make a Frank Hardie and not a bearded Aristotelian of however superior a vintage. I do agree with what you imply, even although you do not state it, namely that a philosopher *pur sang*[2] is indispensable and not merely a very intelligent man who is interested in and competent at philosophy as a hobby, however absorbing. If Hart is willing, firstly, to teach these extra logical subjects and, secondly, to acquire at any rate the rudiments of the Russell 'positivist' language, which I believe he could do without outrage to his convictions, he would be, I feel sure, the best man the College can get for this purpose if it wishes to elect before the end of the War and the return of the armed forces.

(b) Hart would, of course, make an admirable colleague, College tutor,

---

1 James Opie Urmson (b. 1915), CCC classics 1934–8, Senior Demy, Magdalen, 1938–9, Fellow 1939–45, Lecturer, Christ Church, 1945–6, Student 1946–55.
2 'Thoroughbred'.

etc., being a born dean with much of the required gravitas. What I do doubt is whether he would remain at the University during the rest of his working life, and equally whether he would write anything very memorable (far be it for me to cast scorn on that myself, who has not done it either). I do not recollect his having spoken to me about an anti-Ayer book, although he was obviously taken with the idea of doing something about and against the doctrines in question. The late Mr Justice Holmes[1] once divided good lawyers into 'razors' and 'good kitchen knives'. Doubtless this omits many other varieties – guillotines (like Cecil Radcliffe),[2] rapiers with not much edge but the finest points (like John Sparrow), etc., but under that classification Herbert Hart is a slender bread-knife, and any work he produces will resemble the solid pedestrian tramp of Ewing or Broad and will not provide glimpses of something new and exciting; or of something old seen with disturbing freshness, whether veridical or not, i.e. will be useful and part of the staff of life and by no means to be sneezed at, but not original or infected with that non-common-sense fanaticism that seems to me to be a necessary ingredient of philosophers who cut ice. I do not mean that he will be an eloquent amateur (like Father D'Arcy)[3] or a merely worthy hack: he will be at least as good as, let us say, Mabbott,[4] and possibly very much better, but he will probably stay outside the central stream of whatever the younger Oxford philosophers may constitute, a very respected figure but neither a leader nor a follower of the new fashion. Dear me, I seem to be writing an obituary for the *Oxford Magazine*.

On all these grounds I therefore think, without for a moment forgetting the truth of your proposition (with which I entirely agree) that this is a very important matter and that the intellectual reputation of the College will largely depend upon our choice – that, given a sharp and original 'modernist' colleague, Hart would provide the best obtainable tutor in philosophy, given that the entire Greats curriculum must be properly [provided] for within the College. One thing, I feel, is fairly certain: if he feels that he is not abreast of all that is going on and is struggling in a backwater of some sort, he will be the first to insist on leaving us himself. These are the grounds for my cable to you, but I feel that rather than urge the reason for my choice upon you, it

1 Oliver Wendell Holmes, Jr (1841–1935), Justice of the Supreme Court 1902–32; outstanding expert, in theory and practice, on the US legal system and constitution, noted for the incisiveness and wit of his opinions; his extensive and finely phrased writings remain eminently quotable.

2 IB must mean Cyril John Radcliffe (1899–1977), Fellow of All Souls 1922–37, 1st Viscount Radcliffe 1962, barrister, QC; MOI 1939–45, Director General 1941–5.

3 The Revd Martin Cyril D'Arcy (1888–1976), SJ, philosopher, leading apologist for Roman Catholicism (Evelyn Waugh's confessor); Master of Campion Hall, Oxford, 1932–45.

4 John David Mabbott (1898–1988), philosopher, Fellow of St John's 1924–63, Tutor 1930–63, then (1963–9) President.

would be best to reply to the questions which you ask, upon which I agree the right answer should depend:

(1) The candidate's understanding of the Russell language. I think that he would not be maddened by it, and could be induced to learn it sufficiently.

(2) Has he any views of his own on the theory of knowledge and the relevant logic? I think so. That is, his views are Cook Wilsonian, and not original, but not destructive, as Joseph's were, though somewhat old-fashioned. Such as they are, they are firmly held and well defended. Sufficient exposure to Austin ought to achieve the necessary training.

(3) I know nothing of his views on morals or metaphysics.

(4) Will he produce good books and articles? I am sceptical about a book, but, if he sticks to the subject, he may well produce articles of a level varying between those of, say, the elder Gallie,[1] and considerably better than those, say, of Professor Laird.[2]

Dear me, am I conveying any sense? I think I know (if I may use such an expression) precisely what it is that is worrying you about the case of a man nearing forty, who is about to embark on a subject where the professional and the amateur touch are so very distinguishable, and who has lived in the world for so long. If he were to be the sole philosopher of New College, I should be inclined to share your doubts. As it is, I think the virtues outweigh the defects. In any case, the candidate will not be a Wildon Carr[3] nor yet a Crossman. I think I have it at last. He will be a Carritt. I really do think that you may safely proceed upon some sort of basis as that. All empirical judgement is liable to err, but the analogy with Carritt seems to me to be the closest. I do not think I can do any better. Perhaps he will be much tougher-minded than our present Warden (I am very glad about that choice).

This letter is far too long and rambling, I am sure, to be read out to a meeting. I should, therefore, be grateful if, on the plea of length or personalia, you could convey its contents, if that is necessary, to Cecil and Wade-Gery and the Warden and whoever else may be relevant. Best of all if, upon enquiry, you could convey the impression which this letter will have produced upon your own consciousness, but if you feel that extracts should be quoted, you are, of course, free to put it to any use you please, provided it does not fall within the hands of the candidate himself.

Guy [Chilver] is well and sends you his greetings. He has a detailed knowledge of our economic relationships as well as of the components and

---

1 Ian Gallie (1907–48), elder (but not eldest) brother of Bryce Gallie (157/3); Exeter classics 1926–30, Fellow and philosophy Lecturer, Wadham, 1931–41, then joined Civil Service.

2 John Laird (1887–1946), Regius Professor of Moral Philosophy, Aberdeen, 1924–46; author of *An Enquiry into Moral Notions* (London, 1935), of which chapter 16, 'The Comparison of Goods', may have some relevance to IB's pluralism.

3 Herbert Wildon Carr (1857–1931), Professor of Philosophy, King's College, London, since 1918.

effects of foodstuffs, which stagger me, who am merely concerned with the lighter topic of politics. Richard C[hilver] came here recently, and between them they displayed an acquaintance with the politico-economic scene which will be the envy of the Master of Balliol himself,[1] lacking neither in acuteness or earnestness and full of surprising political passion. I hope I shall return to you in March, this time for good, with a set of entirely new and unfamiliar reproducible images culled from my immediate surroundings of the kind which, we are told, is precisely that designed to exacerbate relations between us and our great allies, because dwelling on aspects about which they feel particularly. In addition to this, I have an acquaintance with diplomatic prose, which in certain respects is a more adequate instrument, because so delicately cautious and non-committal as well as so precise in the evocation of the required degree of affective or conative inclination, for the expression of our imperfect knowledge of the external world; thus I was more than once tempted throughout this letter to observe in answer to your query about Hart's likelihood to write a notable book that I should hesitate to advance the suggestion that circumstances might not arise under which it would not be true to conjecture that such might, indeed, prove to be the case, although I was not clear that there was any adequate reason at present for supposing that such circumstances were, in fact, necessarily likely to arise, although there was, as yet, equally no reason for ruling out such a contingency, which it would be well to bear in mind if any steps were, in fact, being contemplated to meet a situation which might conceivably develop in regard to the topic under discussion. That means 'no'.

I have the honour to be, Sir, with great respect your most humble and obedient servant,

Isaiah Berlin

TO DONALD HALL
Foreign Office

8 January 1945 [*carbon*]

British Embassy, Washington

My dear Donald,

[. . .]

As for myself I really am most grateful to you for your noble efforts. I do not know if the FO itself is possible or desirable, but I cannot stomach the idea of even an hour in FORD. I know its members and its organisation well, and it is, as it has been since 1940, a most unhappy family, ill-governed by the

1 A. D. Lindsay.

high minded but impracticable [Arnold] T[oynbee], and forms a kind of dreary basement to the FO, a sorry collection of broken figures, some, of course, much better than others, but all in a state of hopeless moral inferiority, a kind of collection of troglodytes trembling at their master's word, and yet with a donnish feeling of intellectual superiority and, therefore, full of repressed indignation. When I was in London I called on the Russian section and my friend Hill[1] and not only was it quite dead but I am sure incapable of reanimation, because of the open and probably deserved contempt with which it was treated by its master. So I would really much rather accept a far more menial task at Oxford than any which, in fact, awaits me than moulder away in that fearful sink. Please do not think me tiresomely choosy; in 1940 I would have done this because of the all-hands-to-the-pump atmosphere; and perhaps later; but in 1945 it would be a particularly useless kind of self-abasement; despite all that they may have said to you about influence etc., I know too well what the attitude to FORD is. If I were a professional like [Alan] Dudley, I suppose I should have to consider it; fortunately I am not. So do tell them, if the matter ever crops up, that I am most appreciative of the suggestion, which I am sure was made in excellent faith, but that I should rather not be considered for that post, although it is always flattering to be offered anything. 'Unearthly ballets of bloodless categories.'[2] Do you really see me performing on that stage and with that company? But please do not think that I am not beholden to you for throwing out this cable; and do not think too ill of me for preferring to remain on my South Sea island to sharing the life of the poor slaves below the hatches. Do not, I beg you, convey these taunting phrases to your easily shockable colleagues, but I have always suffered a horror of T.'s organisation ever since I did a little work for it in 1940. I expect I am being unjust to those admirable men ('some of my best friends are in FORD') but I still have a slight sense of nausea whenever I think of them. And so, I believe, do you. Do you [not?] really, really? So you must not go on persecuting me like this.

As things are now, Archie Mackenzie is to visit London this month, to return in January or February and so make me free to go home in March. Other things being equal, I should naturally go straight to Oxford without a

1 In 1945 Christopher Hill was working on the Russian desk of the FO Northern Dept.
2 In a hitherto unpublished early paper on 'Matter' IB writes: 'Bradley declares towards the end of one of his great perorations: "It may come from a failure in my metaphysics, or from a weakness in the flesh which continues to blind me, but the notion that existence could be the same as understanding strikes as cold and ghost-like as the dreariest materialism." And "the sensuous curtain is a deception and a cheat, if it hides some colourless movement of atoms, some spectral woof of impalpable abstractions, or unearthly ballet of bloodless categories. Though dragged to such conclusions, we can not embrace them. Our principles may be true but they are not reality."' The quotations are from F. H. Bradley, The Principles of Logic (London, 1883), p. 533 [book 3, part 2, chapter 4, § 16].

pang or any sense of grievance (this really is perfectly genuine). Roger Makins, obviously at the instigation of M. Wright, did ask me whether I had any objection to his talking to someone in the F.O. about the possibility of me doing something about the Library. I said that I had no objection if this was something compatible with my continuing at Oxford in some way, since I have no objection to something semi-academic at the F.O. which can be turned into anything if one has a will to do it and does not convert one into an excessively despised hack, and that I would think about something of that sort very seriously if it were ever offered to me. But it would, I think, be better if you said nothing to anyone about this at present. I really dread the thought of string-pulling about something so unimportant and do not wish to become the object of universal concern like J. W. W[heeler-]B[ennett], when I have something perfectly good to go back to at home and do not suffer from a hankering to remain in public service at all costs. So if nothing comes of all this, I shall not mind. Certainly better a decent competence and honest life at Oxford (which has now formally asked me to return) than a desperate clinging to the outer skirts of public life. I am sure you will agree.

    Yours ever,
        Isaiah Berlin

TO LADY DAPHNE STRAIGHT
Ministry of Information

    10 January 1945 [*carbon*]

                  British Embassy, Washington

Dearest Daphne,
    [. . .]
    Please thank Mr D.C.[1] most warmly for his handsome offer, which did a great deal to set me up after a far more squalid secret offer from D. Hall (but not a word about this to anyone please) to join FORD, that ghastly cemetery of academic ghosts, rattling their bones with a cracking of Gladwyn [Jebb]'s whip, with a few kicks from the Sexton Webster. I really do not feel that so much demotion is my due. Anyway, I am not penniless and not in crying need of a job, so I propose to decline relatively politely and scream about it, as always, only to you. As for Paris, that would be delightful, but (a) I do not really know French. Ten thousand Englishmen speak it like natives. (b) I am a hopeless publicity executive, and should hate to be a Press Attaché anywhere, but particularly in France, which I do not really

---

    1 Duff Cooper, at that time British Ambassador to France, had offered IB the job of Press Attaché in Paris (cf. pp. 504 above, 519 and 538 below).

understand, where relations are likely to be conducted through a thousand other channels directly from London, directly from Paris, between old friends and in all sorts of ways. (c) I do not really understand or like the French, although I admire, respect and worship them. I consulted only one person – Sir R. Campbell – and he agreed that he did not see me in that position.

[. . .]

Yours ever,

Isaiah Berlin

TO A. J. TOYNBEE

FORD

11 January 1945 [*carbon*]

British Embassy, Washington

Dear Toynbee,

Thank you very much for your letter of 28 December, to the contents of which I have given as much careful thought as I could. I know, of course, how valuable is the work which the Research Department is doing, and fully understand the need for securing an expert to deal with the USSR portion of it; and it is this that makes me wonder whether I am really the man for you. I feel that to do a real job of interpretation of what is going on in that country at present, even on the relatively meagre evidence available in London, one has to have more or less contemporary knowledge of, at any rate, some portion of that country, and I have not been there since childhood (in 1919).[1] Although I know the language and have always taken an absorbed interest in Russian affairs, I could not really claim to be regarded as any kind of specialist on it, even in the limited sense in which I might be regarded as being one by now on the USA, and if I am to do any work that is useful, I feel that I should have to be allowed to go there first for a few months in some capacity before setting up shop in London. There may well be valid objections to this from you or the Foreign Office's point of view, and if the alternative is to base political reports on purely paper material divorced from any kind of autopsy, someone better trained in pure research of that type would probably suit your purpose better. I have consulted one or two of my senior colleagues here on this topic, and they feel on this somewhat as I do. I hope you will forgive me for setting out these loose reflections before you – the reason for this is that I am still somewhat at sea as to what to say in reply to your interesting and generous proposal, and should, therefore, be most

1 He in fact left in 1920.

grateful if you could let me know whether you think the above reflections at all just and pertinent. My principal reason for leaving the Embassy is, of course, not connected either with any personal reasons or with the nature of my work: nobody, I am sure, has been treated better or with more confidence by his colleagues than I have had the good fortune to have experienced here; as for my work, it has proved most fascinating throughout and has allowed me access to information, and personal access to remarkable or historically important individuals, and in general given me a glimpse of the workings of political history for which I cannot be too thankful. I am leaving only because four years in the United States is a morally exhausting process, at any rate to some people, and because I feel that, having produced well over a hundred political summaries, I must be getting somewhat stale in the process and would like a change of climate and occupation. I should be quite happy to go straight back to Oxford without further ado, although I must confess to you, with the war taking the turn which it is,[1] I should perhaps still feel a certain amount of guilt at the very easy life which still flows there, when my contemporaries are engaged upon work involving so much danger, and, what can sometimes be worse, dreary tedium of the most soul-destroying kind.

I do hope that I have conveyed how very deeply I appreciate your selection of me for this very responsible work, whether or not it proves to be of a kind for which I should be suitable. I should, therefore, be grateful if you would let me say neither yes nor no until I have received your reply to this letter. Naturally if there is any urgency, and you feel you must appoint someone at once, I shall quite understand it if you put me out of your thoughts and give it to someone probably more accurate as a researcher and better versed in the details of the subject.

    Yours ever,
      Isaiah Berlin

TO SIR ANTHONY RUMBOLD
Foreign Office

    II January 1945 [*carbon*]

                        British Embassy, Washington

Dear Tony,

    How are you? I had a scrappy account of you from Freddie Ayer and a better one from Roger Makins, who was very flattering about your

---

1 The Luftwaffe and German ground forces had launched several fierce attacks in various areas, virtually their last offensive actions before being forced on to the defensive.

judgement, competence etc. I hope to be in London in March and to see you and Felicity then.

In the meanwhile be kind to Marquis Childs,[1] who will be coming soon and has grown to be very important here. Barbara Wace[2] will no doubt bring you together.

I have a very great deal of gossip to communicate but propose to attend to my own interests first, if you will forgive me, since I find that, curiously enough, whenever there is a crisis in my fortunes, in 1940 and 1942, you turn out to be the architect of their war-time progress in the most satisfactory fashion. The thing is this: I announced some time ago that I could not bear being here any longer (although everyone was very kind to me, the work fascinating still and access to papers and individuals unlimited; but I have now written about 150 political summaries, and this obviously cannot go on). When I was in Oxford in April, I thought how delightful it was, and wish [to go] straight back there and prepare myself to write an enormous work on European history from 1815 to 1848 which would keep me going for the rest of my life (25 volumes or so). I obviously need something of this kind to keep me going and thought the earlier I got on to it the better, before all hacks come home from the war and flood me. On the other hand, I feel distinct guilt about going off to the even now delightful life of Oxford when everyone else is doing what they are. Consequently I talked to D. Hall earnestly about all this when I was in London in April, and he said he would look around and let me know. The upshot of all this was a letter from him, and a letter from Toynbee, offering me a job as head of the USSR Section of FORD. At first I felt frightfully insulted at so dreary an offer – as Felicity can tell you. My image of FORD is of a dim basement filled with chained professors, drudging away at handbooks on Bosnia (with Max [Beloff?]), which appear periodically in the prints and are not read by anyone much. I cannot myself read either their political summaries or their specific works with any degree of profit or pleasure, the former because, since they are shown to Americans, they are written so innocuously, and the latter because they are *pedantisch* research at its worst. Gladwyn Jebb told me that FORD

---

1 Marquis William Childs (1903–90), influential journalist with the *St Louis Post-Dispatch*, wrote the 'Washington Calling' column. The transcript of an FBI wiretap on Edward Prichard's phone records IB and Prich agreeing later this year that Marquis Childs is 'a complete dope – but a nice dope': FBI 'technical log' on Prichard, 9 July 1945, cited in Tracy Campbell, *Short of the Glory: The Fall and Redemption of Edward F. Prichard Jr.* (Lexington, 1998), p. 105, note 11 (on p. 296).

2 Barbara Wace (1907–2003), British journalist, worked 1940–3 for BPS, NY, and the British Embassy, Washington; from July 1944 covered the aftermath of the Normandy landings for the Associated Press, including the siege of Brest, where she was one of the first female journalists on the front line (though a male colleague received the credit for the story); when her clothes were stolen, her telegram to AP read: 'Lost skirt, Brest fallen.'

had been, and to some extent still was, an unhappy family under the not too competent administration of Toynbee,[1] and from what I saw of it myself, I should judge that it was a frightful dead end. So I am inclined to refuse. The thought passed through my head that I might accept on condition that they let me go to Russia first, then come back and develop temperamental incompatibility after a bit and resign, but this seems too gross a piece of cheating.

Meanwhile Duff Cooper offered me a job as Press Attaché in Paris, which is difficult enough in itself and not suited to my talent (I have turned down this already), and Michael Wright seems convinced that I ought to become librarian of the FO.[2] This last sounds a much cosier thing, since it is compatible with remaining at New College and All Souls, and writing history books, too, particularly as the Library takes over certain FORD functions after the war, and while the hacks continue hacking, one might put a little life into the rest of the work and do more about educating embassies abroad, etc. So far this is merely an idea in Wright's head, although he said he would write to David Scott, but I do not like to ask if he has. Ronnie Campbell, who is going home shortly, said he would see about that. I do not really want to appear to be angling for a FO job, since my original idea was that I should be perfectly happy and contented at Oxford as from April next, and, indeed, I do not see why I should not be. At the same time, if there were anything interesting to do (e.g. in the Northern Department), I should be prepared to do it for six months or a little longer. D. Hall says that nobody is moving out of there and that this is not practical and that the FORD job is frightfully influential, powerful etc., which sounds like a bogus build-up to me. What I should be most grateful for would be if you could tactfully sound out D. Scott and/or Roddie[3] about this and not appear to be crossing lines with my direct correspondence with Toynbee. I enclose a copy of my letter to him, which is designed to keep doors open, but you had better not have received this, but rather have heard from me privately about my general state of mind and musings about my fate. I would have written to Toynbee to say that I should not be leaving my interesting and quite real job here but for a desire to leave public service altogether – and have politely rejected his offer on those grounds – if this had been true. The fact is that if it were possible to end my war career with something interesting in London

1 The FO's own history of its Research Dept observes: 'Some of his former colleagues have criticised Toynbee's weak grasp of administration and extreme sensitivity to criticism, but he was undoubtedly hard-working and dedicated.' Robert A. Longmire and Kenneth C. Walker, *Herald of a Noisy World – Interpreting the News of All Nations: The Research and Analysis Department of the Foreign and Commonwealth Office – A History* (London, 1995), 14.

2 The FO Library was without a permanent Head of Dept 1943–6.

3 Roderick Barclay (434/6), formerly a colleague of IB's in Washington, was now at the FO in Personnel under David Scott.

(Ronnie C. talked about the Cabinet Secretariat) before finally lapsing back to Oxford, and then retain some sort of semi-academic connection with the FO, that would tempt me greatly. The only other person to whom I have spoken about it – Roger Makins – said he would talk about the Library when he got back to London and find out if it is not too dreary, and if it is, advise me to reject it. But he is not going back now for some three months (until Jock Balfour gets here), so he won't be doing anything much. I have not answered D. Hall's letter and may not do so for a bit, preferring to write to you rather than to him, since with all his excellent characteristics he is something of a bumbler and does not know much about what is what in the hierarchy. I am, as you will recognise, in that awkward state where I should prefer to be wooed rather than solicit, in the same agreeable fashion as Deric Hoyer Millar once at your instance prised me out of New York, with fairly happy consequences to everyone, so far as I can tell, so do sound the relevant people out tactfully and let me know as rapidly as you can whether the Toynbee thing is as awful as it sounds or whether anything else (e.g. the Library) seems feasible. If I could do the Library as well as Toynbee's thing, that might be an honourable solution, particularly if I could go to Russia as well – then come back and do a spell of memoranda-writing for Toynbee – then the Library. I should appreciate it if you could talk to G. Jebb as well, since I am on good terms with him and he would not mince matters about the depressed conditions of nebulims [*sic*] – springing to [ ] life at the crack of Gladwyn's whip – which surely no one who had the least desire to give me benevolent advice would want me to suffer.

Will I apologise for putting upon you so? I long to see you more than I can say. I am chock-a-block with local gossip and have been taking active part from a distance in Oxford intrigues, having, by a series of tremendous manoeuvres, secured the election of the right warden for New College.[1] As you observe, I am becoming megalomaniac, due no doubt to my sudden increase of access to local worthies here both on the British and the American side (on the latter, my chief ally is Chip Bohlen, who is now liaison between the State Department and the President, and as such fascinating to know). It may be immodest, but you do see how unpleasant is the prospect of descending from a Foster-like licence to talk to everyone about everything into the dark pit of the despised researchers? I knew that, having tasted blood, I should find a vegetarian diet difficult to bear. I only now realise how much blood I am daily consuming.

     Yours ever,
     Isaiah Berlin

1 A. H. Smith.

TO SIR ANTHONY RUMBOLD
Foreign Office

24 January 1945 [*carbon*]

British Embassy, Washington

Dear Tony,

I enclose a copy of my letter to Prof. Toynbee.[1] Would you show it, if he feels any desire to see it, to D. Hall, alternatively don't have seen it at all. As D. Hall started the whole business, he is, I suppose, entitled to the pp. of the case.[2] But better say nothing at all. I have a notion that Lord H[alifax] is going to try to use flattering pressure to retain my services. If so, I don't know what to do – possibly if I exact sufficient conditions, I may [stay]. Anyhow, nothing has happened yet.

I furnished Chip Bohlen, who has gone to England with H. Hopkins, with a letter for you, although he claimed to know you well. It is thoroughly worth your while to do something about him, since he is not only nice and intelligent but is very genuinely a key man just now, as liaison between the State Department and the White House, and is an exceedingly sure-footed junior official with whom I, at any rate, find it most agreeable and profitable to discuss matters of common interest. He is, I think, genuinely well disposed towards us, and things can obviously be said to him which cannot be said at a higher level quite so easily, and are then sure to be tactfully reported upwards. So that if, besides yourself, there is anyone in the FO or the Cabinet Secretariat of adequate intelligence and proper views, the investment is very worthwhile indeed. His general idea, with which I think I agree, is that the Russians have no concrete plans about Western Europe and that anything we present will be seriously considered; with suspicion, indeed, but still taken as the basis for discussion; whereas if we wait for them to speak, or settle everything bit by bit, their suspicions will merely multiply per number of cases for solution, and the aggregate will make any set general settlement impossible, if you see what I mean. If this is too obscure, ignore it and ask for his views direct. He is still pretty touchy about Russia, like everyone who has sat there, particularly with Bullitt, but is thoroughly excited about the President's 'Great Design'[3] for a real permanent alliance, thinks the adventure well worth risking since there is no other alternative,

---

1 Presumably the letter of 11 January 1945, a copy of which was to have been enclosed with the letter of the same date to Rumbold, but must have been omitted in error.

2 'pp.' was Civil Service shorthand for 'previous papers' – i.e. the file or papers relating to the matter in hand.

3 FDR's plans for a post-war settlement, encompassing the setting up of a new international organisation of States, and crucially depending on the co-operation of the USSR, to secure which was a key objective of his foreign policy during the war.

and is prepared to be very liberal and bold. We have it that the non-Communist Left alone are worth supporting in Europe. Mr [Richard] Law also is prepared to support them provided they are not called NCO,[1] since he dislikes 'Left' and is not prepared to align himself with non-Communists, despite all our explanations about the profound difference between this and anti-Communism. Anyhow, do have a good talk with C.B. yourself.

This shower of notes from me will now cease. Love to Felicity.

Yours ever,

Isaiah Berlin

TO MARIE AND MENDEL BERLIN

25 January 1945

British Embassy, Washington

My dear parents,

It was very nice to get your two sets of letters – one grave, because of my silence, one gayer, because of my letter. I perfectly understand what occurs when I do not write, but I am physically incapable of writing when there is nothing to say, and you must forgive me for my long silences and assume from cables and the reports of stray travellers that I am really in blooming health.

Now I have a good deal to report: firstly, serious matters, then gay. I have discovered a doctor in Johns Hopkins Hospital in Baltimore, which is probably the best hospital which this country can produce, a man who I really think can do something about my sinus, having suffered from this himself for over 20 years and having finally cured himself. His advice is that I should come to him for a week in the hospital proper and receive daily treatment (involving no operation) and thereafter stay in Baltimore for another fortnight, in a hotel, and receive treatment three times weekly. Although Baltimore is nearer Washington than Reading to Oxford, he rightly says that if I keep on coming by train, the exhaustion and the dust may undo the work. He appears supplied with penicillin, etc., and I have great confidence in him. I have a mad rich friend in Baltimore called Mrs Garrett,[2] wife of an ex-Ambassador in Rome, who, although in many ways

1 Non-Communist Organisation.
2 Alice Warder Garrett (1877–1952), eccentric widow of John Work Garrett (1872–1942), US Ambassador to Italy 1929–33. The Garretts were wealthy collectors and patrons of the arts, and their 48-room house in Baltimore, Evergreen, contained several libraries and a private theatre. Alice Garrett was renowned as a hostess to diplomats, writers, artists and musicians, and so many distinguished guests had stayed at the house that part of it was known as the 'Genius Wing'. The Garretts had no children, and Evergreen, with all its contents, was bequeathed to Johns Hopkins University.

an absurd old woman, is obviously the queen of Baltimore and lives in a vast house in which I have stayed, and she swears by him, and in such matters is completely reliable (only the very best is good enough for the American very rich). So I propose, since the only risk involved is financial, to go to Baltimore at the beginning of February, say on about the 6th or 7th, and re-emerge from there towards the end of the month. Then to take a train down to Mexico where my friends the Morgans are at present recuperating in ex-Ambassador Dwight Morrow's[1] house in an agreeable town called Cuernavaca, an hour and a half from Mexico City, for two or three weeks of total rest, then come back towards the end of March. ⟨I am in particularly splendid health now – best time for a cure I think, not when one is exhausted.⟩

At first I intended to come to England for good immediately after that, but the Ambassador has cracked his whip, and I have, therefore, decided, rather than argue with him about whether or not I should stay here until September, as he would like, to promise to stay until May; by that time I gather that Warden Smith will be here (late in March) on an Oxford expedition to the US, and I can discuss details of return with him. This seems to me a very shrewd and sensible plan, involving no decisions of principle.

Meanwhile, however, the hospital, and the very expensive doctor, may cost something; consequently I may make application for conversion of some more sterling into dollars, so could you please be so good as to place £500 into my account in my Oxford bank. Please do not forget. I repeat my proposed itinerary: February 6–13, Johns Hopkins Hospital; 13–27, residence in Baltimore hotel; 27 February to end of March, journey to Cuernavaca and back. We are expecting Wheeler-Bennett at any moment. Perhaps he will come down to Mexico, too.

Heaven knows what else I am to relate to you about my 'serious' life. I met Mr Morgenthau at dinner the other day at the Embassy, and he is an infinitely shy man, who, if you look at him for more than two minutes on end, blushes automatically and looks for help to his wife. I met him because he demanded to see me, and as Felix proved somewhat inactive in the matter (though later apologetic) he, Morgenthau, applied to the Ambassador direct to duly summon me. I was told to 'drop in to the Treasury' at any time. I doubt if so general an invitation can be literally accepted, but I have no doubt he meant exactly what he said. He is an uncle or cousin of Arthur Goodhart, the Professor with whom I am at present on very flourishing terms, since being a snob he satisfied himself on his last visit here that I was a suitable person to be agreeable to.

1 Dwight Whitney Morrow (1873–1931), lawyer, banker, diplomat, successful US Ambassador to Mexico under Calvin Coolidge 1927–30, Republican Senator 1930–1. See also 540/1.

By this time you will have seen my right-hand Archie Mackenzie, and he will have told you how well I am, look, etc.

As for Miss McGeachy's marriage, I cannot but think it comical. Her husband is a very smooth opportunist, an Austrian Jew or half-Jew, with a passion for English bankers, too great in one so young to be entirely disinterested. Together they will make a very flourishing firm: the rate of progress up the ladder ought to be doubled now that there is so much combined energy there, and yet I am told that they are madly in love with each other. Everything is possible. Certainly the Warden of All Souls has been completely taken in by both. Without any dislike for either of them, I do not really want them in my life much, nor, I feel, do they.

I have received two very nice letters from Mary and David – the last particularly gave all the gruesome details of Mr and Mrs Boult's deaths. Please remember me to them and say how grateful I am and that I shall be writing.

As for my future stay here, I shall obviously have to haggle a good deal with the Ambassador, who knows a good workhorse when he has one; and why should I go away, anyway? My most recent bouquet came from a certain Mr [Alan] Lascelles,[1] apparently the King's private secretary, who thought well of a particular telegram I sent. Who he is I do not know, but I suspect I must be going very conservative to please such people. Please do not report this or enquire about it, as that would seriously embarrass me. But as the Embassy in general get the credit, I see their point. Yet I am very nostalgic and determined to come home fairly early this year, but expect I shall not get away now before the end of May. As for the sinus, I am sure, if I am to have it treated at all, it is best to have it done here and not in England. I must also get myself some clothes made before I return.

Now that we are dissolving into trivialities (talking of that, I think Brodetsky[2] may be giving you regards from me), I must finish my comic Apter story.[3] After the receipt of the socks, which must be regarded as an oriental gift of a sheep or two in advance of the real proposals, I was incessantly telephoned to from New York and curiously enough was always either out, or at a meeting, or else confined to my house (nobody knew the telephone number) with an imaginary indisposition. This went on for some time until it was finally decided to seize the bull (me) by the horns, and

1 Sir Alan Frederick Lascelles (1887–1981), Private Secretary to King George VI 1943–52; described by Frances Donaldson as 'Aristocratic by birth and temperament . . . an exactly typical figure of the old "establishment" ': *Edward VIII* (London, 1974), 102. It is odd that IB had not heard of him.

2 Selig Brodetsky (1888–1954), Ukrainian-born mathematician and Zionist, Professor of Mathematics, Leeds, 1924–48, President of the British Zionist Federation from 1948, President of the Board of Deputies of British Jews 1939–49.

3 See letter of 12 December 1944, pp. 505–6 above.

Konstantin Markovich duly appeared in Washington, apparently on business. Unfortunately I was not able to dine with him. But he came to see me in the office, and talked a great deal of nonsense about the 'general political situation' but with much more genuine affection about both of you. He is really quite a nice man, and his business, I think, is going quite well, but still pompous, vain and magniloquent. After about an hour of aimless chatter of this type (which I was most careful not to divert), he asked me whether I intended to remain a bachelor to the end of my days. I said that such, indeed, was my present intention – one never knew, of course, I might fall madly and hopelessly in love, but this was very abstract and unlikely. He looked slightly gloomy at that point, I thought, but at the time said no more about it. On the next day he pressed me to come to breakfast, lunch, tea, dinner, any or all, although he would have to put off practically the President himself (incidentally, he did not think highly of Liberman's book,[1] as, of course, he knew the important persons concerned much more intimately). Finally he reappeared in my office, and after immense amount of gulping and saying that he was an honest blunt fellow, and did not like beating about the bush, he consulted me about my feelings for his daughter, who he said was not indifferent to me – I feigned immense surprise (not altogether unreal, since his daughter, poor girl, positively dislikes me, if only because I cannot bear her, and in her pathetic condition, sent like a lamb to the slaughter, that is a very disagreeable attribute in somebody you have been ordered to like) – and, indeed, had said that of all the young men of her acquaintance I was perhaps the 'best informed' (wonderful reason for a lifelong association). I did my best to contain myself but was almost overpowered by internal giggles, but kept a straight face and said that she was very young, much younger than I, and that really I did not think that it was a very suitable suggestion. Relieved of his immediate burden, doubtless imposed on him by his remorseless wife, cousin K. went on for about an hour to explain that his feelings were those of a father, but, of course, I would understand that he only wished his daughter's and my own good, that he was in a position to give her quite a suitable dowry ... but that, of course, if there was nothing doing, there was nothing doing, and he hoped that this would not alter relations between us. He kept on returning to the possibility as we walked towards the omnibus, and I was very friendly and gently patted him on the back and wished him well and said that I would come to see him in New York (which I have no intention of doing), but laugh about it still when I think of it (my cousin Liliana is one of the most awful girls in the world, and quite apart from our unfortunately close relationship, I should not recommend any friend of mine to allow himself to be bored by her – it is not

1 See 504/1.

even passive boredom but a repulsive active grinding down by a combination of her mother's coarse driving force and her father's nonsense, together
with a painful awareness of both qualities in her parents and general
bitterness arising from it). I would much rather marry mother's landlady. I
thought you would like to know about this comic episode, since it has given
me so much pleasure. Next week I may go to New York and I shall definitely
pay a visit to the Holdsteins to whom I shall mention the point. ⟨Please
don't worry about that. It shall be done.⟩

I am about to be transferred to the Foreign Office and will, therefore, fall
outside Nicholas's jurisdiction – this had better not be said to him as they all
seem to resent it a little, since the FO is rightly considered smarter, and I
have no doubt that I am suspected of social climbing.

No more for the present, but this ought to be enough to go on with.
Please give Smith my love, and tell him that I am delighted I shall see him so
soon.

⟨All my love, & perhaps two more months of separation (till May) but
then – ah then – happiness.

Isaiah.⟩

TO ROBIN CRUIKSHANK

1 February 1945 [*carbon*]

British Embassy, Washington

Dear Robin,

You can imagine my terror when your very kind and sympathetic cable
arrived enquiring after my health – visions of my aged parents once more in
the throes of frustrated panic, the Evening Standard giving the most
gruesome details of the terrible disease,[1] against which science itself is
impotent, which has me in its grip, etc. The facts are these:

As you know, I am prey to very tiresome sinus attacks, which, without
sending me to bed, debilitate one by settling a load of about 200 [pounds]
weight on one's head and thus making concentration impossible and action
sluggish and intermittent. When I thought that I was returning to England in
March, I decided to try to get rid of this while still in this country, and after
copious enquiries settled on Johns Hopkins as the place. As hospitals are
immensely overcrowded at present, a time was finally fixed for 5 February
and until the 26th, when I am to be kept incommunicado by the doctor in
question. When I tried to shift this in order not to incommode Archie too
much, I found that the shift was not possible. I have in fact been reduced to

---

1 He is referring to the report reproduced on p. 405–6 above.

ghastly inactivity by the more and more frequent attacks of this disagreeable, and all the more maddening because not dangerous, malady and could not face the prospect of continuing like this for ever. Hence the telegram. But there is nothing perilous in my condition. Do show Nick[1] this letter; I have written my parents more or less on the above lines, omitting only the fact that there is an operation involved (which is sure to frighten them out of their wits) and stating specifically, Heaven help me, that there is not. So that is the party line as far as the worthy Berlins are concerned.

I now gather that Archie may be back by the date required. I cannot make out whether we are under you or the FO – it makes no difference in any case as everything, including Grant McKenzie, remains the same. The present persecution of the latter is a separate story; we have set our fiercest retriever, John Russell, on him, but as H. B. B[utler] correctly maintains, nothing will cause him to go.

The Ambassador's sledgehammer has had the effect of keeping me here until May, when told that, in the absence of a solid job in London, my sole motive for going must be dissatisfaction with local conditions, and that soldiers in trenches, not to speak of himself, are doubtless equally dissatisfied by theirs. I really do not know what I can return. Perhaps I will think of something by the beginning of May. I long to get back and would be most touchingly grateful for an adequate excuse with which to meet an attack on moral grounds such as HE does not scruple to make. Perhaps the infinitely wise Warden of New College, due here in March, will provide it.

I hear distant reports of dull fighting on the [Alan] Dudley–[Cyril] Radcliffe–Bruce Lockhart front, with Grubb biding his time, before joining the brigade of guards. I expect John Wheeler-Bennett will tell us all about it.

Meanwhile, I am genuinely sorry that Landau cannot be invited, as it is all a matter of amour propre, and I have frequently told him in the past that he will be warmly welcomed if he came under his own steam, but he won't. Yet he would have done a very useful job for us on the Palestine front, since he can be bought for sixpence, has no principles, and great, and to me, inexplicable devotion to HMG (perhaps more explicable in the light of past financial arrangements). I therefore regret that so useful a tool should be thrown aside for the sake of general rules, and although we shall doubtless still win the war and be allowed a voice in the peace, I feel, as Lord Winster[2] wrote to the editor of the *Baltimore Sun*, profoundly discouraged.

1 H. G. Nicholas.
2 Reginald Thomas Herbert Fletcher, 1st Baron Winster (1885–1961), politician (Labour from 1929), Parliamentary Private Secretary to First Lord of the Admiralty 1940–1, Minister for Civil Aviation under Attlee 1945–6.

Lord Winster also informed Mr Owens[1] that Barbara Ward,[2] an hysterical and naive girl, wrote the famous *Economist* editorials, and not Crowther[3] at all. Be that as it may, they have had quite a good effect, although they have shaken the reputation of *The Economist*, which is now regarded as an excusably but nevertheless markedly nationalist journal.

I hope people will be polite to Judge Rosenman when he comes. His mission is bogus, and he himself very boring and second-rate, but he responds rapidly to kindness and can be a great nuisance if rubbed the wrong way.

The operation on IB's nose took place as planned in the Johns Hopkins Hospital, Baltimore.

TO MARIE AND MENDEL BERLIN

14 February 1945 [*manuscript*]

Johns Hopkins Hospital, Baltimore

Chérissimes Parents,

I cannot conceive of a more blissful mode of life. One is not ill, not in pain, living in secluded comfort (a little expensively it is true, but not so very) Breakfast arrives punctually, one's life is regulated, all is peace, books, radio, no telephone (I cannot describe how much that contributes to peace) no visitors or v. few – Mackenzie has just left – he was sorry not to see you, but as he pointed out with a certain sharpness, he had to cut his whole stay short because I summoned him back so imperiously – true enough – in order to have him replace me in Washington while I came here – & I chose the date in order – but it may not come off – to go to Mexico with [sc. where] the Morgans & Wheeler Bennett now are – Morgan having had a kind of physical collapse in early January, & Wheeler Bennett also not feeling strong,[4] they all went to the rich & eminent теща's[5] estate in Cuernavaca,

1 (James) Hamilton Owens (1888–1967), editor, *Baltimore Sun*, 1938–43, editor-in-chief of the *Sun* papers, 1943–56.
2 Barbara Mary Ward (1914–81), later (1976) Baroness Jackson, development economist, author, at the time assistant editor of *The Economist*.
3 Geoffrey Crowther (1907–72), Editor of *The Economist* 1938–56; late in the war introduced into *The Economist* an American survey intended to inform non-American readers about American affairs, but which acquired a large readership within the US.
4 In addition to chronic health problems and exhaustion, he was recovering from severe jaundice and a demanding Atlantic crossing.
5 'Teshcha' ('mother-in-law'). Elizabeth Reeve Morrow, née Cutter (1873–1955), was a poet. Aubrey Morgan married first the Morrows' eldest daughter, Elisabeth, who died in 1934, and then her sister Constance. Their other daughter, Anne, married Charles Lindbergh.

about an hour by car from Mexico City, where her husband, Dwight Morrow, was once a famous U.S. Ambassador. I am sure I shall be welcome enough there, but if Morgan plans to return circa March 15 & I do not get there much before March 1, is it worth it? I think probably yes, if I travel all the way in a "bedroom"[1] which is v. comfortable. The change is so terrific, the climate so good for my sinus, & the prospect [of] staying till the 21st March (say with Wheeler Bennett even if Morgan departs) that I'll try. I'll never be in Mexico again probably, & everyone says it is most fascinating. Now as for my treatment here under the eminent Dr Polvogt[2] (he must be a Dane or Norwegian by Origin) all that happens is that every day I call on him & he removes something from my nose & then sprays & fiddles about with various injections & lets me go. He says that the Xray proves that my (forehead) sinuses & antrums an sich[3] are perfectly in order: that the cause of evil is inside the left nostril entirely, & that I keep worrying it because there is a slight twist inside the nose, of the central inner ridge, so to speak, which instead of being – is ∼, & has led to a slight swelling inside the left nostril (Snowman[4] diagnosed this in 1932, but as usual, recommended no action) which can be removed by his methods: after which all will be well forever. We shall live & see, meanwhile no risk is involved, and the rest & quiet are clear gain. Meanwhile what of my immediate future? To my surprise Lord Halifax suddenly objected to my leaving on the grounds that I was perfectly well off where I was (he meant this more from his than from my point of view, but let us be lofty & say in the public interest) & why should I go? roughly a kind of "еиди и не ригайся"[5] point of view. Now if I had a govt. job in London, I could, however unplausibly or dishonestly try to argue that it, the London job, is much the more important of the two. But having in effect rejected Toynbee's offer & Cooper's also, I cannot play that card, & have only New College to advance. But then they wd not really want me much before autumn, particularly since they now have Hart (very verjudet[6] even without Falk). So I propose (did I write all this to you before?) to wait till Smith gets here – he is coming I take it? – & get the matter thrashed out between him & Lord H. I wonder if I can get myself to

1 A two-berth compartment in a Pullman car.
2 Leroy Matthew Polvogt (1924–70), Associate Professor of Laryngology and Otology, Johns Hopkins Hospital.
3 'In themselves'.
4 Probably Dr Jacob Snowman (1871?–1959), the Berlins' General Practitioner, a well-known Hampstead family doctor and *mohel*, i.e. a Jew trained in the ritual and practice of circumcision (of which his most celebrated case was Charles, Prince of Wales); or possibly his son Leonard, also a doctor and much in demand for circumcisions.
5 'Eidi [a mistake for 'edi'] i ne rigaisya [a mistake for 'rugaisya']' ('Go and don't make a fuss about it').
6 'Jewified'.

San Francisco[1] on the 25th April – it will take a bit of wangling, but I'll try – I was asked if I wd do press relations of it; God forbid; all the leaks are traced to the press officer whose chief job is to say nothing & secure favourable comment for his country. Not my métier. So anyway I stay here till early May as you desire; then we'll see. I shd like terribly to go for 3–4 months to Moscow with some job: I gather the F.O. are vaguely sounding out possibilities about that.

Meanwhile I wrote you that Prof. Brodetsky came to see me – he, & his friends from the Holy Land all come, all a little suspicious of what exactly I am & do, the British inclined to defend themselves against my possible snobbery & Grand Seigneurism – but all cannot resist an interview. I enjoy it v. much. The F[elix] F[rankfurter]s are very well – so am I – really nothing to write.

All my love to you
Shaya

I propose to send this via F.O. by Bag with a 2½ stamp affixed by me here. Wd you, in replying try to do the same – without stamp – without calling me First Secretary – put on envelope I. Berlin Esqre, British Embassy, Washington D.C., on top 'by favour of Bag' & send it to F. Office Bag Room. See what happens. It will go by sea bag, but still.

I.B.

TO CRESSIDA RIDLEY

14 February 1945 [*manuscript*]

[as from] British Embassy, Washington

Dear Cressida

I have wished to write ever since receiving your letter months ago. And although there is in a sense nothing to say one cannot bear to say nothing. And I was, in spite of being, as all Bubbles's[2] friends were, prepared for it, I was most terribly & permanently upset, & am so still. I have never been in love with anyone who died, nor even lost a parent: so I really do not know what you must feel & won't pretend: but I would do anything in the world which I thought you might like in this connexion – what I do not myself

---

1 An international conference was to be held at the end of April in San Francisco to draft the Charter of the UN and to inaugurate the organisation.
2 As Jasper Ridley was known to his (especially London) friends.

know – write something – endow something – do something not too insufficient.[1]

I am quite clear that I have never liked anyone more in my life, or valued the friendship of, or found more wonderful & thrilling. I have [not] had conversations with anyone such as with him, or hope to: not only did he understand everything one said, but the words blossomed much more rapidly & fantastically, the air became full of magic of every{thing} sort & rope tricks began to occur. But you know this better than me & possibly thought there was too much of it sometimes & not enough of something else. Never enough for me, I admit. I don't mean of course that his main attributes were for me virtuosity and brilliance and zigzags & so on. But I did adore them – the quality of magic, of first handness, of territory not trodden by anyone else or before, of what there is in Berlioz[2] & E. T. A. Hoffmann.[3] It would be absurd to go into a list of characteristics – although if nobody else has, then I should like to write a memoir if only for my own benefit & it can be published, if any good, in the Balliol gazette or whatever: I did conceive almost a culte for him, & why should I keep it under a bushel. I should in a way hate doing it, partly because I think every word I write is vile & always have, partly because in this sense all I say wd seem particularly meretricious or vulgar, however genuinely conceived. So do discourage me if you can. But I do anyhow wish to say to you that such a combination of fantasy & passionate incorruptibility of feeling about everything, has not been seen since Alexander Herzen (with whom he v. characteristically wrote me that he had fallen in love & wished to have a child by) & indeed belongs, not as his father seemed to fear, to decadences, but to the most developed, forward marching, positive moments of both individuals & cultures (I am getting pompous & 'vile' again, & this must stop). His very frustrations were unsqualid to the least possible degree – with Oxford & with the bar, + the necessity of serving the public in some way, old fashioned public spirit & Russian moral sentiment & a most painful fastidiousness of taste about his own position & what he was doing & why. Marriage seemed to me to make him much happier (& saner) & to those who didn't think so before, nicer (he was preternaturally nice acc. to me always; in so far as he was a Nijinsky[4] he

1 In the event he dedicated *The Hedgehog and the Fox* (1953) to Ridley's memory.

2 For example, Berlioz included movements representing opium-induced hallucinations of 'A March to the Scaffold' and of a 'Witches' Sabbath' in his *Symphonie Fantastique*.

3 Ernst Theodor Amadeus Hoffmann (1778–1822), German public official, novelist, composer, and writer of bizarre and uncanny short stories; three of them form the basis for Offenbach's opera *The Tales of Hoffmann*. He replaced his original third name, Wilhelm, with Amadeus, in honour of (Wolfgang Amadeus) Mozart.

4 Vatslav Fomich Nijinsky (1888–1950), virtuoso Russian ballet-dancer and choreographer, famous for his apparently effortless high leaps. IB once defined genius thus: 'I am sometimes asked what I mean by this highly evocative but imprecise term. In answer, I can only say this:

leapt less high but much farther: & when I thought of life in England after America I thought of him as embodying everything the absence of which is so awful here. The beginning of our acquaintance had the elements of a romance: a lot of wooing, & anxiety to please on both sides, & consequent waves & crests & troughs and a great deal of self dramatization & nonsense & elaborate intellectual emotion only possible in places like Oxford – then it all settled down comfortably, & I thought of you both as much the most enviable & admirable persons I knew & passionately longed to get married & thought (sententiously) of how good exciting virtue was, how much more than exciting vice. & I am sure he was killed in the minefield gripped by one of the acute frustrations which you know – which used to lead sometimes to the most terrific lightnings, sometimes to mere half swallowed rumbling & self-eating (auto-cannibalism – when I see you I must tell you how I nearly came to do that – quite literally – myself) – when in that state he always, surely, jumped – with, as he thought, calculation, but determined to leap, never not to react, given a crisis there was always a romantic, a true unbogus romantic fatalism, Byronism, a desire to burn boats & above all not plod or drag or be engulphed or close eyes. Oh dear is all this nonsense? have I constructed an artificial entity? I believe in it irredeemably. And then the wonderful, pure intense moral passion about everything connected with music – when as in his case bravura was the crest of immense fathoms & fathoms of moving water, very thin & narrow & deep & marvellously elegant & sharp & poetical – what could be better & rarer & so on? I mustnt go on & on saying what you know but I never have before & it is a great relief. Meanwhile I sit doomed here, with a promise to be allowed to return last November & this January & this March, & now it is to continue till May & possibly beyond, but I don't think so because beyond all my complacencies & appeasements I am ultimately tremulous & liable to go peacefully mad if persecuted too much, so, although my work is fascinating & my colleagues most considerate & kind (Donald Mclean[1] is very very nice. I've had a row with him, funnily enough, & then we made it up – I was the aggrieved party as always alas, & although I cannot really forgive him I like him v. much), I cannot cannot bear it. So I shall be home before long, & telephone you if I may, & perhaps you'll come to London or to Oxford & I would write Mrs Ridley too but you see that I've nothing to say except that I

the dancer Nijinsky was once asked how he managed to leap so high. He is reported to have answered that he saw no great problem in this. Most people when they leapt in the air came down at once. "Why should you come down immediately? Stay in the air a little before you return, why not?"' PI2 217.

1 Donald Maclean (1913–83), a friend of CR, and later revealed to have been a spy for the Russians, was at the time a colleague of IB's at the Embassy. The row between them had taken place at a dinner party, when Maclean criticised IB's friendship with Alice Roosevelt Longworth on the grounds of her 'horrible views' (MI Tape 7).

shall miss Bubbles all my life & madden people (including I expect yourself)
with recitals of his matchlessness so perhaps Mrs R. will forgive me, &
perhaps you will too, dearest Cressida, for having written all these silly pages
which I cannot bring myself to re-read (apart from their illegibility, which
may be just as well). I can only plead that I am in hospital with an enormous
nose (more like Gogol's[1] than like Cyrano's) & in a lamentable state. You
wouldnt want to come here, would you? to the Embassy I mean? for I have a
job still (at about 3000 dollars a year) which you cd do after I am gone home.
You might live with the Macleans, & your child[2] might enjoy the vitamins
– but if not not, & I shall assume not unless you say before the end of April. I
have a favour to ask – if you think ill of it for some reason don't hesitate for
one second to say so – I have no faith in my own desires – but I should very
greatly like to have (a) a photograph of Bubbles (b) a book with his autograph
in enormous letters.[3] I wish I could convey in staid terms how warmly &
affectionately I think of you – & my love to Mrs R.

    Yrs
      Shaya.

You *will* let me exercise a sinister intellectual influence on your child when
it has grown? you *won't* want it to be *too* sane & ponderé & against
irresponsibility & pedantic nonsense & words?

TO HERBERT HART
War Office

23 February 1945

              [as from] British Embassy, Washington

My dear Herbert,

    I cannot write to you for I am confined to bed with a tiresome
undangerous ailment (not what you think, whatever that is), but I cannot
wait before letting you know how genuinely exhilarated I am by this news,
which no one else gave me.[4] Of course you must identify yourself with the
life of the College in the most violent and ubiquitous way at once and form
that famous bridge between the Junior and the Senior Common Rooms of
which Crossman proved so treacherous a version and I never even tried to

---

1 Gogol had a long nose himself and wrote a short story, *The Nose*, about a man whose nose
  abandons him to live its own life. The long nose of Savien Cyrano de Bergerac (1619–55) was
  immortalised in Edmund Rostand's verse-drama *Cyrano de Bergerac*.
2 Adam Nicholas Ridley (b. 1942), economist and banker.
3 Jasper Ridley had distinctive large handwriting.
4 HLAH's appointment as a Fellow of New College to teach philosophy.

volunteer to be. The lives of undergraduates must be open books to you; and you must not confine yourself to the better-born or better-looking either; in fact I foresee a realm of mutual persecution which is bound to yield a great deal of perverted pleasure in one way or another.

As for work, of course, I shall try to devolve all the subjects I know nothing about or hate on to you; at the moment I know nothing any more. Consequently your field is universal. But I hate Plato, Aristotle, ethics, politics (and even Kant) particularly deeply ⟨but not a word to the W[arden] on this⟩; consequently will you please take them at least for your province? Otherwise the boys will simply not get taught (don't tell Cox about the tone or contents of this terrible letter). I do not think that a journey to the now somewhat senile Moore and Russell will be at all useful. But I will send you the works of Prof. Morris Cohen,[1] the Joseph of America with all that that implies in the way of greater slickness and up-to-dateness with the same maddening qualities. You can certainly attend your colleagues' lectures, but it is likely to be a doubtful pleasure in most cases. I would fish out Major [J. L.] Austin out of your own department and force him to talk to you – no man has greater powers of awakening the full capacity for the philosophical forces of the interior. He is argumentative in the most useful and maddening sense, but I admire him more than any other of my professional contemporaries (if you see what I mean). Don't do anything very silly like going to the Aristotelian Society or thinking about Prichard.[2] For God's sake, read a little Plato and Aristotle and at least the rudiments of ethics or we are all sunk. But what will Jenifer do? Commute? It is unthinkable. I understand her feelings about Oxford only too well. As D. Cecil once said, little knowing his own future fate, 'Bringing a wife to Oxford is like bringing her to the Gold Coast – conditions are colonial.'

As soon as I recover I shall write you a sane letter.

Yours ever,

Isaiah

---

1 Morris Raphael Cohen (1880–1947), Russian-born US logician and philosopher, professor at the City College of New York 1912–38, then at Chicago.
2 Harold Arthur Prichard (1871–1947), White's Professor of Moral Philosophy, Oxford, and Fellow, CCC, 1928–37.

TO WALTER TURNER
Britain in Pictures[1]

23 February 1945 [carbon]

[Baltimore]

My dear Walter,

Much as I love you, no, no, no! If I did this for anyone, I would do it for your series, which I like very much, but I propose neither to write a book nor special articles nor anything else on this terrible topic which has formed the object of my official thoughts but is certainly not going to be allowed to corrode my private life as well. Perhaps H. G. Nicholas at the Ministry of Information could do it for you – he knows this country well and is a readier writer. The best person to consult would be Robin Cruikshank, the Director of the American Division of M. of I., whom I expect you know and who is a very humane, unbureaucratic and perceptive man, or perhaps Granville Barker[2] would – I could forward a letter from you to his address in New York, which I cannot for the moment lay my hands on. It would, at any rate, be very elegantly done and literature would not be forgotten.

I have not used your kind letter of introduction to Schnabel[3] yet but I will – his playing is, astonishingly enough, considering the usual effect of local audiences, as magnificent as ever – he plays all too rarely. The favourite composer of this country is Rachmaninoff (so he is in the USSR, I understand – a very significant and sinister thought).

Yours ever,

Isaiah Berlin

When his medical treatment was finished, IB joined the Morgans and John Wheeler-Bennett at Casa Mañana, the Morrows' villa in Cuernavaca, Mexico, to recuperate. A fortnight of relaxation, sun and

1 Series of books published by Collins during and after the war (1941–50), covering all aspects of British history, culture, life and society and forming an important part of the British propaganda effort. They were beautifully illustrated, with accompanying essays of around 30 pages written by distinguished contributors including Elizabeth Bowen (*English Novelists*, 1942), Edmund Blunden (*English Villages*, 1941), David Cecil (*The English Poets*, 1941) and Sylvia Lynd (*English Children*, 1942). W. J. Turner (338/1) was an editor of the series as well as the author of eight volumes, including *English Music* (1941). He had presumably asked IB to contribute a book on some aspect of Anglo-American relations (see also IB's further letter to Turner of 12 June 1945, pp. 579–80 below).

2 Harley Granville-Barker (1877–1946), English actor, producer, director, dramatist and Shakespeare scholar, author of *Prefaces to Shakespeare* (1927–48); spent most of the war in the US; worked for the British Library of Information, NY, and lectured at Harvard.

3 Artur Schnabel (1882–1951), Polish-born pianist and composer who did much to popularise Beethoven's previously under-appreciated piano music (see 148/3).

congenial company appears to have fortified his sense of humour, as John
Wheeler-Bennett later recalled with affectionate exasperation:

We began our return to our various jobs in the middle of March, the
first stage taking us as far as St Louis, Missouri, a four days' rail journey.
We crossed the border into the United States at Laredo, Texas, where we
encountered the vigilance of the Immigration Service and the FBI.
Though our papers were in perfect order we had to answer a
questionnaire giving the more intimate details of our lives.

   'Where were you born?' an official asked Isaiah. 'In Riga,' was the
unexpected reply. 'Where is that?' came the suspicious query. Isaiah was
feeling puckish that day. 'It is', he replied with literal accuracy, 'a port of
the Eastern Baltic.' 'Who does it belong to?' With the air of one
delivering a lecture to a backward class, Isaiah answered, 'My native
country of Latvia, when I was born in it in 1909, was indeed a part of the
Russian Empire. However, during the First World War it was annexed,
along with the other Baltic States, by Germany under the Treaty of Brest-
Litovsk, but only, as you doubtless recall, for a short time. At the Peace
Conference the independence of these States was recognised and they
remained in this happy state until re-annexed by Russia in 1940. However,
they were re-occupied by the Germans in 1941.' 'Are you a German then?'
the FBI man interrupted. 'Certainly not,' was Isaiah's emphatic answer.

The discussion of the past, present and future diplomatic status of Latvia
continued, until finally IB's inquisitor posed the right question:

'[A]re you a Soviet citizen?' 'Certainly not,' repeated Isaiah with immense
dignity. 'I am a subject of His Britannic Majesty, and if you will look at
my passport, which you are holding in your hand, you will see that I am
an official of the British Foreign Office.' [. . .] I note from my diary that
our halt in Laredo occupied ten hours. I attribute most of this delay to
Isaiah's sense of humour.[1]

TO SIR DAVID SCOTT

23 March 1945 [*carbon*]

                                        British Embassy, Washington, DC

Personal and Confidential

Dear Sir David,
   Thank you very much for your letter of 22 February, which reached me
late, as I was temporarily out of action with a minor operation. I fear that

1 John Wheeler-Bennett, *Special Relationships: America in Peace and War* (London 1975), 197.

since our correspondence appears to occur only when I am in one hospital or another, you will begin to think of me as an incurable hypochondriac. I admit that the splendid privacy and remoteness of a whitewashed room of these splendid institutions are a relief and a wonder in this floodlit country, but I cannot deny that at other times I have a taste for the world, and, I fear, the flesh, too. Not for the devil – there is in any case no trace of him in this very hygienic and extrovert country. You would have to go at least as far as Mexico (as I did) to find him.

I apologise for all this chatter. What I should really like to say is that I can give you every assurance that I shall not commit myself to anything until I come home – and that I hope that in my letter to Toynbee, which I expect he will have shown you, I did not imply that I longed to commit myself to him; I made my letter, naturally enough, as civil as I could, considering that he was, at any rate from his point of view, making a very proper and handsome offer; but to you and in confidence I may say that the prospect of slipping into what seemed to me in 1940, still more in 1942 and 1944, a sunless cave of inhibited professors did not allure me over much. Everyone I have spoken to here seems to take an even gloomier view of the death-in-life atmosphere of the Research Department; and possibly I have tasted a little too much of the blood – if so thin a liquid may be so called – of actual political intercourse to be able to acclimatise myself easily to so subterranean a life. Perhaps I am not fair to it: but my best-loved colleagues now in it seemed to me in 1944 either to have taken refuge in immersion in unworldly pedantries or else to have developed a nervous dread of Gladwyn's curt command; perhaps the Old Stationery Office[1] has that effect on all its inmates: or perhaps I am simply being too snooty: but neither the Minister of State – nor anyone else whom I asked – was encouraging on the subject. If I am to cut myself off from affairs, I should prefer to be thoroughly remote, i.e. at Oxford. On the other hand, I am, of course, ridden with guilt about returning to that more leisurely life while everyone else goes on grinding away. Hence my uncertainty as to what to do. And my anxiety [not] to be too choosey. But my main difficulty is how to get away from here at all. The Earl of H., after receiving the news of my impending departure without any noticeable reaction in November, suddenly, it seems, began to rumble somewhat on this topic in February. He has not spoken to me about it yet, but I learn from Michael Wright that he sees no reason for my departure, and proposes, if I show signs of restiveness, to 'use the sledge-hammer', in his own phrase, and weld me into the local machine beyond all hope of redemption. This sounds very terrifying. As he

1 On Broad Sanctuary, opposite Westminster Abbey. FORD had moved there in summer 1943, shortly after its formation as a new Dept within the FO and the transfer of most of its staff from Oxford to London.

and I have been away lately, the interview with the Warden of the College – for such he still continues to be – has not yet taken place. His reasons seem to me simple enough – he looks on me, doubtless, as a fairly adequate work-horse which performs certain regular tasks – and cannot see why this routine should be disturbed. I dread the interview at which he is bound to look at me sternly (for he is quite able to do that) in the immense gloom of the Warden's study, and ask me whether I propose to desert at such a moment. If I had some other government job in London or elsewhere, I could at least try to represent it as a thousand times more important than my very peripheral activities here; since I have not, even I, trained as I am in most specious Oxford dialectic, should find it embarrassing, to say the least, to maintain that the urgency of my duties at Oxford overrides any possible work which I may be doing here. Hence, to avert the interview, the sledge-hammer etc., I have feebly agreed to stay on until the end of May. But the problem has merely been shelved until then. Unless I have a sound excuse for leaving, I do not quite know, short of a row which I feel temperamentally quite incapable of working up, how I am to extricate myself. Anything on your side which would provide me with an honourable reason either for leaving, or, at any rate, for a visit to London in the near (I should like to say very near) future would, therefore, be received with much relief and touching gratitude by yours devotedly.

PS I do apologise for pouring all this out upon you so; besides Toynbee's troglodytes, the only other offer of employment which I have had came by devious means from Duff Cooper; but since it involved 'public relations' in Paris, I didn't feel that I should do that at all well, and refused, this time with genuine expressions of appreciation. I really hope that you will take this as vox clamantis – de profundis,[1] etc. If you could provide me with even a temporary bridge, or should I say a ladder, however rickety, leading to the outer world, and particularly to London, I should be ever so grateful, and should climb it, be it ever so precarious. I believe that I am formally under your jurisdiction now. I therefore have no hesitation in throwing myself upon your mercy and your wisdom.

On 26 March IB attended John Wheeler-Bennett's wedding[2] at the University of Virginia, Charlottesville.

1 'The voice of one crying – from the depths'. Biblical phrases, from the Gospels and Psalm 130.
2 To Ruth Harrison Risher.

4 April 1945

British Embassy, Washington

My dear parents

This is a new type of brief letter. I am in tremendous health and must acknowledge the healing effects of medical science. The precise nature of the 'operation which was not an operation' I shall describe to you when I see you. Meanwhile, the Mexican trip was a great success. I am delighted to have seen that strange, wild, inhibited D. H. Lawrency[1] country full of cruelty and a kind of barbarian imagination, but I do not wish ever to go back there again. Mrs Morrow was very kind to me and I must write to thank her.

I am plotting to come back in June either for good or for a visit and shall let you know more about that. No sign of Smith, but a very amusing letter from Dr Bowra, who is very displeased about Hart's election and dislikes Sumner's election[2] to All Souls as much as I do. He is a very dismal man, though good-looking in an El Greco way. The Ambassador is obviously reluctant to let me go, the F.O. drops mysterious hints about wishing to discuss this or that scheme with me, nothing will become clear until I get to London.

Please give David and Mary my love – I am glad that you went to Bournemouth. I am looking forward to Charles's arrival later this month. My last communication with the Holdsteins yielded, as I wrote to you, very satisfactory results.

There is really nothing more to tell you except that my health is as good as I could wish yours to be. I am sure I will see you again before the summer is out in one way or another. I am not going to San Francisco, as somebody has to continue to write political reports from here. On the whole, I am glad this is so, as accommodation is very terrible with three-a-room at present and the significance of the occasion does not seem likely to be as great as had been predicted. So when I was asked whether I wished to go, I at first hesitated and then declined. I am sure that staying here quietly will be much better from every point of view – particularly if I am to pay you a visit in the summer – than a very exhausting six weeks to no purpose.

I can only say again that I feel tremendously well – am in excellent spirits – and have not a care in the world at the moment. Au revoir.

Isaiah

1 D(avid) H(erbert) Lawrence (1885–1930) lived for a time in Mexico in the 1920s, and his 1926 novel *The Plumed Serpent* is a vivid evocation of Mexico and of Aztec religion.
2 In succession to Adams.

TO ELISABETH MORROW

4 April 1945 [*carbon*]

[British Embassy, Washington, DC]

Dear Mrs Morrow,

I began to write this letter by hand and swiftly realised that, nicer though manuscript is than anything printed or typed, and more genuine, this method would have the grave defect of remaining unread, or at least undeciphered, by the reader, for if my speech is unintelligible enough, my handwriting is much much obscurer than even that. So I resort to a more modern, but I still think a less nice, and more frigid, method to say how profoundly and lastingly grateful I am for my fortnight at Casa Mañana.[1] I really was in a very dilapidated condition when I arrived and might have been so still but for the delicious, and, so far as I was concerned, most peaceful days at Cuernavaca. I only hope that I did not exhaust other people too much – I do talk so, I fear.[2] But Aubrey and John, who were perhaps the chief victims, seem up and about; I attended the wedding at Charlottesville, and it went off in gallant style in the midst of the most overwhelming Southern hospitality; and perhaps it is all really all right.

I came back full of the most conflicting emotions about Mexico and Mexicans – they were much darker and fiercer than I expected, full of really medieval barbarism and superstition, and richer temperaments and a more secret inner life than the sunny, gay and, I suppose, empty other Latin Americans who one comes across in Washington. The soil in Mexico is obviously very rich and rank and capable of the most luxuriant vegetation, but the looks on people's faces rather terrified me. I could respect them and admire them, but I do not think ever feel comfortable among them. How bright and civilised was life at Casa Mañana; oh, and the pleasure of being allowed to read books and talk about general subjects without a perpetual feeling of guilt about neglecting unreadable official reports stacked on one's desk. I really am ever so grateful to you.

I am still reading the awful Dr Hayek.[3] He is in New York now, I

1 Their house in Cuernavaca (on a street subsequently named after Dwight Morrow) contained a fine collection of folk art built up by the Morrows. It is now a restaurant specialising in Mexican cuisine.

2 John Wheeler-Bennett recalled: 'We sat in the gardens either gossiping, arguing or just being silent together [. . .], though when Isaiah arrived [. . .] there was not quite that same degree of hushed contemplation': op. cit. (536/1), 196.

3 Friedrich August von Hayek (1899–1992), Austrian-born economist known for conservative views and criticisms of the Keynesian Welfare State, Professor of Economic Science and Statistics, London, 1931–50; later (1974) shared Nobel Prize for Economics with Gunnar Myrdal. Hayek's *The Road to Serfdom* (London and Chicago, 1944) had just been published in condensed form in the *Reader's Digest*.

gather, and causing a certain feeling of jealousy in the breast of his old Viennese mentor, Dr von Mises,[1] who is just as much of a dodo, if not more so, and used to be the principal influence behind the more reactionary writings of Mr Henry Haslett[2] in the editorial columns of the New York Times. Dr von Hayek is now competing for Mr Haslett's soul with Dr von Mises: and a great jealousy has sprung up between the two.

Meanwhile, a fearful thing has happened: I wrote a short but bitter paragraph about Dr Hayek's book and influence and the way it was being used by the *Reader's Digest* and the Scripps Howard papers,[3] only to discover that Mr H. Butler presented the book with every mark of praise and admiration to the BIS Library and strongly recommended its doctrines to everyone here. Alas, I fear this fact has given Aubrey too much pleasure. Poor Mr Butler. In the recent election to the Wardenship of All Souls, for which, I fear, he sighed wistfully, his name was not, we are told, even mentioned. And he is not to go to San Francisco. Still, he has not the troubles of Mr A. MacLeish, who sadly asked me what was to become of his announced new policy of candour with the people if secret agreements were continually being hatched. I told him I thought one of his duties was to educate the public to the need of the secrecy of some negotiations, but he obviously felt this was no task for a poet and a tribune, rightly perhaps.

Once more, thank you very much and I hope we may meet before I finally return to England.

Yours ever,
Isaiah Berlin

TO HERBERT NICHOLAS

4 April 1945 [*carbon*]

British Embassy, Washington, DC

Dear Herbert,

It is possible that medicine really helps, since undoubtedly I feel better. I try not to, but there is no denying it – I take more pleasure in the external world. The internal world remains as barren as ever. I was much touched by the very nice letters which you all sent me – particularly by Robin's splendid

---

1 Ludwig Edler von Mises (1881–1973), Austrian-American free-market economist, taught in Vienna (where Hayek was among his students) 1913–38, and at New York University during the war.

2 Henry Stuart Hazlitt (*sic*) (1894–1993), author and journalist, outspoken champion of free-market economics, was influenced by Ludwig von Mises and Friedrich Hayek, whose *Road to Serfdom* he reviewed in the *New York Times* (for which he wrote editorials and reviews 1934–46).

3 WD 534–5.

masterpiece, first to Aubrey and then to myself. I shall reply to him separately. My parents, too, seem to have behaved unhysterically and not to be in need of those crude lies which I so mercilessly tried to force you to take upon your conscience. So that's all right.

I shall not be going to San Francisco since, with Archie there (as requested by FO), somebody must continue to send Political Summaries from here, and the local turmoil is certainly sufficient to justify continued residence. I have had my second interview with HE, who rode an even higher moral horse, spoke of honour, conscience, duty etc. Nevertheless, I am determined to return if only on a visit in mid-summer if that is possible. If that is refused, then for good and to Oxford. That institution seems to have got completely out of hand with the dismal Sumner at All Souls, the moronic Alington and the scarcely more impressive Wild[1] at Univ., the denationalisation of Jesus, the mad attempt to appoint E. H. Carr to the Professorship of Russian, the dim figure of Mr Bullock[2] at New College, etc.: time to go back and strike a blow for reason, I feel, don't you?

As for things here, the Korda party expedition shows no signs of arrival. Their names are on none of the incoming craft. If they left on the 10th, where are they? Even a raft should have arrived by this time.

Politics are getting madder and madder here: Messrs Lyttleton[3] and Llewellin say they have nobody to talk to about food: even Byrnes[4] was suddenly whisked away under their very noses, leaving the sound and benevolent but uninformed Vinson.[5] Americans first asked for three votes in the Assembly, then said they didn't want them.[6] Gloom about Russia is, to say the least, immense. Mr Boothby[7] has been campaigning against

1 For Alington and Wild see p. 694.

2 Alan Louis Charles Bullock (1914–2004), later (1976) Baron Bullock of Leafield, historian, Fellow, Dean and history Tutor, New College, 1945–52. IB later revised this uncharacteristic misjudgement, probably based on insufficient direct evidence.

3 Oliver Lyttelton (sic) (1893–1972), later (1954) 1st Viscount Chandos; Conservative MP 1940–54, President of the Board of Trade 1940–1, Minister of Production 1942–5.

4 James Francis Byrnes (1879–1972), influential lawyer and politician, Democratic Senator 1931–41, Associate Justice, Supreme Court, 1941–2, Director of Economic Stabilization 1942–3, Director, Office of War Mobilization (a central agency supervising the domestic war effort), 1943–5, Secretary of State 1945–7.

5 Frederick Moore Vinson (1890–1953), Chief Justice, Emergency Court of Appeals, 1942–3, Director, Office of Economic Stabilization, 1943–5, and Office of War Mobilization, 1945; later (1946–53) Chief Justice, US Supreme Court.

6 From 4 to 12 February FDR, Churchill and Stalin had met at Yalta in the Crimea to plan the final stages of the war against Germany and Japan, and the post-war spheres of influence of the US, the UK and the USSR. At this conference FDR and Churchill had agreed that Ukraine and Belorussia should be members of the General Assembly of the United Nations, thus giving the Soviet bloc three votes (in place of the sixteen they had claimed). FDR reserved the right to seek two more votes for the US, but did not exercise it.

7 Robert John Graham Boothby (1900–86), later (1958) Baron Boothby of Buchan and Rattray Head, Conservative MP 1924–58.

Bretton Woods[1] and claims to have killed it anyhow pro tem. Was he sent here by the Beaver[2] as a hatchet man? 'I will not', he said, 'be made a martyr or a scapegoat by your damned Embassy.' 'Scapegoat for whom? For himself? He really has done quite a bit of damage. His company is exhilarating and amusing and he does not disguise either his methods or his motives. If he were not such a naked mischief-maker, I should, for all his caddishness, be inclined to rather like him, if only for his resemblance to John L. Lewis, of whom he is a kind of jolly variant.

Mr Ridsdale[3] is amongst us with no specific function save that of staying with Ferdie Kuhn,[4] who seems to have invited him. I cannot conceive of anything emerging from a combination of two such weak elements. Aubrey, mightily bearded and correspondingly fierce, is doubtless giving him a piece of his mind even now. The arrival of Roger Makins here has made all the difference in the world to the general morale of this Embassy. There is a limit to ungeniality and M. Wright has easily reached it.

As for your specific enquiry – about Communications – New York is to send you clippings, while I shall forward by the usual bootleg methods copies of the regular reports which the Chancery send to the FO, plus any telegrams – they are very rare – which may be exchanged. In the meanwhile, Nicoll tells me that you offered some sort of commercial newsletter, regarded as very valuable by the Chancery, on this topic, costing $100 a year, which you invited us to try and find other customers for, e.g. the Post Office, to share the cost, and that no reply had yet been received upon the subject from the Treasury. So I suppose nothing can be done on that score.

Prof. Hayek has arrived; *Reader's Digest*, Scripps Howard etc. have made much play with his book, which is being used powerfully against us. I need not add that Mr Butler has warmly praised it and presented it to the BIS Library. The latter is in a very pathetic condition re San Francisco etc. I think it is wicked of Robin not to be coming and have told the Russians that this is revenge for their not sending Molotov. They seemed a little dazed but will doubtless report this to Moscow and the counterattack will duly appear in *War and the Working Class*.[5]

1 The United Nations Monetary and Financial Conference held in 1944 at Bretton Woods, New Hampshire, to make financial arrangements for the post-war world resulted in the setting up of the International Monetary Fund and the International Bank for Reconstruction and Development, which began operations in 1946 after the required number of governments had ratified the agreement.

2 Lord Beaverbrook.

3 William Ridsdale (1890–1957), Head of FO News Dept 1941–53.

4 Ferdinand Kuhn, Jr (1905–78), journalist, *New York Times*, 1925–40, chief London correspondent 1937–9, assistant to Secretary of the Treasury 1940–2, Deputy Director, Overseas Branch, and head of British Division, OWI, 1943–5.

5 A Moscow fortnightly, renamed *New Times* in 1945.

Mr MacLeish is frightfully unhappy, and wants to know what is to become of his new policy of candour with the people. However, the President has managed to stroke him down a bit, and like the house cat that he is, he is purring again. If the President dies[1] or retires, will US foreign policy be managed by Messrs Truman and Stettinius?[2] On this interesting note, I close. I shall soon write again.

    Yours ever,
      Isaiah Berlin

TO SIR DAVID SCOTT

4 April 1945 [carbon]

British Embassy, Washington

I have just had an interview with the Ambassador about which I feel that I ought to inform you. He sent for me and declared that rumours had reached him that I wished to depart, and then said that he would greatly regret this, etc., that it was a matter concerning which I must look deeply into my conscience, consult my sense of duty, and otherwise conduct a moral self-examination of the most profound and searching order. If this operation revealed that I still considered it my bounden duty to go, we were to discuss it again, preferably after San Francisco. I['ve?] suspected for some time that a very high moral horse, this time, would sooner or later be ridden and, indeed, did not know what to reply. I was wondering whether the best thing would not be for me to stay here, say, until the end of San Francisco (since I have anyway contracted to stay until the end of May), then go to London, at any rate on a visit, to consider the future in the light of whatever claims and suggestions might occur there, promising to return here to wind up finally and return for good, whether to Oxford or not, in the late autumn. I do not like to suggest this course spontaneously as my own plan at this end because I have just been away at Johns Hopkins and on a fortnight's leave and am obviously expected either to stay for a long continuous bit or else – if I can square it with my conscience, etc. – to go for good. But if I were summoned from London – I am now formally transferred to Chancery and my department is, therefore, the FO – that would be another matter, and I do not think any objection would arise here. If the idea smiles to you at all, perhaps it could be arranged that I return with the bulk of the San Francisco

---

1 FDR died within two weeks.
2 Edward Reilly Stettinius, Jr (1900–49), Chairman, War Resources Board, 1939–41, Administrator of Lend-Lease and Special Assistant to the President 1941–3, Under-Secretary of State 1943–4, Secretary of State 1944–5, US representative to the UN 1945–6.

party whenever and however they are returning. Please forgive me if this is putting so much[1] on your last letter, but I should be most grateful if a summer visit to London could be arranged.

The only person I have spoken to here about the matter is Roger Makins, who thinks it a good idea and agrees that a summons had better arrive from London. I do hope that Toynbee does not really count upon me too much. I feel awfully conscience-stricken about that distinguished and sensitive man.

Yours ever,

TO LADY DAPHNE STRAIGHT

9 April 1945 [*carbon*]

British Embassy, Washington, DC

My dear Daphne,

The skies are blue again, the sun shining. In my private world, I mean, in particular with respect to the disturbed relations between your Division and myself. A honeyed letter from Nick, two splendid oeuvres from Robin, and your own unfailing quality have worked that tremendous change. I love you all again most warmly. Incidentally, with regard to Robin, although you had better not say this to him, he appears to have been scattering honeyed cakes with a prodigal hand, since Graham Hutton, Ben [Thomas], Aubrey, and heaven knows who else besides myself, have received the most flattering encomia, and Graham has conducted a kind of general survey on the situation and much pleasure and amusement has been caused by this grand wave of good feeling stimulated from your end. Despite the irony of the above, the effect has undoubtedly been good, and even Graham, who professes not to need such douceurs, is secretly gratified. In his case, a small but neat decoration from a grateful government would be better still, but I doubt if the Minister would agree.[2]

My operation and the subsequent days in Mexico all went off very nicely. I have exchanged discomfort in my sinus for a peculiar feeling in the secret regions of my nose, but the exchange is probably worth it. As for my own return, it is as you say. The Ambassador once more sent for me, rode more high moral horses and said we would discuss it all again in the middle of May. Of course I could flatly break off relations and come back; I should prefer to use Robin's trick and go away on leave to London this summer and

1 i.e. too much weight.
2 Hutton received an OBE in the 1946 New Year Honours List from the new Labour Government.

perhaps not return, or really return only for a month to pack up and finally go. As I am now, I suppose, a slave of the FO (which drops the most mysterious hints about their plans for me but won't say anything concrete – I am not curious since I do not propose to accept any of their offers be they never so alluring), I secretly wrote to Sir David Scott asking him to summon me, at any rate to have a talk sometime this summer. On this my only hope is therefore pinned. If nothing happens by, say, June, I shall, I expect, go away in any case. If I ask to be allowed to go home once a month they will certainly tire of a battle of attrition. If there is anything you can do to cause somebody to call me officially, I should be delighted. I must obviously stay here until San Francisco ends, otherwise there will be no Political Summaries with Archie away at SF. But that should be over by the end of May.

The peculiar figure of Mr Boothby shot across my trail. He is up to no good and was obviously sent here by the Beaver to wreck Bretton Woods, which he claims to have done. I cannot deny that I found the evening I spent with him agreeable and stimulating, although he is himself undoubtedly a most abandoned scamp and up to every kind of mischief. He sent me a wonderful account of himself as put out by his lecture agent, in which his brilliance is compared with that of Shakespeare and the Bible. To do him credit, he knows the truth about himself and does not hesitate to put all his cards on all the tables all the time. The Ambassador was supposed to have taken a stern line with him, but on his own showing, and more particularly that of Mr B, took a line of nervous amiability which led to Mr B's going away under the impression that nothing terrible would happen to him however many beans, real and invented, he spills here and at San Francisco, where he is to represent the *News of the World*. Opie is naturally in a great flap about his nefarious activities and so is Dr Harry White[1] of the US Treasury.

Meanwhile, the next big cloud is in connection with colonial trustee-ships. We are popularly credited, perhaps rightly, with being against any liberalisation of the colonial and mandates system, and Colonel [Oliver] Stanley's recent visit has strengthened this impression very considerably. The Americans certainly believe that the mandatory system was a step in the right direction, whereas we, despite all our talk about regional commissions, have given the impression that we do not. At the moment there is a violent row occurring between Service departments, who want to annex various atolls, and the State Department, who want to internationalise. But we are not likely to gain much advantage from a row between the liberals and the jingos, since both are equally against us on this in any case. Meanwhile, we

---

1 Harry Dexter White (1892–1948), Keynesian economist; US Treasury 1934–46, Assistant Secretary 1945–6, (first) US Executive Director, International Monetary Fund, 1946–7; accused of being a Communist agent, which he denied under oath.

appear to have no line of our own as usual, except to keep what we have and add to it, which won't go down at all. All other departments seem to regard the Colonial Office as absolutely bloody about this, and I dare say they are.

There is a fine fuss going on about the American three votes. Stettinius seems to be implying that this was done on the advice of Messrs Byrnes and Flynn[1] at Yalta;[2] Byrnes hisses that he left Yalta the day before this was discussed and had nothing to do with it, etc. Never was a conference conceived in a mood of greater pessimism as to its outcome. I do not understand why the dominions do not squawk more loudly than they do about being represented as obedient stooges to HMG. Why can't someone be stimulated to emit a shriek, supported by statistical evidence of their League votes?

What more is there to tell you? Too many nice people have been killed lately – poor Twentyman[3] was a really very nice man and left his wife and children wildly uninsured; Bob Brand's son,[4] whom I met and thought very nice: Bob himself is in the most appalling shattered state. And did you ever know David Wallace[5] who was in Athens? I liked him very much and had the most touching tribute paid to him by Mr Sedgwick[6] of the *New York Times*, who has returned from Athens burning with pro-British feeling. He defends Leeper[7] passionately, thinks we made no mistakes[8] except for those made by Casey,[9] of whom he has the lowest opinion, and is lecturing

1 Edward Joseph Flynn (1891/2–1953), lawyer, close friend and supporter of FDR and the New Deal, known as 'Boss of the Bronx', Secretary of State of NY 1929–39, National Chairman of the Democratic Party 1940–2.

2 542/6.

3 Possibly Edward Twentyman (c.1888–1945), civilian of Chatham, d. 27 March, listed by the Commonwealth War Graves Commission under 'Air Crashes at Sea'.

4 (Robert) James Brand (1923–45), a Lieutenant in the Coldstream Guards, had died in action in Germany on 30 March. It was the second tragedy for Bob Brand within a few years, his wife Phyllis (Nancy Astor's sister) having died in 1937.

5 d. 17 August 1944.

6 Alexander Cameron Sedgwick (1901–96), reporter for the *New York Times* from 1925; became their correspondent in Athens, where he settled with his Greek wife.

7 Reginald ('Rex') Wildig Allen Leeper (1888–1968), Australian-born diplomat, former head of FO News Dept and Political Intelligence Dept, head of propaganda section of SOE 1940–1; on executive committee of PWE from its formation in August 1941 until 1943; Ambassador to the Greek government in Cairo 1943–4, in Athens 1944–6; Ambassador to Argentina 1946–8.

8 During the German occupation, Greek Communists had formed a major part of the Resistance movement, while at the same time conducting a virtual civil war against non-Communist partisan groups. The withdrawal of German forces in October 1944 allowed the government of national unity to return from exile to Athens, accompanied by a contingent of British troops. The Prime Minister, Georgios Papandreou (1888–1968), soon called for the total disarmament of Communist forces. Opposition to this led in December to the first phase of the Greek Civil War between the Communist ELAS (548/1) and the government, supported by the British; although confined to Athens the conflict was violent and many thousands died. British military and diplomatic pressure brought a (temporary) end to the fighting and a cease-fire was agreed in February 1945.

9 Presumably William Joseph Casey (1913–87), American lawyer, at that time based in London in

against the EAM[1] all over the place. He seems sure that once the mails are open and the Greek restaurateurs here find out about what has happened to their relations in Greece our stock will bound upwards. Maybe. Mr Sedgwick's dislike of the other correspondents in view of their integrity and general methods is very red hot too. Naturally I nodded with approval and shook him warmly by the hand.

San Francisco is really going to be very queer. Not only is every political body, every organisation of political pressure groups, every European party and every crackpot outfit going to send droves of representatives there, but the mere presence of 140 British, 160 French, 280 American officials, etc., is not going to improve matters. Besides which Mrs Longworth and Mrs Beale are opening a house in San Francisco as an official salon in which gossip will be exchanged at various rates. The general atmosphere, despite Stettinius's gallant efforts to support a failing market, is jittery. However, the Oxford Dons have arrived, and I must to them.

    Much love,
        Isaiah Berlin

PS One more thing. This will call for your highest tact and consideration. Mary Cooke:[2] Having promoted peaceful relations with everyone else it is now the duty of your section to establish a modus vivendi with the Survey in BIS. Remembering as I do that I am no longer one of you (ha!) and have no formal authority in the matter, I can only privately relate the following: It is evidently not to be that a British subject is to be established as the head of that section in New York. Mary Cooke is fully aware (or perhaps exaggeratedly so) of the suspicion entertained of her in London as the voice of respectable US Republicanism rather than an agent of the British people. However, if you want to get the best out of her and her girls and boys, and she is clearly still the best person in that section, one of two things should be done: Either she should be sacked or she should be impressed with the fact that she is, in fact, trusted and liked, otherwise she will continue to bubble much as she does at present. On the one hand, Nick, probably rightly, complains that the surveys are deteriorating again and that the wrong

charge of the clandestine operations being conducted in occupied Europe (including Greece) by OSS, the predecessor of the CIA, of which he was later (1981–7) Director. The OSS did not have a high reputation at the time, partly because of its persistent failure to liaise with other organisations.

1 Ethnikon Apeleftherotikon Metopon (National Liberation Front), Greek resistance movement; a coalition of five socialist parties forming the political wing of the Communist-controlled guerrilla organisation ELAS (National People's Liberation Army).

2 Mary Munroe Cooke (b. 1907), US national; Junior Assistant (Survey), BPS New York, 1941–4, Assistant Section Head, BIS New York, 1944–5 (resigned December 1945).

approach has been adopted towards the facts reported. On the other hand, Mary is aware that the only answer to her, so she says, polite letters to Nick, are replied to merely by somewhat testy telegrams complaining of the inadequacy of this or that product. I sympathise with both sides, and so, I dare say, do you. Obviously she cannot be better than she is, and Con, who is well aware of all this, cannot forget the international tension allegedly introduced by Nick on his visit here precisely on the issue of Americans working for BIS in this province. Mary Cooke apparently was somewhat scarred by this experience, and the approach I should recommend is that given, as it inevitably must be, that Americans do continue to do this work for us, we had better adopt the attitude that their product should be criticised strictly on its merits and not because of its source of origin. Naturally you must complain whenever you feel real grievances with what you get from New York, but it would be a good thing if Mary were finally confirmed in her position as head of Survey unless someone is definitely to be sent from London to replace her, and, having been confirmed, that a friendly and uninhibited correspondence should spring up between her and someone in your section, whether Nick or yourself. Wonders would be worked if a little gratuitous butter were dispatched by you to the BIS Survey, and if, with every sharp criticism, a few roses were thrown in. That is only my advice as an old appeaser and now himself appeased. But I am sure you can grasp what the situation is and perhaps you would have a word with Robin about it, who might spontaneously arrange things with Nick. I do not much relish my role as mediator, since Nick's case is probably very good and I do not want to seem unappreciative of it. I think this is a case for the most delicate diplomacy, of which we cannot deny that you are infinitely capable. So I leave matters in your hands. The steady reports from London, emanating from Robin, that the Survey is perhaps the most valuable part of the BIS from London's point of view – that films or exhibitions or anything is worth sacrificing to its efficiency – merely served to irritate Aubrey, inasmuch as they imply a criticism of his system of values. So if I were you, I would either shut the door or open it wide, i.e. either sack Mary and send a British agent or display great confidence. What do you think yourself about this? The ideal would be if Nick himself would write a letter praising heavily whatever is in the least praiseworthy about the Survey's efforts and only then qualifying this by recommendations of change. But I know how difficult this is to do from London, and if there is anything that I can do by way of tactfully conveying what desirable reforms are thought possible within the present framework of the Survey, I should be glad to execute a mission of this sort. There. Could anything be more sweetly reasonable?

As the diplomatic world converged on San Francisco for the conference to draft the charter of the United Nations, IB's eventual disappointment at having to stay in Washington was tempered by an intriguing suggestion. As IB remembered:

And then Clark Kerr, who was the British Ambassador in Moscow, rather a card, [. . .] came to Washington en route to San Francisco, to which he was summoned – part of the general entourage – and we had lunch together. For some reason he had heard about me from the Americans, and so I was asked to lunch [by] the Ambassador – Halifax – to meet him. I sat next to him, we chatted, and we got on, and he said, 'Look, I'm told you speak Russian like a native, in fact you are a native. [. . .] Nobody in my Embassy talks much Russian. Would you like to come and work for me for a bit? – because I'd like nothing better. I'll see if I can fix it.'[1]

TO MARIE AND MENDEL BERLIN

5 May 1945 [*manuscript*]

British Embassy, Washington

My dear parents

And why not? why not go to Moscow, I mean? Sir A. Clark Kerr, a charming man, full of wit & cleverness is very persuasive: his minister, Mr J. Balfour, has just come here as Minister to replace Sir R. Campbell, after 2 years in Moscow, & paints a very attractive picture. The arrangement is to last only 3–4 months in all. Plan is that I leave here in July, come to Oxford in early Aug, leave early Sept. stay in Moscow ½ Sept, Oct, Nov, Dec., ½ Jan & return in January (end of) to New College & peace. An opportunity surely not to be missed? how long have I panted to go? & the Russians so quick with a diplomatic visa?[2] surely I shall be better off with an intimate friend there – i.e. Crosthwaite – than with strangers – & the fascination is enormous. I am in the best of health (as Smith must have told you) my nose no longer feels anything, & so far I have had no sinus trouble at all yet except once when I caught an ordinary cold which passed in 2 days – so that I am really much better than I have been for I don't know how long. I am sick & tired of Washington, as you know, & to stop rotating all at once is not too agreeable, so this final spin via Moscow will be just right.

1 MI Tape 21.
2 A letter dated 23 April 1945 from N. Konikov to Frank Roberts at the British Embassy in Moscow reports that, in response to Sir Archibald Clark Kerr's letter of 20 February to V. M. Molotov, People's Commissar of USSR Foreign Affairs, the Soviet Embassy in London 'has been instructed to issue a visa to Mr Isaiah Berlin'.

I'll discuss it all with you v. thoroughly when I see you in July–Aug – when I arrive + I hope Inecto No 3[1] – but as always I shall be pretty obstinate (you sigh deeply) – Clark Kerr says that nobody can want to stay more than 3–4 months, & New College really seems to need me – so provided I don't stay there too long it seems a good idea. And perhaps I'll see Petrograd too, or whatever of it remains in Leningrad – via Ostashkov, Andreapol, Toropetz . . . not to be thrown away if I can travel in 'diplomatic' comfort.[2]

I saw your Mr Korner[3] – very nice very polite. To-morrow I dine – for the sake of old times – with Leib Yaffé,[4] with whom I shall talk about Russian poetry of his youth – Khodasevitch,[5] Blok, Bryusov,[6] & even a man now in New York (tell Rach) Boozlyook.[7] What more is there to say? I assiduously cultivate the local Soviet 1st Secretary[8] (question: is he ex nostris?[9] his wife certainly is. After dinner he says "ну наелись?"[10] he gave me a cigar (вы кубинские лубите?')[11] out of which a small white worm dropped out 'чего вы так смотрите? а? ненравит[ь]ся'[12] *very* difficult obviously the directive is to mix a little more with 'foreigners' & people like me who may be 'useful sources of information'. A bientôt[13] – I must go to bed. I saw Rosa Raskin the other day – still nice – longs to go back – her mama not well – her uncle[14] says nobody left in Riga so far as he knows – but all the people returning from Jerusalem (for San Francisco) say that Yitz. & Ida are very well.

What more to tell you? An immense economic operation will have to be

1 A product sold by Inecto Ltd, distributors of cosmetics, especially for hair colouring and care; Marie Berlin had dyed her hair since starting to go grey at the age of twenty-four.
2 St Petersburg had been renamed 'Petrograd' in 1914, the traditional name being thought too German; in 1924 the name was changed to Leningrad. Ostashkov, Andreapol and Toropetz are small towns in the Tver region of Russia, north-west of Moscow. They are all on the railway line to Leningrad. The Berlins had lived briefly in Andreapol (1915–16) before moving to Petrograd.
3 Eric Korner, né Erich Körner (1893–1980), Austrian-born banker at Warburgs in London (one of the original directors of the firm, which began life as the New Trading Company) who dealt with IB's parents, and then with IB.
4 Leib Jaffe (1876–1948), Russian Zionist leader, writer, poet, emigrated to Palestine in 1920.
5 Vladislav Felitsianovich Khodasevich (1886–1939), poet and literary critic, emigrated to Berlin in 1922, wrote little poetry after 1927.
6 Valery Yakovlevich Bryusov (1873–1924), leading Symbolist poet, critic and literary scholar.
7 Possibly David Davidovich Burlyuk (1882–1967), Futurist poet and painter who settled in the US in 1922.
8 Anatoly Gorsky, alias Gromov (506/4).
9 'One of us', sc. Jewish.
10 'Nu naelis'?' ('Well, have you had enough to eat?').
11 'Vy *kubinskie* lyubite?' ('Do you like *Cubans*?').
12 'Chego vy tak smotrite? a? nenravit'sya?' ('What are you looking like that for? Eh? Don't you like it then?')
13 'Until soon.'
14 Probably her father's brother.

carried out when the division of property between Guy Chilver & me takes place when my boxes are packed to go by sea (while I go by air) – financial complications about ownership, e.g. of ½ carpets: & so on. I propose to bring back sheets, blankets, & everything washable: & I have just cashed a cheque for £150 on the Midland Bank to defray my recent "operation" + holiday in Mexico. I may cash another such sum to buy clothes etc. before I leave as I am pretty threadbare (the two suits made in London at father's tailor's are too vulgar to be worn at home – here anything passes).

If there is anything I am likely to bring de trop write & tell me & I'll not bring it. Write via F.O. addressed to me here ("By favour of Bag). I am looking forward{ing} immensely to home & you & the long talks. When I return I'll spend at least 1 week in Oxford incognito before reporting to F.O. (now my masters) – & then to Moscow maybe via Paris–Cairo–Jerusalem–Teheran–Tiflis! *chudno budet!*[1]

   love
      Isaiah

TO HERBERT NICHOLAS

   8 May 1945[2]

                              British Embassy, Washington

Personal

Dear Herbert,

   Thank you for your two most interesting and informative letters. I should be delighted if I were half as well as your letters suggest that I am thought to be (God, John Wheeler-Bennett's wedding, the bride . . .). But although far from ill, I seem to be neither much better nor much worse than during the past 30 years. The newest thing in my life is that I am definitely returning to England at the end of July or the first week in August at the latest, and in September am to go for three to four months to Moscow whither the cynical but very worthwhile Sir A. Clark Kerr has successfully lured me (by the simple but irresistible device of waving a visa in front of me while passing through Washington to San Francisco). I am to be back in Oxford for good towards the end of January and it has so been fixed with Smith who could not have been more delightful. I may bring back Prichard for a year as a freak law tutor at New College but tell no one of this as yet. I am extremely glad that the obvious has happened and that Exeter have

   1 'It'll be wonderful.'
   2 VE Day.

finally come up to scratch[1] (Coghill[2] told me). I can't conceive why they shilly-shallied for so long; I think Exeter Senior Common Room is becoming much too good; I am not sure that Assembly powers are entitled to quite so much strength which should be reserved for the big three (Christ Church, Balliol, New College). Do you think that Magdalen is France?[3]

As for San Francisco, I have no real gossip for you. Indeed, I wish I had been sent there, since in Washington we hear little else than you do in London. But it appeared otherwise to my betters and here I am. Therefore, as you suggest, I shall concentrate on Truman. My last piece was adjudged to be too hot for the summary and I enclose it. In general, the bootleg sheets[4] have stopped coming because the arrangement was discovered and a quiet, but vigorous, demarche made to me personally. However, I had better continue to do this on a sporadic basis, i.e. when something conspicuously interesting does not get in (this particular item is to go as a letter to Sir O. Sargent).[5] As there was a leak about Stettinius (about which he made a terrible fuss at the exact date of the demarche which could only have come (a) from London and (b) from the unincluded part of my Summary draft), I thought it best not to make a stand on this particular issue but I shall not leave you narrowly confined to the official fare. The truth about the White House is that while Truman is clearly sincere, decent ('I know he is decent', said Mr Ickes on the night of Mr Roosevelt's death,[6] 'but can anyone mention any other attributes?') and liberal in a provincial Midwestern way, the best kind of American legionnaire, unexpectedly businesslike, brisk, crisp and capable of getting on with people like Eden and Lyttelton, the whole thing is on such a minute scale, such a Dutch interior, that all these virtues cannot provide for the first really big crisis which general principles do not solve. Truman's predilection is quite simply for respectable, unfrightening hacks. He will probably get rid of Ed [Stettinius] because he must have someone to lean on in the matter of foreign policy, but voices are already whispering about Byrnes, 'Are you going to be president or is he?', so it may

1 By offering HGN a Fellowship.
2 Nevill Henry Kendal Aylmer Coghill (1899–1980), Fellow and English literature Tutor, Exeter, 1925–57.
3 An allusion to the Yalta Conference, to which France was not invited. The 11 February dispatch to the FO had reported: 'De Gaulle's announcement that any decisions made there would not be binding upon France until she had had an opportunity to discuss them on a basis of equality and his demand for French predominance from one end of the Rhine to the other, are regarded in certain quarters as tiresome and unreasonable' (WD 513).
4 Uncensored versions of IB's official political reports, sent to London by covert means.
5 Sir Orme Garton Sargent (1884–1962), FO Counsellor 1926, Deputy Under-Secretary of State, FO, 1939; nicknamed 'Moley'.
6 12 April.

be someone like Senator Hatch[1] or Barkley[2] or some good but enormously limited crony. It won't be someone like Coolidge because Truman has
a genuine desire to help the little man and hates Big Business and doesn't like
Nelson Rockefeller[3] (the latter has all the ruthlessness of his grandfather and
the smoothness of his father, and has our poor, mad, Hadow[4] thoroughly in
willing tow). But it will be tremendously low level and humdrum. I wrote to
you or to Daphne about what binds him to Wheeler – it seems that it no
longer does; both Wheeler and Krock, who are polite about him in public,
describe him as 'just a hack politician' in private. 'Maybe I ought to have
been a piano player in a whorehouse and not President of the United States',
he amiably observed to a friend of mine, but Irving Brant[5] in the *New
Republic*[6] (not to be confused with Pete Brandt[7] of the *St Louis Post-Dispatch*),
who is a kind of older Dilliard,[8] with memories of La Follette[9] instead of
Norris,[10] is very glowing about him as a flaming liberal but sounder than the
New Deal. You can take your choice.

I will write again to you soon, will not expect an answer, and look
forward with genuine feeling to a great discussion in Oxford in August.

Yours ever,

[signed p.p.]

P.S. The rumoured appointment of Judge ex-Senator Schwellenbach[11] is
pretty typical. S. was in some trouble about some dairies or fisheries or

1 Carl Atwood Hatch (1889–1963), Democratic Senator from New Mexico 1933–49.
2 Alben William Barkley (1877–1956), Senator from Kentucky 1927–48, Majority Leader of the
  Senate 1937–47, famed orator, Vice-President 1948–52.
3 Nelson Aldrich Rockefeller (1908–79), grandson of John D. Rockefeller, Sr, founder of Standard
  Oil, son of philanthropist John D. Rockefeller, Jr; Co-ordinator of Inter-American Affairs
  1940–4, later (1974–7) Vice-President to Gerald Ford.
4 Robert Henry Hadow (1895–1963), Counsellor, FO, 1942; British Embassy, Washington, 1944.
5 Irving Newton Brant (1885–1976), newspaper editor and author; foreign correspondent,
  Chicago Sun, 1945.
6 Liberal journal founded by Willard and Dorothy Straight in 1914: see 318/1.
7 Raymond Peter Brandt (1896–1974), Chief of the Washington Bureau of the *St Louis Post-
  Dispatch* 1934–61.
8 Irving Dilliard (1904–2002), chief leader writer for *St Louis Post-Dispatch*, specialising in civil
  liberties and constitutional law.
9 Probably Robert Marion La Follette, Sr (1855–1925), crusading progressive reformer, Senator
  from Wisconsin 1906–25, a lifelong liberal on domestic issues but keenly isolationist, opposed
  to trusts and corruption and a campaigner for tax reform and workers' rights; his son Robert
  Marion La Follette, Jr (1895–1953), isolationist and ardent New Dealer, who was Senator
  1925–47 in succession to his father, seems not to be the La Follette referred to here.
10 George William Norris (1861–1944), Republican Senator from Nebraska 1913–43, 'father' of the
  Tennessee Valley Authority, advocate of federal power projects and farm-relief measures.
11 Lewis B. Schwellenbach (1894–1948), Democratic Senator from State of Washington 1935–41;
  federal judge 1940–5; Secretary of Labor 1945–8.

something in the State of Washington some years ago. He is pro-Labor, anti-isolationist, a good North-Western radical, but not personally too honest and a man of no stature at all, who sat on a back bench with Truman and steadily voted for progressive legislation in a cosy humdrum way with a lot of loyalty to the local machine and a lot of suspicion of 'the Frankfurters and the Tugwells'.[1]

[*enclosure*]

THE PRESIDENCY

Although it is too early to give a long-term estimate of the general quality and prospects of the new regime, certain contours are becoming discernible. The President, both in his public utterances and his administrative acts, is conceded on all sides to be acting with honesty, firmness and dispatch, and to be carrying on faithfully along the general lines so firmly developed by his predecessor. Moreover, his relations with Congress (and the press) are conspicuously better than were Mr Roosevelt's, particularly during his two last terms. He has also shown a tendency to back individuals and institutions liable to attract indiscriminate public attack, in a clear and straightforward fashion which Mr Roosevelt usually failed to display, preferring to leave each agency to defend its own sector of the front by means of its own unaided resources, with relatively little open support from the White House. Thus his public rebuke of its detractors has arrested the traditional attack on the much-abused Office of Price Administration (by no means the most inefficient of US Federal agencies); he has scotched the rumours that 'Southern Bourbons' led by the die-hard Senator McKellar[2] (whom Truman has tactfully welcomed into the Cabinet) would finally succeed in killing or crippling their bogey, the Tennessee Valley Authority, by refusal to confirm its celebrated Chairman David Lilienthal.[3] After a visit of protest from Senators McKellar and Stewart[4] of Tennessee, Truman rapidly announced his reappointment of the justly admired Lilienthal, which will now probably go through the Senate more easily than might have been the case in Roosevelt's day. Similar firmness is to be expected in the case of other

---

1 Rexford Guy Tugwell (1891–1979), economist, member of FDR's 'Brain Trust', chairman of New York City Planning Commission 1938–40, Governor of Puerto Rico 1941–6.
2 Kenneth Douglas McKellar (1869–1957), right-wing Democratic Senator for Tennessee 1917–53.
3 David Lilienthal (1899–1981), lawyer, model public servant, Director of the Tennessee Valley Authority 1933–46, Chairman of the Atomic Energy Commission 1946–50.
4 Arthur Thomas ('Tom') Stewart (1892–1972), lawyer (prosecutor at famous 1925 case in which a Tennessee schoolmaster was tried for teaching evolution), Democratic Senator for Tennessee 1939–49.

domestic agencies in whose operations Truman took an active interest as a Senator. Notwithstanding his warm relations with Congress he has shown an unwillingness to be put upon by imposing his veto on the attempt to exclude agricultural labourers as such from military service. He has incidentally pleased the public and press by the common-sense forthright way in which he dismissed the premature peace rumour.

A less promising side to the picture is to be found in a perhaps unavoidable lowering of the general administrative level in Washington. The men whom the new President has chosen for his personal staff are of blameless enough reputation but dim and provincial to a degree. His chief administrative assistant, McKim[1] (an old 'war buddy' who served in Truman's battery in the 129th Regiment of US Artillery in the last war), is a blunt but undistinguished Missouri insurance man, who acted more or less as Truman's bodyguard during his Vice-Presidential election campaign. His personal assistant, Matthew Connelly[2] (see Political Summary No 2769),[3] is a colourless individual but doubtless a competent enough secretary; his military aide, Vaughan,[4] is also a Battery mate (all of which leads *Time* magazine to gibe about 'Government by cronies'). The Party boss, Hannegan,[5] now duly elevated to the traditional post of Postmaster General (regularly held since 1932 by Roman Catholic, Irish, Democratic Party Chairmen), has secured the appointment of Ed Pauley,[6] a slick oil magnate and the financier of the Party, to represent the United States on the Reparations Commission; the two remaining principal appointments – Snyder[7] as

---

1 Edward Daniel McKim (1895–1969), Omaha insurance executive, close friend of Truman since they were soldiers together in the First World War, accompanied him on Vice-Presidential campaign 1944, but lasted only two months as his *soi-disant* 'Chief Administrative Assistant'.

2 Matthew J. Connelly (1907–76), Truman's appointments secretary 1945–53, and also his poker companion; described at WD 547 as 'a moderate Roman Catholic from Massachusetts of apparently neutral flavour'; later (1956) convicted for conspiracy to defraud the government.

3 The dispatch of 21 April, printed at WD 544–9. The number cited by IB does not relate specifically to the Political Summaries, but to the numbering of telegrams sent out from the Embassy in Washington.

4 General Harry Hawkins Vaughan (1893–1981), old friend of Truman and his military aide 1945–53, later criticised for improprieties, including the questionable acceptance of freezers sent to government officials. The pianist and humorist Victor Borge used to announce thereafter in his concerts: 'My next number will be a classic by Beethoven – the Deep-Freeze Concerto, by Harry S. Beethoven. [*pause*] You will recognise the beat – Vaughan-two, Vaughan-two.' Robert H. Ferrell, *Harry S. Truman: A Life* (Columbia/London, 1994), 361.

5 Robert Emmet Hannegan (1903–49), Democratic National Committee Chairman 1944–9, had played a vital part in placing Truman on the ticket; Postmaster-General 1945–7.

6 Edwin Wendell Pauley (1903–81), Californian oilman, Treasurer, Democratic National Committee, 1944–5, US representative, Reparations Commission, 1945–7.

7 John Wesley Snyder (1895–1985), banker, conservative; Administrator, Federal Loan Agency, 1945, Director, Office of War Mobilization and Reconversion, 1945–6, Secretary of the Treasury 1946–53.

Federal Loan Administrator and Ross[1] as Press Secretary – both went to men from Missouri. These new placemen are a collection, at best, of worthy and honourable mediocrities. The general span of Mr Truman's appointments seems to extend no wider than from that of an unexciting but honest man like Snyder, with whom the liberals find no fault, to pure and unashamed acts of Party patronage like that of Pauley, which has met with a good deal of quite harsh criticism. No more than routine interest attaches to Truman's 'ouster' of Milligan,[2] the prosecutor of his old patron, Pendergast,[3] from Missouri politics and to his possible appointment of his old Missouri friend and rival, the isolationist Champ Clark,[4] to some well paid Federal job.

More serious, however, than the foregoing developments, which amount in the aggregate to blameless if uninspiring kleinmalerei,[5] is the uncertainty that still prevails with regard to the conduct of foreign affairs. One does not have to go to the full length of Lippmann's intensive campaign against Stettinius to realise that the new President needs, and will sooner or later become convinced that he needs, a Secretary of State with sufficient experience and authority to carry weight with Congress, with the public, and indeed with himself. It is unlikely that great use is likely to be made of Hopkins, who is recuperating in his Washington house. Byrnes, on the other hand, is still a favourite for this post. While carrying more weight with Congress and the country than Stettinius, the latter, despite his senatorial experience and his visit to Yalta, is scarcely a man of wide or deep direct experience in foreign affairs. Consequently, despite the new President's obvious integrity and very sound general views on international affairs, and the good influence upon him of such sincere internationalists as Senators Hatch and Barkley, a period is likely to ensue, not indeed of drift or apathy, but at any rate of a passive absence of the vast purposes and energetic drive provided by the late President. If Mr Stimson were ten years younger he could perhaps have filled the gap. As it is, we are likely to witness missed opportunities and neglected acts, not so much through any deliberate change

1 Charles Griffith Ross (1885–1950), Truman's school classmate; chief Washington correspondent, *St Louis Post-Dispatch*, 1918–34, on editorial staff 1934–45; Truman's Press Secretary and confidential adviser 1945–50.
2 Maurice Morton Milligan (1884–1959), US District Attorney for the Western district of Missouri 1934–40, 1940–5, successfully prosecuted Thomas Pendergast on corruption charges 1939; defeated by Truman for US Senate 1940.
3 Thomas Joseph Pendergast (*c*.1870–1945), Democratic boss of Kansas City, Missouri, arguably the most powerful boss of his generation; active in politics from 1911, and dominant in the State 1932–8; supported Truman for the Senate 1934; jailed 1939 for tax evasion.
4 Joel Bennett ('Champ') Clark (1890–1954), Democratic Senator from Missouri 1933–45, unsuccessful candidate for renomination in 1944.
5 'Miniatures'.

of the Roosevelt policies, as because of the sudden disappearance of that combination of political genius and passionately held aims in the foreign field which promised to make so notable an impact on world affairs during Mr. Roosevelt's Fourth Term. Sentiment in the country is of course still overwhelmingly in favour of world collaboration. The weakness is not now principally in public opinion, nor even in the Senate, but in the fact that the Executive, despite its excellent general attitude, lacks men and ideas large enough to cope with the exacting demands of the time. In the meanwhile, and whatever the future may hold, we have no cause to complain at the line taken by Mr. Truman in dealing with day to day problems. His approach so far has been firm, courageous and quick.

TO MOORE CROSTHWAITE

12 May 1945 [*carbon*]

[British Embassy, Washington, DC]

My dear Moore,

I write in haste since I want this to travel in your Ambassador's own baggage. Only to say that I look forward with vast eagerness to arrival in Moscow in early September (or according to Sir A. Clark Kerr in late August, whichever is the more feasible and the earlier the better). As you know, I have like all the Three Sisters been saying 'To Moscow, to Moscow'[1] for goodness knows how long, and probably have exaggerated ideas about how exciting it all will be. I shall arrive armed with every resource for the maintaining of civilised life that I am allowed to bring by air (as I hope). Insecticides, shoe leather, a sealskin cap, and goodness knows what, but if there is anything which you think it particularly necessary to bring beyond the regular objects of which Mr Bolton has spoken to me, do write and tell me – I expect to be leaving here towards the end of July. I have squabbled and haggled with New College to let me stay in Moscow till, at any rate, mid-January, and that seems in the bag. Be prepared to move heaven and earth if and when I disappear spurlos[2] somewhere around about 31 August.

You will be interested to hear that the notorious Mr Drew Pearson, in a broadcast some four weeks ago, said that the negotiations of the Commission on the Polish Government broke down largely because Sir A. Clark Kerr

---

1 In Chekhov's *Three Sisters*, first produced in 1901, the Prozorov sisters Olga, Masha and Irina, and their brother Andrey, long to relieve the boredom of life in a town in the Russian provinces by returning to Moscow, their childhood home.
2 'Without trace'.

was incapacitated by disease, and the negotiations were therefore in the hands of the well-known anti-Soviet diplomat P. M. Crosthwaite, who poured sand into the works with a lavish hand. Bohlen and I thought of sending you a congratulatory telegram since pillory by Mr Pearson is the highest tribute to virtue obtainable in this country. In the end we thought better not. Still you are immortalised and your dossier is probably being inspected with peculiar care.

I have not been particularly well lately and have taken to bed for an odd form of flu on several occasions, but Sir A. Clark Kerr tells me that this will not be permitted in Moscow and that you run things more severely there, and the weaknesses of the flesh are systematically dismissed. My parents, doubtless getting wind from you of my movements, cabled to ask whether 'this journey was very necessary' – in the words of a poster[1] much displayed both here and in England. To them the Union is doubtless a compound of typhus and the Bing Boys[2] (what a splendid thing that is by your Mr Eldridge). However, I look forward to the whole thing immensely.

Much love, and do tell me whether you want anything brought to you. I shall endeavour to see your family before I leave.

Yours,

TO CHRISTOPHER COX

14 May 1945

British Embassy, Washington, DC

My dear Christopher,

Alas, the Götterdämmerung Competition and Raffle arrived about three days before VE and two days before AP[3] day. I duly filled it in but think it not worth returning my document as I now find that every single entry has been falsified by the facts (with the exception of Hess,[4] which was a sitter); as between the alternatives of demonstrating complete incapacity for predicting the future development of anything (which, as I am leaving this establishment anyhow, may not do me so very much damage) and cheating so outrageous that even you would doubt that I was capable of it, I decided to do nothing – if you would like me to spend a beautiful shining sixpence for

---

1 'Is your journey really necessary?'
2 The hit musical *The Bing Boys Are Here* was produced at the Alhambra Theatre in London, in 1916, to be followed the next year by *The Bing Boys Are There* and in 1918 by *The Bing Boys On Broadway*.
3 Perhaps the deadline set by the Associated Press for return of the form.
4 See p. 694.

you here, do let me know what you would like and I swear to bring back an object of appropriate value. I do not know if Michael Wright did anything with a copy with which I provided him; after some debate it was decided not to forward one to the Ambassador at San Francisco.

Meanwhile, your office is coming in for a good many brickbats here for alleged (as we always say in government documents) absence of progressive thought or intentions and is blamed heavily by disgruntled British officials for all our troubles about Trusteeship. Be that as it may, I continue to drive home my unpopular comparison between the youthful vigour of the CO jingoes as opposed to the weary resignation of the old young men in the Foreign Office, which still continues to cause gratifyingly sharp reactions. I am intensifying my campaign in anticipation of leaving them altogether in July. Will you be in England in August? I sincerely hope and trust so. I shall linger in Oxford for a month and then off for another three or four months to you-know-where (if you don't, ask the Warden of New College. Do ask him, too, about my candidate for law tutor for one year – a splendid figure).

I hear your brother David[1] is here but do not know where or in what post – indeed, when he was thought to be coming to see me a very different figure telephoned and said he was 'Sub-Lieutenant Russell'.[2] A few minutes later a dwarf walked in, smiled, and sat down on a chair, wordless. Upon further pressure he yielded up a note which said: 'This is to introduce my son, known to the law as Lord Amberley. Although he is my son, I think he is quite pleasant. Russell.' But your brother never did turn up after all, and if he continues to fail to appear, I shall lodge a formal protest with the new Master of Univ. (I am truly shocked by the goings on of that College). Balliol seemed to be continuing to roll down the Gadarene slopes faster than usual. What a frightful disaster the Master really seems to be. And I do not suppose you like the All Souls election [of Sumner] much more than I do. It was the face that did it, doubtless, but I should have preferred Hancock[3] infinitely, and so, curiously enough, would the All Souls mandarins – Halifax, Brand etc., here gathered, or so they said. But I am babbling on and on and must stop at once.

Why do you not get yourself out here before I go for good? The more officials from your office come here, the better, and surely there must be a

---

1 (Anthony) David Machell Cox (1913–94), medievalist; Fellow and Praelector, Univ., 1939–80; a keen mountaineer who spent most of the war as an army mountain warfare instructor in Canada, the Lebanon, Jordan and Wales.

2 John Conrad Russell (1921–87), later (1970) 4th Earl Russell, son of Bertrand Russell; schizophrenic, becoming increasingly ill from his late twenties onwards.

3 (William) Keith Hancock (1898–1988), historian, first Australian Fellow of All Souls (1924–30), Chichele Professor of Economic History and Fellow of All Souls 1944–9.

very good reason for talking to Americans about colonial education, considering that they are to send out a mission on this subject to the Commonwealth and Empire. Say the word, and I shall, as my last conscious act, leave it as a sacred legacy with M. Wright to see to it that you reach these shores before the year is out. I must clearly stop.

Yours ever,

Shaya

New College Archive

TO BARONESS LAMBERT[1]

28 May 1945 [*carbon*]

[British Embassy, Washington, DC]

Dear [Hansi?]

Thank you very much for my really full and rich super weekend. I scarcely remember ever before having had so many vivid impressions of so many varied people coming up simultaneously leaving a great exciting unassimilated mass which I took hours and days in Washington to sort out and arrange in the filing system. I only hope I was not too much of a nuisance as a guest and did not exhaust you all – the Walkers[2] seemed to me in a very limp and feeble state by Thursday night when they dined with me, and we all went to bed peacefully and early and full of grateful memories.

I shall, if I may, telephone you when next I am in New York, which may be next Tuesday – thank you again.

Yours sincerely,

Isaiah Berlin

PS I believe I left a copy of the new Soviet National Anthem[3] handsomely inscribed to me in Russian by my new master – I shall call for it, if I may, while I am in New York. Its sentimental value is clearly considerable.

1 Baroness Johanna ('Hansi' to her friends) von Reininghaus Lambert (1899–1960), Austrian-born widow of her second husband, Baron Henri Lambert (1887–1933). The Baron owned the Banque Lambert, above whose premises they lived, facing the Royal Palace in Brussels, at 24 Avenue Marnix. Having fled to the US with her three young children on the eve of war, the Baroness lived mostly in a rented apartment in New York, presumably the venue for IB's weekend stay. She also bought as an investment and modernised a farm in Virginia (where she was known as 'Jeanne'); friends from Washington sometimes visited her there. She returned to Brussels after the war.

2 John Walker (1906–95), Chief Curator, National Gallery of Art, Washington, 1939–56, later (1956–69) Director, and his wife Lady Margaret (Gwendolen Mary) (1905–87), née Drummond, daughter of the 16th Earl of Perth.

3 See 473/3.

PPS Is M. Makinsky really the son of a ruling khan on the shores of the Caspian?[1] I find that very chic.

PPS Alikki[2] cabled me the Dodecanese[3] – should I have replied? I didn't.

TO R. VENNELL

28 May 1945 [*carbon*]

[British Embassy, Washington, DC]

Dear Mr Vennell,

You were kind enough to tell me when we spoke on the telephone some two or three weeks ago – when I thanked you for sending me a special shoe stamp – that I might apply to you once more before finally leaving this country with an additional request of the same type. I am now the happy possessor of one brand new pair of shoes obtained through your kindness, but I fear that, bound as I am for wintry Moscow, where, one is told, one is expected to bring one's own shoe leather, let alone shoes, one single pair of new shoes will scarcely carry me through the rigours of that fearful climate. Nor is there any hope of obtaining any redress in shoeless London. And I have been improvident enough to have brought only one pair of shoes during my entire four years' stay in the United States, so my position is grave. I should, therefore, be most grateful if you could be so kind as to let me have two further stamps – I have, as I promised, remembered you in my prayers already. I promise to treble the effort in appreciation of your bounty.

I enclose the last relics of my mutilated Ration Book No 3.

Yours sincerely,

Isaiah Berlin

1 'Makinsky' was the surname of the ruling family of the Khanate of Maku in southern Azerbaijan, of which the capital city was Maku (now in north-west Iran), about 250 miles west of the Caspian Sea. IB may have been referring to Alexander Khan (Prince) Makinsky (1902–88), or to his brother Kyrill Khan Makinsky (1910–91). Their father Pasha (Paul) Khan Makinsky (1862–1934) had emigrated to France *c.*1920 but had presumably technically been the 'ruling khan' until the Khanate was abolished in 1922.

2 Aliki Diplarakos (1912–2002) married John Russell (315/4) in December 1945; she had previously been married to Commandant Paul-Louis Weiller (1893–1993), French war hero, industrialist and patron of charities and the arts.

3 Group of islands – including Rhodes, Kos, and Karpathos – in the Aegean Sea, off the south-western coast of Turkey; part of the Ottoman Empire until 1912, thereafter held by the Italians, then (1943–5) by the Germans. Three weeks before this letter was written the Dodecanese had been handed over to a British military administration, which remained in control until the islands were ceded to Greece in 1947.

TO CHRISTOPHER HILL

29 May 1945 [*carbon*]

British Embassy, Washington, DC

Dear Christopher,

I have a good many accumulated things to tell you, only some of which can be compressed into a letter. I shall, therefore, try to sort them out and be unexpectedly brief.

(1) I shall be coming to call on you officially to talk to Mr Warner[1] and Geoffrey Wilson[2] and yourself about this sudden visit to the USSR which Sir A. Clarke Kerr appears to have arranged behind my back and with my [ex] post facto warm approval. I am not quite clear as to why I am going or what I am expected to do when I get there. Nor yet what I am going as, under what description, emoluments etc., but I expect that your department will have that all cut and dried by the time I get to you. The situation here vis-à-vis Russia is very extraordinary. You will not find much of it in cables from San Francisco because one of your colleagues has been very steadily removing all the meat from the telegrams which one of my colleagues has been industriously packing into the cables, and relatively little will, therefore, have reached you through any official channels. I shall, if there is any curiosity on this subject, endeavour to tell you what has been happening here, particularly in the State Department and the White House, when I arrive. In New York the situation in 'opinion-forming' circles is that of a shrinking damsel before a particularly aggressive suitor – i.e. a mixture of a desire to flee, resist and yield, which produces a very schizophrenic result. I am engaged on an intensive campaign of demonstrating to the few persons I know well that a desire to go to war with Russia could only lead to one of two consequences: (a) America defeats Russia, (b) Russia defeats America. The undesirability of the latter they see for themselves, but I find it less easy to demonstrate to them the horrors of the former. However, a little steady progress is achieved every day. There is a fearful flap in the Communist press as a result of M. Duclos' attack on Browder,[3] but I expect you know all about that.

(2) There are at present various emissaries here such as Dodds and Miss

---

1 Christopher Frederick Ashton Warner (1895–1957), diplomat, at the time Head of Northern Dept, FO, which was responsible for the USSR.

2 Geoffrey Masterman Wilson (b. 1910), a colleague of Christopher Hill in Northern Dept, working for Christopher Warner.

3 Jacques Duclos (1896–1975), Acting Secretary of the French Communist Party, had written an article criticising Earl Russell Browder (1891–1973), Secretary-General of the US Communist Party, for 'revisionism'. Browder was subsequently expelled from the Party, which thereafter adopted a more hardline stance.

Galton[1] investigating the teaching of Slav languages etc. The choice of
Konovalov[2] at Oxford seems to me somewhat depressing. I do not know
him personally but have always thought of him, perhaps mistakenly, as
chiefly interested in a modest second-rate way in Russian social history and
economics and not in language and literature except perforce. He is
obviously better than the miserable Struve,[3] but that is not saying much.
However, what is done is done, and I am obsessed by the idea that if
anything is to be made of Russian studies in England, some distinguished
persons will have to be got over to become centres of pilgrimage from the
continent of Europe. There is only one such person I have so far discovered –
Roman Jakobson.[4] You may remember his rather stupid-looking brother[5]
in Chatham House and in Sir B. Pares's[6] establishment. The brother is also
here, working in the Library of Congress, and although not very talented is
at least professionally competent and better than the decayed White
Guards[7] who are supposed to supervise the vast Russian collection at the
Library of Congress, the greatest outside Russia but at present uncatalogued
and some of the best bits in unopened and rotting crates. It is really a very
surprising situation. The White Guards, aided by a meek and depressed

1 Dorothy Galton (1901–92), secretary to Bernard Pares (note 6 below) 1928–32, Administrative
   Secretary of the School of Slavonic and East European Studies, London, 1932–61; visited US
   and Canada in 1945 to report on Slavonic studies there.
2 Sergey Aleksandrovich Konovalov (1899–1982), Russian-born economist and political scientist;
   Professor of Russian, Birmingham, 1929–45, Editor, *Memoranda* of Birmingham Bureau of
   Research on Russian Economic Conditions, 1931–40, Lecturer in Slavonic Studies, Oxford,
   1930–45, Professor of Russian 1945–67.
3 Gleb Petrovich Struve (1898–1985), Russian-born literary historian, translator, critic and poet;
   Lecturer in Russian Literature, SSEES, 1932–43, Reader 1943–6.
4 Roman Osipovich Jakobson (1896–1982), Russian-American philologist, literary critic and
   historian of literature; left Russia 1920, taught in Czechoslovakia 1933–9, in Scandinavia
   1939–41; settled in US 1941, Professor of General Linguistics, École Libre des Hautes Études
   (the Franco-Belgian university in exile), New York, 1942–6.
5 Sergey Osipovich Yakobson (he did not anglicise his name as 'Jakobson', unlike his brother)
   (1901–79), born in Russia, moved to Germany after the Revolution, then to England (1933),
   where he became librarian and honorary lecturer in Russian history at SSEES; at the
   beginning of the war he translated Russian broadcasts for the British MOI; specialist on Slavic
   history and languages at the Library of Congress 1941–71.
6 Sir Bernard Pares (1867–1949), father of Richard Pares; eminent Russian historian; Professor of
   Russian History, Language, and Literature, London, 1919–36, Director of SSEES 1922–39;
   author of the long-standing classic *A History of Russia* (London, 1926); spent much time in
   Russia and published *My Russian Memoirs* in 1931; head of the Soviet Section of FRPS (339/5)
   1939–40.
7 The nucleus of the extensive Russian collection in the Library of Congress is the library of
   80,000 volumes bought in 1906 from Siberian vodka-maker Gennady Vasil'evich Yudin
   (1840–1912), but this was substantially enlarged in the 1930s with volumes bought from the
   Soviet Government. Accounts of the development of this collection are notably silent about
   progress at the time of this letter. White Guards were the private forces of pre-Revolutionary
   landowners, who opposed the Soviet redistribution of land; IB is presumably implying a
   reluctance to share the collection's treasures with the public.

priest, are really Fascist beasts if ever there were any. However, to return to R. Jakobson, he is, by all those competent to know, said to be the greatest Slavist outside Russia, a view which Miss Galton appears to support. I know nothing about technical Slav studies, but there is no doubt that he is a most remarkable figure, obviously a dedicated scholar who can infuse interest into a discussion of the lyrical tradition among a tribe of some 200 individuals of Northern Sakhalin[1] (unwritten but naturally full of genius). He appears to me to have a vast knowledge of ordinary Russian literature of the eighteenth and nineteenth centuries, and was obviously on good terms with practically everybody in Moscow before 1918. He left, I understand, shortly after and was an émigré in Prague and is married to a Czech wife. I do not think his relations with the Union are particularly dark. I thought that perhaps Birmingham might offer him a professorship, or, absurd though it must sound, Konovalov might take him as his linguist assistant, since he knows nothing about the language side of his chair himself. We shall get a situation of a hack theoretically presiding over a scholar of international reputation, but I dare say that could be worked out. I am really writing all this to you in case you go down to Oxford and see any relevant person about it – Humphrey Sumner or whoever. The objection of all English universities seems at present to be [to] the appointment of refugees, émigrés etc. I can see that there might be [an] objection if they were politically marked men, but as the British scholars on the subject are miserably lacking, and there are no native Americans, e.g., who are much good (Mr Simmons[2] is the best, and Sir B. Pares swears by him, but he is really not much, believe me), that objection ought not to stand. Wherever J. goes, he is bound to attract other luminaries to assist him, and if there are to be summer schools etc., and general fanfare about the Russian studies, he would easily be the most prizewinning poodle of them all. So do make some propaganda for him if you can. I hardly know him but am vastly impressed by this unique figure. I shall get Dodds to lunch with him. Miss Galton is a fervent convert already. The thing to do, I am sure, is to stop British universities electing local hacks; otherwise we shall never be out of the wood. Nor can one exaggerate the apparent silliness of the Oxford electors in writing to their Soviet candidate direct instead of through channels. But that is a long story.

(3) I am distressed about Stuart Hampshire, who tells me he has received a letter from your Master saying that he is of a type not wanted by Balliol

1 Easternmost province of Russia, comprising Sakhalin Island and the Kuril Islands chain.

2 Ernest Joseph Simmons (1903–72), Russian specialist, literary historian and critic, taught at Harvard 1936–9, Cornell 1941–6, Columbia 1946–58; publications include the highly-regarded biography *Leo Tolstoy* (Boston, 1945–6). IB later contributed 'Herzen and Bakunin on Individual Liberty' (reprinted in RT) to a book edited by Simmons, *Continuity and Change in Russian and Soviet Thought* (Cambridge, Mass., 1955).

College. I should have thought that he was precisely of the type that was. However, you know your Master and do not need me to go about screaming at you about him. I gather the chief objection is that Hants is (a) a co-respondent (b) not 'social' enough. I do not know what other fellowships in philosophy are going at Oxford, but Hants says he wants to go into the Foreign Office or the like. I will talk about him to Sir D. Scott when I get to England, since he is a very nice man and can be told the truth. Otherwise I do not know what I can do. It seems to me the greatest pity for Oxford to let him go, and All Souls seems obviously anxious to pack him off. If you have a chance you might raise him with Sumner and see what he thinks. I shall probably worry you on that subject in London.

(4) I am sure you will not think it eccentric of me not to have grasped the chance of succeeding Brigadier Scaife[1] in Prof. Toynbee's shop. I did not know how to use language calculated not to offend T. and yet indicate quite clearly that I would rather be unemployed and starve than work in the atmosphere in which I discovered you all to be enveloped in 1944. I was told that I was needed for 'peace-making and the drawing up of Eastern European frontiers'. It all sounds incredibly silly from here; I do not know how it looks in London. I have just finished reading a column which tells me that General Okulicki[2] is a very gallant man disgracefully treated by us and the Russians (this is written by a good left-wing New Dealer) side by side with a beautiful piece by Mr Sulzberger telling me that the real power behind Lublin[3] is M. Saul Amsterdam, also known as Amsterdamski and Saulski etc. – a Zionist in 1917, a Communist in 1919, born in Radek's[4] village, probably put away at about the same time and functioning in Poland since 1941. As always, he is described as small, unobtrusive, greying etc. There are fewer and fewer of such members of the old brigade left, and not one of them has written his memoirs. Do you think I could ask to see him if and when I am in Moscow? Our two names go well together, and we could reminisce happily about Zionism in 1917. I must stop.

Yours ever,

Isaiah Berlin

1 Brigadier Eric Ommaney Skaife (1884–1956), Military Attaché, Moscow, 1934–7, Soviet Section, FORD, 1941–4.

2 Major-General Leopold Okulicki (1898–?1946), leader of the Polish Home Army, one of a group of 16 Polish leaders offered political talks by the Soviet authorities in March 1945 and then arrested. After a show trial in Moscow they were sentenced in June to long terms of imprisonment. Okulicki's sentence was 10 years, but he probably died, or was executed, in 1946.

3 Where a Communist-inclined provisional government, rivalling the exiled Polish government in London, had been set up in 1944.

4 The Polish-Jewish revolutionary Karl Berngardovich Radek, né Sobelsohn (1885–c.1939), born in Lemberg (a city, not a village) in Austrian Poland (now Lvov in the Ukraine), was arrested in 1937 and sentenced to ten years in prison.

6 June 1945 [*carbon*]

British Embassy, Washington

Dear Stuart,

You will not expect me to go on at length to you about my thoughts on the behaviour of the Master. But I cannot agree that the behaviour of Balliol need or should affect your future at Oxford. My thoughts automatically turn to New College, where I suppose I myself resume operations next year, having promised them to go on teaching philosophy for, at any rate, a year or two before switching to other fields. With Hart there, there may, indeed, be room for part-time teaching, but I do not suppose that you will want to continue on somewhat [Ian] Bowen-like[1] conditions at All Souls since it is a precarious and not sufficiently dignified life. Of course, if they gave you a proper research fellowship at All Souls, it would be quite different, and in that case something might be done about New College. As to that you can only discover via Sumner, I suppose, whom I think you should beard, if that is the term (for some reason a somewhat peculiar Persian miniature suggests itself to me – a long Mongolian beard and a hairless face), forthwith.

As to the civil service, the source of all appointments is Sir D. Scott, with under him Ivor Mallett[2] and a number of smaller fry, some of whom I know. Here I can be of some use, I think. I have mentioned the matter to Ashton Gwatkin,[3] who is not directly concerned but has something to do with Establishments, and he spoke of Scott and Mallett. I know Scott quite well (he is, I believe, a deputy Under-Secretary or something of the kind now) and have been in fairly amiable correspondence with him apropos of a job he wished me to take and which I have refused, perhaps with too much vehemence. I shall be in London in July and shall then, if you instruct me, talk to him, also to Law if you wish me to, who may not pull very much weight ordinarily about such things, but whose help may add something in an auxiliary way.

I do not believe that Harold Nicolson is any use at all – I may be wrong – but I believe that what you or I think of him is what everyone else thinks of him, i.e. that his words have no intrinsic weight whatever. I do not know Eden at all, really, having spoken to him about twice, but I suppose I do by now, having been transferred to that office myself off the sinking ship of the Ministry of Information some months ago, know some of the so-called

1 Ian Bowen was now a Lecturer at Brasenose, but perhaps had access to All Souls facilities.

2 William Ivo (*sic*) Mallet (1900–88), FO Counsellor; in 1945 Head of the FO's Personnel Dept, whose Superintending Under-Secretary was Sir David Scott.

3 Frank Trelawny Arthur Ashton-Gwatkin (1889–1976), Senior Inspector of HM Missions, with rank of Minister, FO, 1944; writer of adventure fiction under the pseudonym John Paris.

senior officials. So do count on me to do a certain amount if you really want that. I shall also buzz round Oxford on the matter since I suppose you can afford not to make up your mind until, say, September, when I shall once more be going off, this time I gather to Moscow, although that is supposed to be moderately secret.

I know nothing about any other government departments. I agree that Duff Cooper is not much use, but while here I have talked to Roger Makins, who enquired about your marital status, was reassured by me, and said he would write to Messrs Mallett and Barclay (our age), from Cambridge – dim, but civilised and in a gentle way quite good and shrewd. Makins proposes to tell them that their experience with All Souls has been very good – Beckett,[1] Reilly, O'Neill and himself being the instances – and urge the virtues of induction by simple enumeration upon them. They are likely to be careful, however, in that office about background, the political character of anyone you may wish to marry, etc., which you may find disagreeably inquisitive and exasperating. I shall also write to Smith at New College – I think you should talk to Ryle, or if you prefer to let me do that, wait until my return if there is no very great hurry. I should have thought that, as Professors, he and Price ought to be able to make plain to, say, Christ Church or Oriel (I am told but I do not know how true it is that Maclagan is not returning, but then, of course, there is Ross).

Besides the Foreign Office, which, if your political convictions are really becoming well-defined and passionate, is likely to madden and frustrate you very considerably – the good in it no less than the bad – the Treasury was the other place of real influence, and indeed interest. There the obvious persons seem to be (a) Mynors,[2] who could certainly do something, particularly if bullied by Maurice, (b) Sir E. Bridges,[3] the new head of it, who ought to do it out of straight party solidarity, (c) Dennis Rickett,[4] who although not a member, could, I am sure, pull a string or two, and finally (d) Eddie Playfair,[5] whom I know and Guy Chilver knows and who is the ablest and most trusted of their young men. Also there is Lord Keynes, whom I do not know well enough to intrigue with, but who ought not to be so very inaccessible via Roy or, indeed, Sparrow or someone like that. All these

---

1 (William) Eric Beckett (1896–1966), lawyer, Fellow of All Souls 1921–8, Legal Adviser, FO, 1925–53.

2 Roger Mynors was appointed a temporary Principal in the Treasury in 1940.

3 Edward Bridges (1892–1969), Fellow of All Souls 1920–7, 1954–68; Treasury 1919–38, Secretary to the Cabinet, 1938–46, Permanent Secretary, Treasury, 1945–56.

4 Denis Hubert Fletcher Rickett (1907–97), Fellow of All Souls 1929–49, Principal Private Secretary to Oliver Lyttelton (Minister of Production) 1943–5, Personal Assistant to Sir John Anderson (Chancellor of the Exchequer) 1945.

5 Edward Wilder Playfair (1909–99), Treasury 1934–46.

persons are of much greater weight than Harold, particularly Keynes, who likes clever young men in a way in which the FO can't really be said to.

I am amused to see that [Christopher] Hill is now in the Northern Department dealing with the 'Soviet Union and Baltic Republics' together with Geoffrey Wilson,[1] who used to be Cripps's Secretary. They must make an ideological island of a very different colour to their surroundings.[2]

As for myself, my desire to return to Oxford is passionate to a degree, and my nostalgia worse than ever. Mr Churchill says that we know our duty more clearly than our interest and act on the assumption that the disagreeable is more likely to be right than the agreeable. I keep on allowing myself to be pulled about this way and that by my superiors here, by Sir A. Clark Kerr and by the FO, stipulating only that I be back in Oxford for good early in 1946. There is now a plan to send me to Moscow, then back to Washington, then finally to Oxford. I have expressed distaste particularly for the return to America (to do a 'lapidary' dispatch to guide British policy for ever and ever and be studied by Woodward[3] for years to come) but let them fight it out as being on the whole better than losing blood myself in the process. I long to see you and shall at any rate in August.

Yours ever,

TO ALIC SMITH
Warden of New College

6 June 1945 [*carbon*]

British Embassy, Washington

My dear Warden,
    This is but to tell you the background to an approach which may yet be made to you by the Foreign Office if they ever get around to it. All seemed amicably settled by the time when you left the US, when our new Minister, Jock Balfour, appeared from Moscow and soon afterwards started agitating for my retention, evidently labouring under the old illusion of my alleged indispensability, to which some of his more simple-minded colleagues, believe me without sufficient reason in all cases, have fallen prey. After an

---

1 Wilson had previously been posted to the British Embassy, Moscow, under Cripps.
2 Hill was a Marxist and a member of the Communist Party (until 1957). Wilson had been Chairman of the Oxford University Labour Club, so his political views, if not as incongruous in the FO as Hill's, would nevertheless have been more left-wing than those of most of his colleagues. (There has been much speculation – on which he never commented in public – about Hill's wartime career: was he a member of SOE, for instance? After his death there were allegations that he was a Soviet 'mole'.)
3 E. L. Woodward had been called back to the FO in 1939 to work on the history of British foreign policy.

immense amount of renewed toing and froing about this, telegrams to Lord Halifax at San Francisco, etc. etc., it was decided to send a telegram to London advocating that I be allowed to go to Moscow as originally planned and still demanded from that end, but that after that I be hoisted back here, say, in December (i.e. to go to Moscow in September from London, to stay there October, November and half December), and remain here, say, until 1 April 1946, 'for special duties', the precise dates of London–Moscow, Moscow–London, London back to Washington being left somewhat elastic, but the general arrangement to terminate in April 1946, otherwise, I pointed out, I might as well leave Oxford for ever and ask for a pension. Moreover, I did not indicate any enthusiasm for this scheme and was duly lectured about my placing of my own, or, at best, the College's and University's interest before my plain duty as man and citizen – here was the most important British Embassy in the world, and I was leaving the ship at the climacteric of Anglo–US–Soviet relations, when I was uniquely qualified, etc. etc. Upon my pressing them as to what exactly they would wish me to do during my few months' return here, it emerged that (a) I was to be relieved of routine duties, e.g. the drafting of my present documents, and was to act as a 'general adviser' on a number of problems which by that time, it was assumed, would be very acute and urgent, (b) as the need for this might go on indefinitely and not cease on 1 April 1946, there was a specific job which I was to do, i.e. write what Laski would call a 'lapidary' dispatch on US foreign policy for the last five or six years in relation to Britain and Russia, which, by getting the facts into their true proportions, would act as a corrective (and it was hoped a tonic) to irritable officials in London apt to go up in flames at every new swerve and obtuseness in US policy. The dispatch was to be a very grand affair, an object of reference to all officials for all time, and by tracing the true course of American policy was to keep them sober and, it was hoped, not too discontented with the bits and pieces of it with which they individually came into collision. I could not deny that I saw the necessity for such a document and that whoever wrote it would have to compose it here rather than in London, since it would be advisable to have talks about the topics contained, very informally and privately, to such eminent Americans, official and unofficial, as the author already happened to be on confidential terms with, and that it would probably not take anyone who had been here for the last three or four years more than two months to compile the 50–60 pages required rather than the three volumes which the subject doubtless deserves. All this I interspersed with complaints that I was being kept a prisoner, etc., for the new Minister (an old New College man, he assures me) – brushed aside with torrents of appeal to my better feeling.

If either the FO or the College do not think particularly well of this, my responsibility will be removed and I shall peacefully return in February as arranged. When faced with a conflict of duties (pace Ross and Prichard)[1] I can only leave decision to higher authority and abide by the result of the battle of the giants. I thought I would just let you know that this is what is contemplated, although not all of it – certainly not the last bit about the dispatch – has been communicated to the FO and had better, therefore, remain confidential to yourself. Why the last bit has not been told to the FO I do not quite know unless it be that the need for putting London straight may seem more obvious at this end than it is in London, and they do not, therefore, wish to risk a tart rejoinder on this, just yet. The scheme seems harmless enough.

I have received a funny letter from the Warden of Wadham complaining that if the other (Edward) Prichard comes 'he would (a) know no English law, and (b) he would be an American'. I attach little importance to that, however, as I expect you do, and would be glad of a word from you as to whether you still want him.

I also received various letters about poor Stuart Hampshire, an admirable philosopher, rejected by Balliol on account of his views, as to whether he could do half-time teaching in New College, etc. As to that, again I assume that there is not much opening with us, but again, if there is, I should be awfully grateful if you could tell me, and finally about the Baron Lambert,[2] a candidate as a commoner about whom I recently wrote to you. Please forgive me for treating you like a senior tutor – the most rapid scribble would be perfectly adequate. I hope you flourish exceedingly and that Sir A. Korda[3] is coming along nicely and providing a rich and fructifying stream.

Yours ever,

⟨Please treat as v. confidential – best of all destroy after reading, as theoretically this is not for private ears; but you must know what is going on otherwise my plans will seem too mysterious.⟩

---

1 Both Ross and Prichard discussed whether prima facie conflicts of duties were genuine, and suggested ways of resolving them; but it is not entirely clear that they would have opposed deference to political authority as a practical way out of such conflicts.

2 Baron Léon Jean Gustave Samuel Lambert (1928–87), son of the late Baron Henri Lambert and Baroness Johanna Lambert (561/1), New College (at IB's suggestion) Hilary–Trinity 1946, no degree (but awarded diploma in political and economic sciences, University of Geneva, 1949; subsequently partner in, then head of, the Banque Lambert).

3 I have been unable to interpret this reference to Korda.

TO MAURICE BOWRA

7 June 1945 [*carbon*]

British Embassy, Washington

My dear Maurice,

Thank you for your most enjoyable letter. You can imagine the effect of any real voice in the monotonous patter which surrounds one. You will have seen Guy and therefore have heard all the local gossip, but I will endeavour to explore whither your colleague Hart's[1] (as opposed to my colleague Hart's) new ambitions are leading him. The two Harts should be brought together as soon as possible to see which knocks out which – they have certain qualities in common.

You will be interested to hear that your friend Finley[2] has been made a full Professor at Harvard – my friend Prof. Quine,[3] who met Freddie in Vienna and liked him, is almost as good a man and is capable of discussing philosophy for eight hours without ceasing in a most agreeable and useful way. He is in the Navy Department and we have evenings about logical positivism. You will doubtless also have seen – but in case you have not I enclose – Edmund Wilson's[4] extraordinary piece about England, which starts sweetly enough and then suddenly goes sour in the usual way.

Your passage about Walt Whitman[5] and Whyte Melville[6] rings very real to me – alas, but even so clever a man as Mr Wilson in some ways is should so obviously have not a spark. The Portuguese in New York were much excited by the knowledge that someone in England could quote Portuguese poetry and immediately identified Wilson's interlocutor as my new Minister Jock Balfour. I proved useful in dispelling this illusion. Balfour

---

1 William Ogden Hart (1903–77), lawyer, Fellow and Tutor, Wadham, 1926–46; Head of British Merchant Shipping Mission, Washington, 1944–6.

2 John Huston Finley, Jr (1904–95), US classicist, taught at Harvard 1942–76, Eliot Professor 1942–74; influential and popular teacher and mentor.

3 Willard Van Orman Quine (1908–2000), leading US philosopher and logician, taught at Harvard 1936–42, 1945–78; naval intelligence officer, Washington, 1942–5.

4 Edmund Wilson (1895–1972), leading US literary critic, essayist and social commentator, wrote for the *New Republic* and the *New Yorker*; author of books and essays on a huge range of subjects. IB refers to his 'A Reporter at Large: Notes on London at the End of a War', *New Yorker*, 2 June 1945, 42–57, repr. 'in a revised and expanded form' (p. v) as 'Notes on London at the End of the War' in Wilson's *Europe Without Baedeker: Sketches, Among the Ruins of Italy, Greece & England* (NY, 1947).

5 Walt(er) Whitman (1819–92), American poet most famous for his collection *Leaves of Grass* (first published 1855 but revised and added to by Whitman in many subsequent editions); rejected literary and social conventions, writing in free verse and colloquial language, often on subjects (such as physical love) hitherto considered unsuitable for poetry.

6 George John Whyte-Melville (1821–78), British romantic novelist known for his descriptions of sport, especially fox-hunting; fought in the Crimean War as a volunteer major in the Turkish irregular cavalry; died in a hunting accident.

is a charming man, quite mad (although not fundamentally), who talks Russian rather well, has met Pasternak[1] in Moscow, has produced the last volume of his verses, which is fascinating (more on this below), and is the first civilised person to come here full of literary passions, Russian, German, French etc., and with remarkable imitations of certain important but hitherto unimitated foreign personalities of Pasternak's nationality.

I had never heard of Chukovsky[2] but knew all about the other – Marshak,[3] the writer of children's verses of great genius, though not as good as Chukovsky's – I can imagine Mr [Raymond] Mortimer's review of them as 'enchanting bibelots' all too well.

My plans are in a fearful state. I made it quite clear that I wished to return to Oxford last November. Pressure was applied and I stayed till March. More pressure was applied, then I stayed till May. Then Clark Kerr – a charming man full of desire to make mischief among his staff and very good with the Russians – offered me a visa secured under remarkable conditions from M. Molotov[4] – I was then invited by the Soviets to their party to celebrate 'complete victory' and the thing was done. I return to Oxford first (which the Berlins have now left, I gather) in late July to go to the Sov. Onion in September for two or three months at the most. There is then a plan to get me back to the US to write an immense dispatch about everything which is to guide the FO for ever and ever on all topics, but I think I can scotch that. In general, I am pleading quite hard to be released but am regarded as indispensable by friendly parties and as too clever by half by the rest. The indispensability springs almost entirely from the extraordinary terror of intellectual activity by the professionals. In order to avoid the fate of the 16 Poles,[5] I propose to attach myself to the powerful Ashton Gwatkin, who may be travelling to those parts, as his dragoman.

As for Prichard, I still think it a good idea: Law is not a subject and he knows a lot of American law, and, after all, Goodhart knew no other when

---

1 Boris Leonidovich Pasternak (1890–1960), Nobel Prize-winning Soviet author of *Doctor Zhivago* (1957). He studied music (which he also composed) and philosophy before turning to poetry, publishing his first collection, *Bliznets v tuchakh* ('Twins in clouds') in 1914. From the mid-1930s he came increasingly under official attack and ceased publishing his poetry, turning to translation work. Partial rehabilitation came after his death, but *Doctor Zhivago* was not published in the USSR until 1989.

2 Korney Ivanovich Chukovsky (pseudonym of Nikolay Vasil'evich Korneichukov) (1882–1969), literary critic, translator, writer for children; head of Anglo-American literature at the World Literature publishing house in Petrograd/Leningrad since 1918.

3 Samuil Yakovlevich Marshak (1887–1964), poet, essayist, children's writer, head of the children's department at Leningrad's State Publishing House since 1924.

4 Molotov's letter of 3 April 1945 is in FO 181/1000 with associated papers.

5 566/2.

he went to Cambridge. He is much thinner than he was and no longer resembles Davison[1] quite so much, although he now bears a peculiar resemblance to Molotov, particularly when he puts on Felix's pince-nez. If he is to become Senator from Kentucky and rescue us all from the local Fascists when this will be much needed at a none too distant future date, he must withdraw to Europe before leaping back. He will make friends and enemies at Oxford, will not stay long, inject some much needed blood into my terrible common room. Admittedly he would be an American, but, after all, so are Price and Plaskett[2] and no one minds. He will undoubtedly persecute the sxxxts,[3] and help in that quarter is to be welcomed wherever it may come from. He is a very gay and neurotic figure and a great deal of trouble to me at all hours, which makes it my duty to encourage his coming. He will not get on with C. K. Allen[4] or Curtis or Sumner but will be more than Lightfoot can manage. Roy can tell you about his latest exploits.

I hear that Roy is standing for Parliament. Surely he ought to have stood as University candidate against the traitor Salter?[5] Salter's move is not regarded with much approval here, since he is thought to have done it merely in order to be able to say that he had been in the Cabinet and is thought mainly due to his unspeakable wife Ethel.[6]

Akhmatova[7] lives in Leningrad and is very inaccessible on account of being a survival of an older day, although not exactly a Fascist beast.

---

1 Presumably J. A. Davison (502/1).

2 Price was only half-American, through his mother. Harry Hemley Plaskett (1893–1980), Savilian Professor of Astronomy and Fellow of New College 1932–60, FRS 1936, worked on experimental navigation for Ministry of Aircraft Production 1940–4; he was in fact Canadian.

3 *sic* in carbon: 'sophists'?

4 Carleton Kemp Allen (1887–1966), Australian, Professor of Jurisprudence, Oxford, 1929–31, Oxford Secretary to Rhodes Trustees and Warden of Rhodes House 1931–52.

5 In the General Election of 5 July Arthur Salter was re-elected as Independent MP for Oxford University, a position he held from 1937 until the abolition of the University seats in 1950. He had not actually been in the Cabinet, but had Cabinet rank in Churchill's caretaker government from May to July 1945, as Chancellor of the Duchy of Lancaster. Presumably the betrayal is to have fraternised with the Tories.

6 In 1940, at the age of nearly 60, Salter had married Ethel Mather Bullard (d. 1969), née Bagg, widow of Arthur Bullard, a former colleague of Salter's. US-born but with wide experience of the world, Mrs Salter owned a house in Washington and was acquainted with a number of prominent members of the US government.

7 Anna Akhmatova, pseudonym of Anna Andreevna Gorenko (1889–1966), outstanding Russian poet and national icon, revered for the tenacity with which she survived Stalinist persecution to produce some of the finest poetry of the Soviet era. A member of the Acmeist group of poets before the Revolution, Akhmatova was denounced in 1922 as 'bourgeois' after the publication of her collection *Anno Domini MCMXXI*. She was officially ostracised as a poet throughout Stalin's rule, but survived to publish her greatest work, the cycle *Requiem* (written 1935–40), as her personal testament to the suffering she and others experienced during the Purges. The encounter between IB and Akhmatova during IB's visit was a deeply significant

Your new book on Dante and Camões[1] is not procurable here yet, although Felix, of course, knows all about it. The Portuguese Minister, Senor de Bianchi,[2] his wife, Mrs Skidelsky, and his Press Attaché, P. P. Bon de Sousa Pernes (Jr) are all very excited about it. His friend Alex Böker,[3] you will recall as the friend of the late sainted Trott, appeared in Washington as correspondent of the *Chicago Journal of Commerce* and produced some very unsuitable sentiments about the undesirability of destroying Germany, etc., the brutal bombings of German civilians, insufficiently offset by the fact that his mother was in a concentration camp for some time. Mark my word, the new good Germans will be much worse than the old bad ones of the corresponding period.

Duff Cooper is really behaving like a brave good man and is obviously an admirable ambassador. It seems a pity that his Minister, whom you did not like, should have lingered over his lunch – at least that is my surmise – so long as to have caused the Prime Minister to have had to apologise to the General.[4]

Relations between Marion and Felix are slightly improved and she is no longer quite so rude to him during Sunday luncheon. She is sorry she told you that I was socially prominent and agrees that she will have to find subtler avenues for her malice. She is a very nice woman. Certainly the nicest face here.

James Pope Hennessy[5] likes America very much, particularly the South, and with Bertie's[6] son (I had a letter from him introducing him thus, 'He is known to the law as Lord Amberley and, although my son, is, I believe, quite nice') is one of the odder members of the armed forces here. The succulent McDougall[7] nearly made Platnauer[8] lose his aeroplane and is at a discount consequently in certain quarters.

Do you know William Clark,[9] late of Oriel? He claims to know you and

experience for them both, as recounted by IB in PI, where he (strangely?) writes as if he didn't know that Akhmatova was still alive.

1 *From Virgil to Milton* (London, 1945), though Dante is not a principal subject. Luis Vaz de Camões (c.1524–80), Portuguese poet whose epic *The Lusiads* celebrates Portugal's history.
2 Dr João A. de Bianchi, then Portuguese Ambassador to the US.
3 (Robert) Alexander Herbert Böker, CCC 1934–7.
4 De Gaulle.
5 (Richard) James Arthur Pope-Hennessy (1916–74), English writer best known for his biographies; served in British Intelligence during the war; posted to Washington 1943–5.
6 Bertrand Russell. For this story cf. p. 560 above.
7 Unidentified. 'Succulent' was the term invented by the mathematician Hardy at New College for attractive young men.
8 Maurice Platnauer (1897–1974), classicist, Vice-Principal of Brasenose 1936–56; he never married.
9 William Donaldson Clark (1916–85), journalist, civil servant, author; Oriel history 1935–8, lecturer in Chicago from 1938, BIS Chicago 1941–5, Press Attaché, British Embassy, Washington, 1945–6, later (1950–5) diplomatic correspondent of the *Observer*.

is in for a Studentship at Christ Church. An able man of not entirely nice character. As he pushed me very hard for a job in the Chicago University which I did not want, I cannot say anything hostile about him. He is worried about addressing the Dean as Mr Lowe[1] instead of Low Esq., but I have reassured him.

Your softness about Highet[2] I deplore, as he makes trouble wherever he goes and is in no sense, believe me, a friend and is second only to Crossman in the degree of loyalty to his old friends. His wife, with all her faults, though intolerable, has a less dangerous character.

Now we come to the grave case of Hants. Of course the Master [of Balliol] would do that and is now really the ruin of his College, Boy Brig[3] or no Boy Brig. I have written to Smith about him, but hold out no hopes since I do not suppose that All Souls would much care to keep him on those conditions, and it would be a Bowen-like status which he himself would dislike very much. He has reached a time of life when he must be a full Fellow engaged on a task commanding his colleagues' confidence and not hang on precariously. However, I have written none of this to Smith and simply recommend him warmly. On the other hand, so long as I am there and Hart continues, there is no room for a full third philosophy Fellowship. Like Catlin,[4] I say what of Oriel? Whither I hear Maclagan is not returning. I suppose Ross is the obstacle. What about Christ Church? What about Queen's, to continue as before? If Queen's eliminates Hants, it will be almost impossible to get Smith to adopt him. The thing to do is to prevent him from starting on the frightful downward MacIver[5] path, and Smith is, anyway, devoted to McKinnon if there is another job going. If McKinnon follows Meiggs to Balliol, Hants will, I fear, not consider the vacancy at Keble. He tells me that he wants to go to the FO and to marry. The objections are (a) he is over-age for the examination, (b) he says he has political views for which the FO is the least suitable domicile, (c) That Woman.[6] The FO expel you for co-respondence, but I dare say might take an ex-co-respondent

1 Revd John Lowe (1899–1960), Dean of Christ Church 1939–59.
2 Gilbert Arthur Highet (1906–78), British classicist (took US citizenship 1951), Fellow and Tutor, St John's, 1932–8, Professor of Greek and Latin, Columbia, 1938–50; with British mission in US and Canada 1941–3, British Army 1943–6; married to novelist Helen MacInnes (1907–85).
3 Edgar Trevor ('Bill') Williams (1912–95), Merton history 1931–4, Harmsworth Senior Scholar 1934–5, Junior Research Fellow 1937–9; army service 1939–45 (became Chief Intelligence Officer to Montgomery, with the rank of Brigadier); Fellow of Balliol 1945–6, Fellow and politics and history Tutor 1947–80.
4 George Edward Gordon Catlin (1896–1979), political theorist, journalist, Professor of Politics, Cornell, 1924–35, husband to author Vera Brittain, father of politician Shirley Williams.
5 Arthur Milne MacIver (b. 1905), New College classics 1924–8 (Double First, John Locke Prize [22/3]) taught at various colleges without securing a full-time post.
6 Renée Ayer.

provided that they felt sure that no further trouble would be given in that direction. Can I guarantee that? Yes, and will. But with a clear conscience? No. It is an example of the duty to disobey one's conscience which would much interest Ross and the high-minded Cambridge colleagues. I have consequently got Makins to write to the FO and recommend Hants, which can do no harm even if they don't take to him or he to them and will myself do nothing until I get back, when I will take advice from all concerned. The real place for Hants is Magdalen when Weldon[1] is finally shown up and Austin takes him as his colleague. Still, if there is anything I can do from here, I should, as they say, be glad to oblige. I have written to Hants and told him about the FO and who to go to. He asked whether Harold Nicolson or Duff Cooper were any help – both are worse than useless with the bien-pensants; Ryle, for example, is much more influential, although Sylvester [Gates] might talk to Mr Law and Henry Moss[2] to Gladwyn.

The next item on the agenda is the Russian professorship. Konovalov, though doubtless a nice good fellow, corresponds to your view of Hart and knows little of the language or the literature. He has specialised in mild social and economic views by unimportant Russians (no good Russian economists or philosophers are known to history). However, what is done is done, and we must reconstruct. It would really be rather nice if something serious were done about the Russian studies at Oxford, and this could be done if K. were suitably modest and prepared to employ talent superior to his own. Sumner's line to me that Anglo-Saxons must be appointed is patently absurd, since there are no good ones anywhere – Simmons at Cornell is a hack fellow-traveller, and about the local British ones, whether Russian or English, the facts speak for themselves. I have, however, discovered in New York a certain Roman Jakobson, whose silly brother at one time worked for Sir B. Pares's shop, who, it is apparently agreed, is the best Slavist living. Certainly his translation into Russian of the *Slovo o polku Igoreve*[3] was very first-rate. He is obviously a philologist of the greatest eminence but also knew all the Futurists in 1917 and had a particularly high opinion of Khlebnikov.[4] He is obviously some sort of genius and would scarcely do a Fraenkel. As London Universities seem intent on inviting Professor Vernadsky[5] as Professor of Russian history – at which he will be perfectly

1 Thomas Dewar Weldon (1896–1958), Fellow and philosophy Tutor, Magdalen, from 1923.
2 See p. 694.
3 Medieval Russian epic, variously translated as *The Tale of Igor's Campaign*, *The Lay of the Host of Igor* etc.
4 Viktor Vladimirovich ('Velimir') Khlebnikov (1885–1922), Russian poet and linguistic theorist, leader of the Cubo-Futurist movement in pre-Revolutionary Russia.
5 George (Georgy) Vladimirovich Vernadsky (1887–1973), Russian-born historian, emigrated to US 1927, Research Associate with rank of Professor, Yale, 1927–46, Professor of Russian History 1946–56; best known for his *A History of Russia* (New Haven, 1929).

competent – Jakobson thinks that in conjunction with him he could cover all needs in England, and I strongly believe that he would attract stars from abroad to visit at his shrine and so automatically create a centre of culture and of light wherever he might be. There is, I believe, a vacancy in Birmingham, also at Manchester. The old arguments that émigrés are no good is absurd – he was originally at Prague and, being a Jew, fled with his Czech peasant wife (she is perfectly nice, however, and cooks beautifully) to Sweden, Norway etc., and so to Columbia. His relations with the Sov. Union are not disturbed and he is not a Fascist beast. I tried to interest Dodds in him, who is here on some sort of bogus expedition about Far Eastern languages, but Dodds assured him that pure research would be frowned upon at Oxford in the future and that only things good for the community would be encouraged, which distressed Jakobson enormously. He is really at his best when quoting (in Russian) the lyrics of a small tribe in Sakhalin, of whom there are only 2,500 surviving and who have, alas, no written language but the best images of love in the world. He complains, quite rightly, that all the literature on his subjects in the Library of Congress is in unopened crates from which the cobwebs are not swept off by the decayed White Guards whom Mr MacLeish unsuccessfully tried to unseat, and whose chief character is hatred of all literatures everywhere all the time. Perhaps Jakobson would be appeased in Birmingham with dear Bakhtin,[1] but if Konovalov can use the £1,200 so improvidently placed at his personal disposal to hire assistants partly on Jakobson (say £800) with, say, a Laming[2] Fellow in Russian from Queen's supported by, say, the extra £300, with £100 for professional expenses, something might be done and we should genuinely be the gainers. So do give the matter your deepest thought, as otherwise K. will hire humbler hacks than himself, and the whole thing will go to the devil and you will have to write more letters to *The Times* about D'Anthes.[3] Sumner, who I suppose will now inevitably be mixed up in all these things, knows only the wrong or stupid Jakobson (Sergey) and must on no account be allowed to drag him in as a red herring. I see the possibility, with my friend about, of a lengthy summer school or something of the kind in Oxford, which one need not go to but can if one wants to, with various Miss Starks about, presided over by all the Slavonic lights of Europe, which I

1 In the event Jakobson never took an academic post in England. Nikolay Mikhailovich Bakhtin (1894–1950) was at the time teaching Russian phonetics in the Dept of Linguistics at Birmingham.

2 Pronounced 'Lamming'.

3 Baron George Charles D'Anthès (1812–95), an officer in the Russian horse guards, fought a duel on 27 January 1837 with the poet Pushkin after being accused of an affair with Pushkin's wife. Pushkin was mortally wounded and died two days later.

think would be (don't you?) rather enjoyable, particularly if the Russians, as they inevitably must, send someone to preach the new life.

I have met your friend Mr Prokosch,[1] who is like a very nice Austrian; his works seem to me a trifle bogus – still, better he than Koestler,[2] who is regarded by some here as the greatest genius of our age. I have also met Mr Henry James[3] – a very nice but somewhat null personality who had nothing of interest to say about either his father or uncle and admired the Prime Minister and General Smuts,[4] but regretted that Smuts was too addicted to outdoor plumbing.[5] Mr George Rublee,[6] who also attended, is the spit image of the late Warden Fisher and could not understand a word I said but remained serene throughout. Mr James said he had heard much about you and had intended often to make your acquaintance and sent his warmest regards. Very courtly and unlike any Americans of our age.

Interesting that Christopher Hill is in the Soviet Department of the Foreign Office. I cannot really see eye to eye with Sir Orme Sargent.

Yours ever,
Isaiah Berlin

TO WALTER TURNER
Britain in Pictures

12 June 1945 [*carbon*]

British Embassy, Washington

My dear Walter,

I think I have found the man at last – it is, I fear, no use expecting me to

---

1 Frederic Prokosch (1908–89), American novelist and poet whose exotic themes and settings emerge from his travels to many parts of the world.

2 Arthur Koestler (1905–83), Hungarian-born British novelist, journalist and social philosopher; influential Communist journalist in Berlin in the 1930s, imprisoned by Franco's forces in the Spanish Civil War and briefly by the Vichy Government in France in 1940, then moved to England; best known for his novel *Darkness at Noon* (London, 1940), which expresses his break with Communism as a result of the Stalinist purges.

3 Henry James (1879–1947), son of psychologist and philosopher William James (1842–1910) and nephew of novelist Henry James (1843–1916).

4 Jan Christiaan Smuts (1970–50), South African soldier and statesman; Minister of Justice in South African coalition government 1933–9; Prime Minister 1939–48; widely respected and influential in government decision-making during the war, which he spent mainly in London; made honorary Field-Marshal in the British Army 1941. He was the only person to sign the peace treaty after both World Wars, and was active in the establishment of the United Nations.

5 Presumably a reference to Smuts's renowned physical toughness.

6 George Rublee (1868–1957), lawyer, adviser to Woodrow Wilson and to FDR, who appointed him chairman of the Intergovernmental Committee on Refugees 1938.

do my duty, however sacred, since I shall not be in London long this summer. I shall only come to rest next year, which will, I am sure, be far too late for you, and in any case I am really most unsuitable for the task despite all your and Cruikshank's sinister flattery on the subject – I am a hopeless dilettante about matters of fact really and only good for a column of gossip, if that. The man I mean is one William D. Clark, who was assistant chief of the M. of I. outpost in Chicago, a historian by profession, who is angling for an Oxford Fellowship now, and whom the University of Chicago have requested, so he told me, to write a really full-scale history of Anglo-American relations some time. He has the whole topic well in his head and is the master of a lucid and reasonably lively and even epigrammatic style and would love to do it. He is at present here (in Washington) and can be reached via British Information Services, 1336 New York Avenue, NW, Washington 5, DC. I think he really is the right person to do what you want and will deliver a perfectly adequate consignment of goods.

Meanwhile, I am fresh from recitals by Heifetz and Horowitz and lunch with Virgil Thompson.[1] Of these the last was really the most satisfactory. Thompson is one of the very few people, among whom you would be perfectly right to include yourself, who have something to say on the subject of music and say it with great feeling and style and freshness and, indeed, truth. Heifetz is really a terrible experience: he is very bored by Bach and Beethoven and only becomes excited in the former when there is a difficult thing to do, when he slightly warms up to show himself and you what he can do. As for the latter, he is very sensational – the last living descendant of Paganini and of great value in the way in which real virtuosi always have been. The experience is not really musical or artistic at all but it takes one's breath away in the way in which an acrobat or racing motorist might – you have the feeling that if you paid him another 10,000 smackers (I think that is the word) he would go faster and clearer and in a more dynamo-motor way still. Consequently his treatment of good music is a desecration and very hollow, but Liszt and Prokofiev are thrilling and splendid.

I shall be back I hope in August and will see you then.

Yours ever,

Isaiah Berlin

In mid-June IB was summoned, after all, to San Francisco for the last two weeks of the conference, to assist Chip Bohlen in vetting the Russian

1 Virgil Thomson (*sic*) (1896–1989), US composer, conductor and music critic (for *New York Herald Tribune* 1940–54).

version of the UN Charter. Archie Mackenzie had been there throughout,
in the press officer role IB had turned down, and well remembered the
positive atmosphere, which contrasted with the deep foreboding about
Soviet intentions already felt in Washington and London:

The optimism was quite extraordinary. I think it was a mixture of all
these delegates, hundreds of them, coming from countries that were still
under war conditions, with blackouts and food rationing; and they
suddenly found themselves in San Francisco with all the American
generosity and the Californian sunshine, and the fact that the war was
very obviously coming to an end, and it generated tremendous euphoria.
[. . .]
    So it was an extraordinary conference. Probably we were too
optimistic. We didn't face all the facts because even then – it was while
we were in San Francisco that the Polish crisis[1] blew up, and other
Eastern Europe troubles. And Churchill wrote that letter to Truman,
which we didn't know about in San Francisco, but saying, 'I'm afraid
there's an iron curtain coming down in Europe.'[2]

TO MARIE AND MENDEL BERLIN

    26 June 1945 [*manuscript*]

The United Nations Conference on
International Organization,
San Francisco

My dear parents,
    I have spent ten extremely agreeable days here on a job for which my
origins particularly qualify me. The situation was *full* of humours which one
day I shall describe to you – I would not have missed it for *anything*. Now I
return to Washington via New York & shall be there on about the 29th June.
I plan to leave U.S.A. circa 25–30th July. By boat I agree, preferably. Quieter,
more restful, with luggage. I am glad you liked Nabokov – he is a dis-
appearing type of Russian intelligent,[3] & worth enjoying while he survives.
I shall certainly bring (a) all my blankets, sheets etc. (b) father's collars &

1 Concerning the future government of Poland (see 566/3). After lengthy negotiations
  a government of national unity was established under the leader of the Lublin provisional
  government, and the US and UK withdrew their recognition from the London-based government in exile.
2 Interview with William Powell, 31 May 1985 (Oral History Collection, UN Archive). In a
  telegram dated 12 May Churchill had written to Truman: 'An iron curtain is drawn down
  upon their front. We do not know what is going on behind' (cf. 623/3).
3 The Russian word 'intelligent' means 'member of the intelligentsia'.

shirts (c) mother's aids to beauty and the stockings which K[onstantin]
wishes me to take as a gift to her, and anything else which anyone may wish
to send by me. As for further journeyings on my part we can discuss that at
leisure, but as you rightly guess, my heart is set on something which may not
be feasible at a later date with such status (which in that country is essential –
quintessential: I see that by their behaviour here) & while my health so v.
good. As I shall see you really so v. soon no more to say at present. I think
you will find that I have made all my dispositions, private and public, quite
sensibly and will have no ground for serious complaint. Possibly Beeley who
saw me here will get hold of you & tell you how well I really am – the
Bowen–Wint informations were false at the time & I can't think why you
use them as a standard. I do *not* ask my friends to tell you anything but what
they choose. I only ask them to *communicate*.

    Love,

      Shaya

*IB's plans for how and when he would return to Britain were overturned
by another interesting suggestion. On this occasion the outcome was less
satisfactory, as he later described:*

On the way back from San Francisco, Mr Bohlen travelled in an
aeroplane with Halifax – same plane – and he told Halifax that I was the
only person who really understood the American point of view on Russia
and many other things, and that at the Potsdam conference[1] I'd be
invaluable as the link. So when I came back to Washington, Halifax said,
'It's a jolly good idea, I'll see what I can do.'

And then I suddenly received a summons from the Foreign Office,
saying would I act as interpreter for Eden at Potsdam? It was the only
way in which I could be got to Potsdam. I accepted with alacrity. Then
I had most frightful 'flu, and I was in bed – quite high temperature – and
I thought, 'No, shall I really go? I don't think I can, quite.' The doctor
came and saw me; and then Halifax called at my bedside and said, 'Look,
do go. If you don't go to Potsdam, we'll never know what happened
there, we'll never be told: we need you to go as a spy for the British
Embassy.'

I saw what he meant; and so I picked myself up and took an
enormous number of antibiotics, and got put on to a plane and flew to
London; and I was interviewed by the head of the American

---

1 The conference held at Potsdam (near Berlin) between 17 July and 2 August 1945, at which
Truman, Stalin and Churchill (replaced during the conference by Attlee, the new Prime
Minister) negotiated the terms of the peace conditions to be imposed on Germany.

Department,[1] and by a man called David Scott, who [. . .] said this and that, where I was to go; I was to come back to the Foreign Office and be fitted out with certain documents next day.

So I appeared on the second day. I was living in the Ritz Hotel, I think, by this time; I came the second day and David Scott, who was an awfully nice man, said, 'I'm very sorry, I'm afraid you're not going to Potsdam.'[2]

William Hayter remembered IB's disappointment:

I was going to the Potsdam Conference as secretary to the delegation, and Isaiah was supposed to be coming too, and one day Isaiah appeared on the doorstep [. . .] shaking his fist in the air; he'd been banned from the Potsdam delegation by Eden, who said, 'I can't have Isaiah chattering round the place.'[3]

In a mood of despondency, IB even attempted to back out of his trip to Moscow:

I wrote to Clark Kerr saying, 'The Foreign Office doesn't want me to go to Potsdam, perhaps I am altogether untrustworthy, I'd better not come to Moscow either.' And he wrote back saying, 'Don't be a bloody fool, the plane goes on 4 September.'[4]

So while the Potsdam conference was taking place IB remained in London, fighting off the 'flu from which he had been suffering, and visited at home in Hampstead by Patricia de Bendern. On 26 July, while he was staying at her country cottage, they celebrated the announcement of the Labour Party's victory in the election that had been held three weeks earlier.[5] Soon afterwards, the atomic bombs dropped on Hiroshima and Nagasaki brought victory over Japan.

Before leaving for Moscow IB was surprised to be summoned to Lord Beaverbrook's penthouse and offered a job writing a weekly political article for the Evening Standard. *Lord Beaverbrook was equally surprised – and displeased – by IB's instant refusal on the grounds that 'I'm not really a very good journalist and I'd find it a very difficult thing to do, I don't think it's my sort of thing at all.'[6]*

---

1 Philip Mainwaring Broadmead (1893–1977), head in 1945 of what since 1941 had been called 'North American Dept'.
2 MI Tape 21.
3 Interview with MI, 28 April 1994.
4 MI Tape 21.
5 The result of the election was not known until the votes of members of the armed forces serving overseas had been counted.
6 MI Tape 21.

TO HENRY LUCE[1]
Time Inc.

12 August 1945 [*cable*]

New College

IN VIEW OF CHARACTER OF MY OCCUPATION NEXT FEW MONTHS SHOULD BE
PARTICULARLY GRATEFUL IF NO REFERENCE OF ME COULD BE MADE IN
YOUR PUBLICATIONS AT ANY RATE UNTIL MY RETURN WASHINGTON
DECEMBER MAY I REGARD THIS IF ONLY AS PURELY PERSONAL FAVOR
WARMEST REGARD
    ISAIAH BERLIN

Time Inc. Archives

Luce sent a cable in reply on 13 August: 'WOULD HAVE BEEN GLAD TO
CARRY OUT YOUR SUGGESTION BUT STORY WAS PUBLISHED IN LAST
WEEKS ISSUE STOP IT IS ENTIRELY PLEASANT STOP DO YOU STILL
WISH OBSCURITY STOP ALL REGARDS HARRY LUCE.'[2] *The entirely
pleasant story read as follows:*

I. BERLIN

Isaiah Berlin once opined that Washington is not a city: 'It's more like a
vast, temporary headquarters during a campaign . . . Washington is a
bivouac.'

After three years in the Washington bivouac, rumpled, tubby,
articulate Isaiah Berlin had left the British Embassy staff last week and gone
home to London. As one of the Embassy's First Secretaries, he had for a
time contributed more than any other one person to official British
knowledge of the current US.

Dark-skinned, raven-haired Berlin's main job was to compile weekly
reports on the US scene, which he accumulated in part in an interminable
round of dinners and cocktail parties. Hostesses and guests were charmed
by his Oxford-accented observations on the world and its great; Reporter
Berlin was charmed with what he learned. His sparkling accounts became
'must' reading for policy-making Britons. Winston Churchill once
entertained Composer Irving Berlin at lunch without learning that he
was not the 'I. Berlin' who signed those fascinating reports from
Washington.

Son of a Riga timber merchant, Berlin emigrated to Britain as a

---

1 Henry Robinson Luce (1898–1967), strongly Republican publisher of *Time* (and other
magazines) from 1923, and editor-in-chief until 1964.
2 Time Inc. Archives.

young man and spent most of his adult life in or near Oxford. He speaks English, German, Russian, French, is an authority on Karl Marx, Greek philosophy, Russian literature and music, the US Congress and politics. He was one of few men at the Embassy who foresaw Britain's Labor victory.[1]

1 *Time*, 13 August 1945, 30; © 1945 Time Inc., reprinted by permission.

MOSCOW

You arrived soon after the armistice, expecting to be sent to Potsdam. However Mr Eden intervened and you were left out. You were very disappointed. You passed a few months with us, then went to Moscow for four months – a time, I think, you greatly enjoyed. Your curiosity in many respects could be satisfied. You had an opportunity of meeting my brothers and sister and their families, all very novel and out of the ordinary. Your knowledge of Russian affairs, their literary and cultural activities [were] much clarified and I think this visit, the books you acquired there and the interest roused in you was the cause to a large extent of your concentrating on past Russian ideas and literature, and led you finally to lecture on these subjects in Harvard in 1949.

Mendel Berlin, family memoir

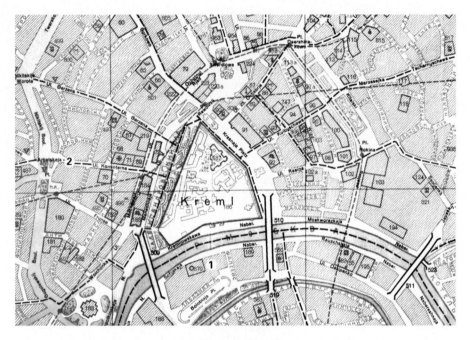

*Central Moscow, showing the British Embassy (1), the Kremlin
and Komintern Street (2)*

Early in September IB set off for the USSR. First he flew to Berlin:

You couldn't walk along the streets because the paving blocks were ruined. The Germans were running about like frightened rabbits – looking humble and frightened; and the waiters in the hotel where we were put up trembled before everybody and brought things and shivered. I had never seen such a terrified lot of people. There I met the present Lord Annan,[1] my old friend Goronwy Rees, and other characters of the British Intelligence, because there was a kind of British canteen at which we all ate [. . .] It's a lunar spectacle, the Germans are terrified, terrified little animals running about – people with things on their backs and not dressed and carrying parcels.[2]

Then on to Moscow. This was IB's first visit to the USSR since he had left it in 1920, aged eleven, and the capital city was new to him. In terms of physical damage, Moscow seemed to have suffered less than Berlin or London in the War:

It hadn't been bombed, there were no destroyed buildings that I could see. The streets were dirty, the inhabitants wore rags, to some extent. Shops contained no goods; the only shops of interest were the second-hand bookshops, the *antikvarii*, where you could pick up things, particularly because so many people died during the war and their books found their way to these shops. The Bolshoy was booming – particularly for the benefit of foreigners, but anyway – theatres were functioning, they were full [. . .]

By '45 everything had been restored [. . .] it was restored [. . .] once Soviet troops began to fight abroad [. . .] and I think you would find that if you read the memoirs of people, too, at that time. You don't get the impression of a devastated city in any way, not like London. I don't think it's ever been shelled, I don't think it was bombed much, and it was never taken; there must have been quite a lot of destruction, but slave labour restores things rather fast.

The damage inflicted by Stalin on Russian society was far greater. Even staying in an Embassy flat with Moore Crosthwaite and Eddie Tomkins[3] gave IB a taste of the paranoia and suspicion that were a constant feature of Soviet life at the time, since the domestic staff worked for the NKVD and he was followed when he went out:

On the third day I wanted to know where my father's relation lived. [. . .]

1 Noël Gilroy Annan (1916–2000), Baron Annan 1965; War Cabinet Offices and Military Intelligence 1940–4; War Office, France and Germany, 1944–6; General Staff Officer First Class, Political Division, British Control Commission, 1945–6; Fellow, King's College, Cambridge, 1944–56; later (1956–66) Provost.

2 MI Tape 21, from which the other quotations in this headnote are also taken.

3 Edward Emile Tomkins (b. 1915), 2nd Secretary, British Embassy, Moscow, since 1944.

So I went to one of those little kiosks that gave out addresses on payment of two roubles. There's no telephone book, because that had been destroyed [. . .]. You paid them roubles and they looked up things in some document they had, and they told you – if you gave them the name. So I said, 'Professor Berlin' – he did dietetics – 'Professor Lev Borisovich Berlin.'[1] But they didn't give it me at once: [I had to] come back in two hours. It was clear that I was followed by some sinister figure, which made it clear that I couldn't be served in the ordinary way. However I did come back absent-mindedly in about two hours, and then they gave it to me. [. . .] I came back with a little fiche containing their names and addresses in my pocket. The next day I had an attack of 'flu, so I didn't get up for two days. When I got up everything was there except this little bit of paper. That had gone.

IB's letters home give little indication of these pressures, no doubt from fear of interception as well as because of his normal practice of omitting what might worry his parents. And they ignore some key events, such as IB's first visit, soon after his arrival, to Boris Pasternak, then living in the writers' colony of Peredelkino.

TO MARIE AND MENDEL BERLIN

Thursday 13 [September 1945, *manuscript*]

[British Embassy, Moscow]

My dear parents,

This is written in an immense hurry as the last bag leaves to-night & then there won't be one for 8 days, I am told. I am very comfortable in Moore's flat in the Skatertny Pereulok (off what is now called Ulitza Vorovskavo) on the Arbat.[2] The food is more delicious than any I have had for 2 or 3 years. Life is simple & peaceful. The sights & sounds (& even smells) are most nostalgic & affecting. I don't know that I shall stay quite as long as I intended, but meanwhile I am enjoying myself.

Everyone is being agreeable to me. I can assure you that I am being most careful, well behaved, discreet etc. Tell Rach that I have as yet found no occasion, nor am likely to find any, for going for walks at 3 a.m. I retain account of my impressions till we meet.

love

Shaya

1 Leo Berlin, in peacetime Professor of Dietetics at Moscow University, one of Mendel's brothers. He and his family shared a flat with one of the other brothers (probably Leo's twin Samuel) and his family.

2 The Arbatskaya district in central Moscow, with its cafes and open-air exhibitions, was and is a favourite haunt of artists, writers and poets. 'Vorovskavo' is a phonetic rendition of the pre-Revolutionary form 'Vorovskago': the street was by then Ulitsa Vorovskogo.

TO MARIE AND MENDEL BERLIN

19 September [1945, *manuscript*]

British Embassy, Moscow

My dear parents

I wrote to you last week. No developments save that

(1) I eat far better here than either in U.S. or U.K., the food is deliciously done, & diplomats get plenty.

(2) the Mchat[1] performance of Tsar Feodor[2] is magnificent in every way. So is Evgeny Onegin. The number of plays & operas worth visiting is v. great

(3) I do not lose hope of calling on Leo. I think I know how.[3]

(4) Everyone is v. nice & kind & I am fascinated by everything. The conversations in the street & theatres particularly. I had forgotten that such emotions & expressions existed. A bientôt. I am really very well & sleep till 11 a.m. every day (I hear the maid Frossia say: да он спит крепко – крепко. будить его совсем мне невозможно – очень сердит бывает ежели его до одинадцати будят. Совсем не Англичанин?[4] On the other hand – imagine *every day* a hot bath.

love

Shaya

TO MARIE AND MENDEL BERLIN

25 September [1945, *manuscript*]

British Embassy, Moscow

My dear parents

Nothing really to tell you. Gwatkin has left for Warsaw & Berlin & will, I hope, ring you when he returns. I shall try to telephone you to-morrow. I am still in the most interested condition: *everything* is worth looking at: I still intend to stay till sometime in November: & then to return possibly by water i.e. Leningrad–Stockholm–England, as I have never seen Sweden. Good plan don't you think? Have [you] written me? If so nothing has arrived. If you send via F.O. it wd be worth while to ensure via Northern Dept (Brimelow

---

1 'Mkhat' is an acronym of 'Moskovsky Khudozhestvennyi Teatr' (the Moscow Arts Theatre).

2 Play by Aleksey Tolstoy (1817–75) published in 1868.

3 By slipping out of a theatre performance at the interval to avoid being followed.

4 'Da on spit krepko – krepko. budit' ego sovsem mne nevozmozhno – ochen' serdit byvaet ezheli ego do odinadtsati budyat. Sovsem ne Anglichanin?' ('Yes he sleeps soundly – soundly. I absolutely mustn't wake him – he gets very angry if anyone wakes him before eleven. Not at all like an Englishman?')

or Pumphrey)[1] that my name is on the 'bag list.' Otherwise letters may get lost in F.O. When is Father going to Germany?[2] has he gone? If so, if I know where to get him. I could easily phone him from here. The food etc. continue to be *delicious*. For a foreign diplomat life offers no hardships in Moscow. The mushroom soups & pirozhki[3] are particularly good. I shall have much to tell when I return.

Love
    Shaya

I am really bounding with health – better far than either in U.S.A. or in England: it must be the influences of youth & early food.

TO MARIE BERLIN

Friday 28 [September 1945, *manuscript*]

British Embassy, Moscow

Dear Ma

Written in a hurry. I forgot my photograph at home but shall send it by the next bag. Meanwhile no letters from you, so I conclude that you perhaps don't address them right or the Foreign office lose them. My view is that you write like this: but Moore cd tell you.

For Moscow Bag
    Mr. I. Berlin
    Foreign Office etc.

Leo is a Lieut-Colonel (medical). But nothing until I return, & don't tell pa, & what *is* his address in Germany? I am *terribly* well but I propose to leave everything until I come back & talk & talk. Life is v. interesting. I enjoyed my talk with you on the phone very much. I need nothing as Moore cd tell you. Much love I wish I cd think of something to say – love to everyone.
    Shaya

1 Thomas Brimelow (1915–95) was transferred in June from the Embassy in Moscow to the FO's Northern Dept in London (with responsibility for the USSR and the Baltic States), where his colleagues included (John) Laurence Pumphrey (b. 1916), who had just joined the FO after spending the war years in the Army.

2 Mendel Berlin spent September–November in Bad Oeynhausen near Minden in Germany as a member of a commission set up by the British government to study the possibilities of exploiting German forests for British needs.

3 Small pies, usually savoury.

11 October 1945 [*manuscript*]

British Embassy, Moscow

Dear Ma

I am really v. well indeed. I send a photograph originally obtained for diplomatic purposes, but it was made on the 2d day after my arrival here & to-day I look really flourishing – not a day's cold or anything. The food, climate etc. suit me admirably, & so I shall probably not return till the end of Nov. as I obviously must wait for the Ambassador & I have no idea, nor has anyone else, when he (or Moore) are returning.

I received your 2 & father's 2 letters, the last from Bad Oeynhausen. I tried to cable him there but that was not practicable. I go to the theatre or opera practically every night, & eat hot borshch at home at 11 p.m. & go to bed at 11.30 – it is all most exciting & agreeable & I shall be full to bursting with impressions. Please put away The enclosed[1] & carefully do nothing with it till I return & I shall explain who & what.

I hope to get permission to go to Leningrad sometime in November – books are said to be easier to buy there than here, here the foreigners seem to me to have cleaned things out much too thoroughly before I came on the scene. My colleagues are being very agreeable to me, & the man I live with, Edward Tomkins is particularly charming & considerate. I have pure comedy conversations every morning with the maid – the whole thing is most extraordinary & delightful. Oh how much I shall have to say when I return from these, really the fullest weeks of my life. I shall try & telephone on Wednesday as before – if not then, the Wednesday after. Please give all the Oxford people my love, particularly the Warden.

Love

Shaya

24 October 1945 [*manuscript*]

British Embassy, Moscow

My dear parents,

Nothing of substance to say. I am very well indeed & the weather is – from my point of view – magnificent. Need I describe to you the crunching snow, the cupolas of the churches, the crisp air, the peasants, the fur caps, the Russian timbre of speech in the streets the distant sound of Red Army men

---

1 A draft of some early chapters of Boris Pasternak's *Doctor Zhivago*: see Pl2 215.

singing as they march? it is all like an almost vulgarly sentimental Repin[1] illustration to Zimnyaya Moskva,[2] or the like (as you know the kind of picture Russians love: 'spotyknoolas'"[3] or "dyed Moroz"[4] with a woman stumbling, or red cheeked peasants). I enjoy it terribly. On Nov. 9 I go to Leningrad. It is said to have better scientists than Moscow – particularly in medicine where a chair is occupied by a twin called by the same first name as the author of Hadji Murat[5] – he is 49 yrs of age & both the twins are v. nice.

The Tretiakov gallery, full of Repins, Serovs, Vasnetzovs[6] is also full of sentimental memories but as kunst[7] it is really too terrible. One of the ladies painted 7 times by Serov – a Mrs Hirschman I remember seeing in Boston last year as Koussevitzky's amie.[8] All v. strange. Of course the plan to go via Sweden meant by land, not air, & then I suppose to Göteborg or else Copenhagen & thence by sea – but I shall have to see. Chilver cabled what about the house – he is leaving in November – I said I didn't want to keep it alone – he had better box & store my things & I shall live in a hotel for my six weeks in Washington. I am enjoying *every minute* of my stay here, far more than anyone else I've met. I am glad you are both well – I shall try to telephone again some time.

love

Shaya

Although IB's official life in Moscow is absent from his letters home, reports to the FO by Frank Roberts fill in some of the gaps. On 30 October, for instance, Roberts recounts that IB had attended 'a Russian supper party consisting largely of professional writers and their wives, and wartime undemobilised officers', at which the general view was that 'the Labour victory in England made relations with the Soviet Union far worse than Mr Churchill could ever have allowed them to become. A Menshevik government was always a nuisance.'[9] Another such report summarises a

1 Il'ya Efimovich Repin (1844–1930), celebrated painter and academician, famous for works such as *Volga Boatmen* (1873) and *Ivan the Terrible with the Body of his Son* (1885).
2 'Moscow in Winter'.
3 'Stumbled' or 'tripped up' (colloquial: strictly the Russian should be *spotknulos'*).
4 'Grandfather Frost' (i.e. Father Christmas).
5 *Hadji Murat* is a novella by Leo Tolstoy: IB is referring in a rather clumsy code to his uncle Leo Berlin, twin of Samuel.
6 Valentin Aleksandrovich Serov (1865–1911), much-admired society portrait-painter in pre-Revolutionary Russia; Viktor Mikhailovich Vasnetsov (1848–1926), artist well known for historical genre paintings (heavily influenced by Russian folk and epic tales) such as *After Prince Igor's Tale with the Polovtsy* (1880).
7 'Art'.
8 'Girlfriend'.
9 Letter of 30 October to Christopher Warner, FO 371/47858, N15507/18/38.

*conversation between IB and a Soviet official at a party on 7 November.
Their discussions again touched on the Russians' admiration for
Churchill; the official*

observed that Mr Churchill had very cleverly outwitted the Germans in
1941 when he 'stabbed Hitler in the back'. It transpired that in the
opinion of the company in general Mr Churchill had conveyed to Hess
that Britain would 'lay off' if and when Hitler attacked Russia; [. . .] but
that Mr Churchill having successfully involved Hitler with the Soviet
Union thereupon broke his part of the bargain and thereby showed the
brilliant genius which the Russians were the first to acknowledge. Berlin
duly expostulated against all this but the atmosphere was exactly that of
Midwestern American businessmen who are told by a British official that
Australia is not a colony. These Russians raised their eyebrows and
courteously refrained from pressing their point further. [. . .] the party
went on to discuss the devious means used ('Blat')[1] to get theatre tickets
and everything else. Berlin was offered generous facilities in this respect.[2]

TO MARIE AND MENDEL BERLIN

Saturday 10 November [1945]

British Embassy, Moscow

Mes chers,

Only to say that I did *not* go to Leningrad on the 9th because the train was
reserved for returning Kremlin guests after the govt reception (to which I
was alas not asked – Neville's frac[3] was all in vain) so I go on the 12th i.e.
Monday & much look forward. The best doctors are *here*, in Moscow, not in
Leningrad. Anyway I am wonderfully well & have seen all I ever wanted to
see & more, & propose to take Mama's advice & not hurry since I am not
likely to be here again soon. And *everything* is fascinating. I can talk really
only when I get back. I bought a Kuprin minus half Yama[4] in a *Niva*
(Marx)[5] edition of 1912, so the war & postwar things are not in, but there
are v. few of them. It cost 450 roubles = £9. Tolstoy is v. difficult since of the
great Jubilee edition of 96 volumes only about 30 have come out. I'll try &

1 The use of backhanders and string-pulling to obtain luxuries normally denied to those not in
  positions of power; endemic in Russia during the Soviet era and after.
2 Letter of 10 November 1945 to Christopher Warner, FO 371/47925, N16432/627/38.
3 French for 'dress coat'.
4 Aleksandr Ivanovich Kuprin (1870–1938), Russian novelist and short-story writer whose best-
  known works include *Yama* ('The pit'), a sensationalist novel about prostitution written over
  several years (1908–15), which explains why IB's 1912 copy contained only part of the story.
  Kuprin's creative powers diminished after his emigration to Paris in 1919, and he returned to
  the USSR in 1937.
5 The Neva (*sic*) publishing house; presumably the Berlins knew their edition of Marx.

collect them. Premier editions fetch fabulous prices (ours is in Lyoma's[1] hands) – but if there is anything you particularly want tell me quick via F.O. bag (your censored letter took 7 weeks.) & I'll do my best. My plans are for Pushkin, Tolstoy, Chekhov, Blok, possibly a nice Turgenev. But what wd *you* like? Mother spoke of pictures. *Here* & *here* only Serov, Repin etc. fetch enormous prices since the Russians *really* like them. They are cheaper, believe me, in London. What is *not* expensive here is only vodka, which + a little caviar I'll try to bring. The food & general life from my point of view are *delicious*. All my love. I really feel terribly happy. Sir A Kerr is back & *most* kind. Moore arrives soon.

    Shaya

---

1 Mendel's other surviving brother, Solomon Berlin.

LENINGRAD

Long enough I have frozen in fear,
    Better to summon a Bach Chaconne,
    And behind it will enter a man,
He will not be a beloved husband to me
    But what we accomplish, he and I,
    Will disturb the Twentieth Century.
I took him by mistake
    For someone mysteriously bestowed,
    The most bitter of fates.
He will come to me in the Fountain Palace
    To drink New Year's wine
    And he will be late this foggy night.
And he will remember Epiphany Eve,
    The maple at the window, the wedding candles
    And the poem's mortal flight . . .
But it's not the first branch of lilac,
    Not a ring, not the sweetness of prayers –
    It is death that he bears.

Anna Akhmatova[1]

---

1 The 'Third and Last' dedication to her *Poem without a Hero*, written on 5 January (Epiphany Eve) 1956, the tenth anniversary of her most recent meeting with IB: p. 547 in *The Complete Poems of Anna Akhmatova*, trans. Judith Hemschemeyer, ed. Roberta Reeder, 2nd ed. (Boston, Massachusetts/Edinburgh, 1994).

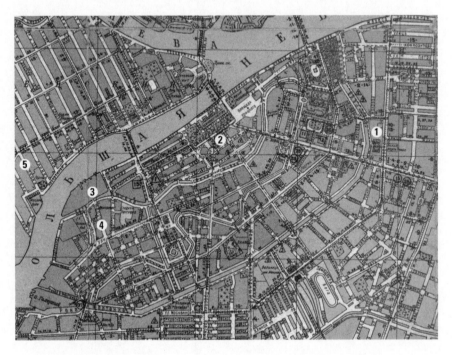

Central Leningrad, showing Fontanny Dom (1) on the Fontanka canal, the Astoria Hotel (2), the Moika canal (3), and the two streets in which the Berlin family lived in Petrograd in 1916–20: Maklin Prospekt (formerly Angliisky Prospekt) (4) and the 22nd line of Vasil'evsky Island (5)

*No letters survive, it seems, from the later part of IB's visit to the USSR.
The gap is partly filled by his own account for the Foreign Office of his
historic visit to Leningrad from 13 to 20 November, not yet two years after
the lifting of the German siege.[1] The following extracts from the diary
kept by his companion on the expedition, Brenda Tripp[2] of the British
Council, set the scene for his vivid memorandum.[3]*

Monday 12 November 1945

Spent the day wondering whether we were going to Leningrad. Finally
settled at 4.15. Train left at 5. Isaiah Berlin called for me at the Metropol.[4]
[I was] wearing Mrs Parnas'[5] fur hat and my thick coat. Cold day but train
very warm & comfortable cabin. We talked a lot at first – then had supper
& went to bed reasonably early – I.B. on top & me below. Priceless
picture of him in his pyjamas dropping his magazines etc. over the edge
like a child in a pram.

Tuesday 13 November: Leningrad

Arrived in Leningrad at 10 a.m. Tiger skin Intourist guide met us and

---

1 The German blockade of Leningrad, generally known as 'the 900-day siege', in fact lasted 872
days, from 8 September 1941 to 27 January 1944. Germany's invasion of Russia, code-named
'Operation Barbarossa', had begun in June 1941, and within less than three months Nazi troops
had reached Leningrad, cut off its communications with the rest of the USSR, and, aided by
Finnish troops from the north, completely encircled the city. Subjected to constant
bombardment from the ground and the air, increasingly desperate shortages, the failure of all
essential services, and an exceptionally cold winter (1941–2), the people of Leningrad showed
extraordinary courage and determination. Opinions vary as to how many died, but the
estimates quoted by IB are far too low; the true figure certainly approaches one million – of a
pre-war population of three million. Most died from starvation, hundreds of thousands from
cold and epidemics of typhoid and other diseases, and as direct casualties of the German
bombardment. The catastrophe would have been even worse but for the famous 'ice road'
across the frozen Lake Ladoga, which allowed limited supplies to be brought in, and the
evacuation of some of the sick, the elderly and the young; in summer supplies were brought
across the lake by barge. The Red Army partially broke the blockade in January 1943 and
conditions improved somewhat, but it was not until January 1944 that the Germans were
finally driven back from the outskirts and Leningrad was liberated. In January 1945 the city was
awarded the Order of Lenin, the USSR's highest national decoration, for its heroism during
the siege.
2 Brenda Muriel Howard Tripp (1906–2004), British Council representative in the USSR
(arranging exchange of non-military scientific articles with the Academy of Sciences), was
formally a FO cultural attaché with diplomatic status, since the British Council was not
officially allowed to function in the USSR at that time.
3 Reproduced below, pp. 601–12.
4 Hotel opposite the Bolshoy Theatre and five minutes from the Kremlin. In the 1940s the hotel
housed members of the British Embassy Press Dept.
5 Wife of the Polish Jewish biochemist Jacob Parnas (1884–1949). The Parnases were in Moscow
because the USSR had offered safe passage to a number of distinguished Poles following the
Nazi occupation of Lvov in 1941 (after which thousands of Jews had been massacred by the
Germans and by Ukrainian nationalists). Parnas was elected an Academician of the Academy
of Sciences of the USSR, but was later arrested and died in prison.

conducted us to the car which took us to the Astoria.[1] We had adjoining
rooms on the first floor – comfortable but rather cold. No hot water.
After coffee we went out to explore and to find Isaiah's birthplace[2] –
walked along the Moika – cold but sunny. Leningrad looked beautiful.

Wednesday 14 November [and following days]
The next day was better still. White hoar frost, brilliant sun, great blocks
of ice piled up on the edges of the Neva, clear water in the middle & the
newly painted palaces gleaming in the sunshine. Then it snowed and later
thawed and the glory had departed from the weather, but the city is
always beautiful, dignified, stately but somehow cruel and relentless, no
mercy anywhere.

  We went to theatres in the evening & Sleeping Beauty Ballet the
first night – & to the moovies & then we parted and I saw King Lear
alone in the theatre down by the Fontanka & then I. went to see A[nna]
A[khmatova] and I stayed at home and went to bed early. Then
Randolph Churchill[3] came & we had a ghastly morning in the
Hermitage[4] which was simply freezing & he came to the Ballet
(Gayaneh)[5] with us and was charming. Then we got up late and spent
days buying books, trudging along in the cold, freezing & thawing streets.
The trams are hell – worse than Moscow.

  [. . .]

  Is. and I had some nice conversations though most of the time his
conversation was so erudite that I remained in complete silence. He
found me boring and ignorant but I liked him: he is very much over-
intellectualised and it is difficult to make any very real contact with him.
He understands too much with his head & not his heart. His relationships
with other people – women at least – are of the subtle, mental, stimulating
kind. There is not much warmth about him. He never touches one or
takes one's arm or seems to be completely natural and friendly. He gave

1 One of the city's most prestigious hotels both before and after the Revolution, and reputedly
  where Hitler planned to hold his victory celebration had Leningrad fallen to the Germans.
2 A misunderstanding: IB was born in Riga, but lived in Petrograd 1916–20, for 2 years on
  Vasil'evsky Island, then on Angliisky Prospekt, the north end of which meets the Moika canal
  just before it joins the Neva.
3 Randolph Frederick Edward Spencer Churchill (1911–68), author, journalist, Conservative
  politician, wartime intelligence officer, only son of the former Prime Minister Winston
  Churchill, who had lost power in the British General Election in July.
4 The State Hermitage museum, founded in 1764 by Catherine the Great, and now among the
  world's greatest art collections, especially of Western European painting; housed on the banks
  of the Neva in interconnected buildings of which the most famous is the Winter Palace
  (completed 1762), but also including the Small, Old and New Hermitages. 'Hermitage' denotes
  a place of relaxation and retreat, fashionable in 17th- and 18th-century European landscape
  gardening. After the German invasion in 1941 the staff of the Hermitage worked day and night
  packing over a million of its treasures for evacuation; others were hidden in basements and
  cellars, and the bulk of the collections survived.
5 See 603/4.

me a frightful feeling of inferiority and inadequacy, chiefly because he was not interested to meet me on my own ground. We once talked about the happinesses of the unhappy [. . .] I think he is really very shy and covers it up with too much talking. By the end we reached a fairly comfortable relationship but I do not think there is any basis for further meeting as his conversation is beyond me.

Wednesday 21 November
Arrived back in Moscow at 11 a.m. with four suitcases and about 9 packages of books: Fortunately Embassy car was there to meet us.

IB did not record his memories of his encounters with Russian writers until thirty-five years later.[1] But he did write two official reports at the time.[2] At the end of his period of duty he compiled a long memorandum on the general condition of Russian culture.[3] He also wrote a more personal account of what he saw in Leningrad, where he had lived as a child. He deliberately underplays, indeed slightly falsifies, his encounter with Akhmatova on (probably) 15–16 November. But the significance he attached to this meeting and its sequel some weeks later emerges in his letter[4] to Frank Roberts, the British Chargé d'Affaires in Moscow, thanking him for his hospitality, as well as in his later account. The Leningrad report follows.[5]

The train left Moscow and arrived in Leningrad very punctually, nor was there any obvious NKVD agent in the compartment on either side of ours. No food was served on the way to Leningrad; moderately attractive *belegte Broetchen*[6] were offered at the usual fantastic prices on the way back. Tea flowed copiously from the guard's samovar during both journeys. Everyone was polite and well behaved; we were not accosted by tipsy Soviet colonels.

The centre of Leningrad shows virtually no destruction, and the restoration and renovation of public buildings, to which much attention has been devoted, seems now to be complete; they glittered with pride and splendour in the clear wintry air. The public statues and monuments are

---

1 See his 'Meetings with Russian Writers in 1945 and 1956', in PI.
2 A letter from Frank Roberts (25 November 1942 to C. F. A. Warner, FO 371/47925, N16819/627/38) summarises a further report by IB of a conversation with 'a rising Soviet star' in Leningrad, who claimed that 'Russians, being by nature kindly, found difficulty in hating their enemies as they deserved [. . .] and much admired the handsome young fair-headed Germans lying dead in the snow.'
3 'The Arts in Russia under Stalin', *New York Review of Books*, 19 October 2000, 54–63 (cut); repr. in full in SM.
4 See p. 619 below.
5 The original text is in the PRO, FO 371/56724, N375/24/38. This lightly edited version first appeared in *The Times Literary Supplement*, 23 March 2001, 13–15, as 'A Visit to Leningrad'.
6 Sandwiches.

once again exposed to view, the Hermitage is open (all save the Spanish, French and English rooms), and is said to be preparing its German acquisitions – apparently for the most part drawings from Dresden and Berlin – for exhibition fairly soon. There is some jealousy about the retention of all the Dresden paintings by Moscow, but this seems to be regarded as inevitable.

People on the streets look shabbier and more emaciated than the Muscovites, doubtless mainly as a result of the blockade which fills all memories and colours every conversation, but probably also because there are not so many peasant types to be seen in Leningrad, and one sees more worn and torn members of the old intelligentsia, or persons who give that impression, upon whom threadbare clothes flapping in the piercing wind and snow look more pathetically tattered than on the cruder and more corn-fed inhabitants of Moscow. The streets are a good deal emptier than in Moscow, save the Nevsky (the main thoroughfare), which at times is as crowded as the Okhotny Ryad in Moscow; the trolley-buses are, as everywhere in the Soviet Union, filled to overflowing. As for trams, they present a grotesque appearance, crawling slowly like gigantic disabled wasps, covered with human barnacles, some of whom tend inevitably to be knocked off by persons attempting to get on or off, and then with loud imprecations and groans hoist and squeeze themselves back on to their very inadequate footholds. In consequence trams are frighteningly close to being literal death-traps, as I almost discovered to my cost. Even at 4 a.m. and 7.30 a.m. I found all seats occupied.

More persons are said to be arriving from the country in Leningrad every day, and the housing problem, although perhaps not quite as acute as in Moscow, is grim enough. Rooms – at any rate those inhabited by the writers I visited – are at once handsomer and emptier than their equivalents in Moscow, the former because Leningrad in general is a better-built city than the more provincial Moscow, the latter because, so I was told, a great deal of furniture, some of it old and beautiful, was used for fuel during the blockade, and there is little likelihood of early replacement. Fuel is conspicuously short in Leningrad still; the Astoria Hotel, not to speak of public museums and galleries like the Hermitage, is not adequately heated, and Miss Tripp found that in one scientific institute there was no heating at all provided in the library, and that such warmth as existed was to be found in two small rooms, yielded by tiny improvised stoves lit by the librarians themselves each morning. Miss Tripp obtained the impression that private individuals could get logs for their stoves only in exchange for bread rations or such belongings as they could sell in the market. Prices appeared considerably lower than those in Moscow (despite rumours to the contrary), from carpets and grand pianos in the Commission shops,[1] and second-hand books (which cost approximately one-third of their price in Moscow), to carrots and sunflower seeds in the market on Vasil'evsky Island.

As for the outskirts, I was informed that Tsarskoe Selo (referred to mostly as 'Pushkin' by Intourist guides) and Peterhof were both still in ruins, Gatchina still gutted; and transport to Pavlovsk, which is a mass of destruction, seemed difficult. At any rate my own suggestion of a visit there was regarded as quite impracticable: 'The trains are very bad and it is very far', though it is only a very few miles beyond Tsarskoe Selo. The poetess Vera Inber[2] said on a later occasion that the Pavlovsk palaces were being very rapidly restored and would be finished by New Year. My suggestion about visiting Oranienbaum was even less well received and I therefore dropped the subject.

Despite the Intourist lady's open scepticism about the quality of the performances, I saw *Ivan Susanin* at the Mariinsky Theatre,[3] now back in its traditional blue and gold; the opera was more poorly sung and acted than anything at the Bolshoy Theatre in Moscow. The orchestra scores still called it *Life for the Tsar* and this was remarked sardonically by my Red Army neighbour. The Leningrad ballet is, however, a notable one. *Sleeping Beauty*, which I saw with Miss Tripp, and *Gayaneh*,[4] an Armenian ballet by the popular composer Aram Khachaturyan, which I saw with Miss Tripp and Mr Randolph Churchill, were superior to the usual Moscow performances, particularly *Gayaneh*, the libretto of which is a fairly normal version of the orthodox kolkhoz–Boy-Scout morality play, brought to life by a series of national dances of the Caucasian and Caspian peoples, danced with very uncommon spirit and skill. This contrasted with the dull pomp and routine competence with which even Tchaikovsky ballets are performed in Russia nowadays, and is rightly put forward by Leningrad today as one of its major claims to fruitful artistic activity.

1 Exclusive shops selling luxury foreign goods to Party grandees and apparatchiks.

2 Vera Mikhailovna Inber (1890–1972), Soviet poet, short-story writer and journalist, survivor of the Siege of Leningrad and winner of the Stalin prize in 1945 for her narrative poem *Pulkovo Meridian* (1942–6).

3 *Ivan Susanin* is the original title of the opera that its composer Glinka renamed *A Life for the Tsar* in honour of Tsar Nicholas I, who attended a rehearsal before the first performance in St Petersburg in 1836; after the Revolution the original title was restored. The Mariinsky Theatre (also known as the Kirov), a famous venue for opera and ballet named after the Tsarina Maria Aleksandrovna, opened in 1860 with a performance of Glinka's *A Life for the Tsar*; its blue and gold auditorium, damaged during the siege, had been restored by the time of IB's visit.

4 *Gayaneh* was the archetypal socialist-realist ballet. The literature of Soviet realism is often caricatured as a 'boy meets tractor' genre; IB's phrase is a variant on this theme, describing the attempt to make something lyrical or romantic out of the often grim and certainly mundane realities of Soviet life. The ballet, premiered in 1945, is set on an Armenian collective farm.

There is a good deal of wounded *amour propre* about Leningrad, a coldly handsome and once arrogant old capital, now viewed as something of a back number by the Moscow *arrivistes,* and responding with sharp but not altogether self-confident disdain. People appear poorer and less cared for than in Moscow; the writers I saw looked less prosperous, and their appearance and general tone was sadder and more genteel and weary than that of their Moscow colleagues. On the other hand life seems politically easier.[1] I was not, so far as I could tell, followed by anyone in Leningrad, and contact with Soviet citizens seemed less difficult than in Moscow. During three long evenings which I was permitted to spend among writers, occasionally tête-à-tête, the most timorous among them told me that he was most careful to avoid foreign contacts in Moscow, and generally to exercise a degree of caution not called for anywhere else, for example in Leningrad. I met these writers through the kind offices of the manager of the Writers' Bookshop in the Nevsky, a ripe character who deserves a few words to himself.[2]

Gennady Moiseevich Rakhlin is a small, thin, gay, baldish, red-haired Jew, noisy, shrewd, immensely and demonstratively affable, and probably the best-informed, best-read and most enterprising bookseller in the Soviet Union. Although, like other managers of State bookshops, he makes no official commission on his sales, and says that he subsists entirely on his official salary, his interest in and passion to promote the sale of books is at least as intense as that of any bookseller in the Western world. As the manager of the two most important bookshops in Leningrad, he is the official dictator of book prices in the city, and is evidently able to get books from other shops at very short notice, and thus to supply the needs of his clients more efficiently than any other known agent. Having certain vaguely romantic literary ambitions, founded on the memory of the famous booksellers of the nineteenth century who acted at once as the publishers, distributors and patrons of literature – his own bookshop is on the site of Smirdin's[3] famous establishment – he has converted one of the rooms in his bookshop into a kind of club for writers and other favoured visitors, and in this room, which Miss Tripp and I were kindly invited to frequent, I was enabled not only to purchase books with a degree of comfort unknown in Moscow, but to make the acquaintance of several well-known literary

1 Because of the relatively autonomous power of Leningrad's city government, which Stalin subsequently purged in the notorious 'Leningrad Affair' of 1949–50.
2 Rakhlin was almost certainly an agent of the NKGB (later the KGB).
3 Aleksandr Filippovich Smirdin (1795–1857), Leningrad publisher and bookseller, famous both for his high publishing standards and for his energy, honesty and generosity, made a crucial contribution to the development of the commercial book trade in Russia.

persons, such as Zoshchenko,[1] Akhmatova, Orlov,[2] Dudin.[3] Whenever I called, there were some three or four people in the room – artists, academic persons, writers – ostensibly looking round the bookshelves, but, as they very rarely carried anything away, perhaps more anxious to meet their friends in a warm room during the winter weather than to make any purchases. Conversation ran easily and freely in this little salon on literary, academic and even political subjects, and it was as the result of an acquaintance formed there that I visited an eminent literary personage[4] at home, and there met other members of the Leningrad intelligentsia. Rakhlin himself took a lively part in these conversations, though it was quite evident that his clients did not look upon him as an intellectual equal, but rather as an exceedingly capable literary factotum (which he is) with whom it was a good thing to keep in, since he acted as a kind of general Leningrad Figaro, procured theatre tickets, arranged lectures, gave monthly literary suppers, carried intelligence, disseminated gossip, and in general performed innumerable small services which made life more interesting, agreeable and indeed tolerable.

Rakhlin, who spoke of his frequent and lavish entertainment in Moscow by Mr Lawrence and Mr Reavey[5] with great gratitude and pleasure, seemed most anxious to continue contacts of this type with members of the British Embassy, and spoke with pride of the number of books which he had succeeded in selling to British and American officials and journalists since 1942. He did display a certain social sensitiveness on the subject and complained, with bitterness, of a British journalist who had made a disparaging reference to him in a recent book, which he thought uncalled for and unjust. He spoke of his plans for opening a bookshop in Moscow with at least five rooms, one of which would be devoted to the foreign colony, whence his foreign buyers would be able to circulate through the other rooms and thus perhaps meet distinguished Muscovites with similar interests. He seemed totally unaware of the kind of difficulties which seemed

---

1 Mikhail Zoshchenko (1895–1958), outstanding Soviet satirical writer, famous for the comic short stories he published in the 1920s. He fell foul of the Soviet authorities for his refusal to conform to the demands of socialist realism, whereby all artistic expression was to be realistic, heroic and optimistic, depicting socialist progress towards a better life. In 1946 he and Anna Akhmatova were the objects of a literary witch-hunt by the Communist Party. Ostracised and destitute, Zoshchenko died a broken man.

2 Sergey Sergeevich Orlov (1921–1977), hack Soviet war poet, best known in his day for his collection *Third Gear* (1946); now largely forgotten.

3 Mikhail Aleksandrovich Dudin (b. 1916), soldier-poet and wartime journalist, remained uncontroversial as an artist in post-war, Stalinist, Russia: his conformist didactic poetry secured his rise through the ranks of the Writers' Union.

4 Anna Akhmatova.

5 John Waldemar Lawrence (1907–99), press attaché, editor of *Britansky Soyuznik*, and George Reavey (1907–76), translator from Russian.

likely to be put in the way of such a project for promoting easier contact between foreigners and Soviet citizens, and indeed such unawareness of the degree of segregation in Moscow seemed to emerge from the conversations of most of the Leningrad writers with whom I spoke.

As Mr Randolph Churchill expressed a desire to see the 'inside of a Soviet home', which he had not succeeded in doing in Moscow, I asked Mr Rakhlin, who happened to be in bed with a cold, whether he would care to be visited by Mr Churchill and talk to him about his experiences during the blockade, on which he is very interesting. Rakhlin seemed to welcome the suggestion and Mr Churchill and I visited him on 16 November at about 3 o'clock in the afternoon. Rakhlin was in bed but talked with irrepressible vivacity about himself and the blockade, and answered all Mr Churchill's questions with great readiness and ease. His wife presently entertained us handsomely with vodka and a solid meal of fish and chicken. The flat, which is off the Nevsky, consisted of three rooms; it was small and gloomily but not uncomfortably furnished, and was approximately such as might have been found in Clerkenwell or Islington, though very much barer, furnished with the heavy German furniture of the 1880s and '90s common in Russia, with no bric-à-brac of any kind. Rakhlin spoke of the days during the siege when 125 grams of bread and no other food was the maximum and total ration allowed civilians, and of the fact that although a great many books were sold to him at that period by families of the dead and evacuated, his customers were too feeble for lack of food to be able to carry away heavy books, and chose either thin volumes or tore chapters out of novels or histories to carry away separately through the frozen streets. He gave gruesome details of the difficulties of burial of the dead, and a very graphic account of the taste of carpenters' glue, which he used to dilute with a little cold water to drink as a soup.

Although stories have reached Moscow that Popkov[1] and not Zhdanov[2] was regarded by the citizens as the saviour of Leningrad, Rakhlin confirmed the general view that Zhdanov was regarded as having been, more than any other man, responsible for keeping up morale in the city, and said that without Zhdanov's convoys across the frozen Lake Ladoga, he,

1 Petr S. Popkov, as First Secretary of Leningrad's Provincial Committee (i.e. mayor of Leningrad), was responsible for maintaining the supply lines across Lake Ladoga, organising rationing and evacuating writers. Stalin, who had always felt threatened by the power of the government in Leningrad, and jealous of Popkov's status as local hero, later had him liquidated – along with most of Leningrad's wartime city government – in the course of the 'Leningrad Affair'.

2 Andrey Aleksandrovich Zhdanov (1896–1948), Soviet government and Communist Party official, secretary of the Leningrad Communist Party 1934, charged, as the city's political boss, with organising its defence during the German siege, which he did energetically and efficiently; close associate of Stalin, later led the post-war purge of Soviet artists, writers and composers in which Akhmatova and Zoshchenko were expelled from the Union of Soviet Writers.

Rakhlin, could not have saved the life of his old mother, who had miraculously survived. Old people and children died in their thousands during this period, everyone assured us, the total number of dead from hunger alone being somewhere in the neighbourhood of 200,000 to 300,000.[1] Among his customers Rakhlin proudly claimed Molotov, Beriya[2] (the head of the NKVD), the Patriarch Alexis,[3] and the Leningrad Rabbi – he said that he himself frequently attended services at the Central Synagogue in Leningrad, which was normally very crowded and was getting a particularly good 'cantor' from Odessa that year – and wondered if he could be invited to England one day to see how 'real' bookshops were run. Towards the end of the visit he presented Mr Churchill with a volume on Leningrad for himself, and one published in 1912 and commemorating the retreat of Napoleon in 1812 for Mr Winston Churchill, who, his son had earlier remarked, was a passionate collector of Napoleoniana.

Rakhlin's harrowing story of the blockade was more than confirmed by others. The critic Orlov told me that virtually all children born during that period had died. He himself had been able to keep alive only as a result of the special rations issued to intellectuals thought to deserve them, for example himself as well as Rakhlin, who was rated for rationing purposes as a 'second-rate writer' (the 'first-rate' and 'classical' authors are relatively well off). The only persons actually evacuated by special aircraft first across the German lines to Moscow and later to Tashkent were Zoshchenko, the short-story writer, and the poetess Akhmatova, on direct orders of Stalin. Both had at first refused to leave but ultimately bowed to authority. They and Orlov said that most of their friends died during the blockade, since, being non-essential civilians, they were virtually condemned to death by the order of priorities for food and fuel. One of them remarked that to him personally Leningrad was now a graveyard. Miss Tripp was told that many people who had been through the blockade were still subject to fits of giddiness, and that general health had steeply declined as a result – a rise in mortality was expected during the next few years, unless nutritional measures are taken to prevent this, which seems unlikely.

All the writers to whom I spoke begged for English books, which they said had been singularly difficult to obtain through VOKS,[4] which was an inefficient and obstructive organisation; and indicated methods by which this might be done. We talked at great length about English and American

1 This figure is too low: see 599/1.
2 See p. 694.
3 Patriarch Aleksey, Metropolitan of Leningrad, born Sergey Vladimirovich Shimansky (1877–1970), was elected Patriarch in February 1945, Stalin having officially re-established the Russian Orthodox Church in 1943.
4 Acronym of 'Vsesoyuznoe obshchestvo kul'turnoi svyazi s zagranitisei' ('All-union society for cultural relations with foreign countries').

literature, and three out of the four writers with whom I had more than casual conversations spoke of Mr Priestley's recent visit and address to the Writers' Club;[1] and indicated very insistently that they did not rate him too highly as a writer, although he did obviously possess a high degree of professional skill. They found it hard to believe that he was really regarded in England as one of the greatest of her authors, and the heir to the great Dickens's mantle – though he told them that that had been said of him. While they found him affable enough personally they thought it queer that in his article for the Moscow *Literary Gazette*, in dealing with the present state of English letters, he should have damned every one of his contemporaries with praise of varying degrees of faintness, conveying throughout that their later works invariably represented a decline from sometimes promising beginnings. One of them finally asked outright why His Majesty's Government should have chosen Mr Priestley, whose achievement as a dramatist is neither ideologically nor artistically so very important (his novels are not known widely), as the literary ambassador of Britain. I tried to explain that it was VOKS and not His Majesty's Government which had arranged Mr Priestley's trip, but this was met with scepticism both in Leningrad and in Moscow, where Mr Priestley's criticisms of the British social order did not seem to register and very similar views of him are to be heard, at any rate among the well-established writers.

During one or two frank conversations about the condition of Russian life and letters which I had with the Leningrad writers, they said that they knew of no exceptionally gifted Russian authors under forty, although there was a great deal of enthusiasm and energy and considerable industry among them. The 'line' at present was to devote attention to the lesser-known parts of the Soviet Union, such as Siberia or Tadjikistan, as the nursery of much

1 In mid-October, at the end of a six-week tour of the USSR by Priestley. A month earlier in Moscow IB had attended the 'dinner in commemoration of the third anniversary of the "British Ally" [*Britansky soyuznik*]', 'the weekly paper produced by the Press Dept of the British Embassy in the Russian language', described by Robert Stern in the *Palestine Post*, 8 December 1947, 4: 'The function was held in the enormous white and gold salon of the pseudo-Moorish-baroque building on Komintern Street, not far from the Kremlin walls, which had been allocated to the Press Dept of the British Embassy, of which I was then a member, for its offices. J. B. Priestley, then in Russia on a lecture tour as the guest of the Soviet Government, was the only speaker. Hairy satyrs and naked nymphs (nine feet tall) looked hungrily down from fresco and cornice on the six-course meal, washed down by vodka and champagne, that was being served below them. Many distinguished Russians were present, for this was one of the officially sanctioned occasions when Soviet citizens were allowed to accept the hospitality of foreigners. At my table were Mme Sofiya Tolstoy, granddaughter of Leo Tolstoy, Isaiah Berlin, Fellow of All Souls and New College, Oxford, then attached to the British Embassy, and Mme Prokofiev, wife of the composer [. . .].' The event must have taken place in the Grand Hall of what is now called Dom Druzhby ('Friendship House'), in which case Stern's description is mildly exaggerated (though the room has since been refurbished). The nymphs are (now) clothed, at any rate.

brilliant new talent about to spring to life with the advance of education and civic consciousness; and that while this might be repaid in the long run, it led for the moment to the encouragement of, and publicity for, a mass of pseudo-archaic lyrics and bogus ballads and epics and official poetry generally, which were driving out whatever originality there was among these primitive or semi-medieval peoples. They asserted with much pride that the Leningrad literary papers were commendably free from this incubus, which cluttered up the pages of the Moscow literary weekly, although they made an exception in favour of Georgian and Armenian literature, which contained works of true genius. For their own part they are not ashamed of the tradition of Pushkin and Blok, Baudelaire and Verhaeren,[1] and would not exchange them for all the poetical treasures of Uzbekistan or Azerbaijan, whatever might be the fashion 'in Moscow'; and more on the same lines.

They spoke of the difficulties of educating their children according to the 'European' standards which they had known before the war, and said that in Leningrad it was in spite of all difficulties easier than in Moscow, because the number of well-educated persons outside the State schools continued to be greater than elsewhere, and that children therefore came under civilised influence, which prevented them from becoming the standardised technical experts – even in literature – which they were otherwise in danger of turning into. There was much talk about the 'values of humanism' and general culture as opposed to 'Americanism' and 'barbarism', which are thought to be the main perils at present. Indeed, I can say from my personal meetings with one young member of the Red Army, lately back from Berlin and son of a person liquidated many years ago,[2] that he was at least as civilised, well-read, independent and indeed fastidious, to the point almost of intellectual eccentricity, as the most admired undergraduate intellectuals in Oxford or Cambridge. But I gathered this case was a very exceptional one, although perhaps less so in Leningrad than anywhere else in the Soviet Union. As the young man in question gave evidence of having read both Proust and Joyce in the original (although he had never left the confines of the Soviet Union), I can well believe that this is so, and that no generalisation can possibly be drawn from one astonishing example.

I cautiously touched with my newly made acquaintances among the writers on the degree of political conformity which they had to observe in order not to get into trouble. They said that the difference between Communists and non-Communists was still pretty well marked. The main advantage of belonging to the Party was the better material conditions, due

1 Emile Verhaeren (1855–1916), Belgian poet.
2 Lev Nikolaevich Gumilev (1912–92), Akhmatova's son by her first husband, Nikolay Stepanovich Gumilev (1886–1921).

to the high proportion of orders placed with reliable Party men by the State publishing firms and literary journals, but the main disadvantage consisted in the duty of grinding out a great deal of lifeless government propaganda at frequent intervals and of appalling length (this was said in a mild, evasive fashion, but the sense was quite unmistakable). When I asked what view was taken, for example, of so faithful a Party member as the poet Tikhonov,[1] the President of the Writers' Union,[2] the answer was that he was 'the boss' (nachalstvo) and consequently undiscussable. I obtained the general impression that there are few real illusions about the actual quality of the work of Soviet writers, and that pretty frank discussions of this went on, but were scarcely ever published in so many words. Thus everyone seemed to take it for granted, for example, that Boris Pasternak was a poet of genius and that Simonov[3] was a glib journalist and little more.

Possibilities of travel were, I learnt, somewhat confined, as no writer could travel, for example, to Moscow of his own free will without a formal invitation from either the President of the Writers' Union or its Communist Party secretary, and although this could of course occasionally be wangled by indirect means, it was humiliating as well as difficult to do so at all frequently. The writers enquired with the greatest eagerness about writers abroad, particularly Richard Aldington[4] and John Dos Passos.[5] Hemingway was the most widely read of the serious novelists in English, and, of the English authors, Dr Cronin,[6] although the highbrows did think him a somewhat commercial author, though superior to some. Knowledge of English literature obviously depends on what is accepted for translation and,

1 Nikolay Semenovich Tikhonov (1896–1979), author of romantic, revolutionary ballads in the early Soviet period. His poetry increasingly took second place to his duties as a literary official for the Writers' Union, and he received three Stalin prizes for his propagandist and jingoistic war poetry.

2 In 1932 the Central Committee of the Communist Party dissolved all existing literary organisations and formed a single writers' union. This set out to impose the new doctrine of socialist realism. Writers who did not belong to the union found it almost impossible to get their work published. Conversely, many untalented hacks who became union officials enjoyed comfortable careers and associated benefits such as dachas, holidays, chauffeur-driven cars and access to the special shops dealing in foreign goods mentioned above (603/1).

3 Konstantin Mikhailovich Simonov (1915–79), Soviet poet, playwright and novelist who wrote love poetry and patriotic verse; war correspondent in the Second World War, author of one of the most popular novels of the war, *Days and Nights* (1944), as well as of numerous undistinguished didactic and propagandist plays; later (1946–54) edited the journal *Novyi mir* ('New world') and became a leading figure in the Writers' Union.

4 Richard Aldington (1892–1962), né Edward Godfree, English writer; one of the Imagist group of poets that included Ezra Pound; much influenced by service in First World War, as reflected in the poetry collection *Images of War* (London, 1919) and in his first novel, *Death of a Hero* (London, 1929). Several of his works were translated into Russian.

5 John (Roderigo) dos Passos (1896–1970), US novelist, author of several influential experimental novels critical of the hypocrisy and materialism of US society, most famously *Manhattan Transfer* (NY and London, 1925) and the *USA* trilogy (London, 1930–6).

6 A. J. Cronin's social realism, as in *The Stars Look Down* (1935), was popular in the USSR.

to a smaller degree, on what VOKS permits to be supplied to individual readers of foreign languages. The results are occasionally eccentric: thus in Leningrad, for example, the names of Virginia Woolf and E. M. Forster (mentioned in Priestley's article) were not known, but everyone had heard of Mason,[1] Greenwood[2] and Aldridge.[3] The source of foreign books was in Moscow, but they were very difficult to obtain even there, and if some method of supplying them with the imaginative literature of the Anglo-Saxon countries could be devised they would be most grateful. Anna Akhmatova was particularly pleased by an article which had appeared in the *Dublin Review* on her verse and by the fact that a doctoral thesis on her work had been accepted by the University of Bologna. In both cases the authors had corresponded with her.

The more eminent Leningrad writers are magnificently housed in the old Fountain Palace ('Fontanny Dom') of the Sheremetevs,[4] a kind of Holland House on the Fontanka, often visited by Pushkin – indeed the most famous of all the portraits of him had been painted in its morning room – a building of the late eighteenth century fronted by an exquisite ironwork grille and gates constructed round a wide quadrangle filled with trees from which thin, narrow staircases go up towards a series of high, well-constructed, well-lighted rooms. The problem of food and fuel is still fairly acute, and the writers I saw there could not be said to be living with any degree of real comfort – indeed their lives were still semi-obsessed by household needs. They hoped, I thought rather pathetically, that, as Leningrad developed into a port communicating with the outside world,

---

1 Alfred Edward Woodley Mason (1865–1948), English novelist, briefly also actor, Liberal MP and wartime intelligence agent; wrote highly successful adventure stories – of which the best-known was *The Four Feathers* (London, 1902), later filmed by Alexander Korda – and detective stories featuring his popular character Inspector Hanaud.

2 Walter Greenwood (1903–74), English working-class novelist, left school at thirteen; while unemployed he wrote *Love on the Dole* (London, 1933) – a story of life in an industrial town in northern England during the Depression – which was an immediate commercial success and remained his best-known work.

3 James Harold Edward Aldridge (b. 1918), Marxist novelist and journalist, Australian by nationality but from 1938 living mainly in UK, war correspondent in Second World War; had by this time published the war stories *Signed with their Honour* (Boston, 1942) and *The Sea Eagle* (London, 1944); his work was popular in Russia in translation, and later (1972) he was awarded the Lenin Prize.

4 The Sheremetevs, renowned as patrons of the arts, were one of Tsarist Russia's wealthiest and most influential noble families. Their palace on the Fontanka canal (whence its name) was first built in 1712, but reconstructed over the years and replaced in the 1740s by a grander building – donated in 1918, with its contents, to the Soviet State. Akhmatova occupied (1933–41, 1944–54) an apartment (now a museum devoted to her life and work) in one wing because she was the wife (and then ex-wife) of the art historian and critic Nikolay Punin (her third husband), who also lived there. A number of the other members of the Union of Soviet Writers lived in another palace owned by the Sheremetevs, almost opposite the Bolshoy Dom on Liteiny (the NKGB Headquarters), not, as IB here assumes, in Fontanny Dom.

more information and perhaps more foreigners would begin to visit their city and so bring them in touch with the world, isolation from which they appear to feel very deeply. My own visits, though arranged quite openly through one of my bookshop acquaintances, had been the first, literally the first, I was told, made by any foreigner since 1917, and I got the impression that it would be as well if I did not mention the fact at all widely. The writers in question said that they read *Britansky soyuznik* with great avidity, and any references to Russian literary achievement in it, for example reviews of books and the like, were most warmly appreciated.

I found no trace of that xenophobia in Leningrad signs of which are discernible in the minds of some of even the most enlightened intellectuals in Moscow, not to speak of Government officials and the like. Leningrad looks upon itself as, and indeed still is to some degree, the home of Westward-looking intellectual and artistic life. The writers in the literary newspapers, the actors in the theatres and the assistants in the half-dozen or so bookshops at which I bought books, as well as passengers in trams and buses, seem slightly better bred and educated than their cosier but more primitive equivalents in Moscow. Any seeds that we could plant in this ground would sprout more gratefully, if my impression is correct, than in any other part of the Soviet Union. Whether this is practical – whether for example, if a British Consulate were established in Leningrad, contact would still be relatively as easy and almost informal as it seems at present, is, of course, another and very real question. Present freedom of circulation may well be due to the absence of resident representatives of foreign institutions and countries, which makes the task of surveillance of those who pass through the inescapable (and surprisingly comfortable) turnstile of the Astoria Hotel relatively easier, and less worrying to the authorities.

WASHINGTON
(reprise)

[N]o town has ever taken itself so seriously with so little reason.[1]

I now know that solemnity and public seriousness are fatal qualities in the conduct of public affairs and shall never believe anything else.[2]

1 IB, of Washington, in a letter of 30 March 1943 to René Janin (not included in this volume).
2 IB in a letter of 11 February 1944 to Joseph Alsop: see p. 488 above.

5th April, 1946.

Dear Sirs:

I should be grateful if you could supply me with 16 resistance coils (2 coils for each appliance listed below) needed for adapting U.S. electrical appliances to British A.C. or D.C. currents of 230 volts. The wattage for each article is:

1 Hot plate   660 watts
1 Iron   1000   "
2 Heating pads   @   50   "
1 Electric clock   2   "
1 Toaster & coffee-pot   650   "
1 Electric Razor   25   "
1 Toaster   550   "

If you will let me know how much this comes to I shall be glad to send you a check by return post.

Yours sincerely,

Isaiah Berlin

Freed Transformer Company,
72, Spring Street,
New York City, N.Y.

The last surviving letter written before IB's return to England

*IB's final departure from the USSR in early January took him again to
Leningrad, and a farewell meeting with Anna Akhmatova, en route to
Finland, Sweden (where he heard that he had been awarded the CBE in
the New Year Honours List) and home. A short trip to Paris, where
Patricia de Bendern and her husband were living, followed almost at once.
IB's subsequent stay in England was brief. By early February, after a
'horrible crossing',[1] he was back in Washington.*

TO DAVID ASTOR[2]

18 February 1946 [*carbon*]

British Embassy, Washington

In connection with our telephone conversation about the American
correspondent for the *Observer*, I really have thought about the matter and
talked to Robin Cruikshank, and I have the following suggestions to make:

There are three people who come to mind, of very different
qualifications: all of them well worth having in my view. The first is the most
eminent of the younger publicists now writing in the United States, namely
Joseph W. Alsop, Jr, who appears to me and to most of his other
contemporaries (he is about 35–6) to be easily the most distinguished young
journalist in America, on a par with Lippmann alone. As you probably know,
he used to publish a column thrice a week in the *Herald Tribune* with a man
called Kintner[3] when his sources of information were particularly good,
since he was President Roosevelt's cousin and was on terms of friendship, or
at any rate easy social intercourse, with most of the members of the
Washington administration. He now publishes this column with his brother
Stewart Alsop,[4] and as he still entertains lavishly and widely and is a
celebrated host, and as his intellectual capacity and literary gifts do not seem
to have been blunted by his war service as a kind of political ADC to General
Chennault[5] in Chungking, his column still seems to me a highly responsible

1 Letter of 4 March 1946 from Marie Berlin.
2 Hon. (Francis) David (Langhorne) Astor (1912–2001), son of 2nd Viscount Astor and his wife
  Nancy; Royal Marines 1940–5; Foreign Editor of the *Observer* 1946–8, later (1948–75) Editor.
3 Robert Edmonds Kintner (1909–80), journalist and television executive, financial reporter, *New
  York Herald Tribune*, 1933–7, columnist 1937–41, co-wrote syndicated Washington political
  column 'The Capital Parade' with Joseph Alsop; from 1944 began a successful career in
  broadcasting.
4 Stewart Johonnot Oliver Alsop (1914–74), political journalist, wrote the syndicated *New York
  Herald Tribune* 'Matter of Fact' column with his brother Joseph 1946–58; Stewart was the more
  liberal of the two.
5 General Claire Lee Chennault (c.1890–1958), adviser to Chiang Kai-shek on the development of
  the Chinese air force 1937–41, founder of the 'Flying Tigers', the American Volunteer Group of
  pilots fighting the Japanese in China 1941–2; Joseph Alsop had been on Chennault's staff in
  China in 1943–4.

and brilliant performance. He would, I am sure, be very willing to contribute a weekly piece, which, since he is a highly well-informed and civilised person, would certainly rise above the standard reached by the ordinary correspondent of any newspaper, and would, at his best, be at least as good as Willmott Lewis was and is at his best. The only drawbacks to him are the fact that he would not exclusively belong to you, which perhaps you may wish, since his column is carried by some 40 newspapers in the United States already, and, secondly, that I am sure he would not wish to displace your present correspondent,[1] in whose newspaper his column appears, and with whom, I surmise, he would not wish to jeopardise his present happy relations. I have naturally not spoken to him on this subject or, indeed, to anyone else here. But so far as your distinction of style and matter and sources of information are concerned, Alsop is, I am sure, wholly in a class by himself.

If you would prefer an Englishman and a correspondent attached purely to the *Observer*, there are two persons you might consider. The first is (1) William Clark, at present working in this Embassy. He was at Oxford after our time, at Oriel I think, and was then a Commonwealth Fellow at Chicago. You might care to look at specimens of his work which have appeared anonymously in the *New Statesman*, e.g. his reviews of Sumner Welles's[2] and Lippmann's (US War Aims)[3] book[s], which seemed to me very good performances. Of all Englishmen available here, he would, I am sure, be best, since he writes with great facility and sharpness and is a pundit on American affairs. I have a notion that he has decided not to be a don at Oxford, which at one time he contemplated (he is a historian), and to undertake instead to be the European editor of the *Encyclopaedia Britannica*, which Marshall Field[4] and the Chicago University manage between them in some sort of way. He used to work as second-in-command in the British Information Services in Chicago under Graham Hutton and Robin C[ruikshank] probably knows him too, but I really have no hesitation in recommending him as a very first-rate correspondent. Learned, accurate, brilliant and an intellectual live wire in the best sense, head and shoulders above the corps of British correspondents at present practising here. I have not spoken to him either –

---

1 Unidentified.

2 W.D.C., 'Sumner Welles's World', review of Sumner Welles, *The Time For Decision* (NY and London, 1944), *New Statesman and Nation*, 18 November 1944, 340–1; hardly anonymous, given the initials (printed at the end of the piece).

3 Walter Lippmann, *US War Aims* (London, 1944), appears not to have been reviewed in the *New Statesman*; nor have I found a review of it by Clark elsewhere.

4 Department store chain named after its founder, dry-goods tycoon Marshall Field (1804–1906), whose original Chicago store, built in 1885–7, was at the time the largest in the world.

if you wish to communicate with him, you could perhaps do so either directly c/o the Embassy or via me. I should be glad to help.

I can also recommend my ex-pupil Patrick Nowell-Smith, who, after New College, in 1937 went to Harvard as a Commonwealth Fellow, knows a great deal about America, and is a very competent person at anything he sets his hand to. He has come back from the army and is being considered for various philosophical Fellowships at Oxford, but will, I imagine, be attracted by the idea of going back to the United States, which is a country obviously fascinating to him. I do not suppose he has done any journalism in the past, but he is one of those highly competent Wykehamists who cannot sink below a certain level, do what they might. I cannot really say what kind of writing he is likely to turn out beyond the fact that it would be based on very solid information, shrewd, serious and polished. Him you could interview in London by getting hold of him at his father's house (the original Nowell-Smith,[1] connected, I believe, with the League of Nations Union, whose address the Oxford telephone book would provide).

All three appear to me each first-rate in his own way, with Joe Alsop as the only solidly-made reputation among them. Indeed, I cannot think why some English daily newspaper does not carry Alsop's column as an American commentary – there is really little need to read anything else either for the general public or for members of the British Cabinet. He has known most of the people at the Washington Embassy well at one time or another, and Tony Rumbold or Hoyer-Millar in the Foreign Office could tell you all about him as a person.

This exhausts my imaginative range. I hope it is the sort of information that you need.

With best wishes,

TO LORD BEAVERBROOK

19 February 1946 [*carbon*]

British Embassy, Washington

Thank you very much for your warm letter,[2] to which I should have replied before if it had not been sent to Moscow a day or two after I had left the Soviet Union. I do not regret the four months which I spent in that

---

1 Nowell (Charles) Smith (1871–1961), Headmaster of Sherborne School 1909–27, Chairman, Committee of Council for Education in World Citizenship, 1939–46.

2 Dated 3 January, and congratulating IB on his CBE. He begins: 'When all other news was bad I knew, in the old days, that I could at least derive amusement as well as profitable information from a certain weekly dispatch from Washington that reached me in the Foreign Office circulation.'

remarkable country; every day had its own peculiar quality, and the conversations in trains and buses are unlike anything to be heard anywhere else on earth.

I shall not linger long in this land of plenty, but will don my gown again on 1 April, All Fools' Day.

Thank you once more for your very courteous letter and all your other kindnesses to me.

TO FRANK ROBERTS

20 February 1946 [*carbon*]

British Embassy, Washington

My dear Frank,

There are many things I should like to thank you for, and the first item is only first because it is the most urgent. I am most grateful for the copy of my rambling discourse on the Russian writers,[1] which seems to me an even darker jungle now that it has appeared in cold type than it had looked in Moscow.

The urgent note is connected with the fact that you say in your covering note that you have enclosed two copies. Jock [Balfour] has received one with a note addressed personally to him and my envelope contained also only one. Is this right? In view of the nature of the document you will more than understand why I should address this anxious enquiry to you. If only one copy was enclosed, that is quite sufficient, as, if they want more here, they can manufacture them on the spot, but if one is really missing ... Horrid speculation as to the fate of X and Y and Z.

In connection with this one only begins to be properly depressed by the irresponsibility and carelessness of people after a visit to the Soviet Union. On arrival in London I discovered that the *News Chronicle* in the course of a ghastly gossip-column about me (shy-making in the last degree, anyhow), said something about my having a close relation who was 'Doctor to the Supreme Soviet'.[2] Inaccurate as this is, it is close enough to the facts to harm my poor relation,[3] since it is bound to be sent by the Sov. Embassy

---

1 See 601/3, and also IB's comments to Harriman, p. 630 below. The memorandum had been printed for circulation.

2 In an article on IB's CBE in the *News Chronicle* diary on 3 January, 'Mr Churchill and the Ragtime King' (p. 3), Ian Mackay had claimed that 'one of his nearest relatives is the medical officer to the Moscow Soviet'.

3 Leo Berlin was arrested in 1952 and accused of belonging to a British spy-ring supposedly including IB and Mendel. He was interrogated and tortured until he 'confessed'. He was released after the death of Stalin, and died soon afterwards of a heart attack upon seeing in the street the man who had interrogated and tortured him.

under cover to Moscow, and every official who receives it will then, as you know better than I, be compelled to take some sort of action, if only not to be accused of negligence. Oh dear, I don't know how the journalist in question, whom I had never met or heard of before, picked this up. Apparently from somewhere in the Foreign Office; all rather depressing.

To turn to nicer things. Thank you very much for innumerable things. I know well what a nuisance emissaries who come on missions which are half-baked can be in well-ordered establishments and how easy it is e.g. in this Embassy to treat them politely but in an offhand way, and am really most appreciative and grateful for the fact that I had so good a time while I was with you in Moscow. I wish I could think of some way of demonstrating that in some concrete fashion – short of warmly repeating my invitation to you and Cella[1] to come to Oxford, where, as from 1 April (All Fools' Day?), I shall be re-established. I can think of nothing; but if there is anything possibly I can do for you here do let me know and I should be delighted to be given the opportunity.

My journey was uneventful save that I repeated the performance with the poetess in Leningrad, who finally inscribed a brand new poem about midnight conversations for my benefit,[2] which is the most thrilling thing that has ever, I think, happened to me. Otherwise nothing occurred until the Finnish frontier, which I crossed with an American [. . .], a temporary clerk at the Moscow Embassy. We were visited by a very high-powered lady in charge of the customs officials, who on inspecting my *laissez-passer* displayed tremendous official courtesy: looked at nothing but said she wished to deliver a short official speech to me. I rose to my feet and bowed, she bowed gravely too and we both sat down. She then said that it was very important for foreign officials leaving the Soviet Union to have their printed materials pre-censored before they left, for such were the regulations of the Soviet Union. If they did not do that, an elaborate search was made necessary at the frontier and documents which appeared innocuous in the eyes of the foreign officials, but which, under Soviet law, customs officials were bound to sequestrate, were liable to be removed from them. In some cases the foreign officials failed to understand this, irritating arguments ensued, and unnecessary bad blood was made between representatives of two countries, particularly unfortunate when they were as great and friendly as were Great Britain and the Soviet Union. All that was necessary in order to avoid this sad state of friction was for British officials leaving the Soviet Union to get the censorship authorities in Moscow to look at their possessions; she understood that it was most inconvenient for them to take all their books

1 FR's wife Celeste Leila Beatrix Roberts, née Pasha (1906–90).
2 The poem is the second in the cycle *Cinque*.

and papers to the relevant Soviet institution – she had no doubt, and here she spoke officially, that were we, the British Embassy, to invite the Soviet authorities on to our precincts and to get them to look through and seal up the printed material to be taken out on the spot, the Soviet Government would have no objection to so convenient an arrangement. The Soviet censors could visit us once a week or more frequently if we so desired (like the barber, I suppose – perhaps the barber could be empowered to do it – the sources of authority must be precisely the same in both cases). Anyhow, I thanked her in my most flowery official language for this communication, which I promised to make known to the Embassy as soon as opportunity offered. She said that I was the highest official (*sic*) she had had the pleasure to encounter on this train for some time, and it was a delight to have had this friendly interchange of opinions on a subject which had given them much trouble in the past. She hoped that my representations would make all the difference between a state of continuing misunderstanding (I expect Bullard[1] or Benham or someone must have fallen foul of her fairly recently before) and that undisturbed harmony which both our countries so strongly desired. The whole scene was most affecting and a source of considerable interest both to my American fellow passenger, the two Russian majors also in the compartment and the three customs officials lined up outside. We shook hands before she departed and the three customs officials then proceeded to ransack the American's luggage in the most minute manner, removing the camera (which they replaced) and all copies of Russian newspapers other than those of Moscow, which he was taking for the Hoover Library[2] in California, such as the *Tashkent Pravda*, etc., since there is apparently a regulation forbidding the export of all but the 'central organs' from the USSR. He made the most tremendous protest with me as an interpreter, but it was of no avail and my original friend, the high-powered lady in charge of the entire train, reappeared and said, in effect, 'There. This is what happens when regulations are not complied with', and spoke to my American in cold and very competent English, pointing out that he had not a legal leg to stand on. She then dramatically pointed to me and said that my having armed myself with appropriate documents made my position very different from his, thus driving the [ ] wedge between Britain and America which, however, we found no difficulty in liquidating after she left us. He

---

1 Sir Reader (William) Bullard (1885–1976), British diplomat, Ambassador to Tehran in 1946 but formerly Consul-General in Moscow (1930) and Leningrad (1931–4). Bullard's diaries from this period were later published by his son and daughter-in-law as *Inside Stalin's Russia: The Diaries of Reader Bullard, 1930–1934*, ed. Julian and Margaret Bullard (Charlbury, 2000).

2 Former President Herbert Hoover (1874–1964) had established the Hoover Institution Library and Archives at Stanford University, California, in 1920 to create and house a collection of primary sources, especially ephemeral ones such as newspapers, on the conflicts and political movements of the age; by documenting war he hoped to promote peace.

was a nice man and a liberal-turned-Fascist-beast, anyway, and lent me some money in Stockholm after I had lent him some in Leningrad, so our relations remained very cloudless. There may be something in the lady's suggestion about pre-censorship on the Embassy ground; anyway, I have now formally communicated with you on the subject.

After this there is nothing notable to relate except that Stockholm was indecently full of everything, and Paris (which I was allowed to visit)[1] seemed like a tomb – clean, beautiful, empty and silent, fearfully depressing, I thought. [. . .]

Here I find everything vastly changed from when I left in July. Truman's stock, which was soaring then, is now pretty low. There isn't that boiling indignation with which Roosevelt used to be assailed, but a kind of awful hard-hearted cynical disillusioned acceptance of machine politics and the poor perplexed little man of the White House. Byrnes is thought to be too much of a compromiser, but with the exception of our colleague Shadow,[2] nobody here in the Embassy thinks that he is anglophobe, although he has obviously been rubbed up the wrong way by Bevin.[3] Lord Halifax, who is very shrewd in such matters, says that in his presence he feels that matters float around him in a vague way and nothing is ever said with great distinctness or sharpness, but that if you treat him like an affable Senator, assume he doesn't know much about what his Department is doing, and talk to him in a man-to-man pseudo-intimate way, he melts easily and one can come to terms, and if you keep him up to the mark he keeps to his side of the bargain fairly well.

The State Department seemed in a very demoralised state largely because there is not much contact between Byrnes, [Ben] Cohen and Acheson[4] on the one hand and the departmental specialists on the other. Durbrow[5] is very exercised about Turkey, Persia, etc.,[6] but doesn't think

---

1 To see Patricia de Bendern.

2 Possibly a nickname for a member of the Embassy staff, alluding to a long-running American radio programme, The Shadow, which featured a mysterious hero who used his powers of remaining unseen in defence of law and order.

3 Ernest Bevin (1881–1951), Labour politician; General Secretary, Transport and General Workers' Union, 1921–40; Minister of Labour and National Service 1940–5; Secretary of State for Foreign Affairs 1945–51.

4 Dean Goodenham Acheson (1893–1971), lawyer, secretary to Justice Louis Brandeis 1919–21, Under-Secretary of the Treasury 1933, Assistant Secretary of State 1941–5, Under-Secretary of State 1945–7.

5 Elbridge Durbrow (1903–97), US diplomat, delegate to 1944 Bretton Woods Conference, head of SD's Eastern European Division 1944–6.

6 Turkey and Persia (Iran) were seen by the Western powers as important barriers against the further spread of Communist influence, and Soviet ambitions in the area aroused increasing speculation and concern during 1946. The key issue in the case of Turkey was the Soviet demand for revision of the 1936 Montreux Convention, whereby Turkey controlled the strategically and commercially vital Bosphorus and Dardanelles straits, so as to give the USSR

he can get his anxieties across to the top. Bill Bullitt asked me if the Turks thought we should stand by them. I said that I had no idea what went on in the minds of HMG but speaking for myself alone I supposed that we should.[1] He then promised, speaking for himself, that the Americans would in that event support us. Bullitt is not in the government or trusted much by anyone now. Nevertheless, I think what he says is truer today than it was even a fortnight ago.

Stalin's speech[2] shook them all surprisingly, and all the weathervanes, Lippmann, Swing, Shirer[3] etc., who before were talking of mediation and twisting our tail for unbridled imperialism, are now either, like Lippmann, wanting to take up a firm position vis-à-vis the Soviet Union, e.g. by acquiring a territory in the Eastern Mediterranean, preventing Russia from going to Tripoli, and generally talking tough, or at least complaining that Russia had once more destroyed their hopes and that maybe, after all, an alignment with the British in defence of the Western world was inevitable. All this seems very healthy to me, and Uncle Joe seems to have performed a considerable service to us by his latest frank utterances. They are still most anxious not to seem to 'underwrite the British Empire' and simply follow in our wake, but if they can perceive themselves that their own interests are being menaced by what goes on in, say, Turkey or China, they will react in a really useful manner. We, I suppose, have too obvious an axe to grind to influence them much directly, and Joe Davies[4] writes notes to HE wanting

joint control over the straits. Further alarm had been caused in the West by the Soviet refusal to withdraw their forces from Iran, which they had occupied jointly with Britain since 1941 on the understanding that they would leave within 6 months of the end of the war. The issue had been raised at the UN in January: the Soviet troops finally left in May, but only after Iran had granted the USSR extremely favourable oil concessions.

1 On the day this letter was written a two-day debate on foreign policy had opened in the British Parliament, during which Bevin expressed his desire for a cordial friendship with the USSR for all time – but also declared (with reference to revision of the Montreux Convention) that he did not want Turkey to become their satellite State.

2 On 9 February, at the Bolshoy Theatre in Moscow, Stalin had given a speech which alarmed the Western powers by its uncompromising defence of the Soviet system and its aggressive stance towards international capitalism, including this assertion: 'The development of world capitalism proceeds not in the path of smooth and even progress but through crisis and the catastrophes of war.' In the light of the speech the SD asked George Kennan to provide an analysis of current Soviet foreign policy; the result was the famous 'Long Telegram' (623/2), which set the tone for the mutual suspicion verging on paranoia which would characterise US–Soviet relations during the cold war.

3 William Lawrence Shirer (1904–93), author, journalist, broadcaster, foreign correspondent for the *Chicago Tribune*, Universal News Service and CBS, best known for his reporting from Berlin in the years before and during the war, and later for his book *The Rise and Fall of the Third Reich* (NY and London, 1960).

4 Joseph Edward Davies (1876–1958), lawyer and diplomat, naively sympathetic ambassador to the USSR 1936–8, Ambassador to Belgium and Minister to Luxembourg 1938–9, Chairman, President's War Relief Control Board, 1942–6.

to know why we can't all get around the table and compose our basic differences and compromise on our basic security needs.

Truman is right out of the whole picture on this and leaves it all to Byrnes and the Senators. Vandenberg[1] told an American Brigadier I know that he thought military government in Germany was an absurdity and the soldiers had better withdraw, but this [view] is not shared by either State or War Department here. The State Department specialists, i.e. Chip and all his friends, take exactly the same view as George Kennan[2] and all the people you know in Moscow, and there there is no basic difference of view with us. If only Bevin or someone could get on slightly easier personal terms – as Winston seems to have done with Byrnes down in Florida this weekend[3] – a great deal of unnecessary suspicion and friction could be eliminated.

Meanwhile I get the feeling that the Middle East is shaping up in the same sort of way as the Balkans and China – the inevitable Tito–Mihailovich pattern[4] – [ ] peasants, discontented intellectuals, corrupt landowners, soldiers and priests will lead to popular discontent, at first 'elemental', then

1 Arthur Hendrick Vandenberg (1884–1951), lawyer, newspaper editor and publisher, Republican Senator from Michigan 1928–51, leading isolationist who reversed his position in 1945, supporting the founding of the UN. Delegate to UN conference, San Francisco, 1945, to UN General Assembly 1946.
2 George Frost Kennan (b. 1904), Soviet specialist, political analyst and diplomat, at the time US chargé d'affaires in Moscow, best known for development of 'containment' policy against Soviet expansion. On 22 February Kennan was to send from Moscow to Byrnes in the SD the 8000-word so-called 'Long Telegram', which argued that there could be 'no permanent peaceful coexistence' with current Soviet policy towards the West. It was to become one of the most influential documents of the cold war, and has been published in *Foreign Relations of the United States 1946*, vol. 6: *Eastern Europe; The Soviet Union* (Washington, DC, 1969), 696–709; the quoted phrase appears on p. 697.
3 Churchill, out of power since his defeat in the 1945 general election, had been in the US since January. He had spent the previous weekend in Florida with James Byrnes and Bernard Baruch, discussing among other things the speech which Churchill, at Truman's invitation, was to deliver on 5 March in Fulton, Missouri. This speech proved to be one of the most famous, and most controversial, of Churchill's career. In it he used again (see 581/2) what was to become the classic cold-war image of an 'iron curtain' that had descended over Europe, and proposed a 'fraternal association of the English-speaking peoples' as the way to preserve world peace and democracy in the face of the Communist threat: op. cit. (336/7), vol. 7, pp. 7290, 7289. Although the speech aroused opposition among those (both in the US and abroad) anxious to preserve the wartime alliance with Stalin, and doubtful about the imperialist overtones of Churchill's 'fraternal association', it was indicative – like Kennan's 'long telegram' – of the growing distrust of Soviet intentions which marked the onset of the cold war.
4 Josip Broz Tito (1892–1980), né Josip Broz, Communist statesman from Croatia, Prime Minister (1945–53) and later (1953–80) President of Yugoslavia; led the Communist partisans against the Nazi occupation after the Axis invasion of Yugoslavia (1941), but also (after initial uneasy co-operation) against the Chetniks, the Serb-dominated royalist guerrilla movement under army officer Dragoljub ('Draza') Mihailovic (1893–1946). The Allies initially backed Mihailovic, but switched their support to Tito as the more effective resistance leader, and after reports of Chetnik collaboration with the Axis forces. Mihailovic was captured by the Partisans in 1946, charged with treason, and executed.

got hold of by a small determined group of ruthless Communist incorrupt-ibles, the huge middle mass will have a choice of either the discredited old right or the grim extremist left, and will on the whole go left because of the patent impossibility of going right, with us caught in between as usual, propping up either the affable and sometimes high-minded and decent Effendis or a knock-kneed liberal centre, and the Soviet Union doing the obvious from its point of view. The Foreign Office has, I know, schemes for mild [subsidy?] of the Middle East, but the Treasury says we have no money and what we have must go to other needs, UK, colonies, British trade with its old customers, payment of liabilities, etc. At that rate the few years which history has given us, since the Middle East is not falling to pieces in the Balkan way yet and the Russians have as yet no material welfare to offer it, will be frittered away in routine support of our 'friends', who are doomed to extinction by economic and social forces anyway.

I must not go on and preach you a sermon or write you a memorandum on this, an obvious subject, but unless we can harness American resources to promote a New Deal in the Middle East and so offer them a method of rapid development superior to and swifter than anything the Union can offer them now, I cannot see how they can fail to penetrate our positions. After all, the holding-off operation – 'non-[ ]' in Turkey or Persia – cannot go on indefinitely against their push, and our positive ideas seems very meagre at the moment. Perhaps Sir A. C. K[err][1] will be able to stimulate them here to something imaginative.

I gave your love to Michael [Wright?] and Jock and Roger Makins, and they all send theirs to you, in particular Roger – in the Foreign Office, too, they all spoke with the greatest warmth of you – I have a notion that they will need you in London in the not too distant future if they are to hold the machine from coming apart at the seams.

I hope your new Ambassador[2] is learning nicely and believing what he is shown. I am sure that with you and George Bolsover[3] there, no ambassador is humanly capable of straying far from the glaring facts, if facts may be said to glare – they certainly do in Russia.

It all seems remarkably remote and unreal here. The Americans are frightfully worried and keep on wondering when war is coming. Do please write a juicy dispatch before I am gathered to my fellow dons in April. I still long and long to know what the reaction is e.g. to the arrest of the spies[4] in

1 Who had just been transferred from Moscow to the Washington Embassy as Ambassador in succession to Halifax.
2 Sir Maurice Drummond Peterson (1889–1952), previously British Ambassador to Turkey, had replaced Archibald Clark Kerr in Moscow in January.
3 George Henry Bolsover (1910–90), 1st Secretary, British Embassy, Moscow, 1943–7.
4 On 15 February the Canadian authorities had arrested a number of people on suspicion of

Canada and so does everyone here.

Thank you once more for all your manifold kindnesses – I am grateful to you for remembering my wish to go back in summer – and my love to Cella. I hope to write to Moore and Edward [Tomkins] separately one of these days.

TO ANGUS MALCOLM

20 February 1946 [*carbon*]

British Embassy, Washington

Your letter was most infinitely welcome. Cabbage patch or no, I continue to have the most passionate memories of Italy, towards which I feel somewhat, I am afraid, as the Germans probably do, i.e. a mixture of fearful nostalgic *sehnsucht*[1] and juvenile enthusiasm. Indeed, despite the unreliable character of the inhabitants, I think I could live there much more happily than e.g. in France, where I admire almost everything and like practically nothing.

But in general I am dazed with too much impressions too rapidly absorbed. First Washington, then London, then Berlin, then Moscow, and Stockholm, then Paris, then London, then Washington again. Moscow is fantastic, and tiresome though it sounds, the essence can scarcely be grasped unless one (a) stays there, (b) knows enough of the language to discover what the inhabitants say in streets and buses. I cannot, alas, get away from specious analogies, but what the Soviet Union seemed to me most like was the severe type of English public school – say Wellington. It isn't a prison or a reformatory because that depends to some degree upon the feeling of the inmates, who feel hideously confined but not exactly imprisoned. But everything else falls too neatly into the familiar categories. The school is divided into houses which are not allowed to intercommunicate too much without special permission. The boys are cold and hungry, but, as in school, they expect to be cold and hungry, and although they may not like it, they take it as part of school life. They are very proud of the strength and prestige of the establishment and Lenin is Dr Arnold[2] who started a new idea in schools (let it be Rugby, then).

spying for the USSR. Further arrests were to follow, making a total of 39 suspects of whom 18 were convicted, including a Canadian MP and the British nuclear scientist Alan Nunn May. This followed the defection from the Soviet Embassy in Ottawa in September 1945 of Igor Gouzenko, a cipher clerk and intelligence agent. Gouzenko brought with him documents proving the existence of a large spy ring in Canada, an alarming discovery for Western governments, hitherto unaware of the scale of Moscow's espionage operations.

1 'Longing'.

2 Dr Thomas Arnold (1795–1842), English educator and historian; Fellow of Oriel 1815–19;

The press is exactly like a school magazine, which, after all, you would not expect to discuss let alone criticise the head master and the masters, and it confines itself to reports of matches won, school events, the latest jolly outing of the Field Club, an occasional gentle 'self-criticism' – *The Wings of a Dove* was sung none too well last week, something must really be done about the tenors, although the basses are not too bad – you do get in the Soviet press occasional references to e.g. the fact that three trainloads of demobilised soldiers have been forgotten somewhere between Odessa and Rostov and had actually frozen to death – this really must not be allowed to happen again.

Marxism is like a school of religion, early morning services for which the boys are allowed to turn out in the bitterest weather. It may not mean very much to most of them and they may dislike attending, but if it were suddenly abolished they would feel a loss of prestige and emptiness and mind not being like other schools. Everything is out of bounds, but if you can get permission to go away for a night or two, that is very sought after and envied.

Politics is exactly like sex at school – discussion of the subject except in the most conventional terms is forbidden, everyone talks about it a little on the sly, if you are caught doing it you not only are but expect to be punished, and the threat of punishment is precisely what makes such forbidden fruit particularly attractive and exciting.

The boys do not exactly believe in the principles of their school with passionate conviction, but they largely take them for granted and acquiesce. Life is really quite tolerable for the conformist majority and hell for the eccentric and sensitive who at worst are expelled – as this happens only in the cases of the most flagrant offences, such a thing is scarcely ever discussed and regarded as too awful to be mentioned except in a whisper by the braver boys.

And so on. One could go on developing this like all other facile similes. There appears to be no particular mystery about their [ ] and promises. To the perpetual question 'Where will they stop?' the proper answer is 'Where they are stopped by the others' – at present they are rolling down a rough but steeply inclined plane, but if a serious obstacle occurred they would stop there with more or less good humour.

Their attitude towards the British Empire seems to me as it might be

innovative Headmaster of Rugby School 1828–42; concurrently Regius Professor of Modern History, Oxford, 1841–2. Arnold transformed the status of Rugby as a school: his reforms were widely copied and his outspoken commitment to liberal Anglicanism influenced the ethos of the English public school system for generations.

[towards] rheumatism – the German war was something like typhus – high temperature, fear of death, a crisis when they did nearly perish, then slow recovery, all very dramatic and tremendous, during which other ailments are forgotten. England is an old chronic complaint: every day in the afternoon in the left knee and the left leg below the kneecap, tiresome, annoying, not bad enough to go to bed with, probably incurable and madly irritating but not necessarily likely to lead to a really serious crisis unless complications set in.

But I do not mean to write you a political summary, although it is obviously a habit too obsessive to get out of easily. Anyway, I am only here for another few weeks to round things off and then on 1 April, All Fools' Day, back I am in the academic groves as if no political problems existed and Senator Vandenberg were not the centre of intense unceasing interest. I went through Oxford this last time, and I cannot describe to you how alluring it still seems, no Congress, no Zionists, no files, and no appalling discretion about practically everything, which ultimately must make one guarded with oneself, which God forfend. I shall be there in April and surely you will come home on leave [then] or thenabouts. Come to Oxford, and I promise to take your mind off the fearful welter in which you obviously live, with the decent and the scrupulous continually yielding before the shock tactics of the bad and bold.

Here, the situation has really degenerated into the honest Harding[1] regime which even those who predicted it did not really believe would come about – but I musn't slip back into my official patter. Paris I did see, and that seemed ominously dead and empty, and Berlin is a lunar spectacle, and Joe Alsop tells us all to put on sackcloth and ashes and lament for a world which is doomed, doomed, doomed. If so I prefer the relative euthanasia of Oxford.

Please come and see me soon.

TO SUSAN MARY PATTEN

26 February 1946 [*carbon*]

British Embassy, Washington

Dear Susan Mary,

I was more than sorry to miss you in Paris, and as I was told firmly that Bill was also away – I was given the precise date and manner of your joint departure, perhaps altogether fictional – I did not see him during my 36 or so hours. I cannot say how depressed I was about that, for I can think of no one who would be more amused by some of the very odd and comic things of which I was the none too unhappy victim. Moreover, Paris seemed terrifying

1 See 441/3.

to me – so cold and abnormally clean and empty and more beautiful than I have ever seen a city be – more so than Leningrad and I cannot say how much that means – but empty and hollow and dead, like an exquisite corpse; the metaphor is vile and commonplace but I can think of nothing else.

How I wish I could have talked about the extraordinary condition of the British Embassy to you – perhaps when I return to England for good at the end of March or beginning of April – to Oxford, for ever I hope – you will be passing through England or I shall be allowed to go to Paris again. I should then be able to describe to you my most enjoyable journey to London via Dieppe and Newhaven with the Lady D[iana] Cooper and the unforgettable moment (but do not say so to her) at luncheon in the pullman car on the English coast.[1]

Here everything has turned topsy-turvy and I feel like Rip Van Winkle. It does not need Joe to come daily and say doom, doom, doom – like the old gentleman in one of Peacock's novels,[2] who used to come in through the garden window saying, 'The devil is amongst us: have great wrath', and then drift out again. The President, who was so popular in July, now seems a pathetic figure; everything seems to be declining into a pseudo-normalcy, without the spirit and the violent irresponsibility of the mad '20s, into a kind of dead apathetic disenchantment fed on nostalgic memories of one kind or another (as in Evelyn Waugh's last book,[3] which seems to me to start so well and peter out into such vulgarity). I am sure that Walter Lippmann will soon follow Clare Luce[4] into the Roman Church, and I can see Arthur Krock's last confession – I should hate to be the priest who received him into the bosom of any faith.

[. . .] So you see how the prevailing atmosphere has got me down. If it were not for my beloved hosts the Bohlens,[5] I should go about spreading gloom and discontent among His Majesty's subjects abroad.

---

1 The conductor asked her for her ticket, which she either didn't have or couldn't find; she told him with some hauteur that this was so, and expected him to accept it without question; there was an argument, but in the end she was too much for him, and he had to admit defeat.

2 *Nightmare Abbey* (1818) by Thomas Love Peacock (1785–1866). The old gentleman is Mr Toobad, a 'Manichæan Millenarian', who utters at every opportunity the warning in Revelations 12: 'Woe to the inhabiters of the earth and of the sea, for the devil is come among you, having great wrath.' Episodes of the kind described by IB recur throughout the book – in chapter 5, for instance: 'The conversation was interrupted by the re-appearance of Mr Toobad, covered with mud. He just showed himself at the door, muttered "The devil is come among you!" and vanished.'

3 *Brideshead Revisited* (London, 1945).

4 Clare Boothe Luce (1903–87), editor, playwright, politician, journalist, diplomat, wife of publisher Henry Luce, Republican Congresswoman 1943–7, later (1953–6) US Ambassador to Italy. She became a Roman Catholic in 1946.

5 Chip Bohlen had married Avis Howard Thayer (1912–81) in 1935.

Please write to me – here if before the end of March; to New College, Oxford, if after – I should like to see you both very much.

TO MARIE AND MENDEL BERLIN

5 March 1946 [*carbon*]

[Washington]

Dear Pa and Ma,

I regret not to have written[1] but really there is absolutely nothing to say. I shall deliver my political lecture when I arrive, personal details there are none.

I am sailing I hope on the Queen Mary on 7 April from New York, which makes me slightly late for Oxford but not very. Shirts are remarkably difficult to get and colourless ones impossible but I shall do my best. Other items are being suitably looked after, so rest assured all is well under control and I have successfully avoided Cousin Apter to date. I may ring him up shortly before departure but that will be all.

Apart from one eccentric enquiry from a would-be relation named Simon, who assures me I had a grandmother called Rifka – I have rejected the attribution[2] – I have nothing amusing to report.

I am living with the Bohlens in peace and content.

Love,

TO AVERELL HARRIMAN[3]

26 March 1946 [*carbon*]

British Embassy, Washington

That monster of discretion, Chip, kept me in deadly ignorance of your new appointment until it was virtually out, and long after more privileged observers, such as the journalists, were in possession of that very valuable

1 In a letter (dated 4 March) which crossed with this, Marie Berlin complained of the total absence of letters since his departure from England (and hence of information about his return), and threatened 'No gossip until we get a nice letter.'

2 Too hastily: the would-be relation may have been Simon Ginsburg, son of IB's great-aunt Rivka Fradkin by her second marriage, and hence half-brother of Yitzhak Sadeh (see p. liii above).

3 William Averell Harriman (1891–1986), businessman, politician, diplomat, closely associated with the New Deal and the Democratic Party, Lend-Lease Co-ordinator, London, 1941–3, US Ambassador to the USSR 1943–46, to Great Britain April–October 1946, Secretary of Commerce 1946–8.

and vastly encouraging fact. I need not tell you what a splendid thing I think this is and how fortunate for both London and Washington – and, indeed, although I doubt whether they will see it in the same light, Moscow too. I am sure, if you will forgive me for saying so, that you must yourself know that of all possible representatives of the USA you are virtually alone in possessing both the required understanding of the issues and the moral insight into the factors and personalities responsible for the future both of Russia and of England, not to speak of the USA. Long may you hold this appointment to the pleasure and advantage of everyone concerned. Everyone here is genuinely glad to hear this news, with not one dissentient voice.

PS I enclose a long and badly written report on Russian literature etc. which I am instructed to forward to you by Frank Roberts. I doubt whether there is anything in it that is either new or arresting – here only Jock Balfour has read it, in the Foreign Office I doubt if anyone will. It is confidential only because of the well-known consequences to the possible sources of the information contained in it, should its existence ever become known to 'them'. I should be grateful if you could return it to me via the Foreign Office bag addressed to New College, Oxford, in the dim recesses of which I shall think with some nostalgia but no regret of the world to which I do not think I shall ever be recalled.

I do really wish to send you my very best wishes for this very crucial task – how crucial you will know so much better than many of those to whom you are accredited.

A fortnight later IB returned to Oxford to take up his own post-war tasks.

FREEDOM

In the present century, more than ever before, it is true that men called themselves free but are everywhere in chains.[1]

I

IT IS IMPORTANT that this aspect of freedom be grasped: namely, that such terms as 'liberty' and 'bondage' are in no sense metaphors from the physical world transposed into the spheres of aesthetics and ethics, but that in ethics and aesthetics, in theology and art, 'slavery' and 'freedom' are terms which are contained in the essence of our conception of these things, and in every department of human activity the same antithesis will be found, like a great rift which divides the whole accumulated mass of human experience into two irreconcilable opposites.

To conceive the universality of this antithesis a large and unclouded objectiveness of vision is required, a remoteness from all purely local or national loyalties; hence it was not until Greece was politically enslaved that it discovered to the West the true nature of freedom in its universal sense: for the Stoics were the first Europeans to establish and propagate those twin principles which remained the bases of all Western conceptions of freedom. These principles Zeus brought with him from the Semitic East, but the West has claimed them for its own for upward of twenty centuries: they consist of the assertions that God or the Universe is consciously tending towards an ideally good state, and that Man's highest freedom consists in self-identification with that aim: the further he identifies his ends with those of the Universe, the nearer he comes to the Ideal of Absolute Good, the freer he becomes. For thereby he has emancipated his soul.

This conception belongs to the moralist's rather than to the politician's or economist's cosmogony; and here a radical difference, the difference between the ethical slave and the economic slave, arises before us, and must be clarified before we can proceed further in our enquiry.

The moralist asserts that one man who stands to another man in the relation of servant to master may yet be free in the full sense of the word. The economist, whose field of enquiry lies wholly in the region of 'circumstance', cannot admit that a man who serves anyone but himself, or

1 The subject assigned for the Truro Prize Essay, St Paul's School, 1928. IB's entry, 'abridged by kind permission' from a lost original, was published in a school magazine: 'The Truro Prize Essay (1928)', *Debater* No 10 (November 1928), 3, and No 11 (July 1929), 22 (with another version of this remark as a title). IB was eighteen when he wrote the essay.

the projection and enlargement of himself (e.g., his family or town or country, or humanity at large), is in any sense of the word free.

The differences between the modern economic world and the ancient are not of degree or kind; and it is well-nigh impossible to compare the new with the old where there are few common characteristics: we may, for instance, declare that the factory has made slaves of those who would have been free had there not been, as there were not in the pre-industrial world, any factories. And therein the world of our ancestors was presumably freer. And we may say parallelly that the institution of feudal serfdom has no counterpart amongst us, and then our times would seem to be more free. It is obvious that any attempt to weigh one against the other must, in this case, be futile and yield false results, because the feudal system and the factory system cannot be compared in any true and fruitful manner. On the other hand, no revolution has taken place in ethics which has affected the bulk of mankind as the Industrial Revolution has affected it: Truth and Goodness and Justice and Courage are essentially the same concepts to Professor Santayana to-day as they were to Shakespeare and Socrates. We venture to assert that Liberty, which undoubtedly belongs to the vital essentials of Moral Science, conjures up substantially the same image in thinkers old and new: that when Plato spoke of the ὄντως ἐλεύθερός τε καὶ καλὸς κἀγαθός[1] he meant by 'really free' not a democrat of his own time, but the same emancipated, Socratic spirit as that which Cervantes extolled, Rousseau preached, and Mazzini sought to create by means of countless essays and pamphlets and speeches. Here, then, we have found a common basis upon which to compare data, for though the methods of living have changed, the material of Life itself, and the apprehension of its values, is curiously similar in the new world and in the old.

II

Every great liberating movement in the history of human culture begins with a great burst of enthusiasm among whole strata of men, enthusiasm for the natural material which they discover around them, in the mood which Watts-Dunton has called 'The Renascence of Wonder'. Perhaps 'The Rediscovery of Unity' is a truer name. For what these men saw was, not a new world, but a synthesis of the parts in a whole, and the relations and proportions of the parts to each other and to the whole; thus in the creative work of the great sons of these epochs, no single devotion to one quality, and one only, will ever be found; neither Beauty nor Liberty nor Pure Might is ever raised to such gigantic proportions as to dwarf its fellow attributes,

---

1 'Man who is really free and a gentleman'. Untraced in Plato or elsewhere.

because to have done so were to have lied against their maker's vision of the Universe and its harmony. There were few freer men than Leonardo or Erasmus; neither panegyrised freedom, because to single it out and devote oneself to its especial pursuit were to lose it.

History seems to show that after every great creative era comes an age during which the great heritage is meticulously examined, divided, classified and labelled, in which the macrocosm is neglected for an infinity of microcosms which are credited with leading separate existences in it, and the wood is ignored because of the exquisite interest felt in the individual trees. The world has not altered in its component parts: but it has lost that which made them an organism, which gave them a common life and purpose. The research of scholars becomes exquisitely fine and exquisitely unimportant because the true nature of the various members cannot be apprehended if the fact that they form an organism be forgotten. The typical sons of the age (the eighteenth century) who thought themselves more and more advanced on the path of Progress and Freedom, the more closely they scrutinised the minutiae of Life, became more and more closely bound by these minutiae; they ceased to look upon Life as material to be moulded, but were dominated and moulded by it. Then came the reaction. Rousseau, however wildly he blundered, spoke with the full authority of the entire human experience behind him when he cried that 'Falseness and slavery are eventually one and the same; freedom and truth can be found only in a return to Nature.'[1]

It remains for us to consider whether our age is the Alexandrine aftermath of the nineteenth century, and, if it be so, what are the symptoms and peculiarities of its particular bondage.

III

No luxury and no comfort, no delight and no pleasure, no new liberty and no new discovery, no praise and no flattery, which we may enjoy on our journey will mean anything to us if we have forgotten the purpose of our travels, and the end of our labours.

Emerson[2]

History moves not in continuous straight lines, but in folds. These folds are not of equal length or substance, but if we venture to examine the points in which these folds touch one another, we will often find strong and real similarities between the points. If we attempt to look through our own age at the layers which are, as it were, in a vertical line below it, we shall see the eighteenth century, and the Roman world in the third century AD, and the

1 Apparently an extrapolation rather than a direct quotation. The fullest discussion of slavery by Rousseau can be found in his *Social Contract*, book 1, chapter 4.
2 Untraced.

Alexandrine culture in the third century BC; the comparison must not be pressed too hard, but the resemblance between these periods and ours is peculiarly profound and precise in this, that the spirit of slavery and convention rests on all.

Convention does not in itself imply slavery; it is largely that instinctive law that arises out of men's fear of anarchy, which is as far removed from freedom as tyranny itself. In this function convention is often a safeguard of inner liberty, creating as it does a broad external disciplinary equality which leaves room for complete inner non-conformity. It hurts no man to conform if he knows that conformity is only a kind of manners, a sort of universal etiquette. It was so, as far as we can judge, in the sixteenth century in Europe, during the Athenian Renaissance in Greece, in the two centuries surrounding the birth of Christianity in Palestine, that is, largely, unconscious and unnoticed. The rebels Giordano Bruno, Euripides, St Paul, bitterly though they attacked the bases of current morality, yet markedly adhered to the current conventions of their age; Euripides accentuates the rigid formalities of Athenian drama; St Paul observed the law all his days; this could happen because they rebelled in an essentially free age; men were not afraid to look ideals in the face, however vast and comprehensive they might be. It is only when the comprehensive ideal is lost sight of, the intellectual and ethical horizon narrows, and inner liberty is lost, that concrete convention grows disproportionate, looks on by force, as it were, of inertia, and having lost all harmony with the inner activity of society, becomes meaningless and stationary; that which was itself but the fences of freedom, a personal importance. The tool begins to be regarded as the treasure. Then it is that the rebels raise their voices in protest; for by this time convention has come to articulate human slavery as loudly as before it expressed the presence of human freedom. The outcry against the tyranny of convention is one of the surest signs of a diseased state of a culture; it means that men are neither in harmony with themselves, nor with their surroundings, that they obey these surroundings, though they cannot understand the real relationship between themselves, their surroundings and the mutual ultimate aim, simply because otherwise they must perish. Without the final purpose their existences become essentially ephemeral, they are at life's mercy, and obey it blindly and miserably that they may live yet another day. The struggle for material existence submerges all other desires and tendencies; in men, as in animals, the dominant motive becomes the desire to live. And this is the deeply-rooted characteristic of the slave.

The eighteenth century suffered this degeneration, but our own age seems to be afflicted by a far more virulent form of it. What Locke and Newton commenced Spencer and Huxley deepened and developed; the eighteenth century preserved a shadow of universal purpose in its deism, such as it was; the modern rationalistic universe is purged even of the shadow; the materialistic philosopher of our days delights in expelling every vestige of purposive, free co-ordination from the world; in destroying all possible illusion that, in any respect save the purely concrete, the universe is an organism and not a piece of machinery. The psychologists intensify this confession of bondage; on the one hand Freud, on the other Bergson (who seldom otherwise agree), insist that conscious human activity is largely determined by influences which operate unconsciously, and which are the products of impressions unconsciously or subconsciously imbibed. Over his subconscious mind, man has ordinarily little or no control, so that in addition to being dominated by external circumstance, there would seem to exist an internal mechanism which obtains equally implicit obedience; those biologists who emphasise the irresistible influence of heredity, based on Mendelian principles, make this mechanism even more despotic. The slave is bound with yet another chain.

This view of the mechanical universe is the boldest and the most merciless self-depreciation which man ever enunciated. It is not surprising, therefore, if few are found to pursue its premises relentlessly to their rational conclusion; for courage – and ruthless introspection of this kind, when it is not merely morbid, requires high, if perverted, courage, – is not a servile quality. So, when faced with the spectacle of a tyrannous universe, which is far worse than hostile, which is insensible, many of its slaves chose, as slaves will, to forget it in sheer weariness, in so far as they could, to do their task with closed eyes in an, as it were, spiritual intoxication, and, having ridded themselves of the consciousness of the external world, to conjure up images of a more harmonious existence, or, if not harmonious, at least sensible and endowed with organic life. The first originated that wave of theosophic mysticism which is at present sweeping the world; the second, who expressed themselves chiefly in art, inherited the traditions of the Romantics (who were free because they were denied the earth), and created distorted semblances of freedom in the works of many Impressionists and Futurists and Cubists and Symbolists. Both ways of escape, that of art and that of religion, became too easily ways of bondage. This hungry quest for liberty outside the confines of common humanity is one of the most pathetic pieces of evidence of human degradation, of the darkening of its spirit. It was not unrelieved; men arose, such as Van Gogh and Rodin, who consciously rebelled against the surrounding slavery; but whereas great men, even great rebels, in free ages, however greatly they tower above the common herd, are nevertheless sublime embodiments of the common type; in enslaved ages such men stand strange and solitary, like beings from another epoch.

We do not wish to imply that mysticism, and every form of what we may call 'other-worldliness', are in themselves signs of the decadence and slavery of the age; in every age there are men out of harmony with its spirit, who create their own worlds. Nor are they the least honoured among the representation of the age; Germany is proud of its Meister Eckhart, and England of William Blake. It is the sudden and rapid spread and wide extent of what is, after all, an essentially anti-social phenomenon that points to a degeneration. When great companies of human beings find the outer world unfit to work in, find it, moreover, oppressive and false and dead (i.e. mechanical), then we must conclude that they are in the position lamented by the Latin poet. 'Propter vitam vivendi perdere causas';[1] that the material which was theirs to mould, moulds and subdues them, and that because they have forgotten the distinctions between ephemeral psychical concrete circumstance and perpetual spiritual values, they have forgotten the terminology of free men, and have begun to apply their titles, which can apply only to their slavish conceptions, to ancient and free doctrines; the conviction of unreality which the true, free mystic held about life, about the world of space and time, has, in their hands, been allowed to invade the very spirit by whose power alone the external world could be convicted of unreality. Thus, communists today call Plato to their aid, and refuse to realise that what Plato wished to see was a society of which each member was so far spiritually developed that he did not need the physical independence to assert his individuality, and could sacrifice such liberty – the mere husk of freedom – wholeheartedly, without regret, to the common weal. This was, *mutatis mutandis*, the ideal of the Essenes and of the medieval monastic Orders. It was in all cases an apotheosis of the spiritual freedom of men. What the modern communist stresses is the exact opposite; the overwhelming, and indeed, exclusive importance of the physical or economic life, and the sacrifice of its independence to the community, expressly so that individualism might be utterly eradicated, that all things should at once be concreticised and nationalised.

'Les extrêmes se touchent',[2] but in words alone. Platonic, Hebrew, Christian communism denies freedom to the concrete, and exalts in the spiritual world; modern economic communism reduces the spiritual to complete dependence on concrete freedom, and then condemns it in the individual. Communism is therein different from non-political forms of slavery, that it does consciously regard convention as a treasure and not a tool; it looks on its chains with open eyes, and raises them into an ideal. The others, as we have attempted to show, strive to ignore them.

1 Juvenal, *Satires* 8. 83: 'to lose the reasons for living for the sake of staying alive'.
2 'Extremes meet' (proverb).

The world is divided into the two camps; those who, be they Russian Communists, American industrialists, or Italian Fascists, work to achieve an essentially collectivist State, whose dominant characteristics shall be equality and impersonality, who must be opposed to individual freedom as being, in a *mechanical* world, a disruptive, because centrifugal, force, and who, since they cannot break their chains, will worship them; and those who strive at all costs to preserve their personal spiritual ego, even though it should mean a total abdication of their rights as citizens of any human polity, and a wilful self-blinding to their actual condition. By constant repetition to themselves that in reality they are free, they have succeeded in persuading themselves that their chains are, if not totally non-existent, yet really incidental and somehow unimportant. By dint of not moving, not grasping at any vital ideal, by remaining quite motionless, the chains may be slackened until they are hardly felt at all. Therefore, let us sit quite still and lull ourselves into a torpid sleep, and, perhaps, we may dream of freedom, and be happy yet. The two camps are far removed from each other; but one characteristic they have in common, and that is that both are equally bound with chains. 'Freedom', said Aristotle, 'is a mean between two extremes: slavery and licence';[1] slavery, which is the product of tyranny imposed from outside, whether by man or circumstance, and licence, which is slavery which comes of tyranny imposed from within by passing fears and desires. Both deny eternal standards, within or without. These are the two struggling forces, which, between them, have subdued the greater part of the civilised world; whether from their strife a new unity and freedom will be born, and a new Renaissance of the human spirit come about in our days, none can tell; for destructive and disintegrating forces die slowly. But as to the eventual issue there can be no doubt, or there is no truth in poetry or religion. And to deny them is to deny the accumulated inner experience of mankind as an empty illusion, and to stultify its whole existence in the world.

I. M. BERLIN

---

1 Another extrapolation, it seems: from *Politics* 5. 9, 1310a25–36.

REPORTS FOR FABER & FABER

IB's reports[1] for Faber & Faber appear together here as an appendix rather than in their chronological position in the main text, for reasons explained on page 37 above.

TO GEOFFREY FABER

4 January 1932 [*manuscript*]

49 Hollycroft Avenue

Dear Mr Faber,

I must apologise for delaying my reply for so long. Your secretary sent me 'Das Ende des Kapitalismus'[2] about a fortnight ago and said that you wanted me to read it and give my opinion as to whether it was worth translating into English. The book interested me greatly, I read it carefully and I am glad of an opportunity of saying something about it, but I must confess to two shortcomings which are bound to detract from the value of anything I may say: my knowledge of German is not perfect, and I probably miss all the finer nuances; and my acquaintance with sociology is distinctly slight: two facts which I must ask you to discount fairly heavily against any conclusions I have to report. Having owned to this I can start with a clear conscience.

The first and strongest impression which the book makes is that of a vigorously, earnestly, and not overscrupulously written pamphlet. Someone once told me that Ferdinand Fried was the name not of an individual, but of a group of semi-intellectual littérateurs with Nazi sympathies who between them write the 'Tat', a nationalist periodical. I do not know whether this is true; but if it is it explains a good deal. It explains all the inconsistencies in the book, notably the central and glaring contradiction which must offend anyone who reads the book – on the one hand there is an unconditional wholesale acceptance of Marxio-Sombartian premises with regard to the

1 I have deliberately treated IB's reports as if they were academic publications: that is to say, I have not annotated them exhaustively, which would, it seemed, be even more open to the charge of heavy-handedness than some of the annotation of the letters.

2 'The end of capitalism'. This book by (Ferdinand) Friedrich Zimmermann (1898–1967) was published in Jena in 1931 under the pseudonym 'Ferdinand Fried'. It was turned down by Faber, who paid IB one guinea for his report, and was not translated into English. Fried was a German journalist and author specialising in economic affairs, who in the late 1920s and early 1930s was closely associated with the journal *Die Tat*, at that time an influential exponent of Nazism; he also became a member of the SS.

death of individualism, growth of mass production, collectivism etc., and from these the natural conclusion is drawn that since collectivism is coming anyway, it might as well be dealt with efficiently and fairly by being converted from Trust-collectivism into State-ownership of the means of production. All this is of course the most orthodox German Social-Democratic Marxism, nor is there anything original or peculiarly striking in either matter or manner of presentation. In contrast with this one unexpectedly comes across sudden explosions of individualist nostalgia: hatred of all mass production and organized labour, medieval romanticism expressed in terms which remind one of Chesterton at his very worst, stretches of sentimental yearning for the old days in which kitchen utensils, e.g., were not standardised but wrought with loving care by the master-craftsman, and bought no less lovingly by the individualist housewife. And now none of these things are any longer. Etc. etc. etc. and it is all the fault of capitalist enterprise which is the villain throughout.

One can obviously sympathise with the romanticisms of Chesterton or William Morris, but in a book which purports to be a scientific analysis of a sick world, this sort of ranting obviously cheapens the issues; and it is particularly surprising to meet with it after a long stretch of cool, realistic Marxism which prepares one for anything rather than sentimentality. But it becomes understandable if there is a real Homeric question here: if the book is by various hands, and only superficial agreement – a common hatred of big business or the like – is sought.

As against this very considerable fault one may balance the fact that the account of the actual economic position of Germany at the moment seems to be – to me at least who probably know no better – first class. It is clear, concise, overdramatic perhaps, but this is not a fault in a work which is obviously fervent and controversial, not sober and authoritative. The figures which are occasionally quoted, seem suspicious to me, but again I could not prove them wrong because I don't know enough about the sources; if they are correct they are very convincing.

Frequently – and this again is a fault – the argument sinks into the narrowest parochialism. Pages on pages are spent on tracing the fortunes of various scions of big business houses, a wealth of detail is provided, and masses of names which simply cannot interest non-Germans, and even to intelligent Germans this part of the book must seem uncommonly small change, almost City gossip. If the book is ever translated into English something will, I suggest, have to be done about this small talk.

The book is obviously written for Germany and not for the world: the collapse of capitalism is traced with anything like completeness in Germany alone: das Ende des Deutschen Kapitalismus would be a very much fitter title.

The economics of the book seem to me – and as I said before I am not very competent to judge – somewhat primitive. The author or authors obviously have no profound knowledge of the workings of e.g. international credit, the complexity of the subject and the technical knowledge required frightens them, so that a certain spurious simplification of issues is carried out which makes everything easier for writer and reader, but does violence to the facts. The same uneasiness in the face of the impenetrable maze of international exchange, coupled, of course with conviction of Germany's inability to pay Reparations, and a spirit of nationalism which is admitted to be irrational, inclines the authors to see the solution in a Central European Zollverein,[1] with vast tariff barriers against the rest of the world: the argument being that if you break off all economic relations with the creditor countries, you cease being dependent on them, and so can repudiate all debts & obligations with impunity; otherwise Germany will share the fate of Carthage.

I imagine that the figures, the arguments involving particular economic theories, and the solution offerred[2] could easily be pulled to pieces by any competent economist. But, (and this is the most important point which I wish to make), this is by no means a conclusive argument against the English publication of the book, for its strength and its importance lie in something different: It is the only adequate expression of the present state of the average middle-class German mind which I have ever come across, it is even more an ardent and characteristic account of the beliefs of that section of the average German intelligentsia which finds in Hitlerism an exaggerated form of its own sense of injury and indignation. As a contribution to knowledge, as a scientific prognosis, the book is very mediocre: it is clear and quite acute, but unoriginal and not outstanding in any way. But it is of the greatest importance as a psychological document, as an expression at a popular level of feelings and convictions, many of them founded on errors perhaps, but if so on widespread, and therefore 'important' errors, which every self-conscious German feels to some extent, and which are responsible for a great many of the phenomena to-day observable in Germany: the disappointment in and contempt for liberalism, the growth of Anti-Reason and authoritarianism alike in e.g. the Stahlhelm[3] and the Catholic revival, and much else. Other books have been written and translated – Schacht's book, or Einzig's indictment of French policy, or Wyndham Lewis's

1 Customs union.
2 *sic*: IB often misdoubled letters in his earlier years; cf. 12/2.
3 Association of ex-servicemen (literally 'Steel Helmet').

'Hitler':[1] but all these were books by individuals expressing an, on the whole, individual point of view: the last of these books, 'Hitler', was downright stupid in my opinion, explained nothing and was used by its author as an excuse for a particularly loud and pointless brawl. The other books were sensible, but written by experts. This book, however, differs from the others precisely in the fact that it is written for the widest public by someone whose intuitions and arguments and prejudices are approximately on the same level as those of his audience. And this makes it a peculiarly interesting document for the sociologist, the practical politician, and the intelligent reader.

I believe that if the book is to be published in England, it is advisable (1) to omit or modify the pages filled with excessively detailed descriptions of the economic adventures of families some of which must be obscure even in Germany, which is the sort of semi-private information that merely confuses and irritates foreign readers and (2) to add an English preface with the purpose of disarming many potential critics among the economists who might otherwise find the prey too easy; this can and ought to be done by pointing out that the importance of the book consists in its *representativeness*, in its clear and vigorous presentation of the intellectual and even emotional bases of pro-Nazi feeling among the decent sections of the population; what should be avoided above all (I feel this very strongly, but I simply am not a good enough economist to be able to defend my views successfully) is any advertisement of the book as a masterpiece of sociological dissection. It is broad but it is not deep, in places even transparently shallow.

With these qualifications and modifications, I think the book may be very well worth publishing: it is, if only from the popular way in which it is written, and from the obvious earnestness of its tone, fairly certain, I think, to find an extensive audience among the more intelligent people: and the immediate present is obviously the right moment for publication, both because the public for it is growing daily, and because its interest is ephemeral.

Your secretary mentioned the fact that various German critics had praised the book very highly. I confess that I am surprised: their attitude is understandable if they praised it as Germans, as patriots anxious to let everyone hear their grievances. It is more difficult to understand their praise in their capacity of critics: the intellectual inadequacies must be plain to anyone of moderate intelligence who is not blinded by sentiment; the only original argument (and that is not genuinely so, I believe) which I have been

---

1 Hjalmar Schacht, *The End of Reparations: The Economic Consequences of the War* (London, 1931); Paul Einzig, *The World Economic Crisis, 1929–31* (London, 1931); Wyndham Lewis, *Hitler* (London, 1931).

able to find runs thus: Capitalism depends on the expansion of individual enterprise: expansion depends on inventions: the era of great inventions is now definitely over (this last is stated as being self-evident), hence it follows that capitalism, being unable to grow, must die. This is an argument which is central in this book, and I wish to suggest that as an instance of acute perception of the state of things, it is, prima facie at least, a failure. The same lack of understanding is shown in the respectful terms applied to Spengler: he and the author of this book, and many of those who dabble in Kulturphilosophie in German to day are often merely diluting and cheapening the writings of Georg Simmel, whose influence they all recognize, who was a really great man, and whose excellent works still deserve to be translated into English far more than those of his epigoni. This is a very irrelevant digression and I apologise.

To end this excessively lengthy letter I should like to recapitulate: first I must repeat the warnings about my lack of expertness, and after that to give this as my considered opinion:

The book well deserves being translated, and ought to find a ready enough market if it is deparochialised and broadened, if it is understood to deal in reality with Germany alone, and with the rest of the world only as a background and source of analogies, if excessive claims are not made for it, if it is advertised as the only book in English which conveys at all adequately the full sense of indignation and the genuine idealism which lie behind German Nationalist movements, the only book which reveals the broad intellectual background of Naziism which is, for foreigners at least, obscured by the louder elements of xenophobia, antisemitism, and general ochlocracy which characterise all the public acts of the party, and finally a book which shows why Nationalism in Germany has become National-*Socialism* and not Fascism or the Lappo movement or any bourgeois conservatism. And this, I think ought to be sufficient to recommend any book.

I hope this does not arrive too late to serve your purpose.

I sincerely hope to have another opportunity of meeting you in Oxford sometime next term.

yours sinc.

I Berlin

15 January 1932 [*manuscript*]

n.p.

Report on 'Film als Kunst' by Rudolf Arnheim (Ernst Rowohlt Verlag, Berlin.)[1]

I have read the Times Lit. Sup. review[2] of this book, and, in my opinion, though it is very complimentary, it does not praise its virtues sufficiently, and, on the other hand, mentions no defects at all; and yet these latter, though they are the defects of virtues, exist, and ought to be remarked.

It is, as the T.L.S. says, a brilliant book. But it is very much more. It is a successful attempt to approach the film from every possible standpoint, to explore and correlate all its various constituents which tend to be treated separately from each other, & are to that extent distorted. It is monumentally painstaking, the author is obviously possessed of an intellectual integrity which drives him on to examine all avenues of approach, however he may dislike some of them personally, and to give reasoned and accurate accounts and refutations of views to which he is opposed, even the most banal and unintelligent, which other critics often do not stoop to, even if only to crush them. This depth & comprehensiveness of treatment gives this book almost unique value as a critical treatise.

It begins with and continues through a fairly lengthy analysis of the technical apparatus of film-making: the significance of every device is shown not only in its relation to the actual effect which the director wishes to produce, but together with a justification of that effect, with an explanation, that is, of what it is in the aesthetic purpose of the film which necessitates this effect, this device, and no other. The result of such a mode of treatment is that the technical exposition, which is a sine qua non of any book on films, and which tends to be treated as a necessary evil, is included reluctantly, and is allowed to be as boring as such expositions usually are, is in this book turned into a genuinely fascinating dissection of the film into its constituent factors carried out wittily, intelligently, often excitingly, for the benefit of a reader who is assumed to have seen films, to know nothing, but to be highly sensitive and intelligent. Nothing better could be desired: the discussion flows on lightly and pleasantly, nothing very original or revolutionising is said, but the whole context is so unfamiliar (to me at least)

---

1 Published in German in 1932, and in English as *Art as Film* by Faber in 1958.

2 'Art in the Cinema', *Times Literary Supplement*, 31 December 1931, 1052.

and attractively revealed, every page so teems with life and intelligence, that one is carried on and on, not in [the] least despite oneself, but on the contrary, with the best will in the world, into the depths of this delightful discussion. I do not wish to give the impression that this is merely the pleasing dallying of an enlightened dilettante: it is not Clive Bellish in the least: the author displays his wares very attractively, but the wares would be appreciated for their sheer intrinsic value even had they been more carelessly exhibited; I am merely trying to express the pleasure which I felt, and which I believe everyone else must feel, in finding that what one had been wanting to discover for so long, is here provided so intelligently so copiously, and yet with so light a touch.

I do not know how great a public there is for books on films: if it is not large – and I suspect it must be comparatively narrow – the fault is largely with the books so far provided for it in English. The only ones which I have seen are those by Paul Rotha, Miss Lejeune, and Pudowkin.[1] The first two are not overendowed with intelligence: Rotha is a narrow specialist who writes clumsily and not very coherently for his own small and technically minded milieu of experts. Miss Lejeune has written a book for the masses, but it makes no attempt to evaluate the film as a form of art: it is simply a catalogue of films she liked with reasons why they pleased her: a collection of critical articles with no attempt to connect them on any objective basis, to present them as illustrating the diverse phases of a phenomenon whose general nature has been previously analysed described, and evaluated. The result is unimpressive. As for Pudowkin's book, that concerns itself with Russian films alone, and though it is admirably written and is full of interest, its English translation is really execrable: nobody who reads it can conceive the excellence of the original. This brings me to the question of translation, which in the case of 'Film als Kunst' is really important. The book is very well written and, so far as I can see, would be bound to have an enthusiastic reception: but this depends to an enormous extent on how it is translated. The German, for all its occasional longwindedness which is inevitable in that language, is so nimble and alive, and derives its charm and acuteness so largely from the exact appropriateness of its metaphors and its adjectives, that a dull translator could kill it with the greatest ease. And that would seal the fate of the best foreign book of this type: it is written not meditatively and massively, as most German books on aesthetic theory, but with greatest liveliness: the subject is conceived by the author not as a corpse for post

1 Paul Rotha, *The Film Till Now: A Survey of the Cinema* (London, 1930), and/or *Celluloid: The Film To-day* (London etc., 1931); C. A. Lejeune, *Cinema* (London, [1931]); V. I. Pudovkin, *On Film Technique* (London, 1929).

mortem dissection, but as a burning question whose essence must be grasped rapidly and vigorously, and the answer to which is never final, but changes with every new formulation. A competent translator, however, who would not be hypnotised by the length and apparent unwieldiness of the German periods into similar excesses in English (in German the words have a lengthy rhythm & swing of their own, in English this is not reproducible), could, in my opinion, produce a book which would score a considerable success with the intelligent and the semi-intelligent public. I repeat once more that the question of style is here as vital as in the case of a novel.

The author does all he sets out to do with great determination and success: when he attacks problems which seem to him important, he succeeds in convincing the reader of their gravity: and where he turns satirist, his sting is very well aimed and the wit is mordant and entertaining. His examination of the ethical and sociological effects of, and beliefs entertained by the makers of, the average commercial film, of what he calls the 'Konfektions film', is serious in intention, but nevertheless extremely amusing. Throughout this section of this book, and indeed everywhere else a strong socialist bias keeps on reappearing: though this is not particularly welcome in a book on aesthetics, yet in the present temper of Germany, it is difficult to expect political or social detachment: and a great many of his political asides seemed to me to be borne out by the nature of the material examined, and to be in no sense gratuitous.

The book is admittedly lengthy: but a good book on this subject is so badly needed in England, and the ardour and vivacity of the author carry one at so rapid a pace that it is hardly a fault: the analysis of the fitting of means to ends (which is what the whole book is mainly about) is throughout masterly. And there is a spirit of 'objectivity' inherent in the book, a systematic adduction of evidence for every view expressed, which is bound to bring relief to a public which has been fed, in this country at least, very largely on the undefended expression of personal reactions by critics of dubious intelligence.

There are only two defects which I should like to put on record, and neither of these militates against the advisability of publishing it:

The first is comparatively slight, and consists in omissions of various characteristic developments of the film, as e.g. the French realistic film, silhouette films, etc. but the book is so full that perhaps it is absurd to cavil.

The second is a personal objection which may not be shared by people more competent than I to speak on such matters. It seemed to me that in a work so comprehensive, so anxious to establish the theoretical basis of the film before amplifying, & filling in the scheme with concrete detail, some attempt ought to have been made by the author to explain his view on aesthetics in general, on all art as such, and then only, after exhibiting the place, which in his opinion, the film occupies in the general scheme, to begin elaborating his particular thesis. Herr Arnheim explicitly forswears such a method: he is determined to start with no theoretical presuppositions at all and merely to record what he finds as & when he finds it. The approach is to be purely psychological, purely empirical and pragmatic. And this to me seems impossible: it is clear that every theorist presupposes something or other, however vague & general: the 'purely' psychological approach is an illusion: and it would be more helpful, & make the book architectonically more satisfying, if the author stated his premises instead of saying that there weren't any, i.e. letting him find out indirectly for himself.

But that is clearly a private objection and is perhaps irrelevant to this report.

Minor faults from an English point of view are also the tendency to dwell on German examples for illustration: but then so much interesting work has been done in Germany in film production, that it is, on the whole, unobjectionable to treat the problem Germanocentrically. Also the book has only one illustration: the author gives his reasons for this: relevant illustrations are difficult to obtain, and art-journals are anyhow so flooded with them that there is on the whole no dearth of them for those who want to see: to include pictures for their own sakes, is pointless: our age is said to suffer from a morbid craze for pictures & illustrations everywhere: to this passion of the mob the author refuses to pander. He is obviously justified in supposing (as, I think he must) that those whose interest in films is genuine do not, at this stage, need illustrations: while those who will not read such a book without them have no genuine interest in the subject, & would not read the book anyhow.

Finally I should like to repeat my impression of the book as very agreeable to read, very acute, intelligent and suggestive, abounding in stimulating theories, exceptionally detached and fair in its judgments, singularly free, for a German book, from any real axe-grinding or pet-theory mongering, and written by one intelligent man of wide culture for other unprofessionals like him. There is a complete absence of technical jargon, and the whole is written in a winged style which only a sensitive & skilled translator with a complete mastery of English can reproduce: provided this last condition is carried out, the book ought to find an eager market: and I therefore very strongly recommend it for publication.

I. Berlin

TO FABER & FABER

21 November 1932 [*Mendel Berlin's manuscript with additions by IB*]

49 Hollycroft Avenue

Report
Wages and Labour Policy by Hugh Gaitskell & I. Durbin[1]
by I. Berlin

I am afraid I have not been able to read this book with the attention it deserves, owing to the fact that I was taken ill while reading it. Also I am not a professional economist and cannot trust myself to make significant judgements about it from that point of view.

It seemed to me a very readable book, written in a language which, although it is not over-technical, cannot be called popular either. Some elementary knowledge of economics is necessary in order to be able to understand it; it is a lucid and forcible presentation of the case against the policy of gradual establishment of socialism by means of wage-raising policies on the part of Labour Governments or Trade Unions, or indeed any policy of gradualism. It is divided into three parts: in the first part, Mr Gaitskell examines various theories of the relation of capital and wages from the standpoint of pure economic theory, and also the probable effects of rises and falls in the wage & price levels – this is done very clearly without any conspicuous originality, as it might be in any competent textbook on Economics. In this part, as indeed in the whole book, Marxism is skated over far too lightly. Considering the multitude of variant interpretations of it, too much seemed to me to be taken for granted. In the second part, Mr Durbin examines current theories of the relation between wages, saving, investment and purchasing power, this not from a theoretical standpoint, but with a view to seeing whether the capitalist system is as inwardly rotten and moribund as it is often said to be, and reaches the conclusion that it is not, and unless steps are taken to kill it, it will not die, but may have many more years of successful life.

In the third part (the specific author is not mentioned) an attempt is made to prove that nothing short of a definite social revolution (although its difficulties are stressed) can establish socialism in England. This part seems to be less well argued and altogether less impressive than the other two, which strike one with the impartiality of their reasoning, [the] openness of their socialist bias and their freedom from the conventional patter of socialist publicists.

---

1 In fact Evan Durbin (433/2); apparently the book was not published.

The book interested me personally, from which I conclude that it may interest others like me, of whom there must be a fair number scattered up and down universities and colleges. On the other hand, since I read very little current economic literature I do not know how many other such books hold the field already: the most attractive quality of the book is the clear insistence on the part of the authors that the ground of their socialism is belief in equality and the necessity of redressing social injustice for its own sake; they do not therefore try and torture their facts into showing that under socialism the prosperity of the worker will necessarily and immediately increase; on the contrary they adduce arguments to show that this will probably not be so, and discuss this fact, which throughout is treated as essentially irrelevant to the socialist position, as likely to be unpopular with the masses, on whose support the creation of the new world will depend. This alone will show how far this work is removed from average socialist propaganda.

From the publisher's point of view it must, I think, be admitted that its audience cannot be large: it is a book by socialists and addressed to socialists, the truth of the general premises of socialism is taken for granted. If its economics is sound enough, and it certainly seems to me to be so – I repeat I am no expert – radicalising economic dons at the universities will buy it and make their pupils buy it. The same applies to socialist educational institutions and the rather scattered body of individuals who are generally interested in the problem. What militates against the possibility of any wider circulation is the fact that both the subject and the language presuppose a level of knowledge which the man in the street definitely does not possess. It is not a book of great originality or depth, but it is clear, honest, vigorous and single-hearted in its purpose and its faith, and characterised by singularly intense desire to reject all dubious or irrelevant doctrines which have become associated with socialism in the popular mind, and which, though they may make it seem more attractive, adulterate the purity of the genuine socialist creed. This Tawneyian character of the book is, I think, in itself a reason for publishing it, apart from the scientific value which, as far as I can see, it definitely possesses.

Though its appeal is to the intelligentsia and educated workman alone, I do not think that it will be a financial failure, although it may do little more than cover its own cost. It is bound to be more or less respectfully reviewed even when it provokes animated criticism. I hope I have not talked too much beside the point – I really know very little about economics. I was exhilarated by the book: on any socialist premise its conclusions seem to me to stand: the effect it may well have on many of its most sympathetic readers would be to make them aware of the fact that they are not & cannot be socialists. Which seems to me to be a very excellent effect for a book to have.

TO FABER & FABER

[Before 7 January 1937,[1] *manuscript*]

n.p.

Report on 'The Metamorphosis of Speculative Philosophy' by J. O. Wisdom.[2]

I have read this MS. carefully, and with it the letters of H. H. Price & of Longman's Reader (who from internal evidence can hardly be Price again), I enjoyed the former and disagreed with the latter. The book is not original, and the author is not a philosophical scholar of the first order. Nor did I find the thesis exciting (cf. Price). Perhaps I ought to give a schematic account of its contents. It is divided into three distinct sections. The first gives a rapid bird's eye view survey of the history of modern philosophy from Descartes to the 19th century idealists. The second discusses the notion of philosophical analysis derived from Moore, Russell, and the so-called Viennese Circle, which in the author's view is the only possible method applicable in philosophy. The third section, which Wisdom himself regards as his chief contribution to the subject, puts forward a psychological hypothesis to account for the fact that metaphysicians, although demonstrably uttering meaningless propositions, were and are apparently intelligible to other metaphysicians and even laymen. The hypothesis, which presupposes the possibility of psycho-analysing the characters of writers long dead and gone by means of a technique borrowed from current Freudian practice, is adumbrated only, and not discussed in detail. If the technique were perfected and applied, then, the author believes, we should be able to determine precisely what physical and mental states are indicated by the nonsense-statements of which metaphysics is largely composed: the illusion of meaning arises because nonsense statements do in fact succeed in indirectly conveying to others some awareness of the states of mind of their authors, much as a gesture, or even a thermometer-reading might to persons sensitive to, or experienced in interpreting symptoms of this kind (these illustrations are my own). So much for the thesis.

I feel bound to say that in spite of sympathy with Wisdom's views and a natural desire to see the truth prevail, I do not think that this book is of absolutely outstanding merit. It is well above the average of the books on philosophical subjects that succeed in getting published: the author is at least neither confused nor obscurantist: he knows what he thinks philosophy is about and what kinds of answer he is looking for, though he never succeeds

1 The date of the typewritten copy made for office circulation.
2 Published in Cairo in 1947 by the Al-Maaref Press.

in working them out at all conclusively. If this thesis (for this [is] what it is at present) were submitted as a Fellowship dissertation, it would have to be very seriously considered. It is written in a gay and easy style without any pretensions to style. I do not think I have ever, or am ever likely, to see a more cheerfully written work on philosophy; this breeziness is very exhilarating and carries the reader on through pages of agreeable, quasi-journalistic, but never quite positively vulgar writing. The book ought not to be too difficult for the layman. How much interest it would have for him I do not know. That there is a market for popular philosophy is shown by the success of Joad's book.[1] But I doubt if this book, even if the title were altered is of a kind to capture this market. This is, I suppose, a point in its favour.

About the first part of the book, the brief history of modern philosophy, though it is not devoid of illuminating ideas, I feel that it is too compact and allusive to be of much benefit to the layman and not thorough enough to satisfy the specialist. The second part is much better. I wish there were more of it in proportion to the rest of the book. Anyone reviewing this book professionally would be justified in complaining that the author does not go deeply enough into the question how far the methods of analysis pursued by Moore, John Wisdom (a cousin of the author whom he frequently quotes) and the Viennese Circle embody a difference of aim, how far analysis is purely formal, what is meant by saying that it is concerned only with the meaning of words etc. It does not seem {a} wholly sufficient to answer [that] this is precisely what none of the major exponents of analysis have [occupied] themselves in doing.

The part about Psychocentrics is interesting and entertaining. It is much the most amusing section of a book which is never tedious. The distinction between directly and symptomatically expressing facts is not new, even in the field of English philosophy, but there is no harm in stressing it again. Again the impartial reviewer will have to note that Wisdom exaggerates its fruitfulness. It is easy enough to say roundly that the metaphysics of Absolute idealists show that they were suffering from sexual repression or what not, but could even the most experienced psycho-analyst translate every 'metaphysical' sentence in 'Appearance and Reality' into a significant sentence about Bradley. It seems very doubtful.

All the same I should like to see the book published, although I should prefer someone else to bear the responsibility for having recommended it. The general quality of it is something like βa.[2] It is obviously the work of

---

1 Presumably his *Guide to Philosophy* (London, 1936).
2 i.e. BA, a mixture of second- and first-class, the former predominating. For a full note on the use of the Greek alphabet in marking academic work, see 93/1.

a very young man of considerable intelligence, vitality and enthusiasm for a new doctrine which has suddenly revealed to him the true nature of philosophy. Such, at any rate wd be my 'psycho-centric' analysis of the author from the evidence provided. And it is, of course, a magnificent achievement for one whose previous reputation was made as a Golf-blue. But it is not an epoch-making work, nor even strikingly original. If it is to be published (like Price, I hope someone will) and the author can endure to rewrite it any more, I suggest that he greatly amplifies the second part, gives concrete examples of the method he advocates in the third part (and also states precisely what difference there is between metaphysics and poetry on his analysis. He says there is one, but does not indicate it clearly) and finally modifies, or even cuts out the first part. If this were done I should recommend it without hesitation to you or any other firm. As it is, I can only do so with considerable misgivings; but having put these on record, and because I believe that the virtues outweigh the defects, I am, in this qualified sense, prepared to recommend it for publication. I should appreciate it if you would treat this document as confidential.

I. Berlin

Presumably IB was asked to amplify some of his recommendations, and responded as follows.

TO FABER & FABER

[Before 27 April 1937,[1] *manuscript*]

All Souls

The Metamorphosis of Philosophy

With regard to Mr Wisdom's book:
It seems to me that the whole first part is too sketchy for the professional philosopher and too allusive for the common reader: I quite see the necessity for a quasi-historical introduction to an unfamiliar subject: and as the chapter on dualism is much the best part of the introductory section, perhaps it could be incorporated: not indeed as an autonomous dissertation, but as a definite introduction to the rest, a sine qua non canter through fairly familiar territory. The section which Mr Wisdom says he owes to the Dublin School is stimulating philosophical journalism of the best type, but of too light a texture to deserve inclusion in a serious book. The real task of the author is, I take it, to elucidate what is meant by Analysis, and to examine its practice. This section ought not merely to be expanded: but must do what [at] present

1 This letter is referred to in a letter from Faber dated 27 April 1937.

it does not do convincingly enough: i.e. it must clearly state what Analysis is; what the various practitioners of it, e.g. Moore, Wittgenstein, the Viennese, the Poles, the Americans (a) are doing (b) say they are doing; what the differences between them are and how far they spring from differences of purpose; finally, give concrete instances of successful or unsuccessful analyses, classifying both the types of analysis they embody and their exact relevance in superseding more traditional philosophical methods.

The subject of analysis, its nature and worth, is at present so much canvassed in academic circles, and so much superficial or misleading matter has been published on it – e.g. by Joad and other widely read commentators, that it is of the highest importance to make any new exposition as unambiguous and as thorough as possible. I am sure that Mr Wisdom, who, I believe, has had the advantage of the teaching both of Moore and of Wittgenstein, is admirably qualified to do this. But he must bear in mind the responsibility in which such a task necessarily involves him: and must provide his own clear answers to the questions set out above: it matters far less that they should be true than that they should look like genuine, full, efficiently equipped answers to the questions asked. By the success of this section of the book the entire work will, so it seems to me, stand or fall, whether with professional critics or the general public.

As for the third section, if it is decided to include this, it must certainly not be left to stand in its present state. At present it is an expanded version of the dogmatic proposition that whatever does not successfully pass the Analyst's test of significance, is literally nonsensical, though it is a symptom of the emotional state of {the} its utterer. This may or may not be true. Baldly asserted, without evidence, it is merely likely to enrage the readers of Bradley unnecessarily and do little to enlighten them.

To be at all convincing Mr Wisdom must indicate how the psychocentrician is to carry out a specific enquiry: e.g. how, taking a passage from Hegel or the later Whitehead, one begins to establish verifiable hypotheses as to the state of mind of which the meaningless passage in question is the expression or by product: and also, of course, of the states of mind of those to whom it seems to be a profound revelation of the nature of reality. Unless something concrete is worked out on these lines, the whole thesis will seem a mere piece of dogmatism, & highly paradoxical at that. Whereas it may quite possibly be true, & should not suffer from undernourishment with evidence. If the author is not prepared to do this, he ought, in my opinion considerably [to] abbreviate the last section since the essential thesis can be stated with great brevity: distinguish metaphysics from poetry and either from cries of pain or string quartets (as it is they all answer to the description 'symptom of emotional state, capable of communicating it to others), and explicitly indicate that this part of the book consists of an undeveloped suggestion, not a full blown theory.

If all this is done, and the author gives us a really new analysis of that vexed subject, Analysis, the book will undoubtedly be notable. Otherwise it risks falling between a great many stools: the professional old world philosophers, the analysts who think the subject has been treated too lightly, the uninstructed and bewildered general public, finally the indignant old Greats men who write in reviews & Sunday newspapers, who are usually the worst informed and most irritating of all. Mr Wisdom has chosen his side: he must be induced to arm himself with weapons sufficiently formidable to impress & frighten off the incompetents.

I very much hope that the book, in an amended form, will be published and cause a stir: there is no reason why it should not, it would be excellent from all points of view if it did. This depends, as I have stressed throughout, more on the author's patience than on his more than adequate competence for the task.

DISPATCHES FROM WASHINGTON

Introduction to H. G. Nicholas (ed.), Washington Despatches 1941–45: Weekly Political Reports from the British Embassy *(London, 1981: Weidenfeld and Nicolson; Chicago, 1981: Chicago University Press)*

This volume consists of a number of dispatches, selected, edited and annotated by Professor Herbert Nicholas, which were sent by the British Ambassador in Washington to the Foreign Office in London during the war years 1941–5. The purpose of these Weekly Political Summaries, as they came to be called, was to provide the Foreign Secretary and members of his Department with information about changing attitudes and movements of opinion in the USA on issues considered to be of importance to Anglo-American relations. They were circulated more widely – to other ministers (including the Prime Minister) as well as to a considerable number of other British officials at home and abroad. My sole qualification for providing this prefatory note is that in the spring of 1942 I was seconded to the Embassy in Washington and charged with the task of preparing the first drafts of these weekly reports.

The reader may well ask himself why this particular job should have been entrusted to me. I doubt whether the explanation of this somewhat puzzling fact will satisfy those who believe that specialised tasks, particularly at critical times, should be performed by experts trained for the purpose; it is certainly a vivid illustration of the way in which appointments of temporary officials were made in Britain in wartime. My qualifications for this function were not obvious. Apart from such impressions as I gained in the course of friendly relations with American colleagues and pupils at Oxford, and an unbroken addiction, perhaps somewhat rare in England in those days, particularly in academic circles, to such American periodicals as the *New Yorker* and *Time* magazine – the latter since my first term at Oxford in 1928 – I had no particular knowledge of the United States. I had never been, or thought of going, there, at any rate; nor did I have any special knowledge or understanding of international affairs in general, or of Anglo-American relations in particular. In the summer of 1940, while still teaching philosophy at Oxford, I was asked by Mr (later Sir Harold) Nicolson, then Parliamentary Secretary of the Ministry of Information, whether I would consider going to Moscow as Press Attaché of the British Embassy: it was put to me, by Mr Gladwyn Jebb (later Lord Gladwyn) of the Foreign Office, who was concerned with such appointments, that, with my knowledge of Russian and interest in Russian culture, I could be of use at the Embassy in Moscow. I accepted, and was ordered to go to the capital of the USSR via the USA and Japan. By the time I arrived in Washington on what I supposed to be the first lap of my journey to Moscow, I was informed by the British Embassy that a message had been received in London from the British Ambassador to the Soviet Union, Sir Stafford Cripps, that he had no need of my services, since whatever tasks a Press Attaché could perform at that time (it was the particularly dark period of the Soviet–Nazi Pact) were being attempted already, and that my presence would therefore be totally superfluous; consequently the Foreign Office did not require me to proceed any further, and, upon being asked what it wished me to do, replied that my further plans were of no interest to it. My friends at the British Embassy in Washington put all this to me as tactfully as they could, and it was, I feel sure, largely due to their initiative that the Press Counsellor, Mr Stephen Childs, offered me a job in his under-manned Embassy office. I thanked him for his kindness and trust, but said that in the circumstances I preferred to return to the United Kingdom. He then asked me whether I would, at any rate, stay for six or seven weeks in order to analyse and write a report on the dispatches of American correspondents of the Associated Press in Britain, which seemed to indicate, after the fall of France, a degree of depression and even defeatism in Britain which was not warranted by the facts, and some of which seemed to be having a deleterious effect on the public opinion of a country of whose goodwill and material aid we stood in desperate need. I agreed to do this provided I was allowed to go home after I had finished. In due course, having read a great many American newspapers in the New York office of the British Library of Information, I produced a report which to a considerable degree bore out the Embassy's initial impression. As a result, some representations in this connection were, so I was told, made to senior executives of the Associated Press: whether these had any effect I do not know.

I returned to Oxford at the beginning of the autumn term and resumed my work as a tutor at New College. In late November I received a letter from the Ministry of Information, informing me that I was overstaying my period of home leave and was required to be at my post in the Ministry's New York office. I said that I was not aware of holding any government post and I was a don doing his job at the university. A correspondence followed, in the course of which I learnt that, on the strength of my AP report, and the recommendations of one or two highly placed Americans whom I had known in the past, I had been appointed to a post in the newly created office of the British Information Services (BIS), charged with the task of providing material about the British war effort in the American press and radio. The new office was headed by Alan Dudley of the Foreign Office, with John Wheeler-Bennett and Aubrey Morgan as its effective directors (an account of this is to be found in Sir John Wheeler-Bennett's published memoirs, *Special Relationships*). Everyone in the BIS and the American section of the Ministry of Information seemed to know of my appointment, I alone had not been informed. As this was the only wartime government post offered to me, I accepted it gladly, and worked in New York during the greater part of 1941 as an information officer. My task was to supply details of the British war effort to the press and other media connected with various social groups and religious minorities, such as labour unions, Jews, and some of the smaller Christian denominations. One of the most obvious functions of the BIS was to provide a survey of the press, radio and other media of communication over the entire spectrum of American opinion. This was regarded as being indispensable by those in the Ministry of Information in London who prepared the data for dissemination, especially in order to counter what was thought most damaging to Britain, and was needed no less by British officials in the USA engaged on tasks of this kind. In the course of my work I wrote reports on the attitudes to public issues in general, and to Britain in particular, of various groups whose views I studied (and some of whose representative figures I met and came to know), and to assess, so far as possible, the effect of these attitudes, both public and private, on American public opinion. In particular, I was concerned with the attitudes of the labour unions and their leaders, divided between the American Federation of Labor with its ties to the TUC, and its great rival, the Congress of Industrial Organizations, which for various reasons was at that time a good deal less friendly to Britain. It is, incidentally, this part of my activity that, so I was told, came to the notice of officials in the British Embassy in Washington, and after Pearl Harbor, when I once more expressed a wish to return to England (since most of my 'clients' in America had by now become firm supporters of Britain and the war), moved them to ask for my transfer to Washington to take charge of political surveys.

The drafting of the Weekly Political Summaries had in earlier years been entrusted to relatively junior members of the British diplomatic mission in Washington, who performed it in such time as they could spare from their normal duties. Once, however, America had entered the war, the need to provide somewhat fuller information about the American scene was recognised, and this, in turn, was thought to require the services of at any rate one or two full-time employees, instructed to analyse and interpret congressional, administrative and public opinion and the influence upon it of individuals and groups in the USA in general and in Washington in particular.

The creation of a special Survey Section of the Embassy was a minute element in the great expansion of British activities in wartime Washington. New missions were established to represent the Treasury, the Ministries of Supply, Food, Aircraft Production, Political and Economic Warfare, Information, and other departments; almost every Ministry in London had representatives, in one form or another, in Washington or New York. Some of these British missions, in liaison with corresponding US departments, operated independently; others, whose functions brought them into closer contact with the work of the Embassy, formed new sections of it, strictly understood to be temporary. The creation of these sections, as well as such other departures from tradition as the addition of, for example, a Labour Attaché (Professor R. H. Tawney was the first, and none too happy, holder of this office), were accepted by the Foreign Office with commendable stoicism, much as the classical public schools accepted the need for 'modern subjects', without undue efforts to resist the inevitable. There had been invasions during the First World War, although on a far smaller scale. The result was the creation in the American capital, at the beginning of the 1940s, of what was, in effect, a short-lived microcosm of Whitehall, the relationship of which with the relevant departments of the United States Administration turned out to depend to a high degree on the nature of the personal relations established between British and American officials. The new wartime auxiliaries, whom the various Ministries in London succeeded in persuading the Foreign Office to attach to the British Embassy, were relegated to a hastily constructed and ramshackle barrack which, for all its ungainliness, had its own quality: the atmosphere was one of agreeable informality, in contrast with the stiffer and more dignified atmosphere of the Chancery and the Ambassador's personal staff, and this may have had some influence on the more easy-going prose style of the Weekly Summaries and other reports of the Section to which I was attached.

The Survey Section, which prepared these reports, consisted of about three members. The material on which the Weekly Political Summary was based came in part from the surveys of the American press prepared in New York for the Ministry of Information in London. In addition, we made use of consular reports from various key posts in the country and those of BIS offices in New York and several other important cities, and, not least, exchanges with well-informed observers of the Washington scene – officials, politicians, journalists, diplomats – as well as such information as members of the British Embassy and other British Missions came by in the course of their regular work. All this was assessed in the light of our constantly growing knowledge of the character, connections, outlooks, allegiances, policies, interests, attitudes and personal feelings of individuals, government departments and political and social groups and movements in the USA. Our work was not secret: it resembled that of any foreign correspondent worth his salt, save that the reports, some of them in code, went to a far smaller and more carefully selected group of readers. Some of these surveys were written in response to specific enquiries transmitted by the Foreign Office; such enquiries were, as a rule, answered in special dispatches which were not part of the Weekly Political Summary series, and are therefore not included here.

There was far less secrecy during the war on matters not connected with national security in Washington than, so it seemed to me, there was in London; even official American society had a far looser texture and was more open than that of older, less socially mobile countries. This was, no doubt, partly due to the fact that a far higher proportion of amateurs – businessmen, lawyers, social workers, academics, and so forth – came to Washington to serve the Government, not only during the war or the immediately preceding period of 'preparedness' (as in Britain), but since 1933, with the New Deal.

The war transformed normal life in the United States far less than in the United Kingdom, indeed, it was one of the main tasks of my Section to convey to the Government at home, where everything was centralised and totally subordinated to the war effort, that in the USA this was not so; that political and economic life to a considerable degree continued as before, and that this fact, in particular some of the pressures and internecine feuds between individuals and power blocs, inherited from the New Deal and even earlier times, continued to characterise it, and themselves affected the war effort. In London this was not always sufficiently understood, especially when it manifested itself in the attitude of Congress, which in this respect was very different from that of Parliament.

The individuals to whom my colleagues and I talked about matters of public interest for the most part knew quite clearly what we were doing, nor did we intend to conceal this from anyone. American officials who worked in the State Department or the White House with whom I discussed general issues did not tell me what they preferred the British Government not to know, nor did I expect them to do so; unlike a journalist, I sought no scoops; on the other hand, where they were not bound by the need for secrecy, they often discussed matters freely. This was, of course, even more true of journalists and others not bound by considerations of security; such conversations led to free exchanges of view and friendships which long survived the war, and have been a source of lasting pleasure and abiding interest to me; they certainly taught me more about America than newspapers or official documents or any other published material could possibly have done. My conversations, and indeed personal relations, with lawyers, bankers, academics who held wartime posts in the Washington hierarchy, as well as labour leaders, politicians, writers, journalists and public figures of all kinds, opened windows with far wider vistas than the political pages of newspapers or information contained in diplomatic cables or dispatches, and supplied that (mistakenly so called) 'background' knowledge which anyone who seeks to understand any country or society must have. A certain reciprocity obtained in these matters: American officials occasionally wished the British Government to be made aware of feelings and attitudes, and even specific policies, which they did not wish to formulate officially, in order not to provoke reactions or rejoinders that might complicate relationships in some sphere of delicate negotiation. The dispatches of my Section could act as a channel for informal communications of this kind without committing anyone to anything, and thus occasionally proved useful in promoting understanding and clearing the air. It was as a result of these personal contacts that I soon learnt that politics in Washington were not only more open but far more personal and less institutional than they were in Whitehall. The State Department did have an institutional personality and continuity – its members spoke not so much of what this or that official thought, as of the attitude of 'the Department'; this was to a lesser, but still significant, degree true also of the US Treasury. But it did not hold for a number of important agencies: if you asked a Washington government official what his job was, he was more likely to answer 'I work for Mr Ickes (or Mr Forrestal, or Mr Nelson)' than 'I am in the Department of the Interior (or Navy, or the War Production Board)'. The relationships between the powerful satraps who governed provinces of the Administration, and between the groups of officials who 'worked for' them (and their relationships to individual journalists) seemed to me to be far more important than relations between established institutions, knowledge of which was indispensable to the understanding of the ways in which the British Civil Service, and, to some degree, British Ministers too, thought and functioned. I sometimes wonder whether things have changed in this respect; after more than thirty years during which I have had no connection with government or current policies anywhere, I cannot tell.

There were trends of American, and in particular Washington, opinion and public comment in which the Foreign Office and the Ministry of Information, naturally enough, took a special interest, and this accounts for the relative frequency with which they crop up in these dispatches (as well as the regular quarterly and special reports for which my Section was initially responsible): among them were such topics as Lend-Lease (and 'Reverse

Lend-Lease'); Isolationism and Pacific Firstism; American expansionist ambitions; British imperial policies, especially in India and the Far East, Hong-Kong and Singapore, in the Middle East and particularly Palestine, all of which were objects of traditional, sharp, well-organised criticism in the USA, as well as American policy on oil, civil aviation, foreign trade; post-war plans, and the like. Occasionally we had to answer questions raised via the Foreign Office by some of our other clients – the Cabinet, the Colonial Office, the Service Departments, the BBC, and so on – to which it was important to convey certain differences which existed between the American Departments with which Britain had direct relations, and similar institutions in London; in particular, to describe and account for the alliances of interest which were constantly forming and re-forming between various political and economic groups; the tensions which arose between the old pre-war power blocs; the ideological differences which divided the New Dealers, with their social aims and policies, on the one hand, from those, on the other, for whom the exigencies of mobilisation of resources for the war took the first place; and the corresponding changes of power centres, of relationships of leading personalities, and in the entire alignment of forces which was determined by all these processes.

The Foreign Office occasionally complained that it was being told more than it wished to know; it was not lack of succinctness, but the sheer number of topics covered, and their ramifications, which led to mild protests, usually thinly disguised as a desire to ease the burden of its overworked cypher section. The Ministry of Information had a far greater appetite for the pabulum we provided, and if, in obedience to the Foreign Office, the supply grew thinner there were anguished cries from, e.g., Denis Brogan, the *doyen* of Americanists then at work as adviser to the North American Service of the British Broadcasting Corporation, who described the Weekly Political Summaries as his Ariadne's thread through the labyrinths of American politics, without which proper understanding of that complex field was in England totally unobtainable. Nevertheless, our master was the Foreign Office, and its wishes could not be disregarded. Consequently, we did report a good deal less than we believed or knew or regarded as worth knowing. Some of this residue spilt over into the private correspondence between Herbert Nicholas (of the American Division of the Ministry of Information) and myself, and may at times have been rather more interesting than the content of the official telegrams, though it did, perhaps, presuppose a somewhat more intimate knowledge of the American political scene than the majority of our readers could be expected to possess.

It should not, however, be inferred from this that the officials to whom these telegrams were circulated were for the most part unduly critical of their contents – on the contrary, we received much encouragement, and a good deal of informal praise; in retrospect (which cannot fail to reveal avoidable errors of observation, judgement, emphasis, or sheer shallowness of assessment) much of it now seems to me a good deal more than our due.

To turn to the dispatches themselves. The majority of those in this volume were drafted in the first instance by myself, but by no means all. I was away for relatively long periods in London; I occasionally took leave for a week or two, and I was sometimes away from my office, either through illness or because I had been sent away on special missions to inspect British consulates or to attend conferences; during those periods the dispatches were drafted with great shrewdness and skill by Mr A. R. K. Mackenzie, Mr Alan Judson and occasionally by Mr Paul Scott Rankine.[1] I was responsible only for the original drafts of the dispatches. The dispatches themselves were subject to various controls: I was naturally expected to exercise discretion – anything which I inadvertently disclosed that was considered at all likely to ruffle the sensibilities of important persons whose goodwill it was deemed politic to retain, had to be omitted or drastically modified; thus the relative absence of character sketches of individuals, or accounts of their careers and origins, is mainly due to the fact that the Foreign Office showed no eagerness for such vignettes; we were given to understand that they were best confined to highly confidential reports sent by couriers, and not included in the telegrams. Inevitably, leakages occurred; although scarcely anything in these dispatches was genuinely secret, the Embassy did not wish its comments on events, attitudes or persons to reach the American personalities concerned, and such leakages sometimes caused mild irritation. In addition to such self-censorship, my drafts, on occasion, went through a good deal of transformation: I delivered them, I think, on Thursday afternoons, to the Head of Chancery of the Diplomatic mission. He tended to show various portions of the draft to relevant officials in case they wished to urge some omission or alteration, or he might introduce these himself. The Minister, and in particular the Ambassador (who was the official source of all these messages), might from time to time add or subtract something. Such sentences as 'This story is supported by language used by Cordell Hull in conversation with myself . . .' or the like clearly do not come from my pen. The late Sir Michael Wright, as Head of Chancery, was particularly

1 To the best of my recollection I was away from Washington from June 1942, when I went to London, until late January 1943; between 26 September and 2 November 1943; between 18 March and 16 May and between 15 July and 4 August 1944; and between 9 February and 4 April 1945. I was in San Francisco during the last fortnight of the conference in 1945. In July 1945 I left Washington to join the British Embassy in Moscow, and returned for a short while in 1946, some time after the dispatches collected in this volume had come to an end. [The accuracy of IB's recollection is variable: see the Chronology, which bases its account of his movements on a range of evidence.]

active in cutting out, altering and adding to the text. Nevertheless, I own to responsibility for the greater part of what is contained in these pages. After this length of years, I have little recollection of precisely what either I, or others in the Embassy, removed or altered; the extant letters exchanged with Professor Nicholas occasionally remind me of it.

To re-read after many years documents in which one has had a hand is an exceedingly odd experience: one becomes aware, rather too often for comfort, how far one failed to realise the relative importance, or unimportance, seen in a longer perspective, of this or that view or development; it is a very chastening experience. What it does bring back most vividly is how things seemed to one at the time. If this collection helps the interested reader to recreate the view of the political scene which, during years that now seem so remote, was common to some of the servants of the British Government during the war in Washington, it will have done something to help to reconstruct the past.

ZIONIST POLITICS IN WARTIME WASHINGTON

A Fragment of Personal Reminiscence

This text is the basis of the first Jacob Herzog Memorial Lecture, delivered by IB in Jerusalem in 1972

I

I OFTEN discussed with my friend Jacob Herzog the complexity of the web of history, the perils, when trying to anticipate the future, of extrapolating it too mechanically from the present and the recent past, of not allowing sufficiently for the role of the incalculable and the fortuitous, in particular for the influence on public events of individual character and individual behaviour – factors which, at least in the short run, are liable to upset perfectly reasonable expectations, and destroy apparently safe and widely accepted assumptions that sometimes turn out to rest on shifting sands. We used to discuss, Jacob Herzog and I, the relative influence of leaders of different psychological formation on events: for example, of men of inflexible and even fanatical conviction who, intent upon their goal, shut their ears to prudent advice, ignore dangers and drive on fearlessly and relentlessly – in contrast with men of cautious temper, mature judgement, moderation, instinctive revulsion from overstepping accepted moral bounds, humane men endowed with practical wisdom, suspicious of heroic attitudes – Shimon Bar Giora versus Yochanan Ben Zakkai. The situation I propose to try to describe – one small corner of wartime Anglo–Zionist–American relations with which I was personally acquainted – seems to me to illustrate the interplay of such factors. But first I must explain my own qualifications for discussing these things at all.

II

Almost the whole of my life, since I came of age, has been spent in academic work. Almost, but not entirely, for in the summer of 1940 I obtained leave from my Oxford College to accept a wartime post offered me by the British Ministry of Information. In 1941 I was sent to New York as a 'specialist' attached to the new British Information Services in that city. My 'specialism' (for which I had no kind of preparation) consisted in trying to induce some of the 'minority' groups in the United States – for example, organised labour, the Jewish press, some of the smaller Protestant sects – to include in their publications some information about the British war effort, and to counter the anti-British or isolationist trends strong among some of them. Catholics, blacks and the rest of the 'hyphenated'-American press were left to others.

My task was not too difficult, since the anti-Nazi sentiments of most of my 'clients' were not in doubt. The American Federation of Labor, with its close ties with the British TUC, knew where it stood. Its great rival, the CIO – the vast body of partly skilled industrial workers – was less friendly. This arose partly out of rivalry with the AFL and a corresponding lack of connections in Britain and among her allies, and partly because it was subject to both Communist and isolationist influences, which, before the attack on the Soviet Union, tended to converge. As for the Jewish press, it was, by this time, openly, solidly and warmly pro-British. The war found the majority of the American-Jewish population, especially those of Eastern European origin, in a pro-Zionist mood. The British White Paper of 1939, which condemned the Yishuv to remain a permanent minority in Arab Palestine, created depression and anger in wide sections of the American-Jewish community. Nevertheless the declaration of war, and British heroism in 1940, created a vast wave of sympathy and enthusiasm for Britain in America, which, for obvious reasons, the Jewish community felt most passionately. Despite the anti-immigration measures of the Palestine administration, and the dreadful fate of the refugee ship *Struma*, which moved to shame some even in the Colonial Office, Zionist attacks on the British Government virtually died down, save for the campaign for the Jewish Army, conducted most vehemently by revisionists and their allies, both among Jews and among their sincere liberal gentile sympathisers. The virtual rejection of the plan by the British Government at the end of 1941 was a bitter disappointment to moderates as well as extremists; no one was taken in by the reason officially given in London – that there was insufficient equipment. Political reasons – mainly fear of upsetting the Arabs – were clearly paramount. Nevertheless, by contrast with the situation in 1914–17, American-Jewish support for Britain was almost unanimous: almost, for there were, of course, Jewish individuals and groups who were nervous of appearing to be war-mongers, or of being accused of putting their sectional interests before the national ends of the United States. Some among these became members of isolationist groups, which contained a handful of prominent and wealthy Jews whose position *vis-à-vis* the rest of the Jewish community ceased to be embarrassing only after Pearl Harbor. In addition to these there were small groups of Jewish Marxists who regarded the war as one between two imperialisms, the outcome of which was, at least in theory, a matter of moral indifference to dedicated internationalists save as a force promoting a revolutionary situation. Some of these, though not all, changed their line after the attack on the Soviet Union.

My chief mentors in these matters were drawn from very different worlds. One was an honourable and gifted Yiddish journalist, Judd Teller, who helped me with the Yiddish press. The other, whom I saw but twice, was the eminent Justice of the Supreme Court, Louis D. Brandeis, then in the last year of his long life. He expounded to me the sociology of the American-Jewish community with the moral charm and lucidity that were characteristic of him. 'Make no mistake,' he said, 'the majority of the Jewish community is with us [that is, Zionists]. They won't emigrate in any numbers, but they know that they have got to be a majority somewhere, have a country of their own, if they are to hold their heads high among other loyal American citizens of recent European origin. They know that. Some of them are pretty ignorant people, but they will learn, and will support the Palestine experiment with all their might. Unfortunately, the majority haven't much money, and they aren't politically organised in the way the Catholics are, so the influence they will be able to have on American policy may not be great; in fact, I think they won't be able to do much that way, only contribute what they can, and give all their hearts and hopes and fears to "the movement" [as he called Zionism]. It's pretty much like the Labour movement in England before the First World War; only they may not have the same success.' (I do not, of course, vouch for the verbal accuracy of this, for I kept no diary, but I did make a note of these conversations for the benefit of Felix Frankfurter, who wished me to tell him what Brandeis had said. I have lost my notes, but the mere fact of making them imprinted their substance on my memory.)

Brandeis went on to add that the money and the influence belonged to the rich and politically prominent among the Jews, some of whom were, in his view, hopelessly ignorant and prejudiced, but, above all, fearful of seeming to attempt to rock the boat of American policy in some Jewish direction. Still, there were some good and brave men among them too: Felix Frankfurter, for example, or Ben Cohen; Henry Morgenthau was a decent, warm-hearted man, in contrast to his vain and narrow father; even Bernard Baruch could be a foul-weather friend. However, the run-of-the-mill Zionist propagandists were, in Brandeis's view, politically terribly inept. They made a great deal of noise, but lacked sense and were much too generous with other people's time and patience. The majority of them were more of a liability than an asset to the Zionist cause. Brandeis spoke with deep feeling of the decency of the lower-middle-class and poor Jews, ill-informed, but with their hearts in the right place, and returned to the contempt which he felt for the behaviour of some of the richest and most powerful and prominent. This was obviously a deeply held conviction. He told me to take no notice of these people – their very cravenness would immobilise them and put them out of account. He mentioned no names, but anyone who knew the American scene at this time could easily identify some of the individuals whom this cap fitted.

I have never before or after met anyone who combined such pure and intense moral feeling, dignity and charm with so uncompromising and ironical a sense of reality, which cut through all cant and rhetoric, and dealt solely in hard facts – brass tacks, no matter how many or how small. The Justice's manner was somewhat impersonal: that of a man engaged in an unswerving pursuit of concrete truth, with little respect for persons. Yet the truth may sometimes have eluded even him. It is to him, I think, that I must, at least in part, attribute my mistaken view that the opinions of five million American Jews would, in the end, have little influence on American foreign policy, and that the only persons in the Jewish community who might affect it would be eminent individuals – men of standing, not unlike himself, on whom he based his principal hopes. It was not, perhaps, a grave error, for in the end the views of these leaders and of the masses coalesced. But it took some major blunders on the part of the British Government, as well as rigid intransigence by pro-Arab officials both in Britain and America, to achieve this unanimity. The situation looked very different in 1941, and remained fluid till the end of the war. After that, things altered dramatically, in a manner that neither I nor, I suspect, others had anticipated; nor, I suspect, Weizmann or those who thought like him, among whom, unofficially, I counted myself at all times. I had a long conversation about this with Ben-Gurion in 1941. He proved to be right, and my friends and mentors mistaken, as I hope to explain.

In 1942 I was transferred to the British Embassy in Washington, with a completely different job – that of reporting on the political scene in the United States in general, and in Washington in particular. My task was, in effect, that of a political observer, a foreign correspondent, with one or two differences – that my drafts were liable to be modified or altered by various Embassy officials through whose hands they passed, up to and including the Ambassador, in whose name they were dispatched; that they were, in theory at least, confidential; and that my audience consisted entirely of British government officials in London and elsewhere. Zionist activities, so far as I can recollect, played a very minute part in these reports, for they were altogether marginal to the movement of general American or Washington opinion. Zionists were regarded at the Embassy as, at best, embarrassing allies; at worst, simply as a minor political nuisance. Until Zionist agitation greatly increased in 1943–4, it was not taken too seriously: Zionists were neither encouraged nor parried, even when their attacks on British policy grew in violence. I was, of course, deeply interested in these matters. My sympathies had been pro-Zionist since my schooldays. When I read in the memoirs of my intimate friend and Oxford colleague Maurice Bowra that my pro-Zionist views seemed to him, in the years before the war, the most prominent and characteristic of all my political convictions, this came as no surprise to me.

I used to argue about Zionism with anyone who showed interest. Despite what appeared to me to be cogent reasoning, I fear I made no converts. One of my pre-war American pupils at Oxford became one of the most fiercely anti-Zionist American officials in the State Department; nor do my efforts appear to have made the faintest impression on my old friend, Sir Harold Beeley, whom neither I, nor Sir Charles Webster, were ever able to shift an inch from his well-known convictions on this subject. Weizmann, whom I first met in 1938, gave shape to my views. His realism, his moderation and his political genius lifted him above any other statesman I ever knew well. I remained devoted to him to the end of his days, and adhere to his principles and outlook to this day. In Washington he and his immediate followers seemed to me to be at once the most far-sighted and the most effective of the Zionists. The extremists, both of the right and of the left, who, out of bitterness or for temperamental reasons, advocated ruthless policies, I never found congenial; they seemed to put the satisfaction of their own emotional needs above the attainable goals of the cause which they supported. The extremists regarded the moderates as craven, the moderates repaid them by regarding them as lunatics. This is perhaps the situation in every movement that seeks to promote radical change against great odds. I knew where I stood. The politics of the extremists seemed to me politics of despair at a time when sanity could still prevail; their goals seemed to me utterly Utopian, their methods horrifying, and likely to lead to results which only fanatics could desire. I was, and remain, an incurably sceptical liberal, a convinced gradualist. The attractiveness to me, therefore, of Weizmann's outlook was obvious.

I had no executive functions in the Embassy, and my work there did not involve me in any kind of Zionist politics. I never spoke of my work to my Zionist friends and acquaintances, and, to do them justice, they never asked me to reveal its nature, though it was not secret; nor did they ask me to give them confidential information. Even Weizmann, in his most intimate moments, never made the slightest attempt to use me in this way. I was a servant of the British Government for the duration of the War, and he did not wish to embarrass me; nor did Moshe Sharett, nor David Ben-Gurion, nor other Zionist leaders whom I met in the United States. They talked about Palestine and Zionism, of course, and their hopes and fears, and although each side probably, now and then, reached the edge of discretion, neither side overstepped it. They did not reveal their secrets, nor expect me to reveal mine. I made no effort to conceal my views from my British or American colleagues, and used to argue for a solution of the Jewish problem on Weizmannite lines with some of my friends in the Embassy, the White House and the State Department; they did not seem in the least surprised by such opinions on my part – indeed, they seemed to them perfectly natural, though they frequently disagreed with them. Like the British Ambassador, Lord Halifax, they were not much interested in the subject; like him, they saw it as a movement that occasionally grew troublesome, but was not of ultimate importance in Anglo-American relations. The Foreign Office was not exactly a pro-Zionist organisation, and had by this time decided to back the Arab horse; but this was not a subject on which total conformity was demanded. So, for example, Oliver Harvey (Lord Harvey of Tasburgh), during the war Eden's Principal Private Secretary, was consistently pro-Zionist and remained a personal friend of the Weizmanns, and there were three or four other officials who were mildly sympathetic to Jewish aspirations in Palestine. As for the Department of State in Washington, the officials in charge of Near-Eastern affairs were, one and all, solidly hostile to the Zionist cause. Among the other American career officials no one, so far as I knew, favoured it; certainly none of my friends among them showed the slightest signs of doing so; they simply thought Zionism was foolish and Utopian in the face of inexpugnable, undilutable Arab hostility. Among the 'political' officials there was some division: Sumner Welles was considered a friend by the Zionists, Acheson was known to be opposed and had agreed never to discuss it with his great friend Felix Frankfurter, with whom he used to walk downtown every morning; Adolf Berle was, as in all things, ambivalent; the Secretary of State, Cordell Hull, appeared to take little interest in foreign affairs unless he was compelled to do so, and followed the President's line. As for the President himself, whether for political or personal reasons, he clearly wished to give the impression, at any rate to some of his Jewish advisers and visitors, of being favourable to Zionist goals, as indeed did one or two White House officials. In this regard there existed (as perhaps there still does) a certain difference of attitude, or at least of degree of flexibility, between the Department of State and the White House.

The executive officials in the British Embassy derived much of their information about American attitudes from their opposite numbers in the Department of State and other American officials with whom they did their business. Consequently they were, quite understandably, at times liable, so it seemed to me, to overestimate the value of impressions obtained from such official sources in their own assessments of American policy in a wide variety of fields. But, as any politician or journalist knew, there were plenty of other influences at work, personal and sectional, stemming from lobbies and pressure groups, as well as evidences of public feeling, and it was one of my functions to bring some of these factors to the attention, through the Embassy, of the Government at home. In this web, a strand, though not a very important one, was the attitude of the great Jewish community in the USA. By 1942, with America in the War, Zionist and Zionist-inspired attacks on British policy in Palestine began to grow in frequency and violence. The refusal to authorise the creation of a Jewish fighting force, and the increasingly rigid implementation of the White Paper policy by the Mandatory authorities in Palestine, exacerbated this feeling. I remember a public occasion on which Weizmann, whose son had lost his life while serving with the Royal Air Force, delivered a strong and characteristic protest against this agitation. He said that to denigrate Churchill's Britain at such a moment was not decent; Britain-baiting was unworthy of a self-respecting movement. Only an Allied, that is, a British victory could save the Zionist cause: this was the cardinal issue – attacks on Britain must cease. To speak of two hundred thousand Jewish volunteers for a National Jewish Army was, he declared, wildly unrealistic – a harmful and dangerous day-dream – a badge, a flag, fifteen to twenty thousand men, was the maximum at present feasible. So long as he was in charge of the movement there would, he declared, be no breach with Britain: without her, the movement was doomed. As for the Arabs, he was ready to negotiate with them if they gave tongue: so far only Jews seem to have spoken on their behalf; let them speak for themselves; then Jews and Arabs could talk to one another. Lord Moyne had accused him of embarrassing the British Government by his public criticisms in London; this charge was quite monstrous; nevertheless to attack Britain in America was odious and counter-productive; one could do this in London or Jerusalem, not in New York.

These forthright sentiments were not well received by Weizmann's audience. He was accused, as so often, before and after, of Anglomania, of feeble 'parliamentarism', of appeasement of his British friends at the expense of the movement. But his prestige was vast, and his position was not shaken. I saw him a good deal at this time, and remember well what he thought. His position rested on certain assumptions which few, if anyone, at the time openly questioned. In the first place he thought it beyond argument that to win the war against Hitler was a goal that transcended all other considerations; that even if the policies of the Churchill Government were unjust or mistaken, no one had the moral right – least of all Jews – to give comfort to the enemies of that Government, in the USA or elsewhere, at this time. When the war was won, Britain, in his view – and who did not believe this at the time? – would surely remain the dominant power in the Middle East. The future of Zionism and of the Jewish settlement – its very survival – were, for better or worse, bound up with England and her goodwill: a final breach would be fatal to Jewish hopes. That this was not impossible the White Paper had made plain: the Foreign Office had killed the Peel partition plan, and would kill Zionism if it could; but the Foreign Office was not everything: the Prime Minister was Winston Churchill, whose sympathy for Zionism was and remained real; the movement had influential friends in Parliament and in the Cabinet, especially the War Cabinet, which was not dominated by the pro-Arabs or anti-Zionists in the Foreign Office – Leo Amery, Archibald Sinclair, Duff Cooper, to some degree Oliver Stanley, Smuts, the Labour ministers (Attlee's steady anti-Zionism was not known about at the time; Bevin's role still lay in the future). To inflame British feeling by irresponsible attacks, and seek disreputable alliances with Britain's critics in America, certainly was immoral and insane.

By this time Weizmann favoured the creation of a Jewish State. His famous article in *Foreign Affairs* showed this clearly. But he believed that it would need to be closely associated with a Great Power if it was to survive politically or indeed physically: it depended on such association for its minimum security, otherwise it might be overwhelmed by the Arabs and their allies. One could not expect America to become this protective power: she would surely not want to assume responsibilities in a region with which she had no traditional ties, and would reject any such suggestion, as she had done after the First World War. Besides, Weizmann did not really want an American protectorate in place of a British one: American policies were too unstable, open to too many internal pressures; and there were too many anti-Semites in high places in that country. Whom else could he look to? The British might be driven to abandon the Jews – this was not at all impossible. But the Jews must not let this happen – it spelt suicide.

These seem to me to have been among the basic considerations that swayed Weizmann till the end of the War. And there were more personal ones, too. He did like and admire the British, their combination of courage and moderation, the civilised quality of their domestic politics, more than the character and life of any other nation. The Jews had more to learn from them than from any other society: association with the British Empire, despite all the obvious disadvantages and the frequently painful character of Anglo-Jewish relations in Palestine in the inter-war years, was nevertheless a desirable fate for a politically inexperienced, unruly, stiff-necked people like the Jews. The White Paper was, as its implacable critic Churchill saw it, a temporary aberration, a pathetic and desperate step taken in a moment of panic. It would pass away. The Jews would obtain a State in Palestine with British help, or not obtain one at all. The British needed the Jewish genius and skills, even if they did not seem to be aware of this; but with time, Weizmann believed, they could be brought to be so. As for the Jews, they needed the British even more. To scream abuse at England, as some Zionists appeared to delight in doing, was a luxury which they could not begin to afford either morally or politically. Weizmann was a British subject by design; he believed in the British connection. He told Lord Halifax that he would keep him informed of any formal conversations he might have with American statesmen. The British Government repaid him with a kind of reluctant admiration: it knew that his purposes were those of every Zionist; but his approach and his means were different and compelled respect. Consequently, British politicians trusted him, took him into their confidence, discussed details of partition plans with him and with him alone. As for America, Zionists should, of course, in Weizmann's view, seek to influence her in their direction by every legitimate means, above all by his own conspicuously successful method of patient diplomacy: by persuading influential persons in the administration and legislature. Marches, petitions, resolutions, advertisements in the Press with signatures of prominent persons, fiery philippics – all this might impress the Jews, but it would not succeed in moving Washington. Weizmann believed this, I feel sure, throughout the war. It divided him from conservatives like Rabbi Abba Hillel Silver and from revisionists and their proto-Irgun allies, and it was far too soft a line for the militants in other Zionist groups as well. But he was Weizmann: he was recognised as the greatest Jewish personality of his time, and little could be done with him. He stuck to his guns: not to alienate Churchill and the pro-Zionists in the British Cabinet; to talk and talk again to responsible people. This is how the Balfour Declaration had been secured. Weizmann's experience and temperament, his moral and political beliefs, made this the only way in which he could function. His immediate collaborators supported him in this – Nahum Goldmann stood by him loyally and ably; so did Louis Lipsky; Meyer Weisgal did much drafting for him and acted as his ambassador to various Zionist groups; even Stephen Wise restrained his natural exuberance out of respect for the great leader.

I must admit that Weizmann's arguments seemed to me unanswerable. To win the war was plainly the supreme common goal. To sow dissension among the Allies was both foolish and wrong. The case of the Jews, despite everything, was bound up with that of Britain. Churchill and Roosevelt would not, once the war was over, sell out the Jewish national cause. America was in any case not a possible substitute for Britain. Extremist tactics – violent agitation (full-scale terrorism had not yet been heard of), impossible demands – were irresponsible, and, with Hitler at the gates, mad and self-defeating. As for Jewish opinion in the United States, even if it were far better organised politically and whole-heartedly favourable to the Jewish State in Palestine, surely it would not achieve as much as key figures in Washington. Roosevelt was the idol of the great majority of Jewish voters; votes mattered in election years – in 1944, for example – but they were not sufficient by themselves to determine major US policies, as was shown by the disregard of Polish or Bohemian feelings in 1940. It was dubious whether the Zionist cause could be made to affect American public opinion, as, say, that of India or Ireland had done; thus far – I am speaking of 1942–3 – the critics and enemies of Britain had not made use of this stick to beat the British with. Weizmann was surely right: only an *Erfüllungspolitik*, Strese-mann's gradualism when he conducted the foreign policy of Weimar Germany – this was the only hope for a movement which had considerably fewer battalions than even the Pope. Politically influential American Jews who stood outside the Zionist movement but helped it when they could – Morgenthau, Frankfurter, Ben Cohen, Herbert Lehman, Judge Rosenman – were of the same mind. It was this, and not craven feeling, or fear of the spectre of double allegiance, that caused such men to wince when the more unbridled Zionist leaders embarrassed the American Administration by excess of zeal or disregard for the truth or by breaking the rules of politically decent conduct. Pro-Zionist American-Jewish officials felt this very strongly. I remember their feelings when the notorious March of Rabbis took place in Washington. It was not Roosevelt only who was moved to fury by such antics.

On the evidence of the years 1942–4 this seems to me, even now, to have been a valid position. The events which later transformed the situation and put Weizmann out of power were still in the unknown and, I believe, unknowable future. There is, however, no doubt that in the light of these later events the assumptions we all made, and the deductions drawn from them, proved mistaken; or that there was a certain sense in which Weizmann was wrong and Ben-Gurion nearer to understanding the forces at play.

I had a long and fascinating conversation with Ben-Gurion on a Sunday in December 1941; so long and so fascinating that when we rose from lunch it was well after 5 pm; and it was only then that I learnt from the cab-driver that the news of Pearl Harbor had been announced some hours before. I kept no notes of conversations with eminent Jewish leaders from Palestine – David Ben-Gurion, Moshe Sharett, Eliahu Elath and others. I must rely only on my very uncertain memory. Ben-Gurion, too, seemed to me to believe in the British connection, both as inevitable and as desirable. But he sharply dissented from Weizmann in several respects: despite his immense admiration for Churchill (not so much on account of his pro-Zionism, but as a man of supreme courage who, like Tito and de Gaulle, stood up and fought against enormous odds), he put no faith in princes, neither in Churchill nor in Roosevelt nor in any other gentile leader or party or country. He believed that the Jews of Palestine would by themselves be able to repel unavoidable Arab attacks, at least for a time; and he put great faith in the support of the Jews of America. The Jewish masses – not the leaders, who were in his view men of little faith or character, but the masses, fired by the image of an independent State – would prove far stouter-hearted and more effective allies than the powerful politicians whom Weizmann might persuade or charm.

When Ben-Gurion spoke in this vein, in short, sharp bursts, punctuated by even more intense, absorbed, brooding silences, it was as if the apocalyptic vision by which he was possessed outran his powers of expression. Jewish opinion must be mobilised everywhere, and particularly in the United States; that alone would help. If it came to a crisis the Jewish settlement in Palestine would know how to stand up for itself as the British did in 1940. Diplomacy – Weizmann's patient appeals to history and to reason – was an obsolescent weapon; the statesmen of the world listened but did nothing. I tried to argue with him: American Jews, even non-Zionists, favoured immigration into Palestine, both from idealistic motives and, whether consciously or not, as a self-protective measure. They knew that Congress would never dream of opening American gates to Jewish refugees; it was not cowardice, it was mere realism, they thought, not to demand this. But to demand a Jewish State – how much support could this muster? The number of committed American Zionists was a minority of the Jewish population. If the American Government, and especially Roosevelt, declared (as they might easily do) that it was not in the national American interest to quarrel, for the sake of Jewish national aspirations, with England or the Arabs or both – that Zionist pressure was an embarrassment to the foreign policy of the United States – would they not recoil from the prospect of being thought to obstruct the policies of their Government, particularly of the great President for whom many of them felt profound admiration and, in some cases, deep personal loyalty? Ben-Gurion waved this away. Let Weizmann go on courting Roosevelt and Sumner Welles; in the end such men, even such proven friends as Churchill and Smuts and Amery and the rest, would inevitably pursue the national interests of their countries; they would not be ready to help the Jews through thick and thin; through thin, perhaps; but not through thick. Only the Jews themselves, only their massed strength in the USA and Palestine, would stand up – in the end it was upon them alone that the movement could count. I argued that American Zionists vastly overestimated the power of the American-Jewish population to influence the foreign policy of the United States. To rely on this, and to fail, was to court a disaster that might set the entire movement back for a generation. So we argued in circles: on the evidence of the war years my thesis does not seem to me unreasonable even now. It proved mistaken. Ben-Gurion's faith in the masses proved justified. But the turn of events which altered the situation was still invisible, at least to me.

I now knew Ben-Gurion's mind. The Biltmore Resolution of 1942 became a rallying-cry for Jewish feeling and proved to be the first step in the mounting ascendancy of Zionism over American-Jewish opinion, culminating in the American-Jewish Conference, of which Weizmann was the principal architect. The Biltmore demand for a Jewish State was variously interpreted, and attacked only by small anti-Zionist groups. Ben-Gurion's 'maximalist' interpretation of it seemed to me Utopian: in the event his passionate faith proved to be politically justified. At the time it looked almost as unrealistic as Theodor Herzl's visionary words more than forty years before.

In the mean while, the defeat of Rommel in North Africa seemed to put Palestine out of immediate danger. By 1943 the Allies were advancing. Britain was no longer beleaguered. Attacks on British policy by American Zionists increased in intensity. The British authorities were increasingly irritated by the mounting stream of denunciation at Zionist banquets, in newspaper advertisements, and in resolutions passed by various humanitarian and political associations; so was the deeply anti-Zionist, not to say anti-Jewish, Near-Eastern section of the State Department, which argued that sooner or later this would upset the Arabs to the detriment of the Allied war effort and of the policy of American-Arab friendship. There was an attempt to damp down the public expression of Zionist views by a joint statement to be issued by the Prime Minister and the President, declaring that a settlement in the Middle East must await the end of the War, and that until then political demands could only inflame an already uneasy situation – in short, that the Zionists must pipe down. But meanwhile there had taken place, for some time, a noticeable rise in pro-Zionist sentiment on the part of prominent Jewish personalities in Washington; whatever their ideas about a Jewish State, they were united in opposition to the White Paper and in a desire for enlarged Jewish immigration into Palestine, which both Jews and Arabs knew to be the nub of the problem. The plan to issue a statement on these lines became known to some of them,[1] and was killed, to the annoyance of some British and American officials, by the intervention, so it was rumoured, of Henry Morgenthau, Felix Frankfurter and Bernard Baruch,

1 443/3.

who had been moved to genuine indignation by the idea of singling out the Jews for reproof from among the various pressure groups in the United States.

I recollect that I tried to convey to my superiors at the Embassy that the Zionist movement was making friends and influencing persons in official Washington. There was mounting sympathy for Zionist ideas in the upper ranks of the American Government, whatever the relevant officials of the State Department might feel or say. Some among the old New Dealers in the Administration had had their imaginations fired by the idea that a million Jewish immigrants, backed by adequate capital and armed with energy and skills, could, by applying the methods whereby marshes had been drained in Palestine and arid lands made to flourish, transform the entire Middle East socially and economically. Bold, well-conceived, large-scale plans, of which the harnessing of the waters of the Jordan, hydroponics, development of the Negev were potential examples, could lead to vast irrigation, electrification, re-afforestation schemes and new industries that would create a new and better life for all the peoples of the region. On a more personal level, Sumner Welles gave his Zionist visitors the impression that he sympathised with their political aims. So did Edward Stettinius, who might indeed be something of a lightweight, but probably reflected the liberal and increasingly generous attitude to the Jewish question in ruling circles in America. Weizmann felt this too. He made it plain over and over again that he was ready to talk to Arabs if Anglo-American diplomacy paved the way, and if it were made plain that minimum Jewish claims were beyond discussion. He thought that Ibn Saud might be ready to help (this proved a total delusion), and that the Arabs would be ready for some rational compromise if they did not feel that the British were so strongly on their side. By this time Weizmann must have known something of the scheme for a new partition of Palestine that was being discussed by a British Cabinet Committee. He asked me, I recollect, what I thought was the likelihood of the abrogation of the White Paper. Unlike him, I had not then heard anything of the ideas on partition (which he did not reveal to me), and answered that I saw no sign of change in the Palestine policy of my Government. He evidently did not believe much in the Cabinet conversations at that time, for in the middle of 1943 he seemed depressed and frustrated. He gave me the impression of feeling impotent so long as the MacMichael administration remained in charge; relations between the British and the Jews in Palestine, in his view, were becoming more tense and unfriendly than at any period in the past. He had had his differences with Herbert Samuel twenty years before, but now he sighed after that time as a golden age.

I received a far more sanguine impression of Zionist progress from my friend Nahum Goldmann, of whom I saw something at this time, and I tried to convey some of this to my colleagues in the light of what that civilised and sagacious man would tell me from time to time about Zionist hopes and attitudes. He revealed no secrets, but his *tours d'horizon* used to fascinate me. He was at this time one of the representatives of the Jewish Agency in Washington, and used to see two or three Embassy officials besides myself; his friendliness, ebullience and good nature, as well as his Weizmannite views, contrasted favourably, in their eyes, with the thunder and lightning of the formidable Rabbi Silver of Cleveland, whom they did not know personally, but who occasionally sought interviews with Lord Halifax. I, too, was entranced both by the content and the exhilarating quality of Goldmann's expositions, and suspect that his tone proved irresistibly infectious. I remember my efforts to convey to my colleagues the sharp contrast between the buoyant mood of even that most moderate of Zionists, who, like his collaborators, met with encouragement in Washington, and the stonewalling tactics of the British Government, which all of us in the Embassy were obliged to reflect, and the Diplomatic Mission to implement. This seemed to me to be based on a continuing lack of attention to the realities of the situation. The Zionists knew perfectly well that however little satisfaction they got from the Foreign Office or the Embassies, they had a staunch friend in Churchill; he might not be able to do much while all his energy and thought were directed to winning the War, but he made no secret of his views. Stories reached us about how, when taxed by some shocked Cabinet Minister with expressing pro-Zionist sentiments to some visitor – Jan Masaryk, or Smuts, or indeed Weizmann himself – he would formally deny the charge of talking indiscreetly, and then add characteristically, 'I did not say anything of this kind, of course, and he is not authorised to repeat it, but it is exactly what in fact I think.' So, too, President Roosevelt, one gathered, had said to Eugene Meyer, the greatly respected Republican elder statesman and publisher of the *Washington Post*, that Churchill was still as much as ever against the White Paper, and so, indeed, was he, Roosevelt; he wished the Jews trusted him more – he would see them through and get the Arabs to make it up with them after the war. By this time it had become known to Weizmann's lieutenants that partition schemes were being discussed in a British Cabinet Committee, that Smuts and Amery and some of the Labour ministers, and to a degree the Colonial Secretary, Oliver Stanley, too, favoured the idea of a Jewish self-governing territory in Palestine. The Foreign Office might scoff at the idea, but Zionists believed that Churchill would not permit a scheme accepted by the Cabinet and Parliament to be sabotaged again, as the Peel Plan had been. My colleagues, despite occasional efforts on my part to bring these facts to their notice, at least in conversation, could not bring themselves to consider the issue as one of more than peripheral interest. And indeed, in the context of other great events, it did not perhaps appear to be so. What the (on the whole) deeply anti-Zionist Foreign Office thought of it all, I have no notion – they appeared to be mainly concerned, as all Foreign Offices always are, with lowering temperatures, evading awkward issues, waiting for Cabinet decisions that did not come, and in the mean time preventing indiscretions or, if they did not succeed in this, trying to dissipate their consequences.

Inevitably there were differences between Zionists. Weizmann and Sharett did not always see eye to eye with Ben-Gurion, and relations were at times pretty tense; Wise and Goldmann did not like it when Silver visited Lord Halifax and did not tell them what had passed (anyone who knew Lord Halifax could be sure that nothing of the slightest importance could have taken place on a topic that he regarded as at once so unimportant and so unsafe). Sharett used to complain bitterly of the apathy of American Jews, on whom Zionism, despite the professions of their official representatives, had not made sufficient impact, and who seemed unaware of plots against Zionist aspirations meditated by their enemies among British or American officials. My colleagues seemed to me to pay no attention to increasing sympathy with Zionist aims in 1943–4 on the part of leading personalities in Washington and elsewhere; the pro-Arab faction in the Administration was by no means having it all its own way; Welles, Stettinius, Winant (at that time Ambassador in London), perhaps (so it was said, although without any genuine evidence) even the President's intimate adviser Harry Hopkins, looked with disfavour upon the views and activities of *arabisant* officers of the State Department such as Wallace Murray and those of like mind. The pro-Zionist and anti-White-Paper speeches or resolutions of Senators and Congressmen and other well-known persons might not amount to much in concrete terms, but even if they were mere expressions of goodwill and no more, they tended to inhibit officials from going too far, for fear of being attacked by name in Congress and in the Press.

There were pro-Zionist pointers in London too. Had not Weizmann been told by Churchill himself that he would presently 'extract a real plum out of the Palestine pie' for him, with which Attlee, who had been present at this meeting, had not disagreed, although he did complain of excessive Jewish pressure in America? And was not Amery said to have confirmed to Weizmann that a new partition scheme – more acceptable to the Jews than even the Peel proposals – was ripe, and would soon be offered him by the Cabinet? And so on. It was true that Zionist agitation, particularly when stimulated by irresponsible extremists from abroad – some of them from Palestine – was said to irritate President Roosevelt greatly, especially when they mobilised his Republican opponents against the policies of his Administration. Moreover, even friendly figures like Stettinius seemed to share the conviction of the British military authorities that pro-Zionist resolutions in the United States could have a dangerously upsetting effect on the Arabs – indeed, Silver made it known that Stettinius had told him to hold his horses until at least the Allied invasion of Europe had begun; still, this was only a question of when these horses would be allowed to gallop, not whether they ever would. These rumours, even if they were taken with more than one pinch of salt, and the estimates based on them, even if they sprang from over-optimism on the part of the more sanguine Zionist leaders, nevertheless indicated real diplomatic progress on their part. Palestine was not, however, in the forefront of attention; it was of no use to treat such rumours as being more than what they were. My job was to describe the entire American public scene, and keep things in their due proportions. I found it only too tempting in dealing with Washington politics to adopt at times a somewhat satirical and irreverent (and on occasion slightly flippant) tone, particularly in dealing with personalities. I found that this style was well received by all but the most solemn and humourless of my superiors. Nevertheless, the substance remained serious, and I interpreted my duties strictly.

III

Weizmann, throughout 1943–4, became more and more critical of the shrillness of Zionist propaganda in the United States. The mounting sound and fury of the rhetoric of Wise and Silver, particularly the latter, representing the Democratic and Republican interests respectively, seemed to him only to make his task of pressure and persuasion in London more difficult, without any corresponding advantage: it irritated even the friends of Zionism in England and had not the slightest effect upon their policies. Like Moshe Sharett, he noted with concern that these tactics had little effect upon general public opinion in the United States, which, despite the writings of pro-Zionist journalists like Edgar Ansel Mowrer, or Dorothy Thompson, and counterblasts from critics and opponents of the movement, in the New York Times or the Reader's Digest, remained uninterested in the Zionist issue; all that Zionist agitation did was to widen the gulf between Britain and the Jews, and this seemed to Weizmann a dangerous and, indeed, a fatal trend. I remember a conversation with Silver about this. I asked him whether he did not think that these assaults on British policy were not counter-productive: what was the use of attacks violent enough to exasperate one's opponent, without, however, deflecting him from his policy? What was the use of ineffective sanctions? And did he think that Roosevelt would be as friendly if he was re-elected to a fourth term in 1944, as he now seemed likely to be? I cannot recollect what, if anything, Silver answered: I suspect that he was mainly concerned with preserving the momentum of American Zionism. Relations with Britain he left to others; Britain would doubtless follow her own national interests – hard words broke no bones, particularly in so subtle and resistant an organism. About this I agreed, as so often, with Weizmann. American Zionists had little to fear from the anti-Zionist faction in America, a collection of feeble mice trying to bell the huge Zionist cat. But if the American Government made it plain that they were not prepared to quarrel with Britain over the Jewish issue, would the majority of American Jews really be ready to come out openly against their Government?

I remained sceptical. It seemed to me that, by contrast with India or, at an earlier time, Ireland, the question of Palestine did not begin to be a key issue in US politics. Some attributed this to the incurable timidity of influential Jewish groups; some to the countervailing force of widespread American anti-Semitism; some to the interest in preserving Arab goodwill on the part of the big oil concerns and other big business enterprises with a stake in the Middle East, and its influence on the government and the public media, and to the corresponding fear that, if America intervened in that part of the world, it would be expected, indeed it might find itself compelled, to send troops to implement policies against Arab opposition, something that no American could favour. Whatever the explanation, this seemed to me to be a fact. Early in 1944 I became convinced that Silver, Neumann and other Zionist leaders vastly overrated Jewish, and more specifically Zionist, political influence in the United States. One could get political and religious leaders and well-known liberals to sign letters and petitions, sponsor resolutions, speak at public gatherings, and in this way do something to inhibit open expressions of anti-Zionism by some of its opponents in government departments, but this was the limit of the effectiveness of this activity. There were few political public polls in those days, but press surveys, reports by British consular and other officials, travellers' tales, Senators' freely expressed views about sentiment in their States, and general Washington talk seemed to me to show that, despite some appearances to the contrary, public opinion in America in 1944 was, by and large, little concerned with the Zionist issue. So far as general American reactions went, the Foreign Office, in my view, had little to fear. Opinion within the Jewish community was, of course, another matter. I still believe that this impression was not inaccurate so far as the situation during the War was concerned, although some of the implications of this view turned out in the end to be misleading. At any rate I was convinced of its validity, and said so, in and out of season, in private and in public, to Jews and gentiles, Zionists and non-Zionists, then and later.

I was in London in the early summer of 1944 when a series of anti-British attacks, indeed a steady campaign of vituperation, was being mounted in a good many Zionist organs in the United States. This was faithfully reported by the British press surveys and probably some British correspondents, and caused a great deal of irritation in government departments in London, not so much those concerned with the Middle East as those which dealt with Anglo-American relations. Liberal-minded and by no means anti-Zionist officials were labouring under a sense of outrage. If any war could ever be just, this was surely the most justified of all wars: the stake of the Jews in allied victory was literally a vital one; bad blood between the allies could only harm the common cause, perhaps delay the date of victory; besides, some of the charges made by Zionists were false and deeply insulting. Americans in London, officials and journalists, offered encouragement and concrete help if the British decided to initiate a counter-offensive in the American press and radio – mere self-defence would, they were assured, not prove effective. They felt hesitant before engaging in open warfare with the Jews of America; yet the offer was a tempting one: there were American observers in the Middle East who reported that Jewish Palestine had become a militarised, almost totalitarian, camp. There were American journalists and officials, particularly in Cairo, who had espoused the Arab cause, and saw the Jews as a disruptive factor in the region. These men sympathised with British difficulties and should surely be encouraged to counter what could be described only as an anti-British Zionist offensive. Were there not anti-Zionists, or at least non-Zionists, among American Jews who might sympathise with such a move? What did I think?

I understood the feelings of decent and patriotic Englishmen, some of whom I knew to be as deeply ashamed of the White Paper as they had been of Munich, who thought that the Jews should be the last persons to denigrate England while she was fighting for her life, and for their lives too; as for the Zionists, but for England their cause would lack all political reality: no matter how much they hated the White Paper, how could they, I was asked, bring themselves to say the things they did, when, but for England, Palestine would have fallen prey to the Nazis? I remember explaining that so far as public opinion in the United States was concerned, it took far less interest in the Palestine issue than in India, or the Far East, or imperialism, or the class structure of Britain, or the future shape of Europe. A concerted anti-Zionist campaign would, in my view, serve no British purpose. Non-Jewish opinion did not need it; as for the Jews, so long as the White Paper remained in force the vast majority of American Jews would remain implacably opposed to

British policy in Palestine; whatever their individual views of a Jewish State, however they conceived it, on the issue of immigration they were virtually united and would remain so, whatever the press or radio might say. So long as the Palestine policy remained unaltered, the political chasm between them and Britain would be unbridgeable. Even non-Zionist Jews were not prepared to go against the pro-Zionist current, if only for fear of appearing, and, indeed, being, heartless or disloyal. On the immigration issue, quite apart from protective self-interest, the great majority of American Jews gave free vent to their deep and genuine Jewish feelings. Some might, indeed, be worried by reports of American journalists who spoke of the grimly disciplined organisation of Jewish Yishuv, the forming of secret armies to be used against the British, the Arabs and so on. But passionate opposition to the entire White Paper policy animated them all; if the British Government persisted in its attitude, it could expect no lowering of temperature among the vast majority of articulate American Jews; if the Government's plan was to create a Palestinian State with a permanent Arab majority it could defend it in America only by sending emissaries, British or Arab or whoever it might be, to plead the anti-Zionist case in influential quarters, but its quarrel with the Jews – all but the most stubborn anti-Zionists, who were a negligible group – would be total. If, however, it contemplated some change in a pro-Zionist direction (as rumours in London and elsewhere insistently suggested), and if it wanted American support for this, it had a task to perform. General American opinion might be neutral, but there were eminent Jewish personalities of great standing, with considerable influence, particularly in Washington, and more especially with the White House and Congress. If the new scheme were at all equitable and met the minimum Zionist requirements, these persons could be of great help in preventing an open breach with American Zionists. If the British Government launched its new scheme without preparing the ground in Washington, American Zionists might feel bound to oppose it in so far as it did not meet their official programme, much as they opposed the Peel Plan in 1936–7; then there was a real danger that the scheme, which might satisfy basic Zionist needs, might nevertheless go down in a terrible shambles of mutual recrimination. The Jews might well lose more than the British, but both sides would suffer greatly and needlessly. But if the plan was of such a kind that men of stature, such as the Secretary of the Treasury, Henry Morgenthau, Justice Felix Frankfurter of the Supreme Court, Governor Herbert Lehman of New York, Benjamin Cohen, who had helped to draft the original Palestine Mandate, and other highly placed and honourable Jews could be informally consulted, and were prepared to approve or even to acquiesce in such a plan, then Jewish, and indeed moderate Zionist, opinion, which felt respect for these distinguished men, with whom Weizmann was in regular contact, and who, indeed, accepted his position, could at least consider the new scheme with initial sympathy. The kind of people whom I mentioned appeared to me to enjoy far more influence at the White House and in Congress and the Cabinet, and among many of those who moulded American opinion, than did Zionist or pro-Zionist organisations up and down the country. If these people could be brought into the picture, there would be a possibility of arriving at a solution acceptable to the moderates: only the most extreme and intransigent Zionists and anti-Zionists would then be left isolated. This would avert a destructive collision between Britain and Jewry, would allay the increasing annoyance and indignation in London with what was regarded as a campaign of falsehoods and libels against a country engaged in a war against the deadliest enemy of the Jewish people, and, since Britain and the Jews were destined, willy-nilly, to march together in Palestine (this was the old Weizmannite thesis), would surely make this complicated and sometimes agonising process easier. Such a development seemed to me to be in the best interests of both Britain and Zionism. To rely on the Jewish battalions in the United States – or anywhere else – to establish a sovereign Jewish State in the whole of Palestine by developing a degree of pressure that would cause the American government to overcome British opposition to this, seemed to me indulgence in a dangerous delusion.

I remember giving an account of the apparent strength but actual weakness of the Zionist forces in America at a meeting in London – I cannot recollect either the auspices under which this meeting was held or, I am afraid, its date. All I remember now is that in the audience was Balfour's niece and biographer, Blanche Dugdale, a very distinguished and fervent Zionist, who, so I was later told (again I cannot recollect by whom), described my talk as 'supercilious, cynical, and not spoken like a Zionist'. I was, to say the least, taken aback by these harsh words. The first two adjectives might have been occasioned by disapproval of the somewhat disparaging manner in which I had probably spoken of the motives and character of some of the American Zionists' more dubious allies, on whom, in my opinion, they relied too much. But 'not spoken like a Zionist' – that cut me to the quick. My purpose was to draw a realistic contrast between Zionist influence on the one hand in America at large, and in the Jewish community and Jewish circles in Washington and New York on the other. My views were identical with those of such proven friends of Zionism, Jews and gentiles, as Felix Frankfurter, Horace Kallen, Reinhold Niebuhr, Charles Webster (who was in New York during part of the war), and, whether I was right or wrong, implied too much, rather than too little, concern on my part with the fate of the movement. I complained to Lewis Namier, who was one of Blanche Dugdale's most intimate friends. He said that my account tallied with his impressions, especially, I seem to remember, with regard to the counter-productive effect of the antics of Zionist extremists in Washington and of their moral standards. He said that he agreed with my analysis. He thought that what had shocked Mrs Dugdale was my excessively ironical and detached manner. No doubt, said Namier characteristically, four years in an Embassy tends to desiccate one's style and petrify one's feelings. It seemed to me that there was a good deal, as always, in what Namier had said. At any rate, apart from one week with the Marshall Plan Conference in Paris in 1947, I never again worked for a government, and returned with relief to private life.

Meanwhile I stuck to my guns. Mere pressure on the American government, without any attempt at negotiation with men who had some sympathy with Zionist aims and understanding of the Jewish predicament, would surely end in frustration. Attempts to pass pro-Zionist resolutions in the Senate would, if they had real teeth, be inevitably blocked by President Roosevelt's Administration. This, indeed, proved to be the case when, towards the end of 1944, General Marshall and Secretary of State Hull caused a strongly pro-Zionist resolution to be defeated in Congress. The Zionist Organisation of America had received a sharp rebuff which exposed the ineffectiveness of its traditional tactics. A return to Weizmann and patient negotiation seemed to me the only constructive alternative.

I do not wish to give the impression that I played any part in Anglo-Zionist relations at this, or any other, period. I did not. But I occasionally met politicians, administrators and government advisers, and they sometimes talked about the Palestine problem. Such very different men as Lord Cranborne and Sir Stafford Cripps, Leo Amery and Maynard Keynes, Sir William Battershill (then in the Colonial Office) and Lord Jowitt (in charge of post-war planning) all wondered whether, if the White Paper were 'modified' (only Amery spoke of outright abrogation), the new version might not be rejected by both Arabs and Jews; and, if so, whether the new policy might not fare worse than the old; if Weizmann accepted it, would the American 'extremists' overthrow him? I could give no clear answer to this. I would stress Weizmann's unique ascendancy in the entire Jewish world, and especially in America, and thought that if he was offered something that he could honourably consider, this would at least form a basis for discussion, which did not exist at present, and in which his influence might prevail. They must hope for the best. But I would make it clear that I was a British official and not in the councils of the Zionist movement; if they meant business they must approach, or get someone else, say a British Jew of adequate standing and respected by Zionists, to approach, men like Morgenthau and

Frankfurter, who were at once sympathetic to Zionism and genuinely Anglophile; their judgement would be of obvious value. My suggestions were not, so far as I know, taken up by anyone. Things went on, or failed to go on, as before.

These conversations and thoughts were based on assumptions on my part, some of which were objective and shared by many others, while others were more clearly subjective. I should like to say something about both. Let me begin with an attempt to recapture my state of mind at this time, avoiding, so far as I am able, the distorting influence of hindsight. Natural loyalty to England certainly played its part in my attitude, and would have done, without question, even if I had not been a government servant; moreover, the ends of the War overrode all other considerations. The White Paper was an iniquitous document, and led to acts of brutal inhumanity. Few Jews doubted this. Neither reasons of State nor pro-Arab sentiment could justify this unilateral abandonment of the Mandate, which seemed to put out the last rays of hope of the homeless Jewish masses in their hour of mortal danger. I could not expect my colleagues, however generous and humane, to understand fully the bitterness of Jewish despair before the apparent indifference of the world to a mass murder carried out on a scale too terrible to be believed; in the face of this the zeal with which the Palestine administration applied White Paper anti-immigration policy seemed monstrous. Nevertheless it was Britain who had alone stood up to Hitler in 1940; she and she alone had saved our lives; her cause was just, her war was the war of the entire human race against the worst enemy it had ever known; whatever her shortcomings – and her Palestine policy was an inglorious surrender to expediency – she surely did not deserve the ceaseless and undiscriminating vituperation poured out against her by exasperated American Jews. The steady campaign of denigration conducted by my fellow Zionists seemed to me often exceedingly unjust, still more often irresponsible, ignorant and counter-productive, and likely to breed only anger and the acts of folly which spring from anger.

I mention these subjective feelings because I have no doubt that they deeply coloured my assessment of the situation; I do not wish to claim to be a model of dispassionate objectivity. Yet, even if subjective reactions can do something to account for this or that prognosis or policy, it is the objective assessments in the assumptions made by Weizmann and his followers (which I accepted) that alone can justify them. There were four of particular importance. First, England would remain the dominant power in the Middle East, if only because France was too greatly weakened and its rule discredited, while America, whatever its economic ambitions, would not be ready to take over political, still less military, responsibilities in a region which lay so far from its traditional sphere of influence. The Soviet Union was not to be thought of. Consequently the future of the Jewish settlement in Palestine, and a fortiori of any viable Jewish State, was bound up with that of Britain. Ben-Gurion accepted this no less than Weizmann: so, for that matter, had Jabotinsky.

Secondly, the British connection was not only inevitable, but also desirable. The physical security of the Jewish settlement, still more of the Jewish State (or Commonwealth, as the American Zionists preferred to call it), would plainly need protection against its Arab neighbours, who could scarcely, in view of past history, be expected to look with favour on its creation; and it would require political and economic aid far beyond what it could itself, even with the aid of the Zionist movement, be expected to supply. Moreover, Weizmann, and those who agreed with him, wished to believe that bygones would become bygones; that Britain had had, and would continue to exercise, a politically civilising influence on a community not notable for calm judgement or political wisdom or avoidance of bitter party strife; and that despite the difficult, and at times profoundly unhappy, relationship between Jews and the English in Palestine between the two wars, their co-operation was essential both in the imperial interest of Britain, and for the national survival of the Jews. True, officials of the Colonial Office (and of the Foreign Office) tended to look on the Jews in Palestine as aggressively self-assertive, shrill, touchy, neurotic, cliquish, devious, ill-mannered, ungrateful, contemptuous of their Arab neighbours, unutterably tiresome and exhausting to deal with. The Jews, in their turn, looked on the British governors as arrogant, remote, snobbish, pompous, oppressed by guilt about the injustice which, they mistakenly believed, their policy did to the Arabs, whom they openly favoured, regarding them as the helpless victims of the wicked Jews, whom they viewed with unconcealed distaste. This accounted for the fact, which caused deep bitterness among the Jews, that whenever the Arabs in Palestine made murderous attacks upon the Jews, the Mandatory administration always rewarded the Arab aggressors with concessions, and punished the victims simply because they were Jews; the White Paper was the natural culmination of this policy. These reciprocal stereotypes did not seem to hold out much promise for fruitful collaboration in the future. Yet, notwithstanding all this, the alliance must go on. For there was no real alternative; beggars could not be choosers, and the advantages, in Weizmann's view, of the British connection, indeed, the absence of alternatives to it, made it the indispensable basis of the Zionist movement. It is my belief that Ben-Gurion accepted this too: though possibly with less enthusiasm.

Thirdly, it was supposed – virtually by everyone during the War (not least by Stalin) – that Churchill would continue his glorious Periclean rule, if not for ever, at any rate for some time after the end of hostilities. He was the most powerful and faithful friend of Zionism to be found anywhere. Under him the Jews would at last obtain a national home. The Foreign Office would resist, but the Cabinet and Parliament were fair-minded and not unfriendly – more reliable than Congress or Roosevelt.

Fourthly, it was assumed, at least by the Weizmannites, that patient diplomacy alone would yield results, as it had in the past. The mobilisation of the Jewish masses, however successful, could be only an aid to, never a substitute for, negotiation, for such collective pressure could never be influential enough to sway America, let alone Britain, from their traditional objectives. The American-Jewish vote, however well organised, even if it was supported by humanitarian feeling on the part of the liberal-minded, could never by itself prevail against the oil interests and other big-business lobbies. Without government support the Zionist movement might go on and even gain strength, but could scarcely become powerful enough to attain even its minimum goals. The possibility of using violence – of terrorist methods – had not then, so far as I knew, entered the thoughts of the Zionist leadership.

I believe these to have been the principal objective premises on which Weizmann built his policies. These assumptions were disputed both from the right and from the left, and the last was not fully accepted by Ben-Gurion; but the moderate centre of the Zionist movement, especially outside America, felt, not without justification, that its outlook embodied a widely accepted view of political reality; and therefore that only on such foundations could a structure be built that would provide a just and lasting political solution of the ancient Jewish problem. Although I thought about Zionist affairs a good deal, it occupied a very small portion of my official horizon. I was occasionally asked by Zionist friends how long the White Paper policy could go on: I was not optimistic. Alternatively, British officials would wonder (although this occurred seldom) how strong American Zionism really was; I would say that it was more influential in official circles in Washington than the State Department liked, or wanted to believe, and that it was the only positive force in Jewish opinion and had come to dominate it. In this way I managed to depress both sets of enquirers.

To my colleagues, British and American, very few of whom took the faintest interest in Jewish affairs, I must have appeared, I think, to be what indeed I was: a moderate Weizmannite, a convinced believer in the Anglo-Zionist connection. To American Zionists, at least to the fiercer among them, I must have seemed a compromiser, a British official concerned to defend his government against hostile attacks, foolishly convinced that a total Anglo-Zionist breach would ruin the Zionist cause, that a solution that would give the Jews self-government, including wide possibilities of immigration, even if this fell short of complete sovereignty, was preferable to a head-on collision. This, too, did not misrepresent my position. I spoke in these terms to most of my friends among Zionist leaders; I do not think that they thought me utterly mistaken. Silver did not disagree. He believed in confrontation, in forcing the American government to resist Britain not merely on the White Paper, but on and on, until the Jewish State in the whole of Western Palestine came into being. I believed this to be suicidal zealotry: Masada was not a victory.

Within the next two or three years the assumptions on which belief in a special relationship with Britain was founded were blown away by events. How far the roots of what occurred had been discerned by sharper eyes than mine, I do not know. It took a dramatically rapid transformation of the historical scene, and one which, so far as I can tell, no one had foretold, or even foreseen, to make the ideas of those who, like Weizmann and his followers, hoped for survival of the British connection, seem obsolete and irrelevant. But even now, after all that has happened, I should maintain that although our prognosis was falsified by events, the policy founded upon it was correct, and its more vehement critics mistaken. If Weizmann had lent himself to a policy likely to lead to an open rupture with the British, this would, I believe, have caused an unavoidable conflict with the American government too. The price that the Zionist movement would in that event have had to pay for this in the post-war years might have been very heavy indeed. It was the relatively unaggressive line taken by Wise and Goldmann, with Weizmannite encouragement, *vis-à-vis* the American government, particularly in 1943–6, that paved the way for President Truman's policies. Weizmann may have paid a very heavy personal price for his faith in the British, for on this issue he lost his undisputed leadership; but he saved the movement. Without him and his policy, a trial of strength before circumstances made it inevitable might have done irremediable damage to the Jewish cause. Weizmann had his hour, as Ben-Gurion had his; neither was dispensable. Without Weizmann's policies during the War the State of Israel could scarcely have come into existence. His position in 1944, which I fully shared, still seems to me to have been both honourable and right. But let me return to the events which altered everything.

IV

Late in 1944 Lord Moyne was assassinated in Egypt by members of the Lekhi organisation, known in the West as the Stern Gang. He was an old personal friend of the Prime Minister, who was profoundly upset, indeed outraged, and in a speech in the House of Commons used harsh and menacing words about the Zionist use of terrorist methods. The Cabinet Committee, I believe, continued to discuss partition schemes. Only the Prime Minister could have put through a radical new plan. But Churchill seemed personally alienated by Moyne's assassination, declined to see Weizmann, and averted his gaze from the entire issue. Nothing, he curtly informed Weizmann some months later in 1945, was to be decided until the War was over. No statement, no hint of things to come, was to be given. The entire issue for the time being, so far as Churchill was concerned, hung fire. This seems to me to have been a critical turning-point in the entire story.

In addition to this, shortly after the meeting at Yalta, where Palestine seems to have been but lightly touched upon between Roosevelt and Stalin and no minute of the discussion made, Roosevelt met King Ibn Saud, and was profoundly impressed by him. He declared that he had learnt more about Palestine from this brief encounter than during the previous years. He was alleged to have made pro-Zionist remarks to Stephen Wise even after this, and political exigencies might have made so mercurial a personality change his mind, or at least his words, again, or at any rate pretend that he had done so. Yet one member of his intimate entourage whom I knew well was very clear that the conversation with the Arab King had turned Roosevelt in a sharply anti-Zionist direction. If ever the Zionists had had a backer in him, they lost him then. With Churchill's withdrawal and Roosevelt in an *arabisant* mood, Zionist prospects declined precipitously.

Soon after this President Roosevelt died. A few months later, after the San Francisco Conference, where no decisions about Zionism were reached, Churchill lost the British elections. Zionist hopes for even more support from the Labour Party, the platform of which contained a super-Zionist plank, were swiftly and cruelly dispelled. Attlee had, in his uncommunicative way, been stonily anti-Zionist for many years (although this had not become clear until he was in power). Ernest Bevin became increasingly infuriated by Zionist claims and attitudes; Cripps was no friend; Dalton thought about other things; there was no one in the Labour Cabinet willing or able to stand up to these powerful figures. Even if Roosevelt had lived it seems wholly improbable that he would have pressed the issue against so sharp a mood in London; at most, he might have sought escape, as so often, in vague generalities and done his skilful best to keep the American Jews from boiling over. Zionism grew to be the only cause the appeal of which rivalled that of Roosevelt's personality in the minds and hearts of American Jews. If he had shown reluctance to support Zionist aspirations, this would have disturbed Jewish sentiment profoundly, and might have divided the American-Jewish community.

In addition to this, three further phenomena seem to me to have changed the course of events. The first was the experience of those who saw the death-camps in Germany and Poland, Dachau or Belsen or Auschwitz. The impression made upon them was terrible beyond description. Statistics of the murdered Jews, then accumulating, appalled their fellow Jews; but they took time to sink into the conscience of mankind. It was difficult to believe that they could be true; and with twenty or more million Russian dead, and who knew how many others on both sides in the War, it was not figures that most deeply devastated the imagination of the world, but the physical sight of the dead and the dying in the camps, the photographs and films of the skeletons and the emaciated corpses, the children with swollen bellies and the pitiful heaps of broken human possessions. A vast wave of horror and compassion and outraged human feeling spread over the earth. This went, if anything, deeper than even the emotion caused by the martyrdom of the men and women in the resistance movements who had been tortured and killed. Sympathy for refugees, displaced persons, but above all for the Jews, for their desperate search for a permanent home from which they could not be driven like cattle, or exterminated by the hostile populations in the midst of which they lived – indignation on their behalf and warm-hearted feeling towards them – sprang up everywhere, most strongly among the inhabitants of what had been Nazi-occupied Europe, but scarcely less powerfully in America and elsewhere. It passed Bevin and his officials by, but it changed the temper of British opinion for a while. The rejection by the British Government of the recommendations on immigration of the Anglo-American Commission of 1945–6 disappointed liberals; Bevin's ill-concealed suspicion that Truman's support for it sprang from cynical motives irritated the President. The rescue of the survivors of the Holocaust by the opening of doors to Palestine seemed the least that could be done to begin to redress a terrible wrong. Illegal Jewish immigration was helped in France and Italy (and other territories liberated from Nazi occupation) by many gentile sympathisers out of a simple sense of solidarity with victims of bullies and oppressors. Bevin and his advisers overplayed their hand, and provoked a reaction against their policies which less brutal behaviour might have avoided. The episode of the *Exodus* caused worldwide indignation, but the decision to return the refugees to Germany was only the most notorious expression of a consistent attitude, and it played its part in the events that led to the decision of the United Nations in 1948. The Foreign Office gravely underestimated the force and content of outraged liberal feeling in those post-war years. The Arab case did not go by default; Arab representatives protested at Lake Success, and in the capitals of the world. But the wrongs of the Jews, above all the immigration issue, dwarfed all others. The death-camps and Bevin's ham-fisted anti-Zionism were two among the unpredicted and novel factors that altered the situation. To these must be added the rise of Jewish terrorism in Palestine itself. Liberal democracies, unlike tyrannies, by their very natures cannot generate continuous counterfrightfulness for any length of time, at least in dependent territories. So it was in Palestine, in Cyprus, in Kenya, in Batavia, in Algiers. The sense of nightmare induced by the campaign of the Irgun and the Sternists and even the Haganah was clearly a real, even if not the decisive, factor in the British decision to abandon Palestine.

Let me recapitulate. With Churchill antagonised by the assassination of Lord Moyne, the British Cabinet Committee's partition scheme was shelved till the end of the war. Churchill fell from power. Terrorism in Palestine enormously diminished all chances of co-operation. The horror of the Nazi death-camps transformed American, and indeed world, opinion. Attlee and Bevin adopted the White Paper policy in its entirety and, by making Arab consent a necessary condition for any new plan, shut all doors to the Jews. This radicalised the Zionist moderates overnight. By 1947 we were all at one: Weizmann and Silver, Frankfurter and Emanuel Neumann, Goldmann and Ben-Gurion, and those to the left and right of them – indeed, every Jew with the faintest sympathy for Zionism – all were moulded into a united whole. The Labour Government's flat rejection in 1946 of the American proposal to admit a hundred thousand refugees into Palestine made total resistance to its policies unavoidable. The Jewish Samson, in his agony, might have no alternative but to bring the entire temple of the Philistines crashing down upon himself and his persecutors: Weizmann, I remember, said this to me in a state of bitter despair. It may be, as Montesquieu observed, that without the operation of general causes, small changes cannot generate great ones. But, equally, these contingent small causes, when conditions are ripe, can lead to huge upheavals. I know of no one who in, say, 1944 could have predicted the roles played by Ernest Bevin and Harry Truman in the birth of the State of Israel. Without Bevin's pig-headed obstinacy, Truman's personal goodwill, and the political miscalculations of their chief advisers, things might have turned out very differently. This, indeed, is the principal moral of my entire tale.

Everyone now knows that it was President Truman who saved the Jewish cause. Votes may have had something to do with Truman's decision, but the fact that he started without any apparent sympathy for Zionism, held back for so long, and acted so late in the day, speaks against the hypothesis that it was the need for the Jewish vote that swayed his mind. Truman's capacity for swift decision and his freedom from his great predecessor's inclination to be all things to all men showed themselves throughout his life:

in his activity as head of the wartime Truman Committee, his decisions about the atom bomb, the Marshall Plan, the Korean War, the recall of General MacArthur, Truman made up his mind about what he considered the right course to follow and then acted without hesitation. On the Palestine issue, he decided that 'the Old Doctor' (as he called Weizmann) had more justice on his side than his opponents. He thought him right about the Jewish State, right about the Negev, about what the Jews were and what they needed. This turned the scale. The new President conceived a genuine admiration for the old leader of the Zionist movement, and supported him against the advice of most of his own officials. It was the last great service, perhaps as great as that thirty years earlier, that Weizmann was able to render his people by the use of the methods he understood best.

By this time another of my most sceptical and strongest beliefs – that which had so greatly shocked Mrs Dugdale – had been falsified by the facts. The Jewish population of the United States proved stronger, more united and more courageous than I had dared to believe. Wartime Zionist propaganda may not have made a significant impact on general public opinion, but it did put heart into the Jews of America. Consequently they remained unshaken by the opposition of powerful American political leaders – James Forrestal, for example, or, to a lesser degree, General Marshall, or Dean Acheson and others among the President's trusted advisers. About this Ben-Gurion's instinct proved sound. It was mass enthusiasm in America and the discipline and the strength of the Yishuv itself, not the British connection in which I had so strongly believed, that were decisive in the creation of the mood in which Palestine Commissions were set up, Britain reappraised its strategic position and abandoned Palestine, the United Nations vote took place, the war of 1948 was won.

And yet: if Moyne had not been killed, if Churchill had continued in power after the war had ended, if a new British plan acceptable to the Zionists, at least Weizmann and the centre, had been accepted and implemented in 1945, if the British Commonwealth had put its umbrella over the new State – would the Arab States have attacked a victorious Britain? Would the Irgun have attempted a civil war, and would not Ben-Gurion have averted it? Might not such a development have saved much blood, prevented much bitterness and, above all, the conditions of beleaguerment in which the State of Israel has led its entire existence? Alternatively, it may be asked whether this could have occurred: would Ben-Gurion then have played the part of de Valera to Weizmann's Griffith, Mazzini to Weizmann's Cavour, only with greater success? Must a Moses always be followed by a Joshua? I do not know. Nor do I know whether the State of Israel would have come into existence if Attlee had accepted the recommendations of the Anglo-American Commission in 1946; or whether, if it had, it could have developed in association with the British Commonwealth; even if the ties had been loose, this would still have involved the surrender of independent defence and financial and foreign policies; could this have lasted, or ended (as it did, say, in West Africa) without a revolt? And if it had, would the Arabs have acquiesced in this British act, as Weizmann used to believe? Can a nation be created, or, as in this case (in the words of Moses Hess), rise from the grave, by the bounty of others? Does the State of Israel owe its vitality to the fact that it won its independence by its own efforts, by the blood of its heroes and martyrs? Has it, in the end, all been for the best?

These may be idle speculations. Yet it is these unfulfilled possibilities that Jacob Herzog and I used to discuss at length in our leisure hours. He too, I remember, thought that what did happen was not inevitable. If there had been a little less blindness on the part of Foreign Offices and State Departments, a better understanding of the peculiar status of a people whose martyrdom resembles that of no other, and whose moral claims the nations seemed to recognise during the brief dawn which followed the terrible night of slaughter; if this had happened – and it did not seem too unrealistic to suppose that it could have happened in the mood and circumstances of the time – would things not have turned out to better advantage for everyone? But it was not to be. The hopes and fears of 1942–5 which I have described are now a mere historical memory. It is for historians to say whether the beliefs and policies of those whose followed Weizmann – the men of the centre, amongst whom I count myself – were written in water, built on shifting sands. 'Things and Actions are what they are,' said a famous English Bishop, 'and the Consequences of them will be what they will be: Why then should we desire to be deceived?'[1] Was Weizmann, were we who followed him, deceived? Were the prophecies of those who disagreed with him, Ben-Gurion and the activists, self-fulfilling, that is to say, themselves decisive factors in bringing to pass that which they predicted? And if they were, is that of the essence of all prophecy, which is not so much objective prediction as the expression of an active attitude towards the world, a commitment to radical change? And do those who are thus committed see the shape of the future more clearly or more deeply than detached observers? To these questions I volunteer no answer. All I have tried to do is to describe my own impressions of Zionist attitudes in the context of British and American policies and opinion in the war years, and of the fantastic transformation of the scene in the two years that followed.

The Jews are a peculiar and difficult people in many ways, not least

1 Joseph Butler, *Fifteen Sermons Preached at the Rolls Chapel* (London, 1726), sermon 7, p. 136 [§ 16].

because their history has contradicted most of the best known and most admired theories of historical causation. Herzog and Zalman Aranne and I used to discuss this when we met. After our friend the Minister of Education died, we continued to talk about these topics and remembered him with love and admiration. And now Jacob, too, has been gathered to his fathers, and I, who am left, salute the memory of my friend Jacob Herzog, *zikhrono livrakha.*[1]

Jacob (Yaacov) Herzog (1921–72), rabbi, legal expert, scholar, served as Israeli Ambassador to Canada and adviser to four of his country's Prime Ministers. Son of a chief rabbi (of Ireland, then of Palestine/Israel), and brother of a future President of Israel, he was remembered by IB for his 'cool, subtle and powerful brain, a pure and warm heart, nobility of character and a simple and untroubled moral vision that sustained and preserved him in the inner conflicts that must, sooner or later, afflict all sensitive persons caught in the problems of public life'.[2]

---

[1] 'Of blessed memory'.

[2] From 'Yaacov Herzog: a Tribute', preface to the published text of the above lecture (Jerusalem, 1972), 3–6, at 3; repr. in Misha Louvish (ed.), *A People that Dwells Alone: Speeches and Writings of Yaacov Herzog* (London, 1995), 14–15, at 14.

SUPPLEMENTARY NOTES

The absence of the information given here was noticed too late for it to be included in its proper place.

p. 200 Edward Hallett Carr (1892–1982), socialist historian; FO 1916–36, Wilson Professor of International Politics, University College of Wales, Aberystwyth, 1936–47; wrote leaders for *The Times* during the war.

p. 542 Giles Alington (1914–56), son of Cyril Alington; history Praelector, Univ., 1944–56, Dean 1945. He was central to Univ. life in the 1940s and '50s, and the former Prime Minister Harold Wilson and his wife Mary named their son Giles after him.

Revd John Herbert Severn Wild (1904–92), Chaplain-Fellow, Univ., 1933–45, Master 1945–51, later (1951–73) Dean of Durham. In 1940 an unbalanced undergraduate borrowed a rifle, and from his room in the main quadrangle took potshots at a group of people coming out of Hall after lunch – a group with whom he had had a violent argument at breakfast that day. One student was killed and two others wounded. Wild, with enormous bravery, went up the stairs to meet him, and fortunately the undergraduate was willing to give himself up. During the war, as the only young Fellow not on active service (he had a heart condition), Wild more or less kept the College together. Neither Alington nor Wild were intellectually distinguished (which explains IB's comments), but they both arouse very fond memories in those who knew them. A collegiate system may benefit from such persons in a quasi-pastoral capacity.

p. 559 Rudolf Hess (1894–1987), Hitler's deputy in the Nazi Party, parachuted into Scotland in May 1941 in an apparently unauthorised attempt to broker peace between England and Germany, so that they could join forces against the USSR. He was held captive for the rest of his life.

p. 577 Presumably Henry St Lawrence Beaufort Moss (1896–1960), graduate of New College and author of *The Birth of the Middle Ages, 395–814* (Oxford, 1935).

p. 607 Lavrenty Pavlovich Beriya (1899–1953), member of the Central Committee of the Communist Party from 1934, head of the NKVD and its successors 1938–53, a deputy prime minister from 1941, member of the Politburo from 1946; one of the most powerful and ruthless men in the USSR; executed as a result of the struggle for power that followed Stalin's death.

CHRONOLOGY 1909–1946

Compiled by Serena Moore and Jennifer Holmes

6 June 1909		Born at 2a Albert Street, Riga, to Mendel and Marie
June 1915	(**aged 6**)	To avoid a German offensive near Riga, the family withdrew to Andreapol, District of Pskov, Russia
Early 1916		The family moved on to addresses in Petrograd
February 1917	(7)	The Social-Democratic Revolution, in which IB witnessed an act of violence that stayed with him for life
October	(8)	The Bolshevik Revolution
October 1920	(11)	The family moved back to Riga

20 February 1921		IB and Marie arrived in England to join Mendel
March		Entered Arundel House School, Surbiton
December	(12)	After living in various flats in the Surbiton area, IB and his parents moved into the Royal Palace Hotel, Kensington, preparatory to buying their own house
5 January 1922		The Berlins took possession of 33 Upper Addison Gardens, Kensington, London W14
June	(13)	Gained a place at St Paul's School, but failed the scholarship examination
September		Entered St Paul's School
Spring 1927	(17)	Sat, and failed, the entrance examination for Balliol College, Oxford
July	(18)	Sat, and passed, Higher Certificate examinations (equivalent of A Level) in Classical Studies, with English literature as a subsidiary subject
15 December		Elected to an entrance scholarship at Corpus Christi College, Oxford
1 May 1928		The Berlin family took up residence once more at the Royal Palace Hotel, Kensington, while between houses
July	(19)	Re-took Higher Certificate in the same subjects, this time gaining Distinctions in Latin and Greek; awarded a St Paul's leaving exhibition in classics
26 July		Noticed in *The Times* as the winner of the St Paul's School Chancellor's Prize and Medal for an English essay,

		and the Butterworth Prize for English Literature
1 October		The family moved to 49 Hollycroft Avenue, London NW3
		———
October		To Corpus Christi College, Oxford, as a Scholar, to read Greats (after the initial hurdle of Pass Mods, an easier course than the usual Honour Mods, chosen because of his relative weakness in languages)
December		Successful in Pass Mods
January 1929		Started Greats course
August	(20)	In Dresden (where he heard of the massacre of Jews in Hebron)
August 1930	(21)	In Salzburg with Stephen Spender, Michael Corley and Walter Ettinghausen for the Festival
July 1931	(22)	Awarded a First in Greats
August		In Salzburg, with Spender
September		Possible job as a journalist with the *Manchester Guardian* under discussion
October		Started course in Philosophy, Politics and Economics (PPE); rented a house in St John Street for the year with Bernard Spencer and two others
November		Shared the John Locke Scholarship in Mental Philosophy with Sidney Budden; won the Haigh Scholarship, a Corpus prize awarded for outstanding performance in final degree examinations
June 1932	(23)	In Holland, waiting for the PPE viva (oral examination); awarded a First in PPE after only one year
July		In Salzburg with Frank Hardie
October		Took up post as Philosophy Lecturer at New College
3 November		Elected a Fellow by Examination at All Souls, the first Jew to be admitted as such; soon returned home, overcome by nervous excitement
December to January 1933		A restorative break in Amalfi with his parents before returning to Oxford; continued to teach for New College while a Fellow of All Souls
Late June to early July 1933	(24)	In Southern Ireland on a motoring holiday with Mary Fisher, Maire Lynd and Christopher Cox; the party called on Elizabeth Bowen at Bowen's Court, Co. Cork
July		With Mendel in le Touquet; in Italy (Portofino, Garda, Bolzano) with Sigle and Maire Lynd, Roy Harrod,

	Harrod's mother Frances, Thomas Hodgkin and (eventually) Teddy Hodgkin
Early August	Via Innsbruck to Marienbad, then on to Salzburg, where he rejoined the Hodgkin brothers
Late August	On to Ruthenia with Goronwy Rees and Shiela Grant Duff
5–10 September	At the Urquhart Chalet des Mélèzes in the French Alps as a member of an all-male New College reading party of nine. Then home to London at last
October	Started teaching Rachel 'Tips' Walker at the request of her Somerville tutor
November	At request of H. A. L. Fisher, undertook to write a book on Karl Marx
30 November	A guest at a dinner party in the Warden's Lodgings, New College, to meet Virginia Woolf
March 1934	A week in Devon with Humphry and Madeline House
22 June (25)	At the New College dinner in Commemoration of the Founder
July	In Ireland (Belfast, Co. Donegal and Co. Galway) with Christopher Cox, Mary Fisher and Maire Lynd; a brief visit to Marie at a hotel in Droitwich
August	In Brighton with his parents; then to Verona, from where, with Tony Andrewes, he made a brief visit to Salzburg (not revealed to his parents until afterwards); most of his friends had already left Salzburg by the time they arrived; from there to Venice
September	On, with John Foster, via Egypt, to Palestine for a month
April 1935	With Guy Chilver to Paris to visit Rachel 'Tips' Walker; to the opera with them and Mary Fisher
June (26)	To Ireland again with Christopher Cox, Mary Fisher and Maire Lynd
July	In Oxford, working hard on his book about Karl Marx
August	In the Acland Home, Oxford, with a quinsy; then to Salzburg to join a party that included Mary Fisher, Maire Lynd and Richard Pares; Spender and Sally Graves came later, Christopher Cox was expected; heard Toscanini's famous performance of Beethoven's *Fidelio*; moved on to Achensee in the Tyrol
September	Saw Rachel Walker at London Zoo, where they had a defining conversation

March 1936		In Nice with Marie and Mendel for Passover, and working on Marx
5 August	(**27**)	Submitted to the Warden of All Souls a memorandum[1] on the state of psychological studies in 1936 because, having recently established a chair in social anthropology, the College was contemplating appointing a psychologist as well; still working intensively on Marx
26 August		To Ireland for a two-week touring holiday with Stuart Hampshire and Con O'Neill which concluded, in early September, with an eventful weekend house-party at Bowen's Court
8–15 September		In Keswick, Cumberland, staying on a farm with Spender
11 October		Back in Oxford, threw a large lunch party, at which Spender met Somerville graduate student Inez Pearn (they were married on 15 December)
Late February 1937		In a nursing home for a month with complications following flu
April		To Italy with his parents, visiting Merano, Vicenza and Venice, and making a first visit to La Scala, Milan (*L'Elisir d'Amore*)
July	(**28**)	At the Hotel Metropole, Brighton, alone, working on Karl Marx
August		In Salzburg with Stuart Hampshire and Elizabeth Bowen; the gang this year included Francis Graham-Harrison, Jasper Ridley and Cressida Bonham Carter, Sally Chilver, and Richard and Janet Pares
September		To Paris on the way home
January 1938		On the French Riviera with Marie and Mendel, working 'ferociously'[2] on Karl Marx
August	(**29**)	At the Hotel Metropole, Folkestone, alone, 'to cut 30.000 words out of my MS. in 4 days'[3]
August/September		In Co. Galway, Ireland with Christopher Cox, Mary Fisher and Maire Lynd; a night at the Shelbourne Hotel, Dublin, where he observed 'Mr Yeats chanting verse in a corner to a young woman',[4] then on to Bowen's Court, where the Marx MS was finished
end September		Moved out of All Souls and into New College, having

1 187/1.
2 See p. 262 above.
3 See p. 276 above.
4 See p. 277 above.

		resigned his seven-year All Souls Fellowship by Examination a year early
26 October		Formally elected a Fellow of New College
Autumn 1939	(30)	*Karl Marx: His Life and Environment* published in UK by Thornton Butterworth
Mid-June 1940	(31)	Offered his services, as a Russian speaker, to the British Foreign Office
Late June		Visited by Guy Burgess, who claimed that the FO wanted IB to become Press Attaché in Moscow
1 July		Issued with a FO Courier's Passport to Moscow, via the USA and Japan, and back to London
10 July		Sailed, with Guy Burgess, on the *SS Antonia* for America
18 July		Disembarked at Quebec; spent the weekend in New York before continuing to Washington
27 July		FO in London recalled Burgess and denied the existence of a job for IB in Moscow
August		Obliged to hang around, waiting, for weeks, while attempting to obtain agreement that he should continue to Moscow
September		Carried out an analysis of Associated Press dispatches for the British Library of Information in New York; discussions under way on a possible long-term role in the US
Mid-October		Returned to England by sea-plane via Lisbon, where he was delayed for nearly a week
November		Returned to Oxford and resumed teaching
late November		Received letter from MOI saying he was overdue for the post he had been appointed to in New York
Early January 1941		Returned to New York, by air to Lisbon, then by sea.
January		Appointed as a 'specialist attached to the British Press Service'[1] on the 44th floor of 30 Rockefeller Plaza, New York (BPS soon became part of the new British Information Services); his role was principally to present the British point of view to special interest groups, initially Jews; organised labour, Negroes (as they were then called) and various Christian denominations were later added to his remit (but see p. 644)
Late June	(32)	In hospital being treated for sinusitis

1 See p. 356 above.

July		Convalescent holiday in Vermont
August		Three weeks in Washington
Mid-November		In Detroit for a Labour convention, then on to Chicago
Early 1942		Met Patricia de Bendern at a dinner party
Spring		Appointed Head of Political Survey Section at the British Embassy, Washington, until July splitting his week between New York and Washington
Early August	(33)	Returned to England for consultations and leave
August–September		In London and Oxford, on leave
Late September		Return journey to US involved a week's delay in Ireland, where he became ill but continued his journey; went to hospital the day after arriving in New York
October		In the New York Hospital, having treatment for 'sinusitis' (actually viral pneumonia); officially appointed as a diplomat, with the local rank of First Secretary
Early November		A brief convalescent holiday with the Weizmanns at Grossinger's Hotel in the Catskill Mountains, near New York
January 1943		Back in Washington
June	(34)	Left the Shoreham Hotel for a rented house in Georgetown, shared until August with Edward Prichard
September		Moved into another rented house, also in Georgetown, sharing with Guy Chilver
26 September to 2 November		On holiday: travelling via Chicago to Aubrey Morgan's farm in Washington State for two weeks, then a long trip via San Francisco, Los Angeles, the Grand Canyon, Arizona, New Mexico, Texas and New Orleans
November		Visited Harvard
9 February 1944		Irving Berlin in England: Churchill mistook him for IB, and cross-questioned him over lunch at 10 Downing Street
late March to mid-May		Another trip home, including four days at New College negotiating a change of subject from philosophy to the history of ideas, and a stay in London for talks with Donald Hall and others at the FO
mid-July to mid-August	(35)	On holiday in the US, staying in the mountains, calling at Princeton and Harvard, and visiting his friend Alix de Rothschild at Cape Cod
Early 1945		Officially transferred from MOI to FO

January	Refused Arnold Toynbee's offer of the headship of the USSR section at FORD; also Duff Cooper's offer of the job of Press Attaché in Paris
Early to end February	In Baltimore for three weeks, receiving treatment at the Johns Hopkins Hospital for sinusitis
Early to mid-March	In Cuernavaca, Mexico for two weeks of 'total rest';[1] back at work in Washington by 23 March and negotiating a return to the UK
May	Learned that he was to achieve the longed-for trip to Moscow, for three–four months in the autumn
Late June (36)	In San Francisco during the last fortnight of the two-month Conference held to draft the Charter of the UN and inaugurate it
Early July to early September	Returned early to England in the disappointed hope of attending the Potsdam Conference; in London and Oxford for a few weeks; refused Lord Beaverbrook's offer of a regular column in the *Evening Standard*
Early September	Travelled via Berlin to Moscow, on secondment to the British Embassy as a temporary First Secretary
Mid-September	The *British Ally* dinner, at which he met J. B. Priestley and a number of Russian writers
Late September	To Peredelkino to see Boris Pasternak
?End September	Clandestine visit to Leo Berlin and other relatives
13 November	Arrived in Leningrad
c.15/16 November	First visit (in two parts) to Anna Akhmatova
21 November	Back in Moscow
1 January 1946	Created CBE in New Year Honours List
5 January	Second visit to Anna Akhmatova
6 January	Left Leningrad for England, travelling via Finland and Stockholm
?15–16 January	In Paris; visited Patricia de Bendern
Early February	Back in Washington
31 March	Appointment as First Secretary in Washington ended
7 April	Sailed from New York on *SS Queen Mary*, for England – and Oxford

1 See p. 523 above.

SELECT BIOGRAPHICAL GLOSSARY

THESE notes on some important and/or frequently mentioned dramatis personae include rather more information than is appropriate in a footnote. The existence of these supplementary notes is flagged by asterisks attached to the relevant surnames on their first occurrence in a footnote, and in the index, thus: *Berlin. As in the footnotes, coverage is in general limited to the period covered by the present volume.

Adams, (William) George Stewart (1874–1966), Gladstone Professor of Political Theory and Institutions, Oxford, 1912–33, Fellow (1910–33) and Warden (1933–45) of All Souls. Married Muriel Lane 1908. IB remembered him as 'a thoroughly nice man [. . .] who was like an old farmer, he was by nature kindly and courteous';[1] according to Harry Hodson he was 'eclectic in outlook and never ready to take a difference of opinion as opposition'.[2]

Alsop, Joseph Wright (1910–89), Connecticut patrician, 'young Boston Brahmin',[3] related to the Roosevelts. Journalist with the *New York Herald Tribune* 1932–7, then syndicated newspaper columnist. US Navy 1940–1; transferred to American Volunteer Group (Flying Tigers) on staff of General Claire Chennault until he was captured by Japanese in Hong Kong; released in an exchange of prisoners August 1942; Chief of Lend-Lease Mission to China December 1942; in 14th (China) Air Force and once more on Chennault's staff 1943–5, after which he resumed his career as columnist and political commentator. Co-author of *The 168 Days* (1938), *Men Around the President* (1939) and *American White Paper: The Story of American Diplomacy and the Second World War* (1940).

Austin, John Langshaw (1911–60), Fellow of All Souls 1933–5, Fellow and philosophy Tutor, Magdalen, 1935–52 (then White's Professor of Moral Philosophy and Fellow of Corpus 1952–60). Subject of a study in PI; talking to Michael Ignatieff, IB added: 'Cleverest man I ever knew, apart from Keynes, whom I didn't know at all well. [. . .] Became a great friend. He was entirely honest, he was very vain, [. . .] rigorous, and extremely kind by nature. I thought he was admirable, he really was dedicated to his subject; and very sceptical about himself.'[4]

Ayer, Alfred ('Freddie') Jules (1910–89), Christ Church classics 1928–32; Lecturer in Philosophy, Christ Church, 1932–5, Research Student, 1935–44; Fellow of Wadham 1944–6; later Grote Professor of the Philosophy of Mind and Logic, London University (1946–59), Wykeham Professor of Logic and Fellow of New

---

1 MI Tape 20.
2 http://www.athelstane.co.uk/hvhodson/hvhbiogr/hvhbiogr.txt, accessed 21 October 2003.
3 IB to Washington colleagues, 9 November 1943.
4 MI Tape 6.

College, Oxford (1959–78). Married 1932 (divorced 1942) (Grace Isabel) Renée Lees (1909–80). IB later commented that Ayer wrote 'in excellent English, no repetitions, lucid, best English philosophical prose style since Mill, I would say – and never had an idea in his life'.[1] *Language, Truth and Logic* (1936), *The Foundations of Empirical Knowledge* (1940).

Berlin, Isaiah [Mendelevich] (1909–97), St Paul's School, London, 1922–8; CCC classics 1928–31, PPE 1931–2; Prize Fellow, All Souls, 1932–8; Lecturer in Philosophy, New College, 1932–8, Fellow 1938–50; war service with Ministry of Information in New York, 1941–2, at British Embassy in Washington, 1942–6, at British Embassy, Moscow, September 1945 to January 1946. *Karl Marx: His Life and Environment* (1939).

Berlin, (Mussa) Marie (1880–1974), née Volshonok ('Wolfson'), IB's mother, first cousin of her husband Mendel, but according to her son 'socially a class below my father'.[2] IB described her as 'full of humour, strong temperament, lively, imaginative and colossally frustrated by being married to a dull, decent, friendly husband, when she really wanted a lover[3] [. . .] [She] was an absolutely uncompromising, intransigent Jewish nationalist by temperament. Nothing anti-Semitic must be allowed.'[4] And although he was irritated by her domineering character and parsimony, at her death he freely acknowledged her enormous influence on him:

> My dogmatic confidence in my own judgment, which used to irritate Maurice so, comes from my mother (she liked Maurice *very* much) [. . .] no doubt her scrutiny of basic values was sharpened by being in such absolute exile: Sir George [Weidenfeld], Goronwy, Burgess, were shot down at once; Rachmilevich for lack of heart; Scholem for vanity and envy; & so on: Herbert H. she *pitied*; you [Stuart Hampshire] passed with flying colours (Freddie too was sent spinning): she had enormous vitality, fantasies of what she might have been, passionate love of Ibsen, Hamsun, D. H. Lawrence, Gorky's lower Depths, Verdi, Carmen, all forms of full blooded self assertion, and like Maurice, dislike of those who shush people, recoil from coarse vitality, and display refined, thin lipped disapproval. [. . .] I suppose I do owe my Judaeocentricity [. . .] to her & her world & Russian-Jewish cultural roots, to her: my father had none of that.[5]

Berlin, Mendel [Borisovich] (1884–1953), timber and bristle trader, IB's father. IB's memories of his 'anglo-maniac'[6] father are of a 'sweet, innocent [. . .] quite amusing, rather ungrown-up sort of man'[7] who was 'very able' and 'very

---

1 ibid.
2 MI Tape 2.
3 'He loved her, yes, to the end; she not, no.' MI Tape 22.
4 MI Tape 2.
5 Letter to Stuart Hampshire, 23 February 1974.
6 MI Tape 4.
7 MI Tape 22.

timid [. . .] He never made much money, and wasn't liked by the enterprising Jewish merchants, some of whom he knew, because he didn't play cards, didn't have any temperament, wasn't adventurous. He could have made an excellent civil servant. He had an excellent brain, but he was timorous. He knew what he was doing. He never did anything dangerous, so he always was comfortably off – not very comfortably, fairly comfortably.'[1] But in contrast Mary Bennett later recalled Mendel as 'a very robust and admirable character' with 'a sort of no-nonsense quality' about him, whom she could imagine 'in his gumboots walking about buying forests'.[2]

Bowen, Elizabeth Dorothea Cole (1899–1973), novelist and short-story writer, chatelaine of Bowen's Court, County Cork, Ireland, where IB revised *Karl Marx* in 1938; married 1923 Alan Charles Cameron (1893–1952). IB described her as 'a wonderful talker, highly intelligent, very sympathetic, charming and interesting and agreeable [. . .] she was Christian, she was religious, she liked mainly men, she liked joking and she voted Conservative and wanted people to be masculine and no nonsense, hated pacifists and vegetarians and that kind of thing [. . .] she wanted a sort of clashing of swords'.[3] Despite his enthusiastic comments on her novels in his letters in the 1930s, he said later that he found her books 'unreadable'.[4] *The Hotel* (1927), *The Last September* (1929), *Friends and Relations* (1931), *To The North* (1932), *The Cat Jumps* (1934), *The House in Paris* (1935), *The Death of the Heart* (1938), *Bowen's Court* (1942), *Seven Winters* (1943).

Bowra, (Cecil) Maurice (1898–1971), classicist; New College, Oxford, 1918–22; Fellow and Tutor, Wadham, 1922–38, Warden 1938–70. Later Professor of Poetry (1946–51) and Vice-Chancellor (1951–4), Oxford. After Bowra's death IB described him as 'a tremendous liberator in our youth'[5] and remembered:

He did a very great deal for me when I was very young – he was the most talked-about person in Oxford, parents trembled about the wicked influence he might have on their children, although he was always very positive and a major-key sort of figure, and all that shouting staccato utterance and special style [. . .] was due to a fearful inner insecurity. When one came to know him he was a very sweet and touching man, and genuinely life-giving and warm-hearted, but he must have been wounded early in his youth, and the rest of his life was emotionally with the poachers, even when he officially crossed over to the gamekeepers, and that is what made him ultimately a friend and an ally – he never did join the pompous establishment, the majority. He was for what he called the 'immoral front' – all the minorities who were disapproved of by the stolid

1 MI Tape 2.
2 Interview with MI, 1 February 1994.
3 MI Tape 13.
4 ibid.
5 Letter to A. J. Ayer, 20 July 1971.

'silent majority'.[1]

Writing to Noel Annan, IB recalled Bowra's inconsistencies:

[He was] capable of saying to X that Shelley was a muddled watery mess, and five minutes later to Y (D. Cecil, say) that he was the noblest poet in the English language. This cost him, apparently, nothing: it was part of a wild, impulsive, careless playing: he was easily carried away by poetry, by painting, by people, he adored the momentary crest of a wave, he hated careful, cautious, calculation [. . .] but *integrity* was an empty concept to him. He lied like a trooper, to win, to enhance life, to humiliate an enemy, to do good to a friend, to get out of a corner: and was terrified of being found out.[2]

Also the subject of a study in PI. *Tradition and Design in the Iliad* (1930), *Greek Lyric Poetry* (1936), *The Heritage of Symbolism* (1943), *Sophoclean Tragedy* (1944), *From Virgil to Milton* (1945), *The Creative Experiment* (1945).

Cecil, Lord (Edward Christian) David (Gascoyne) (1902–86), Fellow of Wadham 1924–30, Fellow of New College 1939–69, later (1948–69) Goldsmiths' Professor of English Literature. Married 1932 Rachel Mary V. MacCarthy (1909–82), daughter of literary critic Desmond MacCarthy (124/1). Subject of a study in PI. IB described him as 'highly intelligent, full of charm, imagination and a very good talker [. . .] a sceptical conservative', but very patriotic, 'violently anti-egalitarian', 'very sensible' and 'in no way sentimental, nothing gooey'.[3] *The Stricken Deer* (1929), *Sir Walter Scott* (1933), *Early Victorian Novelists* (1934), *Jane Austen* (1935), *The Young Melbourne* (1939), *Hardy the Novelist* (1943).

Chilver, Guy Edward Farquhar (1910–82), Merton classics 1932–4; Fellow and Praelector, Queen's, 1934–63; Ministry of Food, 1940–5; British Food Mission, Washington, 1943–5, sharing a house with IB, who recalled his 'extreme scrupulousness and liability to genuine moral indignation about dishonourable or dubious behaviour' as well as his dislike of reactionaries and Roman Catholics, and considered him 'a civil servant by nature, who might have written admirable Roman history on the side', 'gallant and charming [. . .] very courteous, very affectionate [with] a very civilised heart'.[4]

Cox, Christopher William Machell (1899–1982), ancient historian, 'lively and amusing and sensitive and very good company and a tremendous human being';[5] Fellow of New College 1926–70, Sub-Warden 1931, Dean 1934–6; Director of Education, Anglo-Egyptian Sudan, and Principal of Gordon College, Khartoum, 1937–9; Educational Adviser to the Secretary of State for the Colonies 1940–61.

1 Letter to Rowland Burdon-Muller, 19 July 1971.
2 Letter to Noel Annan, 31 August 1971.
3 MI Tape 15.
4 Letter to Mary Warnock, 14 October 1982.
5 MI Tape 5.

Crossman, Richard Howard Stafford (1907–74), New College classics 1926–30, Fellow and Tutor in Philosophy, 1930–7; Assistant Editor, *New Statesman and Nation*, 1938–55; Leader of Labour group, Oxford City Council, 1934–40; later a Labour politician. Married 1932 (divorced *c.*1935) Erika Susanna Glück (née Landsberg; previously married to, first, Theo Simon, second, Gustav Alois Julius Glück); secondly 1937 Inez ('Inezita' / 'Zita') Hilda Baker (1900–52) (née Davis, previously married to John Randal Baker). IB later recalled: 'he didn't really believe in anything very much. He wasn't bogged down. Politically what repelled me was that he was a left-wing Nazi [. . .] He was anti-capitalist – quite genuinely – hated the civil service, hated respectability, hated conventional values [. . .] what he wanted was young men singing songs, hearty, vulgar students with linked arms drinking beer [. . .] Nazi marches, torch-lit. [He had] a strong Fascist streak [. . .] liked power, hated mildness, liberalism, kindness, amiability. It provoked him.'[1] *Plato Today* (1937), *Socrates* (1938), *Government and the Governed* (1939), *How We Are Governed* (1939).

Crosthwaite, (Ponsonby) Moore (1907–89), CCC classics 1926–30; Laming Fellow, Queen's, 1931–2; Diplomatic Service from 1932 (FO Central Dept 1932–4, Baghdad 1934–7, FO Eastern Dept 1937–43, Moscow 1943–6, Madrid 1946–7). According to IB, 'a fairly notorious homosexual'[2] and 'a great, great friend'.[3]

Fisher, Herbert Albert Laurens (1865–1940), historian, statesman; MP 1916–26, President of the Board of Education 1916–22, Delegate to the League of Nations 1920–2, OM 1937, Warden of New College 1925–40. IB remembered him as 'very cynical about the University in general, very detached [. . .] slightly sardonic [. . .] highly intelligent [. . .] a superior person. [. . .] He believed in what might be called intellectual values and academic values very, very strongly. Didn't like mediocrity.'[4] Works include *The Medieval Empire* (1898), *The History of England: From the Accession of Henry VII to the Death of Henry VIII (1485–1547)* (1906), *Bonapartism* (1908), *The Republican Tradition in Europe* (1911), *Studies in History and Politics* (1920), *A History of Europe* (1935), *England and Europe* (1936), *Pages from the Past* (1939).

Fisher, Lettice (1875–1956) née Ilbert, historian and economist; married H. A. L. Fisher (q.v.) 1899; Founding Chairman of the National Council for the Unmarried Mother and her Child (1918–55); after her husband's death was asked by New College to go on running the Lodgings,[5] in which various senior members who had been evacuated from London would be housed, until a new Warden should be elected. Works include *Getting and Spending: An Introduction*

---

1 ibid.
2 Interview with Brian Harrison, 19 October 1992.
3 MI Tape 21.
4 Interview with Brian Harrison, 25 April 1988.
5 A phrase proposed by Mary Bennett, who writes to the editor (23 October 2003): 'I think "running the Lodgings" covers all that standing in queues for cakes to feed undergraduates, which occupied at least as much time & energy as seeing to housemaids.'

to Economics (1922), *The Citizen: A Simple Account of How we Manage our National and Local Affairs* (1927), *Mothers and Families* (1932), *The Housewife and The Town Hall: A Brief Description of What is Done by Our Local Councils and Public Services* (1934), *Life and Work in England* (1934), *An Introductory History of England and Europe, from the Earliest Time to the Present Day* (1935), *Twenty-One Years: 1918–1939* [a history of the National Council for the Unmarried Mother and her Child] (1939).

Fisher, Mary Letitia Somerville (b. 1913), daughter of H. A. L. and Lettice Fisher (qq.v.), Somerville classics 1931–5 (living at home in the Warden's Lodgings, New College, for her last year); Joint Broadcasting Committee 1940–1 (which she described as 'a front organisation for getting recorded material into Germany');[1] Transcription Service of BBC 1941–5; Colonial Service 1945–56. Married John Bennett 1955; later (1965–80) Principal, St Hilda's.

Foster, John Galway (1904–82), lawyer; Fellow of All Souls 1924–82, First Secretary, British Embassy, Washington, 1939–43, then legal adviser, SHAEF; Conservative MP 1945–74. IB described him thus to Michael Ignatieff:

John Foster, [. . .] a legal adviser [to the British Embassy] who had been a Fellow of my College; he was a very agreeable, remarkable, very odd man [. . .] he was a very free spirit, lacked certain human qualities, benevolent, amusing, not exactly an adventurer, but full of vitality and fun, couldn't understand why poetry was written, why words were put in this funny way together; had never read a novel in his life because he didn't want to read false statements about reality when you could read history and newspapers, and he couldn't imagine living in a world that didn't have telephones, for example. He didn't smoke, didn't drink; he went to bed with more ladies than anybody in the twentieth century. His promiscuity was total. He didn't know the meaning of the word 'love', I think. He was like a very nice dog, a very frisky dog who didn't happen to have a human soul. He had a heart, a nervous system and a very good quick brain. Terribly benevolent. He was a pure Benthamite Utilitarian. He believed in maximising human pleasure. He was altruistic. But pleasure to him meant physical pleasure. Therefore medicine he was prepared to back because that minimised pain. But [. . .] research into, I don't know what, crusaders of Malta, seemed to him to be mad, absolute rubbish. But since people enjoyed it, he didn't want to stop them, because pleasure was all right and they took their pleasure in these funny ways. His natural friends were the slightly dubious Jewish lawyers in Brooklyn [. . .].[2]

Frankfurter, Felix (1882–1965), born in Vienna, Byrne Professor of Administrative Law, Harvard, 1914–39, George Eastman Visiting Professor, Oxford, 1933–4, Associate Justice of the US Supreme Court, 1939–62. Prominent in the

---

1 loc. cit. (705/2).
2 MI Tape 20.

unsuccessful campaign on behalf of Italian-born anarchists Nicola Sacco and Bartolomeo Vanzetti, who were controversially convicted of murder and robbery in 1921 and executed in 1927. A supporter of FDR and the New Deal, and a liberal by conviction, Frankfurter nevertheless maintained that it was for the legislature, not the courts, to set the law, and therefore became alienated from other liberals who favoured greater court intervention. Works include: *The Case of Sacco and Vanzetti* (1927), *Mr Justice Holmes and the Constitution* (1927), *The Public and its Government* (1930), *The Commerce Clause under Marshall, Taney and Waite* (1937), *Mr Justice Holmes and the Supreme Court* (1938), *Law and Politics: Occasional Papers of Felix Frankfurter, 1913–1938* (1939), ed. Archibald Macheish and E. F. Prichard.

Frankfurter, Marion A. (1890–1975), née Denman, daughter of a Presbyterian minister. Married Felix Frankfurter (q.v.) 1919. Co-edited *The Letters of Sacco and Vanzetti* (1928), and edited her husband's non-juridical writings after his death. Frankfurter's biographer, Liva Baker, described the couple as 'completely different and completely complementary. Her reserve set off his ebullience. His indulgence was matched by her toughness. His tastes were legal; hers, literary.'[1] And the *New York Times*[2] recalled that she 'was known for her wit and ability to deflate her husband on occasion. Speaking of his limitations as a public speaker, she once said: "There are only two things wrong with Felix's speeches: He digresses and he returns to the subject."'

Grant Duff, Shiela (b. 1913), St Paul's Girls School, LMH PPE 1931–4 (she met IB at Oxford through her friend Goronwy Rees, q.v.); then Foreign Correspondent in Germany and Czechoslovakia; FRPS 1939–41, BBC Foreign Service 1941–4; married to (1) Noel Francis Newsome 1942–52, (2) Micheal Sokolov (who changed his name to Sokolov Grant before the marriage) from 1952 until his death in 1998. *German and Czech: A Threat to European Peace* (1937), *Europe and the Czechs* (1938), *A German Protectorate: The Czechs under Nazi Rule* (1942).

Hampshire, Stuart Newton (b. 1914), Balliol classics 1933–6, philosopher, Fellow of All Souls 1936–40, philosophy Lecturer, Queen's, 1936–9, military intelligence 1940–5; Personal Assistant to Minister of State, FO, 1945. Later Lecturer in Philosophy, University College London (1947–59), Grote Professor of Mind and Logic, London (1960–3), Professor of Philosophy, Princeton (1963–70), Warden, Wadham (1970–84). Married Renée Ayer 1961.

Hardie, William Francis ('Frank') Ross (1902–90), Fellow and philosophy Tutor, CCC, 1926–50, later (1950–69) President; married Isobel Macaulay 1938. *A Study in Plato* (1936), *Aristotle's Ethical Theory* (1968). IB said of him:

I had an absolutely wonderful tutor– an exhausting sort of teaching – extremely clever, modest, sharp – one couldn't get away with a single piece of rhetoric, however harmless, without explaining exactly what one

1 Liva Baker, *Felix Frankfurter* (NY, [1969]), p. 89.
2 11 June 1975, 46.

meant, very clearly. Extremely deflationary; all the same, just and kind [. . .] to whom I owe a great deal. Son of a classical scholar. Classical scholar himself, brother of another one [Colin], got all the prizes from Balliol in his day. Modest, shy, rather repressed, Scottish – from Edinburgh, strong Scotch accent. Written a few books, which are not particularly praised, on Plato and Aristotle. Knew a lot of Greek, but was a very minute tutor, and extremely careful and clear; never humiliated one, merely corrected one; said 'This can't be right, because you say so and so, but in what way do you mean that? But that can't be right, can it, because . . .?' All done with extreme gentleness and firmness. I never knew anyone else like that. That had a profound effect on me: then clarity became an obsessive value to me. One might be shallow, one might be superficial, but obscurity and pretentiousness, and sentences which [*slaps wrist*] doubled over themselves, became a horror to me, from then till this moment.[1]

This description is echoed by J. O. Urmson in a piece written on Hardie's retirement as President of Corpus:

Mr Hardie, when a tutor, turned out many more first-rate philosophers than most, so that his method was certainly successful; but he was certainly inclined to judicious questioning rather than to imparting information or propagating his own views. One had very little idea what his views were. An essay beginning with a confident assertion of some generality would be greeted with a low, but agonised, moan. One would be required to say what one meant, what were one's grounds, how one would deal with this and that objection.[2]

Harrod, (Henry) Roy Forbes (1900–78), economist, Student (i.e. Fellow) of Christ Church 1924–67. Son of novelist and painter Frances Harrod, née Forbes-Robertson (1866–1956), and main victim of her exhausting emotional demands and melancholy; married 1938 Wilhelmine ('Billa') Margaret Eve Cresswell (b. 1911), on whom Nancy Mitford reputedly based the calm and sensible character of Fanny Logan in *The Pursuit of Love* and *Love in a Cold Climate*. IB met him as an undergraduate in 1929 or 1930 at Christ Church via their mutual friends Maurice Bowra and John Sparrow. *International Economics* (1933), *The Trade Cycle* (1936).

Hart, Herbert Lionel Adolphus (1907–92), New College classics 1926–9, Chancery Bar 1932–40, War Office 1940–5; married Jenifer Williams (q.v.) 1941; Fellow and philosophy Tutor, New College, 1945–52; later Professor of Jurisprudence, Oxford (1952–68), Principal, Brasenose (1973–8).

Hart, Jenifer: see Williams, Jenifer.

Hodgkin, Thomas Lionel (1910–82), Balliol classics 1928–32; Senior Demy (i.e. graduate scholar), Magdalen 1933, based in Palestine 26 December 1932 to 24

1 MI Tape 5.
2 J. O. Urmson, 'W. F. R. Hardie: President 1950–1969', *Pelican* 1 No 1 (Michaelmas 1969), 4.

July 1933 pursuing archaeological research; Assistant Secretary, Palestine Civil Service, May 1934 to summer 1936; Education Officer, Cumberland Friends' Unemployment Committee, 1937–9; Staff Tutor in North Staffordshire, Oxford University Tutorial Classes Committee, 1939–45; Secretary to the Oxford University Delegacy for Extra-Mural Studies, and Fellow of Balliol, 1945–52. IB remembered him as 'left-wing, sentimental, pro-native' and 'a secret Communist, [. . .] a 1,000 per cent anti-Zionist'.[1]

House, (Arthur) Humphry (1908–55), Hertford history 1925–30; schoolmaster, Repton School, 1930–1; Fellow and English Lecturer, Wadham, 1931–2; deacon in the Church of England 1931–2, after which he reverted to lay status; Special Assistant Lecturer in Classics, University College, Exeter, 1933–5; married Madeline Edith Church (1903–78) 1933; Professor of English, Presidency College, Calcutta, 1936; Lecturer in English, University of Calcutta, 1937; William Noble Fellow, Liverpool, 1940. Described by IB as 'dark, heavy, with a lowering brow, formidable, talked slowly and deliberately [. . .] by nature highly susceptible [. . .] a friend to whom I was devoted: but [. . .] a man of passionate nature, which he had little wish to control.'[2] Wrote *The Dickens World* (1941).

Hutchinson, Jeremy Nicolas St John (b. 1915), lawyer, son of Mary Barnes Hutchinson, brother of Victor Rothschild's first wife Barbara; Magdalen PPE 1933–6 (had lodgings in Beaumont Street with Stuart Hampshire and Ben Nicolson), Harmsworth Law Scholar 1937, called to Bar 1939; married Peggy Ashcroft 1940 (divorced 1966); later QC (1961), Baron Hutchinson of Lullington (1978).

Jay, Douglas Patrick Thomas (1907–96), economist and politician; Fellow of All Souls 1930–7; married Margaret ('Peggy') Christian Garnett 1933 (divorced 1972); journalist 1929–40 (*The Times* 1929–33, *The Economist* 1933–7, *Daily Herald* 1937–40); Ministry of Supply 1940–3; Board of Trade 1943–5; Personal Assistant to Prime Minister 1945–6; later Labour politician, Baron Jay of Battersea (1987). Tam Dalyell telephoned IB for comments before writing his obituary of Jay,[3] in which he quotes IB's description of Jay as 'highly eccentric, idiosyncratic and unyielding', and his observation that 'Douglas was often foolish and certainly fanatical on any subject. Once he had made up his mind nothing would dislodge his opinion. He had fixed habits, never to be altered.' In a letter[4] to Jay's widow (his second wife, Mary), IB praises Jay's talents, achievements and character in the strongest terms, and explains that he had talked to Dalyell 'at great length. The passages he attributed to me were, I am afraid, spoken by me, but they seem unduly critical taken out of context and not accompanied, as they might have been, by all the admiration and love I conveyed. He was

1 MI Tape 10.
2 Letter to Maire Gaster, January 1982.
3 *Independent*, 6 March 1996, 18.
4 Letter to Lady Jay, 8 March 1996.

fanatical and idiosyncratic in some ways, but there were only minor aspects of a much larger, more interesting and noble character.' *The Socialist Case* (1937), *Who is to Pay for the War: And the Peace* (1941).

Lehmann, Rosamond Nina (1901–90), novelist; married Hon. Wogan Philipps 1928 (divorced 1944); guest of Elizabeth Bowen at Bowen's Court with IB and Stuart Hampshire in September 1936 (began affair with Goronwy Rees during that stay; they then lived together until Rees married in 1940). Works include *Dusty Answer* (1927), *Invitation to the Waltz* (1932) and *The Weather in the Streets* (1936).

Lynd, Maire (pronounced 'Moira'; nicknamed 'BJ', which stands for 'Baby Junior') (1912–90), daughter of the Irish nationalist writers Robert and Sylvia Lynd, younger sister of Sigle/Sheila; a friend of the whole 1930s circle, starting at St Paul's Girls School; Home Student reading Classics at Oxford 1930–4, living for her first year with the Joachims, and then, when Mary Fisher went to Somerville, replacing her as daughter of the house at the Warden's Lodgings, New College; after graduating, worked for the publishers William Heinemann as a reader for some fifty years; married Jack Gaster (b. 1907) in 1938. She was IB's pupil (reading Greats) when she and Christopher Cox organised the first of a series of summer holidays (1933, 1934, 1935, 1938) in Ireland for themselves, IB and Mary Fisher. She and her sister were both, in their different ways, exceptionally beautiful, and both – Sigle first (and more ardently, though less enduringly)[1] – became members of the Communist Party. BJ later became somewhat uncomfortable with Communism but made no formal break, concentrating on the peace movement, and organising intensive marmalade-making to raise funds for causes she thought deserving. Tony Gifford wrote in his obituary: 'What she strove for in the world was reflected in what she gave to her family, friends and neighbours– generosity, serenity, love and concern for others.'[2]

Lynd, Sigle (or Sheila, pronounced the same; on her birth certificate the spelling is 'Sighle') (1910–76), Somerville chemistry and biology 1929–30, left after four terms (too busy dancing); elder sister of Maire (q.v.); worked for the publisher Victor Gollancz (a very close working relationship brought to an end by political differences on the outbreak of the Second World War); married Peter Wheeler 1939. Described by Mary Bennett as 'talkative, amusing, laughing, and fair'.[3]

Morgan, Aubrey Niel (1904–85), Welsh grandson of the founder of the David Morgan department store in Cardiff; Survey Section, British Library of Information, 1939–40; BPS 1940–2 (Special Assistant to the Director-General of BIS 1941–2); Deputy Director-General of BIS and head of BIS NY 1942–5. Married first 1932 Elisabeth Reeve Morrow (1904–34), eldest daughter of Dwight

---

1 She left in 1956 after the suppression of the Hungarian revolution.
2 *Guardian*, 1 October 1990, 37.
3 loc. cit. (705/2).

Morrow, former US Ambassador to Mexico, and subsequently (1937) her youngest sister Constance Cutter Morrow (1913–95). John Wheeler-Bennett describes him as 'utterly fearless, full of initiative and imagination, ruthless when necessary', and also 'warm, loyal, supremely dependable', and applauds the contribution that 'his zeal for action, his contempt for all pomposity, official or unofficial, and his tendency for driving clean through any difficulty' made to establishing a more effective British propaganda organisation in the US at the start of the Second World War.[1] IB confirmed that, whoever was nominally in charge of the British propaganda machine in the US during the war, Morgan and Wheeler-Bennett were 'the ever-present powers behind the throne'.[2]

Nicholas, Herbert George (1911–98), New College classics 1931–5, Commonwealth Fund Fellow in Modern History, Yale, 1935–7, politics Lecturer, Exeter College, 1938, Fellow 1946–51, later (1969–78) Rhodes Professor of American History and Institutions and Fellow of New College. Writing to IB, Daphne Straight explained that his 'unfortunate and facetious prose style which so often conveys an impression of unkindness and sarcasm when it is only actually intended to be funny [. . .] his pen and sometimes sharp tongue are his only defensive weapons to conceal a complicated inferiority complex (particularly in his relations with you) and a very kind heart'.[3]

Nicolson, (Lionel) Ben(edict) (1914–78), historian of art; son of Harold Nicolson and Vita Sackville-West, Balliol history 1933–6; Deputy Surveyor of the King's Pictures 1939–47; served in the Intelligence Corps during the war; from 1947 editor of *The Burlington Magazine*.

Price, Henry Habberley (1899–1984), Fellow and Lecturer in Philosophy, Trinity, 1924–35; Wykeham Professor of Logic and Fellow of New College, 1935–59; President of the Society for Psychical Research 1939–40. *Perception* (1932), *Hume's Theory of the External World* (1940).

Prichard ('Prich'), Ed(ward) Fretwell (1915–84), educated at Harvard, brilliant New Deal lawyer; briefly shared a house with IB in Washington during the summer of 1943; worked for FDR on the US wartime economy; imprisoned in 1949 for ballot-stuffing in Bourbon County, Kentucky, in 1948; later a notable champion of higher education.

Rees, (Morgan) Goronwy (1909–79), journalist and author; New College history, then after his first year PPE, 1928–31; Fellow of All Souls 1931–46, later (1951–4) Estates Bursar; after Munich, joined the Territorial Army and later became a Staff Officer in France and Germany; married Margaret ('Margie') Ewing Morris 1940; later (1953–7) Principal, University College of Wales, Aberystwyth. Left-winger, friend of Guy Burgess, controversially a Communist sympathiser

---

1 *Special Relationships* (325/3), 75.
2 loc. cit. (309/1).
3 Letter to IB, 27 February 1945.

or more at one stage: according to Christopher Andrew and Vasili Mitrokhin,[1] Rees was recruited to the CP by Burgess and given a code name; see also Jenny Rees's biography of her father, *Looking for Mr Nobody*.[2] IB's recollection was that Rees was 'extremely good-looking and full of charm, a rogue but delightful; clever, agreeable, great friend'.[3] *The Summer Flood* (1932), *A Bridge to Divide Them* (1937).

Ridley, Jasper Maurice Alexander (known to his London friends as Bubbles) (1913–43), son of banker also named Jasper Ridley, mother a Benckendorff; friend of Stuart Hampshire as an undergraduate at Balliol; married 1939 (Helen Laura) Cressida Bonham Carter (1917–98); killed while fighting in Italy. Music was the main bond with IB, whose *The Hedgehog and the Fox* is dedicated to his memory. See Philip Toynbee, *Friends Apart: A Memoir of Esmond Romilly and Jasper Ridley in the Thirties* (London, 1954).

Rothschild family. During the Napoleonic wars the five sons of Mayer Amschel Rothschild (1743–1812), a merchant banker living in the Frankfurt ghetto, made the family into the leading financiers of Europe. Three of the sons settled abroad, founding Rothschild financial dynasties in London, Vienna and Paris which because of business ties and intermarriage remained closely linked. Members of each of these branches appear in this volume:

English branch
(Lionel) **Walter** Rothschild (1868–1937), 2nd Baron Rothschild 1915, great-grandson of Mayer Amschel; his younger brother was
(Nathaniel) **Charles** Rothschild (1877–1923), married Rozsika von Wertheimstein (1870–1940), lived at Ashton Wold near Peterborough; the eldest of their children is
Miriam Louisa Rothschild (b. 1907), entomologist and conservationist, married 1943 George Henry Lane (né Lanyi) (divorced 1957); her brother was
(Nathaniel Mayer) **Victor** Rothschild (1910–90), 3rd Baron Rothschild 1937; zoologist; Research Fellow, Trinity College, Cambridge, 1935–9; Intelligence Corps 1939–45; married 1933 (divorced 1946) Barbara Judith Hutchinson (1911–89), daughter of Mary Barnes Hutchinson and brother of Jeremy (q.v.) (Barbara later married Rex Warner, then Niko Ghika).

Austrian branch
Eugène Daniel de Rothschild (1884–1976), soldier and art connoisseur, great-great-grandson of Mayer Amschel.

French branch
Guy Edouard Alphonse Paul de Rothschild (b. 1909), great-great-grandson of Mayer Amschel; banker; left France for the US 1941 (having served in the French Army, winning the Croix de Guerre, before the defeat of France);

1 *The Mitrokhin Archive: The KGB in Europe and the West* (London, 1999), 104–5, 111–2.
2 London, 1994.
3 MI Tape 13.

joined Free French under de Gaulle in London 1943; married 1937 (divorced 1956) Alix Hermine Jeannette Schey de Koromla (1911–82).

Baron **Edmond** James de Rothschild (1845–1954), grandson of Mayer Amschel, established a programme of agricultural settlements for Jews in Palestine; his son was

James ('Jimmy') Armand Edmond de Rothschild (1878–1957), settled in England; Liberal MP, Isle of Ely, 1929–45; Joint Parliamentary Secretary, Ministry of Supply, 1945; lived at Waddesdon in Buckinghamshire; ardent Zionist.

Rumbold, Sir (Horace) Anthony (Claude) (1911–83), diplomat, FO 1935–7, Washington 1937–42, FO 1942–4, Seconded as Minister Resident, Allied Forces HQ, Mediterranean Command, 1944; FO 1944–7. Married 1937 (divorced 1974) Felicity Ann Bailey (1917–84), of whom IB admitted 'I was faintly in love with her [. . .] When her husband went off with another lady in Washington, I was living with them as a paying guest – I had to hold the hand of the abandoned wife'.[1]

Salter, Sir (James) Arthur (1881–1975), Gladstone Professor of Political Theory and Institutions and Fellow of All Souls, 1934–44, MP (Independent) for Oxford University 1937–50, head of the British Shipping Mission in Washington 1941–3, later (1954) 1st Baron Salter of Kidlington. Married 1940 Ethel Mather Bullard, née Bagg (1883–1969). Harry Hodson remembered him as 'an experienced man of world affairs, cautious, methodical (I remember his mood of melancholy resignation when his American wife, whom he had married late in life, set about rearranging, to suit her own pictorial ideas of order, all the books in his rooms at All Souls), trained as a civil servant to keep his feet firmly on the ground.'[2] Works include *Allied Shipping Control: An Experiment in International Administration* (1921), *The World's Economic Crisis and the Way of Escape* (1932), *Recovery, the Second Effort* (1932), *Political Aspects of the World Depression* (1932), *The United States of Europe: And Other Papers* (1933), *Modern Mechanization and its Effects on the Structure of Society* (1933), *The Framework of an Ordered Society* (1933), *China and the Depression: Impressions of a Three Months Visit* (1934), *World Trade and its Future* (1936), *The Dual Policy* (1939).

Schapiro, Meyer (1904–96), art historian, artist, polymath and inspirational teacher, with particular interests in Romanesque sculpture and the art of the late nineteenth century and the early twentieth; born in Lithuania and emigrated to the US as a child; taught in the Department of Fine Arts and Archaeology, Columbia University, as Lecturer 1928–36, Assistant Professor 1936–46, Associate Professor 1946–52; also lectured at New York University (1932–6) and the New School for Social Research (1936–52); married paediatrician Dr Lillian Milgram (b. c.1903) 1928. The *New York Times* commented that:

He regarded all forms, schools and systems of knowledge as interrelated

1 MI Tape 12.
2 loc. cit. (703/2).

and interdependent. As far as he was concerned, he had been put on earth to know, and to make known, the correspondences between them all. And he addressed himself not to the insider, but to the generality of intelligent human beings. [. . .] New York made him welcome, nourished his fiery and agile intelligence, and made it possible for him to master one discipline after another with a speed and a thoroughness that have had few parallels in our century.[1]

Smith, Alic Halford (1883–1958), Scottish Office 1906–19, Fellow and philosophy Tutor, New College, 1914–44, Acting Warden 1940–4, Warden 1944–58, Vice-Chancellor, Oxford, 1954–7. Roy Harrod remembered 'his originality, his humanity, his blend of philosophy and gaiety, his blend of scholarship and aestheticism'.[2] E. C. Yorke described Smith as 'of subtle and supple mind, endowed with an unusual measure of practical wisdom', an 'enthusiastic and discriminating connoisseur of the fine arts [. . .] boyishly unassuming, winningly courteous'.[3] John Sparrow recalled: 'he was a controversial figure [. . .] so in the sense that he loved a battle, and in battle he was selfless, tireless, fearless, and, in a good cause, shameless. [. . .] his love for the College, like everything else about him, was unsentimental, austere, selfless, and without thought of any return'.[4] *A Treatise on Knowledge* (1942).

Sparrow, John Hanbury Angus (1906–92), classicist, barrister, prolific reviewer, homosexual; Fellow of All Souls 1929–52, then (1952–77) Warden; War Office 1941–50 (Washington, DC, February–December 1941). In IB's words:

His wit, his irony, his charm, his sheer intelligence, indeed his brilliance, and his total lack of fear, moral and physical, and his independence, were unique in my experience. [. . .] in College, to which he was in a sense devoted, his principal achievement was blocking, with the greatest ingenuity, style and brilliance, the slightest change in its arrangements. He had deep friendships, not many, but very genuine, throughout his life, and some acute hatreds, particularly among his colleagues in All Souls, which the latter naturally returned in kind. But it was, of course, his sexual life which dominated him to a profound degree and affected his attitudes to life and people and literature and politics to quite a high degree [. . .] He was, as you know, easily bored, and responded to vitality, wit, charm and, above all, youth, and was profoundly bored by worth, virtue, serious dedication to academic life. His values were worldly – he respected statesmen, politicians, judges, bankers much more than dons. He wanted to be admired and amused. Personal relations meant far more to him than

1 *New York Times*, 4 March 1996, pp. A1, D10.
2 Obituary Notice in *The Oxford Magazine*, 6 November 1958, 78.
3 E[ric] G. [sc. Cecil] Y[orke] (338/1), obituary notice in *Oxford*, December 1958, 70.
4 'Extract from a speech delivered at the Gaudy on 4 July, 1958 (nine days before the death of A.H.S.) by J. H. A. Sparrow, Warden of All Souls', in *Alic Halford Smith, 1883–1958, Scholar, Fellow, and Warden of New College and Vice-Chancellor of the University of Oxford*, 'a collection of tributes published by direction of the Warden and Fellows of New College' [Oxford, n.d.], 5–10, at 5 and 10.

academic ones.'[1]

Half-Lines and Repetitions in Virgil (1931), *Sense and Poetry: Essays on the Place of Meaning in Contemporary Verse* (1934).

Spender, Stephen Harold (1909–95), poet and critic; Univ. PPE 1927–30; co-editor of *Horizon*, 1939–41, then served as a fireman 1941–4; later (1953–67) co-editor of *Encounter*. Married (1) 1936 (divorced 1941) Marie Agnes ('Inez') Pearn (1913–76), (2) 1941 Natasha Litvin (b. 1921). A lifelong friend of IB, who remembered: 'he was absolutely charming, he was very good-looking and very friendly [. . .] naïve and generous-natured [. . .] I met him in my first year, in his second year and we made great friends and we used to go for walks together on Hampstead Heath because we lived there. [. . .] the poetry he wrote at that time and for a few years after was very, very good. [. . .] he was a very good critic, a very candid and penetrating critic [. . .] there's nothing between him and the object. [. . .] He was a man of the left as we all were, but he had no doctrines and he didn't have an analytic mind [. . .] he had general sympathies.'[2] *Twenty Poems* (1930), *Poems* (1933), *The Destructive Element* (1934), *Vienna* (1934), *The Burning Cactus* (1936), *Forward from Liberalism* (1937), *Trial of a Judge* (1938), *Poems for Spain* (1939), *The Still Centre* (1939), *Ruins and Visions* (1942), *Life and the Poet* (1942), *Citizens in War, and After* (1945).

Straight, Lady Daphne Margarita (1913–2003), née Finch-Hatton, daughter of the 14th Earl of Winchilsea (brother of Karen Blixen's lover Denys Finch Hatton), married to the American-born Whitney Willard Straight, and thus sister-in-law of Michael Whitney Straight (318/1), had worked with IB in the BPS in New York and was now a secretary in the American Division of the MOI in London. IB was very fond of her (as she was of him) and admired her abilities; in addition, as she understated it herself in a letter to IB of 14 August 1943, 'I am reasonable to look at.' Their correspondence was evidently greatly valued by both of them, though unfortunately most of IB's personal letters to DS have not survived (the letter of 26 November 1942,[3] not having been sent, at any rate in this form, is a happy exception); many of hers to him have, however, and they are among the best incoming letters among his papers – as she wrote to him on 20 July 1943, 'I always seem to write my mind to you.'

Trott zu Solz, Adam von (1909–44), Balliol PPE (Rhodes Scholar) 1931–3 after a doctorate in international law in Germany; visited the US (twice) and China 1937–9;[4] joined German Foreign Office 1940 and used his post to gain support for the opposition; arrested when his leading role in the 1944 attempt to assassinate Hitler (the 'July plot') was disclosed; executed 26 August 1944. Married Clarita Tiefenbacher (b. 1917) 1940. IB wrote the following tribute to

---

1 Letter to John Lowe, 27 February 1989.
2 MI Tape 9.
3 See p. 423.
4 IB told Nicholas Cull (309/1) that no one really knew what Trott was doing when he visited Washington (in 1939), where he was attached to the Institute of Pacific Relations.

von Trott, about whom he had ambivalent views (contra David Astor, Diana Hopkinson and others), in 1986:[1]

I knew Adam von Trott best during the early 1930s, when he was a Rhodes Scholar, and I was a graduate student and then at All Souls. We met at lunch in [Balliol], at the end of which he suggested that we might go for a walk that afternoon. We became friends almost at once. He had exceptional charm, great distinction of mind and manner, was extremely handsome, had both wit and humour, and was, at all times, a most delightful companion. I was completely captivated. He had a far wider view of history and culture than most of my Oxford friends: his conversation was interspersed with references to Schiller, Hegel, Kleist, Goethe – not names often mentioned in those days by students of the school of PPE, and he aroused in me an interest in these thinkers which has stayed with me ever since. Oddly enough he did not, so far as I can remember, talk to me about contemporary politics, either then or, with one or two exceptions, later, as he evidently did to others of his friends. In 1931–3 he seemed to me gay, carefree and invariably exhilarating. Even with Hitler's rise to power, he did not speak to me about it. If I brought up the subject, he tended to wander into fascinating, somewhat general, historical disquisitions.

He went to Germany, and returned to Oxford, some time in 1933. The philosopher R. G. Collingwood gave a party to welcome him. On this occasion, when we all crowded round him and asked him what was going on in Germany, he said 'My country is very sick', and not much more (to the best of my recollection). I received the impression that he saw a vast transformation going on in Europe, a kind of fateful historic mutation, to which the ordinary categories did not apply, terrifying, sinister, but unlikely to be intelligible to academics like myself, encapsulated, so it may have seemed to him, in the excessively self-centred, cosy Oxford world.

I did not see him often after that. I remember one incident. After he returned to Germany for good he wrote a letter to the *Manchester Guardian* which somewhat upset me. It was in response to a report by the *Guardian*'s correspondent in Germany, F. A. Voight, who said that justice in German law courts was weighted against Jews. Adam, I seem to recollect, denied this, and said that in the court where he practised, in Cassel, this was not so. I was ready to take his word for this, but I thought that the obvious implication – that the harassment of Jews was not as great as was commonly supposed – could not be valid and wondered why he had chosen to publish it. He was evidently told of my feelings by one of his friends, wrote to me reproachfully and, when he was next in Oxford, told me that, while he understood my feelings and sympathised with them,

---

1 'A Personal Tribute to Adam von Trott (Balliol 1931)', *Balliol College Annual Record* 1986, 61–2. See also Catherine Andreyev, review of Hedley Bull (ed.), *The Challenge of the Third Reich* (Oxford, 1986), ibid., 62–4.

what he had written in the letter was in fact true, and needed saying. In any case, we remained friends. I gave him a letter to Professor Felix Frankfurter, of Harvard, whom he visited and duly charmed, as he did us all. I did not see him again until 1938, when he dined in All Souls as Humphrey Sumner's guest. He then said to me – virtually the only spontaneous political statement he ever addressed to me – that unless England and France stood up to Hitler, war would come and Hitler might win it. I asked what he thought should be done: 'Germany must be surrounded and stopped. This must be done very soon. German expansion must not occur.' I never saw him again.

On his last visit to England, in 1939, perhaps wisely, he did not communicate with me. The Warden of All Souls, Dr Adams, told me that he had received a message from Adam that in the event of war he might feel obliged to fight in his country's army; but I never saw this letter. I was told that he spoke to others about what his friends in Germany, and perhaps wider circles, hoped to do to avert war, but, for whatever reason, he did not speak to me of this. He may have felt doubtful about my discretion, or thought, perhaps rightly, that I could be of little political use to him. At any rate, he did not confide in me at any time. Thus I had no direct knowledge of what he thought or did after the mid-1930s, in China, Germany or the US. Our relations had been affectionate and familiar but not intimate. All I heard about him after the war had begun came from John Wheeler-Bennett, until 1941, and even that was very little. That Adam was anti-Nazi was always absolutely clear to me; but I knew nothing about his precise political ideas, actions, ambitions, hopes, or the risks he took, which ended in his terrible martyrdom. David Astor, who was far closer to him than anyone in England, and perhaps others, know more about this.

When researchers write to me and ask about Adam von Trott's life and political activities, I can give them little concrete information: I can say no more than than he was a brave and honourable man, a passionate patriot, incapable of anything ignoble or unworthy, and that he served what he regarded as being the deepest interests of his own countrymen and of decent people everywhere.

Walker, Rachel ('Tips') (1913–92), Somerville PPE 1931–4; pupil and close friend of IB, hoped to marry him in 1935; later became mentally ill. Mary Bennett writes:

Tips was quite exceptionally clever and vivid, always flawlessly dressed and very much the centre of her circle of friends. She was a keen rider to hounds – knew Jorrocks as well as T. S. Eliot – introduced us to Picasso and to Strauss waltzes, and made us laugh unendingly. It is easy to see how she and IB stirred each other up when she was his pupil, and initially she may well have failed to perceive that his manner was to a large extent the same as his manner to every intelligent and presentable young woman, and so believed it special to herself. I have no doubt that she believed that he was in love with her, and may well have thought that it was only his

Jewishness and complete difference of background – hers was conventional English upper middle class – that prevented him from coming forward.

The year after she left Oxford to read philosophy in Paris (where she was on the verge of accepting the passionate advances of a philosopher [Jean Cavaillès] at the École normale, later shot by the Germans), she came to the conclusion that he was the man she wished to marry. During that year, and more rapidly afterwards, she became increasingly unbalanced, and a few years later was confined to a mental hospital. She was hospitalised until her death.

Tips herself wrote in a letter to her friend Barbara Stancliffe postmarked 25 March 1935, a few months before IB extricated himself:

The excitement in the middle of which I splashed the last letter to you abated, for M. Cavaillès proposed to me and I realised it was not that I really wanted. I don't know. He is cleverer, stronger, purer than I, I admire him, I love him; but he is austere and mathematic to the point of frightenning [sic] away all of me that Shaya stimulated, the humane sweep of Europe, Don Giovanni, Budapest, Elliot [sic], El Greco – the aristocrat swirling down the marble staircase to the Blue Danube. Yes, all that I can't cut away. Shaya comes in a fortnight with Guy Chilver and Mary to chaperone us. Whisk hey and with a pirouette I discard them both . . . and stay free. Genius is within me and for its burning alone I stay.

Wallace, David John (1914–44), son of Conservative chief whip Euan Wallace; Balliol classics 1933–6; married Prudence Major 1939, killed in action, in Greece, by a stray bullet. Wallace had lived in Athens and travelled through the Balkans, Greece and Turkey photographing archaeological sites; he had been in SOE with the rank of Major, and was killed while attached as an observer to the 10th Greek Division; they subsequently raised a memorial to him whose inscription reads (in translation): 'Here rests amongst his guerrilla comrades an Englishman, Major David Wallace [. . .] The soil of Greece is honoured to give shelter to this hero.'

Warburg family. The Warburg banking family from Hamburg became well known because of the achievements of five brothers:

Aby Warburg (1866–1929) rejected banking to become an influential art historian.

Max Warburg (1867–1946) became head of the family firm of M. M. Warburg & Co, and one of the leading Jews in Hamburg, until forced to flee to the US in 1938.

Paul Warburg (1868–1932) and **Felix** Warburg (1871–1937), also bankers, both married American wives and moved to the US; Paul became the prime mover behind the setting up of the Federal Reserve Board; Felix worked for his father-in-law's firm Kuhn, Loeb, but became increasingly involved in fund-raising for (particularly Jewish) charities.

Fritz Warburg (1879–1962) remained in the family bank in Hamburg until 1938, when he moved to Sweden after Aryanisation of the German banks; he died in Israel.

Among the next generation were:

Edward Mortimer Morris Warburg (1908–92), Felix's son, a noted connoisseur of the arts, after his father's death continued many of his philanthropic activities.

Ingrid Warburg Spinelli (1910–2000), Fritz's daughter, studied in Oxford during 1932, when she met IB; she went to the US in 1936, became active in refugee organisations, married Veniero Spinelli in 1941 and, after the War, settled in Italy.

Fredric John Warburg (1898–1981), left-wing publisher, belonged to a distant branch of the family long established in England (he was third cousin once removed of the five brothers); worked in educational publishers George Routledge & Sons 1922–35 (Joint Managing Director 1931–5); with Roger Senhouse, bought firm of Martin Secker 1936; Chairman of Martin Secker & Warburg 1936–71 and hence publisher of many of George Orwell's books, including *Animal Farm* (1945); married 1933 as his second wife Pamela de Bayou (1905–78), dress-designer and painter, described by a colleague of her husband as 'strikingly handsome, warm-hearted and totally uninhibited'.[1]

Weizmann, Chaim (1874–1952), chemist and statesman; President, World Zionist Organisation and Jewish Agency for Palestine 1921–31, 1935–46; Chairman, Board of Governors of the Hebrew University in Jerusalem, 1932–50; later (1949) first President of Israel. Married Vera Chatzman (1881–1966) 1906. Subject of a study in PI. IB recalled:

He was a great flirt, Weizmann. If he wanted to capture people, he proceeded to do so [. . .] He was head of the movement, highly intelligent, very amusing and a statesman. He was a great man of an obviously powerful kind and what he said was extremely interesting. Cosy he was not – he was with me, later – quite jolly, not solemn, cynical about politics and so on, and funny, and not at all kind; if he didn't need people, he threw them into the gutter, rather like Winston.

Wheeler-Bennett, John Wheeler (*sic*) (1902–75), attached to British Library of Information, NY, 1939–40; Assistant Director, BPS, NY, 1940–41; Special Assistant to Director-General of BIS in the US 1941–42; Head of NY Office of British Political Warfare Mission in the US 1942–44; Intelligence Dept, FO, 1944, Assistant Director-General 1945; Assistant to British Political Adviser to SHAEF 1944–5. Suffered from frequent health problems, often exacerbated by exhaustion. Married 1945 Ruth Hamilton Risher. His obituary in *The Times*, based on a draft by IB, includes these remarks on his wartime service:

He was one of the triumvirate charged by the Ministry of Information with the task of overhauling the peacetime British information machinery in

1 David Farrer, *The Warburgs* (London, 1975), 233.

New York, and with A. N. Morgan and Alan Dudley established the British
Information Services in New York, an institution which played a significant
part in the evolution of American opinion during the Second World War.
[. . .] In 1942 he became the representative in America of the British
Political Warfare organisation, and later European adviser and Assistant
Director General of the Political Intelligence Department. He worked in
the Political Adviser's Department in SHAEF in the last year of the war,
and was attached to the British Prosecution Team [sent] to the Nüremberg
War Criminals Tribunal in 1946. He had no doubt that these trials were
wholly just, and this caused a rift between him and some of his old anti-
Nazi German friends. In the same year he was appointed British Editor-in-
Chief of the captured archives of the German Foreign Ministry, and was
retained as general adviser to the Foreign Office on publications of this
type.[1]

Works include *The Disarmament Deadlock* (1934), *Hindenburg: The Wooden Titan*
(1936), *Brest-Litovsk: The Forgotten Peace, March 1918* (1938), *The Treaty of Brest-
Litovsk and Germany's Eastern Policy* (1939).

Williams, Jenifer Margaret (b. 1914), Somerville history 1932–5; Civil Service
1936–47; married Herbert (H. L. A.) Hart 1941; close and lifelong friend of IB.
Her father was John Fischer Williams, not hyphenated, though it was often
thought that 'Fischer' was part of the family's surname; hence Jenifer was at
times called 'Miss Fischer-Williams' (and variants). She first met IB at the
H. A. L. Fishers' in 1934. Because application to the Civil Service was not
permitted until the age of 22, she studied in Oxford until 1936, when she took
the exam, and did very well indeed. She met Herbert Hart in 1936, lived with
him from 1937 (married women were not normally allowed in the Civil
Service), and married him by special dispensation in 1941. For more information
see her autobiography, *Ask Me No More* (London, 1998). This volume is
dedicated to her.

1 *The Times*, 10 December 1975, 19.

INDEXES

Compiled by Douglas Matthews

INDEX OF CORRESPONDENTS

The style of the names follows that of the headings to the letters. Fuller identifications appear in the General Index.

GENERAL INDEX

Page numbers in italic identify pages on which footnotes – usually the first for the person or subject in question – give fuller information. An asterisk preceding a name indicates an entry in the Glossary. Works by IB appear directly under their titles, works by others under their authors' names. The Chronology is not indexed.

Athena's owl takes wing only as dusk falls.

G. W. F. Hegel [*see page xlviii above*]